advanced computer architectures

A DESIGN SPACE APPROACH

Dezső Sima, Terence Fountain, Péter Kacsuk

PEARSON

The programs in this book have been included for their instructional value. They have been tested with care but are not guaranteed for any particular purpose. The publisher and authors do not offer any warranties or representations nor do they accept any liabilities with respect to the programs.

Many of the designations used by manufacturers and sellers to distinguish their products are claimed as trademarks. Pearson Education has made every attempt to supply trademark information about manufacturers and their products mentioned in this book. A list of the trademark designations and their owners appears on page xxiii.

Publishers' Acknowledgements
The publishers would like to thank the following for permission to reproduce thec items listed below:
Table 4.2, Figure 4.13 and Table 4.3 (Stephens et al., 1991); Table 4.5 (Lamm and Wilson, 1992); Table 4.6 (Aiken and Nicolau, 1988); Table 4.6 (Lam, 1988); Table 4.8, Figure 4.21 and Figure 4.22 (Wall, 1991); Figure 5.9 (Burgess et al., 1994); Figure 5.28 (Butler et al., 1991); Figure 5.53 (Chang et al., 1991); Table 8.10 and Figure 8.28 (Yeh and Patt, 1992); Figure 9.20 (Fisher et al., 1984); Figure 16.22 (Nikhil and Arvind, 1989); Figure 16.23 and Figure 16.24 (Nikhil et al., 1992) © Association for Computing Machinery, Inc. Reprinted by permission.
Figure 17.25 appears courtesy of BYTE / McGraw-Hill.
Figure 5.16, 5.48 and the conditional move instructions on p. 363 reproduced with the permission of Digital Equipment Corporation.
Figures 5.7, 9.7, 9.8, 9.9, 17.33, 17.34 and 17.35 appear courtesy of International Business Machines Corporation.
Figure 16.13 reproduced with permission of Massachussets Institute of Technology (MIT).
Figures 7.66, 7.68, 7.73 and 8.43 reprinted with permission of MicroDEsign Resources, Sebastopol, California.
Table 18.2 appears courtesy of SiliconGraphics Computer Systems.
Figure 17.27 appears courtesy of SGS Thomson Microprocessors (Inmos).
Figure 11.15 appears courtesy of Thinking Machines Corporation.
Table 1.1 reprinted by permission of John Wiley & Sons Ltd.
Although we have tried to trace the Copyright holder for Figures 17.30 and 17.31, we chave not been successful. Should you have any information that would enable us to do so, please contact the publishers at the address given above.

ISBN 978-81-317-0208-6

First Impression, 2006
Twenty-First Impression, 2013
Twenty-Second Impression, 2014

Published by Dorling Kindersley (India) Pvt. Ltd., licensees of Pearson Education in South Asia.

Head Office: 7th Floor, Knowledge Boulevard, A-8(A), Sector-62, Noida – 201309, U.P, India.
Registered Office: 11 Community Centre, Panchsheel Park, New Delhi 110 017, India.

Printed in India by Pushp Print Services.

Preface

Why yet another textbook on computer architectures?

With excellent textbooks on computer architectures already available for example, Hwang (1993) and Patterson and Hennessy (1990), is there any need for yet another one?

Our answer is a definitive yes for two main reasons. First, the past few years have seen dramatic changes in the world of computer architectures. In addition to superscalar processors becoming predominant in the market, a plethora of new concepts have emerged, including predecoding, dynamic branch prediction, instruction reordering, speculative execution of loads, and implementing CISC processors by means of a RISC core. These new ideas have become widely used in the lastest generation of superscalars, such as the PentiumPro, Power PC 620, α 21164, UltraSparc and R10000, but have not yet been covered by earlier textbooks.

Second, in our textbook we use a novel approach to presenting architectures and related concepts. Our approach is to identify and explore the *design space* of the architecture classes and concepts discussed. The design space is an excellent means to point our significant design aspects, relevant design choices as well as to show trends. For example, when we describe the concept of speculative branch processing, we first present the *design aspects* pertaining to this concept (Figure 1).

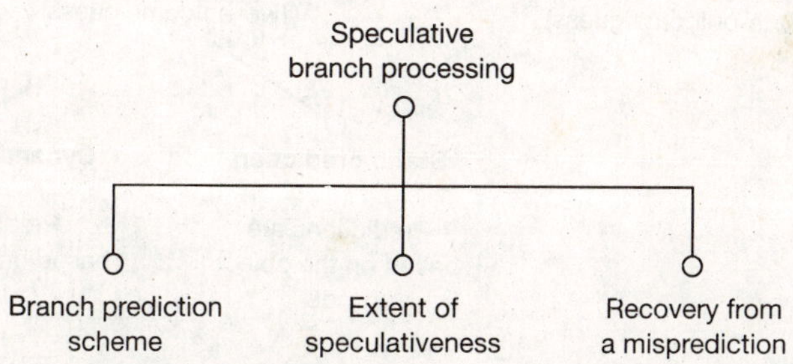

Figure 1 Design space of branch processing policies.

For these design aspects we then indicate the relevant *design choices*. For example, in Figure 2 we show the range of major design choices for branch prediction schemes.

A significant advantage of the concept of design space is that it is open-ended and a top-down approach. By going on to further levels of detail, step by step, any concept can be discussed to a reasonable depth, as shown in Figures 2 and 3. To represent design spaces we use a concise graphical means called *DS-trees*. DS-trees, as shown in Figures 1–3, are introduced in Section 2.5.3. Together, design spaces and DS-trees allow a clear presentation of relevant information in a well structured manner.

We have taken considerable effort to show how concepts are implemented in a range of representative processors. By considering subsequent processors, significant *trends* become clear, from these trends, superseded and current concepts can easily be identified. For example, Figure 3 shows current trends in branch prediction schemes. Consequently, an informative picture emerges to illustrate the rise and fall of concepts used. This also demonstrates how misleading it can be if the description of a concept is restricted to a single possible implementation (design choice), as is often done.

We are convinced that the inclusion of design spaces and DS-trees, which is unique amongst textbooks in this area, will help readers to build up a well structured, enlightening and dynamic knowledge on advanced computer architectures.

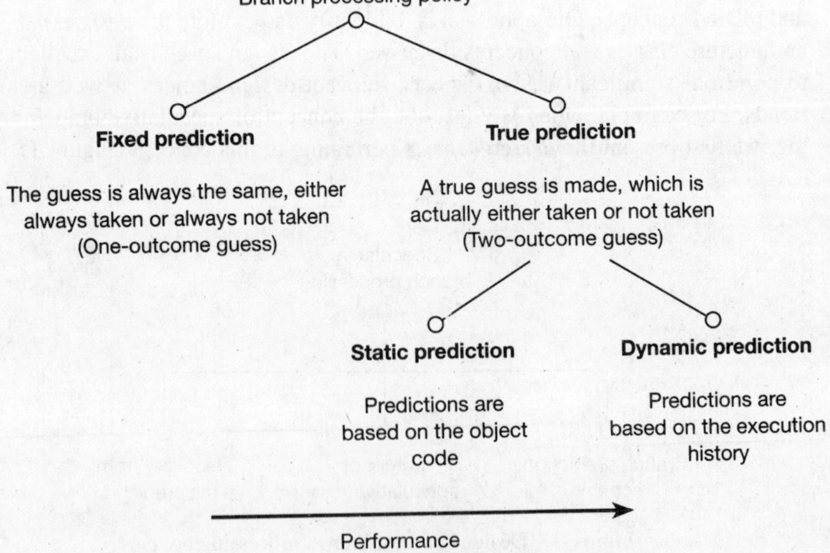

Figure 2 Basic kinds of branch predictions.

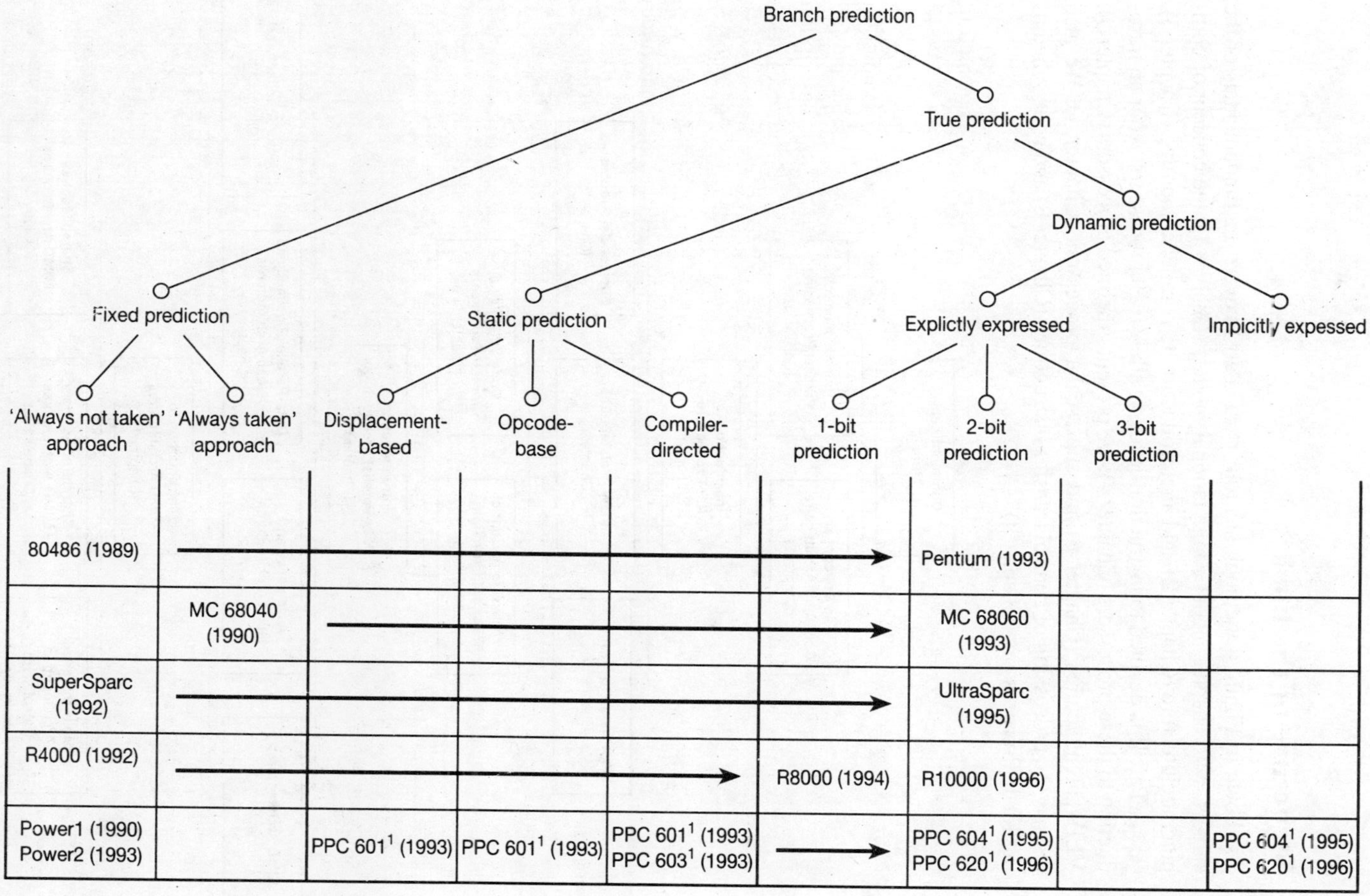

Figure 3 Branch prediction trends as indicated by subsequent models of particular processor lines. [1]PowerPC is abbreviated here as PPC.

Structure of the book

As shown in Figure 4 the book has four parts. Part I covers the fundamentals of the subject, with chapters about computational models (Chapter 1), the concept of computer architecture (Chapter 2), and an introduction to parallel computing (Chapter 3).

Part II is devoted to instruction-level parallel (ILP) processors. After an introduction to these processors (Chapter 4), we present pipelined processors (Chapter 5), VLIW architectures (Chapter 6) and superscalar processors (Chapter 7). We also discuss the processing of control transfer instructions (Chapter 8) and code scheduling for ILP-processors (Chapter 9).

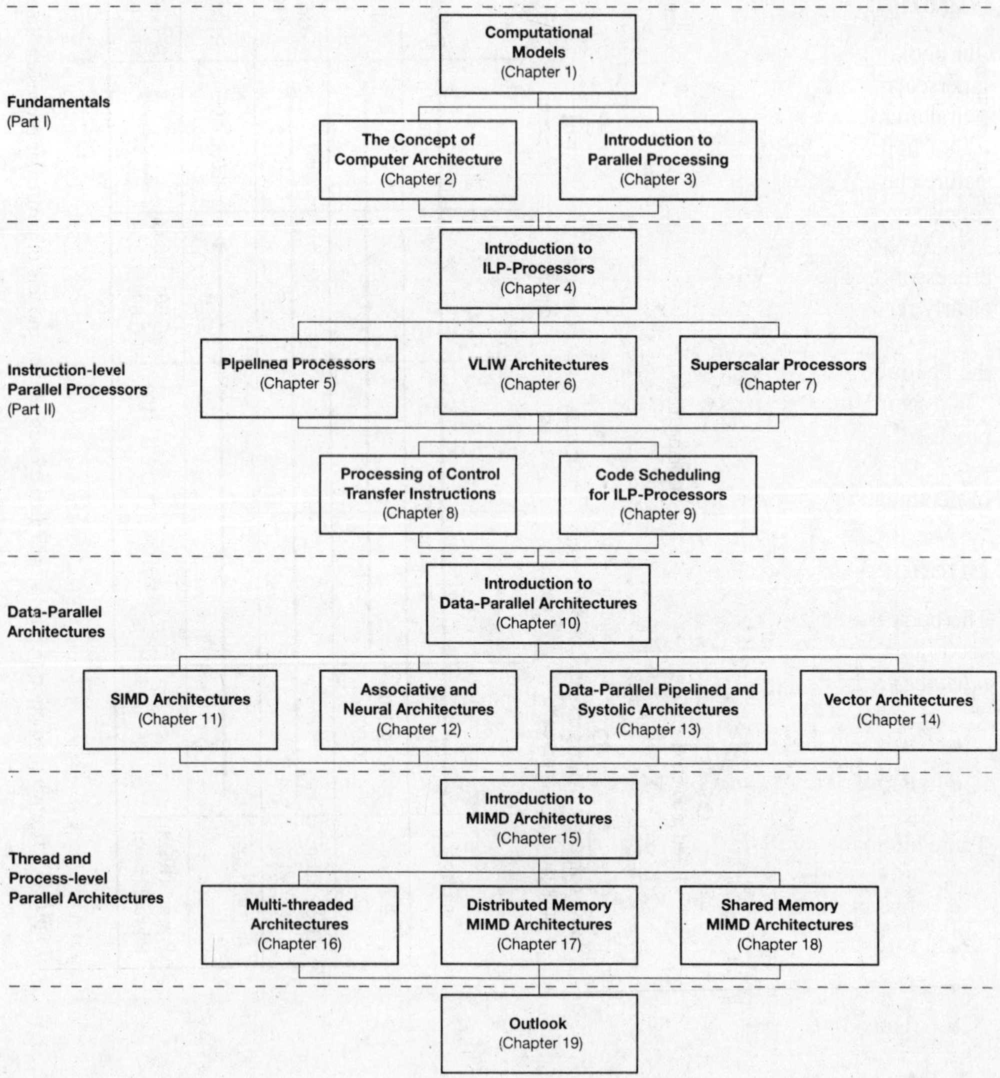

Figure 4 Structure of the contents.

Part III is concerned with data-parallel architectures. After introducing these architectures (Chapter 10), we present SIMD architectures (Chapter 11), associative and neural architectures (Chapter 12), data-parallel pipelined and systolic architectures (Chapter 13) and vector architectures (Chapter 14).

Part IV acquaints the reader with thread- and process-level parallel architectures. After an introduction to MIMD architectures (Chapter 15), we describe multi-threaded architectures (Chapter 16), distributed memory MIMD architectures (Chapter 17) and shared memory MIMD architectures (Chapter 18). The book concludes with a look ahead to future architectural developments.

Highlights of the book

Our book gives an up-to-date overview of significant architecture classes, including superscalar, multi-threaded, shared and distributed memory MIMDs, associative and neural architectures.

In presenting the material we show and explore the design spaces of the architecture classes and related concepts. This gives a framework for a well-structured and concise presentation of all the important points associated with the material covered.

We identify which concepts and design choices have been used in important processors. Based on this, significant trends become apparent and the reader can clearly recognize both superseded and currently predominant concepts.

Case studies show microarchitectural details of relevant processors, such as the PentiumPro, PowerPC604, PowerPC 620, R10000, and so on.

Numerous tables summarize the microarchitectural details of different processors, allowing miscellaneous comparisons to be made.

Furthermore, we believe that this is the first book on the market to contain an in-depth and up-to-date overview of superscalar processors.

Intended readership

The book is intended for both academic use and for practitioners in the field. It can serve as a textbook for either *advanced overview courses* or *in-depth courses on advanced topics*. We suggest two possible overview courses:

- Advanced computer architectures (Chapters 1, 2, 4, 6, 7, 10, 15)
- Parallel architectures (Chapters 1, 3, 10–18)

There are many options for in-depth courses on advanced topics, including:

- Instruction-level parallel architectures (Part II)
- Superscalar architectures (Chapters 4, 7, 8, 9)
- Data-parallel architectures (Part III)
- Thread- and process-level parallel architectures (Part IV)

The book is as a source from which a lecturer or instructor can easily select material for a lecture series. Students will find both well-structured material (concepts, their trends and implementations in recent processors) and background information for comparisons and for a bettcr understanding.

We also recommend our book to practitioners interested in recent architectural concepts, processors and related trends. We are confident that the concise presentation of the material will enhance its understanding.

Readers are assumed to be familiar with conventional architectures and programming concepts to the level of an introductory course.

Miscellaneous

In order to support a dynamic view, many figures include the *birth date* of the processors mentioned. The birth date is represented by the first year of volume shipment, if available, like PA 8000 (1996). If this date was not available or not applicable, because, for instance, a proposed processsor never reached the market, we mark it with a 'p' after the year of the related publication; for example, Lightning (1991p). In a few cases there is some uncertainty associated with the chronological data. Nevertheless, we feel that these data are very useful for orientating the reader as to where a given processor belongs in the main line of evolution.

Advanced Computer Architectures is the result of a long-standing collaboration between the three authors. Parts I and II were written by D. Sima (Chapter 3 was co-authored with P. Kacsuk), Part III and Chapter 19 by T. Fountain, and Part IV by P. Kacsuk.

In spite of extensive reviews and proofreadings of our book, errors and shortcomings undoubtedly remain for which the authors are fully responsible. We encourage the reader to contact the authors with details of any errors they find, and we welcome any suggestions for a future edition. The authors can be contacted using the following e-mail addresses:

sima@alphal.obuda.kando.hu (D. Sima)
kacsuk@sunserv.kfki.hu (P. Kacsuk)
t.fountain@ucl.ac.uk (T. J. Fountain)

Acknowledgments

Many people have helped with the production of this book. Although it is not possible to mention everyone, the authors would particularly like to thank the following individuals for their help.

For providing us with valuable source material: Dr Balázs Szabó, IBM Hungary; Sándor Nacsa, DEC Hungary; Dr Frank Baetke, Convex Computer GmbH Germany; András Neményi, Euro Trend Ltd, Hungary; Clarke Hoyle, Sparc International.

For reviewing parts of the manuscript and for their valuable comments: Dr Frank Baetke, Convex Computers GmbH; Michael Mahon, Hewlett-Packard USA; Prof. Michael Duff, UCL England; Dr Ferenc Vajda, Hungarian Academy of Sciences.

For their efforts in improving our English: Dr John Corn, Middlesex University, England and Susan Kutor.

For drawing many of the figures, and for helping to correct the manuscript: P. Földesi, Gy. Harkai, E. Hirling, L. Martinkovics and Z. Szabó.

For their hard work in bringing the manuscript to publication: Simon Plumtree, formerly of Addison Wesley Longman, and Karen Mosman and Mark Ralph of Addison Wesley Longman.

Common abbreviations

The following common abbreviations are used in the book:

ALU	arithmetic and logic unit
CC-NUMA	cache-coherent non-uniform memory access machine
CDG	control dependency graph
CISC	complex instruction set (architecture/processor/etc.)
COMA	cache-only memory access machine
DDG	data dependency graph
EU	execution unit
FP	floating point
FX	fixed point
ILP	instruction-level parallel processor
ISA	instruction set architecture
MIMD	multiple instruction streams multiple data streams machine
NUMA	non-uniform memory access machine
RISC	reduced instruction set (architecture/processor/etc.)
ROB	reorder buffer
RS	reservation station
SIMD	single instruction stream multiple data streams machine
UMA	uniform memory access machine
VLIW	very large instruction word (architecture/processor/etc.)

Summary of Contents

Contents

Trademark notice

Part I

Fundamentals

1 Computational Models

In this chapter we introduce computational models. Section 1.1 describes the concept and relates it to programming languages and computer architectures. Section 1.2 introduces six computational models and Section 1.3 describes one of them, the von Neumann computational model, in detail. Finally, Section 1.4 discusses granularity and typing, two key concepts of computational models.

1.1 The concept of a computational model

1.1.1 Introduction

It is widely observed that certain computer architecture classes and programming language classes correspond to one another, for example von Neumann architectures and imperative languages, or reduction architectures and functional languages. For this to be the case the corresponding architecture and language classes must have a common foundation or paradigm called a *computational model*. For instance, von Neumann architectures and imperative languages have a common foundation which we call the von Neumann computational model, while reduction architectures and functional languages are based on the applicative computational model. In fact, most existing architectures and languages follow one of only a few computational models.

The concept of a computational model represents a *higher level of abstraction* than either the computer architecture or the programming language alone, and covers both, as shown in Figure 1.1. The abundance of different computer architectures and programming languages can best be surveyed and classified using this powerful high-level abstraction.

As the term 'computational model' is one of the most fundamental concepts in computing, we first give a short overview of how this concept has evolved (Figure 1.2), before discussing its interpretation.

Originally the term 'model for parallel computation' was introduced in the 1960s to express possible concepts for sequencing and for the semantics of parallel operations. Almost a decade later the concept of a 'model of computing system' was introduced to designate the underlying model of computer languages. Subsequently, the concept of a computational model was introduced, initially to designate the underlying model of computers. This was later expanded to include both computers and computer languages. The latter interpretation originates from Treleaven et al. (1987), who identified eight parallel models of computation. Treleaven's specification of the associated programming styles and languages is shown in Table 1.1.

In this book, we interpret the concept of a computational model in the same way as Treleaven. However, we go a step further and give a detailed interpretation as well.

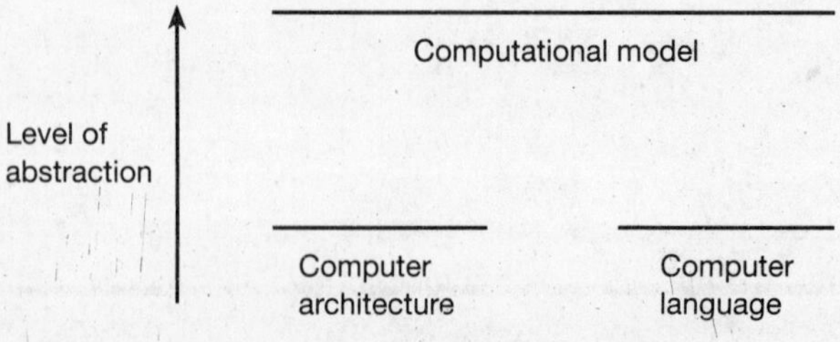

Figure 1.1 Interpretation of the computational model concept as a high-level abstraction.

Evolutionary path →				
Model for parallel computation	**Model of computing system**	**Computational model**	**Computational model**	**Computational model**
Sequencing and semantics of operations	Underlying model of computer languages	Underlying model of computers	Underlying model of both computer languages and computers	Same as previous, but interpreted as covering: basic items of computation; problem description model; execution model
(Karp and Miller, 1996) (Rodriguez, 1967) (Adams, 1968) (Peterson and Bredt, 1974)	*(Backus, 1978)*	*(Treleaven and Hopkins, 1981) (Dally and Wills, 1989)*	*(Treleaven et al., 1987; Treleaven, 1990)*	

Figure 1.2 Main steps in the evolution of the computational model concept.

Table 1.1 Parallel models of computation identified by Treleaven (1990).

Programming style	*Programming languages*	*Models of computation*
Procedural	Ada, Occam	Control flow
Object-oriented	Smalltalk, POOL	Object-oriented
Single assignment	ID, SISAL	Data flow
Applicative	Pure Lisp, MIRANDA	Reduction
Predicate logic	Prolog, GHC	Logic
Production system	OPS5	Rule-based
Semantic network	NETL	Cellular array
Neural network	SAIC ANSpec	Neurocomputer

1.1.2 Interpretation of the concept of a computational model

In our interpretation the concept of a **computational model** comprises the set of the following three abstractions (Figure 1.3):

- the basic items of computation,
- the problem description model and
- the execution model.

Contrary to initial thoughts, the set of abstractions that should be chosen to specify computational models is far from obvious. A smaller number of criteria would define fewer but more basic computational models, while a larger number of criteria would result in a relatively large number of distinct models. In this chapter our aim is to introduce the most basic computational models and to choose, accordingly, the minimal set of required abstractions.

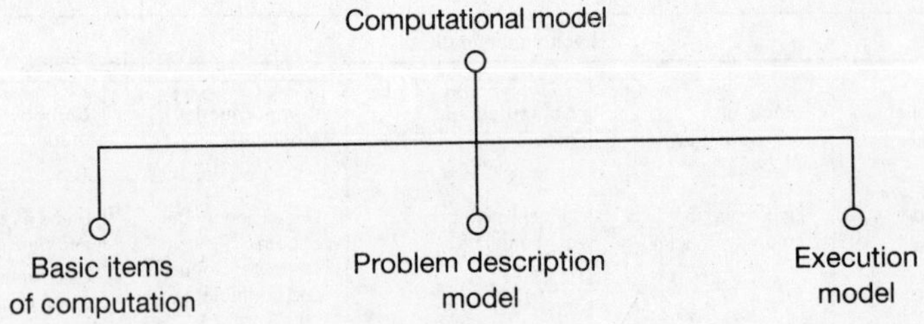

Figure 1.3 Interpretation of the computational model concept as covering three abstractions.

The first abstraction identifies **the basic items of computation**. This is a specification of the *items* the computation refers to and the *kind of computations* (operations) that can be performed on them.

For instance, in the von Neumann computational model the basic items of computation are data. This data will typically be represented by named (that is, identifiable) entities in order to be able to distinguish between a number of different data items in the course of a computation. These named entities are commonly called **variables** in programming languages and are implemented by memory or register addresses in architectures.

All the best known computational models, namely:

- the Turing model,
- the von Neumann model and
- the dataflow model

are based on the *concept of data*.

In contrast, there are a number of models which are *not* data based. In these models the basic items of computation are:

- objects or messages sent to them requiring an associated manipulation (as in the object-based model),
- arguments and the functions applied on them (applicative model),
- elements of sets and the predicates declared on them (predicate-logic-based model).

The **problem description model** refers to both the style and the method of problem description, as shown in Figure 1.4.

The **problem description style** specifies how problems in a particular computational model are described. The style is either procedural or declarative, as depicted in Figure 1.5.

In a **procedural style** the algorithm for solving the problem is stated. A particular solution is then declared in the form of an algorithm. For instance, an algorithm to calculate 'n' factorial could be given using a Pascal-like syntax as in Figure 1.6. For the sake of simplicity the declaration part is omitted.

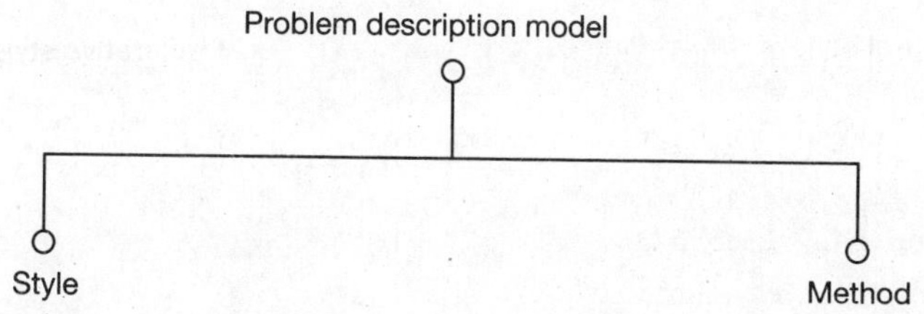

Figure 1.4 Interpretation of the problem description model.

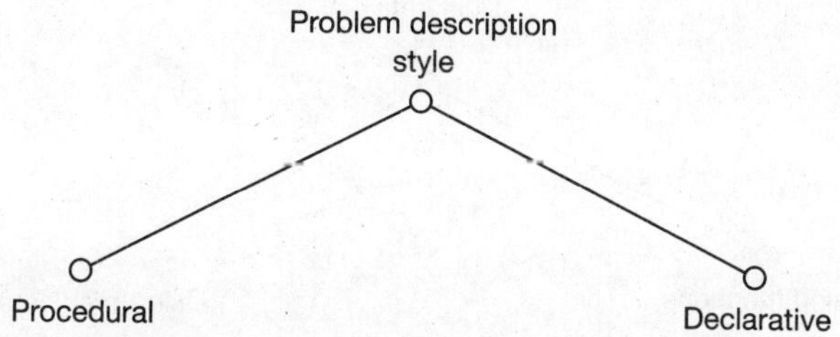

Figure 1.5 Different problem description styles.

If a **declarative style** is used, all the facts and relationships relevant to the given problem have to be stated. There are two methods for expressing these relationships and facts (Figure 1.7). The first uses functions, as in the applicative model of computation, while the second states the relationships and facts in the form of predicates, as in the predicate-logic-based computational model.

In order to illustrate the declarative style we will calculate 'n' factorial using functions, as in the applicative model (see Figure 1.6). To calculate, say, three factorials, that is fac(3), we first look for the appropriate function definition and then substitute the given argument into the right side of the definition. We continue repeating the substitution for as long as possible. Finally, we evaluate (reduce) the result numerically. In our example this requires the following calculations:

fac(3) = ?
fac(3) = 3 ∗ fac(2) = 3 ∗ 2 ∗ fac(l) = 3 ∗ 2 ∗ 1 = 6

Note that in the declarative style the sequence of the statements has no significance, in contrast to the procedural style, where it does. Thus, in Figure.1.6 we could reverse the sequence of the two statements without suffering any consequences.

While stating the relevant relationships and facts that specify a particular problem, the declarative style expresses what the problem is. This is in sharp contrast to the procedural style which articulates one specific solution to solving the given problem. Obviously, when using the declarative style, problems are described at a higher level of abstraction than in the case of the procedural style and usually in a more elegant and concise way.

Procedural style

```
if n := 0 then
   fac := 1
   else_fac := 1;
      for i := 1 to n do
         fac := i * fac;
end;
```

Declarative style

```
fac (0) := 1
fac ( n>0 ) := n * fac ( n-1);
```

Figure 1.6 Contrasting the procedural and declarative styles of problem description.

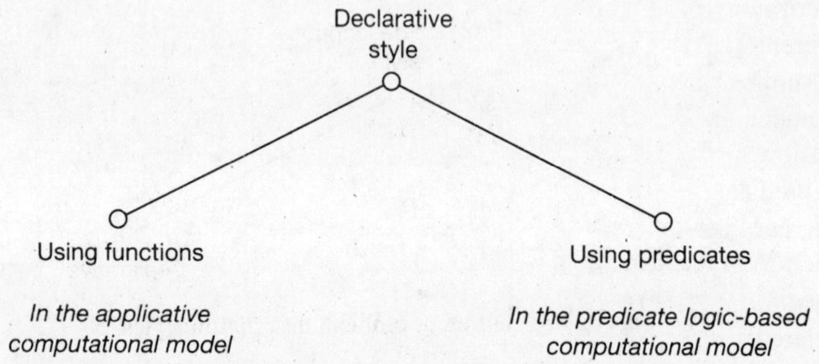

Figure 1.7 Fundamental methods of declarative problem description.

The other component of the problem description model is the **problem description method**. It is interpreted differently for the procedural and the declarative style. When using the procedural style the problem description model states how a *solution* of the given problem has to be described. In contrast, while using the declarative style, it specifies how the *problem* itself has to be described. For instance, in the von Neumann computational model a problem solution is actually described as a sequence of instructions expressing an appropriate algorithm. In the applicative model, a problem itself is described by stating a particular set of functions which expresses the relationships and facts characteristic of the given problem. The problem description methods for each of the basic computational models are summarized in Section 1.2.

The third, and last, element of the computational model outlines the **execution model**. It consists of three components, as shown in Figure 1.8.

The first component declares the **interpretation of the computation**, which is strongly related to the problem description method. The choice of problem description method and the interpretation of the computation mutually determine and presume each other. Consider the case of the von Neumann computational model where the problem is described as a sequence of instructions specifying data and control manipulations. The computation has to be interpreted as the execution of the given sequence of instructions. This component is examined in more detail in Section 1.3.

The next component of the execution model specifies the **execution semantics**. This can be interpreted as a *rule* that prescribes *how a single execution step* is to be performed. This rule is, of course, associated with the chosen problem

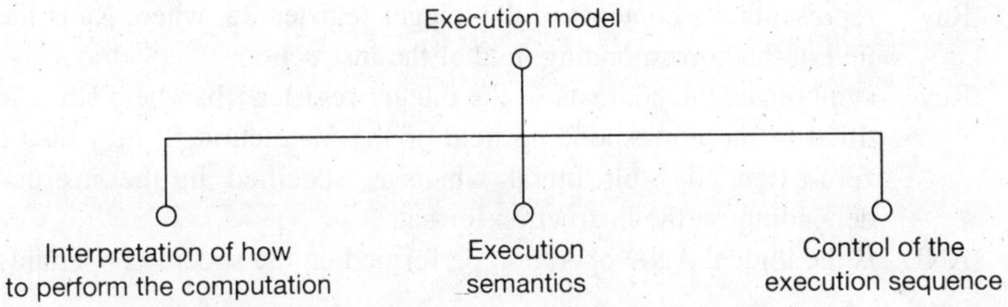

Figure 1.8 Interpretation of the execution model.

description method and how the execution of the computation is interpreted. The different kinds of execution semantics applied by the basic computational models are summarized in Figure 1.9. *State transition semantics* is used in the Turing, von Neumann and object-based models, *dataflow semantics* in the corresponding dataflow model, *reduction semantics* in the applicative model and *SLD-resolution* in the predicate-logic-based computational model. Here, we do not go into details the different kinds of semantics mentioned, but refer to related publications.

We can illustrate the concept of execution semantics by briefly outlining *state transition semantics*. State transition semantics presumes that the concept of state is declared for the model in question. Then, the state transition semantics states, for each instruction, how the actual state will be modified. This is declared, for example in the von Neumann model for a given processor, by the semantic definition of the particular instructions, usually in a processor-specific description language. For instance, in case of DEC's Alpha architecture the semantics of an AND instruction is specified in the following way (Sites, 1992):

```
Rc | Rav AND Rbv
```

where

Rc is the contents of a specified integer register. Rc is identified in the corresponding field of the instruction.

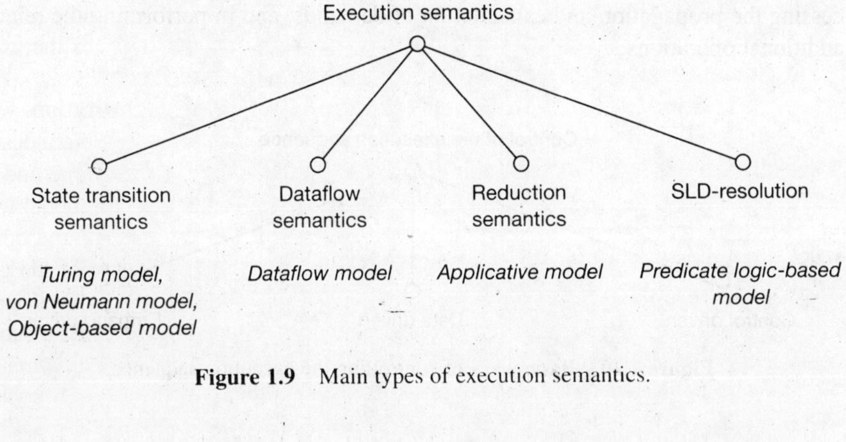

Figure 1.9 Main types of execution semantics.

Rav represents the contents of the integer register Ra, where Ra is identified in the corresponding field of the instruction.

Rbv symbolizes the contents of the integer register Rb, where Rb is identified in the corresponding field of the instruction. It may also be a zero-extended 8-bit literal which is specified in the instruction, depending on the instruction format.

AND is the logical AND operation performed on the specified operands.

Here, the modification of the contents of Rc is only part of the state modification. The value (that is, the state) of the Program Counter will also be modified (incremented by 4). In general, state modification can also include the setting of declared status bits or condition codes in a prescribed way.

The last component of the model specifies the **control of the execution sequence**. In the basic models, execution is either control driven or data driven or demand driven (Figure 1.10).

For **control-driven execution** it is assumed that there exists a program consisting of a sequence of instructions. The *execution sequence* is then *implicitly* given by the order of the instructions. However, *explicit control instructions* can also be used to specify a departure from the implied execution sequence. In the von Neumann model and the object-based computation model, control-driven execution is taken for granted.

Data-driven execution is characterized by the rule that an operation is activated *as soon as all the needed input data is available*. This mode of sequence control is also called **eager evaluation** for obvious reasons. Data-driven execution control is characteristic of the dataflow model of computation.

In **demand-driven execution** the operations will be activated only when their *execution is needed* to achieve the final result. This mode of execution control is also called **lazy evaluation** because the 'delayed until needed' philosophy is applied. Demand-driven execution control is typically used in the applicative computational model.

Comparing the data- and demand-driven modes of execution control, we see that data-driven computation activates a great deal of unnecessary computation by evaluating all conditional operations. Demand-driven computation, on the other hand, avoids superfluous computation, but it usually incurs a high overhead in processing the propagation and cancellation of demands, and in performing the related additional operations.

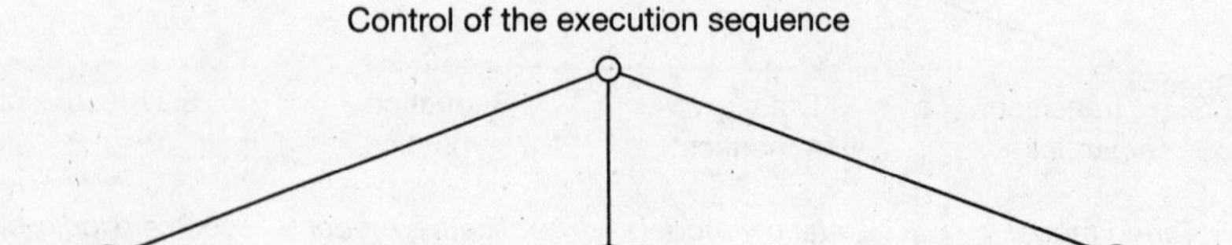

Figure 1.10 Basic ways of controlling the execution sequence.

1.1.3 Relationships between the concepts of computational model, programming language and architecture

As we have seen, the concept of a computational model is a higher-level abstraction than the concepts of programming language and computer architecture. A *programming language* can be thought of as a *specification tool* making possible the formulation of a computational task whereby a particular computational model is presumed. A *computer architecture* may be looked upon as a *tool to implement a computational model*, or to execute a given computational task expressed by means of a programming language, whereby a particular computational model is given (see Figure 1.11).

In order to illustrate these relationships we will examine the basic features of the programming languages and computer architectures that correspond to the *von Neumann computational model.*

A programming language corresponding to this model should allow variables to be declared and their values to be manipulated (altered) by means of a proper set of instructions as many times as required during computation (according to the state transition semantics briefly discussed earlier). Furthermore, the language should provide control instructions to allow explicit control of the execution sequence. Languages fulfilling these requirements are called **imperative languages**. The most widely used languages, such as C, Pascal, Fortran and so on, are all imperative languages.

It can easily be shown that **von Neumann architectures** suit the von Neumann computational model. Variables are implemented as addressable locations in memory, or registers, and, therefore, their values can be altered as many times as required. Sequence control is implemented by storing the instructions in memory and declaring a pointer, called the Program Counter, which indicates the instruction to be executed next.

Finally, it should be pointed out that new computational models, and their corresponding programming languages and architectures, usually evolve in the following sequence: computational model, programming language, computer architecture (Figure 1.12).

To emphasize this point, we quote the publication dates of literature on the dataflow principle of operation (Karp and Miller, 1966), dataflow (single assignment)

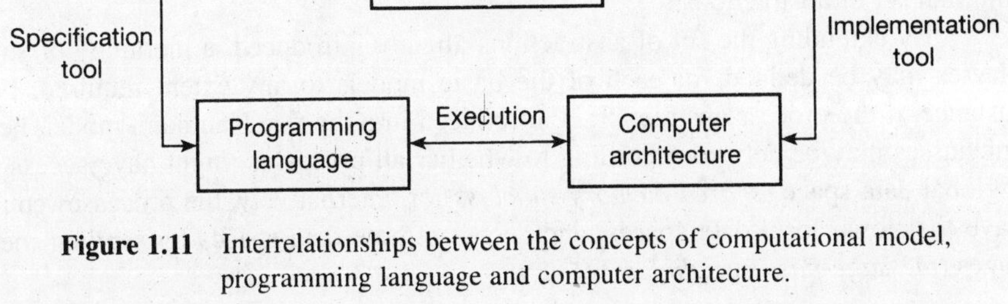

Figure 1.11 Interrelationships between the concepts of computational model, programming language and computer architecture.

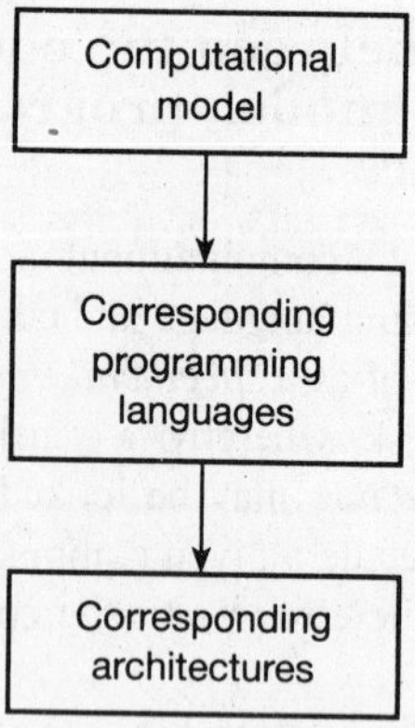

Figure 1.12 Typical evolution sequence of a computational model and the corresponding languages and architectures.

languages (Tesler and Enea, 1968) and dataflow architectures, as paper designs (Dennis and Misunas, 1975; Arvind and Gostelow, 1977) and as working experimental machines such as DDM1 in 1977 (Davis, 1978) or LAU in 1979 (Gurd et al., 1987).

Summing up, we can state that a number of basic computational models can be declared, each covering corresponding classes of language and architecture. In the next section we give an overview of the basic computational models along with the corresponding language and architecture classes.

1.2 Basic computational models

In this chapter we identify the following six basic computational models:

- Turing
- von Neumann
- dataflow
- applicative
- object based
- predicate logic based.

These models are called *basic models* because they may be declared using a minimal set of abstractions.

By extending the set of abstractions already introduced, a hierarchy of subclasses may be defined for each of the basic models to any extent required. For instance, if the process abstraction is introduced into the von Neumann model, new subclasses may be defined according to whether all processes might have access to a global data space *(shared memory subclass)* or, alternatively, the processes could have their own local data spaces, and access remote data spaces by sending messages *(message-passing subclass)*.

Table 1.2 Computational models, languages and architecture classes.

Computational model	*Language class*	*Architecture class*
Turing	'Type 0' languages	–
von Neumann	Imperative	Von Neumann
Dataflow	Single assignment (dataflow)	Dataflow
Applicative	Functional	Reduction
Object based	Object-oriented	Object-oriented
Predicate logic based	Logic programming	So far unnamed

In Table 1.2 we indicate the basic computational models and their corresponding languages and architecture classes. In order to give an overview and allow comparisons, the key features of the basic computational models are condensed in Figure 1.13, using the framework outlined in Section 1.1.2. Thus for each model we specify

- the basic items of computation,
- the problem description model and
- the execution model.

It is interesting to note that most basic models using a procedural problem description are inherently sequential, while others which use a declarative method of problem description are parallel. Here, we understand the inherent mode of concurrency to be that mode which fits the assumed execution model of the computational model considered. However, as already mentioned, all sequential models may be properly extended to provide concurrent execution. On the other hand, an inherently parallel model may also be implemented sequentially to reduce complexity (as, for example, in the early implementations of reduction architectures such as SKIM).

Although it would be tempting to summarize all the basic models mentioned, this would be beyond the scope of this book, so we confine ourselves to the brief description of the most salient basic model to date, namely the von Neumann computational model (Section 1.3).

1.3 The von Neumann computational model

1.3.1 Description of the model

We designate the underlying model of von Neumann computers and the corresponding languages as the **von Neumann computational model**. The key features of this oldest and most widely used data-based model may be summarized as follows (Figure 1.14).

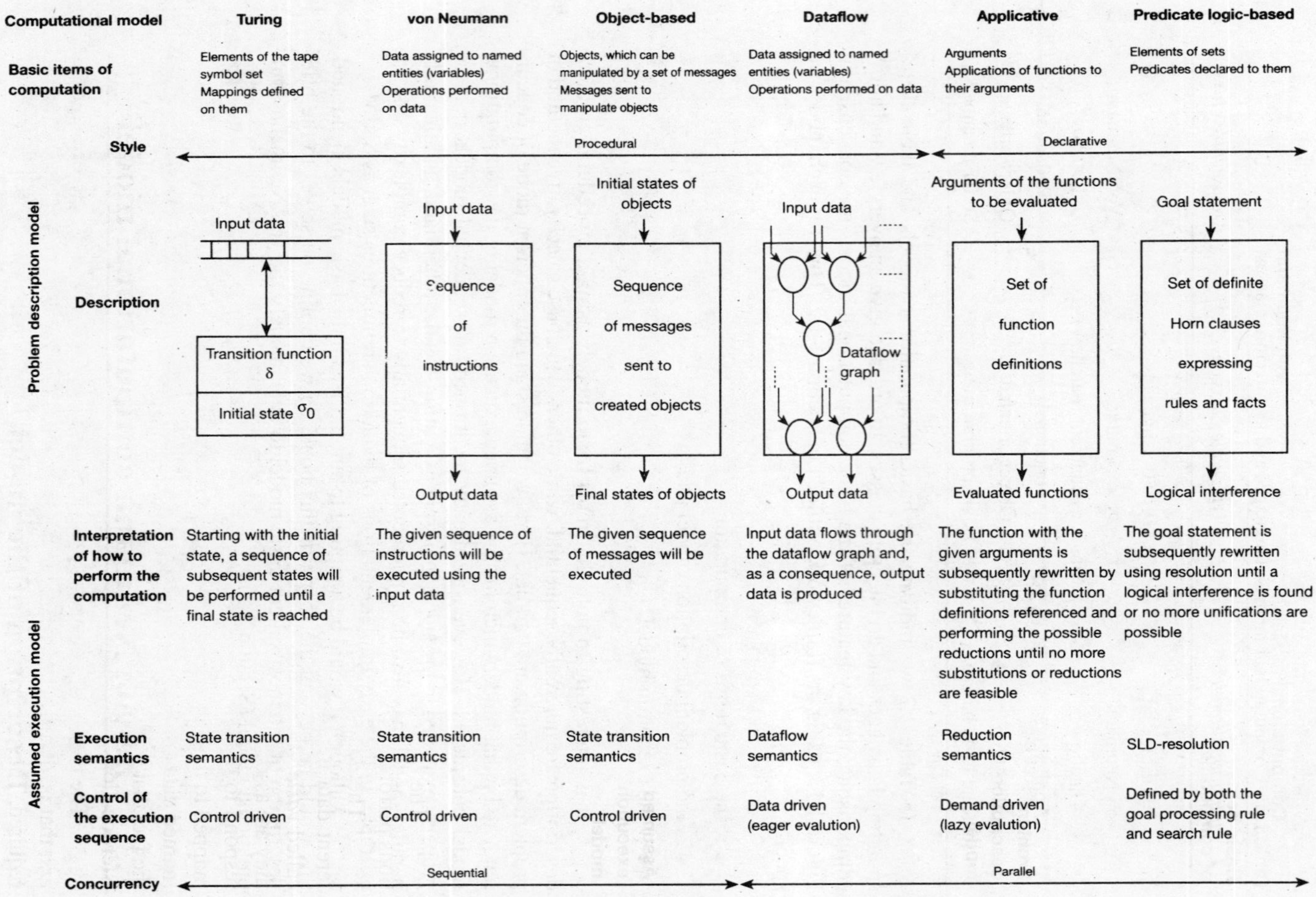

Figure 1.13 A summary of the key features of the basic computational models.

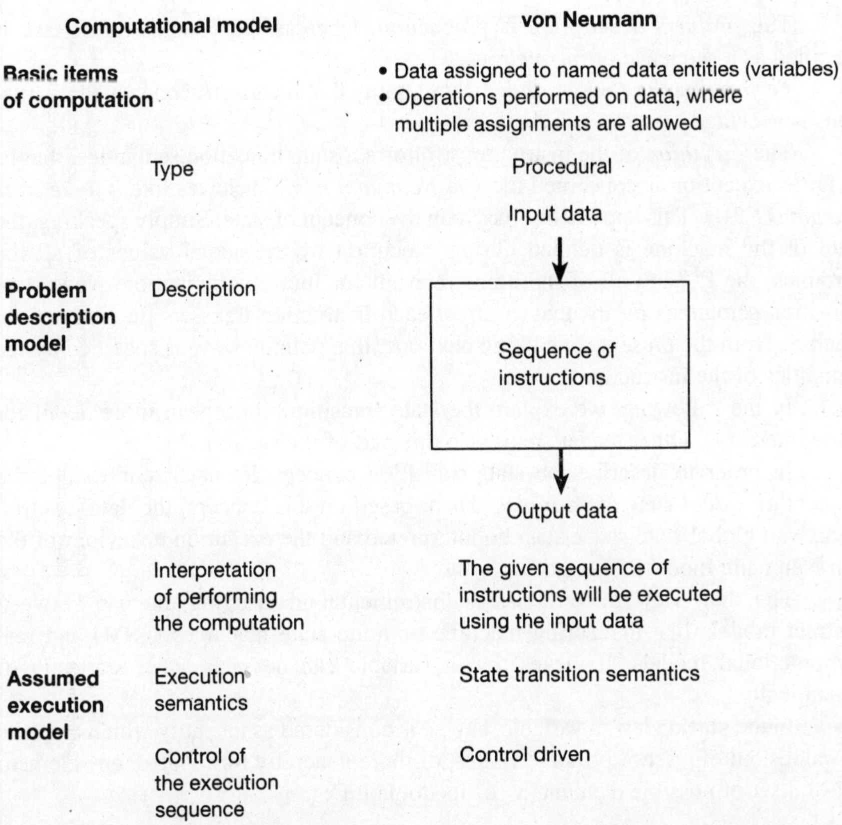

Figure 1.14 Key features of the von Neumann computational model.

The *basic items of computation* are data, where computation means operations performed on data.

The *data items* are identified by names in order to distinguish between different data items used in the same computation. These **named data entities** are called *variables* in programming languages. In architectures, during a computation they are associated with selected *memory or register locations* whose addresses correspond to the names of the variables. Memory and register addresses are usually mapped to the variable names by the compiler. In the following, instead of the term 'named data entity' we use the term 'variable' for ease of understanding, neglecting the fact that in architectures named data entities are implemented by memory or register locations rather than by variables.

The peculiarity of named data entities is that they behave like *data containers*; that is, during a computation they can be assigned new values as many times as required. They can keep the value they already have until a new value is assigned to them. This behaviour is expressed by saying that **multiple assignments** of data to variables are allowed, or in short, that multiple data assignments are allowed. In contrast, in the dataflow model of computation variables may be associated with data values only once (single assignment principle).

The *problem description* is procedural, whereas the computational task is specified as a sequence of instructions.

Performing the computation means simply that the given sequence of instructions is executed.

The *execution* of the instructions follows a state transition semantics; that is, as far as execution is concerned the *von Neumann model* behaves like *a finite state machine (FSM)*. This approach is based on the concept of state. Simply speaking, the state of the machine is defined during execution by the actual values of all the variables, the PC and all of the items relevant for future computation. Now, state transition semantics means that in effect each instruction transfers the state of the machine from the present state to the next one, in a definite way, as specified by the semantics of the instructions.

In the following, we explain the state transition concept in more detail for those interested. Other readers may skip this part of the section.

In order to describe the state transition concept, let us first introduce the concept of a *dual view of variables*. Then, based on this concept, the data, control, status and global state spaces can be interpreted and the execution behaviour of the von Neumann model discussed.

The dual view of variables is instrumental in bridging the gap between abstract models like the Turing machine or finite state machines (FSM) and real computational models. It means that a variable can be seen either statically or dynamically.

In the **static view**, a variable, say v_i, is considered as an entity which can take on values out of a set of possible values, or more generally formulated, any element out of a set of possible elements v_{ij} of its domain D:

$$\mathbf{v_i \in D_i \qquad D_i = \{ v_{i1} \ldots v_{ik}, \ldots v_{in} \} \ \forall_{i,j}} \qquad \textbf{(1.1)}$$

For example, if v_i is an 8-bit signed binary integer, then in the static view v_i is seen as a variable which can take on any integer value out of its domain, that is, out of the set of integers $D_i = \{-128, -127, \ldots -1, 0, 1, \ldots 127\}$.

On the other hand, a variable, say v_i, can also be considered *dynamically*, that is, during the execution of a computation. In this respect v_i will be seen as initialized, say at a time t_1 to v_i^1, and subsequently its value will be modified at $t_2, t_3, \ldots t_k, \ldots t_m$ to $v_i^2, v_i^3, \ldots v_i^k, \ldots v_i^m$, respectively, where

$$\mathbf{v_i^k \in D_i \qquad (i = 1, 2, \ldots m)} \qquad \textbf{(1.2)}$$

as indicated in Figure 1.15.

This dynamic behaviour is expressed by saying that a variable also has a **dynamic view**. It means that a variable v_i can have different *states* during execution. The *set of possible states* that v_i can take on is called **the data state space** (Figure 1.16). It is determined by the domain of the variable $D_i = \{ v_{i1}, \ldots v_{ij}, \ldots v_{in} \}$.

During computation, at $t_1, t_2, \ldots t_k, \ldots t_m$ v_i takes the states $v_i^1, v_i^2, \ldots v_i^k, v_i^m$, which correspond to the actual values of v_i, say to $v_{i3}, v_{il} \ldots$, respectively, as depicted in Figure 1.17.

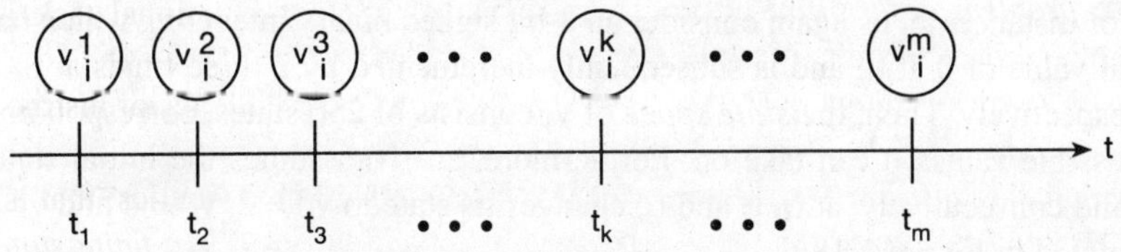

Figure 1.15 Dynamic view of a named entity v_i during computation.

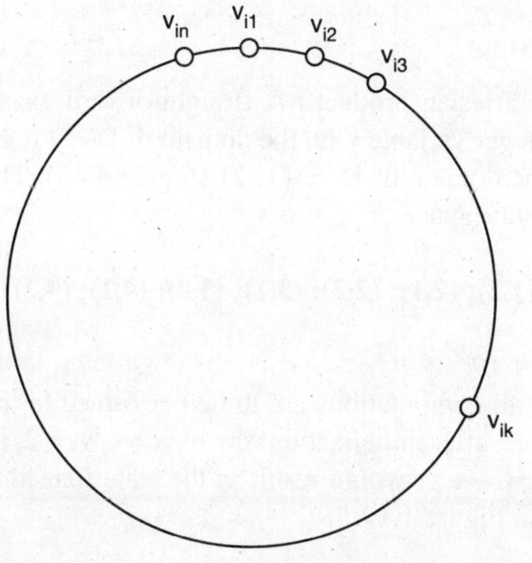

Figure 1.16 The state space of a named entity v_i according to the dynamic view.

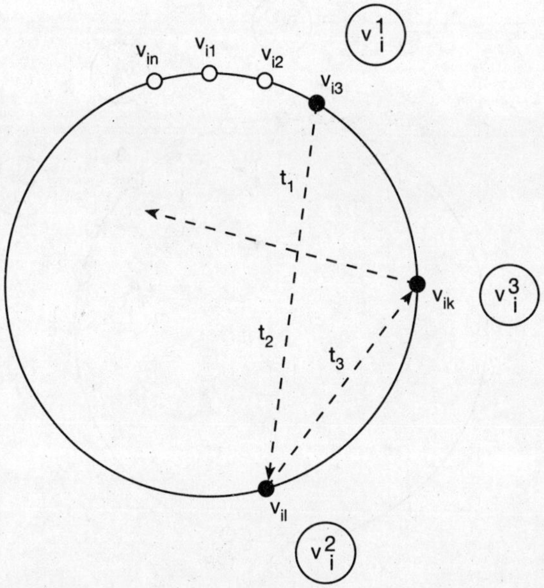

Figure 1.17 Dynamic view of a named entity v, during computation.

For instance, let us again consider an 8-bit signed binary integer v_i, which has the initial value of 0 at t_1, and is subsequently incremented by 2 three times at t_2, t_3 and t_4, respectively. Then, the *state space* of v_1 consists of 256 states, corresponding to the possible values it can take on. Furthermore, at t_1 v_i assumes the initial state, $v_i^1 = 0$, and consecutively, at t_2, t_3 and t_4, changes its state to $v_i^2 = 2$, $v_i^3 = 4$ and $v_i^4 = 6$, as depicted in Figure 1.18.

Next, let us consider two variables v_i and v_k, each with domain D_i and D_k. Then these two variables constitute a *data state space* D of:

$$\mathbf{D = D_i \times D_k} \qquad (1.3)$$

(This denotes the Cartesian product.) A straightforward example should illustrate this. Let v_i be an integer variable with the domain of $D_i = \{1, 2, 3, 4\}$ and v_k an integer variable with the domain of $D_k = \{1, 2\}$ (Figure 1.19). Then v_i and v_k together constitute the data state space of

$$\mathbf{D = \{(1,1); (1,2); (2,1); (2,2); (3,1); (3,2); (4,1); (4,2)\}} \qquad (1.4)$$

as shown in Figure 1.19.

In this case, all computations are to be performed in the specified data state space D. For example, after initialization, say to $v_i = 1$, $v_k = 2$, the initial state is (1,2) and an addition $v_i := v_i + v_k$ would result in the state transition to the new state of (3,2), as indicated in Figure 1.19.

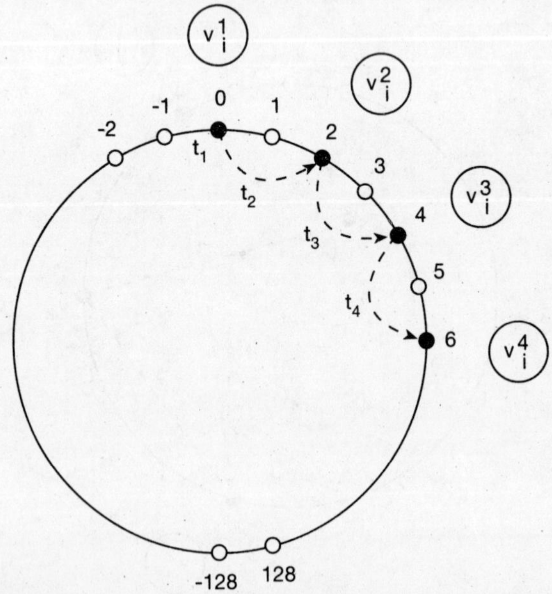

Figure 1.18 State transitions of a named entity v_i during computation.

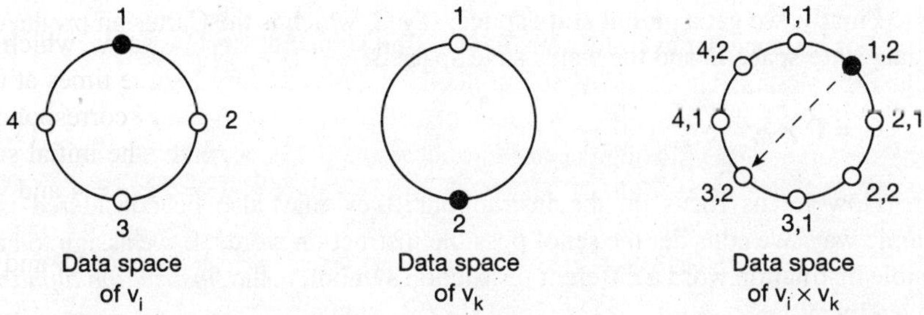

Figure 1.19 State spaces of v_i, v_k and $v_i \times v_k$, as well as the state transition after initialization (v_i=1, v_k=2) and performing $v_i := v_i + v_k$.

Now, we can extend the concept of the data space for any set of variables. A a set of variables, say v_i (i = 1, ..., m), constitutes a **data state space D** as follows:

$$\mathbf{D = v_1 \times \ldots \times v_i \times \ldots \times v_m} \qquad \textbf{(1.5)}$$

As well as the data state space we have to take into account the **control state space**. This is the state space which is spanned by the possible states during controlling the execution. Let us identify the instructions with the integers 1,2,...,i,...,n. Then the set of possible control states C, that is, the control state space, is given by:

$$\mathbf{C = \{1,2,\ldots,i,\ldots,n\}} \qquad \textbf{(1.6)}$$

where n is the largest instruction identifier. Here, the actual state of the control state space is the identifier of the instruction under execution.

There is also a third possible component of the state space, which we call additional status space. This kind of state space is often declared in low-level languages or architectures for testing and for the processing of exceptions, errors and so on. The additional status space in composed of all the flags (conditional codes and so on) which indicate specific or exceptional conditions during execution (such as overflow, carry, sign and so on).

Let us suppose that the additional status space consists of additional *status entities* (say, flags) $f_1,\ldots,f_i\ldots,f_v$, each of which is given as a set of allowable values

$$\mathbf{F_i = \{ f_{i1},\ldots,f_{ij},\ldots,f_{iw} \} \quad i = 1, 2, \ldots, v \text{ and } v_j} \qquad \textbf{(1.7)}$$

Then the **additional status state space**, say F, is given by

$$\mathbf{F = F_1 \times F_2 \times \ldots \times F_i \times \ldots \times F_v} \qquad \textbf{(1.8)}$$

Thus, the overall **status state space**, say S, may be expressed as

$$\mathbf{S = C \times F} \qquad \textbf{(1.9)}$$

Finally, we get a **global state space**, say G, which is the Cartesian product of the data state space D and the status state space S:

$$\mathbf{G = D \times S} \tag{1.10}$$

Now let us focus on the instructions, they may also be considered in a dynamic way. We consider the set of possible instruction words. If we assign to each possible instruction word a different instruction symbol, ι_i, the *'instruction alphabet'* is given by

$$\iota = \{\iota_1, \iota_2, \ldots \iota_i, \ldots \iota_f\} \tag{1.11}$$

Let us assume that the program consists of the instruction sequence i_p.

$$\mathbf{i_p} = \iota^1, \iota^2, \ldots \iota^i, \ldots \iota^z \tag{1.12}$$

Then each instruction i^i brings about a new global state G^{i+1}, according to the semantics of the executed instruction i^i:

$$G^{i+1} \leftarrow (G^i, i^i) \tag{1.13}$$

Now we are in a position to state that instruction execution in the von Neumann model of computation is carried out according to a final state machine (FSM):

$$\mathbf{FSM} = \{\, \iota, G, \delta, G_0, G_f \,\} \tag{1.14}$$

in which

- ι: the input alphabet, given as the set of the instruction alphabet;
- G: the set of the (global) states;
- δ: the transition function δ, which specifies for each instruction and actual value of the global state space (G) the new value of the global state space, that is, the value of the data state space (result), control state space (next instruction) and the additional status state space (flags or condition code):

$$\delta: \iota \times G \rightarrow G, \text{ with } G = D \times C \times F \tag{1.15}$$

- G_0: the initial state;
- G_f: the final state.

Thus, the *execution semantics* of the von Neumann computational model can formally be defined as *a state transition semantics*.

This consideration is obviously only of theoretical interest because of the enormous and unmanageable complexity of the global state space involved.

However, it pinpoints the equivalence of the inherent execution mechanism of the von Neumann computational model and that of an FSM.

As a last remark, it is probably worth noting that the concept of an FSM (attributed to McCulloch and Pitts (1943), see also Hopcroft and Ullmann (1969)) preceded by only two years von Neumann's seminal publication which describes the principle of operation of computers (von Neumann, 1945).

The execution sequence is control driven, as discussed in Section 1.1.2.

1.3.2 Key characteristics of the von Neumann model

The main attributes of the model follow from the possibility of multiple assignments of data as well as from the control-driven execution.

Consequences of multiple assignments of data

A consequence of multiple assignments is that the values of the variables may be modified during the execution of each data manipulation instruction. This means that the actual values of the variables are **history sensitive**, that is, they are dependent on the actual sequence of the executed instructions.

Obvious examples of history sensitivity are loop variables. Another way of expressing history sensitivity is to say that the variables **are not referentially transparent**. This expression stresses the fact that the actual values of the variables are not independent of the actual point of execution.

There exists a special case of history sensitivity called **side effects**. In the context of the von Neumann model of computation, it is usually interpreted as an unwanted, marginal modification of the state, for example of global variables. As an example, consider the case when a procedure invocation modifies the value of a variable which is out of the scope of the programmer.

An illustrative example of side effects is given by Field and Harrison (1988), shown below. Let us consider the following short program using Pascal syntax:

```
program example(output)
var flag : boolean;
function f( n : integer ):integer;
begin
if flag
  then f := n
  else f := 2*n;
flag := not flag;
end;
begin
  flag := true;
  writeln(f(1) + f(2));
end.
```

The execution of this program results in the printout:

f(1) + f(2) = 5
f(2) + f(1) = 4

In everyday mathematical reasoning we would expect that

$$f(1) + f(2) = f(2) + f(1)$$

because of the commutativity of the addition. However, the marginal operation

flag := **not** flag;

causes the side effect indicated in the printout listed above.

History sensitivity and, especially, side effects put a heavy burden on the programmer, particularly during program testing.

State transition semantics presumes the existence of **state**, which means that the variables have a *dynamic* nature; that is, they can take on new values as often as required and they preserve those values until new values are assigned. The state transition semantics also presumes the possibility of multiple assignment of data to the variables. To put it another way, state transition semantics and multiple assignments are interchangeable concepts.

Consequences of control-driven execution

Because the computational task is specified as an ordered sequence of instructions and the execution sequence of these instructions is control-driven, this model of computation is basically a *sequential* one. Such an essentially sequential problem description forces sequential processing even in those cases where the problem is inherently parallel, for example:

$$z = (a + b) * (c + d)$$

In this case the terms (a+b) resp. (c+d) could obviously be calculated in parallel. Nevertheless, the computational model enforces a serialization which could be expressed something like:

$z_1 = a + b \qquad z_2 = c + d \qquad z = z_1 * z_2$

This imposed serialization often hides potential parallelism inherent in the problem and gives rise to serial and, therefore, time-consuming execution. Serial execution is often intolerable, in particular for massively parallel problems such as numerical problems using vector or matrix calculus.

1.3.3 Related languages

Languages implementing the von Neumann model of computation should allow the declaration of variables with multiple assignments of data values, offer an adequate set of operations on them, and provide a proper set of control statements to implement the control-driven mode of execution. These languages are often called **imperative languages**, emphasizing the possibility of multiple assignments, or sometimes **procedural languages**, pinpointing the procedural nature of the problem description that they support. Because the procedural style of problem description is used in more than one computational model, in the following we prefer to use the term '*imperative languages*' to denote the language class corresponding to the von Neumann computational model. Examples of imperative languages are C, Pascal, ALGOL, Fortran, and so on.

Architectures with the underlying von Neumann model of computation are called **von Neumann architectures**. They should provide a memory with addressable and rewritable locations to implement variables with multiple assignment and preserve their states. Furthermore they should maintain a pointer, called the Program Counter, which points to the instruction to be executed to implement the control-driven mode of execution. Lastly they should contain adequate data and control manipulation facilities (processing unit, control unit) to implement the state transition semantics.

Von Neumann architectures are, at present, the most widely used class of architectures because of their relative simplicity and effectiveness for general computational tasks. Examples are all the well-known architecture families like the IBM 360/370 series, DEC PDP/11 and VAX families, or all the widely used microprocessors such as the Intel 80x86 and Pentium processors, Motorola 68000 and 88000 families, the MIPS R series, the Sparc processors, members of the PowerPC family, and others.

Both imperative languages and von Neumann architectures inherit the fundamental *drawbacks and limitations* of their underlying model of computation, namely

- history sensitivity (side effects, lack of referential transparency)
- basically sequential nature of execution (word-at-a-time execution).

However, this model has, from the architectural point of view, a significant *advantage*: it can easily be implemented. This seems to be the main reason for the clear dominance of the von Neumann model of computation at present, in spite of fierce criticism and a huge amount of research and development work carried out on alternative models.

1.3.4 Extensions of the von Neumann computational model

The basic von Neumann model may be enhanced in many directions by extending the set of abstractions already considered, so that we have subclasses, sub-subclasses and so on of the basic model. For example, the fundamental constraint of sequentiality can be relaxed by introducing a new abstraction of *parallelly executable pieces of computation*, usually called *processes* or *threads*. For parallel execution, proper mechanisms must be provided for communication, synchronization and data sharing (see Chapter 3).

The **communication mechanism** allows the transfer of data (parameters) between executable units. The most widely used mechanisms are (see Andrews and Schneider (1983)):

- unprotected shared (global) variables,
- shared variables protected by modules or monitors,
- message passing, and
- rendezvous.

The **synchronization mechanism** allows us to impose restrictions on the execution sequence of the executable units.

Commonly used methods are (again according to Andrews and Schneider (1983)):

- semaphores
- signals
- events
- queues
- barrier synchronization.

A **data sharing mechanism** is needed to declare whether parallel executable units (processes) are allowed to access a common data space (**shared variable concept**), or whether distinct processes have access only to their local data spaces. Also, a communication mechanism should be provided for accessing data pertaining to other processes (often termed the **message-passing concept**).

Thus, by extending the set of abstractions and taking into account key aspects and possible approaches to cope with them, we can arrive at a large number of subclasses of the basic model.

1.4 Key concepts relating to computational models

1.4.1 Granularity

As discussed earlier, one of the vital decisions relating to a computational model concerns the types of item that the computation should be performed on and the kinds of operation allowed on them. Possible alternatives are data, objects, sets and so on, along with the declared operations. These items and operations may, however be, of quite different *complexity*. In order to reflect the complexity of the items of computation, it makes sense to introduce the concept of **granularity**. Then items of computation can be informally classified as *fine-grained* or *coarse-grained*, according to their complexity; in some cases *middle-grained* items of computation can also be distinguished. Accordingly, as far as von Neumann architectures are concerned, RISC, conventional CISC, HLL and application-oriented architectures may be distinguished as *subclasses with increasing granularity* (Figure 1.20).

The concept of granularity was introduced in connection with parallel architectures as well. In this case the granularity refers to the size of the computations that can be executed in parallel without any synchronization or communication. Usually, the parallelism of individual operations is designated as fine-grain parallelism, while parallelism at the thread or process level is called coarse-grained parallelism. Examples of this interpretation are the fine-grain and coarse-grain dataflow and reduction architectures given in Table 1.3.

Table 1.3 Examples of fine-grain and coarse-grain dataflow and reduction architectures.

Architecture type		*Examples*
Dataflow	**Fine grain**	Dataflow machines such as: The Manchester Dataflow Computer (e.g. Gurd et al., 1987), SIGMA-1 (Hiraki et al., 1987)
	Coarse grain	LGDG (Dai and Gilois, 1990 The Stallmann Data Flow Machine (Glück-Hiltrop et al., 1989), ADAM (Maquelin, 1990)
Reduction	**Fine grain**	Reduction machines such as: Flagship (Watson et al., 1987), GRIP (Pyton Jones et al., 1987)
	Coarse grain	Dutch Parallel Reduction Machine (Hertzberger and Vree, 1989)

Clearly, the computation/communication ratio is better in coarse-grain systems. On the other hand, the exploitable parallelism is usually much less in coarse-grain systems than in fine-grain parallel systems.

It is useful to introduce the concept of granularity at a higher abstraction level as well, that is, in connection with computational models. Concerning computational models, the granularity will be understood in a more general sense than discussed before. This means that in sequential environments the granularity is interpreted as the complexity of the items of computation, whereas in parallel environments as the size of parallel computations. This interpretation is vague and imprecise, but concerning granularity it yields a unified framework for both architectures and languages.

In Figure 1.20 we give an overview of the unified interpretation of granularity for different architecture classes.

Concerning languages, conventional *assembly languages* can be thought of as fine-grained, while conventional *high-level languages* are coarse-grained (Figure 1.21).

Granularity	Architecture class: von Neumann	Dataflow	Reduction
Low	RISC	Fine grain	Fine grain
	Conventional		
		(Medium grain)	(Medium grain)
	CISC		
	HLL	Coarse grain	Coarse grain
High	Application-oriented		

Figure 1.20 The interpretation of granularity for different architecture classes.

1.4.2 Typing

Typing is another concept which is worth introducing at a higher level as it is often used in connection with programming languages. If the concept of typing is introduced at the abstraction level of the computational model, typing of languages and tagging of architectures are closely associated.

In **typed languages** there exists a concept of *data type* and the language system (compiler or interpreter) may check the consistency of the types used in expressions, function invocations and so on. If the language is **strongly typed**, a type mismatch will cause an error. In **weakly typed** languages, a type mismatch is allowed under given circumstances, namely if the types involved are consistent.

LISP and FP are examples of untyped languages. Pascal, Miranda and HOPE are strongly typed languages, whereas the single assignment language Sisal is weakly typed.

Typed architectures are commonly called **tagged**. They provide a mechanism for typing the data being stored or processed, by extending the data word by a **tag**. The tags (usually 3–5 bits long) contain the type-identification.

Granularity	Language class
Low	Conventional assembly languages
High	Conventional high-level languages

Figure 1.21 The interpretation of granularity for programming languages.

Table 1.4 Typing-related concepts of languages and architectures.

Computational model		*Typed items*	*Languages*	*Architecture*
Data-based	**Typed**	Data types	Typed (strongly, weakly)	Tagged
	Untyped	–	Untyped or typeless	Untagged
Object-based	**Typed**	Object classes	Intrinsically typed	Intrinsically typed
	Untyped	–	–	–

Tagging first appeared towards the end of the 1950s in architecture proposals and implementations such as the Merlin Machine (1957), the RICE computer (1959) and the Burroughs B5000 (1960), as stated in the surveys of Feustel (1973) or Levi (1986). Tagging was considered as a means to bridge the gap between the untyped von Neumann architectures and the widely used typed languages. Tagging results in comprehensible storage dumps, and it makes run-time type checking feasible. Thus, tagging can considerably shorten the time needed to test programs.

However, tagging never attained mainstream status. General-purpose mainline computer families such as IBM/360, IBM/370, DEC PDP-11, VAX, 80x86 or the more recent Sparc, DEC Alpha and PowerPC lines remained untagged.

When typing is understood already at the level of the computational model, typed languages and tagged architectures appear as implementations of typed computational models, and vice versa. Accordingly, in Table 1.4 we summarise the typing-related concepts of languages, architectures and computational models. Here we take into account only data- and object-based computational models.

In the table the Turing and predicate-logic-based models are omitted since, to the best of the authors' knowledge, typing has not been introduced for languages or architectures belonging to these models.

The object-based model is inherently typed. This feature will obviously be inherited by object-oriented languages and architectures.

2 The Concept of Computer Architecture

In Section 2.1, we describe briefly how computer architectures evolved and then discuss the more recent interpretation of the concept of computer architecture, which is seen as a number of levels of abstraction. Section 2.2 describes these levels in detail. Section 2.3 introduces the concept of computer architecture as a multilevel hierarchical framework and Section 2.4 extends this to higher levels of abstraction, including operating systems. Section 2.5 looks at how computer architectures are described, including the use of architecture description languages (ADLs) and design-space (DS) trees.

2.1 Evolution and interpretation of the concept of computer architecture

Although the concept of computer architecture is unquestionably one of the basic concepts in informatics, at present there is no general agreement about its definition or interpretation. In the following, we first describe how this important concept has evolved. Then, we state our definition and interpretation.

2.1.1 Evolution of the concept

As far as the evolution of the concept of computer architecture is concerned, there are four major steps to be emphasized, which will be overviewed as follows.

The term '*computer architecture*' was coined in 1964 by the 'chief architects' of the IBM System/360 (Amdahl et al., 1964) in a paper announcing the most successful family of computers ever built. They interpreted computer architecture as 'the structure of a computer that a machine language programmer must understand to write a correct (timing independent) program for a machine'. Essentially, their interpretation comprises the definition of registers and memory as well as of the instruction set, instruction formats, addressing modes and the actual coding of the instructions excluding implementation and realization. By *implementation* they understood the actual hardware structure and by realization the logic technology, packaging and interconnections.

Bell and Newell made an important contribution to the concept of computer architecture by introducing a *hierarchical, multilevel description* (Bell and Newell, 1970). They identified *four levels* that can be used for describing a computer. These are the *electronic circuit level*, the *logic design level*, the *programming level* and the *processor-memory-switch (PMS) level*. The third level refers to the concept of architecture mentioned above. The fourth level is a top-level description of a computer system based on the specification of the basic units like the processor, memory, and so on, as well as their interconnections.

The next step in refining the concept of computer architecture was *to extend* the concept of architecture equally *to both the functional specification* and *the hardware implementation* (Sima, 1977; Dasgupta, 1981).

Since the authors just quoted also made use of the multilevel description approach, they introduced a *'two-dimensional' interpretation*. Here, one of the 'dimensions' is the level of abstraction, in much the same way as introduced by Bell and Newell (1970). The other, orthogonal 'dimension' is the scope of interest. Here, they differentiate at each level between a black-box-like *functional specification* and the description of the *implementation*. Correspondingly, they distinguish between 'logical' and 'physical' architecture (Sima, 1977) and endo- and exo-architecture (Dasgupta, 1981), respectively.

As pointed out later in this section, the two dimensions considered by these authors, constitute single, hierarchical description framework with increasing levels of abstraction.

Although this interpretation of the architecture concept is quite useful for a broad range of computers, it has a deficiency. It assumes the use of the von Neumann model of computation. Therefore, in order to generalize the concept of computer architecture, we shall include in its definition a '*third dimension*', *the model of computation used*. We describe this in the next section.

2.1.2 Recent interpretation of the concept

We interpret the concept of computer architecture at a number of levels of increasing abstraction. At each level the architecture will be described by stating the underlying computational model, the functional specification as well as the actual implementation. Thus, our interpretation covers three aspects, as indicated in Figure 2.1: the underlying computational model, the level of consideration and the scope of interest.

First, we briefly overview the underlying computational model. A couple of years ago the term '*computer architecture*' was inherently interpreted as a von Neumann architecture. Subsequently, when novel architectures based on a model of computation other than the von Neumann model were introduced, these architectures were properly labelled, for example dataflow architecture, reduction architecture and so on. However, at present it is evident that the concept of computer architecture should include the specification of the underlying computational model as well. Here, we refer to Chapter 1, where the basic models of computation are discussed. Figure 2.2 recalls the most important models relating to architectures.

Concerning the level of consideration, there are mainly three levels of interest (in increasing degree of abstraction):

- the micromachine level (in microprogrammed processors),
- the processor level, and
- the computer-system level

as shown in Figure 2.3.

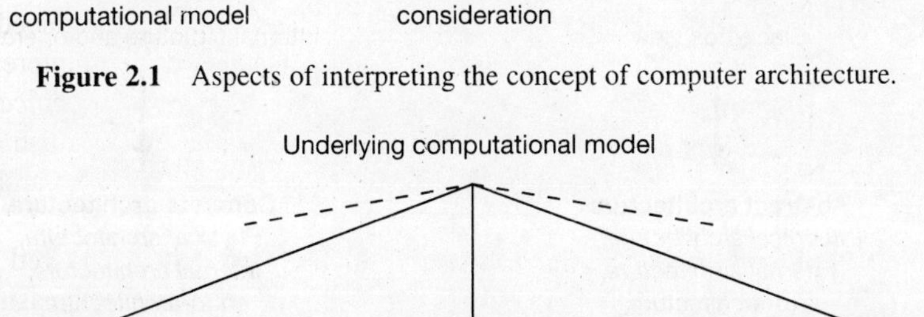

Figure 2.1 Aspects of interpreting the concept of computer architecture.

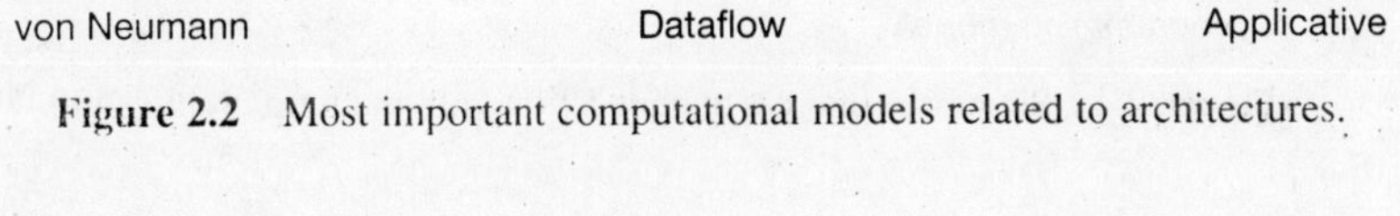

Figure 2.2 Most important computational models related to architectures.

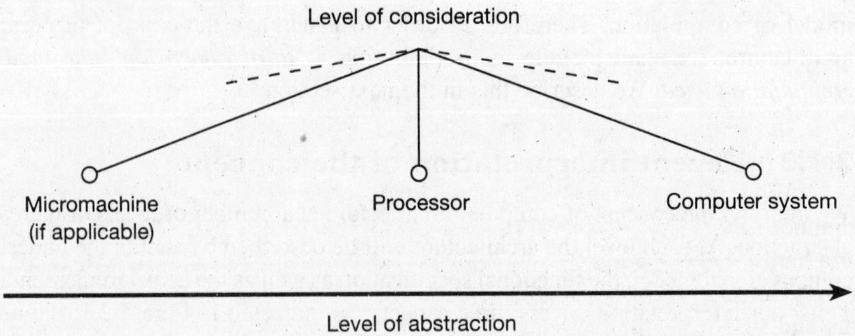

Figure 2.3 Levels of consideration in interpreting the concept of computer architecture.

The term 'architecture' can be used at each level of consideration with two distinct scopes of interest, as indicated in Figure 2.4. If we are interested in the *functional specification* of a computer, we are dealing with its **abstract architecture**. Or, if we are interested in its *implementation*, we are concerned with its **concrete architecture**. Evidently, the abstract architecture reflects the black-box view whereas the concrete architecture covers the description of the internal structure and operation.

The *abstract architecture* is also referred to as an *exo-architecture*, an *external* or *logical architecture*, *a black-box description*, or in certain contexts as a *programming model* and *behavioural description*.

The abstract architecture is a black-box specification

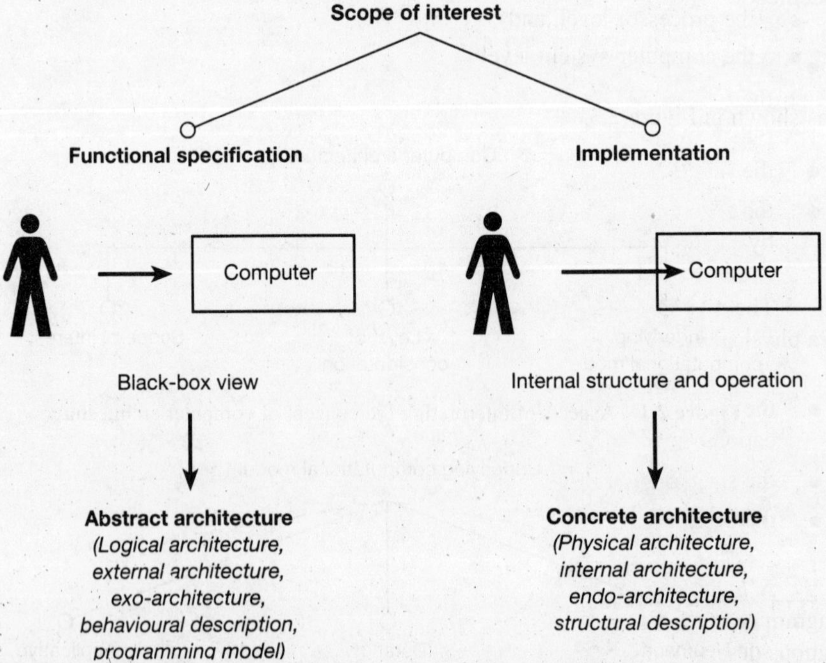

Figure 2.4 Scopes of interest in connection with the term architecture.

- either from the *programmer's point of view*, or
- from the hardware *designer's point of view*.

In the first case we are dealing with *the programming model*, in the second with the *hardware model*.

While the **programming model** is a black-box specification from the programmer's point of view, the **hardware model** is viewed as a black-box description for a hardware designer.

The latter must incorporate additional specifications such as interface protocols and so on. Therefore a more precise interpretation of the concept of abstract architecture should also include an indication of whether this term is to be understood from the programmer's viewpoint or from the hardware designer's viewpoint, except when this is self-explanatory.

Concrete architecture is designated by different authors as an *endo-architecture*, or sometimes as an *internal* or *physical architecture* or a *structural description*. It specifies how a computer is implemented at a particular level of abstraction, whereby a particular computational model is taken for granted. By *implementation* we mean the internal structure and operation, which may be given by specifying a set of components and their interconnections as well as the possible data- and control-flows.

The *concrete architecture* can also be considered from two different points of view: *logic design* or *physical design*.

The **logic design** is an abstraction of the physical design and precedes it. Its specification requires:

- the declaration of the logical components used (actually the declaration of their black-box behaviour, that is, of their abstract architecture), such as registers, execution units and so on,
- the specification of their interconnections, and
- the specification of the sequence of information transfers, which are initiated by each of the declared functions (operation, microinstruction or instruction).

The **physical design** is based on concrete circuit elements. The specification of a physical design covers:

- the declaration of the circuit elements used, which also includes the specification of signals,
- the specification of their interconnections, and
- the declaration of the initiated signal sequences.

A *logic design* will usually be described informally by means of a block diagram or formally by means of an ADL language (Section 2.5.2). A formal, unambiguous description is required when the logic design has to be passed on as input to a CAD package. The physical design is typically the output of a CAD package.

Usually, both the logic and physical design are described in terms of the next lower level of components. For example, the concrete architecture of a processor would be best described in terms of functional units such as register files, execution units, buses and so on.

Considering the variety of applicable computational models, levels of consideration and scope of interest, the concept of computer architecture covers a multitude of interpretations which are summarized in Figure 2.5.

For the reader who is interested in a more precise discussion of the concept of computer **architecture**, we make the following short discourse.

Formally the concept of computer **architecture** can be described at a given level i by the 3-tuple:

$$\mathbf{A_l := \{ P_i, S_{i,p}, I_{i,p} \}} \qquad \textbf{(2.1)}$$

where

- A_l: interpretation of the concept of architecture at level l;
- P_l: underlying computational model at level l;
- $S_{l,p}$: functional specification of the architecture assuming computational model P_l;
- $I_{l,p}$: implementation of the architecture, assuming the specification $S_{l,p}$;
- l: refers to one of the levels: micromachine level, processor level or computer system level.

If only the specification is of interest and points of implementation can be neglected, we speak of **abstract architecture** or simply architecture $A_{a,l}$:

$$\mathbf{A_{a,i} := \{ P_i, S_{ip} \}} \qquad \textbf{(2.2)}$$

If only the implementation is of concern, we are dealing with the **concrete architecture** $A_{c,i}$:

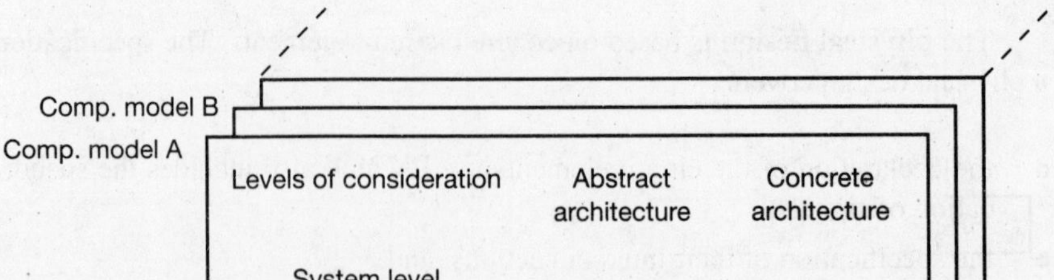

Figure 2.5 The multitude of interpretations of the concept of computer architecture.

$$\mathbf{A_{c,i} := \{ P_i, I_{i,p} \}} \quad (2.3)$$

As a consequence, the concept of **architecture** includes both views:

$$\mathbf{A_i := A_{a,i} \cup A_{c,i}} \quad (2.4)$$

2.2 Interpretation of the concept of computer architecture at different levels of abstraction

In this section we overview the most important particular interpretations of the concept of computer architecture. These are the concrete architecture at the system level, the abstract and concrete architecture at the processor level and the abstract and concrete architecture at the micromachine level. For simplicity, in our subsequent discussion we assume the von Neumann model as the underlying model of computation.

2.2.1 Concrete architectures of computer systems

At the *system level* the description of the concrete architecture is based on processor-level building blocks, such as processors, memories, buses and so on. Its description includes the specification of the building blocks, of the interconnections among them

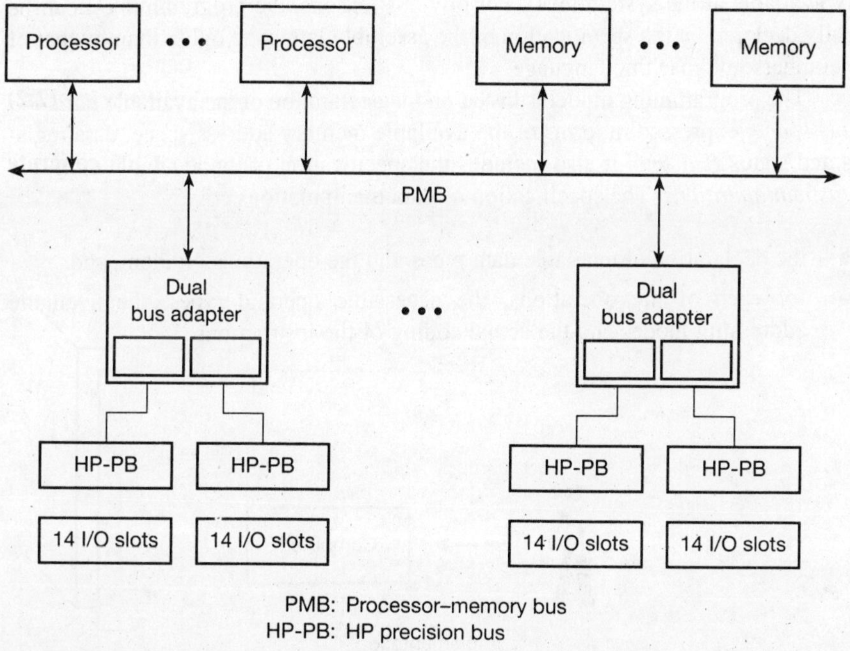

Figure 2.6 An example of concrete architecture at the system level (HP 9000 Corporate Business Servers (Chan et al., 1993)). © 1993 IEEE

and of the operation of the whole system. Figure 2.6 shows as an example the system-level concrete architecture of the HP 9000 Corporate Business Servers.

We note that the concept of concrete architecture of computer systems corresponds to the PMS level of description introduced by Bell and Newell (1970).

2.2.2 Abstract architecture of processors (architecture)

The **abstract architecture of a processor** is often referred to as simply the **architecture** of the processor. It reflects the black-box description of a processor, as indicated in Figure 2.7.

As mentioned previously, the black-box description can be considered from either the programmer's or the hardware designer's point of view. Thus, when speaking about the processor-level abstract architecture, we are concerned with either the *programming model* or the *hardware model* of a particular processor.

The *programming model* is equivalent to the description of the machine language. Consequently, our interpretation of the concept of architecture includes the original definition (as given by Amdahl et al., 1964). Thus, the original definition turns out to be the abstract architecture of the processor, when considered from the programmer's point of view, assuming the von Neumann model of computation.

The programming model, which is given by the machine language, is often described at two different privilege levels: the *user level* and the *system level*. Instructions such as I/O instructions and some status manipulation instructions are only available at the system level. For obvious reasons, the programming model is usually declared by the specification of the assembly language rather than by that of the cumbersome machine language.

The programming model is based on the declaration of the available *data and status space*, expressed in terms of the available memory address space, data registers and status registers. It also includes the specification of the available *data and status manipulations*. The specification of data manipulations covers:

- the declaration of available data types and the operations on them, and
- for each of the operations, the accessible operand types, the available addressing modes and the actual coding of the instructions.

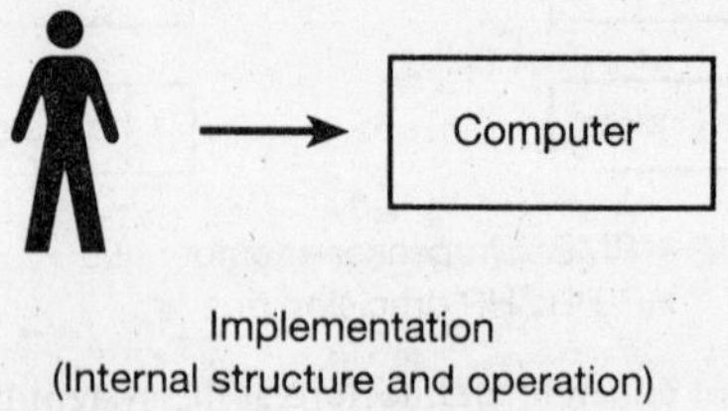

Figure 2.7 The interpretation of the processor-level abstract architecture.

The specification of status manipulation comprises:

- the declaration how status registers (such as flags) are set during instruction execution, and
- the declaration of control transfer instructions as well as further status manipulation instructions.

By contrast, the *hardware model of the processor* is a description from the hardware designer's point of view. Here, the processor is considered as a building block of a computer system. This can be specified by three interfaces: *the programming interface, the interrupt interface* and *the I/O interface* (Figure 2.8).

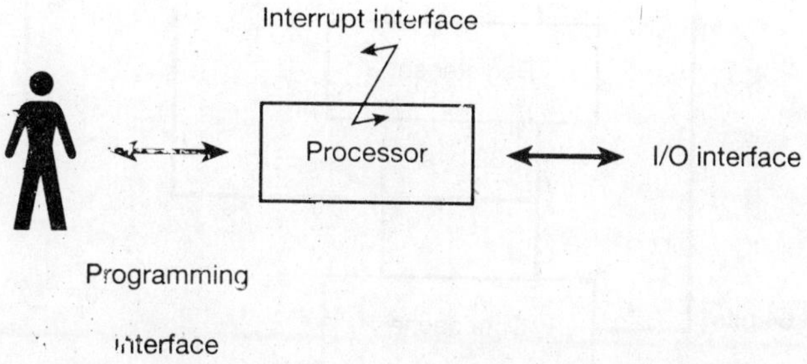

Figure 2.8 The abstract architecture of the processor viewed as a building block.

The programming interface is equivalent to the programming model. The other two interfaces specify the behaviour of the interrupt system and the I/O system, respectively. Here again, we do not go into details, but instead refer to introductory textbooks, such as Patterson and Henessy (1990), Baron and Higbie (1992) or Stone (1993).

2.2.3 Concrete architectures of processors (microarchitecture)

The **concrete architecture of a processor** is often referred to as the **microarchitecture**. In publications, the microarchitecture of processors is usually given as a *logic design*.

Usually, this is informally described by means of a block diagram, through the specification of a set of functional units (such as register blocks, buses, execution units and so on) and their interconnections, and by declaring the operation of the whole processor. Figure 2.9 shows as an example the simplified microarchitecture of the Pentium processor.

The microarchitecture as a *physical design* is usually detailed in technical documentation, which is in most cases proprietary information.

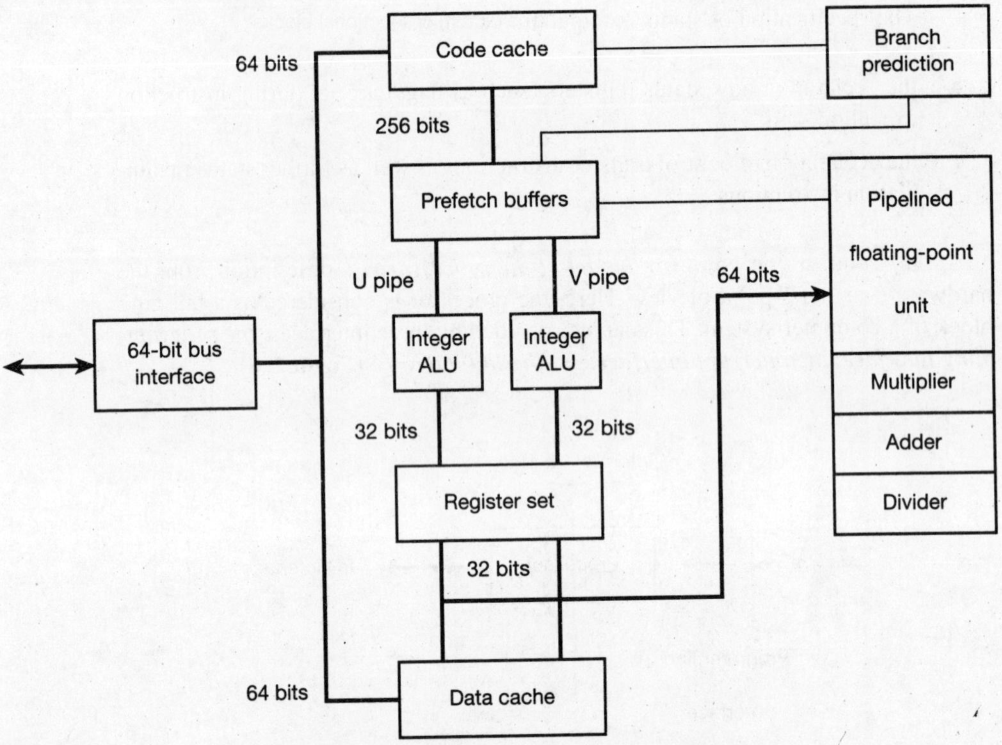

Figure 2.9 Simplified microarchitecture of the Pentium, given as a logic design (Alpert and Avnon, 1993). © IEEE 1993

2.2.4 Abstract and concrete architecture at the micromachine level

If the computer is microprogrammed, the **micromachine level** is also of interest. **The abstract architecture at the micromachine level** specifies the *microprogramming model* whereas the **concrete architecture at this level** describes the internal structure and operation of the micromachine.

The micromachine level was of much interest in connection with sequential microprogrammed computers. Recently this level has lost its importance.

2.3 The concept of computer architecture as a multilevel hierarchical framework

We remind the reader that the concrete architecture at a given level is usually described in terms of its components. Thus, the description of the concrete architecture at a given level is based on the abstract architectures of its components. As a consequence, the concrete architecture at a particular level is a description at a

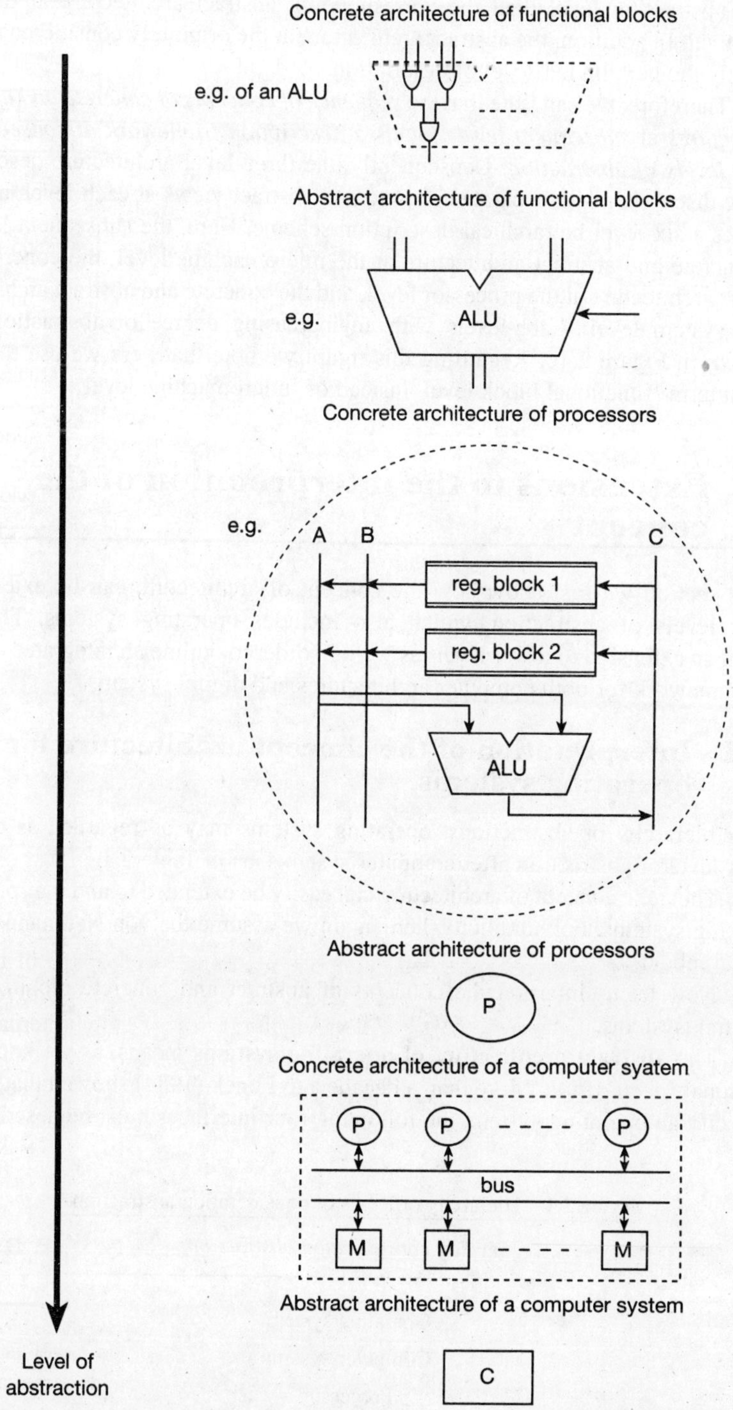

Figure 2.10 Architecture concepts at increasing levels of abstraction.

higher abstraction level than the corresponding abstract architecture at the next lower level. In addition, the abstract architecture at the originally considered level is evidently the next higher level of description.

Therefore, we can state that the *sequence of concepts of concrete and abstract architectures* at *subsequent levels* yields *a description framework at consecutively higher levels of abstraction.* Consequently, the three-level architecture description scheme discussed, with separate concrete and abstract views at each level, actually provides a six-level hierarchical description scheme. Here, the subsequent levels – the concrete and abstract architecture at the micromachine level, the concrete and abstract architecture at the processor level, and the concrete and abstract architecture at the system level – are levels with an increasing degree of abstraction. This is shown in Figure 2.10. Regarding this figure we note that here we use the more general term 'functional block level' instead of 'micromachine level'.

2.4 Extensions to the interpretation of the concept

In this section we first show how the concept of architecture can be extended to higher levels of abstraction, which also includes operating systems. Then, we present an extension to lower levels as well, in order to outline an integrated description framework for both computer architectures and digital systems.

2.4.1 Interpretation of the concept architecture for operating systems

In our hierarchy of abstractions, operating systems may be regarded as the next higher level of abstraction after computer systems, as in Table 2.1.

Thus, the concept of architecture can easily be extended to and interpreted for operating systems. For simplicity, here again we assume the von Neumann computational model.

Now let us interpret the concepts of abstract and concrete architecture of operating systems.

The **abstract architecture of operating systems** means, as we know, their functional *specification*. More than a decade ago Funck (1984) showed that in order to specify an operating system, the following four interfaces must be described:

Table 2.1 Hierarchy of levels of consideration/abstraction.

Level of consideration/abstraction
Operating system
Computer system
Processor
Micromachine (functional unit)

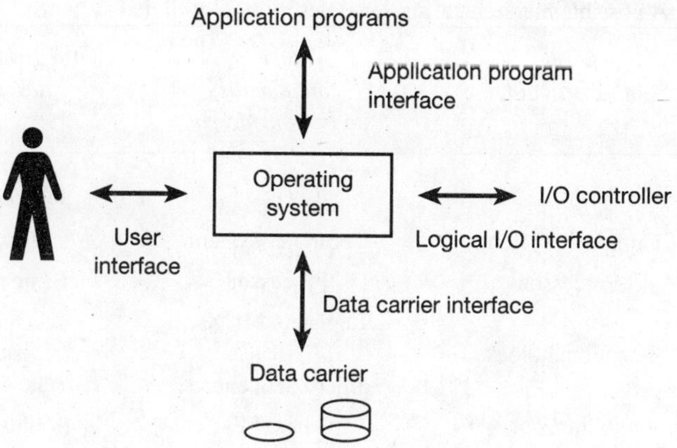

Figure 2.11 Abstract architecture of an operating system.

- *the user interface* (command language),
- *the interface to application programs* (set of system calls),
- *the logical interface to peripheral control units* (format of I/O requests, description of I/O devices in the form of device tables), and
- *the data carrier interface* (how data is represented and accessed on floppy disks, hard disks and so on).

Thus, the *abstract architecture of an operating system* can be interpreted as consisting of four interfaces as indicated in Figure 2.11.

In order to interpret the **concrete architecture of an operating system**, its building blocks, their interconnections and its operation have to be specified. In this case, the building blocks are the main components of the operating system, such as memory management, processor management, I/O management, and so on. Obviously, in this case, the interconnections are the communication mechanisms between the components of the operating system.

2.4.2 Integration of the hierarchical description of computer architectures and digital systems

It is unquestionably useful to consider digital systems at many successive levels of abstraction and to integrate their description, as suggested by Bell and Newell (see Section 2.1.1). In this way, systems can be considered at a whole spectrum of abstraction levels, from the circuit element level to the operating system level.

Integration with digital system description can easily be achieved when the considered levels of abstraction are extended also to lower levels. This means that below the functional block level, the circuit level and the circuit element level have to be considered. Table 2.2 shows the resulting six-level hierarchical description framework.

This hierarchical description framework differs slightly from that introduced by Bell and Newell (1970). The table also indicates correspondence with the concept

Table 2.2 A possible hierarchical six-level description of digital systems.

	Level of abstraction	*Basic components to be considered*	*Behavioural description by*
Computer Architecture	OS	OS	OS commands
	Computer system	Computer system	Instructions
	Processor	Processor	Basic instructions
	Functional block	Registers/MUXs, ALUs, micro-sequencer	Operations (register transfers, state sequencing)
	Circuit	Gates, FFs	Boolean equations
	Circuit element	Transistors etc.	Differential equations

of computer architecture. As discussed earlier, the concept of computer architecture is usually understood as covering both the computer system and the processor levels (see Table 2.2). In a sense, the functional block level may also be associated with the concept of computer architecture. This is indicated by the dotted line in Table 2.2.

2.5 Description of computer architectures

2.5.1 Alternative methods of description

Particular computer architectures are usually described *informally*, for example in processor handbooks, using a convenient method of presentation. An *informal description* is also used in most papers introducing a new architecture or in papers comparing existing architectures.

However, a *formal description* is required if a precise, unambiguous representation is needed, such as for inputting architecture specifications into a CAD package. This may be required in order to perform a verification, simulation or analysis based on the given structural or behavioural description.

The usual method of formally describing an architecture is by using an **architecture description language (ADL)**. Sometimes *ADLs* are also called *hardware description languages* (HDLs), or *computer hardware description languages* (CHDLs). A further concept, which is also used, is *register-transfer languages* (RTLs). RTL designates a particular type of ADL, which is confined to the processor level. Occasionally, ADLs and HDLs will be distinguished on the basis of the level of abstraction they cover. HDLs are considered as low-level and ADLs as higher-level description languages. However, we disregard this difference, and here-

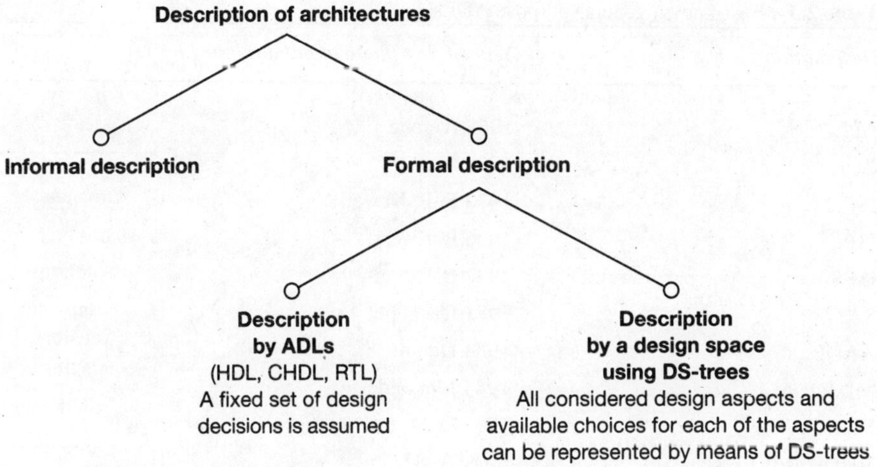

Figure 2.12 Overview of the ways of describing architectures.

after we use the term ADL to refer to the whole class of the above-mentioned description languages.

When using ADLs, one point should be underlined: ADLs are appropriate for the description of a *particular design*, that is, one whose design decisions have been fixed in the design process. Thus, the input into an ADL presumes a fixed set of parameters concerning the design decisions.

A design process, however, usually involves an optimization. It is often carried out by simulation and scanning the design space for the best or for a good enough set of design decisions. Therefore, it is of considerable importance to be able to *represent the design space* in a way that is appropriate to describe all possible design choices, or more precisely, all design choices considered. In Section 2.5.3 we discuss design spaces. There, we introduce a *graphical representation* of design spaces called *DS-trees*.

Finally, it should be pointed out that the design space and ADLs can be considered as being two complementary ways of describing architectures, in the sense that the design space is suitable for representing all the design choices considered, whereas ADLs are applicable to a fixed design, that is, to a set of design choices that are at least temporarily fixed. Figure 2.12 summarizes this section.

2.5.2 A brief overview of general-purpose ADLs

If we consider HDLs as being low-level ADLs, then by the beginning of the 1980s there had already been more than 200 ADLs published (Shiva, 1979). However, only a few deserve to be mentioned as widely used or known general-purpose HDLs.

These languages, their developers and the year of their first publication are summarized in Table 2.3.

We do not go into details of the ADLs listed in Table 2.3, but restrict ourselves to the following comments:

- All the languages mentioned support the von Neumann model of computation.

Table 2.3 Best-known general-purpose ADLs.

Designation	*Year of first publication/developed by*
APL	1962 Iverson
CDL	1965 Chu
ISP	1970 Bell, Newell
ISPL	1976 Barbacci
ISPS	1977 Barbacci
SA*	1981 Dasgupta
AADL	1984 Damm
MIMOLA	1984 Marwedel
VHDL	1985 DoD, Intermetrics, IBM, Texas
VHDL as IEEE standard	Since 1987
VHDL as ANSI standard	Since 1989

- All earlier ADLs were confined to *one particular level* only. For example, ISP, ISPL and ISPS are concerned with the processor level. To be more specific, these languages were developed to describe the abstract architecture of processors. This fact is also stressed by their common use of ISP in their names, since ISP stands for Instruction Set Processor. ISP was the original language introduced by Bell and Newell in 1970 to describe processor architectures. ISPL (Barbacci, 1976) is a subset of ISP, whereas ISPS is an update of ISPL (Barbacci, 1977).
- MIMOLA is a two-level HDL, primarily conceived to describe microarchitectures for retargetable high-level microcode compilers. (A retargetable microcode compiler is capable of generating microcode for a given set of target architectures.) A first version was published in 1979; the newer version (Marwedel, 1984) became part of the MSS hardware design environment.
- More up-to-date languages like SA*, VHDL or AADL already support a *hierarchical view*. For example, *VHDL* (VHSIC Hardware Definition Language) is intended to support the design of very high speed integrated circuits (VHSIC) and, therefore, it comprises a set of levels (five, actually) from the circuit level up to the architectural level (Table 2.4). AADL (an acronym for Axiomatic Description Language) also supports five levels of abstraction from the chip level up to the operating system level within one conceptional framework.
- Current languages also provide means for both structural and behavioural description (for instance, VHDL or AADL).
- VHDL is the most widespread HDL; it became an IEEE standard in 1987 and an ANSI standard in 1989.

Table 2.4 Levels of abstraction in VHDL (Nash and Saunders, 1986). © 1986 IEEE

	Behavioural domain	*Structural domain*
Architectural level	Performance specifications	CPUs Memories Switches Controllers
Algorithmic level	Algorithms (manipulation of data structures)	Hardware modules Data structures
Functional block level	Operations Register transfers State sequencing	ALUs MUXs Registers Microsequencer Microstore
Logic level	Boolean equations	Gates, latches Flip-flop
Circuit level	Differential equations	Transistors Capacitors Resistors

Finally, it should be pointed out that ADLs belong to the broader class of *specification languages*.

2.5.3 Design space and its representation by DS-trees

Early in the 1970s Bell and Newell introduced the concept of the 'computer space' (Bell and Newell, 1970) saying: 'There are, then, three main ways to classify or describe a computer system: *according* to its *function*, its *performance*, or its *structure*. Each consists in turn of a *number of dimensions*. It is useful to think of all these dimensions *as making up a large space* in which any computer system can be located as a point.' The objective of this concept was to have a means of classifying computers. The point of introducing the computer space is that it allows all the relevant aspects (dimensions) and corresponding design choices concerning computers to be clearly presented. Furthermore they point out that 'The *virtue of thinking* of such a space is *to abstract to a small number of dimensions*, and to *select those* that *are most relevant*'.

Bell and Newell identified about 30 dimensions and gave the possible numerical values or the sets of available choices for each dimension. They also interpreted the entirety of the dimensions as an *n-dimensional space* where each computer may be represented by one particular point.

For illustration, Figure 2.13 shows a simple computer space which consists of only three dimensions, where in dimensions CA_1, CA_2, CA_3 in turn 2, 3 and 4 choices (called attributes) are available. The point P_1 then represents a computer class or a particular computer having the attributes (1,1,2) in the dimensions considered.

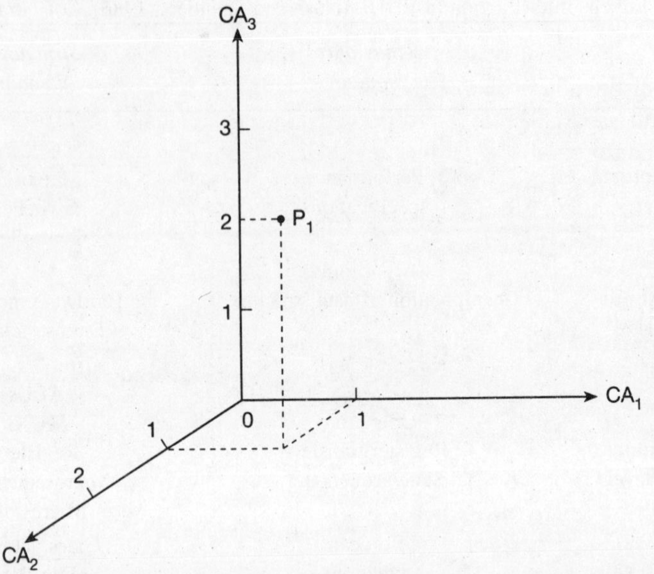

Figure 2.13 A simple computer space with three orthogonal classification aspects (CA) where for each decision aspect in turn two, three and four design choices are available, respectively.

For instance, let us consider a computer space with the following three dimensions and possible attributes:

Dimension 1: purpose of the computer:
 Possible attributes: 0: dedicated
 1: general purpose
Dimension 2: word length of the computer:
 Possible attributes: 0: 16-bit
 1: 32-bit
 3: 64-bit
Dimension 3: technology of the computer:
 Possible attributes: 0: first generation
 1: second generation
 2: third generation
 3: fourth generation

The attribute triplet (1,1,2) represents the general-purpose, 32-bit, third-generation computers.

The abstraction of computer space may be considered as a pioneering work in classifying and describing computers. Furthermore, it paved the way to the concept of design space.

However, the computer space as introduced has a few shortcomings. First, the computer space involves aspects which refer to the whole system (such as application domain or performance), and also aspects of subsystems (such as the processor or input/output). An additional problem is that in the concept of design space no distinction is made between structural aspects (concrete architecture) and behavioural aspects (abstract architecture). Instead, all these aspects are taken into account undifferentiated. A further major shortcoming is that the available alternatives of the aspects considered are supposed to be exclusive. This is unsatisfactory if it is reasonable to make multiple choices, such as in the case of data types, or the data word length of an architecture.

A more appropriate concept for the description of computer architectures is the *design space*. This concept was introduced more than two decades ago (Barbacci and Siewórek, 1973). In early interpretations, the design space was used mostly for the representation of a range of one or a few notable design parameters (for example, Haynes et al. (1982)). In later publications (for example, Bartoli et al.; 1993, Gfeller; 1992) it came to be used in a more general sense to represent all of the design aspects considered.

This concept is conceptually more coherent than that of computer space, since it covers independent and consistent aspects. Nevertheless, its interpretation as stated above lacks the possibility to represent non-exclusive design choices or a hierarchy of design aspects.

Next, we want to introduce a general interpretation and representation of the concept of design space, which allows the consideration of non-exclusive design choices and a hierarchy of design aspects as well. In addition, we provide an appropriate graphical representation of design spaces which we call **DS-trees** (design-space trees). Here, we note that design spaces can be favourably used in discussing any decision problem. Moreover, by using DS-trees the essentials of decision problems may be represented in a lucid and concise way. Therefore, we use DS-trees throughout the book while describing architectures or any design issues related to architectures.

A **design space** should allow the representation of the following basic design elements:

- orthogonal design aspects,
- exclusive design choices for a given design aspect,
- non-exclusive design choices for a given design aspect,
- logically consecutive design choices or aspects.

In the following, we briefly discuss each of the design elements mentioned and give their graphical representations.

- In order to be able to represent **orthogonal design aspects**, a relation called *'consists of'* should be introduced. Then the relation A 'consists of' B and C means that the design aspect A covers two orthogonal sub-aspects B and C. This is represented by the symbolism shown in Figure 2.14.

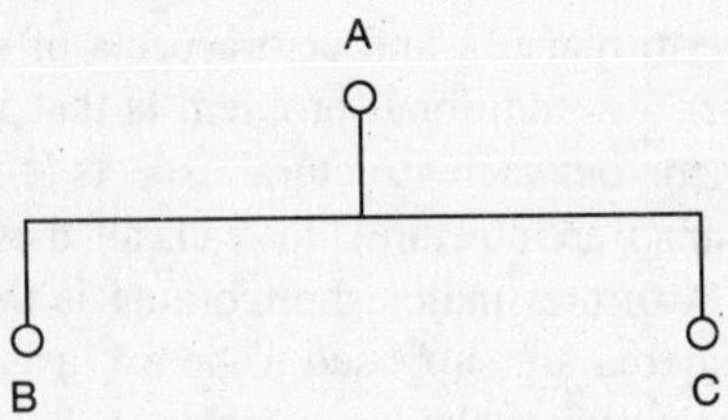

Figure 2.14 Representation of the relation A 'consists of' B and C.

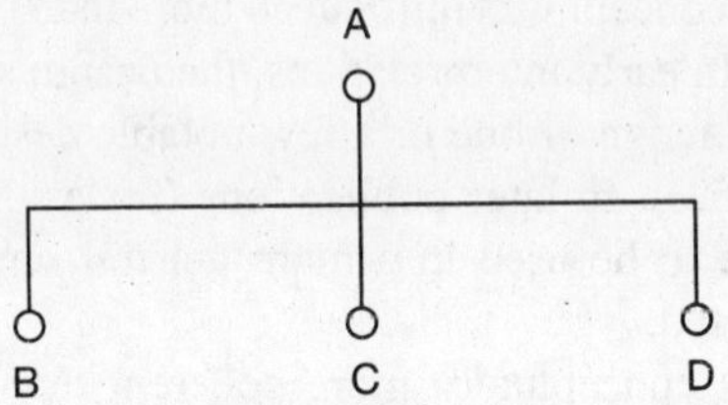

Figure 2.15 Representation of the relation A 'consists of' B and C and D.

Relations with more than two constituents can be interpreted and graphed in a similar way. Thus, if A had three constituents B, C and D, the corresponding graphical representation would be as shown in Figure 2.15.

For example, let us consider a kind of branch processing policy called *speculative branch processing*. As explained in Section 8.4.3, speculative branch processing covers three independent design aspects: the branch prediction scheme, the extent of speculativeness and the scheme used to recover from a misprediction. This fact can be expressed graphically using DS-trees, as shown in Figure 2.16.

- **Exclusive design choices** are expressed by the relation *'can be exclusively performed by'*. Here the designation *'performs'* also stands for terms like accomplish, realize. For instance, E *'can be exclusively performed by'* F or G. This relation can best be expressed graphically by a tree, where the exclusiveness of the design choices is indicated by crossed circles (Figure 2.17).

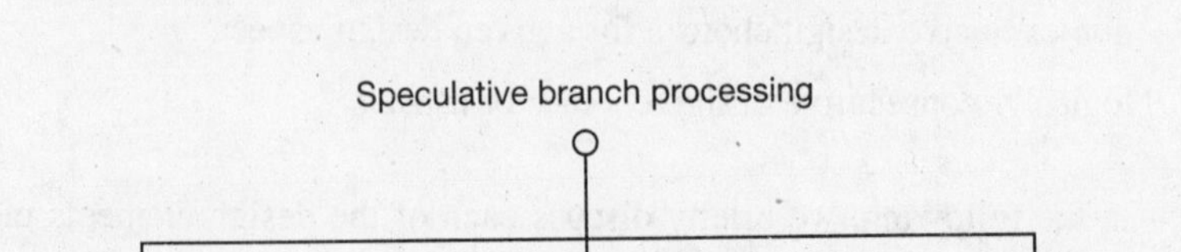

Figure 2.16 Representation of three orthogonal design aspects of speculative branch processing.

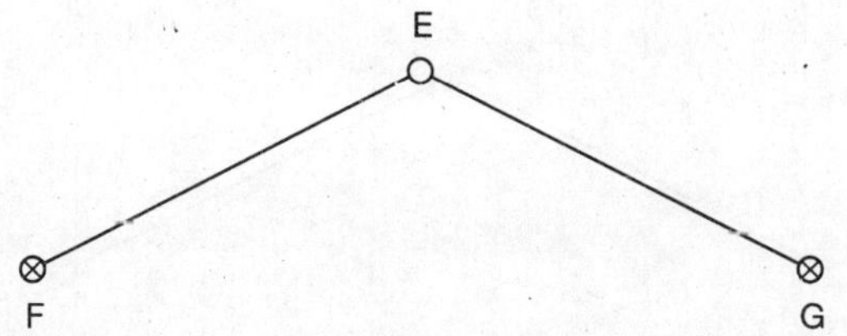

Figure 2.17 Representation of the relation E 'can be exclusively performed by' F or G.

For instance, let us consider branch prediction schemes, mentioned above. As discussed in Section 8.4.4, processors employ one of two schemes, termed as fixed prediction and true prediction. A fixed prediction is a one-outcome guess, which is always the same, that is either always taken or always not taken. In contrast, a true prediction is a two-outcome guess, which is either taken or not taken. These exclusive design choices are graphed by means of DS-trees as indicated in Figure 2.18.

Here, we note that it is often desirable to explain briefly the design choices (or aspects). So we extend the graph with a brief explanation, for example as shown in Figure 2.19.

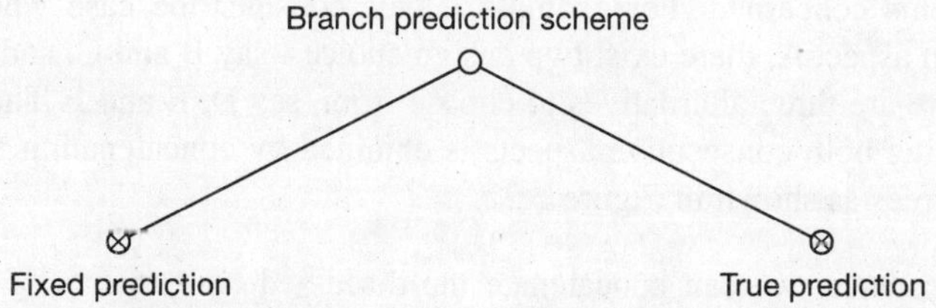

Figure 2.18 Representation of exclusive design choices.

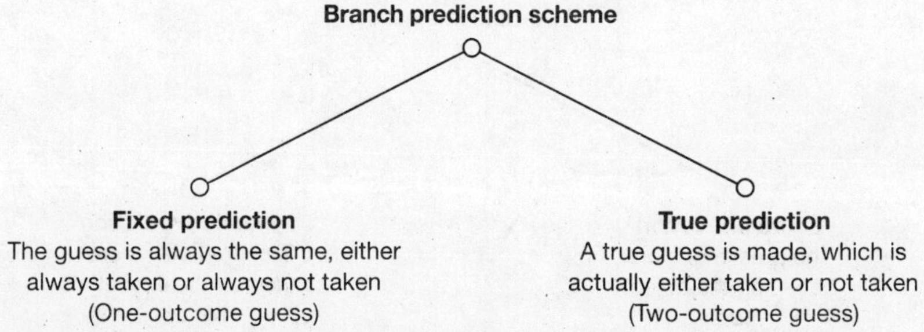

Figure 2.19 Including brief explanations in the DS representation.

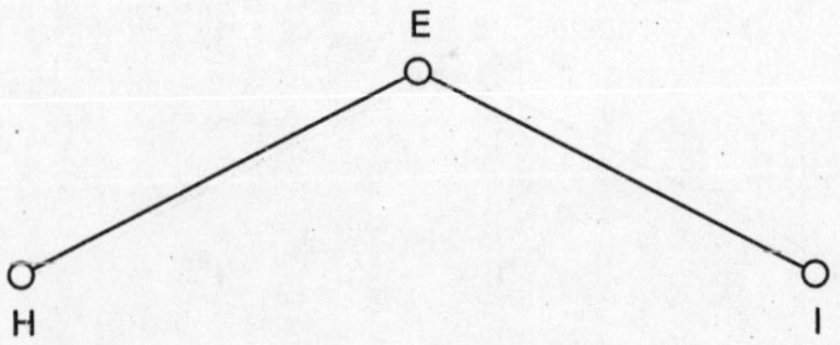

Figure 2.20 Representation of the relation E 'can be performed by' the alternatives H or I.

- **Non-exclusive design choices** represent the *'can be performed by'* relation. A simple example is E *'can be performed by'* the alternatives H or I. This relation can again best be represented by using a *tree* (Figure 2.20).

As a further example let us turn to the design choices of true branch prediction, discussed previously. Here, we have two basic possibilities to make a true prediction: perform a static prediction or a dynamic one, as described in the related section. A static prediction is based on the object code, whereas a dynamic prediction is made according to the branch history which is stored for each conditional branch. If we assume that processors may use both prediction techniques at the same time, as in a few cases, we can graph these design choices as non-exclusive ones (Figure 2.21).

- **Logically consecutive design choices or aspects**. If there are logically consecutive design choices or aspects, we can graph them by concatenating the elements concerned. For example, let us consider the case when, for the design aspect A, there exist two design choices, say B and C, and in turn for C there are three alternatives to choose from, say D, E and F. Then, the tree covering both consecutive aspects is obtained by concatenating the component trees as shown in Figure 2.22.

For instance, we can concatenate the discussed components of the design space of speculative branch processing to the representation shown in Figure 2.23.

By using the basic components discussed so far, we describe design spaces in the form of **DS-trees**.

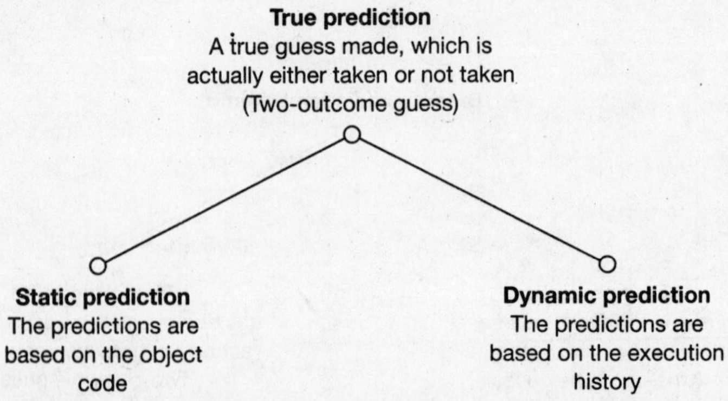

Figure 2.21 Representation of non-exclusive design choices.

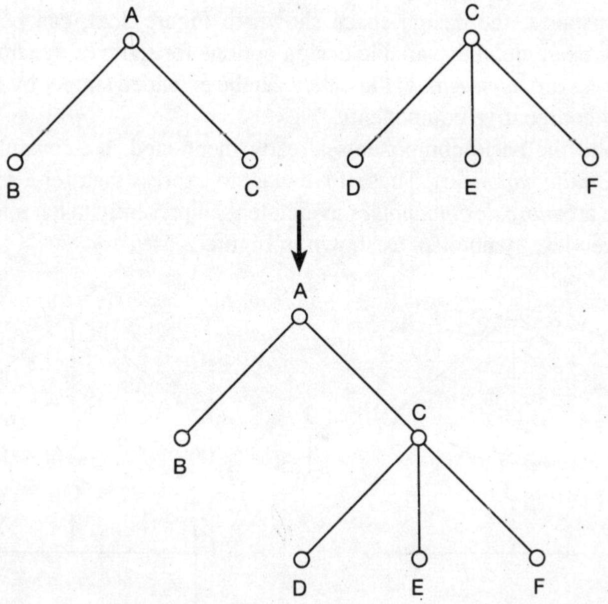

Figure 2.22 Representation of logically consecutive design aspects by concatenation.

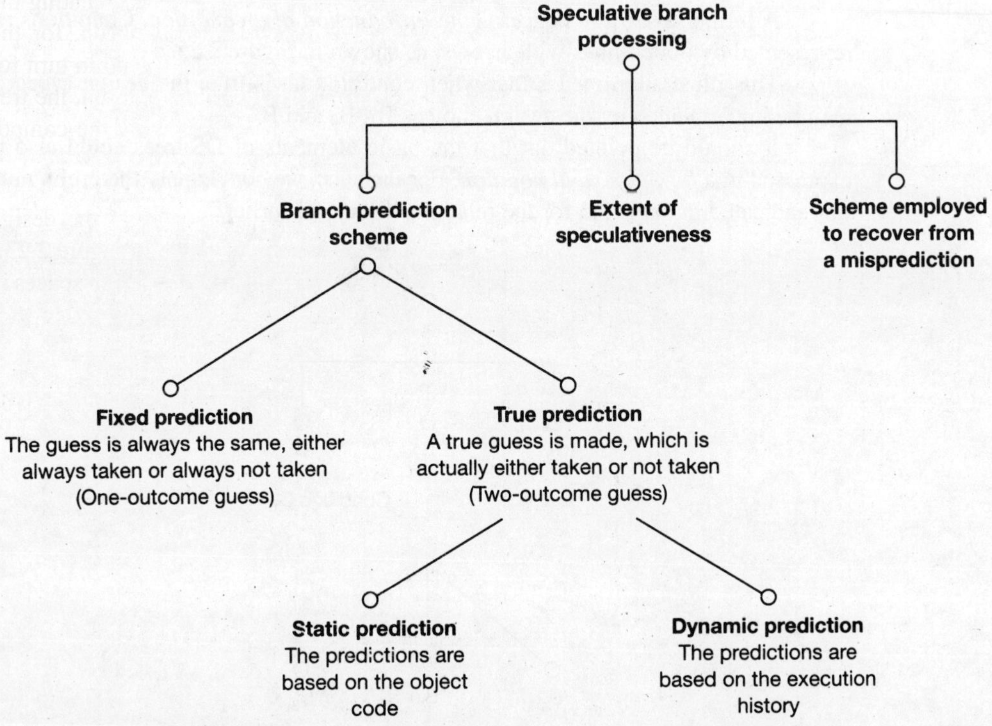

Figure 2.23 Representation of logically consecutive design aspects and choices.

For instance, the design space shown in Figure 2.23, can be extended by detailing, for example, the available design options for static or dynamic prediction.

DS-trees are *open-ended*; thus, they can be extended simply by concatenating the logically consecutive components.

Beyond the basic components already mentioned, it is useful to introduce some *additional components*. Thus, if we want to express that, for a selected design aspect, there are *more design choices* available than presently taken into account, we use the broken line symbolism as shown in Figure 2.24.

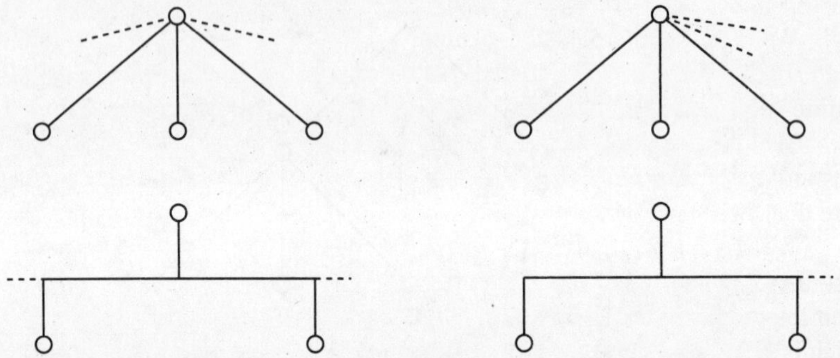

Figure 2.24 Representation of further, not explicitly specified design choices in DS-trees.

A further extension concerns *the introduction of a condition*. Conditions are represented by dotted lines with arrows, as shown in Figure 2.25.

This illustration means that when condition C_1 is true, the design aspect B may be implemented by the design choices B_1, B_2 and B_3.

It should be pointed out that the basic elements of DS-trees could also be expressed in a *formal textual notation*. For instance, we could apply the prefix notation indicated in Table 2.5 for the relations discussed earlier.

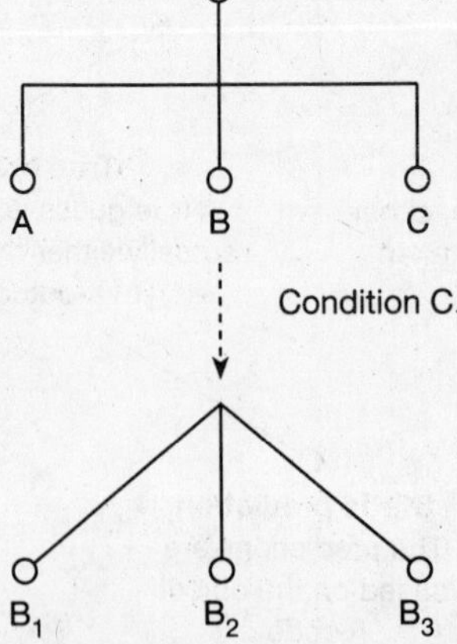

Figure 2.25 Representation of conditions in DS-trees.

Table 2.5 Possible textual notation for the relations introduced.

Relation	*Notation*
A *'consists of'* B and C	A := con (B, C)
A *'can be exclusively performed by'* B or C	A := pex (B, C)
A *'can be performed by'* B or C	A := per (B, C)

We note that there is an appealing analogy between the basic relations introduced and the corresponding logical functions of Boolean algebra. For example, the relation A := per (B, C) is obviously analagous to the Boolean function $A = C \vee B$.

Table 2.6 summarizes the relations, their graphical and textual representations and the analogies to Boolean functions for two 'operands'. An extension for more than two 'operands' is evident.

We emphasize that design spaces can be utilized for two different purposes. First, they can be used to represent the *entirety of design aspects* and *design choices* taken into account. Second, they can also be used to represent a *particular design*, which is given by a chosen set of design decisions (selected design choices).

Figures 2.26(a) and (b) show both possibilities. Figure 2.26(a) illustrates, as an example, the design space of a given design problem, where empty circles repre-

Table 2.6 Summary of the relations, their graphical and textual notations and analogies to Boolean functions.

Relation	*Graphical notation*	*Textual notation*	*Analogy to the Boolean functions*
A *'consists of'* B and C	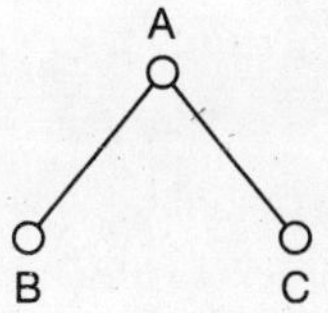	A := per (B, C)	$A = B \vee C$
A *'can be exclusively performed by'* B or C	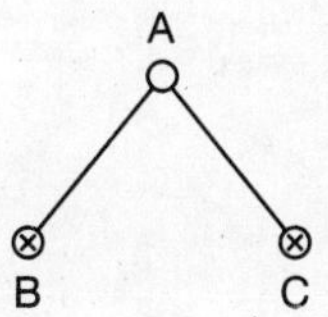	A := pex (B, C)	$A = B \oplus C$
A *'can be performed by'* B or C	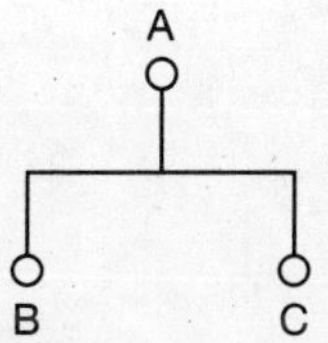	A := con (B, C)	$A = B \wedge C$

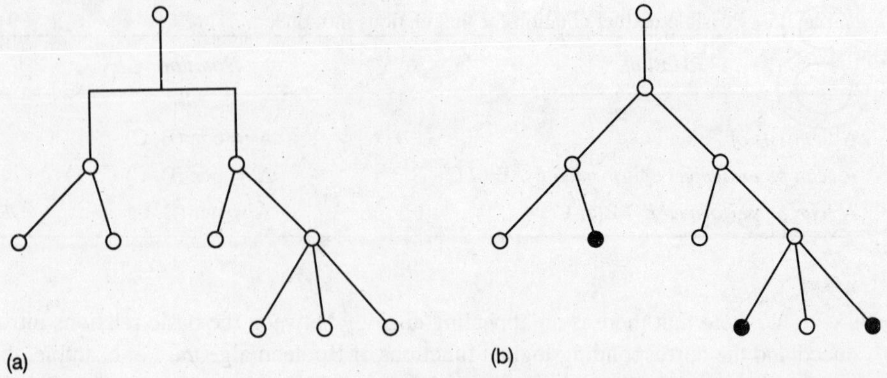

Figure 2.26 (a) Design space of a design problem; (b) a particular design represented in the design space.

sent possible design choices. Figure 2.26(b) depicts a particular design chosen from this design space. Filled circles indicate design decisions taken (chosen).

Although we have introduced the concept of design space in connection with the description of architectures, the concept has a far wider importance: it can be used to expose the relevant aspects and design choices of *any complex decision problem.* Therefore, throughout this book we use *design spaces* and their *DS-tree representations* to present relevant aspects and design choices of any design problem discussed.

3 Introduction to Parallel Processing

There are a number of concepts concerning parallel execution whose understanding is crucial in the following chapters, such as the notions of program, process, thread, concurrent and parallel execution, or kinds of concurrency and parallelism. Section 3.1 reviews these notions. Section 3.2 introduces the types and levels of parallelism. Section 3.3 proposes a major extension to Flynn's classic scheme for categorizing architectures, while Section 3.4 describes pipelining and replication, the two basic ways of exploiting parallelism. Finally, Section 3.5 discusses the relationships between programming languages and parallel architectures.

3.1 Basic concepts

3.1.1 The concept of program

From the programmer's perspective a program is an *ordered set of instructions*. On the other hand, from *the point of view of an operating system*, it is an *executable file* stored in secondary (auxiliary) memory, typically on a disk. For example, Figure 3.1 shows the program P1.EXE as seen by the programmer and by the operating system. The file P1.EXE is stored in secondary memory and can be accessed through the corresponding directory entry and file description.

3.1.2 The concept of process

In operating system terminology, the notion of **process** is used in connection with execution instead of the term 'program'. It designates a commission or job, or a quantum of work dealt with as an entity. Consequently, the resources required, such as address space, are typically allocated on a process basis.

As a comparison, imagine a car repair shop. A car coming in for repair is parked in the repair shop's car park. This car is like a program stored in auxiliary memory. Then, the owner goes to the counter and asks the service station to repair the car. When the dispatcher accepts this request, a new job is created. A worksheet is filled in with all the relevant information, such as registration number, owner's name and so on. From then on, the repair jobs are represented by the worksheets and the dispatcher deals solely with the worksheets as far as scheduling the work is concerned. Evidently, repair jobs correspond to processes. Processes are created similarly and described by appropriate tables. Staying with our example, before work can start on repairing a car, a depot and a mechanic have to be allocated to

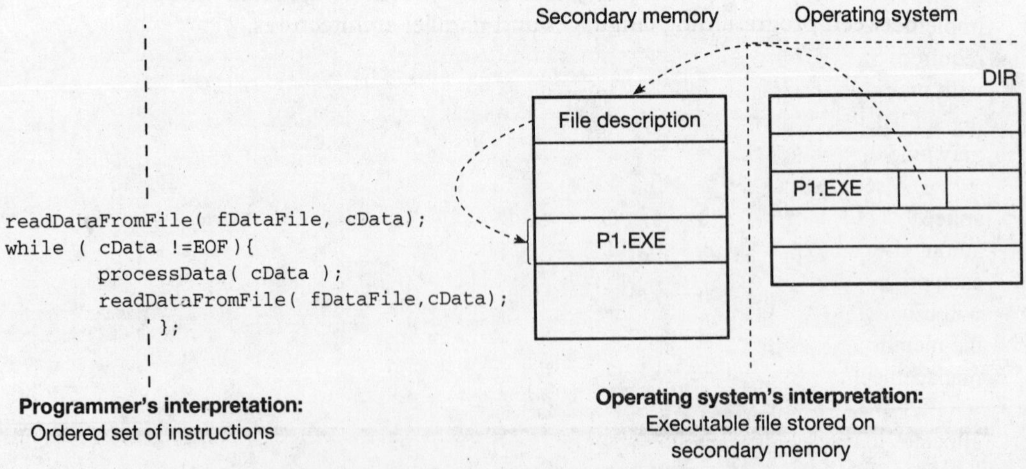

Figure 3.1 Dual interpretation of the notion 'program'.

the job. Furthermore, if additional resources, such as a hydraulic car lift, are required, these should also be allocated. Similarly, in process creation, memory space and, if necessary, additional resources such as I/O devices should be allocated to a process. Lastly, to execute a process, a processor is allocated. This is expressed in operating system terminology by saying that the process is scheduled for execution.

Earlier operating systems, such as the IBM/360 operating systems /DOS, /MFT, /MVT and so on, used the term **task** in the same sense as more recent operating systems use the notion of a process. Each process has a *life cycle*, which consists of creation, an execution phase and termination.

In order to execute a program a corresponding process is created. A process will be created using system services (system calls or supervisor macros). For example, in OS/2 processes are created by means of the system call DosExecPgm, where the name of the executable program file is given as a parameter, such as P1.EXE. Creating a process means commissioning the operating system to execute a program.

Process creation involves the following four main actions:

- setting up the process description,
- allocating an address space,
- loading the program into the allocated address space, and
- passing the process description to the scheduler.

Usually, operating systems *describe* a process by means of a description table which we will call the *Process Control Block* or *PCB*. Different operating systems use different designations for the process description table, for example *Process Table* in UNIX, *Process Control Block* in VMS, *Process Information Block* in OS/2, and Task Control Block in IBM mainframe operating systems.

A PCB contains all the information relevant to the whole life cycle of a process. It holds *basic data* such as process identification, owner, process status, description of the allocated address space and so on. It also provides space for all the implementation-dependent, process-specific *information* that may additionally be required. Such information may be needed for process management, in connection with memory management, scheduling and so on; examples are page tables, working set lists, various timers relating to the execution of the process, and so on. This may amount to a considerable amount of information.

A second major component of process creation is the **allocation of address space** to a process for execution. There are two approaches: *sharing* the address space among the created processes (*shared memory*) or allocating distinct address spaces to each process *(per-process address spaces)*. Subsequently, the executable program file will usually be *loaded* into the allocated memory space. How this is done depends on the memory management system; the file will be partly loaded when virtual memory management is used or in its entirety when real memory management is used.

Finally, the process thus created is *passed to the process scheduler* which allocates the processor to the competing processes. The process scheduler manages processes typically by setting up and manipulating queues of PCBs. Thus, after creating a process the scheduler puts the PCB into a queue of ready-to-run processes.

Summing up, process creation essentially consists of setting up the PCB, allocating a shared or a per-process address space to the process, loading the program file and putting the PCB into the ready-to-run queue for scheduling (Figure 3.2).

However, there are *two submodels* for process creation to be mentioned. In the simpler submodel a process cannot generate a new process, whereas in the more advanced submodel, a process is allowed to establish new processes. Usually, this latter possibility is called **process spawning** (for example, in UNIX or VMS) or **subtasking** (in IBM terminology).

Earlier operating systems, such as IBM/PCP or earlier versions of IBM/360/DOS or OS/MFT did not allow process spawning, so a program was represented as one process. In the more advanced submodel a process may create a new process, called a *child process* (for instance in VMS or UNIX) or a *subtask* (in IBM operating systems). Child processes can be created by the programmer using the standard mechanisms for process creation. Spawned processes form a *process hierarchy,* also termed a **process tree**. Figure 3.3 illustrates a program where process A spawns two processes B and C, and B spawns another two processes, D and E.

Processes spawning results in *more concurrency* during execution. That is, more processes belonging to the same program are competing for the processor and if the running process becomes blocked, another ready-to-run process pertaining to

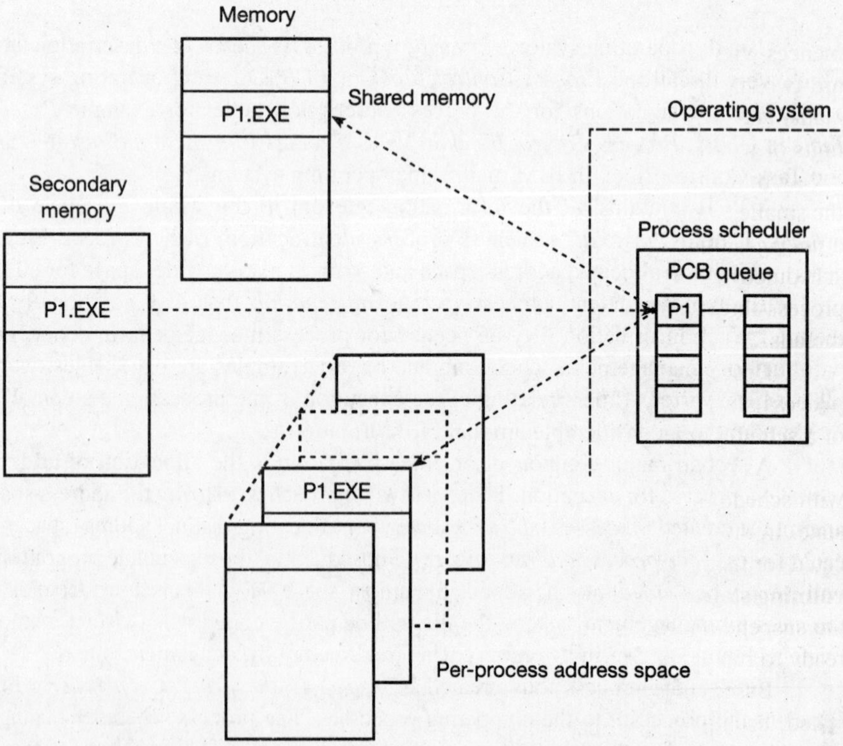

Figure 3.2 Description and location of a process after creation.

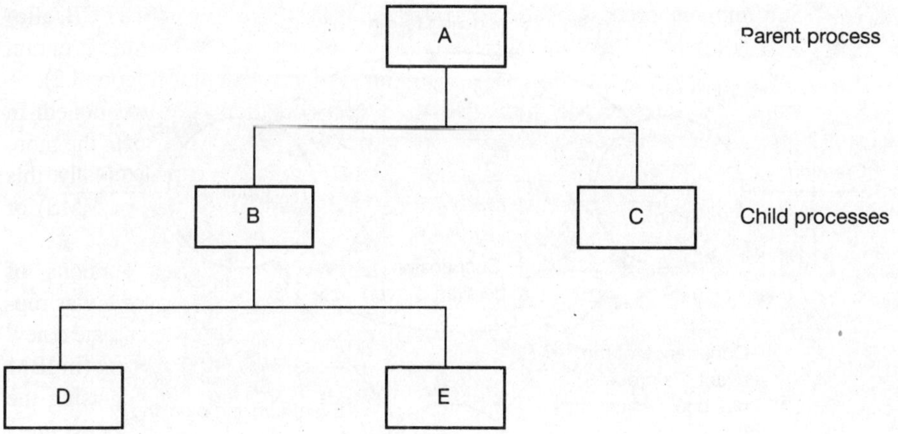

Figure 3.3 Process spawning.

the same program can be scheduled to execution. However, the price of ensuring concurrency is the effort required to create multiple processes and to plan carefully their communication and synchronization.

The execution phase of a process is under the control of the scheduler. It commences with the creation of a process and lasts until the process is terminated. There are two basic scheduling models used by operating systems, termed the *process model* and the *process-thread mode*. They differ essentially in the *granularity* of the units of work scheduled as one entity.

In the **process model** scheduling is performed on a *per-process* basis, that is, the smallest unit of work to be scheduled is a process. The **process-thread model** is a *finer-grained* scheduling model, where smaller units of work, called *threads*, are scheduled as entities. In the following we will outline the process model; the process-thread model will be briefly discussed in connection with the description of threads.

Process scheduling involves three key concepts: the declaration of distinct **process states**, the specification of the **state transition diagram** and the statement of a **scheduling policy**.

As far as **process states** are concerned, there are *three basic states* connected with scheduling: the *ready-to-run* state, the *running* state and the *wait* (or *blocked*) state. In the **ready-to-run** state processes are able to run when a processor is allocated for them. In this state they are waiting for the processor to be allocated. In the **running state** they are in execution on the allocated processor. In the **wait state** they are suspended or blocked waiting for the occurrence of some event before getting ready to run again.

Based on these states, the possible *state transitions* and their conditions are stated, usually in a **state transition diagram**. For the straightforward case represented by the basic states, the state transition diagram of the scheduler could be specified as shown in Figure 3.4.

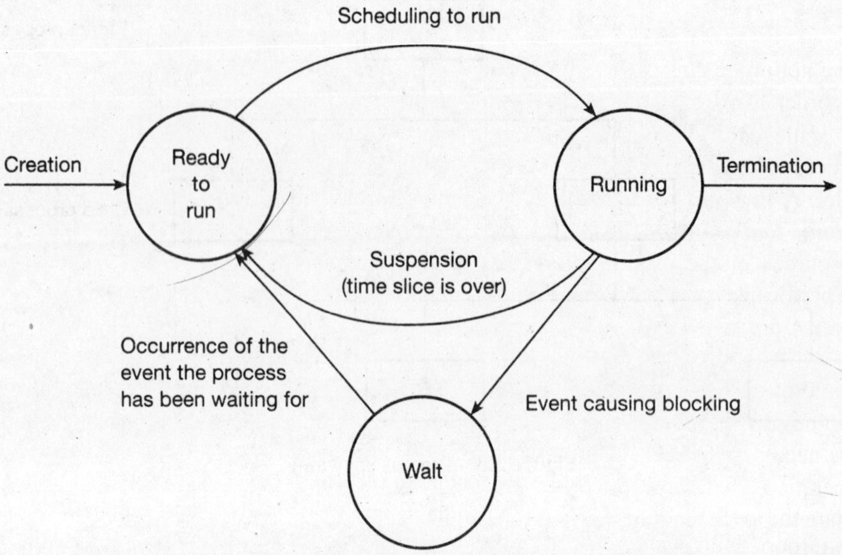

Figure 3.4 State transition diagram for the basic states.

When the scheduler selects a process for execution, its state is changed from ready-to-run to running. The process remains in this state until one of the following three events occurs:

(1) In compliance with the scheduling policy the scheduler decides to cease execution of the process (for instance, because its allocated time slice is over) and puts it into the ready-to-run queue again, changing its state accordingly.

(2) The process in execution issues an instruction that causes this process to wait until an event takes place. In this case the process state is changed to the wait state and its PCB is placed in the queue of waiting (or blocked) processes.

(3) If the process reaches the end of execution, it terminates.

Finally, a process in the wait state can go into the ready-to-run state, if the event it is waiting for has occurred. Real operating systems have a number of *additional states*, in the order of ten, introduced to cover features like swapping, different execution modes and so on.

The last scheduling component specifies rules for managing multiple competing processes; this is usually termed the **scheduling policy**. Basic scheduling policies will be overviewed in connection with concurrent execution later in this chapter.

When the process finishes execution it is terminated, releasing all the allocated resources. Many operating systems are based on the process model (such as IBM/360 /DOS, OS/MFT, OS/MVT and so on, UNIX, VMS).

3.1.3 The concept of thread

The notion of thread was introduced in the framework of the process-thread model in order to express and utilize more parallelism than in the process model. This is achieved by declaring smaller chunks of code, called *threads* (lightweight processes), within a process as entities that can be executed concurrently or in parallel. A **thread**, like a process, is a sequence of instructions. Threads are created *within, and belong to*, processes. All the threads created within one process share the resources of the process, in particular the address space. Of course, scheduling is performed on a per-thread basis. In other words, the process-thread model is a *finer-grain scheduling model* than the process model.

Although this model is far more affordable than the process model, it has numerous other *advantages*. Evidently, with finer-grained entities more parallelism can be exposed than in the case of processes. In addition, the creation of threads and the necessary communication, synchronization and switching are far less expensive operations than those for processes, since all threads belonging to the same process share the same resources. Therefore, most operating systems introduced in the 1980s and 1990s are based on the process-thread model, such as OS/2, Windows NT or SunOS 5.0. Recently, the thread interface has been standardized (IEEE POSIX 1003.40). Some operating systems, such as SunOS 5.0, are already following this emerging new standard.

Threads have a similar *life cycle* to the processes and are mainly managed in the same way. Initially each process is created with a single thread. However, threads are usually allowed to create new ones using particular system calls. For instance, in OS/2 new threads can be created by issuing the DosCreateThread system call. Then, a thread tree is typically created for each process (Figure 3.5).

During creation each thread is declared by a data structure usually called a *Thread Control Block (TCB)*. The scheduling of threads is performed in a similar way as described above for processes. Correspondingly, threads can be basically in

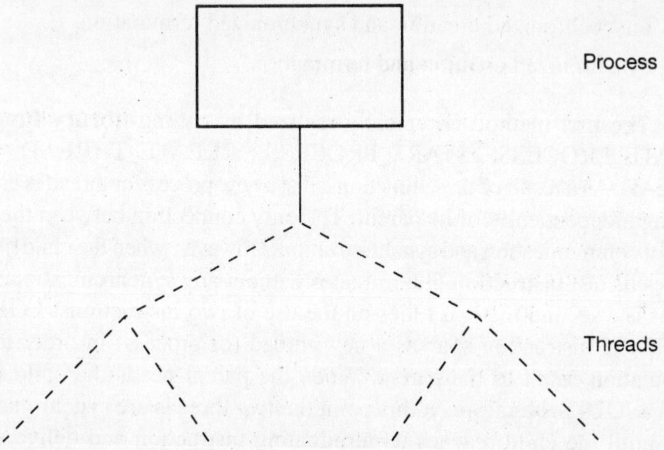

Figure 3.5 Thread tree.

one of *three states*: running, ready to run, or waiting (blocked). Of course, each operating system additionally maintains a number of system-specific states. For instance, Windows NT distinguishes the following additional states: initialized, terminated, standby (selected for execution but not yet in execution) and transition (a special wait state indicating unavailability of resources). Again, a *state transition diagram* describes possible state transfers. Thread management is performed by setting up TCB queues for each state and performing state transitions according to the state transition diagram and the scheduling policy. The scheduling part of the operating system takes on the responsibility of managing all these queues in much the same way as for processes. At the end of thread creation the TCB is placed in the queue of ready-to-run threads and competes for the processor.

3.1.4 Processes and threads in languages

So far, processes and threads have been described as operating system entities that can be managed by system calls. However, there are a large number of concurrent and parallel programming languages that enable parallelism to be expressed at the language level by providing language tools to specify the creation of processes and threads. Moreover, these languages also contain language constructs to describe the synchronization and communication of processes and threads.

As in operating systems, different languages use different terms (task, process, module, and so on) for processes and threads. Unfortunately, there is an ambiguity between operating system processes and concurrent language processes. Most of the concurrent and parallel languages (Ada, Concurrent Pascal, Occam-2, and so on) mean threads even if they use the term 'tasks' or 'processes'. One of the rare exceptions is 3L Parallel C which uses 'task' to specify processes and 'thread' to describe threads in compliance with operating system terminology.

There are three basic methods in concurrent languages for creating and terminating threads:

- unsynchronized creation and termination,
- unsynchronized creation and synchronized termination,
- synchronized creation and termination.

The first method is typically realized by calling **library functions** such as CREATE_PROCESS, START_PROCESS, CREATE_THREAD and START_THREAD. As a result of these function calls, a new process or thread is created and starts running independently of its parent. The only connection between them is the possibility of communication and synchronization. However, when the child process or thread reaches its last instruction, it terminates without any synchronization with its parent.

The second method relies on the use of two instructions: **FORK** and **JOIN**. The FORK instruction spawns a new thread (or process) in order to deliver some computation result to the parent. When the parent needs the child's result, it performs a JOIN instruction. At this point the two threads are synchronized. The parent waits until the child reaches its terminating instruction and delivers the requested result.

The typical language construct to implement the third method is the **COBEGIN/COEND** structure:

```
.., COBEGIN, T1, T2, …, Tn, COEND, …
```

The threads between the COBEGIN/COEND brackets are executed in parallel. The work of the parent thread is suspended until all the child threads are terminated. At this point the parent can continue its progress by executing the instruction that follows COEND. A semantically equivalent construct called the **PAR** construct is used in the Occam-2 language.

The first two solutions represent an undisciplined programming style. Though they are more efficient than the third method, they can lead to ambiguous process graphs whose verification is nearly impossible. However, compilers can use them in a disciplined way, resulting in efficient parallel code. The situation is similar to the use of the GOTO instruction. Compilers can use it to realize higher-level program constructs like loops, but its direct use by programmers led to unmaintainable software products.

The comparison of the FORK/JOIN and COBEGIN/COEND constructs is illustrated by the thread graphs of Figure 3.6. The special characteristic of the COBEGIN/COEND construct is that it can always be included in a black box which has only one input and one output arc. This property enables reasonably easy debugging of individual threads in these programs. Overlapped FORK/JOIN constructs prohibit this property, rendering the verification of these programs difficult. The

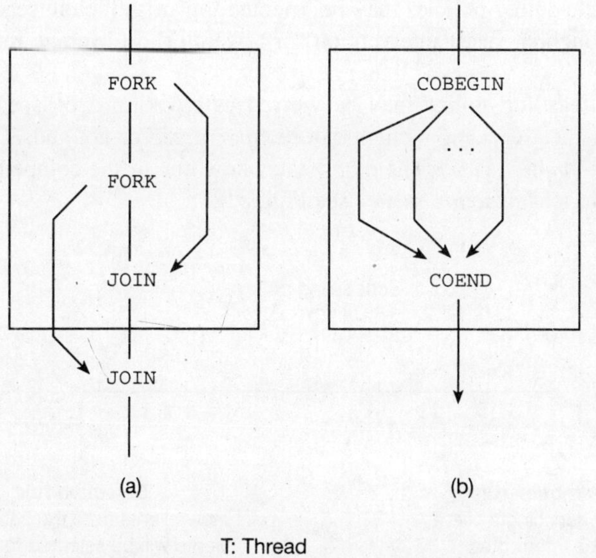

Figure 3.6 Thread graphs of language constructs to create and terminate threads. (a) FORK/JOIN; (b) COBEGIN/COEND.

FORK/JOIN construct is a lower-level one than the COBEGIN/COEND construct since the former can be used to implement the latter but not vice versa. Usually, lower-level language constructs are more efficient to implement but more difficult and dangerous to use.

3.1.5 The concepts of concurrent and parallel execution

Although the adjectives 'concurrent' and 'parallel' are often used as synonyms, it is often desirable to make a distinction between them.

Concurrent execution is the temporal behaviour of the *N-client 1-server model* (Figure 3.7) where one client is served at any given moment. This model has a dual nature; it is *sequential* in a small time scale, but *simultaneous* in a rather large time scale.

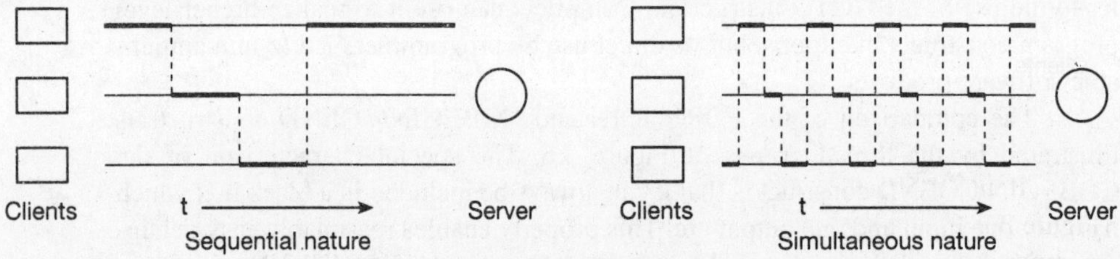

Figure 3.7 N-client 1-server model with concurrent execution.

In this situation the key problem is how the competing clients, let us say processes or threads, should be scheduled for service (execution) by the single server (processor). Scheduling policies may be oriented towards efficient service in terms of highest throughput (least intervention) or towards short average response time, and so on.

The **scheduling policy** may be viewed as covering two aspects. The first deals with whether servicing a client can be *interrupted* or not and, if so, on what occasions *(pre-emption rule)*. The other states how one of the competing clients is *selected for* service *(selection rule)* – see Figure 3.8.

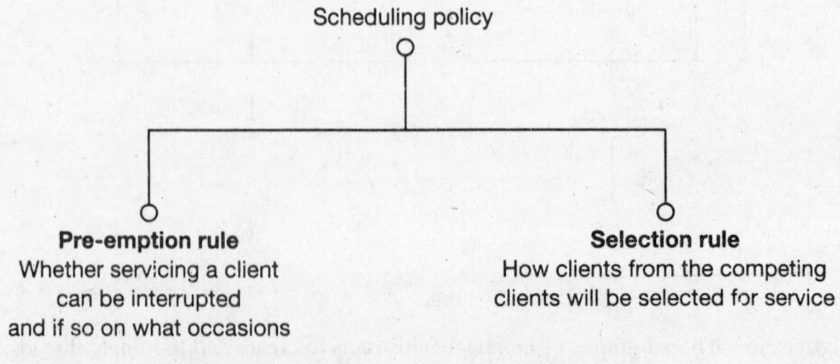

Figure 3.8 Main aspects of the scheduling policy.

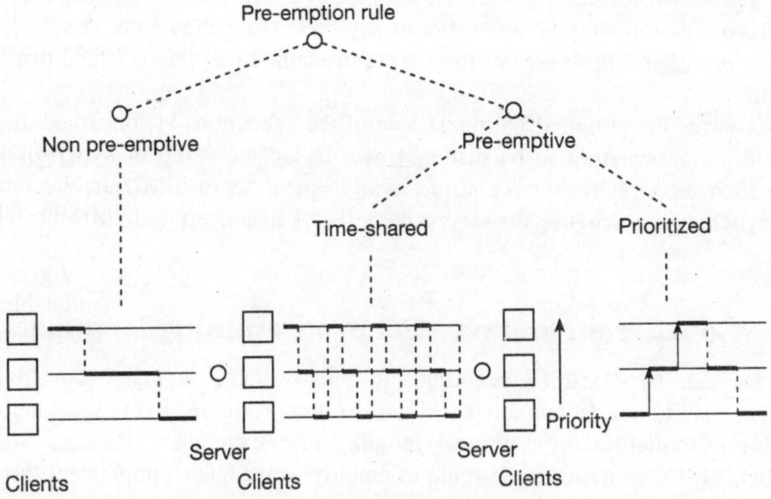

Figure 3.9 Basic pre-emption schemes.

If pre-emption is not allowed, a client is serviced for as long as needed (Figure 3.9). This often results in intolerably long waiting times or in the blocking of important service requests from other clients. Therefore, pre-emptive scheduling is often used. The **pre-emption rule** may either specify *time-sharing*, which restricts continuous service for each client to the duration of a time slice, or can be *priority based*, interrupting the servicing of a client whenever a higher priority client requests service, as shown in Figure 3.9.

The **selection rule** is typically based on certain parameters, such as priority, time of arrival, and so on. This rule specifies an algorithm to determine a numeric value, which we will call the *rank*, from the given parameters. During selection the ranks of all competing clients are computed and the client with the *highest rank* is scheduled for service. If more than one client have the same rank, arbitration is needed to choose one (for example, on a FIFO basis).

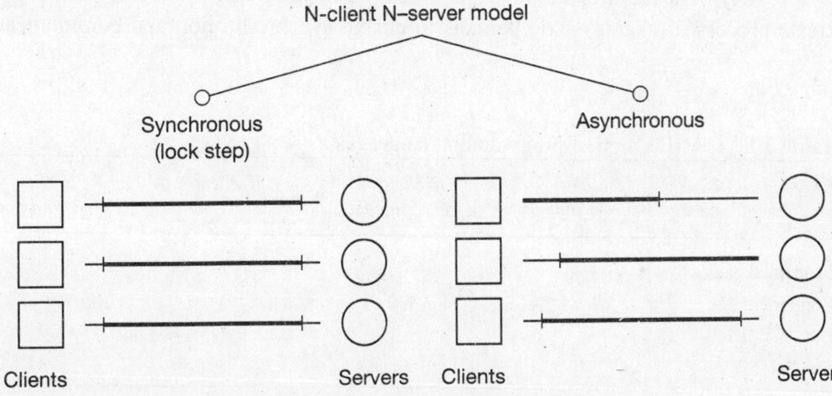

Figure 3.10 N-client N-server model.

Parallel execution is associated with the *N-client N-server model* (Figure 3.10). Having more than one server (let us say processor) allows the servicing of more than one client (processes or threads) at the same time; this is called parallel execution.

As far as the temporal harmonization of the executions is concerned, there are two different schemes to be distinguished. In the **lock-step** or **synchronous scheme** each server starts service at the *same moment*, as in SIMD architectures. In the **asynchronous scheme**, the servers do not work in concert, as in MIMD architectures.

3.1.6 Concurrent and parallel programming languages

Languages can be classified according to the available language constructs. Languages that do not contain any constructs to support the N-client model belong to the class of **sequential** (or traditional) **languages** (for example, C, Pascal, Fortran, PROLOG, LISP). **Concurrent languages** employ constructs to implement the N-client 1-server model by specifying concurrent threads and processes but lack language constructs to describe the N-server model (for example, Ada, Concurrent Pascal, Modula-2, Concurrent PROLOG). **Data-parallel languages** introduce special data structures that are processed in parallel, element by element. They also apply special mapping directives to help the compiler in the optimal distribution of parallel data structures among processors (for example, High Performance Fortran, DAP Fortran, DAP PROLOG, Connection Machine LISP). Finally, **parallel languages** extend the specification of the N-client model of concurrent languages with processor allocation language constructs that enable the use of the N-server model (for example, Occam-2, 3L Parallel C, Strand-88). Table 3.1 summarizes the relationship between language classes and client–server models.

In Section 3.1.4 the constructs of concurrent languages supporting the N-client 1-server model were described. Additionally to those constructs, parallel languages contain tools to specify the relationship between processes and processors; that is, the programmer can impose processor allocation on the compiler and run-time system.

A typical parallel language is Occam-2, which contains PAR constructs to create processes (clients) and channels to enable synchronization and communication

Table 3.1 Classification of programming languages.

Languages	*1-client 1-server model*	*N-client 1-server model*	*1-client N-server model*	*N-client N-server model*
Sequential	+	–	–	–
Concurrent	–	+	–	–
Data-parallel	–	–	+	–
Parallel	–	+	–	+

+ means that the language class supports the client–server model.

between processes. These language features support the N-client model. Occam-2 also has a configuration part that does not affect the logical behaviour of the program but enables processes to be arranged on the processors to ensure that performance requirements are met (INMOS Limited, 1988). **PLACED PAR, PROCESSOR** and **PLACE AT** commands are introduced for this purpose. In 3L Parallel C a separate **configuration language** is defined for a similar purpose.

Though parallel languages contain more types of language constructs than concurrent languages, it does not mean that they are superior to concurrent or sequential languages. On the contrary, the configuration part of parallel languages represents an extra burden for the user. It is much more convenient for the programmer if the configuration task is performed either by the compiler or by the run-time system.

3.2 Types and levels of parallelism

3.2.1 Available and utilized parallelism

Parallelism is one of the 'hottest' ideas in computing. Architectures, compilers and operating systems have been striving for more than two decades to extract and utilize as much parallelism as possible in order to speed up computation.

In our subject area the notion of parallelism is used in two different contexts. Either it designates **available parallelism** in programs (or, in a more general sense, in problem solutions) or it refers to parallelism occurring during execution, called **utilized parallelism**. First, let us overview available parallelism.

3.2.2 Types of available parallelism

Problem solutions may contain two different kinds of available parallelism, called functional parallelism and data parallelism. We term **functional parallelism** that kind of parallelism which arises from the logic of a problem solution. It occurs in all formal descriptions of problem solutions, such as program flow diagrams, dataflow graphs, programs and so on, to a greater or lesser extent. However, in the following we will restrict our attention to available functional parallelism inherent in programs expressed in traditional imperative languages.

There is a further kind of available parallelism, called **data parallelism** (Hillis and Steele, 1986). It comes from using data structures that allow parallel operations on their elements, such as vectors or matrices, in problem solutions. Data parallelism is inherent only in a restricted set of problems, such as scientific or engineering calculations or image processing. Usually, this kind of parallelism gives rise to a massively parallel execution for the data-parallel part of the computation. Thus, the actual values for the achievable speed-up depend heavily on the characteristics of the application concerned.

From another point of view parallelism can be considered as being either regular or irregular. *Data parallelism* is *regular,* whereas *functional parallelism*, with the exception of loop-level parallelism, is usually *irregular*. Intuitively, parallelism is called weak, when the extent of the available or exploited parallelism remains in the *one-digit range*. This is the typical case for irregular parallelism. Regular parallelism is often **massive**, offering several orders of magnitude in speed-up.

3.2.3 Levels of available functional parallelism

Programs written in imperative languages may embody functional parallelism at different levels, that is, at different sizes of granularity. In this respect we can identify the following four levels and corresponding granularity sizes:

- parallelism at the instruction level (fine-grained parallelism),
- parallelism at the loop level (middle-grained parallelism),
- parallelism at the procedure level (middle-grained parallelism), and
- parallelism at the program level (coarse-grained parallelism) as shown in Figure 3.11.

Available **instruction-level parallelism** means that particular instructions of a program may be executed in parallel. To this end, instructions can be either assembly (machine-level) or high-level language instructions. Usually, instruction-level parallelism is understood at the machine-language (assembly-language) level. While considering instruction-level parallelism we will confine ourselves to instructions expressing more or less elementary operations, such as an instruction prescribing the addition of two scalar operands, as opposed to multi-operation instructions like those implying vector or matrix operations.

Parallelism may also be available **at the loop level**. Here, consecutive loop iterations are candidates for parallel execution. However, data dependencies

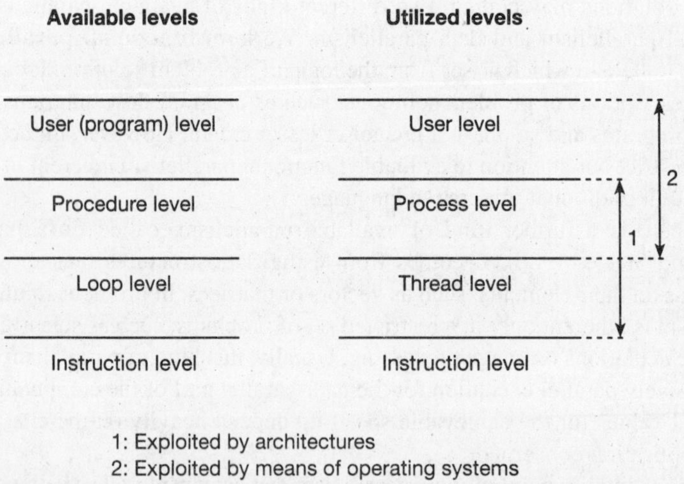

Figure 3.11 Available and utilized levels of functional parallelism.

between subsequent loop iterations, called **recurrences**, may restrict their parallel execution. The potential speed-up is proportional to the loop limit or, in the case of nested loops, to the product of the limits of the nested loops. Loop-level parallelism is a promising source of parallelism.

Next, there is **parallelism** available **at the procedure level** in the form of parallel executable procedures. The extent of parallelism exposed at this level is subject mainly to the kind of the problem solution considered.

In addition, different programs (users) are obviously independent of each other. Thus, **parallelism** is also available **at the user level** (which we consider to be coarse-grained parallelism). Multiple, independent users are a key source of parallelism occurring in computing scenarios. Evidently, in a problem solution different levels of parallelism are not exclusive but may coexist at the same time.

3.2.4 Utilization of functional parallelism

Available parallelism can be utilized by architectures, compilers and operating systems conjointly for speeding up computation. Let us first discuss the utilization of functional parallelism. In general, functional parallelism can be utilized at four different levels of granularity, that is, at instruction, thread, process and user level (see again Figure 3.11).

It is quite natural to utilize available functional parallelism, which is inherent in a conventional sequential program, **at the instruction level** by executing instructions in parallel. This can be achieved by means of architectures capable of parallel instruction execution. Such architectures are referred to as **instruction-level function-parallel architectures** or simply **instruction-level parallel architectures**, commonly abbreviated as **ILP-architectures**. Since available instruction-level parallelism is typically hidden, that is, implicit in traditional sequential programs, prior to execution it must be detected either by a dedicated compiler (usually called a parallel optimizing compiler) or by the ILP-architecture itself.

Available functional parallelism in a program can also be utilized at the **thread** and/or at the **process level**. As discussed earlier, threads and processes are self-contained execution entities embodying an executable chunk of code. They are constructs to expose parallel executable pieces of code. Processes are higher-level constructs than threads, that is, they expose coarser granular parallelism.

Threads and processes can be created either by the programmer using parallel languages or by operating systems that support multi-threading or multitasking. They can also be automatically generated by parallel compilers during compilation of high-level language programs. Available loop- and procedure-level parallelism will often be exposed in the form of threads and processes.

There are two different ways to execute threads and processes. On the one hand, they can be executed in parallel by means of specialized architectures referred to as **multi-threaded** and **MIMD architectures**, respectively. Multi-threaded architectures are typically specialized processors able to perform very fast context switching. Since they are employed as processors of MIMD architectures solving the remote memory access problems of MIMD machines, they are described in Part IV dealing with MIMD architectures. The other way to execute threads and processes concurrently is to use architectures that run threads or processes in sequence, under the supervision of a multi-threaded or multitasking operating system.

In general, lower levels of available parallelism are likely to be utilized directly by parallel architectures in connection with parallel optimizing or parallel compilers whereas the utilization of higher levels of parallelism usually relies more heavily on operating systems supporting concurrent or parallel execution in the form of multitasking or multi-threading. Figure 3.11 shows the relationship between the available and utilized levels of functional parallelism.

3.2.5 Concurrent execution models

In order to round out the picture we will briefly outline below high-level concurrent execution models such as *multi-threading*, *multitasking*, *multiprogramming* and *time sharing* (Figure 3.12). Note that all these concurrent execution models refer to *different granularity* of execution, also termed different levels. Typically, they are implemented by means of the operating system on a single processor (that is, on a SISD, in Flynn's taxonomy). It is important to note, however, that all these notions can also be interpreted in a broader sense, as notions designating the execution of multiple threads, processes or users in a concurrent or parallel way. Nevertheless, the interpretations below are focused on the narrower scope of concurrent execution.

Thread-level concurrent execution is termed **multi-threading**. In this case multiple threads can be generated for each process, and these threads are executed concurrently on a single processor under the control of the operating system.

Multi-threading is usually interpreted as *concurrent execution at the thread level*. Multi-threading evidently presumes that a process has multiple threads, that is, a process-thread model is used to represent and schedule units of work for the processor. Multi-threading is supported by recent operating systems (such as OS/2, Windows NT or SunOS 5.0) as well as by multi-threaded architectures (Chapter 16).

Process-level concurrent execution is usually called *multitasking*. All current widely used operating systems support this concept. **Multitasking** refers to concurrent execution of processes. Multiple ready-to-run processes can be created either by a single user if process spawning is feasible, or by multiple users participating in multiprogramming or in time-sharing. Multitasking was introduced in operating systems in the mid-1960s, including, among others, the IBM operating systems for the System/360 such as /DOS, OS/MFT and OS/MVT. Almost all recent operating

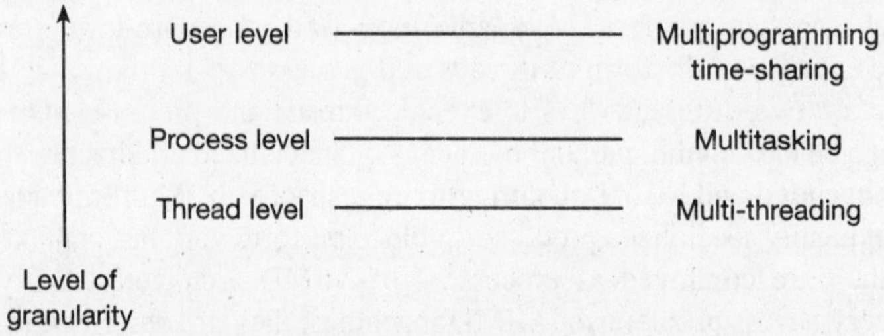

Figure 3.12 Concurrent execution models.

systems provide this feature. MIMD architectures support process-level parallel execution (see Chapters 17 and 18).

Finally, user-level concurrent or parallel execution can be either *multiprogramming* or *time-sharing*. **Multiprogramming** aims at the effective utilization of the processor by creating multiple ready-to-run processes, each belonging to different users. If the process actually running becomes blocked, because it has to wait for a particular event, such as completion of I/O, the processor will be scheduled to another ready-to-run process (if one exists). This mode of operation was supported by multiprogrammed operating systems such as those mentioned in the preceding paragraph. Notice that multiprogramming is implemented *internally* as *multitasking* for *independent tasks* arising from different users.

On the other hand, **time-sharing** has the objective of offering computer *services of adequate quality* to a number of users through terminals. This mode of operation is intended to guarantee a *short access time* to all users instead of striving for the effective utilization of the processor. In this case a number of ready-to-run processes are created, again by different users. Scheduling has to be performed in such a way that a proper response time can be guaranteed for each user. Time-sharing evolved as a response to the lengthy turnaround times of efficiency-oriented and user-unfriendly multiprogrammed systems in the 1960s (TSS, MAC and so on).

3.2.6 Utilization of data parallelism

Data parallelism may be utilized in two different ways. One possibility is to exploit data parallelism directly by dedicated architectures that permit parallel or pipelined operations on data elements, called data-parallel architectures (DP-architectures). The other possibility is to convert data parallelism into functional parallelism by expressing parallel executable operations on data elements in a sequential manner, by using the loop constructs of an imperative language.

3.3 Classification of parallel architectures

3.3.1 Flynn's classification

Flynn's classic taxonomy (Flynn, 1966) is based on the number of control units as well as the number of processors available in a computer. Accordingly, he introduced the notions of:

- single instruction stream (that is, the architecture has a single control unit producing a single stream of instructions), abbreviated as **SI**;
- multiple instruction streams (that is, the architecture has multiple control units, each producing a distinct stream of instructions), abbreviated as **MI**;
- single data stream (that is, a single processor is available which executes a single stream of data), abbreviated as **SD**;

- multiple data streams (that is, multiple processors are available each executing a distinct stream of data), abbreviated as **MD**.

Based on these notions he categorized computers combining the possible instruction streams and processing aspects (Figure 3.13).

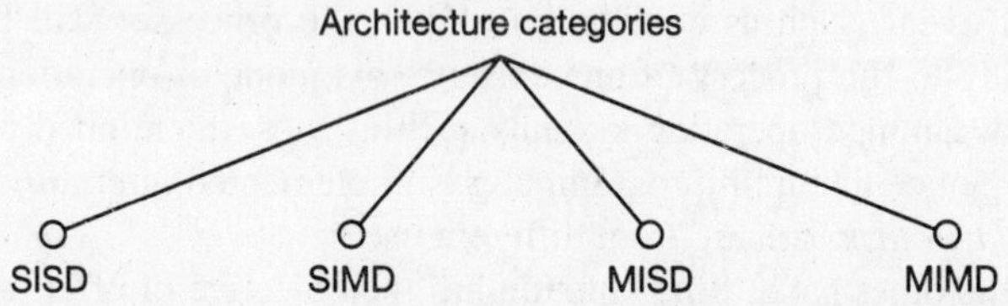

Figure 3.13 Architecture categories introduced by Flynn.

Although this is a lucid and straightforward scheme, it does not reveal or cover key aspects such as what kind of parallelism is utilized, at what level or how parallel execution is implemented. In the following we will present a classification scheme covering all these points of view.

3.3.2 Proposed classification

The proposed classification of parallel architectures is based on the kind of parallelism exploited and takes into account the granularity of the functional parallelism utilized, as shown in Figure 3.14.

Subject to the kind of parallelism utilized, first we differentiate between **data-parallel** and **function-parallel architectures**. Based on their principle of operation, data-parallel architectures may be subdivided into **vector**, **associative and neural**, **SIMD** and **systolic processors**. These architectures are discussed in Part III. Function-parallel architectures may be categorized according to the granularity of the parallelism they utilize. Thus, we can distinguish **instruction-**, **thread-** and **process-level parallel architectures**. Instruction-level parallel architectures are referred to as **ILP-architectures**. We describe ILP-architectures in detail in Part II. Thread- and process-level parallel architectures are equivalent to the class of **MIMD-architectures** as introduced by Flynn. However, we emphasize the special features of thread-level architectures and use the distinguishing term **multi-threaded architectures** for them. Part IV focuses on multi-threaded and MIMD architectures. Each of the major architecture classes may be subdivided into a number of subclasses. According to their principle of operation ILP-architectures can be classified into three major subclasses: **pipelined**, **VLIW** and **superscalar processors**. Process-level architectures are subdivided into two basic classes: **multicomputers** and **multiprocessors**. They are also designated as **distributed memory computers** and **shared memory computers**, referring to the implementation of their memory system. Because of the software model supported by multicomputers, they are often called **message-passing machines**. The classification tree of parallel computer architectures is given in Figure 3.14. A separate chapter in this book is devoted to each of the leaves of the classification tree, explaining in detail their main

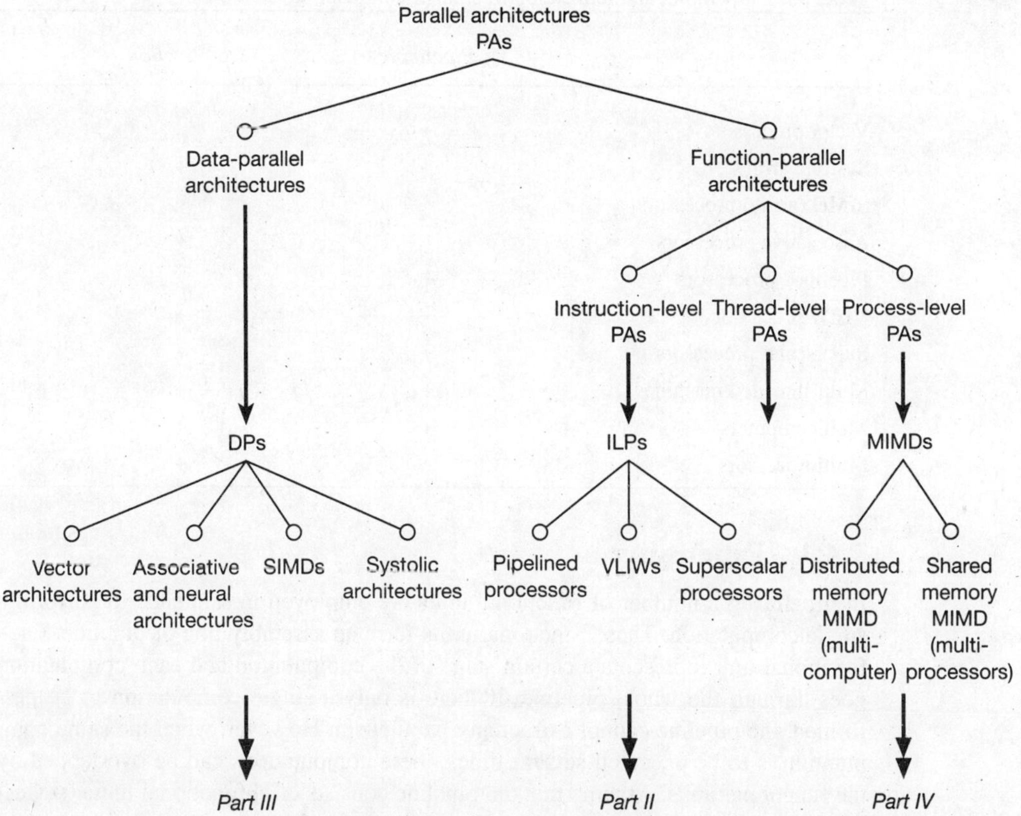

Figure 3.14 Classification of parallel architectures.

features. In those chapters these architecture classes are further subdivided, based on their design space.

We feel that the classification presented here is a more suitable one than the well-known Flynn's taxonomy, introduced in 1966. In our opinion, an up-to-date classification has to cover aspects such as what kind of parallelism is utilized and at what level, as well as how parallel execution is implemented, as our scheme does.

3.4 Basic parallel techniques

There are two basic ways of exploiting parallelism in parallel computer architectures:

- Pipelining
- Replication

These parallel techniques are extensively used in various parallel computer architectures as summarized in Table 3.2. In the following subsections a detailed explanation of Table 3.2 is given.

Table 3.2 Pipelining and replication in parallel computer architectures.

	Pipelining	*Replication*
Vector processors	+	
Systolic arrays	+	+
SIMD (array) processors		+
Associative processors		+
Pipelined processors	+	
VLIW processors		+
Superscalar processors	+	+
Multi-threaded machines	+	+
Multicomputers	+	+
Multiprocessors		+

3.4.1 Pipelining

In **pipelining** a number of functional units are employed in sequence to perform a single computation. These functional units form an assembly line or pipeline. Each functional unit represents a certain stage of the computation and each computation goes through the whole pipeline. If there is only a single computation to be performed, the pipeline cannot extract any parallelism. However, when the same computation is to be executed several times, these computations can be overlapped by the functional units. Assume that the pipeline consists of N functional units (stages) and that the slowest requires time T to execute its function. Under such circumstances a new computation can be started at every Tth moment. The pipeline is filled up when all the functional units are working on a different computation. Once the pipeline is filled up, a new computation is finished at every Tth moment. Accordingly, a full pipeline results in speed-up N if the time necessary to fill the pipeline is negligible compared to the amount of time when the pipeline is full. A detailed description of pipelining can be found in Chapter 4.

Pipelining is a very powerful technique to speed up a long series of similar computations and hence is used in many parallel architectures. It can be used inside a processor (micro-level) and among the processors or nodes (macro-level) of a parallel computer. A member of the oldest class of parallel computers, the vector processor, is a good example of applying the pipeline technique inside a processor. The elements of two vectors enter the vector unit at every time step. The vector unit, consisting of several functional units, executes the same operation on each pair of vector elements. Modern pipelined processors and superscalar processors also use the pipelining technique to overlap various stages of instruction execution. The processors used in multi-threaded architectures are usually built on the pipelining principle, too.

Another classical example of applying pipelining can be found in systolic arrays. However, here the processors of the array form the pipeline in either one or two dimensions. The wavefront array is an asynchronous version of the systolic array, where data is transferred according to the dataflow principle but the pipeline mechanism of systolic systems is preserved. An interesting and powerful application of pipclining can be found in the wormhole router of message-passing computers. The introduction of the wormhole routing technique, which is a special form of pipelining, resulted in three orders of magnitude reduction in communication latency and led to a new generation of both multicomputers and multiprocessors.

Dataflow machines apply pipelining both inside and among the nodes. The dataflow nodes contain several functional units that form an instruction pipeline similarly to the pipelined processors of RISC machines. Different nodes of a dataflow machine execute different nodes of the corresponding dataflow graph. In tagged-token dataflow machines the nodes of the dataflow graph can be activated in a pipeline manner and hence the executing nodes of the dataflow machine are also used as a pipeline.

3.4.2 Replication

A natural way of introducing parallelism to a computer is the replication of functional units (for example, processors). Replicated functional units can execute the same operation simultaneously on as many data elements as there are replicated computational recources available. The classical example is the array processor which employs a large number of identical processors executing the same operation on different data elements. Wavefront arrays and two-dimensional systolic arrays also use replication alongside pipelining parallelism. All the MIMD architectures employ replication as their main parallel technique. Inside the processor, both VLIW and superscalar processors can apply it. Some multi-threaded processors are also designed to exploit replication.

However, not only processor units but also memory banks can be replicated. Interleaved memory design is a well-known technique to reduce memory latency and increase performance. Similarly, I/O units can be advantageously replicated resulting in higher I/O throughput. The most trivial case of replication is the increase of address and data lines in processor buses. Microprocessor buses have developed from 8-bit buses to 64-bit buses and this progress will not be stopped in the near future.

3.5 Relationships between languages and parallel architectures

Although languages and parallel architectures could be considered as independent layers of a computer system, in reality, for efficiency reasons the parallel architecture has a strong influence on the language constructs applied to exploit parallelism.

Vector processors do not often impose special language constructs, rather they require special compiler support to exploit loop parallelism related to identical operations on elements of vectors or matrices. Vectorizing compilers have been successfully employed for Fortran programs in the field of scientific and engineering applications.

Another way to exploit loop parallelism relies on the **SPMD (Single Procedure Multiple Data) execution model**. SPMD represents a generalization of the SIMD execution model where basically only one thread of execution is applied but from time to time this thread can split into N threads that work on different invocations of the same loop. When the whole loop is finished the threads are merged again into a single thread. All the N threads execute the same code, similarly to the SIMD model where all processors execute identical code. However, in the SPMD model, threads can execute the same code at different speeds; that is, in a given moment they can perform distinct instructions. In the SIMD model an instruction-by-instruction synchronization is applied, whereas in the SPMD model it is sufficient to synchronize the parallel threads at the end of the loop when they are merged again into a single thread. This type of synchronization is called **barrier synchronization** and its efficient implementation requires hardware support. The SPMD execution model is typically employed on MIMD parallel architectures where processors are able to execute distinct instructions.

Similarly to the vector machines, neither systolic arrays nor associative processors require language support. The only data-parallel architecture that is sensitive to languages is the SIMD (array processor) machine. Data-parallel languages developed for SIMD computers typically contain parallel data structures like 1-, 2- and more dimensional arrays that are handled as single objects. This means that an operation on such an object is performed in parallel at each element of the object without applying the usual loop constructs. For example, to add two 2-dimensional arrays requires two nested loops in Fortran, while it is programmed by a single statement in DAP Fortran as shown in Figure 3.15.

There is only one common control unit for all the processors in SIMD machines and hence, each processor executes the same code. However, there are situations when only a subset of the elements of an array is involved in an operation. A new language construct, called the mask, is needed to define the relevant subset of arrays. The mask technique is a crucial part of data-parallel languages. Again a DAP Fortran example illustrates the use of masks compared to conventional Fortran programs in Figure 3.16. Both programs assign value zero to those elements of the 2-dimensional array A that are less than 3. In Fortran, this simple operation is realized by two nested loops. In DAP Fortran, a single assignment is sufficient to define the

Fortran code	**DAP Fortran code**
`do 2 j=1, n`	
`do 1 i=1, n`	
`C (i,j) = A (i,j) + B (i,j)`	`C = A + B`
`1 continue`	
`2 continue`	

Figure 3.15 Programming sequential and parallel data structures.

Fortran code	**DAP Fortran code**
`do 2 j=1, n`	
`do 1 i=1, n`	
`if (A (i,j).It.3.0) A (i,j) = 0.0`	`A (A.It.3.0) = 0.0`
`1 continue`	
`2 continue`	

Figure 3.16 Mask technique in DAP Fortran.

operation. The mask on the left-hand side of the assignment ensures that only the chosen elements of array A will be updated.

Finally, data-parallel languages contain language constructs to specify the allocation of processors for the elements of the parallel data structures. While the application of parallel data structures and masks simplifies and shortens the program text, the allocation constructs lead to the expansion of programs. All three new techniques require a special way of thinking significantly different from conventional Fortran and that is one of the main reasons why SIMD machines could not gain real popularity.

As already mentioned, ILP-architectures are not supported by special language constructs. Intelligent optimizing compilers are necessary to exploit that level of parallelism.

A particularly efficient way of programming multi-threaded machines relies on the data-driven execution model and applicative programming languages. In this case there is no need of any explicit specification of parallelism, since compilers can easily exploit inherent parallelism from the program text. However, coarse-grain multi-threaded architectures are usually programmed similarly to process-level MIMD machines by either concurrent or parallel languages.

Beyond the creation and termination of threads, concurrent and parallel languages provide tools for communicating between and synchronizing these threads. Figure 3.17 illustrates the progress of synchronizing tools from low-level to high-level constructs. The two main lines correspond to shared memory and distributed memory MIMD machines.

Processes and threads in shared memory MIMD computers use shared data structures to communicate. Simultaneous access of shared data structures must sometimes be prohibited and hence, they require synchronization. Obviously, a shared data structure must not be read while it is being updated. The writer and reader processes should access the shared data structure in a mutually exclusive way. This problem, called **mutual exclusion**, is one of the main synchronization problems. For such synchronizations the lowest-level (machine instruction level) language tool is the **test_and_set operation** which should be implemented by hardware on any machine. Based on the test_and_set mechanism various **semaphores** and

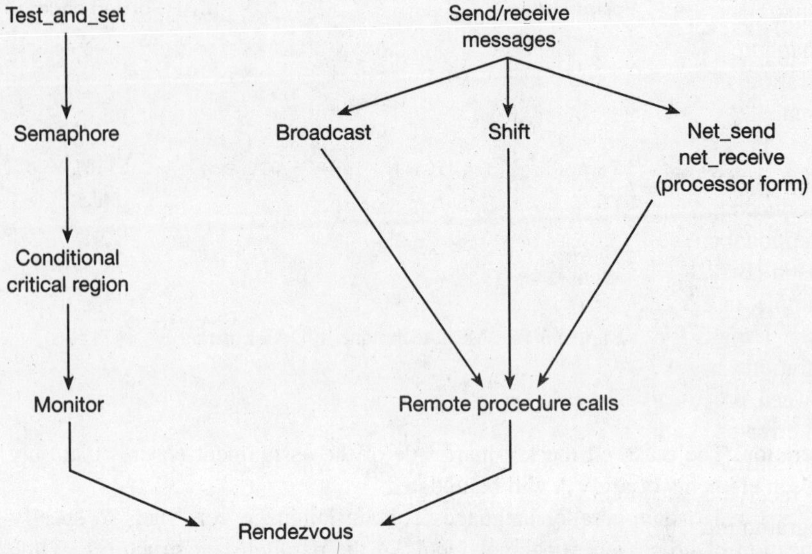

Figure 3.17 Progress of language constructs used for synchronization.

semaphore operations (P and V) can be defined (Dijkstra, 1968a,b). The two most well-known versions are the **binary semaphore** and the **queue-semaphore**. The mutual exclusion problem and its solution by a binary semaphore is shown in Figure 3.18. The main difference between the two types of semaphore comes from the scheduling mechanism behind the P-operation. In the case of binary semaphores the test phase of the P-operation is executed in a busy-wait fashion. The process keeps

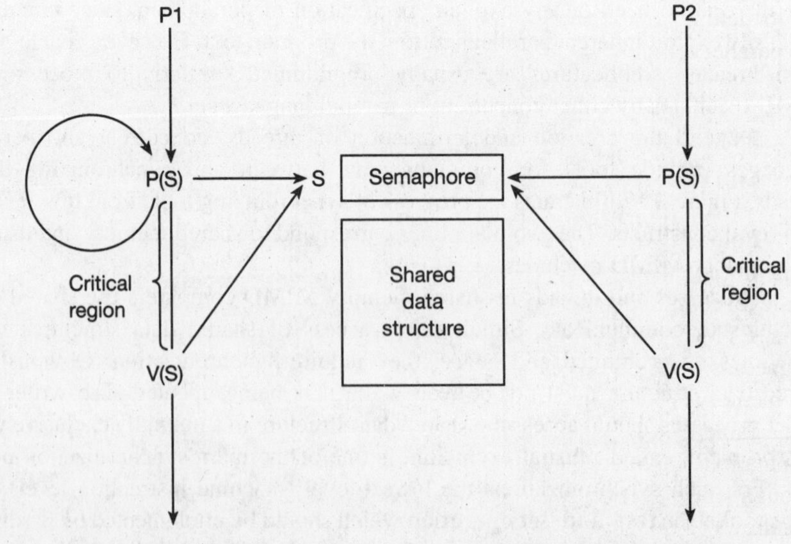

Figure 3.18 Using a semaphore to solve the mutual exclusion problem.

the processor busy as long as the requested semaphore is locked. Queue-semaphores enable the process that executes a P-operation to be suspended on a locked semaphore. When the semaphore is unlocked by another process executing a V-operation, the suspended process can acquire the shared resource and becomes ready to run.

Programming process communication by semaphores is very error-prone and hence, several higher-level synchronization constructs have been proposed and introduced into concurrent and parallel languages. The two most notable ones are the conditional critical region (Brinch Hansen, 1973) which was applied in the language Edison (Brinch Hansen, 1981) and the monitor (Hoare, 1974) which appeared, for example, in Concurrent Pascal (Brinch Hansen, 1975).

Languages to program distributed memory architectures use message-passing operations like *send* and *receive* to specify communication and synchronization between processors. Like the semaphore operations they represent very low-level and error-prone operations and hence, higher-level language constructs like broadcast, shift, net_send and net_receive have been introduced. The net_send and net_receive constructs appear in 3L Parallel C and they support the processor farm programming technique. A further step in the safe programming of distributed memory architectures is the introduction of remote procedure calls (RPCs). Application of RPCs significantly reduces the main problem of message-passing architectures, namely the creation of deadlock situations where processors mutually wait for one another. For example, Occam-3 introduced the RPC concept in order to make Transputer programming safe.

The two main lines of synchronization tools lead to the rendezvous language construct which combines the features of remote procedure calls and monitors. The rendezvous concept could be implemented on both shared and distributed memory machines. The most well-known language employing the rendezvous concept is Ada (Dept. of Defense, 1983).

Recently, many efforts have been devoted to avoiding machine dependencies and to defining parallel interfaces that can be easily ported to various MIMD-type parallel computer architectures. The two most famous and celebrated interfaces are:

- PVM (Parallel Virtual Machine) (Geist et al., 1994)
- MPI (Message-Passing Interface) (Gropp et al., 1994).

Both are based on the message-passing programming paradigm and provide a rich library of send/receive-type commands. Additionally, MPI realizes many high-level communication constructs that simplify the programming of MIMD computers. PVM is intended primarily to support workstation clusters, while MPI was designed as a standard programming interface for massively parallel (both distributed memory and distributed shared memory) computers.

Table 3.3 summarizes the relationships between explicit language constructs, computational models, languages and parallel computer architectures. A very thorough study of concurrent programming languages and techniques can be found in Andrews (1991).

Table 3.3 Summary of forms of parallelism.

Specification of parallelism	*Execution model*	*Language*	*Parallel architecture*
Loops	Vector execution	Conventional procedural	Vector computers
Loops	SPMD	Conventional procedural	MIMD architectures with barrier synchronization
(1) Explicit declaration of parallel data structures (2) Explicit allocation of parallel data structures to processors	SIMD	Data-parallel	SIMD (array processors)
No explicit specification	Instruction-level function-parallel	Imperative	ILP-architectures
No explicit specification	Data driven	Dataflow	Multi-threaded architectures
(1) Explicit partitioning of program into parallel processes (2) Explicit synchronization among processes	Processes communicating through shared data	Concurrent	Shared memory MIMD machines
(1) Explicit partitioning of program into parallel processes (2) Explicit messages among processes (3) Explicit allocation of processes to processors	Processes communicating by message passing	Parallel	Distributed memory MIMD machines

References and Further Reading for Part I

References

Adams D. A. (1968). A computational model with dataflow sequencing. *PhD Thesis*, TR/CS 117, Dept. of Computer Science, Stanford University, CA

Alpert, D. and Avnon, D. (1993). Architecture of the Pentium microprocessor. *IEEE Micro*, June, 11–21

Amdahl G. M., Blaauw G. H. and Brooks F. P. (1964). Architecture of the IBM System/360. *IBM Journal of Research and Development*, **8**(2), April 87–101

Andrews G.R. (1991). *Concurrent Programming: Principles and Practice*. Redwood City, CA: The Benjamin/Cummings Publishing Company, Inc.

Andrews G. R. and Schneider (1983). Concepts and notations for concurrent programming. *ACM Comp. Surveys*, **15**(1), March, 3–43

Arvind and Gostelow, K. P. (1977). A computer capable of exchanging processors for time. In Information Processing 77 (Gilchrist B., ed.), pp. 849–53. Amsterdam: North Holland

Backus J. (1978). Can programming be liberated from the von Neumann style? A functional style and its algebra of programs. *Comm. ACM*, **21**(8), Aug., 613–41

Barbacci M. R. (1976). The Symbolic Manipulation of Computer Descriptions: ISPL Compiler and Simulator. TR Dept. of CS, CMU

Barbacci M. R. and Siewiorek D. P. (1973). Automated exploration of the design space for register transfer (RT) systems. *Proc. First Ann. Symposium on Computer Architecture*, pp. 101–6.

Barbacci M. R. et al. (1977). *The ISPS Computer Description Language*. Dept. of Computer Science, CMU, Pittsburg

Bartoli A. et al. (1993). Wide-address spaces exploring the design space. *Operating Systems Review*, **27**(1), 11–7

Bell C. G. and Newell A. (1970). The PMS and ISP descriptive systems for computer structures. In *Proc. Spring Joint Computer Conference*, pp. 351–74

Bell C. G. and Newell A. (1971). *Computer Structures: Readings and Examples*. McGraw-Hill Book Company

Brinch Hansen P. (1973). Concurrent programming concepts. *ACM Computing Surveys*, **5**, Dec., 223–45

Brinch Hansen P. (1975). The programming language Concurrent Pascal. *IEEE Trans. on Software Engr.SE-1*, **2** (June), 199–206

Brinch Hansen P. (1981). Edison: a multiprocessor language. *Software Practice and Experience*, **11**(4), April, 325–61

Chan K., Alexander T., Hu C., Larson D., Noorden N., VanAtta Y., Wylegala T. and Ziai S. (1993). Multiprocessor features of the HP Corporate Business Servers. In *Proc. COMPCON 1993*, pp. 330–7

Chu Y. (1965). An Algol-like computer design language. *Comm. ACM*, Oct., 607–15

Dai K. and Giloi W. K. (1990). A basic architecture supporting LGDG computation. In *Proc. 1990 Int'l. Conference on Supercomputing*, pp. 23–33

Dally W. J. and Wills D. S. (1989). Universal mechanism for concurrency. *Proc. PARLE*. In

Lecture Notes in Computer Science, vol. 365. Berlin: Springer-Verlag, pp. 19–33

Damm W. (1984). Automatic generation of simulation tools: A case study in the design of the retargetable firmware development system. In *Advances in Microprocessing and Microprogramming*, (Myrhaug B. and Wilson D. R., eds), pp. 165–76. North Holland

Dasgupta. S. (1981). SA*: A language for describing computer architectures. In *Proc. the 5th Intl Symposium on Computer Hardware Description Languages and their Applications* (Breuer M. A. and Hartenstein R., eds.), Sept., pp. 65–78. Amsterdam: North-Holland

Davis A. L. (1978). The architecture and system methodology of DDM1: A recursively structured data driven machine. *In Proc. 5th Ann. Symposium on Computer Architecture*, pp. 210–15

Deitel H. M. and Kogan M. S. (1992). *The Design of OS/2*. Reading, MA: Addison-Wesley

Dennis J. B. and Misunas D. P. (1975). A preliminary architecture for a basic data flow processor. In *Proc. 2nd Ann. Symposium on Computer Architecture*, pp. 126–32

Dept. of Defense (1983). *Reference Manual for the Ada Programming Language*. New York, NY: Springer-Verlag

Dijkstra E.W. (1968a). The structure of the 'THE' multiprogramming system. *Comm. ACM*, **11**, May, 341–6

Dijkstra E.W. (1968b). Cooperating sequential processes. In *Programming Languages* (Genuys F., ed.). New York: Academic Press

Feustel E. A. (1973). On the advantages of tagged architectures. *IEEE Trans. on Computers*, **C-22**(7), July, 644–56

Field A. J. and Harrison P. G. (1988). *Functional Programming*, Wokingham: Addison-Wesley

Flynn M. J. (1966). Very high speed computing systems. *Proc. IEEE*, **54**, Dec., 1901–9

Funck G. (1984). Component-based operating system works in real time. *Computer Design*, July, 203–11

Geist A. et al. (1994). *PVM Parallel Virtual Machine, A User's Guide and Tutorial for Networked Parallel Computing*. The MIT Press

Gfeller M. (1992). Walks into the APL design space. *APL Quote Quad*, **23**(1), July, pp. 70–7

Glück-Hiltrop E., Ramlow M. and Schürfeld U. (1989). The Stollman Data Flow Machine. In *Proc. PARLE 1989*, LNCS 365, pp. 433–57. Springer-Verlag

Gropp W., Lusk E. and Skjellum A. (1994). *Using MPI, Portable Parallel Programming with the Message-Passing Interface*. The MIT Press

Gurd J., Kirkham C. and Böhm W. (1987). The Manchester Dataflow Computer System. In *Experimental Parallel Computing Architectures* (Dongarra J. J., ed.), pp. 177–219. Elsevier North Holland

Haynes L. S., Lau R. L., Sieworek D. P. and Mizell D. W. (1982). A survey of highly parallel computing. *Computer*, **15**(1), 9–24

Hertzberger L. O. and Vree W. G. (1989). A coarse grain parallel architecture for functional languages. *Proc. PARLE*. In Lecture Notes in Computer Science, vol. 365. Berlin: Springer-Verlag, pp. 269–85

Higbie, L. and Baron R. J. (1992). *Computer Architecture*. Reading, MA: Addison-Wesley

Hillis W. D. and Steele Jr G. L. (1986). Data parallel algorithms. *CACM*, **29**(12), Dec., 1170–83

Hiraki K. et al. (1987). The SIGMA-1 dataflow supercomputer: a challenge for new generation supercomputing systems. *J. Info. Processing*, **10**(4), 219–26.

Hoare C.A.R. (1974). Monitors: an operating system structuring concept. *Comm. ACM*, **17**, Oct., 549–57

Hopcroft J. E. and Ullmann J. D. (1969). *Formal Languages and Their Relation to Automata*. Reading, MA: Addison-Wesley

INMOS Limited (1988), *Occam 2, Reference Manual*. Prentice Hall International Series in Computer Science

Intel Corp. (1996)

Iverson K. E. (1962). *A Programming Language*. New York, NY: Wiley

Iverson K. E. (1962). A common language for hardware, software and applications. *AFIPS Proc. FJCC*, **22**, 121–9

Karp R. M. and Miller R. E. (1966). Properties of a model for parallel computations: determinancy, termination, queuing. *SIAM Journal of Applied Math*, **14**(6), Nov., 1390–1411

Levi H. M. (1986). *Capability-based Computer Systems*. Digital Press

Maquelin O. C. (1990). ADAM: a coarse-grain dataflow architecture that addresses the load balancing and throttling problems. In *Proc. Joint Conference on Vector and Parallel Processing*, Sept., pp. 265–76

Marwedel P. (1984). A retargetable compiler for a high-level microprogramming language. In *Proc. 17th Ann. Workshop on Microprogramming, ACM SIGMicro Newsletter*, **15**(4), Dec., 267–274

McCulloch W. and Pitts W. (1943). A logical calculus of the ideas imminent in nervous activity. *Bull. Math. Biophys.*, **5**, 115–133

Nash J. D. and Saunders L. F. (1986). VHDL critique. *IEEE Design & Test*, April, 54–65

Patterson D. A. and Hennessy J. L. (1990). *Computer Architecture, A Quantitative Approach*. Morgan Kaufmann Publishers Inc.

Peterson J. L. and Bredt T. H. (1974). A comparison of models of parallel computation. In *Proc. IFIP'74*. North-Holland Publishing Comp.

Peyton Jones S. L., Clack C., Salkind J. and Hardie M. (1987). GRIP – a high performance architecture for parallel graph reduction. In *Proc. the Functional Programming Languages and Computer Architecture Conference* (Kahn G., ed.), Lecture Notes in Computer Science 274, pp. 98–112. Berlin: Springer Verlag

Rodriguez J. E. (1967). A graph model for parallel computation. *PhD Thesis*, Dept. of EE, MIT, Sept.

Shiva S. G. (1979). Computer hardware description languages, tutorial. In *Proc. IEEE*, **76**(12), Dec., pp. 1605–15

Sima D. (1977). Formale Beschreibung der logischen Architekture von Rechnern. *Wissenschaftliche Beiträge der Ingenieurhochschule Dresden*, no. 5, 2–11, no. 6, 2–13

Sites R. L. (1992). *Alpha Architecture Reference Manual*. Digital Press

Stone H. S. (1993). *High Performance Computer Architecture*, 3rd edn. Addison-Wesley

Tesler L. G. and Enea H. J. (1968). A language design for concurrent processes. In *Proc. SJCC*, pp. 403–8

Treleaven P. C., ed. (1990). *Parallel Computers*, Chichester: Wiley

Treleaven P. C. and Hopkins R. P. (1981). Decentralized computation. In *Proc. 8th. Ann. Symp. on Comp. Arch.*

Treleaven P. C. et al. (1987). *Computer Architectures for Artificial Intelligence in Future Parallel Computers*, Lecture Notes in Computer Science, vol. 272. Berlin: Springer-Verlag

von Neumann J. (1945). *First Draft of a Report on the EDVAC*. Moore School of Electrical Engineering, University of Pennsylvania

Watson I., Sargeant J., Watson P. and Woods V. (1987). Flagship computational models and machine architectures. *ICL Technical Journal*, **5**, May, 555–74

Further reading

Aburto A. A. Jr (1988). Problems and pitfalls. *BYTE*, Jun. 217–24

Aho A. V., Hopcroft J. E. and Ullmann, J. D. (1974). The Design and Analysis of Computer Algorithms. Reading, MA: Addison-Wesley

Anderson P., Kelley P. and Winterbottom, P. (1990). The feasibility of a general-purpose parallel computer using WSI. *Future Generation Computer Systems*, **6**, 241–53

Annot J. K.and den Haan P. A. M. (1990). POOL and DOOM: The object-oriented approach. In *Parallel Computers* (Treleaven P.C., ed.) Chichester: Wiley. pp. 47–81.

Apt K. R. and van Emden M. H. (1982). Contributions to the theory of logic programming. *J. ACM*, **29**(3), July, 841–62

Austin T. M. and Sohi G. S. (1992). Dynamic dependency analysis of ordinary programs. In *Proc. 19th AISCA*, pp. 342–51

Bacon D. F., Graham S. L. and Sharp O. J. (1994). Computer Science Division, University of California. *ACM Computing Surveys*, **26**(4) Dec., 345–420

Balboni G. P., Bosco P. G., Cecchi G., Melen R., Moiso C. and Sofi G. (1990) Implementation of a parallel logic + functional language. In *Parallel Computers* (Treleaven P.C., ed.), pp. 175–214. Chichester: Wiley

Barbuti R., Bellia M., Levi G. and Martelli M. (1984). On the integration of logic programming and functional programming. In *Proc. IEEE 1984 Int'l. Symposium on Logic Programming*, pp. 160–6

Baron R. J. and Higbie L. (1992). *Computer Architecture* pp. 25–30 Addison-Wesley

Brunner R. A. (1991). VAX Architecture Reference Manual. Digital Press

Burstall R. M., McQueen D. and Sanella D. (1980). HOPE: An experimental applicative language. In *Proc. 1st International LISP Conference*, Stanford, pp. 136–43

Butler M., Yeh T.-Y., Patt Y., Alsup M., Scales H. and Shebanov M. (1991). Single instruction stream parallelism is greater than two. In *Proc. 18th AISCA*, pp. 276–86

BYTE editorial staff (1987). High-tech horsepower. *Byte*, Jul., 101–8

Case B. (1995). SPEC95 Retires SPEC92. *Microprocessor Report*, Aug. 21, 11–14

Chakravarthy U. S., Kasif S., Kohli M., Minker J. and Cao D. (1982). Logic programming on ZMOB: a highly parallel machine. In *Proc. Int. Conference on Parallel Processing*, IEEE, pp. 347–9

Church A. (1936). An unsolvable problem of elementary number theory. *American Journal of Mathematics*, **58**, 345–63

Church A. (1941). The Calculi of Lambda-conversion. Princeton, NJ: Princeton U. Press

Clark K. L. and Gregory S. (1983). PARLOG: a parallel logic programming language. *Imperial College Research Report 83/5*, May

Clarke T. J. W., Gladstone P. J. S., MacLean C. D. and Norman A. C. (1980). SKIM – The S, K, I reduction machine. In *Lisp Conference Record*, Stanford University, pp. 128–35

Colmerauer A. (1982). Prolog and infinite trees. In *Logic Programming* (Clark K. L. and Tarnlund S. A., eds). New York, NY: Academic Press

Colmerauer A. (1987). Opening the Prolog III universe. *Byte*, July

Colmerauer A., Kanoui H., Pasero R. and Roussel P. (1972). Un système de communication homme-machine en francais. *Rapport preliminaire*, Groupe de Researche en Intelligence Artificielle, Universitè d'Aix-Marseille, Luminy,

Culler D. E. and Papadipoulos G. M. (1990). The explicit token store. *J. of Parallel and Distributed Computing*, **10**, 289–307

Custer H. (1993). *Inside Windows NT*. Microsoft Press

Dahl O.-J. and Nygaard K. (1966). SIMULA, an ALGOL-based simulation language. *Comm. ACM*, **9**(9), Sept. 671–8

Dahl O.-J., Nygaard K. and Myhrhaug B. (1968). The SIMULA 67 Common Base Language. Oslo: Norwegian Computing Centre

Duden (1989). "Informatik". Mannheim: Dudenverlag

Duff C. (1990). *ACTOR Programming*. Evanston, Il: The Whitewater Group Inc.

Feldman Y. and Shapiro E. (1992). Spatial machines: a more realistic approach to parallel computation. *Comm. ACM*, **35**(10), Oct., 61–73

Fortune S. and Wyllie J. (1978). Parallelism in random access machines. In *Proc. 10th Annual ACM Symposium on Theory of Computing*, pp. 114–18

Fox R. (1988). Why MIPS are meaningless. *BYTE*, Jun. 225–34

Goguen J. and Meseguer F. (1987). Models and equality for logical programming. In *Proc. TAPSOFT 87*, LNCS vol. 250. Berlin: Springer Verlag

Goldberg A. and Kay, A., eds (1976). Smalltalk-72 Instructional Manual. *Xerox PARC Technical Report*, March

Goldberg A. and Robson D. (1983). *Smalltalk-80, The Language and its Implementation*. Addison-Wesley

Goldenberg R. E. and Kenah L. J. (1991). *VAX/VMS Internals and Data Structures*. Digital Press

Gordon M. J. C., Milner R. and Wadsworth C. (1979). *Lecture Notes in Computer Science*, **78**, Edinburgh LCF. Berlin: Springer-Verlag

Grafe V. G. and Hoch J, E. (1990). The EPSILON-2 Multiprocessor System. *Journal of Parallel and Distributed Computing*, **10**, 309–18

Green C. (1969): Application of theorem proving to problem solving. In *Proceedings of IJCAI*, Washington DC, pp. 219–39

Grohoski G. F. (1990). Machine organization of the IBM RISC System/6000 processor. *IBM Journal of Research and Development*, **34**(1), Jan., 37–58

Guo Y., Lock H., Darlington J. and Dietrich R. (1990). A classification for the integration of functional and logic languages. TR Dept. of Computing, Imperial College London and GMD Forschungsstelle an der Univesität Karlsruhe, March

Gurd J. and Watson I. (1977). A multilayered data flow computer architecture. In *Proc. Int'l Conf. on Parallel Processing*, IEEE, p. 94

Gwennap L. (1995). Processor performance climbs steadily. *Microprocessor Report*, Jan. 23, 17–24

Harrison P. G. and Reeve M. J. (1987). The parallel graph reduction machine, ALICE. In *Graph reduction, Proc. a Workshop Santa Fé* (Fasel J. H. and Keller R.M., eds.), Lecture Notes in Computer Science, pp. 181–95. Berlin: Springer-Verlag

Hewitt C. et al. (1973). A universal modular actor formalism for artificial intelligence. *Proc. of IJCAI*, pp. 235–45

Horn A. (1951). On sentences which are true of direct unions of algebras. *J. of Symbolic Logic*, **16**, 14–21

Ingalls D. H. H. (1978). The Smalltalk-76 Programming System: Design and implementation. In *Proc. the 5th Annual ACM Symposium on Principles of Programming Languages*, Tucson, Jan.

Intel Corp. (1981). *Introduction to the iAPX432 architecture*. Manual, order number 171821, Intel Corp.

Jones A. K. and Liskov B. H. (1976). A language extension for controlling access to shared data. *IEEE Transactions on Software Eng.*, **SE-2**(4), Dec., 277–85

Jouppi N. P. (1989). The nonuniform distribution of instruction-level and machine parallelism and its effect on performance. *IEEE Trans. on Computers*, **38**(12), Dec., 1645–58

Kacsuk P. and Wise M. J., eds (1992). *Implementations of Distributed Prolog*, Wiley pp. 469

Kowalski R. (1974). Predicate logic as programming language. In *Proc. IFIP'74*, pp. 569–74. North-Holland Publ. Comp.

Kuck D. J., Muraoka Y. and Chen S.-C. (1972). On the number of operations simultaneously executable in Fortran-like programs and their resulting speed up. *IEEE Trans. on Computers*, **C-21**(12), Dec., 1293–1310

Kurfeß F., Pandolfi X., Belmesk Z., Ertel W., Letz R. and Schumann J. (1990). PARTHEO and FP2: Design of a parallel inference machine. In *Parallel Computers* (Treleaven P.C. ed.), pp. 259–97. Chichester: Wiley

Lam M. S. and Wilson R. P. (1992). Limits of control flow on parallelism. In *Proc 19th AISCA*, pp. 46–57

Leler W. (1989). Specification and generation of constraint satisfaction systems. *PhD Thesis,* The University of North Carolina, Feb.

Levi G. (1986). Logic programmirg: the foundations the approach and the role of concurrency. In *Current Trends in Concurrency*, LNCS 224, pp. 396–441. Berlin: Springer-Verlag

Levi H. M. (1986). *Capability-Based Computer Systems*. Digital Press

Lieberman H. (1987). Concurrent object-oriented programming in Act 1. In *Object-Oriented Concurrent Programming* (Yonezawa A. and Tokoro M., eds), pp. 9–36. The MIT Press

Liskov B. H. (1976). An Introduction to CLU. *Computation Structures Group Memo 136*, Lab. Computer Science, MIT , Feb.

Liskov B. and Zilles S. (1976). Programming with abstract data types. In *Proc. ACM SIGPLAN Notices*, **9**(4), 50–9

Lloyd J. W. (1984). *Foundations of Logic Programming*. Berlin: Springer-Verlag

Lock H. C. R. (1988): Guarded term ML. In *Workshop on Implementations of Lazy Functional Languages,* Aspenas, Sweden, Sept.

Magó Gy. (1980). A cellular computer architecture for functional programming. In *Proc. IEEE COMPCON*, pp. 179–87

Intel Corp. (1990). *Microprocessors,* Intel Corp.

MiniDAP: DAP FORTRAN Language (1985). London: Pero Business Centre

Minsky M. (1975). A framework for representing knowledge. In The *Psychology of Computer Vision* (Winston P., ed.). NY: McGraw-Hill

Moiso C., Giovannetti E., Levi G. and Palmidessi C. (1986). Kernel leaf: An experimental logic plus functional language – its syntax, semantics and computational model. *ESPRIT Project 415*, Second Year Report

Nadatur G. and Miller D. (1988). An overview of λ-Prolog. *Technical Report*, Computer and Information Science Dept., Univ. of Pennsylvania, March

Nicholls B. (1988). That "B" world! *BYTE*, Jun. 207–12

Nicolau A. and Fisher J. A. (1984). Measuring the parallelism available for very long instruction word architectures. *IEEE Trans. on Computers*, **C-33**(11), 968–76

Papadopoulos G. M. and Traub K. R. (1991). Multithreading: A revisionist view of dataflow architectures. In *Proc. 18th Ann. Int'l. Symposium on Computer Architectures*, pp. 342–51

Post E. L. (1936). Finite combinatory processes–formulation 1. *The Journal of Symbolic Logic*, **1**(3), Sept., 103–5

Reese B. and Boes B. (1992). Standard cell design. In *Anatomy of a Silicon Compiler* (Brodensen R. W. ed.). Boston: Kluwer, pp. 87–101

Riseman E. M. and Foster C. C. (1972). The inhibition of potential parallelism by conditional jumps. *IEEE Trans. on Computers*, **C-21**(12), Dec., 1406–11

Sakai S., Yamaguchi Y., Hiraki K., Kodama Y. and Yuba T. (1988). An architecture of a dataflow single chip processor. In *Proc. 16th Ann. Int'l. Symposium on Computer Architectures*, pp. 46–53

Saltzer J. H. and Schroeder M. D. (1975). The protection of information in computer systems. In *Proc. IEEE*

Sanderwall E. (1973). Conversion of predicate-calculus axioms, viewed as non-deterministic programs, to corresponding deterministic programs. In *Proc. IJCAI-3*, pp. 230–4

Shapiro E. Y. (1983). A Subset of Concurrent Prolog and its Interpreter. *Technical Reports TR-003*, ICOT

Simpson D. (1990). The trouble with benchmarks. *Systems Integration*, Aug., 37–45

Stephens C., Cogswell B., Heinlein J., Palmer G. and Shen J. P. (1991). Instruction-level profiling and evaluation of the IBM RS/6000. In *Proc. 18th ISCA*, pp. 137–46

Stroustrup B. (1986). The *C++ Programming Language.* Addison-Wesley

Subrahmanyam P. A. and You J.-H. (1984). Conceptual basis and evaluation strategies for integrating functional and logic programming. In *Proc. IEEE 1984 Int'l. Symposium on Logic Programming*, pp. 144–53

Taylor S., Lowry A., Magulre Jr G. Q. and Stolfo S. J. (1984). Logic programming using parallel associative operations. In *Proc. IEEE 1984 Int'l. Symposium on Logic Programming*, IEEE, pp. 58–68

Tjaden G. S. and Flynn M. J. (1970). Detection and parallel execution of independent instructions. *IEEE Trans. on Computers*, **C-19**(10), Oct., 889–95

Townsend P. (1987). Flagship hardware and implementation. *ICL Technical Journal*, May, 575–94

Turing A. M. (1936). On computable numbers, with an application to the Entscheidungsproblem. In *Proc. of the London Mathematical Society*, Series 2-42, pp. 230–65

Turner D. A. (1979). A new implementation technique for applicative languages. *Software-Practice and Experience*, **9**, Sept., 31–49

Turner D. A. (1985). Miranda: A non-strict functional language with polymorphic types. In *Proc. Functional Programming Languages and Computer Architecture* (Jouannaud, J. P. ed.). pp. 1–16. Berlin: Springer-Verlag

Wall D. W. (1991). Limits of instruction-level parallelism. In *Proc. ASPLOS IV*, pp. 176–88

Warren D. H. D. (1983). *An Abstract Prolog Instruction Set*. SRI International, AI Center, Menlo Park, California

Warren H. S. (1990). Instruction scheduling for the IBM RISC System/6000 processor. *IBM J. Research and Development*, **34**(1), Jan., 85–92

Weicker R. P. (1984). Dhrystone: A synthetic systems programming benchmark. *Proc. ACM*, **27**, Oct. 1013–30

Weicker R. P. (1990). An overview of common benchmarks. *Proc. IEEE*, Dec., 65-75

Wulf W. A. (1974). HYDRA: The kernel of a multiprocessor operating system. *CACM*, **17**, June, 337–45

Wulf W. A., London R. L. and Shaw M. (1976). An introduction to the construction and verification of Alphard programs. *IEEE Transactions on Software Eng.*, **SE-2**(4), Dec., 252–65

Yokote Y. and Tokoro M. (1987). Concurrent programming in Concurrent Smalltalk. In *Object-Oriented Concurrent Programming* (Yonezawa A. and Tokoro M, eds). The MIT Press

Yonezawa A. and Tokoro M., eds. (1987). *Object-Oriented Concurrent Programming*. The MIT Press

Part II

Instruction-level Parallel Processors

4 Introduction to ILP-Processors

This chapter is built up of five sections. In Section 4.1 we introduce the basic ILP-classes. We emphasize both their common and distinctive characteristics, and also point out the sequence of their evolution. Next, in Section 4.2 we give an overview of possible dependencies between instructions of a program. We are concerned with three kinds of dependencies: data, control and resource dependencies. As dependencies are common to all ILP-classes, we discuss them jointly. Dependencies impose constraints on the parallel execution of instructions. In Section 4.3 we overview how dependencies can be detected and resolved by instruction scheduling and at the same time how ILP-execution can be optimized. Section 4.4 is devoted to the question of preserving sequential consistency; in other words, preserving the logical integrity of a program despite parallel execution of the instructions. Finally, in Section 4.5 we investigate how much speed-up potential is embodied in instruction-level functional parallelism.

4.1 Evolution and overview of ILP-processors

The evolution of von Neumann processors can be attributed to two areas of development: improvements in technology, marked by increasing clock rates, and the functional evolution of processors. Functional evolution has been achieved primarily by increasing the degree of parallelism of the internal operations, the issue and execution of instructions. This occured in three consecutive evolution phases. The first phase is represented by *traditional von Neumann processors*, which are characterized by sequential issue and sequential execution of instructions. This is illustrated in Figure 4.1.

The search for greater performance gave rise to the introduction of parallel instruction execution. Parallel execution was achieved by using one of two orthogonal concepts: by the introduction of multiple (non-pipelined) execution units, or by pipelining. Consequently, *instruction-level parallel processors (ILP-processors)* emerged. Because early ILP-processors used sequential instruction issue, the second phase of the evolution is characterized by *scalar ILP-processors*.

In the course of this evolution, the degree of parallel execution was increased even further by making use of multiple pipelined execution units. Although this increased the parallelism of the execution, it soon became clear that sequential instruction issue was no longer able to feed enough instructions to pipelined execution units operating in parallel. Consequently, instruction issue became a bottleneck, as Flynn (1966) had foreseen long before. Thus, the third phase in the evolution of von Neumann processors became inevitable when sequential instruction issue had to be replaced with parallel issue. As a result, *superscalar ILP-processors* began to appear. They were first implemented as statically scheduled VLIW-architectures, which issue multi-operation instructions. Later, more complex,

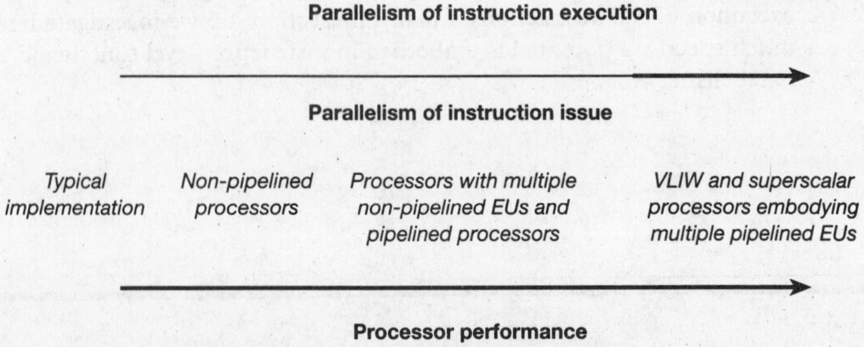

Figure 4.1 Evolution of von Neumann processors.

dynamically scheduled superscalar processors emerged that were capable of issuing multiple instructions in each cycle.

Clearly, instruction issue and execution are closely related. The more parallel the instruction execution, the higher the requirements for the parallelism of instruction issue. Thus, the evolution of von Neumann processors is marked by the continuous and harmonious increase of the parallelism of instruction issue and execution.

In the following section, we will discuss the principle of the operation of ILP-processors. However, out of the four ILP-processor classes existing, we cover only three: pipelined, VLIW and superscalar processors. The fourth ILP-processor class (processors with multiple non-pipelined EUs) is only of historical importance and should be disregarded in our discussion.

The internal principle of operation of pipelined processors differs significantly from that of VLIW and superscalar processors. Whereas *pipelined processors* work like an *assembly line*, both *VLIW and superscalar processors* operate basically *in parallel*, making use of a number of concurrently working EUs, as shown in Figure 4.2.

In describing the *principle of operation* of pipelined processors, for simplicity we confine ourselves to a straightforward pipelined processor which executes integer, RISC-like, register–register instructions. Pipelines like these operate along the following lines:

- Instruction processing is subdivided into a number of successive subtasks: instruction fetch (F), decode (D), execute (E) and writeback of the result (W), as shown in Figure 4.3(a).
- Each subtask is performed by an associated pipeline stage. In our example we call them the F, D, E and W stages (Figure 4.3(b)). The operation in each stage is implemented by dedicated hardware. The F stage fetches instructions from the cache or from memory. The D stage decodes the fetched instructions and performs, if needed, some additional tasks, such as checking for pipeline hazards. In the E stage the required operation is executed using the fetched

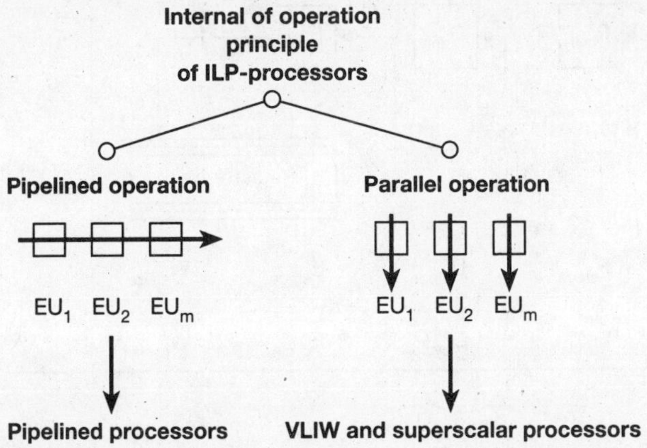

Figure 4.2 Internal principle of operation of ILP-processors.

register operands. This is accomplished by means of the E unit, which, in our case, is a traditional integer ALU. Finally, in the W stage the result is written back into the specified destination register. This operation does not require additional hardware; it is performed simply by a write operation into the register file.

- All the pipeline stages operate like an assembly line, with synchronous timing. This means that at the beginning of every pipeline cycle each stage accepts a new input and at the same time delivers its output to the next stage; except the last stage which writes the result into the specified destination (Figures 4.3(b) and 4.3(c)).

A significant feature of pipelined execution is that *in each cycle a new instruction* can enter the pipeline, as depicted in Figure 4.4. Clearly, if an instruction has completed the last phase of its execution, it retires. Thus, as many instructions can be executed in parallel as there are pipeline stages; in our example, four.

Pipelining offers higher performance at a cost of increased hardware complexity. Accordingly, pipelined processors were first employed in very expensive super and vector processors, around 1970. Subsequently, pipelined instruction processing became the standard implementation in mainframes and, in the 1980s, in microprocessors. Most dedicated functional units, such as FX or FP EUs, also became pipelined. At present, pipelined EUs are commonly used as building blocks of advanced processors, like VLIWs or superscalar processors. For example, the PowerPC 601 has three pipelined EUs, one each for FX, FP and branch execution.

The *number of pipeline stages* used depends on the kind of operation to be performed. In general, pipelines have two to ten stages. For instance, the pipelined EUs of the PowerPC 601 use two to six stages, as depicted in Figure 4.5 (Becker et al., 1993).

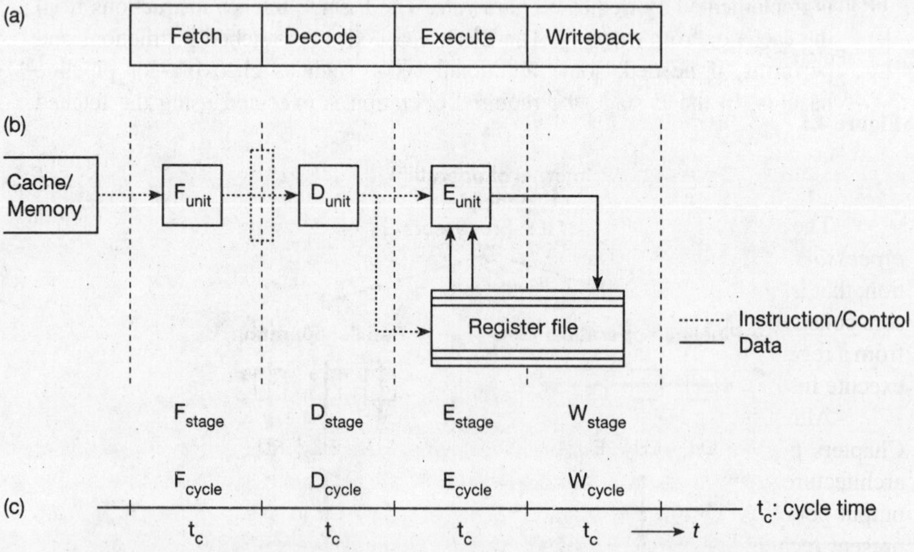

Figure 4.3 (a) Subtasks of instruction execution for integer register–register operations; (b) basic structure of an integer pipeline; (c) timing of the execution.

	t_1	t_2	t_3	t_4	t_5	t_6	t_7
Instr. 1	F_1	D_1	E_1	W_1			
Instr. 2		F_2	D_2	E_2	W_2		
Instr. 3			F_3	D_3	E_3	W_3	
Instr. 4				F_4	D_4	E_4	W_4
Instr. 5					F_5	D_5	E_5
Instr. 6						D_6	D_6
Instr. 7							F_7

Figure 4.4 Parallel execution of instructions in a straightforward pipelined processor.

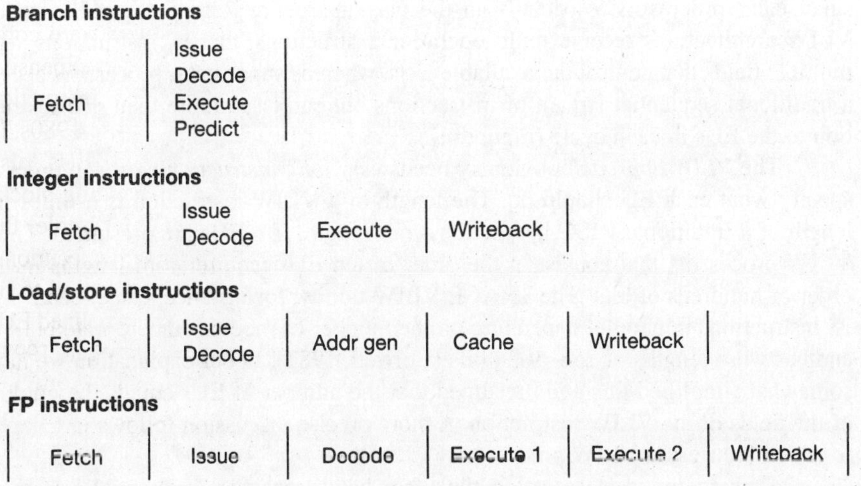

Figure 4.5 Number and kind of pipeline stages in the pipelined EUs of the PowerPC 601. © 1993 IEEE

The other class of ILP-processors, consisting of *VLIW and superscalar processors*, differs substantially from pipelined processors in that they use replication, that is, multiple EUs. The basic structure of both VLIW and superscalar processors consists of a number of EUs, each capable of parallel operation on data fetched from a register file, as shown in Figure 4.6. In both kinds of processors, multiple EUs execute instructions and write back results into the register file simultaneously.

Although the details of single v. multiple register files will be discussed in Chapters 6 and 7, a significant characteristic is that both VLIW and superscalar architectures require highly *multiported register files*. This means that usually one output port and two to three input ports are required for each EU. Considering that present technology restricts register port numbers to fewer than 20, the common basic structure of VLIW and superscalar processors has an inherent limitation on the maximum number of EUs.

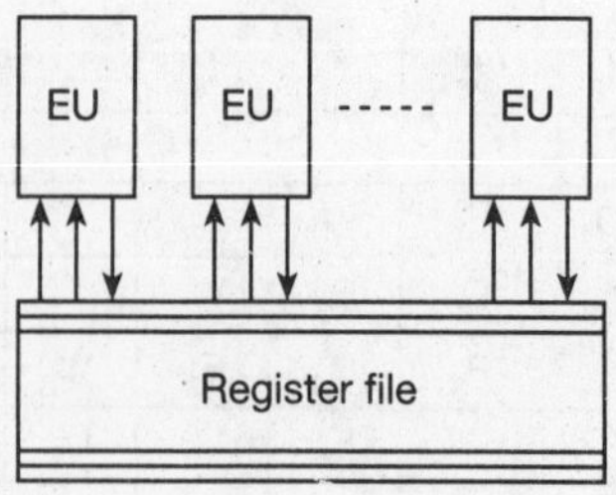

Figure 4.6 Common basic structure of conventional VLIW and superscalar processors.

Assuming pipelined EUs, the maximum number of instructions that can be executed in parallel in a VLIW or superscalar processor is the sum of the instructions that may be processed in parallel in each of the available units.

Despite these similarities, there are also basic *differences* between VLIW and superscalar processors, especially in the way instructions are presented to them. VLIW architectures receive multi-operation instructions, that is, instructions with multiple fields that control the available EUs, whereas superscalar processors accept a traditional sequential stream of instructions but can issue more than one instruction to the EUs in each cycle (Figure 4.7).

The *VLIW approach* obviously needs *very long instruction words* in order to specify what each EU should do. The length of a VLIW instruction is n-times the length of a traditional RISC instruction word length, if n EUs are presumed. Thus, VLIW processors that consist in the order of ten EUs require word lengths in the order of hundreds of bits. The TRACE VLIW family, for instance, can execute 7 to 28 instructions in parallel depending on the number of modules incorporated (1–4), and has word lengths of 256–1024 bits (Colwell, 1987). In our explanation we have somewhat simplified this and presumed that the number of EUs equals the number of the fields of the VLIW instruction. A more precise discussion follows in Chapter 6, which focuses on VLIW processors.

Superscalar processors, on the other hand, receive a sequential stream of conventional instructions. The Decode and issue unit then issues *multiple instructions* for the multiple EUs in each cycle. Current superscalar processors issue anywhere from two to six instructions per cycle. The DEC α 21064 and Intel Pentium issue two instructions, the PowerPC 601 three, and most recent processors like the Power1 (RISC/6000) or PowerPC 604 and PowerPC 620 issue four. The Power2 tops the list by using six instructions per cycle.

A further significant difference between VLIW and superscalar processors is that VLIW processors expect dependency-free (multi-operation) code, whereas superscalar processors typically do not expect this (see Section 6.1). Instead, superscalar processors cope with dependencies themselves using hardware. Clearly, superscalar processors with the same degree of parallel execution are considerably more complex then VLIWs. This explains why VLIWs preceded superscalar processors in the main line of evolution by about a decade.

Concluding this preliminary description we note that parallel instruction execution has certain *constraints* common to all ILP-processor classes. These constraints arise from the fact that, although ILP-processors allow instructions to be executed in parallel, they have to take into account dependencies among the instruc-

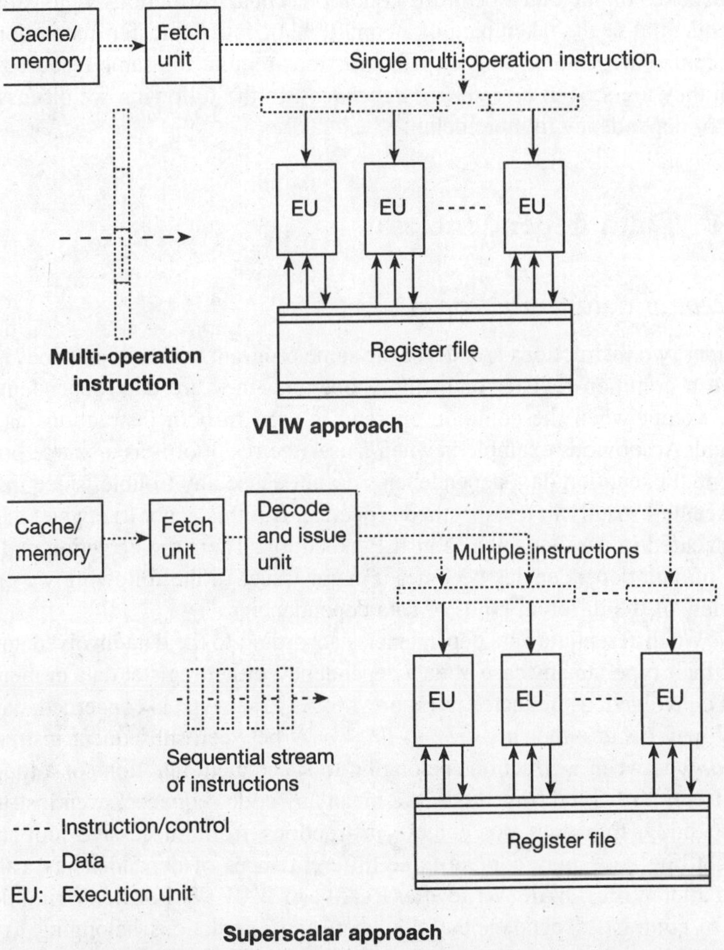

Figure 4.7 Distinction between VLIW and superscalar processors.

tions as well as *preserve* the *sequential execution semantics*. The corresponding issues are discussed in the following sections.

4.2 Dependencies between instructions

In a program, instructions often depend on each other in such a way that a particular instruction cannot be executed until a preceding instruction or even two or three preceding instructions have been executed. For instance, such a dependency exists if an instruction uses the result of the preceding instruction as a source operand.

There are three possible kinds of dependencies between instructions. If subsequent instructions are dependent on each other because of data, we term this *data dependency*. If a conditional transfer instruction is met, the subsequent execution path depends on the outcome of the condition. Thus, instructions which are in either the sequential or the taken path of a conditional control transfer instruction are said to be *control dependent*. Finally, if instructions require the same resources for execution they are said to *be resource dependent*. In the following we discuss all three types of dependency in more detail.

4.2.1 Data dependencies

Concept of data dependencies

Consider two instructions i_k and i_l of the same program, where i_k precedes i_l. If i_k and i_l have a common register or memory operand, they are data dependent on each other, except when the common operand is used in both instructions as a source operand. An obvious example is when i_l uses the result of i_k as a source operand. In sequential execution data dependencies do not cause any trouble, since instructions are executed strictly in the specified sequence. But this is not true when instructions are executed in parallel, such as in ILP-execution. Then, the detection and fair handling of data dependencies becomes a major issue. In the following we provide an overview of the different kinds of data dependencies.

We differentiate data dependencies according to the data involved and according to their type. In any case of data dependency, either register data or memory data may be involved, as indicated in Figure 4.8. As far as type is concerned, data dependency may occur either in *'straight-line code'* between subsequent instructions, or in a *loop* between instructions belonging to subsequent iterations of a loop (Figure 4.8). Here, by 'straight-line code' we mean any code sequence, even instructions of a loop body, that does not contain instructions from successive loop iterations. Straight-line code may contain three different types of dependencies, called *RAW* (Read after Write), *WAR* (Write after Read) and *WAW* (Write after Write) dependencies. In contrast, dependencies found between instructions belonging to different loop iterations are termed recurrences, which will be discussed later in this section.

Data dependencies in straight-line code

In the following discussion we will restrict ourselves to *register data* in our examples. Data dependencies for memory data can be interpreted in the same way.

RAW dependencies Consider two assembly language instructions:

```
i1:    load    r1, a;
i2:    add     r2, r1, r1;
```

Here, instruction i2 uses r1 as a source. As a result, i2 cannot be correctly executed until r1 has been loaded by i1. Therefore, i2 is said to be *RAW-dependent* on i1.

In general, an instruction il is said to be **RAW-dependent** on another instruction i_k, if i_l references as a source a data value which will be produced by i_k. RAW

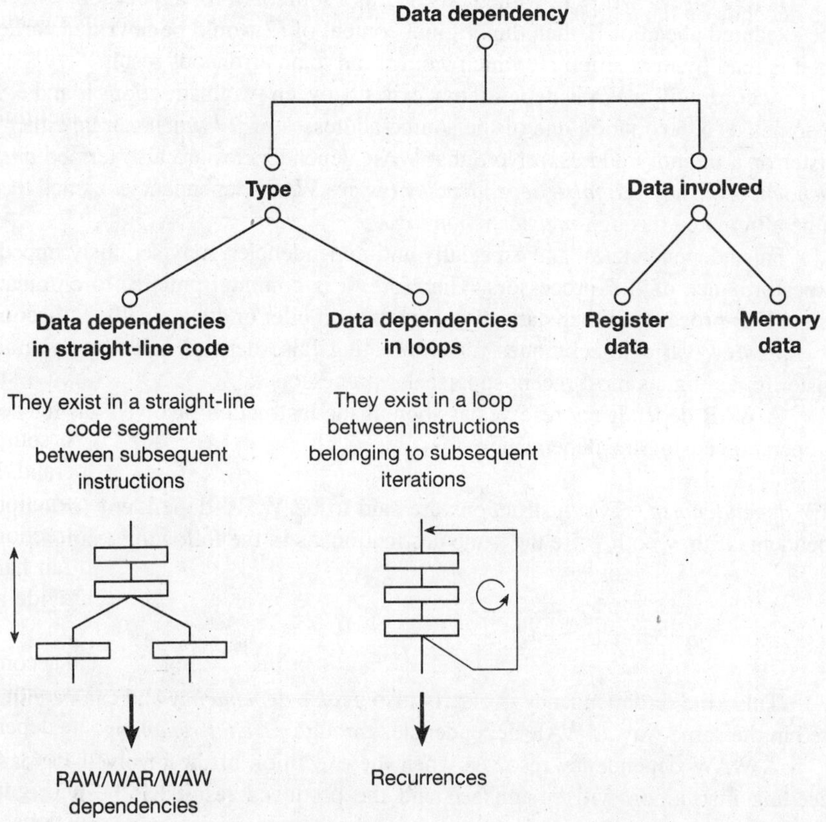

Figure 4.8 Main aspects of data dependencies.

dependencies are also called *flow dependencies*. They are *true dependencies*, since they cannot be abandoned. This is in sharp contrast to WAR and WAW dependencies, which can be circumvented.

RAW dependencies can be broken down into load-use and define-use dependencies. In the above example the requested source operand has to be *loaded* first. In this case we are dealing with a **load-use dependency**. By contrast, if the requested source operand is *defined* in the preceding instruction, in the instruction sequence,

```
i1:  mul  r1, r4, r5;
i2:  add  r2, r1, r1;
```

this kind of RAW dependency is designated as **define-use dependency**.

WAR dependencies Consider the execution of the following instructions:

```
i1:  mul  r1, r2, r3;
i2:  add  r2, r4, r5;
```

In this case i2 writes r2 while i1 uses r2 as a source. If, for any reason, i2 were to be executed ahead of i1 then the original content of r2 would be rewritten earlier than it is read by instruction r1, which would lead to an erroneous result.

Accordingly, a **WAR dependency** exists between two instructions i_k and i_l, if i_l specifies as a destination one of the source addresses of i_k (which can be either a register or a memory address). Note that WAR dependencies are also termed *anti-dependencies*. They are *false dependencies* (as are WAW dependencies) since they can be eliminated through *register renaming.*

False dependencies, and especially anti-dependencies, may seriously impede the performance of ILP-processors. Therefore, it is common practice to eliminate them in ILP-processor either statically using the compiler or dynamically. In Section 7.5 we review various techniques for eliminating false dependencies by dynamic register renaming, as most recent superscalar processors do.

A WAR dependency resolves as soon as the instruction involved has fetched the operand causing the dependency.

WAW dependencies Two instructions are said to be **WAW-dependent** (or output dependent) if they both write the same destination, as in the following example:

```
i1:  mul  r1, r2, r3;
i2:  add  r1, r4, r5;
```

This kind of dependency is clearly also a *false dependency* and can be eliminated in the same way as WAR dependencies through *register renaming.*

A WAW dependency resolves when the execution of the involved logically preceding instruction will be finished and the produced result has been used to update the program state (that is the result has been written into the referenced register or memory location).

In summary, Figure 4.9 reviews the terms relevant to data dependencies in straight-line code.

Data dependencies in loops

As we have seen in the previous section, the instructions of a loop body may have RAW, WAR or WAW dependencies among themselves. But beyond this kind of data dependency in loops, instructions belonging to a particular iteration may also be dependent on instructions belonging to previous loop iterations. We term this kind of data dependency **recurrence**. The terms *inter-iteration data dependencies* or *loop-carried dependencies* are also used.

From another point of view, recurrences are references in loop bodies to values that have been computed in previous iterations. For instance, look at the high-level language loop below:

```
do I   = 2, n
  X(I) = A*X(I-1) + B
enddo
```

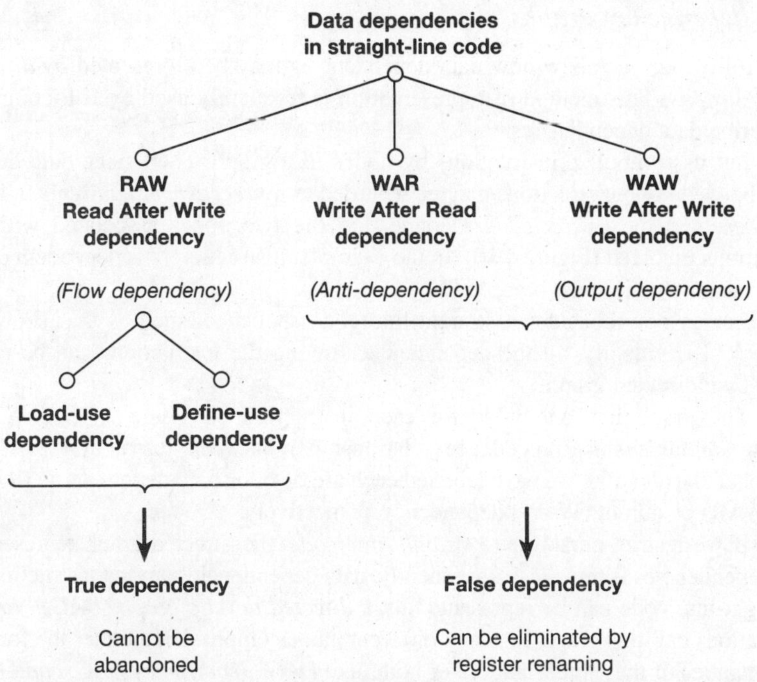

Figure 4.9 Terms relating to data dependencies occurring in straight-line code.

There is a recurrence in the loop since in order to compute the value of X(I) we need the value of X(I–1), the result of the previous iteration.

In general, a **recurrence** is said to be **of k-th order**, if the associated computation needs results which have been computed in the preceding k iterations, such as:

$$X(I) = f(A(I), X(I-1), X(I-2), \ldots , X(I-k))$$

The most common form of recurrences is *first order linear recurrences*, like the one shown in the loop above.

A **first order linear recurrence** has the general form:

$$X(I) = A(I) * X(I-1) + B(I)$$

Recurrences may be a major concern for some types of architecture, and may pose problems for some methods used by compilers. This is always the case when the result of a previous iteration of a loop is required before its computation has been completed. For instance, recurrences can inhibit vectorizing loops in vector processors. A further example where recurrences occur is the modulo scheduling technique of software pipelining (see Section 9.3.3). In this case recurrences considerably complicate the algorithm.

Data dependency graphs

In the following, we show how data dependencies may be represented *by directed acyclic graphs*. This method of representation is frequently used by ILP-compilers to describe data dependencies.

Let us symbolize instructions by nodes of a graph. Then since data dependency between two instructions may be regarded as *a precedence requirement*, it can be represented by a *directed arc* connecting the two nodes associated with the instructions involved (Figure 4.10). In the example, instruction i2 is dependent on i1, which means that i1 must precede i2.

Let us now consider a straight-line code sequence, such as that shown in Figure 4.11. Evidently, all the dependencies among the instructions can be represented by a directed graph.

The graph has one node for each instruction considered. *Directed arcs* indicate *dependencies* (precedence relationships) between instruction pairs. As additional clarification, we have labelled each arc δ_t, δ_a or δ_o to denote a true (RAW), anti (WAR) or output (WAW) dependency, respectively.

If we restrict ourselves to *straight-line code*, the directed graph representing data dependencies is *acyclic*. Consequently, data dependencies among instructions of a straight-line code can be represented by a *directed acyclic graph* **(DAG)**. Various publications call this graph by many different names emphasizing either the form or the semantics of the representation, or both, like *DAG*, *dependency DAG*, *code DAG*, *dependency graph*, or *data dependency graph*. With some minor differences, they all indicate the same: dependency, or precedence, relations among the instructions or operations concerned. Therefore, we call this a **data dependency graph (DDG)**.

Instruction i2 is dependent on i1

Figure 4.10 Representation of a data dependency between two instructions by a directed graph.

```
i1: load  r1, a;
i2: load  r2, b;
i3: ad    r3, r1, r2;
i4: mul   r1, r2, r4;
i5: div   r1, r2, r4;
```

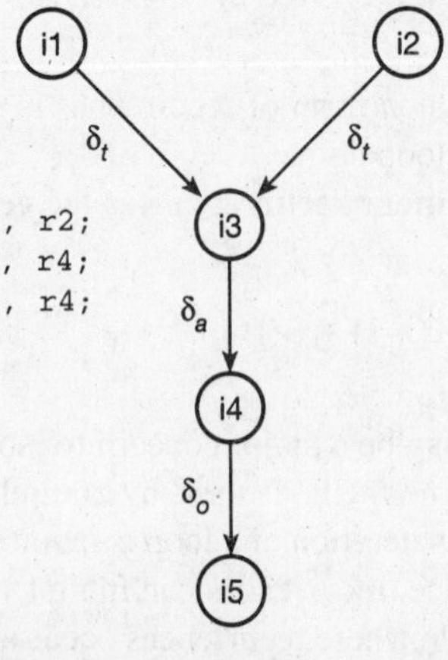

Instruction interpretation: r3← (r1) + (r2) etc.

Figure 4.11 A straight-line assembly code sequence and its corresponding DDG.

A DDG differs in two respects from a dataflow graph (DFG). First, a DDG does not comprise control structures, as do DFGs. Furthermore, a DDG shows all possible dependency relations among operations, or instructions (that is, all RAW, WAR and WAW dependencies), while a DFG indicates only RAW dependencies because of the single assignment character of the dataflow model of computation.

Usually, both traditional optimizing compilers and ILP-compilers (see Chapter 9) construct a DDG for each *basic block*.

Basic block is a concept arising from compiler technology. It denotes a straight-line code sequence that can only be entered at its beginning and left at its end. Conditional branches and branch target addresses break programs into basic blocks. Figure 4.12 shows an assembly-level basic block and its graphical representation.

The principle of the construction of a DDG is straightforward: examine all possible instruction pairs for dependencies, and if a dependency exists between the two instructions considered, construct the graph accordingly.

In the case of a *basic block* with 'n' instructions, $(n^2 - n)/2$ such examinations are required. The construction of a DDG is clearly the most time-consuming task of schedulers (Warren, 1990). For details of DDG construction see, for instance, Landskov et al. (1980).

```
i1:  calc: add r3, r1, r2;
i2:        sub r4, r1, r2;
i3:        mul r5, r3, r4;
i4:        mul r7, r6, r6;
i5:        sub r8, r7, r5;
i6:        jn negproc;
```

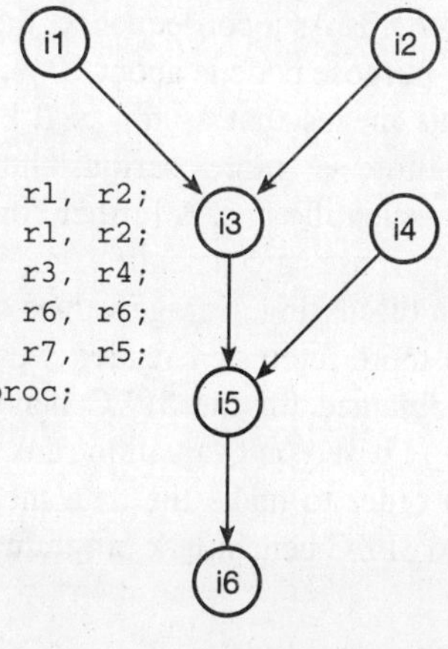

Figure 4.12 An assembly-level basic block and the corresponding DDG.

4.2.2 Control dependencies

Concept and impact of control dependencies

Consider the following code sequence:

```
        mul    r1, r2, r3;
        jz     zproc;
        sub    r4, r7, r1;
        :
zproc:  load   r1, x;
:
```

In this example, the actual path of execution depends on the outcome of the multiplication. This means that the instructions following a conditional branch are dependent on it. In a similar way, all conditional control instructions, such as conditional branches, calls, skips and so on, impose dependencies on the logically subsequent instructions, which are referred to as **control dependencies**.

As we will show later in this section, conditional branches can seriously impede the performance of parallel instruction execution. Therefore, it is important to examine how frequent conditional branches actually are.

Published data evaluating execution traces (Lee and Smith, 1984; Stephens et al., 1991; Yeh and Patt, 1992) show that general-purpose programs behave quite differently from scientific/technical programs, as far as the frequency of branches, or conditional branches, is concerned. The term **general-purpose program** stands for compilers, operating systems or non-numeric application programs. For a brief overview, we have compiled the published data into a single table (Table 4.1). The data indicates that **general-purpose programs** have a very high percentage of branches, *up to 20–30 %*. In contrast, **scientific/technical programs** contain far fewer branches; the probable frequency is as low as *5–10 %*. The ratio of conditional branches to branches seems to be quite stable in different programs, remaining within the range *75–85 %*. As a consequence, the expected frequency of conditional branches in general-purpose code is about 20 %, whereas in scientific programs it is merely 5–10 %. This means that as far as ILP-processors are concerned, control dependencies constitute a more serious hurdle in speeding up a general-purpose code than a scientific one. A further conclusion is that it makes more sense to discuss general-purpose and scientific code separately as regards conditional branches rather than discussing average values of both.

For the more interested reader, we show in Figure 4.13 a set of more detailed statistics, obtained for the SPEC benchmark programs (SPEC, 1990) by Stephens et al. (1991) based on evaluation runs on the Power1 (IBM RS/6000).

However, in order to make the data more informative, we first present the basic features of the SPEC benchmark programs used in Table 4.2 and Figure 4.13.

Table 4.1 Published branch statistics.

	Ratio of branches (%)		*Ratio of cond. branches to branches (%)*		*Total ratio of cond. branches (%)*	
	general-purp.	*scientific*	*general-purp.*	*scientific*	*general-purp.*	*scientific*
Yeh and Pat (1992)						
MC88100	24	5	78	82	20	4
Stephens et al. (1991)						
Power1 (RS/6000)	22	11	83	85	18	9
Lee and Smith (1984)						
IBM/370	29	10	73	73	21	8
PDP/11-70	39		46		18	
CDC 6400		8		53		4

Table 4.2 Basic features of the SPEC benchmark programs (Stephens et al., 1991). © 1991 ACM

Program	*Description*	*Characteristics*	*Dynamic instrs*
doduc	Monte Carlo simulation of nuclear reactor	Fortran, floating point	$1060 * 10^6$
eqntott	Boolean equation to truth table transistor	C, integer	$979 * 10^6$
espresso	Logic minimization package	C, integer	$2180 * 10^6$
fpppp	Quantum chemistry simulation	Fortran, floating point	$1040 * 10^6$
li	XLISP interpreter solving 8 queens problem	C, integer	$5779 * 10^6$
matrix 3000	Matrix operations on 300*300 matrices	Fortran, floating point	$1110 * 10^6$
nasa 7	Seven FP kernels from NASA	Fortran, floating point	$4860 * 10^6$
spice 2g6	Device-level circuit simulator	Fortran, floating point	$14780 * 10^6$
tomcatv	Vectorized mash generation	Fortran, floating point	$744 * 10^6$
gcc	GNU C compiler	C, integer	N/A

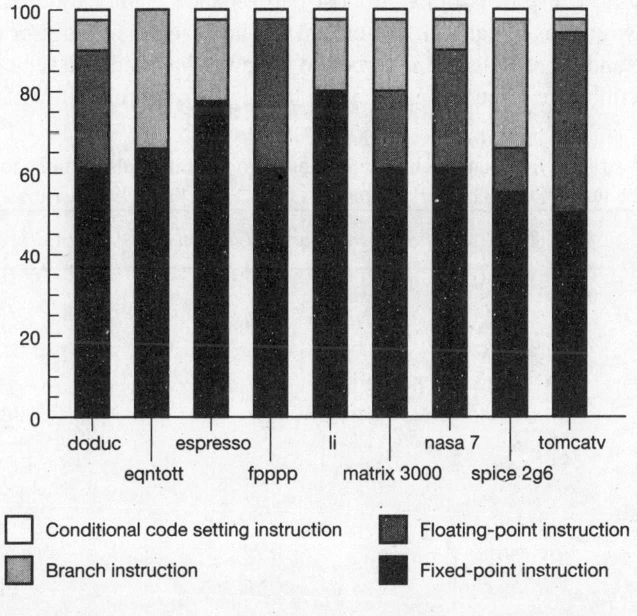

Figure 4.13 Ratio of the main instruction types for the SPEC benchmark programs, as evaluated from running them on the IBM Power1 (RS/6000) (Stephens et al., 1991). © 1991 ACM

These tables show that the original SPEC set of benchmarks is composed of four integer (eqntott, espresso, li, gcc) and six FP programs. Somewhat arbitrarily, we regard the integer programs as general purpose and the FP programs as scientific, a distinction we shall continue in this chapter.

Table 4.3 shows the average dynamic branch distance and the ratio of branch instructions for eight of the ten original SPEC benchmarks. We have excluded the results obtained for fpppp as the authors report that these data are not comparable with the others because of certain problems encountered during evaluation. Furthermore, we have slightly rearranged the table in order to group the general-purpose (integer) and scientific (floating-point) benchmark programs.

In Table 4.3 the distance between branches includes the branch instruction itself.

The data shows that for general-purpose (integer) and scientific (floating-point) programs the average ratio of branches varies considerably. General-purpose programs clearly contain more branches than scientific ones, as we have pointed out previously. The simple mean values of the average branch distances in general-purpose and scientific programs are 4.6 and 9.2 respectively. The related values of branch ratios are 21.9 % versus 10.9 %.

All in all, in running a general-purpose code for operating systems or non-numerical applications, we can expect every 3rd–6th instruction, on average, to be a conditional branch. By contrast, while executing scientific programs, every 10th–20th instruction on average is likely to be a conditional branch.

Frequent conditional branches impose a *heavy performance constraint* on ILP-processors. ILP-processors can boost performance mainly by executing more and more instructions in parallel. To achieve this however, the processor must incorporate more and more EUs and is forced to raise the instruction issue rate. But the more instructions are issued in each cycle, the higher the probability of encounter-

Table 4.3 Average dynamic branch distance and ratio of branch instructions for eight of the ten SPEC benchmarks (Stephens et al., 1991). © 1991 ACM

Program	*Type*	*Average branch distance* *	*Average branch ratio %*
eqntott		2.86	35.0
espresso	General purpose	4.81	20.8
li		6.05	16.5
Average		**4.57**	**21.9**
doduc		10.59	9.4
matrix 3000		5.05	19.8
nasa 7	Scientific	10.72	9.3
spice 2g6		3.27	30.6
tomcatv		16.28	6.0
Average		**9.18**	**10.9**

* Average branch distance includes the branch instruction itself.

ing a conditional control dependency in each cycle. For example, let us consider a code sequence where every sixth instruction is a conditional branch, as indicated in Figure 4.14. Furthermore, let us assume that the code sequence does not contain any data or resource dependencies, so the instruction issue mechanism can issue two, three or six instructions at will. When the issue rate will be increased from two instructions/cycle to three or to six instructions/cycle, each third, second, or even every issue will contain a conditional branch, giving rise to possibly more and more severe performance degradation.

Control dependencies are clearly a *major obstacle* to increasing the performance of ILP-processors. Consequently, one of the focal points of recent research in this class of processors is how to cope with control dependencies. This question will be discussed in detail in Chapter 8.

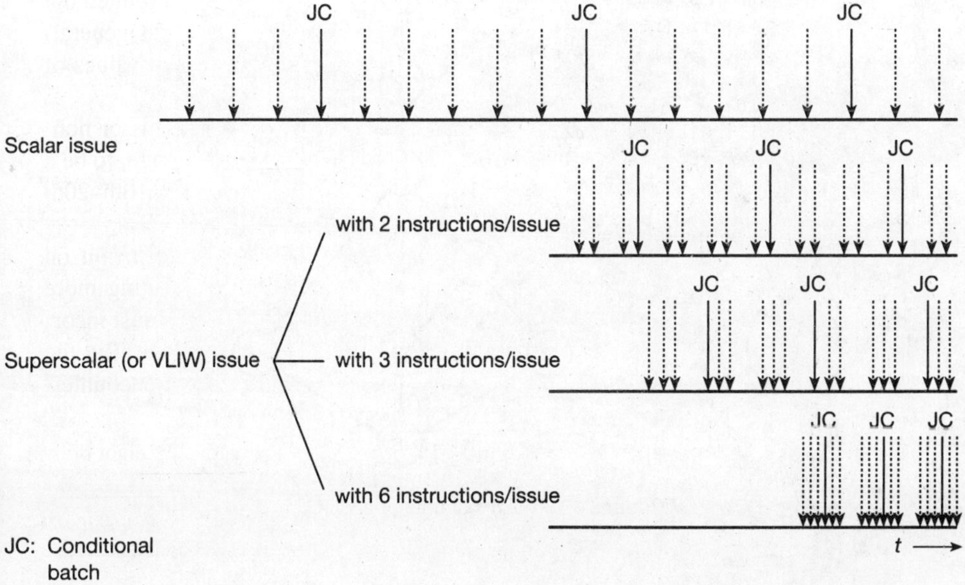

Figure 4.14 Impact of increasing the instruction issue rate on the frequency of conditional branches per issue.

Control dependency graphs

Like data dependencies, control dependencies can also be represented by directed graphs.

Instructions carrying control dependencies are basically represented by nodes with two successor arcs, as depicted in Figure 4.15. The outgoing arcs represent the true (T) and false (F) paths, and are usually labelled accordingly.

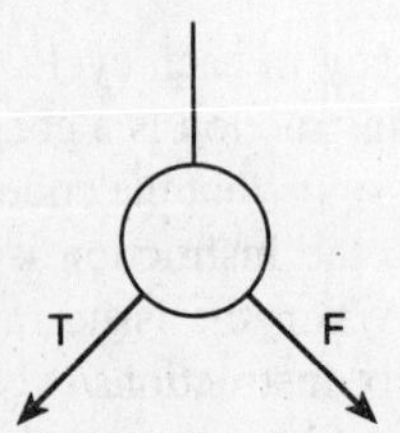

Figure 4.15 Representation of a control dependency.

```
i0: r1 = op1;
i1: r2 = op2;
i2: r3 = op3;
i3: if (r2 > r1)
i4:     if (r3 > r1)
i5:         r4 = r3;
i6:     else r4 = r1}
i7: else r4 = r2;
i8: r5 = r4 * r4
```

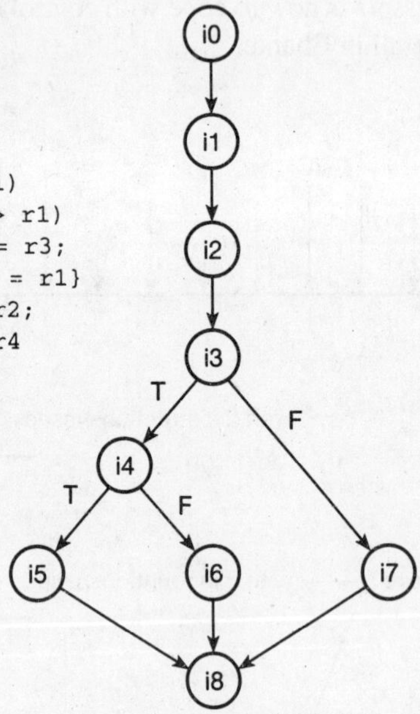

Figure 4.16 An example of a CDG.

Nodes with only one outgoing arc represent either an operational instruction or a sequence of conditional branch-free operational instructions (straight-line code). The usual term for directed graphs expressing control dependencies **is Control Dependency Graph (CDG)**. Alternative terms (often with minor differences in their interpretation) are *Program Flow Graph*, *Program Graph* and *Program Control-Flow Graph*. An example of a CDG is shown in Figure 4.16.

4.2.3 Resource dependencies

An instruction is **resource-dependent** on a previously issued instruction if it requires a hardware resource which is still being used by a previously issued instruction. If, for instance, only a single non-pipelined division unit is available, as is usual in ILP-processors, then in the code sequence

```
div  r1, r2, r3:
div  r4, r2, r5;
```

the second division instruction is resource-dependent on the first one and cannot be executed in parallel.

Resource dependencies are constraints caused by limited resources such as EUs, buses or buffers. They can reduce the degree of parallelism that can be achieved at different stages of execution, such as instruction decoding, issue, renaming, execution and so on. In general, with the evolution of integrated circuit technology, more and more hardware resources are becoming available in processors, and related constraints will impede performance to a lesser extent than at present.

4.3 Instruction scheduling

When instructions are processed (that is, issued, renamed, executed, and so on) in parallel, it is often necessary to detect and resolve dependencies between instructions. In this book, we usually discuss dependency detection and resolution as it relates to processor classes and the processing tasks involved separately. Nevertheless, the question of whether these tasks are expected to be performed by the compiler or by the processor deserves special attention.

The *two basic approaches* are termed static and dynamic (Figure 4.17). *Static* detection and resolution is accomplished by the compiler, which avoids dependencies by reordering the code. Then the output of the compiler is reordered into dependency-free code. Note that VLIW processors always expect dependency-free code, whereas pipelined and superscalar processors usually do not.

In contrast, *dynamic* detection and resolution of dependencies is performed by the processor. If dependencies have to be detected in connection with instruction issue, the processor typically maintains two gliding windows. The *issue window* contains all fetched instructions which are intended for issue in the next cycle, while instructions which are still in execution and whose results have not yet been produced are retained in an *execution window*. The width of the issue window equals the issue rate. In each cycle, all the instructions in the issue window are checked for data, control and resource dependencies with respect to the instructions in execution. There is also a further check for dependencies among the instructions in the issue window. As a result of the dependency checks, zero, one or more independent instructions will be issued to the EUs. For pipelined processors the instruction issue unit attempts to issue one independent instruction in each cycle, whereas for superscalar processors it tries to issue as many independent instructions as demanded by the specified issue rate.

It must be emphasized that this is only one possible method of dependency detection. In general, detection and resolution is part of the instruction issue policy of the processor. Related details are discussed in Section 7.3.

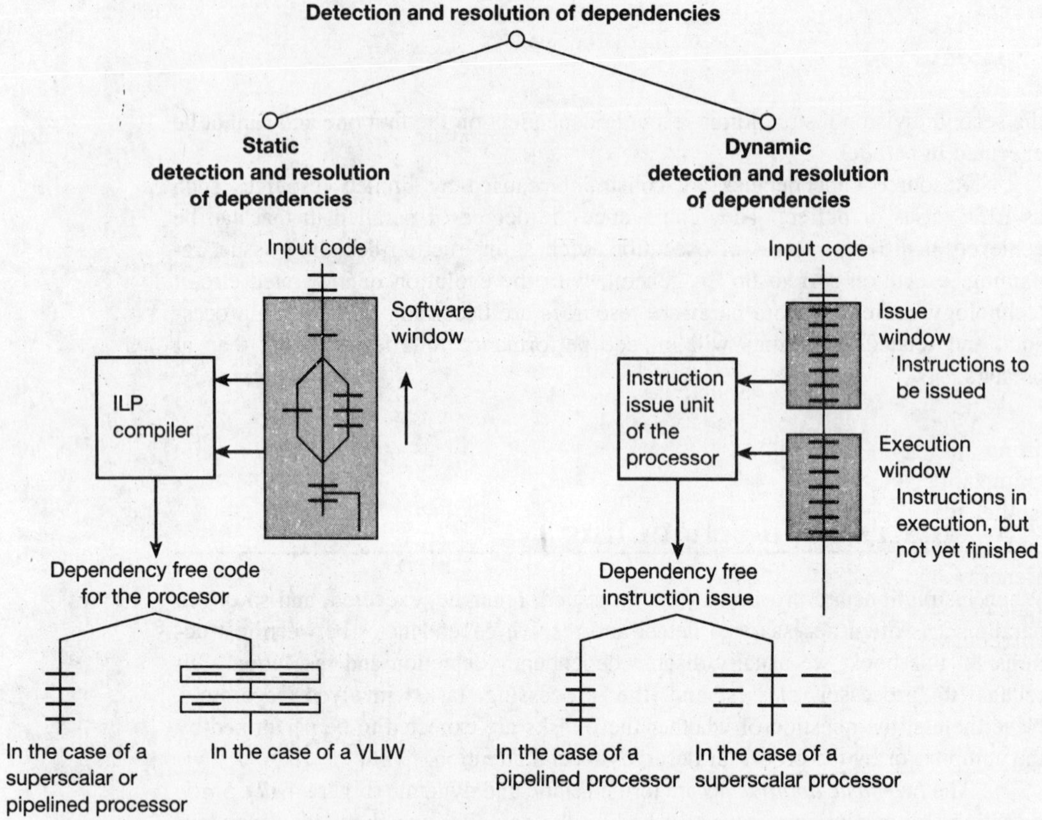

Figure 4.17 Basic approaches to instruction scheduling.

The performance of an ILP-processor can be significantly increased by parallel code optimization. If dependencies are detected and resolved statically by a compiler, clearly the compiler has to be enhanced to perform parallel code optimization as well. If, however, dependency detection and resolution is dynamic, code optimization has to be carried out previously by the compiler in connection with object code generation. Parallel optimization goes beyond traditional sequential code optimization. It is achieved by reordering the sequence of instructions by appropriate code transformations for parallel execution (also known as code reorganization or code restructuring). This means, for instance, moving instructions that are not data- or control-dependent forward to utilize unused EUs.

All in all, there are two correlated general tasks concerning ILP-processors the detection and resolution of dependencies and parallel code optimization. Now we introduce the term **ILP-instruction scheduling** to cover both (Figure 4.18).

The two aspects considered for ILP-instruction scheduling give rise to four possible approaches. Of these, the three used in connection with ILP-processors are summarized in Figure 4.19.

In *static scheduling boosted by parallel code optimization* it is the exclusive task of a compiler to detect and to resolve data, control and resource dependencies

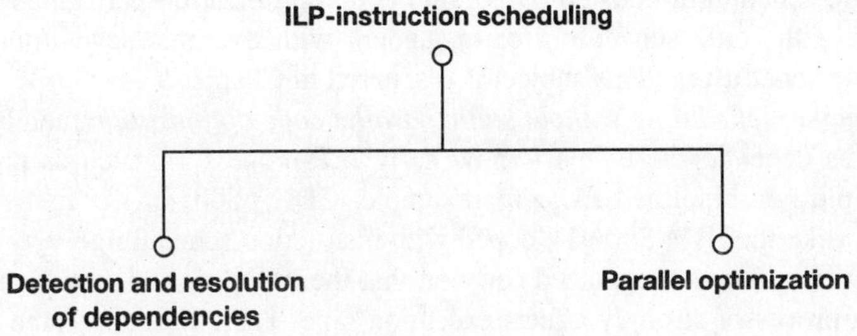

Figure 4.18 Interpretation of the concept of instruction scheduling in ILP-processors.

during code generation. Moreover, the compiler also performs parallel code optimization. That is, the compiler generates dependency-free optimized code for parallel ILP-execution. As mentioned before, VLIWs are entirely statically scheduled. Further examples of statically scheduled pipelined processors are the MIPS (Henessy and Gross, 1983) and MIPS-X (Chow and Horowitz, 1987). Another statically scheduled superscalar architecture proposal is the TORCH from Stanford University (Smith et al., 1990).

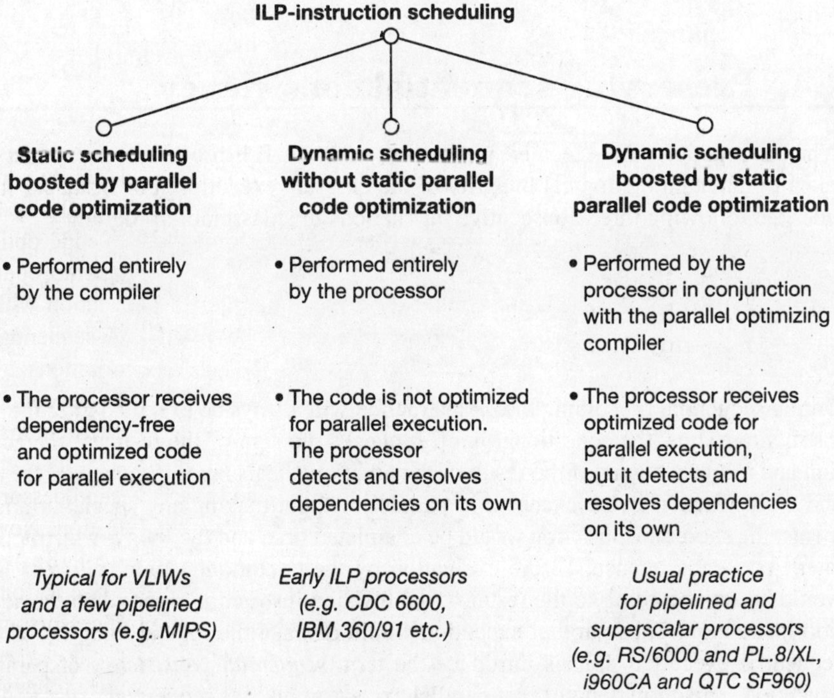

Figure 4.19 Basic approaches to ILP-instruction scheduling.

Static scheduling boosted by parallel code optimization performed either in connection with static scheduling or in tandem with dynamic scheduling is also termed **code scheduling**. This subject is discussed in Chapter 9.

Dynamic scheduling without static parallel code optimization merely detects and resolves dependencies. This is how early ILP-processors, such as processors with multiple non-pipelined EUs (for example, CDC 6600) or the first pipelined processors (like the IBM 360/91), coped with instruction scheduling.

However, it was recognized early on that the order of the instructions passed over to the processor strongly affects execution time. Therefore, it became *common practice to boost* the performance of *dynamic scheduling using static parallel code optimization.* Here, parallel code optimization part is performed either by a separate post-pass code optimizer which follows the traditional compiler, or by enhancing the traditional compiler with parallel code optimization (see Figures 9.1(c) and (d)). The first application of boosting the performance of a dynamically scheduled processor by a preceding parallel optimization, was probably the CYBER 200 FORTRAN compiler for the scalar unit of the CDC CYBER 205 (about 1981). This scalar unit consisted of six EUs operating in parallel, of which five were pipelined, and it was scheduled dynamically. Nowadays, this approach is typical for superscalar processors like the Power1 (RS/6000) with the PL.8 or the XL families of compilers (Warren, 1990).

Finally, we note that dependency detection and resolution is a means to extract *parallelism.* This is how instruction-level functional parallelism, which is implicit, is made explicit.

4.4 Preserving sequential consistency

When instructions are executed in parallel, as in an ILP-processor, care must be taken to maintain the logical integrity of the program execution. For instance, consider the following three consecutive instructions in an assembly program:

```
div  r1,  r2,  r3:
ad   r5,  r6,  r7;
jz   anywhere;
```

During sequential processing the *ad* instruction will always be executed after the *div* instruction. Thus, the conditional jump *jz* checks the sign of the result of the addition and initiates a jump if the result of the addition equals zero. If, however, the *div* and *ad* instructions were executed in parallel, without making any special arrangements, the short *ad* instruction would be completed first, and the long *div* instruction later. As a consequence, before evaluation by the conditional jump, the zero flag would be set according to the result of the division instruction rather than the addition instruction. Thus parallel execution would damage the logical integrity of the sequential execution. Let us introduce the term *sequential consistency* of parallel execution. This term denotes that parallel execution mimics sequential execution as far as the logical integrity of program execution is concerned.

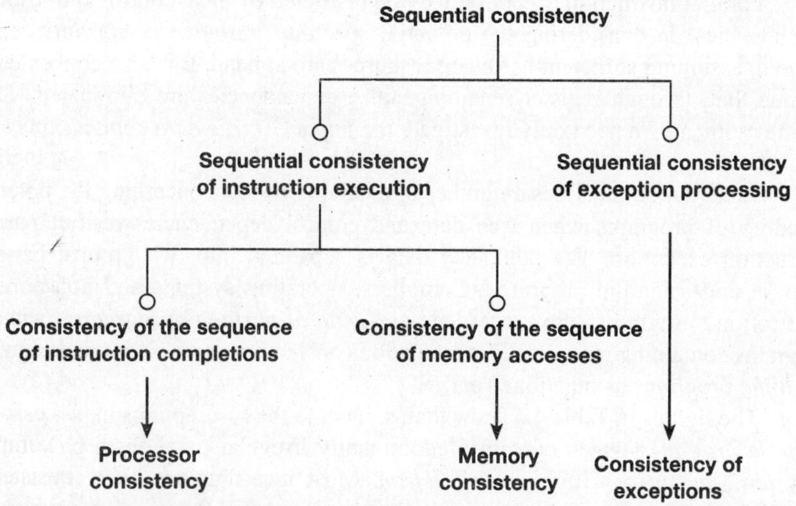

Figure 4.20 Implementation of the concept of sequential consistency.

However, sequential consistency may be interpreted for both instruction execution and exception processing (interrupt processing) as indicated in Figure 4.20. Furthermore, the sequential consistency of instruction execution covers the sequence of both instruction completions and memory accesses. In the first case we are concerned with *processor consistency* and in the latter with *memory consistency*.

For the details concerning sequential consistency we refer you to Section 7.7, where sequential consistency of superscalar execution is discussed. The only point we now emphasize is that sequential consistency may be either strong or weak in each of the cases mentioned. A *strong consistency* denotes exactly the same sequence of operations as during sequential execution, whereas a *weak consistency* means an operation sequence which can differ from the sequential one, but which does not damage the logic of the sequential operation. For instance, in the case of a weak processor consistency, instructions which are not dependent on preceding ones may be executed earlier than in the sequential case. Again, Section 7.7 has further details.

4.5 The speed-up potential of ILP-processing

In this section, we discuss the extent to which instruction-level parallelism is available in programs. This is a crucial point regarding ILP-processors, since it indicates the limits of how far traditional sequential computation can be speeded up by means of ILP-compilers and ILP-processors.

Our discussion is based on the considerable number of papers that have been published on this topic since the early 1970s.

Parallel instruction execution may be restricted by data, control and resource dependencies. In considering the potential speed-up, *resource constraints* can be ignored, assuming sufficient hardware resources are at hand. It is also convenient to assume that, through register renaming, false dependencies are eliminated. Thus, for the moment, we need only investigate the *impact of true data dependencies and control dependencies*.

Table 4.4 summarizes a number of available results concerning the potential speed-up of programs when true data and control dependencies restrict parallel instruction execution. The published data is separated into two groups: general-purpose and scientific programs. Compilers, operating systems and non-numeric application programs are regarded as *general-purpose programs*, whereas programs containing massive FP computations on vectors or matrices are designated *scientific programs* as mentioned earlier.

The figures in Table 4.4 show that, subject to the assumptions made, *general-purpose programs* which contain predominantly irregular parallelism have only a *very low amount of available parallelism*. Most investigations have revealed an astonishingly low potential speed-up in the range of 1.2–3.0 with an *average* value of *about 2*. The corresponding speed-up values for scientific programs are in a slightly higher range of 1.2–17 with an average of about 2–4. The extremely large figure indicated by Lam and Wilson (1992), which is due to the open-handed evaluation technique used, is not taken into account.

This data is quite disappointing and would certainly discourage any motivation to develop ILP-processors relying on potential speed-up values like this. But why are the speed-up figures so astonishingly low? The reason for these results is that a low-efficiency method was used to extract parallelism, called *basic block scheduling*. As we mention in Section 9.2, when basic block scheduling is used parallelism is extracted piecewise, separately for each basic block. Note that basic

Table 4.4 Published data on potential speed-up when parallel instruction execution is restricted by true data and control dependencies.

Paper	Benchmark	*Speed-up for general programs*		*Speed-up for scientific programs*	
		range	*average*	*range*	*average*
Tjaden and Flynn, 1970	31 library programs			1.2–3.2	**1.9**
Kuck et al., 1972	20 Fortran programs			1.2–17	**4**
Riseman and Foster, 1972	7 Fortran/ assembly programs	1.2–3.0	**1.8**	1.4–1.6	**1.6**
Jouppy, 1989	8 Modula-2 programs	1.6–2.2	**1.9**	2.4–3.3	**2.8**
Lam and Wilson, 1992	6 SPECmarks + 4 others	1.5–2.8	**2.1**	2–293	

block scheduling cannot cope with control dependencies. Basic blocks are, however, relatively short. For several C benchmarks on a RISC II architecture, DeRosa and Levy (1987) measured basic block lengths of 3.5–6.3, with an overall average of 4.9. In another instance, Lam and Wilson (1992) obtained somewhat higher basic block lengths for MIPS 3000 programs quoted in Table 4.5. Their results also show that scientific programs apparently contain longer basic blocks, on average 31.6, than do general-purpose programs, with an average of 7.5. This is in accordance with the data on the average branch distance listed in Table 4.3.

Obviously, for RISC-style as well as scientific programs, the basic block size is somewhat longer than for CISC programs or for general-purpose programs. Therefore, the small number of instructions available in a basic block for scheduling restricts the *speed-up* potential of basic block scheduling to low values of *about 2* for general-purpose and 2–4 for scientific programs. Techniques for basic block scheduling and parallelism extraction at basic block level are presented in Section 9.2.

There are, however, two encouraging possibilities to follow. The first is to utilize *regular parallelism*, that is, potential speed-up embodied in loops. The second is based on the *proper handling of control dependencies.*

It has been shown that *loops* are a promising source of parallelism when exploited by proper techniques such as *software pipelining* (see Section 9.3.3). Published data on potential speed-ups of loops assuming piplined processors and obtained figures are summarized in Table 4.6.

According to the table, *potential speed-up* values for the first 14 Livermore Loops amount to a figure of *more than 50 on average* assuming unlimited resources

Table 4.5 Basic block lengths of six SPEC benchmarks and four other programs, measured on a MIPS 3000 (Lam and Wilson, 1992). © 1992 ACM

	Program	*Basic block length*	
		General-purpose programs	*Scientific programs*
	awk	7.8	
others	ccom	7.5	
	irsim	7.7	
	latex	10.4	
	eqntott	4.4	
	espresso	7.0	
specmarks	qcc (cc1)	8.9	
	matrix 3000		21.0
	spice 2g6		14.1
	tomcatv		59.8
	Average	**7.8**	**31.6**

Table 4.6 Potential as well as actual speed-up values achieved for the first 14 Livermore Loops ([1] Aiken and Nicolau, 1988, [2] Lam, 1988). © 1988 ACM

Loop	*Potential speed-up*[1]					*Actual speed-up*[2] *obtained*
	For limited processors		*For an ideal schedule*			
	1 processor	*2 processors*	*Processors*	*Registers*	*Speed-up*	
LL1	3.4–5.6	6.3–11.1	13	82	44	8.25
LL2	2.5–4.3	5–7.5	16	105	40	3.25
LL3	2.2–2.8	2.8–3.2	5	8	3.8–5.7	2.71
LL4	2.6	3.3	5	8	4.5	2.71
LL5	2–2.5	2.5–2.6	3	5	2.6	1.12
LL6	0.7–2	0.7–2.5	5	8	0.7–3.3	2.86
LL7	1.8–2.5	3.5–4.9	36	243	64	6.00
LL8	3.6–5	7.2–10	60	363	218	2.29
LL9	2–2.8	4–5.7	39	264	80	4.27
LL10	1.8–2.5	3.6–4.8	40	210	72	5.31
LL11	1–2.2	1–2.7	4	4	1–3.2	1.30
LL12	3.2–5	6.7–10	6	37	20	4.00
LL13	2.7–3	5.5–6	50	376	140	2.63
LL14 (avg)	3.5–4.5	6.2–7.7	28	161	67.5	3.32
Average	**2.3 – 3.5**	**4.3 – 6.2**			**54.2–54.7**	**3.6**
Harmonic mean	**1.8 – 2.8**	**2.5 – 4.7**			**3.5–7.5**	

and an ideal schedule. In order to exploit this huge amount of parallelism a large number of processors (in the region of 50) and a considerable number of registers (in the region of 400) would be required. If, however, resources are constrained, potential speed-up may be severely limited. For instance, if the number of processors is restricted to one or two, the potential speed-up declines sharply to average values of two to six. In addition, the second part of the table indicates actual speed-up values obtained by *software pipelining* on the WARP machine (Lam, 1988). The speed-up values obtained fall into the range of 1.1–8.2 with a mean value of 3.6. Software pipelining is described in Section 9.3.3.

The second promising possibility concerns the *appropriate handling of control dependencies*. Riseman and Foster recognized as early as 1972 that control dependencies severely restrict parallel execution. They investigated the potential speed-up assuming a *perfect oracle* for each conditional statement as well as *removal of false data dependencies*. Their results, as well as the results of similar investigations, are compiled in Table 4.7.

Table 4.7 Published data on upper limits of speed-up assuming a perfect oracle for conditional statements.

Paper	*Benchmark*	*Speed-up for general-purpose programs*		*Speed-up for scientific programs*	
		range	*average*	*range*	*average*
Riseman and Foster, 1972	7 Fortran/ assembly programs	8–100	**42**	30–120	**75**
Nicolau and Fisher, 1984	22 numerical programs			3–988	**12**
Kumar, 1988	4 Fortran programs			475–3500	**1839**
Butler et al., 1991	9 SPEC benchmarks	38–200	**170**	17–1165	**509**
Wall, 1991	6 SPEC benchmarks,	16-41	**28**	57–60	**59**
	13 others	7–37	**24**	6–27	**18**
Austin and Sohi, 1991	SPEC benchmarks	13–942	**288**	51–33 749	**6188**
Lam and Wilson, 1992	6 SPEC benchmarks,	174–3283	**1400**	844–188 470	**64 500**
	4 others	47–265	**229**		

This data indicates that *control dependencies* are *the real obstacle* in utilizing instruction-level parallelism. If we were able to make perfect oracles, and could assume the availability of sufficient hardware resources, we could expect speed-up values on the order of 10 to 100, in some cases even higher. In practice, of course, neither perfect oracles nor unlimited resources exist. An apparent substitution for an oracle would be to pursue all possible execution paths by multiple, multiway branches. This would require following both (or all) possible paths for each conditional branch and at the end of the computation discarding all paths except the one which turned out to be the all-true one. This approach would require the execution of computations along 2^n paths for a chain of 'n' conditional statements. Obviously, pursuing an exponentially increasing number of paths would be an unrealistic approach. However, based on this approach, a number of applicable approximations have been developed, either by guessing the most probable path (*branch prediction*) or by pursuing both possible execution paths (*multiway branching*) for a single conditional branch or for a restricted number of subsequent branches. These techniques are discussed in Chapter 8.

A crucial question is how close *real systems* can come to the upper limits of speed-up. The remarkable results published by Wall are presented in Table 4.8 and Figure 4.21.

Wall's investigations show that ambitious systems can expect to achieve speed-up figures of *about 4–6 for general-purpose programs* and *around 10–20 for scientific programs*. An ambitious system in his interpetation predicts conditional branches, has 256 integer and 256 FP (floating point) registers, eliminates false data

Table 4.8 Characteristics of the test programs used (Wall, 1991). © 1991 ACM

	Lines	*Dynamic instructions*	*Remarks*
Livermore	268	22 294 030	Livermore loops 1–14
Whetstones	462	24 479 634	Floating-point
Linpack	814	174 883 597	Linear algebra (3)
Stanford	1 019	20 759 516	Hennessy's suite (5)
sed	1 751	1 447 717	Stream editor
egrep	844	13 910 586	File search
yacc	1 856	30 948 883	Compiler-compiler
metronome	4 287	70 235 508	Timing verifier
grr	5 883	142 980 475	PCB router
eco	2 721	26 702 439	Recursive tree comparison
ccom	10 142	18 456 797	C compiler front end
gcc1	83 000	22 745 232	Pass 1 of GNU C compiler
espresso	12 000	135 317 102	Boolean function minimizer
li	7 000	1 247 190 509	LISP interpreter
fpppp	2 600	244 124 171	Quantum chemistry
doduc	5 200	284 697 827	Hidrocode simulation
tomcatv	180	1 986 257 545	Mesh generation

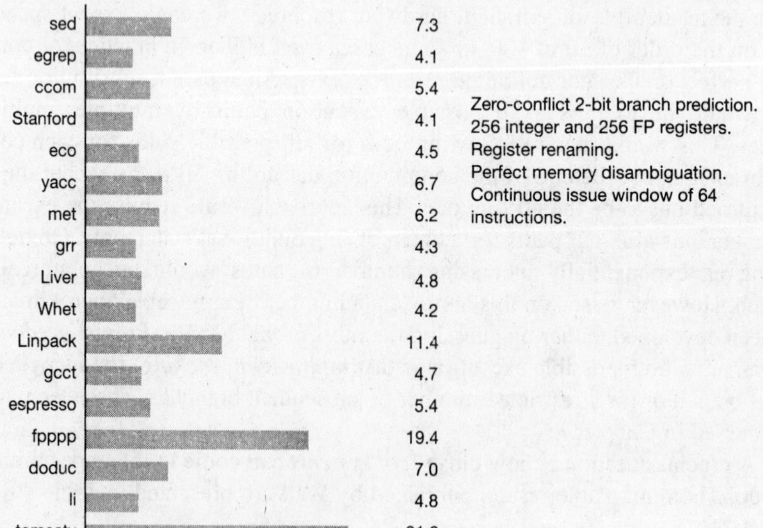

Figure 4.21 Expected limits of speed-up for ambitious IFP-processors (Wall, 1991). © 1991 ACM

dependencies through register renaming, performs a perfect memory disambiguation and maintains a gliding instruction window of 64 items. For the time being, both his hypotheses concerning an ambitious machine and the obtainable speed-up figures seem to demarcate the real limits.

5 Pipelined Processors

Chapter 4 demonstrated that there are *two fundamental parallel concepts* at the instruction level that can be used to increase the performance of traditional sequential processors: pipelining and replication. *Pipelining* boosts performance by executing instructions like an assembly line. *Replication* means using multiple EUs operating in parallel. Evidently, pipelining is the principle behind pipelined processors, while replication is the foundation for VLIWs and superscalar processors.

We emphasize that pipelining and replication are two orthogonal concepts. Thus both approaches can be applied at the same time to achieve a cumulative effect. In practice, this means that an additional performance increase can be achieved using *multiple pipelined EUs*. This arrangement is typical for both VLIWs and superscalar processors.

Pipelining appeared at the end of the 1960s as an effective FP number crunching technique in the first supercomputers of that time, such as the IBM 360/91 (1967) and the CDC 7600 (1970). At the beginning of the 1970s this technique became a common feature in the emerging vector processors, like the CDC STAR 100 (1973) or the TI ASC (1973). The use of pipelining also spread to instruction processing to increase performance. This happened first in mainframes like the B7700 (1970) in the 1970s, and then also in microprocessors from the beginning of the 1980s. Pipelining is now the standard instruction processing technique. Furthermore, pipelining has penetrated into the functional units of processors. Nearly all recent EUs operate on this principle.

This chapter is devoted to this important topic. In the first section we introduce the basic concepts of pipelining, such as principles of operation, general pipeline structure, performance measures and application scenarios. Section 5.2 goes on to explore the design space while the remaining sections give an introduction to the practice of pipelining. First, in Section 5.3 we discuss how this technique is used for overall instruction processing. Then in Sections 5.4 and 5.5 we give an insight into how FX and load/store instructions are pipelined in current processors.

5.1 Basic concepts

5.1.1 Principle of pipelining

As stated earlier, the term '*pipelining*' refers to the temporal overlapping of processing. *Pipelines* are nothing more than assembly lines in computing that can be used either for instruction processing or, in a more general sense, for performing any complex operations. Note that pipelining can be utilized effectively only for a sequence of the same or similar tasks, much the same as assembly lines.

In this first section, we restrict our discussion to a straightforward pipeline which we call a **basic pipeline**. Subsequently, we expand on several additional aspects of this concept.

A *basic pipeline* processes a sequence of tasks, such as instructions, according to the following principle of operation:

- Each task is subdivided into a number of successive subtasks, as shown in Figure 5.1. For instance, the execution of register–register instructions may be broken down into instruction fetch, decode, execute and writeback.
- We assume, furthermore, that there is a pipeline stage associated with each subtask which performs the required operations. In our example, these are labelled Stage 1 to Stage n.
- For a basic pipeline we assume that the same amount of time is available in each stage for performing the required subtask.
- All the pipeline stages operate like an assembly line, that is, receiving their input typically from the previous stage and delivering their output to the next stage. The very first stage, of course, accepts the input of the pipeline and the last stage delivers its output.
- Finally, we assume the basic pipeline operates *clocked*, in other words *synchronously*. This means that each stage accepts a new input at the start of the

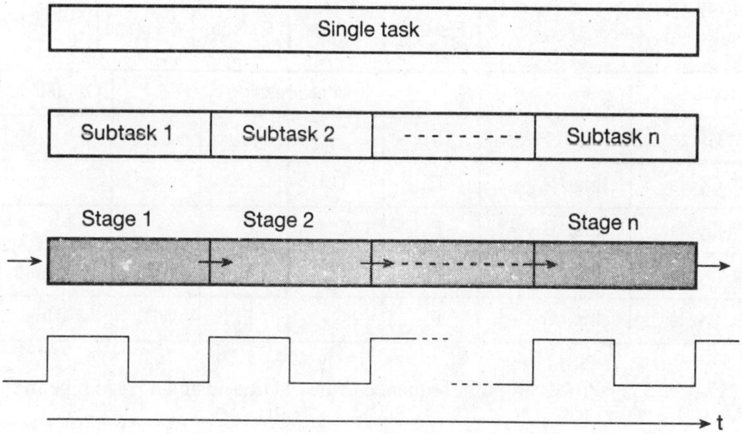

Figure 5.1 Basic principle of pipelining.

clock cycle, each stage has a single clock cycle available for performing the required operations, and each stage delivers the result to the next stage by the beginning of the subsequent clock cycle.

Consider, for example, the pipelined processing of simple FX or logical instructions given in register–register format (Figure 5.2). Here, the processing of each single instruction can be broken down into four subtasks, each of which can be performed in approximately the same period of time: instruction fetch, decode, execute and writeback. A corresponding basic pipeline will consist of four associated stages (F stage, D stage, E stage and WB stage).

Next, let us consider how performance is increased when a sequence of instructions is executed using pipelining (Figure 5.3).

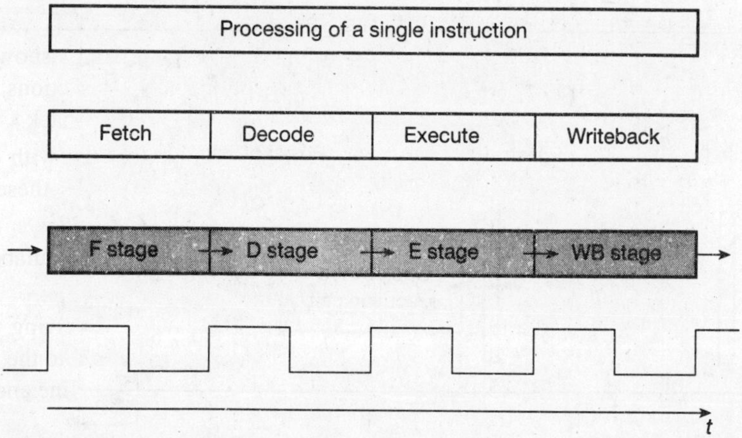

Figure 5.2 Principle of pipelining as applied to the processing of FX or logical instructions of register–register format.

Cycle	In	In processing				Out (Finished)
		F stage	D stage	E stage	WB stage	
1. Cycle	Instr 1 →	F_1				
2. Cycle	Instr 2 →	F_2	D_1			
3. Cycle	Instr 3 →	F_3	D_2	E_1		
4. Cycle	Instr 4 →	F_4	D_3	E_2	WB_1	→ Instr 1
5. Cycle	Instr 5 →	F_5	D_4	E_3	WB_2	→ Instr 2

Figure 5.3 Processing of a sequence of instructions using a basic pipeline.

In the first clock cycle instruction 1 is fetched by the pipeline. In the second cycle, instruction 1 is decoded and the following instruction (instr. 2) fetched. Subsequently, in the third cycle, instruction 1 starts execution, instruction 2 is decoded and instruction 3 fetched. In the fourth cycle the result of the execution of instruction 1 is written into the register file, instruction 2 is executed, instruction 3 decoded and the next instruction (instr. 4) fetched. Note that beginning with this cycle, all four stages are operating in parallel with four instructions in execution at the same time.

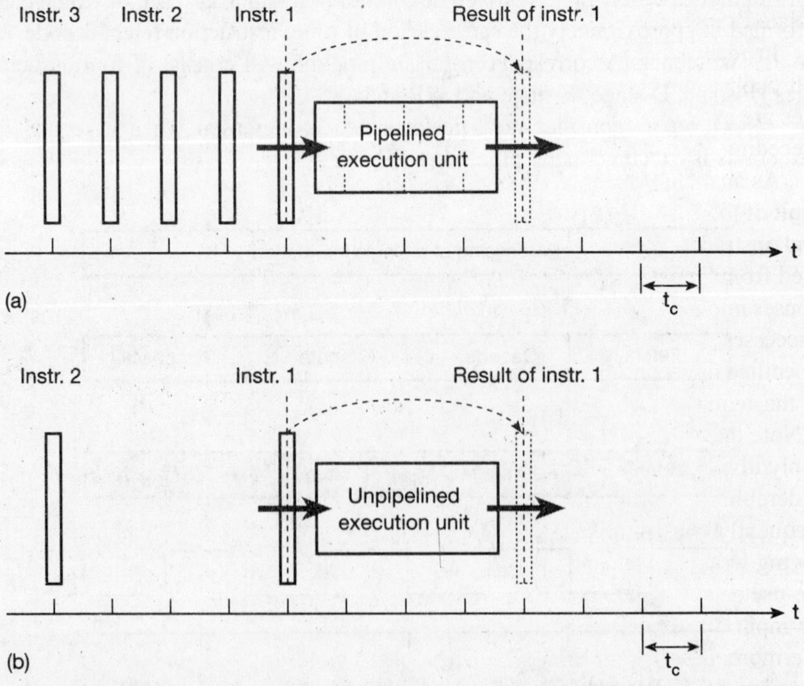

Figures 5.4 Contrasting (a) pipelined and (b) unpipelined processing.

Owing to its principle of operation, a basic pipeline can accept a *new task*, such as processing a new instruction, *in each* successive *clock cycle* (t_c), as indicated in Figure 5.4(a). This is a significant improvement in comparison with traditional unpipelined processing where the processing unit is occupied for the entire period of the execution time, as depicted in Figure 5.4(b). In the unpipelined case, a new task can be started only after the previous one is completed. Here, for ease of comparison, we assume that both the pipelined and unpipelined EUs need four cycles to produce the result.

In conclusion, we mention that a real pipeline may include a few *extensions* to basic pipelines. For instance, real pipelines can also be used for tasks whose subtask structure is more general than a linear sequence. Pipelined execution is also often performed using half-cycles. For an example see Figure 5.38. And in certain cases, one or more pipeline stages may have to be recycled to accomplish a given task, as depicted in Figure 5.33. These additional cycles may be required to perform certain complex arithmetic operations, like FP multiplication, or to calculate addresses in complex addressing modes.

5.1.2 General structure of pipelines

A straightforward pipeline consists of a number of *stages*, one for each subtask (Figure 5.5). The stages are decoupled from each other by registers, called *latches*. As each clock cycle ends, the latches gate in their inputs and forward them into the associated stage where the required operation will be performed.

In reality, each stage is often implemented by a number of different EUs which cooperate in performing the required operations, as Figure 5.6 shows. The latches are extended with multiplexers that select and transfer data from the outputs of preceding EUs to the inputs of subsequent EUs.

As an example, Figure 5.7 shows the structure and pipelined operation of the FX unit of the IBM Power1 (RS/6000) (Grohoski, 1990). This unit executes FX and logical instructions, typically in four cycles. In the fetch cycle, instructions are fetched from the on-chip instruction cache (not shown in the figure) via the instruction buses into the instruction buffer. The decode cycle decodes the fetched instruction and accesses the referenced register values. Then, in the next cycle (execute cycle) the specified data manipulation is performed. This stage provides three EUs that perform the required data manipulation: an adder, a logic unit and a multiply/divide unit. Note that the first two units need only one cycle to accomplish the result. The multiply/divide unit, however, does not operate in a pipelined mode and requires a considerable number of cycles to complete a multiplication or a division. Subsequently, the result is written back into the register file via the T-latch during the following writeback cycle. It is worth noting that, in order to shorten or to eliminate define-use delays, the result of the execute stage can be directly returned (bypassed) to the input of the execute stage (the A-, B- and S-latches) through the result bus. Furthermore, the FX unit provides an additional stage for processing load and store instructions, which operates in the cache-access cycle. In this cycle, data may be written into or read from the cache.

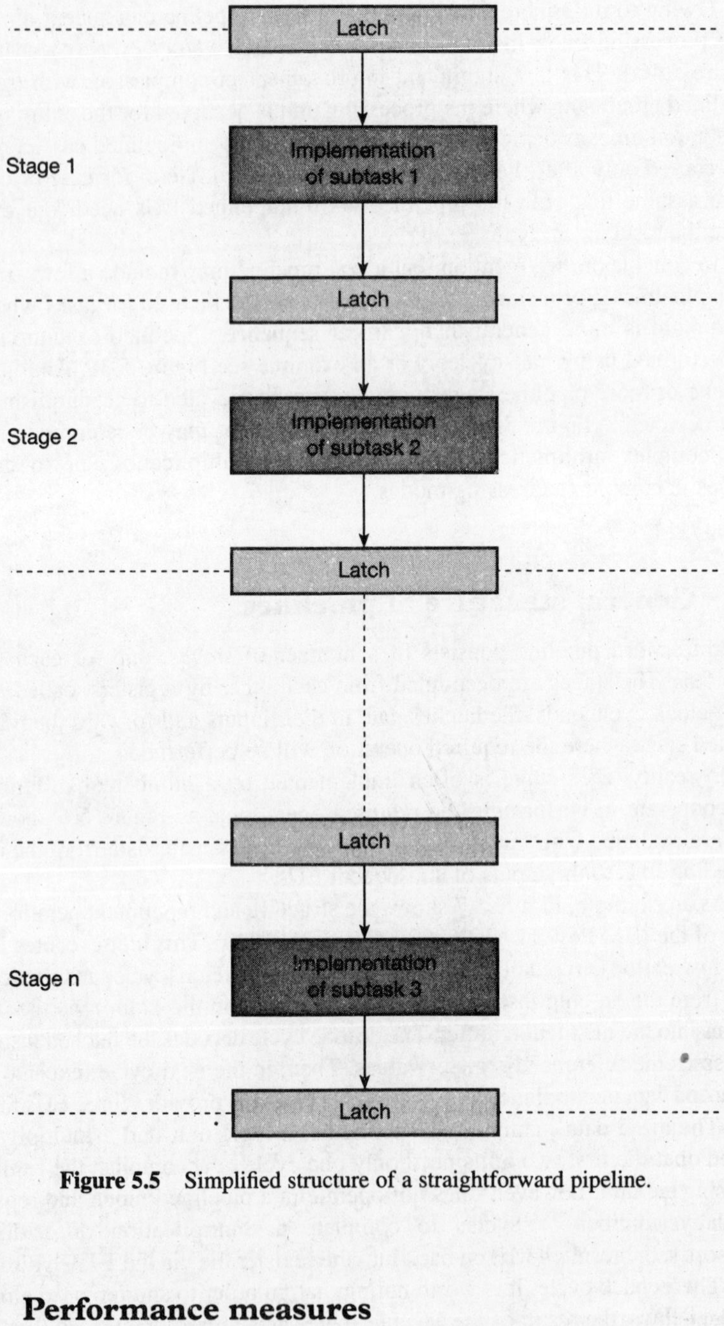

Figure 5.5 Simplified structure of a straightforward pipeline.

5.1.3 Performance measures

Performance in an unpipelined processor is characterized by the cycle time and the execution times of the instructions. In the case of pipelined execution, instruction processing is interleaved in the pipeline rather than performed sequentially as in non-pipelined processors. Therefore, the concept of the execution time of instruc-

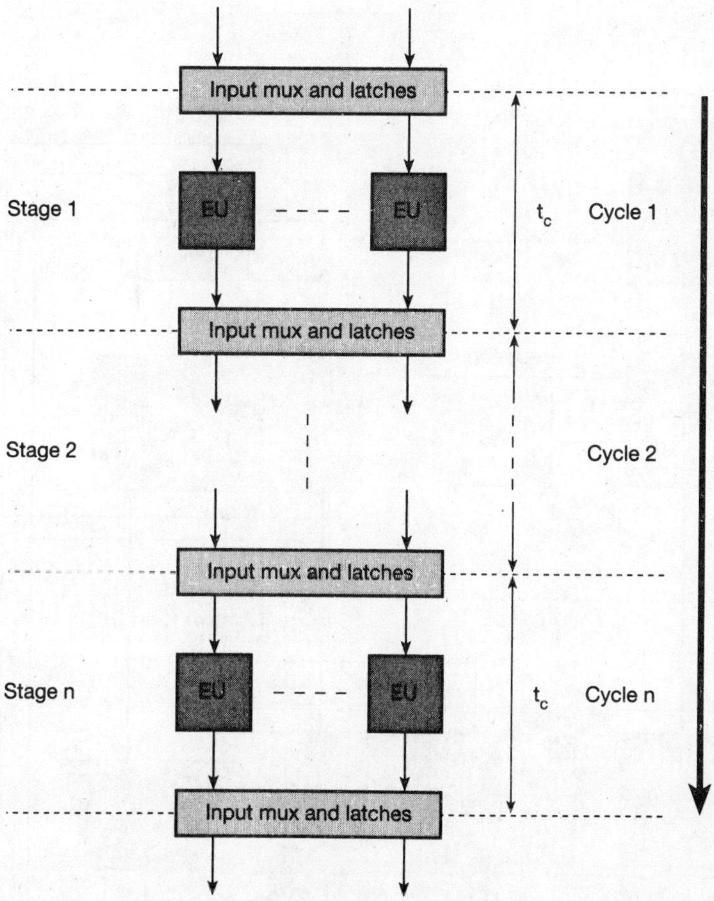

Figure 5.6 Structure of a straightforward pipeline.

tions has no meaning, and an in-depth performance specification of a pipelined processor requires three different measures: the *cycle time* of the processor and the *latency* and *repetition rate* values of the instructions.

The **cycle time** specifies the time available for each stage to accomplish the required operations. The cycle time of the processor is determined by the worst-case processing time of the longest stage. Currently pipelined processors generally operate with cycle times in the range of 2–20 nsec. (For actual values of several current processors see Table 5.1 later in this section.)

The term *latency* is used in the context of processing subsequent RAW-dependent instructions. **Latency** specifies the amount of time that the result of a particular instruction takes to become available in the pipeline for a subsequent dependent instruction. Usually, latency is given as multiples of the cycle time. If the latency of a particular instruction is one cycle, its result is available for a subsequent RAW-dependent instruction in the next cycle. In this case a RAW-dependent

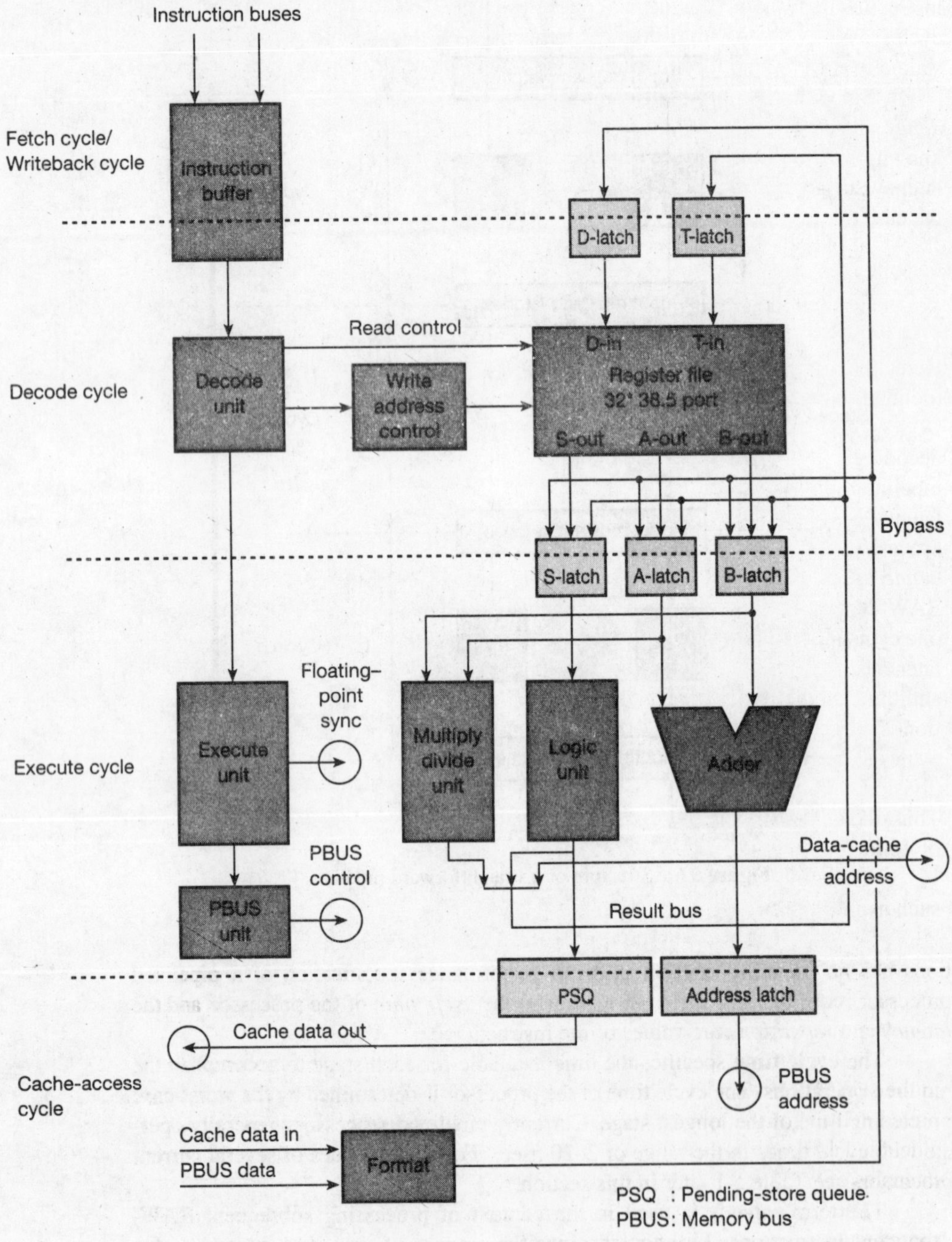

Figure 5.7 Structure and pipelined operation of the FX unit of the IBM Power1 (RS/6000).

instruction may be processed without any delay. If the latency is more than one cycle, say n-cycles, an immediately following RAW-dependent instruction has to be stalled in the pipeline for n–1 cycles.

Since there are two different kinds of RAW dependency, *define-use dependency* and *load-use dependency*, there are two corresponding kinds of latencies, known as *define-use latency* and *load-use latency*. (See Figure 5.8.) Define-use latency is interpreted in the context of two define-use dependent instructions, as in the case of

```
mul  r1, r2, r3;
 ad  r5, r1, r4;
```

Here, the *ad* instruction uses as its source the value of r1, which is produced (defined) in the preceding *mul* instruction.

The **define-use latency** of an instruction is the time delay occurring after decoding and issue until the result of an operate instruction becomes available in the pipeline for a subsequent RAW-dependent instruction. If the value of the define-use latency is one cycle, an immediately following RAW-dependent instruction can be processed without any delay in the pipeline. Related terms are *define-use delay* and *define-use penalty*. The **define-use delay** of an instruction is the time a subsequent RAW-dependent instruction has to be stalled in the pipeline. The define-use delay is one cycle less than the define-use latency. Recent processors usually have one-cycle latencies, that is, no define-use delays for straightforward operations, such as FX addition, subtraction, logical operations and so on. However, in the case of FP addition, subtraction and multiplication, there is typically a define-use latency of a few cycles as seen in Table 5.1. Here, we note that division and all operations based on division, such as square root calculations, are not currently pipelined in processors. Thus, the define-use latency and delay of such operations are quite high, in the order of 10 to 100 cycles.

The term *load-use latency* is interpreted in connection with load instructions, such as in the sequence

```
load  r1,x;
  ad  r5,r1,r2;
```

In this example the result of the *load* instruction is needed as a source operand in the subsequent *ad*. The notions of **load-use latency** and **load-use delay** are interpreted in the same way as define-use latency and define-use delay. See Figure 5.8 for a detailed explanation. Table 5.1 shows that recent processors usually have load-use latencies of 1–3 cycles, that is, load-use delays of 0–2 cycles.

The latency of an instruction being executed in a pipeline is determined by the execute phase of the pipeline. We illustrate this with the FP pipeline of the PowerPC 603 (Burgess et al., 1994), which is shown in Figure 5.9.

Figure 5.9 indicates that the PowerPC 603 processes FP additions/subtractions or multiplications in three phases. Two cycles are needed for the instruction fetch, decode and issue phase. The subsequent execution phase takes three cycles.

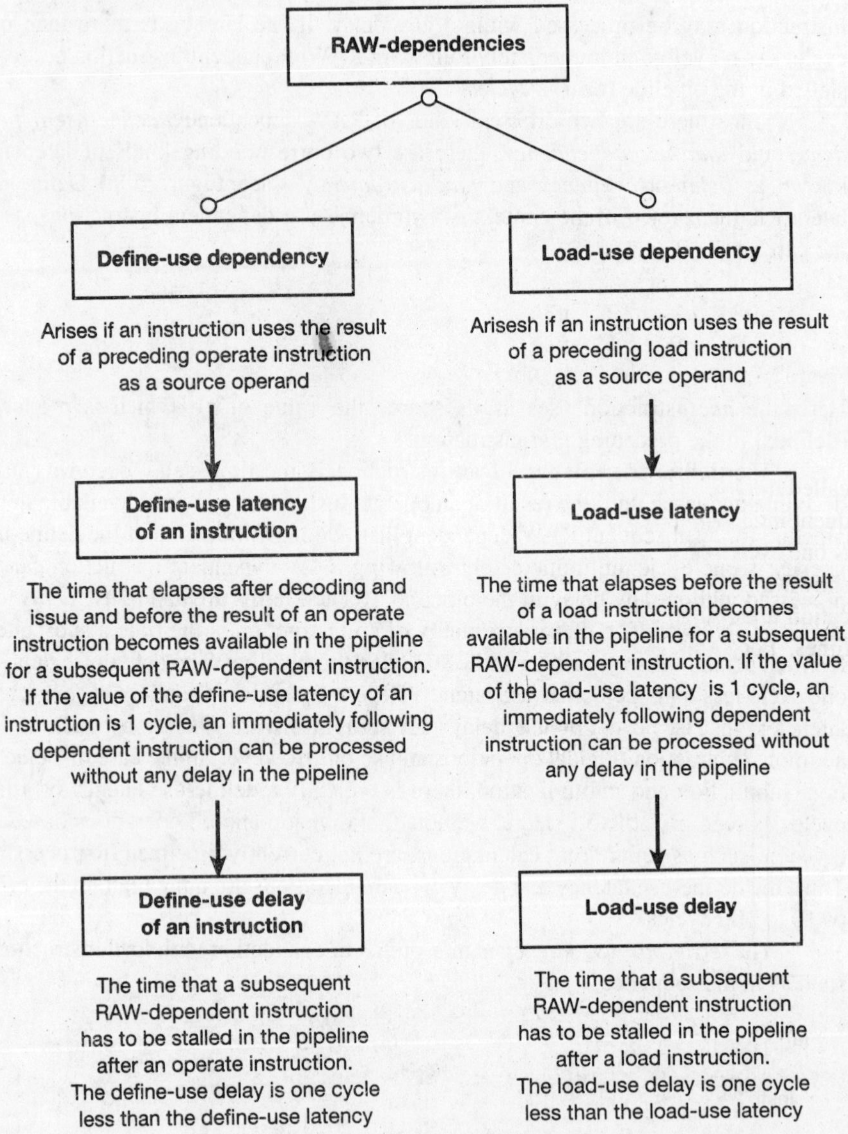

Figure 5.8 Define-use and load-use dependencies, latencies and delays.

At the end of this phase the result of the operation is forwarded (bypassed) to any requesting unit in the processor. Finally, in the completion phase the result is written back into the architectural register file.

As seen in Figure 5.9, when bypassing is used the latency comprises only the execution phase of the instruction processing. After this the result is available and may be used by a subsequent RAW-dependent instruction. Similary, most other processors employ bypassing in order to shorten or eliminate define-use delays. Bypassing is discussed in Section 5.2.2.

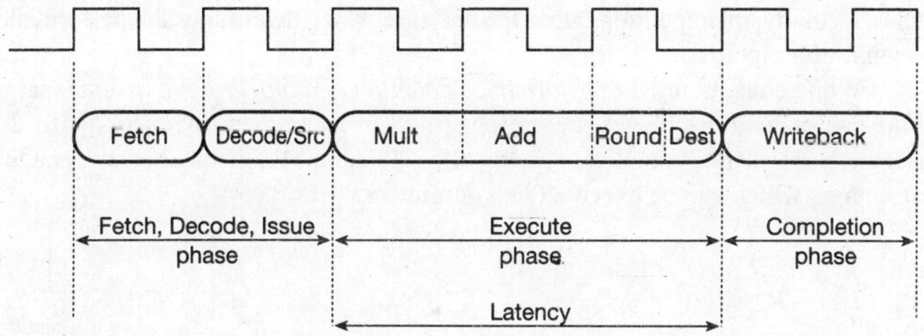

Figure 5.9 Pipeline cycles and latency of the FP pipeline in the PowerPC 603. © 1994 ACM

The third performance measure used in pipelining is the **repetition rate**, also called the *throughput*. It specifies the shortest possible time interval between subsequent independent instructions in the pipeline. The repetition rate of a basic pipeline is one cycle, since in this case a new instruction can be started in each new cycle, as shown in Figure 5.10. However, for more complex operations such as FP multiplication a particular pipeline stage, or a few stages, are often recycled, one or more times. For these operations a pipeline has repetition rate values of two or more

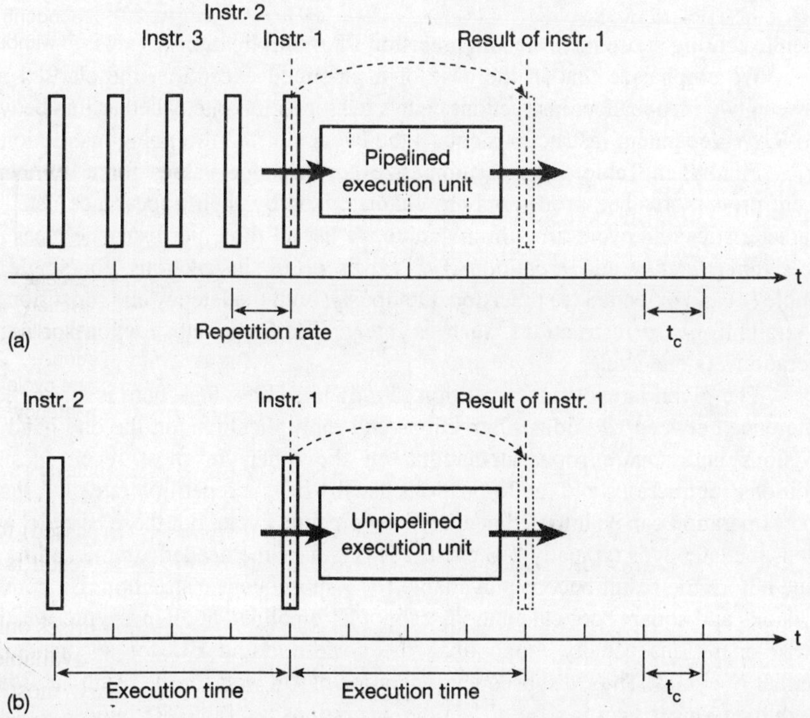

Figure 5.10 Repetition rate of a pipelined processor v. execution time of an unpipelined processor (a) Pipelined processing; (b) Unpipelined processing.

cycles. Actually, the repetition rate is the measure which determines the performance potential of a pipeline.

While considering the *performance potential of a pipeline*, we assume that no define-use or load-use delays are present between subsequent instructions. In this case, the performance potential of the pipeline (P) equals the number of independent instructions which can be executed in a unit interval of time:

$$P = \frac{1}{R * t_c} \tag{5.1}$$

where:

R: is the repetition rate of the pipeline in cycles

t_c: is the cycle time of the pipeline.

For instance, consider the FP pipeline of the PowerPC 603 when performing double precision multiplications. In this case, the repetition rate is two cycles and the cycle time is t_c = 12 ns. Thus, this processor has the performance of

$$P = \frac{1}{R * t_c} = \frac{1}{2 * 12 \text{ nsec}} = 44.6 \text{ MFLOPS} \tag{5.2}$$

when executing subsequent double precision FP multiplications.

We emphasize that in the case of a pipelined execution, the elapsed time between two independent instructions equals the repetition rate, whereas that between two RAW-dependent instructions equals the latency of the foregoing instruction.

Finally, in Table 5.1 we summarize performance values for a number of recent processors. The processors are characterized by their appearance date, key characteristics and cycle time. In this table we list all three performance measures: *cycle time*, *latency* and *repetition rate* values of FP instructions, for single (s), double (d) and extended (e) precision. Obviously, both the latency and repetition rate of straightforward instructions, such as integer additions, substractions or logical operations, is one cycle.

The given latency and repetition rate figures show that there is a significant difference between additions/subtractions and multiplications on the one hand and divisions and square root calculations on the other. In most recent designs, additions/subtractions and multiplications usually have a repetition rate of 1, that is, a new operation can be initiated in every new pipeline cycle. For these 'simple' operations the latency is typically 2–3 cycles. This is the time needed after decoding and issue before the result becomes available for a subsequent instruction. By contrast, divisions and square root calculations cannot be pipelined at all at the present time. These operations usually monopolize the corresponding EU for a considerable number of cycles. Thus, a subsequent operation has to wait for the result an order of magnitude longer than in case of 'simple' operations, as Table 5.1 indicates.

We note that latency is usually specified assuming ideal conditions during execution. This presumes that there are no cache misses either for the referenced

Table 5.1 FP latency/repetition rate figures of processors.

Processor type	*Appearance*	*Key characteristics*	*Cycle time (nsec)*	*Precision*	*FADD*	*FMUL*	*FDIV*	*FSQRT*
MC 68040	1990	CISC, scalar	40	s	7/3	9/5	42	107
				d				
SuperSparc	1992	RISC,	30/25/20/	s	1/1	3/1	6/4	8/6
		superscalar	/17	d			9/7	12/10
α21064	1992	RISC,	7/5	s	6/1	6/1	34	–
		superscalar		d	6/1	6/1	63	–
HP PA 7100	1992	RISC,	16/10	s	2/1	2/1	8	8
		superscalar		d	2/1	15	15	15
PowerPC 601	1992	RISC,	20/15	s	4/1	4/1	17	–
		superscalar		d		5/2	31	–
MC 88110	1993	RISC,	20	s	5/1	6/1	30	–
		superscalar		d	6/2	9/2	60	–
PowerPC 603	1993	RISC,	15/12	s	3/1	3/1	18	–
		superscalar		d	n.a.	4/2	33	–
Power2	1993	RISC,	18/15/14	s	2/1	2/1		27
		superscalar		d	2/1	2/1		
Pentium	1993	CISC,	16/15/11	s	3/1	3/1	39	70
		superscalar	/10/7.5/6/5	d	3/1	3/1	39	70
				e	3/1	3/1	39	70
PentiumPro	1995	CISC,	7.5/6.7/5	s	3/1	5/2	18	29
		superscalar		d	3/1	5/2		
				e	3/1	5/2		
PowerPC 604	1995	RISC,	10/7.5/6.7	s	3/1	3/1	18	–
		superscalar		d	3/1	3/1	31	–
HP PA 8000	1996	RISC,	5.6	s	3/1	3/1	17	17
		superscalar		d	3/1	3/1	31	31

– not implemented; n.a. not available

data or for address translations and so on. For a more precise performance specification, the penalties for at least the most frequent irregularities should also be given in processor descriptions.

Finally, we want to mention a technique which is used to double performance potential, **multiple-operation instructions**. Its basic idea is to allow the specification of two operations in the same instruction and to execute them in parallel. However, this is by no means a novel concept for doubling performance. Early vector processors, like the TI ASC (1973) or CDC STAR 105 (1973), made use of it. From the more up-to-date superscalar processors, the HP PA 7100 and the Power and PowerPC families include this performance boosting feature, although in a slightly different way. The HP PA 7100 allows a three-operand FP multiplication and an independent two-operand FP addition or subtraction to be specified as a single instruction, such as

```
FMPYADD      RM1, RM2, RM3, RA1, RA2
```

(Asprey et al., 1993). Here, the first three operands specify a multiplication with RM1 and RM2 as sources and RM3 as the destination. RA1 and RA2 are the oparands for an independent addition with RA1 as source and RA2 as both source and destination. An FP-unit executes both operations simultaneously.

The Power and PowerPC processors pursue a slightly different course. Here, an FP multiplication and a dependent add operation can be specified as a single instruction (called FMA), performing (A∗C) + B. In this case, too, both operations will be executed in the same pipeline run. Actually, the FP units of the above-mentioned processors are designed with this aim in mind.

5.1.4 Application scenarios of pipelines

Pipelining can be used principally in three different scenarios, as depicted in Figure 5.11.

- The first is to use pipelining for the *execution of a sequence of the same operations*, such as adding the values of two vectors. In this case pipelining is used to execute vector instructions in a vector processor, as described in Chapter 14 of Part III.
- The main application of pipelining is *general instruction processing*. This issue is detailed in Section 5.3.

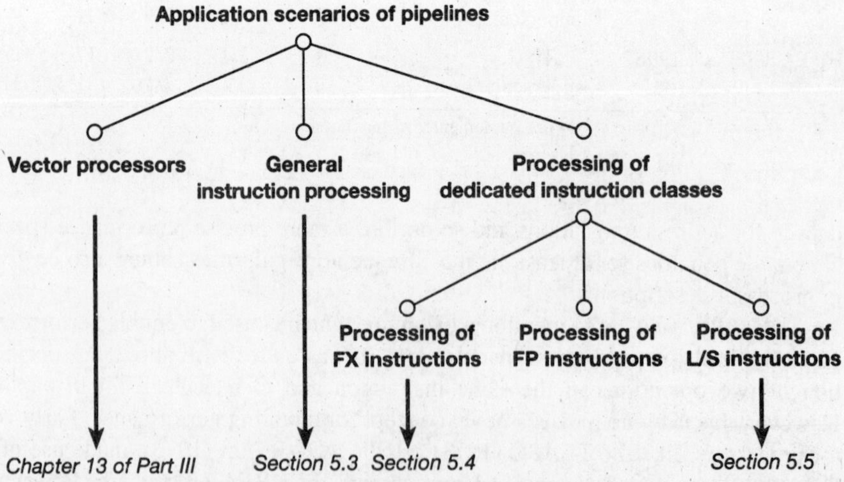

Figure 5.11 Application scenarios of pipelined processors.

- A further scenario is to use a pipeline for the *execution of a dedicated instruction class*, such as FX, FP or L/S instructions. Sections 5.4 and 5.5 are devoted to this while discussing how FX and L/S instructions are pipelined.

5.2 Design space of pipelines

5.2.1 Overview

In this section we explore the design space of pipelines in general. Here, we stress that the design space comprises the following two salient aspects: the basic layout of the pipeline and the method of dependency resolution, as shown in Figure 5.12. These aspects are discussed in the following two sections.

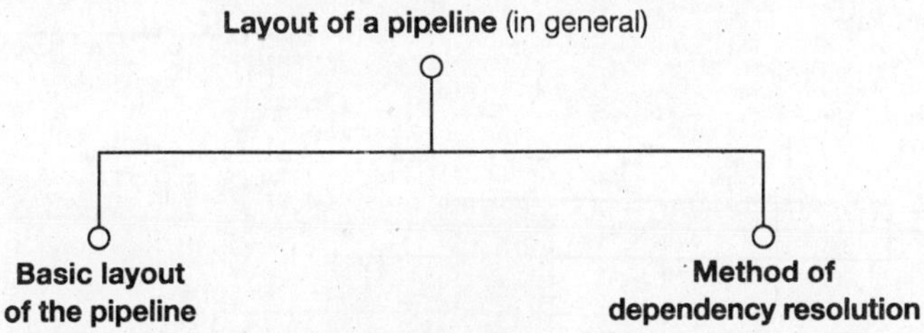

Figure 5.12 Key aspects of the design space of pipelines.

5.2.2 Basic layout of a pipeline

Here, we identify and discuss those decisions which are fundamental to the layout of a pipeline:

- the number of pipeline stages used to perform a given task,
- specification of the subtasks to be performed in each of the pipeline stages,
- layout of the stage sequence, that is, whether the stages are used in a strict sequential manner or some stages are recycled,
- use of bypassing, and
- timing of the pipeline operations, that is, whether pipeline operations are controlled synchronously or asynchronously (Figure 5.13).

In the sequel we will discuss each of the aspects mentioned.

The *number of pipeline stages* is one of the fundamental decisions. Evidently, when more pipeline stages are used, more parallel execution and thus a higher performance can be expected, as depicted in Figure 5.14.

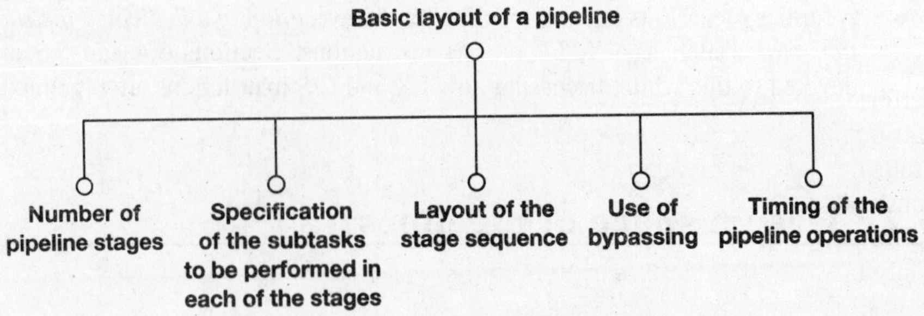

Figure 5.13 Design space of the overall stage layout.

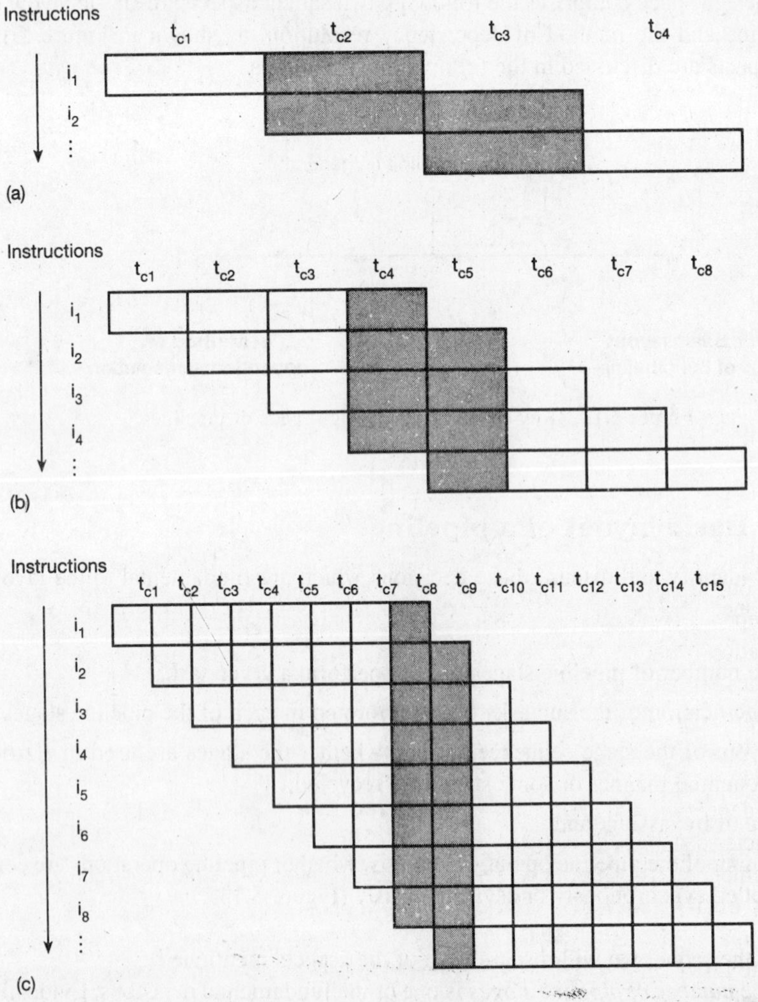

Figure 5.14 Increasing the degree of parallelism during execution by raising the number of pipeline stages (a) Two-stage pipeline; (b) Four-stage pipeline; (c) Eight-stage pipeline.

However, several problems arise when a pipeline is made deeper. First, data and control dependencies occur more frequently, which directly decreases performance. Furthermore, while increasing the number of pipeline stages, the partitioning of the entire task becomes less balanced and clock skew grows. This limits the possible increase of the clock frequency to a less than linear extent. As a consequence, by increasing the depth of a pipeline, at first we expect an increase in performance. However, after a maximum is reached, the performance would certainly fall, due to the reasons mentioned above, as outlined in Figure 5.15.

Early microprocessor instruction processing pipelines for FX and logical instructions consisted of only 2–3 stages, such as the RISC I (2 stages, 1982) or RISC II (3 stages, 1983).

Contemporary instruction pipelines contain in most cases 5–10 stages. As an example, see the number of pipeline stages used by the DEC α 21064 in Figure 5.16 (DEC, 1994b). As further examples, the pipelines of the Pentium, the PowerPC 601 and PowerPC 604 processors are shown in Figures 5.31, 5.22 and 5.33. Note that pipelines for processing FX and logical instructions typically contain 4–6 stages (see Section 5.4), whereas those for FP execution usually have one or two stages more.

Pipelining with more than the usual number of stages is said to be **superpipelining** (Jouppi and Wall, 1989). Examples of superpipelined processors are the DEC α line of processors, such as the α 21064, α 21064A, α 21164, or the Intel Pentium, having, for instance, 6 and 7 stages for FX processing as well as 8 and 10 stages for FP processing, respectively. Further examples are the MIPS R4000 (8 stages) and the MC 68060 (9 stages).

The second aspect is the *specification of the subtasks to be performed in each of the pipeline stages*. The specification of the subtasks can be done at a number of levels of increasing detail. For example, see Figures 5.36 and 5.38 for two different specification levels.

The next aspect of the basic layout of a pipeline is the *layout of the stage sequence*, which concerns how the pipeline stages are used (Figure 5.17).

While processing an instruction, the pipeline stages are usually operated successively one after the other. In some cases, however, a certain stage is recycled, that is, used repeatedly, to accomplish the result. This often happens while performing a multiplication or division. Recycling allows an effective use of hardware resources, but impedes pipeline repetition rate.

Bypassing (data forwarding) is the fourth aspect mentioned. **Bypasses** are intended to reduce or eliminate pipeline stalls due to RAW dependencies. As described in Section 4.2.1, there are two kinds of RAW dependencies: define-use and load-use dependencies. In the following, we discuss bypasses for both types of dependencies separately.

Remember that *define-use* dependencies occur when an instruction uses the result of a preceding operate instruction, such as an arithmetic or Boolean instruction, as a source operand. Unless special arrangements are made, the result of the operate instruction is written into the register file, or into the memory, and then it is fetched from there as a source operand. Evidently, this approach causes two cycles of superfluous delay for an immediately following dependent instruction. Bypassing is the correct way to avoid this. When bypassing is employed the result

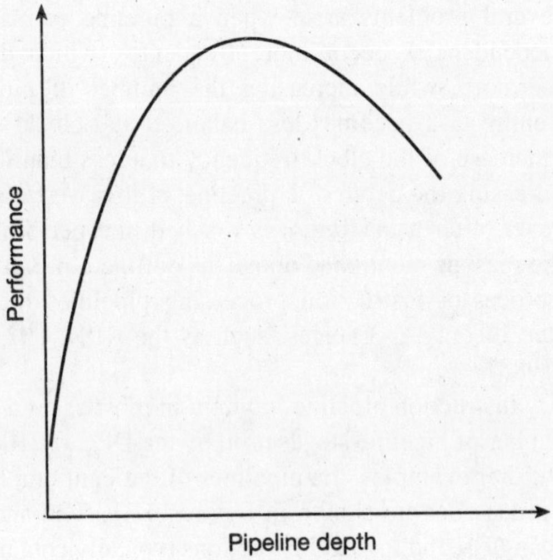

Figure 5.15 Performance v. pipeline depth, principal tendency.

of the EU is immediately forwarded to its input for use in the next pipeline cycle, as shown in Figure 5.18. *Bypassing*, also called *data forwarding*, is commonly employed in both FX and FP pipelines. Its implementation requires an additional data bus for forwarding the result of the execution stage to its input and an appropriate extension of the associated input multiplexers and latches. As an example, look at the FX pipeline of the Power1 (RS/6000), shown in Figure 5.7. Here, the result bus is bypassed to the input latches of the EUs.

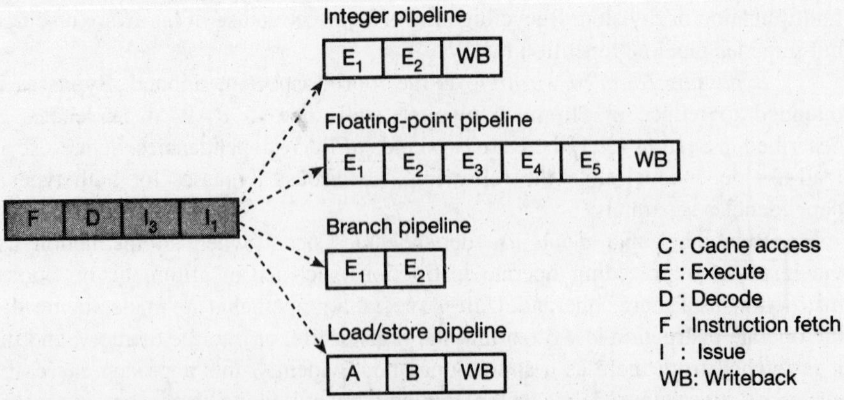

Figure 5.16 Pipelines of the DEC α 21064.

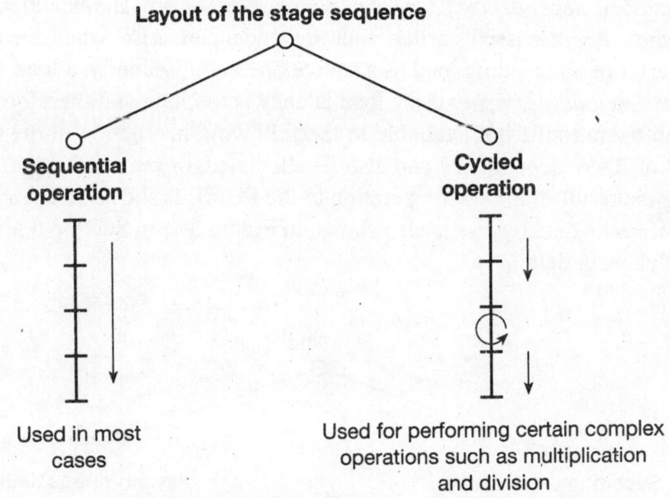

Figure 5.17 Possibilities of using the pipeline stages for instruction processing.

By means of bypassing, define-use delays of straightforward operations are eliminated in most recent processors. A notable exception is the deeply pipelined DEC α 21064, which has a one-cycle define-use delay for the basic FX logical operations. On the other hand, define-use delays of FP operations are reduced in most processors by means of bypassing by one cycle. Actual figures of FP define-use latencies are given in Table 5.1. The define-use delays (penalties) can be obtained by decrementing the latency figures by one.

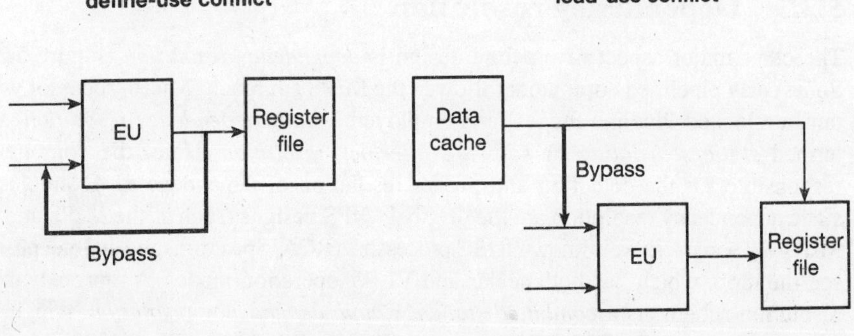

Figure 5.18 Principle of bypassing in define-use and load-use conflicts.

Load-use dependencies (see again Figure 5.18) are another kind of RAW dependencies. As discussed earlier, such dependencies arise when an instruction uses the result of a preceding load as a source operand. Evidently, a load-use dependency causes a *ioad-use delay* if the load latency is too long and therefore the result of the load operation is not available to the following instruction at the right time. This kind of RAW dependency can also be alleviated, or removed, by immediately bypassing the result of the fetch operation to the EU(s), as shown in Figure 5.18. An example of cache data bypass is also shown in Figure 5.7. In Section 5.5 we discuss load-use delays in detail.

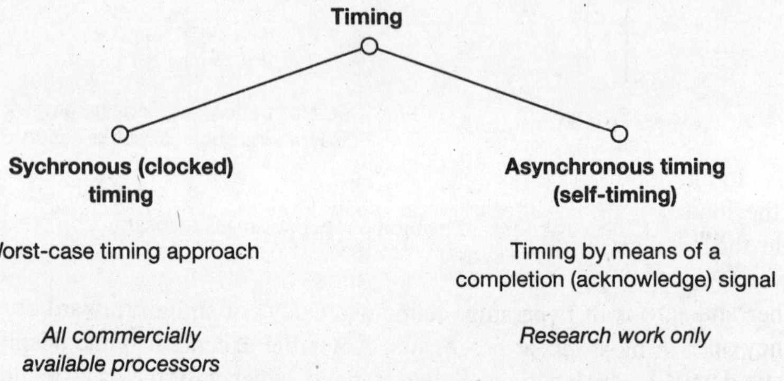

Figure 5.19 Possibilities for the timing of pipeline operation.

The last aspect of the basic pipeline layout is the *timing* of the pipeline operation, as depicted in Figure 5.19. There are two principal methods available here: the *clocked (synchronous)* and the *self-timed (asynchronous)* approaches (Franklin and Pan, 1993). In addition, a synchronous timing may be either *one-* or *two-phase clocked*. At the present time, to the authors' knowledge, all commercially available processors employ clocked pipelines, mostly with two-phase clocking schemes. However, asynchronous timing of pipelines is also considered as a promising approach in future developments (Franklin and Pan, 1993).

5.2.3 Dependency resolution

The other major aspect of pipeline design is *dependency resolution* (Figure 5.20). Some early pipelined computers followed the MIPS approach (Microprocessor without Interlocked Pipeline Stages) and employed a *static dependency resolution*, also termed *static scheduling* or *software interlock resolution*. Here, the compiler is responsible for the detection and proper resolution of dependencies. Examples of static dependency resolution are the original MIPS designs (such as the MIPS and the MIPS-X), some less well-known RISC processors (RCA, Spectrum) and an Intel processor, the i860, which has both scalar and VLIW operation modes. A more advanced resolution scheme is a *combined static/dynamic dependency resolution*, which has been employed in the MIPS R processors (R2000, R3000, R4000, R4200, R6000).

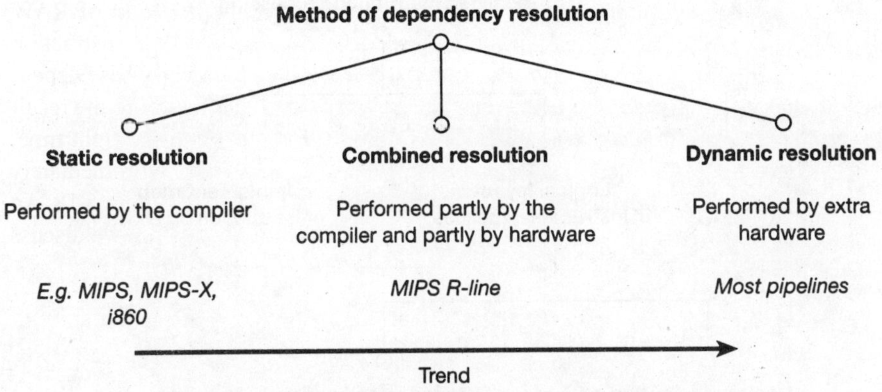

Figure 5.20 Possibilities for resolving pipeline hazards.

In the first MIPS processors (R2000, R3000) hardware interlocks were used for the long latency operations, such as multiplication, division and conversion, while the resolution of short latency operations relied entirely on the compiler. Newer R-series implementations have extended the range of hardware interlocks further and further, first to the load/store hazards (R6000) and then to other short latency operations as well (R4000). In the R4000 the only instructions which rely on a static dependency resolution are the coprocessor control instructions.

In recent processors dependencies are resolved *dynamically*, by extra hardware. Nevertheless, compilers for these processors are assumed to perform a parallel optimization by code reordering, in order to increase performance, as detailed in Chapter 9.

5.3 Overview of pipelined instruction processing

In this section we give a framework of pipelined instruction processing. After presenting its design space we give an overview of the most common implementations. Finally, we describe how instructions are processed using pipelining in the Pentium and PowerPC 604.

5.3.1 The design space

To start, we overview the design space of pipelined instruction processing with reference to Figure 5.21. The design space covers two key aspects, namely the specification, or logical layout, and the implementation of instruction pipelines.

The *logical layout* specifies the tasks to be accomplished. This includes:

- the declaration of the pipelines to be implemented, and
- for each of the pipelines a detailed specification of the subtasks to be performed and their execution sequence.

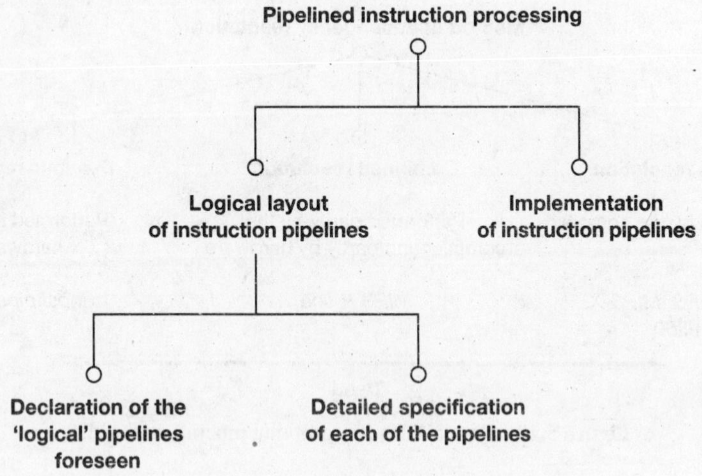

Figure 5.21 Design space of pipelined instruction processing.

In recent processors different pipelines are declared for each of the major instruction classes. There are usually separate pipelines for the processing of FX and logical data, called the **FX pipeline**, for FP data, the **FP pipeline**, for loads and stores, the **L/S pipeline**, and finally, for branches, the **B pipeline**. Obviously, for the processing of additional data types (for instance, pixels) further pipelines could be specified. We note furthermore that recent processors often provide two or even more separate pipelines for FX or FP data. For instance, the DEC α 21164 provides two types of FX pipeline, a simple one for the straightforward integer and logical operations (where multiplication and division are not included) and a full one, capable of performing all operations mentioned.

The *detailed specification of a pipeline* includes the statement of the pipeline stages as well as the specification of the subtasks to be done in each of the stages. As an example, Figure 5.22 shows the declared 'logical' pipelines and their stages in the PowerPC 601 (Becker et al., 1993).

A *description of the subtasks* can be done at a number of levels with an increasing degree of detail. For instance, the data manipulation subtasks of an FX pipeline could be specified at a high level, as depicted in Figure 5.23. Obviously, in an actual case all of the subtasks mentioned have to be described in full detail.

Now let us turn to the *implementation*. Logical pipelines can be implemented in various ways: either by using the same hardware pipeline for all logical pipelines, or by implementing each logical pipeline as a dedicated pipeline or otherwise. This is the point which makes it worthwhile distinguishing between logical layout and implementation (Figure 5.21).

As far as the *implementation* of instruction pipelines is concerned, there are *three significant aspects* which have to be considered, as shown in Figure 5.24. These aspects are the layout and the multiplicity of the physical pipelines, as well as how sequential consistency is preserved in case of multiple physical pipelines. In the following we deal with these aspects in more detail.

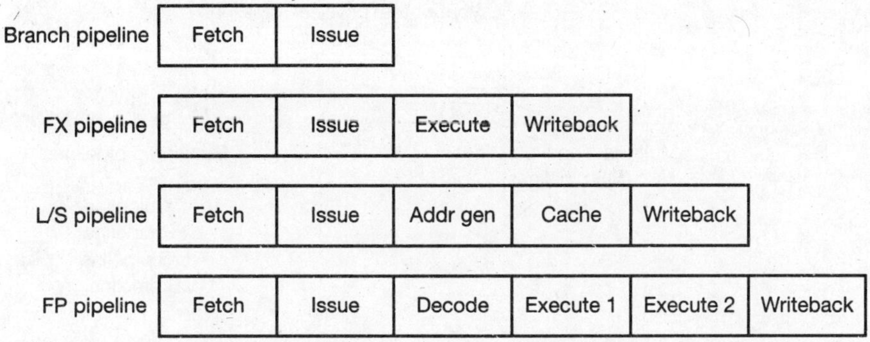

Figure 5.22 Overall layout of the pipelines of the PowerPC 601. © 1993 IEEE

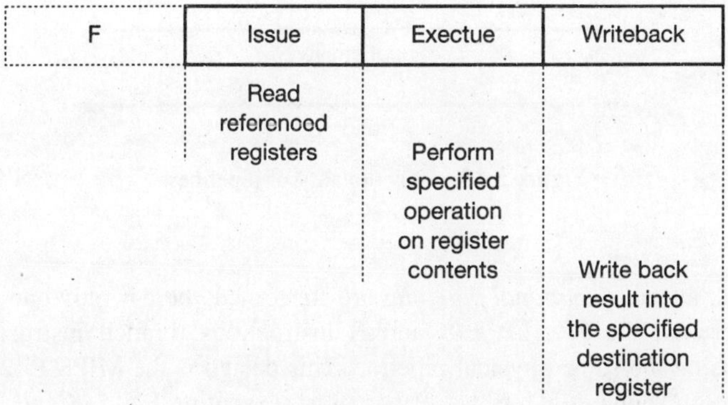

Figure 5.23 Description of the data manipulation subtasks for an FX pipeline.

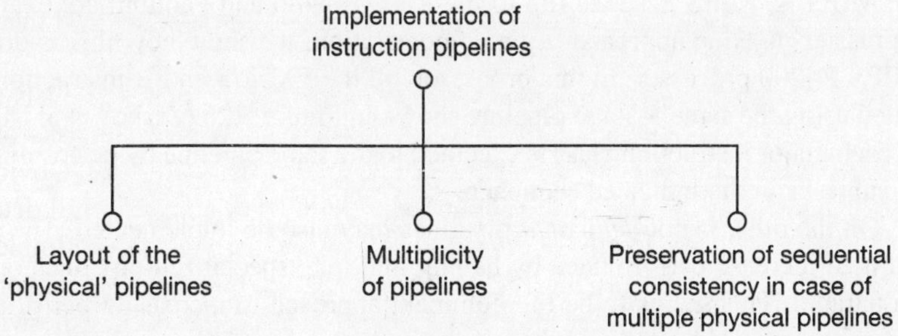

Figure 5.24 Significant aspects of the implementation of instruction pipelines.

First let us discuss the *layout of the 'physical' pipelines* with reference to Figure 5.25. As shown in the figure, the main point here is whether the logical pipelines should be implemented with minimal hardware, by a multifunctional pipeline, or be performance oriented, by using multiple dedicated pipelines.

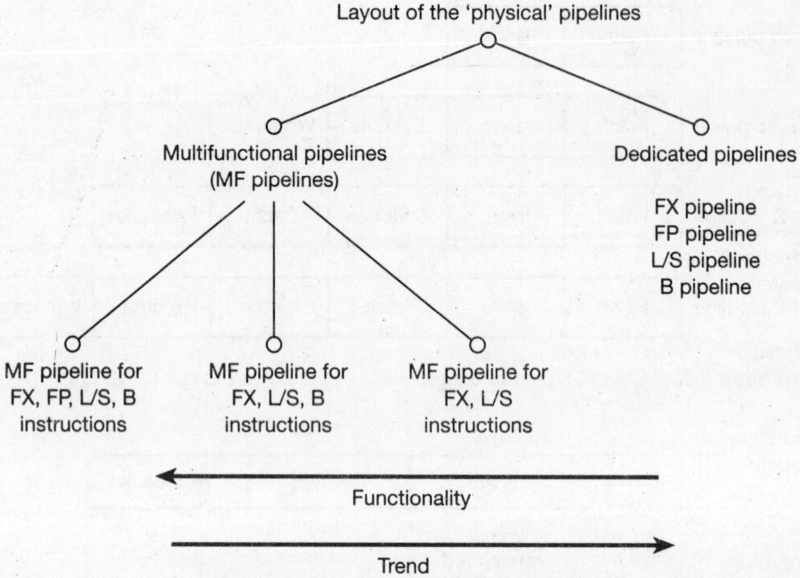

Figure 5.25 Functionality of pipelines.

As far as *multifunctional pipelines* are concerned, there is only one published design where all the FX, FP, L/S and B instructions (branch instructions) are processed using the same physical pipeline. This design is the MIPS R4200, introduced in 1994 (Yeung et al., 1994). By contrast, executing FX, L/S and B instructions on the same pipeline is a frequently employed 'classical' approach, The *master-pipeline* approach. Here, the adder of the FX pipeline is also used for the address calculations needed when executing L/S and B instructions. The IBM 801, MIPS, MIPS-X, MIPS R-series (up to the R6000), i486 and Pentium are examples of the master-pipeline approach. As a demonstration, we show how this is done in the MIPS R4200 processor. In this processor, all the FX, L/S and B instructions are executed using the same 5-stage pipeline shown in Figure 5.26 (Zivkov et al., 1994). Here, each major instruction class is executed in the same pipeline by performing the given subtasks in the indicated sequence.

On the other hand, *dedicated* pipelines may also be implemented. The motivation is to increase performance by having multiple, specialized pipelines operating in parallel. This seems to be the dominant approach to increasing performance nowadays. Thus, dedicated pipelines are applied more and more frequently in current processors like the PowerPC 603, PowerPC 604, DEC α line and so on. Let us consider, for instance, the processor PowerPC 604, shown in Figure 7.42. It has altogether six implemented pipelines: two FX pipelines for straightforward FX and logical operations, one for FX multiplication and division, another one for FP operations, and two further pipelines for the execution of branches as well as load/stores. These six autonomous units operate in parallel to enable the PowerPC 604 to achieve a superscalar issue rate of 4.

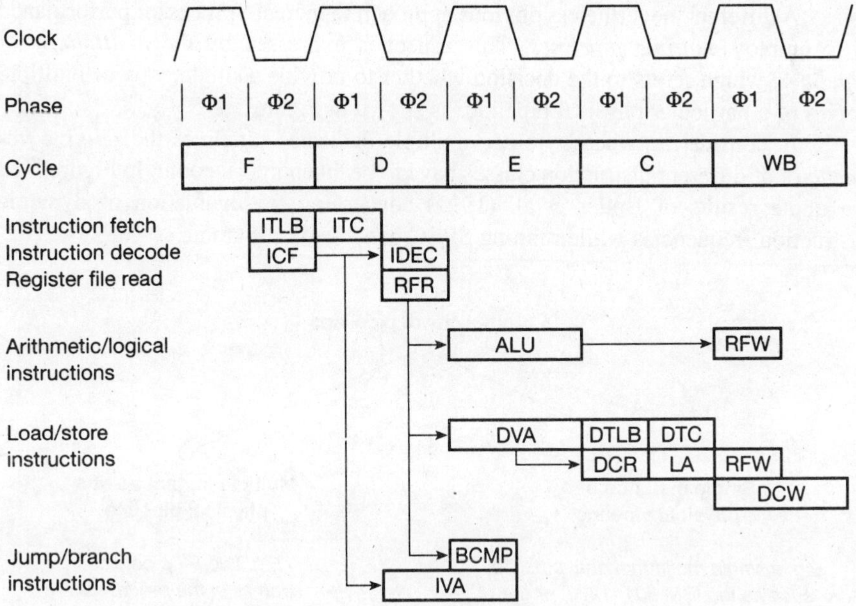

Cycle	Phase	Mnemonic	Description
	Φ1		
F	Φ2	ICF	Instruction Cache Fetch
		ITLB	Instruction micro-TLB read
	Φ1	ITC	Instruction cache Tag Check
D	Φ2	RFR	Register File Read
		IDEC	Instruction DECode
		IVA	Instruction Virtual Address calculation
	Φ1	IVA	Instruction Virtual Address calculation
E		BCMP	Branch CoMPare
	Φ1, Φ2	ALU	Arithmatic/Logic operation
		DVA	Data Virtual Address calculation
	Φ1	DCR	Data Cache Read
C		DTLB	Data joint-TLB read
	Φ2	LA	Load data Alignment
		DTC	D-cache Tag Check
WB	Φ1	RFW	Register File Write
	Φ1, 2	DCW	Data Cache Write

Figure 5.26 Required subtasks for the pipelined implementation of FX, L/S and B instructions and their implementation using the same physical pipeline in the MIPS R4200. © 1994 IEEE

A different, nevertheless obvious approach to increase processor performance is to employ *multiple pipelines*. This aspect is expressed by the *multiplicity of pipelines*, which refers to the decision whether to provide a single copy or multiple copies of a particular physical pipeline, as shown in Figure 5.27.

In considering whether to use multiple dedicated pipelines the *relative frequencies* of different instruction classes have to be taken into account. In Figure 5.28 we quote results of Butler et al. (1991) concerning the evaluation of dynamic instruction frequencies while running SPEC benchmark programs.

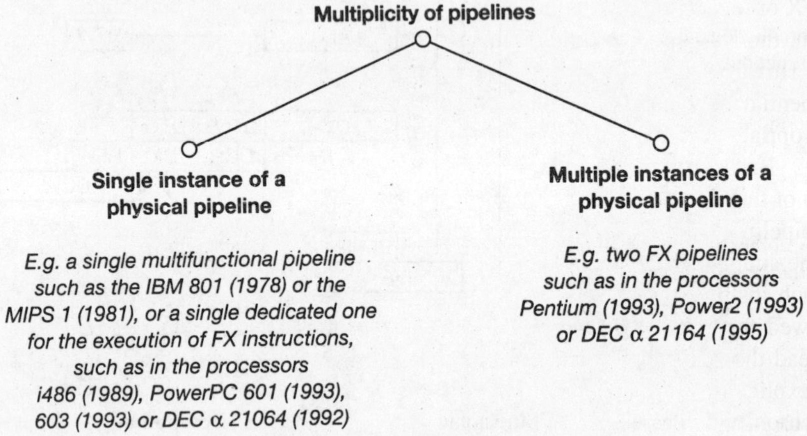

Figure 5.27 Multiplicity of pipelines.

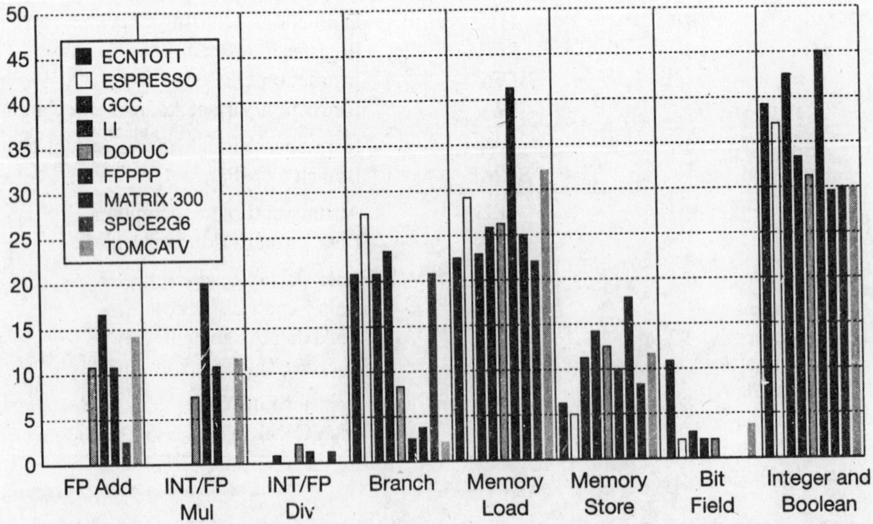

Figure 5.28 Relative frequency of distinct instruction classes, measured while running SPEC benchmark programs. © 1991 ACM

This figure shows that the most frequent instructions are simple integer and Boolean instructions. They account for about 30–40% of all executed instructions. Loads and stores also occur often; they have relative frequencies of about 25% and 10%, respectively. Branches are frequent instructions as well, as already discussed in Section 4.2.2. Therefore, when considering the multiplication of dedicated pipelines, the first candidates are those pipelines which execute the most frequent instruction classes.

The last aspect concerns only multiple pipelines. In this case, instructions may be completed out of order, since subsequent instructions may be executed by different pipelines of different length. Consider, for instance, the case when a long latency instruction, such as an FP instruction, is followed by a short latency one, like an FX or logical instruction, and both instructions are executed in separate pipelines. Then, the simple FX or logical instruction is completed earlier than the preceding one. However, out-of-order instruction completion would cause a deviation from the sequential method of execution. Therefore, in the case of multiple pipelines, an appropriate technique is needed to *preserve sequential consistency.*

Basically, there are three methods to achieve this, as shown in Figure 5.29. Two of these are applied mostly when there are two pipelines, that is, an FX and an FP pipeline, whereas the third method is used typically for more than two pipelines. In the simplest case, we assume having a multifunctional pipeline for FX, L/S and branch instructions as well as a distinct FP pipeline. Here, the FP pipeline is not allowed to write back the results into the register file or memory autonomously. Instead the *writeback* operation is performed under *software control* as a result of an explicit instruction. For instance, this is how earlier FP coprocessors were synchronized with the master FX pipeline.

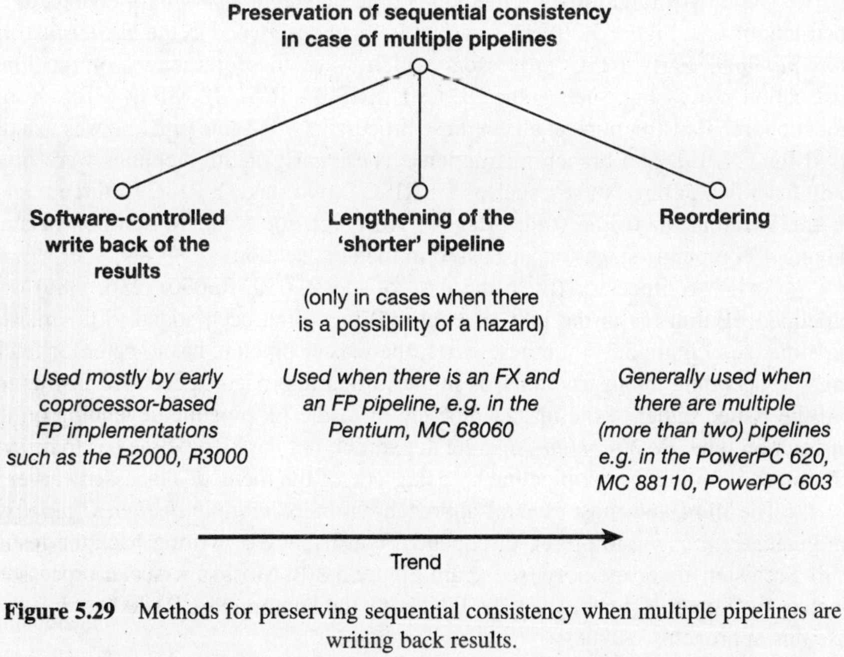

Figure 5.29 Methods for preserving sequential consistency when multiple pipelines are writing back results.

In the second method we again assume two lock stepped operating pipelines, a master FX and an FP pipeline. Here, in-order completion of the instructions is achieved by properly *lengthening the shorter FX pipeline*, by introducing unused cycles (bubbles) into it, if necessary. A more relaxed variant of this method checks for possible hazards (such as possible exceptions related to FP execution) and triggers a delay only if a hazard is likely. This latter variant is used, for instance, in the Pentium processor.

The third method is *reordering*. It is usually applied if there are more than two pipelines. By reordering, the pipelines are not allowed to write back the results directly into the architectural registers or into memory. Instead a mechanism is provided such that the results of the instructions are written back in program order, despite being generated in an out-of-order fashion. Reordering takes place in a so-called completion stage. For more details of reordering, see Section 7.7.3. We emphasize that we have discussed the schemes for preserving sequential consistency in the same sequence as their trend line. Thus, recent processors almost exclusively use reordering to retain sequential consistency. Finally, we refer to Section 7.7 where the question of sequential consistency is discussed more comprehensively.

5.3.2 Most frequently used implementations of pipelined instruction processing

Although there are more variations, pipelined instruction processing is implemented in most cases along three prevailing lines, as summarized in Figure 5.30.

The most straightforward method is to use a *single pipeline* for all except FP instructions (see Figure 5.30). This variant is often designated as the *master instruction pipeline*. Early RISC processors which were the forerunners of pipelined instruction processing, such as the IBM 801, RISC I, RISC II, MIPS, MIPS-X, did not support FP instructions at all. In these processors, the same pipeline was usually used for FX, L/S and branch instructions. These early RISC pipelines were often built from two or three stages, such as the RISC I (two stages), RISC II (three stages) or the Pyramid 9000 line (three stages). However, the standard solution became having 4–5 pipeline stages, as discussed in the next section.

An FP coprocessor (as in the case of the R2000, R3000, i286, i386) or a pipelined FP unit (as in the i486 or Pentium) has often been added to this master pipeline (see Figure 5.31). In these cases, the master pipeline has to cater for fetching and decoding the instructions, as in the former approach. A decoded instruction will be issued either to the master pipeline or to the FP pipeline depending on the instruction type. *Both pipelines* operate in parallel, but the FP pipeline has to be synchronized with the master pipeline by using one of the methods discussed earlier.

The third and most general approach assumes *multiple dedicated pipelines* and using *reordering* to preserve sequential consistency of writing back the results into a register file or memory (see again Figure 5.30). Most superscalar processors, such as the PowerPC line (except the PPC 601), the Pentium Pro, PA8000 or R10000, use this approach.

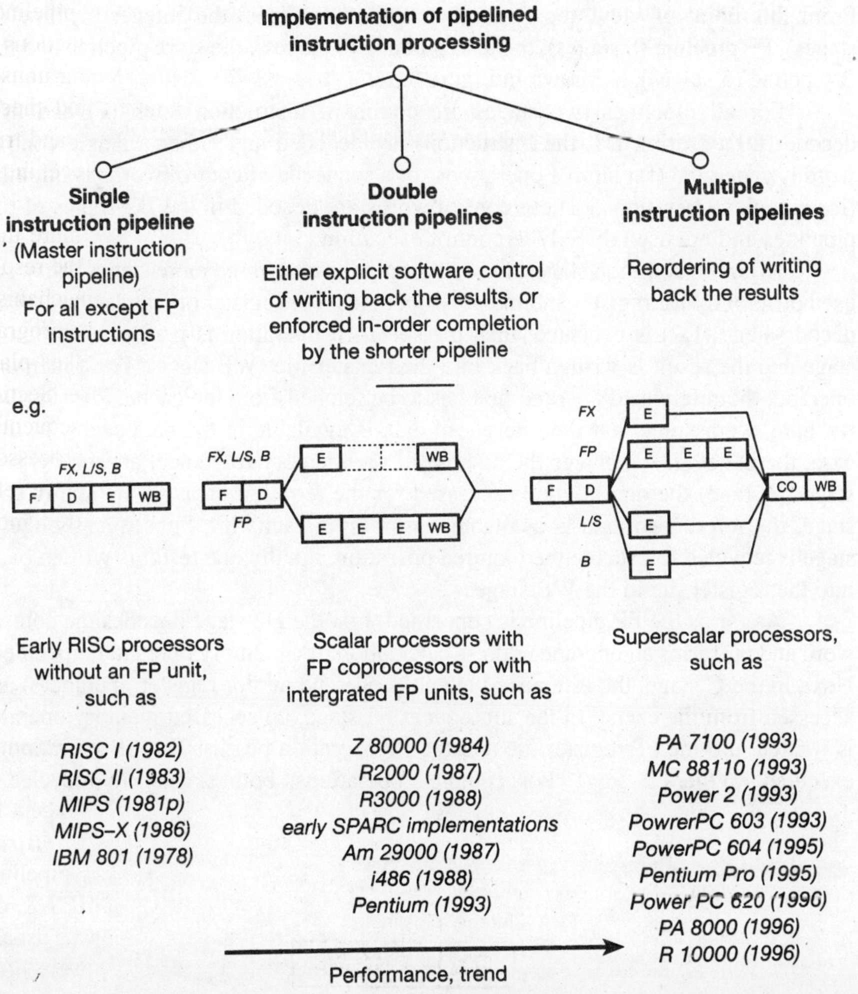

Figure 5.30 Main approaches to implementing pipelined instruction processing. (Note that in the figure both the number and naming of pipeline stages are hypothetical; they are indicated only for illustration, thus they do not necessarily match the processors listed as examples.)

5.3.3 Case studies

In concluding this section we present two examples of the overall layout of pipelined instruction processing: the Intel Pentium and the PowerPC 604.

Pipelined instruction processing in the Pentium

In the Pentium, the logical layout and physical implementation of the pipelines have to be sharply distinguished. First, we describe the logical layout of its pipelines.

From this point of view, the Pentium has five pipelines: the Integer pipeline (5 stages), FP pipeline (8 stages), the load pipeline (5 stages), the store pipeline and the B pipeline (5 stages), as shown in Figure 5.31.

For all pipelines two stages are common: instruction fetch (F) and first decode (D1). During D1, the instructions are decoded and either a single control word is generated (for simple operations) or a sequence of control words is initiated (for complex operations). These control words are decoded in the D2 stages of the pipelines and are used directly to control execution.

After the common stages, the integer pipeline has three more stages. They are used differently for register and memory operands. For register operands, the second decode stage (D2) is executed, then the specified operation is performed in the E stage and the result is written back into the register file (WB stage). For a memory operand, the referenced operand first has to be fetched from the cache. For simplicity, here, we assume that the referenced data is available in the data cache. In this case, the D2 stage calculates the address of the memory reference, and in the next stage (E stage) the data cache is accessed for the required data. At the end of this stage, the referenced data is available, assuming a cache hit. Subsequently, the E stage is recycled to execute the required operation. Finally, the result is written back into the register file in the WB stage.

As far as the FP pipeline is concerned, first the D2 stage decodes the control word and performs an operand address calculation, if a memory operand is specified. Next, in the C stage, the referenced memory operand and/or register operand(s) are accessed from the cache. In the subsequent E1 stage, an accessed memory operand is written into the FP register file and the FP operation begins. The FP operation is executed in the E2 stage. For complex operations, both stages are recycled a

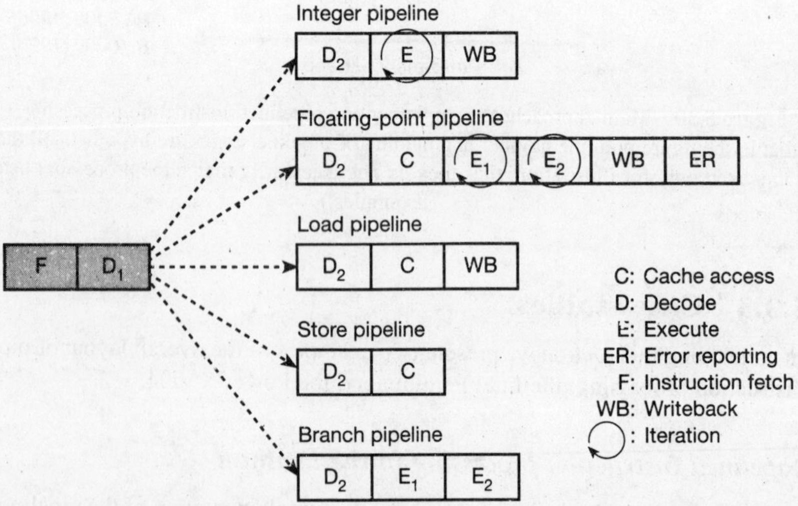

Figure 5.31 Logical layout of Pentium's pipelines.

number of times. In the WB stage the FP operation is completed and the result is written into the FP register file. Finally, in the ER stage, the FP unit reports on possible exceptions and the FP status word will be updated.

Load and store operations are performed in five and four stages, respectively (assuming a data cache hit). The dedicated pipeline stages cater for address calculation (D2 stage), cache access (C stage) and writing the accessed data into the register file (WB stage).

Here, we do not go into the details of branch processing, but instead refer to Section 8.4.4 where this point is discussed in detail.

In contrast to the logical pipelines discussed above, physically the Pentium has two master pipelines (called the U and V pipes) and a pipelined FP unit which operates in conjunction with the U pipe, as shown in Figure 5.32 (Alpert and Avnon, 1993). Both pipes can execute FX, L/S and B instructions. Furthermore, the U pipe is used to execute the first five stages of the FP pipeline, while the remaining three stages are executed by the FP unit.

In the Pentium processor, sequential consistency and precise interrupts are achieved by appropriate delay of the shorter pipeline, that is, by using the delay method described earlier in this section.

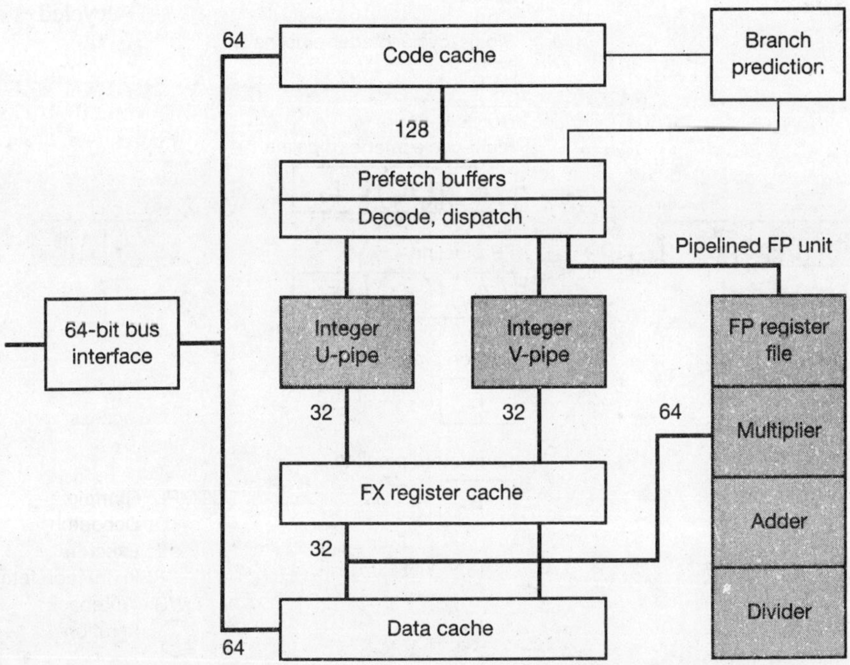

Figure 5.32 Simplified block diagram of the Pentium. © 1993 IEEE

Pipelined instruction processing in the PowerPC 604

The logical pipelines of the PowerPC 604 are somewhat different from the Pentium, as indicated in Figure 5.33 (IBM/Motorola, 1994). Here, there are three stages in common: the instruction fetch stage (F), the decode stage (D) and the instruction issue stage (I). The I stage can issue up to four instructions per cycle. The subsequent execution can comprise multiple pipeline cycles, as for FP or multi-cycle integer execution.

In all cases, however, at the end of the last execute stage the result is written into a rename buffer rather than into the appropriate architectural register file. (Here we note that renaming is used to eliminate false data dependencies, as introduced in Section 4.2.1 and discussed in depth in Section 7.5.) Two common pipeline stages follow: the completion stage (CMPL) and the writeback stage (WB). These common stages are required to ensure sequential consistency as well as precise interrupts. Refer to Chapter 7 for related background information.

In the PowerPC 604 each of the logical pipelines is implemented by a separate unit. Figure 5.34 shows an overview of the internal structure of the PowerPC 604, where the pipelined EUs are highlighted (IBM/Motorola, 1994). Here, our aim is only to demonstrate the overall implementation of the pipelines; a detailed description of this processor may be found in Section 7.4.5.

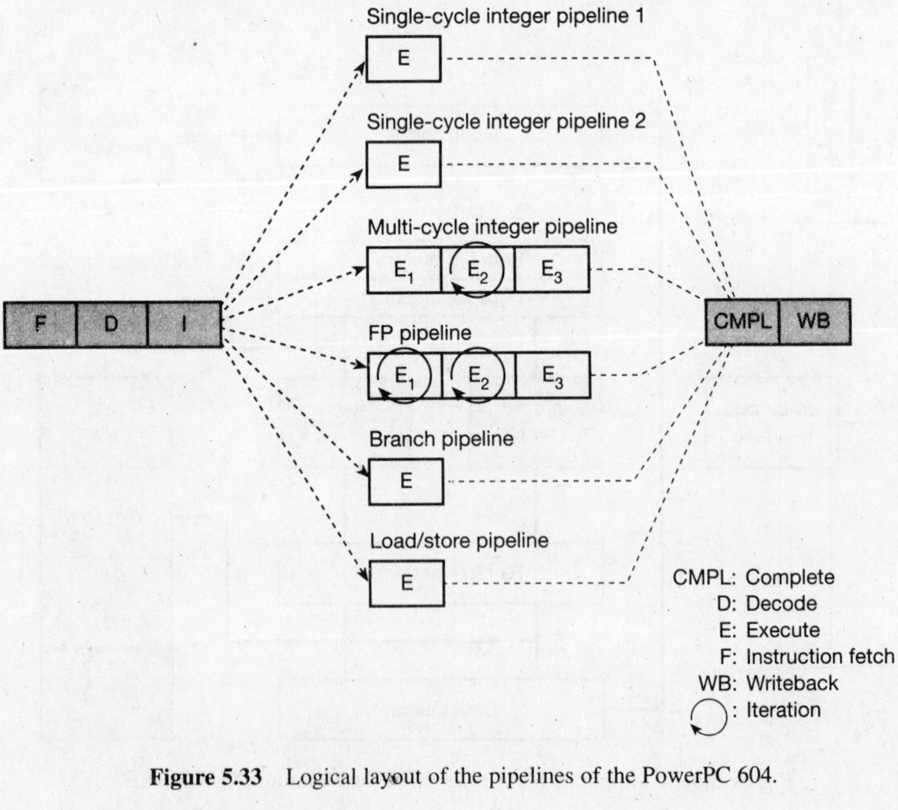

Figure 5.33 Logical layout of the pipelines of the PowerPC 604.

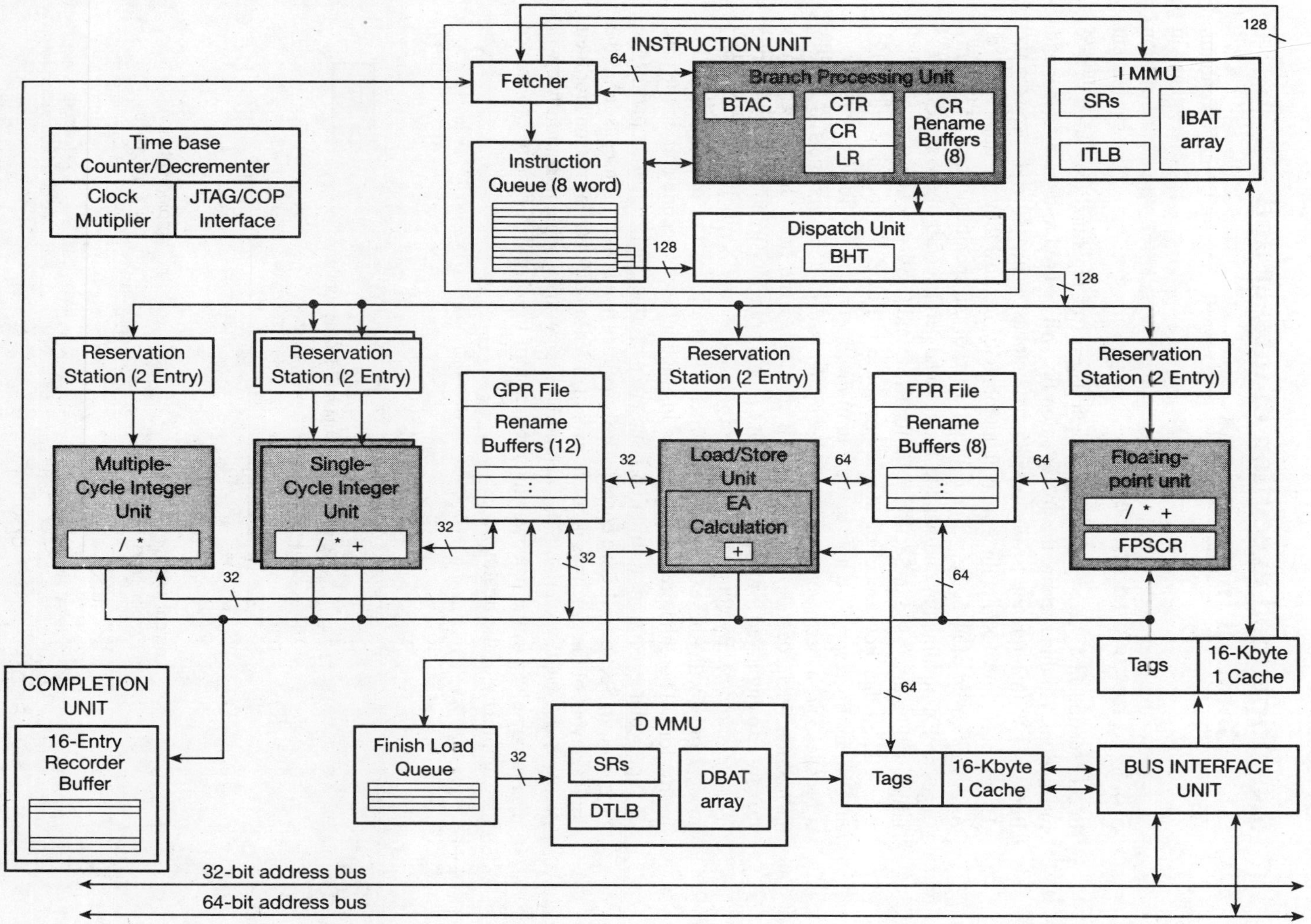

Figure 5.34 Simplified block diagram of the PowerPC 604.

5.4 Pipelined execution of integer and Boolean instructions

5.4.1 The design space

In this section first we overview the salient aspects of pipelined execution of FX instructions. (In this section, the abbreviation FX will be used to denote integer and Boolean.) With reference to Figure 5.35 we emphasize *two basic aspects* of the design space: how FX pipelines are laid out logically and how they are implemented. A *logical layout* of an FX pipeline consists, first, of the specification of how many stages an FX pipeline has and what tasks are to be performed in these stages. These issues will be discussed in Section 5.4.2 for RISC and CISC pipelines.

The other key aspect of the design space is how FX pipelines are *implemented*. In this respect we note that the term *FX pipeline* can be interpreted in both a broader and a narrower sense. In the *broader sense*, it covers the full task of instruction fetch, decode, execute and, if required, write back. In this case, it is usually also employed for the execution of L/S and branch instructions and is termed a *master pipeline*. By contrast, in the *narrower sense*, an FX pipeline is understood to deal only with the execution and writeback phases of the processing of FX instructions. Then, the preceding tasks of instruction fetch, decode and, in the case of superscalar execution, instruction issue are performed by a separate part of the processor. In Section 5.4.2 we consider FX pipelines in a broader sense, as far as the logical layout of the pipelines is concerned, in order to point out the reasons for their design. However, in Section 5.4.3, while discussing their implementation, we will restrict ourselves to the narrower interpretation of the term FX pipeline, to reduce the complexity of the treatment.

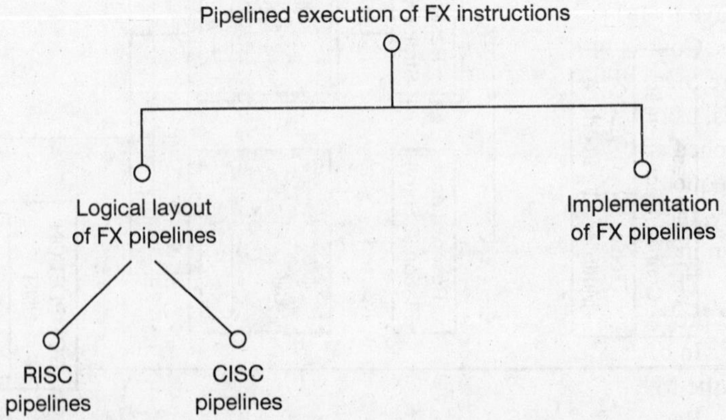

Figure 5.35 Design space of the pipelined execution of FX instructions.

5.4.2 Logical layout of FX pipelines

Integer and Boolean instructions account for a considerable proportion of programs. Together, they amount to 30–40 % of all executed instructions (see Figure 5.28). Therefore, the layout of FX pipelines is fundamental to obtaining a high-performance processor.

In the following, we discuss how FX pipelines are laid out. However, we describe the FX pipelines for RISC and CISC processors separately, since each type has a slightly different scope. While processing operate instructions, RISC pipelines have to cope only with register operands. By contrast, CISC pipelines must be able to deal with both register and memory operands as well as destinations.

RISC pipelines

A *traditional FX pipeline* in RISC processors is modelled on the execution of register–register instructions. Consider here that the execution of register–register instructions includes the following subtasks:

- fetch the instruction,
- decode the instruction,
- fetch the referenced registers,
- execute the specified operation, and
- write back the result into the register file.

If we assume that

- instruction decoding and register fetch are short latency operations compared to all others mentioned, and thus can both be performed in the same pipeline cycle, and
- each of the other subtasks is assigned a separate cycle

we have the traditional RISC pipeline.

Consequently, a **traditional RISC pipeline** has four stages, as depicted in Figure 5.36. These are the fetch (F), decode (D), execute (E) and writeback (WB) stages, as mentioned already. The pipeline operates as follows. First, the instruction is fetched and decoded in the F and D cycles; in the D cycle, register data is fetched. Subsequently the required operation is performed in the following E cycle and, finally, the result is written back into the register file in the concluding WB cycle, as shown in Figure 5.36.

The Sparc, SuperSparc, MC 88110 and the PowerPC line are examples of RISC processors which use this arrangement for FX pipelines.

In certain processors there are some minor variations in cycle duration, such as in the MC 88110 or SuperSparc processors (see Table 5.2).

Besides this traditional layout there is another approach which we term the **traditional MIPS-pipeline**. It is typified by the MIPS line of processors (except the

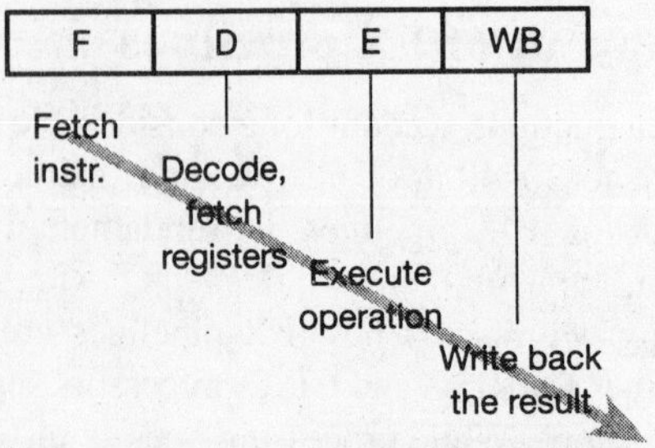

Figure 5.36 Traditional FX pipeline of RISC processors.

Table 5.2 Variations in pipeline cycle duration in traditional FX pipelines.

	F	D	E	WB
Most processors	1	1	1	1
MC 88110	1	1/2	1	1/2
SuperSparc	1	3/2	1	1/2

R8000 and R10000) as well as by the HP 7100 processor. Here, the traditional FX pipeline is extended by a data cache access cycle, which is inserted after the E cycle (Figure 5.37).

This extension of the pipeline is surprising at first, since the execution of simple register–register instructions does not require cache accesses. The rationale behind this layout is to simplify design by using a unified pipeline scheme for both the FX and L/S instructions. With reference to Figure 5.28 we note here that FX and L/S instructions together cover about 60–70% of all executed instructions. As an example, Figure 5.38 shows how the unified pipeline of the MIPS R4200 (Zivkov et al., 1994) is used to execute FX and L/S instructions.

Finally, Figure 5.39 summarizes the main approaches to the layout of FX pipelines in RISC processors.

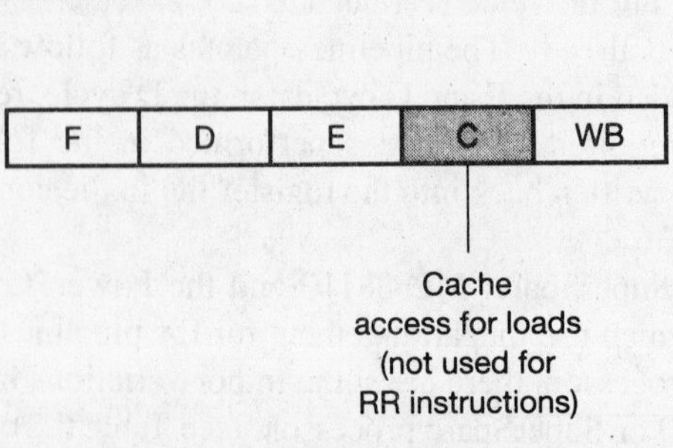

Figure 5.37 Typical layout of FX pipelines in the MIPS line of processors (except the R8000 and R10000).

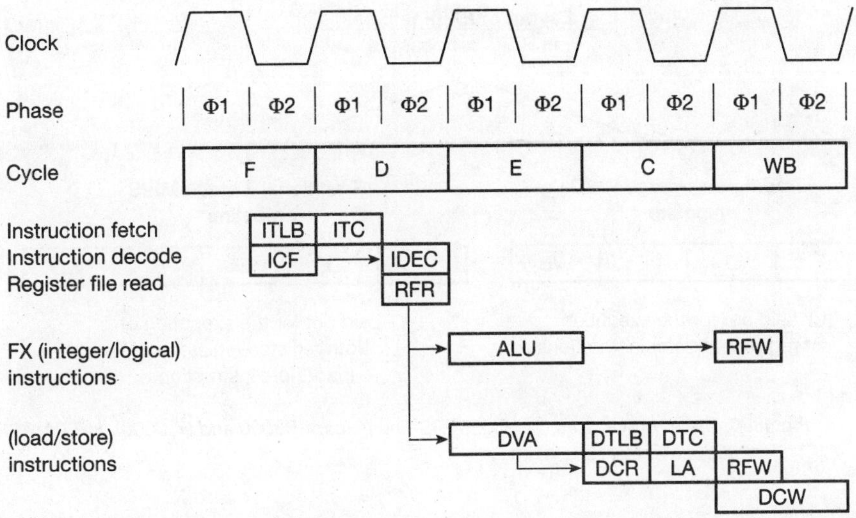

Cycle	Phase	Mnemonic	Description
	1		
F	2	ICF	Instruction Cache Fetch
		ITLB	Instruction micro-TLB read
	1	ITC	Instr cache Tag Check
D	2	RFR	Register File Read
		IDEC	Instruction DECode
		IVA	Instruction Virtual Address calculation
E	1, 2	ALU	Arithmatic/Logic operation
		DVA	Data Virtual Address calculation
	1	DCR	Data Cache Read
C		DTLB	Data joint-TLB read
	2	LA	Load data Alignment
		DTC	D-cache Tag Check
WB	1	RFW	Register File Write
	1, 2	DCW	Data Cache Write

Figure 5.38 Layout of the FX and L/S pipelines in the MIPS R4200. © 1994 IEEE

CISC pipelines

Next, we overview the layout of FX pipelines in CISC processors. CISC pipelines differ from RISC pipelines, mainly in that CISC pipelines must be able to process both register and memory operands and destinations.

In order to access a memory operand (which is supposed to be in the cache), two additional subtasks are carried out: calculating the operand address and fetching the operand (presumably from the cache). Therefore, a **traditional CISC pipeline**, which is laid out to execute *register–memory* instructions effectively, contains two

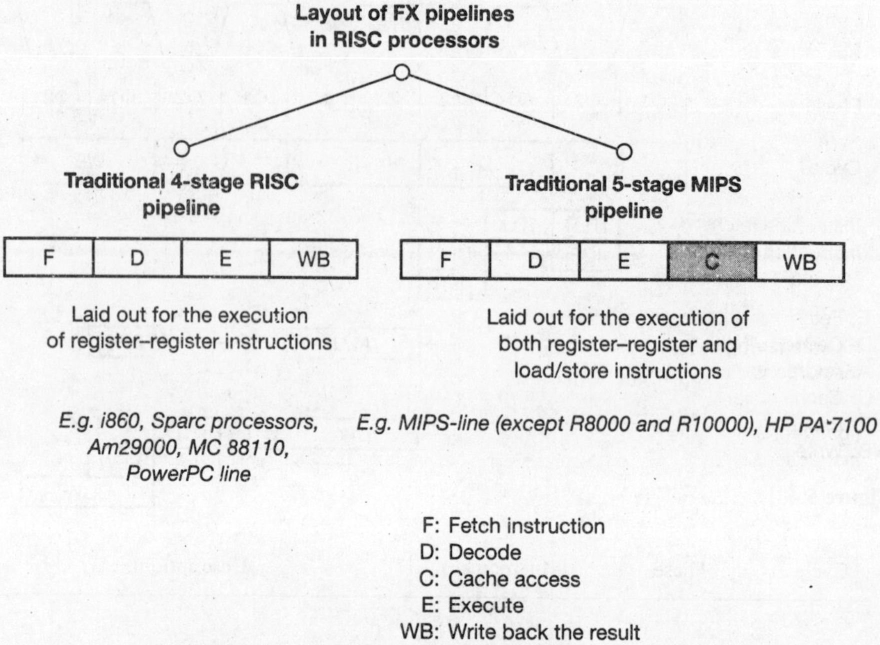

Figure 5.39 Layout of FX pipelines in RISC processors.

more stages than a traditional RISC pipeline. As illustrated in Figure 5.40, such a pipeline consists of the following six stages: instruction fetch (F), decode (D), address calculation (A), cache access (C), execute (E) and writing back the result into the register file (WB). It is used by several CISC processors such as the MC 68040 and MC 68060.

Apparently, this pipeline can also be easily used to execute register–register and load/store instructions (Figure 5.41). In order to execute *register–register* instructions, the referenced register operands are fetched in the D cycle, while the A and C cycles remain unused. Subsequently, the required operation is perfoımed in the E cycle, and the result is written back into the register file during the concluding WB cycle. We note here that unused internal cycles do not directly affect performance, since they do not cause pipeline stalls. Nevertheless, in reality, a slight performance decrease can be expected because of the increased frequency of dependencies due to the higher number of pipeline stages.

For *load* instructions, the referenced address registers, if any, are fetched in the D cycle, and the memory address is generated in the A cycle. Then, the addressed data is fetched from the cache in the C cycle, and during the WB cycle the fetched data is written into the register file. Here, the E cycle remains vacant. In the case of *store* instructions, the content of the specified address registers is fetched in the D cycle, the memory address is generated in the A cycle and execution is completed in the C cycle by writing the fetched data into the cache.

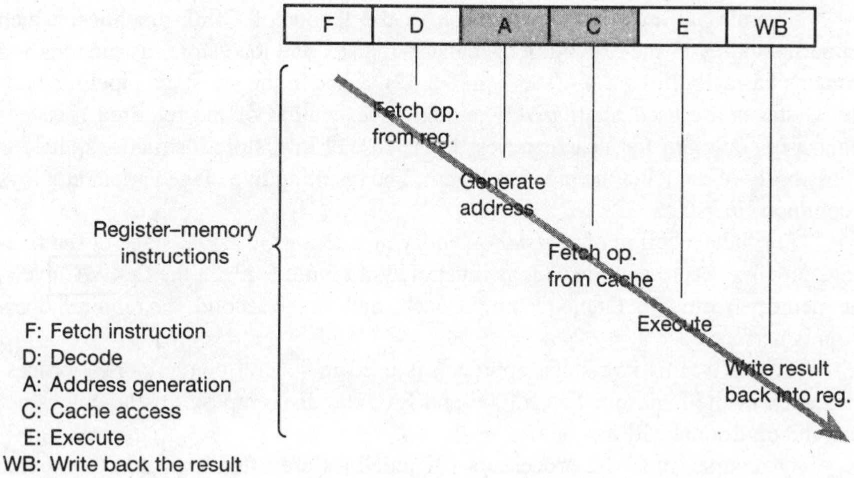

Figure 5.40 Layout of a traditional CISC pipeline and the execution of register–memory instructions.

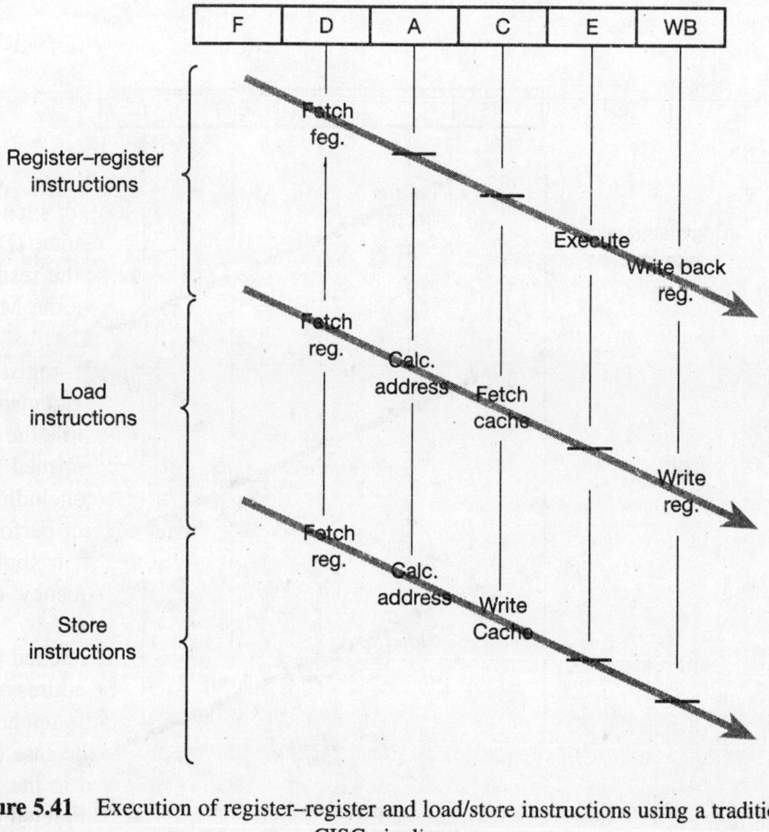

Figure 5.41 Execution of register–register and load/store instructions using a traditional CISC pipeline.

There is an *alternative approach* to the layout of CISC pipelines, which primarily addresses the execution of register–register and load/store instructions and contains basically *five stages* (see Figure 5.42). Since in the six-stage pipeline the E and C stages are used alternatively, either for execution of the required register–register operation or for a cache access in the case of load/store instructions, there is a possibility of reducing the pipeline length. The resulting five-stage variant employs a common E/C stage.

For the execution of *register–memory* instructions, the E/C stage of the five-stage pipeline has to be recycled, as illustrated in Figure 5.43. In the first E/C cycle, the memory operand is fetched from the cache and, in the second, the required operation is performed.

Basically, this five-stage approach is used in several contemporary processors, such as the Pentium. The R8000 and PA 7100 also employ this layout, rather than the traditional MIPS scheme.

Of course, in CISC processors FX pipelines are often expected to execute more complex operations. Typical examples are memory–memory instructions, or storing the result into the memory, or more complex integer operations such as multiplication and division. For *memory–memory* instructions, a CISC pipeline is easily extended to include one or two additional stages for performing the address

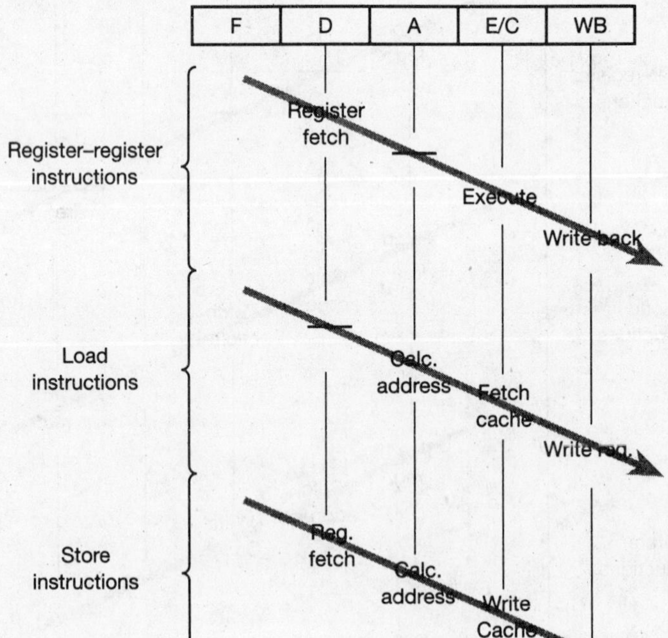

Figure 5.42 Layout of a five-stage CISC pipeline and the execution of register–register and load/store instructions.

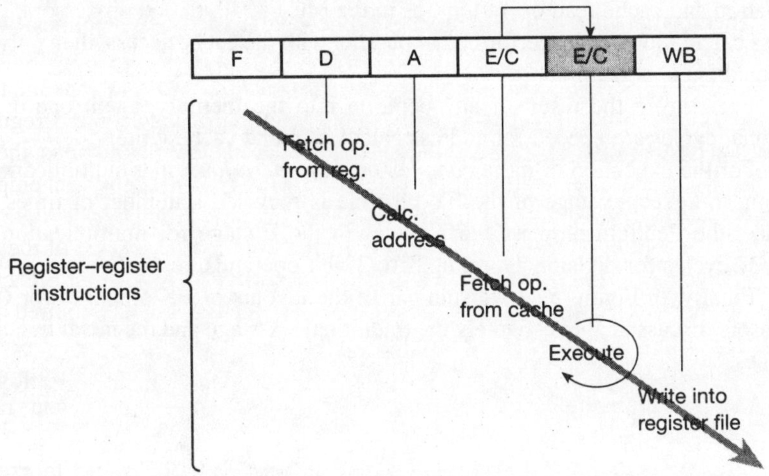

Figure 5.43 Execution of register–memory instructions using a five-stage CISC pipeline and recycling of the E/C stage.

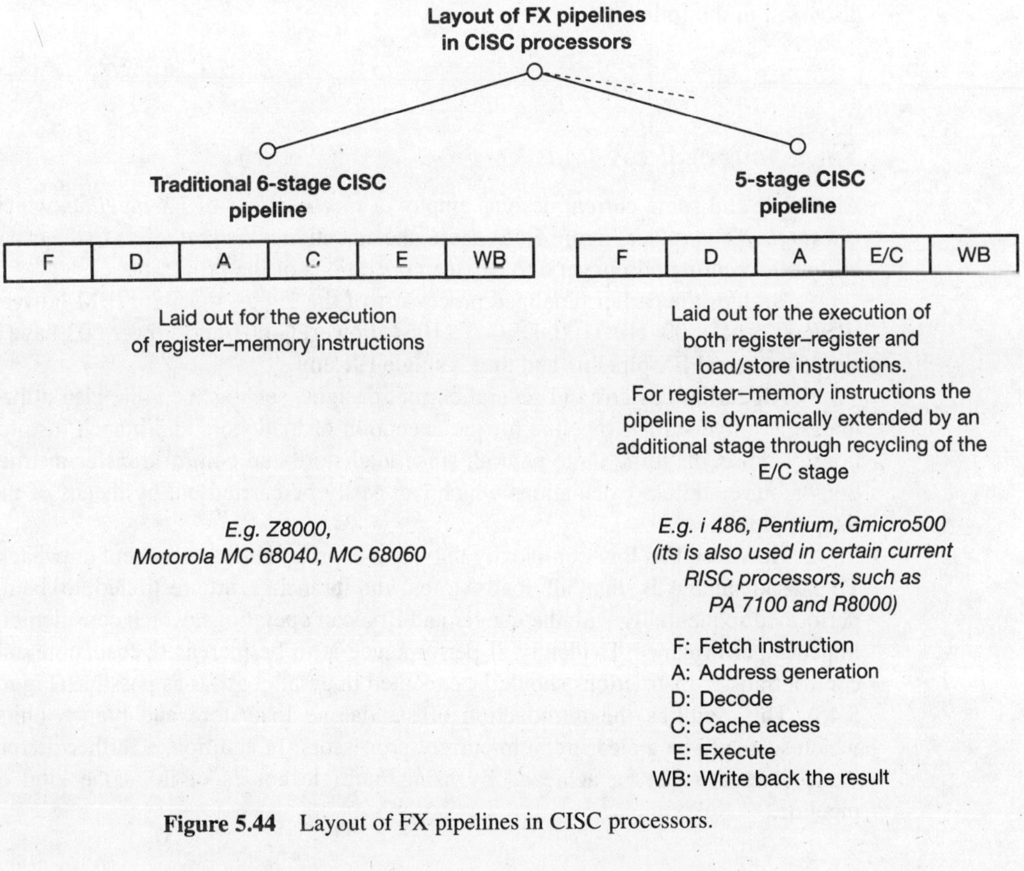

Figure 5.44 Layout of FX pipelines in CISC processors.

calculation and cache read operations, as in the MC 68040, 68060 processors. If the address calculation can be performed in parallel with the cache access, then only one additional cycle is required.

For *storing* the result of an operation into the memory, again one or two additional cycles are needed for address calculation and cache write.

For the execution of more *complex integer operations*, like multiplication or division, the execute stage of the FX pipeline is recycled a number of times. For instance, the Pentium requires 6/6/7 cycles in the E stage for multiplication and 13/21/37 cycles for division assuming 8/16/32-bit operands, respectively.

Finally, in Figure 5.44 we summarize the layouts of FX pipelines for CISC processors discussed above, namely the traditional six-stage and the novel five-stage pipelines.

5.4.3 Implementation of FX pipelines

As depicted in Figure 5.45, FX pipelines may be implemented as either universal or dedicated FX units. Furthermore, a processor may incorporate either a single universal unit or multiple universal units. These implementation variants are discussed in the following.

Single universal FX units

All earlier and some current designs employ a *single universal FX pipeline*, which is a *single FX unit* (see Figure 5.45). Here, the adjective *universal* refers to the capability of executing all integer and Boolean operations of the processor.

Besides the earlier pipelined processors of the 1980s, the i486, IBM Power1 (RS/6000), R 4000, HP 7100, DEC α 21064, PowerPC 601 and Power 603 have a single universal FX pipeline and thus a single FX unit.

All earlier designs and several current designs, such as the i486, also utilize the same universal FX pipeline for the execution of load/store and branch instructions. This seems to be quite natural, since load/store and control transfer instructions require address calculations which can easily be carried out by means of the integer pipeline.

However, this low-complexity universal approach has an apparent drawback. The disadvantage is that all loads/stores and branches are restricted to being performed sequentially with the integer and Boolean operations, which considerably impedes performance. Evidently, if performance is to be increased, load/store and control transfer instructions should be executed in parallel as far as possible (Figure 5.46). This requires the introduction of standalone load/store and branch units, which seems to be a clear trend in current processors. In addition, a further performance increase can be achieved by using multiple copies of the same kind of pipeline.

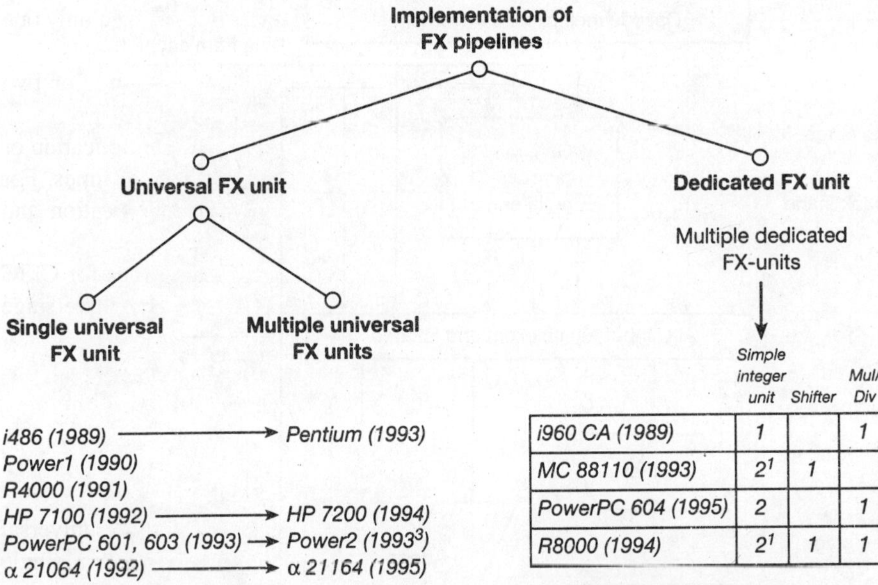

	Simple integer unit	Shifter	Mul/Div	Mul	Div
i960 CA (1989)	1		1		
MC 88110 (1993)	2[1]	1		1[2]	1[2]
PowerPC 604 (1995)	2		1		
R8000 (1994)	2[1]	1	1		

[1]: Without shift operations
[2]: For both FX and FP operations
[3]: Second adder doesn't contain a Mul/Div unit

Figure 5.45 Main approaches to the implementation of FX units.

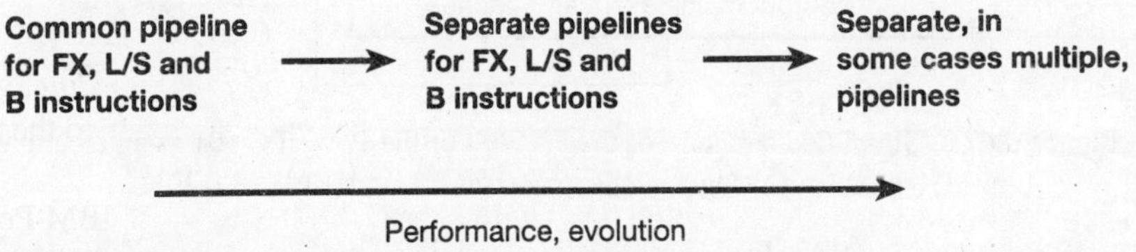

Figure 5.46 Major trend in increasing the performance of pipelined instruction execution.

Next, we show an example of a universal FX unit. Figure 5.47 depicts the simplified structure of the FX unit of the PowerPC 601 (Becker et al., 1993).

The operation of this unit is straightforward. We shall demonstrate it by describing how register–register operations are performed. Referenced operands are fetched from the register file in the decode stage. The requested operation is performed in the execute stage using the available adder, shifter and logic unit. Some instructions, like multiply and divide, require several iterations at this stage. In order to shorten latencies for define-use instruction sequences, the unit forwards the result of an operation to all possible destinations (the input latch of the execute stage, branch unit, MMU, data cache). Finally, the writeback stage ensures that the result is written back into the register file.

Here, we point out that the FX unit of the PowerPC 601 is also used for load and store operations by utilizing the adder for address calculations. The only required extensions, therefore, are two buses used to send the effective address to the

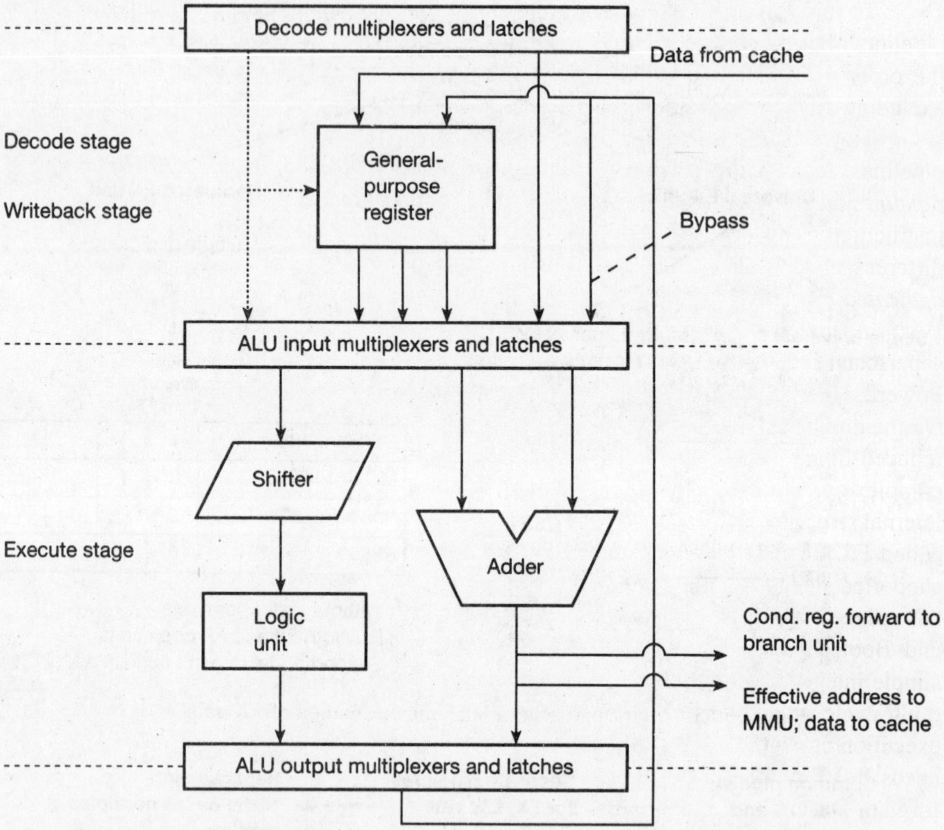

Figure 5.47 Simplified structure of the FX unit of the PowerPC 601 as an example of a processor using a single universal FX unit. © 1993 IEEE

MMU, as well as to send and to receive data to and from the data cache. Furthermore, we note that the PowerPC 601 already provides a separate branch unit to increase performance.

A second example of a processor having a single universal FX unit is the Power1 (RS/6000), which is depicted in Figure 5.7.

Multiple universal FX units

A further step in boosting performance may be achieved by applying *multiple FX pipelines*, that is, multiple pipelined FX units. As far as the number of FX units is concerned, it is worth referring to dynamic instruction distributions, which show that 30–40% of all executed instructions are integer and Boolean, as shown in Figure 5.28. Therefore, in order to exploit more parallelism, providing more than one FX unit seems inevitable. All the more so, since a single FX unit could be busy for a relatively long time while performing a multi-cycle operation and thus become a real resource bottleneck.

In this respect, it should be pointed out that integer division is usually not pipelined. For all processors, division requires a considerable number of cycles (in the order of 10–100). During or about this time, division monopolizes the unit, excluding all other operations.

However, there are *two possible approaches* to multiplying the number of FX pipelines. As shown in Figure 5.45, the first approach is to use *multiple universal pipelines* and thus *multiple universal FX units* for all supported integer and Boolean instructions. The other possibility is to employ *multiple dedicated pipelines* for different classes of integer and Boolean instructions, implemented as *multiple dedicated FX units*.

As indicated in Figure 5.45 several high-performance members of current superscalar processor families provide *two universal FX units*, such as the Pentium, Power2, HP 7200 or DEC α 21164. However, these units are usually not identical. On the one hand, there is a fully fledged universal unit, and on the other, a second, reduced-functionality FX unit, which lacks the capability of performing more complex operations, such as multiplication or division. As an example, we show the internal structure of the α 21164 in Figure 5.48. The α 21164 contains two FX units, called FX EUs. One of the units has full functionality, capable of performing all supported integer and Boolean instructions (Unit 1), whereas the other (Unit 2) has reduced functionality, capable of performing only integer additions/subtractions and Boolean operations. Thus, double units can be used either to execute two simple integer or Boolean operations in each cycle or, while Unit 1 is executing a multi-cycle integer instruction such as a multiplication, Unit 2 can proceed with the execution of simple integer or Boolean instructions. For example, the DEC α 21164 needs 8–16 cycles for performing integer multiplications, depending on operand format. During this time, Unit 2 can continue executing simple instructions. Somewhat surprisingly, this processor does not support an integer division instruction in hardware.

Dedicated FX units

The other approach is to use a *set of dedicated units*, such as simple FX units, multiplier/dividers, or separate multipliers and dividers, shifters and so on. As shown in Figure 5.45, the early i960 CA, the first superscalar processor, or several high-end superscalar processors such as the PowerPC 604, PowerPC 620 or R8000 serve as examples of this approach. Except for the early i960 CA, these processors usually contain two simple FX units (not providing multiply/divide capabilities) and implement the multi-cycle integer operations either by means of a common dedicated multiplier/divider unit (such as the PowerPC 604 or the R8000) or by a couple of separate multipliers and a separate divider, such as the MC 88110. As shown in Figure 5.45, two of the models mentioned use separate shifter units (MC 88110 and R8000). Furthermore, the MC 88110 has two additional units for graphics. As a further example we refer to Figure 7.42, which shows the internal structure of the PowerPC 604. This processor contains two single-cycle FX units to perform simple integer and Boolean instructions as well as a multi-cycle FX unit for integer multiplications and divisions.

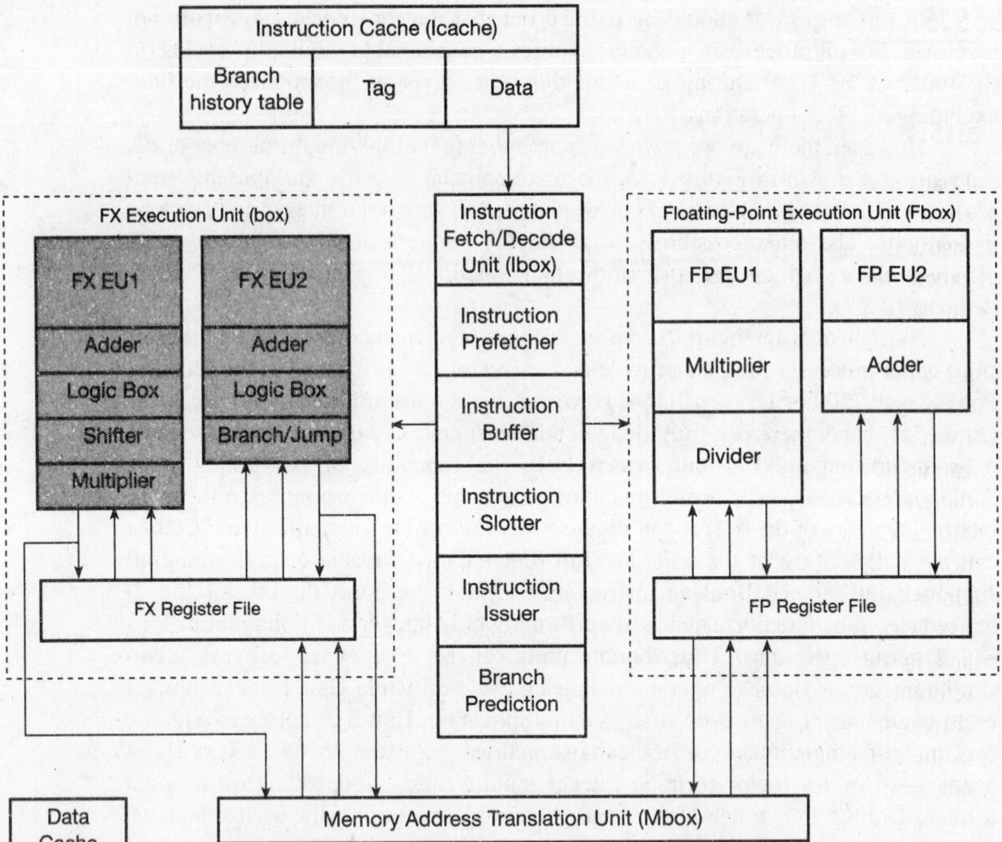

Figure 5.48 Internal structure of the DEC α 21164 as an example of a processor employing multiple universal FX units (DEC, 1994a).

5.5 Pipelined processing of loads and stores

5.5.1 Subtasks of L/S processing

Loads and stores are frequent operations, especially in RISC code. As Figure 5.28 shows, while executing RISC code we can expect to encounter about 25–35 % load instructions and about 10 % store instructions. Thus, it is of great importance to execute load and store instructions effectively. How this can be done is the topic of this section.

To start with, we summarize the *subtasks* which have to be performed during a load or store instruction (see Figure 5.49). Let us first consider a load instruction. Its execution begins with the determination of the effective memory address (EA) from where data is to be fetched. In straightforward cases, like RISC processors, this can be done in two steps: fetching the referenced address register(s) and calculating the effective address. However, for CISC processors address calculation may be a difficult task, requiring multiple subsequent register fetches and address calculations, as for instance in the case of indexed, post-incremented, relative addresses. Once the effective address is available, the next step is usually, to forward the effective (virtual) address to the MMU for translation and to access the data cache. Here, and in the subsequent discussion, we shall not go into details of whether the referenced cache is physically or virtually addressed, and thus we neglect the corresponding issues. Furthermore, we assume that the referenced data is available in the cache and thus it is fetched in one or a few cycles. Usually, fetched data is made directly available to the requesting unit, such as the FX or FP unit, through bypassing. Finally, the last subtask to be performed is writing the accessed data into the specified register.

For a store instruction, the address calculation phase is identical to that already discussed for loads. However, subsequently both the virtual address and the data to be stored can be sent out in parallel to the MMU and the cache, respectively. This concludes the processing of the store instruction.

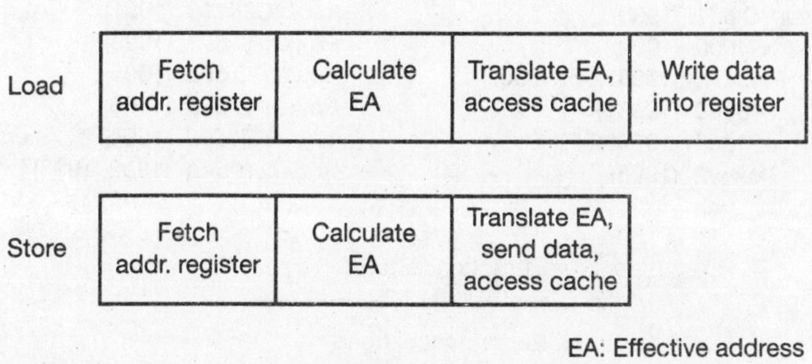

Figure 5.49 Subtasks of executing load and store instructions.

5.5.2 The design space

While considering the design space of pipelined load/store processing we take into account only one aspect, namely whether load/store operations are executed sequentially or in parallel with FX instructions (Figure 5.50).

In traditional pipeline implementations, load and store instructions are processed by the *master pipeline*. Thus, loads and stores are executed *sequentially* with other instructions (Figure 5.50). In this case, the required address calculation of a load/store instruction can be performed by the adder of the execution stage. However, one instruction slot is needed for each load or store instruction.

Representatives of this low-cost implementation approach are, in addition to earlier designs, the MIPS R4000, Pentium (with two integer units), PowerPC 601, Power2 and DEC α 21164 (also with two integer units). At first glance, it is surprising that the α 21164 uses a sequential load/store processing technique when the preceding α 21064 and α 21064A provided a dedicated autonomous load/store unit. This unexpected departure from the parallel approach is surely an implementation trade-off caused by the limited chip area.

A more effective technique for load/store instruction processing is to do it *in parallel* with data manipulations (see again Figure 5.50). Obviously, this approach assumes the existence of an *autonomous load/store unit* which can perform address calculations on its own. In addition, in order to be able to perform both address calculations and arithmetic operations in parallel, the corresponding units should

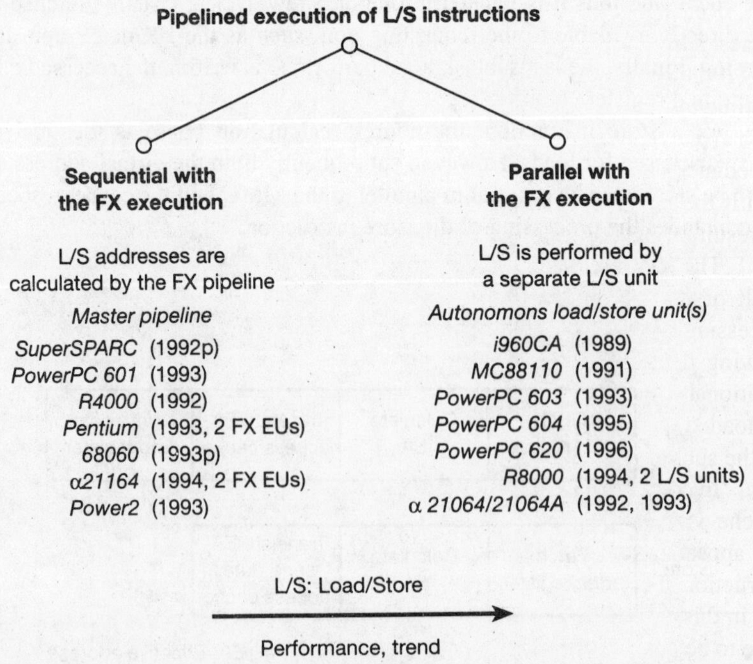

Figure 5.50 Sequential v. parallel execution of load/store instructions.

receive register data in parallel. This requires two additional output ports at the register file.

There are an increasing number of superscalar processors that implement an autonomous load/store unit. Examples of early designs are the i80960 CA or MC 88110. More recent examples are the DEC α 21064, DEC α 21064A, PowerPC 603, PowerPC 604, PowerPC 620 and MIPS R8000.

Autonomous load/store units can either be operated lock-stepped with the processing of other instructions or work decoupled. In *lock step,* load and store requests to the memory (cache) are issued in order. Alternatively, the execution of loads and stores can be *decoupled* from the execution of other instructions in order to boost performance. This can be achieved by providing queues for pending loads and stores and executing these operations from the queues. However, decoupling load and store operations raises a number of issues, such as preserving sequential consistency in respect of instruction execution or memory accesses. These points are more relevant to superscalar processors and will be discussed in Section 7.7.

5.5.3 Load-use delay

In this section, we are concerned with an important performance measure of pipelined load/store processing, namely load-use delay. The value of the load-use delay is a characteristic attribute of pipelined execution of loads. Large load-use values can seriously impede processor performance, especially in superscalar processors.

Remember from Section 5.2 that *load-use delays* arise from load-use dependencies, a kind of RAW dependency. *Load-use dependency* gives rise to a load-use delay if the result of the load instruction cannot be made available by the pipeline in due time for the subsequent instruction.

We note that a load-use delay does not occur only in situations when the load immediately precedes the instruction that uses it. There may be a load-use delay even if the load precedes the utilizing instruction by more than one instruction but the result of the load is not available in due time.

The load-use delay is understood as the difference between the time when the result of the load operation is available and the time when it is needed during processing of the subsequent consumer instruction. Figure 5.51 illustrates this by showing the pipelined execution of a load–add instruction pair and assuming a traditional four-stage pipeline. On the left-hand side of this figure, we assume that the loaded data is available at the end of cycle c_{i+2}, just in time to be used as input for the subsequent add instruction. Thus, there is no load-use delay at all.

In contrast, on the right-hand side of this figure we indicate a situation when a cache with a longer access time is used and, therefore, the result of the load instruction appears only one cycle later, at the end of cycle c_{i+3}. Since the subsequent add instruction requires the result of the load earlier, namely at the beginning of cycle c_{i+3}, in this case there is a load-use delay (LUD) of one cycle. Apparently, if nothing were to be done to prevent it, the add instruction would fetch a wrong register value, namely the value prior to loading the requested one. Figure 5.52 shows what can be done to prevent sequential inconsistency due to a load-use delay.

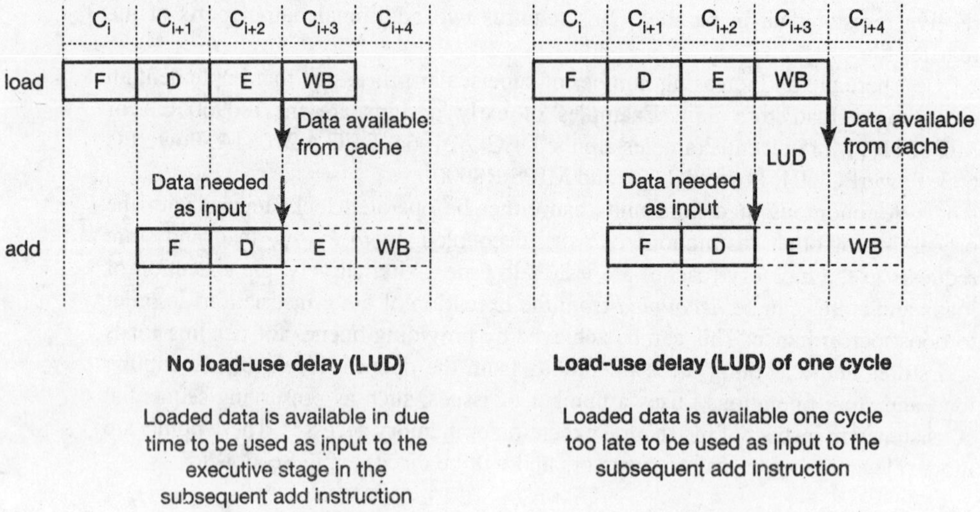

Figure 5.51 The interpretation of load-use delay.

A load-use delay can be handled either statically or dynamically. If *static resolution* is used, the compiler tries to insert as many independent instructions as necessary between the load instruction and the consumer instruction to compensate for the load delay. In the example shown, there is a load-use delay of one cycle, thus it is sufficient to put a single instruction in between. The consumer instruction comes next and thus requests the result of the load only at the end of cycle C_{i+3}, a time when it is available. If the compiler cannot find an independent instruction to insert, it generates a NOP.

Early MIPS computers, such as the R2000 and R3000, are examples of handling load-use delays by static scheduling. Here, the compiler is assumed to insert a load delay slot after all load instructions. This slot is filled by the compiler either with an independent instruction or with a NOP.

The other most frequently used technique for handling load-use delays is *dynamic scheduling* (see again Figure 5.52). Here, dedicated hardware is responsible for detecting and resolving hazards that can harm sequential consistency.

In general, the *value of the load-use delay* depends on the pipeline layout and on the implementation of caches. How it depends on the pipeline layout will be discussed later in this section. As far as caches are concerned, most current processors implement two-level caches with separate, on-chip first-level caches. We note that most processors have a load-use delay of one cycle, and a few have two or three cycles (Table 5.3). However, there are several processors in which load-use delays are eliminated, such as the Intel i486, the Pentium, the SuperSparc and the R8000.

How severely do load-use delays *limit* processor performance?

For traditional *scalar processors* load-use delays of one cycle are quite acceptable, since a parallel optimizing ILP-compiler will frequently find independent instructions to fill the slot following a load. However, *for superscalar processors* with instruction issue rates of 2 and higher, it is much less probable that the

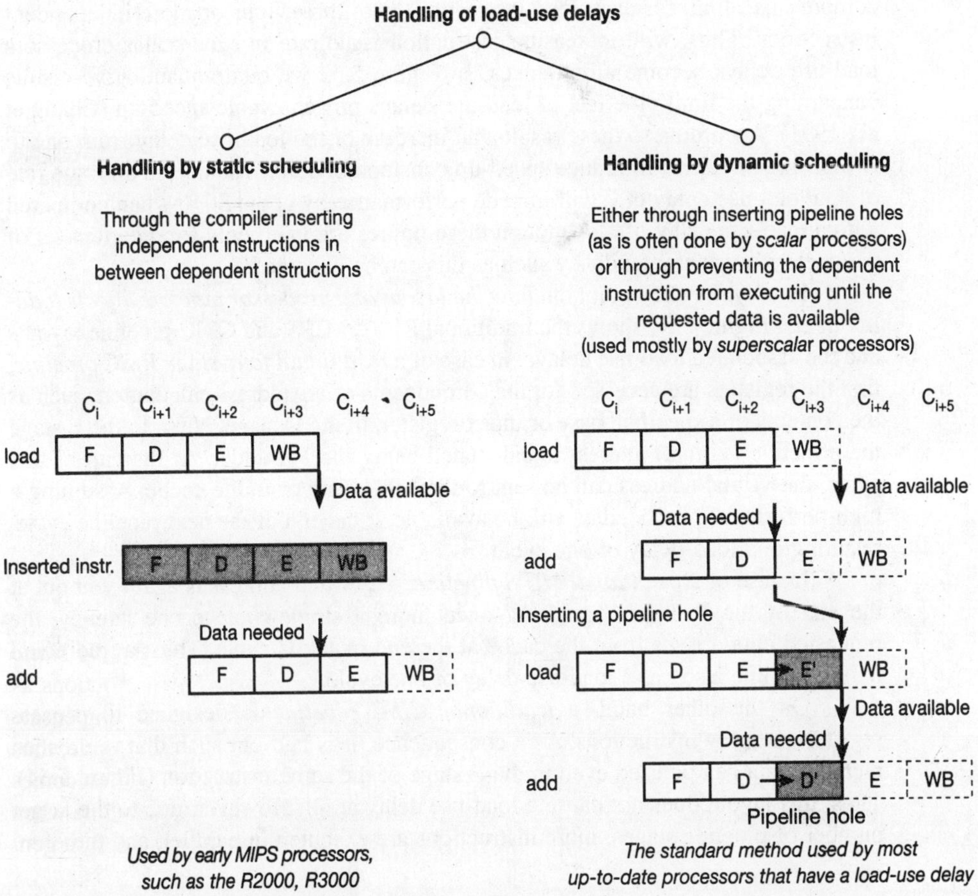

Figure 5.52 Basic approaches to cope with a load-use delay. Note that in the example shown a load-use delay of one is assumed.

Table 5.3 Values of load-use delays (in cycles) for current processors.

	Load-use delay (in cycles)	
0	*1*	*2 or 3*
i486	MIPS X	MC 88100
Pentium	R2000, R3000	R4000
SuperSparc	R6000	α 21064 (3 cycles)
R8000	PA 7100, PA 7200	α 21164 (2/3 cycles)
	Power1 (RS/6000)	
	PowerPC 601, 603	
	Power2	

compiler can find, for each load instruction, two, three, four or more independent instructions. Thus, with increasing instruction issue rate in superscalar processors load-use delays become a bottleneck. In Figure 5.53 we quote quantitative results concerning the limiting effect of load-use delays on achievable speed-up (Chang et al., 1991). According to these results, an increase of the load-use delay from one to two or three cycles will reduce speed-up considerably. For instance, at an issue rate of 4, a load-use delay of 2 will impede performance by about 30 % when compared with a load-use delay of 1. Although these figures are valid only for a certain set of parameters, a general tendency such as this can be expected.

Finally, we shall point out *how the layout of a processor pipeline affects load-use delay*. Figure 5.54 shows the traditional RISC, MIPS and CISC pipeline layouts and the associated load-use delays. In case of a *traditional four-stage RISC pipeline*, first the registers are accessed for the components of an address calculation, such as the contents of a specified base or index register, in the D stage. Next, in the E stage the effective (virtual) address is calculated using the FX adder. At the end of this cycle, the virtual address can be sent to the MMU and/or to the cache. Assuming a high-performance cache, data will be available at the end of the next pipeline cycle, resulting in a load-delay of one cycle.

In case of a *traditional MIPS pipeline*, the virtual address is again sent out at the end of the E stage. Assuming once more a single-cycle cache latency, the requested data arrives from the cache at the end of the C cycle. Thus, a traditional MIPS pipeline also has a load-use delay of one cycle.

On the other hand, a *traditional CISC pipeline* is designed to process register–memory instructions. As a consequence, it is laid out such that referenced memory data can be used even in the E stage of the same instruction (Figure 5.54). Thus, this layout does not cause a load-use delay at all. However, due to the larger number of pipeline stages, more instructions are executed in parallel, and therefore

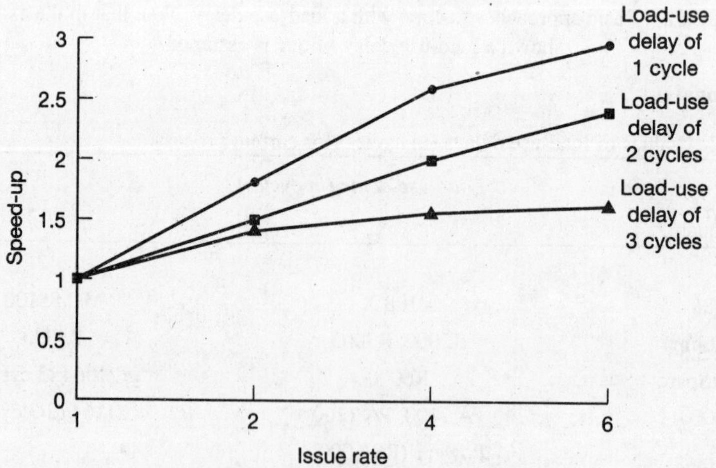

Figure 5.53 Effect of the load-use delay on possible speed-up (Chang et al., 1991). © 1991 ACM

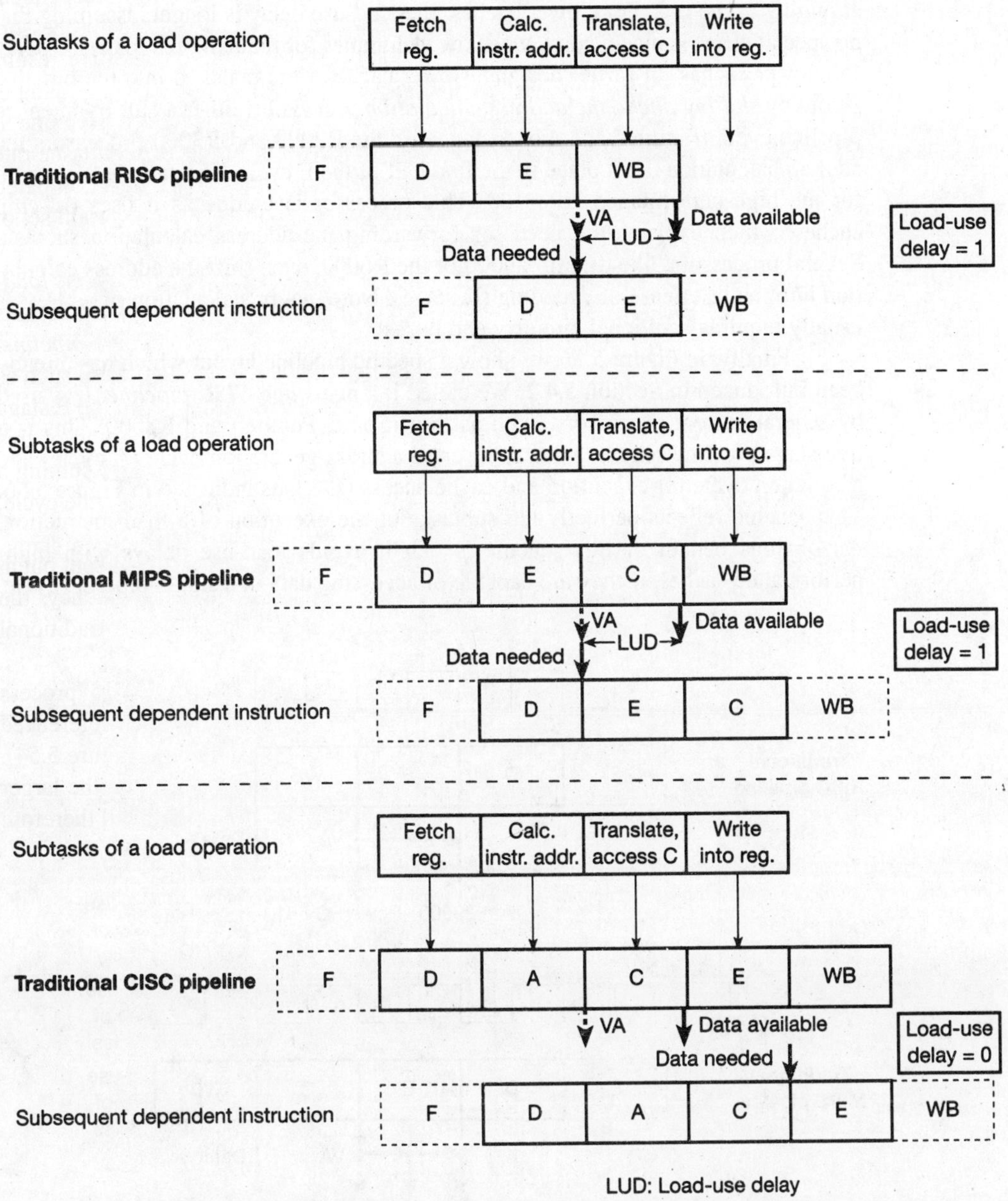

Figure 5.54 Execution of load instructions by traditional RISC, MIPS and CISC pipelines and the associated load-use delays.

more dependent instructions can be expected to occur than in case of four- or five-stage pipelines. This fact can unfavourably affect performance.

For the above discussion, we have assumed high-performance caches capable of accessing data in one cycle, including address translation (if needed), and assuming cache hits. For slower caches, the load-use delay is longer, assuming that no special effort is made. Next, we show techniques for reducing the load-use delay for slower caches. In earlier designs, slower caches were matched into the pipeline layout by *shifting ahead the address calculation process* by either a half or an entire pipeline cycle (Figure 5.55). For instance, in the R2000 and R3000 processors the address calculation takes place in the first half of the E cycle. The same is also valid for the high-performance HP 7100. This processor is unique as it uses off-chip caches, which explains the need for forwarding the address calculation subtask. Several processors, like the Am 29000 or the R6000, even shift the address calculation into the last phase of decoding (D stage). Note that precalculation of addresses usually requires additional circuitry and buses.

Finally, in Figure 5.56 we show a specific pipeline layout which has already been introduced in Section 5.4.2. We called it a *five-stage CISC pipeline*. It is used by several current processors, such as SuperSparc, Pentium and R8000. This is a five-stage pipeline scheme with an inserted address-generation cycle (A cycle) and a common cycle for execution and cache access (E/C), as indicated in Figure 5.56. This scheme reflects perfectly the subtasks of the execution of a load instruction. An obvious benefit of this scheme is that it avoids load-use delays with high-performance caches, if they are capable of accessing data in a single pipeline cycle.

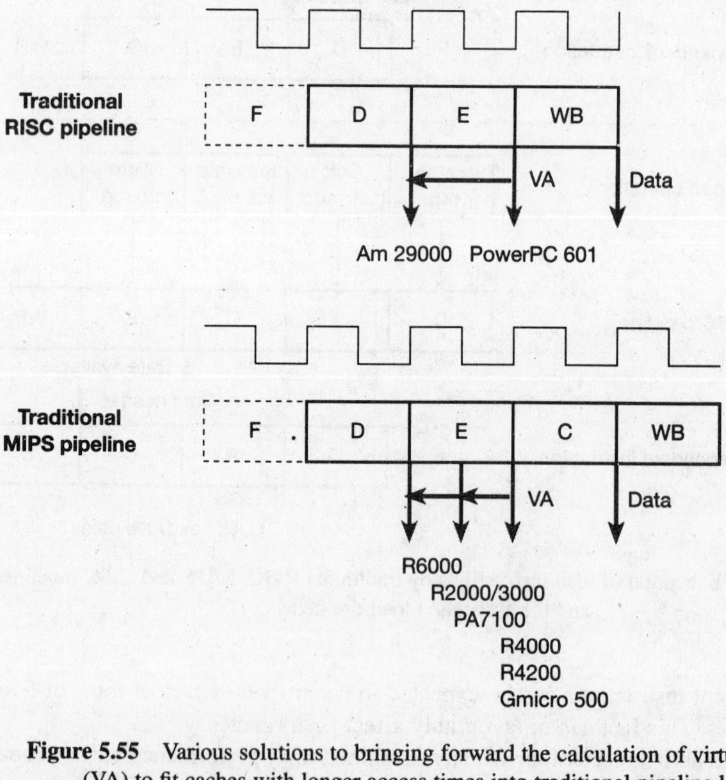

Figure 5.55 Various solutions to bringing forward the calculation of virtual addresses (VA) to fit caches with longer access times into traditional pipeline layouts.

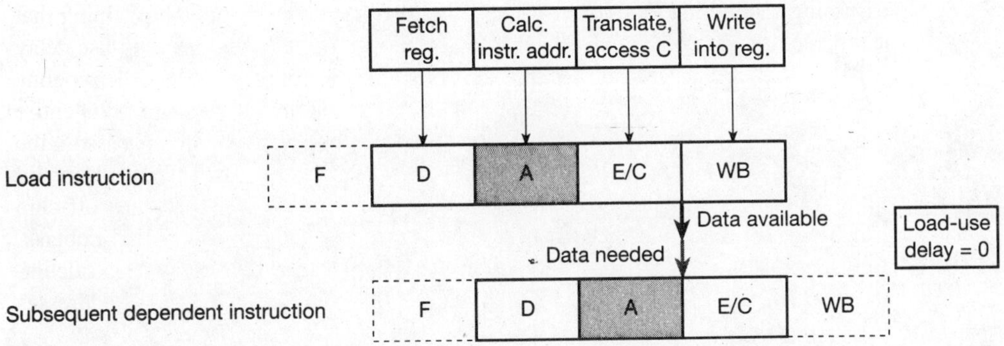

Figure 5.56 The five-stage CISC pipeline layout which is often used in current processors, e.g. i486, Pentium, SuperSparc and R8000, to avoid load-use delay for high-performance caches.

At first glance, our foregoing discussion is relevant only to sequential load/store processing. However, for *parallel load/store processing* the same principles remain valid. The only difference is that the load-use delay can be determined by comparing the FX pipeline as well as the FP pipeline with the load pipeline. An example is the PowerPC 603 which has a standalone load/store unit. Figure 5.57 shows the load, FX and FP pipelines as well as the resulting load-use delay (LUD). Note that in the figure the load instruction is assumed to be immediately preceding the integer and FP operate instructions.

Concluding this section, we note that in case of *decoupled architectures*, load-use delays do not have the same interpretation as for processors with lock-stepped L/S processing. In decoupled architectures load queues allow load-use delays to be probabilistic in character, rather than having fixed values of 0, 1, 2 and so on. Here, the actual values also depend on the features of the application running on the processor.

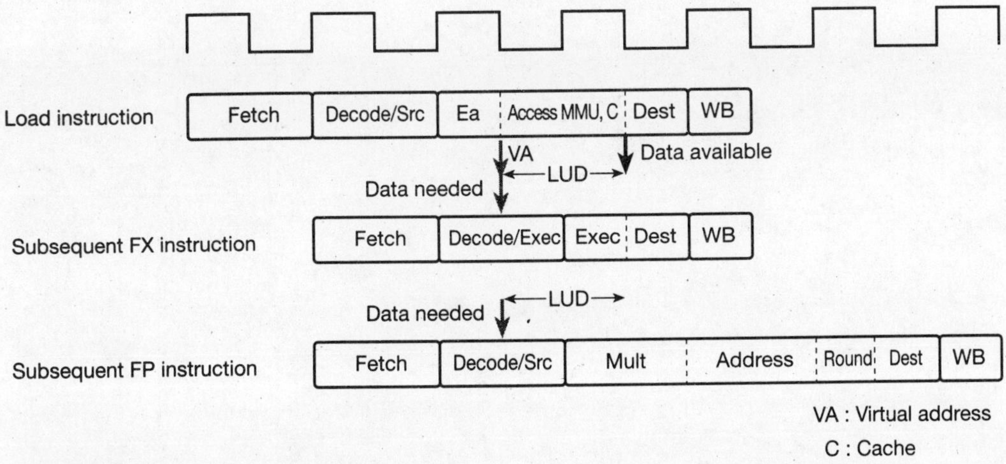

Figure 5.57 Layout of the FX, FP and load pipelines in the PowerPC 603, which has a separate load/store unit for parallel execution.

6 VLIW Architectures

In this chapter we present a short overview of **VLIW (Very Long Instruction Word) architectures**. Unlike other chapters, however, here we confine our description to the distinctive features of this architecture class rather than presenting and discussing its design space. We have simplified our description since at the moment it is questionable whether VLIW architectures have a promising future. There are two main reasons for this. VLIWs have several inherent constraints, which will be discussed in Section 6.1. Also their fiercest competitors, superscalar processors, have achieved tremendous progress in increasing performance in the past couple of years. At the end of this chapter we give an overview of proposed or marketed VLIW machines and describe the Trace 7/200 VLIW architecture as a case example.

6.1 Basic principles

As already mentioned in Chapter 4, VLIW architectures are closely related to superscalar processors. Both aim at speeding up computation by exploiting instruction-level parallelism. Both have nearly the same execution core, consisting basically of multiple execution units (EUs) operating in parallel, and employing either a unified register file for all data types or distinct (split) register files for FX and FP data, as depicted in Figure 6.1.

For the sake of simplicity, the *common basic structure* shown comprises only the execution core. At this point, we are not interested in either the cache/memory connection or possible additional features like shelving, renaming or reordering.

The two main *differences* between VLIW and superscalar processors are *how instructions are formulated* and *how scheduling is carried out.*

Whereas superscalar architectures are designed to receive conventional instructions conceived for a sequential processor, VLIW architectures are controlled by long instruction words comprising a control field for each of the execution units available, as indicated in Figure 6.2 for the unified register file layout.

The length of the VLIW instructions depends on two factors: the number of execution units available and the code lengths required for controlling each of the execution units. VLIWs usually incorporate a considerable number of execution units, say 5–30. Each unit requires a control word length of about 16–32 bits. This results in word lengths of about 100 bits – 1 Kbit for a VLIW processor. For instance, the Trace 7/200, which is capable of executing seven instructions/cycle, has a word length of 256 bits. At the other end, a four-module Trace 28/200 needs a word length of 4*256 bits = 1 Kbit. Another example is the ELI 512, one of the pioneer VLIW machines, which had a word length of 512 bits. This is indeed an **E**xtremely **L**ong **I**nstruction word!

The other important difference between VLIW and superscalar processors relates to instruction scheduling. In general, superscalar processors are assumed to be scheduled dynamically. In contrast, VLIW architectures are scheduled *statically.*

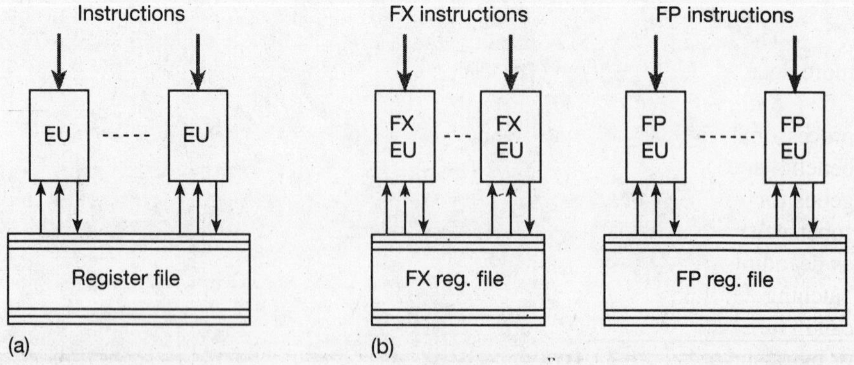

Figure 6.1 Common basic structure of superscalar and VLIW architectures (a) Unified register file; (b) split register file.

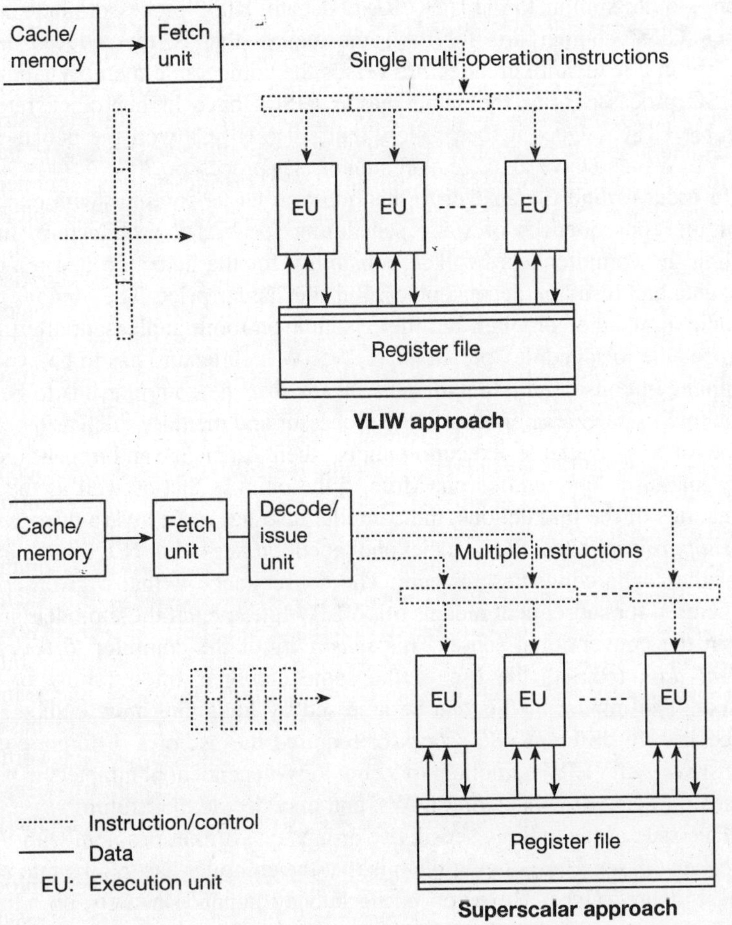

Figure 6.2 Main differences between superscalar processors and VLIW architectures.

The basic differences between these computer classes are worth discussing in more detail. Let us first examine static scheduling.

Static scheduling removes the burden of instruction scheduling from the processor and delegates this task entirely to the compiler. This has both far-reaching benefits and drawbacks. On the one hand, static scheduling is extremely advantageous for VLIW architectures as it *reduces complexity* considerably. Compared to a superscalar processor, a large number of tasks are simpler or even superfluous, such as decoding, data dependency detection, instruction issue, shelving, renaming, dispatching and instruction reordering. The lesser complexity of a VLIW architecture can in turn be exploited for boosting performance, either by increasing the clock rate or by raising the degree of parallelism, or both.

The real advantage of a VLIW design over a comparable superscalar design is the *higher possible clock rate* because of its reduced need for complexity. This situation is quite similar to the CISC/RISC debate. RISC processors have an edge over their CISC counterparts for the same reason, that is, the reduced need for complexity in a load/store architecture versus the comparable memory architecture of a CISC processor. For the same reason RISCs have higher clock rates than comparable CISCs. Does it then follow that since RISCs won the debate against CISCs, VLIWs also have an edge over superscalar processors?

In order to find the answer to this question let us continue with our assessment of the consequences of static scheduling for VLIW architecture. In static scheduling the compiler takes full responsibility for the detection and removal of control, data and resource dependencies. But this has its price. The obvious price is the complexity of the compiler, but there is an even more unpleasant aftermath. In order to be able to schedule operations, the VLIW architecture has to be exposed to the compiler in considerable detail. This means that the compiler has to be aware of all the important characteristics of the processor and memory, such as the number and type of the available execution units, their latencies and repetition rates, memory load-use delay and so on. More to the point is that as well as the syntax and semantics of the instructions, the compiler also has to be aware of *technology-dependent parameters* like the latencies and repetition rates of the EUs or the load-use delay of the cache connected to them. The consequence is that a given compiler cannot be used for subsequent models of a VLIW line, even if these models are compatible in the conventional sense. This *sensitivity* of the compiler to *technology-dependent data* restricts the use of the same compiler for a family of VLIW processors. The impact of this can be assessed by imagining how cumbersome it would be if each different x86 processor required the use of a different compiler. This sensitivity of VLIW compilers to technology-dependent parameters is possibly the most significant drawback of VLIWs, and may decide their future.

The issue of technology sensitivity brings up a further problem with VLIWs, that of *cache misses*. Here, the problem is that the compiler has to take into account worst-case delay values. However, cache latency depends heavily on whether a cache access hits or misses. Actual values could be, for instance, two cycles for a cache hit and five cycles for a cache miss. Then, without any specific measures, the compiler has to take into account the maximum possible value for a cache access, which would impede performance considerably. One possible solution to this problem would be to support the cache misses by speculative loads (see Section 7.7.2).

The second significant difference between VLIWs and superscalar architectures is that VLIWs use a long instruction word, which provides a field for each available execution unit. This kind of instruction layout has some disadvantages, because on average only some of the fields will actually be used. The result is *wasted memory space and memory bandwidth*. For instance, data published on the Trace family has revealed that compiled Fortran code is as much as three times larger for a Trace processor than it is for a VAX architecture (Colwell et al., 1988).

A further important point concerning VLIWs is the degree of parallelism achievable, that is, the number of execution units operating in parallel. In many ways the limits to increasing parallelism are similar for both VLIWs and superscalar processors. In both cases each additional execution unit typically requires two more read and one more write port on the register file. Another similarity is that in order to exploit a large number of available execution units, high-performance optimizing compilers are necessary, such as global schedulers, as discussed in Chapter 9. In this respect the question is whether VLIW architectures can *convert the benefits* they gain from reduced complexity into a higher degree of parallelism. The answer, however, depends on compiler technology and available parallelism in programs. For instance, recent high-end superscalar processors have about 10 execution units operating in parallel. A VLIW would have an appreciable edge over this superscalar processor if it provided, say, 20 parallel units and these units could be appropriately utilized. This, however, would require much more powerful optimizing compilers than are currently available for superscalar processors. Furthermore, it remains questionable whether the application concerned has enough intrinsic parallelism available to be extracted. All in all, it is highly questionable whether the reduced complexity of VLIW architectures can really be utilized for effectively speeding up computation.

We note an additional drawback to VLIWs. Because of the high complexity of the task concerned, they *cannot be programmed in assembly language*. Imagine the difficulty of an assembly programmer having to take into account simultaneously for, say, 10–20 execution units which ones are free or busy, when data is available at each of the execution units, when referenced cache data arrives, and so on. It quickly becomes clear that this is virtually an impossible task to solve manually.

6.2 Overview of proposed and commercial VLIW architectures

Only a few VLIW architectures have been proposed or marketed. We give a brief overview of them here, using Figure 6.3 as a reference.

Although the term **V**ery **L**ong **I**nstruction **W**ord computer was only coined in 1983 (Fisher, 1983), VLIW architectures appeared on the market as early as 1975. The first VLIW machine was Floating Point Systems' *FPS-120B*, a VLIW with two FP units operating in parallel. The FPS-120B was an attached processor, called

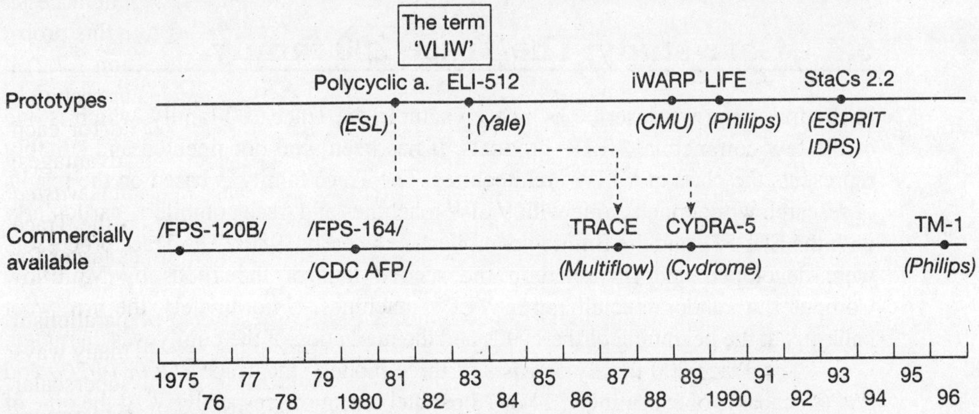

Figure 6.3 Overview of proposed and commercial VLIW machines.

an array processor, which was used to speed up FP operations in scientific code. Two similar commercial VLIW machines followed, the *FPS-164* and the *CDC AFP*.

A notable prototype development was the Polycyclic architecture from ESL (Rau et al., 1982), which evolved into the commercial product *CYDRA-5* from Cydrome around 1990 (Rau et al., 1989). Probably the most far-reaching development within this class of computers was the prototype machine called *ELI-512*, which was developed at Yale around 1983 (Fisher, 1983). This project had its origin in optimizing horizontal (parallel) microcode. The Yale machine and its compiler, which was based on trace-scheduling (see Section 9.4.3), called *Bulldog*, has become widely known. This project spawned the term VLIW. In addition, a commercial product line based on ELI-512, the *Trace family* of VLIW machines, was developed by Multiflow around 1987 (Colwell et al., 1987). The Trace family is described in more detail in Section 6.3. We note that both Multiflow and Cydrome, two firms which were established to produce and market VLIW machines, went bankrupt at the beginning of the 1990s, mainly due to management problems.

Subsequent developments such as the *iWarp* at CMU (Cohn et al., 1989), the *LIFE* from Philips and the *StaCs* 2.2 at C.E.A. France (de Dinechin, 1992) also deserve mention.

Finally, we mention yet another commercial VLIW product, an embedded processor from Philips dubbed *TM-1*, to be introduced in 1996.

It is interesting to note that the first Intel RISC processor, the *i860* (around 1989), has a so-called dual-instruction mode, which operates like a VLIW. In this mode two instructions are fetched from the cache at once, one for the integer unit and one for the FP unit. Despite this, we do not consider the i860 to be a fully fledged VLIW and have not included it in Figure 6.3.

As mentioned earlier, the future of VLIWs is not yet clear. In 1993 Hewlett-Packard revealed plans to develop a VLIW machine about 1997. IBM and Intel are also said to be pursuing such plans (Gwennap, 1994). However, we are rather sceptical of whether these ongoing VLIW developments will actually result in commercial products.

6.3 Case study: The Trace 200 family

In the following we describe as a case example the Trace 200 family, which is one of the few commercial VLIW products. It has been well documented and suitably represents the class of VLIW architectures. The Trace family is based on the results of research work done at Yale with VLIW machines and trace compilers, particularly with the ELI-512 and the Bulldog compiler, in the early 1980s. The Trace processors were developed and marketed in the second half of the 1980s by Multiflow Computer, a vendor specializing in VLIW machines. Unfortunately, the firm went bankrupt at the beginning of the 1990s and the marketing of the family was disrupted.

The Trace 200 family consists of three models, the Trace *7/200*, *14/200* and *28/200*, capable of executing 7, 14 or 28 parallel operations respectively. At the time of its introduction the 7/200 achieved impressive performance figures, an increase in speed of five to six times over that of machines of higher cost, such as the VAX 8700, for a wide range of scientific applications (Colwell et al., 1988). Here, we describe the basic model, the 7/200. Higher numbered models consists of two or four linked 7/200s.

The *7/200* has a split-register 32-bit RISC kernel, as shown in Figure 6.4. The processor is partitioned into an integer part and an FP part and is implemented on two boards (I-board and F-board).

The integer part has 64 32-bit registers and *two integer execution units* (ALU0 and ALU1) capable of performing operations on 16- and 32-bit integers, and bit and byte strings. The integer part also generates the virtual addresses and carries out dynamic address translation to produce the physical memory addresses. The integer execution units operate in minor cycles called 'beats' (65 ns). Simple operations require one minor cycle.

The FP part consists of a 32∗64-bit FP register file, *two FP execution units* (one adder (FADD) and one multiplier/divider (FMUL)), as well as a 32∗32-bit dedicated register file for holding the data of store instructions. The FP execution units perform 64-bit operations in compliance with the IEEE standard. These units are pipelined and can begin one new operation every other minor cycle. The operation latencies for 64-bit FP operations are as follows:

FP add	6 minor cycles
FP multiply	7 minor cycles
FP divide	25 minor cycles

Two 32-bit buses link the FX and FP parts.

In the following, we give some details about the instruction word format as diagrammed in Figure 6.5.

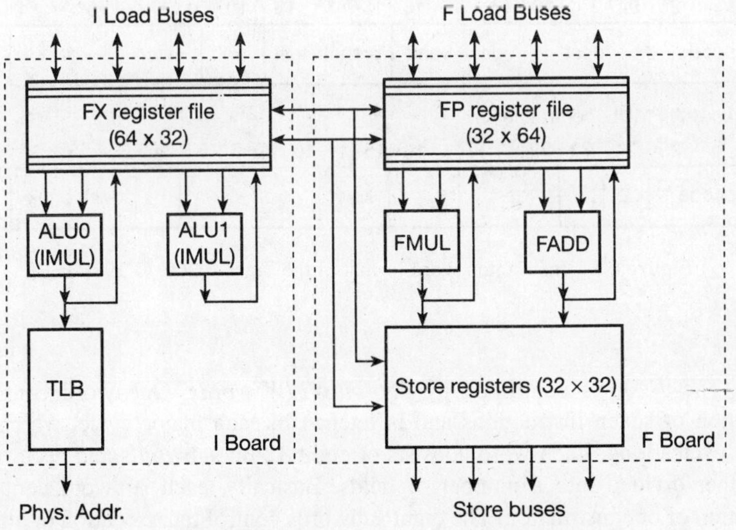

Figure 6.4 Block diagram of the 7/200. © 1988 IEEE

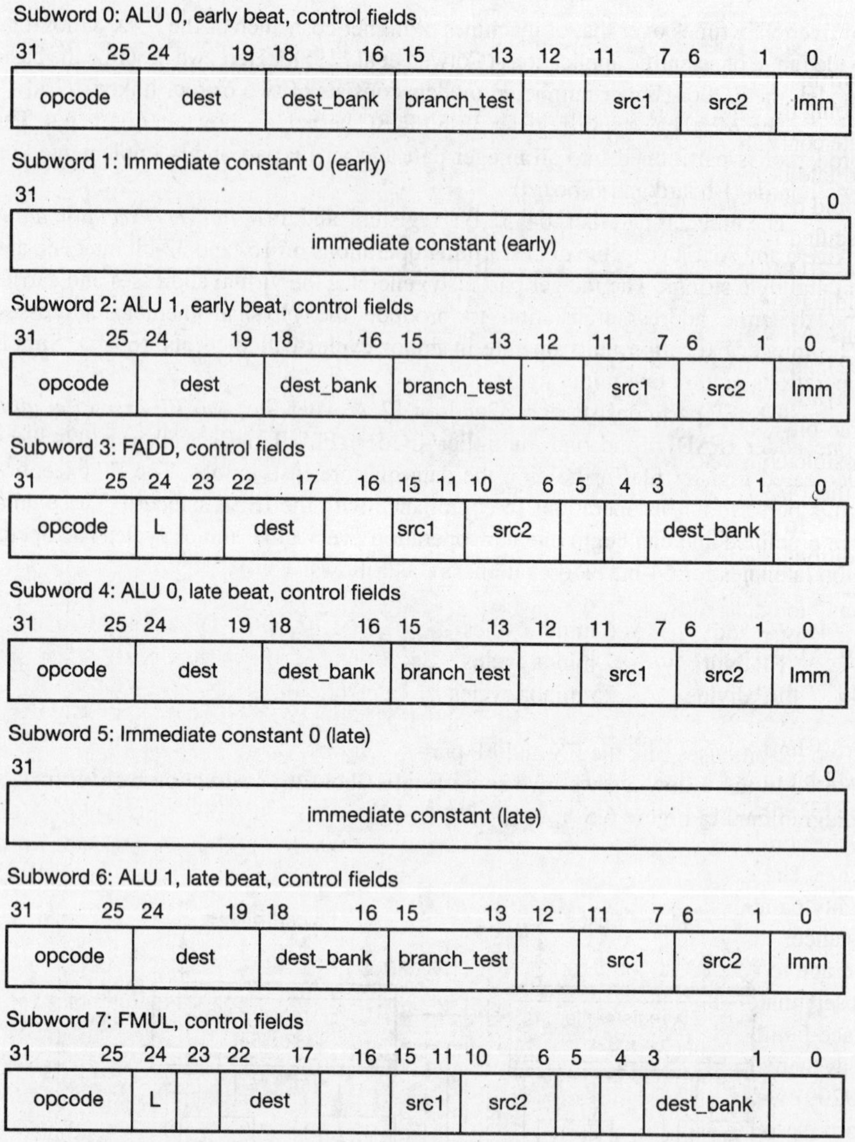

Figure 6.5 Instruction word format of the Trace 7/200. © 1988 IEEE

The 7/200 is controlled by *256-bit VLIW words*. One word controls the execution of seven instructions and is fetched in each major cycle, which is two minor cycles long. Each word consists of eight 32-bit subwords and each subword is further divided into a number of fields. Basically, each subword controls the execution of one instruction. The eight subwords control the execution of altogether four integer operations, two FP operations and a conditional branch.

Now, referring back to Figure 6.5 let us review the *format of the instruction word* in the 7/200. Subword 0 controls ALU0 during the early beat, with subword 4 doing the same for the late beat. Both subwords allow the specification of an immediate constant and a conditional branch. Subwords 2 and 6 control ALU1 in the early and late beats, respectively. Both permit the specification of a conditional branch. It should be noted that even though it seems that up to four conditional branches can be specified in one VLIW word of the 7/200, actually only two may be used.

Of the eight subwords, six are actually control words while two are used for holding immediate constants. The control words are fairly similar to RISC instructions. All words contain a 7-bit opcode, two source operand designations (src1 and src2), and a destination designation (dest_bank, dest). Corresponding to the number of available FX registers, the source and destination fields are six bits wide. The three-bit-wide dest-bank field selects the actual register file for the destination. Some possible choices are the local FX or FP register file, the local store file, or in the case of the 14/200 or 28/200, an FX register file on another board.

In addition, certain control words hold supplementary information. These additional specifications are as follows:

- the declaration of an immediate constant (Imm-field),
- the declaration of the word length of FP operations (L-field), and
- the declaration and specification of branch tests.

In the control words of the integer execution units (ALU0 and ALU1) 6-, 17- or 32-bit immediate constants can be specified in accordance with the operation code. The FP units, on the other hand, can operate either in 32- or 64-bit mode, depending on the content of the L-field. If the L-field contains a '1' the 64-bit mode is selected.

The specification and processing of *conditional branches* is a key issue in a highly parallel ILP-processor since conditional branches have a high frequency. For instance, the designer of the Trace family found every 5th to 8th operation on average to be a conditional branch in a typical program (Colwell et al., 1988). This closely matches the frequency data presented in Section 4.2.3. On the other hand, the Trace family is a highly parallel ILP-architecture, supporting the parallel execution of as many as 7–28 instructions. This means that in a fully configured model (Trace 28/200) about 3–6 conditional branches can be expected to occur in each VLIW word. As a consequence, it is critical that the Trace family provides a sophisticated branching scheme, and it has succeeded in doing so. The Trace family has a *multi-way branching* capability with the following features. In the simplest model, the 7/200, two conditional branches can be coded in each VLIW word, whereas the largest model (28/200) can handle eight. The original sequence of the conditional branches is preserved by using a priority code for each one which corresponds to its relative order among the branches. For instance, the earliest conditional branch has the highest priority, and the last one the lowest. In this way the earliest conditional branch will always determine the next target address. The priority of each conditional branch is specified by the compiler and is hidden in the immediate constant field. For further details of the branching scheme we refer to the original publication (Colwell et al., 1988).

Finally, subwords 3 and 7 control the FP execution units FADD and FMUL, respectively. As mentioned above these control words contain an L-field which determines whether operations are to be performed in 32-bit or 64-bit mode.

Another interesting aspect of the Trace family is *how* the unusually long VLIW *instructions are stored* in the memory. The Trace family concept includes a high bandwidth (984 Mbyte/s) instruction cache, which holds 8 K VLIW instructions. This represents 1 Mbyte cache space for the 28/200. The cache provides one VLIW instruction per cycle. However, the Trace family uses an intricate scheme for saving memory space while storing long instruction words with a relatively large number of empty fields. The solution selected is based on the premise that no empty 32-bit subwords are stored in the memory. Instead, each 1 Kbit VLIW word is associated with a 32-bit mask. This mask indicates which 32-bit subwords are empty and which are not. The mask is stored in the memory, followed by all subwords that are not empty. Thus, a significant saving in the memory capacity required can be achieved. The price of this solution is the high complexity of the cache fill and refill circuitry, which is perhaps the most complex hardware unit of Trace processors.

Finally, we provide further data on code expansion, performance figures and programming of the Trace family. Colwell et al. (1988) revealed that compiled Fortran code for the Trace is approximately three times larger than VAX object code. This is quite a considerable *code expansion*. As far as *performance* is concerned, the Whetstone figures shown in Table 6.1 were published by Colwell et al. (1988).

The published performance data for the Trace processors is impressive indeed. As the data in Table 6.1 shows, the Trace machines outperform the DEC 8700 considerably and approach performance figures measured for the esteemed Cray XMP supercomputer.

Trace family processors run under UNIX 4.3 BSD. Programming was done typically in Fortran, which is quite natural, since VLIW machines require a high degree of fine-grained parallelism which is available particularly in scientific applications. In order to generate the VLIW code, Multiflow developed a highly complex trace-scheduling compiler. The development of this compiler was certainly one of the most challenging tasks of the entire project.

Table 6.1 Performance data for Trace processors compared with that of the DEC 8700 and Cray XMP.

	Instruction issue rate (ns)	*Compiled Linpack (Full precision) (MFLOPS)*
Trace 7/200	130	6
Trace 14/200	130	10
DEC 8700	45	0.97
Cray XMP	8	24

7 Superscalar Processors

In this chapter we deal with superscalar processors. Since these are currently the predominant class of processors, we discuss them in considerable detail.

In Section 7.1 we first give an overview of how superscalar processors emerged and gained a foothold in the market. Then we introduce the design space of superscalar instruction issue. Subsequent sections are devoted to the specific tasks of superscalar processing, such as parallel decoding (Section 7.2), superscalar instruction issue (Section 7.3), shelving (Section 7.4), register renaming (Section 7.5), parallel execution (Section 7.6), preserving the sequential consistency of execution (Section 7.7) and that of exception processing (Section 7.8). We then discuss the implementation of superscalar CISC processors using a superscalar RISC core (Section 7.9). We conclude the chapter with case examples in Section 7.10, highlighting the R10000, the PowerPC 620 and the PentiumPro.

7.1 Introduction

7.1.1 The emergence and spread of superscalar processors

The path to widespread use of superscalar instruction issue in main-line processors took quite some time. As is usual in technology-related developments, superscalar processors *emerged in three consecutive phases*. First, the *idea* was conceived, then a few *architecture proposals* and *prototype machines* appeared, and finally, in the last phase the *commercial products* reached the market.

The **idea** of superscalar issue was first formulated as early as 1970 (Tjaden and Flynn, 1970). It was later reformulated more precisely in the 1980s (Torng, 1982; Acosta et al., 1986).

Superscalar processor proposals and **prototype machines** followed as overviewed in Figure 7.1.

As far as prototype machines are concerned IBM was the first with two significant superscalar developments called the *Cheetah* and *America projects*. The *Cheetah* project (1982–83) and the subsequent *America project* (from 1985 on) were the test beds for IBM to study superscalar execution. The four-way Cheetah machine served as a base for the America processor, which spawned the RS/6000 (1990), that was later renamed the Power1. Actually, the Power1 is almost identical to the America machine (Grohoski, 1990). It is interesting to note that the term 'superscalar' is assumed to have first appeared in connection with these developments in an internal IBM Technical Report (Agarwala, T. and Cocke, J.: High Performance Reduced Instruction Set Processors, 1987).

A second early player in the field of superscalar developments was DEC with its *Multititan project*, carried out from 1985 to 1987 (Jouppi et al., 1989). While the Multititan project was the continuation of project Titan (1984), whose goal was to construct a very high speed RISC processor, this project did not actually contribute

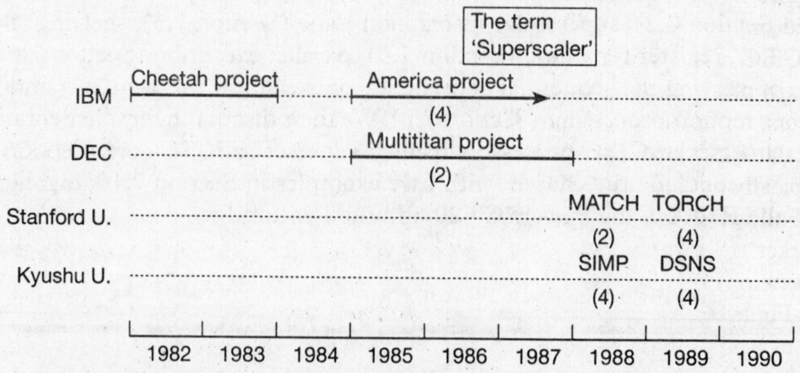

Figure 7.1 Overview of proposed or prototype superscalar processors.

much to the development of the α line of processors. As reported in Comerford (1992), the α development started in 1988 as a totally new project, then code-named RISCy VAX.

Two further projects also deserve mention (Smith et al., 1990). At Stanford University an R2000-based superscalar processor proposal called *Torch* was studied by extensive simulations. Torch was conceived as a two-way superscalar processor which supported global scheduling in hardware. The other Stanford project was code-named Match. This was a simulated architecture proposal of Johnson (1989). Finally, two superscalar prototype machines labeled *SIMP* and *DSNS* were developed at Kyushu University, Japan, around 1988–89 (Kuga et al., 1991).

These research projects paved the way to the **commercial developments**, depicted in Figure 7.2. In this figure we show how superscalar processors (highlighted) appeared in significant processor lines.

As Figure 7.2 shows, the Intel 960CA embedded RISC processor was the first commercial superscalar machine, introduced in 1989. In order to boost performance subsequently all major manufacturers were forced to introduce superscalar issue in their commercial processor lines. We point out that superscalar issue was introduced earlier in RISC than in CISC processors.

Superscalar RISC *processors* emerged according to two different approaches. Some appeared as the result of *converting an existing (scalar) RISC line* into a superscalar one. Examples of this are the Intel 960, MC 88000, HP PA (Precision Architecture), Sun Sparc, MIPS R and AMD Am29000 RISC lines. The other major approach was to conceive *a new architecture*, and to implement it from the very beginning as a superscalar line. This happened when IBM announced its RS/6000 processor in 1990, later renamed the Power1. Other examples are the DEC α line and the PowerPC family from Apple, IBM and Motorola.

Owing to their higher complexity, superscalar *CISC processors* appeared on the market after a considerable delay. Higher than RISC complexity is caused by two reasons. First, in contrast with RISCs, superscalar CISC processors have to decode multiple variable length instructions. Second, it is more demanding to implement a CISC-type memory architecture than a simple RISC-type load/store architecture. The Pentium and the MC 68060 are examples of the first superscalar CISC machines, which have been available since 1993. Both were the result of converting existing CISC lines into superscalar ones. In contrast, the M1 and the K5 processors were designed *from scratch* as x86 compatible superscalar processors. All of these superscalar CISC processors have a low issue rate of around 2 due to the additional complexity of superscalar CISC processors mentioned above. We note that some CISC processors, for instance the Pentium, the Nx586 and the K5, are implemented using a superscalar RISC core, as explained in Section 7.9. In these processors the RISC core typically has an issue rate of 4, which is equivalent to a CISC rate of 'about 2'.

Following their introduction, superscalar processors rapidly conquered the market. In just a few years every major manufacturer was offering superscalar versions of their earlier scalar lines or had introduced a new superscalar family. Figure 7.3 provides an overview of the significant superscalar lines and models as well as their manufacturers. We also indicate the issue rate of the various processors.

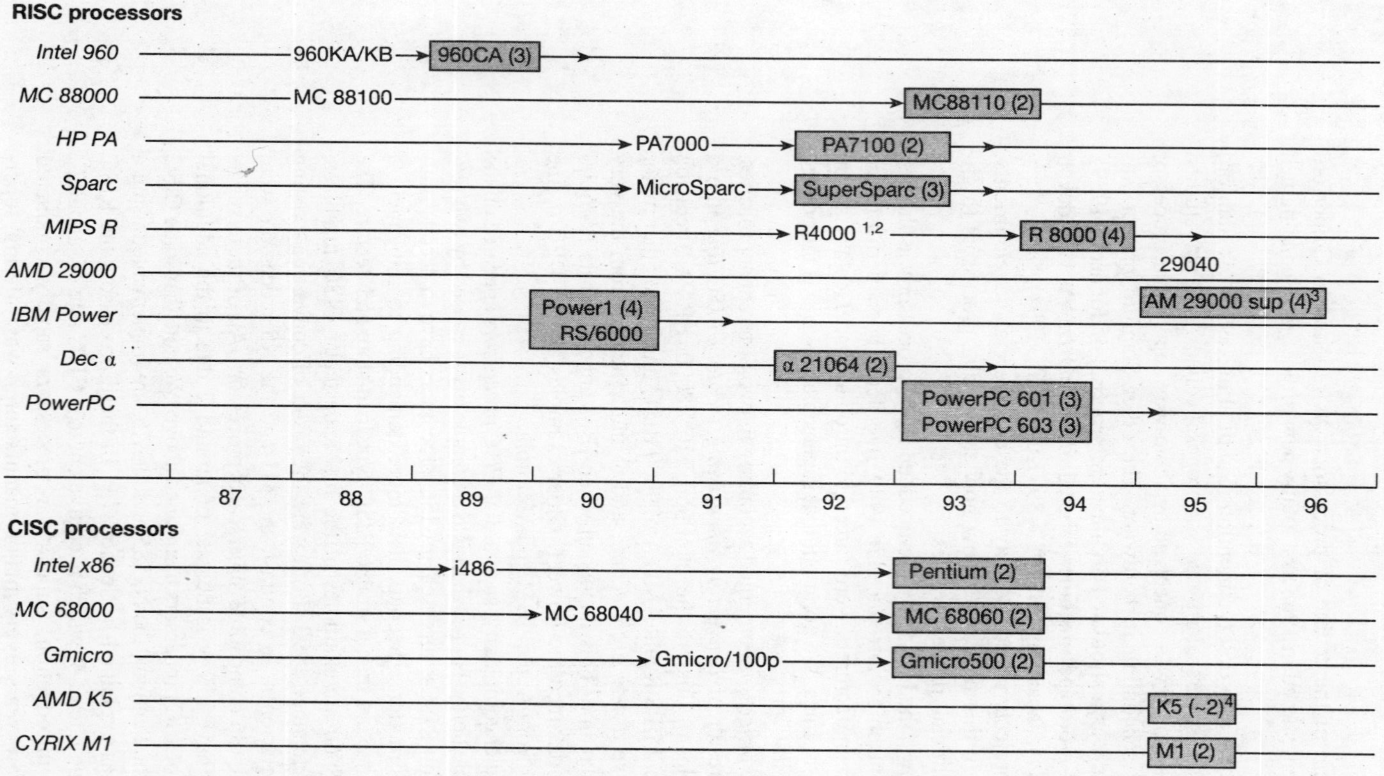

[1]Here we do not take into account the low-cost R 4200 (1994) since superscalar architectures are intended to extend the performance of the high-end models of a particular line.

[2]We also omit Rxxxx compatible processors offered by manufacturers other than MIPS Inc., such as the R 4400 (1994) from IDT, Toshiba and NEC.

[3]The whole Am29000 product line was cancelled at the end of 1995.

[4]The K5 issues 4 RISC-like micro-operations per cycle; this is roughly equivalent to two CISC instructions per cycle.

Denotes superscalar processors

Figure 7.2 The appearance of superscalar processors.

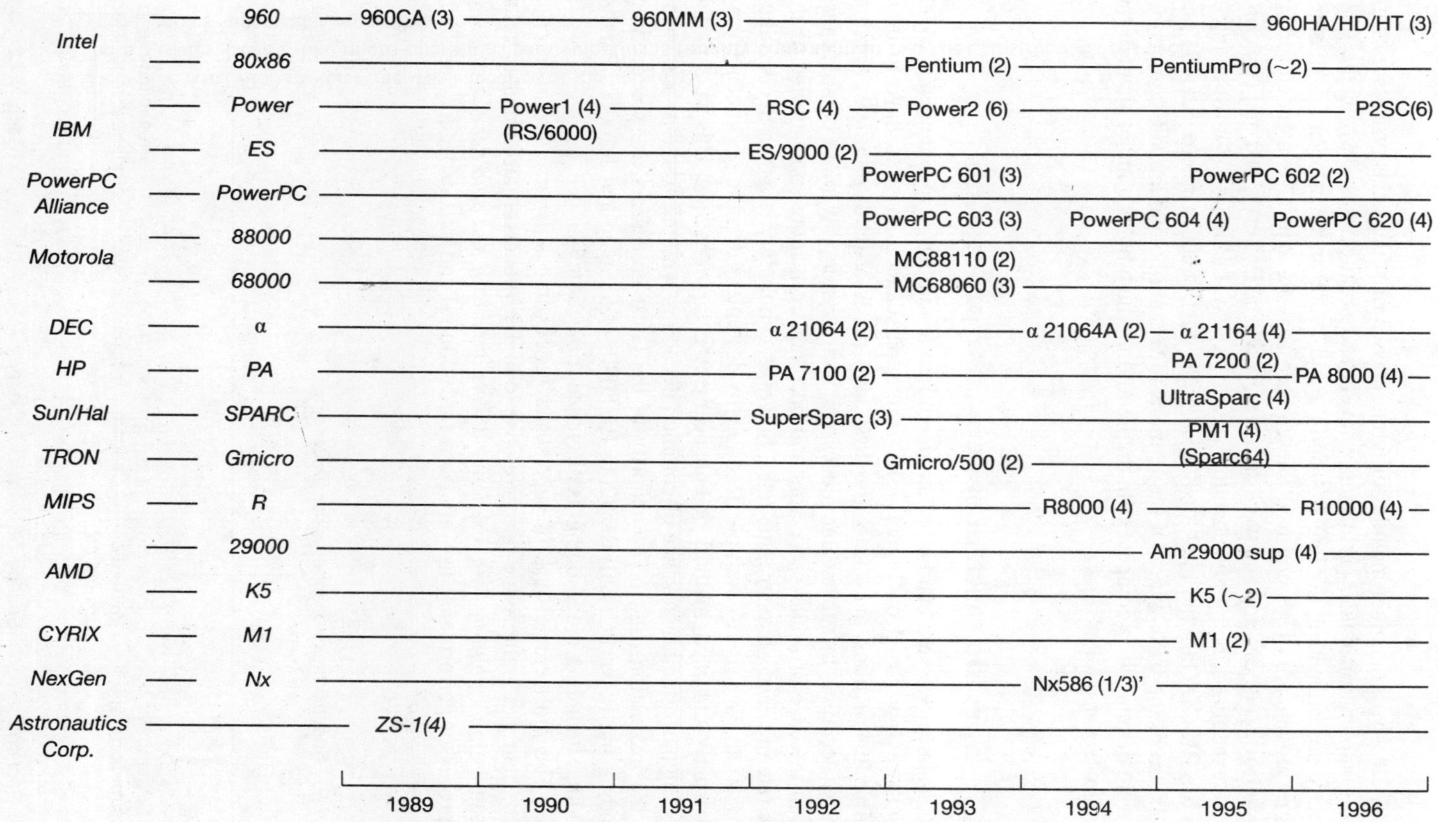

[1]The Nx586 has scalar issue for CISC instructions but a 3-way superscalar core for converted RISC instructions

Figure 7.3 Overview and evolution of commercial superscalar processors.

Clearly, the market includes different classes of superscalar processors with varying application fields, performance levels and architectures. Two of the lines indicated are embedded: the Intel 960 and the Am 29000 superscalar lines. All other lines or models are of general use. These processors are typically intended for the high-performance desktop and workstation market. The PowerPC 602 and PowerPC 603 are exceptions, being low cost, low power models. In Figure 7.3 most architectures are RISCs. Only the Intel 80x86, ES/9000, MC 68000, Gmicro, K5, M1 and the Nx are of the CISC type. Of these, the K5, M1 and Nx586 are x86 compatible and were developed to compete with the Pentium, which holds a major share of the microprocessor market.

7.1.2 Specific tasks of superscalar processing

Superscalar processing can be broken down into a number of specific tasks, which we will review based on Figure 7.4. Since superscalar processors have to issue multiple instructions per cycle, the first task necessarily is *parallel decoding*. Clearly, decoding in superscalar processors is a considerably more complex task than in the case of scalar processors and becomes even more sophisticated as the issue rate increases. Higher issue rates, however, can unduly lengthen the decoding cycle or can give rise to multiple decoding cycles unless decoding is enhanced. An increasingly common method of enhancement is *predecoding*. This is a partial decoding performed in advance of common decoding, while instructions are loaded into the instruction cache. The majority of the latest processors use predecoding, including the PowerPC 620, PA 7200, PA 8000, UltraSparc and R10000. Parallel decoding, including predecoding, is discussed in Section 7.2.

The most crucial task of superscalar processing is *superscalar instruction issue*. Clearly, a higher issue rate gives rise to higher processor performance, but at the same time it *amplifies the restrictive effects of control and data dependencies* on the processor performance as well. As regards control and data dependencies, there

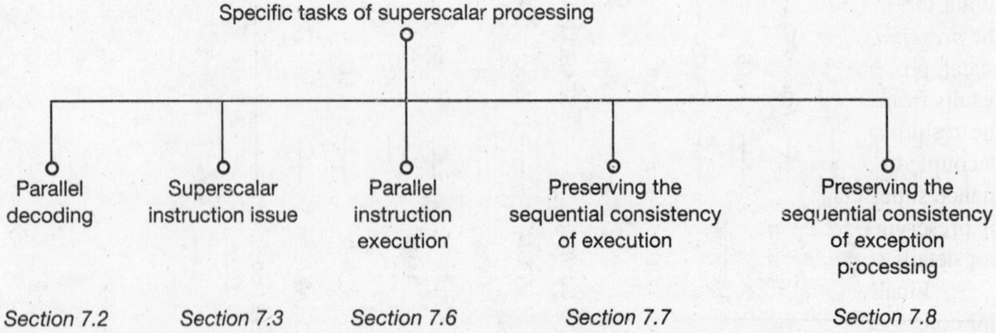

Figure 7.4 Specific tasks of superscalar processing.

are different reasons for this. Control dependencies clearly occur more frequently per issue in a superscalar processor, which issues multiple instructions in each cycle, than in a scalar processor. The frequency increase is roughly proportional to the issue rate of the processor.

As far as data dependencies are concerned, a higher issue rate may also strongly impede processor performance. Consider here that in a scalar processor, for instance in a pipelined processor, issue blockages due to dependencies may be avoided in most cases through the use of a parallel optimizing compiler. The compiler fills otherwise unused instruction slots, called bubbles, with independent instructions. Since for a scalar processor there are usually enough independent instructions available, a smart compiler can fill most otherwise wasted slots. However, when the issue rate is increased, say from 1 to 4, more and more independent instructions are needed to fill each issue slot. Very soon the point will be reached when far more independent instructions would be needed than are available.

This qualitative picture may be quantified as follows. Assuming that a straightforward issue scheme is used, in a general-purpose program, a common parallel optimizing compiler will probably be able to fill most issue slots with independent instructions for a low issue rate of 2. However, when the issue rate is increased to more than 2, issue slots will be filled to an increasingly smaller degree due to the lack of sufficient independent instructions. In other words, while the issue rate is increased to over 2, the effective issue rate, reflecting the mean value of the instructions actually issued, will increase only slightly.

Therefore, in order to achieve higher performance, superscalar processors have introduced intricate *instruction issue policies*, involving advanced techniques such as *shelving, register renaming and speculative branch processing*. As a consequence, the instruction issue policy used becomes crucial for achieving higher processor performance. Section 7.3 is devoted entirely to this topic. Shelving, register renaming and speculative branch processing are dealt with in Sections 7.4, 7.5 and 8.4.4, respectively.

The next task is *parallel instruction execution*, which is a precondition of superscalar processing and is discussed in Section 7.6. However, while instructions are executed in parallel, instructions are usually completed out of order in respect to a sequentially operating processor. Because of this, specific means are needed to retain the logical consistency of program execution. This task is commonly called the *preservation of the sequential consistency of instruction execution*. Recent superscalar processors typically accomplish this by decoupling the generation of the results from writing them back into the specified register or memory location. While the results are generated in parallel by the EUs, the program state is updated in a decoupled manner sequentially in program order. As in the quest for higher performance superscalar processors tend to offer increasingly higher parallelism, the task of preserving sequential consistency also becomes increasingly more demanding. For details see Section 7.7.

Finally, during instruction execution exceptions may arise. Here too sequential consistency is important – and gives rise to the task called the *preservation of sequential consistency of exception processing*. We are concerned with this topic in Section 7.8.

7.2 Parallel decoding

As mentioned earlier, decoding in a superscalar processor is a much more complex task than in a scalar one, and this complexity increases with the issue rate. In order to illustrate this point, we compare the decode and issue tasks of a scalar and a superscalar processor (see Figure 7.5).

A scalar processor has to decode only a single instruction in each cycle as indicated on the left of Figure 7.5. In addition, a pipelined processor has to check for dependencies in order to decide whether this instruction can be issued or not. In comparison, a superscalar processor has to perform a much more complex task. As demonstrated on the right of Figure 7.5 it has to decode multiple instructions, say four, in a single clock cycle. It also needs to check for dependencies from two perspectives: first, whether the instructions to be issued are dependend on the instructions currently in execution and, second, whether there are dependencies among the instructions which are candidates for the next issue. Since a superscalar processor has more EUs than a scalar one, the number of instructions in execution is far higher than in the scalar case. This means that more comparisons have to be performed in the course of dependency checks. Clearly, the *decode–issue path* of superscalar processors is a much more critical issue in achieving a high clock frequency than that of scalar processors. It is little wonder that superscalar processors tend to use two and sometimes even three or more pipeline cycles for decoding and issuing instructions. For instance, the PowerPC 601, PowerPC 604 and UltraSparc need 2 cycles, while the α 21064 requires 3 cycles and the PentiumPro even needs 4.5 cycles. One way to cope with this problem is through *predecoding*.

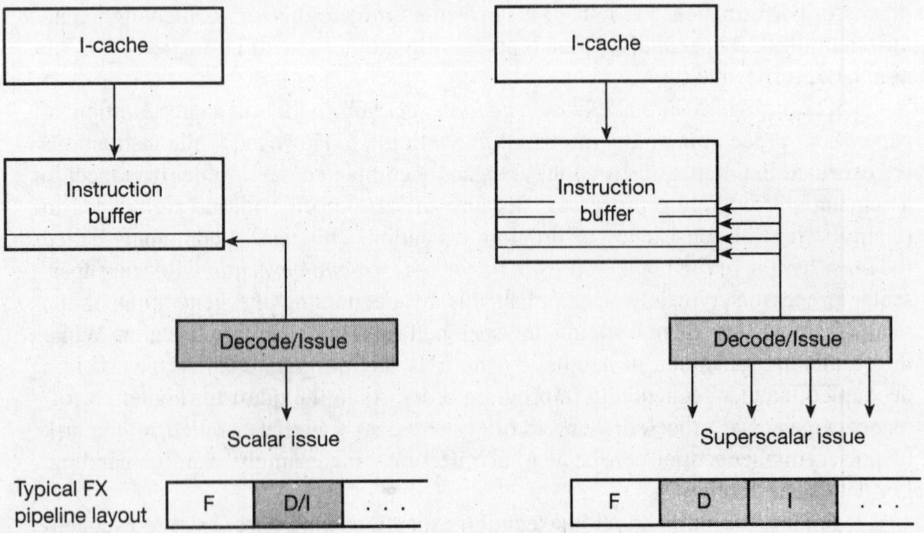

Figure 7.5 Contrasting decoding and instruction issue in a scalar and a 4-way superscalar processor.

Predecoding shifts a part of the decode task up into the loading phase of the on-chip instruction cache (I-cache), as depicted in Figure 7.6.

Here, while the I-cache is being loaded, a dedicated unit, called the *predecode unit*, performs a partial decoding and appends a number of decode bits to each instruction. In the case of RISC processors, for example, 4–7 bits are usually attached which indicate:

- the instruction class,
- the type of resources which are required for the execution, and
- in some processors even the fact that branch target addresses have already been calculated during predecoding (like in the Hal PM1 or in the UltraSparc).

The *number of the predecode bits* used is summarized in Table 7.1.

For a CISC processor such as the AMD K5 predecoding can determine where an instruction starts or ends, where the opcodes and prefixes are, and so on. This requires quite a large number of extra bits. The K5, for instance, adds five extra bits to each byte. Thus, in this case more than 70 % additional storage space is needed in the instruction cache.

The trend towards predecoding is immediately evident when we look at the overview of their introduction in Figure 7.7. Whereas some fairly recent processors, such as the PA 7100, PowerPC 601, PowerPC 604, R8000 and SuperSparc did not

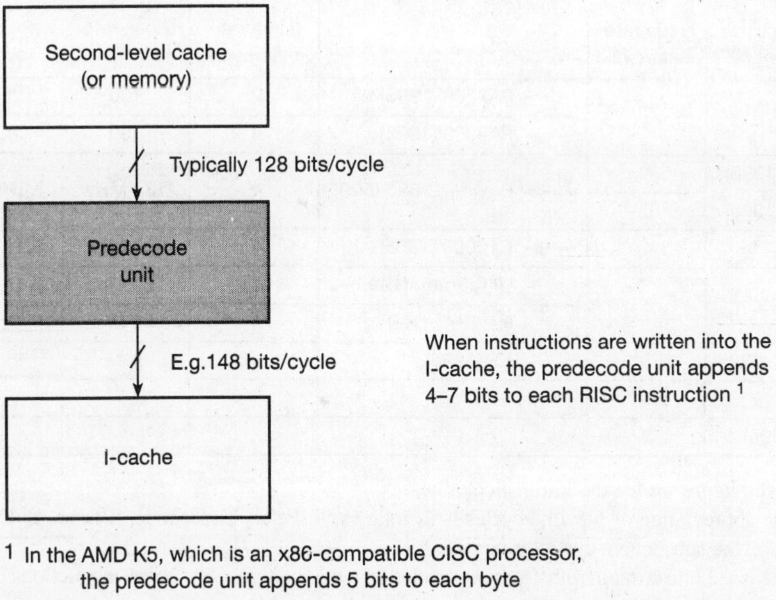

Figure 7.6 The principle of predecoding.

Table 7.1 Number of predecode bits used.

Type/year of first volume shipment	*Number of predecode bits appended to each instruction*
PA 7200 (1995)	5
PA 8000 (1996)	5
PowerPC 620 (1996)	7
UltraSparc (1995)	4
HAL PM1 (1995)	4
AMD K5 (1995)	5[†]
R10000 (1996)	4

[†]In the K5, 5 predecode bits are added to each byte

use predecoding, subsequent processors of the same lines have since introduced it. Examples are the PA 7200, PA 8000, R10000, UltraSparc and Hal's PM1. The K5, a CISC processor without any predecessor, has also introduced predecoding.

Superscalar processors without predecoding | **Superscalar processors using predecoding**

Type/Year of first volume shipment	Issue rate instr./cycle			Issue rate instr./cycle	Clock rate[1] MHz	Pipeline cycles[2]
PA 7100 (1992)	2	→	PA7200 (1995)	2	100	n.a.
			PA8000 (1996)	4	150	n.a.
PowerPC 601 (1993)	4	→	PowerPC 620 (1996)	4	133 MHz	F, D/I, E
PowerPC 604 (1995)	3					
R8000 (1994)	4	→	R10000 (1995)	4	200 Mhz	F, D, I, E
SuperSparc (1992)	3	→	UltraSparc (1995)	4	167 Mhz	F, D, I, E
			Hal PM1 (1995)	4	154 Mhz	F, D, I, E
Am 29000 sup. (1995)	3		K5 (1995)	~2[3]	n.a.	n.a.
α21164 (1995)	4					
PentiumPro (1995)	3					

[1]In the figure we list the initial clock rates.

[2]The abbreviation of pipeline cycles is as follows: F: Fetch, D: Decode, I: Issue, E: Execute. Here, the subsequent cycles are omitted.

[3]The issue rate is 4 microinstructions/cycle, which equals roughly 2 ×86 instructions/cycle

Figure 7.7 The introduction of predecoding.

Precoding is used either to shorten the overall cycle time or to reduce the number of cycles needed for decoding and instruction issue. For instance, through precoding the PowerPC 620, R10000 and Hal's PM1 require only a single cycle for decoding and issue.

Finally, it is worth mentioning that predecoding has not yet been introduced in some very recent processors, such as the α 21164, PentiumPro and Nx586.

7.3 Superscalar instruction issue

7.3.1 The design space

Superscalar instruction issue is the most sensitive task of superscalar operation. It can favourably be discussed within the framework of its *design space*. As Figure 7.8 illustrates, superscalar instruction issue comprises two major aspects, issue policy and issue rate.

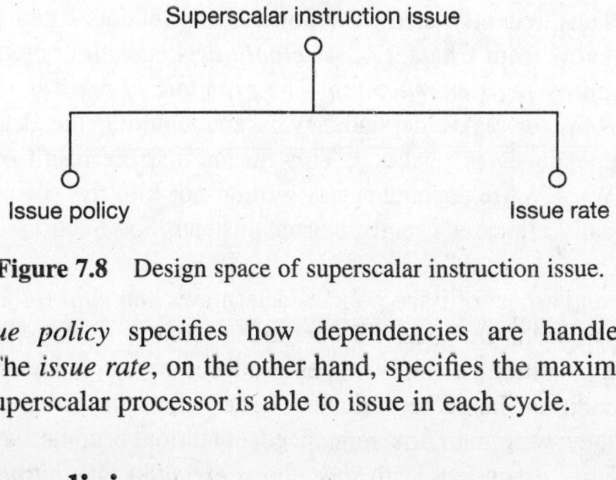

Figure 7.8 Design space of superscalar instruction issue.

The *issue policy* specifies how dependencies are handled during the issue process. The *issue rate*, on the other hand, specifies the maximum number of instructions a superscalar processor is able to issue in each cycle.

7.3.2 Issue policies

The design space of issue policy is considerably complex. As shown in Figure 7.9 it consists of four major aspects. The first two specify how false data and unresolved control dependencies are coped with during instruction issue. In both cases, the design options are either to avoid them during instruction issue by using register renaming and speculative branch processing, respectively, or not. The third aspect determines whether issue blockages will be drastically reduced by the technique of shelving and the final aspect specifies how to deal with issue blockages. In the following we provide a brief overview of the design aspects mentioned.

Within the design space of issue policy the first aspect determines how the processor copes *with false data dependencies*, which occur either between the instructions to be issued and those in execution, or among the instructions to be issued. Specifically, we are concerned with the decision whether WAR (write after read) and WAW (write after write) dependencies occuring between register

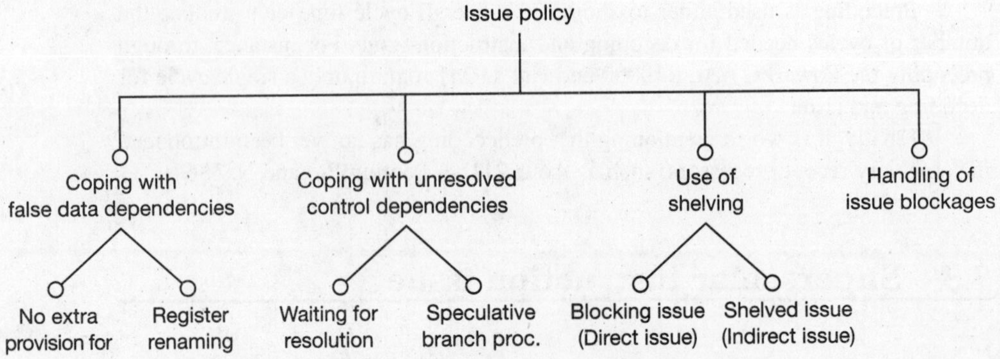

Figure 7.9 Design space of issue policies.

references will be eliminated or not. We emphasize that this aspect is confined to register data dependencies and does not cover possible false data dependencies between memory data. The rationale therefore is that false data dependencies between memory data are much less frequent than those between register data, especially in RISC architectures. Thus, recently used issue policies are not concerned with them.

As we know from Chapter 4, *false data dependencies* between register data may be removed by *register renaming*. The *principle of register renaming* is quite simple. If a WAW or WAR dependency is encountered, the destination register causing the dependency is renamed. This means that the result of the instruction causing a WAW or WAR dependency is written not into the specified register, but into a dynamically allocated 'spare register' instead. See Section 7.5 for details on this technique.

The second aspect of issue policies determines how *unresolved control dependencies* are dealt with. Obviously, a conditional control transfer instruction causes problems if the condition has not yet been produced by the generating instruction by the time the condition should be evaluated. Issue policies handle this in two different ways. Either they wait until the referenced condition becomes available, or they employ speculative execution. With *speculative execution of control transfer instructions*, or *speculative branch processing* for short, a guess is made as to the outcome of each unresolved conditional transfer instruction. Instruction issue is then resumed accordingly. Speculative branch processing is discussed in depth in Section 8.4.4.

The third aspect of issue policy concerns the *use of shelving*, an efficient technique to avoid issue blockages. Simply speaking, the alternatives are either to allow dependent instructions to cause issue blockages *(blocking issue)* or to avoid them through *shelved issue*.

The *blocking issue* (also called direct issue) is a strict approach related to dependencies. In this scheme decoded instructions to be issued are checked for dependencies, as depicted in Figure 7.10. When dependencies occur, instruction issue is blocked.

Checking for dependencies takes place in a so-called *issue window*. The **issue window** is n instructions wide, where n is the *issue rate*. Actually, the issue window comprises the last n entries of the instruction buffer. In the absence of dependencies,

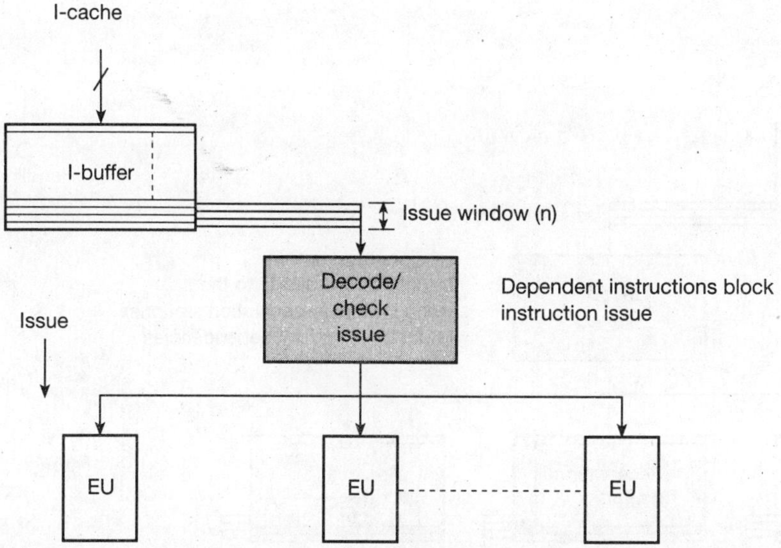

Figure 7.10 Principle of the blocking issue mode. (In the figure we assume a 4-instruction wide issue window.)

all instructions in the window are issued directly to the execution units (EUs). However, when dependencies occur, the issue blockage will be handled as specified by the corresponding aspect of the design space, which is discussed later in this section. Suffice it to say at this point that use of the blocking issue mode heavily impedes issue performance. A more advanced technique which avoids this drawback is to employ shelving.

Shelving (also called shelved issue, indirect issue) decouples instruction issue and dependency checking. This technique presumes that special instruction buffers, often referred to as reservation stations, are provided in front of the EUs. With shelving, instructions are issued first to the shelving buffers with essentially no checks for dependencies, as illustrated in Figure 7.11. In this figure we assume that there are individual reservation stations in front of each EU. Other possibilities for the implementation of shelving buffers exist and will be discussed in Section 7.4.3. At this point we note that even if shelving is used, certain hardware constraints, such as smaller than needed bus widths, or lack of free entries in the shelving buffers, may continue to cause issue blockages. For the sake of simplicity we have ignored these constraints in this introduction.

When shelving is used, no dependency checks are performed between the instructions in the issue window and those in execution. This kind of dependency checking is delayed to a later step of processing called dispatching. Nevertheless, if renaming is employed, an inter-instruction dependency check is needed for the instructions in the issue window (see Section 7.5). During *dispatching* the instructions held in the shelving buffers are checked for dependencies and dependency-free instructions are forwarded to available EUs. Because of their importance, shelving and dispatching are discussed in depth in Section 7.4.

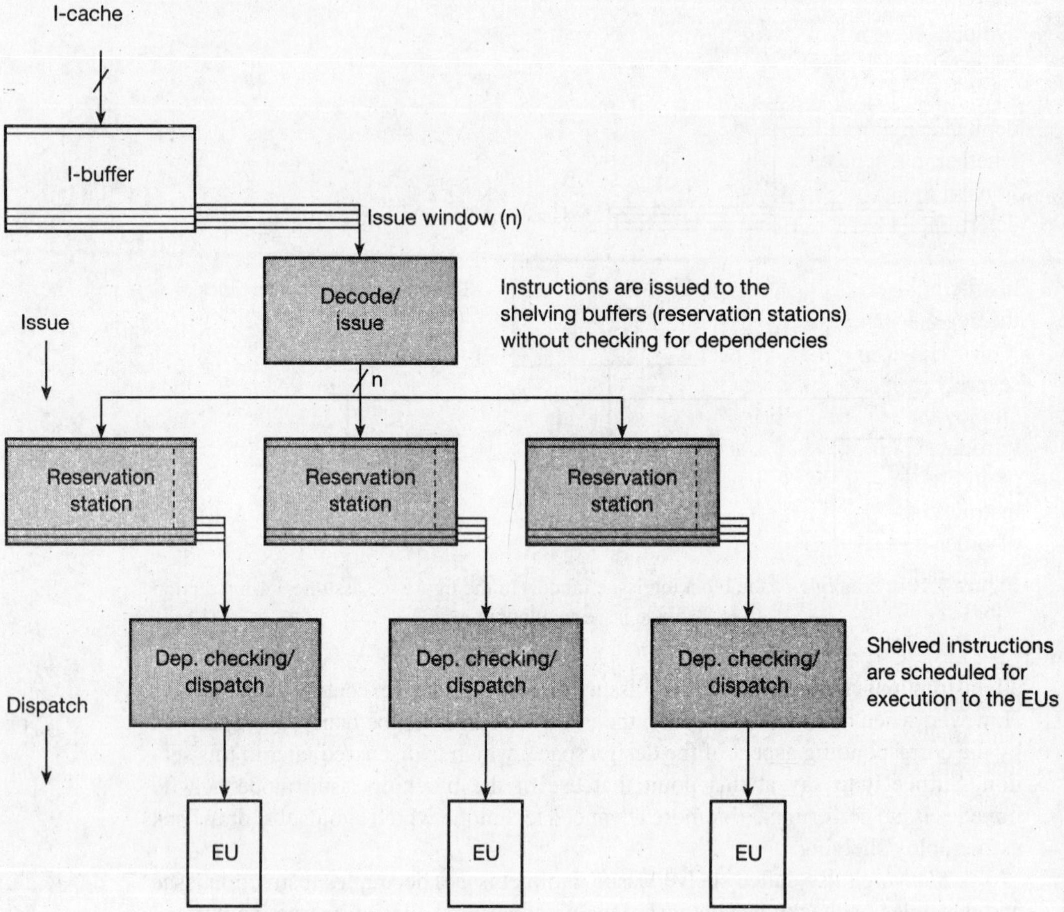

Figure 7.11 The principle of shelving, assuming that dedicated buffers (reservation stations) are available in front of each execution unit (EU).

Here, it is appropriate to make a comment regarding terminology. Note that we have used two different terms, instruction *issue* and *dispatch*, to express different actions. Furthermore, we have also used the term *'issue'* in two different interpretations. Without shelving, that is, when the blocking issue is used, *'issue'* refers to the action of disseminating decoded independent instructions to the EUs. When shelving is used, *'issue'* designates the dissemination of decoded instructions to the shelving buffers. The term *'dispatch'*, on the other hand, is only used in the case of shelving. Here dispatch designates the dissemination of dependency-free instructions from the shelving buffers to the EUs. While useful, this clear distinction is not common in the literature and both terms are used in either interpretation.

The last aspect of the design space of instruction issue declares how *issue blockages* are handled. *Instruction issue* may be blocked in both cases, with or without shelving. As long as shelving is not used, any dependencies encountered in the issue window immediately block the issue of instructions. In contrast, when shelving is used, issue blockages due to data and unresolved control dependencies are avoided. Nevertheless, despite shelving, resource dependencies can restrict the issue of instructions into the shelving buffers, as mentioned above.

The handling of issue blockages can be broken down into two aspects, as depicted in Figure 7.12. The first aspect, called *preserving issue order*, specifies whether a dependent instruction blocks the issue of subsequent independent instructions in the issue window. The second aspect is the *alignment of instruction issue*. It determines whether a fixed or gliding issue window is used.

Figure 7.13 offers more details about issue order. As shown, if a dependent instruction, such as instruction b, blocks the issue of all subsequent instructions until the dependency is resolved, the issue order is called *'in-order'*.

However, restricting subsequent independent instructions from issue can severely impede performance. Therefore, a few superscalar processors which employ the blocking issue mode, such as the MC 88110 and the PowerPC 601, have introduced *out-of-order issue*. This scheme allows independent instructions (such as 'c' in Figure 7.13) to be issued from the issue window even if a preceding dependent instruction ('b' in the figure) cannot yet be issued. In both processors mentioned out-of-order issue is only partially allowed, that is, only for particular instruction types. For instance, the PowerPC 601 issues branches and FP instructions out-of-order, whereas the MC 88110 does so only for FP instructions.

At first sight it is surprising how few superscalar processors use out-of-order issue. There are two reasons for this. First, preserving sequential consistency for out-of-order issue requires a *much higher effort* than for in-order issue. Second, *processors with shelving* have almost *no motivation* for using *out-of-order issue*. Consider here that with shelving, the issue of instructions is rarely blocked (only due to resource

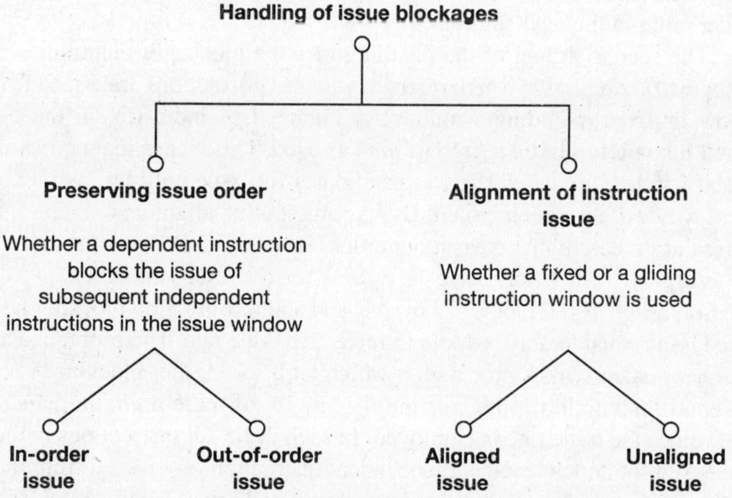

Figure 7.12 Design aspects and design choices concerning the handling of issue blockages.

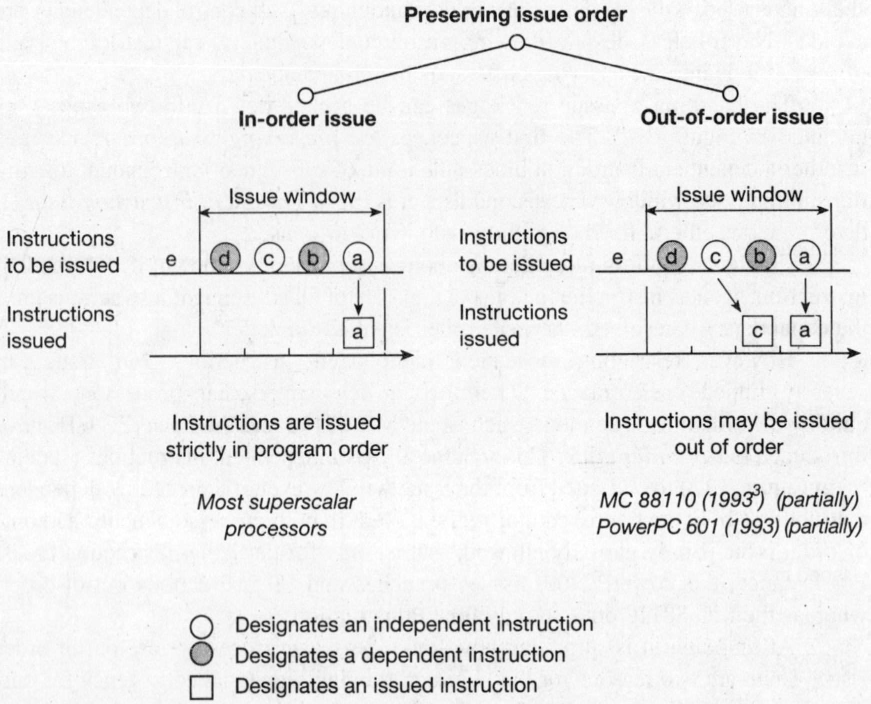

Figure 7.13 Issue order of instructions. A 4-issue in-order superscalar processor is assumed.

constraints). Therefore, out-of-order issue would only have a marginal benefit. As a consequence, we expect mainstream superscalar processors to continue to employ in-order issue in the near future.

The second aspect of the handling of issue blockages determines the *alignment of instruction issue*, which refers to whether instructions are issued from a fixed window or from a gliding window. As Figure 7.14 indicates, in the case of an **aligned instruction issue** a *fixed window* is used. This means that no instructions of the next window are considered as candidates for issue until all instructions in the current window have been issued. By its nature, issue alignment is relevant only for superscalar processors whereas issue order relates to all ILP-processors.

Aligned instruction issue is typical for the first generation of superscalar processors, such as the i960CA, Power1, and so on. But in the blocking issue mode, aligned issue considerably reduces the effective issue rate. Therefore, in a number of subsequent superscalar processors which still used the blocking issue mode, **unaligned instruction issue** was introduced. In this case a *gliding window* whose width equals the issue rate is employed. In each cycle, all instructions in the window are checked for dependencies. Independent instructions are issued from the window in either an in-order or an out-of-order fashion, as discussed before. After instruction issue, however, the window is refilled. We could say it is 'shifted along the instruction stream' by as many instructions as issued in the last cycle, as Figure 7.14 shows.

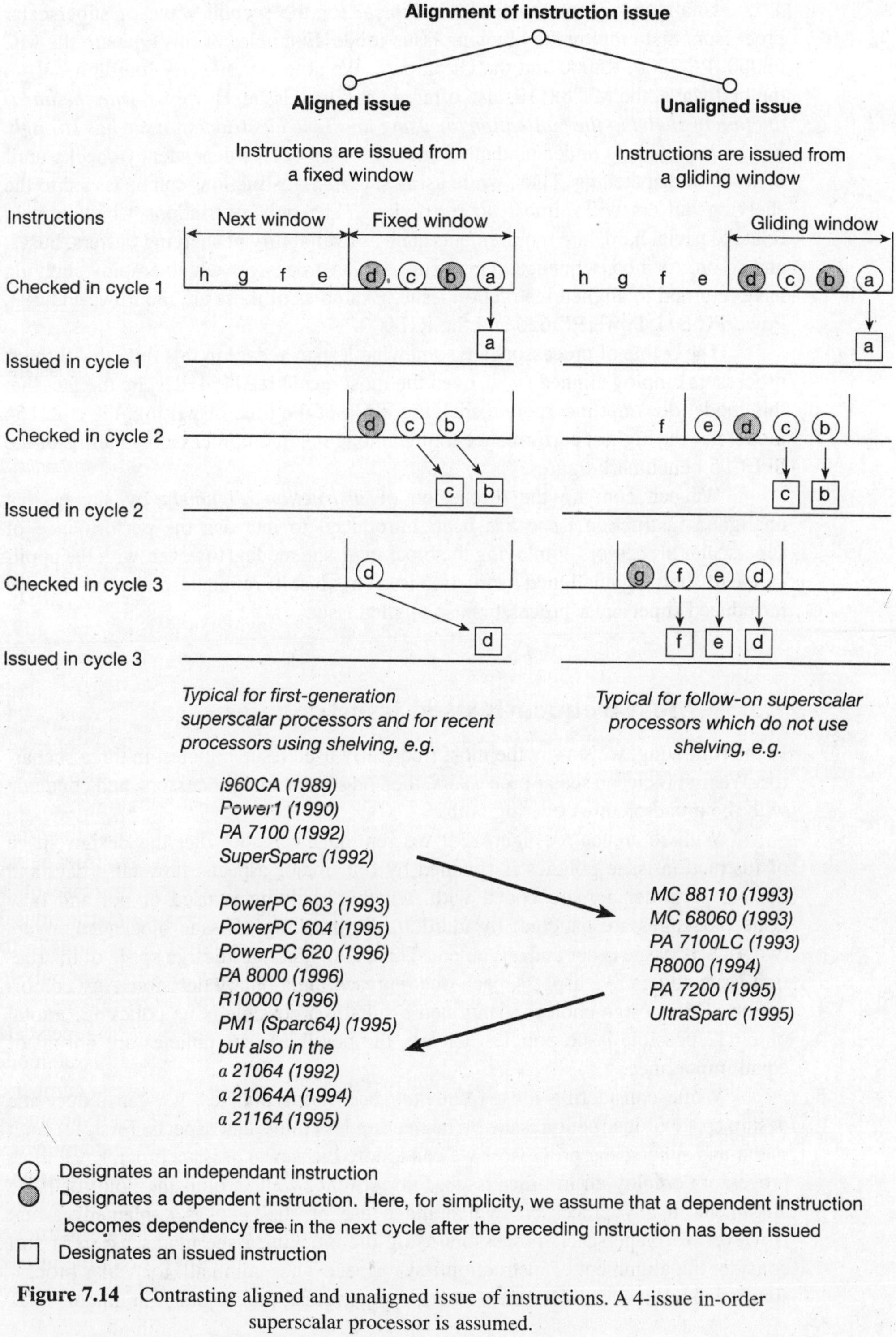

Figure 7.14 Contrasting aligned and unaligned issue of instructions. A 4-issue in-order superscalar processor is assumed.

Unaligned instruction issue is typical for the second wave of superscalar processors that employ the blocking issue mode. Examples of this type are the MC 68060, PA 7200, R8000 and the UltraSparc. We note that an early forerunner from the first wave, the MC 88110, also offered unaligned issue. However, *with the introduction of shelving the motivation for using unaligned instruction issue has strongly diminished.* This is understandable, since shelving delays dependency checks until instruction dispatching. Thus, while using shelving, instructions can be issued to the shelving buffers with almost no restrictions. The only restrictions which remain relate to trivial hardware requirements such as availability of shelving buffers, buses, and so on. As a consequence, recent superscalar processors which employ shelving have returned to aligned instruction issue. Examples of these are the PowerPC 603, PowerPC 604, PowerPC 620 and the R10000.

The α line of processors are somewhat a special case in this regard. All the α processors employ aligned issue, even the most recent α 21164, despite the fact that this model does not incorporate shelving. Still, at the time of writing, the α 21164 model has the highest performance figure among the microprocessors in terms of the SPEC95 benchmark figures.

We can sum up the discussion of *instruction alignment* by saying that unaligned instruction issue has been introduced to increase the performance of superscalar processors employing the blocking issue mode. However, with the application of shelving unaligned instruction issue has lost its rationale, and most recently introduced superscalar processors use aligned issue.

7.3.3 Most frequently used issue policies

In the following, we survey the most frequently used issue policies, in three scenarios. We first focus on scalar processors, then on superscalar processors, and conclude with the broad picture covering both.

With reference to Figure 7.9 we remind the reader that the design space of instruction issue policies is spanned by four major aspects: how false data and control dependencies are coped with, whether shelving is used or not and how issue blockages are handled. In addition, the handling of issue blockages covers two aspects: issue order and alignment. Thus, altogether, the design space of instruction issue covers five aspects, each one representing a binary decision. Any combination of the design choices mentioned results in a possible issue policy for a total of $2^5=32$ possible issue policies. Clearly the possible issue policies are not all of equal importance.

While considering most frequently used issue policies, we can reduce the design space of instruction issue by neglecting less important aspects. First, for both scalar and superscalar processors we can ignore the aspect of issue order, since most processors employ an in-order issue. Furthermore, we can omit the point of issue alignment in any processors which make use of shelving, as explained earlier. However, for superscalar processors using the blocking issue mode, we must still consider the alignment of instruction issue aspect. Thus, all in all, for scalar processors we have to consider three and for superscalar processors four major issue aspects. In the following sections we point out the most frequently used issue policies in the simplified design spaces for scalar and superscalar processors.

Instruction issue policies of scalar processors

While discussing instruction issue policies in the case of scalar processors, we have to take into account the three basic issue aspects, that is, whether renaming, speculative execution and shelving are employed or not.

Of the resulting eight possible issue policies, *scalar processors* use predominantly two, as indicated in Figure 7.15. We refer to them as the *traditional scalar issue* and *its enhancement with speculative execution*. In addition, there are two further policies of historical importance, designated as the *traditional scalar issue with shelving* and the *traditional scalar issue with shelving and renaming*.

Early non-pipelined processors issued instructions in sequence. This means that the next instruction was issued only after the previous one had been completed. Obviously, these processors did not use renaming, speculative branch processing or shelving. In our classification this issue mode is designated as the *traditional scalar issue policy*. This issue policy was also employed in early pipelined microprocessors. Examples are the i86, i286, i386 or the MC 68000, MC 68020, MC 68030 and so on.

Later, when ILP-processors, that is, processors with multiple EUs or pipelined processors, emerged the traditional scalar issue policy proved too restrictive on performance. Two approaches were followed to relieve this. One was introduced in the CDC6600, the other in the IBM 360/91. The CDC 6600, a supercomputer of its time, was one of the first ILP-processors. It achieved high performance by introducing *multiple non-pipelined EUs working in parallel*. In this processor, the instruction issue bottleneck was relaxed by *enhancing the traditional issue scheme* with *shelving*. The other approach was pioneered in the IBM 360/91. This processor was a more advanced ILP-processor from that time, built of multiple pipelined FP execution units. It also employed a more advanced issue scheme, involving both shelving and renaming. Although these innovations contributed significantly to the high performance of the processors mentioned, the associated exceptionally high hardware cost was at that time prohibitive for their widespread use. Thus, almost a quarter of a century passed before *shelving* was again employed in processors.

Actually, the main line of evolution of the issue scheme was determined by the spread of *pipelining*. In pipelined processors unresolved conditional branches can considerably reduce performance in the blocking issue mode, since then instructions are prevented from issue at each unresolved conditional branch. Obviously, the performance cut-back increases as the number of pipeline stages increases. Therefore, more advanced pipelined microprocessors, which often were implemented with an increased number of stages, had inevitably to enhance the *traditional scalar issue with speculative execution of unresolved conditional branches*, as indicated in Figure 7.15. Examples of this type are the i486, MC 68040, R4000 and the MicroSparc.

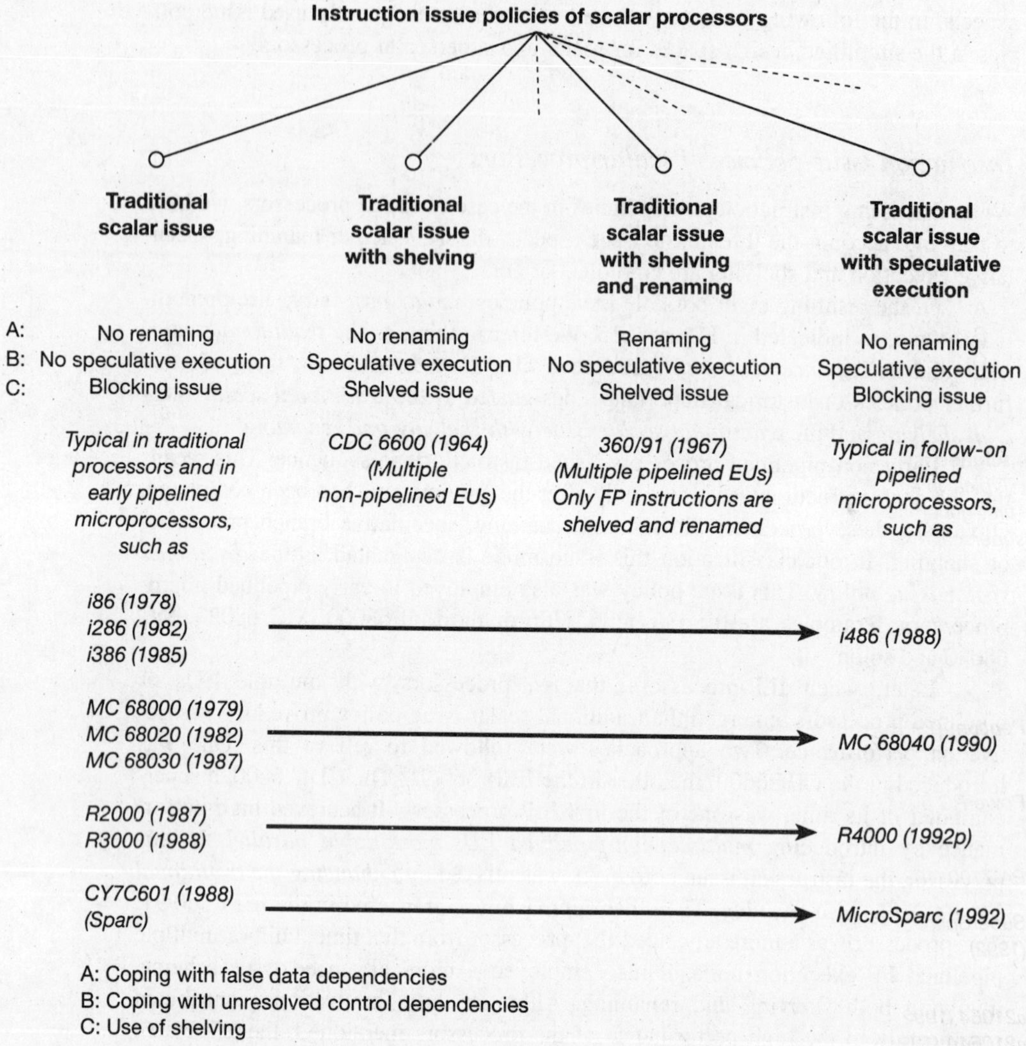

Figure 7.15 Most frequently used instruction issue policies of scalar processors.

Instruction issue policies of superscalar processors

When we expand our discussion of instruction policies to superscalar processors, we have to take into account, beyond the three basic issue aspects considered above, issue alignment as well. This results in 12 feasible issue policies. Of these, superscalar processors employ mainly five. As Figure 7.16 shows, they are designated as the *straightforward superscalar issue* with and without issue alignment, the *straightforward superscalar issue with shelving*, the *straightforward superscalar issue with renaming* and the *advanced superscalar issue*.

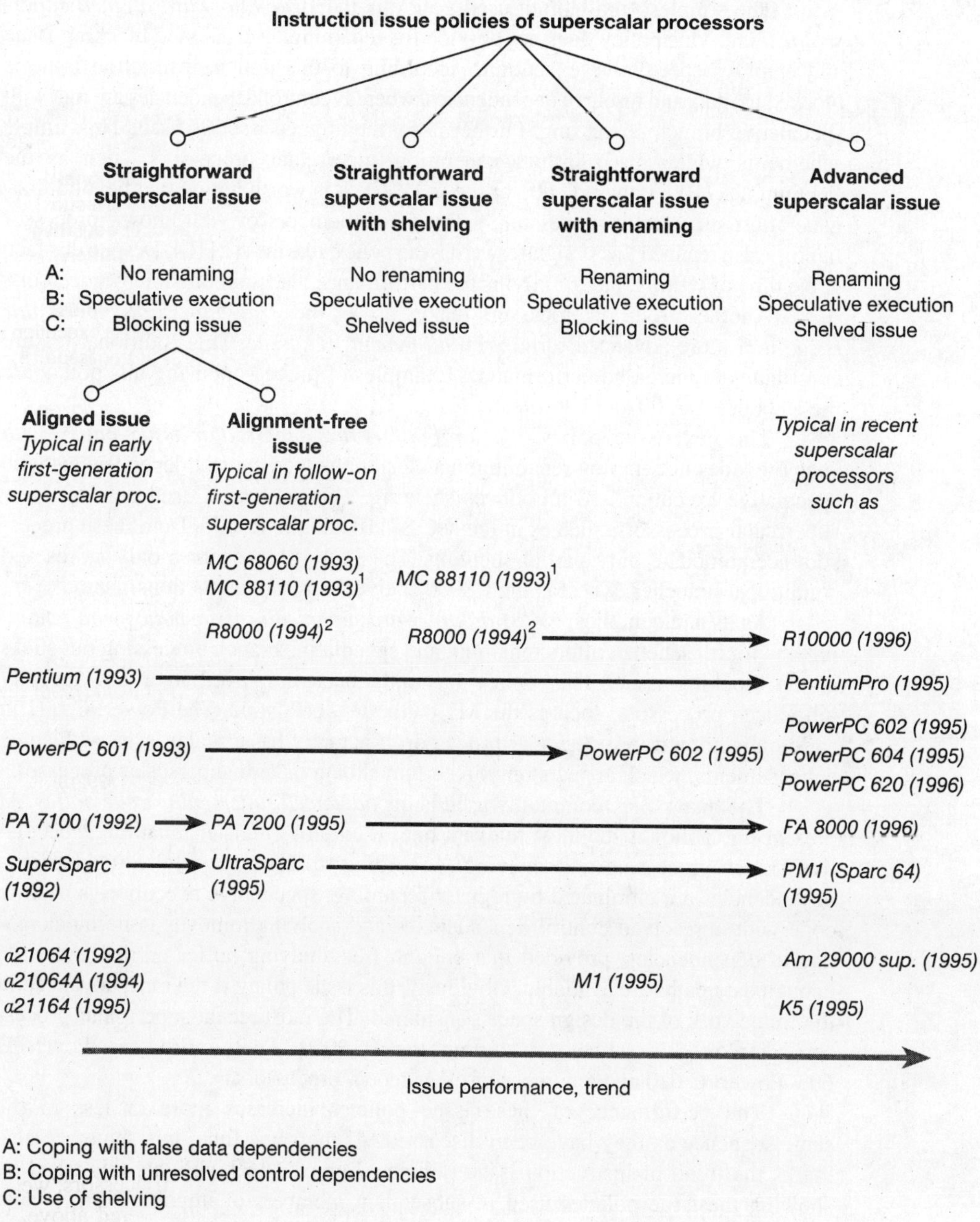

[1] Stores and conditional branches are shelved
[2] FP instructions are shelved

Figure 7.16 Most frequently used instruction issue policies of superscalar processors.

The simplest, most often used policy is the *straightforward aligned superscalar issue*. This policy does not provide for renaming, uses aligned blocking issue and employs speculative execution. According to this policy, instruction issue is blocked for data and resource dependencies, whereas control dependencies are met with speculative branch processing. Furthermore, the aligned issue is used. This simple scheme is widely used in first-generation superscalar processors, such as the Pentium, PA7100, PowerPC 601 or the α 21064. It is worth noting that beyond first-generation superscalar processors, a few later members of well-known processor families also retained this straightforward issue policy, like the α 21164. Despite this fact, at the time of writing, the α 21164 is the performance leader among microprocessors.

Another group of processors makes use of the *straightforward superscalar issue*, in a more advanced form, with *alignment free issue*. This additional feature contributes to increased performance. Examples of processors using this policy are the R8000, PA 7200 and UltraSparc.

The next issue policy, the *straightforward superscalar issue policy with shelving*, does not employ renaming, handles unresolved control dependencies with speculative execution and introduces shelving. This scheme is used only in a few superscalar processors, such as in the MC 88110 and the R8000. Both these processors accommodate only partial shelving, The MC 88110 shelves only stores and conditional branches, whereas the R8000 shelves only FP instructions.

As its name implies, the *straightforward superscalar issue policy with renaming*, the fourth scheme, offers renaming and speculative branch processing but sticks at the blocking issue. This policy has only been employed in a few recently introduced processors, such as the M1 or the PowerPC 602. The PowerPC 602 in addition is not a true superscalar processor. It actually has a scalar issue with some enhancements, which appears only in certain situations as a superscalar processor.

The final policy commonly used is the *advanced superscalar issue policy*. At present this policy is the most relevant one. It employs register renaming, speculative branch processing and shelving. According to this policy, false register data dependencies are eliminated by register renaming, speculative execution is used to cope with unresolved control dependencies and shelving removes issue blockages due to dependencies, provided that enough free shelving buffer entries and wide enough data paths are available. Obviously, this issue policy is the most advanced in the framework of the design space considered. The most recent superscalar processors employ this scheme, including the R10000, PentiumPro, the PowerPC 603–PowerPC 620 and a number of other recent processors.

The performance of these issue policies increases more or less in the same sequence as they have been discussed. At the same time, this sequence also marks the trend of instruction issue policies. Figure 7.16 highlights this trend by showing the issue policies used in subsequent members of important superscalar processor families.

The trend in instruction issue policies

In Figure 7.17 we summarize the most frequently used issue policies both in scalar and superscalar processors. These policies are: the traditional scalar issue, the traditional

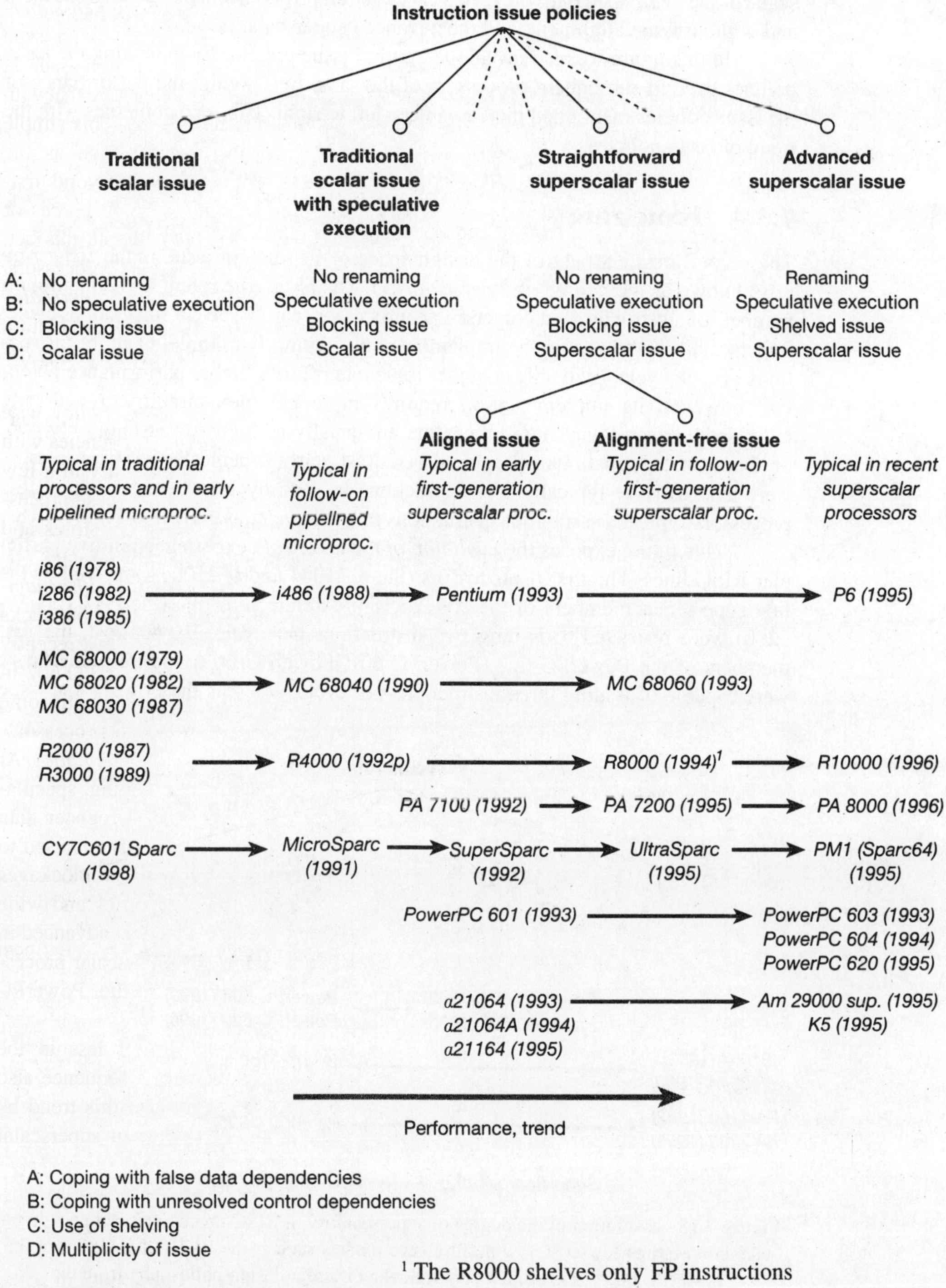

Figure 7.17 Most frequently used instruction issue policies and their trend.

scalar issue with speculative execution, the straightforward superscalar issue with and without issue alignment, and the advanced superscalar issue.

In this figure we also reveal the trend of issue policies by indicating the issue policies used in subsequent processors of the same line. Again, the performance of the issue policies mentioned increases from left to right. This also coincides with the trend of issue policies.

7.3.4 Issue rate

The second major aspect of the design space of instruction issue is the *issue rate* (also known as the *degree of superscalarity*). The *issue rate* refers to the maximum number of instructions a superscalar processor can issue in the same cycle. Superscalar operation may be implemented by issuing two, three, or more instructions in each cycle. Evidently, a higher issue rate offers a higher performance potential; however, its implementation requires more complex circuitry. As already mentioned, superscalar CISC processors are usually restricted to issuing only two, or about two, instructions per cycle. In contrast, early superscalar RISC processors were able to issue typically 2–3 instructions in each cycle, whereas recent RISC processors typically issue four instructions in each cycle, as shown in Figure 7.18.

This figure exposes the *evolution of the issue rate* experienced in five particular RISC lines. The first α processors (the α 21064 and α 21064A) as well as the first superscalar members of the HP Precision Architecture line (the PA 7100, PA 7200) were restricted to issuing two instructions per cycle. By contrast, the first members of the PowerPC line (PowerPC 601, PowerPC 603) and the SuperSparc were capable of issuing three instructions per cycle, whereas the Power1 can issue

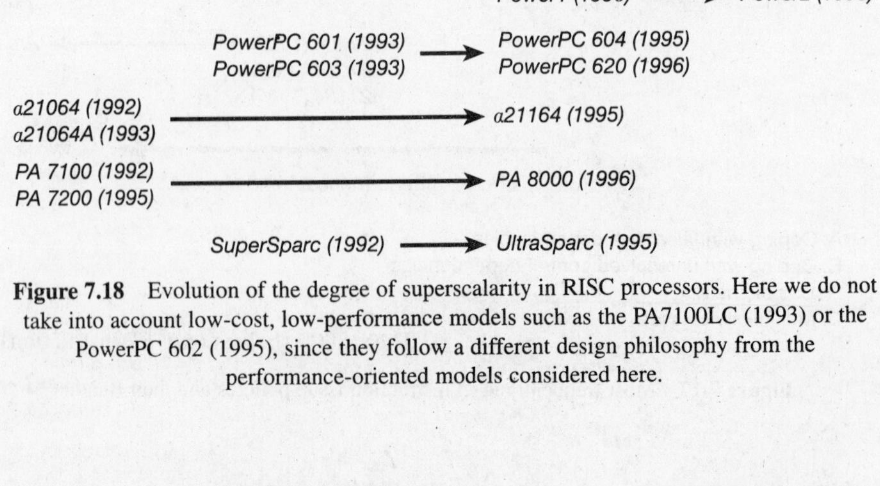

Figure 7.18 Evolution of the degree of superscalarity in RISC processors. Here we do not take into account low-cost, low-performance models such as the PA7100LC (1993) or the PowerPC 602 (1995), since they follow a different design philosophy from the performance-oriented models considered here.

four instructions. For the time being all upcoming models of the lines mentioned except the Power2 are four-issue superscalar processors. The Power2 can even issue six instructions per cycle while executing a sequential path. However, after a guessed branch, while starting the execution of the target path, the processor issues only four instructions. Thus, the Power2 is now the issue-rate leader.

7.4 Shelving

Recall that with a straightforward issue policy dependencies block instruction issue, as indicated in Figure 7.19.

In Section 7.3.2 we introduced the concept of shelving. This is an advanced issue mode, which is employed to eliminate issue blockages due to dependencies. Shelving makes use of dedicated instruction buffers, called **shelving buffers**, in front of each EU. In Figure 7.20 and in the subsequent description of the operation, we assume that individual shelving buffers are associated with each EU. As we shall detail in Section 7.4.3, other possibilities for the layout of shelving buffers also exist. Nevertheless, this does not affect the principle of how shelving is carried out. Therefore, our description of shelving assumes individual reservation stations as seen in Figure 7.20.

Shelving decouples dependency checking from the instruction issue, and defers it to the dispatch phase. More precisely, with shelving decoded instructions are issued to the shelving buffers *despite data or control dependencies* or *busy EUs*. This eliminates the issue bottleneck of the blocking issue.

Nevertheless, certain *resource constraints* can restrain the processor to issue fewer instructions in a cycle than its issue rate is. There are two typical resource constraints: *lack of free entries* in the targeted shelving buffer, in the rename register file or in the ROB; *data path restrictions* and limiting the number of instructions which

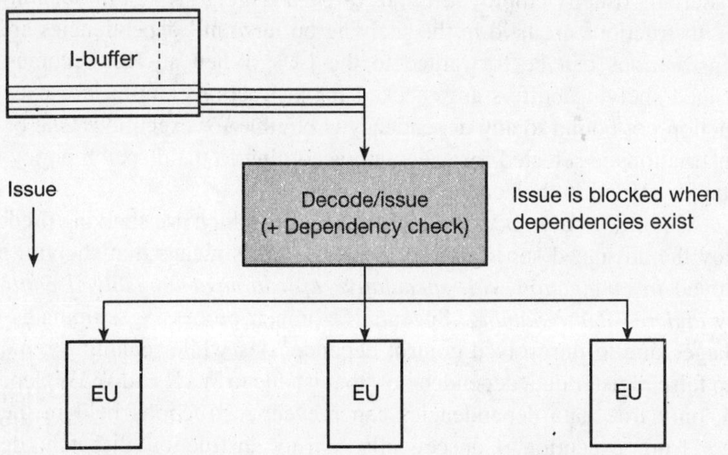

Figure 7.19 Principle of a straightforward issue policy.

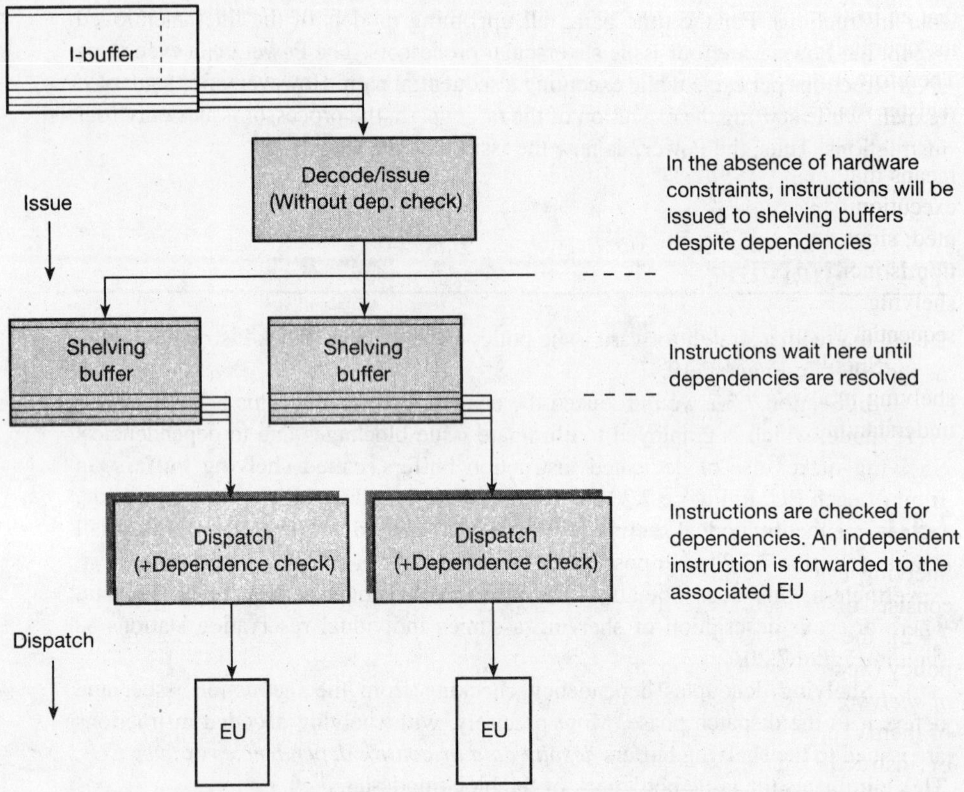

Figure 7.20 The principle of shelving.

can be transferred in one cycle to the allocated shelving buffer. This point is discussed in more detail in Section 7.4.3. In the case of an *issue blockage*, processors with shelving usually employ *in-order*, *aligned issue*, as stated in Section 7.3.2.

Instructions are held in the shelving buffers until dependencies are resolved and instructions can be forwarded to the EUs. When an EU becomes free, the associated shelving buffers are checked for instructions eligible for execution. An instruction not bound to any dependency is eligible for execution. One of the eligible instructions is selected for execution according to the dispatch policy used, and will be forwarded to the connected EU.

As pointed out in Section 7.3.3, processors which use shelving predominantly employ the advanced superscalar issue policy. This means that shelving is usually employed *in connection with speculative execution of unresolved control dependency and register renaming*. Speculative branch processing eliminates execution blockages due to unresolved control dependencies while renaming removes those due to false register data dependencies, that is, due to WAR and WAW dependencies. Then, only true data dependencies can prevent instructions held in the shelving buffers from execution. Consequently, during instruction dispatch, dependency checking is reduced to checks for true data dependencies (RAW dependencies). Thus that an instruction held in a shelving buffer becomes eligible for execution when all its operands are available. This is exactly the *dataflow principle of operation*. Therefore, a superscalar processor with shelving, speculative branch processing and register renaming executes instructions on the dataflow basis.

A last remark concerns the preservation of *sequential consistency*, which means that the logical integrity of the execution has to be sustained despite parallel execution of instructions. But, in a sense, shelving makes processing more distributed, since with shelving the number of instructions which are available for execution is increased by the number of instructions held in shelving buffers. Therefore, shelving is typically used *in connection with* an advanced method of retaining sequential consistency called *instruction reordering*, which is explained in Section 7.7.3.

Shelving is quite a complex topic. Recent superscalar processors implement shelving in a variety of ways. This section gives a framework for overviewing and understanding this challenging diversity.

7.4.1 The design space of shelving

Shelving has a fairly complex design space, which is depicted in Figure 7.21. It consists of the following four main components: the scope of shelving (Section 7.4.2), the layout of the shelving buffers used (Section 7.4.3), the operand fetch policy (Section 7.4.4) and the instruction dispatch scheme (Section 7.4.5). The *scope of shelving* declares whether shelving covers all data types or is restricted to a few of them. The *layout of the shelving buffers* specifies the infrastructural background of instruction buffering after issue. The *operand fetch policy* decides whether operands are fetched in connection with issue or, in contrast, along with instruction dispatch. Finally, the *instruction dispatch scheme* specifies the details governing the selection and forwarding of instructions for execution.

7.4.2 Scope of shelving

The **scope of shelving** specifies whether shelving is restricted to a few instruction types or is performed for all instructions, as indicated in Figure 7.22.

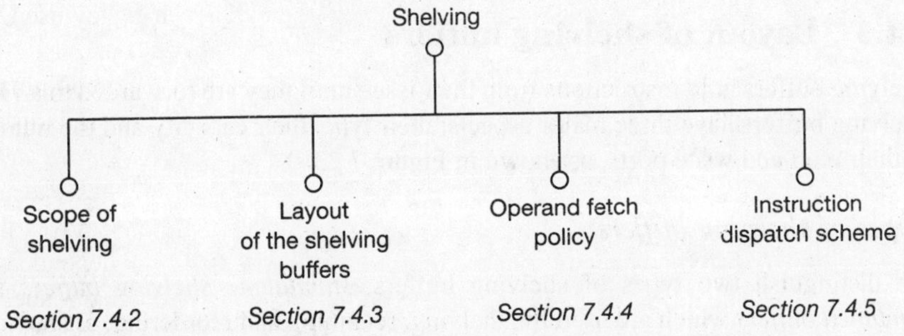

Figure 7.21 Design space of shelving.

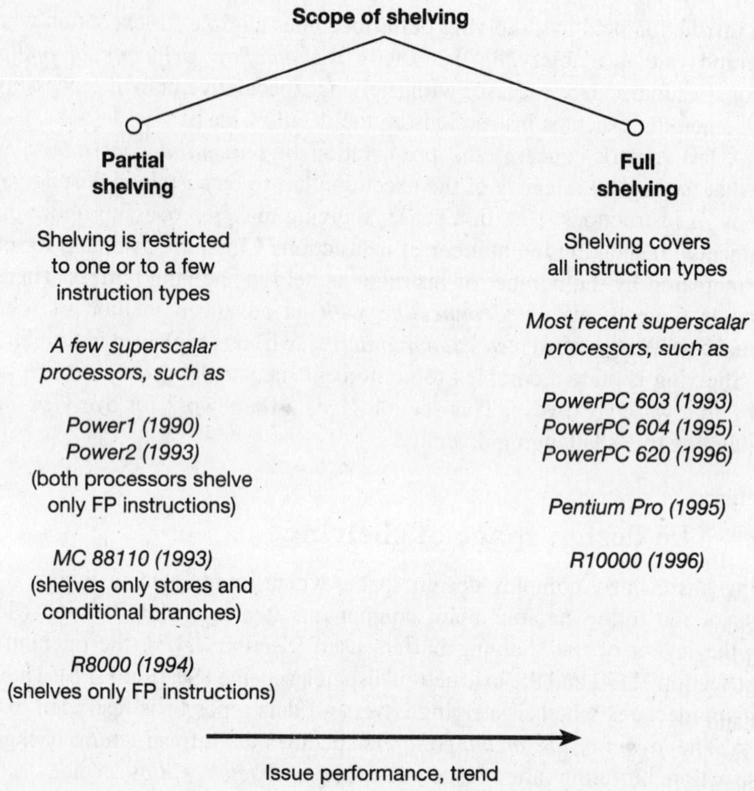

Figure 7.22 Scope of shelving.

Partial shelving is only used in a few superscalar processors. As pointed out in the figure, three of the processors mentioned restrict shelving to FP instructions, whereas the MC 88110 shelves stores and conditional branches.

Partial shelving is evidently an incomplete solution to the problem eliminating issue blockages caused by dependencies. Therefore, most recent superscalar processors employ **full shelving**, including the PentiumPro as well as those shown in the figure.

7.4.3 Layout of shelving buffers

Shelving buffers hold instructions from their issue until they are forwarded to an EU. Shelving buffers have three major aspects: their type, their capacity and the number of their read and write ports, as shown in Figure 7.23.

Types of shelving buffers

We distinguish two types of shelving buffers, *standalone shelving buffers* and *combined buffers* which are used for shelving, renaming and reordering, as shown in Figure 7.24.

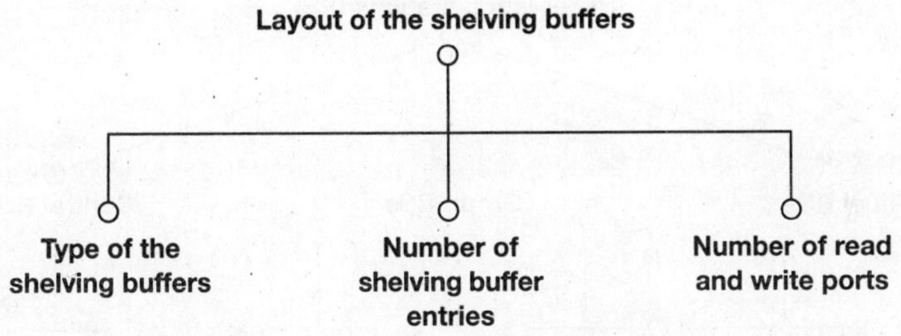

Figure 7.23 Layout of the shelving buffers.

In most cases shelving buffers are implemented as *standalone shelving buffers*, that is, buffers which are used exclusively for shelving. This type of shelving buffer is usually designated a **reservation station**. In superscalar processors reservation stations are implemented using one of three basic schemes, as indicated in Figure 7.25.

In the simplest case, **individual reservation stations** are used in front of each EU. Instructions issued for execution in a particular EU are transferred into the individual reservation station of that EU. Usually, individual reservation stations provide space to hold only a small number of instructions, say two to four. For instance, in the PowerPC 620 the reservation stations in front of the three integer units and the single FP unit can hold two instructions each, whereas those associated with the load/store unit and the branch processing unit have places for three and four instructions, respectively. (See Figure 7.69 for details of the microarchitecture of the PowerPC 620.)

Both the early implementations of shelving employed individual reservation stations. The CDC 6600 provided one-entry stations before each EU, and in the IBM 360/91 the FP Add unit was equipped with a two-entry station and the FP Multiply unit with a three-entry station. Further examples of superscalar processors using individual reservation stations are shown in Figure 7.25.

In an alternative approach, reservation stations are implemented as **group stations** (see Figure 7.25). Here, the same reservation station holds instructions for

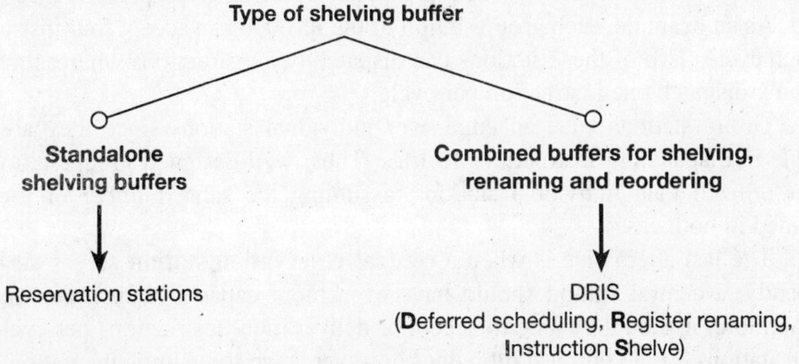

Figure 7.24 General layout of the implementation of shelving buffers.

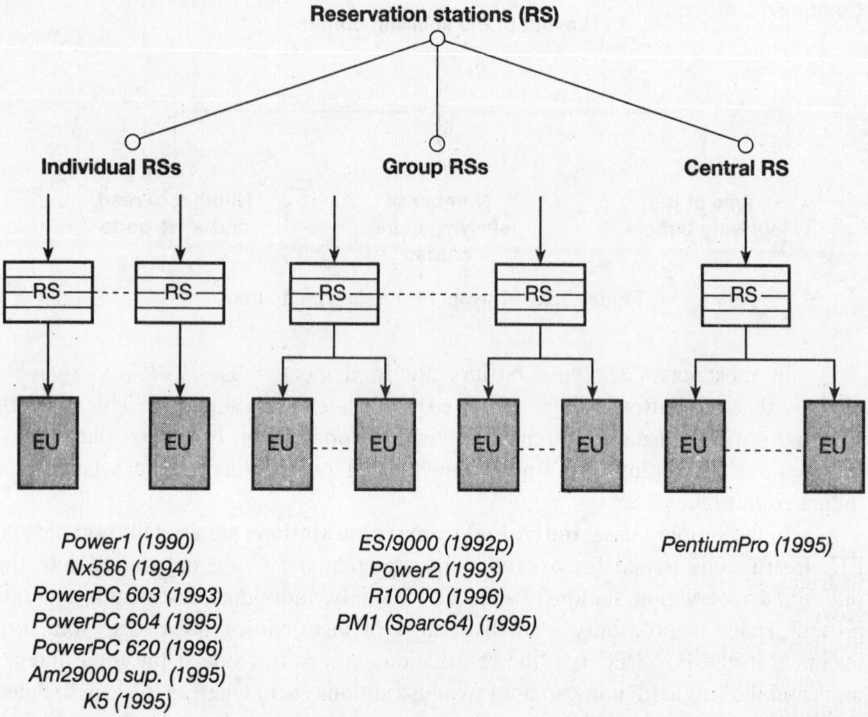

Figure 7.25 Basic variants of shelving buffers.

a whole group of EUs, each of which execute instructions of the same type. For instance, the R10000 has three group stations. As illustrated in Figure 7.67, one of these serves two FX ALUs, another a single address unit, and the third group station four FP units.

Evidently, group stations must have more available buffer space than individual stations. For instance, the R10000 has three group stations with 16 positions each; the PM1 has four group stations with 8 or 16 entries each. Furthermore, since group stations serve more than one EU, they must be capable of shelving or dispatching more than one instruction in each cycle to avoid performance bottlenecks. As an example, each group station of the R10000 can accept four instructions in each cycle. Two of these stations can dispatch two instructions whereas the third can only dispatch one instruction per cycle.

Group stations have an edge over individual stations since they are *more flexible* in dispatching instructions to EUs. Thus, well-designed group stations are better utilized than individual stations, assuming the same number of locations provided in both cases.

The last alternative is when a **central reservation station** serves all ALUs. Evidently, a central station should have even more capacity than group stations. Furthermore, it should be able to accept or deliver more instructions per cycle than group stations do. A central station does however, have some implementation disadvantages. First, it must have a word length equal to the longest possible data word.

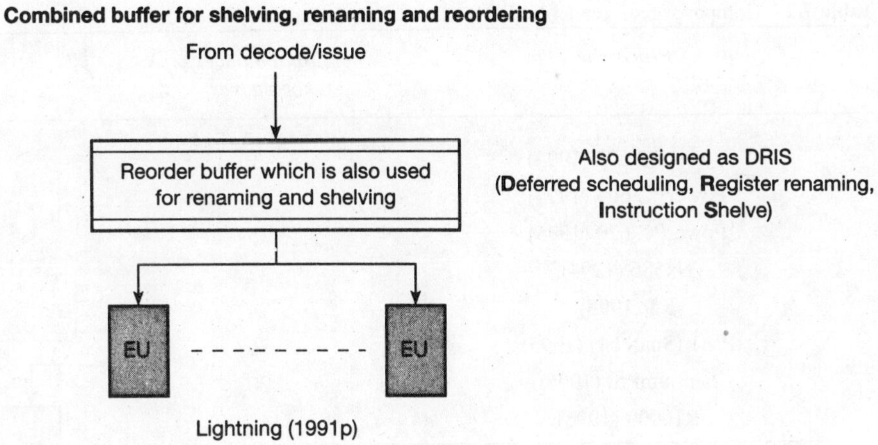

Figure 7.26 Using a combined buffer for shelving, renaming and reordering.

Second, as central stations are expected to be able to accept and dispatch more instructions per cycle than group stations do, they are more expensive to implement. Nevertheless, the PentiumPro opted for a central station whose 20 entries serve all available EUs (10 altogether). For more details consult Figure 7.72.

A quite different approach to the implementation of shelving buffers is to use a **combined buffer** *for shelving, renaming and reordering* as shown in Figure 7.26.

In this case, the *reorder buffer* (ROB), which assures the logical integrity of the program execution, is extended such that it is used for shelving and register renaming as well. (See Section 7.7.3 for a discussion of the reorder buffer.) An example is the Metaflow Lightning processor (1991p) which was announced but never reached the market. In the Lightning the combined structure was designated **DRIS** (**D**eferred scheduling, **R**egister renaming, **I**nstruction **S**helving). Despite its complexity, the efficiency of this approach makes it attractive. In the future, we expect further processors to use this design option.

Finally, a comment on our terminology. When we use the term *'shelving buffer'* we refer to all possible implementations, including reservation stations and DRIS. By contrast, the terms *'reservation stations'* and *'DRIS'* refer to the particular type of implementation.

Number of shelving buffer entries

As a rule of thumb, individual, group and central reservation stations have to provide an increasing number of shelving places. Typically, individual reservation stations shelve 2–4 instructions, group stations have 6, 8, 12 or 16 entries, while the only implementation so far of a central reservation station (the PentiumPro) has room to hold 20 instructions. The total number of entries in the reservation stations provided restricts the number of instructions waiting in shelving buffers to be dispatched. Recent processors have typically between 15 and 40 shelves, as Table 7.2 indicates.

Table 7.2 Comparison of available shelves in recent superscalar processors.

Processor	*Total number of shelves*
PowerPC 603 (1993)	3
PowerPC 604 (1994)	12
PowerPC 620 (1995)	15
Nx586 (1994)	42
K5 (1995)	14
PM1 (Sparc64) (1995)	36
PentiumPro (1995)	20
R10000 (1996)	48

Number of read and write ports

The last component of the layout of shelving buffers is the **number of read and write ports**, which specifies how many instructions may be written into or read out from a particular shelving buffer in a cycle. First, let us consider the expected number of read ports (output ports). Clearly, individual reservation stations only have to forward a single instruction per cycle. A group or central reservation station, on the other hand, should deliver multiple instructions per cycle, ideally as many as there are EUs connected to it. Thus, while individual reservation stations have a single read port, each group station is expected to provide multiple read ports, and central reservation stations should have even more read ports than group stations have.

Similarly individual, group and central reservation stations require increasingly more write ports (input ports). So processors with individual reservation stations often allow only one instruction per cycle to be issued into any one reservation station. Examples are the PowerPC 604 and the Nx586. In contrast, recent superscalar processors with group reservation stations permit the transfer of more than one or even all issued instructions into any of the reservation stations. For instance, the PM1 (Sparc64), which is a four-issue processor, can issue up to two FP, two load/store, one branch and four integer instructions into the corresponding group reservation stations but not more than two integer instructions may be complex ALU operations (such as shifts, multiplications or divisions). In the four-issue R10000, all four instructions issued can be forwarded into any of the three group stations.

7.4.4 Operand fetch policies

Basic fetch policies

Closely connected with shelving is the policy governing how processors fetch operands. The fetch policy is either *issue bound* or *dispatch bound*, as indicated in Figure 7.27.

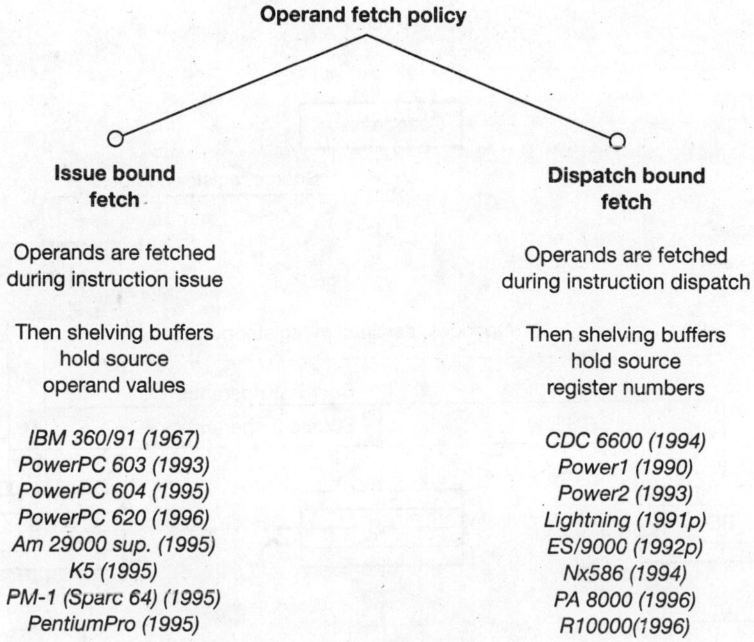

Figure 7.27 Operand fetch policies.

The **issue bound fetch policy** means that operands are fetched during instruction issue. In this case shelving buffers have to provide entries long enough to hold source operands. The other basic operand fetch policy is the **dispatch bound fetch *policy***, when operands are fetched during dispatching. In this case shelving buffers contain short register identifiers instead of long operands.

In the following, we describe both these operand fetch policies in more detail, assuming individual reservation stations. This assumption does not affect the principles discussed here and allows us to focus on the vital points. First, we describe both policies assuming the simplest case, that is, when a single register file is employed for both FX and FP data and no renaming is used. Subsequently, we extend our discussion to the case when split register files or renaming is used.

Figure 7.28 shows the principle of the *issue bound operand fetch policy.* During instruction issue, the source register numbers of the issued instructions are forwarded to the register file for fetching the referenced operands. In addition, the operation codes, the destination register numbers of the issued instructions and the fetched operand values (Source 1 and Source 2 operands in the figure) are written into the allocated reservation stations.

Figure 7.29 shows the *dispatch bound* operand fetch policy, in which *operands* are fetched *in connection with instruction dispatch*.

In this case, the reservation stations hold the instructions, including the *source register numbers*. During dispatch, the operation codes and destination register numbers of the dispatched instructions are forwarded from the reservation stations to the associated EUs, and the source register numbers are passed to the

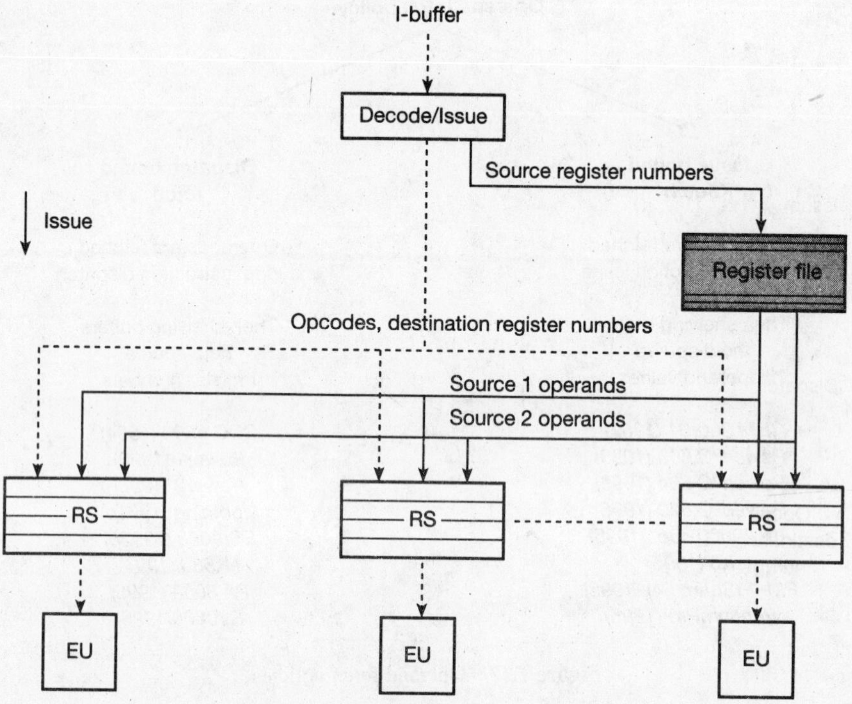

Figure 7.28 Operand fetch during instruction issue, assuming a single register file for both FX and FP data.

register file. After a delay, the fetched source operand values appear at the inputs of the EUs and are gated into the requesting EUs.

Now, let us *compare* the operand fetch policies. If operands are fetched during instruction issue, the register file must be able to supply operands for all issued instructions at the same time. Assuming two referenced operands per instruction, this requires twice as many read ports in the register file as the maximum issue rate. For instance, under the assumptions made, a four-issue superscalar processor requires a register file with eight read ports.

If operands are fetched during instruction dispatch, ideally the number of read ports should equal the dispatch rate. Since the maximum dispatch rate is usually higher than the maximum issue rate (see Section 7.4.5 and Table 7.3), the dispatch bound operand fetch policy usually requires more read ports on the register file than the issue bound policy. The same relationship is true for the number of operand buses required. This fact is a drawback of the dispatch bound operand fetch policy.

On the other hand, the dispatch bound operand fetch policy has two advantages over the issue bound policy: the critical decode/issue path is shorter, and the shelving buffers are less complex, since register numbers require considerably less buffer space than operand values.

As the benefits and drawbacks of the basic fetch policies are roughly in balance, there is no clear trend in their use at the moment. A number of processors

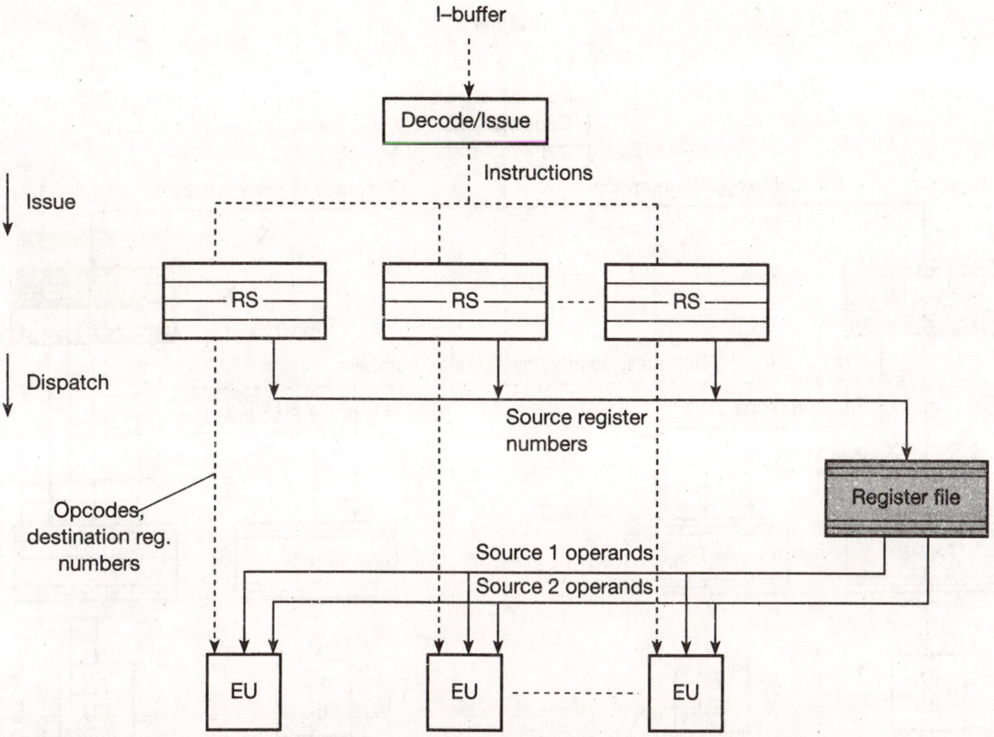

Figure 7.29 Operand fetch during instruction dispatch assuming a single register file for both FX and FP data.

use the issue bound operand fetch policy, and a similar number employ the dispatch bound policy. Examples are given in Figure 7.27.

Operand fetch assuming split register files for FX and FP data

Our simplified introduction to operand fetch policies assumed a common register file for FX and FP data. However, in practice, most processors use *distinct register files* for *FX and FP data*. Figure 7.30 revisits the *issue bound operand fetch policy assuming distinct register files for FX and FP data.*

In fact, the microarchitecture now has a *symmetrical internal structure*. FX instructions and FX data on the one hand, and FP instructions and FP data on the other, are processed by two distinct and more or less symmetrical parts of the processor.

The situation is much the same for the other fetching policy. Figure 7.31 shows the principle of the dispatch bound operand fetch policy assuming split register files.

Again we see a symmetrical internal structure with distinct FX and FP parts. In this case, the FX and FP register files supply the operands directly to the EUs rather than to the reservation stations.

Actually, most recent architectures declare *separate register files* for FX and FP data, such as the PowerPC, x86, R and PA architectures. Accordingly, superscalar implmentations of these architectures which make use of shelving, such as the

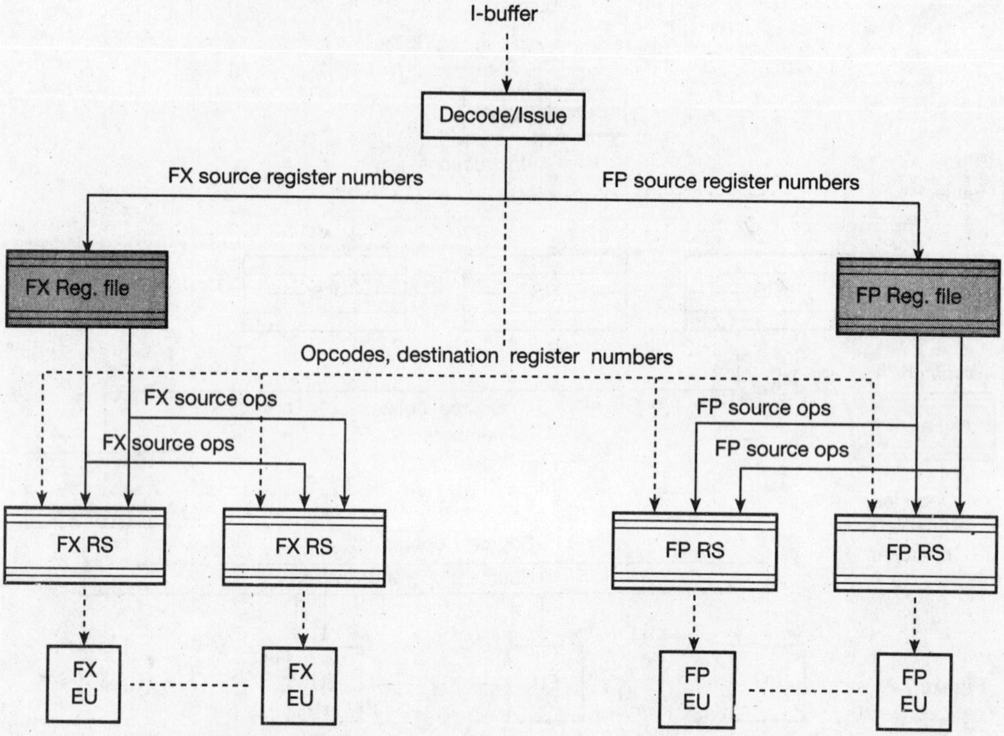

Figure 7.30 Issue bound operand fetch assuming distinct register files for FX and FP data.

PowerPC line of processors, the PentiumPro, R10000 and the PA 8000, fetch operands in principle as indicated in Figures 7.30 and 7.31. We note that some embedded processors, like the Am29000 superscalar, support only FX data, and consequently have only a single FX register file. Other processors, such as the Nx586, implement only the FX part of the architecture in the main processor, while the FP part is realized by an FP coprocessor chip, called the Nx587.

Operand fetch using renaming

Without renaming, all required operands are supplied by the architectural register file(s). When register renaming is used we encounter a quite different picture since additional register space is needed for storing renamed values. Then, required *operands* may be *either in the architectured register file(s)* or *in the register space used for renaming*. In this case also, the same two basic operand fetch policies are used. (See Section 7.5.1 for a discussion of further issues related to register renaming.)

Most frequently used combinations of shelving buffer types and operand fetch policies

In conclusion, we will give an overview of the most frequently used combinations of shelving buffer types and operand fetch policies. All possible combinations are given in Figure 7.32 along with the choices made in recent processors.

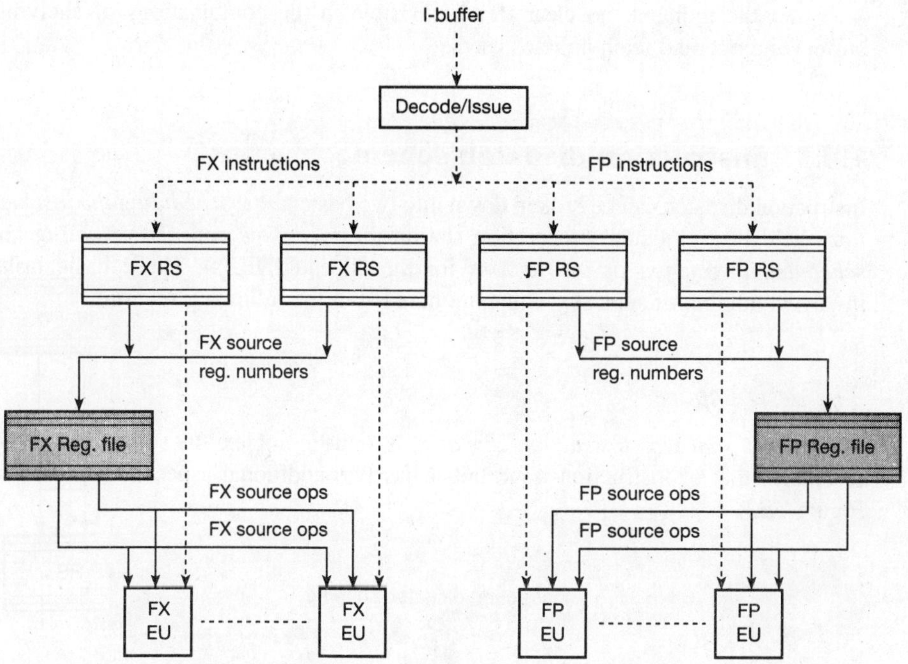

Figure 7.31 Dispatch bound operand fetch assuming distinct register files for FX and FP data.

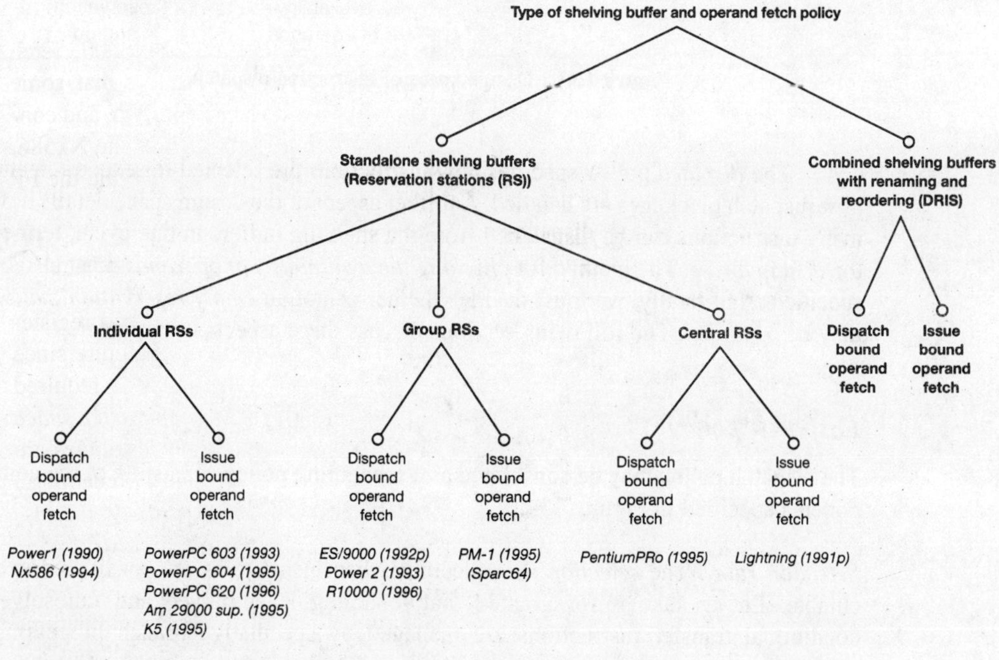

Figure 7.32 Most frequently used combinations of shelving buffer types and operand fetch policies.

At the moment, no clear trend is visible in the combinations of shelving buffers and operand fetch policies used.

7.4.5 Instruction dispatch scheme

Instruction dispatch can be broken down into two basic tasks: *scheduling the instructions* held in a particular reservation station *for execution*, and *disseminating the scheduled instruction* or *instructions* for the allocated EU(s). These basic tasks involve a number of subtasks which are detailed in the following sections.

The design space

The design space of instruction dispatch is quite complex. In some respects it resembles that of instruction issue but it has two additional aspects, as shown in Figure 7.33.

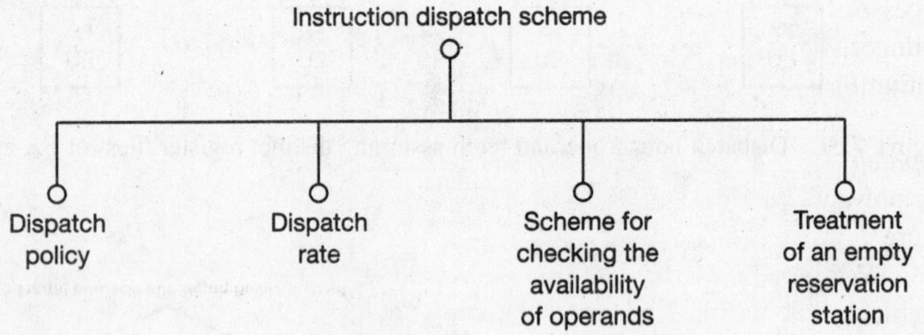

Figure 7.33 Design space of instruction dispatch.

The *dispatch* policy specifies how instructions are selected for execution and how dispatch blockages are handled. A further aspect of the design space details how many instructions can be dispatched from the shelving buffers in one cycle, termed the *dispatch rate*. The method for *checking the availability of operands* must also be specified. And finally, we must decide whether or not an *empty reservation station* may be *bypassed*. The following sections discuss these aspects in more detail.

Dispatch policy

The dispatch policy may be considered as a scheduling policy consisting of the components specified in Figure 7.34.

Selection rule The *selection rule* specifies when instructions are considered executable. Let us take it for granted that renaming is employed and unresolved conditional transfer instructions are managed by speculative branch processing.

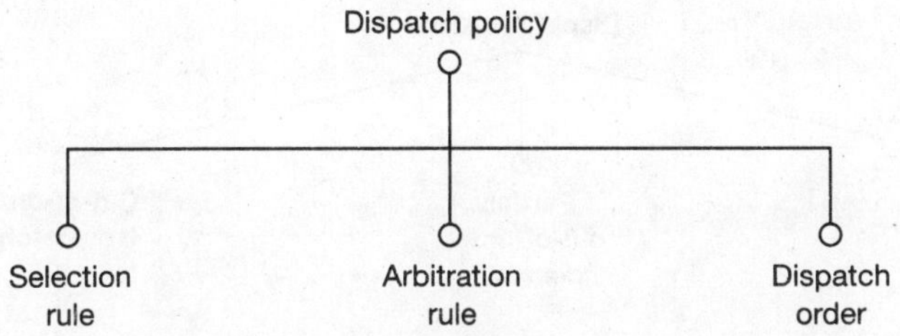

Figure 7.34 Design space of instruction dispatch.

Then, assuming availability of the EU, those instructions whose operands are available are executable. In this case the selection rule is the same as the *dataflow principle of operation* introduced in Section 1.2. In other cases, the selection rule must include further dependency checks.

Arbitration rule We also need an *arbitration rule* for the case when more instructions are eligible for execution than can be disseminated in the next cycle. Most processors use a straightforward arbitration rule that prefers 'older' instructions over 'younger' ones. The Power1, Power2, PowerPC 620, PM1 (Sparc64) and PentiumPro are examples that use this arbitration rule.

Dispatch order The dispatch order determines whether a non-executable instruction prevents all subsequent instructions from being dispatched, as summarized in Figure 7.35.

When an **in-order dispatch scheme** is employed, a non-executable instruction blocks any further dispatch. Thus, even if subsequent instructions were available for execution, they could not be dispatched. Obviously, in-order dispatching impedes performance.

A slight performance increase may be achieved using a **partially out-of-order dispatch**. The Power2, PowerPC 604 and PowerPC 620 are processors using this approach. The Power2 shelves only FP instructions, and allows a single non-executable FP instruction to be skipped by an executable FP instruction during dispatching. The PowerPC 604 and PowerPC 620 dispatch instructions from particular reservation stations in-order and from others out-of-order. Thus, the PowerPC 604 performs in-order dispatch from the Branch, Load/Store and FP reservation stations, whereas it dispatches instructions out-of-order from the three FX reservation stations (see also Figure 7.42). The dispatch scheme of the PowerPC 620 is slightly improved over that of the PowerPC 604, since the Load/Store reservation station is converted to an out-of-order dispatch fashion (see Section 7.10.2). All the other reservation stations dispatch in the same manner as the PowerPC 604, as indicated in Figure 7.35.

The most advanced scheme is clearly the **out-of-order dispatch**. Here, a non-executable instruction does not block the dissemination of subsequent executable instructions. Instead, any executable instructions held in the shelving buffer are eligible for dispatch. From the implementation point of view, all or at least a large number of shelving buffer entries have to be inspected for executable instructions.

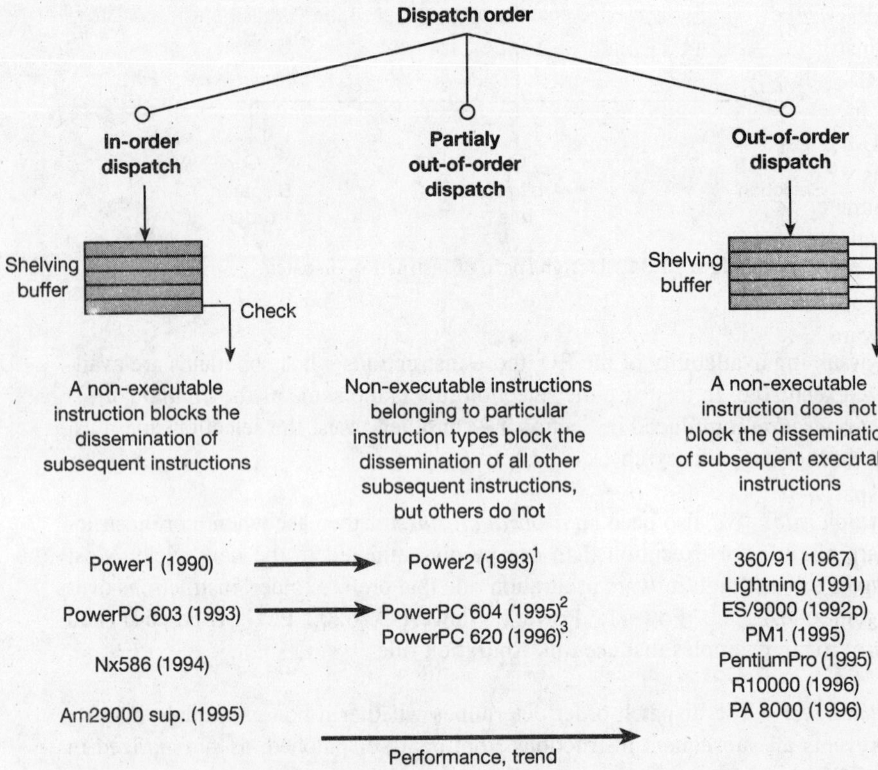

[1] In the Power2, only a single pending (not executable) FP instruction can be skipped.

[2] Out-of-order dispatch from the three integer reservation stations, but in-order dispatch from the Branch, Load/Store and FP reservation stations.

[3] Out-of-order dispatch from the three integer and Load/Store reservation stations, in-order dispatch from the Branch and FP reservation stations.

Figure 7.35 Dispatch order.

By contrast, in an in-order dispatch scheme it suffices to check only the last buffer entry. A very early forerunner of out-of-order dispatch was the IBM 360/91 processor. Further examples followed more than two decades later, such as the Lighting and the ES/9000. The majority of most recent processors employ out-of-order dispatch.

As we know, group and central reservation stations have to supply executable instructions for multiple EUs. If a non-executable instruction blocked the dispatch of subsequent executable instructions in these cases, performance could be impeded to a considerable degree. Therefore, we expect processors with group reservation stations or a central station to use the out-of-order dispatch scheme.

Dispatch rate

Unlike individual reservation stations, a group or central reservation station, or a DRIS, must be capable of dispatching more than one instruction in each cycle. In these cases, the design space needs an additional component that determines how many instructions can be dispatched from each of the reservation stations, or from the DRIS, per cycle. This component is called the **dispatch rate** (Figure 7.36).

Ideally, a shelving buffer must be capable of dispatching one instruction to any EU connected to it in each cycle. Obviously, this is easier to achieve for group stations with two to three EUs than for a central station or a DRIS with a considerable number of EUs connected to it. The R10000, for instance, employs *group reservation stations*. Its FX reservation station can dispatch two instructions per cycle, one each to the EUs served. In contrast, its FP reservation station serves four FP EUs, but can only dispatch up to two instructions per cycle. One instruction can be forwarded to the FP Adder, and one to either the FP Multiplier, FP Divider or FP Square root unit. These dispatch rate limitations are mainly due to data path or register port limitations aimed at reducing complexity. (See Figure 7.67.)

In the case of a *central reservation station*, or *DRIS*, higher dispatch rates are clearly required than for group reservation stations. For instance, the PentiumPro can dispatch five RISC instructions (called nop-s) per cycle, as indicated in Figure 7.72. Here, it may be noted that port 0 is shared by six EUs. This is a design trade-off. In the PentiumPro, FP data requires 86 bits internally. Considering that each FP unit needs at least two operands and delivers at least one result, a considerable saving can be achieved in the die area by sharing one complex input/output port.

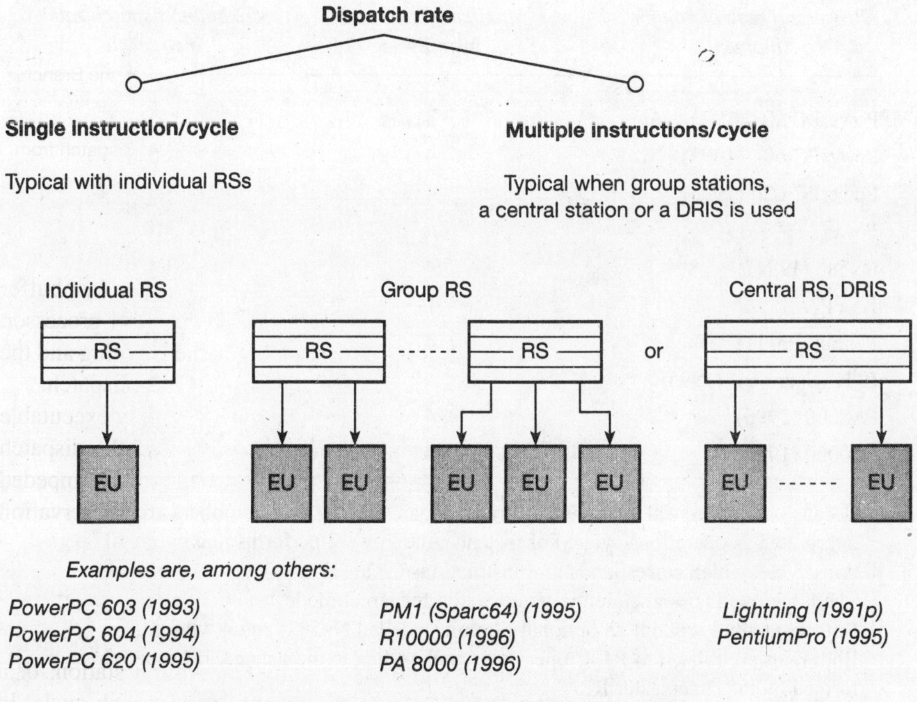

Figure 7.36 Multiplicity of dispatched instructions.

tor counts, we expect fewer hardware restrictions imposed on data path and port limitations, and thus higher dispatch rates than in recent processors.

For an overview, we have compiled the maximum issue and dispatch rates of superscalar processors with shelving, as shown in Table 7.3.

As Table 7.3 shows, in some cases both rates are the same, for instance in the PowerPC 603 and PA 8000 processors. However, in most cases superscalar processors with shelving are capable of dispatching more instructions for execution than of issuing them for shelving. For example, the PowerPC 604 and PowerPC 620 issue up to four instructions but are able to start the execution of up to six operations in each cycle. As other examples, Hal's PM1 (also termed the Sparc64) and the Power2 issue up to four and six instructions respectively, whereas they are in a position to start the execution of up to eight and ten operations per cycle, respectively.

The motivation for setting *higher dispatch rates than issue rates* is the following. Shelving allows the maximum number of instructions, as specified by the issue rate, to be issued in most cycles. By contrast, complex instructions such as division, square root calculation, and so on cannot be started immediately one after the other. Thus, for a balance of instruction issue and dispatch the processor should be capable of dispatching more instructions to available EUs per cycle than it issues to the shelving buffers.

Table 7.3 Maximum issue and dispatch rates of superscalar processors with shelving.

Processor/Year of volume shipment	*Maximum issue rate instr./cycle*	*Maximum dispatch rate[1] instr./cycle*
PowerPC 603 (1993)	3	3
PowerPC 604 (1995)	4	6
PowerPC 620 (1996)	4	6
Power2 (1993)	4/6[2]	10
Nx586 (1994)	3/4[3,4]	3/4[3,4]
K5 (1995)	4[4]	5[4]
PentiumPro (1995)	4	5[4]
PM1 (Sparc 64) (1995)	4	8
PA8000 (1996)	4	4
R10000 (1996)	4	5

[1] Because of address calculations performed separately, the given numbers are usually to be interpreted as operations/cycle. For instance, the Power2 performs maximum 10 operations/cycle, which corresponds to 8 instructions/cycle.

[2] The issue rate is 6 for sequential mode and 4 for target mode.

[3] Both rates are 3 without an optional FP unit (labelled Nx587) and 4 with it.

[4] Both rates are related to RISC operations (rather than to the native CISC operations) performed by the superscalar RISC core.

Scheme for checking the availability of operands

The availability of operands has to be checked in two scenarios. When operands are fetched from the register file, a scheme is needed to check whether requested contents are available in the register file. A similar scheme is needed during instruction dispatch to check whether all the operands of the instructions held in the shelving buffers are available. In discussing possible solutions to this, we make use of a technique which is generally employed to indicate the availability of register operands, called scoreboarding.

The term **scoreboard** was introduced in connection with the CDC 6600 (1964) to denote the complex circuitry used in this processor for controlling parallel operation. Recently, this term has been generalized and reinterpreted to designate a technique for checking the availability of register operands. Figure 7.37 demonstrates the principle.

The scoreboard is actually a status register consisting of one-bit entries. Each of the entries may be envisaged as a one-bit extension of the corresponding register. The scoreboard bits indicate whether data in the associated register is valid, that is, available. Usually, a '1' designates available data. When an instruction is issued, the scoreboard bit of the corresponding destination register is reset to 0. This indicates to all subsequent instructions requesting the contents of the register in question that its value is not yet available. Later, when the instruction in question has been executed and the result is written into the destination register, the corresponding scoreboard bit is set to 1. From now on, the appropriate register content is available to all requesting instructions.

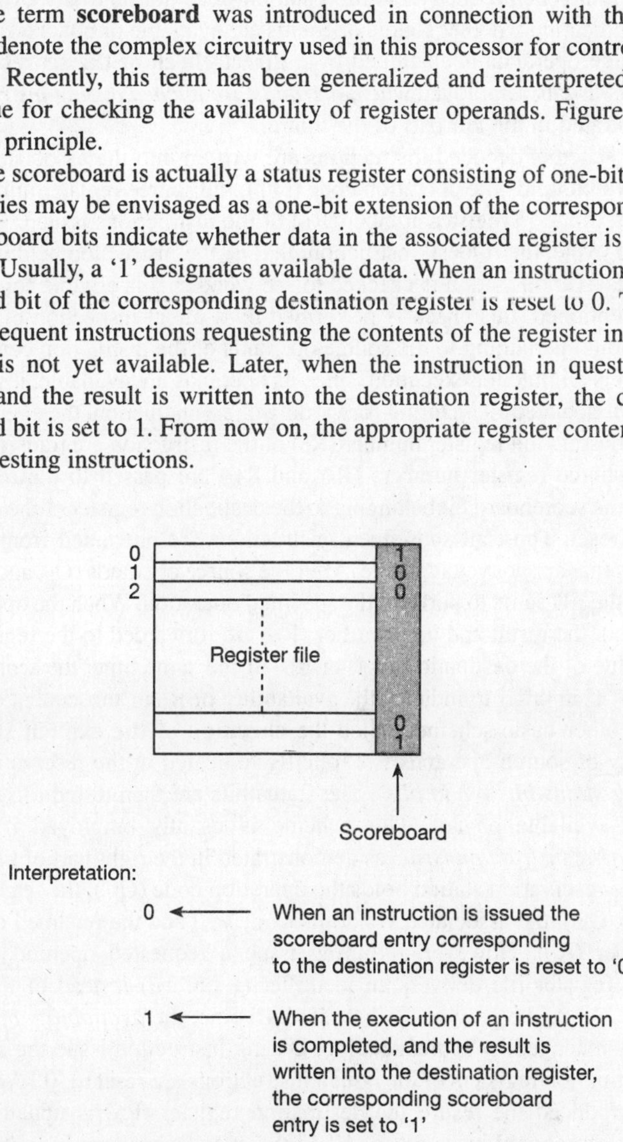

Figure 7.37 The principle of scoreboarding.

As Figure 7.38 shows, there are two basic schemes for checking the availability of operands.

In the first, the *scoreboard bits are directly checked* for the availability of operands, whereas in the second scheme *explicit status bits are maintained* and checked.

Figure 7.38 demonstrates both schemes. For the sake of simplicity, we assume an individual reservation station with in-order dispatch as well as a single register file for all data types. Also for simplicity, we do not take renaming into account.

In the first scheme, the reservation station does not hold any explicit status information indicating whether source operands are available or not. Thus, the availability of source operands is examined by a **direct check of the scoreboard bits.** This scheme is usually employed *when operands are fetched during instruction dispatch*, as illustrated in the left part of the figure.

In this scheme, decoded instructions are written into the associated reservation station, which holds the operation code (OC), the source register numbers (R_{S1}, R_{S2}) and the destination register number (R_D) of the instructions issued.

In each cycle, the 'oldest' instruction, that is, the instruction held in the 'last' entry of the reservation station is checked to see whether it is eligible for execution. As already mentioned, this check is performed by a direct inspection of the scoreboard bits (V-bits) pertaining to the source operands of the instruction considered. If the instruction is eligible for execution, since its operands are available, it will be forwarded to the associated EU. During forwarding of an instruction, the operation code (OC) and the destination register number (R_D) of the instruction are transferred to the EU, and the source register numbers (R_{S1} and R_{S2}) are passed to the register file. Furthermore, the scoreboard bit belonging to the destination register of the dispatched instruction is reset. Thus, all subsequent instructions are prevented from accessing register values that are not yet available. After the source operands (O_{S1} and O_{S2}) have been fetched, the EU starts to perform the specified operation. When the operation has been completed, the result and its identifier (R_D) are forwarded to the register file to update the value of the destination register R_D. At the same time, the scoreboard bit of R_D is set to '1' in order to indicate the availability of R_D in subsequent checks.

In the other basic scheme, called the **checking of the explicit status bits,** the availability of source operands is explicitly indicated in the reservation station by introducing *status bits (valid bits)*. The status bits are then tested to see whether operands are available or not. This scheme is usually employed *if operands are fetched during instruction issue*, as demonstrated in the right part of Figure 7.38. In this case the reservation station holds the operation code (OC), the fetched source operands (O_{S1}, O_{S2}), the associated valid bits (V_{S1}, V_{S2}) and the renamed destination register number (R_D). However, if during issue a requested operand is not yet available, the register file delivers an identifier (I_{S1} or I_{S2}) instead of the missing operand value. As in the previously discussed scheme, the *availability of the register contents* is managed by *scoreboarding*. During instruction issue the scoreboard bits of the destination registers of the issued instructions are reset to '0'. Again, when the EU has produced the result, the destination register (R_D) is updated and the corresponding scoreboard bit is set to '1'. In this way, subsequently issued instructions can access the produced result value.

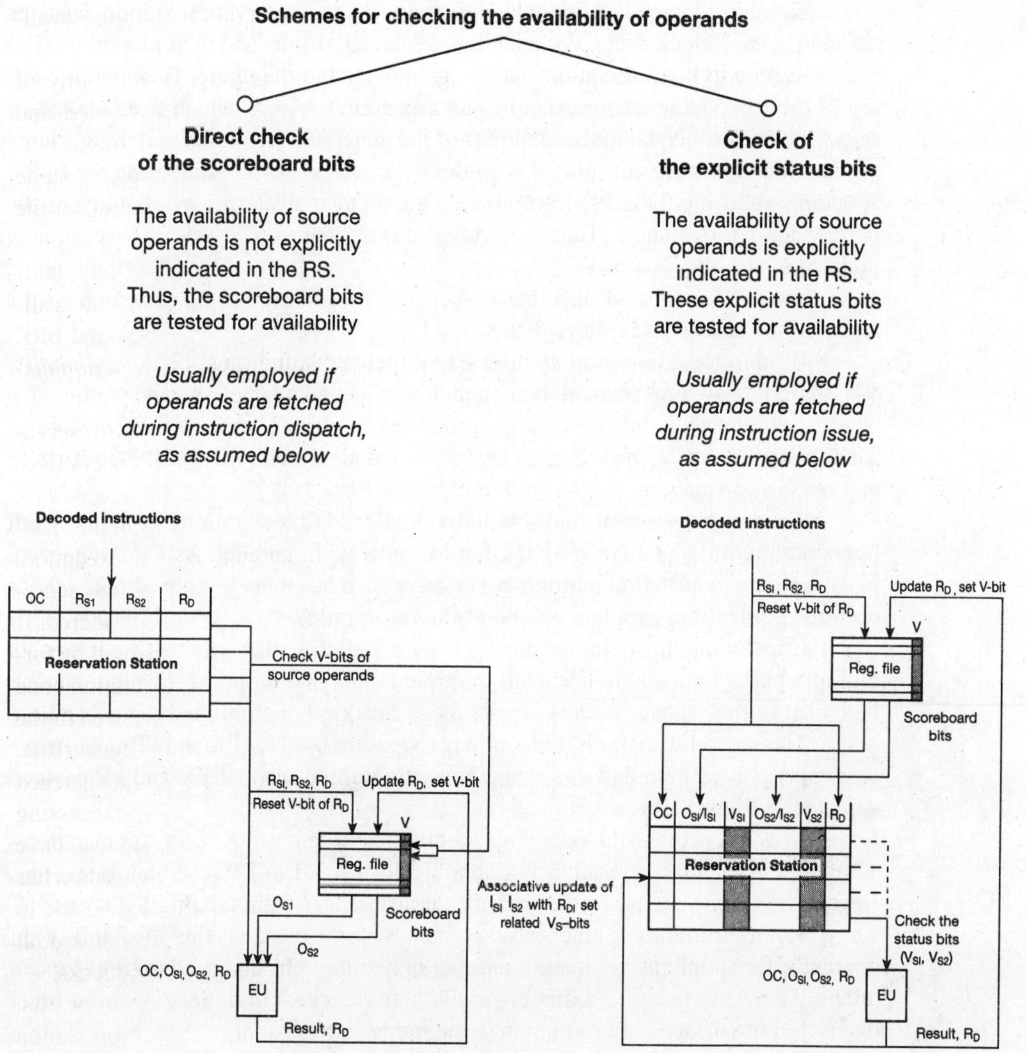

OC:	Operation code
R_{SI}, R_{S2}:	Source register numbers
R_D:	Destination register number
O_{SI}, O_{S2}:	Source operand values
I_{SI}, I_{S2}:	Source operand identifiers (tags)
V_{SI}, V_{S2}:	Source operand valid bits
RS:	Reservation station

Figure 7.38 Schemes for checking the availability of operands.

In this scheme, additionally the status of the reservation station must be updated in each clock cycle. For updating, generated results and their identifiers (R_D) are forwarded to the reservation station, as indicated in the figure. However, *updating* of the reservation stations requires an *associative search*, which finds all source register identifiers equal to the identifier of the generated result. All matching source register identifiers are substituted with the result value. At the same time the corresponding valid bits (V_{S1}, V_{S2}) are also set to '1' to indicate the availability of the corresponding operands. Thus, checking during the next cycle meets already updated status bits (V_{S1}, V_{S2}).

Two extensions of this basic scenario must also be examined: multiple reservation stations and split registers.

If *multiple reservation stations* exist, their updating must be done *globally*. We should take into account here that a not yet available operand value in a reservation station is not necessarily produced by the EU that is connected to it. Thus, for updating, all results must be forwarded along with the result identifiers to any reservation station, as indicated in Figure 7.39.

Thus, in the case of multiple individual reservation stations as many result buses are required as there are EUs that can operate in parallel. As a consequence, in each reservation station multiple associative searches must be carried out, one for each result identifier supplied by one of the result buses.

Concluding this point we redraw Figure 7.39 in such a way that we represent multiple buses by a single line with multiple inputs and outputs (see Figure 7.40). Note that in this chapter usually we are using this kind of simplified representation.

The second scenario is when split registers are used for FX and FP data. In this case, operand fetching and updating are separated into distinct FX and FP parts as depicted in Figure 7.41.

Now FX results and associated identifiers are sent to FX reservation stations, whereas FP results and result identifiers are forwarded to FP reservation stations. Beyond this, there are no further significant differences from the original scenario.

While introducing the basic schemes for checking the availability of operands, for simplicity we made a number of assumptions that need to be expanded upon. We recall that we assumed individual reservation stations with in-order dispatch. Furthermore, we did not take renaming into account.

First, let us consider using group or central reservation stations. Then the dispatch scheme should be extended to provide, instead of a single instruction, multiple executable instructions to available EUs. In this case multiple availability checks are required, a maximum of as many in each cycle as the dispatch rate of the RS being considered.

Both schemes may be extended to out-of-order dispatch. However, register naming has then to be presumed and all instructions in the reservation stations have to be checked in parallel for availability and execution. Furthermore, in the direct checking scheme the scoreboard bits belonging to the destination registers of the issued instructions have to be reset during instruction issue rather than during instruction dispatch.

When renaming is used, operands are fetched either from the rename buffers or from the architectural registers as explained in Section 7.5.1. Another difference

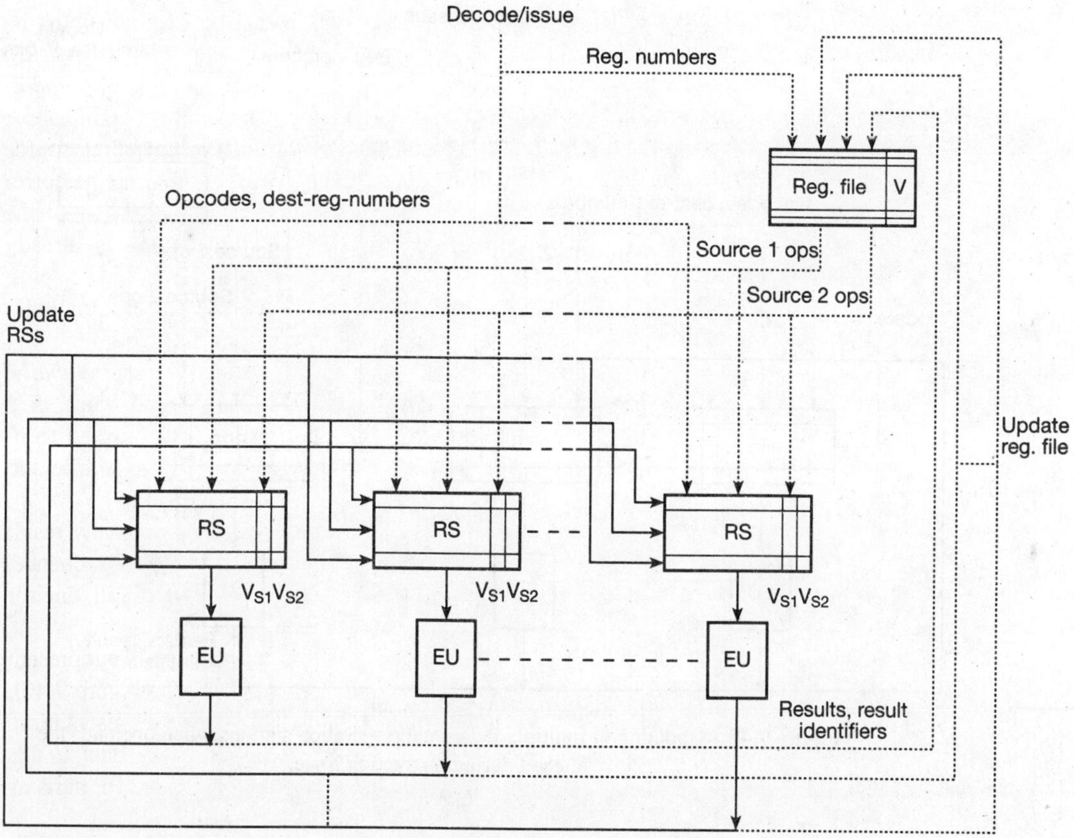

Figure 7.39 Use of multiple buses for updating multiple individual reservation stations.

is that, in the case of renaming, the rename buffers are updated with the generated results rather than the architectural registers.

Finally, we show a case example to demonstrate how operand availability checks are integrated into processor operation. Our example is the PowerPC 604 whose internal data paths are depicted in Figure 7.42, which is based on IBM/Motorola (1994).

The PowerPC 604 uses split registers for FX and FP data, and, as do most recent processors, employs renaming. As discussed in Section 7.5.3, there are separate register files for rename and architectural registers. This processor has six EUs altogether. In addition to the branch processing unit (BPU), there are three FX units (2× SCIU, MCIU), a load/store unit (SU) and an FP unit (FPU). Two of the FX units, called single-cycle integer units (SCIU), are straightforward FX ALUs executing instructions in one cycle. A third FX unit executes multi-cycle FX operations (MCIU). The load/store unit (L/SU) computes addresses and processes loads and stores. Thus, as indicated in the figure, four FX result buses altogether are available. In front of each execution unit there is a reservation station with two entries.

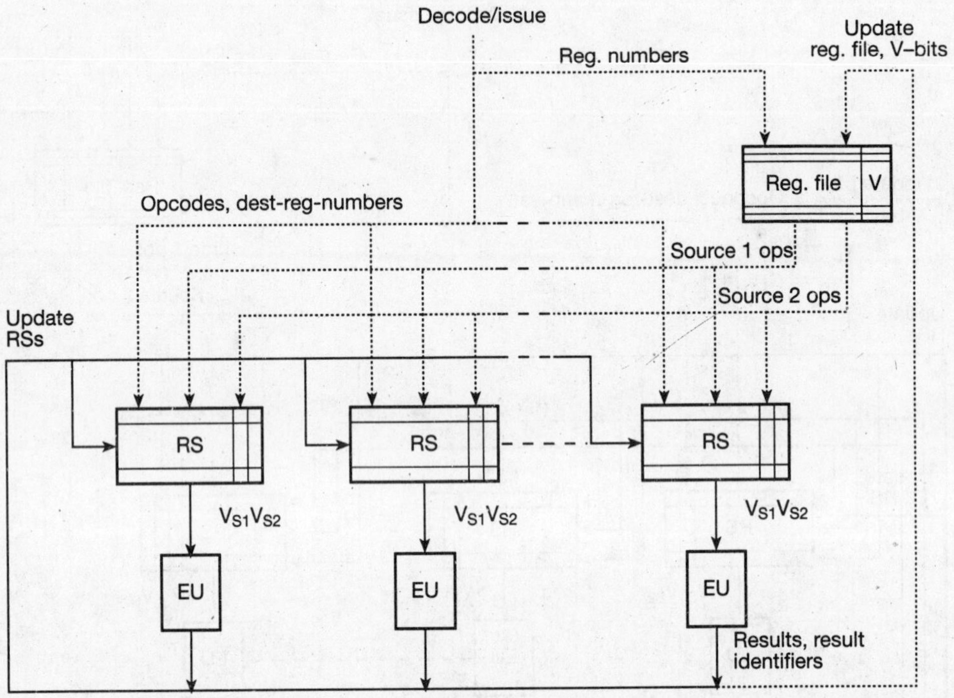

Figure 7.40 Updating of multiple individual reservation stations when operands are fetched during instruction issue.

The other part of the microarchitecture covers FP processing. Here, there is a single FP unit available (FPU) with a two-entry reservation station in front of it. Note that the L/SU also delivers FP results. Thus, two FP result buses are needed to pass the FP results for updating both the FP reservation station and the FP rename register file.

In this architecture up to four predecoded instructions are decoded and issued into the appropriate reservation stations in each cycle. As indicated in the figure, during issue up to eight FX operands and three FP operands are fetched from the register files, if available. Here, rename and architectural registers are accessed in parallel. (See Section 7.5.3 for further details.)

Operand availability is explicitly indicated in the reservation stations. If a referenced source operand is available, the operand itself is read into the reservation station. If the operand is not available an identifier is latched instead of the operand and the availability bit is set accordingly. Instructions held in the reservation stations are inspected in each cycle to see whether they are executable by checking the corresponding availability bits of the source operands. Instructions are dispatched from the reservation stations partly in-order (BPU, FPU), partly out-of-order (remaining units), up to one from each station in each cycle.

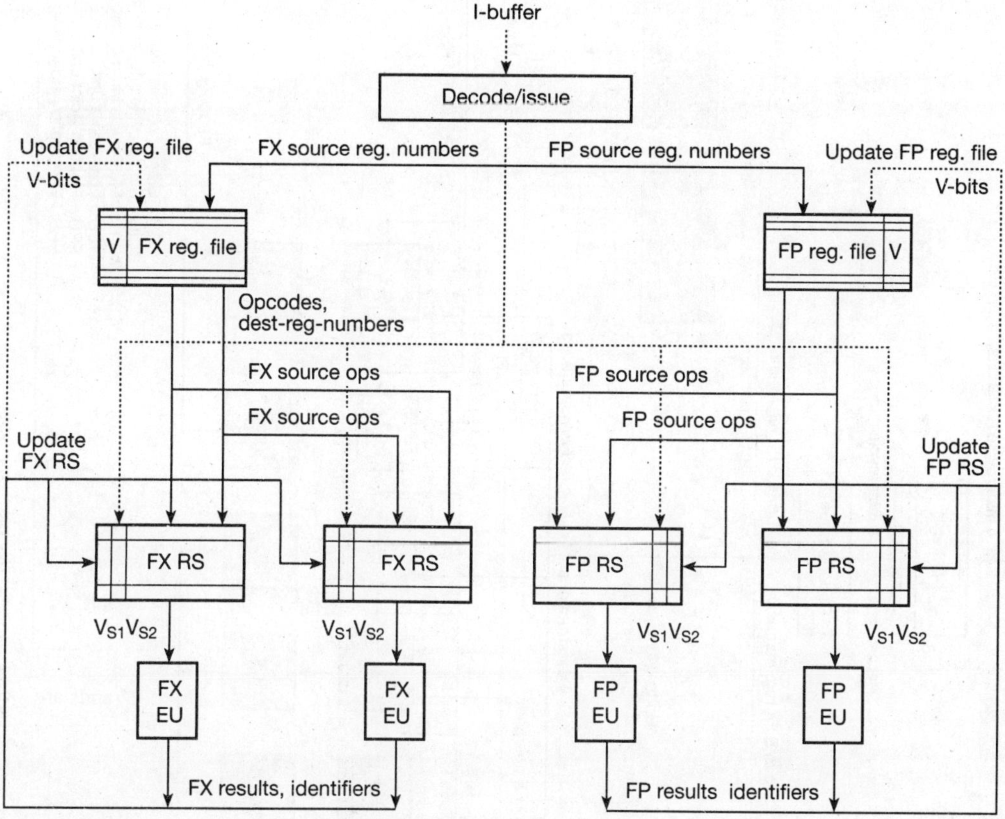

Figure 7.41 Updating of reservation stations in case of split FX and FP register files.

The generated results are used to update the reservation stations and the rename registers. Four FX and two FP result buses transfer result values and their identifiers to the reservation stations and rename registers. In the reservation stations an associative search is conducted to see whether generated results are waiting in any reservation station. If there is a match, the appropriate result is latched and the associated availability bit is set. Section 7.5.3 details the updating of the rename registers.

Treatment of an empty reservation station

When instructions arrive at an empty reservation station, superscalar processors follow two different aproaches (see Figure 7.43). The **straightforward approach** is to process the instructions in the same way as with a partially filled reservation station. However, entering instructions have to stay for at least one cycle in the empty station before they are dispatched. The Nx586 is an example of a processor that treats an empty reservation station in this way.

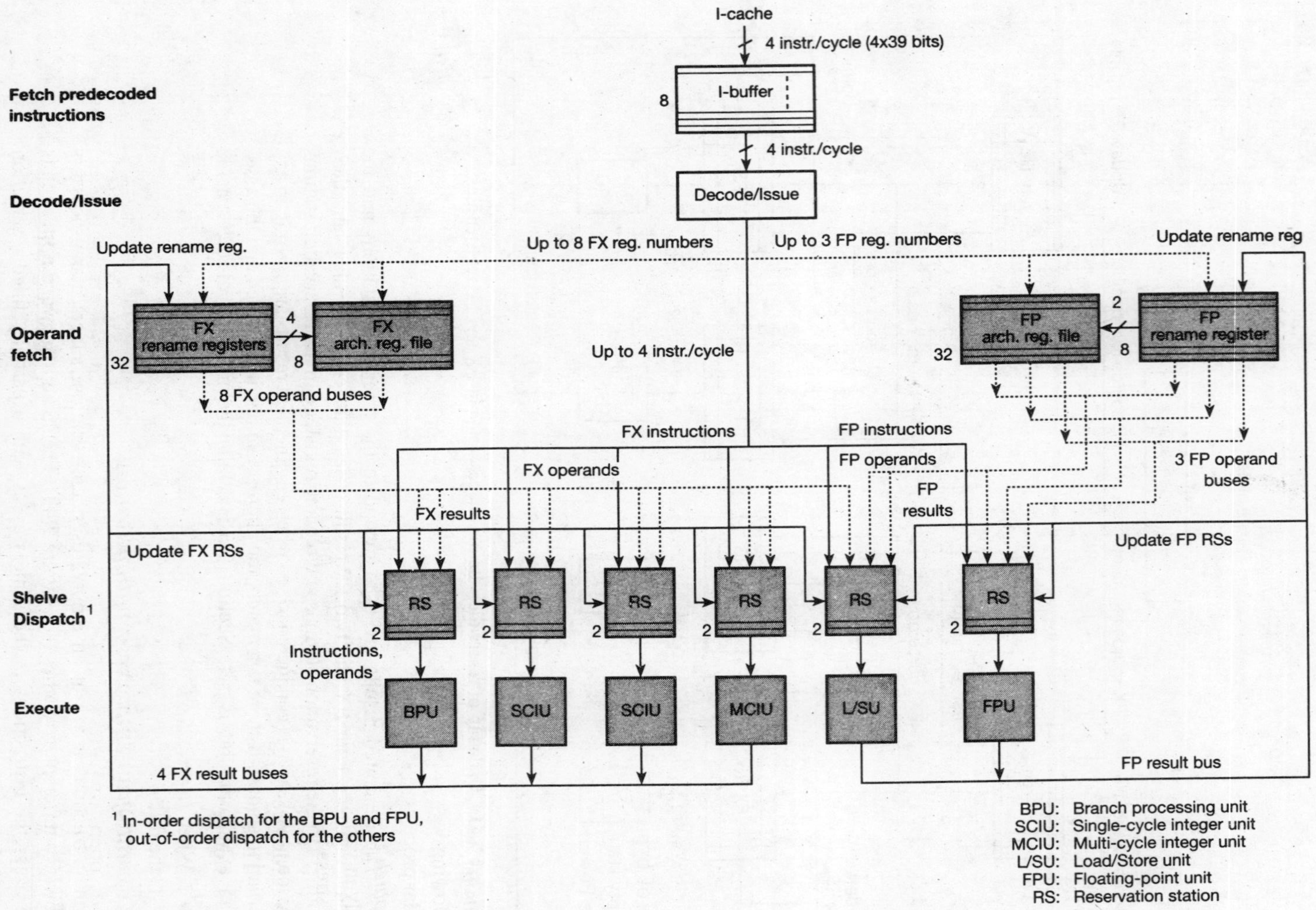

[1] In-order dispatch for the BPU and FPU, out-of-order dispatch for the others

Figure 7.42 Internal data paths of the PowerPC 604.

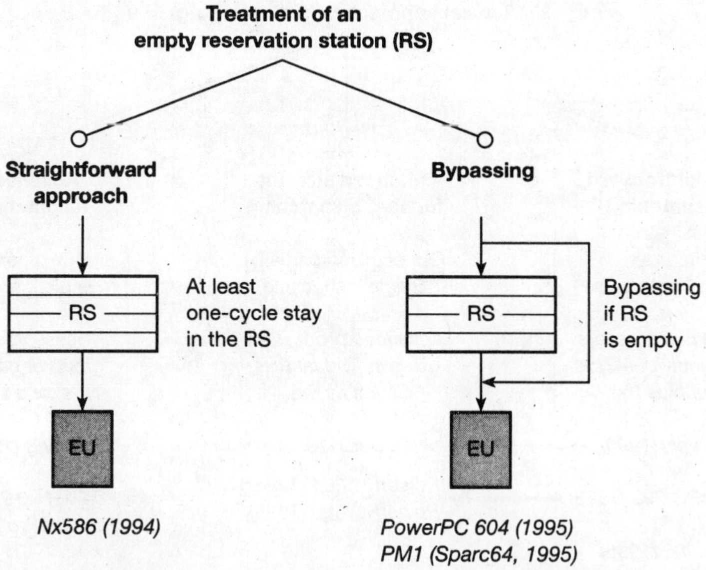

Figure 7.43 Treatment of an empty reservation station.

A more advanced approach for treating empty reservation stations is the use of **bypasses**. Here, some additional circuitry permits instructions to bypass an empty station and be immediately forwarded to the EUs without any additional delay. The PowerPC 604 and the PM1 (Sparc64) employ this more efficient approach.

Typical dispatch schemes

Thus far, we have discussed the individual components of dispatch schemes. In the following we point out which dispatch schemes are used most frequently in superscalar processors. For simplicity in our discussion, we focus on only two aspects, the *dispatch order* and the *dispatch rate*. These are the aspects which are used differently in various superscalar processors. Regarding other aspects of the design space we stress the following typical solutions:

- Most recent processors employ register renaming and speculative execution. Thus, the dataflow selection rule is used most often, with the oldest instruction preferred if an arbitration is needed.
- When operands are fetched during instruction dispatch most processors use the direct checking method. Alternatively, when operands are fetched during instruction issue, explicit status bits are typically maintained and checked for operand availability.
- An empty reservation station is usually bypassed.

If we focus only on the dispatch order and the dispatch rate, three typical approaches can be identified in recent superscalar processors, which are summarized in Figure 7.44.

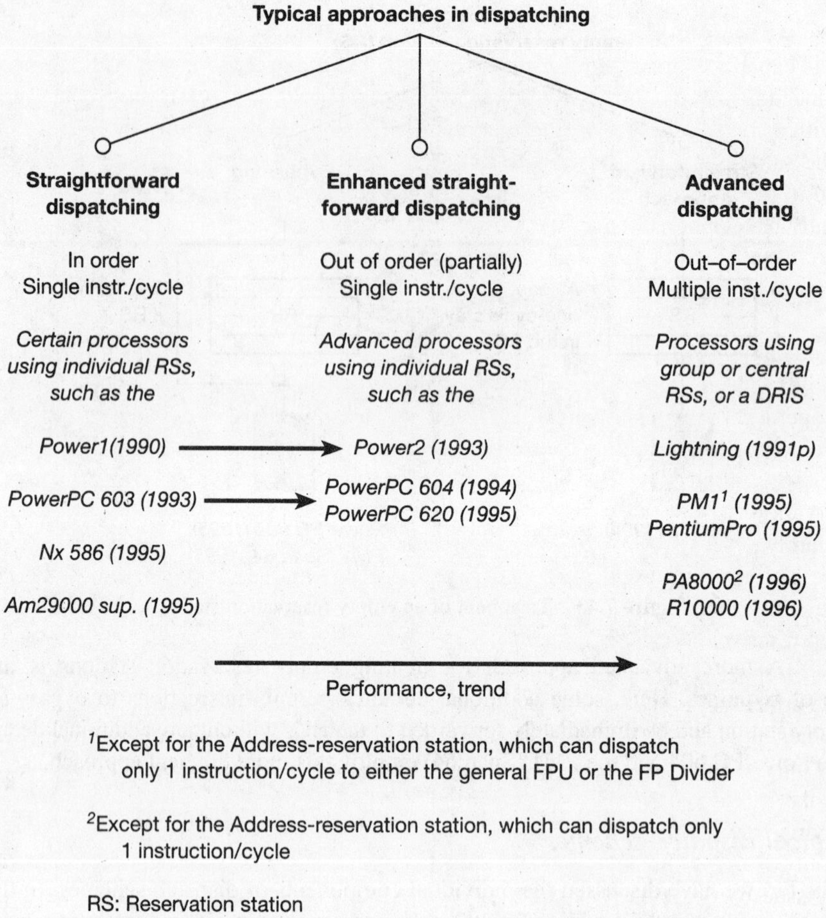

Figure 7.44 Typical approaches in dispatching.

In **straightforward dispatching**, instructions are dispatched one at a time. In this simple approach an instruction that is not yet executable *blocks* further dispatching until this instruction becomes executable. Some processors using *individual reservation stations* employ this straightforward but inefficient approach.

The efficiency of this simple approach can be increased by introducing out-of-order dispatching for particular reservation stations. We call this approach **enhanced straightforward dispatching**. In this case, the reservation stations use an out-of-order dispatch, and subsequent executable instructions can *bypass* an instruction that is not yet executable. Obviously, this results in a performance increase over the basic approach. This approach is typically employed in advanced processors using *individual reservation stations*.

Advanced dispatching is the most powerful. It allows *out-of-order dispatch* and is capable of forwarding *multiple instructions* per cycle to available EUs. This advanced dispatch policy is employed in processors with *group reversation stations* or with a *central reservation station* or with a DRIS. Usually, subsequent processors of the same line tend to use more powerful approaches for dispatching. Thus, the trend in dispatching corresponds to the sequence of our discussion of the most frequently used approaches.

7.4.6 Detailed example of shelving

As indicated in Figures 7.21–7.27, 7.33–7.36 and 7.38 shelving has an extremely complex design space. Consequently, there is a puzzling variety of possible ways it can operate. From the large number of possible layouts, in the following we demonstrate how shelving is carried out in one of the most frequently used scenarios while executing a short piece of code. Our selected layout of shelving assumes individual reservation stations, issue bound operand fetching and explicit indication of operand availability. This model is used basically in the PowerPC 603–620, and in some sense also in the K5 and Am29000 superscalar processors. Shelving also operates quite similarly in the PM1 (Sparc 64), the main difference being that the PM1 has group reservation stations.

Before getting down to details, let us first describe the assumptions we have made concerning the microarchitecture, instruction issue, shelving and dispatching scheme. As far as the architecture is concerned, for the sake of simplicity, we consider only a single FX EU with a split FX register file. Concerning instruction issue, we take it for granted that the advanced superscalar issue policy is used providing shelving, renaming and speculative execution of unresolved conditional branches. In our example no issue blockages can occur, therefore it does not matter how issue blockages are handled. As regards shelving buffers, we assume an individual reservation station in front of the FX EU which has four entries and is capable of accepting at most two instructions per cycle. Furthermore, we assume that operands are fetched during instruction issue. Finally, for the dispatch policy we assume the dataflow selection rule in accordance with the advanced superscalar issue policy chosen. From the FX reservation station instructions should be dispatched out of order, at most one instruction per cycle, with the oldest instruction is preferred when more than one instruction is executable. We assume that the availability of operands is explicitly indicated by valid bits in the reservation station. Lastly, we suppose that an empty reservation station is not bypassed. To summarize the salient points, we assume individual reservation stations, issue bound operand fetching and explicit indication of operand availability.

Overview of the operation

As indicated in Figure 7.45(a), in our example decoded, issued (and renamed) FX instructions are written into the FX reservation station, up to two per cycle. According to our assumption, the source operands of the instructions will

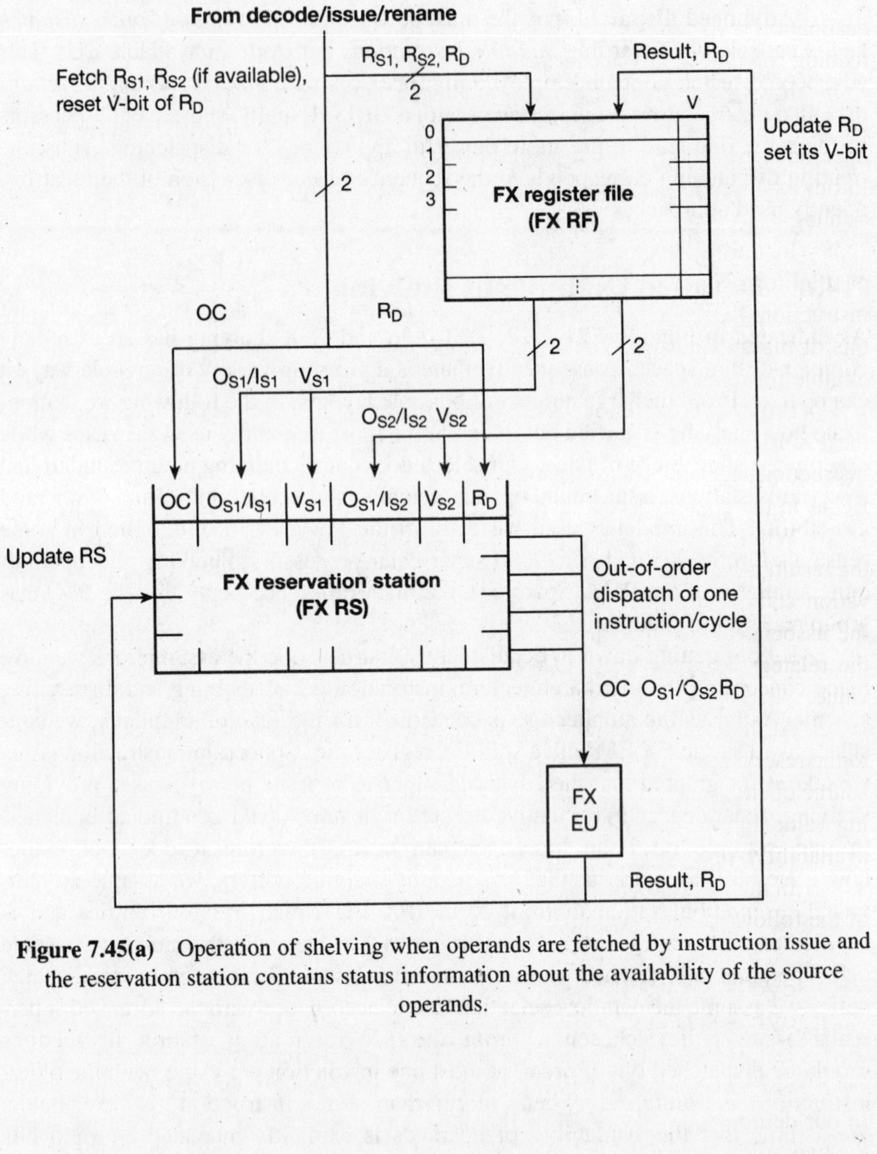

Figure 7.45(a) Operation of shelving when operands are fetched by instruction issue and the reservation station contains status information about the availability of the source operands.

be fetched during issue, if available. Therefore, the source operand identifiers (RS_1, RS_2) of up to two instructions are sent during issue to the FX register file. The register file maintains scoreboard bits (V-bits) associated with each of its entries in the same way as described above. Thus, during instruction issue the availability of the referred register operands can be checked by inspecting the corresponding V-bits. Available source operands are written into the corresponding fields of the reservation station, which are designated by O_{S1} and O_{S2} in Figure 7.45(a). At the same time the associated valid bits (V_{S1} and V_{S2}) are set and the scoreboard bits of the destination registers R_D are reset in order to prevent all subsequent instructions from reading referenced but not yet available data.

If a source operand is not available (which is indicated by the reset value of the corresponding V-bit), a tag is stored (labelled as I_{S1} and I_{S2}) instead of the source operand itself. This tag usually identifies where the missing operand will come from. In our example let us suppose that the destination register identifier, R_D, will serve as a tag.

In the next step, all instructions in the reservation station are checked in parallel to find any instructions whose source operands are available and, thus, the instruction is executable. The check is performed simply by investigating the valid bits of the operands (V_{S1} and V_{S2}). If both are set, the corresponding instruction is eligible for dispatching.

Provided that a single executable instruction is found, it will be forwarded to the FX EU connected to the reservation station. When more than one executable instruction is available, the 'oldest' one will be selected and transmitted to the FX EU as in the preceding example.

When the instruction which has been dispatched to the FX EU is completed, the result, along with its identifier (R_D), is sent to both the register file and the reservation station for updating. After the register file has received the identifier and the associated result value, the corresponding R_D entry is updated. Furthermore, the related scoreboard bit is set to 1 to indicate the availability of the associated value.

At the same time the result value and the result identifier are also forwarded to the reservation station. Here, an associative search is needed to find any matching source operand identifiers. Matching identifiers are substituted with the corresponding value and the related status bits (V_{S1} and V_{S2} bits) are set to 1 to indicate their availability.

In the next section we detail the operation just overviewed assuming the issue of the following short code sequence:

```
cycle i:     mul   r1, r2, r3;   r3←(r1)*(r2)
cycle i+1:   ad    r2, r3, r5;   r5←(r2)+(r3)
             ad    r3, r4, r6;   r6←(r3)+(r4)
```

In our demonstration we assume that the 'mul' instruction is issued in cycle i, and the two 'ad' instructions in cycle i+1.

Issue of the 'mul' instruction into the reservation station in cycle i

After decoding and renaming, the 'mul' instruction

```
mul   r1, r2, r3
```

is issued into the reservation station (Figure 7.45(b)).

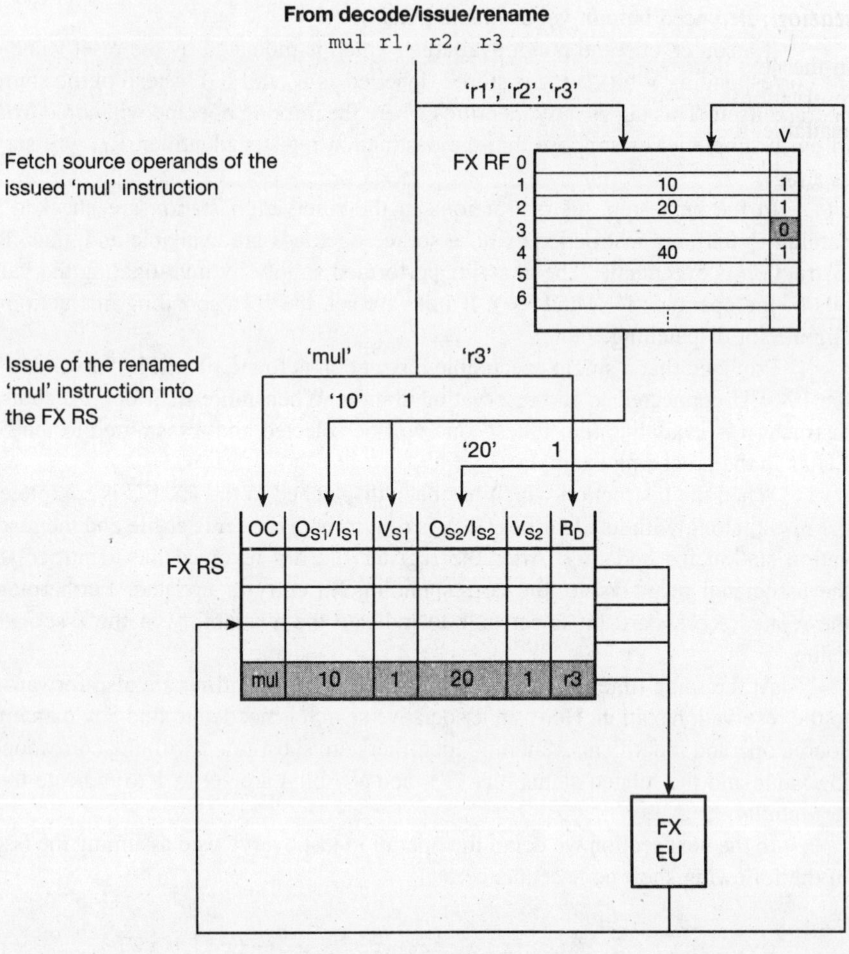

Figure 7.45(b) Issue of the 'mul' instruction into the reservation station in cycle i and fetching of the corresponding operands.

The operands of the 'mul' instruction (r1 and r2) will already be fetched during instruction issue from the register file. As the associated V-bits indicate, both values are available and thus, the fetched values (r1 = 10, r2 = 20) are sent to the matching fields of the FX RS. In addition, the valid bits of the operands (V_{S1}, V_{S2}) are set and the scoreboard bit of r3 is reset to prevent any further access to it.

Dispatching of the 'mul' instruction from the reservation station and issue of the subsequent two 'ad' instructions into the reservation station, in cycle i+1

In the next cycle (cycle i+1), the valid bits (V_{S1} and V_{S2}) of all instructions in the reservation station are checked (Figure 7.45(c)) Since both source operands are available, the 'mul' instruction is passed to the FX EU for execution.

In the same cycle, the next two 'ad' instructions

```
ad  r2, r3, r5;
ad  r3, r4, r6;
```

arrive, as Figure 7.45(d) indicates.

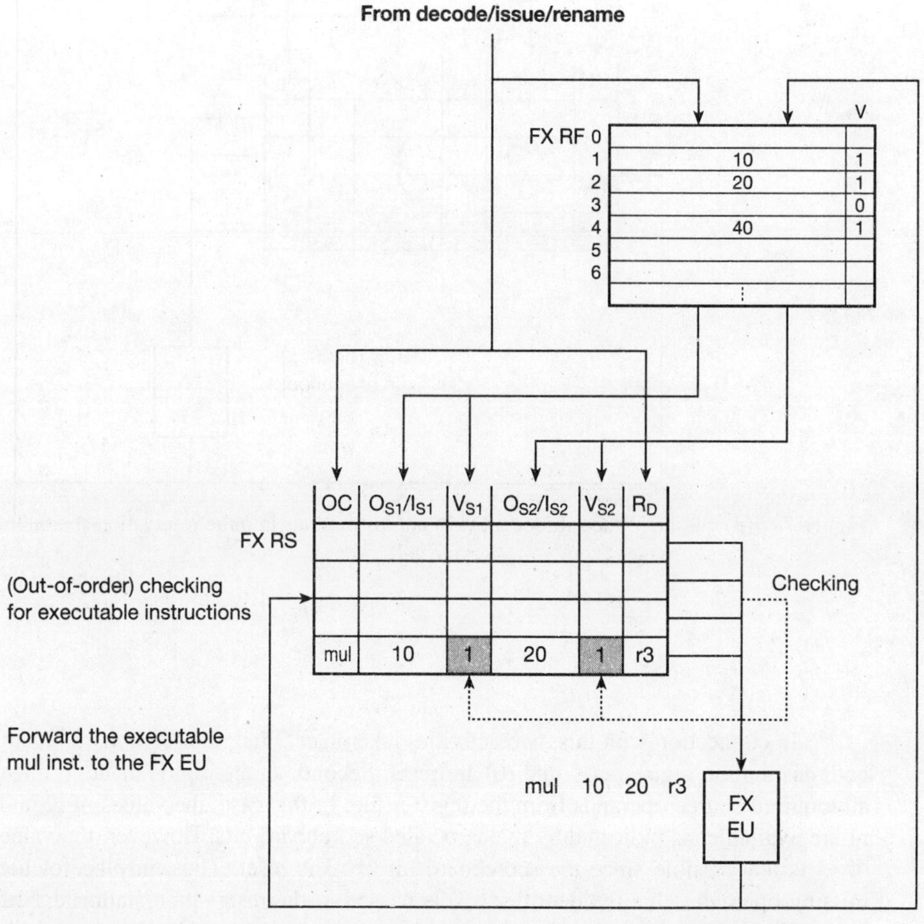

Figure 7.45(c) Checking for executable instructions and dispatching of the 'mul' instruction in cycle i+1.

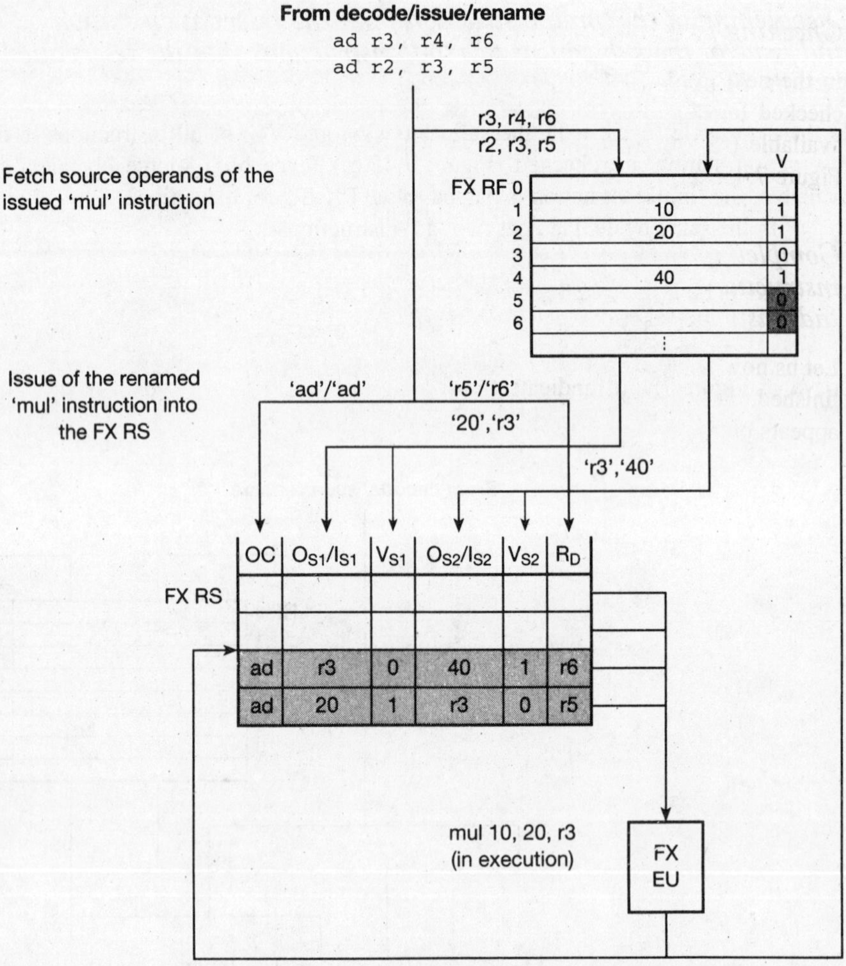

Figure 7.45(d) Issue of the subsequent two 'ad' instructions into the reservation station in cycle i+1.

In connection with this, two activities take place. First, the scoreboard bits of both destination registers (r5 and r6) are reset. Second, an attempt is made to fetch all required source operands from the register file. In this case, the values of r2 and r4 are available, as indicated by the associated scoreboard bits. However, the value of r3 is inaccessible since the scoreboard bit of r3 is reset. Thus, in place of the missing operand value its identifier (r3) is passed to the reservation station. In the reservation station the status bits of the source operands (V_{S1} and V_{S2}) are set accordingly ('0' for a not available source operand and '1' for an available one).

Checking for executable instructions in cycle i+2

In the next cycle (cycle i+2), again, all instructions in the reservation station are checked for eligibility for dispatching. Since one of the operand values is not yet available (r3), no new instruction can be dispatched in this cycle, as indicated in Figure 7.45(e).

Completing the computation of the 'mul' instruction, checking the instructions held in the reservation station and forwarding the 'older' 'ad' instruction for execution, in cycle i+3

Let us now assume that the execution of the 'mul' instruction in this cycle has been finished. Then the result of the operation (200) and the associated identifier (r3) appears on the result bus, as seen in Figure 7.45(f).

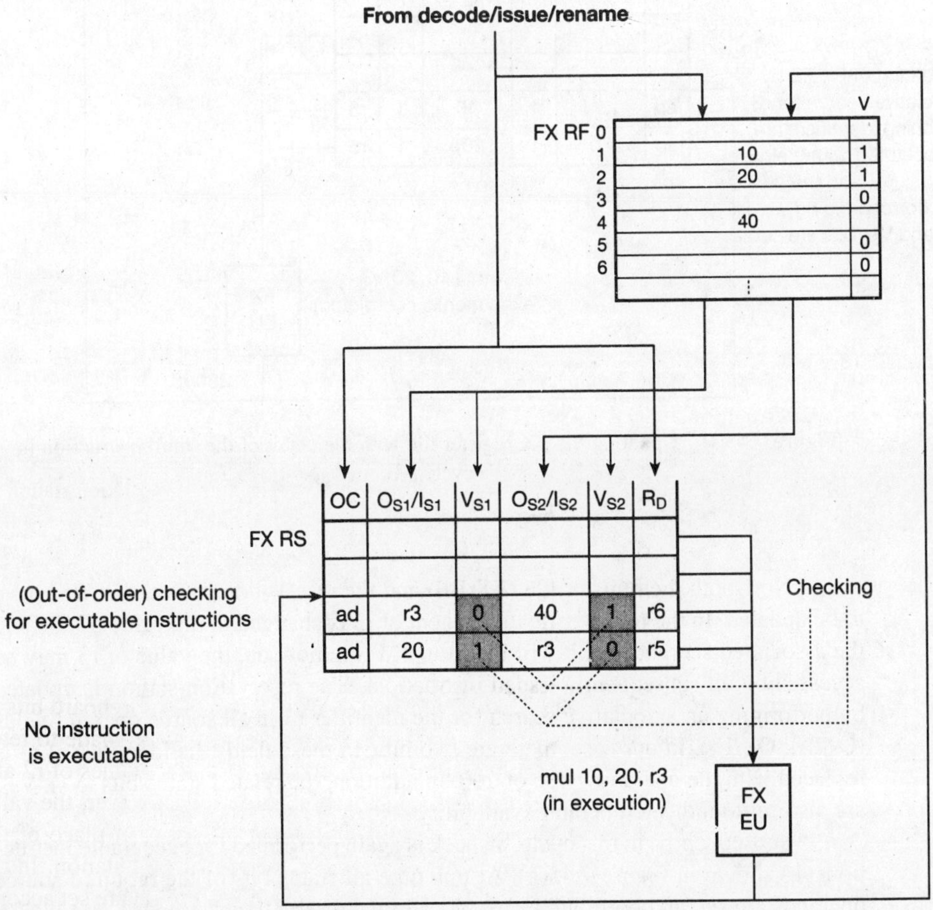

Figure 7.45(e) Checking for executable instructions in cycle i+2.

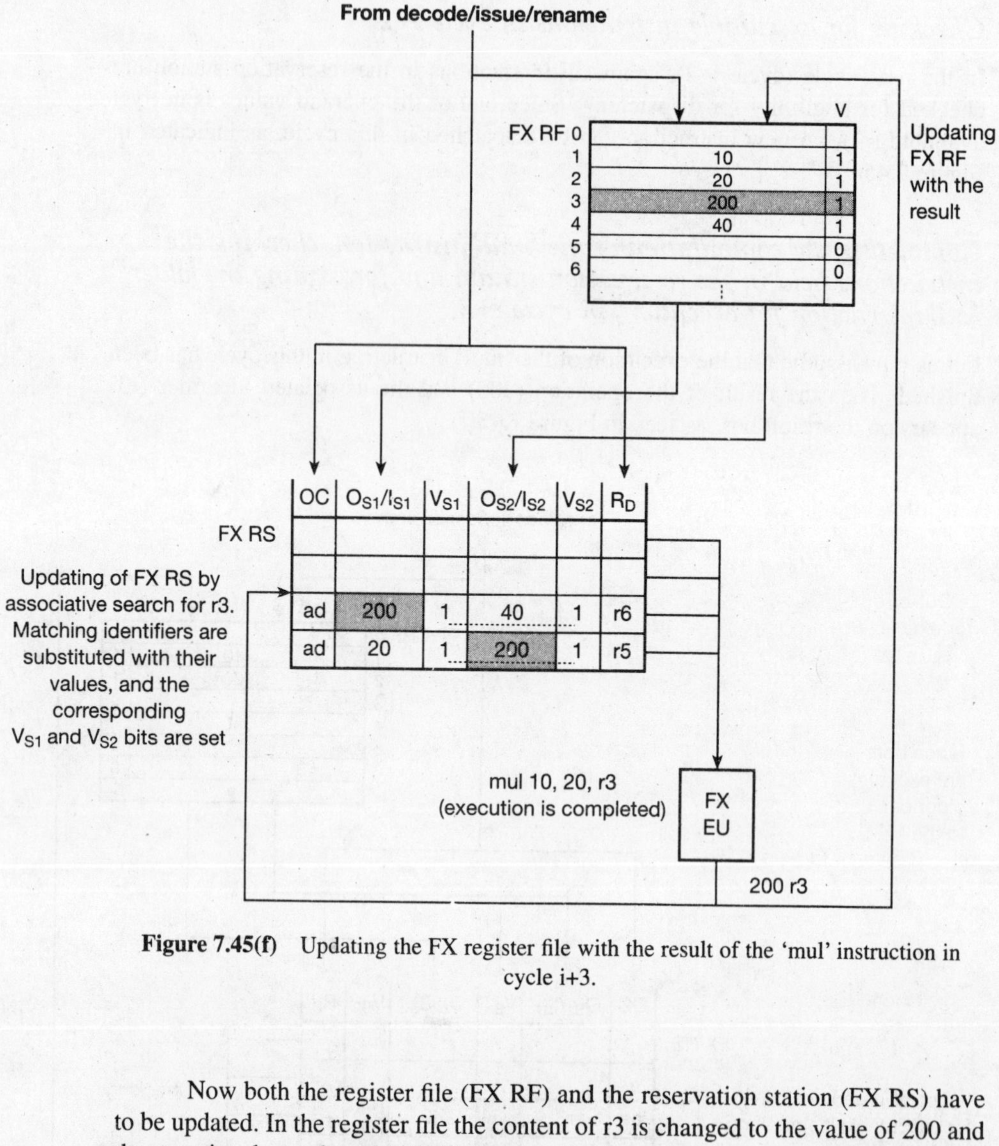

Figure 7.45(f) Updating the FX register file with the result of the 'mul' instruction in cycle i+3.

Now both the register file (FX RF) and the reservation station (FX RS) have to be updated. In the register file the content of r3 is changed to the value of 200 and the associated scoreboard bit will be set to 1. From now on, the value of r3 may be accessed by all subsequently issued instructions. The reservation station is updated by performing an associative search for the identifier r3 in all source operand fields (O_{S1}/I_{S1}, O_{S2}/I_{S2}). In our case, there are two hits. In these fields the identifier of r3 is replaced with the operand value of 200. In addition, the related status bits (V_{S1}, V_{S2}) are also set to indicate operand availability.

Subsequently, in this cycle, a check is again performed for executable instructions, as shown in Figure 7.45(g). At this time all status bits of the required source operands are set, and both 'ad' instructions in the reservation station are eligible for execution. Since more than one executable instruction was found, the arbitration rule

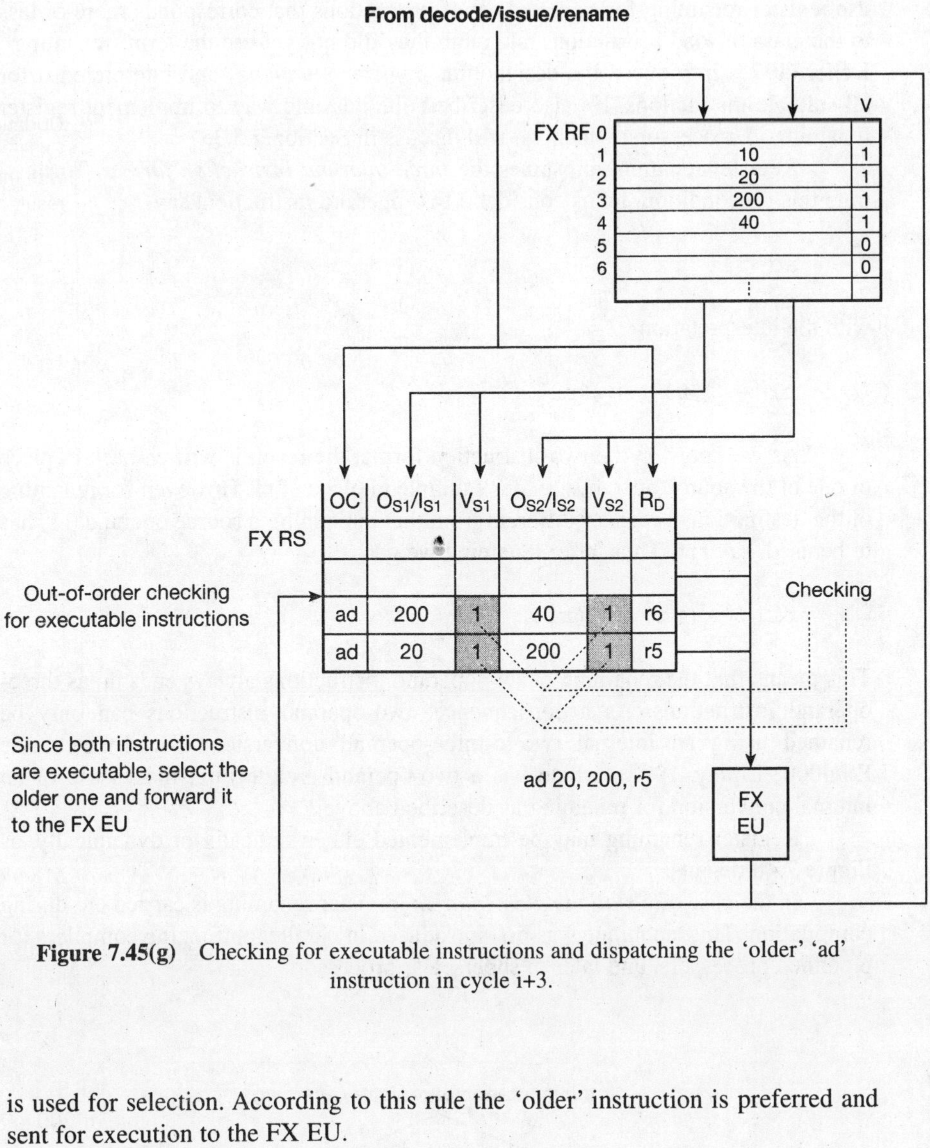

Figure 7.45(g) Checking for executable instructions and dispatching the 'older' 'ad' instruction in cycle i+3.

is used for selection. According to this rule the 'older' instruction is preferred and sent for execution to the FX EU.

This concludes the description of our demonstration example, since all subsequent processing steps are more or less trivial.

7.5 Register renaming

Register renaming, introduced earlier in Section 7.3.2, is a standard technique for removing false data dependencies, that is, WAR and WAW dependencies, among register data. It was first suggested by Tjaden and Flynn in 1970. They intended to use register renaming for a limited set of instructions that corresponds more or less to the class of load instructions, although they did not yet use the term 'renaming'. Keller (1975) introduced the designation *'register renaming'* and interpreted it for all suitable instructions. He also described one possible way to implement register renaming in processors, which we will discuss in Section 7.5.3.

Register renaming presumes the *three-operand instruction format.* To illustrate this precondition, let us consider a two-operand instruction, say

```
ad r1, r2
```

with the interpretation

```
r1 ← (r1) + (r2)
```

As we know, in the two-instruction format the result is written back in place of one of the source operands, in our example in place of r1. However, for renaming of the destination, a register different from that containing a source operand (r1) has to be used, say r11. Thus, after renaming we get

```
r11 ← (r1) + (r2)
```

This means that the renaming of two-operand instructions always ends up as three-operand instructions. As a consequence, two-operand instructions can only be renamed using an internal two-to-three-operand conversion. For instance, the ES/9000 (Liptay, 1992), which has a two-operand architecture, makes use of an internal conversion for renaming as described above.

Register renaming may be implemented either statically or dynamically, as Figure 7.46 depicts.

In the case of a *static implementation*, register renaming is carried out during compilation. This technique was first introduced in parallel optimizing compilers for pipelined processors, and later in superscalar processors.

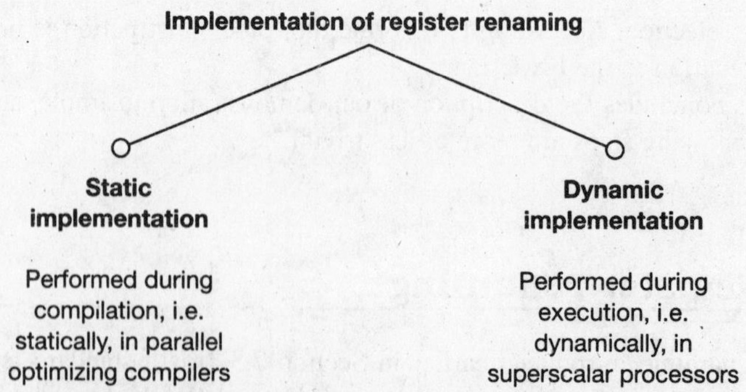

Figure 7.46 Implementation of register renaming.

When register renaming is implemented *dynamically*, renaming takes place during execution. Obviously, this requires extra circuitry in terms of supplementary register space, additional data paths and logic. Dynamic renaming has been used in advanced superscalar processors since the early 1990s, as shown in Figure 7.47. Renaming was clearly introduced in two stages. In the first stage renaming was only partially implemented. Here, renaming is confined to one or a few particular data types, as discussed in Section 7.5.2. For instance, the Power1, Power2, PowerPC 601 and Nx586 processors employ partial renaming. Full renaming has emerged in the second stage, since about 1992.

In both stages IBM was the first vendor to introduce renaming, initially in its Power-line with the Power1 (RS/6000) and later in the high-end processors of its ES/9000 family. IBM continued to implement full renaming in the Power-based PowerPC-line with the exception of the first model, the PowerPC 601. All vendors of significant superscalar processors have introduced renaming in their most recent models, except DEC in its α-line and Sun in the UltraSparc. Thus, register renaming is now almost a standard feature of superscalar processors.

As pointed out in Section 7.3.2, most superscalar processors use shelving and renaming at the same time. Only a few processors employ renaming but do not use shelving, such as the M1 and the PowerPC 602.

In the following section we focus on the technique of register renaming, emphasizing its design space and actual practice.

7.5.1 The design space

The *design space of register renaming* resembles that of shelving. As Figure 7.48 shows, it consists of the following main components: the scope of register renaming, the layout of the rename buffers, the operand fetch policy, and the number of renames per cycle. These components are discussed in the following sections.

7.5.2 Scope of register renaming

Most first-generation superscalar processors, like the PA 7100, SuperSparc, α 21064, R8000, Pentium and others, did not employ renaming. In the first stage of introduction, a few early superscalar processors introduced **partial renaming**. In this case, renaming is restricted to a particular instruction type or to a few types. Examples are the Power1 (RS6000), Power2 and Nx586. Of these, the Power1 (RS6000) renames only FP loads, whereas Power2 extends renaming to all FP instructions. We note that the Power1 has only one FP unit, and hence it executes FP instructions in sequence. FP instructions do not need to be renamed. On the other hand, the Nx586 is an FX processor, thus it renames only FX instructions.

The next stage in the introduction of register renaming is **full renaming**. In this case, renaming is carried out for all eligible instruction types. As Figure 7.49 demonstrates, virtually all recent superscalar processors employ full renaming. Noteworthy exceptions are DEC's entire α-line, including the recent α21164, and Sun's UltraSparc. These processors do not use renaming at all.

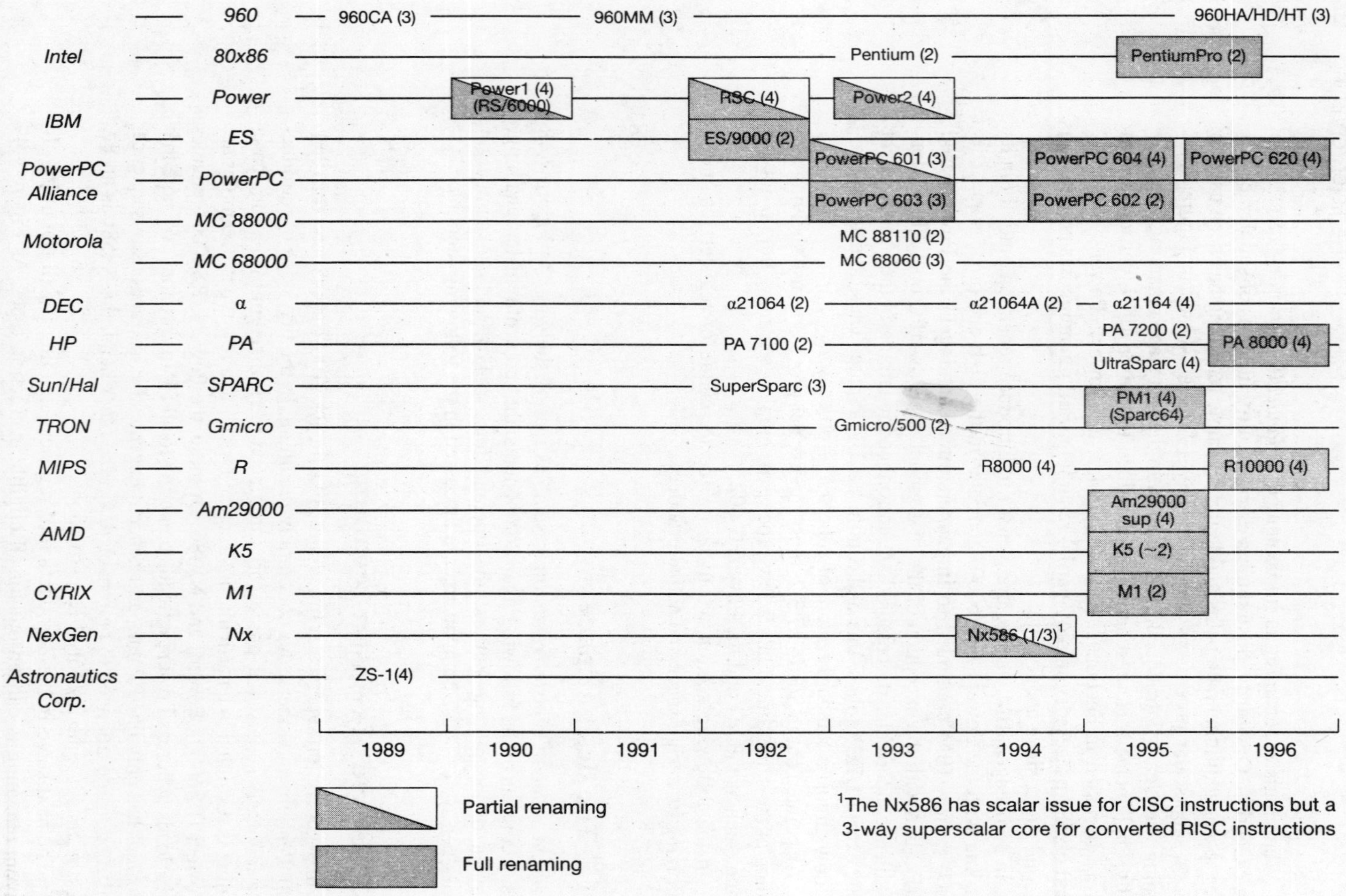

Figure 7.47 Chronology of introduction of renaming in commercial superscalar processors.

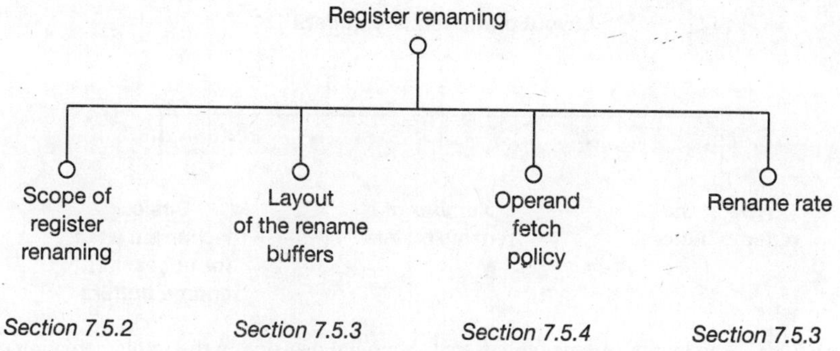

Figure 7.48 Design space of register renaming.

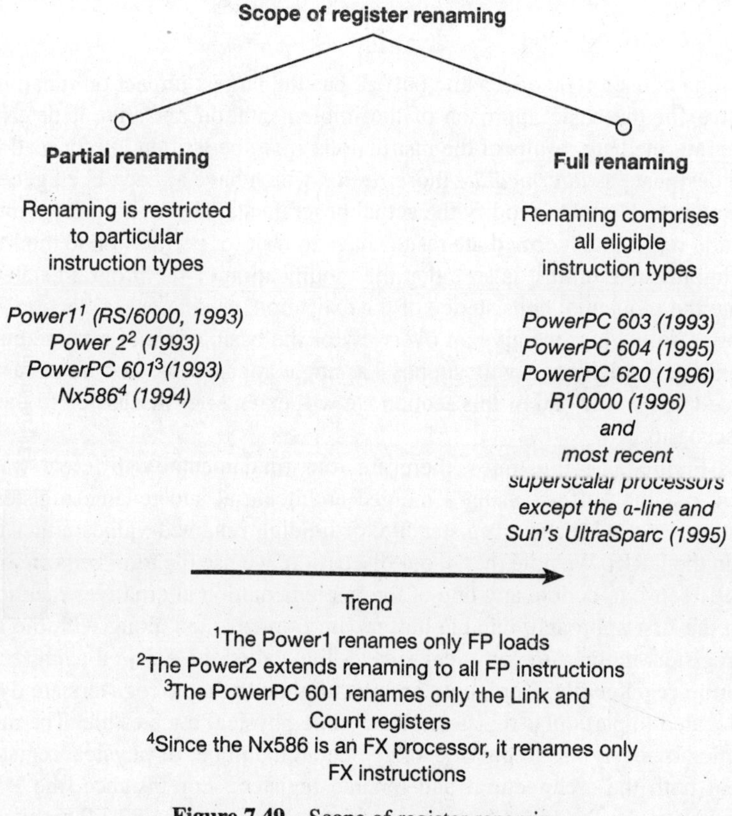

Figure 7.49 Scope of register renaming.

7.5.3 Layout of the rename buffers

The layout of the rename buffers establishes the actual framework for renaming. Its three basic components are the type and the number of the rename buffers as well as the basic mechanism which is used for accessing rename buffers, as shown in Figure 7.50.

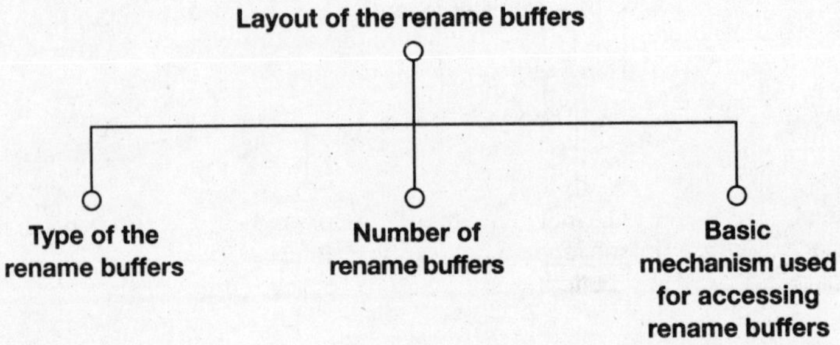

Figure 7.50 The layout of rename buffers is a crucial decision in the implementation of register renaming.

Types of rename buffers

Certainly, the chosen type of rename buffers has the largest impact on renaming. It is definitive for the basic approach of the implementation and thus it determines where the intermediate results of the instructions are to be written into or read from. Here, we designate as *intermediate* those *results* which have already been generated but are not yet qualified to modify the actual program state by writing them into the architectural registers. Intermediate results have to wait for permission to modify the actual program state until it is sure that the modification of the program state does not violate the sequential consistency of the execution, as detailed in Section 7.7.

In the following, we give an overview of the basic types of rename buffers. For simplicity, initially we will suppose a single register file for all data types processed. Then, at the end of this section we will extend our discussion to the split register scenario.

As Figure 7.51 illustrates, there are four fundamentally different ways to implement rename buffers: using a merged architectural and rename register file, employing a separate rename register file, or holding renamed values either in the ROB or in the DRIS. We note that in our discussion, we use the term **rename buffer** in a generic sense to denote any one of the implementation alternatives mentioned.

In the first approach, rename buffers are implemented along with the architectural registers in the same physical register file, called the **merged architectural and rename register file**. Here, both architectural and rename registers are dynamically allocated to particular registers of the same physical register file. The merged register file obviously has to provide a large enough number of physical registers to implement both the architectural and rename registers. For instance, the Power1 provides 40 and the R10000 64 physical registers for renaming 32 FP architectural registers.

This scheme operates in the following way. Let us assume that at a given moment the architectural registers are associated with a particular set of physical registers. Now, for each *destination register* specified in an instruction, a free physical register is allocated, if available. In this way, the architectural registers are represented by a dynamically changing set of physical registers. The actual allocation of the architectural registers to physical registers is tracked in a *mapping table*.

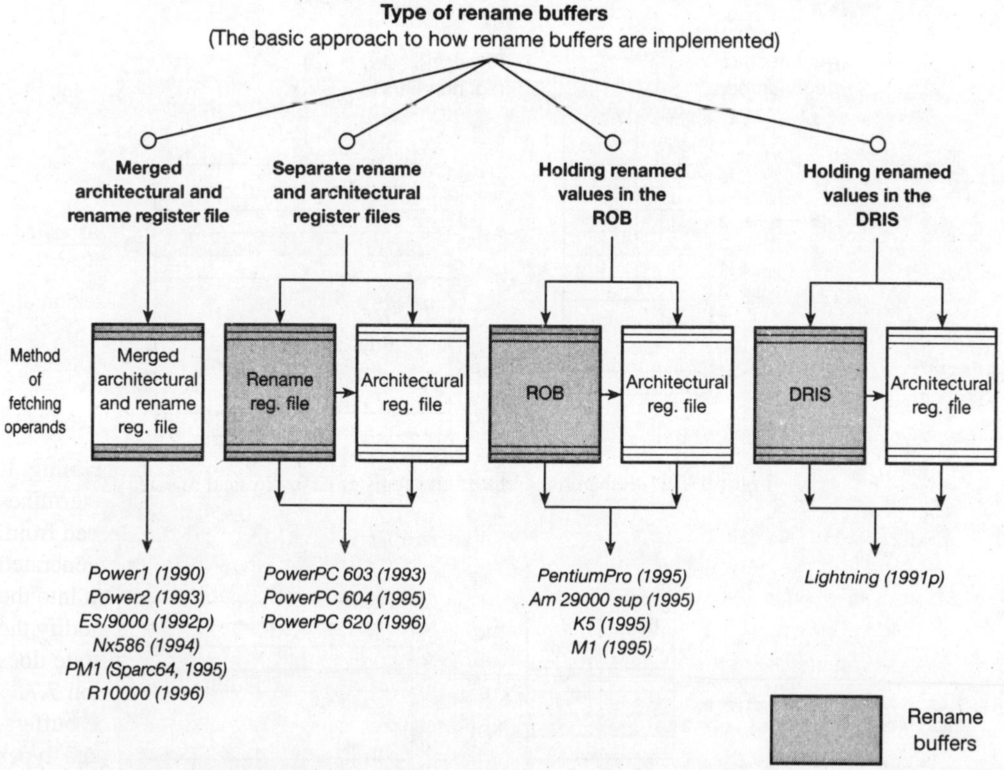

Figure 7.51 Type of rename buffers.

For instance, let us assume that the rename process allocates to the destination register of the instruction

```
ad  r2,  ...,  ...
```

that is, to r2, the physical register p3. An entry is then set up in the mapping table, as shown in Figure 7.52. The first part of the entry is the entry valid bit. If this bit indicates a valid entry the second part is interpreted as the rename buffer index (RB index), which points to the physical register used as a rename register. In our case this is p3.

After renaming we get:

```
ad  p3,  ...,  ...
```

As described before, *source operands* are renamed simply by substituting the architectural register numbers with the physical register numbers found in the corresponding RB index fields. Figure 7.53 illustrates this for the instruction:

```
ad  ..., r0, r1
```

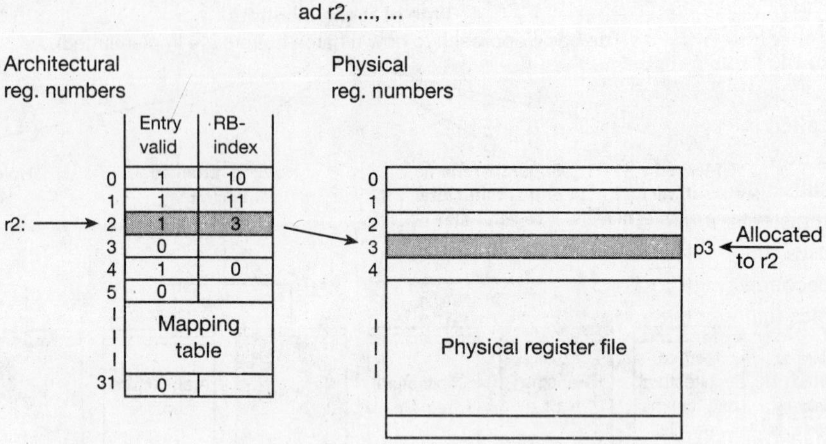

Figure 7.52 Renaming architectural register r2 to physical register p3.

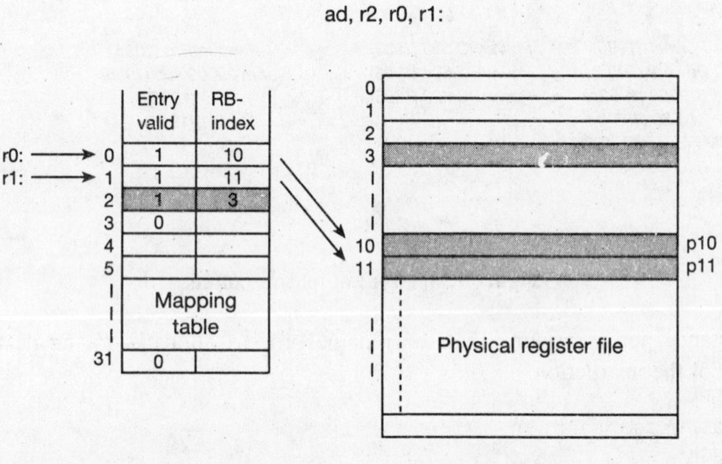

Figure 7.53 Renaming the ad …, r0, r1 instruction to ad … p10, p11.

In this way, the renaming of the instruction ad r2,r0,r1 results in

```
ad  r2, r0, r1
```

An additional scheme is required in order to *reclaim physical registers* no longer in use. In the case of a merged register file, reclaiming is a rather complex task, which we do not discuss. For a possible solution we refer to Grohoski (1990).

Renaming in this manner was first proposed by Keller (1975). Most early superscalar processors which introduced register renaming employed this scheme, including the Power1 (RS 6000), Power2, ES 9000 and Nx586. Further examples of using merged register files are the recent PM1 (Sparc64) and the R10000.

In *all other types* of renaming, rename buffers are implemented separately from the architectural registers. In these cases rename buffers are realized either as a separate rename register file, as an extension of the reorder buffer (ROB) (see Section 7.7.3) or as part of the DRIS (see Section 7.4.3). All three alternatives operate basically in the same manner, the only difference being the location of their implementation.

When rename register values are held in a separate register file, this file is called the **rename register file**. Here, each time a *destination register* is referred to, a new rename register is allocated to it. This allocation remains valid until either a subsequent instruction refers to the same destination register and the architectural register is reallocated to a different rename register or until the instruction which uses that particular destination register completes (retires) and the allocation becomes invalid. The PowerPC processors PowerPC 603–PowerPC 620 are examples that employ a rename register file.

A further possibility is to use the **reorder buffer** (ROB) to implement rename buffers. As described in Section 7.7.3, while using a ROB each issued instruction will be allocated a separate ROB entry. Thus, it is quite natural to store the generated (intermediate) result of that instruction in the same entry as well. All that is needed is to extend each ROB entry with appropriate fields. Examples of processors which use the ROB for storing intermediate results are the Am29000 superscalar, K5 and the PentiumPro.

In the final method of implementation, the **DRIS** is used in the same manner as the ROB. The Lightning made use of this alternative.

In all three cases, intermediate results are held in the respective rename buffer until their retirement. During retirement the content of the rename buffer (rename register entry, ROB entry or DRIS entry) is written back into the architectural register file. In this way, the architectural register file is updated and the rename buffer is reclaimed for further use.

Seen from another point of view, the type of rename buffer also specifies how operands have to be fetched. (See 'Basic mechanisms' below.)

For simplicity's sake in our discussion so far, we assumed that all data types are stored in the same register file. However, processors *usually* provide *distinct register files* for FX and FP data. Then there are distinct register files for FX and FP data in the case of merged or separated architectural and rename registers, as depicted for instance in Figures 7.67 and 7.69.

The situation is quite different when renaming takes place *within the ROB or the DRIS*. Since in both cases a *single mechanism* is maintained for preserving the sequential consistency of the execution, renamed FX and FP data must be held in the same place. Because of this, the ROB and the DRIS ordinarily provide fields that are long enough to hold either FX or FP data.

Number of rename buffers

Table 7.4 gives an overview of how many rename buffers are provided by recent processors. Each of the three sections of the table covers a different implementation type. In the first section we list processors that use a *merged register file* for architectural and rename registers. Of course, in these processors we find quite a large number of additional registers which can be used for renaming. The number of rename buffers ranges from 8 in the Power1, up to 32 in the R10000 and even 38 in

Table 7.4 Number of rename buffers provided.

Implementation of renaming		*Number of rename buffers*	
Processor type		FX	FP
Merged rename and arch. register file			
Power1	(1990)		8 (32 arch. + 8 rename)
Power2	(1993)	–	22 (32 arch. + 22 rename)
ES/9000	(1992p)	16 (16 arch. + 16 ren.)	12 (4 arch. + 12 rename)
PM1	(1995)	38 (78 arch. + 38 ren.)	24 (32 arch. + 24 rename)
R10000	(1996)	32 (32 arch. + 32 ren.)	32 (32 arch. + 32 rename)
Separate rename register file			
PowerPC 603	(1993)	n.a.	4
PowerPC 604	(1995)	12	8
PowerPC 620	(1996)	8	8
Renaming within the ROB			
Am29000 sup	(1995)	10	
K5	(1995)	16	
PentiumPro	(1995)	40	

the 64-bit Sparc-processor PM1 (Sparc64). Processors in the next section employ *separate rename registers* and use between 4 and 12 dedicated registers for renaming. Finally, processors that implement *renaming within the ROB* use between 10 and 40 rename buffers, the number of ROB entries provided.

We stress again that in the first two alternatives, distinct register files are typically used for the renaming of FX and FP data. In contrast, when renaming is accomplished by means of an ROB, available ROB entries are used for all types of data processed.

Basic mechanisms used for accessing rename buffers

Rename buffers need to be accessed for several purposes, such as to fetch operands, to update them or to deallocate them. Here, we deal with how operands can be accessed from rename buffers. There are two entirely different *access mechanisms* available: an *associative mechanism* and an *indexed access mechanism*, as Figure 7.54 shows.

A typical layout of the **associative access mechanism** is depicted on the left of Figure 7.54. Rename buffers with associative access hold typically three kinds of information: the destination register numbers, their values and necessary status

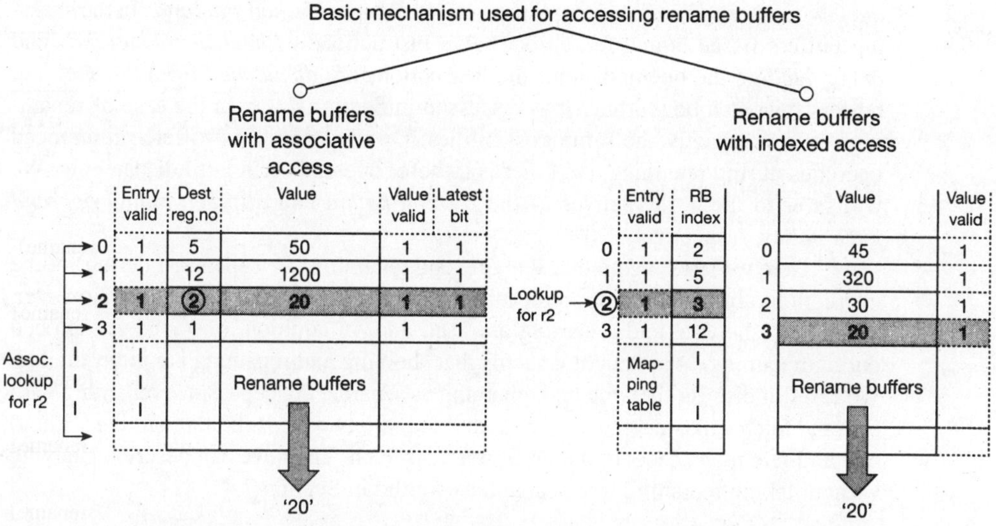

Figure 7.54 Basic mechanisms for accessing rename buffers.

information. In this scheme, when a register content is to be fetched, say that of r2, all entries are looked up *associatively* to find the particular entry whose destination register field matches r2. In the figure, this is entry no. 2. Thus, the corresponding value of '20' will be fetched.

In addition, *multiple instances of the same register* may exist; that is, two or more entries can belong to the same architectural register. Evidently, this complicates the operation considerably. How this situation can be handled is explained in the detailed renaming demonstration in Section 7.5.8.

The other, fundamentally different access mechanism is the **indexed access mechanism**. In this case a **mapping table** is used to obtain the actual *index* into the rename buffer file. On the right of Figure 7.54, the mapping table contains for register r2 the index '3'. Thus, the register value of '20' will be accessed from the corresponding entry no.3 in the rename buffer. We note that the mapping mechanism provides a unique index into the rename buffer file which always corresponds to the most recent instance (renaming) of the destination register concerned. Thus, multiple instances of the same register do not occur.

As far as operand fetching is concerned, let us take into account that a required source operand is either an intermediate result or a final result. Intermediate results are held in a rename buffer, whereas final results are stored in the architectural register file. Thus, while looking for an operand, both places have to be accessed at the same time and the access mechanism has to provide the right selection. This requires a priority access. If both the architectural and the intermediate register contents exist, then the intermediate content is delivered as the operand value.

7.5.4 Operand fetch policies

In our introduction to shelving we discussed possible operand fetch policies. As explained there, processors employ one of two possible policies: fetch operands *during instruction issue* and store instructions along *with their operands* in the shelving buffers (issue bound fetch), or shelve instructions *without their operands* and delay *fetching* the operands until the instructions are *dispatched* from the shelving buffers (dispatch bound fetch), as discussed in Section 7.4.4. In the case of renaming we have exactly the same possibilities. One possibility is to fetch referenced operands during renaming, the other is to defer operand fetch until dispatching. We will refer to these alternatives as the *rename bound* and *dispatch bound operand fetch policy*, respectively.

Here we stress again that shelving and renaming (as well as reordering) of the instructions are usually common features of recent superscalar processors. However, when both shelving and renaming are used and, in addition, operands are fetched during renaming, at first sight it seems that shelving and renaming are intermingled. We can still discuss shelving and renaming as separate concepts since renaming with operand fetch can conceptually be subdivided into two steps: first, renaming without operand fetch, and second, the usual operand fetch. Thus, we can describe shelving without taking renaming into account, as we did in Section 7.4.

7.5.5 Rename rate

The **rename rate** is the maximum number of renames per cycle that a processor is able to perform. In order to avoid bottlenecks the rename rate usually equals the issue rate. Recent processors can often issue up to four FX or FP instructions or any mix of the two. We expect these processors to rename up to four instructions in each cycle. This may require a large number of ports at register files and mapping tables. For instance, the R10000 performs renaming by using a merged file, which holds both the architectural and renamed register values. This processor fetches the operands during dispatching and accesses the merged register file via a mapping table. In order to be able to map four FX or FP instructions, the FX mapping table has 12 read ports and 4 write ports, whereas the FP table is equipped with 16 read and 4 write ports. This many ports are needed since FX instructions can refer to up to three and FP instructions up to four operands.

Another example worth looking at is the PM1, also called Sparc64. This four-way superscalar processor implements renaming in the same way as the R10000 with one difference: PM1 fetches operands during renaming. In this case, both the FX mapping table and the merged FX register file have 10 read and 4 write ports while its FP counterpart has 6 read and 3 write ports. According to Asato et al. (1995), the 14-port 116-word 64-bit merged FX register file has a remarkably high complexity of 371K transistors. In comparison, the whole Intel 8086 processor has a complexity of about 30K transistors, and even the i386 has no more than about 275 K transistors (Crawford, 1990).

7.5.6 Further issues

As we know, shelving makes it unnecessary to check for data and control dependencies as well as for busy EUs during issue. Nevertheless, during renaming we do need to *check for data dependencies among the instructions issued in the same group*. For instance, the PowerPC 620 and the R10000 check whether there are data dependencies among the four instructions issued in the same group, and if dependencies are encountered, the rename logic has to be modified accordingly. Let us consider true data dependencies (RAW dependencies) between two instructions, as in the following example:

```
mul r2, ..., ...
ad  ..., r2, ...
```

Here, the 'ad' instruction uses the result of the 'mul' instruction as a source operand. Furthermore, let us assume that the 'mul' instruction is renamed to

```
mul p12, ..., ...
```

Then, because of the true data dependency, r2 in the 'ad' instruction also has to be renamed to p12 rather than to the register number corresponding to r2 before the 'mul' instruction was renamed.

Similarly, if there are WAW dependencies among the instructions issued in the same group, as, for instance, between the instructions

```
mul r2, ..., ...
ad  r2, ..., ...,
```

special care has to be taken during renaming. This means that despite simultaneous renaming of all instructions in the same issue group in this case, different rename buffers have to be allocated to the destination registers of the 'mul' and the 'ad' instructions.

7.5.7 Most frequently used basic implementation alternatives of register renaming

In the preceding section we acquainted the reader with the design space of renaming. Here, we present the most frequently used implementation alternatives. By taking into account all four essential aspects (scope of register renaming, the layout of shelving buffers, the operand fetch policy and the rename rate) and possible alternatives for each of them, we arrive at a large number of feasible *implementation alternatives*.

In our discussion of the basic implementation alternatives we will take only two aspects, the *layout of rename buffers* and the *operand fetch policy*, into account. We ignore the scope of shelving, since recently most processors implement full shelving, and also the issue rate component, since it is only of a quantitative nature. As far as the layout of rename buffers is concerned, here we will take into account only the type of rename buffers used and their access mechanism. We ignore the number of rename buffers for obvious reasons. Thus, for the discussion of the basic implementation alternatives, we consider three aspects as vital: the type and access mechanism of rename buffers and the operand fetch policy.

Figure 7.55 depicts the corresponding *reduced design space* of renaming. Each of the leaves represents a basic implementation alternative. In this figure we also show which basic alternative is employed in relevant superscalar processors, as well as some references to when certain basic alternatives were proposed.

As Figure 7.55 shows, there are *six basic renaming alternatives* which are currently used in processors. In the following we overview these. A number of processors employ a *merged register file* for both architectural and rename registers, as was proposed by Keller a long time ago (1975). Since a merged register file requires a large number of registers, all processors which have opted for this implementation alternative use a *mapping table* for accessing the merged file. Most of them postpone operand *fetching* until *dispatching*, but the PM1 (Sparc64) *fetches operands during renaming*.

The next important alternative employs a *separate rename register file*, accesses it *associatively* and *fetches operands in connection with renaming*. The PowerPC models shown follow this method of implementation.

The *use of the ROB for renaming* seems to be an appealing alternative, since for most issued instructions both a new ROB entry and a new rename buffer have to be allocated. However, while a new ROB entry has to be allocated to each issued instruction, not every instruction has to be renamed. Renaming is needed only for instructions that write into architectural registers. Thus, when buffer space is provided along with each and every ROB entry, a part of the ROB space is wasted. This is a slight drawback of this alternative.

The principle of renaming within the ROB was first described by Smith and Pleszkun as early as 1988 and later also by Johnson (1991). Processors utilizing this alternative access the ROB *associatively*. It is worth noting here that the cited author was the principal architect of both AMD processors. Another recent processor which has chosen this implementation alternative, while accessing the ROB via a *mapping table* and *fetching operands during issue*, is the PentiumPro.

The final basic alternative implements *renaming within the DRIS*, accesses it in an *associative way* and *fetches operands during dispatching*, as proposed by Sohi and Vajapeyam (1987). This variation was selected for renaming by the architects of the Lightning processor, which never reached the market. Probably the high complexity requirement of its implementation turned out to be prohibitive for manufacturing at that time.

7.5.8 Detailed example of renaming

Next we describe in depth how renaming is accomplished in one of the basic alternatives, which features a *separate rename register file* with an *associative access* and *operand fetching during renaming*. Processors employing this basic alternative are the PowerPC 603–PowerPC 620.

In this demonstration we show how the following short instruction sequence

```
mul  r2, r0, r1
ad   r3, r1, r2
sub  r2, r0, r1
```

is renamed.

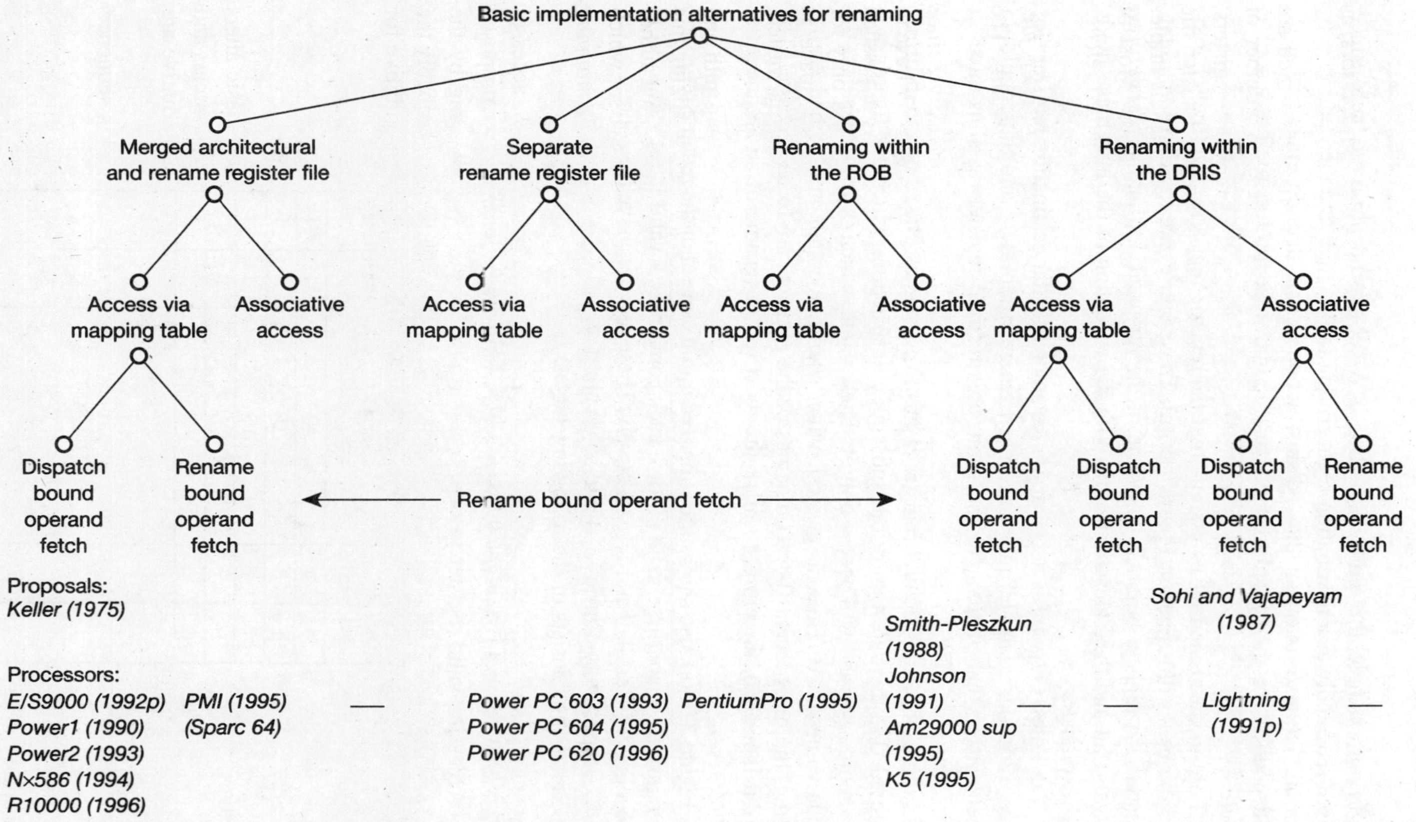

Figure 7.55 Basic implementation alternatives for register renaming.

In our example, the 'mul' instruction is WAW-dependent on the 'sub', since r2 is used repeatedly as a destination register, first in the 'mul' and then in the 'sub' instruction. We also note that the 'ad' instruction is true data-dependent, that is, RAW-dependent, on the preceding 'mul' instruction, since it refers to r2 as a source operand.

For our discussion let us assume that the rename registers have five characteristic entries, as illustrated in Figure 7.56(a). These entries are the Entry valid bit, the Destination register number, the Value of the renamed destination register, the Value valid bit and the Latest entry bit. With the exception of the last, these fields are self-explanatory.

The Latest entry bit is necessary since any particular destination register (for instance, r2 in our example) may have been renamed repeately and thus, multiple rename registers may belong to the same architectural register, as illustrated in Figure 7.56(b).

In this case, architectural register r1 has two renames. Based on the information provided in the Latest entry bit, subsequent instructions which ask for register r1 as a source operand will access only its latest value, which is 15, rather than the previous value of 10. Thus, in general, when source operands are fetched during renaming, the most recent (latest) renames of the registers are to be accessed. The Latest bit is needed, therefore, to mark the most recent rename of an architectural register.

Figure 7.56(a) also shows the supposed initial content of the rename registers. In the figure there are three valid entries, each containing a valid latest value of the architectural registers 4, 0 and 1, respectively. These registers have the content of 40, 0 and 10, respectively. Entries 3, 4 and so on are free.

Renaming consists of the following subtasks:

- Allocation of a free rename register to a destination register.
- Accessing valid register values.

	Entry valid	Dest reg.no.	Value	Value valid	Latest bit
0	1	4	40	1	1
1	1	0	0	1	1
2	1	1	10	1	1
3	0				
4	0				
⋮	⋮		Rename registers		

Figure 7.56(a) Structure of the rename buffers and their supposed initial contents.

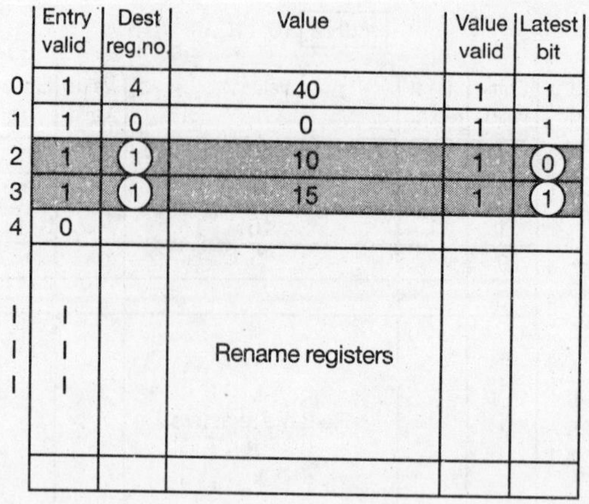

Figure 7.56(b) Multiple subsequent renames belonging to the same architectural register (r1).

- Accessing a register value that is not yet available
- Reallocation of a destination register
- Updating a particular rename buffer with a computed result
- Deallocation of a rename buffer that is no longer needed.

In our demonstration example we assume that the given instructions are renamed one after the other. Obviously, superscalar processors perform multiple renames per cycle, as discussed in Section 7.5.3. Nevertheless, for better understanding we describe renaming of the example instructions as if it were performed in sequence.

Allocation of a free rename buffer to a destination register

Each time an instruction is issued which references a destination register, a new rename register needs to be allocated to the destination register concerned. This allocation is performed by looking for and reserving a free entry, and properly initializing its fields. Usually, rename registers are handled as circular buffers. Then a head pointer designates the first free entry and a tail pointer indicates, say, the last one (see the top part of Figure 7.56(c)).

When a new entry is required, the entry indicated by the Head pointer (in our case entry 3) is selected for use and the pointer is stepped. If an entry is no longer needed, this entry is deallocated by updating the Tail pointer.

During allocation of a new rename register, the following updates have to be accomplished: setting the Entry valid and Latest entry bits, copying the destination register number into the corresponding field and resetting the Value valid bit. Figure 7.56(c) demonstrates this in connection with the renaming of the destination register of the 'mul' instruction (r2). The upper part of this figure displays the initial content of the rename registers in accordance with Figure 7.56(a).

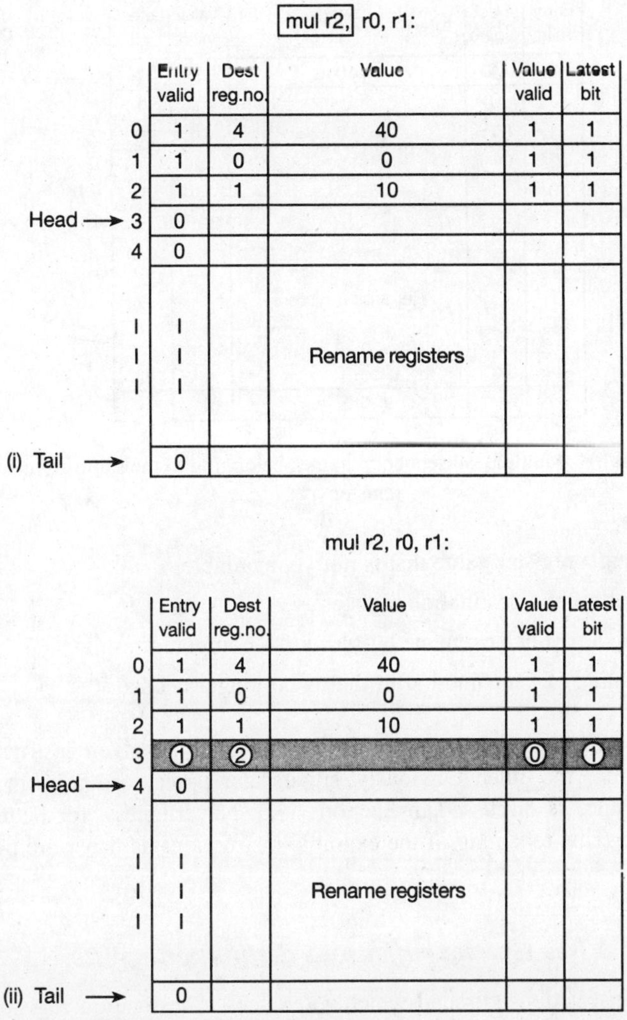

Figure 7.56(c) Allocation of a new rename buffer to destination register r2. (i) Supposed initial content of the rename buffers before renaming of the destination register of the 'mul' instruction; (ii) content of the rename buffers after renaming the destination register of the 'mul' instruction.

The lower part of the figure shows what happens after allocation. As depicted, the next free entry, that is, entry no. 3, will be allocated to register 2 and the status fields of the allocated entry are initialized as discussed before. Here, we note that for simplification in the subsequent figures, we do not indicate the Head and Tail pointers.

Accessing valid register values

Let us now consider how valid operand values are fetched from the rename buffers. This is the case when, in our example, the source operands of the 'mul' instruction,

r0 and r1, are fetched. Remember here that, in the basic variant considered, rename registers are accessed associatively. So for accessing a referenced operand value, all rename registers have to be looked up associatively for the latest value of the specified register number, that is, for r0 and r1 (see Figure 7.56(d)). If there is a matching entry and in this entry both the Value valid and the Latest bits are set, the latest valid register value has been found. It is then fetched and appropriately marked as valid, as illustrated in Figure 7.56(d), for the referenced registers r0 and r1.

Of course, both renaming of the destination register and fetching the specified source operands are accomplished in the same cycle.

Accessing a register value that is not yet available

When an accessed register value is not valid, since it has not yet been computed, the register value cannot yet be fetched. Instead, the entry identifier is fetched with an appropriate marking.

Figure 7.56(e) demonstrates this by showing what happens when the second instruction

```
ad  r3, r1, r2
```

is renamed.

The first subtask is to allocate a new rename register to r3; this is entry no. 4. This allocation is done in the same way as described earlier. In addition, the contents of r1 and r2 are to be fetched. Since the latest rename of r1 holds a valid value, it can be fetched, as discussed before. However, r2 has not yet been computed. Therefore, in place of the requested value, the index of the associated rename buffer (which in our example is 3) is forwarded to the reservation station, as illustrated.

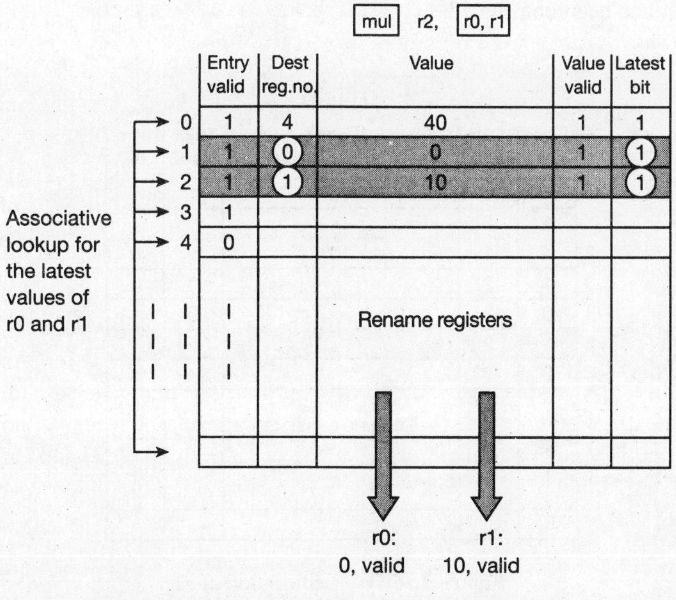

Figure 7.56(d) Accessing available register values.

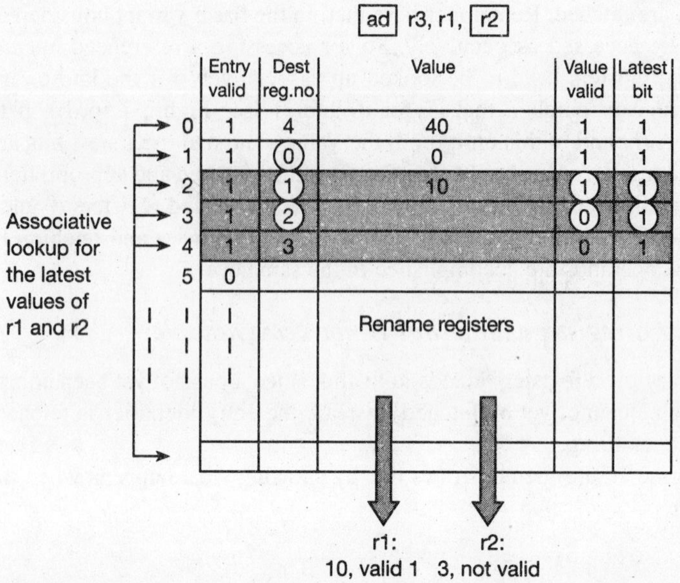

Figure 7.56(e) Accessing a register value that is not yet available.

Reallocation of a destination register

Obviously, during program execution the same architectural register may be used repeatedly to hold results. Therefore, it can happen that multiple valid rename entries belong to the same register. For instance, in Figure 7.56(f) we show what happens when the next instruction, that is, the 'sub' instruction, is issued before the 'mul' instruction has been completed.

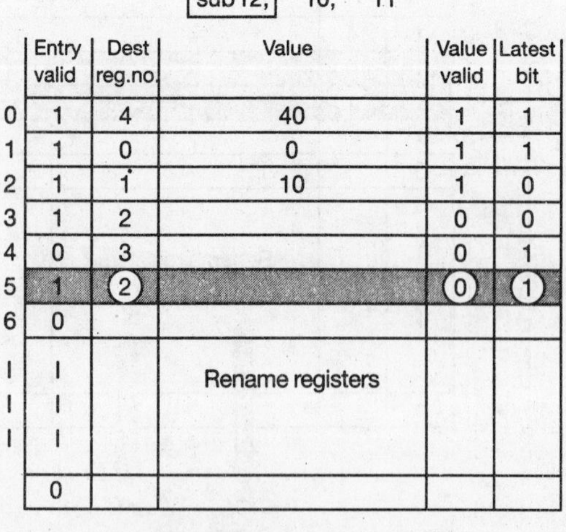

Figure 7.56(f) Reallocation of r2.

As the figure demonstrates, in this case a second entry has to be allocated to register r2. For this reason a new free entry is selected (entry no. 5) and the corresponding Value valid and Latest bits are set appropriately. At the same time, the latest bit of the previous r2 entry (entry no. 3) has to be reset. Thus, from now on all subsequently issued instructions will access the latest r2 value from entry no. 5 instead of the previous one. This remains true until a subsequent instruction is issued whose destination register is again r2. Then a new rename becomes the latest one and so on. We note that, in our example, resetting the Latest bit of the previously allocated rename register requires an associative search for the latest r2 allocation.

Updating a particular rename buffer with a computed result

If an instruction is finished, the destination register concerned has to be updated, so that subsequently issued instructions will be able to access the generated result. Updating is based on the result identifier, which is supposedly the index of the rename register which is allocated to the destination register in question.

In our example, let us assume that the 'mul' instruction has been finished. Then the result (0) is governed by the identifier 3, which means that the result has to be written into rename register 3 (Figure 7.56(g)).

Entry no. 3 can be directly accessed and updated. Then the Value valid bit is set. This indicates that the value of register 2 has become available. Here we note that this value is not the latest one and it is no longer needed in the rename register file. Nevertheless, it can be needed to update failing operand values in the reservation station.

Deallocation of a rename buffer that is no longer needed

The final logical step in the renaming process is the deallocation of an entry that is no longer needed, as demonstrated in Figure 7.56(h). Deallocation is usually

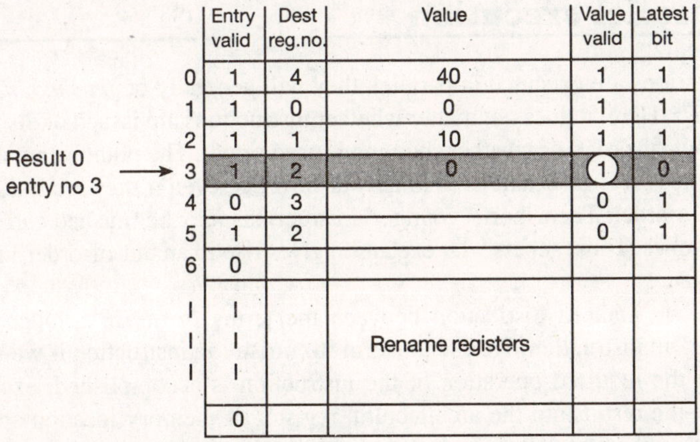

Figure 7.56(g) Updating the rename buffers of register 2 with the result, 0.

Deallocation of entry no. 0 → 0

	Entry valid	Dest reg.no.	Value	Value valid	Latest bit
0	(0)	4	40	1	1
1	1	0	0	1	1
2	1	1	10	1	1
3	0			0	0
4	0	3		0	1
5	1	2		0	1
6	0				
⋮	⋮		Rename registers		
	0				

Figure 7.56(h) Deallocation of the rename buffer no.3.

performed in conjunction with the ROB, as detailed in Section 7.7.3. The ROB assures sequentially consistent program execution through allowing instructions to retire only in strict program sequence. When an instruction retires, the corresponding rename buffer entry can be deallocated. This is carried out by assuming that the index of a no longer needed rename buffer entry is provided by the ROB.

In our example, let us assume that the instruction whose result is in entry 0 retires. Thus, the ROB requests the deallocation of the associated rename register. Deallocation is accomplished simply by resetting the corresponding Entry valid bit, as Figure 7.56(h) demonstrates. Thus, this entry again becomes available for allocation. At the same time the tail pointer is stepped by 1 to point to the last free entry in the rename register file. Here we note that the ROB retires instructions in strict program order, so deallocation will be accomplished in the sequence of increasing indices.

7.6 Parallel execution

When instructions are executed in parallel, they will generally be *finished in out-of-program order*. Here, it does not matter whether instructions are issued or dispatched in-order or out-of-order, or whether shelving is used or not. The point is that unequal execution times force instructions to finish out-of-order, even if they are issued (and dispatched) in-order. Then short, 'younger' instructions may be finished earlier than long, 'older' ones. Thus, superscalar execution gives rise to an out-of-order finishing of instructions.

Here, we make a distinction between the terms *'to finish'*, *'to complete'* and *'to retire'* an instruction. We use the term **'to finish'** an instruction if we want to indicate that the required operation of the instruction is accomplished, except for writing back the result into the architectural register or memory location specified and/or updating the status bits. In contrast, we employ the term **'to complete'** an instruction if we want to refer to the last action of instruction execution, which is writing back the result into the referenced architectural register. Finally, in connection with the ROB, instead of the term 'to complete' we say **'to retire'** since in this case two tasks have to be performed, to write back the result and to delete the completed instruction from the last ROB entry. Nevertheless, we use both terms interchangeably. We note furthermore that there is no generally accepted use of these terms and the terminology differs from processor to processor. Thus, care must be taken in the interpretation of the literature.

Under special conditions, instructions *finishing out-of-order* can be *avoided* in spite of multiple EUs. The conditions are as follows: instructions must be issued in-order and all EUs operating in parallel must have equal execution times. These conditions may be fullfilled by using a *dual pipeline* and *lock-stepping* them, that is, lengthening the shorter pipeline by introducing unused extra cycles ('bubbles') into it, as described in Section 5.3.2. Evidently, these prerequisites are overly restrictive and impede performance. Therefore, there are only a few superscalar processors which avoid out-of-order completion in this way. Examples are the MC 68060 and the Pentium, both of which employ lock-stepped dual pipelines.

7.7 Preserving sequential consistency of instruction execution

7.7.1 Sequential consistency models

As discussed above, in superscalar processors, or in a more general sense in processors with multiple EUs operating in parallel, instructions *finish* in general in an *out-of-order fashion*. Nevertheless, overall instruction execution should mimic sequential execution, that is, it should preserve *sequential consistency*. Although, as stated before, the problem of preserving sequential consistency relates to a broader class of processors than superscalar ones, for the sake of consistency with the recent chapter, in the following we confine our discussion to superscalar processors.

Sequential consistency of instruction execution relates to two aspects: first, to the *order in which instructions are completed*; and second, to *the order in which memory is accessed* due to load and store instructions or memory references of other instructions, as indicated in Figure 7.57.

Concerning the first aspect we are interested in whether instructions in a superscalar processor complete in the same order as in a sequential processor. Here, we use the term *'complete'* as explained in the previous section. We use the term **processor consistency** to indicate the *consistency of instruction completion with sequential instruction execution.*

As far as processor consistency is concerned, superscalar processors preserve either a *weak* or a *strong consistency*. A **weak processor consistency** means that instructions *may complete out-of-order*, provided that *no data dependencies are sacrified*. In this case, instructions may be reordered by the processor only if no dependencies are violated. In order to achieve this, data dependencies have to be

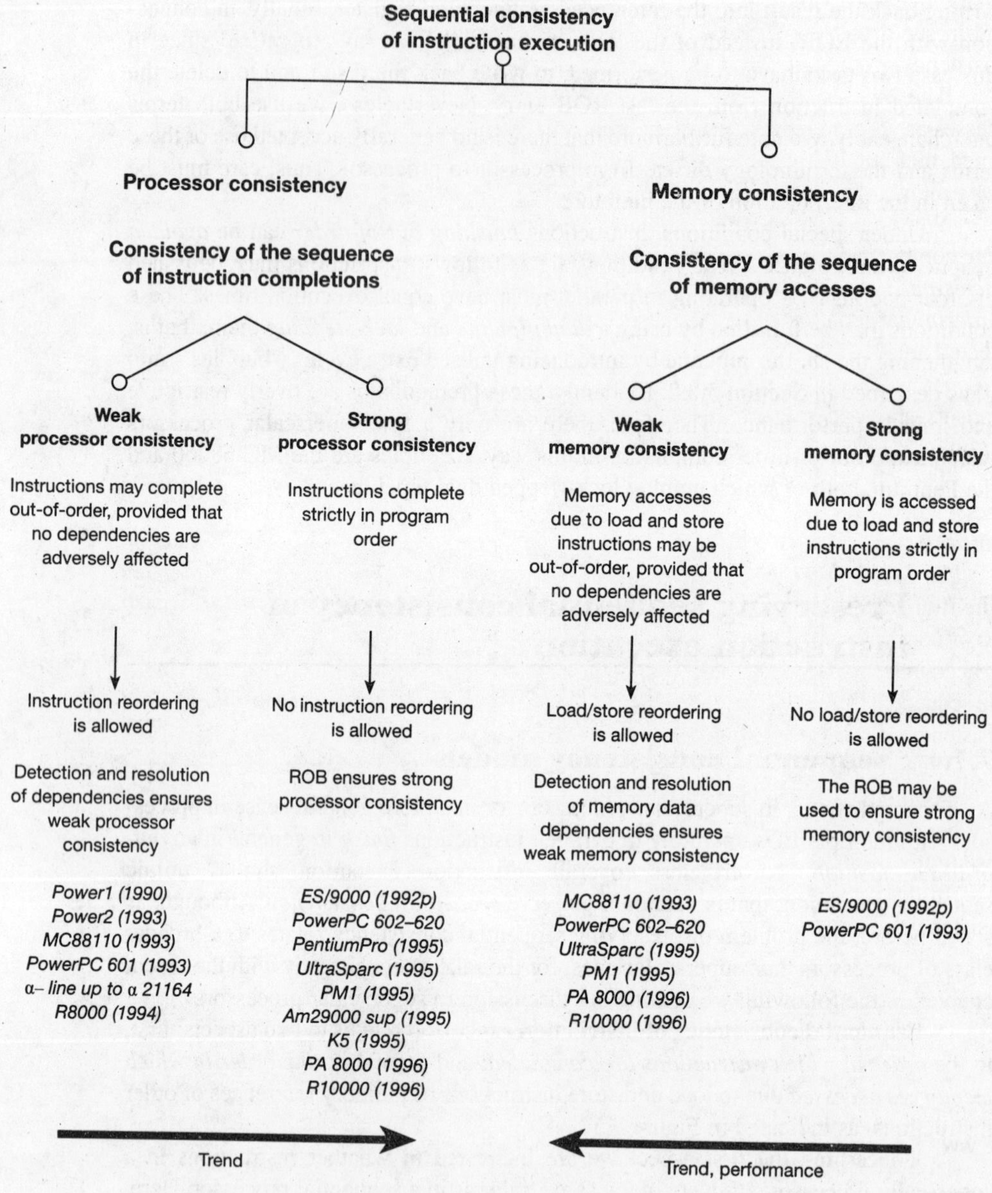

Figure 7.57 Interpretation of the concept of sequential consistency of instruction execution.

detected and appropriately resolved during superscalar execution. Early superscalar processors usually provided a weak processor consistency, as indicated in Figure 7.57.

In the case of **strong processor consistency**, instructions are forced to *complete in strict program order*. Usually, this is achieved by employing a reorder buffer (ROB). The ROB is a very practical tool as it can also be used to implement renaming and shelving as well, as emphasized earlier, and ROBs are now widely used in superscalar processors. Most recent processors guarantee strong processor consistency, since it is easy to implement.

The other aspect of superscalar instruction execution is whether memory accesses are performed in the same order as in a sequential processor. This aspect is termed **memory consistency**. Here again, we can distinguish between *weak* and *strong* memory consistency.

We say that **memory consistency is weak** if *memory accesses may be out of order* compared with a strict sequential program execution. However, *data dependencies must not be violated.* In other words, weak consistency allows *load/store reordering* provided that dependencies, particularly memory data dependencies, are detected and resolved.

As we shall discuss in thc following section, weak memory consistency is a means to increase processor performance, so most up-to-date superscalar processors rcly on it.

The other alternative is **strong memory consistency**, in which *memory accesses* occur *strictly in program order*. Strong memory consistency forbids any load/store reordering.

So far, we have discussed processor and memory consistency separately. The **sequential consistency model of a processor** integrates both aspects. It specifies the kind of consistency maintained *by the processor* and *by the memory*. Thus, by taking into account both aspects of processor and memory consistency, we arrive at four possible sequential consistency models (Figure 7.58). These are the **WW**, **WS**, **SW** and **SS** consistency models, where the first character refers to the type of the processor consistency (**W**eak/**S**trong) and the second the type of memory consistency (**W**eak/**S**trong).

As indicated earlier, *strong processor consistency* and *weak memory consistency* have advantages. Consequently, recent processors tend to maintain the **SW consistency model**.

In the following section we will discuss some aspects of the weak memory consistency model.

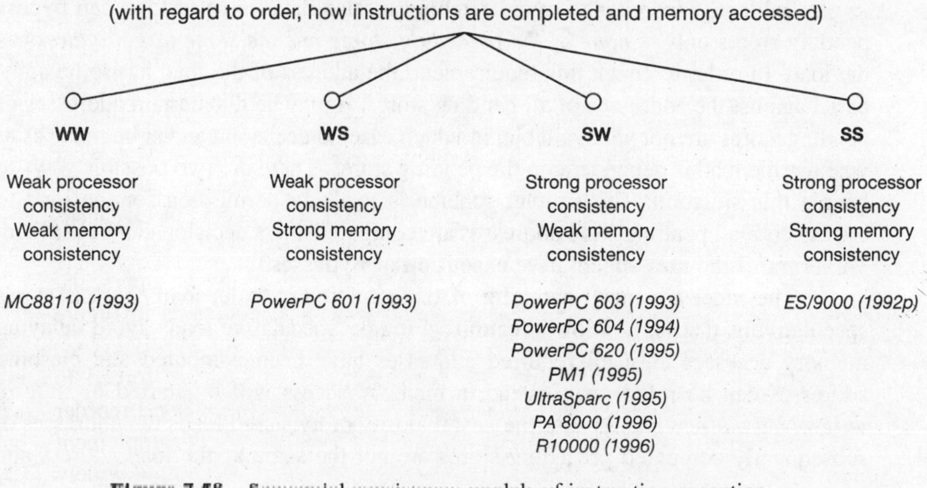

Figure 7.58 Sequential consistency models of instruction execution.

7.7.2 Load/store reordering

Load and store instructions involve actions affecting both the processor and the memory. While executing, both loads and stores must first wait for their addresses to be computed by an ALU or address unit. Then, loads can access the data cache to fetch the requested memory data which is then made available in a register. This is when a load instruction is said to be finished. The load is then completed usually by writing the fetched data into the specified architectural register.

Stores have a different execution pattern. After receiving their generated addresses, stores have to wait for their operands to be available. Unlike other instructions, a store is considered to be finished when operands become available. Now, let us assume an ROB is in use. When the ROB indicates that the store comes next in sequential execution, the memory address and data to be stored are forwarded to the cache and a cache store operation is initiated.

A processor that supports *weak memory consistency* allows the reordering of memory accesses. This is advantageous for at least three reasons:

- it permits load/store bypassing,
- it makes speculative loads or stores feasible, and
- it allows cache misses to be hidden.

Below we discuss these points on the basis of Figure 7.59.

Load/store bypassing means that either loads can bypass pending stores or vice versa, provided that no memory data dependencies are violated. As Figure 7.59 indicates, a number of recent processors allow loads to bypass stores (either non-speculatively or speculatively, as will be explained later) but not vice versa.

Permitting loads to bypass stores has the advantage of allowing the runtime overlapping of tight loops. The overlapping is achieved by allowing loads at the beginning of an iteration to access memory without having to wait until stores at the end of the previous iteration are completed. Notice that this runtime overlapping of cycles is comparable with software pipelining (see Section 9.3.3).

Evidently, in order to avoid fetching a false data value, a load can bypass pending stores only if *none of the preceding stores has the same target address* as the load. In order to check this requirement, the address of the load has to be compared against the addresses of all pending stores. It may be that certain addresses of pending stores are not yet available, in which case no decision can yet be made as to whether the load is dependent on the pending stores. There are two possible ways to handle this situation. The simpler scheme is to delay permission for the load to bypass until all pending store addresses are computed and a decision can be reached. We term this the **non-speculative execution of bypasses**.

The more advanced handling of this situation is to let loads bypass stores speculatively, that is, to allow **speculative loads**. Speculative loads avoid delaying memory accesses until all required addresses have been computed and clashing addresses can be ruled out. Instead, a memory access will be started *in spite of unresolved address checks*. For the vast majority of bypassed loads the addresses of subsequently computed preceding stores are not the same as the load address and

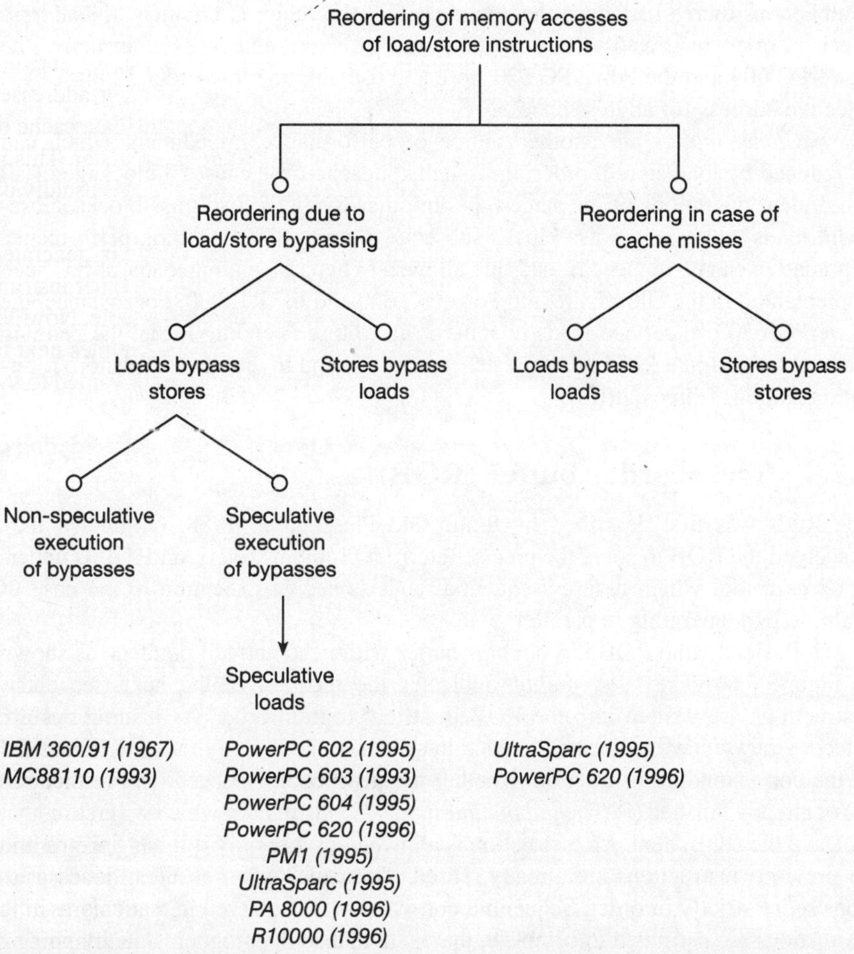

Figure 7.59 Reordering of memory accesses of load/store instructions.

this speculative behaviour is justified. The correctness of speculative loads must be checked in any case and if necessary the speculative load must be undone. This is performed as follows. When store addresses have been computed, they are compared against the addresses of all younger loads. If a hit is found, the corresponding speculative load has fetched an incorrect data value. At this point the load instruction and all subsequent instructions are cancelled and the load is re-executed.

We note that speculative loads are quite similar to speculative branches. Speculative branches (see Section 8.4.4) react in exactly the same way to unresolved condition checks as speculative loads do to unresolved dependency checks. A number of recent processors allow speculative execution of loads, as indicated in Figure 7.59.

The address checks are usually carried out by writing the computed target addresses of loads and stores into the ROB (or DRIS) and performing the address comparisons there. To reduce the complexity of the required circuitry, the address check is often restricted to a part of the full effective address. For instance, the PowerPC 604 and the PowerPC 620 store and use only the low-order 12 bits of the effective address for address checks.

Cache misses are another source of performance impediment which can be reduced by load/store reordering. Usually, a cache miss causes a blockage of all subsequent operations of the same type. In other words, a load miss blocks subsequent loads and a store miss blocks subsequent stores. The resulting performance degradation can be reduced if loads are allowed to bypass pending loads, as has been implemented in the UltraSparc, the PowerPC 620 and the R10000. For instance, the PowerPC 620 can service loads in spite of up to three pending loads; the pending loads are stored in a Load miss register (one entry) and in the three load/store reservation stations (three entries).

7.7.3 The reorder buffer (ROB)

The ROB was first described by Smith and Pleszkun in 1988. Originally, they conceived the ROB to solve the precise interrupt problem. Today, an **ROB** is understood as a tool which assures sequential consistency of execution in the case of multiple EUs operating in parallel.

Basically, the ROB is a *circular buffer* with head and tail pointers, as shown in Figure 7.60. The *head pointer* indicates the location of the next free entry. Instructions are written into the ROB in strict program order. As instructions are issued, a new entry is allocated to each in sequence. Each entry indicates the status of the corresponding instruction: whether the instruction is issued (i), in execution (x) or already finished (f). The *tail pointer* marks the instruction which will retire, that is, leave the ROB, next. An instruction is allowed to retire only if it has finished and all previous instructions are already retired. This mechanism ensures that instructions retire strictly in order. Sequential consistency is preserved in that only retiring instructions are permitted to complete, that is, to update the program state by writing their result into the referenced architectural register(s) or memory.

Here, we note that an ROB can effectively *support both speculative execution* and *interrupt handling*.

As we know, in *speculative execution* the processor carries on executing instructions in spite of an unresolved condition such as an unresolved conditional branch or memory address check. Later, when the condition is resolved, it becomes clear whether the speculatively executed instructions can be affirmed; if not, they have to be cancelled and the correct instructions executed. An ROB easily supports speculative execution. Each ROB entry is extended to include a speculative status field, indicating whether the corresponding instruction has been executed speculatively. In addition, finished instructions may not retire until they are in the speculative state. The whole operation is then as follows. Speculatively executed instructions are marked as such and are not eligible for retirement. Later, when the related condition is resolved, speculative execution is either affirmed or not. For affirmed instructions, in-order completion is maintained as described before. If the speculative execution turns out to be incorrect, the corresponding instructions which

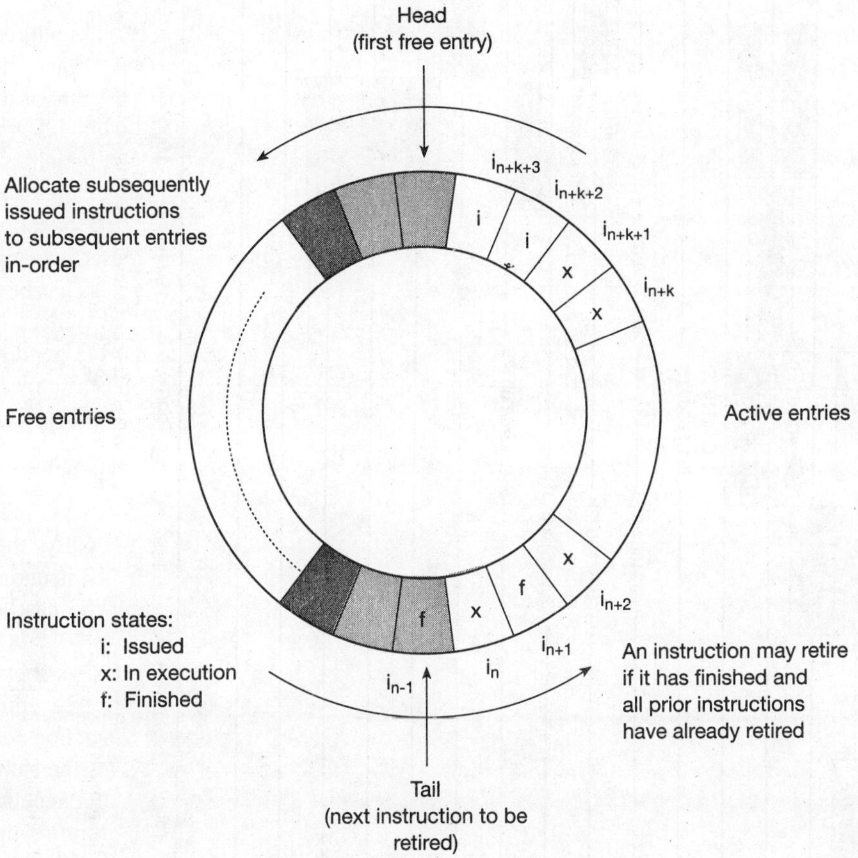

Figure 7.60 Principle of the ROB.

are marked as being speculative have to be cancelled and instruction execution continued with the correct instructions.

An ROB also *assists interrupt handling* in a natural way. Interrupts generated in connection with instruction execution can easily be made precise (that is, handled at the correct point in the execution), by accepting interrupt requests only when the related instruction becomes the next to retire, as discussed in the next section.

ROBs were introduced primarily in connection with shelving and register renaming. Figure 7.61 shows the introduction of ROBs compared with the introduction of renaming. It can easily be seen that, with a few exceptions, renaming and ROBs (and shelving) appeared at the same time in superscalar processors.

Next, we will discuss the *design space of ROBs*. Here, we are concerned with their *basic layout*, the ROB size and retire rate, as shown in Figure 7.62.

Before discussing possible basic layouts of ROBs we introduce the term **'reordering of instructions'**. We use this term to designate the basic function of an ROB, that is, to provide strict in-order instruction completion by reordering out-of-order finished instructions.

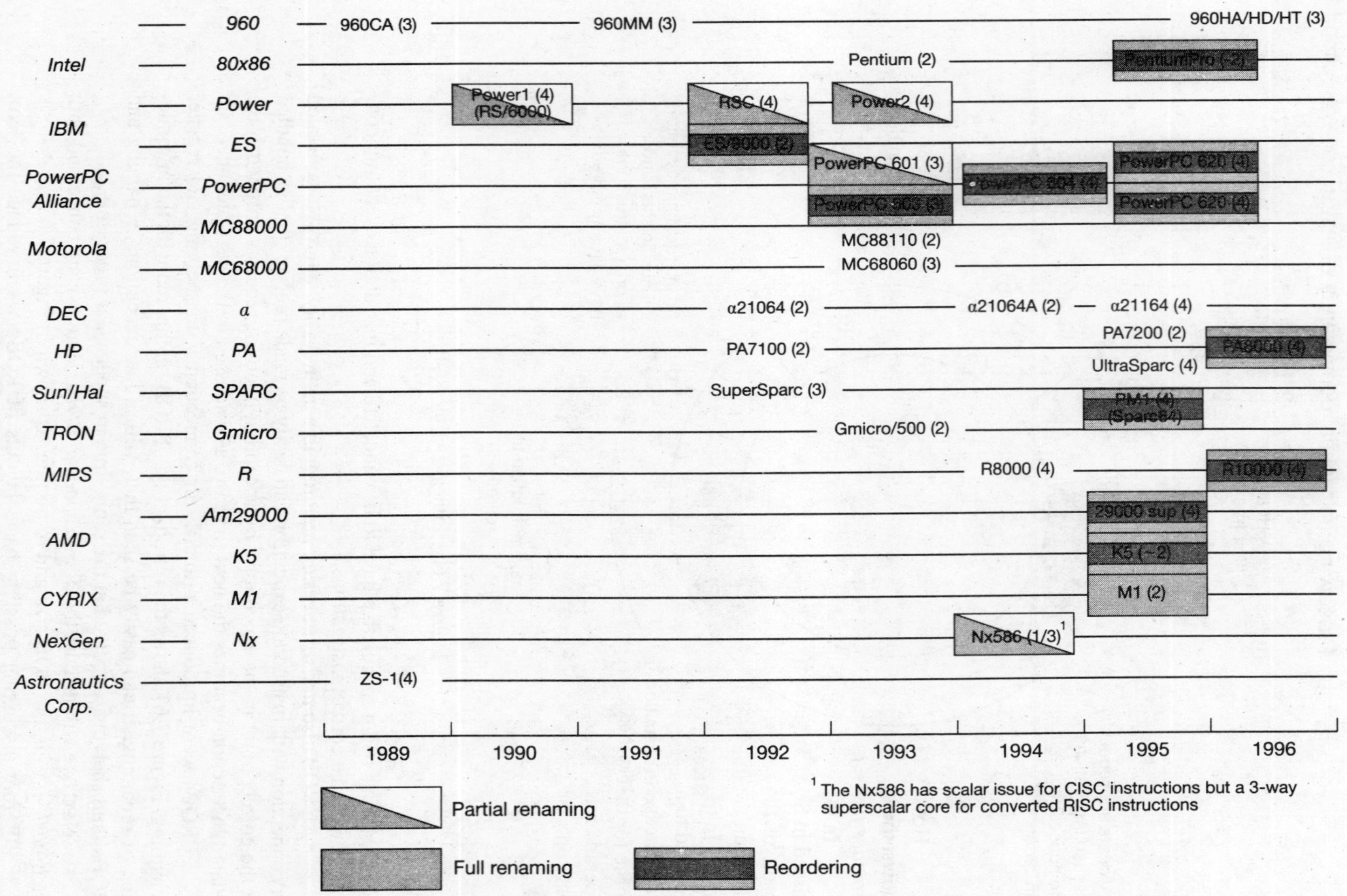

Figure 7.61 Introduction of ROBs in commercial superscalar processors.

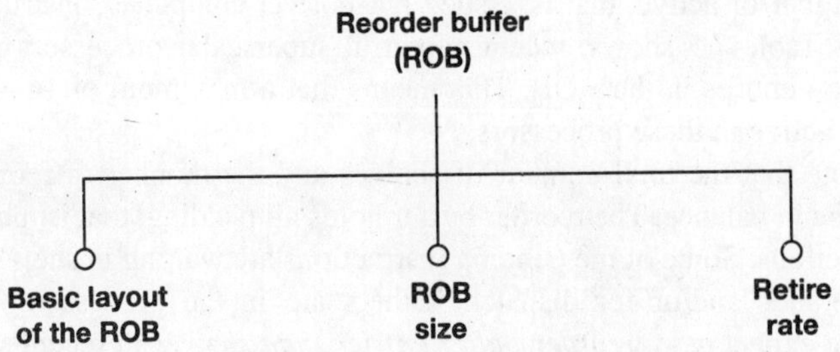

Figure 7.62 Design space of ROBs.

However, as mentioned before, ROBs are more versatile. As Figure 7.63 shows, they can be employed in three different ways. In the simplest layout, an ROB *provides just reordering*, as discussed earlier.

In the next layout, an ROB is *used for both reordering and renaming*, as discussed in Section 7.5. In this case, each ROB entry has to provide space to hold the result of the corresponding instruction as well. Here, we note that in Smith and Pleszkun's original proposal (1988) the ROB also contained the instruction results.

In the third alternative, *the ROB is used for shelving as well*, and is frequently referred to as the DRIS (Deferred scheduling, Register renaming Instruction Shelf). In this case, the ROB also has to provide space for shelving, which means either space for the source register numbers or space for source operands, depending on the operand fetch policy. Although the DRIS is an attractive construct, it is a fairly complex one. So far, the DRIS has only been proposed for one processor, the Lightning. We recall that this ambitious processor never reached the market.

We will briefly discuss two further aspects of the design space. In particular, we are concerned with two implementation details, the *ROB size* and the *retire rate*. The **ROB size** determines the number of entries in an ROB. This parameter

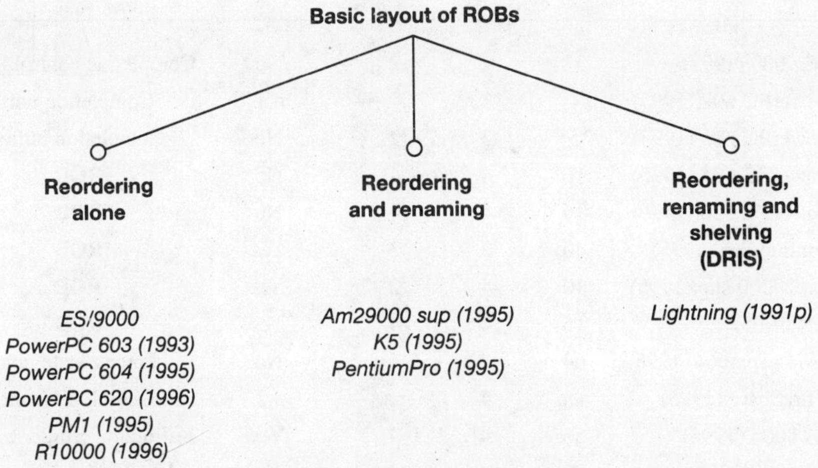

Figure 7.63 Basic layout of ROBs.

limits the number of active, that is, issued but not yet completed, instructions in a processor. As Table 7.5 shows, recent powerful superscalar processors provide as many as 16–64 entries in the ROB. This means that a maximum of 16–64 instructions may be active in these processors.

We note that the total number of shelves and the number of reorder buffer entries must be in balance. The reorder buffer holds all pending, that is, not yet completed, instructions. Some of the pending instructions are waiting in shelving buffers for their operands and/or for dispatch. Others are in the process of execution. Therefore, we expect *more reorder buffer entries than shelves* in recent superscalar processors. As the data in Table 7.6 demonstrates, this is true for most processors listed. Exceptions are the Nx586 and the R10000, where more shelves than reorder buffer entries are available.

The **retire rate** specifies the maximum number of instructions that can be completed by the ROB in each cycle. This value indicates the maximum throughput of the processor.

As far as the *maximum throughput* is concerned, typically, the processor may be considered as consisting of a number of sequentially linked subsystems, which are decoupled from each other by some kind of buffers. These subsystems are: fetch, issue, dispatch (if applicable), execute and retire (or completion). The maximum throughput of the processor as a whole is determined by the 'weakest' subsystem. In a good design, the throughput of all sequentially linked subsystems is balanced. This means that the fetch width, the maximum issue rate, the maximum dispatch rate (if applicable) and the maximum retire rate should be more or less the same. For fine-tuning of these parameters, extensive simulations are needed using benchmark programs.

Table 7.5 ROB implementation details.

	ROB size	*Issue rate*	*Retire rate*	*Intermediate results stored*	*Designation*
ES/9000 (1992p)	32	2	2	No	Completion control logic
PowerPC 602 (1995)	4	2	1	n.a.	Completion unit
PowerPC 603 (1993)	5	3	2	No	Completion buffer
PowerPC 604 (1995)	16	4	4	No	ROB
PowerPC 620 (1996)	16	4	4	No	ROB
PentiumPro (1995)	40	3	3	Yes	ROB
Am29000 sup (1995)	10	4	2	Yes	ROB
K5 (1995)	16	4	4	Yes	ROB
PM1 (Sparc64, 1995)	64	4	4	No	Precise state unit
UltraSparc (1995)	n.a.	4	n.a.	n.a.	Completion unit
PA 8000 (1996)	56	4	4	Yes	Instruction reorder buffer
R10000 (1996)	32	4	4	No	Active list

Table 7.6 Comparison of available shelves and reorder buffer (ROB) entries in recent superscalar processors.

Processor	*Total number of shelves*	*Number of ROB entries*
PowerPC 603 (1993)	3	5
PowerPC 604 (1995)	12	16
PowerPC 620 (1996)	15	16
Nx586 (1994)	42	14
K5 (1995)	14	16
PM1 (Sparc64) (1995)	36	64
PentiumPro (1995)	20	40
R10000 (1996)	48	32

With reference to Table 7.5, let us compare the retire rates and issue rates of the processors. What we see is that with a few exceptions (Am29000 superscalar, PowerPC 603) the retire rate equals the issue rate, which is quite natural.

Finally, we discuss whether intermediate results are stored in the ROB. The definitive aspect is whether the ROB supports renaming. If it does, intermediate results have to be stored there. If not, there is no need to hold intermediate results in the ROB.

We note that the reorder unit has different names in different processors. The most frequently used designation is the reorder buffer. Other terms used are the completion unit (PowerPC 602, UltraSparc), completion buffer (PowerPC 603), completion control logic (ES/9000), active list (R10000) and precise state unit (PM1).

7.8 Preserving the sequential consistency of exception processing

When instructions are executed in parallel, *interrupt requests*, which are caused by exceptions arising in instruction execution, are also generated *out-of-order*. If these requests are acted upon immediately, interrupts occur out-of-order, that is, in a different order than in a sequentially operating processor. In this situation we say that the *sequential consistency of the interrupts is weak*, or in other words that we have to deal with **imprecise interrupts**, as shown in Figure 7.64.

When an imprecise interrupt occurs, the processor is unable to reconstruct the correct state unless appropriate additional mechanisms are employed. For instance, let us assume that the processor executes two subsequent instructions in parallel, an 'older' division (div) and a 'younger' addition (ad). It can happen that the 'younger' 'ad' finishes first and updates the processor state. If subsequently the 'older' 'div'

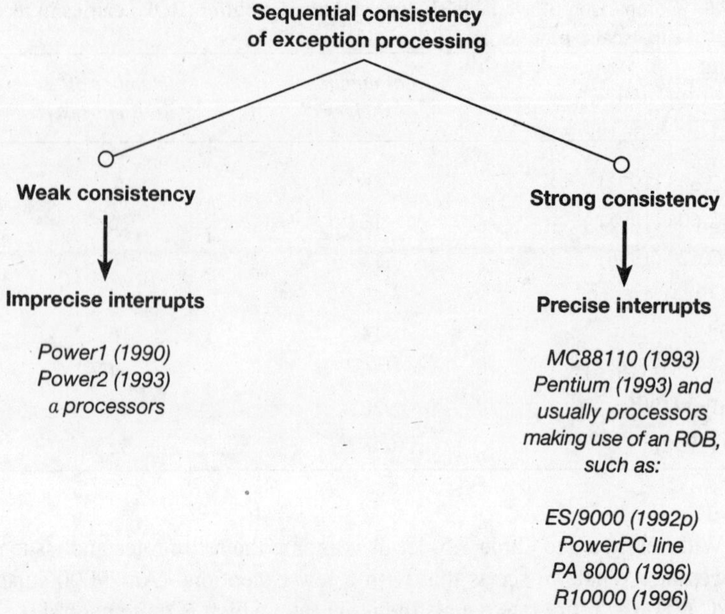

Figure 7.64 Sequential consistency of exception processing.

instruction causes an interrupt, for example because of an overflow, at the time when the interrupt request of the 'div' is accepted the processor state is already 'corrupted' by the result of a later instruction. Thus, without any additional measures, it becomes impossible to reconstruct the correct state of the processor at the time when it accepted the interrupt request caused by the 'div' instruction. In a number of ILP-processors, including early superscalar processors, interrupts can be imprecise, such as in the Power2 or R8000. In both these processors, the FP interrupts are imprecise. A further example is the α architecture, where all arithmetic exceptions are imprecise.

Most advanced superscalar processors maintain *strong sequential consistency with respect to exception processing*, so that after interrupts the state of the processor remains consistent with the state a sequential processor would have. An obvious way to achieve **precise interrupts** is to maintain in-order instruction completion, for instance by using an ROB, and to accept interrupts caused by an instruction only when the related instruction retires. A few earlier and most recent superscalar processors offer precise interrupts, as indicated in Figure 7.64.

7.9 Implementation of superscalar CISC processors using a superscalar RISC core

A trend has become evident in the implementation of superscalar CISC processors. An increasing number of recent CISC processors utilize a *superscalar RISC core*.

Examples are the Nx586, K5 and the PentiumPro. In these ×86 compatible processors, the CISC instructions are first converted into RISC-like instructions during decoding. The RISC-like instructions are then executed using a superscalar RISC core, as outlined in Figure 7.65.

The RISC-like instructions, referred to subsequently as *RISC operations*, are of the load/store type. Thus, many simple CISC instructions are converted directly to a single RISC operation, such as all register-to-register ALU instructions, loads and stores. In contrast, ALU instructions referring to memory operands generate two or more RISC operations. For instance, the x86 (CISC) instruction

```
SUB   EAX, [EDI];
```

which subtracts the content of the memory location [EDI] from the content of the register EAX, would be translated into the following two RISC-like operations:

```
MOV   EBX, [EDI];
SUB   EAX, EBX;
```

Here, the first RISC-like instruction loads EBX with the referenced memory operand. Then the subsequent register–register instruction performs the required substraction.

More complex CISC instructions, such as string or transcendental ones, will be converted into long sequences of RISC operations. However, the frequency of

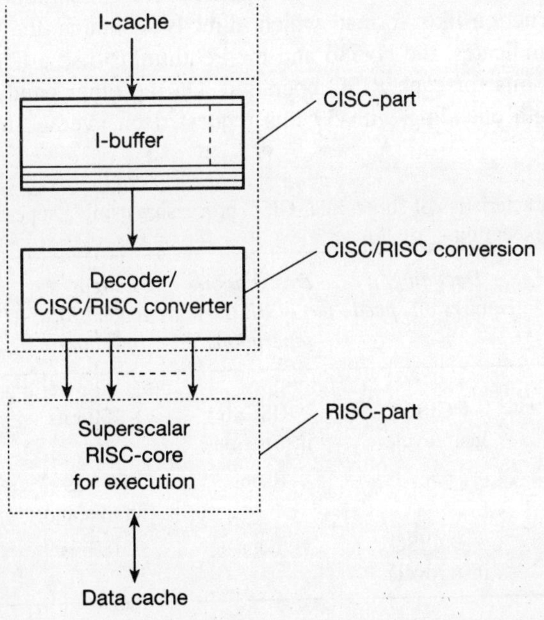

Figure 7.65 The principle of superscalar CISC execution using a superscalar RISC core.

such complex instructions is quite small. On average, one CISC instruction generates 1.5–2 RISC operations (Gwennap, 1995).

Some characteristics of superscalar CISC processors using a superscalar RISC core for execution is summarized in Table 7.7.

The processors listed convert 1–3 CISC instructions per cycle. The Nx586 translates only a single CISC instruction in each cycle while the PentiumPro can handle up to three. Actually, the PentiumPro has three instruction decoders (Figure 7.66). The general decoder can translate any CISC instruction which will be converted into not more than four RISC operations, called *uops*. For more complex CISC instructions needing more than four uops, such as string or transcendental instructions, an uop-sequencer takes over the task of uop-generation. This sequencer, which is in essence a ROM, is capable of generating up to four uops in each cycle.

In the PentiumPro simple decoders are restricted to decoding straightforward CISC instructions like register-to-register ALU instructions. Such instructions can be converted into a single uop. Decoding/conversion is done in program order. Thus, if a simple decoder cannot manage to convert the subsequent instruction, decoding will be blocked. As a result, the PentiumPro decodes and converts more than one CISC instruction in a cycle only when the second (and the third) CISC instruction is a simple one.

In the superscalar CISC processors mentioned above, the RISC operations are designated differently. In the PentiumPro they are called uops, whereas in the Nx586 terminology they are labelled RISC86 instructions; the K5 literature refers to them as R-ops.

We point out that the internal encoding of the RISC operations requires much longer words than those used for traditional RISC instructions. This is due to the microinstruction-like format which directly contains the referenced data. As Table 7.7 indicates, the Nx586 and the PentiumPro use a fixed format requiring about 100 bits for each RISC operation. On the other hand, the K5 employs a variable-length encoding with 59 bits requested on average for a single RISC operation.

Table 7.7 Characteristics of superscalar CISC processors using a superscalar RISC core for execution.

Processor	*Decoding/ conversion speed*	*Designation of RISC-operations*	*Length of encoded RISC-operations*	*Maximum issue-rate of RISC-operations*
Nx586[1] (1994)	1 CISC instr./cycle	RISC86 instructions	~ 100 bits	3–4
K5 (1995)	n.a.	R-ops	59 bits (on average)	4
PentiumPro (1995)	1–3 CISC instr./cycle	uops	118 bits	3

[1]The Nx586 is actually a scalar processor from the point of view of CISC instructions. However, it is a superscalar processor with respect to the RISC operations.

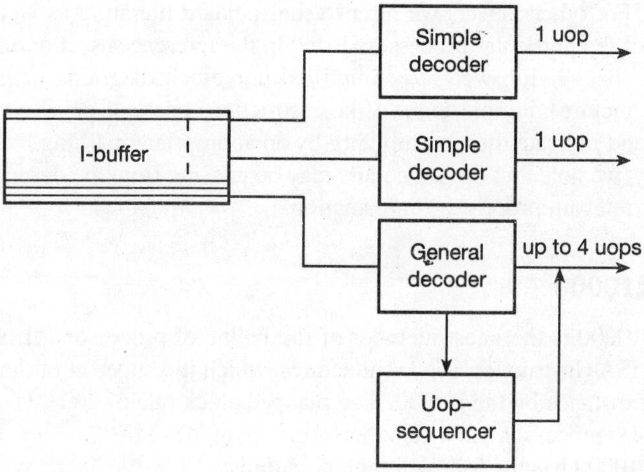

Figure 7.66 Decoding/converting CISC instructions to RISC operations, called uops, in the PentiumPro (Gwennap, 1995).

We conclude our description of superscalar CISC processors with a RISC core by discussing the *maximum issue rate* for the RISC operations (see Table 7.7). The Nx586 and the K5 are capable of issuing four RISC operations per cycle, while the PentiumPro can handle only three. We note, however, that the Nx586 is restricted to converting at most one single CISC instruction/cycle. Thus, the Nx586 is a scalar processor from the point of view of CISC execution, and a superscalar one if we consider the RISC core. In contrast, the K5 and the PentiumPro are roughly dual-issue superscalar CISC processors.

7.10 Case studies of superscalar processors

In this section we describe a number of the latest superscalar processors which use shelving and renaming. We present the microarchitecture and describe the operation of the following processors:

- the *R10000,*
- the *PowerPC 620*, and
- the *PentiumPro.*

In order to facilitate understanding and cross-comparisons, we have followed essentially the same format in our discussion of each.

Our description focuses on the crucial points of up-to-date superscalar operation, that is, on *instruction* issue, *renaming, shelving, dispatching and reordering.* Aspects such as cache and memory implementation, load/store and branch operations and exception handling are omitted. With regard to branch processing, we refer to Chapter 8. For other aspects we refer to the standard literature as well as to the publications of the particular processors listed in the references section for Part II.

For further clarity, we have simplified our block diagrams in places. For example, we picture multiple buses (like instruction, operand or result buses) as single buses and indicate their multiplicity by an appropriate marking.

Finally, we note that certain details may be missing from the descriptions due to the lack of relevant proprietary information.

7.10.1 R10000

The MIPS R10000 is the latest member of the R line of processors. It implements the MIPS IV ISA (Instruction Set Architecture), which is a superset of the MIPS III, supported for instance by the R8000. At a planned clock rate of 200 MHz, this four-way superscalar processor has a peak performance of 800 MIPS.

The R10000 has the following main features:

- It is a four-way superscalar processor with a maximum dispatch rate of five.
- It uses predecoding.
- It has three group reservation stations.
- Operands are fetched in connection with instruction dispatch.
- Renaming is implemented using a merged architectural and rename register file.
- Sequential consistency is preserved by means of an ROB.

We describe the core part of the microarchitecture of the R10000 with reference to Figures 7.67 and 7.68.

As shown in Figure 7.67, the R10000 execution core consists of the following main units: decode/issue unit, FX and FP register mapping tables, three group reservation stations, merged FX and FP register files, seven EUs and the ROB. The EUs are as follows: three FX units and four FP units. The FX units are the IU1, IU2 and the AU. Both IU1 and IU2 can perform a wide range of simple arithmetic and logical instructions. In addition, IU2 can carry out integer multiply and divide operations. The address unit (AU) is an address adder for generating addresses. The available FP units are dedicated to FP addition (FADD), multiplication (FMUL), division (FDIV) and square root calculation (FSQRT).

The R10000 has a short five-stage pipeline for FX operations, consisting of the Fetch, Decode, Dispatch, Execute and Writeback cycles, as depicted in Figure 7.68. This figure also indicates the layout of the load/store and FP pipelines, which are not discussed here.

The R10000 employs predecoding in order to shorten the critical decode/issue/rename path. In each cycle four predecoded instructions are fetched from the I-cache (Fetch cycle). Subsequently, all four instructions are decoded, issued and renamed in the next cycle (Decode cycle). Both decoding and issue are carried out in program order. Decoded register numbers of issued instructions are renamed. Renaming is carried out using separate merged register files and mapping tables for

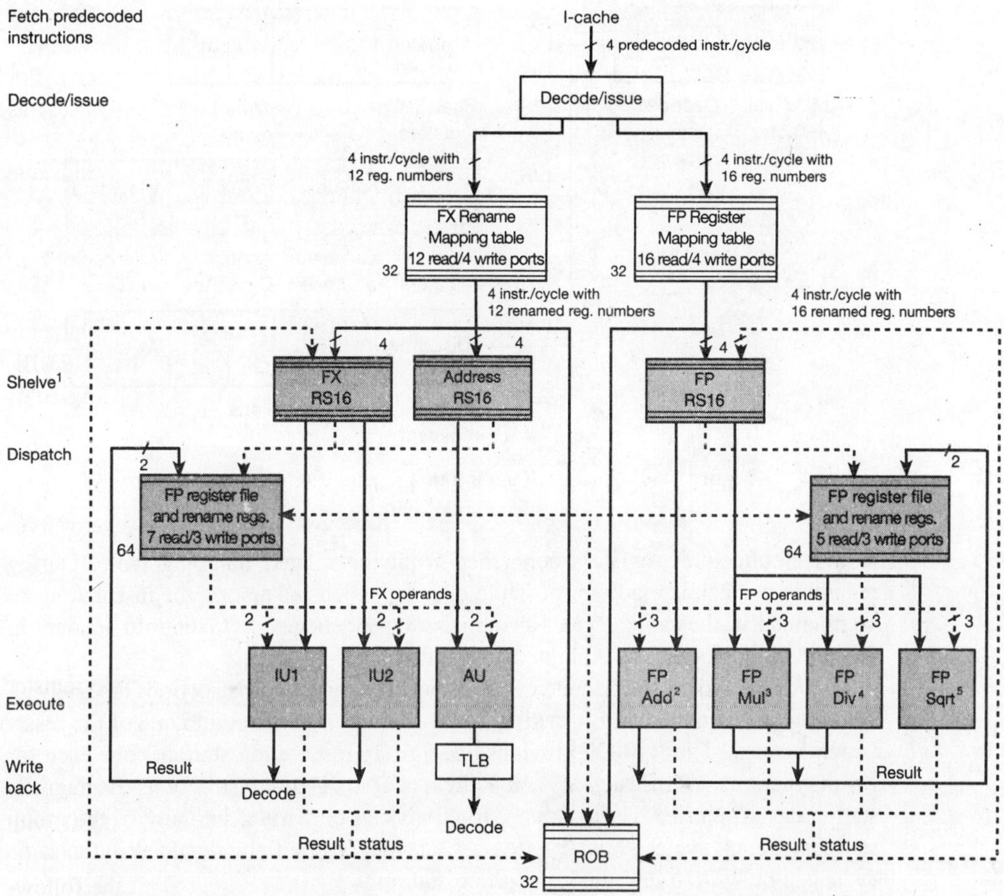

¹In-order dispatch for the AU and FPU, out-of-order dispatch for the others
²FADD
³FMUL
⁴FDIV
⁵FSQRT

AU: Address unit
IU: Integer unit
ROB: Reorder buffer
RS: Reservation station
TLB: Translation-Look-Aside buffer

Figure 7.67 Core part of the microarchitecture of the R10000.

FX and FP instructions. Each mapping table has 32 entries and enough read and write ports to rename up to four instructions of the same type in each cycle. Actually, the FX mapping table provides 12 read and 4 write ports while the FP table has 16 read and 4 write ports. Thus, FX instructions may have up to three and FP instructions at most four operands.

Destination and source register numbers are renamed quite differently. During renaming, each destination register is allocated a new physical register out of the 64 physical registers available in each of the merged FX and FP register files, provided that a free register is at hand. In addition, each table is updated with the newly established mappings of up to four destination registers. Source registers are renamed simply by reading the actual physical register numbers, which are allocated

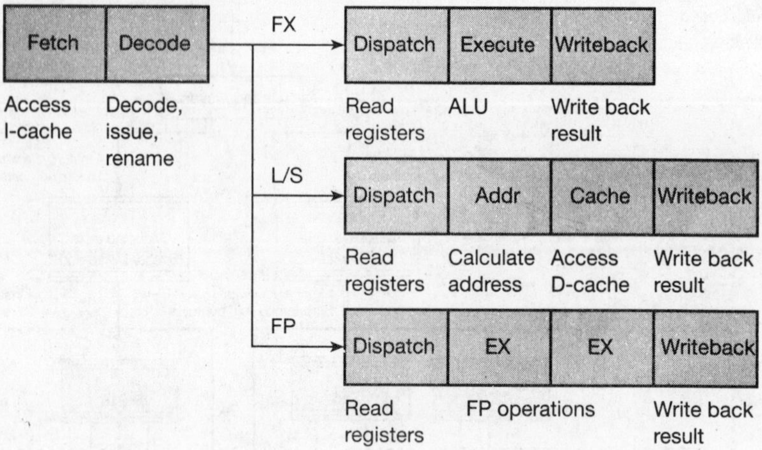

Figure 7.68 Layout of the R10000 pipelines (Gwennap, 1994b).

to the architectural registers concerned from the related mapping table. During renaming a check is made for possible data dependencies among the instructions to be renamed in the same cycle. Recognized dependencies are taken into account in the renaming process, as explained in Section 7.5.6.

At the end of the Decode cycle, issued and renamed instructions are shelved. Shelving is accomplished by writing each renamed instruction into one of the reservation stations. The R10000 provides three group reservation stations, one each for FX instructions, FP instructions and addresses of load/store instructions. Each group station has 16 entries. Up to four instructions can be written into any of the group stations in each cycle. Thus, if necessary, all four instructions renamed in the same cycle can be written into the same group station.

Next, we describe how shelved instructions are dispatched from the group reservation stations. Since the R10000 employs both register renaming and speculative branch processing, only true data dependencies can prevent instructions becoming eligible for dispatching. In other words, dispatching is dataflow-based. Later in this section we return to the question of how availability of the operands is checked in the reservation stations.

Instructions are dispatched from each reservation station in an out-of-order fashion. In this way, older instructions that are not yet ready do not block the dispatching of younger instructions that are ready for execution. In most cases EUs can accept a new instruction in each cycle. Exceptions are the IU2 while performing an FX multiplication or division and the FP units FMUL, FDIV and FSQRT. For illustration, we summarize in Table 7.8 the latency and repeat rate values of the R10000 instructions (Heinnich, 1994).

When dispatching instructions out-of-order, priority rules are needed to break the tie if multiple instructions are ready for execution in the same cycle. As usual, the R10000 gives priority to non-speculative instructions over speculative ones and to older instructions over younger ones. The FX and FP reservation stations can select up to two instructions per cycle, whereas the address reservation station is

Table 7.8 Instruction latencies and throughput values of the R10000. © 1996 MIPS Technologies, Inc.

Instruction		*Latency cycles*	*Repetition rate cycles*
Simple integer and logical instructions		1	1
Load/store integer data		2	1
Load/store FP data		3	1
Integer multiply	32 bit	5/6	6
	64 bit	9/10	10
FP multiply		2	1
Integer divide	32 bit	34/35	35
	64 bit	66/67	67
FP divide	32 bit	12	14
	64 bit	19	21
FP square root	32 bit	18	20
	64 bit	33	35

confined to choosing only one instruction per cycle, as indicated in Figure 7.67. Thus, at most five instructions can be dispatched in every cycle.

Dispatched instructions are forwarded to the corresponding EUs while the operands needed are picked up from the register files. The merged FX register file has seven read ports for simultaneous delivery of two operands for each of three FX instructions and one data value for the cache. The merged FP register file has five read ports to provide two FP instructions with two operands each and to supply one FP data value to the cache. We note that Figure 7.67 shows only the execution engine and does not indicate data paths to and from the cache.

The results are forwarded to the related register files. Two write ports are available for updating each of the merged files with the computed destination register values. Results are accompanied by tags identifying the physical register into which the result is to be written. We note that each physical register contains a 'register value valid' bit (usually called the scoreboard bit). When a new physical register is allocated to an architectural destination register, the 'register value valid' bit of that physical register is reset. Later, when the result has been forwarded, this bit is set to '1', indicating the availability of the corresponding register value. The reservation stations keep track of the availability of the source operands needed based on the 'register value valid' bits.

The R10000 preserves a strong sequential consistency by using an ROB. The ROB holds 32 consecutive active instructions. During issue, up to four instructions are written into the ROB in each cycle in program order. After finishing, they will retire in program order, again up to four instructions in each cycle. However, not more than one store can be retired per cycle due to data path constraints. In order to keep track of instruction execution the ROB gets 'finished' status reports from the

EUs. Furthermore, the ROB is responsible for indicating which FX and FP physical registers can be reclaimed following the retirement of instructions.

7.10.2 The PowerPC 620

The PowerPC 620 is the highest performance model of the PowerPC line. Its microarchitecture is based on the PowerPC 604 which is shown in Figure 7.42, but incorporates certain extensions for achieving greater performance. With its initial clock rate of 133 MHz, the PowerPC 620 offers a peak FX performance rate of 530 MIPS.

The main features of the PowerPC 620 are:

- It is a four-way superscalar processor.
- It employs individual reservation stations.
- Renaming is implemented by separate architectural and rename register files.
- Sequential consistency is maintained using a reorder buffer.

As shown in Figure 7.69, the PowerPC 620 has six EUs capable of parallel operation. These units are as follows: a branch processing unit (BPU), two simple integer units (IU1 and IU2) performing one-cycle integer and logical operations, a single multi-cycle integer unit (MIU) performing mainly integer multiplications and divisions, a load/store unit (L/SU) and an FP unit (FPU).

The PowerPC 620 employs individual reservation stations with two to four buffers. Two buffers are available in the integer and FP units, whereas the L/SU has three entries and the BPU four. We note that the existence of four entries in the BPU reservation station allows speculative execution of up to four unresolved conditional branch instructions.

Renaming is carried out by means of separate architectural registers and rename registers. The PowerPC 620 utilizes eight FX and eight FP rename registers. Sequential consistency of the execution is preserved by a 16-entry reorder buffer (ROB).

The PowerPC 620 has basically a five-stage pipeline, as indicated in Figure 7.70. The processor operates in the following way. Predecoded instructions are fetched in the Fetch cycle from the I-cache into an 8-entry I-buffer, four at a time. In the Issue cycle the processor decodes and issues up to four instructions per cycle into the six individual reservation stations present. Instructions are issued in-order and aligned. However, there are four issue constraints that need to be mentioned:

- Not more than one instruction can be written into a particular reservation station per issue.
- Instructions requiring two FX source operands can only be issued from the first half of the lower four entries of the I-buffer.
- Each instruction to be issued requires a free entry in the ROB.
- If the instruction produces a result value, register renaming must be performed, which requires a free rename register entry.

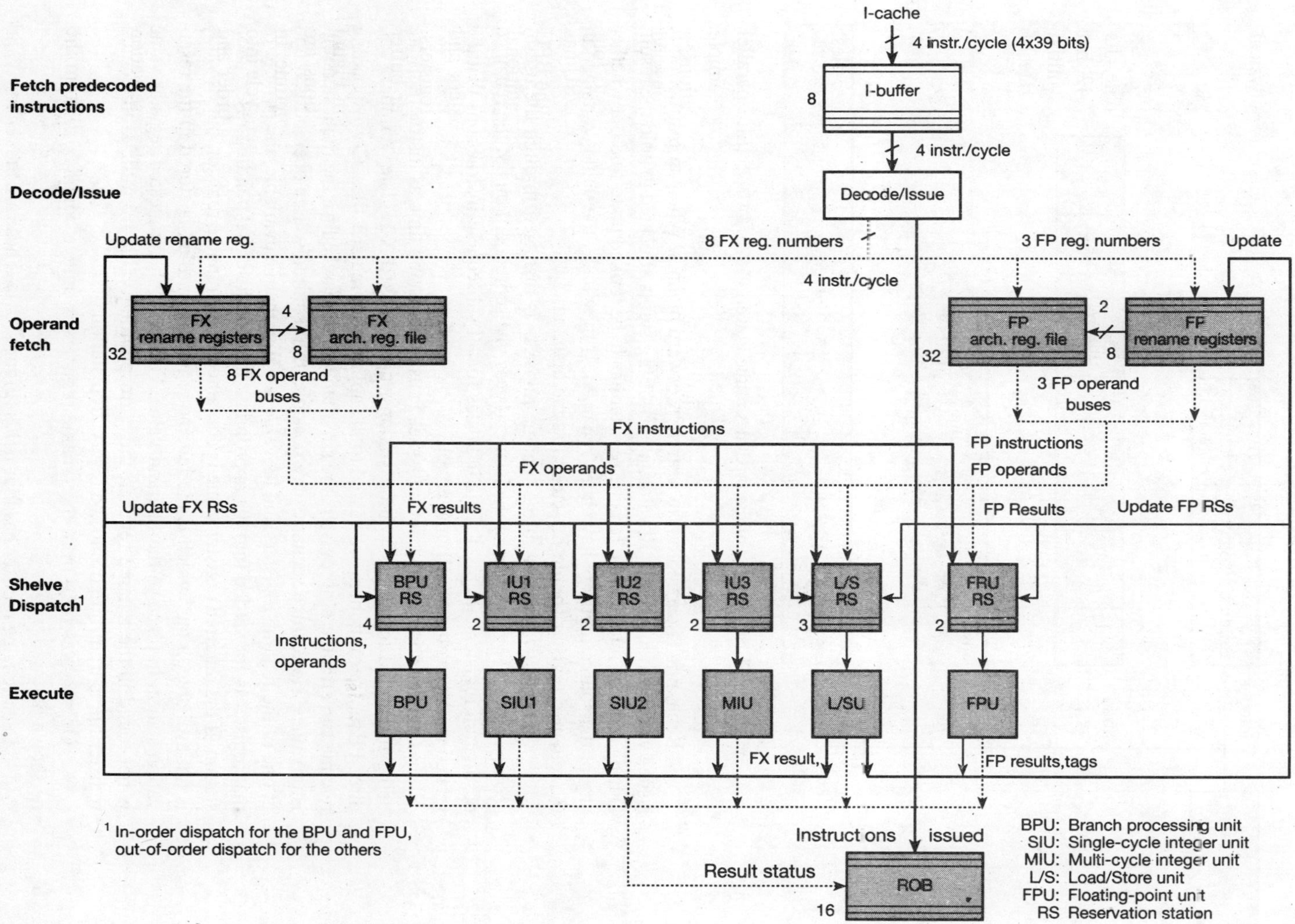

Figure 7.69 Core part of the microarchitecture of the PowerPC 620.

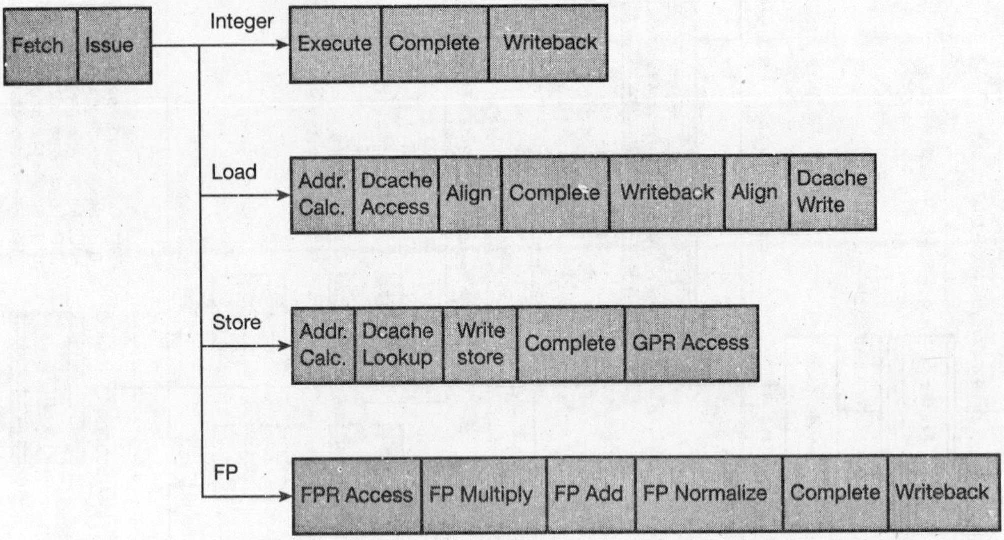

Figure 7.70 Layout of the pipelines of the PowerPC 620. © 1995 IEEE

Renaming is carried out in a straightforward manner. When an instruction is issued which produces a result value, a rename register is allocated to hold the result. During operand fetching the rename register has to be looked up to find out whether any of the source registers have been renamed. If they have, the value contained in the renamed register should be fetched as the operand.

Operand availability in the rename registers is managed through the use of scoreboarding. Thus, as part of the issue process, the scoreboard bits of the renamed destination registers are reset. This indicates for all subsequent instructions that the related register value is still unavailable.

Operands are fetched during issue. Thus, at the same time as instructions are being forwarded to the reservation stations, up to eight FX register numbers and three FP register numbers are passed to the appropriate register files. Corresponding rename and architectural registers are simultaneously searched for the requested register values. Here, three scenarios are possible. If a required source operand is found in one of the rename registers and its value is valid, that is, available, the content of that register is forwarded into the appropriate field of the corresponding reservation station. If the required register value is contained in the rename register, but its value is not available, a tag, which is the rename register identifier, is stored in the reservation station in place of the operand value. Finally, if the requested register value is not found in the rename register, the corresponding value from the architectural register file is transmitted into the reservation station.

Operand fetching from the rename registers is quite a complex task, as will be shown below.

Each rename register has four fields (Figure 7.71). These are the rename valid bit, the register number to which this rename register is allocated, the result value, if available, and the result valid bit.

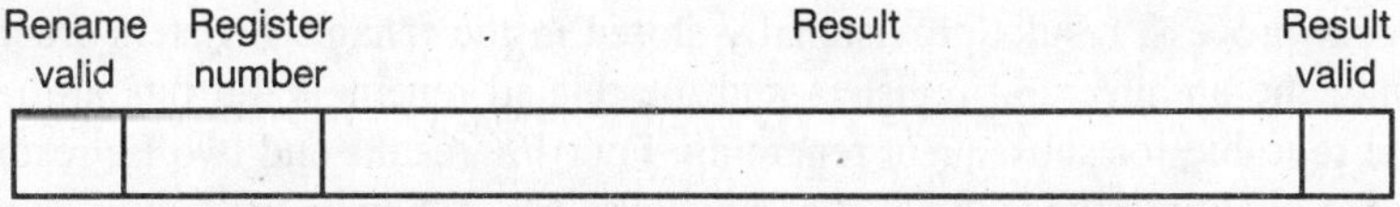

Figure 7.71 Format of the rename register entries.

Fetching operands from the rename registers requires an associative search since the contents of the register number fields must be searched for matching source register numbers. Furthermore, since subsequent instructions may use the same destination register, the architectural register can have multiple renames. During an associative search, clearly, the latest rename is to be accessed. Thus, accessing operands from the rename registers requires an associative search for the youngest renamed value of the requested source register.

Dispatching from the reservation stations is performed partly in-order, partly out-of-order. The reservation stations associated with the BPU and FPU dispatch instructions in-order, whereas the other stations operate out-of-order. An instruction which is held in the reservation station becomes eligible for execution when all of its operands are available. For reservation stations with out-of-order dispatch, arbitration is needed when more than one instruction is eligible for execution. The method used is to select the oldest eligible instruction. Now, the execution cycle can begin. Some operations, such as simple FX operations, are performed in one cycle. More complex operations such as division or multiplication require a number of execution cycles.

If an EU finishes its operation, it forwards its result and the associated tag to the result bus. Results are used to update both the related rename register file and the reservation stations. Updating the corresponding rename register is simple. Since the result is governed by a tag, which is the rename register identifier, the related rename register can be accessed using the tag as an index. Thus, the corresponding rename register is updated with the produced value and the result valid bit is set to '1' to allow subsequently issued instructions to access that value. The reservation stations also have to be updated. This update, however, requires an associative search for the tag (rename register identifier) for each result in all source operand fields of each reservation station concerned. If there is a match, the rename register identifier is replaced with the result value, and is marked as available. Thus, instructions waiting for these operands become eligible for execution during the next cycle. The finishing of an instruction changes its processing state. The information that a particular instruction has finished execution is called the result status.

The ROB ensures the correct ordering of writing back the results into the architectural register files. This is achieved by appropriate controlling of the retirement of the instructions. Retirement is the final step of instruction processing which updates the program state. The ROB lets instructions retire in strict program order by allowing an instruction to retire only if it has been finished and all prior instructions have already been retired.

Once it receives the result ready status, that is, the identifiers of finished instructions, the ROB can retire up to four instructions in each cycle. As part of the retirement process, results provisionally stored in the rename registers are written back into the architectural registers and the related rename valid bits are reset to become reusable for subsequent renaming. Four FX results and two FP results can be written back into the associated architectural file. When an instruction is retired, the allocated ROB entry is also deallocated for further use. This completes our description of the operation of the PowerPC 620.

7.10.3 The PentiumPro

The PentiumPro is the flagship of Intel's x86 line of processors. It features a 133 MHz initial clock rate, which is quite an impressive figure for a CISC processor.

This processor has the following main features:

- It is a superscalar CISC processor with a RISC core.
- It issues up to three RISC operations per cycle, and dispatches up to five RISC operations per cycle.
- It has a unified central reservation station with 20 entries, used at the same time for all types of instructions, such as for FX, FP instructions and so on.
- Strict sequential consistency is retained using a reorder buffer.
- Renaming is implemented in the reorder buffer.

The execution engine of the PentiumPro is shown in Figure 7.72.

The PentiumPro has an extremely long pipeline of at least 14 stages for FX instructions (Figure 7.73).

Like other superscalar CISC processors (see Section 7.9) the PentiumPro first converts the fetched CISC instructions internally into RISC ones, known as uops. Subsequently, a superscalar RISC core executes the uops. Finally, the back-end of the processor ensures the logical consistency of the execution.

Instructions are fetched in 128-bit chunks from the I-cache into the I-buffer. Instructions taken from the I-buffer must first be aligned because of the variable instruction length character of the CISC instructions. Then, up to three CISC instructions are decoded and converted to RISC instructions in each cycle. The conversion is carried out by two simple decoders (D1 and D2), a general decoder (D3) and a microinstruction sequencer (MIS). Both simple decoders can only accept instructions which are converted into a single uop. More complex instructions which translate into maximum four uops are translated by the generalized decoder (D3), and instructions resulting in more than four uops are converted by the MIS. Each uop has a regular format and a fixed length of 118 bits. We emphasize that decoding and conversion is carried out in order.

The next steps of the operation are register renaming, operand fetch and issuing of the renamed uops into the central reservation station.

Register renaming is implemented using a register mapping table while intermediate results of renamed registers are stored in the ROB. The register mapping table (called the register alias table, RAT) is able to map register numbers of three

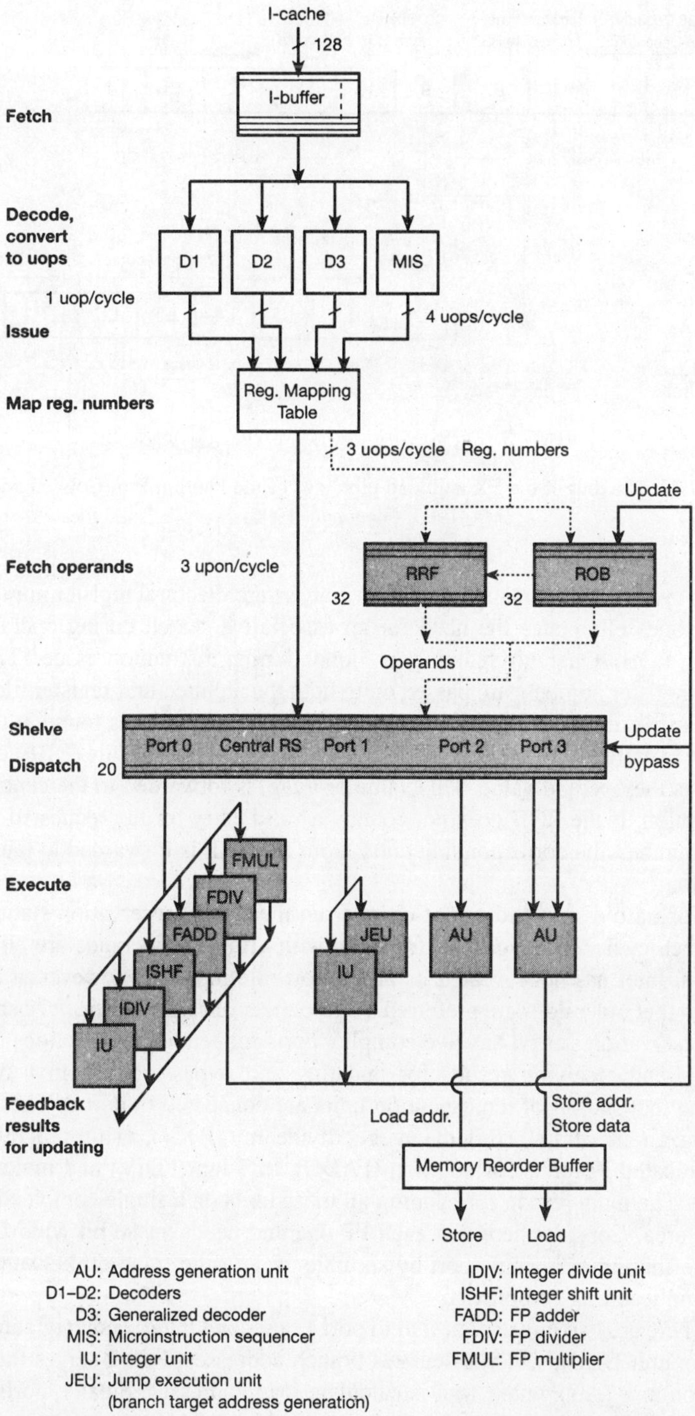

Figure 7.72 Core part of the microarchitecture of the PentiumPro.

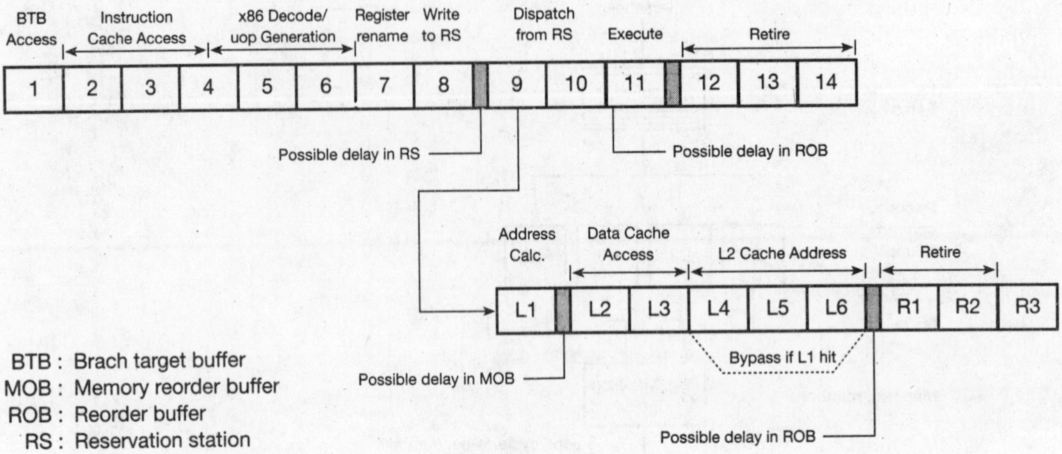

Figure 7.73 Layout of the FX and load pipelines of the PentiumPro (Colwell and Steck, 1995; Gwennap, 1995).

uops in a cycle. Using a mapping table to convert architectural register numbers into renamed ones eliminates the need for an associative search during operand fetch from the ROB. Operand fetching is done during instruction issue. Therefore, renamed register numbers are passed on to both the architectural register file and the ROB. If a valid entry for the required renamed register number is found in the ROB, this entry is preferred to the corresponding architectural register file (RRF) entry and is taken as the operand value. This value or a tag, is forwarded to the central reservation station. If the ROB does not contain a valid entry for the requested renamed register number, the corresponding entry from the RRF is forwarded to the reservation station.

Uops are dispatched out-of-order from the central reservation station, up to five in each cycle. Here again instructions with available operands are eligible for execution. Intel has not revealed its arbitration rule in detail; however, it has been published that older uops are preferred over younger ones. As Figure 7.72 shows, the central reservation station has five complex ports for sending instructions to execution units and receiving results for updating and bypassing. On first sight it is surprising that six out of ten execution units are connected to port 0. These are the following: an integer unit (IU), the integer divide unit (IDIV), a shift unit (SHF), and three dedicated FP units for addition (FADD), division (FDIV) and multiplication (FMUL). The main reason for hanging all these units on a single complex port is to save die area. Consider here that each FP operand needs an 86-bit wide data path. Thus, the sharing of a single port by six units is a design trade-off between performance and resulting complexity.

There are two units connected to port 1, a second integer unit (IU) and a jump execution unit (JEU), which calculates branch addresses. Port 2 serves the address generation unit (AU) whose task is calculate load addresses. Finally, ports 3 and 4 are devoted to the calculation of store addresses by a further address generation unit (AU).

Results and their tags are used to update both the central reservation station and the ROB. Updating of the central reservation station must be done associatively. If shelved instructions contains the same tag as broadcasted by one of the execution units these tags must be replaced with the corresponding result values. In addition, the availability status of the related operands must be updated.

Updating of the ROB serves two purposes. First, the destination register whose value has just been produced needs to be updated for subsequent instructions to be able to fetch this value. The other purpose of updating concerns the need to retain sequential consistency of execution. Through the use of a controlled retirement of instructions the ROB maintains logical consistency in the following way. When an instruction is finished, the ROB lets it retire only after all prior instructions have been retired. An additional requirement for its retirement is that uops belonging to the same CISC instruction are allowed to retire only if all uops belonging to the same CISC instruction are finished.

Retirement of an uop involves writing back the result of the corresponding ROB entry into the related architectural register and deallocating the corresponding ROB entry.

8 Processing of Control Transfer Instructions

Branches seem to be the most straightforward instruction type for a processor, since there is nothing more to do than modify, conditionally or unconditionally, the value of the PC. However, this easy-to-perform operation has turned out to be one of the most serious obstacles to increasing the performance of ILP-processors.

In Section 8.1 we take a close look at branches. Here we overview the major types of branch, the approaches to how conditions can be checked, the reasons why branch handling became a crucial problem of ILP-processors and finally, the measures which are used to indicate the performance of branch processing.

In Section 8.2 we overview the basic approaches to branch handling, which are detailed in the subsequent sections. Section 8.3 is devoted to delayed branching, a concept which arises with pipelined processors and declines with superscalar processors. Section 8.4 is the kernel section of this chapter. Here we are concerned mainly with speculative branch processing, which is one of the cornerstones of all recent superscalar processors.

In the concluding sections we review two further appealing approaches to branch handling: multiway branching (Section 8.5) and guarded execution (Section 8.6).

8.1 Introduction

In this section we first review the basic kinds of branch. Then we discuss two architectural concepts which can be used for checking the results of operations. Here, we identify the problems which arise when parallel instruction execution is introduced. Next, we point out why branch handling is a crucial problem in ILP-processors. Subsequently, we review significant branch statistics, which allow readers to orient themselves in the realm of branch handling. Finally, acquaint the reader with performance measures used to indicate quantitative aspects of branch processing.

8.1.1 Types of branches

Branches are used to *transfer control*, unconditionally or conditionally, to a specified locus of the program (Figure 8.1). Accordingly, we distinguish two types of branch. **Unconditional branches** are always taken. In contrast, **conditional branches** involve a *condition*, and therefore are either taken or not taken, depending on whether the specified condition is true or false.

In Figure 8.1 we show three types of unconditional branches: simple unconditional branches, branches to subroutines and returns from subroutines. **Simple unconditional branches** do not save the return address whereas **branches to subroutines** do. **Returns from subroutines** are dedicated unconditional branches performing a control transfer to the saved return address. Note that in the case of *nested subroutines*, while branching to and returning from the individual sub-routines, the return addresses are saved and used in a last-in-first-out (LIFO) manner.

A special kind of conditional branch is **the loop-closing conditional branch**. These branches are backward branches that are taken for all but the last iteration of a loop. Certain architectures provide means to support the execution of loop-closing branches. For instance, a number of architectures specify a Count Register that can be used as a loop counter, such as the PowerPC architecture.

In Figure 8.1 we also give examples of corresponding branch instructions, as used in the DEC Alpha and PowerPC architectures.

It is worth mentioning that the PowerPC architecture has a nice conception of branches, at least in two respects. First, the architecture does not have different branch and branch to subroutine instructions at the processor level. All branches, whether conditional or unconditional, can be turned into a branch to subroutine instruction by setting a specified bit in the instruction encoding (called the LK bit) to 1. In this case, the return address will be saved in an architecturally defined register, called the Link Register. A Return from Subroutine instruction is implemented simply as a special kind of branch where the target address is taken from the Link Register. Second, this architecture handles conditional and unconditional branches in a unified way. Unconditional branches are simple variants of conditional branches with the condition always met. However, this approach has a drawback, resulting in some odd instruction mnemonics.

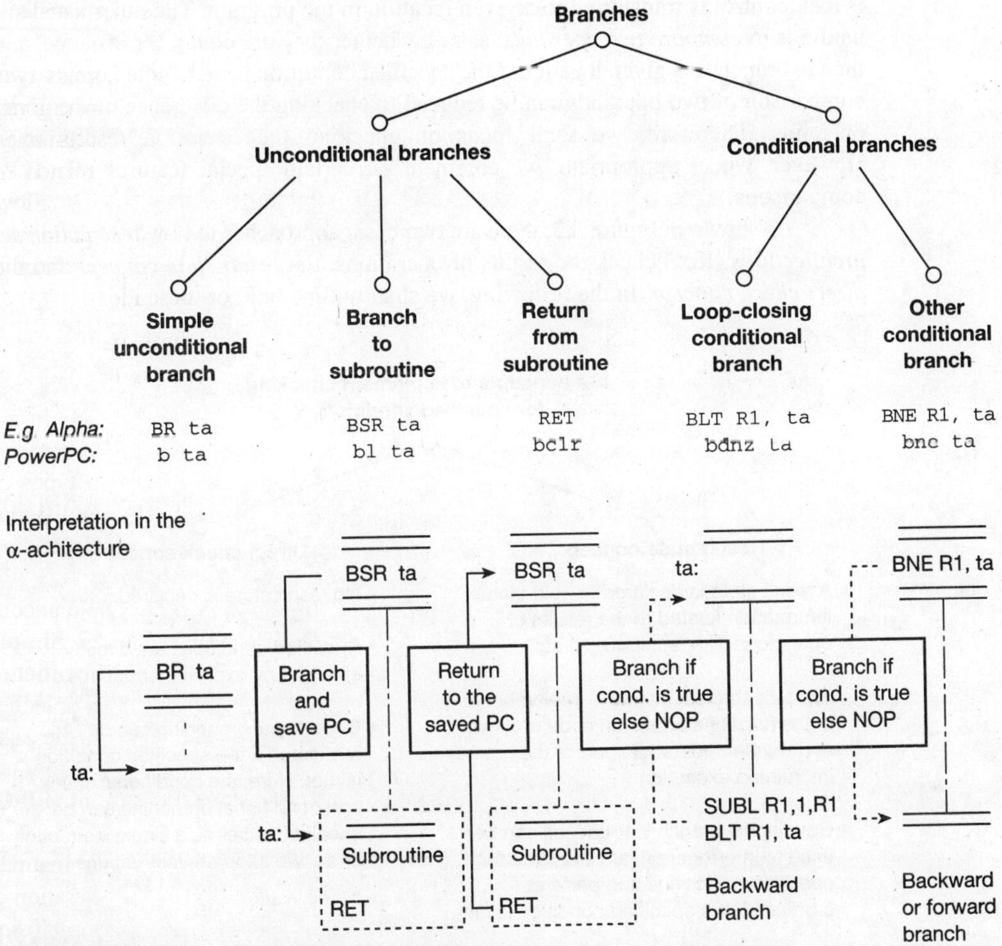

Semantics of the non-self-explanatory instructions:

```
BLT    R1, ta     // Branch if (R1) ≤ 0
SUBL   R1,1,R1    // Decrement R1 by 1,
BNE    R1, ta     // Branch to 'ta:' if (R1) ≠ 0
bl     ta         // Branch to 'ta:' and store next PC into the Link
                     Register
bclr              // Branch to the address stored in the Link Register
bdnz   ta         // Decrement Count Register, branch to 'ta:' if Count
                     Register ≠ 0
bne    ta         // Branch to 'ta:' if Condition Register field (CR1) ≠ 0
```

Figure 8.1 Major types of branches.

8.1.2 How architectures check the results of operations

Conditional branch instructions are used mainly in two situations. Most frequently they are employed to *check the result of an instruction* for a specified condition, such as whether the result equals 0, or if it is negative, and so on. If the specified condition is met, control is transferred to a given location in the program. The other usual situation is to *compare two operands*, asking whether they are equal, for instance, and then to branch to a given location if the specified condition is met. Note here that the comparison of two operands can be reduced to checking the difference of the given operands. Therefore, we shall focus on checking the operation results only. However, where appropriate, we comment on certain special features related to comparisons.

As shown in Figure 8.2, there are two basic approaches to how *instruction set architectures* (ISA) check the results of operations: the *result state concept* and the *direct check concept*. In the following, we shall outline both of these ideas.

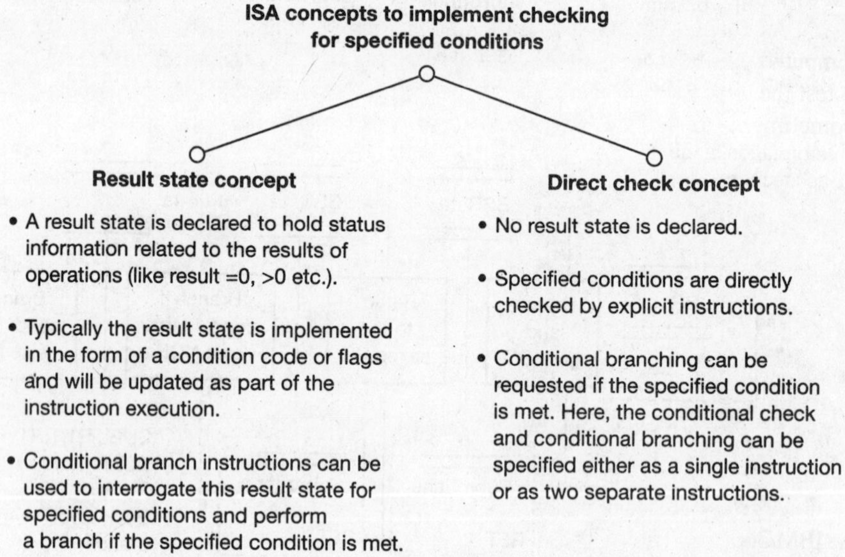

Figure 8.2 Basic alternatives for checking the results of operations for specified conditions (such as checking for result equals 0, if it is negative etc.).

The result state concept

The **result state concept** supposes that a *result state* is declared in the ISA concerned. Usually, it is represented in the form of a *condition code* or *flags*. The **result state** holds relevant information about the results of the operations, such as whether the result is = 0, < 0 and so on. In this concept, the results of operations are automatically checked during instruction execution for specific conditions (like = 0, < 0 and so on). The result state is then updated according to the outcome of these checks. Subsequently, if required, the result state is tested by a conditional branch instruction. If the specified condition is met, a branch is initiated to a given location.

For instance, if the *result of* an addition operation is *subsequently used* in a division as a divisor, the result of the arithmetic operation can be checked as follows:

```
    add  r1, r2, r3;  // r1 ← (r2) + (r3),
    beq  zero;        // test for result equals zero
                         and, if yes, branch to the
                         location 'zero'
    div  r5, r4, r1;  // r5 ← (r4)/(r1),
     :
     :
zero:                 // processing the case if divisor
                         equals zero
```

In addition, the architecture also has to provide some specific instructions *to check for* relevant conditions of *any operand* value *which has been generated earlier*, and to set the result state accordingly.

As an illustration, suppose that in the above example the divisor had been computed earlier in the program and is now held in r1. In this case, we would have to test the contents of r1 before using it as a divisor by employing a *test instruction* (sometimes also called a *compare instruction*) as follows:

```
    teq  r1;          // test for (r1) = 0 and update
                         result state accordingly
    beq  zero;        // test for result equals zero
                         and, if yes, branch to the
                         location 'zero'
    div  r5, r4, r1;  // r5 ← (r4)/(r1),
     :
     :
zero:                 // processing the case if divisor
                         equals zero
```

A great number of main-line architectures use the result state approach, such as the IBM/360 and /370, PDP-11, VAX, x86, Pentium, MC 68000, SPARC and PowerPC.

The result state approach has a number of disadvantages and a slight benefit. The *disadvantages* are:

- The generation of the result state is not straightforward; it requires an irregular structure and occupies additional chip area.
- The result state is a sequential concept. Obviously, this concept cannot be applied without modification in architectures which have multiple execution units (EUs) operating in parallel, such as VLIWs and superscalar processors. For these processors, the result state concept has to be augmented with appropriate mechanisms, to avoid multiple or out-of-order updating of the result state, that is, to preserve sequential consistency.

There are two basic possibilities for *retaining sequential consistency* in superscalar processors or VLIWs, *with respect to condition checking*. First, *multiple sets of condition codes or flags* can be introduced. For instance, there are two sets of condition bits in the x86 and MC68030 architectures. The SPARC architecture defines three sets, while the PowerPC architecture has eight sets of condition bits.

Here, it remains the programmer's or compiler's responsibility to use different registers for results or for the outcomes of checks which are generated by different EUs operating in parallel. Second, the *direct check concept* which will be discussed in the next section can also be used for preserving sequential consistency of the result state in the case of parallel instruction execution.

On the other hand, the result state approach has a *benefit* as well – it saves a small percentage of code length (1% according to Hennessy et al. (1982) – 6–7% according to DeRosa and Levy (1987)). Obviously, the stated drawbacks are more important than the slight benefit mentioned. Therefore, we expect novel architectures to employ the direct check concept more and more frequently; this concept is presented in the next section.

The direct check concept

The **direct check concept** is the other basic alternative for checking the results of operations. In this case, no result state is declared (see again Figure 8.2). Instead, if required, the *results of* the operations are *checked directly* for specified conditions by using dedicated instructions. If the specified condition is met, a conditional branch is initiated.

Direct checking of a condition and a dependent branch can be implemented in architectures in two ways, either by using *two separate instructions* or by employing a *single instruction*. Figure 8.3 shows these possibilities. For ease of comparison and overview, this figure depicts both basic concepts.

When direct checking is implemented by *two separate instructions*, first the result value is checked by an appropriate compare (or test) instruction. This instruction writes the outcome of the check into a chosen register. Subsequently, a conditional branch instruction can be used to test the deposited test outcome and branch to a given location if the specified condition is met, as the following example shows.

```
add   r1, r2, r3;
cmpeq r7, r1;       // r7 ← true, if (r1) = 0,
                       else NOP
bt    r7, zero;     // branch to 'zero': if (r7) =
                       true, else NOP
div   r5, r4, r1;
  :
  :
zero:
```

In this example, the cmpeq (compare for equal) instruction tests the contents of register r1 for zero and if (r1) = 0, sets the Boolean value 'true' into register r7. The subsequent bt (branch if true) instruction interrogates the deposited Boolean value in register r7 and initiates a branch to the label 'zero:' if the stored value is 'true'.

The AMD 29000 is an architecture that provides two separate instructions for direct checking and conditional branching.

In the other implementation of direct checking, a *single instruction* fulfils both testing and conditional branching, as the example at the top of page 302 indicates.

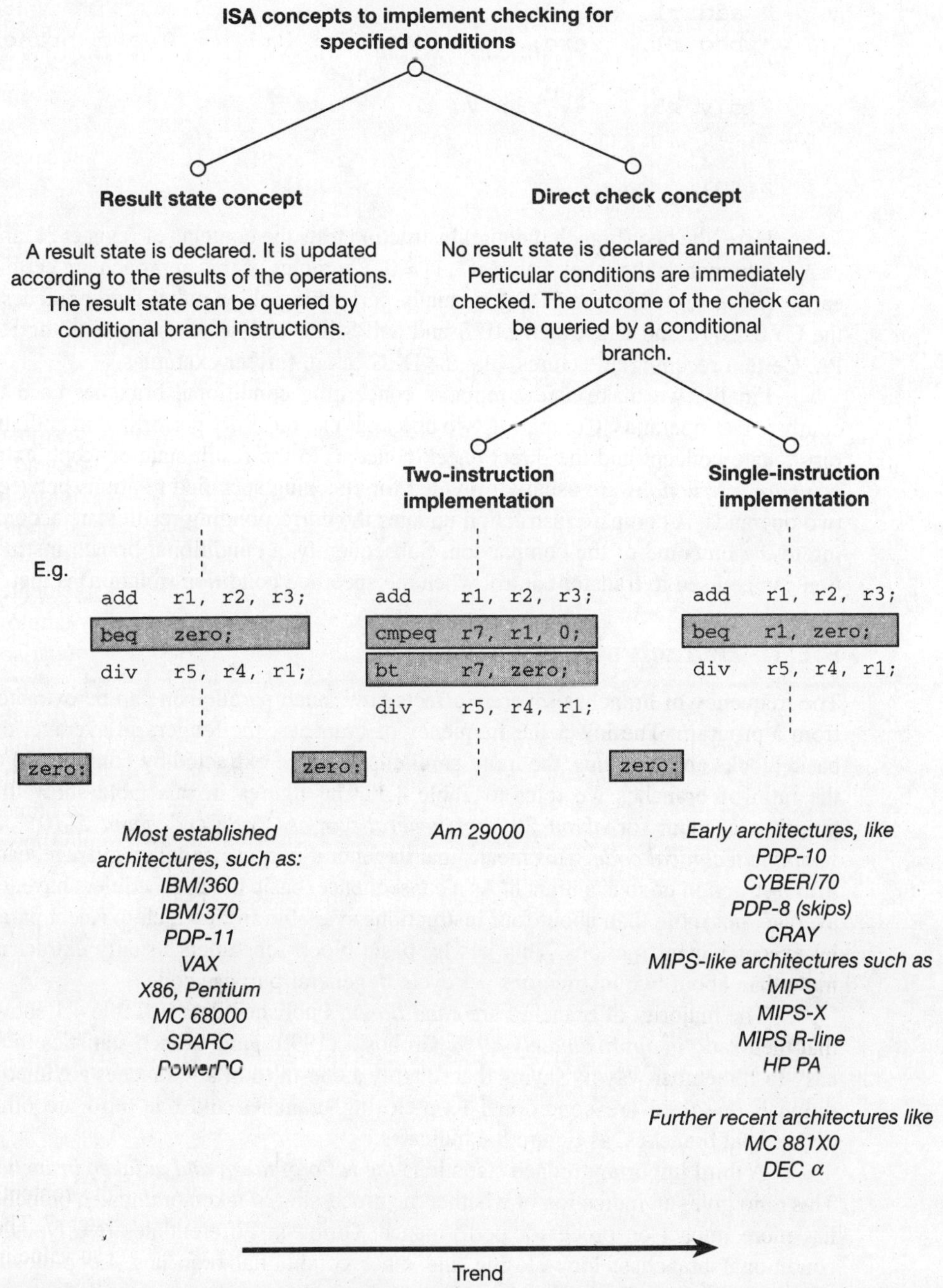

Semantics of the non self-explanatory instructions used in the example:

```
cmpeq    r7,r1,r2;     // r7 ← true if (r1) = (r2), else r7 ← false
bt       r7,null;      // branch to 'null': if (r7) = true, else NOP
cmpbeq   r1,r2,null;   // branch to 'null': if (r1) = (r2), else NOP
```

Figure 8.3 Alternatives for checking the operation results.

```
    add r1,   r2, r3; //
    beq r1,   zero;   // test for (r1) = 0 and branch
                         if true
    div r5,   r4, r1; //
     :
     .
  zero:
```

Here, the beq (branch if equal) instruction tests the contents of register r1, and causes a branch to the label 'zero:' if (r1) = 0. Examples of this approach are certain early architectures like the PDP-8 (actually performing skips rather than branches), the CYBER/70 and Cray, then MIPS and MIPS-like architectures, such as the HP PA. Certain recent architectures, like the DEC α, are further examples.

Finally, we make a few remarks concerning conditional branches used to compare two operands. Comparing two operands can be easily performed in both the result state concept and the direct check concept. In the result state concept, extra *compare instructions* are usually provided for checking specified relations between two operands. A compare instruction updates the corresponding result state according to the outcome of the comparison. Subsequently, a conditional branch instruction can be used to transfer control when the specified condition (relation) is met.

8.1.3 Branch statistics

The frequency of branches severely affects how much parallelism can be extracted from a program. The lower the frequency of branches, the longer, on average, the basic blocks are and, thus, the more parallelism can be extracted by compilers. For the ratio of branches we refer to Table 4.1. The figures in this table show that branches account for *about 20 % of general-purpose code* and *about 5–10 % of scientific/technical code*. This means that in general-purpose code, on average, each fifth instruction or so is a branch. As a consequence, basic block schedulers have, on average, not more than about four instructions available from which to select parallel executable instructions. This is why basic block schedulers usually extract no more than about two instructions per cycle in general-purpose code.

The majority of branches are *conditional*. Published data in Table 4.1 shows that their ratio is *approximately 80 %*. Grohoski (1990) gave branch statistics in an easy-to-remember way by saying that roughly a one-third of all branches are unconditional, one-third are conditional loop-closing branches and one-third are other conditional branches, as Figure 8.4 indicates.

A third important branch statistic is *the ratio of taken and untaken branches*. This ratio gives an indication of whether the processing of taken or untaken branches has more impact on processor performance. Grohoski differentiates two types of conditional branches: loop-closing and other conditional branches. Loop-closing branches are taken for the first (n–1) iterations of a loop being executed n-times. He estimates that the remaining conditional branches are taken, or not taken, almost with the same probability, as indicated in Figure 8.4. Summarizing his estimates, the ratio of taken and untaken branches to the total number of branches is approximately 5/6 and 1/6, respectively. Other publications indicate a measured ratio of about 3/4

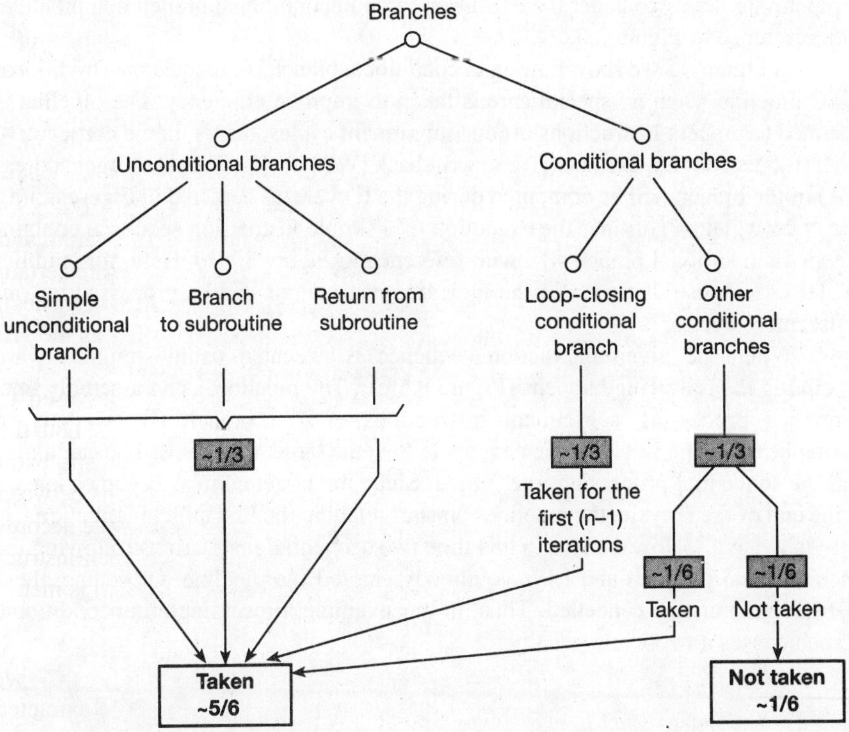

Figure 8.4 Grohoski's estimate of branch statistics (Grohoski, 1990).

Table 8.1 Frequency of taken and not-taken branches.

Reference	*Frequency of taken branches*	*Frequency of untaken branches*
Lee and Smith, 1984	57–99 %	1–43 %
Edenfield et al., 1990	75 %	25 %
Grohoski, 1990	~ 5/6	~ 1/6

and 1/4, respectively, as shown in Table 8.1. Based on this data, we can estimate that around *75–80 % of all branches*, that is, the overwhelming majority of branches, *are taken*. Thus, a well-designed branch processing scheme should lay much more *emphasis on the effective processing of taken branches* than on not-taken ones.

8.1.4 The branch problem

Pipelining is a very effective technique for speeding up instruction execution along a sequential path. But if a branch enters the pipeline and disrupts the sequential processing, the performance of the pipeline will be seriously impeded unless appropriate techniques are used. In order to demonstrate the problems that cause branches in pipelining, let us consider the execution of an unconditional branch in a pipeline, with reference to Figure 8.5.

In Figure 8.5 we show how an unconditional branch is executed on a traditional RISC pipeline when no special care is taken to improve efficiency. The pipeline is assumed to process instructions in four subsequent cycles, that is, in the consecutive fetch (F), decode (D), execute (E) and writeback (WB) cycles. Then the target address (TA) of the branch will be computed during the E cycle, as depicted in Figure 8.5(a).

Now, let us consider the execution of a simple instruction sequence containing an unconditional branch (B), with reference to Figure 8.5(b). Here, for simplicity, let us suppose that each of the indicated instructions can be processed in four consecutive cycles.

When the given instruction sequence is executed using straightforward pipelining the following happens (Figure 8.5(c)). The pipeline, as an assembly line, continues processing subsequent instructions until a branch (B) is detected during its decoding in t_{i+2}. In the next cycle (t_{i+3}) the target address will be calculated and the sequential processing interrupted. Since the target address becomes known at the end of the E cycle, the pipeline can start fetching the first target instruction (i_{t1}) only in cycle t_{i+4}. However, up to this time two sequential instructions following the unconditional jump (i_3 and i_4) have already entered the pipeline. Of course, these instructions must be cancelled. Thus, in our example, processing an unconditional branch causes a two-cycle penalty.

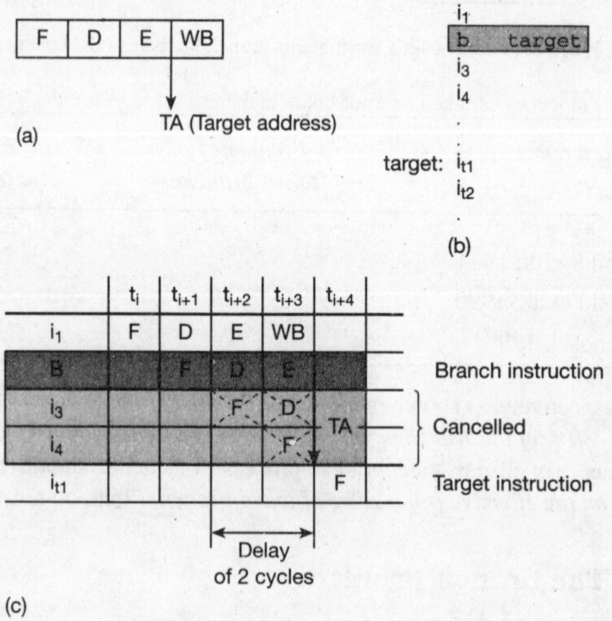

Figure 8.5 The delay caused in pipelining by straightforward execution of an unconditional branch. (a) Straightforward execution of the unconditional branch; (b) the instruction sequence to be executed; (c) resulting execution of the instruction sequence.

Processing a *conditional branch* in a straightforward pipeline could cause an even longer penalty. This would result from the additional task of evaluating the specified condition, which needs an extra cycle. Thus, the next address, whether the incremented sequential one or the branch target address, can only be determined afterwards. The situation is even worse for **unresolved conditional branches**. We term a conditional branch *unresolved*, if the specified condition cannot be evaluated in due time because the result referred to has not yet been produced. Consider here, for instance, a conditional branch intended to test the result of a preceding floating-point division. In this case, a large number of cycles is required, usually 10–50, to get the result. Thus, a subsequent conditional branch remains unresolved for many cycles.

This means that in a pipeline each branch instruction gives rise to a number of *wasted cycles* (called **bubbles**) unless appropriate branching techniques are introduced. As we have discussed in the previous section, branches are very frequent in general-purpose code; on average, we can expect about *each fourth to sixth instruction to be a branch*. Thus, *ineffective branch processing can seriously impede performance*. For instance, if each branch introduced an additional delay of, say, three cycles and, on average, each fifth instruction was a branch, then branches would cause an average additional delay of $3 * 1/5 = 0.6$ cycle per instruction. This would yield a considerable performance degradation in a RISC processor which requires only one cycle for most instructions.

Furthermore, with recent developments in processor technology *branching became the most crucial hurdle* in increasing the performance of processors. There are two reasons for this. First, pipelines became deeper and deeper. Most recent processors often have pipelines with up to 8-12 stages, like the Pentium (8 stages), the UltraSparc (9 stages), the α 21064 (10 stages), and the α 21164 and PentiumPro (12 stages). Thus, using straightforward branch processing, each branch would result in a yet larger number of bubbles as indicated in the four-stage pipeline assumed in our earlier example. Second, in superscalar processors more than one instruction can be issued in each cycle, say two, three, four or even six. As a consequence, we have a much higher probability of encountering a branch in each pipeline cycle than in scalar processors. Since the issue rate tends to increase, the branch problem becomes more and more serious. As a consequence, during the recent development of processors more and more effort is put into efficient branch processing. This chapter is devoted to overviewing the branch techniques developed for pipelined scalar and superscalar processors.

8.1.5 Performance measures of branch processing

In order to evaluate and compare different branch processing techniques, we need a performance measure. Such a measure is the branch penalty, which is introduced next.

As a starting point let us consider the execution of a branch instruction in a four-stage pipeline, with reference to Figure 8.6. If the branch is processed in the same straightforward manner as discussed previously, the branch target address (BTA) will be computed in cycle t_{i+3}. Then the branch target instruction can be fetched in cycle t_{i+4}. Thus, the branch target instruction is fetched with 3 cycles' delay in comparison to the fetching of the branch instruction. This means a 2-cycle

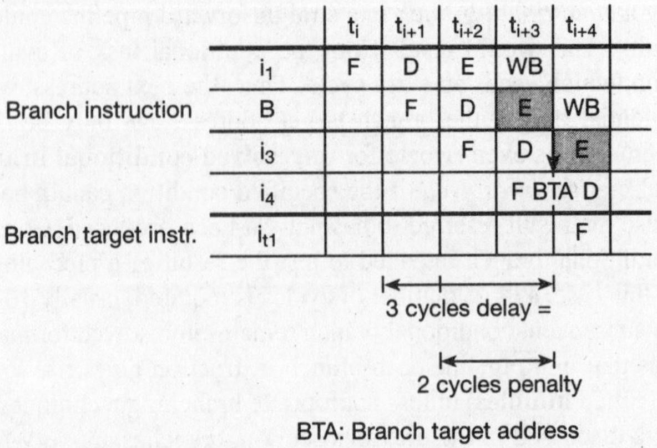

Figure 8.6 Interpretation of the concept of branch penalty.

penalty compared to the sequential processing. Now, in the case of branches, we interpret the number of additional delay cycles occurring until the target instruction is fetched over the natural 1-cycle delay as the *performance measure of branches*. It is referred to as the **branch penalty**. For instance, the branch in Figure 8.6 causes a 2-cycle penalty.

In the following we discuss the performance of branch processing in certain typical situations. First, let us consider the situation when the penalties for taken and not-taken branches differ, as is often the case. Then, obviously, we have to distinguish between taken and not-taken penalties. Let us denote the penalties of 'taken' and 'not taken' branches by P_t and P_{nt}, and the corresponding probabilities (frequencies) of 'taken' and 'not taken' branches as f_t and f_{nt}. Then the *effective penalty of branch processing* P is

$$\mathbf{P = f_t * P_t + f_{nt} * P_{nt}} \qquad \textbf{(8.1)}$$

Next, as examples, we calculate the effective penalties of the 80386 and i486 processors. For the 80386 the values of the taken and not-taken penalties are 8 and 2 cycles, respectively. The corresponding data for the i486 is 2 cycles and 0 cycles, respectively. When the probability of taken branches is assumed to be 0.75 (f_t = 0.75), we get for the effective penalty of branches in the 80386:

$$P_{80386} = 0.75 * 8 + 0.25 * 2 = 6.5 \text{ cycles}$$

This means that the 80386 requires, on average, 6.5 additional cycles for each branch.

In contrast, the i486 has a substantially enhanced branch mechanism. Its effective branch penalty is

$$P_{i486} = 0.75 * 2 + 0.25 * 0 = 1.5$$

which is considerably less than the penalty of the 80386.

A further typical situation is when branch processing uses *branch prediction* (discussed in Section 8.4.4). In this case, a prediction is made for each branch by guessing whether the branch in question will be taken or not. Let us now introduce the following notation:

P_{tc}: penalty for correctly predicted taken branches,
P_{tm}: penalty for mispredicted taken branches,
P_{ntc}: penalty for correctly predicted not-taken branches,
P_{ntm}: penalty for mispredicted not-taken branches,
f_{tc}: probability for correctly predicted taken branches,
f_{tm}: probability for mispredicted taken branches,
f_{ntc}: probability for correctly predicted not-taken branches,
f_{ntm}: probability for mispredicted not-taken branches.

Then, the *effective penalty* of branch processing can be expressed as:

$$\mathbf{P = f_{tc} * P_{tc} + f_{tm} * P_{tm} + f_{ntc} * P_{ntc} + f_{ntm} * P_{ntm}} \quad (8.2)$$

However, we can very often assume a *straightforward* case when the branch penalties for correctly predicted taken and not-taken branches, and for mispredicted taken and not-taken branches, are equal. That is

$$\mathbf{P_{tc} = P_{ntc} \text{ and } P_{tm} = P_{ntm}} \quad (8.3)$$

Furthermore, let us designate the total probability of correctly predicted branches as f_c and that of mispredicted branches as f_m, that is

$$\mathbf{f_c = f_{tc} + f_{ntc} \text{ and } f_m = f_{tm} + f_{ntm}} \quad (8.4)$$

In this straightforward case the *effective branch penalty* can be calculated as

$$\mathbf{P = f_c * P_c + f_m * P_m} \quad (8.5)$$

As an example, let us consider the Pentium processor which uses branch prediction. In this case the penalty for correctly predicted branches is 0 cycle, whereas that for mispredicted branches equals either 3 cycles (if the branch is processed by the U pipe) or 4 cycles (if the branch is executed in the V pipe). For the calculation, let us suppose an average misprediction penalty of 3.5. When we further assume a branch prediction accuracy of 0.9 (that is, $f_c = 0.9$ and $f_m = 0.1$) we get for the effective branch penalty of this processor:

$$P_{Pentium} = 0.9 * 0 + 0.1 * 3.5 = 0.35$$

That is, the Pentium requires, on average, only 0.35 additional cycles for branches. This is a remarkable improvement over the i486 which has a 1.5-cycle effective penalty.

We note that as well as the typical cases mentioned above, there are certain further situations where the effective branch penalty has to be calculated in a more complex way. As an example, consider the case where there are two mechanisms used in parallel for branch prediction (discussed in Section 8.4.4) and, therefore, there are two distinct values for both the correct penalty and the probability of correct prediction. We leave it to the reader to calculate the effective penalty in this case.

Actual values of branch penalties for a number of processors are given in a later section in Tables 8.3–8.5 and 8.15, in connection with the discussion of branch policies.

With reference to performance measures, the concept of zero-cycle branching is also worth mentioning. **Zero-cycle branching** (branch folding) refers to branch implementations which allow execution of branches with a one-cycle gain compared to a sequential execution. This means that the instruction logically following the branch is executed immediately after the instruction which precedes the branch, as Figure 8.7 shows. This figure demonstrates what happens while an unconditional branch is executed in zero-cycle branching. In this case the target instruction (i_t) will be executed immediately following the instruction which preceeds the branch (i_1).

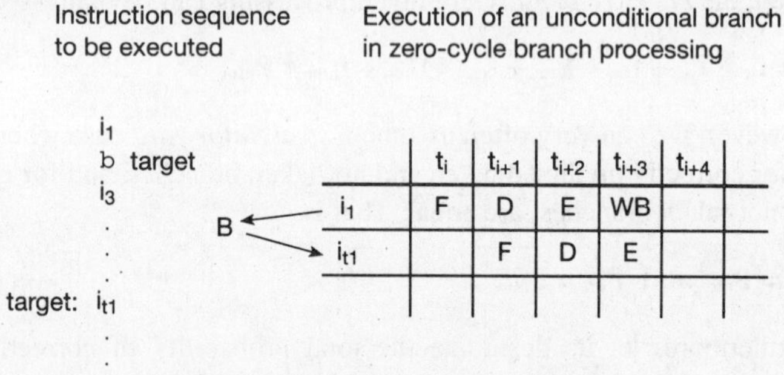

Figure 8.7 Zero-cycle branching.

Zero-cycle branching can also be implemented with conditional branches, when it provides for a seamless execution along both the taken and not-taken paths. That is, after instruction i_1, which precedes the branch, either the first instruction of the target path (i_{t1}) or the next sequential instruction (i_3) will be immediately executed. There are a number of recent processors offering zero-cycle branches, such as members of the PowerPC line or the PA 8000. In Section 8.4.5 we discuss techniques which provide this feature.

8.2 Basic approaches to branch handling

Processors use a large variety of approaches and techniques for branch handling. In this section we overview them.

In Figure 8.8 we summarize the basic approaches employed. As indicated, there are three aspects which give rise to the basic approaches in branch handling. These are:

- whether branch delay slots are used,
- how unresolved conditional branches are handled, and
- whether the architecture provides means to avoid conditional branches.

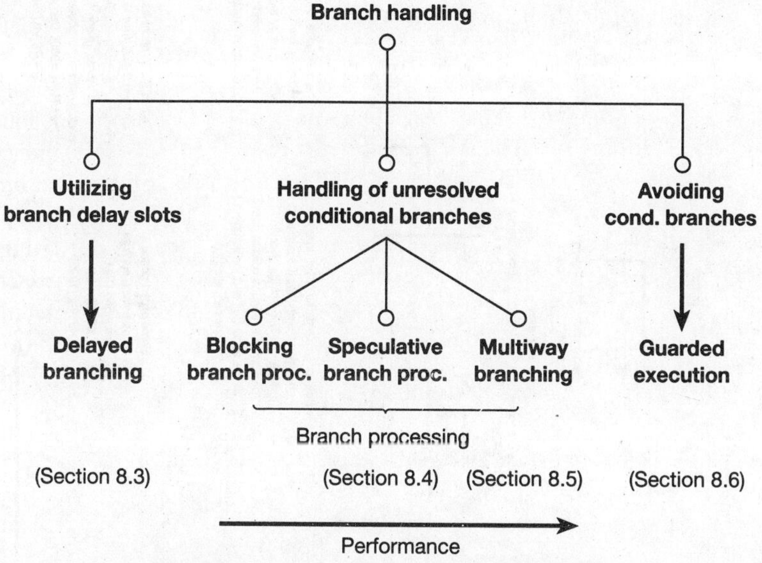

Figure 8.8 Basic approaches to branch handling.

The basic approaches to branch handling reflect these questions. According to how branch handling responds to these questions we distinguish delayed branching, blocking and speculative branch processing, multiway branching as well as guarded execution. These different approaches are discussed in sections 8.3–8.6. Here we note that, for practical reasons, blocking and speculative branch processing are treated in the same section, entitled 'Branch processing'. Next, with reference to Figure 8.9 we overview the aspects mentioned and the associated basic approaches to branch handling.

The first aspect is whether branch delay slots are utilized. If they are, we have *delayed branching*.

We remind the reader that straightforward branch handling usually results in one or two wasted pipeline cycles, called bubbles, after each branch instruction. With delayed branching, otherwise unused bubbles are filled as far as possible with executable instructions. However, for delayed branching the execution semantics of the architecture is so modified that an instruction which is inserted immediately behind a branch is executed before the branch, in the cycle or cycles which would otherwise be wasted. A large number of early RISC architectures and others which followed have made use of this scheme. In Section 8.3 we describe delayed branching in detail.

The second aspect concerns how unresolved conditional branches are handled. As shown in Figure 8.9, processors may use one of three basic approaches. When unresolved conditional branches block the processing of branches until the specified condition can be evaluated, we are concerned with *blocking branch processing*. Early pipelined microprocessors, such as the MC 68020, MC 68030 and 80386 employed this ineffective way of branch handling.

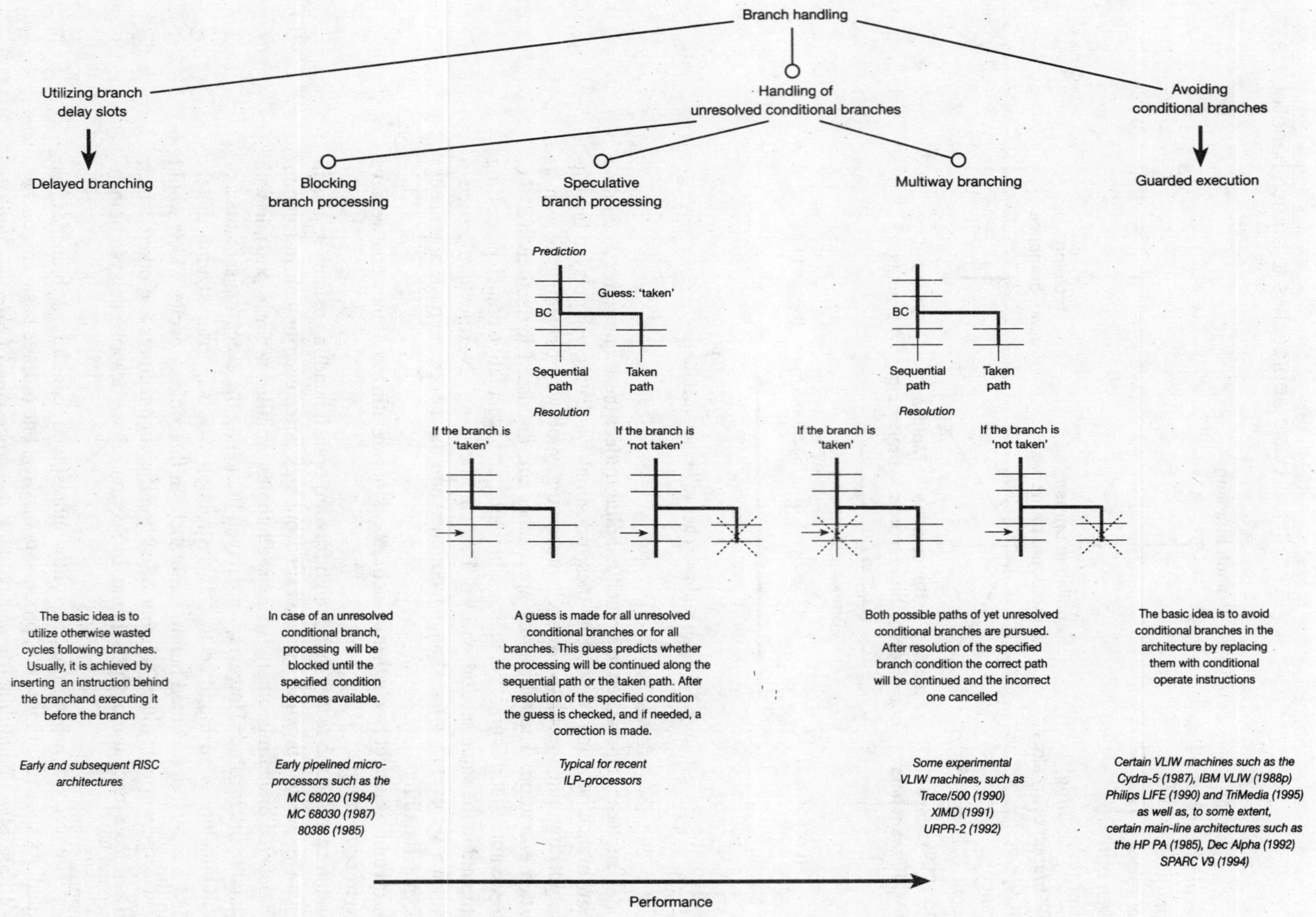

Figure 8.9 Review of the basic approaches to branch handling.

The other approach to cope with unresolved conditional branches is to use *speculative branch processing*. In this case, for each unresolved conditional branch a prediction is made for the outcome of the condition and processing continues along the guessed path. The prediction is a guess as to whether the branch is likely to be taken or not, that is, whether the sequential or the taken path is likely to be followed. After resolution of the specified condition, the guess is checked. If it proves correct, processing continues. If the guess is wrong, all speculatively executed instructions are discarded and the execution is continued along the correct path. Speculative branch processing is the prevailing approach at the present time. It is widely used in recent ILP-processors, especially in superscalar ones. Here, we note that blocking and speculative branch processing are collectively called simply branch processing, to which Section 8.4 is entirely devoted.

The final possibility for handling unresolved conditional branches is to pursue both possible execution paths and discard the incorrect path after resolution of the specified condition. This approach is called *multiway branching* and has been used in some experimental or prototype VLIW machines. This approach is described in Section 8.5.

In reviewing the basic approaches to unresolved conditional branches we note that their performance potential increases in the following order: blocking branch processing, speculative branch processing and multiway branching.

The third and last aspect of branch handling is whether the architecture provides appropriate means to avoid conditional branches, as shown in Figure 8.9. If there are such means available, we have *guarded execution*. This approach is based on substituting conditional branch instructions with conditional operate instructions, called *guarded instructions*. In a sense, control dependencies are replaced by data dependencies. Although guarded execution probably has the highest performance potential among the schemes overviewed, it also has a crucial drawback: it requires either a significant extension to or a redefinition of the instruction set architecture (ISA), as described in Section 8.6. So far, guarded execution has only been introduced in certain VLIW architectures, although a few main-line architectures also provide guarded instructions to some extent, such as the HP PA, DEC Alpha and SPARC V9 architectures. More details of guarded execution can be found in Section 8.6.

8.3 Delayed branching

In this section, first we explain and assess the basic delayed branching scheme. Then, we overview certain extensions which have been adopted by architectures since the second half of the 1980s. At the end of this section, we appraise the delayed branching approach in the light of the currently predominant concept of superscalar execution.

8.3.1 The basic delayed branching scheme

As we know, when branches are processed by a pipeline in a straightforward manner, after each taken branch, at least one cycle remains unused. This is due to the assembly line-like inertia of pipelining, as demonstrated in Figure 8.10(a)–(c). In

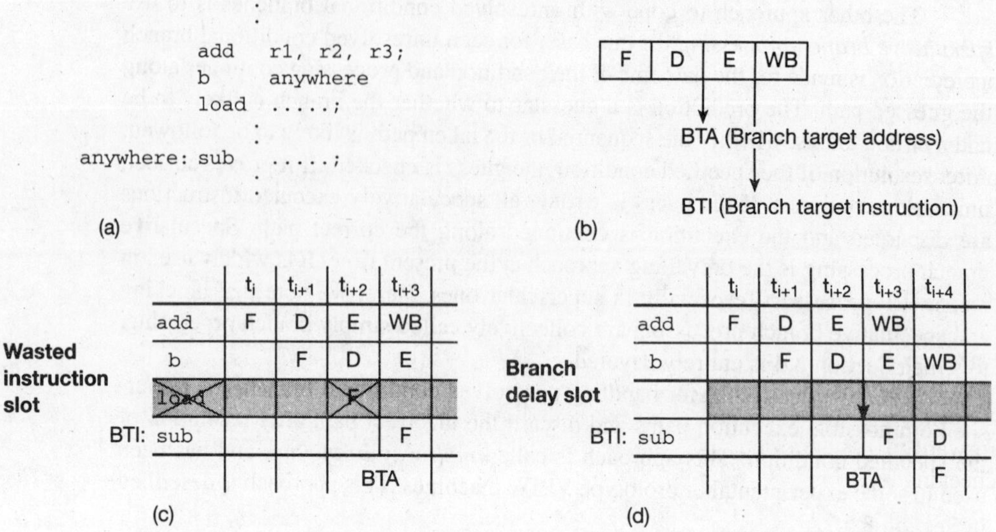

Figure 8.10 Occurrence of an unused instruction slot (bubble) during execution of an unconditional branch and the idea of a branch delay slot. (a) An instruction sequence to be executed; (b) supposed execution of an unconditional branch; (c) execution of the given instruction sequence by the pipeline without delayed branching; (d) the notion of a branch delay slot.

these figures we show how a short instruction sequence involving an unconditional branch is executed by straightforward pipelining. The instruction sequence is given in Figure 8.10(a). For its execution we assume a four-stage traditional RISC pipeline. Furthermore, let us suppose that

- the branch target address (BTA) becomes available at the end of the D cycle, and
- the referenced branch target instruction (BTI) can be fetched in a single cycle (E cycle) from the cache, as indicated in Figure 8.10(b).

Note here that both assumptions indicate a fairly advanced implementation. In a straightforward case, the BTA would be calculated during the E cycle and a cache access could take more than one cycle.

Figure 8.10(c) shows how this instruction sequence is executed by the pipeline. The pipeline fetches consecutive instructions until it detects a branch in t_{i+2}. At the end of t_{i+2} the pipeline discards the already fetched next instruction (load). Then, in t_{i+3} it fetches the branch target instruction (sub) from the calculated address, which corresponds to the label 'anywhere'. Thus, the instruction slot following the branch remains unused; in other words, a *pipeline bubble* occurs.

Instruction slots following branches are called **branch delay slots** (Figure 8.10(d)). Note that similar delay slots can also occur following load instructions; these are termed *load delay slots*. Branch delay slots are wasted during traditional execution. However, when delayed branching is employed, these slots can be at least partly utilized.

With **delayed branching**, the instruction that follows the branch is executed in the delay slot. However, the branch will only be effective later, that is, delayed by one cycle. Figure 8.11 demonstrates this feature.

In Figure 8.11 we move the add instruction of our program segment that originally preceded the branch into the branch delay slot. With delayed branching the processor executes the add instruction first, but the branch will only be effective later. Thus, in this example, delayed branching preserves the original execution sequence:

```
            add      r1, r2, r3;
            b        anywhere;
anywhere:   sub
```

Our example in Figures 8.10 and 8.11 refers to an unconditional branch. Evidently, conditional branches cause similar or longer delays during a straightforward pipelined execution. This is due to the additionally required operation of checking the specified condition.

Thus, delayed branching can be considered as a scheme applicable to branches in general, irrespective of whether they are unconditional or conditional. Another important point is that in the basic delayed branching scheme discussed so far, instructions in the delay slot are always executed. Accordingly, an instruction in the delay slot of an untaken branch will always be executed as well.

We emphasize that delayed branching reverses the execution sequence of the branch instruction and the instruction placed in the delay slot. In other words, delayed branching requires an *architectural redefinition of the execution sequence* of instructions compared with traditional von Neumann architectures. Therefore, delayed branching exemplifies a departure from traditional architectures. Thus this concept could only have been introduced into novel architectures rather than into existing ones.

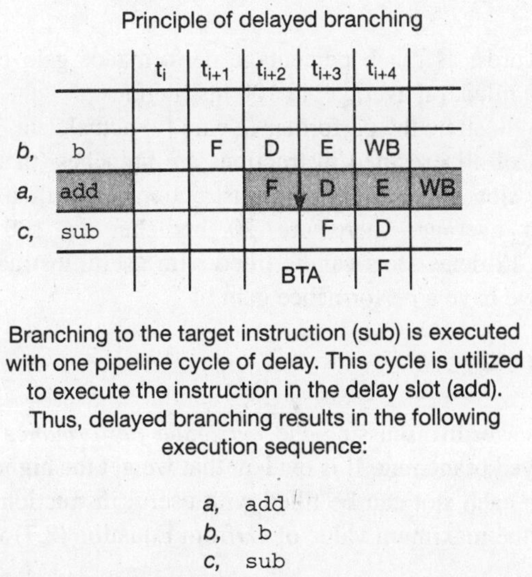

Figure 8.11 Basic scheme of delayed branching.

Delayed branching was first introduced in the MANIAC I in 1952, and was commonly used later in microprogramming (Patterson and Sequin, 1981). At the beginning of the 1980s this scheme was 'reinvented' in the RISC-I (Patterson and Sequin 1981), and used subsequently in a number of RISC architectures emerging at that time, such as the MIPS (1982p), RISC-II (1983), MIPS-R-line (from 1987 on) and AMD 29000 (1987).

Next we discuss how much performance gain can be expected with delayed branching.

The performance gain is achieved by filling the delay slots as far as possible with appropriate instructions and executing them in this slot, instead of leaving the delay slots empty. However, not every instruction is suitable for the delay slot. The only suitable instructions are those which are not dependent on preceding ones and can be executed in a single pipeline cycle, like simple integer or Boolean instructions, can be used. According to the literature, compilers can usually fill 60–70 % of delay slots with useful instructions (Radin, 1982; Ryan, 1988). Obviously, the remaining delay slots are filled with NOPs.

Based on this data, we can estimate the *performance gain* achieved by delayed branching. Let us suppose that during a program run the frequency of branches is f_b and the ratio of those delay slots that can be filled with useful instructions is f_f. Then, on average, 100 instructions have $100 * f_b$ delay slots, and from those n_u

$$n_u = 100*f_b*f_f \qquad (8.6)$$

can be utilized. As a consequence, on average, instead of 100 instructions, $100 + n_u$ useful instructions will be executed. Thus, the performance gain achieved by delayed branching (G_d) is

$$G_d = (100 + n_u)/100 - 1 = n_u/100 = f_b*f_f \qquad (8.7)$$

In other words, as much percentage performance gain can be expected as delay slots can be filled, on average, in 100 instructions.

In order to illustrate the performance gain for actual data, let us suppose that, on average, 20 % of all executed instructions are branches (that is, $f_b = 0.20$) and 60 % of the delay slots can be filled with instructions other than NOPs (that is, $f_f = 0.60$). Then, on average, there are 20 branches in 100 instructions and $100*0.20*0.60 = 12$ delay slots can be filled with useful instructions (that is, $n_u = 12$). In this case we have a performance gain of

$$G_d = 12/100 = 12\ \% \qquad (8.8)$$

Here, it is worth discussing the *maximum performance gain* that may be achieved by delayed branching. It is evident that we get the highest possible performance gain when each slot can be filled with useful instructions, that is, if $f_f = 1$. Then, we get for the maximum value of G_d from Equation (8.7) with $f_f = 1$:

$$G_{dmax} = f_b \qquad (8.9)$$

This means that the maximum achievable performance gain equals the ratio of branches. Thus, recalling the branch statistics given in Section 4.2.2 we estimate that delayed branching can result in a maximum performance gain of 20–30 % in general-purpose programs and about 5–10 % gain in scientific programs.

Finally, we consider the advantages and drawbacks of the basic delayed branching scheme. Evidently the advantage is slightly increased performance, which amounts to an actual value of about 10 %. The disadvantages are:

- Delayed branching requires a redefinition of the architecture.
- Delayed branching gives rise to a slight code expansion due to the NOPs to be inserted. For instance, in our example we would have to insert $100*f_b*(1 - f_f) = 100*0.2*(1 - 0.6) = 8$ NOPs per 100 instructions and thus would have 8% longer code than without delayed branching.
- Interrupt processing becomes more difficult. This is because interrupt requests caused by instructions in the delay slot have to be processed differently from those arising from 'normal' instructions. When a delay slot instruction initiates an interrupt, the preceding instruction, namely the conditional branch, has already been fetched but not yet processed. This situation is quite different from that which occurs in traditional instruction processing where all instructions preceding an instruction that causes an interrupt have always been completed.
- Additional hardware is required to implement delayed branching.

In the following section we consider how the concept of delayed branching can be enhanced to increase performance gain and decrease code expansion.

8.3.2 Extensions of the basic scheme

The foregoing discussion of the basic concept makes it clear that the crucial point in delayed branching is to fill as many delay slots as possible. This is how performance gain can be increased and code expansion decreased. Next, based on Figure 8.12, we overview possible extensions of the basic concept, yielding an increased number of filled delay slots.

As Figure 8.12 shows, there are two possible ways of extending the basic concept: *increase the multiplicity* of delay slots, or *introduce annulment* of an instruction in the delay slot.

Most architectures provide *one delay slot* only. However, there are a few architectures offering *multiple delay slots*, such as the MIPS-X.

The other possibility to fill more delay slots is to introduce **annulment** (also called *nullification* or *squashing*). The basic idea is to introduce options in using delay slots, which can permit more delay slots to be filled than in the case of the basic scheme. In principle, for conditional branches four different kinds of annulment can be introduced, as shown in Figure 8.13. The four variants are distinguished by whether the delay slot is annulled or not for the taken and not-taken paths.

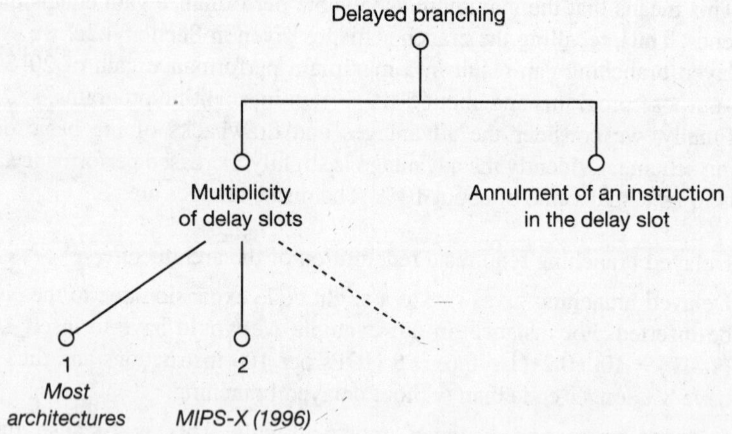

Figure 8.12 Design space of delayed branching.

The variants are:

- no annulment (**Branch-with-execute**),
- annul delay slot if the branch is not taken (**Branch-or-skip**),
- annul delay slot if the branch is taken (**Branch-with-skip**), and
- annul always.

The first variant is designated *branch-with-execute.* It is equivalent to the basic delayed branching scheme. The *branch-or-skip* scheme allows a delay slot to be annulled if the branch is not taken. It can be used, for example, for backward conditional branches, in order to move an instruction from within the loop body into the delay slot (see Figure 8.13). The *branch-with-skip* variant permits annulment of the delay slot if the branch is taken. This is useful for forward conditional branches, to relocate an instruction from the sequential path into a delay slot. Finally, The *annul always* scheme allows optional delayed branching to be introduced.

Architectures with annulment usually provide two of the above-mentioned possibilities, on a select basis, as indicated in Table 8.2. It is worth noting that in most main-line RISC architectures, which emerged in the second half of the 1980s, annulment has been introduced in some form to increase performance. Examples are the HP PA, the SPARC and the MC 88100 architecture.

As Table 8.2 indicates, most architectures that provide an extended scheme for delayed branching offer, in addition to the basic scheme (*Branch-with-execute*), the *Branch-or-skip* option. In practice, this is usually done by providing, for each individual branch instruction, two different forms, one with no annulment and the other with a certain type of annulment. These forms are usually distinguished in assembly language syntax by different mnemonics (like BNZ and BNZX in the MIPS-X), or by an optional suffix (such as .n in the MC 88100 family). Evidently, in the instruction encoding an extra bit is then used to differentiate between the options offered.

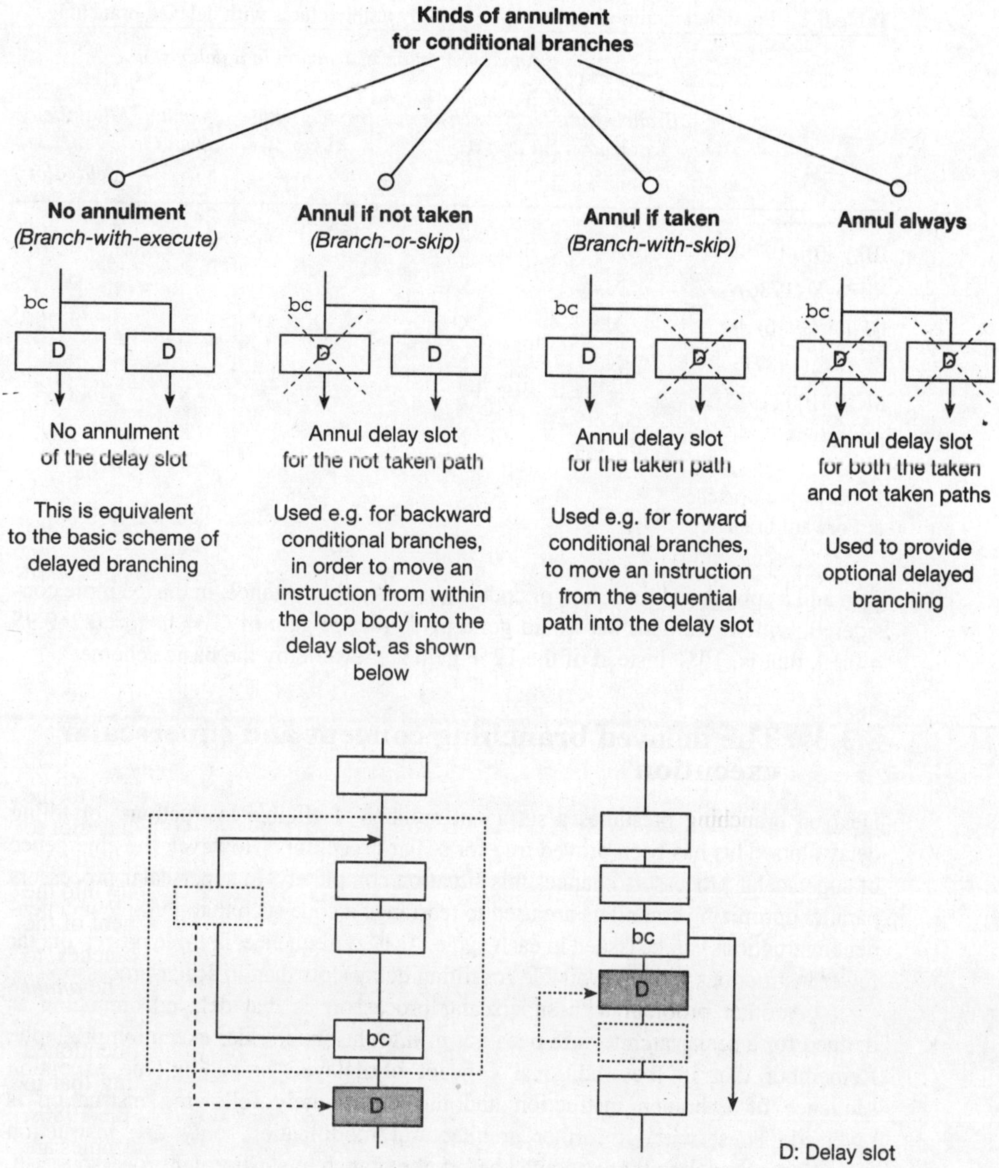

Figure 8.13 Kinds of annulment for conditional branches.

Most architectures listed in Table 8.2 also offer the possibility of annulling the instruction in the delay slot for unconditional branches, for instance the HP PA, SPARC and MC 88100.

How much can performance be increased by annulment? Garner et al. (1988) report, for the SPARC architecture, a 95 % filling of delay slots when annulment is used. Compared with the basic scheme, this is a considerably higher performance

Table 8.2 Possible annulment options provided by architectures with delayed branching.

	Annulment of an instruction in a delay slot				
	Branch-with-execute	*Branch-or-skip*	*Branch-with-skip*	*Annul always*	*Multiplicity of delay slot*
IBM 801 (1978)	X			X	1
MIPS-X (1986)	X	X			2
HP PA (1986)	X	X[1]	X[2]		1
SPARC (1987)	X	X			1
MC 88100 (1988)	X			X	1
i860 (1988)		X		X	1

1: Backward branches
2: Forward branches

gain and a substantial reduction of code expansion. For instance, in the example considered, with annulment we would get a performance gain of $G_d = f_b*f_f = 0.2*0.95 = 0.19$, that is, 19 % instead of the 12 % gain achievable by the basic scheme.

8.3.3 The delayed branching concept and superscalar execution

Delayed branching presumes a sufficient number of eligible instructions for filling delay slots. This has been proved true for scalar processors. However, the emergence of superscalar processors changes this situation completely. In superscalar processors parallel optimizing compilers are used to rearrange a code such that multiple independent instructions can be issued in each cycle. As a consequence, in these processors far fewer instructions remain available for filling delay slots than in scalar processors.

Another problem with superscalar processors is that delayed branching as defined for a scalar architecture does not fit into the superscalar execution principle. Remember that in the traditional concept of delayed branching, the execution sequence of a branch instruction and the immediately following instruction is reversed. Thus, without further architectural modification, only one instruction following a branch will be executed before the branch in superscalar processors also. However, an n-way superscalar processor would be able to issue n instructions ($n > 1$) in the cycle corresponding to the delay slot. This substantially reduces the maximum possible filling rate to a value which equals the reciprocal of the issue rate (n). For instance, in the case of a superscalar processor with an issue rate of four, the maximum possible filling rate is only 1/4, that is, 25 %. As a consequence, the expected gain in performance due to delayed branching diminishes for superscalar processors.

Actually, main-line architectures which have introduced delayed branching in connection with scalar processing are forced to retain architectural compatibility despite introducing superscalar execution. Consequently, in their superscalar implementations, architectures like the HP PA, SPARC and MC 88100 also restrict delayed branching to only one instruction following a branch, irrespective of the issue rate. This, of course, reduces the incentive to use delayed branching.

Thus, delayed branching seems to be a concept with no future. Note that all main-line RISC architectures introduced since the emergence of superscalar processors have avoided delayed branching, such as the i960 (1988), Power1 (RS/6000), DEC Alpha (1992) and PowerPC (1993). It is worth noting that the User's Manual of the superscalar MC 88110 contains a recommendation to avoid the delayed branching option, arguing that future MC 88XX0 processors are likely to implement delayed branching in software (Motorola, 1991).

8.4 Branch processing

The objective of this section is to acquaint the reader with the appealing, but very complex field of branch processing. Here, we refer to two basic approaches: blocking and speculative branch processing. These are commonly used in main-line processors.

As we have stressed many times, effective processing of branches has become a cornerstone of increased performance in ILP-processors. No wonder, therefore, that in the pursuit of more performance, predominantly in the past few years, computer architects have developed a confusing variety of branch processing schemes. After the recent announcements of a significant number of novel processors, we are in a position to discern trends and to emphasize promising solutions.

In this section, first we give an overview of the design space of conventional branch processing. Subsequently, we discuss the 'major dimensions' of the design space.

8.4.1 The design space

Branch processing has two aspects, its layout and its microarchitectural implementation, as depicted in Figure 8.14. As far as its layout is concerned, branch processing involves three major subtasks: detecting branches, handling of unresolved conditional branches and accessing the branch target path.

Thus, the layout part of the design space covers the corresponding aspects, as indicated in Figure 8.14.

The first aspect is *branch detection*. Initially, processors detected branches during instruction decoding. However, the earlier a processor detects branches, the earlier branch processing can be started and the fewer penalties there are. Therefore, novel schemes try to detect branches as early as possible. In Section 8.4.2 we present appropriate methods for doing that.

The next aspect of the layout is the handling of *unresolved conditional branches*. We note that we designate a conditional branch **unresolved** if the specified condition is not yet available at the time when it is evaluated during branch processing. In Section 8.4.3 we give an overview of the basic policies used. Section 8.4.4 is devoted to the predominant policy used in recent processors, called *speculative branch processing*.

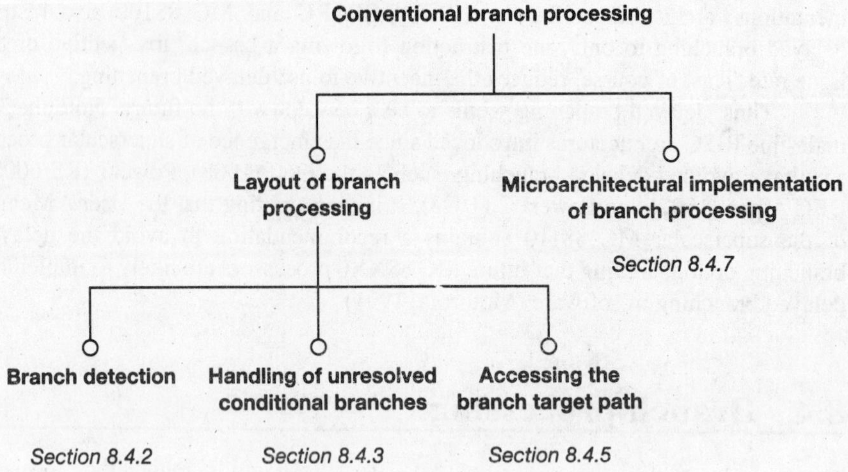

Figure 8.14 Key aspects of the design space of branch processing.

The last aspect of the layout of branch processing is how the branch target path is accessed. Section 8.4.5 reviews the ways used by processors to perform this task. Finally, the design space also covers the *microarchitectural implementation of branch processing*, which is discussed briefly in Section 8.4.7.

8.4.2 Branch detection

Figure 8.15 gives an overview of branch detection methods employed in processors. Early pipelined microprocessors, such as the MC 68020 or the 80386, detect branches during the common instruction decoding (*master pipeline approach*). The obvious drawback of this straightforward approach is that it gives rise to long branch processing penalties.

In order to reduce taken penalties, up-to-date processors usually detect branches earlier than during common instruction coding (*early branch detection*). As Figure 8.15 indicates, there are three methods: in parallel branch detection, look-ahead branch detection and integrated instruction fetch and detection. In the following we introduce these early branch detection schemes.

A number of processors detect and decode branches *in parallel* with the 'common' instruction decoding, as indicated in Figure 8.16 for the PowerPC 601. We call this scheme **in parallel branch detection**. The α line of processors (α 21064, α 21064A or α 21164) serves as further examples.

A slightly more advanced branch detection method is to spot branches from the instruction buffer in parallel with the common instruction decoding as before, but also to look ahead into preceding buffer entries. We call this scheme **look-ahead branch detection**. For instance, as Figure 8.17 shows, the Power1 (RS/6000) detects branches from the last five entries, and the Power2 from the last eight entries, of the sequential instruction buffer. By contrast, instructions other than branches are decoded and issued only from the last four and six entries, respectively. We note here that in order to support a quick recovery from a misprediction (see Section 8.4.4),

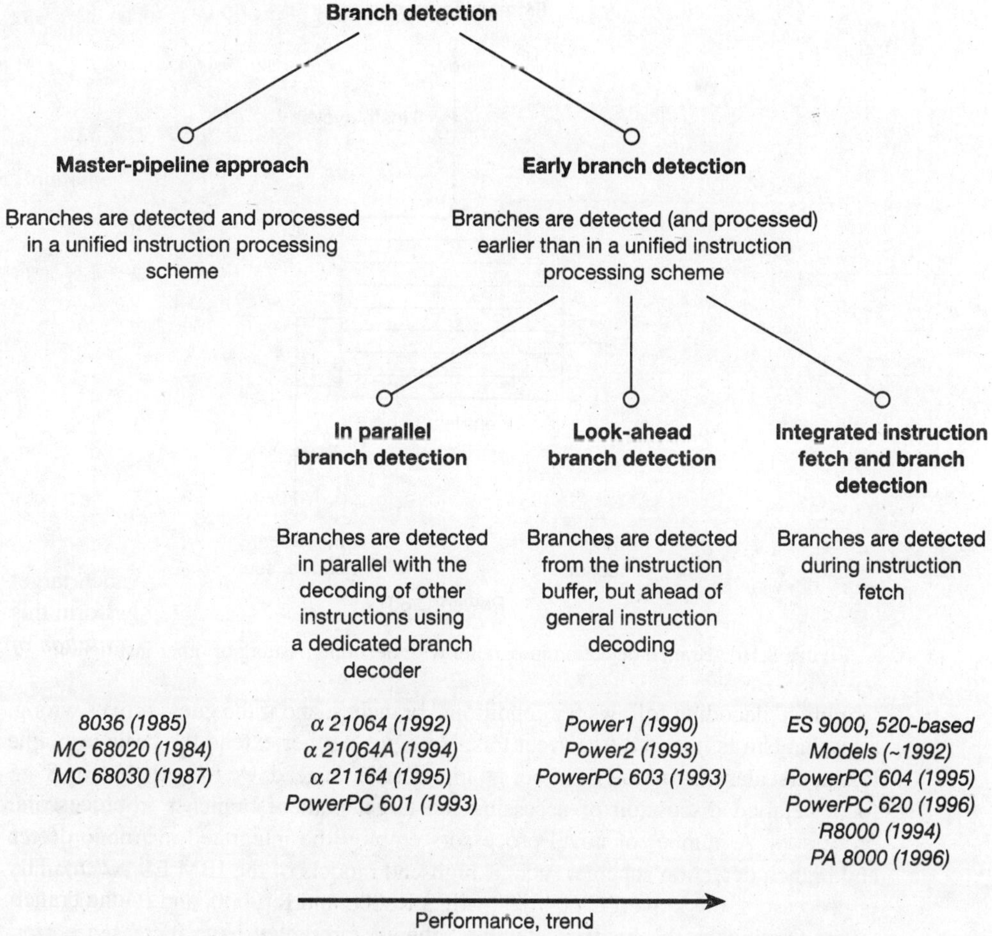

Figure 8.15 Branch detection schemes.

both processors mentioned have two distinct instruction buffers, one for the sequential path and one for the taken path. Nevertheless, in Figure 8.17(a) we consider only how branches are decoded in the sequential path.

A somewhat different variant of branch detection is chosen in the PowerPC 603. In this processor branch detection is *entirely shifted ahead, to the input* of the instruction buffer. A dual decoder checks the instructions read from the instruction cache into the instruction buffer for branches, as shown in Figure 8.17(b).

The most advanced method of branch detection avoids explicit decoding such as described above. Instead, branch detection is integrated into the instruction fetch mechanism. This scheme is called **integrated instruction fetch and branch detection**. For scalar processors its principle is as follows. The instruction fetching mechanism is extended such that it is able to detect whether the next instruction to be fetched is a branch or not. Each detected branch is guessed to be taken and instead of, or in addition to, the next sequential instruction, the target address of the branch or even the target instruction is also fetched in advance. Evidently, in this scheme a

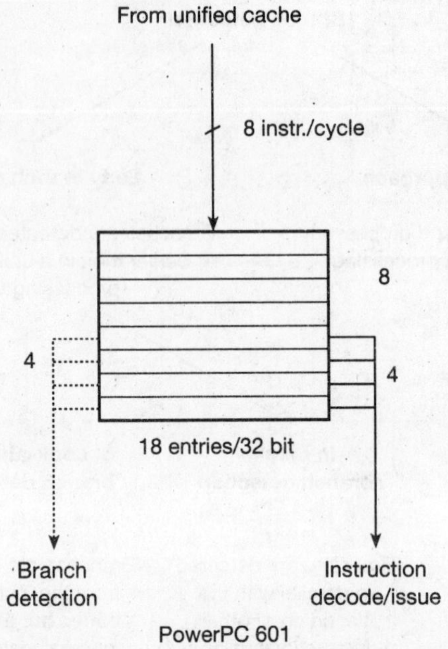

Figure 8.16 Branch detection in parallel with decoding/issuing of other instructions.

'common' decoding follows for conditional branches, and if the guess proves wrong, a mechanism is initiated to correct this. Here, we neither extend the basic principle for superscalar instruction issue nor go into details. Instead, we refer to Section 8.4.5 for a detailed discussion of accessing the target path of branches in superscalar processors. A number of novel processors employ the integrated instruction fetch and branch detection scheme, such as high-end models of the IBM ES 9000 family of processors, the PowerPC 604/620, MIPS R8000 and R10000, and PA 8000.

Obviously, the branch detection schemes presented have increased performance potential according to the sequence in which they are discussed. This sequence also represents the trend of branch detection.

8.4.3 Overview of unresolved conditional branch processing policies

A conditional branch cannot be evaluated before the referenced condition is known. For instance, if the specified condition refers to the sign of the result of the preceding instruction, the precondition of the evaluation is that the preceding instruction has been executed. Until the referenced condition becomes known, the conditional branch is said to be *unresolved*. There are three basic approaches used by processors to cope with unresolved conditional branches: blocking branch processing, speculative execution and multiway branching, as shown in Figure 8.18.

Blocking branch processing is the trivial approach to cope with unresolved conditional branches (Figure 8.18). Execution of the conditional branch is simply stalled until the specified condition can be resolved.

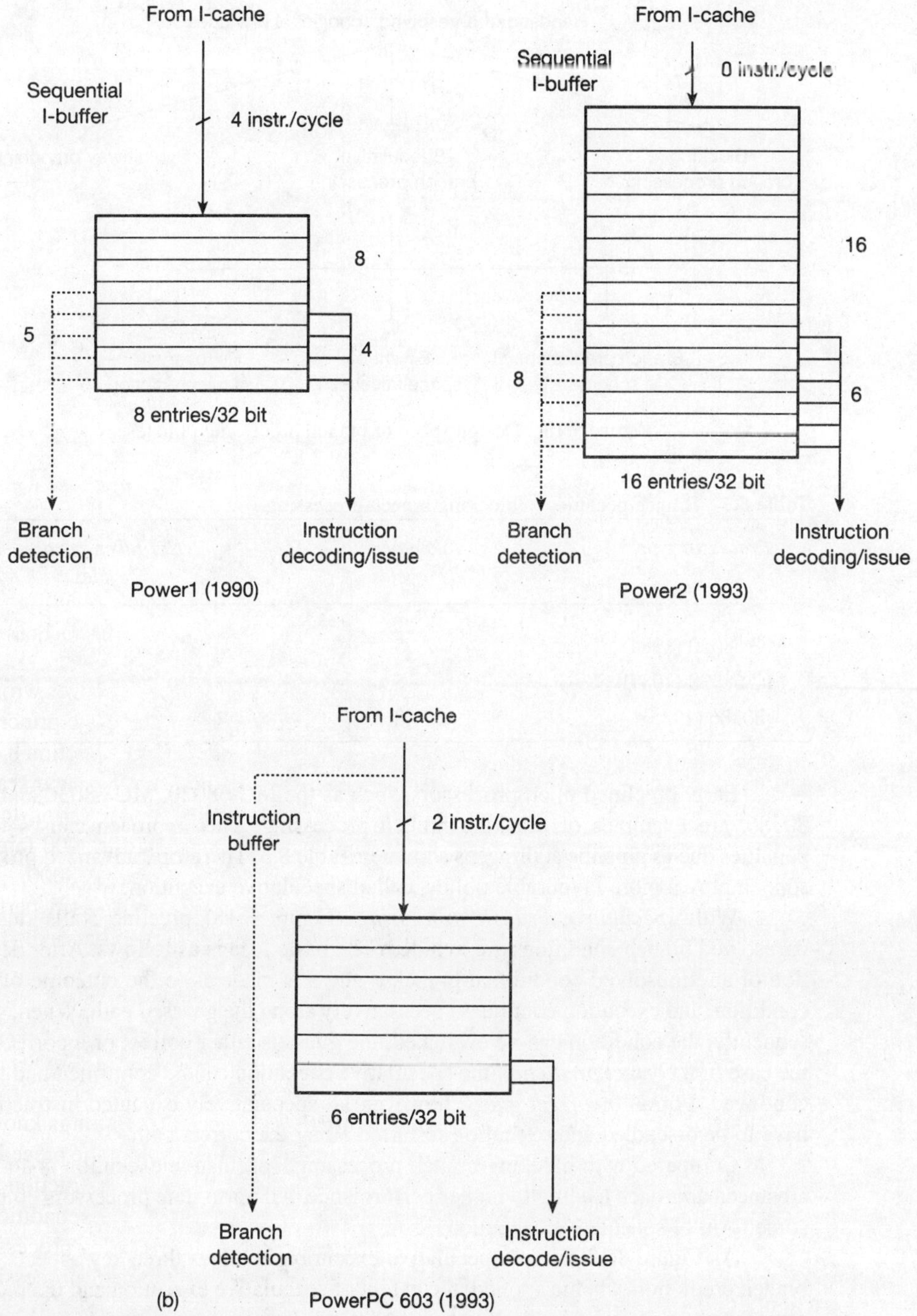

Figure 8.17 (a) Early detection of branches by looking ahead into preceding entries of the instruction buffer; (b) early detection of branches by inspection of the instructions to be read into the instruction buffer.

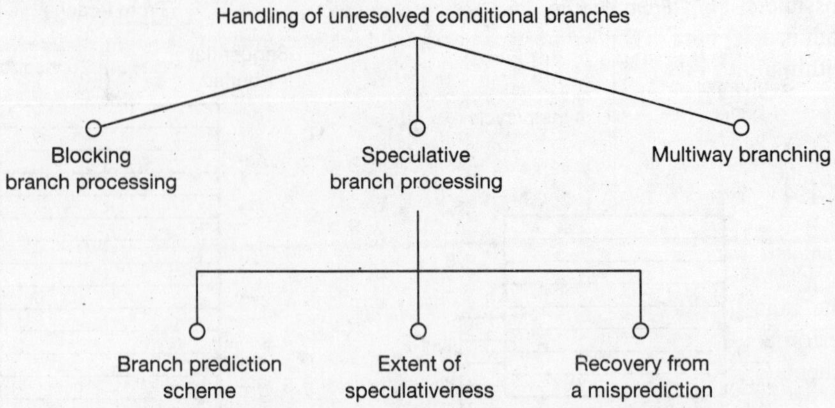

Figure 8.18 Design space of branch processing policies.

Table 8.3 Branch penalties in blocking branch processing.

Processor type	*Taken penalty cycles*	*Not-taken penalty cycles*
MC 68020 (1984)	5	3
MC 68030 (1987)	5	3
80386 (1985)	8	2

Early pipelined microprocessors, such as the MC 68020, MC 68030 and the 80386, are examples of blocking branch processing. This approach causes long penalties due to pipeline stalling, as shown in Table 8.3. Therefore, advanced processors employ a more favourable policy, called speculative execution.

With *speculative branch processing* (Figure 8.18) pipeline stalls due to unresolved branch conditions are avoided. The basic idea is as follows. After detection of an unresolved conditional branch a guess is made as to the outcome of the condition, and execution continues speculatively along the guessed path. When, subsequently, the condition can be evaluated, the guess is either correct or incorrect. In the case of a *correct prediction* the speculative execution can be confirmed and then continued. For an *incorrect guess*, however, all speculatively executed instructions have to be discarded and execution restarted along the correct path.

Compared with blocking branch processing, speculative execution is a more advanced approach leading to higher performance. All up-to-date processors employ some form of speculative execution.

As Figure 8.18 shows, speculative execution involves three key aspects: the branch prediction scheme applied, the extent of speculative execution and the recovery scheme used in the case of a misprediction. These issues are discussed in the related subsections.

Finally, *multiway branching* is the most ambitious scheme to cope with unresolved conditional branches. Here, in case of an unresolved conditional branch both possible paths are pursued. When the specified condition is evaluated the correct path is determined. This path is confirmed and the incorrect path cancelled. We deal with multiway branching somewhat arbitrarily in a separate section (Section 8.5).

8.4.4 Branch prediction schemes

Overview

The branch prediction scheme used in a processor has a crucial impact on its performance. Consequently, much effort has been put into developing an effective scheme. In this section we overview the basic prediction schemes developed so far.

Basically, a prediction may be either a fixed or a true prediction (Figure 8.19). In a **fixed prediction** the same guess is always made, either 'taken' or 'not taken'. This is a *one-outcome* guess.

A **true prediction** has *two possible outcomes*, either 'taken' or 'not-taken' (fall through, sequential path).

With true predictions, we distinguish between *static* and *dynamic* predictions, as indicated in Figure 8.19. The prediction is called **static** if it depends only on the code in question. If the prediction is subject to the previous execution of the same branch instruction, that is, the prediction depends on the execution history, we are dealing with **dynamic prediction**.

Static prediction is more straightforward than dynamic prediction. Here, a guess is made on the fly according to some specific attributes of the branch instruction, for

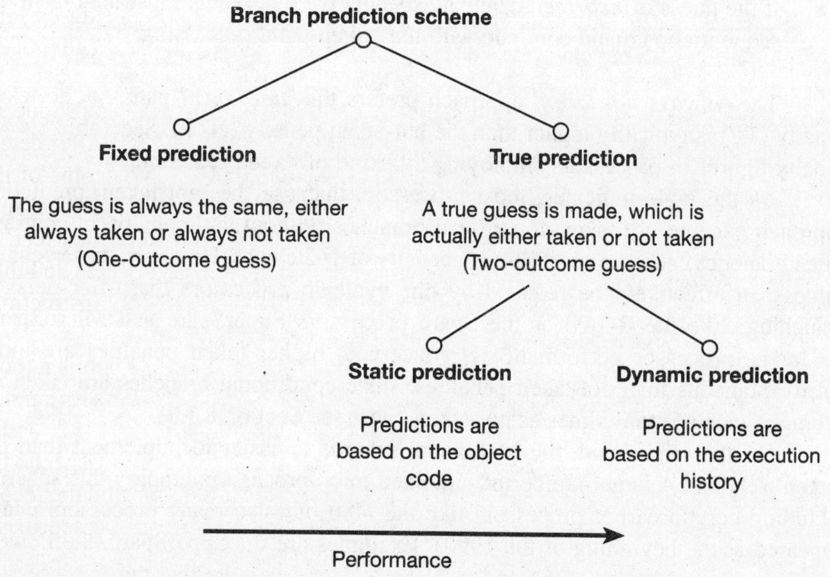

Figure 8.19 Basic kinds of branch predictions.

instance according to the sign of the displacement. In contrast, *dynamic branch prediction* takes into account the outcomes of past branches. This requires the processor to save the outcome of the last, or of the last n, recently executed branches. Consequently, dynamic prediction is more complex than static prediction, but it offers higher potential.

Fixed, static and dynamic predictions have increasing performance potential in that order, as indicated in Figure 8.19. In the following we discuss these prediction schemes in detail. Then, we show some numerical results of prediction accuracy. Finally, we discuss branch prediction trends.

Fixed prediction

Figure 8.20 shows the fixed prediction approach and contrasts its basic alternatives: the '*always not taken*' and the '*always taken*' approaches.

'Always not taken' approach The **'always not taken'** approach (or 'not taken' approach for short) has the following typical processing scheme (see also Figure 8.20):

- Detect an unresolved conditional branch and guess it as *'not taken'*.
- Continue with the execution of the sequential path, but in preparation for a wrong guess, start the execution of the taken path (for example, calculate BTA) in parallel.
- When the condition becomes evaluable, check the guess.
- If the guess is *correct*, continue with the execution of the sequential path, and delete taken path preprocessing.
- If the guess is *incorrect*, delete all speculative by executed instructions in the sequential path and continue with the 'taken path' processing.

The *'always not taken'* approach prefers the *'not taken'* path, so the taken penalty (TP) is typically higher than the not-taken penalty (NTP). See Table 8.4 for penalty figures of processors employing this kind of fixed prediction.

As the table indicates, most processors that use the 'not taken' prediction approach execute not-taken conditional branches without any penalty. In contrast, taken branches cause, in most cases, a penalty of 1–3 cycles. However, these penalty values can effectively be reduced by one cycle in processors that offer delayed branching, like the R4000 or the Sparc processors SuperSparc and MicroSparc. As far as processor performance is concerned, higher taken penalties are more disadvantageous than not-taken penalties, since conditional branches are taken on average twice as many times as not-taken ones (see Section 8.1.3).

On the other hand, the 'not-taken' scheme is easier to implement than the 'taken' scheme. A large number of pipelined microprocessors employ this scheme, including certain earlier processors like the i486 but also many processors which appeared at the beginning of the 1990s. Examples are the SuperSparc, the Power1 and Power2, and the α 21064 and α 21064A. Here we note that the α processors mentioned provide the 'not taken' prediction scheme as an available option.

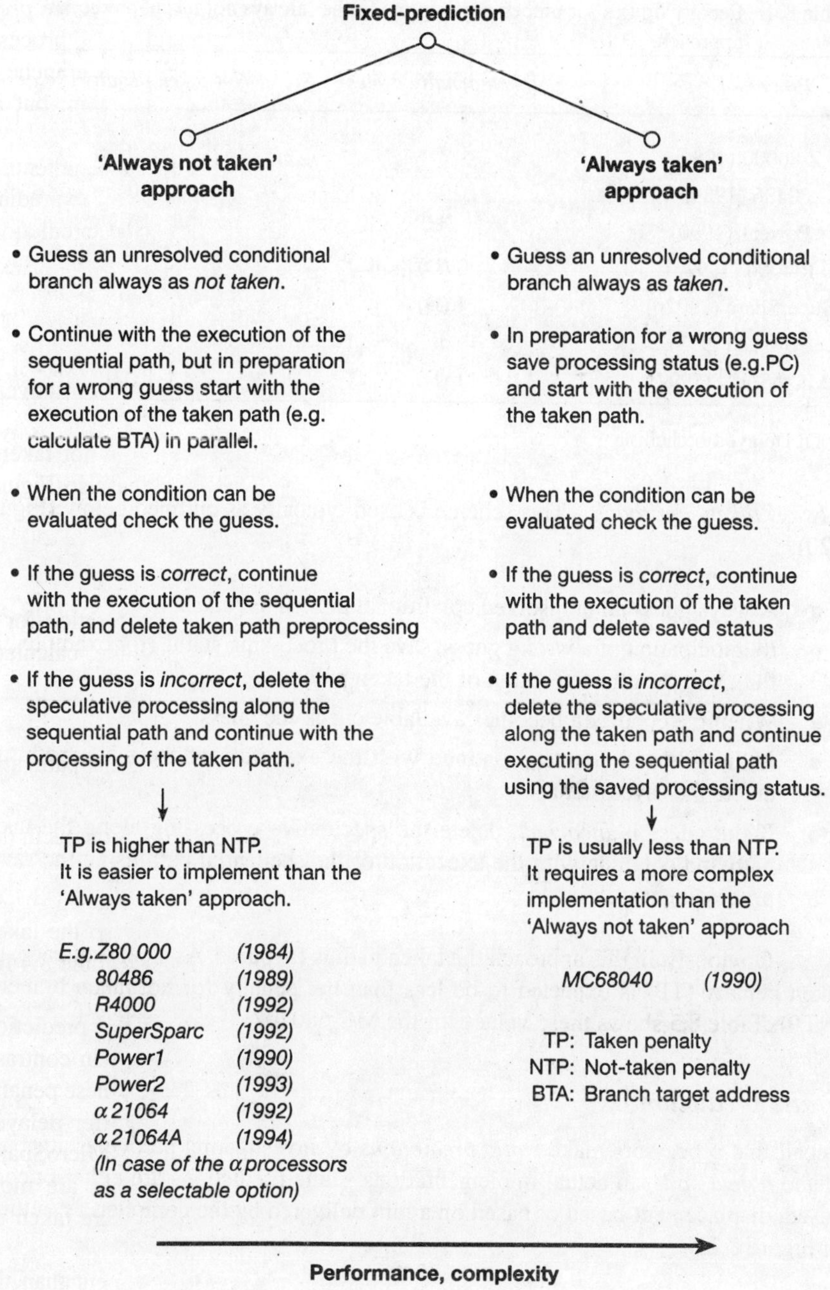

Figure 8.20 The fixed prediction approach.

Table 8.4 Penalty figures for processors employing the 'always not taken' prediction approach.

Processor type	*Taken penalty cycles*	*Not-taken penalty cycles*
Z 80000 (1984p)	3	0
80486 (1989p)	2	0
Power1 (1990)	3	0
R 4000 (1992p)	3 (D)	0
SuperSparc (1992p)	1 (D)	0
Power2 (1993)	1	0
MicroSparc (1992)	1 (D)	1 (D)

D: Delayed branching

'Always taken' approach This scheme is used typically as outlined below (Figure 8.20):

- Always guess an unresolved conditional branch as '*taken*'.
- In anticipation of a wrong guess, save the processing status (for example, the PC), and start the execution of the taken path.
- When the condition becomes available check the guess.
- If the guess is *correct*, continue with the execution of the taken path and delete the saved status.
- If the guess is *incorrect*, delete the speculative processing along the taken path and continue with the execution of the sequential path using the saved processing status.

Obviously, in this approach the taken path is favoured. As a consequence, the taken penalty (TP) is expected to be less than the penalty for not-taken branches (NTP). Table 8.5 shows these values for the MC 68040.

Static prediction

Recall that processors make *static predictions* by investigating particular attributes of the *object code*. In actual implementations, static predictions are either opcode-based, displacement-based or based on a hint delivered by the compiler, as outlined in Figure 8.21.

Table 8.5 Penalty figures for the 'always taken' prediction approach.

Processor type	*Taken penalty cycles*	*Not-taken penalty cycles*
MC 68040 (1990)	1	2

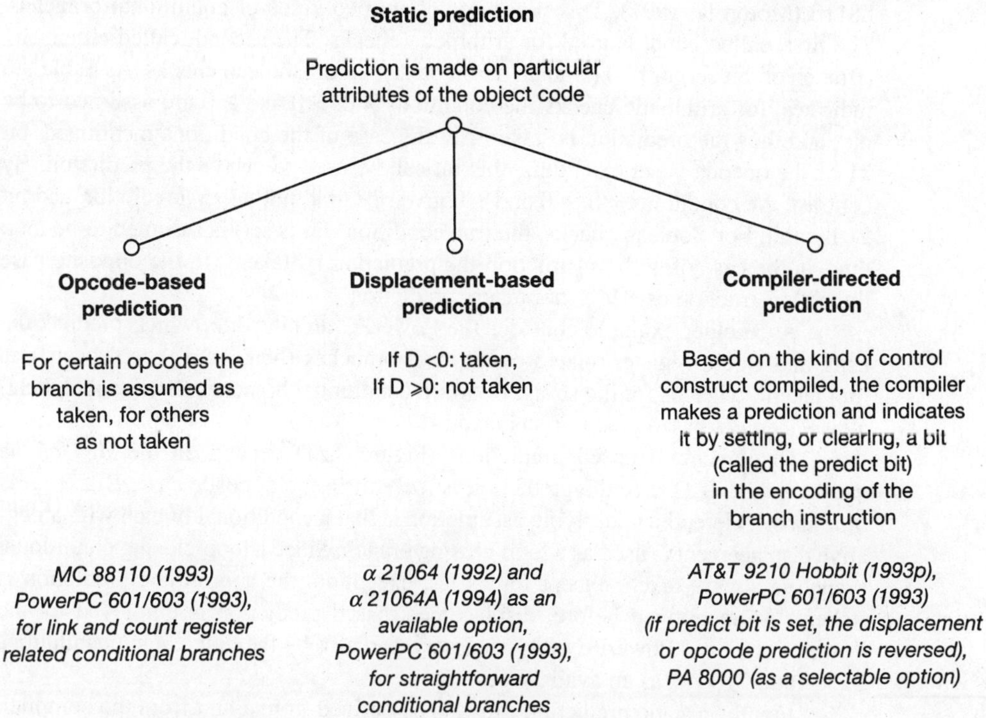

Figure 8.21 Basic alternatives of static branch prediction.

Opcode-based predictions are made by assuming that the branch will be 'taken' for certain opcodes and 'not taken' for others. This prediction technique is used, for instance, in the MC 88110 and PowerPC 601/603 processors. As a demonstration, Table 8.6 shows how opcode-based prediction is accomplished in the MC

Table 8.6 Static prediction as implemented in the MC 88110 (1993).

Instruction	*Condition specified*	*Bit 21 of the instr. code*	*Prediction*
bcnd (Branch conditional)	=0	0	Not Taken
	≠0	1	Taken
	>0	1	Taken
	<0	0	Not Taken
	≥0	1	Taken
	≤0	0	Not Taken
bb1 (Branch on bit set)			Taken
bb0 (Branch on bit clear)			Not Taken

88110 (Motorola, 1991). This processor offers two kinds of conditional branches. The first, called bcnd, is used for arithmetic checks. The second, called either bb1 (Branch on bit set) or bb0 (Branch on bit clear), is for Boolean checks. As Table 8.6 indicates, for arithmetic checks the conditions $\neq 0$, > 0 and ≥ 0 are assumed to be met and thus the prediction is 'taken'. In the case of the conditions mentioned, bit 21 of the opcode is set to 1; thus, this bit can be used to derive the prediction. By contrast, the conditions $= 0$, < 0 and ≤ 0 give rise to a 'not taken' prediction and bit 21 is reset. For Boolean checks, the true condition (bit is set) is assumed to be met; thus, in the case of a bb1 instruction the prediction is 'taken'. In the opposite case the bb0 instruction causes a 'not taken' prediction.

As another example consider the PowerPC architecture, which predicts the Link and Count register-related conditional branches (bclr, bclrl, bcctr, bcctrl) as 'not taken', whereas for the straightforward conditional branches (bc, bca, bcl, bcla) a displacement-based prediction is made.

Displacement-based predictions (Figure 8.21) depend on the *sign of the displacement*. If $D < 0$, the prediction is '*taken*'; in the opposite case, $D \geq 0$, *it is 'not taken'*. Here, the underlying assumption is that a conditional branch with a negative displacement is used as a loop-closing branch. Since a loop-closing conditional branch is always taken, except for its last execution, the appropriate prediction is 'taken'. As mentioned before, displacement-based prediction is employed by the PowerPC 601 and PowerPC 603 processors, and also by the first α implementations 21064 and 21064A as an available option.

Finally, a static prediction can also be derived from a hint from the compiler. This kind of prediction is called **compiler-directed prediction** (Figure 8.20). In this case the compiler makes a prediction according to the kind of control construct compiled or a user-delivered hint (expressed, for instance, as an optional suffix attached to the instruction coding). The compiler's prediction is indicated by setting or clearing a bit (called the **predict bit**) in the encoding of the conditional branch instruction. For instance, in the PowerPC architecture bit 10 of the encoding of conditional branches is the predict bit. When specified as such, the outcome of opcode-based and displacement-based prediction (default prediction) is reversed. Examples of processors using predict bits are the PowerPC 601 and PowerPC 603. Another processor which makes use of compiler-directed predictions is the PA 8000. In this case, compiler-directed prediction is an available option. If specified, it overrules dynamic prediction on a page-by-page basis. This remarkable solution enables the use of static prediction in programs recompiled for the PA 8000 if a higher prediction rate can be expected. On the other hand, older programs like library routines can carry on using dynamic prediction as the default prediction method.

Dynamic prediction

Overview of dynamic prediction techniques *Dynamic prediction* is made on branch history. The basic philosophy of *dynamic prediction* is that branches which were taken at their last occurrence (or last n occurrences) are also likely to be taken at their next occurrence. Evidently, dynamic techniques have a higher performance potential than static schemes. But the price is a more complex implementation, since the processor has to store and update the last outcomes of a large number of branches. By contrast, static schemes neglect branch history, and instead make a code-based prediction on the fly.

There are two different approaches for expressing the history of branches, as shown in Figure 8.22. In the **explicit dynamic technique** branch history is explicitly stated in the form of *history bits*. Actual implementations of this technique use one, two or three bits for expressing the history, as discussed below. The other approach is the **implicit dynamic technique**, in which branch history is implicitly stated by the presence of an entry for a predicted branch target access path. We now discuss how these dynamic techniques work.

1-bit dynamic prediction This is the simplest dynamic technique. In a **1-bit prediction**, a single bit per branch is used to express whether the last occurrence of the branch was taken or not. Accordingly, this technique maintains a straightforward

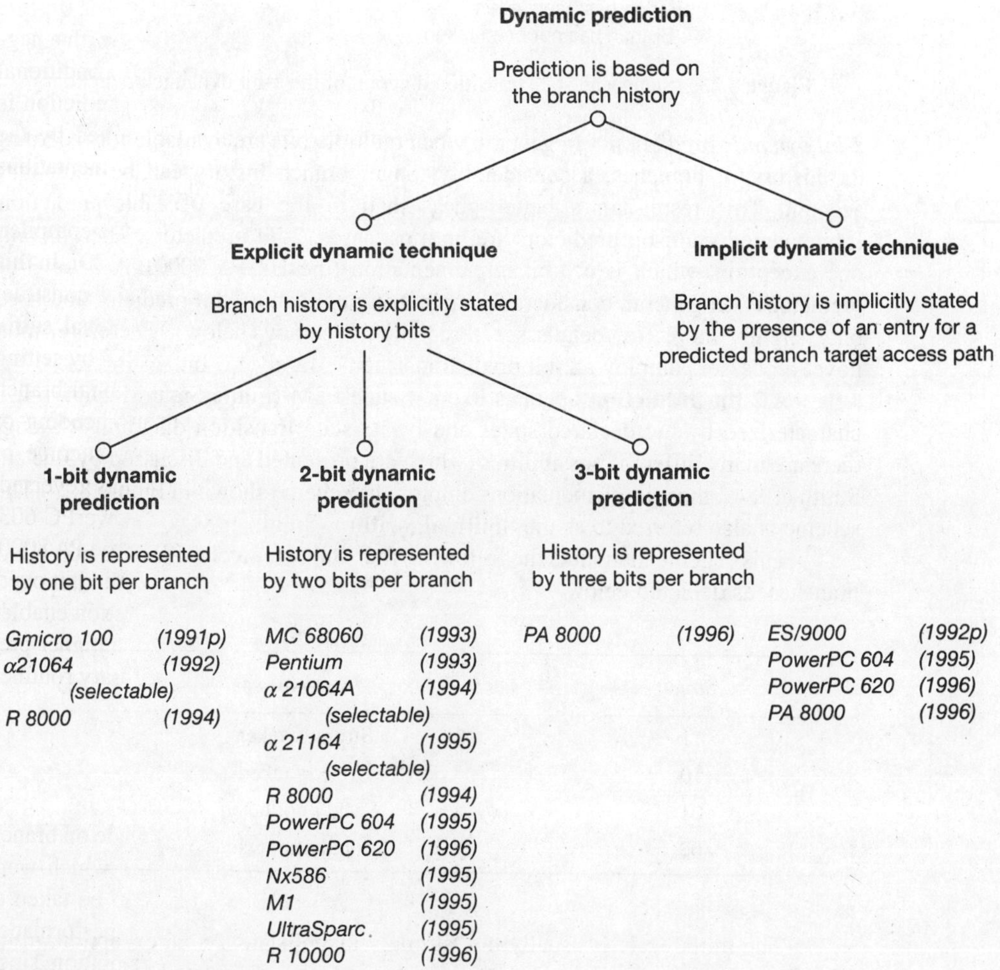

Figure 8.22 Basic types of dynamic branch prediction.

two-state history ('taken' or 'not taken') for a number of branches, as indicated in Figure 8.23. After evaluating the branch, its associated history is updated as a *one-bit saturating counter*. In this case, the prediction is the same as the last outcome of the associated branch.

There are only a few processors which use the 1-bit dynamic prediction, such as the α 21064 as an available option and the R8000 as one of the prediction techniques used.

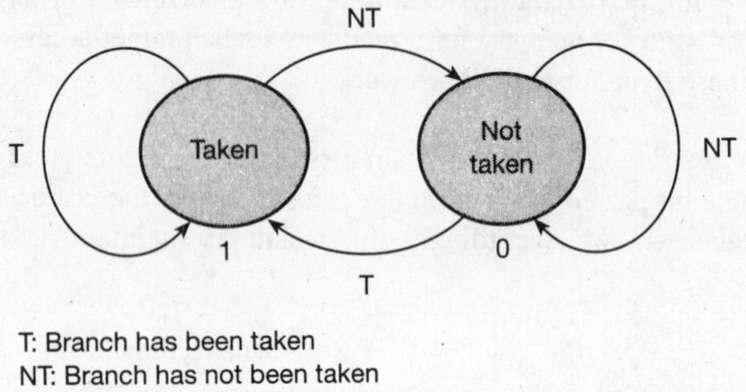

Figure 8.23 States and state transition diagram of the 1-bit dynamic prediction.

2-bit dynamic prediction In general, when multiple bits are available for recording the history of branches, a considerably longer branch history can be taken into account. This results in a better guess than in the case of 1-bit prediction. Implemented multi-bit predictors are, in most cases, 2-bit predictors. There is only one exception, which is a 3-bit implementation (the HP PA 8000). A 2- or 3-bit predictor is, in general, considerably more accurate than a 1-bit predictor and costs only slightly more (for details see 'Prediction accuracy' below). Therefore, most novel processors employ a 2-bit prediction scheme, rarely a 3-bit.

A **2-bit prediction** operates like a 4-state FSM (Finite State Machine). It is characterized by the declared states and by its state transition diagram. Although there are many different possibilities (which are presented and discussed by Lee and Smith (1984), most implementations employ the scheme shown in Figure 8.24. This scheme is also referred to as the **Smith algorithm** (Smith, 1981).

This scheme maintains the following four states for a considerable number of branches, as depicted below:

State	*Designation*
11	Strongly taken
10	Weakly taken
01	Weakly not taken
00	Strongly not taken

The initial state is usually the 'strongly taken' state. As an exception, in the UltraSparc a compiler-delivered 'branch prediction bit' is used to initialize the

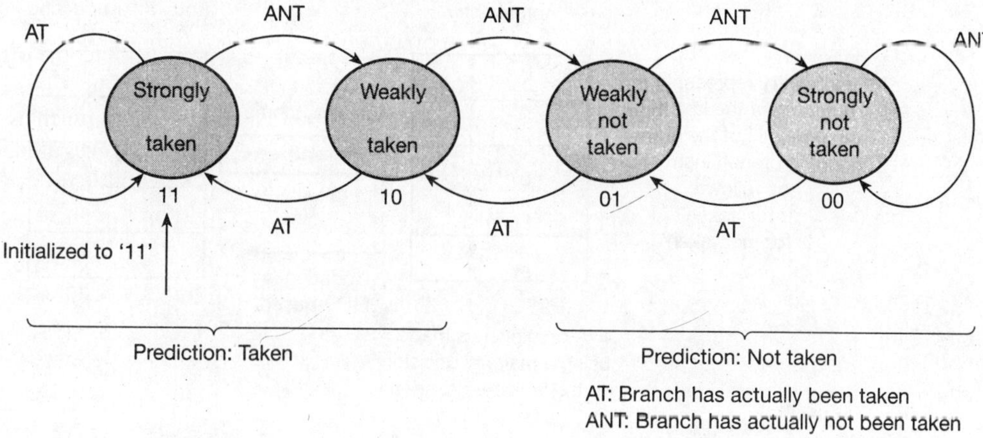

Figure 8.24 Maintained states, initial state and the state transition diagram for the most frequently used 2-bit prediction scheme (Smith algorithm).

branch prediction state. The state transition diagram corresponds to a *2-bit saturating counter* with the states 'strongly taken', 'weakly taken', 'weakly not taken' and 'strongly not taken'. The prediction is made according to the actual state of the counter, as follows. If the actual state is either the 'strongly taken' state or 'weakly taken' state, the prediction is 'taken' but in the two other states it is 'not taken'. Following the predictions, when the actual branch has been resolved, the state of the FSM is updated according to the outcome of the branch.

The overwhelming majority of recent, or recently announced, processors employ the prediction scheme just described. Some processors offer it as an available prediction alternative, like the α 21064A, but most recent, superscalar processors employ it as the standard prediction technique, such as the α 21164, Pentium, and PowerPC 604 and 620. For a more complete list of processors using 2-bit dynamic prediction see Figure 8.22.

3-bit prediction In **3-bit prediction**, the outcomes of the last three occurrences of the branch instructions are stored, as indicated in Figure 8.25. The prediction is made on a majority basis. For instance, if two of the last three branch outcomes were taken, the guess will be 'taken'. Subsequently, after the outcome of the branch becomes known, the corresponding entry is updated. This is done on a FIFO basis, writing a '0' into the entry if the branch has not been taken or a '1' if it has. This scheme is claimed to be simpler to implement than the 2-bit technique, yet results in similar accuracy (Gwennap, 1994).

So far, only the recently introduced PA 8000 processor employs the 3-bit prediction scheme.

Implicit dynamic technique In Section 8.4.5 we will discuss schemes for accessing the branch target path. Among these are two which may also be used for branch prediction. These are the so-called BTAC (Branch Target Access Cache) and BTIC

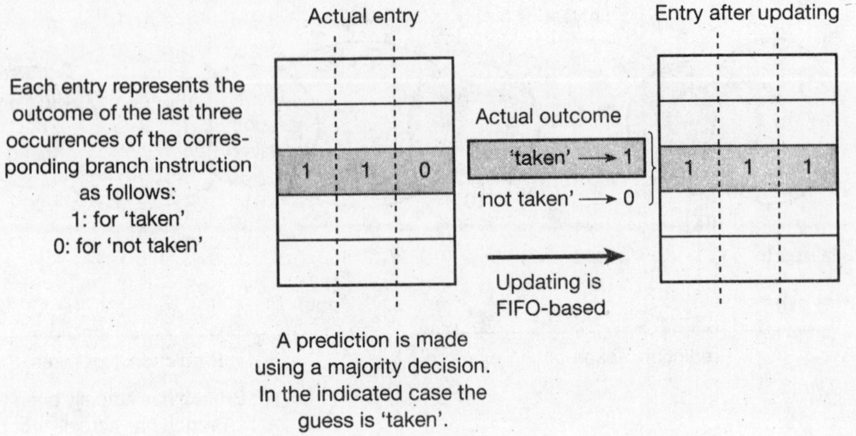

Figure 8.25 Principle of the 3-bit prediction.

(Branch Target Instruction Cache) schemes. In both methods an extra cache is introduced which holds the most recently used branch addresses and either the corresponding branch target addresses (in the BTAC scheme) or the corresponding branch target instructions (in the BTIC scheme). Thus, whenever a branch instruction is fetched, the corresponding branch target address (BTAC scheme) or the corresponding branch target instructions (BTIC scheme) can be made available at the same time. Now, the BTAC and BTIC branch target accessing schemes can be used for prediction too. This is achieved simply by holding entries in the BTAC or BTIC only for *taken* branches. In this case the branch history is indicated implicitly by the presence or absence of a corresponding entry in the BTAC or BTIC. The existence of an entry means that the corresponding branch was taken at its last occurrence and so its next occurrence is also guessed as 'taken'.

It is worth noting that the implicit prediction technique is a *special kind of 1-bit prediction*. At the same time, the implicit prediction is a specific variant of the BTAC or BTIC scheme. Its speciality is that for not-taken branches no entries are maintained in the BTAC or BTIC. Obviously, this type of entry management is more efficient than retaining entries for both taken and not-taken branches in a BTAC or BTIC.

Considering that a 1-bit prediction has a low performance potential, implicit prediction is usually enhanced by a multi-bit prediction which is discussed later in this section.

There are only a few processors employing implicit prediction. Certain processors use it as one element of a multiple prediction technique, such as the PowerPC 604, PowerPC 620 and PA 8000, as shown in Figure 8.22.

Implementation of history bits As discussed earlier, in the 1-, 2- and 3-bit dynamic prediction techniques history bits are used to record branch history. Here, we review their implementation.

Processors employ one of four different schemes to implement history bits (Figure 8.26). In the most straightforward scheme history bits are placed *in the*

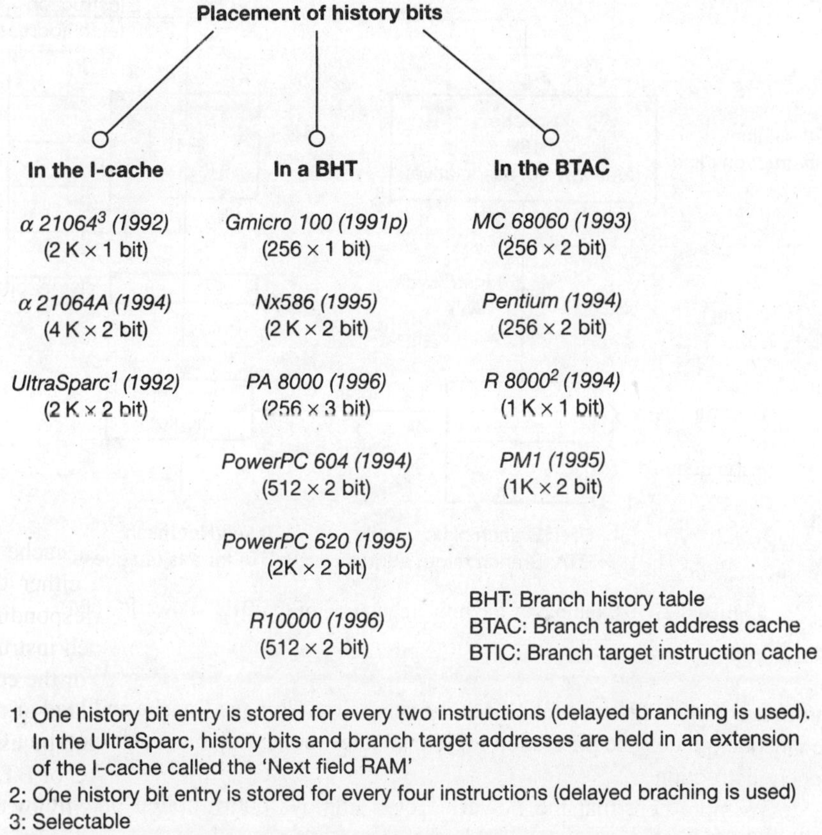

Figure 8.26 Implementation alternatives of history bits.

I-cache. For instance, the α processors provide one (21064) or two (21064A) history bits in the I-cache for each instruction. In contrast, the UltraSparc maintains only two 2-bit entries for each cache line, which contains four instructions. Remember here that the Sparc architecture maintains delay slots, thus not more than two branches (and two delay slots) can occur in four subsequent instructions. Since in the UltraSparc only a single branch target address (actually a 10-bit cache index) is provided per cache line, the compiler is expected to guarantee not more than one branch per cache line.

The next solution is to provide an extra hardware unit, termed the **branch history table** (BHT). The BHT contains 256 to 2 K entries in recent processors, while each entry has one, two or three bits, according to the prediction scheme supported. This table is accessed in parallel with the I-cache and is addressed by the least significant part of the address. Figure 8.27 shows a typical implementation (PowerPC 604, with reference to Song et al. (1994)). In the PowerPC 604 there is a 512-entry BHT organized as 128 × 4 entries with two history bits per entry. The BHT is accessed by the instruction fetch address and delivers four entries belonging to the

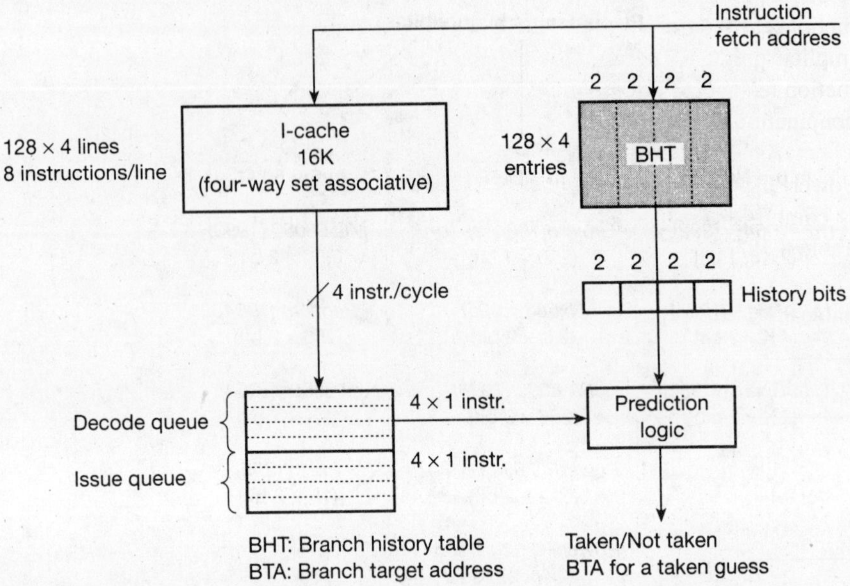

Figure 8.27 Example of the implementation of the BHT (PowerPC 604).

four instructions which are fetched at the same time from the I-cache and loaded into the Decode queue. The prediction logic evaluates the history bits corresponding to a branch instruction.

We note here that the PowerPC 604 employs both implicit prediction and explicit 2-bit prediction as detailed in the next section.

Using a BHT seems to be the most preferred implementation of history bits. Among others, the PowerPC 604, PowerPC 620, PA 8000 and R10000 employ this scheme.

Referring to Figure 8.26 we also mention a further implementation variant. In this variant the history bits are placed into *the BTAC*. The Pentium, MIPS R8000 and PM1 (Sparc69) are examples that place history bits in the BTAC.

At the present time it is too early to assess these novel variants. Some years will have to pass before a proper comparison can be made or trends become noticeable.

Application of multiple prediction techniques in a processor

Implicit prediction is a favoured prediction technique since it allows a correctly guessed taken path to be accessed without any penalty and it is easy to implement. The simplicity of implementation arises from the fact that the presence of a corresponding entry to a branch address in the BTAC or BTIC is interpreted as an indication of a 'taken' guess. The problem with implicit prediction, however, is that it requires a fully associative implementation. But the high cost of fully associative structures restricts the size of the BTAC or BTIC in most current implementations to 32–256 entries, as indicated in Tables 8.12–8.13. As a consequence, implicit prediction alone would result in a low prediction accuracy. Thus, processors using implicit prediction are often also equipped with a more efficient but 'slower' prediction technique. Then both techniques, or in one case three techniques, operate in conjunction as detailed next.

As an example, let us discuss how multiple prediction is implemented in the PowerPC 604 and PowerPC 620 processors. In these processors implicit prediction is combined with 2-bit prediction. The resulting guess is derived as indicated in Table 8.7.

Table 8.7 Combining implicit and 2-bit prediction, as implemented in the PowerPC 604 (1995) and 620 (1996) processors.

BTAC	*Outcome of the 2-bit prediction*	*Overall prediction*
Hit	Don't care	Taken
Miss	Taken	Taken
Miss	Not taken	Not taken

The PowerPC 604 has a 64-entry BTAC and a 512-entry BHT, whereas the corresponding values for the PowerPC 620 are 256 entries in the BTAC and 2 K entries in the BHT. When there is an entry in the BTAC for a referenced fetch address, that is, the BTAC hits, the overall prediction is 'taken', regardless of the outcome of the 2-bit prediction. If, however, there is no corresponding entry in the BTAC, that is, there is a miss, the outcome of the 2-bit prediction is used as the overall guess. We note here that the penalties for the two cases resulting in a taken prediction are different. When the overall 'taken' prediction results from a BTAC hit, the taken penalty is zero in both the 604 and 620. In contrast, if the overall 'taken' prediction is derived, in the case of a BTAC miss, from the 2-bit prediction, the PowerPC 604 has a 'taken' penalty of 1–2 cycles whereas the PowerPC 620 has a penalty of only 1 cycle.

We note that the Pentium and the MC 68060 also employ a combined implicit and 2-bit prediction. Both processors have a 256-entry BTAC with two history bits per entry. However, in these processors the overall prediction is derived differently from the PowerPC 604 and 620, as shown in Table 8.8.

Table 8.8 Overall prediction by combining implicit and 2-bit prediction, as implemented in the Pentium (1993) and MC 68060 (1993) processors.

BTAC	*Outcome of the 2-bit prediction*	*Overall prediction*
Hit	Taken	Taken
Hit	Taken	Not taken
Miss	Don't care	Not taken

In these processors the outcome of the 2-bit prediction is adopted as the overall prediction for a BTAC hit. In the case of a BTAC miss, the guess is 'not taken', no matter what the outcome of the 2-bit prediction is.

Finally, we mention that the PA 8000 combines three prediction methods: implicit, 3-bit dynamic and static compiler-directed prediction. Here, 3-bit dynamic prediction overrides implicit prediction, whereas static prediction if selected, overrides the 3-bit dynamic prediction. We note that static prediction is available on a page-by-page basis.

Prediction accuracy

According to Equation (8.5) the average penalty of predicted branch processing (P) is:

$$\mathbf{P = f_c * P_c + f_m * P_m} \qquad \textbf{(8.10)}$$

where

f_c: Probability of correctly predicted branches
f_m: Probability of mispredicted branches
P_c: Penalty of correctly predicted branches
P_m: Penalty of mispredicted branches

In most cases, recent processors provide advanced branching schemes with no penalties for correctly predicted branches ($P_c = 0$). Then, the average penalty of predicted branches, supposing no penalties for correctly predicted branches (P_0), is:

$$\mathbf{P_0 = f_m * P_m} \qquad \textbf{(8.11)}$$

Now, let us express the probability of mispredicted branches (f_m) by means of the probability of correctly predicted branches (f_c) as follows:

$$\mathbf{f_m = 1 - f_c} \qquad \textbf{(8.12)}$$

Then the average penalty, again assuming $P_c = 0$, is:

$$\mathbf{P_0 = (1 - f_c) * P_m} \qquad \textbf{(8.13)}$$

What Equation (8.10) says is that in this case the average number of additional (penalty) cycles per predicted branch is proportional to $(1-f_c)$. Let us consider, for instance, a processor with

$$\mathbf{P_c = 0 \text{ and } P_m = 4} \qquad \textbf{(8.14)}$$

Then, we obtain for different values of branch accuracy the branch penalty data shown in Table 8.9.

This data shows that prediction accuracy has a large impact on branch penalty. An increase in prediction accuracy from 0.6 to 0.8, 0.9 and 0.95 in turn, reduces the branch penalty each time by 50%. Therefore, branch accuracy is a

Table 8.9 The effect of branch accuracy on branch penalty (for $P_c = 0$ and $P_m = 4$).

Prediction accuracy (f_c)	*Branch penalty (P_0) cycles*
0.6	1.6
0.8	0.8
0.9	0.4
0.95	0.2

Table 8.10 Simulation results of prediction accuracy on the SPEC benchmark suite (Yeh and Patt, 1992). © 1992 ACM

Prediction method	*Prediction accuracy (%)*
Fixed, always taken	62.5
Static, displacement based	68.5
Dynamic, 1-bit	89
Dynamic, 2-bit	93

crucial characteristic of branching schemes. We now present some simulation results and measured figures of prediction accuracy.

Yeh and Patt (1992) evaluated the prediction accuracy of different prediction methods using the SPEC benchmark suit. Their results are quoted in Table 8.10. As the published figures indicate, the fixed, always taken prediction scheme and the static, displacement-based prediction scheme yield considerably lower prediction accuracies (62.5 % and 68.5 %) than the 1- and 2-bit dynamic techniques (89 % and 93 %).

This significant difference between fixed and static predictions on the one hand and dynamic prediction on the other explains why recent systems switched from static methods to dynamic ones (see below for a discussion of branch prediction trends).

In Figure 8.28 we quote further interesting simulation results from Yeh and Patt (1992) concerning the 1- and 2-bit dynamic prediction methods. In this figure we show the prediction accuracies of both methods for four integer and five floating-point SPEC benchmark programs. Furthermore, Figure 8.28 also gives the geometric means of the prediction accuracies separately for the integer and floating-point benchmark programs as well as the resulting total geometric mean values for all benchmark programs. What this data shows is twofold. First, the prediction accuracy has a *considerable range* for the benchmark programs considered. For instance, the prediction accuracy of the 2-bit dynamic prediction varies on integer benchmarks from 86.5 % to 93 % and on floating-point benchmark programs from 91.5 % to 98.5 %. Second, the *prediction accuracy values for floating-point benchmarks are significantly higher than the values for integer benchmarks*. So, for example, the geometric mean of the 2-bit prediction on the floating-point benchmarks is about

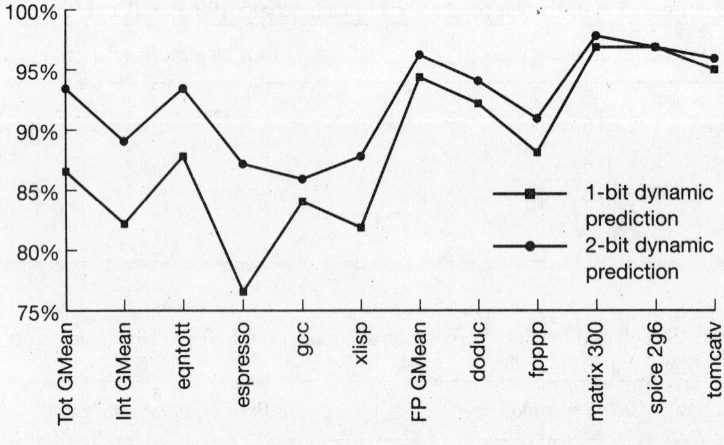

Figure 8.28 Simulated prediction accuracy results on the SPEC benchmark suite for the 1- and 2-bit dynamic prediction (Yeh and Patt, 1992a). © 1992 ACM

Table 8.11 Data on prediction accuracy of recent processors.

Processor	*Guessing method (relevant for prediction accuracy)*	*Implementation*	*Prediction accuracy*	*Reference*
Am 29000 (1987)	Implicit dynamic	32-entry two-way set associative BTIC	60 % for repetitive branches	Weiss, 1987
MC 88110 (1991)	Implicit dynamic, overridden by opcode-based static	32-entry fully associative BTIC	70 % on SPEC	Diefendorff and Allen, 1992
MC 68060 (1993)	2-bit dynamic	256-entry BTAC	> 90 %	Circello and Goodrich, 1993
MIPS R10000 (1996)	2-bit dynamic	512-entry BHT	90 %	Halfhill, 1994
PowerPC 620 (1996)	Implicit dynamic, augmented with 2-bit dynamic	256-entry fully associative BTAC, 2K-entry BHT	90 %	Thomson and Ryan, 1994
PA 8000 (1996)	Implicit dynamic, overridden by 3-bit dynamic or compiler-based static	32-entry fully associative BTAC, 256-entry BHT	80 % on SPECint92	Gwennap, 1994
UltraSparc (1995)	2-bit dynamic	2 K entries in the IC, each shared among two instructions	88 % on SPECint92, 94 % on SPECfp92	Wayner, 1994

BHT: Branch history table
BTAC: Branch target address cache
BTIC: Branch target instruction cache
IC: Instruction cache

96 %, in contrast to 88.5 % on the integer benchmarks. This means that floating-point programs can be run more efficiently on ILP-processors than integer programs (that is, general-purpose programs) due to their more regular control transfer behaviour.

Finally, in Table 8.11 we summarize figures of *branch accuracy values* published for recent processors. This data shows that implicit dynamic prediction with a small number of entries (in case of the Am 29000 or MC 88110) yields very low prediction accuracies (actually 60–70 %). On the other hand, most processors employing 2-bit dynamic prediction show prediction accuracies of about 90 %, in accordance with the simulation results mentioned earlier. For instance, see the prediction accuracies of the MC 68060, MIPS R10000, PowerPC 620 or UltraSparc processors. Here, it is worth noting that the published accuracy figure of the PA 8000 (1995), featuring a 3-bit dynamic prediction, is surprisingly low (merely 80 % on SPECint 92).

Branch prediction trends

In the preceding section we discussed the accuracy of different prediction methods. We pointed out that fixed and static prediction techniques provide substantially lower prediction accuracy than dynamic ones. On the other hand, fixed and static techniques can be implemented much more easily than dynamic methods, since for static methods no branch history has to be stored. Consequently, processors which have introduced branch prediction first employed predominantly *fixed and static* techniques. Examples are the 80486, SuperSparc, R4000, PowerPC 601 and PowerPC 603, as indicated in Figure 8.29.

It is very instructive to inspect subsequent members of the same lines for the prediction technique employed. As Figure 8.29 shows, there is a manifest trend in prediction technique. All subsequent members of the processor families mentioned *switched from fixed or static prediction to dynamic*, like the Pentium, the UltraSparc, the R8000 and R10000, and the PowerPC 604 and PowerPC 620. This switch to dynamic techniques is due to the significantly higher prediction accuracy provided in comparison with fixed or static techniques (see preceding section). Furthermore, it is remarkable that of the available dynamic techniques, most processors employ the 2-bit prediction scheme, due to its performance gain over the 1-bit scheme. A noteworthy exception is the R8000 which uses the 1-bit prediction technique, presumably because of implementation constraints.

Extent of speculativeness

Following a prediction, a processor continues to execute instructions in a speculative fashion until the condition is resolved. However, the time interval between the start of the conditional execution and the resolution of the corresponding condition can vary considerably. Often, the condition is resolved in the immediately following cycle. This happens when the specified condition refers to the result of a simple operation, such as an integer addition, subtraction or logical operation. However, in the case of long operations, such as FX or FP division, a large number of cycles will pass before the condition can be resolved. Furthermore, superscalar processors can issue several instructions in each cycle. Thus, occasionally, during speculative execution scores of instructions are executed before the specified condition becomes

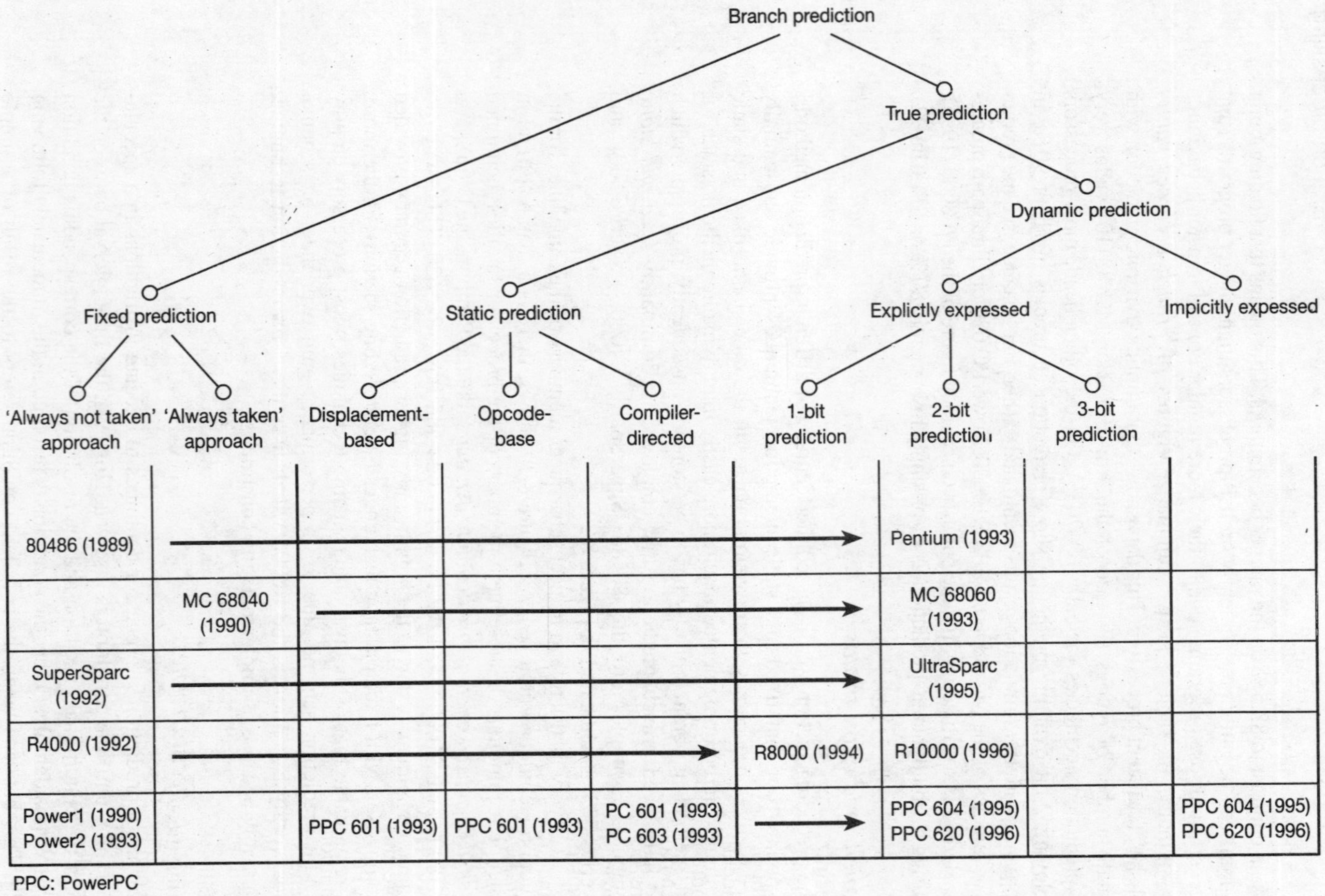

Figure 8.29 Branch prediction trends as indicated by subsequent models of particular processor lines.

evaluable. Moreover, during speculative execution further unresolved conditional branches may occur.

This raises the question of how far a processor should execute instructions speculatively. The answer is not at all trivial. On the one hand, to increase performance, it seems to be desirable to continue speculative execution until the condition is resolved. On the other hand, in the case of a misprediction, all speculatively executed instructions have to be cancelled and processing has to be resumed along the correct path. Obviously, the more speculative execution has been accomplished, the more work has to be discarded when a misprediction occurs and, thus, the higher the penalty for misprediction. As a consequence, the optimal amount of speculative processing depends on the prediction accuracy achieved. In general, the higher the prediction accuracy, the more speculative processing can be performed without reducing the resulting performance.

Below, we briefly overview how far modern processors extend speculative execution. We emphasize two main aspects: the level and the degree of speculativeness, as indicated in Figure 8.30. By **level of speculativeness**, we understand the number of conditional branches that may be executed speculatively in succession. Evidently, it is beneficial for performance if a second, third and so on, unresolved conditional branch does not terminate speculative execution. This requirement is even more imperative for superscalar processors capable of issuing multiple instructions per cycle. The higher the issue rate, the more imperative the requirement. However, if a second, third and so on, speculative conditional branch is allowed, misprediction of all previous branches is a possibility. Therefore, for each predicted branch the execution status has to be saved. Thus, for multiple speculative branches *multiple execution states* have to be saved and maintained. As a matter of fact, at present, most processors accept only a single pending speculative branch; examples are the α 21064, 21064A or the PowerPC 601 or PowerPC 603, see Figure 8.30.

However, novel superscalar processors with higher issue rates tend to allow more and more pending conditional branches. For instance, the Power2 allows two, the PowerPC 620 and the R10000 four and the α 21164 as many as six pending conditional branches. In future, we expect a further increase in the level of speculativeness, especially in superscalar processors with high issue rates.

From another point of view, processors that allow only one pending conditional branch resemble basic block schedulers, which schedule instructions for parallel execution up to the end of the current basic block, while processors that permit multiple pending conditional branches are similar to global schedulers, going beyond basic block boundaries.

When discussing the extent of speculative processing, the other aspect to be considered is the **degree of speculativeness**. This concept relates to how far instructions, other than unresolved conditional branches, are executed following a guessed conditional branch. Here, processors pursue different schemes; see again Figure 8.30. In the simplest case, speculative execution goes no further than *fetching* a number of instructions belonging to the predicted path, such as in the Power1. A higher degree of speculativeness is found when instructions along the predicted path are *fetched and decoded*, or *fetched, decoded and dispatched*, as in the PowerPC 601. Processors with an even higher degree of speculativeness *fetch*, *decode*,

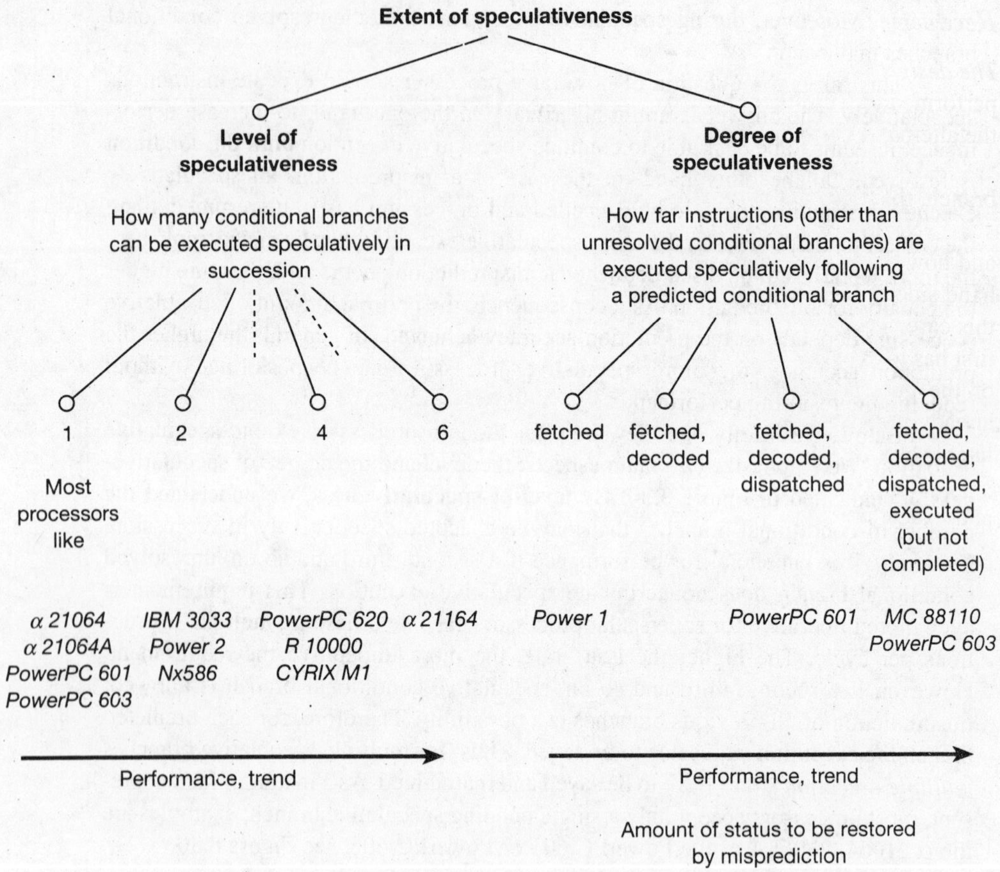

Figure 8.30 Extent of speculative processing.

dispatch and execute instructions after a pending conditional branch, although without completing them, as in the MC 88110 or PowerPC 603.

For instance, the MC 88110 allows instructions to be executed speculatively and provides a mechanism to undo them in the case of a misprediction. Fundamentally, this mechanism aims at retaining sequential consistency for out-of-order execution. It is based on a history buffer and can undo two instructions per cycle.

Obviously, the higher the degree of speculativeness, the higher the performance potential of the scheme considered, but, at the same time, the larger the state to be restored in the case of a misprediction. As a consequence, in future performance-oriented processors, offering improved prediction accuracies, we expect higher degrees of speculativeness than in current processors. However, at the same time we expect novel processors to employ advanced schemes to recover from a misprediction as fast as possible. This is the topic for the next section.

Recovery from a misprediction

The design space After discovering a misprediction there are two basic tasks to be performed: discard the results of the speculative execution and resume execution of the alternative, that is, the correct, path (Figure 8.31).

Of course, when there is more than one pending (predicted) conditional branch, the matching alternative path must be selected and pursued.

Next, we discuss what has to be done to allow recovery from a misprediction and how the recovery procedure can be shortened. First, with reference to the left-hand side of Figure 8.32, let us look at *recovery from a mispredicted taken path.* In this case, as preparation for a possible recovery from a misprediction, the processor first has to save the address of the sequential continuation, before it starts execution of the guessed taken path. The recovery procedure can be further shortened if already prefetched sequential instructions are not discarded but saved for possible later use in the case of a misprediction.

The other situation is when the *sequential path* has been *incorrectly* predicted and executed (right-hand side of Figure 8.32). Here, in conjunction with the 'not

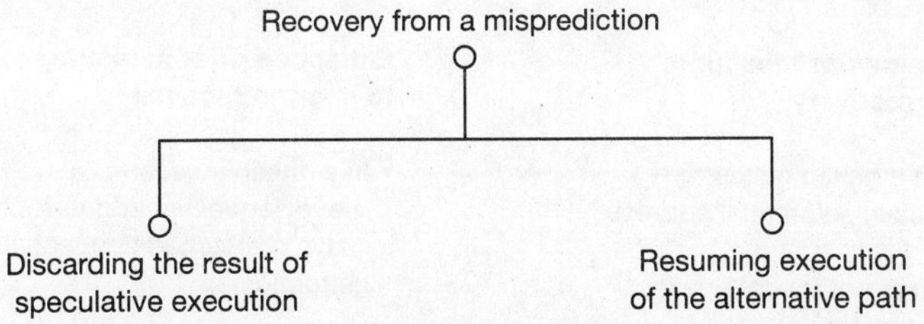

Figure 8.31 Basic tasks during recovery from a misprediction.

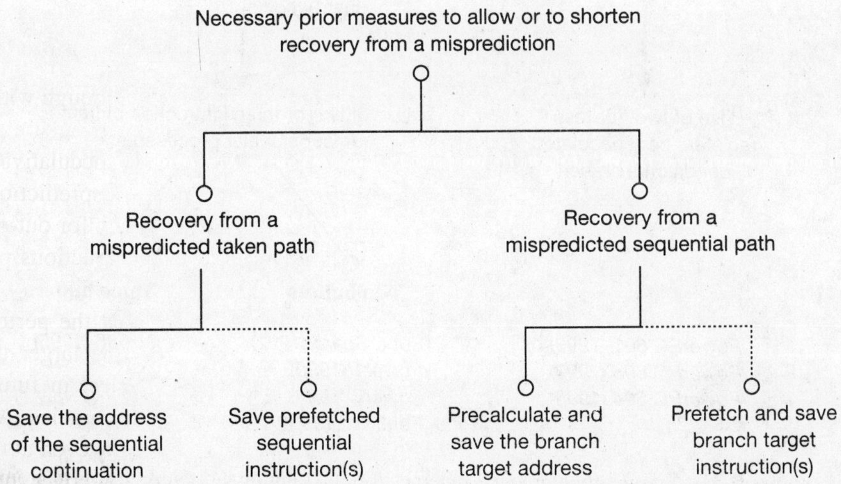

Figure 8.32 Necessary activities to allow or to shorten recovery from a misprediction.

taken' (that is, sequential) prediction, the branch target address should be precalculated and saved to allow a recovery. In this case, the penalty for misprediction can be reduced by prefetching the branch target instruction for a scalar processors, or a number of instructions in the case of superscalar processors. Evidently, this requires additional buffer space as well as additional cache access bandwidth.

From the possible precautionary measures outlined in Figure 8.32, we survey two frequently employed schemes, with reference to Figure 8.33.

In the simplest scheme, during a prediction only those precautionary measures are undertaken which are absolutely necessary for recovery from a misprediction. In Figure 8.33 this scheme is referred to as *basic prior measures for recovery*. The minimal provision for a misprediction covers two activities: for a 'taken' guess save the sequential address; for a 'not taken' guess, precalculate and save the branch target address. This requires *two fetch address registers per speculated conditional*

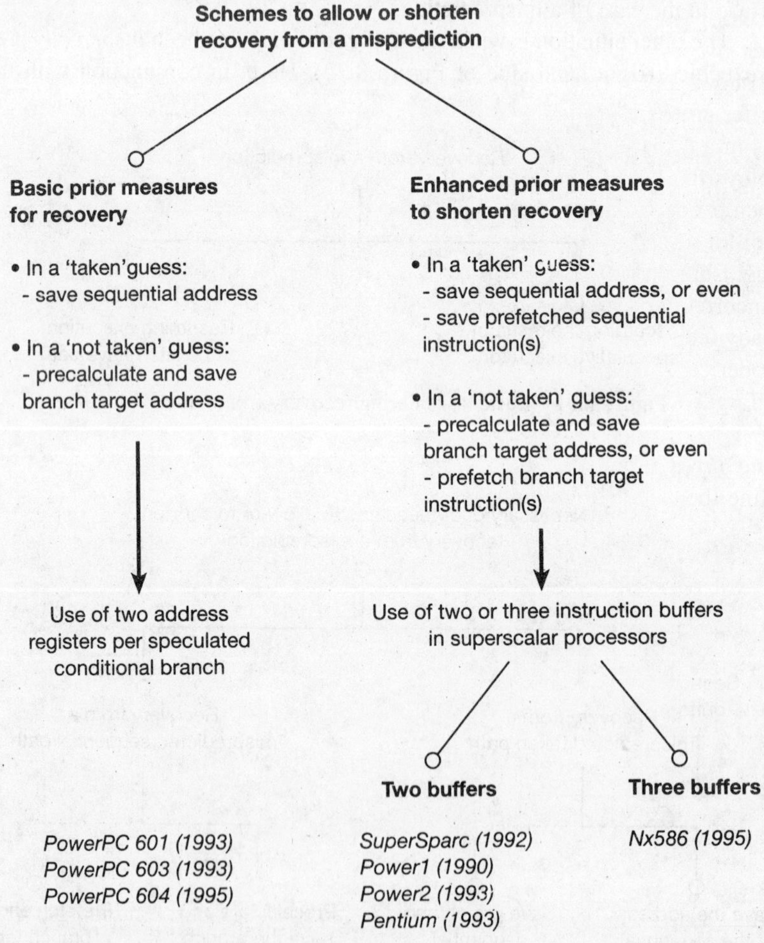

Figure 8.33 Frequently employed schemes for allowing or shortening recovery from a misprediction.

branch in order to store both addresses of the possible continuations. Among others, the PowerPC 601, PowerPC 603 and PowerPC 604 use this basic scheme.

A more advanced scheme involves supplementary actions in order to shorten the misprediction penalty. This is often achieved by saving already prefetched sequential instructions for a 'taken' guess and by prefetching branch target instructions in the case of a 'not taken' prediction. In Figure 8.33, this scheme is designated as *enhanced prior measures to shorten recovery*. Obviously, the implementation of this enhanced scheme requires at least *two instruction buffers* with at least as many entries as instructions can be fetched in a single cycle. Examples of processors providing two instruction buffers to shorten recovery from a misprediction are the SuperSparc, Power1, Power2 and Pentium. The Nx586 provides *three buffers*, a sequential one and two target buffers, to cater for thetwo pending conditional branches allowed. In the following, as an illustration, we describe how two or three instruction buffers are used in the SuperSparc and Nx586.

Using two instruction buffers to shorten recovery in the SuperSparc As Figure 8.34 shows, the *SuperSparc* has two separate instruction buffers called the Sequential I-buffer and Target I-buffer. Both buffers can accept from the I-cache four instructions in a cycle and both have a capacity of four instructions. Since this processor employs the 'always not taken' prediction, in the case of an unresolved conditional branch execution always commences along the sequential path. However, in anticipation of a misprediction, four target instructions will be fetched and saved in the Target I-buffer for every unresolved conditional l ranch. When the guess turns out to be incorrect, the results of the speculative execution are first discarded. Then, the already fetched target instructions can be decoded without any significant delay. The decoder can decode the last three instructions from either the sequential I-buffer or the Target I-buffer.

Using three instruction buffers to shorten recovery in the Nx586 Finally, we outline the *Nx586* solution to reduce the penalty for misprediction. This processor

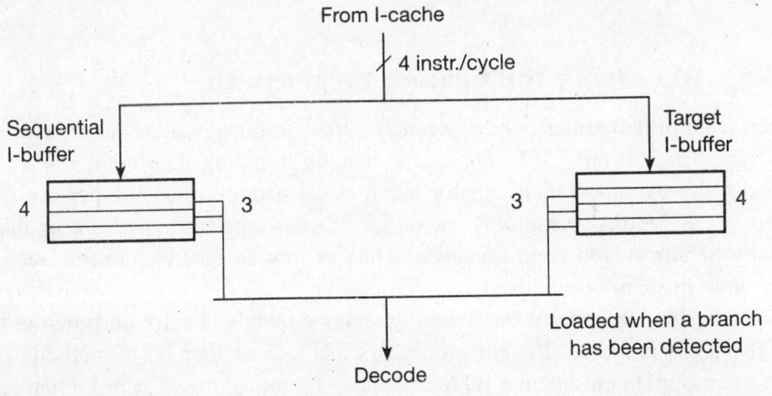

Figure 8.34 Using two instruction buffers in the SuperSparc (1992) to shorten recovery from a misprediction.

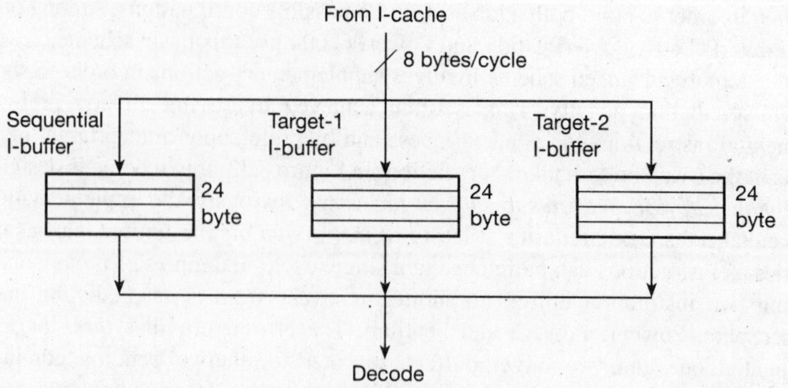

Figure 8.35 Using three instruction buffers in the Nx586 (1994) to shorten recovery from a misprediction.

uses three instruction buffers, as indicated in Figure 8.35. We note here that the Nx586 is a Pentium-compatible superscalar CISC processor and thus it has a variable instruction length. A feature of this processor is that it allows two pending unresolved (that is speculatively executed) conditional branches.

All three buffers provided by the Nx586 have a capacity of 24 bytes each, large enough to store several x86 instructions. One of the buffers, called the Sequential I-buffer, is used to hold prefetched sequential instructions. The remaining two buffers (Target 1 and Target 2 I-buffers) are used to store fetched target instructions for two subsequent speculatively executed conditional branches. Even in the case of two pending speculatively executed conditional branches, using three buffers guarantees a short recovery from a misprediction. Here, when a misprediction is detected, the saved instructions belonging to the preceding correct path can be accessed in the corresponding instruction buffer in a short time.

8.4.5 Accessing the branch target path

Taken conditional branches have a much higher frequency than not taken ones, as indicated in Section 8.1.3. Thus, the penalty for 'taken' conditional branches impedes the overall branch penalty much more strongly than the penalty for 'not taken' ones. For this reason, it is crucial for processor performance to keep the taken penalty of unresolved conditional branches as low as possible. In this section we show how this can be achieved.

The branch penalty for 'taken' guesses depends heavily on how the branch target path is accessed. Recent processors use one of four basic methods (Figure 8.36): compute/fetch scheme, BTAC (Branch Target Address Cache) scheme, BTIC (Branch Target Instruction Cache) scheme and the successor index in the I-cache scheme. Below, we overview these schemes.

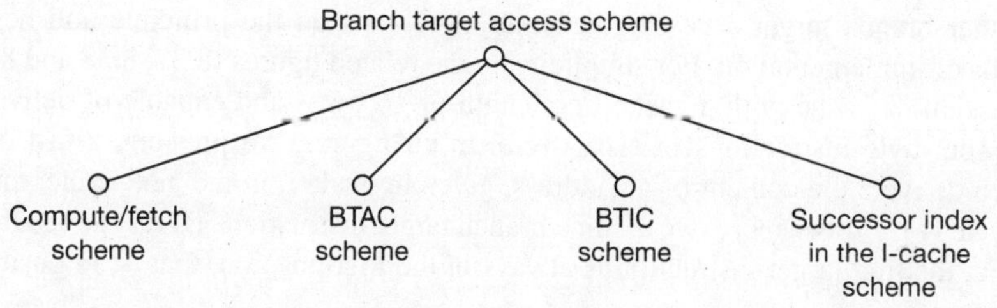

Figure 8.36 Overview of branch target accessing schemes.

The compute/fetch scheme

This scheme (Figure 8.37) is the natural method of accessing branch targets. First, the branch target address (BTA) is *computed* either by the pipeline or by a dedicated adder. Then, the corresponding branch target instruction (BTI) is *fetched.* In recent processors this means an access to the I-cache, whereas in early pipelined processors without an I-cache, the memory is accessed instead.

With reference to Figure 8.37, bits go into the details of the compute/fetch scheme. The instruction fetch address (IFA) is maintained in the *instruction fetch address register* (IFAR), which is usually called the Program Counter (PC) in a sequential environment. In order to start the execution of a particular program, the IFA is set to its initial value, referred to as IIFA (initial instruction fetch address). In the absence of branches, the IFA is incremented after each access to get the next sequential address. When a branch is encountered, the next sequential address is overwritten by the computed branch target address (BTA), and the corresponding instruction cache (I-cache) entry is fetched. Here, and in the following presentation

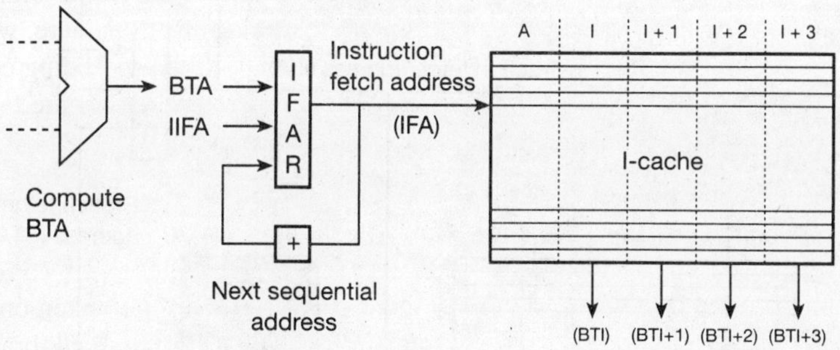

Figure 8.37 Principle of the compute/fetch scheme for accessing branch targets. When a branch is detected, the branch target address (BTA) is computed. In this case the next sequential address is overwritten by the BTA. Thus the BTA becomes the next instruction fetch address (IFA). Then, in the next cycle the corresponding branch target instruction (BTI) is read from the instruction cache (I-cache). This scheme is employed in earlier scalar processors as well as in some recent scalar and superscalar processors, such as: Z 80000 (1984), i486 (1989), MC 68040 (1990), Sparc CY7C601 (1988), SuperSparc (1992p), Power1 (1990), Power2 (1993), Power PC 601 (1993), 603 (1993), α 21064 (1992), α 21064A (1994), α 21164 (1995), R4000 (1992), R 10000 (1996).

of other branch target accessing schemes, we focus on the principle and neglect details of implementation. For simplicity, in the related figures (8.37, 8.38 and 8.42), we assume a cache with a cache line length of 16 bytes and capable of delivering four four-byte instructions in each cycle. In all figures, we presume a fast cache which delivers the content of an address, given in cycle i, in the next cycle, that is, in cycle i+1. Furthermore, we assume branch target instructions (BTIs) to be aligned so that the first target instruction is always in the first position, that is, in position I in Figure 8.37.

The calculate/fetch scheme is straightforward and does not require any additional hardware. This is the *standard* branch target accessing scheme used in all earlier and in some recent scalar processors, such as the i486 and the R4000. A number of superscalar processors also employ this simple scheme, like the Supersparc, Power1, Power2 and the first PowerPC implementations, such as the PowerPC 601 and PowerPC 603, and the α implementations α 21064, α 21064A and α 21164. The obvious *drawback* of this method is the sequential manner of the BTA calculation and BTI access. This can cause a considerable taken-path access penalty, except when branches are detected and BTA calculations are performed early enough. In the following we describe more efficient methods for accessing branch targets.

The BTAC scheme

This scheme employs an extra cache, called the *branch target address cache* (BTAC), for speeding up access to branch targets, as shown in Figure 8.38. The **BTAC** contains pairs of recently used *branch addresses* (BA) and *branch target*

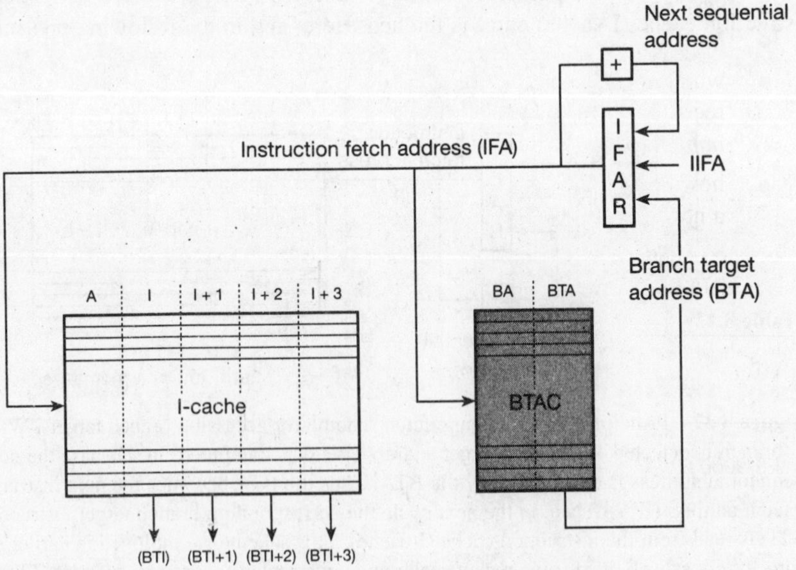

Figure 8.38 Principle of the BTAC scheme for accessing branch targets. The Branch Target Address Cache (BTAC) contains branch target addresses (BTAs). These BTAs are read from the BTAC at the same time as the branch instruction is fetched.

addresses (BTAs) and is accessed associatively. When the actual instruction fetch address (IFA) is a branch address (BA), and there is a corresponding entry in the BTAC, the branch target address (BTA) is fetched along with the branch instruction in the same cycle. This BTA is then used to access the branch target instruction in the next cycle.

In this way branch target instructions (BTIs) may be fetched immediately in succession to the branch instruction, that is *without* any *idle cycles*. Furthermore, the BTAC scheme even has the potential to implement *zero-cycle branching* (see Section 8.1.5). With zero-cycle branching, the first target instruction can be fetched immediately after the last sequential instruction preceding a branch, i.e. without any delay.

For zero-cycle branching the branch target address (BTA) must be accessed along with the instruction preceding the branch. Then the BTAC must contain, instead of the branch address (BA), the instruction fetch address preceding the branch addresses. For a scalar processor with 4-byte instructions this would be the address BA – 4.

The BTAC scheme was proposed by Lee and Smith (1984), and has been called Branch Target Buffer design. This scheme is implemented in a number of recent processors, as shown in Table 8.12. The number of BTAC entries varies from 32 to 4 K.

We note here that there are some differences in the implementation of the BTAC scheme, especially concerning the following issues:

- whether the BTAC is implemented as a 2-way, 4-way of fully associative cache;
- how the BTAC is initialized;
- whether entries are retained in the BTAC for all recent branches or only for recently taken branches (in the latter case the BTAC scheme also performs *implicit dynamic prediction*);
- how to select the entry to be overwritten, if there is no room in the BTAC for a new entry;

Table 8.12 Examples of processors using the BTAC scheme.

Processor	*Number of BTAC entries*	*Implementation of the BTAC*
ES/9000 520-based processors (1992p)	4 K	2-way associative
Pentium (1994)	256	Fully associative
MC 68060 (1993)	256	4-way associative
PA 8000 (1995)	32	Fully associative
PowerPC 604 (1994)	64	Fully associative
PowerPC 620 (1995)	256	Fully associative

- if the processor uses predict bits, whether they are contained in the BTAC or in a separate BHT.

These details cannot be discussed here due to space limitations. The interested reader is referred to the descriptions of the processors mentioned.

The BTIC scheme

This scheme is only used occasionally, in cases when the taken penalty would be untolerably high due to a longer than usual I-cache latency. The basic idea of the **BTIC scheme** (Branch Target Instruction Cache scheme) is to provide a small extra cache which delivers, for taken or predicted taken branches, the branch target instruction (BTI) or a specified number of BTIs, rather than the BTA. Thus, otherwise unused pipeline cycles can be filled with target instructions.

There are two alternative implementations of the BTIC scheme, as indicated in Figure 8.39. In the first, the address of the continuation of the taken path is also stored in the BTIC, whereas in the second it is dynamically calculated.

In the sequel, we overview these implementations based on two selected examples.

BTIC scheme with storing of the taken path continuation We show the principle of this implementation based on the Hitachi Gmicro/200 (1988) processor, referring to Figure 8.40. The Gmicro family of processors has been developed within the framework of the Japanese *TRON project* which was initiated in 1984. TRON is an open architecture defined at a number of layers, among others at the ISA layer (Sakamura, 1987a, 1987b). We note here that the TRON ISA is a CISC architecture. The Gmicro/200 is the first microprocessor which implements the TRON ISA specification. It is a scalar implementation using a six-stage CISC pipeline and an I-cache with a load latency of two cycles.

As Figure 8.40 shows, the BTIC contains entries consisting of three components. These are the addresses of recently taken branches (BA), the corresponding target instructions (BTI) and the addresses of the instructions following the BTIs (designated as BTA+). When there is an entry in the BTIC for the actual instruction fetch address (IFA), the corresponding BTI is fetched from the BTIC and this instruction is selected for decoding, instead of the instruction being read directly

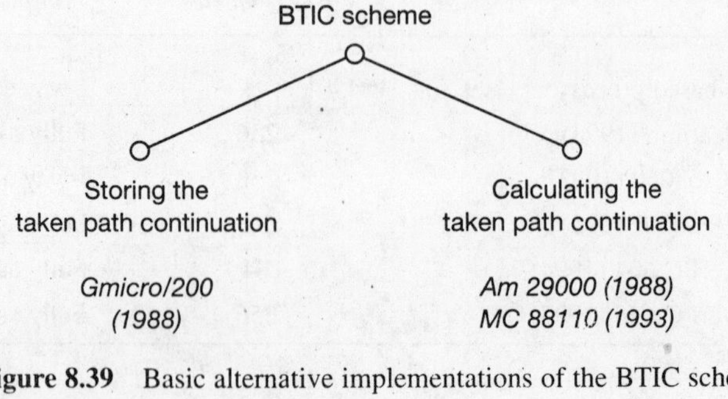

Figure 8.39 Basic alternative implementations of the BTIC scheme.

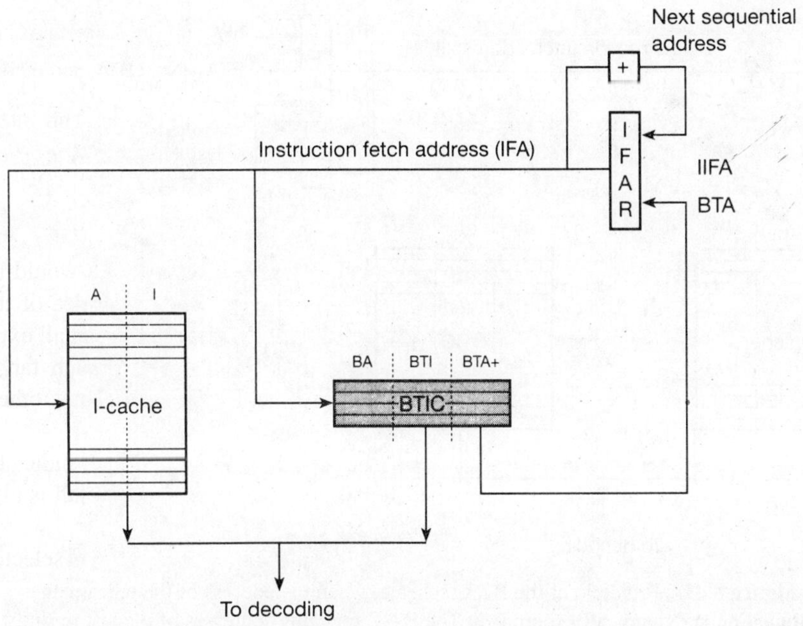

Figure 8.40 Principle of the BTIC scheme, when the address of the taken path continuation is also stored in the BTIC. The BTIC contains the addresses of the last recently taken branches (BA), the corresponding branch target instructions (BTI) and the addresses of the instructions following the BTIs (BTA+). When there is an entry in the BTIC for the actual IFA, the corresponding BTI is fetched from the BTIC and selected for decoding instead of the instruction from the I-cache. The address of the subsequent instruction along the taken path (BTA+) is also read from BTIC and becomes the next IFA. This figure actually shows the Hitachi Gmicro/200 implementation of the scheme.

from the I-cache. The address of the subsequent instruction along the taken path (BTA+) is also fetched from the BTIC. It becomes the next BTA. The BTIC contains only four entries.

BTIC scheme with calculation of the taken path continuation The other variant of the BTIC scheme differs from the one described above in that here the *addresses of the taken path continuations* are actually *computed* rather than stored in and read from the BTIC. Figure 8.41 demonstrates this by showing how it is implemented in the MC 88110 processor.

In this implementation variant, the BTIC contains triplets of addresses of the last recently taken branches (BA) as well as the first two instructions of the corresponding branch target path (BTI and BTI+1). We note here that the MC 88110 is a superscalar processor with an issue rate of two. This fact explains why just two instructions from each taken path are stored in the BTIC.

When the BTIC contains an entry for the actual IFA, the corresponding two target instructions (BTI and BTI+1) are fetched from the BTIC and selected for decoding instead of the two sequential instructions being read from the I-cache. The address of the taken path continuation (BTA+) is calculated from the BTA by incrementation and is used as the next IFA.

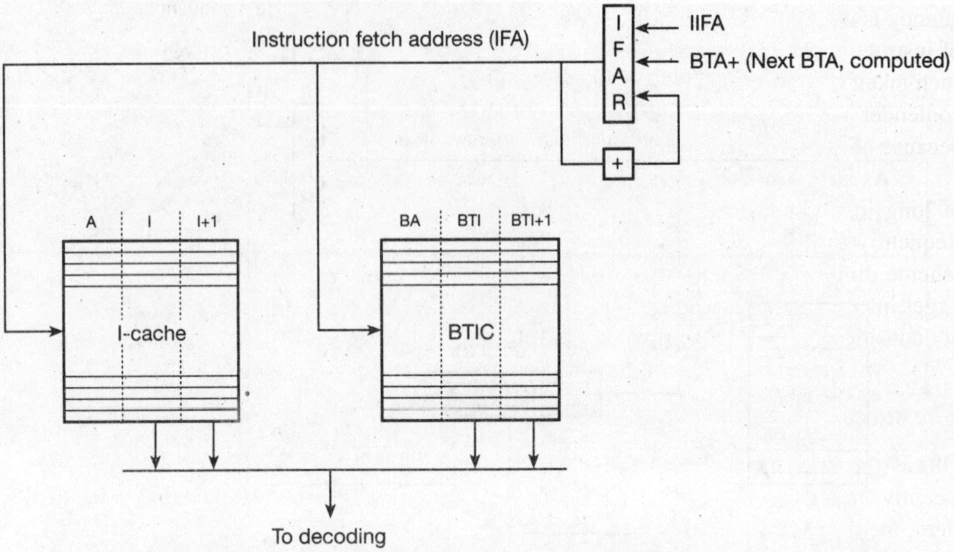

Figure 8.41 Principle of the BTIC scheme, when the address of the taken path continuation is dynamically computed. The BTIC contains addresses of the last recently taken branches (BA) as well as the first two corresponding branch target instructions (BTI and BTI + 1). When the BTIC contains an entry for the actual IFA, the corresponding two target instructions (BTI and BTI+1) are fetched from the BTIC and selected for decoding instead of the two instructions being read from the I-cache. The address of the taken path continuation (BTA+) is calculated from the branch target address and is chosen as the next IFA. This figure actually shows the MC 88110 implementation.

There are only a few processors employing this branch target access scheme. See Table 8.13 for examples and for a sample of basic characteristics of actual implementations.

As Table 8.13 indicates, the implemented BTICs have a relatively small number of entries ranging from 4 to 96. The number of instructions stored in each entry varies from one (Gmicro/200) to four (Am 29000). In the latter case we have a scalar processor without any instruction cache. Therefore, the memory access

Table 8.13 Examples of processors using the BTIC scheme.

Processor	*Number of entries in the BTIC*	*Number of BTIs stored in each entry*	*Determination of the address of taken path continuations*	*Actual designation of the BTIC*
Am 29000 (1987)	32	4	Calculated	Branch Target Cache
Gmicro/200 (1988)	4	1	Stored	Branch Window
MC 88110 (1993)	32	2	Calculated	Target Instruction Cache
Nx586 (1995)	96	24 byte	n.a.	Branch Prediction Cache

latency is comparatively high (four cycles). This is the reason why a large number of instructions is stored in the BTIC. Finally, the Nx586 stores the first 24 bytes of each taken path in the BTIC. We note here that the Nx586 is a superscalar Pentium contender which would have a five-cycle taken penalty without a BTIC, mainly because of the long cache access time.

As already mentioned, the BTIC scheme is employed exceptionally in cases of long instruction access times. Caches, however, are designed more and more frequently to match the processor cycle times; thus, the motivation for using this scheme diminishes. The BTIC scheme also has a drawback: it has to store branch target instructions twice, in the I-cache and in the BTIC. As a consequence, we do not consider that this branch target access scheme has a future.

The successor index in the I-cache scheme

This is the latest scheme introduced to access branch targets, employed in a few, recently announced processors such as the Am 29000 superscalar, K5 and UltraSparc. Here, the basic idea is to append, for each line in the I-cache, a *successor index* that points to the next line to be fetched, as demonstrated in Figure 8.42. In all the processors mentioned, each cache line can contain 16 bytes of instructions. This means that a cache line holds in the Am 29000 superscalar and in the UltraSparc four instructions, whereas in the x86-compatible K5 a variable number of CISC instructions. The successor index is fetched in parallel with the instructions of the same line. It points either to the next sequential line or, if the present line contains a branch which is guessed to be taken, to the line which contains the first taken path instruction.

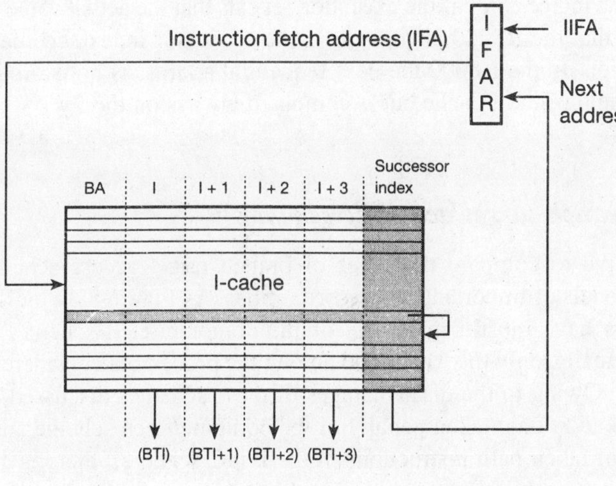

Figure 8.42 Principle of the successor index in the I-cache scheme to access the branch target path. The I-cache contains a successor index that points to the next instruction cache entry to be fetched. The successor index points either to the next sequential line or, in the case of a branch that is guessed to be taken, to the line which contains the first taken path instruction. Examples of processors using this scheme are: Am 29000 superscalar (1995), K5 (1995), UltraSparc (1995).

Again, this scheme can be implemented differently as far as the initialization and handling of the successor index is concerned. As an example, we give some details of how this is done in the UltraSparc, referring to Figure 8.43.

The UltraSparc is the first processor announced which implements the SPARC V9 ISA. It is a superscalar full 64-bit design with an issue rate of four. Here, we are only concerned with the branch target access part of this microarchitecture and do not go into further details.

We emphasize that the UltraSparc includes a *predecode unit*. This seems to have become a common design approach in recent processors to shorten the decode–issue path as discussed in Section 8.2. The main task of the predecode unit is to partially decode instructions and to label them accordingly using 4-bit tags. These tags are stored along with each instruction in the I-cache and allow a quick decoding. As instructions are loaded into the I-cache, the predecode unit detects branches, determines the corresponding BTAs and makes predictions using a hint bit delivered by the compiler. This prediction is used to initialize the prediction bits available for every two instructions (two bits). The prediction bits are updated according to the branch history. The successor indices and prediction bits are actually held in an extra 2 K buffer (called the Next Field RAM), one successor index for every four instructions. If the prediction is taken, the successor index becomes the value of the determined BTA, otherwise the next sequential address is taken as the successor index. The successor index is then used as the next instruction fetch address. Thus, for taken predictions, the successor index redirects execution to the taken path. We note here that the UltraSparc employs a 2-bit dynamic prediction with the history bits placed in the Next Field RAM.

In contrast, the K5 initializes all successor indices to the next sequential value and rewrites the indices only if the execution reveals that the actual value is incorrect. We note here that the R8000 also employs the successor index scheme, albeit in a modified fashion. In the R8000 the next sequential address is not stored in the successor index field of the I-cache but is computed always on the fly.

Trends in branch target accessing schemes

It is informative to compare the types of branch target access schemes used in subsequent models of important processor families. As Figure 8.44 indicates, previous processors have mostly made use of the compute/fetch scheme, with a few processors (actually, only the Am 29000 among the processors considered) using the BTIC scheme. Owing to the disadvantages of these schemes discussed earlier (that is, the implied additional taken penalty of the compute/fetch scheme and the duplicated storing of taken path instructions in the BTIC scheme), there is a clear trend away from these techiques. Recently introduced or announced processors have switched in most cases either to the BTAC or to the successor index in the I-cache scheme. For instance, the Pentium, PowerPC 604 and PowerPC 620 follow the BTAC approach, while the Am 29000 superscalar and the UltraSparc opted for the successor index in the I-cache solution.

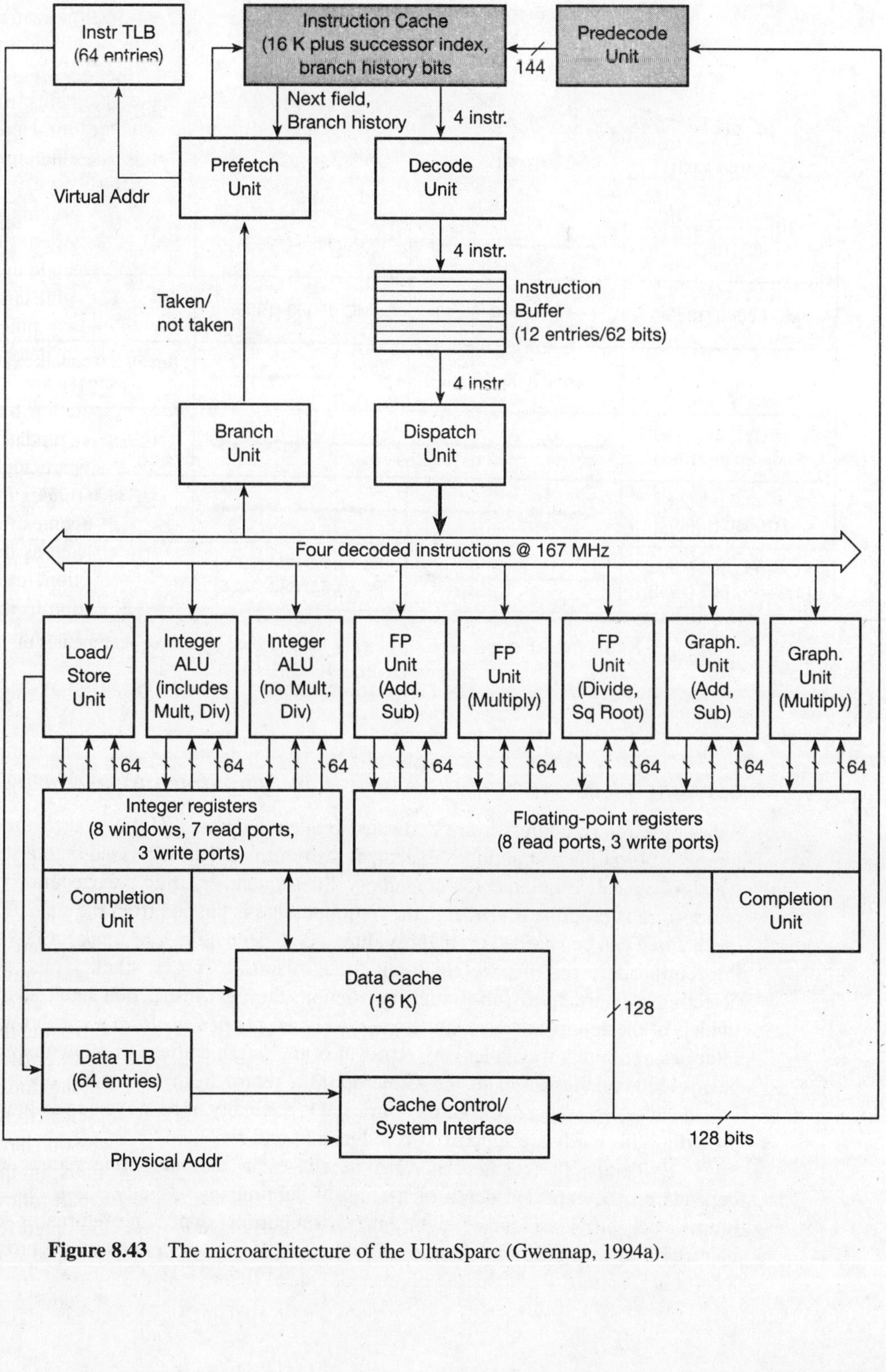

Figure 8.43 The microarchitecture of the UltraSparc (Gwennap, 1994a).

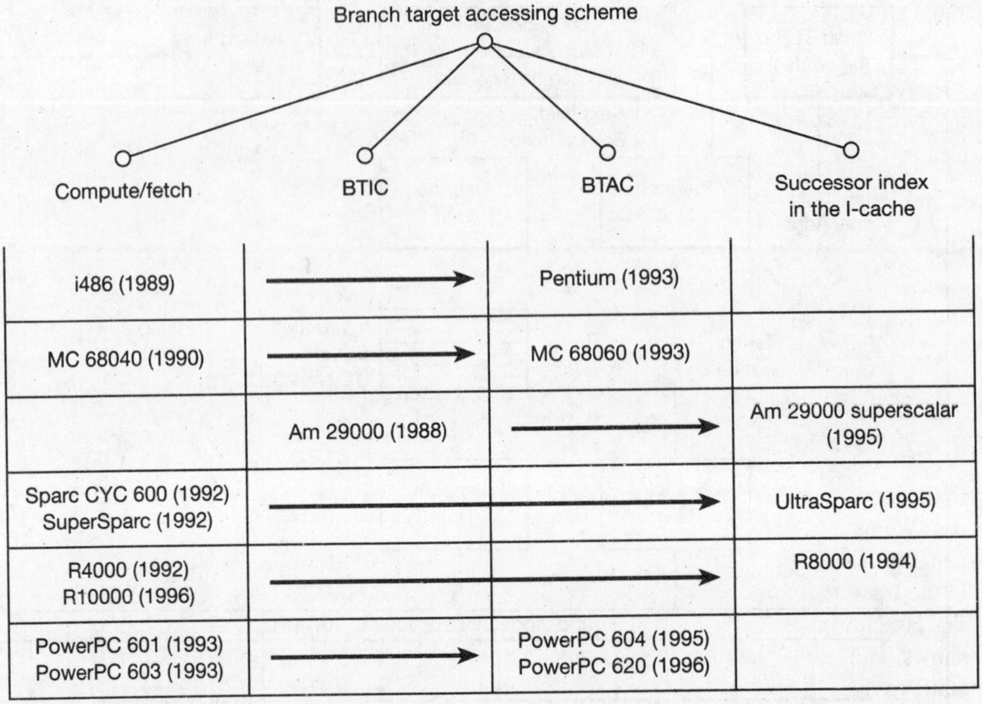

Figure 8.44 Branch target accessing trends as indicated by subsequent models of important processor lines.

Speeding up execution of the return from subroutine instruction

Subroutine return addresses are dedicated branch addresses. Usually, each time a jump to subroutine instruction is executed, the return address is pushed onto a stack which is typically implemented in memory. Subsequently, during the execution of a return from subroutine instruction, the return address is popped from the stack. This mechanism can be speeded up by providing a dedicated *hardware stack* for holding the return addresses that we shall call the **subroutine return stack**. Thus, after detecting a return from sub-routine instruction, the next instruction fetch address (which is the return address) can immediately be popped up from the subroutine return stack. In this way, a lengthy retrieval of the return address from memory can be avoided. For instance, in the Gmicro/500 a return from subroutine operation would cause, without a sub-routine return stack, a penalty of four cycles whereas by providing this hardware support, it is reduced to one cycle.

Evidently, the required number of entries in the subroutine return stack depends on the expected depth of nesting of subroutines. Usually, the subroutine return stack provides four or eight entries, supporting subroutine returns up to a depth of four to eight. For example, in Table 8.14 we list processors which provide a subroutine return stack and the number of entries implemented.

Table 8.14 Processors providing a subroutine return stack for speeding up access to return addresses.

Processor type	*Number of entries*	*Designation*
Gmicro/100 (1991p)	8	PC-stack
Gmicro/500 (1993)	8	Return buffer
α 21064 (1992)	4	JSR-stack
α 21064A (1994)	4	JSR-stack
M1 (1995)	8	Return address stack
R10000 (1996)	1	Return address buffer

8.4.6 Branch penalties of processors using prediction

In the preceding sections we have overviewed techniques for reducing branch penalties. We have seen that there are effective techniques to sharply reduce, or to avoid, penalties for correctly predicted branches, such as the BTAC or the successor index in the I-cache schemes. Moreover, by using these schemes, even *zero-cycle branching* is achievable (see Sections 8.1.5 and 8.4.5), as compiled data in Table 8.15 shows. This table contains data on branch penalties in recent processors that use true static or dynamic prediction. For comparison, Tables 8.3 and 8.5 contain penalty figures for processors employing less advanced branch prediction schemes.

We have also discussed appropriate techniques for reducing the penalties for misprediction, such as fast recovery schemes and restricting the extent of speculative execution. The data in Table 8.15 shows that although these techniques reduce misprediction penalties considerably, most recent processors require at least two or three cycles for recovery. Notable exceptions are the PA 7200 and the R10000 which have, in certain cases, only one or even no penalty cycles. However, how far a misprediction penalty contributes to the effective branch penalty depends heavily on the prediction accuracy. The higher the prediction accuracy, the less a misprediction penalty impedes processor performance. For instance, for 90 % prediction accuracy, a misprediction penalty of two cycles causes only a $0.1*2 = 0.2$ cycle increase in the average branch penalty.

8.4.7 Microarchitectural implementation of branch processing

Branch processing comprises *basic tasks*, such as instruction fetch, decode and BTA calculation, and possibly additional *dedicated tasks* to speed up branch processing. These dedicated tasks may be early branch detection, branch prediction or an advanced scheme for accessing target paths. Usually, the dedicated tasks are executed by means of dedicated hardware, like a BTAC, BTIC or BHT. There are two approaches to the *basic tasks*. All earlier pipelined processors and many recent processors execute branches by utilizing the pipeline stages available for common instruction processing. Examples of this approach are given in Figure 8.45.

Table 8.15 Branch penalties in processors employing static or dynamic prediction.

Processor type	*Penalty of a correctly predicted branch (cycles)*	*Penalty of a mispredicted branch (cycles)*
MC 88110 (1993)	0	2
MC 68060 (1993)	z	7
Pentium (1993)	0	3–4
Gmicro/500 (1993)	z/2[1]	n.a.
PA 7200 (1995)	n.a.	0-1
PA 8000 (1996)	z/2[2,3]	5
R 8000 (1994)	n.a.	3
R10000 (1996)	1[3]	1–4[6]
α 21164 (1995)	0	5
PowerPC 604 (1995)	0[1]/1–2[2]	3
PowerPC 620 (1996)	0[1]/1[2]	2
Nx586 (1995)	z	5[4]–19[5]

1 If the branch address hits the BTAC
2 If the branch address does not hit the BTAC
3 If there are enough instructions in the decoded queue, this latency may be partly or entirely hidden
4 If the reservation station queues are empty
5 If the reservation station queues are full (14 entries)
6 The R10000 allows at most 4 embedded pending predictions. The actual value of the misprediction penalty depends on the 'depth' of misprediction
z means zero-cycle branching

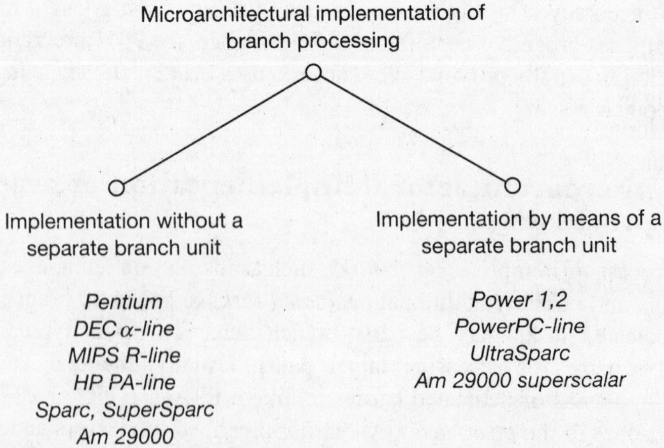

Figure 8.45 Implementation of the basic subtasks of branch processing.

By contrast, a number of recent processors provide a separate unit, usually called a **branch unit**, to execute the basic tasks of branch processing. This approach *decouples* branch processing from general data manipulations and results in a more symmetrical structure of the microarchitecture. Furthermore, this approach also contributes to *increased performance*, since other units (such as an integer unit) are released from subtasks of basic branch processing, such as address calculations. Thus, branches can be processed in parallel with data manipulations. As Figure 8.45 shows, the Power1, Power2 and PowerPC models follow this approach. Further examples are the UltraSparc and Am 29000 superscalar processors. It is worth noting that the latter processors switched to separate branch units in contrast to earlier models of the same lines, which followed the traditional approach. We expect this trend to continue in future implementations of other lines, too.

8.5 Multiway branching

Multiway branching is another possibility for reducing branch penalities, as indicated in Figure 8.9.

With **multiway branching**, both the sequential and the taken paths of an unresolved conditional branch are pursued, as indicated in Figure 8.46. Note that multiway branching requires multiple program counters (PCs) referred to as IFA1 and IFA2 in the figure.

Once the specified condition is resolved, which of the paths is correct becomes evident. If the correct path is the sequential one, its execution will be confirmed and the taken path execution discarded. Consequently, IFA1 contains the correct continuation address. In the opposite case, vice versa.

Obviously, during speculative execution of a conditional branch, a second unresolved conditional branch instruction may occur. Consequently, a more advanced multiway branching scheme should allow *multiple unresolved branches*. As an example, Figure 8.47 shows threefold multiway branching. In this case, four instruction fetch addresses are maintained concurrently (IFA1–IFA4). Obviously, only one of these is associated with the correct path. After all conditional branches have been resolved, the single correct thread is ascertained and all the computations belonging to incorrect paths are cancelled.

Although multiway branching seems to be attractive as a means of increasing performance, especially for highly parallel ILP-processors (like VLIWs), this technique also has significant *drawbacks*. First, multiway branching has a substantially

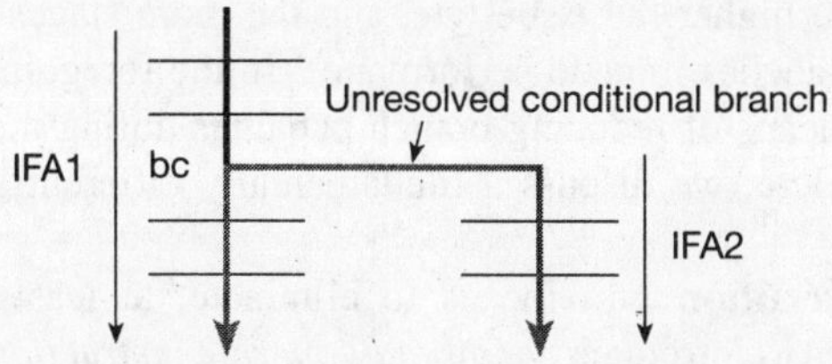

Figure 8.46 The principle of multiway branching.

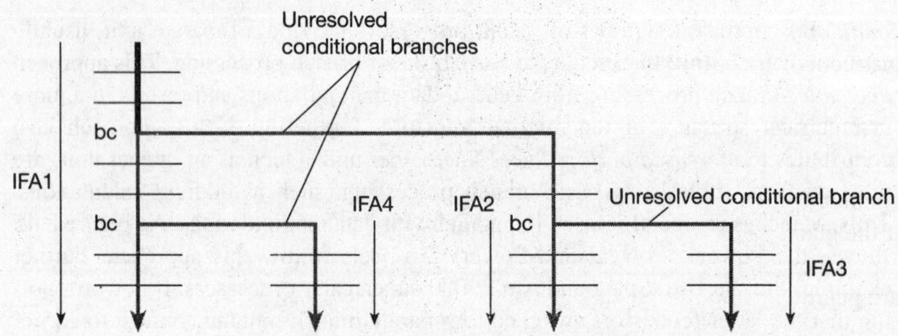

Figure 8.47 Threefold multiway branching.

higher demand for hardware resources (in the first-line execution units) than speculative branch processing. Furthermore, for multiple multiway branching, preserving sequential consistency and discarding superfluously executed computation becomes an increasingly complex and time-consuming task. Therefore, so far true multiway branching has been used in only a few processors. For instance, in the Multiflow TRACE 500 VLIW architecture proposal (Wolfe and Shen, 1991) two paths can be pursued, and two sets of 14 functional units were planned. A second example is the URPR-2, which is an experimental machine (Su et al., 1992). It has nine functional units with separate IFAs, allowing multiple multiway branching. A last example is a novel computational model called XIMD and its first experimental implementation, the XIMD-1 (Wolfe and Shen, 1991). This model enables concurrent execution of multiple paths (threads) and can operate in a number of different modes, one of which can address multiway branching. The experimental implementation has eight identical 32-bit RISC processors, each equipped with its own IFA.

Despite the drawbacks mentioned above, there are some expectations that this brute-force approach to speeding up the processing of unresolved conditional branches still has a future (Brian, 1994). This opinion is based on the rapid development of technology allowing increasingly complex microarchitectures to be realized for approximately the same cost.

8.6 Guarded execution

Recall that conditional branches can severely limit the performance of ILP-execution by causing branch penalties, especially in the case of unresolved conditional branches. The higher the issue rate, and the more stages a pipeline has, the more conditional branches impede performance. In the foregoing sections we have discussed various means of reducing branch penalties during the execution of conditional branches. Here, we discuss a fundamentally different approach to branch handling.

Guarded execution is a means to eliminate; at least partly, conditional branches. The idea is to introduce *conditional operate instructions* into the architecture and use them to replace conditional branches. Conditional operate instructions are called **guarded instructions**. A guarded instruction consists of two parts, a *condition part* called the *guard*, and an *operation part* which is a traditional instruction. It can be expressed, for instance, in the form:

(guard) instruction

The execution of guarded instructions depends (is guarded) on the following condition: if the specified guard is true, the associated instruction will be executed; if the guard turns out to be false, the instruction behaves like a NOP.

For instance, the α *architecture* provides conditional move instructions which are guarded instructions, with the following syntax and semantics (DEC, 1992):

```
cmovxx   ra.rq, rb.rq, rc.wq
cmovxx   ra.rq, #b.ib, rc.wq
```

where

xx	indicates a condition
ra.rq	is an integer, read-only 64-bit operand stored in register ra
rb.rq	is an integer, read-only 64-bit operand stored in register rb
rc.wq	is an integer, write-only 64-bit operand to be stored in register rc
#b.ib	is an integer 64-bit literal

This instruction operates as follows. Register ra is tested. If the specified condition is true, the contents of rb (or the value of the given literal #b) is transferred into register rc.

The instruction mnemonics specify the condition of the guarded execution:

cmoveq	//cmove if the contents of register ra are equal to zero
cmovge	//cmove if the contents of register ra are greater than or equal to zero
cmovgt	//cmove if the contents of register ra are greater than zero
cmovlbc	//cmove if the low bit of register ra is clear
cmovlbs	//cmove if the low bit of register ra is set
cmovle	//cmove if the contents of register ra are less than or equal to zero
cmovlt	//cmove if the contents of register ra are less than zero
cmovne	//cmove if the contents of register ra are not equal to zero

Now, *forward conditional branches can be eliminated* by using guarded instructions with the opposite condition as specified in the corresponding conditional branch. For instance, consider the code sequence

```
beq     ra, label    // if (ra) = 0 branch to 'label',
or      rb, rb, rc   // else move (rb) into rc
```

It can be replaced by

```
cmovne  ra, rb, rc
```

We note that the *SPARC V9* (1994) also offers some similar conditional move instructions. The *HP Precision Architecture* (1985) introduced guarded instructions in a more comprehensive way (and much earlier) than the DEC α. Here, all integer operate instructions are guarded instructions of the form

opcode.cond operands

The given condition (cond) relates to the result of the operation. If the specified condition is true, for instance the result is positive, the *following* instruction will be *nullified*. Note that this is a guarded execution of the following instruction, where the guard is the opposite of the given condition.

Using guarded instructions allows a number of disruptions in the control flow to be eliminated. We quote data published by Pnevmatikatos and Sohi (1994) for the *ratio of the eliminated* branches.

Pnevmatikatos and Sohi examined guarding in 13 general-purpose benchmark programs. Table 8.16 shows the benchmark programs used, the number of instructions run, and percentage of conditional and unconditional branches measured.

In their experimental runs, Pnevmatikatos and Sohi investigated two types of guarding, full guarding and restricted guarding. In **full guarding** all instructions are assumed to be guarded, whereas in **restricted guarding** only operate instructions (ALU instructions) have a guarded form. This restricted form of guarding takes into account the fact that in existing architectures the instruction code space is usually squeezed and in most cases only a few additional bits are available for specifying guard conditions.

The *ratio of eliminated branches* is given in Table 8.17 for both full and restricted guarding. The results indicate that full guarding eliminates, on average,

Table 8.16 Key characteristics of the benchmark programs used and the branch ratios measured (Pnevmatikatos and Sohi, 1994). © 1994 IEEE

Program	*Dynamic instructions (Millions)*	*Branch ratio (%)* Conditional	*Branch ratio (%)* Unconditional
Compress	78.59	14.9	4.0
Eqntott	300.00	30.6	1.2
Espresso	300.00	17.6	1.4
Gcc	128.78	15.6	4.2
Sc	300.00	20.7	3.7
Sunbench	300.00	14.8	6.7
Supermips	300.00	11.1	5.6
Tektronix	300.00	13.6	8.2
TeX	214.69	14.3	5.5
Thissim	300.00	10.5	4.6
Tycho	300.00	12.3	6.1
Xlisp	300.00	15.7	9.1
Yacc	26.37	23.7	2.0

Table 8.17 Percentage of eliminated branches by full and restricted guarding (Pnevmatikatos and Sohi, 1994). © 1994 IEEE

Program	*Percentage of loop branches (%)*	*Percentage of eliminated branches (%)*			
		Full guarding		*Restricted guarding*	
		Cond.	*Uncond.*	*Cond.*	*Uncond.*
Compress	26.48	24.86	84.29	18.24	0.00
Eqntott	29.07	44.55	54.98	40.04	1.02
Espresso	38.08	16.76	29.03	10.17	1.17
Gcc-ccl	24.84	31.92	17.04	9.64	0.37
Sc	24.63	43.07	17.74	9.83	0.18
Sunbench	15.79	35.65	47.10	11.35	0.03
Supermips	5.03	50.69	19.36	17.15	0.60
Tektronix	16.83	37.53	41.60	17.08	7.48
TeX	25.09	12.80	24.03	5.99	1.00
Thissim	11.52	62.31	33.70	23.26	1.43
Tycho	18.28	15.64	33.84	7.10	1.31
Xlisp	27.03	13.64	14.33	13.87	14.14
Yacc	38.64	19.53	38.95	8.18	1.71
Arithmetic Mean	**23.17**	**31.15**	**35.07**	**14.76**	**2.34**

one-third of both the conditional and unconditional branches. In contrast, restricted guarding is much less effective, eliminating only about 15 % of the conditional and 2 % of unconditional branches.

By eliminating a number of branches *the basic block* (BB) *size* is enlarged, as shown in Figure 8.48. With full guarding the average basic block size is increased from about 4.8 to 7.3 for the benchmark programs used. The expansion of basic blocks by 2.5 instructions is considerable.

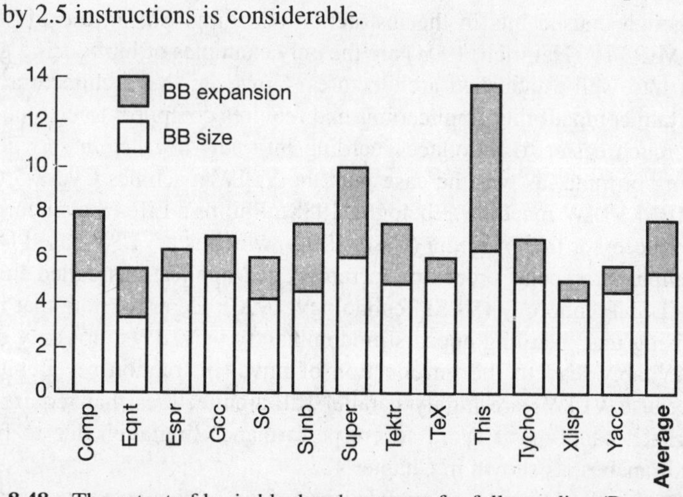

Figure 8.48 The extent of basic block enlargement for full guarding (Pnevmatikatos and Sohi, 1994). © 1994 IEEE

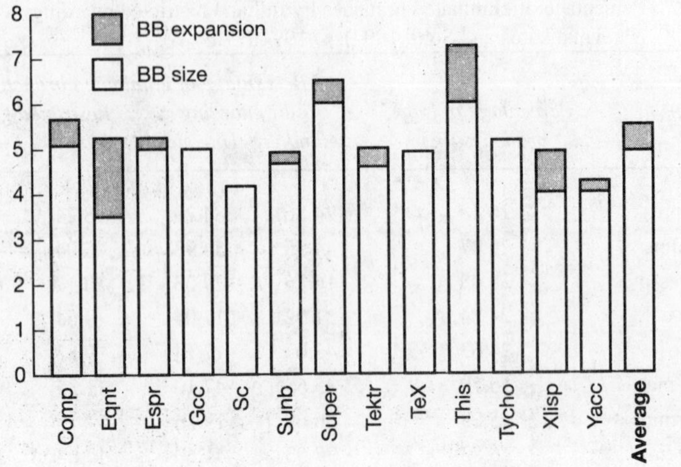

Figure 8.49 The extent of basic block enlargement for restricted guarding (Pnevmatikatos and Sohi, 1994). © 1994 IEEE

By contrast, the basic block enlargement for restricted guarding is much less impressive (Figure 8.49).

Larger basic blocks offer more parallelism for parallel optimizing compilers and contribute to a slight increase in the hit ratios for branch prediction (Pnevmatikatos and Sohi, 1994). However, at the present time, no experimental results are known to the authors regarding the performance increase that may be expected.

Nevertheless, there are several *problems with* guarded execution, which are clearly exposed by Pnevmatikatos and Sohi (1994). The biggest problem is that their integration into existing instruction sets needs an *architectural extension*. In most cases this extension is not at all feasible, because existing architectures usually do not have enough unused bits in the instruction encoding. So far, the SPARC V9 (1994) and MIPS IV (Heinrich, 1994) are the only examples of introducing guarded instructions into well-established architectures. However, this architectural extension has certain compatibility implications and requires compilers to be redesigned.

It is much easier to introduce guarding into *new instruction sets* designed with guarding in mind, as was the case with the VLIW machines Cydra-5 (Rau et al., 1989), IBM VLIW machine (Ebcioglu, 1988), Philips's Life (Slavenburg et al., 1991) or its successor the TriMedia (Case, 1994), which is a VLIW-based DPSP. A further example is a scalar processor for embedded applications called the ARM 610, from VLSI Technology (VLSI Technology, 1993). Here, we note that it is not at all surprising that guarding appears predominantly in VLIWs, not only because VLIWs unevitably lead to the introduction of novel instruction set architectures but also because VLIWs are highly parallel ILP-architectures that require highly effective branch handling to avoid severe performance limitation due to frequent conditional branches, as shown in Chapter 4.

A second disadvantage of guarded execution is that guarding transforms instructions from both the taken and the not-taken paths into guarded instructions.

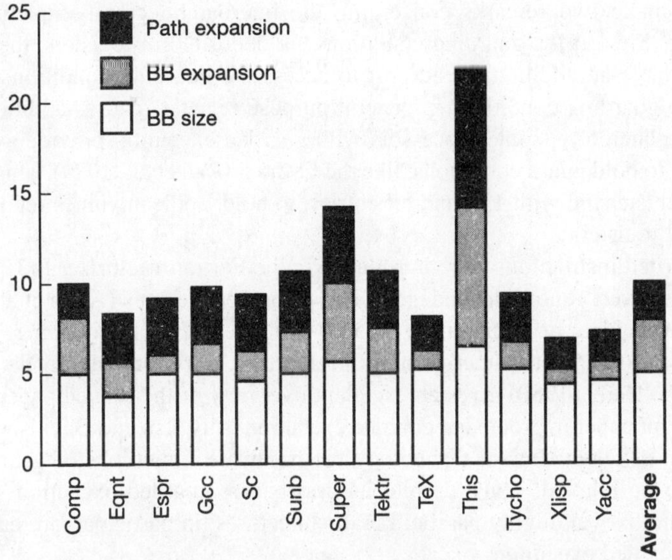

Figure 8.50 The extent of path expansion for full guarding (Pnevmatikatos and Sohi, 1994). © 1994 IEEE

Thus, guarding causes the processor to execute an increased number of instructions. According to published data (Pnevmatikatos and Sohi, 1994), full guarding generates about 33 % and restricted guarding about 8 % *additional instructions* (Figure 8.50 and 8.51). As a consequence, guarding requires *additional hardware resources* if an increase in processing time is to be avoided.

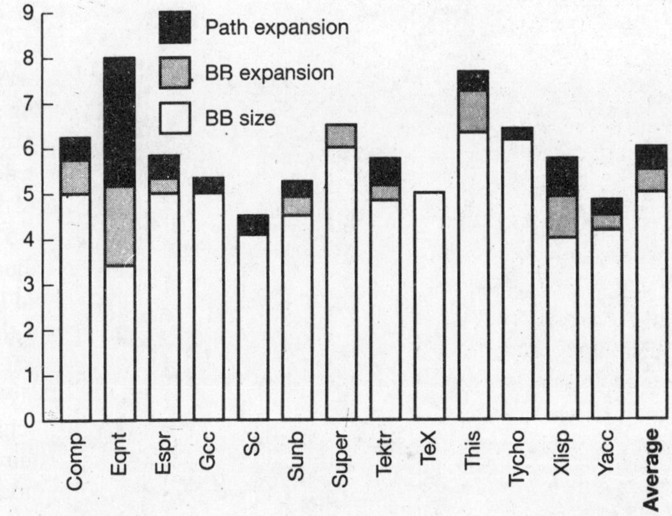

Figure 8.51 The extent of path expansion for restricted guarding (Pnevmatikatos and Sohi, 1994). © 1994 IEEE

We make two remarks concerning the microarchitectural implementation of guarding. First, if the guarding conditions are deposited in registers, the register file has to have an additional read port to access the guarding condition. Second, holding the guarding conditions in general-purpose registers causes additional register usage. Therefore, some processors with guarded execution provide a separate register file to hold guard conditions, like the Cydra 5 (Rau et al., 1989). This processor has a register file with 128 one-bit entries, to hold Boolean values (called iteration control registers).

Guarded instructions were introduced in the Fortran vectorizer PFC in 1983, in order to convert control dependencies into data dependencies (Allen et al., 1983). However, the idea of eliminating GOTO statements by introducing Boolean variables, in order to get a superior program structure, has a long history dating back to the 1960s. Harel (1980) gives an excellent overview of the related papers. A further important paper in proposing guarded execution is by Hsu and Davidson (1986).

With developments in technology the hardware limitations of guarding are expected to be relaxed. Thus, despite its drawbacks, guarded execution seems to have a future. Novel, highly parallel ILP-architectures, in particular, are candidates for using guarded execution.

9 Code Scheduling for ILP-Processors

In this chapter we review how parallel optimizing compilers schedule code for ILP-processors. This job covers two tasks: first, the detection and resolution of dependencies occurring in subsequent instructions, and second, optimization of the object code for parallel execution.

As we mentioned in Section 4.3, smart code schedulers can boost the performance of ILP-processors significantly, since ILP-processors perform, at most, dependency checking and resolution, but do not carry out code optimization for parallel execution.

In Section 9.1 we acquaint the reader with the structure of parallel optimizing compilers, and the main approaches used for code scheduling. Then we introduce the basic code scheduling techniques: basic block scheduling (Section 9.2), loop scheduling (Section 9.3) the global scheduling (Section 9.4). In doing so, we indicate the potential of these complex techniques to speed up processing. Case examples are described and trends identified.

9.1 Introduction

In this introductory section we are concerned mainly with three topics. First, we show how traditional compilers can be enhanced with code scheduling. Next, we identify and introduce the basic approaches conceivable for code scheduling. Finally, we discuss the complexity of the task of code scheduling.

As pointed out in Section 4.3, in instruction-level parallel processing dependencies have to be detected and resolved. This can be achieved either statically or dynamically, or in a concerted way both statically and dynamically. In the case of static scheduling the processor has to deliver dependency-free and parallel optimized code, as in the case of early pipelined processors, or VLIWs. In contrast, during dynamic sheduling the ILP-compiler behaves as a performance booster, and as far as the detection and resolution of dependencies is concerned relies on the processor, as is usually the case with superscalar processors.

As also emphasized in Section 4.3, performance-greedy ILP-processors expect parallel optimization from the compiler as well. During parallel optimization, the compiler identifies independent instructions and reorders code such that independent instructions become executable as early as possible. Thus, hardware resources are better utilized and program execution is speeded up. Evidently, a parallel optimization can be carried out only if dependencies among instructions have been previously identified. Thus, dependency detection and resolution is a prerequisite for parallel optimization. In Section 4.3 we introduced the designation *code scheduling* to cover dependency detection and resolution as well as parallel optimization. In the present chapter we show how code scheduling is performed.

Code scheduling is usually accomplished in conjunction with traditional compilation. A code scheduler accepts as input a set, or a sequence, of executable instructions, and a set of precedence constraints imposed on them, typically in the form of a DAG. As output, it attempts to deliver, in each scheduling step, an instruction which is dependency-free and represents the best choice for the schedule to achieve the shortest possible execution time.

How can code scheduling be included in traditional compiler operation? In order to answer this let us look at how traditional compilers are built up. **Traditional non-optimizing compilers** can be considered as consisting of two major parts (Figure 9.1(a)). The front-end part of the compiler performs scanning, parsing and semantic analysis of the source string and produces an intermediate representation. This intermediate form is usually represented by an attributed abstract tree and a symbol table. The back-end part, in turn, generates the object code (for details see, for example, Zima and Chapman (1990) or Aho et al. (1986)).

Traditional optimizing compilers speed up sequential execution and reduce the required memory space mainly by eliminating redundant operations. Sequential optimization requires a program analysis, which comprises control flow, data flow and dependency analysis in the front-end part, as depicted in Figure 9.1(b). For details see Zima and Chapman (1990).

Now let us turn to **ILP-compilers**, that is, to compilers that incorporate code scheduling. There are *two different approaches* to integrating traditional compilation and code scheduling. In the first, code scheduling is completely integrated into the

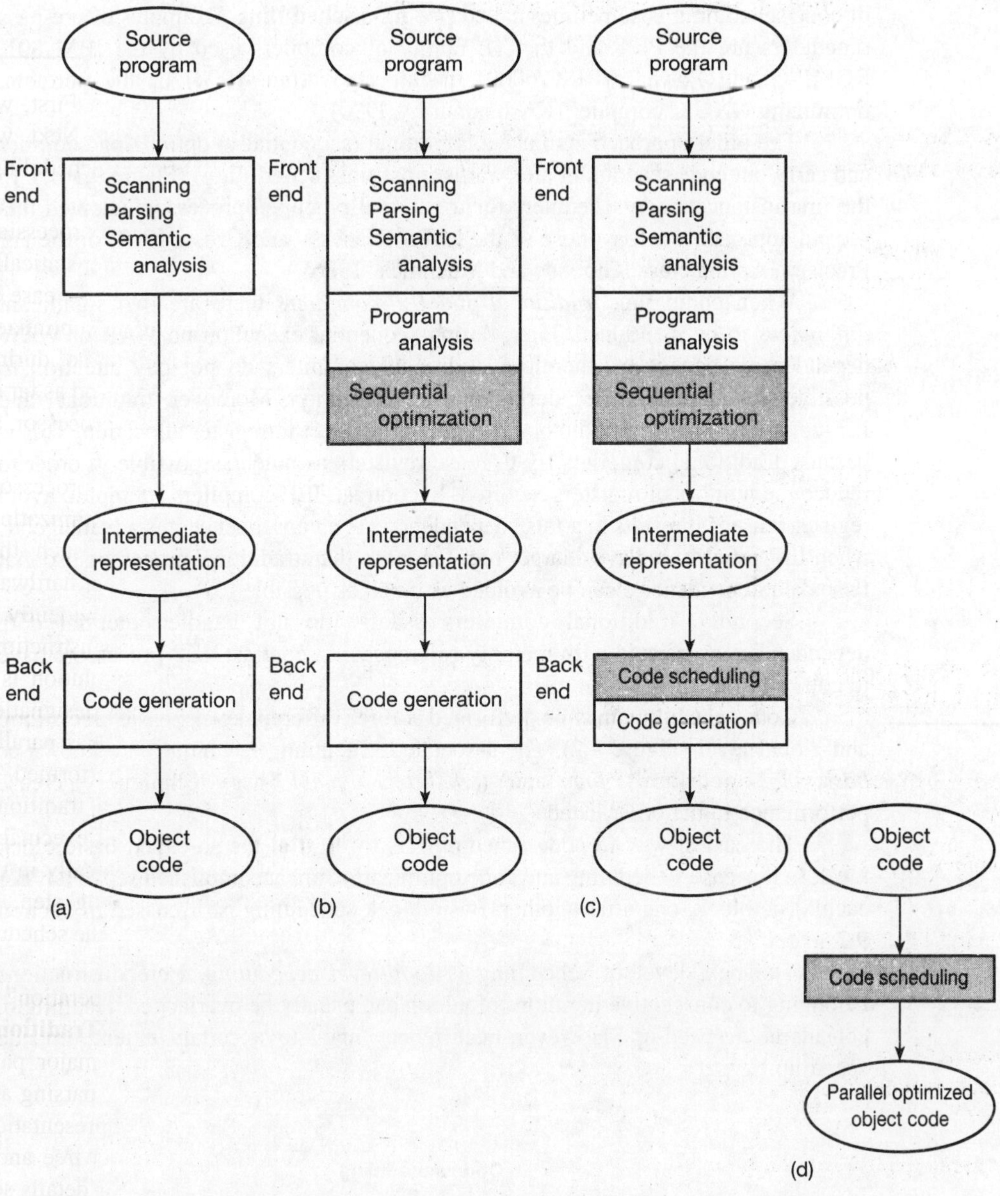

Figure 9.1 Typical layout of (a) a traditional non-optimizing compiler, (b) a traditional optimizing compiler, (c) an ILP-compiler performing pre-pass parallel optimization, and (d) an ILP-compiler with post-pass parallel optimization.

compilation process. In this case, the code scheduler uses the results of the program analysis produced by the front-end part of the compiler. Accordingly, the code scheduler usually follows the traditional sequential optimizer in the back-end part, before register allocation and subsequent code generation (Figure 9.1(c)). This type of code scheduling is sometimes called **pre-pass scheduling**. Examples of pre-pass schedulers are the PL.8 and the XL family of compilers used by the IBM 801, ROMP-C and Power1 (RISC/6000) machines (Warren, 1990) or the portable, optimizing GNU C compiler (Krishnamurthy, 1990).

The other approach is to use a traditional (sequentially) optimizing compiler and carry out code scheduling afterwards (**post-pass scheduling**) (Figure 9.1(d)). In the first instance, code schedulers for traditional pipelined processors adopted this second approach, such as those of the MIPS (Henessy and Gross, 1983) or the HP Precision Architecture (Gibbons and Muchnick, 1986).

When comparing *traditional* and *ILP-compilers* there are two significant *differences* to be mentioned. First, during sequential execution no WAR or WAW dependencies can occur, therefore traditional compilers do not pay attention to possible false dependencies during register allocation. Moreover, traditional and ILP-compilers have contradictory criteria with respect to register allocation. This is because traditional compilers try to reuse registers as much as possible in order to reduce the number of registers required. In contrast, ILP-compilers attempt to avoid register reuse if it results in a false dependency. As a consequence it is advantageous when ILP-processors have a larger register space than traditional processors, so that false data dependencies can be avoided as much as possible.

Secondly, traditional compilers usually do not handle potential data dependencies associated with memory references. In contrast, ILP-processors have to cope with this task.

Code scheduling may be performed at three different levels: basic block, loop and global level (Figure 9.2). The associated scheduling techniques are known as *basic block* (or local), *loop* and *global techniques*. These techniques increase performance in the order listed.

The easiest way to code scheduling is to do it at the so-called basic block level. In this case, scheduling and code optimization are accomplished separately for each basic block, one after another. Basic block scheduling is discussed in Section 9.2.

The next level of scheduling is *loop-level scheduling*. Here, instructions belonging to consecutive iterations of a loop can usually be overlapped, resulting in considerable speed-up. However, recurrences may, to a certain extent, impede speed-up.

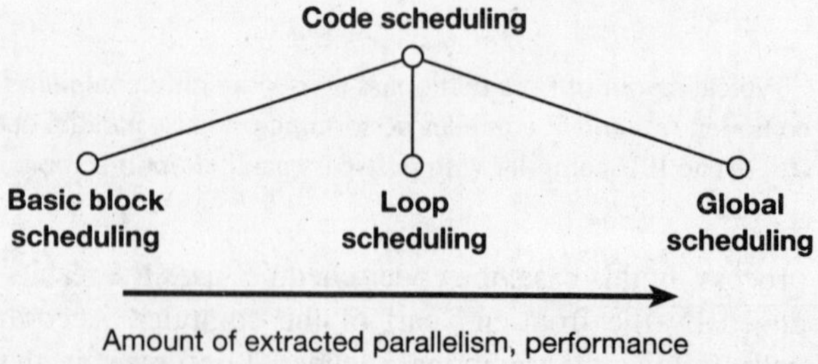

Figure 9.2 Levels of static scheduling.

It is widely accepted that loops are a significant source of parallelism, especially in scientific programs. Therefore, it is apparent that for highly parallel ILP-processors, such as VLIW architectures, compilers should perform scheduling at least at the loop level. Accordingly, a large number of techniques have been developed for scheduling at this level; these are overviewed in Section 9.3.

The most effective way to schedule is to do it at the highest possible level, using *global scheduling techniques*. Here, parallelism is sought and extracted beyond basic blocks and simple loops, in such constructs as compound program sections involving loops as well as conditional control constructs. Evidently, in the case of a chunk of code larger than a basic block, there are many more possibilities for parallelization. However, the price for higher speed is increased complexity (Figure 9.3). Section 9.4 gives an introduction to global scheduling techniques.

We emphasize that code scheduling carried out at a higher level has a higher speed-up potential as well as complexity (Figure 9.3). On the other hand, ILP processors with a higher degree of parallel execution potential require a more powerful scheduler in order to exploit their multiple, pipelined execution units satisfactorily. This means that slightly parallel ILP-processors, such as traditional pipelined processors, can be suitably served by basic block schedulers. On the other hand, highly parallel ILP-processors, such as VLIW or highly superscalar processors, undoubtedly require the use of more powerful scheduling techniques, such as loop or global scheduling.

Almost all instruction schedulers for pipelined processors and the majority of the first-generation schedulers for superscalar processors (such as the schedulers of the PL.8 compiler for the Power1 (IBM RS/6000) or of the GNU C compiler) are basic block (or local) schedulers. Novel ILP-compilers, on the other hand, make increasing use of loop and global scheduling (like the XL compiler, which is a follow-on of the PL.8).

Finally, we briefly discuss the *complexity of code scheduling*. The problem of finding an optimal schedule in the case of resource constraints is known to be *NP-complete*, also called *NP-hard* (Garey and Johnson, 1979).

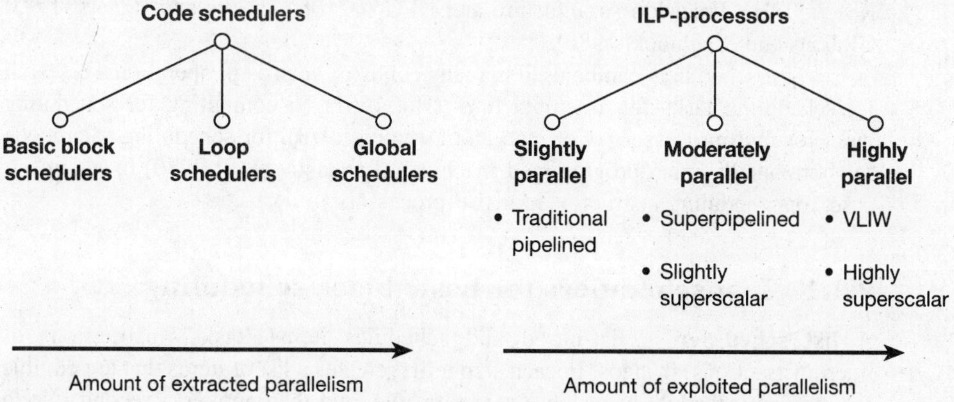

Figure 9.3 Contrasting the performance of code schedulers and ILP-processors.

This general statement can be applied to various special cases of code scheduling. In doing so, it can be proved that particular cases of code scheduling are also NP-complete. Examples are the scheduling of single basic blocks of micro-operations in microprogramming (Dewit, 1976) and, as a consequence, also the scheduling of single basic blocks at the assembly code level (Bodin and Charot, 1990) as well as the scheduling for pipelined processors (Henessy and Gross, 1983) or loop scheduling by software pipelining (Lam, 1988).

NP-complete problems are believed to be of at least exponential complexity, thus these problems are considered practically intractable if an *exact solution* is required. The problem of finding an optimal solution is in practice circumvented by appropriate heuristics yielding *adequate solutions*. In Sections 9.2–9.4 we shall see how heuristics are used for different kinds of code scheduling.

9.2 Basic block scheduling

9.2.1 Introduction

Basic block scheduling is the simplest but least effective code scheduling technique. Here, only instructions within a basic block are eligible for reordering. As a consequence, the achievable speed-up is limited by both true data and control dependencies (see Section 4.2). Thus, the expected average speed-up for general-purpose programs is less than 2 and for scientific/engineering programs most likely not more than 2–4.

Basic block schedulers are typically used for slightly and moderately parallel ILP-processors, such as pipelined and early superscalar processors. Nevertheless, basic block schedulers are currently the most widely used.

Most basic block schedulers for ILP-processors belong to the class of *list schedulers*, like the ones developed for the MIPS processors, Sparc processors, RS/6000, HP Precision Architecture and DEC α 21064 (Kerns and Eggers, 1993; Gibbons and Muchnick, 1986).

List schedulers can be used in many contexts, such as in operational research for scheduling tasks for assembly lines (Hu, 1961), in computing for scheduling tasks for multiprocessors (Coffman and Denning, 1973), for scheduling microcode for horizontally microprogrammed machines (Landskov et al., 1980) or, as in our case, for scheduling instructions for ILP-processors.

9.2.2 List schedulers for basic block scheduling

A **list scheduler** is list-based and schedules items (tasks, instructions or microinstructions) in steps. In each step it first creates a list of items that are eligible for the next schedule by using a selection rule, and then applies a second rule to

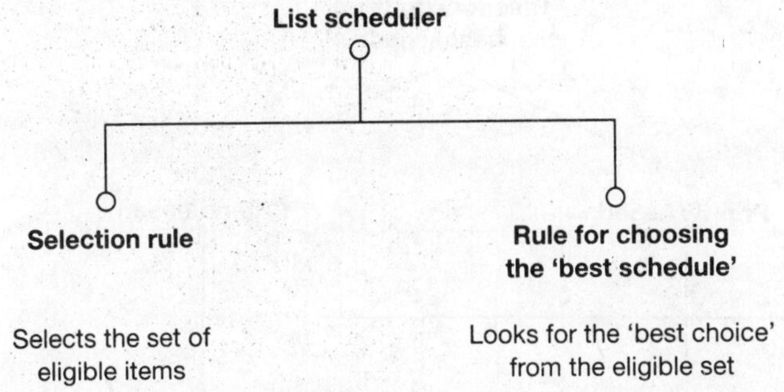

Figure 9.4 Main components of a list scheduler.

make the best choice for the next schedule (Figure 9.4). In each step one or more items are scheduled.

As far as *list schedulers for basic block scheduling* are concerned, the scheduled items are instructions. As far as the number of scheduled instructions per step is concerned, code schedulers for both pipelined and superscalar processors deliver one scheduled instruction at a time.

Now let us turn to the main components of list schedulers. The selection rule selects the set of eligible instructions for scheduling. Eligible instructions are dependency-free, that is, they have no predecessors in the DDG and the hardware required resources are available.

The **rule for choosing the 'best schedule'** is used to look for the instruction most likely to cause interlocks with the follow-on instructions (Gibbons and Muchnick, 1986). This rule is typically a matter of heuristics.

Most schedulers implement this heuristics by searching for the critical execution path in the DDG and choosing a particular node associated with the critical path for scheduling. However, **'critical path'** can be interpreted in a number of different ways and can be selected on the basis of either priorities or criteria (Figure 9.5).

In general, a **priority-based scheduler** calculates a priority value for each eligible instruction (scheduling item) according to the chosen heuristics. In the case of basic block list schedulers for pipelined and superscalar processors, the *'priority value'* of an eligible node is usually understood as the length of the path measured from the node under consideration to the end of the basic block. After calculating all priority values, the best choice is made by choosing the node with the *highest priority value*. Evidently, a *tie-breaking rule* is needed for the case when more than one node has the same highest priority value. Such a rule could give preference, for instance, to an instruction occurring earlier in the original code sequence.

In contrast, **criteria-based schedulers** apply a set of selected criteria in a given order to the items to be scheduled. A 'best choice' is made by finding the first

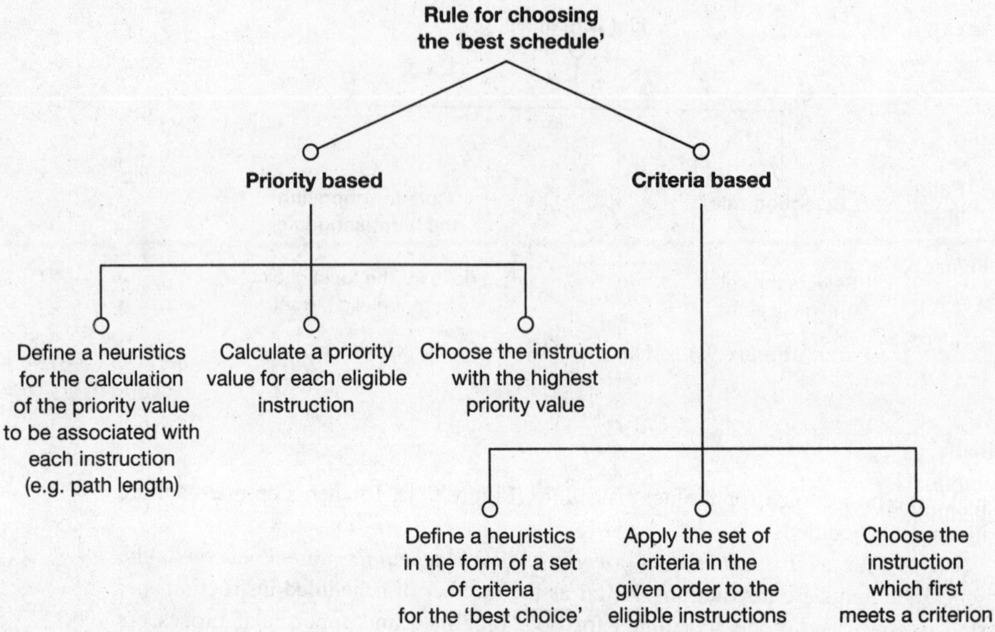

Figure 9.5 Types of rules applied by list schedulers for choosing the 'best schedule' in the case of basic block instruction scheduling.

item that meets the highest possible ranking criterion. Here, of course, the scheduler also has to provide an additional criterion or rule for tie-breaking.

For example, a published prototype version of the scheduler for the HP Precision Architecture uses the following set of criteria (Gibbons and Muchnick, 1986):

- whether there is an immediate successor that is dependent on the instruction in question,
- how many successors the instruction has, and
- how long is the longest path from the instruction in question to the leaves.

These criteria are applied in the order given above.

A number of schedulers employ the priority-based critical path approach, or a similar one, such as schedulers for MIPS-X, i960CA and Power1 (RISC/6000). As far as the **interpretation of the critical path** is concerned, some priority-based schedulers interpret 'critical path' as the *path with the greatest number of node levels*, others as the *path with the longest delay time* to the end of the basic block (Figure 9.6). The first approach is attributed to Hu (see Hu, 1961; Krishnamurthy, 1990).

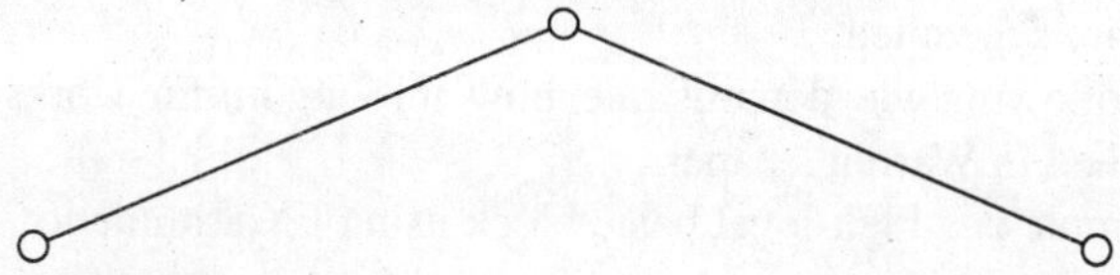

Figure 9.6 Possible interpretations of 'critical path' in priority-based list schedulers for basic block ILP instruction schedulers.

9.2.3 Case study: The code scheduler of the PL.8 and XL compiler families for the Power1 (IBM RS/6000)

Finally, as a case example, we describe the instruction scheduler of the PL.8 and XL compiler families, slightly simplified, with reference to Warren (1990). These schedulers were designed for the IBM Power1 (RISC/6000) processor.

As previously stated, here we are concerned with a list scheduler that produces one scheduled instruction at a time. Initially, a DDG is given and the execution latencies of the nodes are assumed to be known. Now, **Warren's algorithm** schedules the nodes of a DDG step by step as follows: in each step the algorithm selects the set of eligible nodes, chooses one of them for scheduling and removes it from the DDG. In each step the scheduler considers as eligible for schedule a node that

- either has no predecessor (that is, is not data dependent), or
- although it has a predecessor, its predecessor no longer interlocks the execution of the node under consideration (that is, data to be produced by a predecessor node is already available).

This latter requirement is evaluated by maintaining a *system-wide current time* as well as an *earliest time* for the immediate successors of already scheduled nodes. The immediate successors of scheduled nodes are the nodes to be scheduled. At the beginning the current time is set to 0. After each schedule, the earliest time for the successor of the scheduled node is calculated by incrementing the current time by the execution latency of the scheduled node. A successor node is eligible for selection when the current time is equal to, or greater than, the earliest time.

Choosing an eligible node for scheduling is accomplished using the *critical path approach*, where the *longest path* to the end of the basic block is considered to be critical. The path length is interpreted as the sum of the execution latencies of the nodes along the path considered. Thus, out of the eligible nodes, that particular node will be chosen for the next schedule, which is in the longest path. Next, the scheduled node will be removed from the DDG.

Then, the algorithm updates the current time by 1 and calculates the earliest execution time of the successor node as the sum of the updated current time value and the execution latency of the scheduled node. Finally, the successor node is marked by the calculated earliest time. This algorithm is used for the given DDG until all nodes are scheduled.

In the following we demonstrate how this algorithm works by using the example published in Warren's paper.

The example is a high-level basic block using FX arithmetic:

```
A = B + C - D;
IF E > 0 THEN ...
```

From this source code, the front-end part of the compiler generates the intermediate code shown in Figure 9.7. Note that the intermediate form is generated before register allocation, thus all the registers used are virtual registers. Next, the scheduler constructs the corresponding DDG. In the graph LB, LC and so on indicate 'load B', 'load C' and so on; ST.A means 'store A'. The arc between ST.A and BC deserves further comment. In spite of the fact that there is no data dependency between these instructions, the ST instruction must precede BC. Therefore, an arc is placed between them to enforce precedence.

In the given DDG the execution latencies of all instructions involved are marked on the arcs. The *latency values* indicate how many time units the successors have to wait before the result of the predecessor node becomes available.

```
l      r100, b(r200)
l      r101, c(r200)
add    r102, r100, r101
l      r103, d(r200)
sub    r104, r102, r103
st     r104, a(r200)
l      r105, e(r200)
cmp    r106, r105, 0
bc     r106, . . .
```

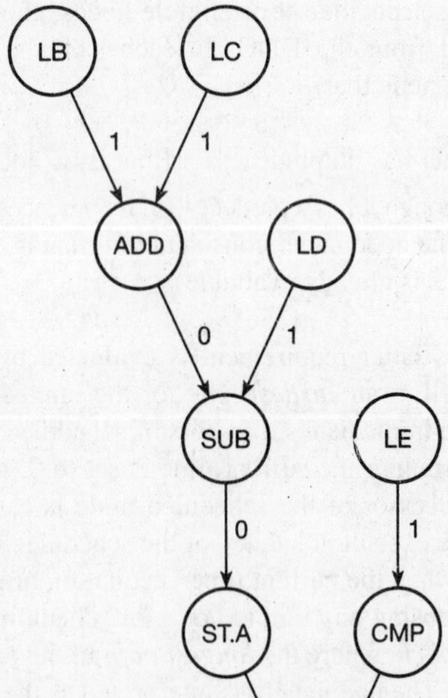

Figure 9.7 The intermediate code and the corresponding DDG of the example program (Warren, 1990).

As far as the scheduling of the DDG is concerned, the successive steps are illustrated in Figure 9.8(a)–(i). When scheduling starts (Figure 9.8(a)) the current time is set to 0. Then, the eligible set is selected by looking for all the nodes that have no predecessor. That is the set {LB, LC, LD, LE}. Note that in the figures eligible instructions are shaded. From this set, the instruction L.E is chosen for scheduling since it is in the longest path – LE has a delay path length of 4, whereas all other eligible nodes have a delay path length of 1 (Figure 9.8(a)).

Next, the chosen node is removed from the graph, and the current time updated by 1 time unit. This results in the new current time of 1 (Figure 9.8(b)). The first scheduling step ends by calculating and marking the earliest time for the successor of the selected node. This is done by summing the updated current time value (1 unit) and the latency of the removed node (1 time unit) and by labelling the CMP node with the resulting value of 2.

In the second scheduling step (Figure 9.8(b)), the eligible set is {LB, LC, LD}. Note that the CMP node cannot be a member of this set yet because its earliest

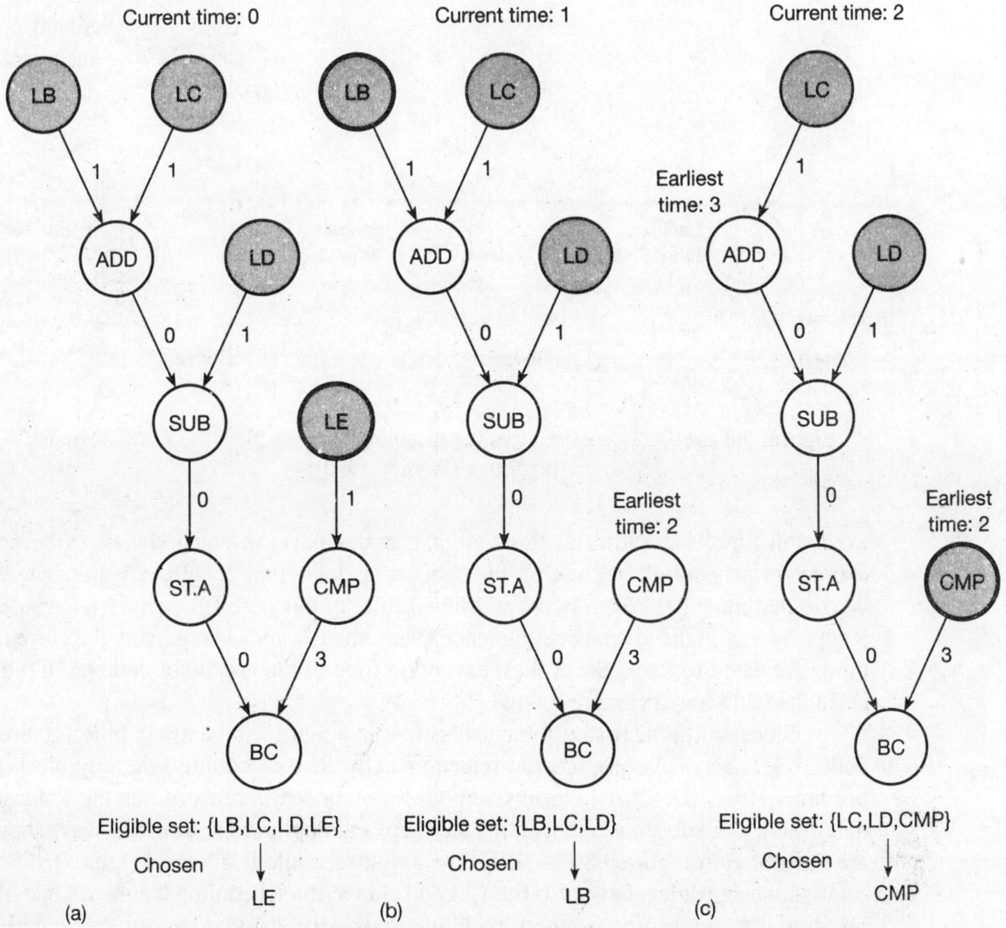

Figure 9.8 The first three steps in scheduling the example DDG using Warren's algorithm (Warren, 1990).

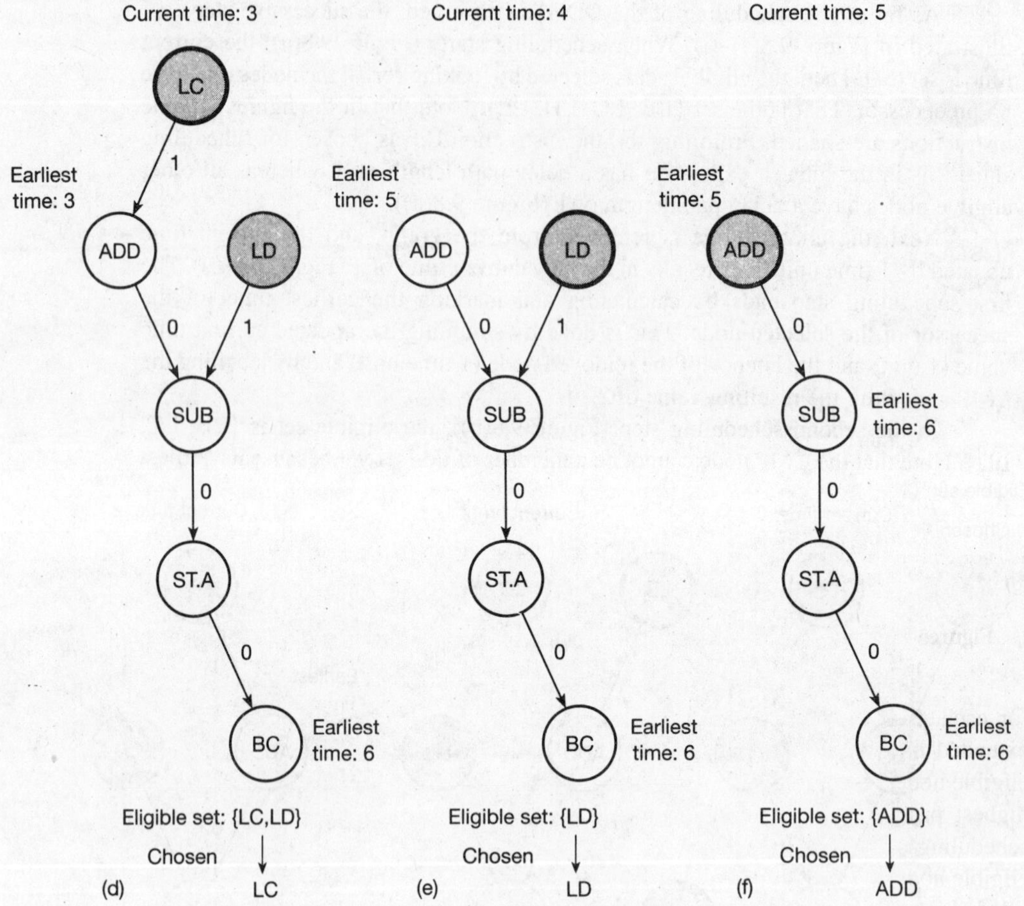

Figures 9.8 cont. Successive steps in scheduling the example DDG using Warren's algorithm (Warren, 1990).

execution time is 2. Now, all three eligible nodes have an equal chance of being chosen for scheduling because all have the same delay path length of 1 unit. There is a tie that must be broken by an additional rule. In this case LB is chosen because it appears first in the given code sequence. Next, the LB node is removed, the current time is updated to 2 and the earliest execution time of the successor node (ADD) is calculated and noted (Figure 9.8(c)).

Since in the next step the current time is equal to the earliest time for this node, CMP becomes eligible for selection as well. Accordingly, the eligible set becomes {LC, LD, CMP}. In this step CMP is chosen because it has the longest delay path. The successive scheduling steps are accomplished in a similar way. They are illustrated in Figure 9.8(d)–(i). The resulting schedule is given in Figure 9.9.

List schedulers have also been a good choice for scheduling the microcode of horizontally microprogrammed machines, usually refered to as **microcode compaction** (see Landskov et al. (1980)). These schedulers differ from the ones described above in that they typically have to choose *more than one* microoperation

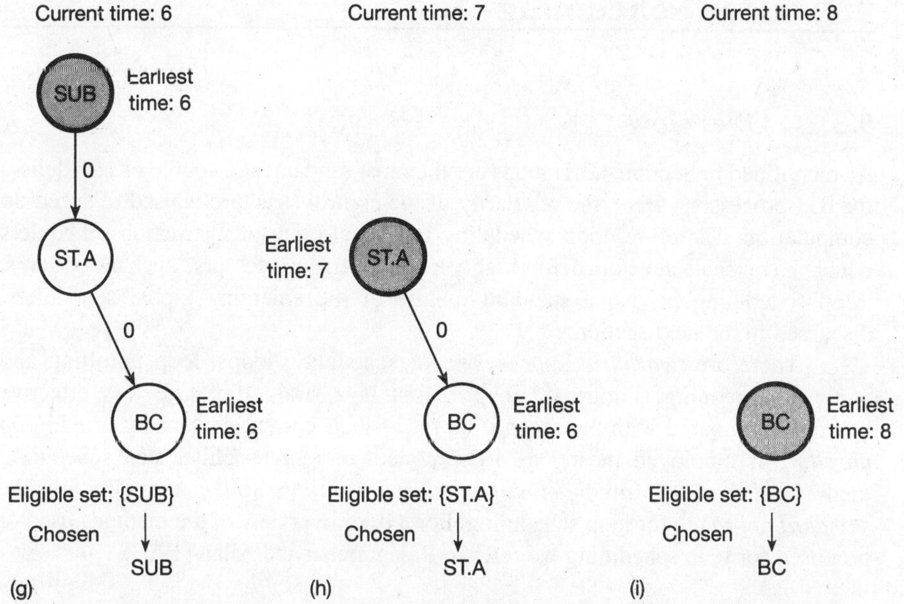

Figures 9.8 cont. Successive steps in scheduling the example DDG using Warren's algorithm (Warren, 1990).

for each microinstruction. Therefore, the rule for choosing the best schedule is extended in such a way that more than one node will be chosen from the list of eligible nodes in each step. This is accomplished by first selecting the node with the highest priority, and then selecting the node with the next highest priority and scheduling it if there is no resource conflict. This process continues until either all eligible nodes have been examined or all possible places in the microinstruction are filled. List schedulers performing microcode compaction usually operate on the basis of priorities (using weights).

Note that although scheduling for horizontally microcoded machines and VLIW processors appears at first sight to be very similar, compilers for VLIW processors do not use list schedulers. This is because VLIW processors require a more aggressive parallelism extraction than basic block schedulers can provide, as pointed out earlier. Therefore, compilers for VLIW machines typically employ global schedulers, discussed later in this chapter (Section 9.4).

```
l    r105, e(r200)
l    r100, b(r200)
cmp  r106, r105, 0
l    r101, c(r200)
l    r103, d(r200)
add  r102, r100, r101
sub  r104, r102, r103
st   r104, a(r200)
bc   r106, . . .
```

Figure 9.9 Resulting schedule for the example DDG using Warren's algorithm (Warren, 1990).

9.3 Loop scheduling

9.3.1 Overview

As mentioned in Section 4.3.1, loops are the most fundamental source of parallelism for ILP-processors. Here, the regularity of the control structure is used to speed up computation. Therefore, loop scheduling is a focal point of instruction schedulers which have been developed for highly parallel ILP-processors, such as VLIWs. Loop scheduling is also a standard feature of the emerging global schedulers, discussed in the next section.

There are *two basic approaches* for scheduling loops, loop unrolling and software pipelining (Figure 9.10). The first is a straightforward, less effective approach compared with the second. As far as their current use is concerned, *loop unrolling* is employed mostly as a component of more sophisticated scheduling methods, such as *software pipelining* or *trace scheduling*. Software pipelining is the *standard approach* for loop scheduling. For a brief overview of the methods used or proposed for loop scheduling we refer to Rajagopalan and Allan (1993).

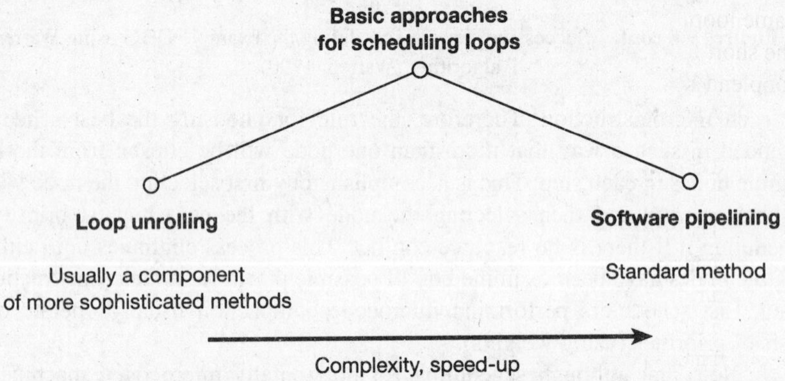

Figure 9.10 Basic approaches for scheduling loops.

9.3.2 Loop unrolling

The basic idea of **loop unrolling** is to repeat the loop body a number of times and to omit superfluous inter-iteration code, such as decrementing the loop count, testing for loop end and branching back conditionally between iterations. Obviously, this will result in a reduced execution time. Loop unrolling can be implemented quite easily when the number of iterations is already fixed at compile time, which occurs often in 'do' and 'for' loops. As an example, let us consider the following simple loop:

```
for i = 1 to 3 do {
 b(i) = 2.0 * a(i)
}
```

Before register allocation and optimization a CISC-like intermediate code for this high-level construct could be something like:

```
      load  r100, a1;             //load starting address of
                                    block a
      load  r200, b1;             //load starting address of
                                    block b
      load  r300; 3;              //load loop count
Loop: fmul(r200), 2.0, (r100); //multiplication with
                                    indirect addressing
      inc   r100, 4;              //increment pointer to the
                                    next data element a(i)
      inc   r200, 4;              //increment pointer to the
                                    next data element b(i)
      decr  r300;                 //decrement loop count
      bnz   Loop;                 //branch back to Loop: if
                                    loop count is not zero
```

Notice that this CISC-like intermediate code uses indirect addressed memory operands in the 'fmul' instruction. In contrast, a RISC-like intermediate code for the same loop would use register operands for the 'fmul' instruction. In this simple case the short loop can be unrolled easily and decrementing the loop count and testing for loop end become superfluous.

After loop unrolling we get:

```
load r100, a1;
load r200, b1;
load r300; 3;
fmul (r200), 2.0, (r100);
inc  r100, 4;
inc  r200, 4;
fmul (r200), 2.0, (r100);
inc  r100, 4;
inc  r200, 4;
fmul (r200), 2.0, (r100);
```

Thus, loop unrolling saves execution time, at the expense of code length, in much the same way as code inlining or traditional macro expansion. **Code inlining** is one of the standard compiler optimization techniques, applied for short, infrequently used subroutines. Code inlining means inserting the whole subroutine body each time the subroutine is called 'at the point of call', instead of storing the subroutine body separately and calling it from the main code if needed.

However, simple unrolling is often not practicable, for example when a loop has to be executed a large number of times, or when the number of iterations is not fixed at compile time. In such cases simple loop unrolling has to be extended. The usual method is to unroll the loop a given number of times, say three times, and to set up a loop for the resulting group of unrolled loops. Then the decrementing, testing for loop end and conditional branching back code is only necessary for each group of unrolled loops. Evidently, some simple 'prologue' and 'epilogue' code is also required to carry out the necessary adjustments.

For example, if we wish to execute the original loop 30 times, using loop unrolling, this could be done as follows:

```
        load  r100, a1;
        load  r200, b1;
        load  r300; 30;
Loop:   fmul  (r200), 2.0, (r100);
        inc   r100, 4;
        inc   r200, 4;
        fmul  (r200), 2.0, (r100);
        inc   r100, 4;
        inc   r200, 4;
        fmul  (r200), 2.0, (r100);
        inc   r100, 4;
        inc   r200, 4
        decr  r300 3;
        bnz   Loop;
```

After loop unrolling we get a larger basic block that will be scheduled as described in the preceding section.

Loop unrolling is sensible to recurrences. When recurrences exist between subsequent iterations, loop unrolling is only feasible if requested and in a preceding iteration calculated data becomes available in due time. This can restrict the merit of loop unrolling considerably.

How much *speed-up* can be achieved by loop unrolling? There are *two sources* of speed-up. First, omitting inter-iteration (loop updating) code immediately results in performance improvement. The resulting speed-up depends on the size of the loop. For larger loop bodies the relative gain is less whereas for shorter ones, obviously, it is more significant. In addition, enlarging the basic block size can lead to a more effective schedule with considerable speed-up.

Weiss and Smith (1987) published simulation results of loop unrolling obtained for the first 14 Lawrence Livermore Loops (McMahon, 1972) on a modified CRAY-1S. These results are worth quoting (Table 9.1).

When interpreting their results, they differentiate three kinds of loops. Loops denoted by * do not have recurrences between loop iterations. Thus, the scheduling of the resulting large basic blocks yields notable speed-up values. In loops labelled with # there are recurrences. However, in these loops memory hazards due to recurrences may be avoided during scheduling. In addition, some memory loads and stores can be removed by forwarding data between iterations through registers. For these loops, again, loop unrolling has a significant benefit. Finally, in loops without any label, the compiler could not resolve hazards between memory operands occurring due to recurrences. Therefore, the unrolled loop bodies could not be scheduled, and the advantage of unrolling is restricted to omitting superfluous inter-iteration code. Not surprisingly, this method has only a slight speed-up which is less for large loops (labelled 8, 13, 14) and greater for the single short loop (no. 4).

Table 9.1 Speed-up produced by loop unrolling for the first 14 Lawrence Livermore Loops (Weiss and Smith, 1987). © 1987 IEEE

	Relative speed-up to the case when no unrolling is used		
Loop	*Unrolled by 2 blocks*	*Unrolled by 4 blocks*	*Unrolled by 8 blocks*
LLL *1	1.82	2.68	2.92
LLL *2	1.48	1.77	1.91
LLL *3	1.62	2.21	2.66
LLL †4	1.14	1.20	1.22
LLL #5	1.20	1.30	1.36
LLL #6	1.23	1.30	1.35
LLL *7	1.42	1.67	1.45
LLL †8	0.92	0.94	0.97
LLL *9	1.26	1.35	1.22
LLL *10	1.49	1.59	1.36
LLL #11	1.74	2.45	3.03
LLL *12	1.74	2.63	2.73
LLL †13	1.03	0.93	0.95
LLL †14	1.03	0.95	0.98
Aggregate	**1.34**	**1.50**	**1.56**
H-mean	**1.37**	**1.56**	**1.62**

* : no recurrences
\# : recurrences, where memory hazards could be resolved during scheduling
† : recurrences, where memory hazard could not be resolved during scheduling

Loop unrolling, albeit by doing it manually, was first proposed by Dongarra and Hinds (1979). This method was used for the STACKLIB Fortran routines, a mathematical package developed for the CDC 6600, 7600 and CYBER 200 machines (CDC, 1981a). Subsequently, automatic loop unrolling has been included in more sophisticated scheduling techniques, such as trace scheduling and, in some cases, even in software pipelining.

We now turn to the more effective but also more complex software pipelining approach.

9.3.3 Software pipelining

Basic concept

Software pipelining is an analogous term to hardware pipelining.

In order to demonstrate the underlying idea let us look at the *most feasible parallel execution* of a loop on an *ILP-processor* which has multiple execution units operating in parallel. For simplification, we shall base our discussion on an example. We take the following high-level loop:

```
for i  = 1 to 7 do {
a(i)   = 2.0 * b(i)
}
```

Furthermore, let us assume a RISC-like intermediate code for the loop body such as:

```
load  r100, b(i);
fmul  r100, 2.0, r100;
store a(i), r100;
```

While demonstrating the principle of software pipelining, we focus only on the loop body, neglecting some prologue and epilogue code.

We make the following assumptions about the ILP-processor. It has separate execution units for FP, FX, load and store instructions, all capable of parallel operation. All execution units should allow a new operation to be initiated in every cycle. Finally, we suppose that the FP unit delivers the result of the fmul instruction in, say, three cycles, whereas loads and stores have an execution latency of one cycle.

Now let us look for the most parallel execution feasible. We achieve it when we unroll the loop and execute subsequent iterations in as parallel a fashion as possible. Let us start with the first iteration. It can be executed as follows:

Cycle	*Instruction*	*Comment*
c	`load r101, b(1);`	`//b(1) is loaded`
c+1	`fmul r101, 2.0, r101,`	
c+2	`decr r200;`	`//decrement loop count`
c+3	`nop`	`//wait for result of fmul`
c+4	`store a(i)+, r101;`	`//store a(i), autoincrement i.`

Here we note that the supposed latency of the fmul operation is three cycles, therefore in cycle c+3 its result is not yet available and a 'nop' has to be inserted.

Under the assumptions made, the second iteration can be initiated in cycle c+1 by loading the second data item, b(2). However, to avoid interference with the first iteration, that is, to avoid a WAW conflict in using r101, in the second iteration r101 has to be renamed, say to r102. Subsequently, both iterations may be executed in parallel. Thus, we get the following execution sequence:

Cycle	*1. iteration*	*2. iteration*
c	`load r101, b(1);`	
c+1	`fmul r101, 2.0, r101,`	`load r102, b(2);`
c+2	`decr`	`fmul r102, 2.0, r102,`
c+3	`nop`	`decr`
c+4	`store a(1)+, r101;`	`nop`
c+5		`store a(2)+, r102;`

We can now proceed with the subsequent iterations in the same way. In Table 9.2 we illustrate the entire execution of the loop. Here, for a better overview we omit the operands of the instructions.

What Table 9.2 actually illustrates is *software pipelining*, which is so called because subsequent loop iterations are executed as if they were a hardware pipeline.

Next, let us consider cycles c+4, c+5 and c+6. These are the ones showing the real merit of software pipelining. The crucial point is that for these cycles the available parallelism between subsequent loop iterations is fully utilized. For instance, in cycle c+4 the parallel operations are as follows:

- storing the result of iteration 1 (that is, a(1)), autoincrementing the index;
- decrementing the loop count, which in maintained in r200, by 1;
- performing the floating-point multiplication with the operands belonging to cycle 4, that is (2.0 ∗ b(4)); and
- loading the operand for iteration 5 (that is, b(5)).

Table 9.2 Most parallel execution of the given loop on an ILP-processor with multiple pipelined execution units.

Cycle	*Iteration number*						
	1	2	3	4	5	6	7
c	`load`						
c+1	`fmul`	`load`					
c+2	`decr`	`fmul`	`load`				
c+3	`nop`	`decr`	`fmul`	`load`			
c+4	`store`	`nop`	`decr`	`fmul`	`load`		
c+5		`store`	`nop`	`decr`	`fmul`	`load`	
c+6			`store`	`nop`	`decr`	`fmul`	`load`
c+7				`store`	`nop`	`decr`	`fmul`
c+8					`store`	`nop`	`decr`
c+9						`store`	`nop`
c+10							`store`

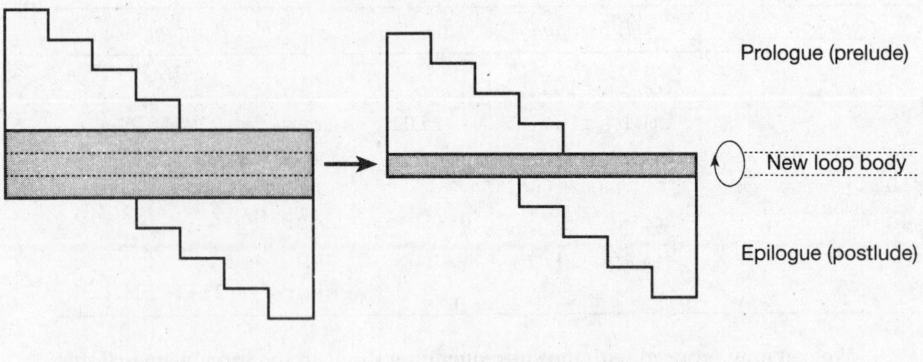

Figure 9.11 Structure of the software-pipelined code.

Notice that cycles c+4 to c+6 have a repetitive pattern of scheduling, therefore they may be replaced by a corresponding loop. Note that each iteration of this new loop contains multiple operations associated with different iterations of the original loop:

```
loop: store i; decr i+2; fmul i+3; load i+4; bc loop;
//the loop has to be executed for i = 1 to 3
```

Actually, what we get after this replacement is software-pipelined execution of the original loop. Software-pipelined code consists of *three parts* (see Figure 9.11). The *main part* is the *repetitive pattern (new loop body)*. It is preceded by some start-up code, which is usually called the *prologue* or *prelude* and succeeded by some finishing code, termed the *epilogue* or *postlude*. Notice that in software pipelining the original loop is essentially replaced by the new loop body. This piece of code is what really determines the efficiency of execution in software pipelining.

In our example, the new loop body can be executed in a single cycle, which is extremely favourable. This is because we chose quite a simple loop for software pipelining on a fairly parallel ILP-processor. In practice, loops to be software pipelined are usually more complex and the resulting loop bodies require more than one cycle to be executed. The real problem in software pipelining is to find the repetitive pattern that can be executed in the shortest possible number of cycles (called the initiation interval).

Finding an optimal schedule using software pipelining is known to be an *NP-complete* problem (Lam, 1988), hence it is a special case of resource-constrained scheduling (Garey and Johnson, 1979); see also Section 9.1. Therefore, all general methods of software pipelining proposed or used are *heuristics* and they produce, in the general case, a solution which is good enough instead of the optimal solution.

Software pipelining was described as early as 1977 by Kogge, as used manually for microprogrammed pipelined processors. Subsequently, automatic software pipelining was introduced into the Fortran compiler for the CYBER 176 machines, and into compilers for the FPS-164 array processors (Touzeau, 1984). The

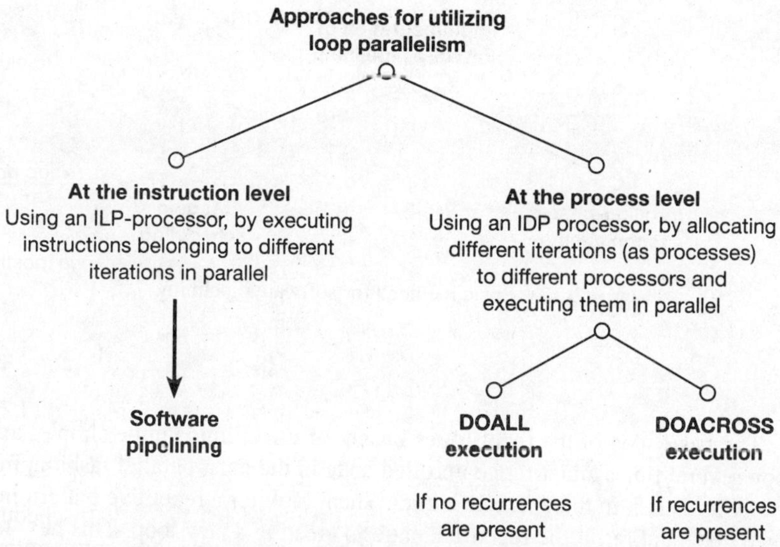

Figure 9.12 Approaches for utilizing parallelism.

latter was one of the first VLIW machines ever built. Software pipelining became widely known in connection with the emerging VLIW architectures in the 1980s as the usual method of instruction scheduling. Further examples of VLIW compilers using software pipelining are those for the iWarp (Lam, 1988), URPR-1 and StaCS2.2.

In concluding our discussion of software pipelining, we emphasize, with reference to Figure 9.12, that software pipelining is used to exploit parallelism at the instruction level, more precisely, *between subsequent iterations of a loop when a single ILP-processor is available*. In contrast, *if* there are *several processors* available (such as in an SIMD machine) each iteration can be allocated to a different processor. Then parallelism is exploited at the process level. By doing so, the temporal parallelism existing between subsequent loop iterations is transformed into a spatial one. In a number of cases, this means that functional parallelism is replaced by data parallelism. This is the case when the loop implements the same kind of manipulation on all elements of a data structure. To distribute computation on a number of homogeneous processors, two constructs, termed DOALL and DOACROSS, can be used. The **DOALL** construct can be applied on parallel processors if no recurrences between loop iterations are present. In contrast, the **DOACROSS** construct provides an additional synchronization mechanism which can be utilized to handle recurrences as well. For details see Zima and Chapman (1990).

Implementation

In practice, software pipelining is implemented either by techniques based on unrolling or by modulo scheduling, as depicted in Figure 9.13.

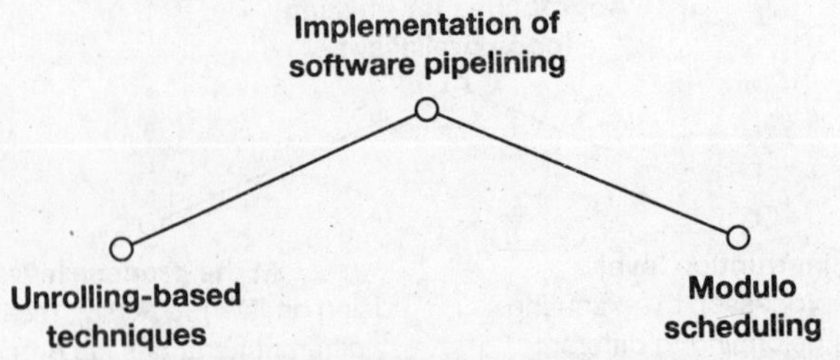

Figure 9.13 Basic methods for software pipelining.

The basic idea of the **techniques based on unrolling** is quite simple: unroll the loop several times and arrange unrolled code in the most parallel fashion, in the same way as shown in the example earlier. Then, look for a repetitive pattern in the arranged code and reroll the repetitive pattern, creating a new loop. This new loop, along with the start-up (prologue) and finishing (epilogue) code sections, represents the software-pipelined instruction schedule.

We illustrate the unrolling method by one of its representatives called *URPR* (**U**n**R**olling, **P**ipelining and **R**erolling). Below, we quote Su et al. (1986) to show the principle of URPR (Figure 9.14).

As Figure 9.14 shows, this variant of the unrolling technique first schedules the original loop body, then unrolls it k times, arranges it for the most parallel execution and searches for a repetitive pattern. Finally, this pattern is rerolled, resulting in the new body. The outcome of the schedule is the new loop body preceded by the prologue code and succeeded by the epilogue code section.

The other major method of software pipelining is *modulo scheduling*. This technique was originally proposed by Rau and Glaeser in 1981 and has been implemented in several compilers for VLIW machines, such as FPS-164 (Touzeau, 1984), CYDRA-5 (Rau et al., 1989) and iWARP (Lam, 1988).

Modulo scheduling is based on a type of list scheduling. In general, this method has an iterative character, and consists of three steps:

- First, a guess is made concerning the minimal required length of the new loop body, commonly called in these methods the *minimum initiation interval*.
- Next, a schedule for this interval is attempted, taking into account data and resource dependencies.
- If the attempted schedule is not feasible, the length of the new loop body is increased and a new schedule for the enlarged interval is prepared.

The designation 'modulo scheduling' emphasizes the *repetitive character* of the schedule with respect to data and resource dependencies. Descriptions of proposed or already implemented algorithms may be found in Rau and Glaser (1981), Touzeau (1984) and Lam (1988).

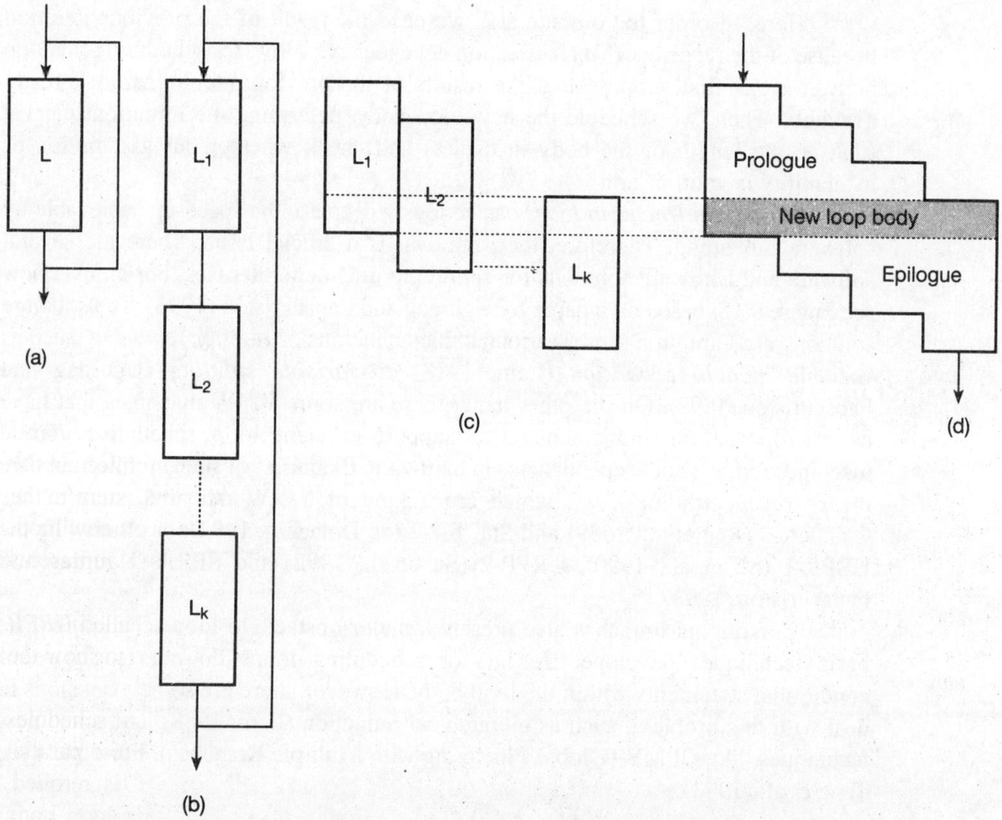

Figure 9.14 Principle of the unrolling-based URPR software pipelining method. (a) The loop body after basic block scheduling; (b) the k times unrolled bodies; (c) most parallel execution of the k bodies; (d) the final rerolled result. © 1986 IEEE

Two remarks are appropriate:

- In the general case, the *basic method* has a *trial and error character*; that is, it is not deterministic.
- As far as recurrences are concerned, the basic software pipelining techniques behave quite differently. Unrolling methods handle recurrences naturally; however, recurrences complicate modulo scheduling algorithms considerably. There are actually recurrences which make the basic method undeterministic. For an explanation, consider a simple loop with a first-order recurrence:

```
for i  = 2 to 10 do {
  a(i) = 2.0 * a(i-1)
}
```

Here, in order to compute a(i), we need the result of the previous iteration because of the recurrence (inter-iteration dependency). Now, for scheduling the loop body, we can first suppose that the results of the previous iterations are already available. Then, we schedule the new loop body, determine the initiation interval (that is, the length of the body in cycles) and check whether our assumption of availability is valid or not.

Anti-dependencies in loops can seriously decrease the speed-up achievable by software pipelining. Therefore, their removal is a crucial issue. There are several software and hardware solutions for **removing anti-dependencies**. For an overview see Figure 9.15, based on a paper by Ugurdag and Papachristou (1993). The software solutions used are, in a sense, various implementations of *register renaming*, such as *variable modulo expansion* (Lam, 1988) or *variable splitting* (Ugurdag and Papachristou, 1993). On the other hand, there are some VLIW machines that have been proposed, or implemented, to support efficient loop scheduling. These machines remove anti-dependencies in hardware. Examples of such architectures are the *polycyclic architectures*, which are a kind of VLIW machine, such as the CYDRA-5 (Rau et al., 1989) and StaCS 2.2 (de Dinechin, 1992), or others like the URPR-1 (Su et al., 1990), URPP-2 (Su et al., 1992) and SFRA (Ugurdag and Papachristou, 1993).

Conditional branches also present a major obstacle to loop scheduling. The basic techniques developed so far for scheduling loops do not take care of conditional statements within the loop body. However, there are some extensions to deal with this problem, such as hierarchical reduction (Lam, 1988), and some new techniques, like GPMB (**G**lobal **P**ipelining with **M**ultiple **B**ranches). For details see Tang et al. (1993).

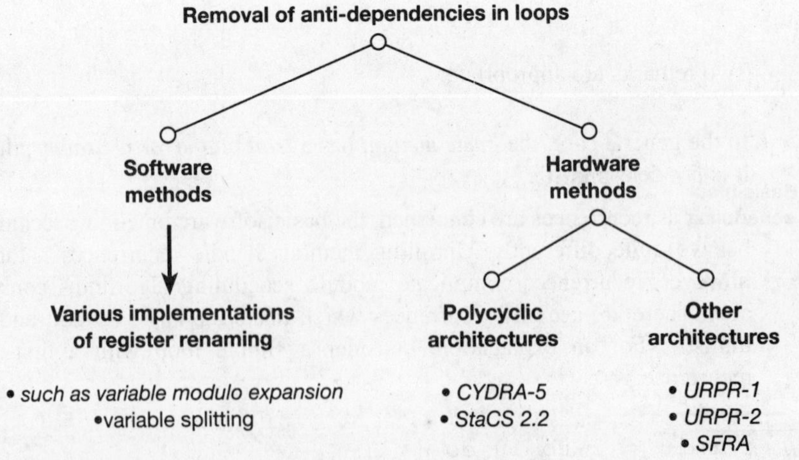

Figure 9.15 Basic approaches for removing anti-dependencies, according to Ugurdag and Papachristou (1993).

9.4 Global scheduling

9.4.1 Introduction

ILP-compilers have to extract sufficient instruction-level parallelism to utilize available hardware resources properly, especially EUs. This is not an easy task for highly parallel ILP-processors, such as VLIW machines or highly superscalar architectures. In particular, general-purpose programs, such as operating systems or application programs, with their small basic block sizes and highly irregular parallelism, characterized by unpredictable branches make this task extremely demanding or even unsolvable. In this case, basic block schedulers cannot be expected to extract enough parallelism to feed highly parallel ILP-processors properly. Consequently, compilers for parallelism-greedy ILP-processors have to utilize the most effective scheduling techniques, called *global scheduling* (Figure 9.16). Global schedulers operate *beyond basic block boundaries* and even *across subsequent loop iterations*, in order to extract as much parallelism as possible. In the following, we first explain their basic concept and then discuss their implementation based on two case examples: the Trace scheduling compiler and the FRGS global schedulers.

9.4.2 Basic concept

Global scheduling is quite a complex task. First, there are *two basic tasks* to contend with: scheduling individual instructions beyond basic blocks and scheduling loops (Figure 9.17). In addition, there are a number of further issues to be considered and managed in order to implement a real global scheduler, such as handling procedure calls within loops, handling control dependencies, and supporting the instruction issue policy of the target machine (see Section 7.3). Of these we shall discuss only the one most typical of global scheduling, which is how instructions can be

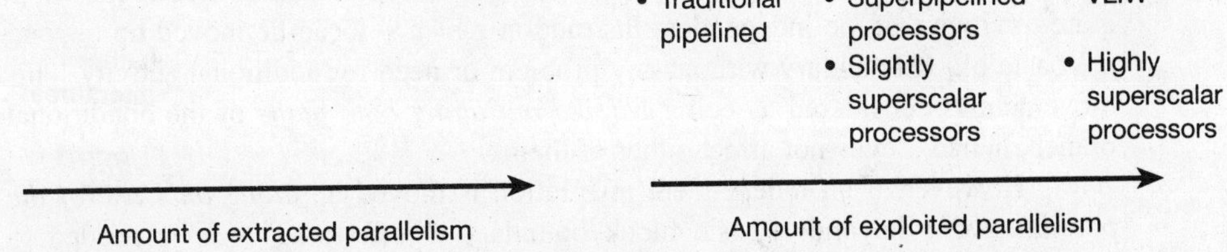

Figure 9.16 Extracted and utilized amounts of parallelism for different kinds of schedulers and ILP-processors.

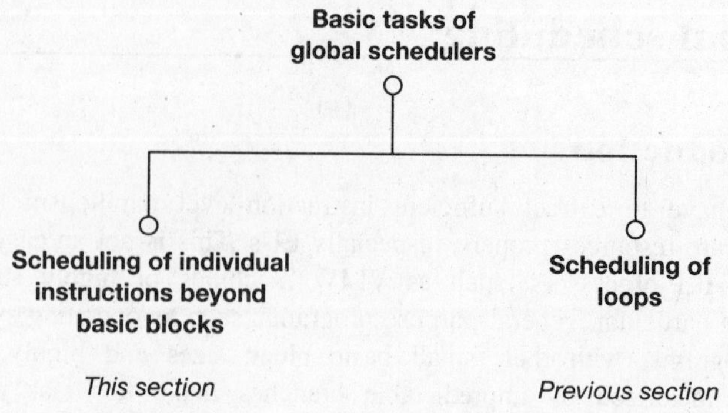

Figure 9.17 Basic tasks of global schedulers.

scheduled globally by code motions across basic block boundaries. For loop scheduling we refer to the previous section.

As we know, basic block schedulers (local schedulers) extract parallelism only within the limits of a basic block. In contrast, a global scheduler tries to identify as many independent instructions in the control flow graph as possible and to move them up along the graph as far as possible, even beyond basic block boundaries, in order to keep multiple EUs in each cycle as busy as possible. The *hard limit* to moving instructions up is *true data dependencies*, since false data dependencies might be eliminated by register renaming, as discussed in Section 7.5.

Typically, global schedulers are not satisfied with the amount of parallelism obtained by just moving independent instructions ahead even beyond basic block boundaries. Moreover, a global scheduler often tries to *make a guess as to the outcome of unresolved conditional statements* as well. Then, instructions along a guessed path will also be considered as candidates for code motions. When, during scheduling, an instruction from the guessed path is moved ahead (assuming that no data dependencies exist), typically an additional compensation code, called **bookkeeping code**, is placed into the other path. This bookkeeping code should be able to undo the moved-ahead operation originally belonging to the guessed path, if the guess is wrong and a path other than the guessed path has to be taken.

In order to get a feeling for code motions across basic block boundaries, let us consider a short piece of code and several typical code motions, with reference to Figure 9.18(a) and (b). Figure 9.18 shows a simple code segment which consists of a conditional branch, of the taken (T) and not taken (F) paths, each one comprising a single instruction, and after merging of both paths, of two further instructions. It is quite obvious that the independent instruction z := u + v can be moved up beyond the basic block boundary without any problem or need for additional activity. This movement is considered as being *carried out along both paths* of the conditional branch, hence it does not affect either of them.

However, if an independent instruction is moved up *along only one of the possible paths* beyond a basic block boundary, *bookkeeping code* is needed to compensate for the additionally executed but not needed operation. Figure 9.18(b) shows an example. Here, the movement of the instruction x := x + 1 before the conditional branch is restricted to the left path. Now, in order to maintain sequential

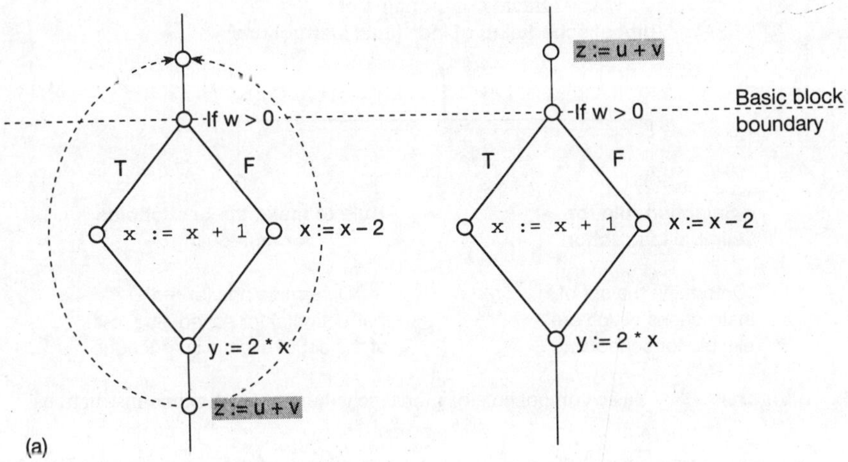

Figure 9.18(a) Moving up an independent instruction beyond a basic block boundary 'along both paths' of a conditional branch.

consistency, a bookkeeping code (`x := x -1`) must be placed into the right path to offset the execution of the moved-up instruction `x := x + 1`.

Code motions which are restricted to only one of the paths of a conditional branch are said to be **speculative** (Moon et al., 1993). This designation stresses the fact that these code motions are made under the assumption that the conditional branch follows the path of the code movement and, thus, the execution of the moved-up instruction will be useful.

Global code motions along guessed paths are sensitive operations. On the one hand, they are a significant source of parallelism but, on the other, if improperly implemented, they can cause considerable code expansion as well as performance degradation. The primary cause of code expansion is bookkeeping code. Executing

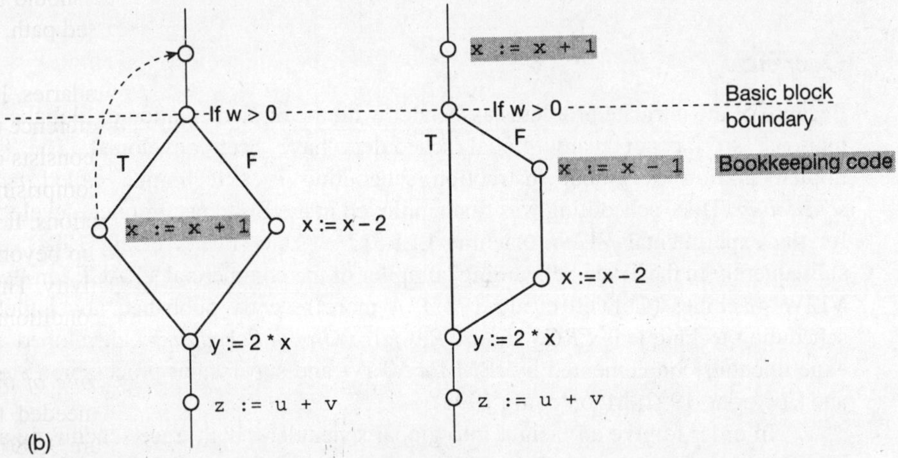

Figure 9.18(b) Moving up an independent instruction beyond a basic block boundary 'along a single path' of a conditional branch.

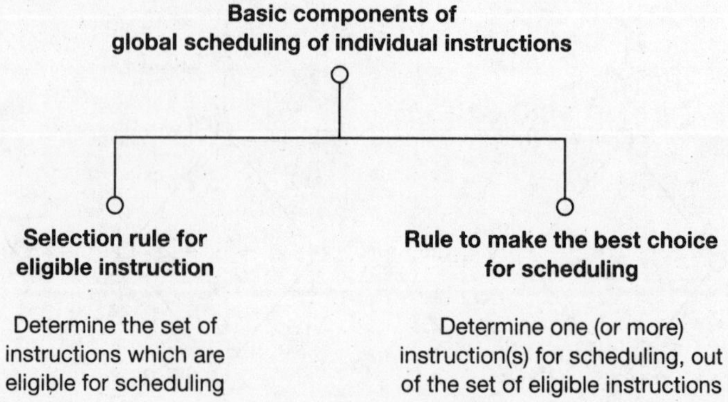

Figure 9.19 Basic components of global scheduling of individual instructions.

useless operations and binding resources necessarily reduce performance. Therefore, how good the guesses are (that is, how high the average hit rate is) and when code motions along guessed paths are initiated are crucial for global schedulers.

Individual instructions will be scheduled by most global schedulers in two steps (Moon et al., 1993), which is similar to what list schedulers do (Figure 9.19).

First, global schedulers have to *select* for each cycle the set of instructions which are eligible for scheduling, according to a chosen heuristics. Second, a further heuristics is needed to *make a choice* from the set of the eligible instructions. The scheduling decision may also involve a code motion.

For scheduling loops, global schedulers use the same or similar methods as discussed in the foregoing section. Loops deserve special attention, since they remain the major source of parallelism for global schedulers as well.

9.4.3 Implementation

Overview

Because of the intricate problems associated with the implementation of global code motions, so far not many global schedulers have been developed. The first implementation of global instruction scheduling is a technique called *trace scheduling*. Trace scheduling was first employed in the Bulldog compiler, developed for the experimental VLIW machine ELI-512 at Yale (Fisher et al., 1984), and subsequently in the Trace Scheduling compiler of the commercial TRACE family of VLIW machines (Colwell et al., 1987). A more recently published novel global scheduling technique is *FRGS (Finite Resource Global Scheduling)*, developed and experimentally implemented by IBM for VLIW and superscalar processors (Moon and Ebcioglu, 1992; Moon et al., 1993).

In order to give an insight into global schedulers, both trace scheduling and FRGS are briefly reviewed.

Trace scheduling

This technique originates, like most instruction scheduling techniques, in scheduling for horizontally microcoded machines (Fisher, 1981). Subsequently, trace scheduling was reimplemented as an instruction scheduling technique for VLIW machines (Fisher et al., 1984).

Trace scheduling is based on the concept of *trace*. A **trace** is an execution path within a loop, such that a trace may include conditional branches and join points. For example, Figure 9.20(a) shows the traces identified in a flow graph.

By and large, a **trace scheduler** first identifies the traces in a program (or more precisely in the associated control flow graph), and then selects the most likely trace and schedules it as an entity. Then it selects the next most likely trace and repeats the process until the whole program is scheduled (Figures 9.20(b)–(d)).

In selecting the most likely trace, the compiler uses dynamic branch predictions as well as hints supplied by the programmer. In our example (Figure 9.20(a)), let us assume that trace no. 3 has the highest probability, and therefore it will be scheduled first (Figure 9.20(b)).

Each trace is scheduled as if it were a single basic block, as depicted in Figure 9.20(c). However, in this case scheduling is global; that is, during scheduling independent instructions can be moved across conditional branches or join points. If necessary, bookkeeping code will also be generated and placed into the appropriate path of conditional branches and joins, as described earlier (Figure 9.20(d)).

After completing the schedule for trace no. 3, the next most probable trace is selected, say trace no. 4, then this trace is scheduled, and so on.

In order to increase exposed parallelism for trace scheduling, inner loops are unrolled, say 32 times, in traces. Nevertheless, an unrolled loop becomes part of the same trace and is scheduled along with the remainder as an entity.

FRGS (Finite Resource Global Scheduling)

This global scheduling method in intended *to avoid* the serious *inefficiency problems* of the existing VLIW compilers caused by long compilation times and code explosion (Moon et Ebcioglu, 1992). It can be applied for both VLIWs and superscalar processors such that this method first delivers a superscalar code and, if required, in a second step VLIW code can be obtained through a local transformation.

It is informative to overview the *target machine* expected by FRGS. This is a VLIW with the following hardware resources. There are 16 general-purpose ALUs, with eight of them able to execute memory load/store operations as well. ALU and load/store operations for the same unit are exclusive. There are 128 general-purpose registers and 16 condition code registers. Sixteen-way branching is foreseen. These hardware resources are considered implementable in the near future.

FRGS is quite a complex method. Instead of going into details, only the basic idea will be mentioned. First, in each cycle FRGS selects all operations available for a schedule (so-called *greedy selection*). Here, a software window is used to limit the required amount of computation. Then, a simple heuristics is used to select operations from the availability list for the next schedule, to utilize the hardware

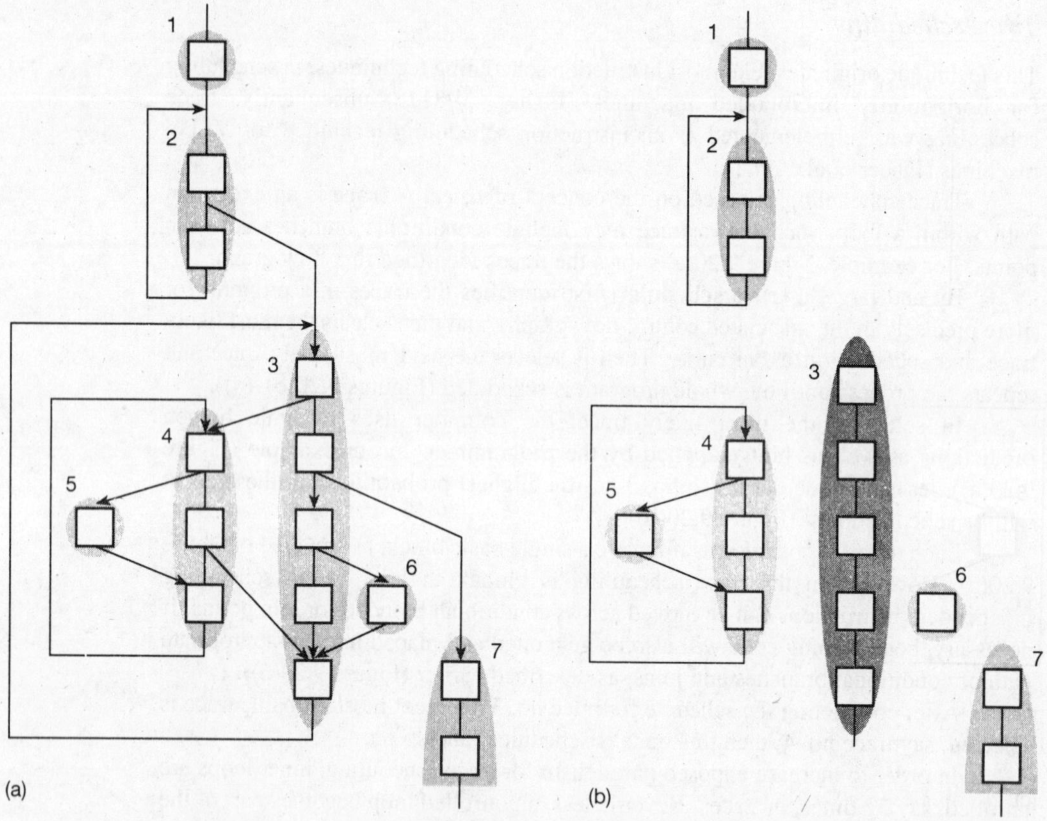

Figure 9.20 (a) A flow graph and its identified traces (Fisher et al., 1984); (b) selection of the trace with the highest probability. © 1984 ACM

resources as far as possible. This heuristics prefers non-speculative operations to speculative ones. In accordance with the selections made, any required code motions are performed and, if needed, bookkeeping codes are generated and correctly placed.

FRGS employs *enhanced pipelining*, which means that it can pipeline nested loops too, starting from inner loops and proceeding towards outer loops.

The authors also published experimental results gained by an implementation of FRGS. They measured *speed-up* and *code expansion rates* by comparing execution times and code lengths for selected benchmark programs on a base machine and on the target VLIW machine with the same cycle time executing the globally scheduled code. In Table 9.3 we quote their speed-up figures measured for four SPEC benchmarks of a general-purpose character. The authors compared the execution times of the compiled benchmark programs on an IBM Power1 (RS/6000) using the PL.8 compiler with the execution times attained for the target VLIW machine executing the globally scheduled object code. Here, the execution times for the target machine are measured by simulation, assuming the same cycle time (40 ns) as the Power1 (RS/6000).

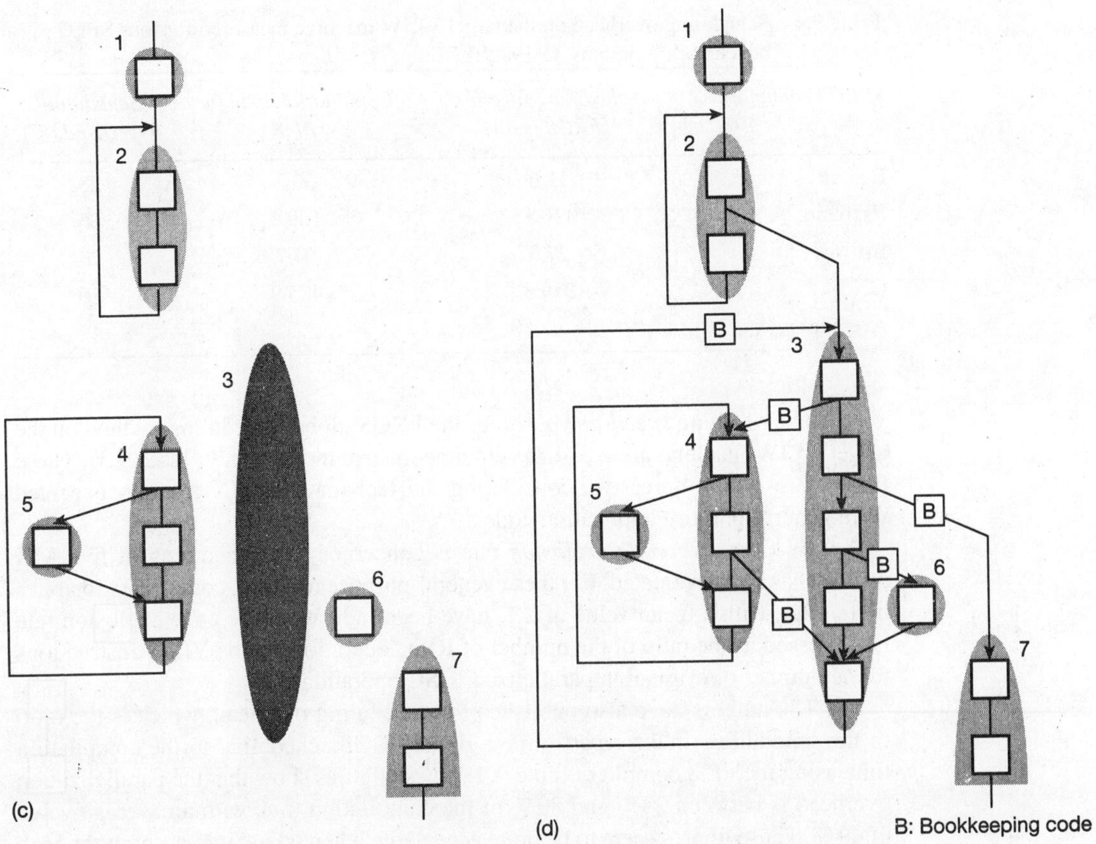

Figure 9.20 cont. (c) scheduling of the selected trace as a single basic block; (d) inserting required bookkeeping code of conditional branches and regions. © 1994 ACM

Table 9.3 Speed-up figures for the globally scheduled code on the target VLIW machine measured for four SPEC benchmark programs. © 1992 IEEE

SPEC benchmark	*Power1 execution time (sec)*	*VLIW execution time using global scheduling (sec)*	*Speed-up*
Eqntott	45.0	9.3	4.8
Espresso	109.5	38.8	2.8
Li	304.0	87.3	3.5
Gcc	78.0	19.9	3.9
Geometric Mean			3.7

Table 9.4 Scheduling overhead on the target VLIW machine measured for four SPEC benchmark programs. © 1992 IEEE

SPEC benchmark	*Scheduling time for FRGS (sec)*	*Compilation time for PL.8*	*Scheduling Overhead (%)*
Eqntott	11.6	50.3	23
Espresso	110.1	169.0	65
Li	27.0	94.7	28
Gcc	349.3	435.9	80
Average			49

The resulting *speed-up values* for the FRGS global scheduling method on the target VLIW machine are 2.8–4.8, with a geometric mean of 3.7 (Table 9.3). These figures are quite impressive, considering the fact that the AIX routines executed were general-purpose application code.

As far as the *code explosion* rate is concerned, the scheduling of five AIX utilities has been evaluated. For these general-purpose routines, code explosion rates of 1.7–2.5, with a mean value of 2.1, have been indicated. The code explosion rate is expressed as the ratio of the number of RISC operations in the VLIW instructions to the number of original unparallelized RISC operations.

The authors have also published the scheduling overhead, which is the ratio of the scheduling time for performing global FRGS scheduling to the compilation time using the PL.8 compiler (Table 9.4). These figures show that the parallelization overhead is between 23 % and 80 % of the compilation time with an average value of 49 %. These figures seem to be quite acceptable when taking into account the high speed-up figures achieved.

References for Part II

References

Acosta R. D., Kjelstrup J. and Torng H. C. (1986). An instruction issuing approach to enhancing performance in multiple functional unit processors. *IEEE Trans. on Computers*, **C-35**(9), Sept., 815–28

Aiken A. and Nicolau A. (1988). Optimal loop parallelization. In *Proc. SIGPLAN'88 Conf. on Programming Language Design and Implementation, SIGPLAN Notices*, **23**(7), 308–17

Aho A. V., Sethi R. and Ullman J. D. (1986). *Compilers: Principles, Techniques and Tools*. Addison-Wesley, Reading, MA

Agerwala T. and Cocke J. (1987). High Performance Reduced Instruction Set Processors. *Technical Report* RC12434 (No. 55845), IBM Thomas J. Watson Research Center, Yorktown Heights, NY

Allen J. R., Kennedy K., Porterfield C. and Warren J. (1983). Conversion of control dependencies to data dependence. In *Proc. Tenth Annual Symposium on Principles of Programming Languages*, pp. 177–89

Alpert D. and Avnon D. (1993). Architecture of the Pentium microprocessor. *IEEE Micro*, June, 11–21

Asato C., Montoye R., Gmuender J., Simmons E. W., Ike A. and Zasio J. (1995). A 14-port 3.8 ns 116 word 64b read-renaming register file. In *Proc. ISSCC95*, pp. 104–5

Asprey T., Averill G. S., DeLano E., Mason R., Weiner B. and Yetter J. (1993). Performance features of the PA7100 microprocessor. *IEEE Micro*, June, 22–35

Austin T. M. and Sohi G. S. (1992). Dynamic dependency analysis of ordinary programs. In *Proc. 19th AISCA*, pp. 342–51

Becker M. C., Allen M. S., Moore C. R., Muhich J. S. and Tuttle D. P. (1993). The PowerPC 601 microprocessor. *IEEE Micro*, Oct., 54–68

Bodin F. and Charot F. (1990). Loop optimization for horizontal microcoded machines. In *Proc. 1990 Int. Conf. on Supercomputing, ACM SIGARCH*, **18**(3), Sept., 164–76

Brian C. (1994). x86 has plenty of performance headroom. *MPR*, Aug., 22, 9–15

Burgess B., Ullah N., Van Overen P. and Ogden D. (1994). The PowerPC 603 microprocessor. *Comm. ACM*, **37**, June, 34–42

Butler M., Yeh T-Y., Patt Y., Alsup M., Scales H. and Shebanov M. (1991). Single instruction stream parallelism is greater than two. In *Proc. 18th AISCA*, pp. 276–86

Case B. (1994). Philips hopes to displace DSPS with VLIW. *Microprocessor Report*, **8**(16), 12–15

CDC (1981). *CYBER 200 FORTRAN Extended Version 4 Reference Manual*. Publication 60497800, CDC Arden Hills, MN

Chang P. P., Mahlke S. A., Chen W. Y., Warter N. J. and Hwu W. W. (1991). IMPACT: An architectural framework for multiple-instruction-issue processors. In *Proc. 18th ISCA*, pp. 266–75

Chow P. and Horowitz M. (1987). Architectural tradeoffs in the design of MIPS-X. In *Proc. 14th ISCA*, pp. 300–8

Circello J. and Goodrich F. (1993). The Motorola 68060 microprocessor. In *Proc. COMPCON'93*, pp. 73–8

Coffman E. G. and Denning P. J. (1973). *Operating Systems Theory*. Prentice Hall, Englewood Cliffs, NJ

Cohn R., Gross T., Lam M. and Tseng P. S. (1989). Architecture and compiler tradeoffs for a long instruction word microprocessor. In *Proc. ASPLOS III*, pp. 2–14

Colwell R. P. and Steck R. L. (1995). *A 0.6 μm BiCMOS Processor with Dynamic Execution*. Intel Corp.

Colwell R. P., Nix R. P., O'Donnell J. J., Papworth D. B. and Rodman P. K. (1988). A VLIW architecture for a trace scheduling compiler.

Comerford R. (1992). How DEC developed Alpha. *IEEE Spectrum*, July, 26–31

Crawford J. H. (1990). The i486 CPU: executing instructions in one clock cycle. *IEEE Micro*, Feb., 27–36

IEEE Trans. on Computers, **37**(8), Aug., 967–79

Dao-Trong S. and Helwig K. (1992). A single-chip IBM System/390 floating-point processor in CMOS. *IBM J. Research and Development*, **36**(4), July 733–49

de Dinechin B. D. (1992). A static control superscalar architecture. In *Proc. MICRO-25* 1992, pp. 282–91

DEC (1992). *Alpha Architecture Handbook*. Maynard, MA: DEC

DEC (1994a). *DEC Alpha 21164 Microprocessor Hardware Reference Manual*, preliminary version. Maynard, MA: DEC

DeRosa J. A. and Levy H. M. (1987). An evaluation of branch architectures. In *Proc. 14th ISCA*, pp. 10–16

Dewit D. J. (1976). A machine independent approach to the production of horizontal microcode. *PhD Thesis*, Univ. of Michigan

Diefendorff K. and Allen M. (1992). Organization of the Motorola 88110 superscalar RISC microprocessor. *IEEE Micro*, April, 40–63

Dongarra J. J. and Hinds A. R. (1979). Unrolling loops in FORTRAN. *Software Practice and Experience*, **9**(3), March

Ebcioglu K. (1988). Some design ideas for a VLIW architecture for sequential natured software. In *Parallel Processing, Proc. of IFIP WG 10.3 Working Conference on Parallel Processing* (Cosnard et al., eds), pp. 3–21. North Holland

Fisher J. A. (1981). Trace scheduling: A technique for global microcode compaction. *IEEE Transactions on Computers*, **C-30**(7), July, 478–90

Fisher J. A. (1983). Very long instruction word architectures and the ELI-512. In *Proc. 10th AISCA*, pp. 140–50

Fisher J. A., Ellis J. R., Ruttenberg J. C. and Nicolau A. (1984). Parallel processing: A smart compiler and a dumb machine. In *Proc. ACM SIGPLAN '84 Symp. on Compiler Construction, SIGPLAN Notices*, **19**(6), June, pp. 37–47

Flynn M. J. (1966). Very high speed computing systems. In *Proc. IEEE*, **54**, Dec., pp. 1901–9

Franklin M. A. and Pan T. (1993). Clocked and asynchronous instruction pipelines. In *Proc. MICRO-26*, pp. 177–84

Garey M. R. and Johnson D. S. (1979). *Computers and Intractability, A Guide to the Theory of NP-Completeness.* Freeman

Garner R. B., Agrawal A., Briggs F., Brown E. W., Hough D., Joy B., Kleiman S., Muchnick S., Namjoo M., Patterson D., Pendleton J. and Tuck R. (1988). The Scalable Processor Architecture (SPARC). In *Proc. Int. Spring Computer Conf.*, pp. 278–83

Gibbons P. B. and Muchnick S. S. (1986). Efficient instruction scheduling for a pipelined architecture. In *Proc. SIGPLAN 1986 Symposium on Compiler Construction, SIGPLAN Notices*, **21**(7), July, pp. 11–16

Grohoski G. F. (1990). Machine organization of the IBM RISC System/6000 processor. *IBM J. Res. Develop.*, **34**(1), Jan., 37–58

Gwennap L. (1994a). UltraSparc unleashes SPARC performance. *Microprocessor Report*, **8**(13), 6–10

Gwennap L. (1994b). MIPS R10000 uses decoupled architecture. *Microprocessor Report*, **8**(14), 18–22

Gwennap L. (1994c). PA-8000 combines complexity and speed. *Microprocessor Report*, **8**(15), 1–8

Gwennap L. (1995). Intel's P6 uses decoupled superscalar design. *Microprocessor Report*, **9**(2), February, 9–15

Halfhill T. R. (1994). T5 brute force. *Byte*, Nov., 123–8

Harel D. (1980). On folk theorems. *CACM*, **23**(7), July, 379–89

Heinrich J. (1994). *MIPS R10000 Microprocessor User's Manual*. MIPS Technologies Inc.

Hennessy J. L. and Gross T. R. (1983). Postpass code optimization of pipeline constraints. *ACM Trans. on Programming Languages and Systems*, **5**(3), July, 422–48

Hennessy J., Jouppi N., Baskett F., Gross T. and Gill J. (1982). Hardware/software tradeoffs for increased performance. In *Proc. ASPLOS*, pp. 2–11

Hicks T. N., Fry R. E. and Harvey P. E. (1994). Power2 floating-point unit: Architecture and implementation. In *PowerPC and Power2: Technical Aspects of the New IBM RISC System/6000*. IBM

Hsu P. Y. T. and Davidson E. S. (1986). Highly concurrent scalar processing. In *Proc. 13th ISCA*, pp. 386–95

Hu T. C. (1961). Parallel sequencing and assembly line problems. *Operational Research*, **9**(6)

IBM/Motorola (1994). *PowerPC 604 RISC Microprocessor Technical Summary*. Motorola Order Number MPC604/D, IBM Order Number MPR604TSU-02

Johnson M. (1989). *Super-scalar Processor Design*. TR No. CSL-TR-89-383, Stanford University

Johnson M. (1991). *Superscalar Microprocessor Design*. Prentice Hall, Englewood Cliffs, NJ.

Jouppi N. P. (1989). The nonuniform distribution of instruction level and machine parallelism and its effect on performance. *IEEE Trans. on Computers*, **38**(12), Dec., 1645–58

Jouppi N. P., Bertoni J. and Wall D. W. (1989). A unified vector/scalar floating-point architecture. In *Proc. ASPLOS III*, 134–43

Jouppi N. P. and Wall D. W. (1989). Available instruction-level parallelism for superscalar and superpipelined machines. In *Proc. ASPLOS III*, pp. 272–82

Keller R. M. (1975). Look-ahead processors. *Computing Surveys*, **7**, Dec., 177–96

Kerns D. R. and Eggers S. J. (1993). Balanced scheduling: Instruction scheduling when memory latency is uncertain. *ACM SIGPLAN Notices*, **28**(6), June, 278–88

Kogge P. M. (1977). The microprogramming of pipelined processors. In *Proc. 4th Ann. Symposium on Computer Architectures*, pp. 63–9

Krishnamurthy S. M. (1990). A brief survey of papers on scheduling for pipelined processors. *SIGPLAN Notices*, **25**(7), July, 97–106

Kuck D. J., Muraoka Y. and Chen S.-C. (1972). On the number of operations simultaneously executable in Fortran-like programs and their resulting speedup. *IEEE Trans. on Computers*, **C-21**(12), Dec., 1293–310

Kuga M., Murakami K., Tomita S. (1991). DSNS (Dynamically-hazard-resolved, Statically-code-scheduled, Nonuniform Superscalar): yet another superscalar processor architecture. *Computer Architecture News* **19**(4), 14–29

Kumar M. (1988). measuring parallelism in computation-intensive scientific/engineering applications. *IEEE Trans. on Computers*, **C-37**(9), 1088–98

Lam M. (1988). Software pipelining: An effective scheduling technique for VLIW machines. In *Proc. SIGPLAN '88 Conference on Programming Language Design and Implementation*, pp. 318–28

Lam M. S. and Wilson R. P. (1992). Limits of control flow on parallelism. In *Proc. 19th AISCA*, pp. 46–57

Landskov D., Davidson S., Shriver B. and Mallett P. W. (1980). Local microcode compaction techniques. *Computing Surveys*, **12**(3), Sept., 261–94

Lee J. K. F. and Smith A. J. (1984). Branch prediction strategies and branch target buffer design. *Computer*, **17**(1), 6–22

Liptay J. S. (1992). Design of the IBM Enterprise System/9000 high-end processor. *IBM J. Res. Develop*, **36**(4), July, 713–31

McMahon F. H. (1972). *FORTRAN CPU Performance Analysis*. Lawrence Livermore Laboratories

Moon S.-M. and Ebcioglu K. (1992). An efficient resource-constrained global scheduling technique for superscalar and VLIW processors. In *Proc. MICRO-25*, pp. 55–71

Motorola (1993). *PowerPC 603 RISC Microprocessor Technical Summary*. Order number MPC603/D

Motorola (1991). *MC88110, Second Generation RISC Microprocessor User's Manual*. Motorola Inc.

Nicolau A. and Fisher J. A. (1984). Measuring the parallelism available for very long instruction word architectures. *IEEE Trans. on Computers*, **C-33**(11), pp. 968–76

Patterson D. A. and Sequin C. H. (1981). RISC-I: A reduced instruction set VLSI computer. In *Proc. 8th ISCA*, pp. 443–57

Pnevmatikatos D. N. and Sohi G. S. (1994). Guarded execution and branch prediction in dynamic, ILP processors. In *Proc. 21. ISCA*, pp. 120–9

Radin G. (1982). The 801 Minicomputer. Proc. ASPLOS, in *ACM SIGARCH Computer Architecture News*, **10**(2), 39–47

Rajagopalan M. and Allan V. H. (1993). Efficient scheduling of fine grain parallelism in loops. In *Proc. MICRO 26*, pp. 2–11

Rau B. R. and Glaeser C. D. (1981). Some scheduling technique and an easily schedulable horizontal architecture for high performance scientific computing. In *Proc. MICRO-14*, pp. 183–98

Rau B. R., Glaeser C. D. and Picard R. L. (1982). Efficient code generation for horizontal architectures: compiler techniques and architectural support. In *Proc. 9th AISCA*, pp. 131–9

Rau B. R., Yen D. W. L., Yen W. and Towle R. (1989). The Cydra 5 departmental supercomputer.*Computer*, **22**, Jan., 112–25

Riseman E. M. and Foster C. C. (1972). The inhibition of potential parallelism by conditional jumps. *IEEE Trans. on Computers*, **C-21**(12), Dec., 1406–11

Ryan D. P. (1988). Intel's 80960: An architecture optimized for embedded control. *IEEE Micro*, June, 63–76

Sakamura, Ken (1987a). The TRON project. *IEEE Micro*, April, 8–14

Sakamura, Ken (1987b). Architecture of the TRON VLSI CPU. *IEEE Micro*, April, 17–31

Sites R. L. (1978). Instruction Ordering for the Cray-1 Computer. *Technical Report 78-CS-023*, Univ. of California, San Diego, July

Slavenburg G. A. et al. (1991). The LIFE family of high performance single chip VLIWs. In *Proc. Hot Chips III*

Smith J. E. (1981). A study of branch prediction strategies. In *Proc. 8th ASCA*, pp. 135–48

Smith J. E. and Pleszkun A. R. (1988). Implementing precise interrupts in pipelined processors. *IEEE Trans. on Computers*, **C-37**(5), 562–73

Smith M. D., Lam M. S. and Horowitz M. A. (1990). Boosting beyond static scheduling in a superscalar processing. In *Proc. 17th ISCA*, pp. 344–54

Sohi G. S. and Vajapayem S. (1987). Instruction issue logic for high performance, interruptable pipelined processors. In *Proc. 14th ASCA*, pp. 27–36

Song S. P., Denman M. and Chang J. (1994). The PowerPC 604 RISC microprocessor. *IEEE Micro*, Oct., 8–17

SPEC Newsletter (1990). Systems Performance Evaluation Cooperative, Spring 1990

Stephens C., Cogswell B., Heinlein J., Palmer G. and Shen J. P. (1991). Instruction level profiling and evaluation of the IBM RS/6000. In *Proc. 18th ISCA*, pp. 137–46

Su B., Ding S. and Xia J. (1986). URPR – an extension of URCR for software pipelining. In *Proc. MICRO-19*, pp. 94–103

Su B., Wang J., Tang Z. and Zhao W. (1990). A software pipelining based VLIW architecture and optmization compiler. In *Proc. MICRO-23*, pp. 17–27

Su B., Zhao W., Tang Z. and Habib S. (1992). A VLIW architecture for optimal execution of branch-intensive loops. In *Proc. MICRO-25*, pp. 119–24

Tang Z., Chen G., Zhang C., Zhang Y., Su B. and Habib S. (1993). GPMB – software pipelining branch-intensive loops. In *Proc. MICRO-26*, pp. 21–29

Thomson T. and Ryan B. (1994). PowerPC 620 soars. *Byte*, Nov., 113–20

Tjaden G. S. and Flynn M. J. (1970). Detection and parallel execution of independent instructions. *IEEE Trans. on Computers*, **C-19**(10), Oct., pp. 889–95

Torng H. C. (1982, 1983). Arithmetic Engines in the VLSI Environment. *Technical Reports EE-CEG-82-7 and EE-CEG-83-3*, Oct. 1982 and July 1983, School of Elec. Eng., Cornell Univ., Ithaca, NY

Touzeau R. F. (1984). A Fortran compiler for the FPS-164 scientific computer. In *Proc. SIGPLAN '84 Symposium on Compiler Construction*, in *SIGPLAN Notices*, **19**(6), June, 48–57

Ugurdag H. F. and Papachristou C. A. (1993). A VLIW architecture based on shifting register files. In *Proc. MICRO-26*, pp. 263–8

VSLI Technology (1993). Advanced RISC Machines, ARM 610 RISC processor. *Document No. ARM DDI 004C*, VLSI Technology

Wall D. W. (1991). Limits of instruction level parallelism. In *Proc. ASPLOS IV*, pp. 176–88

Warren H. S. (1990). Instruction scheduling for the IBM RISC System/6000 processor. *IBM J. Research and Development*, **34**(1), Jan., 85–92

Wayner P. (1994). SPARC strikes back. *Byte*, November, 105–12

Weiss R. (1987). RISC processors: The new wave in computer systems. *Computer Design*, May 15, 53–73

Weiss S. and Smith J. E. (1987). A study of scalar compilation techniques for pipelined supercomputers. Proc. ASPLOS II, in *SIGPLAN Notices*, **22**(10), Oct., pp. 105–9

Wolfe A. and Shen J. P. (1991). A variable instruction stream extension to the VLIW architecture. In *Proc. ASPLOS IV*, pp. 2–14

Yeh T.-Y. and Patt Y. N. (1992). Alternative implementations of two-level adaptive branch predictions. In *Proc. 19th ISCA*, pp. 124–34

Yeung N., Zivkov B. and Ezer G. (1994). Unified datapath: An innovative approach to the design of a low-cost, low-power, high-performance microprocessor. In *Proc. COMPCON 1994*, pp. 32–7

Zima H. and Chapman B. (1990). *Supercompilers for Parallel and Vector Computers*. Addison-Wesley, Reading, Mass.

Zivkov B., Ferguson B. and Gupta M. (1994). A high-performance MIPS microprocessor for portables. In *Proc. COMPCON 1994*, pp. 18–25

Further reading

Barreh J., Dhawan S., Hicks T. and Shippy D. (1994). The POWER2 processor. In *Proc. COMPCON*, pp. 389–98

Chan K., Alexander T., Hu C., Larson D., Noorden N., VanAtta Y., Wylegala T. and Ziai S. (1993). Multiprocessor features of the HP Corporate Business Servers. In *Proc. COMPCON*, pp. 330–7

Edenfield R. W., Gallup M. G., Ledbetter Jr, W. B., McGarity R. C., Quintana E. E. and Reininger R. A. (1990). The 68040 processor. *IEEE Micro*, February, 66–78

Hennessy J. L. and Patterson D. A. (1990). *Computer Architecture: A Quantitive Approach.* Morgan Kaufmann Inc., San Mateo, CA

Hintz R. G. and Tate D. P. (1972). Control Data STAR-100 processor design. In *Proc. COMPCON*, Fall, pp. 1–4

Hsu P. Y. (1986). Highly concurrent scalar processing. *PhD Thesis*, Univ. of Illinois at Urbana-Champaign

Hwang K. (1993). *Advanced Computer Architecture.* McGraw-Hill, New York

IBM (1993). *PowerPC Architecture*, 1st edn. IBM Corp.

McLellan E. (1993). The Alpha AXP architecture and 21064 processor. *IEEE Micro*, June, 36–47

Moon S.-M., Ebcioglu K. and Agrawala A. K. (1993). Selective scheduling framework for speculative operations in VLIW and superscalar processors. In *Architectures and Compilation Techniques for Fine and Medium Grain Parallelism*, (Cosnard M., Ebcioglu K. and Gaudiot J.-L., eds), IFIP Transactions A-23, pp. 229–42. Elsevier Science Publishers B.V.

Popescu V., Schultz M., Spracklen J., Gibson G., Lightner B. and Isaman D. (1991). The Metaflow architecture. *IEEE Micro*, June, 10–13, 63–71

Russel R. M. (1978). The CRAY-1 computer system. *Comm. ACM*, **21**(1), Jan., 26–35

Smotherman M., Chawla S., Cox S. and Malloy B. (1993). Instruction scheduling for the Motorola 88110. In *Proc. MICRO-26*, pp. 257–62

Sun Microsystems (1992). The SuperSPARC Microprocessor. *Technical White Paper*, Sun Microsystems

References to Processors

Alpha 21064/64A (1992/1994)

Comerford R. (1992). How DEC developed Alpha. *IEEE Spectrum*, July, 26–31

DEC (1994b). *DECchip 21064 and DECchip 21064A Alpha AXP Microprocessors Hardware Reference Manual*, EC-Q9ZUA-TE. DEC, Maynard, Massachusetts

McLellan E. (1993). The Alpha AXP architecture and 21064 Processor. *IEEE Micro*, June, 36–47

Sites R. L. (1993). Alpha AXP architecture. *Comm. ACM*, **36**(2), 33–44

Sites R. L. (1992). Alpha AXP architecture. *Digital Technical Journal*, **4**(4), 19–25

Alpha 21164 (1995)

Bannon P. and Keller J. (1995). Internal architecture of Alpha 21164 microprocessor. In *Proc. COMPCON 1995*, pp. 79–87

Bowhill et al. (1995). A 300 MHz 64b quad-issue CMOS RISC microprocessor. In *Proc. ISSCC95*, pp. 182–3

DEC (1994c). *Alpha 21164 Microprocessor Hardware Reference Manual*, EC-Q9ZUA-TE. DEC, Maynard, Massachusetts

Edmondson J. H., Rubinfeld P., Preston R. and Rajagopalan V. (1995). Superscalar instruction execution in the Alpha microprocessor. *IEEE Micro*, April, 33–43

Ryan B. (1994). Alpha rides high. *Byte*, October, 197–8

Am 29000 superscalar (1995)

Case B. (1994). AMD unveils first superscalar 29K core. *Microprocessor Report*, **8**(14), 23–6

Am K5 (1995)

Slater M. (1994). AMD's K5 designed to outrun Pentium. *Microprocessor Report*, **8**(14), 1–11

ES/9000 (1992p)

Liptay J. S. (1992). Design of the IBM Enterprise System/9000 high-end processor. *IBM J. Res. Develop.*, **36**(4), July, 713–31

Gmicro/500 (1993)

Uchiyama K., Arakawa F., Narita S., Aoki H., Kawasaki I., Matsui S., Yamamoto M., Nakagawa N. and Kudo I. (1993). The Gmicro/500 superscalar microprocessor with branch buffers. *IEEE Micro*, October 12–22

HOBBIT (AT&T 9210) (1993)

Argade P. V., Aymeloglu S., Berenbaum A. D., DePaollis Jr M. V., Franzo R., Freeman R. D. et al. (1993). Hobbit: A high-performance, low-power microprocessor. In *Proc. COMPCON 1993*, pp. 88–95

i960-Series (1988p)

Ryan D. P. (1988). Intel's 80960: An architecture optimized for embedded control. *IEEE Micro*, June, 63–76

i960CA (1989)

McGeady S. (1990). The i960CA superscalar implementation of the 80960 architecture. In *Proc. COMPCON 1990*, pp. 232–9

i960MM (1991p)

McGeady S., Steck R., Hinton G. and Bajwa A. (1991). Performance enhancements in the superscalar i960MM embedded microprocessor. In *Proc. COMPCON 1991*, pp. 4–7

i960 H-Series (1995)

Case B. (1994). Intel reveals next-generation 960 H-series. *Microprocessor Report*, **8**(13), 11–15

M1 (1995)

Burkhardt B. (1994). Delivering next-generation performance on today's installed computer base. In *Proc. COMPCON 1994*, pp. 11–16

Gwennap L. (1994). Cyrix M1 design tapes out. *Microprocessor Report*, **8**(16), 1–7

MC 68060 (1993)

Circello J. and Goodrich F. (1993). The Motorola 68060 microprocessor. In *Proc. COMPCON 1993*, pp. 73–8

Circello et al. (1995). The superscalar architecture of the MC 68060. *IEEE Micro*, April, 10–21

MC 88110 (1991)

Diefendorff K. and Allen M. (1992). Organization of the Motorola 88110 superscalar RISC microprocessor. *IEEE Micro*, April, 40–62

Motorola Inc. (1991). *MC88110 Microprocessor Technical Summary*. Motorola Inc.

Metaflow Lightning

Lightner B. D. and Hill G. (1991). The Metaflow Lightning chipset. In *Proc. COMPCON 1991*, pp. 13–18

Popescu V., Schultz M., Spracklen J., Gibson G., Lightner B. and Isaman D. (1991). The Metaflow architecture. *IEEE Micro*, June, 10–13, 63–71

Nx586 (1994)

Draper et al. (1995). A 93 MHz, x86 microprocessor with on-chip L2 cache controller. In *Proc. ISSCC 1995*, pp. 172–3

Gwennap L. (1994). NexGen enters market with 66-MHz Nx586. *Microprocessor Report*, **8**(4), 12–17

Ryan B. (1994). NexGen Nx586 straddles the RISC/CISC divide. *Byte*, June, 76–88

PA 7100 (1993)

Asprey T., Averill G. S., Delano E., Weiner B. and Yetter J. (1993). Performance features of the PA7100 microprocessor. *IEEE Micro*, June, 22–35

PA 7200 (1995)

Gwennap L. (1994). PA-7200 enables inexpensive MP systems. *Microprocessor Report*, **8**(3), 1–4

Kurpanek G., Chan K., Zheng J., DeLano E. and Bryg W. (1994). PA-7200: A PA-RISC processor with integrated high performance MP bus interface. In *Proc. COMPCON 1994*, pp. 375–82

PA 8000 (1996)

Gwennap L. (1994). PA-8000 combines complexity and speed. *Microprocessor Report*, **8**(15), 1–8

Pentium (1993)

Alpert D. and Avnon D. (1993). Architecture of the Pentium microprocessor. *IEEE Micro*, June, 11–21

Saini A. (1993). An overview of the Intel Pentium processor. In *Proc. COMPCON 1993*, pp. 60–71

(1993). Was den Pentium schnell macht, *Chip Special, Inside: Pentium*, 20–34

Asato C., Montoye R., Gmuender J., Simmons E. W., Ike A. and Zasio J. (1995). A 14-Port 3.8 ns 116 Word 64b Read-Renaming Register File. In *Proc. ISSCC95*, pp. 104–5

Colwell R. P. and Steck R. L. (1995). A 0.6 μm BiCMOS processor with dynamic execution. In *Proc. ISSCC95*, pp. 176–7

Gwennap L. (1995). Intel's P6 uses decoupled superscalar design. *Microprocessor Report*, **9**(2), 9–15

Gwennap L. (1995). Hal reveals multichip SPARC processor. *Microprocessor Report*, **9**(3), 1, 6–11

Patkar N., Katsuno A., Li S., Maruyama T., Savkar S., Simone M., Shen G., Swami R. and Tovey D. (1995). Microarchitecture of HaL's CPU. In *Proc. COMPCON 1995*, pp. 259–66

Shen G. et al. (1995). A 64b 4-issue out-of-order execution RISC processor. In *Proc. ISSCC95*, pp. 170–1

Power1/(RS/6000) (1990)

Grohoski G. F. (1990). Machine organization of the IBM RISC System/6000 processor. *IBM J. Res. Develop.*, **34**(1), January, 37–58

Oehler R. R. and Blasgen M. W. (1991). IBM RISC System/6000: Architecture and performance. *IEEE Micro*, June, 14–17, 56–62

Power2 (1993)

Barreh J., Dhawan S., Hicks T. and Shippy D. (1994). The POWER2 processor. In *Proc. COMPCON 1994*, pp. 389–98

Barreh J., Golla R., Arimilli B. and Jordan P. (1994). POWER2 instruction cache unit. In *PowerPC and POWER2: Technical aspects of the new IBM RISC System/6000*, IBM Corp., pp. 19–27

Hicks T. N., Frey R. E. and Harvey P. E. (1994). POWER2 floating-point unit: architecture and implementation. In *PowerPC and POWER2: Technical aspects of the new IBM RISC System/6000*, IBM Corp., pp. 45–54

Shippy D. J., Griffith T. W. and Braceras G. (1994). POWER2 fixed-point, data cache, and storage control unit. In *PowerPC and POWER2: Technical aspects of the new IBM RISC System/6000*, IBM Corp., pp. 29–44

White S. W. (1994). POWER2: Architecture and performance. In *Proc. COMPCON 94*, pp. 384–8

PowerPC 601 (1993)

Becker M., Allen M. S., Moore C. R., Muhich J. S. and Tuttle D. P. (1993). The PowerPC 601 microprocessor. *IEEE Micro,* Oct., 54–68

Potter T., Vaden M., Young J. and Ullah N. (1994). Resolution of data and control-flow dependencies in the PowerPC 601. *IEEE Micro*, October, 18–29

Ogden D., Kuttanna B., Loper A. J., Mallick S. and Putrino (1995). A new PowerPC microprocessor for low power computing systems. In *Proc. COMPCON 1995*, pp. 281–4

Pham D. et al. (1995). A 1.2W 66MHz supercsalar RISC microprocessor for set-tops, video games, and PDA-s. In *Proc. ISSCC95*, pp. 180–1

PowerPC 603 (1993)

Burgess B., Ullah N., Van Overen P. and Ogden D. (1994). The PowerPC 603 microprocesor. *Comm. ACM*, **37**(6), 34–42

Burgess B., Alexander M., Ying-wai H., Licht S. P., Mallick S., Ogden D., Sung-Ho P. and Slaton J. (1994). The PowerPC 603 microprocessor: A high performance, low power, superscalar RISC microprocessor. In *Proc. COMPCON 1994*, pp. 300–6

Gary S., Dietz C., Eno J., Gerosa G., Park S. and Sanchez H. (1994). The PowerPC 603 microprocessor: A low-power design for portable applications. In *Proc. COMPCON 1994*, pp. 307–15

Motorola Inc. (1994). *PowerPC 603 RISC Microprocessor Technical Summary*, MPC603/D. Motorola Inc.

PowerPC 604 (1995)

Gwennap L. (1994). PPC 604 powers past pentium. *Microprocessor Report*, **8**(5), 1–9, 21

Motorola Inc. (1994). *PowerPC 604 RISC Microprocessor Technical Summary*, MPC604/D. Motorola Inc.

Song S. P., Denman M. and Chang J. (1994). The PowerPC 604 RISC microprocessor. *IEEE Micro*, October, 8–17

PowerPC 620 (1996)

Bearden D., Bailey R., Beavers B., Gutierrez C., Kau C-C, Lewchuk K., Rossbach P. and Taborn M. (1995). A 133 MHz 64b four-issue CMOS microprocessor. *In Proc. ISSCC95*, pp. 174–5

Gwennap L. (1994). 620 fills out PowerPC product line. *Microprocessor Report*, **8**(14), 12–16

Levitan D., Thomas T. and Tu P. (1995). The PowerPC 620 microprocessor: a high performance superscalar RISC microprocessor. In *Proc. COMPCOM 1995*, pp. 285–91

Motorola Inc. (1994). *PowerPC 620 RISC Microprocessor Technical Summary*, MPC620/D. Motorola Inc.

Thompson T. and Ryan B. (1994). PowerPC 620 soars. *Byte*, November, 113–20

R4000 (1992p)

Mirapuri S., Woodacre M., Vasseghi N. (1992). The MIPS R4000 processor. *IEEE Micro*, April, 10–22

R4200 (1994)

Yeung N., Zivkov B. and Ezer G. (1994). Unified datapath: An innovative approach to the design of a low-cost, low-power, high-performance microprocessor. In *Proc. COMPCON 1994*, pp. 32–7

Zivkov B., Ferguson B. and Gupta M. (1994). R4200: A high-performance MIPS microprocessor for portables. In *Proc. COMPCON 1994*, pp. 18–25

R8000 (1994)

Hsu P. Y-T. (1994). Designing the FPT microprocessor. *IEEE Micro*, April, 23–33

MIPS Technologies Inc. (1994). *Microprocessor Chip Set Product Overview*. MIPS Technologies Inc., August

R10000 (1996)

Gwennap L. (1994). MIPS R10000 uses decoupled architecture. *Microprocessor Report*, **8**(14), 18–22

Halfhill T. R. (1994). T5: Brute force. *Byte*, November, 123–8

Heinrich J. (1994). *MIPS R10000 Microprocessor User's Manual*, Alpha Draft 11 Oct. MIPS Technologies Inc., Mountain View, CA

MIPS Technologies Inc. (1994). *R10000 Microprocessor Product Overview*, pp. 1–12. MIPS Technologies Inc., October

SuperSparc (1992)

Blanck G. and Krueger S. (1992). The SuperSPARC microprocessor. In *Proc. COMPCON 1992*, pp. 136–41

Sun Microsystems (1992). *The SuperSPARC Microprocessor Technical White Paper*. Sun Microsystems

UltraSparc (1995)

Goldman G. and Tirumalai P. (1996). UltraSparc-II: The advancement of ultracomputing. In *Proc. COMPCON 1996*, pp. 417–23

Greenley D. et al. (1995). UltraSparc: the next generation superscalar 64-bit SPARC. In *Proc. COMPCON 1995*, pp. 442–51

Gwennap L. (1994). UltraSparc unleashes SPARC performance. *Microprocessor Report*, **8**(13), 1–10

Wayner P. (1994). SPARC strikes back. *Byte*, November, 105–12

Part III

Instruction-level Data-Parallel Architectures

10 Introduction to Data-Parallel Architectures

Section 10.1 introduces the concept of data-parallel architectures. Section 10.2 discusses connectivity between processing elements, one of the most important aspects of the design space of data-parallel architectures, and describes several interconnection models. Finally, Section 10.3 introduces the different classes of data-parallel architectures.

10.1 Introduction

Like many of the other paradigms of parallel computing, the idea behind data-parallel architectures is conceptually simple but can be complex in realization. To understand the idea, it is probably easiest to begin by considering a simple von Neumann CPU. Figure 10.1 illustrates a portion of such an architecture at two levels. Figure 10.1 (a) shows a straightforward block diagram including memory, registers and ALU. In this form, there would normally be no suggestion that the architecture is in any way parallel – single computations are taking place sequentially on single words of data. However, consider Figure 10.1 (b), in which the elements are depicted as the aggregates of binary functional units which, in practice, they are. Viewed in this light, the ALU is operating *in parallel* on eight bits of data – it is performing parallel computation. Of course, the user of the system never has to consider its operation at this level. All that is really happening is that the single data items which the user normally works with – the words, which the processor treats as single entities – in truth comprise aggregates of simpler data items – the bits – which the user does not normally consider.

This idea is at the heart of data-parallel computation. In its more usual implementations, the parallel data entities are more complex and more subtle than a single word of eight bits, but the principle of operation is substantially the same. Once a parallel data entity has been defined, the computer treats it (at least conceptually) as a single unit on which it executes instructions (computations) sequentially. Some examples of typical parallel data sets are illustrated in Figure 10.2. Figure 10.2 (a) shows a structure which occurs in many mathematical problems – a matrix. It is portrayed in the figure as a square *array* of data, and this is important, since one of the principal subtleties of data-parallel computation lies in the significance of the relationships between the elements which make up a parallel data entity. In this case, for example, it is well known that the *diagonal* elements of a matrix usually have special significance.

Figure 10.2 (b) shows an image. It is usually the case that, for reasons we shall see later, data-parallel architectures operate on data sets whose degree of internal parallelism is extremely high. One of the main application areas in which such data sets occur is variously known as image processing, machine vision and pattern recognition. All these phrases describe computation on images which can comprise up to 10^6 *pixels* (a pixel is a small area of an image whose data content can be represented by a single number). Obviously, the relative positions of pixels within an image are important in defining the content of the image so, again, spatial relationships within the parallel data entity are significant. This example introduces another point of importance to data-parallel computing – many of the computational operations which take place are unusual and unfamiliar to the ordinary computer user.

Finally, Figure 10.2(c) illustrates an (imaginary) database entry referring to employee records. The use of computers in the fields of accountancy and management far outweighs their use in scientific computing. It is therefore important to consider the use of data-parallel computers in this area. The largest data structures which occur here are databases, which are structured arrangements of data items

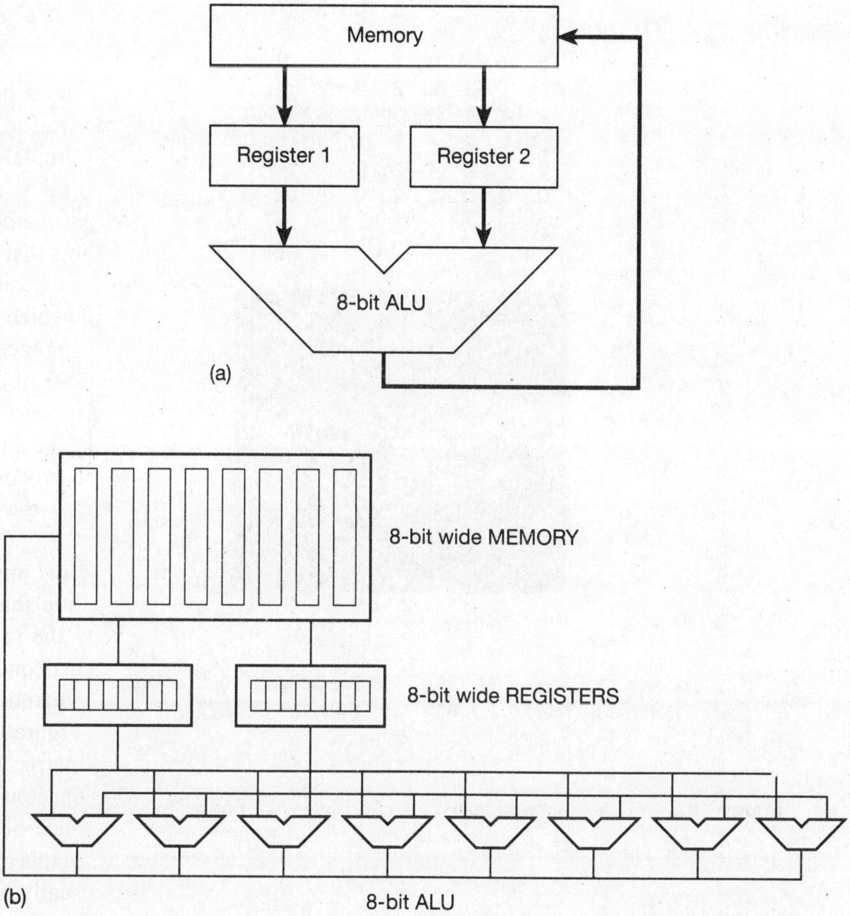

Figure 10.1 (a) What is data-parallel computation? (b) Is this data-parallel?

(the entries) which are themselves structured arrangements of data (the fields of each entry). Furthermore, the position of any individual item in the structure is of significance. The two main conditions for the successful application of data-parallel computing are therefore fulfilled by large databases.

Although highly parallel data sets share many features in common, because they arise in a variety of application fields, both their structures and the operations which are performed on them can differ significantly. In the field of image processing, a single data set frequently undergoes a long sequence of fairly simple manipulations in which the result at each point derives from the values of a significant number of other data items in the set. In scientific computation, results are usually computed from small subsets of data, but the computations themselves are often extremely complex. In parallel database manipulation the main computation involved is usually comparison, but the principal operation which occurs is repeated access to memory.

64	16	4	2	1	0	0	0
8	32	8	4	2	1	0	0
8	16	64	16	8	4	2	1
2	4	8	32	8	4	2	1
2	4	8	16	64	16	8	4
0	1	2	4	8	32	8	4
0	1	2	4	3	16	64	16
0	0	0	1	2	4	8	32

(a)

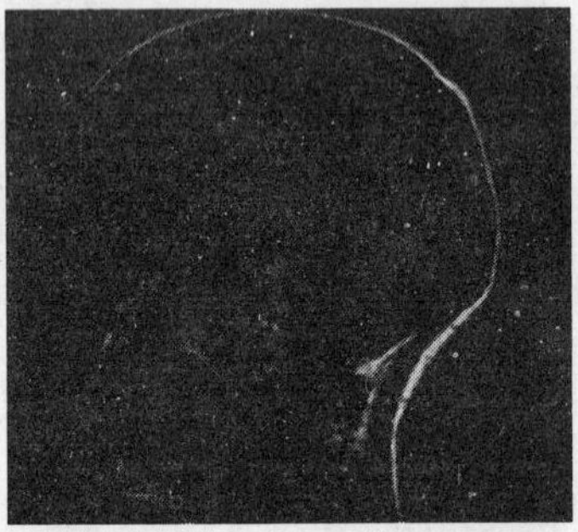

(b)

Doe	Joe	M	36	B.Sc.	30,000	1982	1991
Peterson	Mary	F	42	M.Sc.	42,000	1977	–

(c)

Figure 10.2 (a) A structured matrix; (b) An image; (c) Entries in a database.

10.2 Connectivity

One of the most important aspects of the design space of all classes of data-parallel computer is that relating to connectivity between the processing elements. Because of its importance, and to avoid duplication in the chapters of this section, we deal with the main aspects of this facet here. The scope of the available design space is illustrated in Figure 10.3.

Although any of these interconnection methods can be used for data-parallel computers, certain of them have been found to be more suitable than others for the massive parallelism involved. In particular, the near-neighbour, tree, pyramid and hypercube have all been widely used, whereas the bus, crossbar and multistage networks have proved to be more suitable for function-parallel designs.

10.2.1 Near neighbours

The idea of near-neighbour connectivity as a specific class of arrangement originally arose in the context of mapping spatially coherent data onto SIMD systems

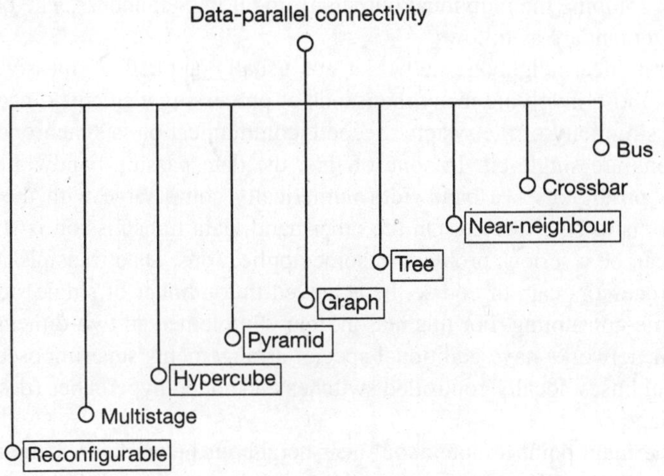

Figure 10.3 The design space for connectivity in data parallel computers.

(see Chapter 11). The importance of the arrangement comes about precisely because data in such sets is spatially correlated, which, in turn, implies that information needs to be assembled over spatially limited areas. In the limit, it is only passed between neighbouring processors.

Although some systems do provide diagonal connections between the elements of a square array, the most common arrangement is to limit the system to so-called fourfold connectivity, in which only neighbours in the North–South and East–West directions are connected. Figure 10.4, which illustrates the more general eight-connected case, shows how each PE has only a single output, but must

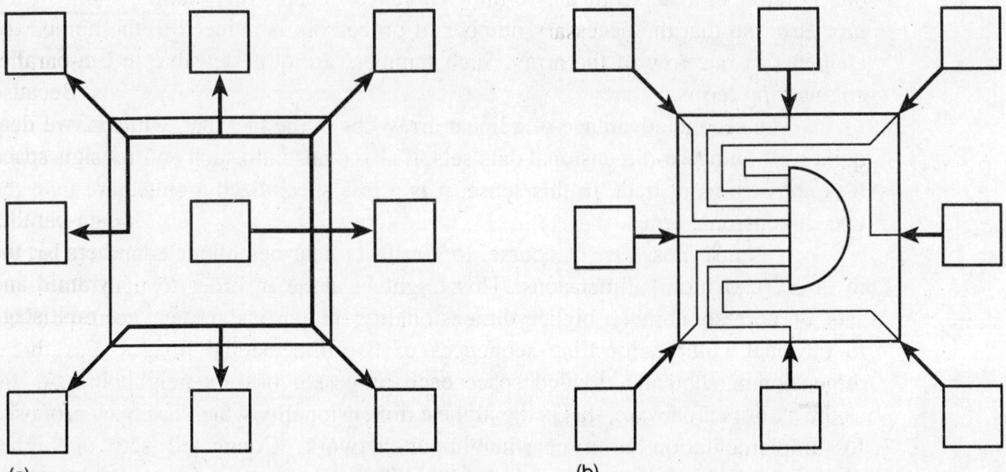

Figure 10.4 Near-neighbour connectivity.

somehow combine the individual outputs from all its neighbours. The properties of the arrangement are as follows.

First, near-neighbour networks are usually applied to massively parallel systems – those involving many thousands of processing elements – because of the technical simplicity of the system. Second, communication is synchronous, and the connections are single-bit. In spite of this, the data passing bandwidth of such a system is prodigious – a bandwidth numerically comparable with the number of processors is to be expected. On the other hand, data transmission is strictly local, and this can be a serious problem in some applications. Data transmission between distant processors can, of course, be achieved in a number of single steps, but this can be time-consuming. For this reason, many implemented two-dimensional near-neighbour networks have additional special arrangements superimposed, including orthogonal buses, locally controlled switches and added hypercubes (described later in this chapter).

The main point to note about near-neighbour networks is their simplicity of implementation – all connections are short and uncomplicated. Of course, this only applies up to a certain maximum size where a planar arrangement of the processing elements can be physically maintained. Beyond this size, the folding of the plane which is required becomes a serious problem.

Finally, it is possible to consider near-neighbour connected networks of dimensionality other than two. A great many so-called linear arrays have been constructed in which each processing element is connected to only two others, forming a one-dimensional system. Naturally, the engineering problems involved in constructing such systems are rather simpler than for the two-dimensional array, but a number of other advantages are perhaps more important. First is the question of data mapping. The underlying assumption in an SIMD system is that one processor is mapped to each data item. For larger data sets (perhaps 4096×4096 elements) this is presently impossible, so that less efficient strategies have to be introduced to map the data set onto the available number of processors. In the case of the linear array, one column of data from a two-dimensional set maps very naturally onto each processor, so that the necessary number of processors is reduced to the number of elements in one row of the array. Such numbers are quite feasible in present-day engineering terms.

The second advantage of a linear array lies in the fact that, while it will map quite well onto two-dimensional data sets, it also maps onto such entities as vectors, lists and strings of data. In this sense, it is a less specialized architecture than the two-dimensional array.

It is also possible, of course, to construct near-neighbour connected arrays in three (and more) dimensions. This might be done in order to map onto data sets of correspondingly higher dimensionality, in particular data corresponding to physical volumes or time sequences of two-dimensional images. For three-dimensional, cubically divided space each processor has six neighbours. As far as the authors are aware, this is the highest dimensionality which has been proposed for implementation as a near-neighbour network. Connected sets of higher dimensionality are always treated in a rather different manner, discussed later in this chapter.

10.2.2 Trees and graphs

Near-neighbour connected systems are usually specialized for image processing applications in particular. The idea of the graph-connected system is perhaps as unspecialized as any idea can be. Any particular problem has a natural expression in the form of a *graph* which embodies the computational and communication requirements of the problem. The connections required to permit the necessary dependencies can be quite irregular, in which case no mathematically definable regular structure implements only the desired connections between nodes. The only completely general structures which would be useful in this context would be those embodying all-to-all connectivity (usually impractical) or *reconfigurability*, which we shall return to later, but for the moment we will consider what fixed structures might be of some use in this context.

If we examine more general types of problems, it becomes apparent that many embody a hierarchical structure of some sort – database searching, model matching and expert systems are all types of problem which can be formulated in this way. This structure, in which many simultaneous processes are executed at a low level, then progressively fewer at higher levels, with the computation at these levels depending on results from lower levels, suggests the type of connectivity shown in Figure 10.5.

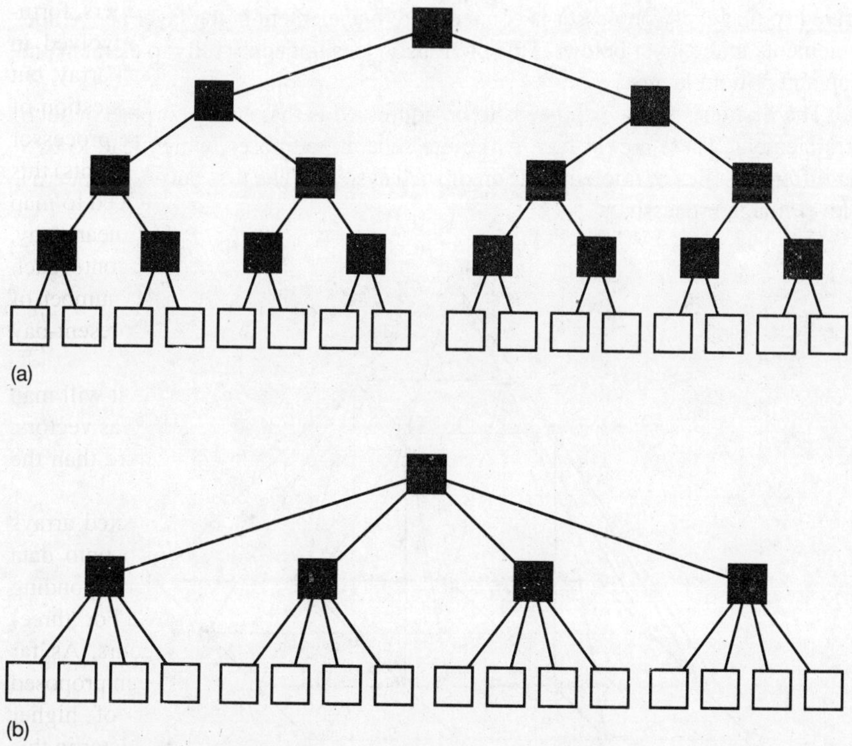

Figure 10.5 Alternative tree connectivities.

Two of the most widely used regular alternatives are shown in parts (a) and (b) of the figure – the *binary tree* and the *quadtree*. The binary tree is particularly attractive in that it is the minimal implementation of the idea and is therefore likely to involve the least number of conceptual problems in use. The quadtree, and other tree structures of higher degree, are favoured because of their increased flexibility, particularly where the convergence of computations in the problem domain is likely to be faster than the repeated factor of two embodied in the binary tree.

There are, however, drawbacks to this structure. Principal amongst these is the problem of data bottlenecks, which occur when information between lower-level nodes needs to be passed through a high-level node. In the quadtree, for example, each node at the second level is the only communication channel for the six possible data routings between the four processors at the first level to which it is directly connected. In addition to this, it is the only channel through which longer-range communication with these processors can be effected.

10.2.3 The pyramid

This interconnection scheme is best envisaged as being a combination of the two-dimensional near-neighbour mesh and the tree (often, but not always, the quadtree). The basic architecture is that shown in Figure 10.6. Each level of the system (except the top layer) is a four-connected mesh. Connections between the layers are contrived so that every processor is connected to one element in the layer above and four elements in the layer below. (This obviously does not apply fully to elements in the top and bottom layers.)

The first question which needs to be addressed is that of the purpose of such an arrangement. There are, in fact, two quite separate purposes, which lead to two rather different styles of implementation of such systems. The first purpose concerns low-level image processing.

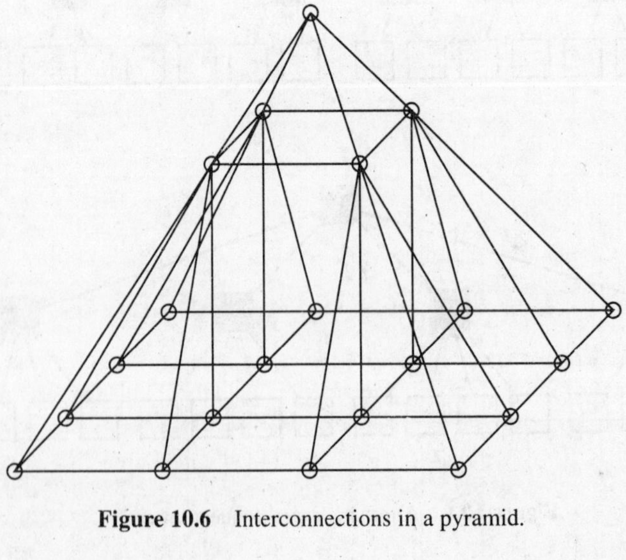

Figure 10.6 Interconnections in a pyramid.

Mesh architectures have two undesirable properties from the image processing point of view – they are slow to pass data over large distances, and they do not lend themselves easily to the manipulation of data at different resolutions. One implementation of the pyramid is designed to overcome both these problems. Consider the question of data passing in an $N \times N$ mesh. As an example, to pass an item of data from one corner of the array to that diagonally opposite demands $2N$ shift operations. However, if the same array forms the base level of a pyramid, the operation can be performed with $2\log_2 N$ shifts, a considerably smaller number, by passing data to the peak of the pyramid and then back down. This level of analysis was, for a time, accepted as indicating that pyramid structures of this sort are generally better at passing data than equivalent meshes. However, it has been demonstrated that, if larger quantities of data are to be moved around the base array, passing the data via the pyramid connections is disadvantageous, as serious bottlenecks occur in the upper layers when, for example, the number of data items exceeds the number of processors in a given layer.

A second advantage does, however, remain. It is frequently advantageous in image processing to deal with a given image at a series of different resolutions. The pyramid architecture facilitates such operations by, for example, allowing each processor in a given layer to compute the average value of the image points held in the four processors directly connected to it in the next lower layer. These average values then constitute a new image, at lower resolution, which retains the same configuration as the previous image.

Systems of the type just described usually comprise identical processing elements at each level of the pyramid. An alternative structure, intended to address the complete vision problem, uses the same connectivity but has processors of different complexities at each level of the pyramid. This arrangement has two advantages. First, there is no longer an assumption that complete images will be passed between layers of the structure, but rather that information derived from images will be communicated. This reduces the load on the more limited communication bandwidth in the upper levels. Second, the individual connections in the upper levels can be of higher complexity, reflecting that embodied in the processing elements, with consequent benefits to communication bandwidth.

10.2.4 The hypercube

The fundamental idea behind hypercube connectivity is as follows. If a system has 2^N processing elements, and each element is allowed N interconnection channels, the elements can be connected together into a hypercube of dimension N. The process can easily be understood with reference to Figure 10.7. For $N = 0$, we have one element and zero connections. For $N = 1$, the number of elements is two, and only one wire is needed to connect them. This pair of elements is a first-order hypercube. When the number of connections per element is two, the number of elements is four, and the resulting structure (a second-order hypercube) can be visualized as either a square or a ring. Note that the total number of connections in the system is now also four. At the next stage, the number of processors is eight, each with three connections to neighbours, and the total number of channels in the system is 12.

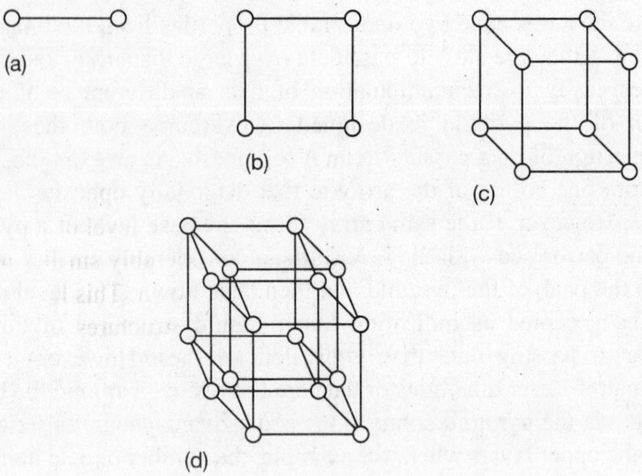

Figure 10.7 Four orders of hypercube.

The resulting arrangement (a three-dimensional hypercube – in fact, simply a cube) can be obtained by replicating the previous order of hypercube and connecting corresponding elements.

The final part of the figure shows a four-dimensional hypercube. There is an alternative representation, shown in Figure 10.8, which demonstrates an interesting property of the hypercube, namely that it incorporates near-neighbour connectivity, with additional long-range channels. It is this combination of short- and long-range connections that makes the hypercube so interesting as a method of connecting a

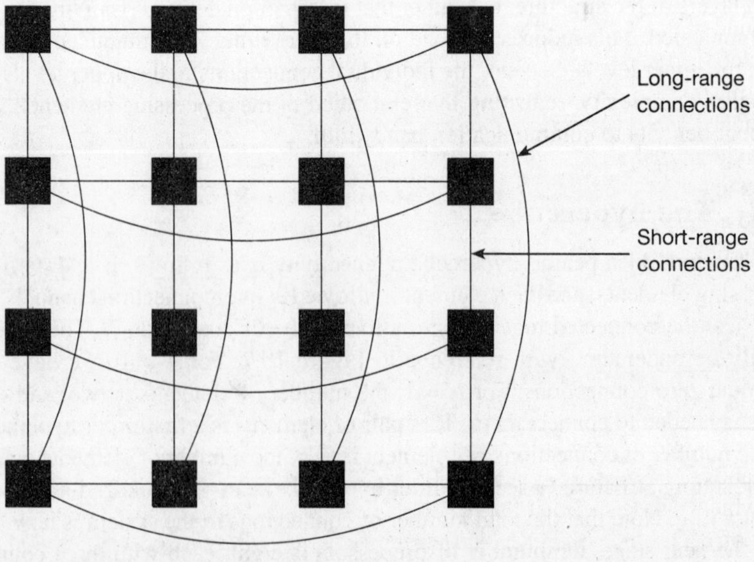

Figure 10.8 Long- and short-range connections in a hypercube.

large number of processors. The corresponding drawback is inevitable – to connect, for example, 4096 elements requires a twelfth-order hypercube and, therefore, 12 connections per element. For numbers of this order or larger, this represents a significant additional complexity for each processor. Furthermore, the incomplete symmetry of the arrangement means that asynchronous communication (message passing) is the most appropriate method within such structures. This naturally carries with it implications for processor complexity and autonomy.

It is generally true that the largest number of steps needed to connect two elements of an *N*th-order hypercube is equal to *N*. The improved distribution of connections over, in particular, the near-neighbour arrangement is apparent. Of course, it is not to be supposed that this improvement is obtained at zero cost – the engineering difficulties of making long-range physical connections and the more complex communications algorithms needed are two of the drawbacks.

10.2.5 Reconfigurable networks

Some of the networks in the overall interconnection design space are intrinsically reconfigurable – they embody sets of switches which can define a variety of configurations according to their settings. Examples of networks of this sort include the crossbar switch and the generalized cube network. In fact, the use of reconfigurability is more widespread than this.

As ever, at the root of this technique lies the desirability of mapping problems closely onto architectures. For those arrangements which embody selectivity in a natural way, it is no real problem to map a variety of applications onto the common architecture since, in fact, the architecture is changed to fit the requirements of the new problem domain. In the case of architectures such as the near neighbour mesh, however, the changing data structures which almost inevitably arise in the course of solving a problem cause considerable difficulties and, usually, inefficiency. Two ways around this problem exist. In the first technique, a local switch allows a particular connection (or set of connections) to be chosen out of those which the hardware makes available. The second technique is rather more general in action. Here, switches allow direct connections to be made between inputs to, and outputs from, individual elements. Using this technique, it is possible to bypass subsets of processors and, for instance, to map all the upper levels of a pyramid, simultaneously, onto a square mesh. In general, allowing reconfigurable connections by these methods in otherwise fixed networks can considerably extend their field of efficient action.

10.3 Alternative architectural classes

From the above examples we can see that there are a number of somewhat different ways in which data-parallel computers can be configured. These are reflected in a number of alternative classes of data-parallel architectures, illustrated in Figure 10.9.

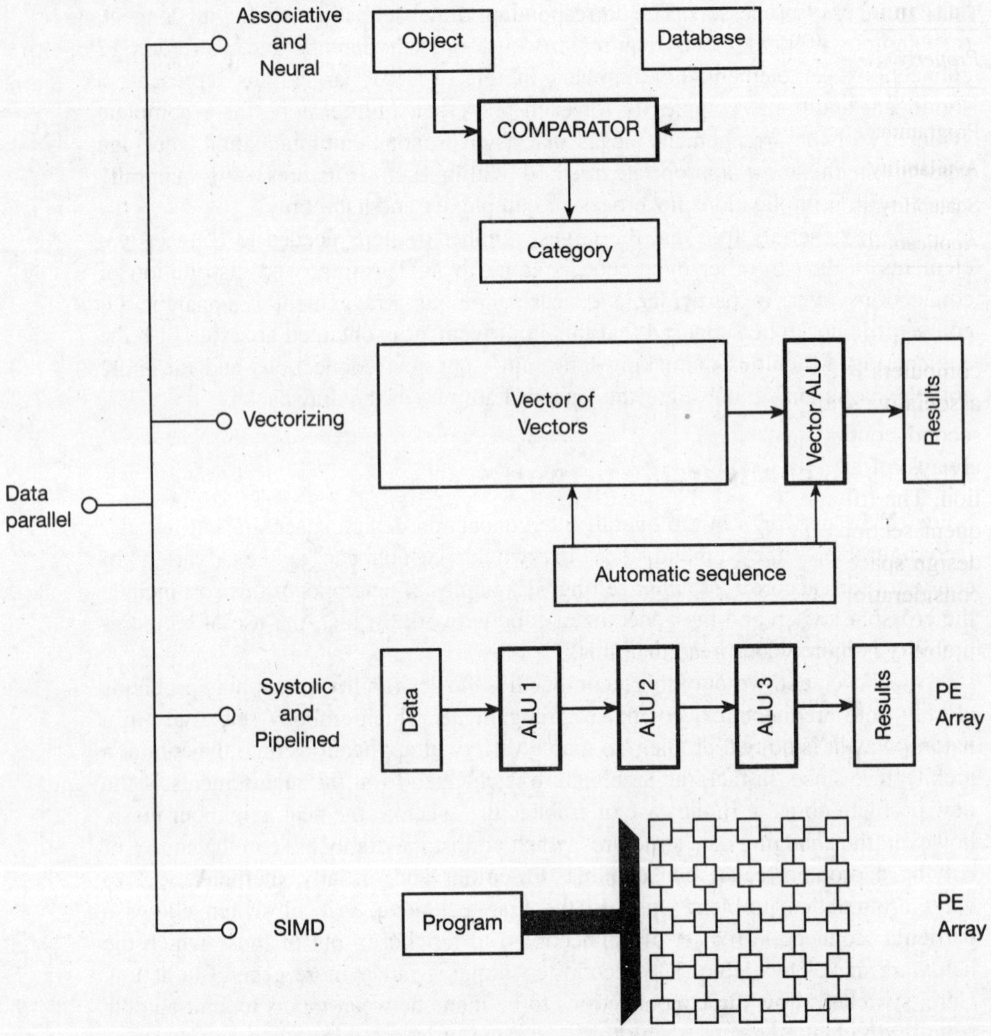

Figure 10.9 Alternative data-parallel approaches.

SIMD systems usually arrange their processing elements into a connectivity which physically matches the configuration of their target data sets. Systolic and pipelined machines take advantage of the repetitive nature of simple calculations on extended data sets. Vectorizing computers utilize a similar method, but incorporate both enhanced programmability and parallelism within the data set. Associative and neural computers exploit the parallelism within databases in executing parallel comparisons.

In the following chapters we consider in detail each of these alternatives, but at this stage it is sensible to summarize the characteristics which differentiate the fundamental types of system. These are presented in Table 10.1.

Table 10.1 The principal characteristics of data-parallel systems.

Property	*SIMD*	*Systolic*	*Pipeline*	*Vectorizing*	*Neural*	*Associative*
Programmability	Good	Fixed	Fixed	Good	Poor	Good
Availability	Good	Poor	Poor	Good	Poor	Poor
Scalability	Good	Fixed	Fixed	Fixed	Fixed	Good
Applicability	Wide	Narrow	Narrow	Wide	Narrow	Wide

It would appear from the table that the design space for data-parallel computers is polarized into two fields – the first containing SIMD, vectorizing and associative systems which are programmable and therefore of wide applicability, the second containing pipelines and systolic and neural devices which are (almost always) of fixed function and defined performance and therefore of limited application. The true situation is much more complex than this, as we shall see in subsequent sections of this chapter. Each of the main categories has its own complex design space, and these spaces overlap to some extent. We commence the detailed consideration of these architectures with SIMD systems.

11 SIMD Architectures

First, Section 11.1 describes the history of SIMD architectures. Section 11.2 describes a number of areas in which design decisions must be made, including granularity, connectivity, processor complexity and local autonomy. Section 11.3 describes fine-grained SIMD architectures, using the Massively Parallel Processor as an example. Finally, Section 11.4 describes coarse-grained SIMD architectures, using the CM5 as an example.

11.1 Introduction

SIMD systems comprise one of the three most commercially successful classes of parallel computers (the others being vector supercomputers and MIMD systems). A number of factors have contributed to this success, including:

- simplicity of concept and programming
- regularity of structure
- easy scalability of size and performance
- straightforward applicability in a number of fields which demand parallelism to achieve necessary performance.

Historically, the roots of SIMD architectures can be traced back to two sources. The first of these was contained in the early ideas of John von Neumann (1951) concerning cellular automata. In a number of papers, he suggested that aggregates of comparatively simple, self-replicating circuits could be effective in executing parallel computation. The second, and perhaps more significant, source of ideas was a paper by Steven Unger (1958), which included the following concepts, still common to most systems of this type today.

- There is a two-dimensional array of processing elements, each connected to its four nearest neighbours.
- All processors execute the same instruction simultaneously.
- Each processor incorporates local memory.
- The processors are programmable, that is, they can perform a variety of functions.
- Data can propagate quickly through the array.

If we add to these concepts a host computer to act as the source of the instruction sequence and, usually, a dedicated system for data input, output and mass storage, then the resulting block diagram, shown as Figure 11.1, can act as the general model for the majority of subsequent and present systems.

From these historical beginnings, it is possible to categorize the development of SIMD systems in three phases:

- Design studies which explored and developed the basic principles
- Prototype implementations which demonstrated the practical applicability of the idea
- Commercially viable systems.

Naturally, there was some overlap between these areas. Figure 11.2 illustrates how various lines of investigation developed over the period 1960 to 1995, and indicates the three phases of development mentioned above.

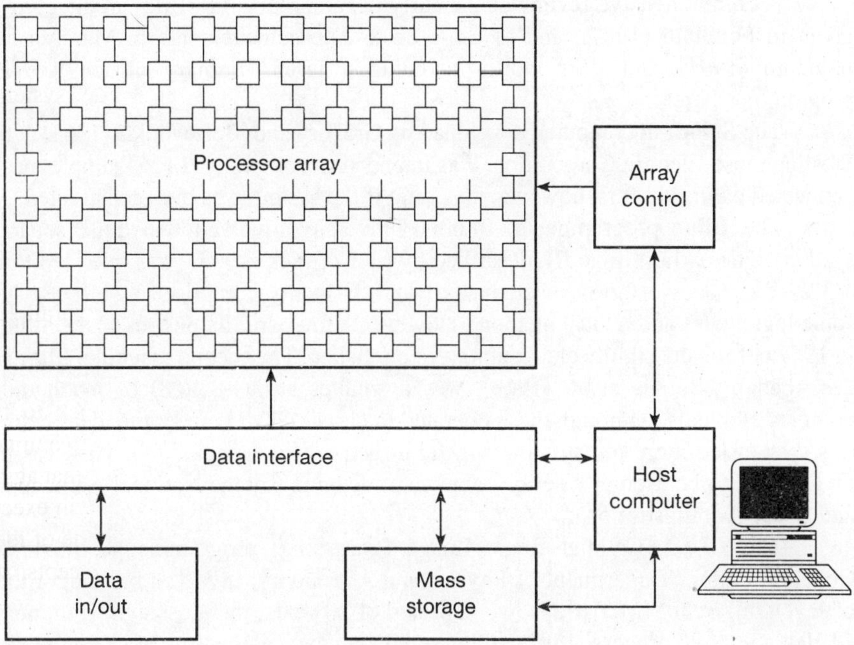

Figure 11.1 The archetypal SIMD system.

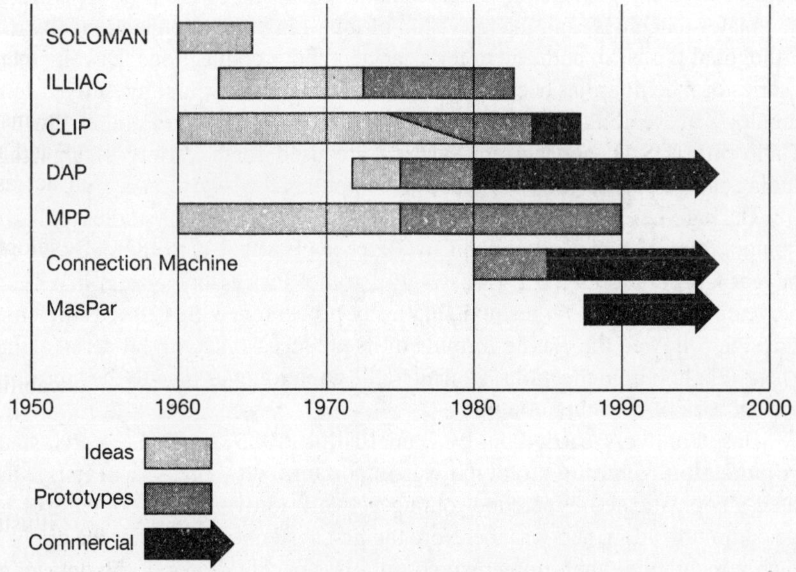

Figure 11.2 The development of SIMD systems.

A comprehensive review of the early developments in SIMD architecture is given in Fountain (1987), and of more up-to-date achievements in Maresca and Fountain (1991), but it is worth including a brief summary of the relevant programmes here.

The **Solomon** computer, developed by Gregory and McReynolds (1963) at the Westinghouse Electric Corporation, was intended to comprise 32 × 64 simple mesh-connected elements. It is, however, uncertain if the system was ever constructed.

The **Illiac** programme at Illinois University involved two quite separate systems. The earlier, Illiac III, described by McCormick (1963), was intended to be a 32 × 32 processor array of elements which basically comprised a shift register, some logic gates and a local memory. However, a fire partially destroyed the system in 1967 before any significant results were published. The second machine, Illiac IV, described by Barnes et al. (1968), was a smaller array (8 × 8) of much more complex elements. Although these operated in classic SIMD mode, the ideas behind this system led more towards the MIMD direction (see Chapter 15). This was the first system to be used as a serious application engine (by the National Aeronautics and Space Administration).

The **CLIP** (Cellular Logic Image Processing) programme at University College London (Department of Physics and Astronomy) involved building a total of seven different SIMD arrays over a period of 20 years, the most significant being CLIP4, a 96 × 96 processor array of bit-serial elements, at the time of its completion in 1980 the largest processor array in the world. This system, described by Duff et al. (1973), proved to be an effective low-level image processing computer.

Workers at ICL, including Reddaway (1973), began work on the **DAP** (Distributed Array Processor) in the early 1970s and had produced a prototype 32 × 32 element system by 1976. The two main aspects of interest concerned the large amount of memory provided at each element (1000 bits in the prototype system – more in later machines) and the provision of long-range interconnections (by means of orthogonal buses) in addition to the near-neighbour connections. Development of this series of machines has been continued to the present day, first by Active Memory Technology of Reading (UK) and subsequently by Cambridge Parallel Processing of California (USA), and current systems are used for a variety of applications including image processing and scientific computing.

During the 1970s NASA commissioned a number of studies of parallel computers, one of which, described by Batcher (1980), led to the delivery of the Goodyear Corporation's **MPP** (Massively Parallel Processor) system in 1983. For some years this was the largest existing array processor, with 128 × 128 elements. The design followed the classic formula of its predecessors, with bit-serial elements and near-neighbour connections. Considerable attention was paid to the increasingly important area of data input/output.

Based on work carried out by Daniel Hillis (1985) while a research student, the **Connection Machine** prototype was important for two reasons. First, it incorporated a sophisticated hypercube routing network to overcome problems of long-range communication, and was therefore the first system to encounter the drawbacks of such a technique when implemented on a large scale. Second, the development spawned a commercial company (Thinking Machines Inc.) which was instrumental in gaining more widespread acceptance of the SIMD approach to parallel computing. The main application area for current systems is scientific computing.

MasPar were the first company since ICL to enter the commercial system arena without a prior gestation within a University or Government laboratory environment. The founders worked on SIMD systems at DEC before setting up their own company. The MasPar systems, described by Blank (1990), were the first commercial machines to be implemented with basic processing elements of greater complexity than one-bit, and the first to implement long-range connections by means of a multi-level crossbar switch.

There is now an increasing number of commercial systems being marketed which can be operated in SIMD mode, some by major companies in computer manufacture such as **IBM**, **Cray** and **DEC**, others by firms dedicated to parallel computing such as **nCUBE**. With the increasing numbers of implemented designs, it has become apparent that there are a number of design aspects where choices can be made which affect the configuration, performance and use of a system. In the next section we consider the choices available in each of the major areas of design.

11.2 Design space

In spite of the conceptual simplicity of the SIMD system, there is a comparatively large number of major design areas in which choices must be made. They are:

- The complexity of the processing element. This includes the natural data types of the processor, the instruction set complexity and the amount of memory.
- The degree to which each processing element is allowed local autonomy within the SIMD paradigm.
- The types of connectivity which are provided between elements in the array.
- The relationship between connectivity network, distribution of memory and processor array configuration.
- The number and connection topology of the processing elements.
- The disposition and method of connection of backup memory.
- The implementation technology.

Unfortunately, these are not independent variables. For example, the number of elements will probably be influenced both by their complexity and by the technology of implementation. This interdependence is reflected in the following sections, which analyse the design features one by one while taking account of other aspects where necessary.

11.2.1 Granularity

The granularity of an SIMD system is defined in terms of the relationship between the number of processing elements and the parallelism of the data sets upon which it operates. A system with few data elements per processing element is regarded as having high granularity and is usually referred to as fine-grained. One with many data elements per processor has low granularity and is referred to as coarse-grained. The difference is illustrated in Figure 11.3. The idea of granularity is in contradiction to the assumption at the heart of the parallel data paradigm – that the parallelism in the computer will be equal to that in the problem, that is, there should be as many processing elements as there are data items in one parallel data set. Although there are a very few application areas where achievement of this ideal is not impossible (for example, in the real-time processing of CCTV images), two factors mitigate against its general achievement within the constraints of present-day technology. The first is the sheer size of many data sets. A single satellite image may well be several thousand pixels square – perhaps tens of millions of pixels in one image. It is impractical at present to conceive of parallel computers having millions of processing elements. The second factor relates to the variability of size of data sets within a single application area. A normal serial computer deals with, for example, matrices of various sizes by providing large amounts of (relatively) inexpensive memory within which any required size of matrix can be accommodated. Providing an SIMD array of a size beyond that which is routinely required is a much more costly exercise, and *changing* the size of an array at any stage is more costly still.

It is therefore apparent that the size (and therefore granularity) of an SIMD array is not usually solely determined by the anticipated size of the application data sets, but by other factors. First, a designer must determine if subsets of data exist in the application whose size can be regularly accommodated by a fixed and acceptable amount of parallelism. If such subsets can be detected, then their size should be

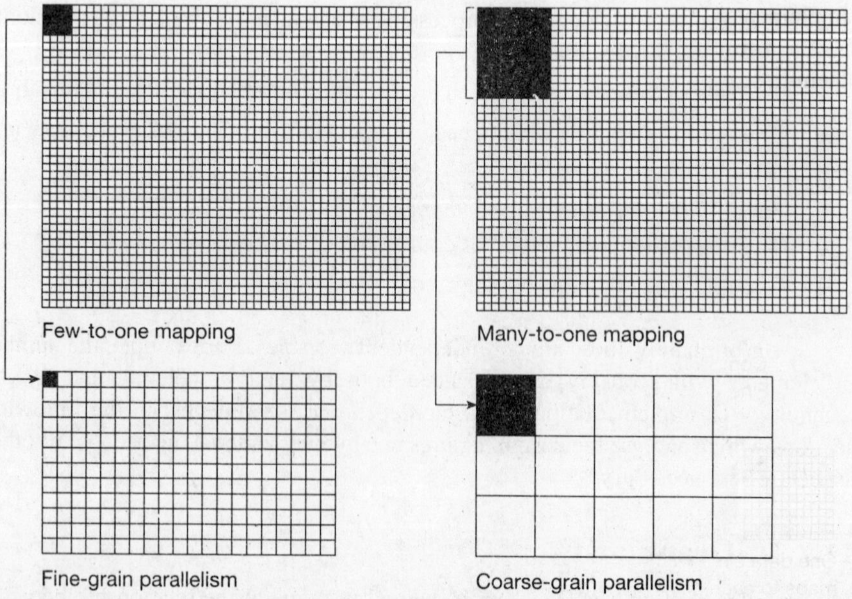

Figure 11.3 Types of granularity.

taken into account in determining that of the array. Second, an examination should be made of the data element types which are most often used in an application area. The complexity or otherwise of these will determine the most efficient processor complexity, which in turn will determine the maximum allowable amount of parallelism within economic or performance constraints. Although there is apparently a spectrum of alternatives, involving various degrees of processor complexity and a corresponding variety of levels of granularity, in fact design decisions usually polarize to the two extremes – high granularity with simple processing elements and low granularity with complex processors. At least a part of the reason for this is that a decision in favour of one extreme or the other encourages conceptual clarity. It is frequently beneficial for an applications programmer to concentrate either on the concept of total fine-grain parallelism or on the quite different ideas used when dealing with the coarse-grain approach. A representation for the design space concerning granularity is therefore that shown in Figure 11.4.

11.2.2 Connectivity

There are a number of conflicting requirements to be addressed in considering the proper connectivity to provide between the elements of an SIMD system. First, the unattainable ideal would be for any processor to be able to communicate with any other in unit time. Second, any desired number of communication events should be able to occur simultaneously. Third, the connectivity network should embody a degree of regularity which permits a straightforward expression of source, destination and routing. Fourth, the network should embody a degree of redundancy or fault-tolerance, in terms of both the connectivity itself and the substitution of faulty array processing elements. Finally, the resulting connectivity network should be implementable in a compact and well-structured form.

Some of these requirements are incompatible, so it is necessary to prioritize them in some way in order to develop a satisfactory design. A first step towards this

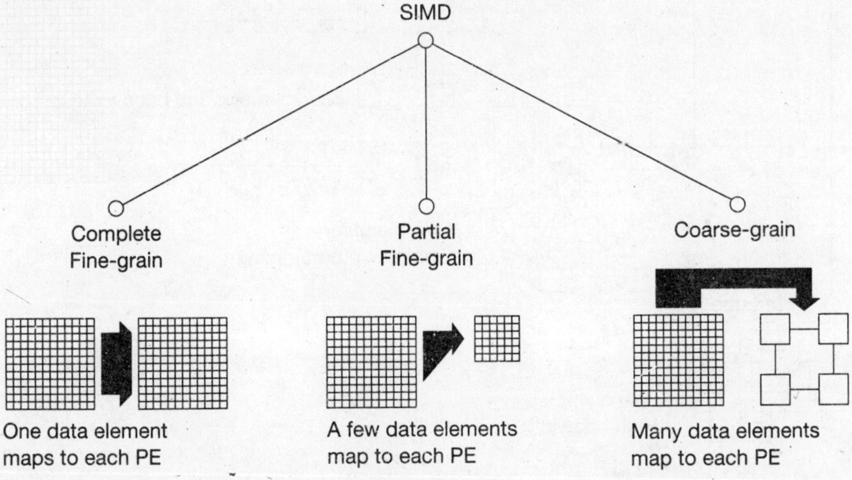

Figure 11.4 The design space for granularity.

process is an analysis of the alternatives which are available in terms of the criteria which they satisfy, and their relative merits in terms of performance and cost-effectiveness. The main alternatives have been described in Chapter 10 and are illustrated in Figure 11.5.

The selection of the appropriate connectivity arrangement for an SIMD system is perhaps the most complex of all the design decisions to be made. It is therefore useful to have a small number of easily compared parameters which may help to guide the initial choice. The first and most useful of these is the minimum number of processor-to-processor steps required to convey information between the physically most remote elements of the system. This parameter is called the *diameter* of the network.

The second parameter which can be readily derived is the total *bandwidth* of the network. This is the maximum amount of data which can be conveyed by the network, between one set of processors and another, in a single operation.

The final network parameter which must be considered concerns the probable degrees of *bottlenecking* and *blocking* which may occur in the network during typical (that is, non-optimum) data transfer operations. Such a parameter is both more loosely defined and more difficult to calculate or measure than the others. Its

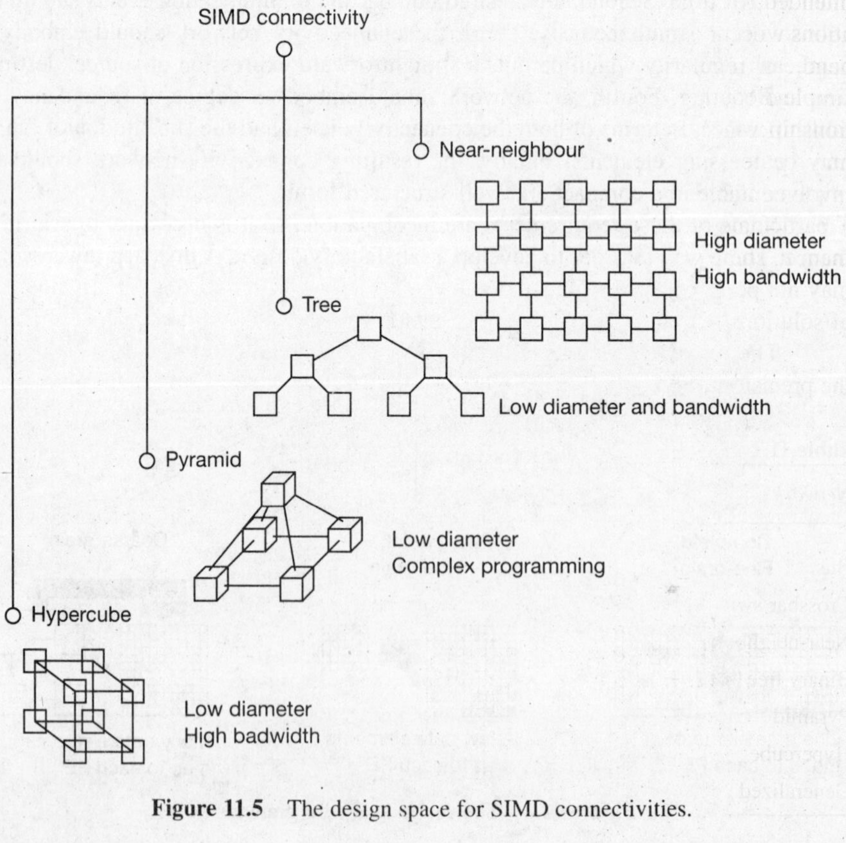

Figure 11.5 The design space for SIMD connectivities.

value depends critically on what are regarded as typical operations in any given context, and is therefore application dependent. For this reason, we make no attempt to calculate values for the networks considered here, although a potential user or designer would need to do so.

Calculated values for the first two parameters mentioned above are presented in Table 11.1. They are calculated for an array of N elements in each case. The reader should, however, regard these figures with caution, as a number of simplifying assumptions have been made in arriving at them. These include the assumption that the connecting links of each network are of identical bandwidth (unlikely to be true), and that one limiting factor on the bandwidth figure is the ability of each processing element to accept only one data item in one cycle (not always true in the case of near-neighbour networks, amongst others). It is therefore true that the performance of a given network will be influenced by the complexity and flexibility of the elements which it connects. These factors are considered in the following sections.

11.2.3 Processor complexity

The second important issue in the design of SIMD computers concerns the complexity of each of the processing elements. To a very significant extent this will reflect the target functionality of the system under consideration. If a system is intended for use in scientific calculations, then in all likelihood floating-point operations will be a *sine qua non* and appropriate units will be incorporated. On the other hand, an image processing system might be most efficiently implemented with simple Boolean logical operators. Often, the only modifier on such a natural relationship will be an economic or technological one. Some desirable configurations may be too expensive for a particular application, and the performance penalty involved in a non-optimum solution may be acceptable. Alternatively, the benefits of a particularly compact implementation may outweigh those of optimum performance. There may even be cases where the generality of application of the system may not permit an optimum solution to be calculated at all. In such cases, a variety of solutions may be supportable.

The first determinant is the precision of the circuits. We do not mean by this the precision of the answers any given circuit could calculate, given sufficient time.

Table 11.1 Relative performance of interconnection networks.

Network	*Diameter*	*Bandwidth*
Bus	1	1
Crossbar switch	1	N
Near-neighbour	$2\sqrt{N}$	N
Binary tree	$2\log N$	$2\log N$
Pyramid	$2\log\sqrt{N}$	$2\log\sqrt{N}$
Hypercube	$\log N$	N
Generalized cube	1	N

Alan Turing's famous work (1937) demonstrated that a very simple computer can execute any required (computable) function. Here, we use the term to indicate the natural precision of data with which a given circuit works – we are all familiar with the concept of an 8-bit microprocessor, or a 32-bit multiplier.

The idea of parallelism tends, at one level, to minimize the complexity of the individual circuits, since a natural impulse is to attempt to increase the number of parallel computation units at (almost) any cost. This impulse led many developers in the field of data parallelism to adopt minimal one-bit circuits as their processors, some of which are described in Fountain (1983). In many cases, there were additional reasons for this decision. SIMD arrays for image processing are required to act upon data elements of differing precision, and a single-bit processing element (PE) is maximally efficient in such an environment – the maximum possible number of circuit elements is always active..

A second type of reason supports the use of single-bit processors for data-parallel systems. The very large number of processors which should be used in the optimum arrangement means that cost per processor should be minimized – single-bit processors are certain to be cheaper than their multi-bit counterparts. Further, large numbers of processors mean large numbers of interconnections. If the bitwise complexity of each interconnection can be reduced to a minimum, then engineering problems can be reduced.

Taken together, these reasons mean that, in some circumstances, a one-bit processor is a very valid choice. However, this is not always so and, when it is not, things become more complicated. One difficulty, mentioned above, which arises in considering the use of multi-bit processors in a parallel system, concerns efficiency. In a single-processor computer system, the cost of even the most complex CPU is likely to be small when compared with the costs arising from the rest of the system. It is therefore relatively unimportant if that processor is somewhat over-specified. If, for example, a 32-bit processor is used in a system where most computation occurs on 16-bit numbers, no great cost penalty accrues from the (mostly unused) extra 16 bits. This argument does not hold in a parallel computer embodying perhaps thousands of such processors. It becomes much more important, in such systems, that the costly computing power should be distributed efficiently – after all, if each processor can be halved in complexity, twice as many processors can be deployed for the same cost.

There is therefore a very complex balance to be struck between the precision of each processor and its efficiency in executing calculations on a broad range of data types. This dilemma is most likely to arise in coarse-grain SIMD arrays, in which, because they incorporate fewer processing elements, the design of each element is correspondingly less constrained.

Other options are available to the parallel system designer which can have similar effects on system costs and efficiency. Thus, there is the possibility of incorporating either hard-wired multipliers or floating-point accelerators at each node of the parallel system, and these could be between 16- and 64-bit precision. Such an approach is perfectly reasonable when maximum total computing power is being sought. However, it is usually the case that the higher the precision of each individual processor, the lower the complexity of the interconnection network through which they communicate. The relationship between communication rates and computation rates is not simple, but an increase in one usually implies a decrease in the other. It is therefore the case that there are a variety of implementations which can validly employ processors having precisions between one and 64 bits. The design space for this factor is depicted in Figure 11.6.

One aspect which might modify the efficiency of any particular choice is the degree to which each processor is allowed to modify its own behaviour. This factor itself is more complex than it appears at first sight.

11.2.4 Local autonomy

Flynn's classical taxonomy of computer architectures embodies the ideas of singular and multiple instruction and data streams and is widely used as the basis of a convenient shorthand method of classifying multiprocessor architectures. From two of the principal categories of classification (SIMD and MIMD) it is usually assumed that only the two extreme modes of control – complete independence (autonomy) or complete synchronization – are possible in an assembly of processors. The advantage of this viewpoint is its simplicity. The disadvantage is that physical implementations of the two extremes differ so enormously in complexity (and therefore cost) that consideration of the best level of autonomy for a particular application is often overwhelmed by the apparent economic consequences. In fact, this degree of polarization is unnecessary. Ideas delineated by Fountain (1988) encompass a sequence of levels of autonomy which permits a much finer and more accurate choice to be made. In such locally autonomous systems, the action carried out at each processor depends, to a greater or lesser extent, on previous results which have been locally determined.

In the following paragraphs a progression from pure SIMD to complete MIMD is described which allows a variety of designs of increasing complexity to be developed. It is important to remember that, no matter how much independence each element in an assembly is allowed, some degree of global control will remain. In the following it is assumed that an appropriate global control is provided and that, usually, selection of the locally autonomous aspects can be either global or local as required. The available levels of local autonomy are as follows.

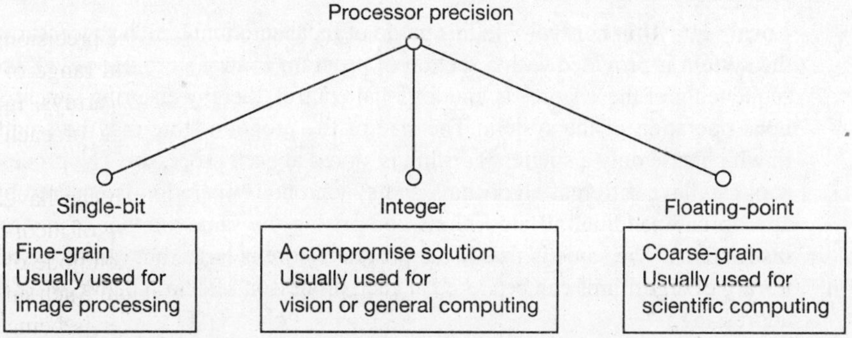

Figure 11.6 The design space for processor complexity.

No local control In order to develop a progression of increasingly autonomous processors, a starting-point should first be defined. Although it ought to be rather easy to propose a processor which embodies no local autonomy, it is, in fact, more difficult than might have been supposed. One example is that of a single-function systolic array, such as those described in Chapter 13. Not only is no local autonomy permitted, but the global function cannot be changed.

Local activity control Many SIMD systems embody very simple local autonomy, namely the ability to locally determine whether or not each processor in the array is active. This can be easily achieved by a variety of means and leads to substantial improvements in performance.

Local data control Processors which embody this type of autonomy allow the source and destination of the data used by a globally determined process to be locally selected. This is usually achieved by calculating a local address (or address offset) for the local data memory. The processor function is under global control.

Local connectivity control Arrays embodying this arrangement, which permits some local variation in the inter-processor connection pattern, fall into two categories. There are those in which the interconnection network itself is intrinsically reconfigurable (for example, arrays in which elements are connected by means of a crossbar switch), and there are those in which the interconnection network is fixed (such as a mesh) but in which the data paths within each processing element can be locally modified to change the effective interconnection pattern.

Local function control The processing elements in a system can be regarded as consisting of two sections, one part concerned with movement of data around the processor, the other part executing some function upon that data. The function generator may be singular (a single-bit ALU) or multiple (ALU, barrel-shifter and multiplier). In either case this stage of local autonomy allows each processor to select which function is to be performed, data movement being under global control. This can be achieved either by storing a previous result and using that to control the function, or by local addressing of a lookup table of functions.

Local algorithm control In this mode of local autonomy, each processor in the system is provided with a section of program control store. However, the sequencing of these stores is under global control, thereby ensuring synchronous operation of the system. The size of the program store may be small, in which case only a single algorithm is stored at each processor. The processors can have different algorithms and synchronous operation is ensured by appropriate padding, all algorithms comprising the same number of microinstructions. The same is true if the program store is large, but in this case a library of algorithms can be stored at each processor, selection being by local addressing.

Local sequencing control Each processor in this type of system not only has local selection of algorithm, but is also able to sequence its own program

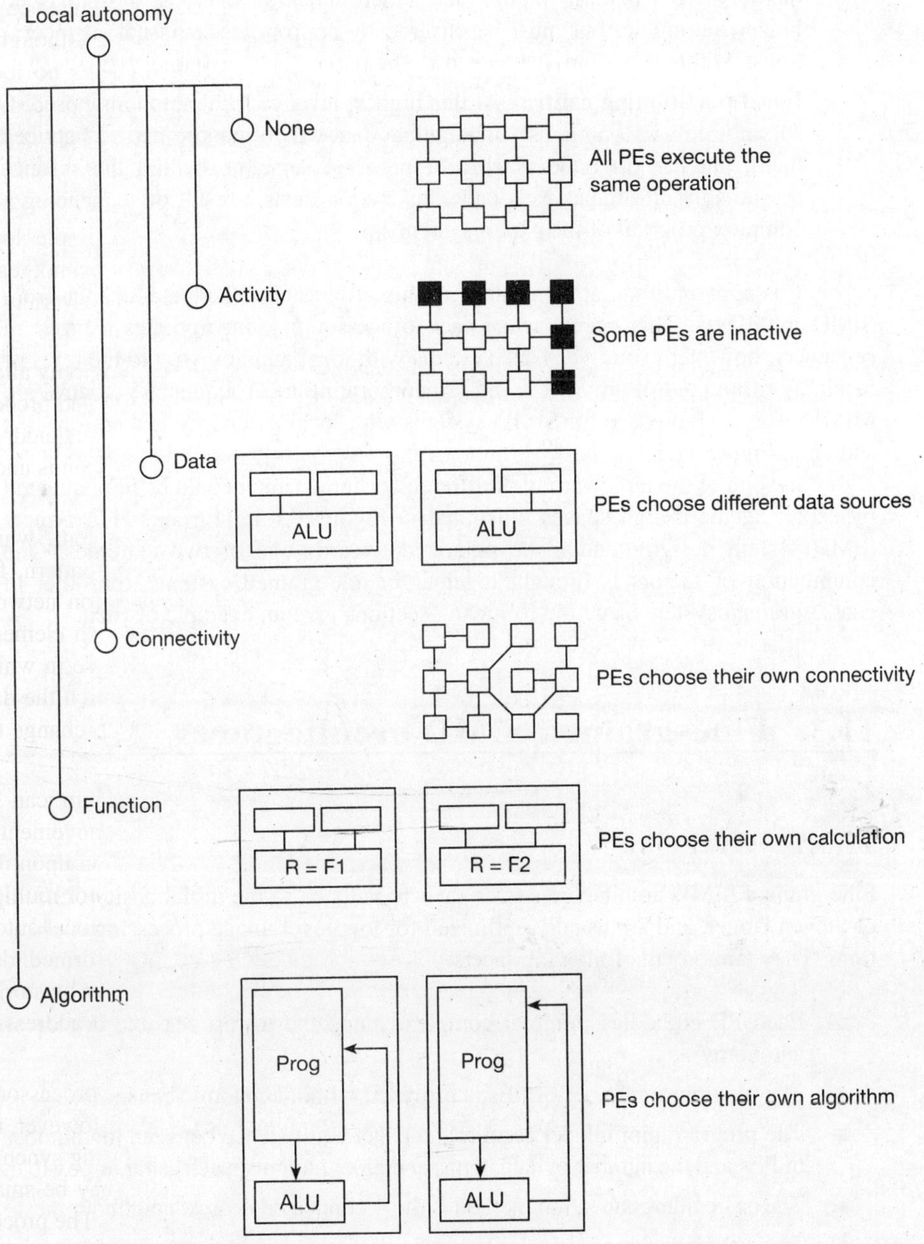

Figure 11.7 The design space for local autonomy.

memory. This in turn implies that synchronization over the system is no longer automatic, but must be ensured by appropriate handshaking operations. At this level, only data needs to be passed between processors.

Local partitioning control At this highest level of local autonomy, processors not only autonomously manipulate data which may be passed between them, but can alter the placing of program segments within the system, presumably on the basis of load equalization or as a result of sequencing a complex program of the expert system sort.

It is apparent that, at some stage in this progression, there is a change from SIMD to MIMD. This occurs when each processor first incorporates a program sequencer, however primitive. Thus systems with local autonomy up to the level of local algorithm control are SIMD, those incorporating local sequencing control are MIMD. The design space for SIMD systems with local autonomy is therefore that shown in Figure 11.7.

In spite of the large variety of different systems which could be implemented by exploring the design spaces illustrated in Figures 11.5, 11.6 and 11.7, typical SIMD system designs tend to be polarized towards one of two extremes. One combination of factors is brought together in fine-grained systems, the other in coarse-grained systems, and the following sections give an example of each.

11.3 Fine-grained SIMD architectures

11.3.1 Overview

Fine-grained SIMD architectures trace their roots back to the initial design scheme of Steven Unger, and are usually optimized for low-level image processing applications. They embody the following facets:

- Each PE embodies minimal complexity and the lowest feasible degree of autonomy.
- The maximum number of PEs is provided within economic constraints.
- The programming model assumes an exact equivalence between the number of PEs and the number of data items, and hides any mismatch as far as possible.
- The basic interconnection method is the 4-connected nearest neighbour mesh.
- The usual programming language is a simple extension of a sequential language with parallel-data additions.

Although this purity of concept is seldom completely maintained in practice, a number of systems come close. They include CLIP4, the DAP, the MPP (all first-generation systems), the CM1 and the MasPar1 amongst later embodiments. Where deviations from the classical model occur, they fall into the following categories:

- Processing element complexity is increased, either so as to operate on multi-bit numbers directly or by the addition of dedicated arithmetic units.
- Enhanced connectivity arrangements are superimposed over the standard mesh. Such arrangements include hypercubes and crossbar switches.

One of the most important architectural developments which has occurred in this class of system over time is the incorporation of ever-increasing amounts of local memory. This reflects the experience of all users that insufficient memory can have a catastrophic effect on performance, outweighing, in the worst cases, the advantages of a parallel configuration.

Perhaps the most modern design which retained the simplicity of the fine-grained approach in classical fashion was the MPP system, and this is examined in detail in the next section.

11.3.2 An example – the Massively Parallel Processor

MPP is not the most recent example of a fine-grained SIMD system, but its design does illustrate the principles of this group in the clearest possible fashion. The overall system design is illustrated in Figure 11.8, in which the following factors are important.

There is a square array of 128 × 128 active processing elements. The square array was chosen to match the configuration of the anticipated data sets on which the

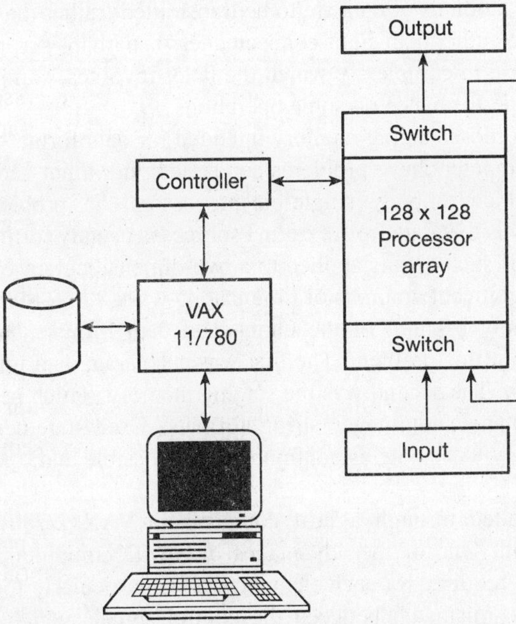

Figure 11.8 The MPP system.

system was intended to work. The MPP was constructed for (and used by) NASA, with the obvious intention of processing mainly image data. The size of the array was simply the biggest that could be achieved at the time, given the constraints of then current technology and the intended processor design (see below). It resulted in a system constructed from 88 array cards, each of which supported 24 processor chips (192 processors) together with their associated local memory.

The array incorporates four additional columns of spare (inactive) processing elements to provide some fault-tolerance. One of the major system design considerations in highly parallel systems such as MPP is how to handle the unavoidable device failures. The number of these is inevitably increased by the use of custom integrated circuits, in which economic constraints lead to poor characterization. The problem is compounded in a data-parallel mesh-connected array, since failure at some point of the array disrupts the very data structures on which efficient computations are predicated. The MPP deals with this problem by allowing a column of processors which contains one faulty element to be switched out of use, while one of the four spare columns is added to the edge of the array to maintain its size and shape. Naturally, if a fault occurs during computation, the sequence of instructions following the last dump to external memory must be repeated after replacement of the fault-containing column.

The processing elements are connected by a two-dimensional near-neighbour mesh. This solution offers a number of significant advantages over possible alternatives, including engineering convenience, easy maintenance of data structures during shifting, high bandwidth and a close conceptual match to the formulation of many image processing calculations. The main drawback of the system is the slow transmission of data between distant processors in the array. However, this is only manifest if relatively small amounts of data are to be transmitted (rather than whole images). The choice of four- rather than eight-connectedness is perhaps surprising in view of the minimal increase in complexity which the latter involves, compared to a twofold improvement in performance on some operations.

There is a special-purpose staging memory intended for data format conversion. All highly parallel computers have problems concerned with input and output of data, and in those which embody single-bit processors the problems are compounded. The difficulty is that data from external sources is usually formatted as a single string of integers. If such data is applied to a two-dimensional array in any straightforward fashion, significant amounts of time can be wasted before effective processing can begin, simply because of the unmatched data format. The MPP incorporated two solutions to this problem. The first was a separate data input/output register described below. The second was the staging memory, which permitted conversions between bit-plane and integer string formats. Used together, these permitted the processor array to operate as continuously as possible and, therefore, with maximum efficiency.

The array is controlled through a host computer (a VAX12/780) and a dedicated array control unit. One of the advantages of SIMD computers is that program sequencers are not required for each element. This is particularly fortunate, since there is an inevitable mismatch between the control signals which can be derived from the output interface of a typical serial computer (always needed to provide the complex but necessary higher-level software structures at reasonable cost) and those needed by the unusual structure of an SIMD array. In common with other contemporary systems, the MPP solved this problem with a dedicated, hard wired local controller. Microcoded controllers did not become commonplace until after the MPP was constructed.

The programming language is either parallel Fortran or parallel Pascal. The MPP software engineers adopted the practice, common at the time and still the most popular approach, of simply adding the data type *data-array* to those of a standard language, and providing a pre-processor to detect instances of the added data type and call specialized subroutines to execute the relevant array operations by directing appropriate control words to the relevant interface. This approach has the great benefit of providing a familiar programming environment for application programmers, although, inevitably, much work is demanded of systems programmers to provide the environment.

Many of the system design aspects considered above can have a significant effect on overall performance (particularly the total number of processing elements). It is probably true, however, that the most crucial aspect of the design is the configuration of the processing element itself, shown in Figure 11.9. Significant aspects of the design include the following:

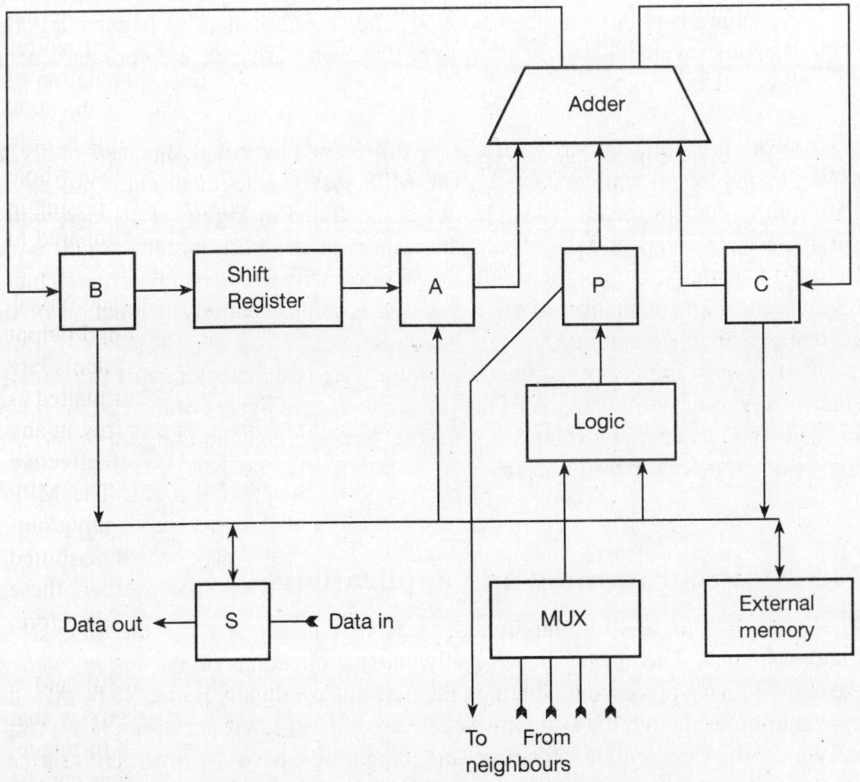

Figure 11.9 The MPP processing element.

- All data paths, registers and functional units are one-bit. This permits a minimal implementation and, therefore, the maximum number of elements in a given integration.
- There are separate adder, barrel shifter and Boolean logic function generator units, all of which can operate in parallel. This permits faster execution of some operations.
- Inputs from neighbours are multiplexed into the Boolean logic unit; there is a single output which is distributed to all neighbours. This is the minimal requirement for neighbourhood connections – some contemporary systems allowed a logical function of the complete neighbourhood to be generated in a single cycle.
- A dedicated register bit (the S register) is linked to the equivalent elements of other processors to form a data input/output shift register which can operate independently of the other elements of the processor, thereby permitting overlapped calculation and data transfer.
- Local memory is provided by a separate device. This has at least two important advantages over the alternative of integrating the memory on the processor chip. The first is that advantage can be taken of the enormous commercial investment in memory design to permit large amounts of fast, reliable memory to be incorporated. The second is that, as larger memories become available and/or desirable, they can easily be incorporated in the system.

This last point is partly a facet of processor element design and partly an aspect of processor implementation. The MPP system integrated eight processors onto a fully custom circuit whose layout is illustrated in Figure 11.10, and whose parameters are listed in Table 11.2. This aspect of the MPP system design is the easiest to quantify but, perhaps, the least informative in general terms. This is because the implementation of such systems is almost entirely a function of the currently available technology.

The most important parameter of Table 11.2 is the clock rate of the circuits, since this permits normalization of the raw performance figures of the system (given in Table 11.3) and thereby comparison of its effective architectural performance with that of other, more modern systems.

11.3.3 Programming and applications

The MPP system was commissioned by NASA principally for the analysis of Landsat images. This meant that, initially, most applications on the system were in the area of image processing, although the machine eventually proved to be of wider applicability. Although the system was delivered in 1983, a user, Strong (1991), still talked of the 'tremendous increase in computing speed … over conventional machines' several years after its installation. At the same time, the applications studies listed below were singled out.

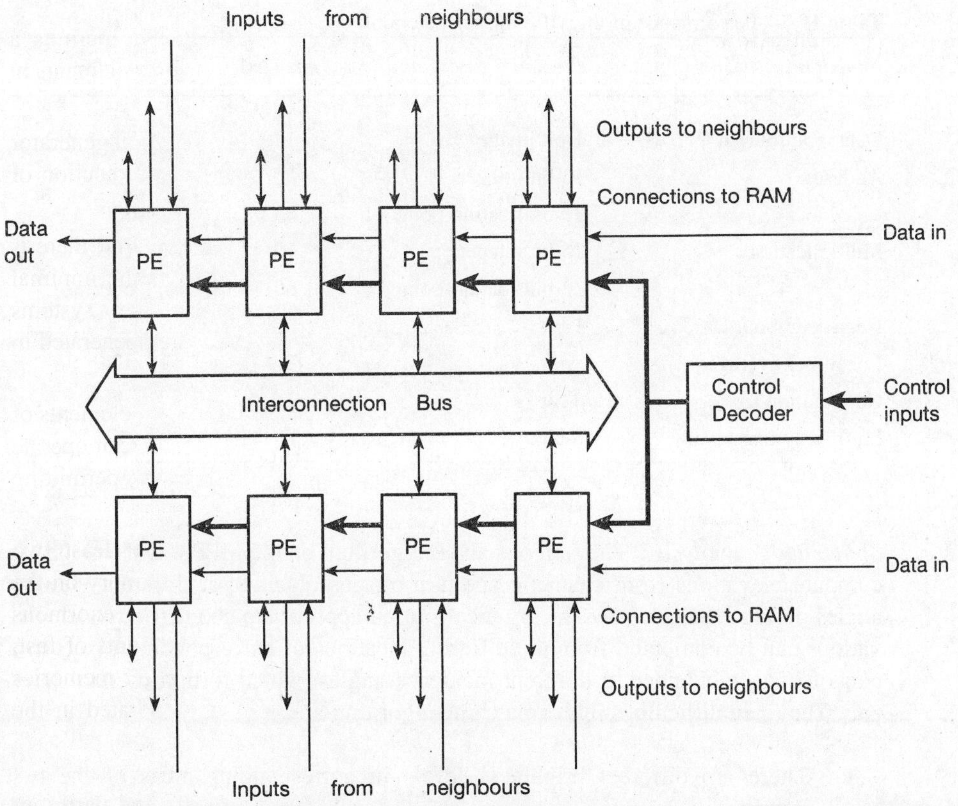

Figure 11.10 The MPP integrated circuit.

Table 11.2 Parameters of the MPP integrated circuit.

Parameter	*Value*	*Unit*
Number of processors	8	
Number of transistors	8000	
Clock rate	10	MHz
Technology	CMOS	
Power dissipation	500	mW
Package size	52	pins

Table 11.3 Performance of the MPP integrated circuit.

Function	*Precision*	*Time (μs)*	*No. of clocks*
Data input/output	1-bit image	0.1	1
Addition	16-bit integer	2.5	25
	32-bit floating-point	33	330
Multiplication	16-bit integer	10	100
	32-bit floating-point	60	600
Near-neighbour	1-bit	1.5	15
Local 3×3 average	8-bit	12.4	124
Convolution (3x3)	8-bit	9.5	95
Shift array one pixel	8-bit	1.7	17

Stereo image analysis The stereo analysis algorithm on the MPP was developed to compute elevations from synthetic aperture images obtained at different viewing angles during a Shuttle mission. By means of an appropriate geometric model, elevations can be computed from the differing locations of corresponding pixels in a pair of images obtained at different incidence angles, which form a pseudo stereo pair. The main difficulties in the matching algorithm are:

- There are different brightness levels in corresponding areas of the two images.
- Images have areas of low contrast and high noise.
- There are local distortions which differ from image to image.

The first two can be overcome by the use of normalized correlation functions (a standard image processing technique) but the third occurs because of the different viewing angles. The MPP algorithm operates as follows.

For each pixel in one of the images (the reference image) a local neighbourhood area is defined. This is correlated with the similar area surrounding each of the candidate match pixels in the second image. The measure applied is the normalized mean and variance cross correlation function. The candidate yielding the highest correlation is considered to be the best match, and the locations of the pixels in the two images are compared to produce the disparity value at that point of the reference image.

The algorithm is iterative. It begins at low resolution, that is, with large areas of correlation around each of a few pixels. When the first pass is complete, the test image is geometrically warped according to the disparity map. The process is then repeated with a higher resolution (usually reducing the correlation area, and increasing the number of computed matches, by a factor of two), a new disparity map is calculated and a new warping applied, and so on. The procedure is continued either for a predetermined number of passes or until some quality criterion is exceeded.

The advantage of this iterative algorithm, and the eventual high-density disparity map which it yields, is the utilization of redundancy to overcome the inevitable matching errors which occur in such a process. This procedure is assisted by applying a continuity criterion to the eventual elevation map, utilizing local averaging and rejection of disparity discontinuities.

Chaos experiments One of the principal uses of powerful computers is in obtaining numerical solutions to mathematical problems in which an analytical solution is difficult or impossible to obtain. Chaotic behaviour is one such area in which the structure of fine-grain SIMD systems is particularly well suited to the desired methods of solution. This particular work concerns a two-dimensional application of the following pair of so-called logistic equations:

$$F(x) = r[x(1-x)] \quad 0<x<1 \qquad (11.1)$$
$$x = F(x)$$

For certain values of r, the value of $F(x)$ converges to the same value (during iteration of the equations) no matter what its original value. This behaviour may be of interest to biological scientists since it mimics the creation of ordered complex entities from random starting conditions.

The experiments carried out on MPP, which evaluated $F(x)$ at each point of a two-dimensional matrix, explore the effects of different amounts of coupling between the neighbours in the matrix. The original expression for $F(x)$ is modified to include a coupling coefficient c:

$$F(x) = r[x(1-x)]+c \quad 0<x<1 \qquad (11.2)$$

The array of values of c is calculated by:

$$c_{i,j} = CP(x_{av}-x_{i,j}) \quad 0<CP<1 \qquad (11.3)$$

where the average value of x is taken over the four nearest neighbours in the matrix. To avoid undesirable edge effects, MPP is connected as a torus for these experiments.

In one experiment, the elements of a 512×512 array are initialized with a set of random variables. After a thousand iterations of the value of $F(x)$, the results are displayed as a grey-level image. Figure 11.11, reproduced with kind permission from Strong (1991), shows how the images of $F(x)$ vary for some selected values of c and r. The images to the lower left are ordered (less variation of $F(x)$ *over the image*), those to the upper right are chaotic (more variation of $F(x)$).

Image segmentation The segmentation of images into coherent areas of significance is a key step in most image and signal processing applications. Segmented areas may be defined by a number of criteria including shape, texture, grey-level spectrum, and so on. A common segmentation technique calculates the relevant criterion for every (predefined) small area of an image, then seeks to iteratively merge

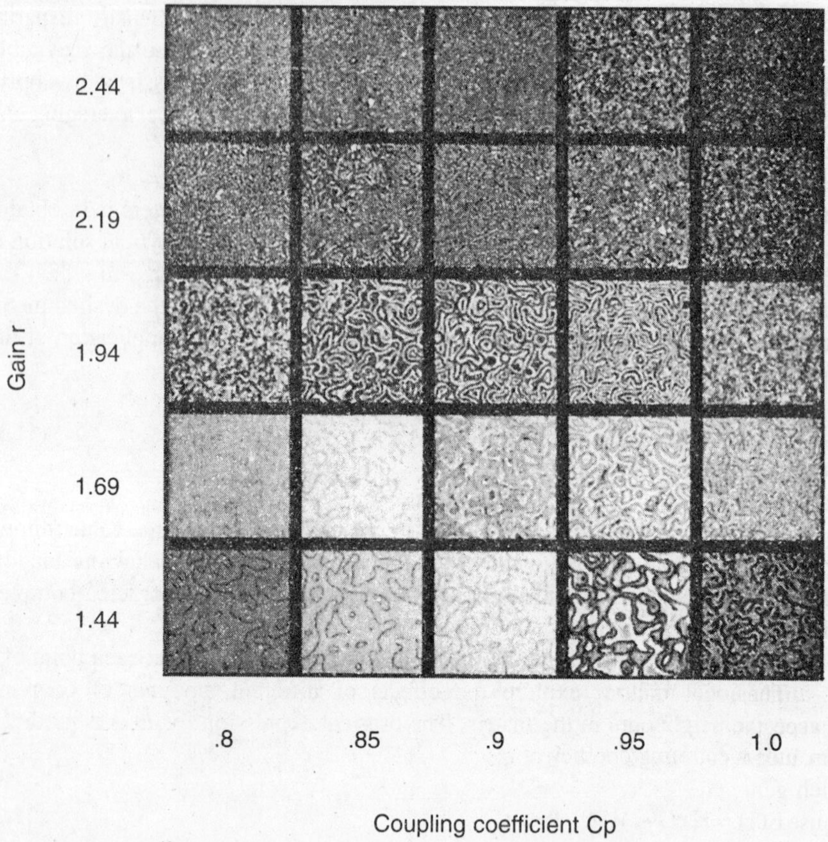

Figure 11.11 The boundary between chaotic and ordered behaviour. © 1991 IEEE

(join) those adjacent areas for which the difference in the criterion values is either a minimum for the image, or is below a predetermined threshold. In some cases, the parallelism of the algorithm is improved by simultaneously calculating a best merge within several regions of the image.

In either case, the main parallel operations required by the algorithm are the calculation of the similarity (or dissimilarity) criterion for each region pair, and the determination of the best value of the criterion over a region. Both of these operations are characterized by the large amount of information which must flow between regions, and therefore between the elements of an SIMD array.

In the MPP algorithm, the criterion used is a measure of the difference between the average brightness values of the two candidate merging regions and the average brightness of the putative merged region. If the two candidate regions i and j have corresponding average brightness value D and numbers of pixels n, and if the total number of pixels in the image is N, then the difference criterion is given by:

$$Difference = [n_i(D_i - D_{ij})^2 + n_j(D_j - D_{ij})^2]/(N-1) \quad (11.4)$$
$$D_{ij} = (n_iD_i + n_jD_j)/(n_i + n_j)$$

These equations imply that the numbers of pixels in a region, and the average grey value in the region must first be calculated and then broadcast to each pixel in the region. This is achieved by calculating a tree of paths by means of which values can be communicated within each region. This pathtree, which includes information on the distance of each pixel from the chosen accumulation pixel, is then used to parallelize the calculations in such a way as to complete the process in a time determined by the diameter of the pixel region rather than the number of pixels it contains. The computation load of the algorithm is reduced by only considering disparities between pixels at the borders of candidate merging regions, since these are the only areas where disparity is greater than zero. Although, in an SIMD architecture, the amount of *calculation* is not thereby reduced, the amount of data to be *communicated* is significantly reduced, and this is an important factor in this type of algorithm.

The results of the region merging algorithm applied to a 128 × 128 pixel segment of a Landsat image are shown in Figure 11.12. Part (a) shows the original image, part (b) the segmentation into 33 regions achieved after 217 iterations, and part (c) the 20-region segmentation achieved after a further 13 iterations (also reproduced by kind permission from Strong (1991)).

These three examples of applications carried out on the MPP illustrate different aspects of the performance of fine-grain SIMD architectures. However, each of them utilizes iteration, and it is frequently this aspect of data-parallel computing which generates the extremely high computational demands which, in turn, justify the use of highly parallel computers. This is often a much more important factor than the apparently simple operations which form each cycle of any given process.

The level of these applications studies reflects the state of algorithmic development at the time when they were carried out but, more significantly, the areas share the common properties of highly parallel data sets and simple, repetitive computations.

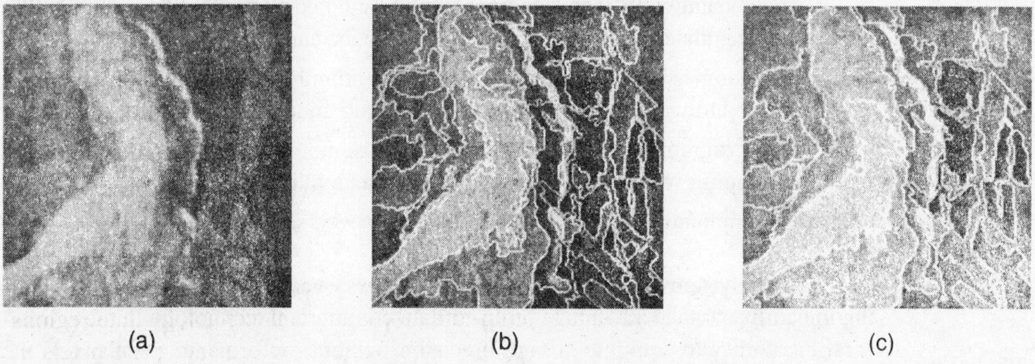

Figure 11.12 Iterative segmentation of a Landsat image. © 1991 IEEE

11.4 Coarse-grained SIMD architectures

It is possible to argue that, because of the technical difficulties in fulfilling completely the fine-grained SIMD ideal of one processor per data element, and the consequent necessity for some method of handling the inevitable data mapping, it is better to begin with the coarse-grained approach and therefore develop a more coherent architecture. This view is currently adopted by a number of manufacturers of parallel computers, including nCUBE and Thinking Machines Inc.

11.4.1 Overview

Coarse-grained data-parallel architectures are often developed by those more familiar with the mainstream of computer design than the application-specific architecture field. They are sometimes the result of MIMD programmes which have discovered the complexities of this approach and seek to mitigate them. The consequences of these roots are systems which can employ a number of different paradigms including MIMD, multiple-SIMD and what is often called single program multiple data (SPMD) in which each processor executes its own program, but all the programs are the same, and so remain in lock-step. As can be seen from the examples given below, such systems are very frequently used in this data-parallel mode, and it is therefore reasonable to include them within the SIMD paradigm. Naturally, when they are used in a different mode, their operation has to be analysed in a different way. Coarse-grained SIMD systems of this type embody the following concepts:

- Each PE is of high complexity, comparable to that of a typical microprocessor.
- The PE is usually constructed from commercial devices rather than incorporating a custom circuit.
- There is a (relatively) small number of PEs, on the order of a few hundreds or thousands.
- Every PE is provided with ample local memory.
- The interconnection method is likely to be one of lower diameter but also lower bandwidth than the simple two-dimensional mesh. Networks such as the tree, the crossbar switch and the hypercube can be utilized.
- Provision is often made for prodigious amounts of relatively high-speed, high-bandwidth backup storage, often using an array of hard disks.
- The programming model assumes that some form of data mapping and remapping will be necessary, whatever the application.
- The application field is likely to be high-speed scientific computing.

Such systems offer a number of advantages over fine-grained SIMD, including the ability to take advantage of up-to-date commercial technology in the processors, the ability to compute at high precision without performance penalty and the easier mapping to a variety of different data types which the lower number of processors and enhanced connectivity allows. The software required for such systems offers at the same time an advantage and a disadvantage. The advantage lies in its closer similarity to normal programming; the disadvantage lies in the less natural programming for some applications.

Coarse-grained systems also offer greater variety in their designs, because each component of the design is less constrained than in a fine-grained system. The example given below is, therefore, less specifically representative of its class than was the MPP machine considered earlier.

11.4.2 An example – the CM5

The Connection Machine family marketed by Thinking Machines Inc. has been one of the most commercially successful examples of niche marketing in the computing field in recent years (one other which springs to mind is the CRAY family). Although the first of the family, CM1, was fine-grained in concept, the latest, CM5, is definitely coarse-grained. The first factor in its design is the processing element, illustrated in Figure 11.13. The important components of the design include:

- internal 64-bit organization;
- a 40MHz SPARC microprocessor;
- separate data and control network interfaces;
- up to four floating-point vector processors with separate data paths to memory;
- 32 Mbytes of memory.

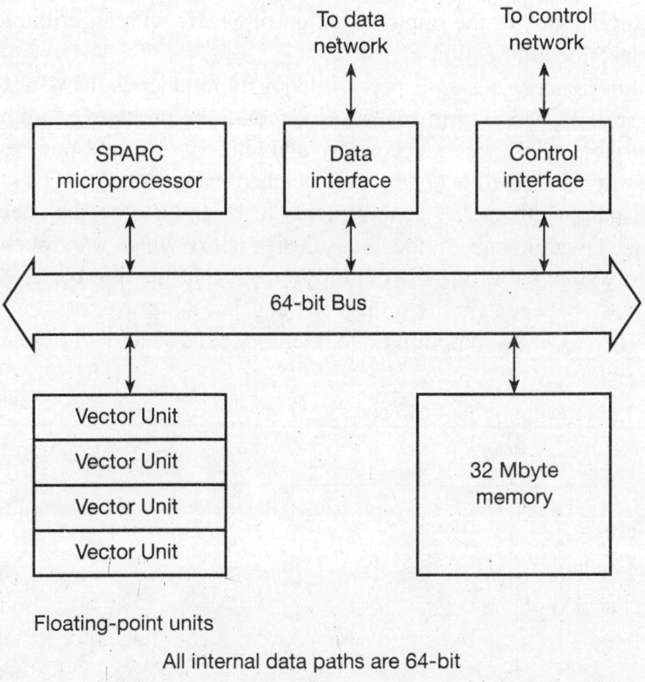

Figure 11.13 The CM5 processing element.

Taken together, these components give a peak double-precision floating-point rate of 128 MFLOPS and a memory bandwidth of 512 Mbyte/sec. Achieved performance rates for some specific operations are given in Table 11.4.

There are three aspects to the system design which are of major importance. The first is the data interconnection network, shown in Figure 11.14, which is designated by the designers a *fat tree* network. It is based upon the quadtree described in Chapter 10, augmented to reduce the likelihood of blocking within the network. Thus, at the lowest level, within what is designated an *interior node* of four processors, there are at least two independent direct routes between any pair of processors. Utilizing the next level of tree, there are at least four partly independent routes between a pair of processors. This increase in the number of potential routes is maintained for increasing numbers of processors by utilizing higher levels of the tree structure. Although this structure provides a potentially much higher bandwidth that the ordinary quadtree, like any complex system, achieving the highest performance depends critically on effective management of the resource.

The second component of system design which is of major importance is the method of control of the processing elements. Since each of these incorporates a complete microprocessor, the system can be used in fully asynchronous MIMD mode. Similarly, if all processors execute the same program, the system can operate in the SPMD mode. In fact, the designers suggest that an intermediate method is possible, in which processing elements act independently for part of the time, but are frequently resynchronized globally. This method is claimed to offer a better compromise than either extreme, particularly since the frequency of global resynchronization can be adjusted between *once every instruction* and *never*. This technique corresponds to the implementation of SIMD with algorithmic processor autonomy, described in Section 11.2.4.

The final system design aspect of major importance is the data I/O method. The design of the CM5 system seeks to overcome the problem of improving (and therefore variable) disk access speeds by allowing any desired number of system nodes to be allocated as disk nodes with attached backup storage. This permits the amount and bandwidth of I/O arrangements to be tailored to the specific system requirements. Overall, one of the main design aims which was pursued for the CM5 system was scalability. This not only means that the number of nodes in the system can vary between (in the limits) one and 16 384 processors, but that system parameters such as peak computing rate, memory bandwidth and I/O bandwidth all

Table 11.4 Performance of the CM5 node.

Function	*Performance (MFLOPS)*
Matrix multiply	64
Matrix-vector multiply	100
Linpack benchmark	50
8k-point FFT	90
Peak rate	128

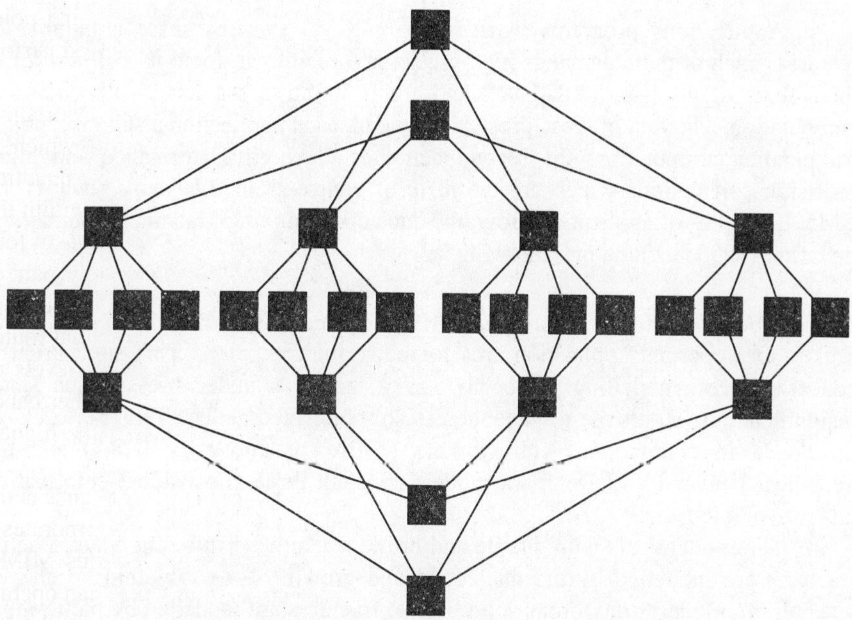

Figure 11.14 The CM5 fat tree connectivity structure.

automatically increase in proportion to the number of processing elements. This is demonstrated in Table 11.5.

11.4.3 Programming and applications

Because of the large investment involved in purchasing a substantial CM5 machine, it is usually viewed as a multi-user system, in which resources (that is, partial systems), once allocated, are fully protected and are independent. This is ensured by a UNIX-based time-sharing operating system and priority-based job queuing. Under this operating system, data-parallel versions of C and Fortran are provided, together with a variety of packages for data visualization and scientific computation.

Table 11.5 CM5 system parameters.

Number of processors	*32*	*1024*	*16 384*
Number of data paths	128	4096	65 536
Peak speed (MFLOPS)	4	128	2 048
Memory (Gbyte)	1	32	512
Memory bandwidth (Gbyte/s)	16	512	8 192
I/O bandwidth (Gbyte/s)	0.32	10	160
Synchronization time (μs)	1.5	3.0	4.0

Applications programs carried out on CM5 systems share a number of features. Each of them demands high-precision three-dimensional modelling. All of them share highly parallel data sets and highly iterative, mathematically intensive computation. The first of these properties renders each application a suitable subject for parallel computation, the second demands the high performance and high-precision calculations which are the *forte* of coarse-grained systems such as the CM5. Examples of application programs quoted in Thinking Machines' commercial literature (1993) include the following.

Irregular finite-element structural analysis The analysis of the behaviour of materials is an important application area for powerful computers. This application is concerned with modelling the behaviour of materials under stress, when small insignificant cracks merge to generate catastrophic fracture. The TeraFrac package developed in conjunction with workers at Brown University (USA) and the Technical University of Denmark models transient three-dimensional deformation under dynamic loads.

The model deals with ductile and brittle fractures in different ways. Ductile fractures are modelled by the nucleation and growth of voids within an elastic-viscoplastic model for a porous solid. Brittle fractures are modelled by partitioning the material into cleavage grains and calculating the volume average of stress over the grain. When this exceeds some threshold value, fracture is assumed to occur. This reflects the actual failure mode of metals at the grain level.

Elements and grains within the model are allocated to processors on the CM5 by a standard library function. Other library functions are used to accumulate and distribute data between the processors, and hence between the appropriate elements of the model. Typical performance within this environment is 26 MFLOPS per node, which implies that the ductile fracture analysis of a $64 \times 64 \times 64$ element volume of material requires about 16 hours to execute on a 1024-node CM5.

Rarefied gas dynamics Modelling the dynamic behaviour of rarefied gases is important for predicting the environment of space vehicles on re-entry. Normal fluid behaviour is modelled by the Navier–Stokes equations, but these are not valid for rarefied gasses. For this environment it is necessary to model the statistical behaviour of aggregates of individual particles by means of the Boltzmann equation. This equation has proved difficult to solve either analytically or computationally, the best results having been achieved by the computationally expensive Monte Carlo methods.

More recent techniques exploit three factors which are well matched to the characteristics of coarse-grain machines such as the CM5:

- Many of the computations involved in calculation of the collision integral are independent, so they can be executed effectively on the separate nodes of a parallel machine.
- Arithmetic operations are comparatively cheap on a parallel machine.
- The data locality inherent in the nature of the problem can be effectively exploited in a parallel machine with efficient communication.

The algorithm implemented on the CM5 for executing this application makes effective use of all these factors to model one-dimensional shock waves, gas flow in ducts, and gas flow around hypersonic bodies.

Molecular dynamics Application of the methods of molecular dynamics to the simulation of the interactions of thousands of particles has, in the past, been limited to unrealistically small systems which do not correctly predict the properties of condensed matter. Researchers at Los Alamos National Laboratory are running code on a CM5 which simulates solid state systems consisting of atoms.

The simulation models molecular space as a rectangular region with periodic boundary conditions. The code divides this space into elements which it assigns to CM5 nodes, seeking to organize the partitioning to minimize eventual interactions between nodes. This has permitted the effective modelling of the hypersonic impact of a projectile onto a block at the atomic level, correctly predicting the observed shock waves and material break-up at a sustained processing speed of 50 GFLOPS on a 1024-node system (Figure 11.15). The motions of the more than one million particles involved in this simulation are shown to be substantially determined by the lattice symmetries of the materials, rather than by the gross physical shapes of the solids.

Computational aerodynamics This work revolves around a three-dimensional finite element program whose code is both parallel and scalable. The goal of the program, which is within one or two orders of magnitude of success, is to perform a full Navier–Stokes analysis of a complete air-frame environment within a period of about ten hours. In its present state, the program has been used in the design of the European space shuttle, Hermes.

A typical application permits the computation of streamlines and local Mach number near to and on the surface of aircraft travelling at near-Mach speeds. This demands computations applied to a three-dimensional mesh of more than 100 000 tetrahedra. A typical performance of 12.2 GFLOPS is obtained from a 512-node machine running this program.

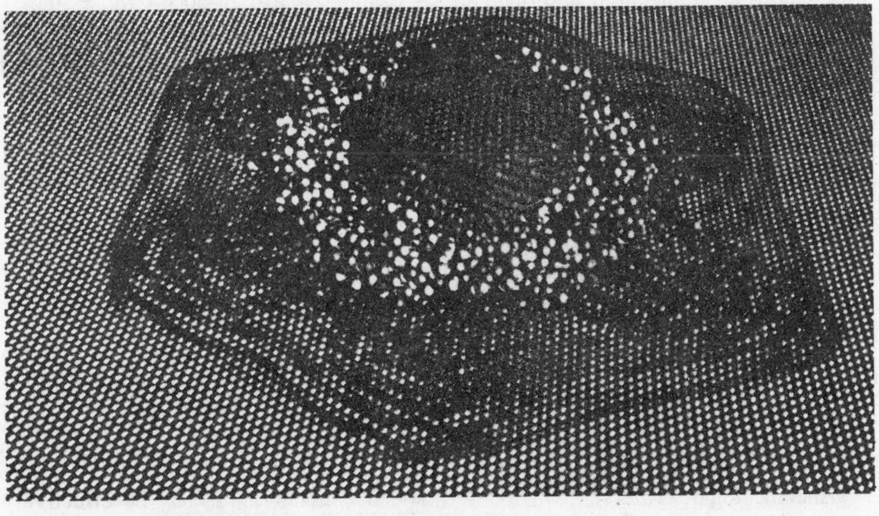

Figure 11.15 Modelling shock-waves in a collision process.

Quantum chromodynamics This theory, which describes how the most fundamental particles so far discovered (quarks and antiquarks) are bound together to form particles such as protons and neutrons, is the basic theory of the strong atomic force. The force is described as being transmitted by gluons (analogous to photons in electromagnetic theory), but the interactions between these gluons make the calculation of the situation more complex.

The problem can be partially solved by a lattice formulation of the theory, opening the possibility of using Monte Carlo simulation methods to study the situation. In this formulation, space-time is modelled as a four-dimensional grid over which the relevant states (of quarks and gluons) are distributed. Predictions of the behaviour of matter are obtained by solving the quark fields over the grid under various conditions, and two methods (the Wilson and Kogut–Susskind methods) are available for doing so.

The major problem in this work is the scale of the computations involved. There are two main reasons why it is desirable to work with the maximum size of grid (and hence the maximum possible number of computations). In the first place, the results of the lattice formulation are only strictly valid when the lattice spacing is reduced to (or at least towards) zero. Secondly, the larger the grid used, the less are the effects of boundary states. Since the kernel of the code used involves multiplying a complex 3×3 matrix-valued field by a complex 3-vector scalar field at each site on each iteration of the program, a system such as the CM5 machine is ideally suited for this application. However, computation of the proton mass (one possible result of this modelling) to 10 % accuracy would take up to a full year on a 1024-node system, so the most valuable results of this program are unlikely to be realized until further advances in computing power become available.

These examples are typical of applications on coarse-grained SIMD systems, most of which combine a high degree of data parallelism, structured data and a requirement for high-precision computation. This last makes it appropriate to measure the performance on various applications in terms of GFLOPS rates. Table 11.6 summarizes figures for the applications described above, running on a 1024-node CM5 system.

The differences between these figures (almost a factor of three) can be explained almost completely by differences in the effectiveness of mapping problem to computing structure, and by differences in the amounts of communication involved in the various programs.

Table 11.6 Application performance of a 1024-node CM5 system.

Application	*Performance (GFLOPS)*
Irregular finite-element structural analysis	26.0
Rarefied gas dynamics	61.0
Molecular dynamics	50.7
Computational aerodynamics	24.0
Quantum chromodynamics	42.0

12 Associative and Neural Architectures

Section 12.1 introduces the basic ideas underpinning associative and neural architectures. Section 12.2 describes how these ideas are translated into practice in associative processing, using the Associative String Processor as an example in Section 12.3, and Section 12.4 briefly discusses the ease of mapping applications onto an associative system. Section 12.5 is devoted to the comparatively new field of neural computers.

12.1 Introduction

The basic ideas which underlie these two approaches to parallel computing are very similar. They arise naturally out of one of the human methods of problem solving, illustrated in Figure 12.1.

The idea is that, given unknown subject matter, it is possible to decide what it is, and therefore what action to take about it, on the basis of its similarity (complete or partial) to known data. Thus, in the figure, an unknown animal is analysed in terms of the components of its anatomy, and the similarity of those to the relevant portions of other animals. By combining these items of partial information, the analyser can suggest that the unknown animal is probably a dinosaur. Each item of partial information is derived by determining the degree of similarity to corresponding elements of a range of known possibilities.

12.2 Associative processing

As far as associative computers are concerned, such operations are carried out in practice as follows. The incoming data may represent any entity or situation at all – an image, a language structure, a mathematical relationship – but, in each case,

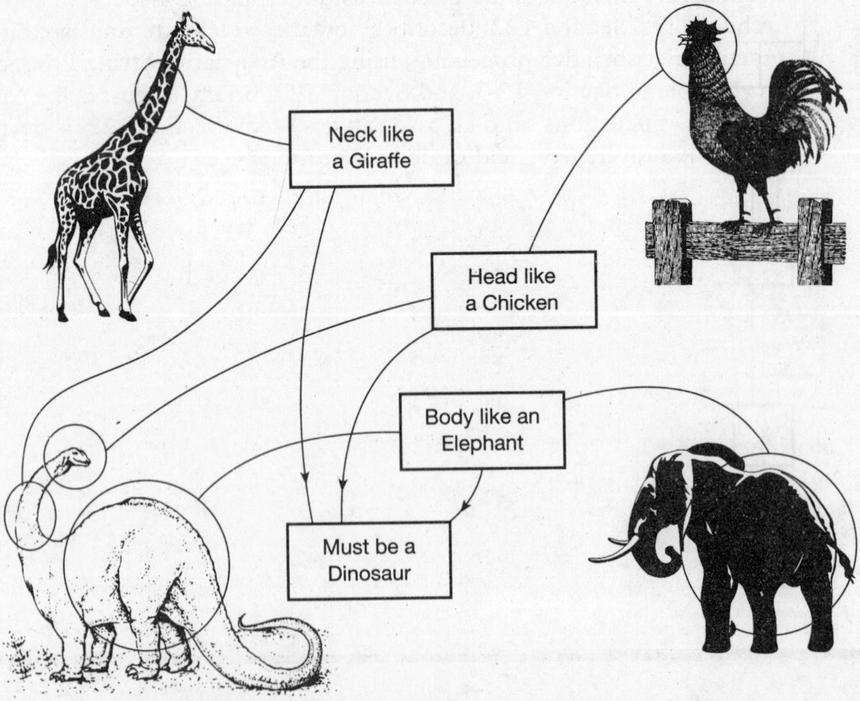

Figure 12.1 The idea of associative problem solving.

it will be encoded for the computer as a set of (ultimately) binary bits. In the data-parallel context considered here, these bits are handled as illustrated in Figure 12.2.

Each bit of data is compared (in parallel) with the relevant bit of a series of known data items. Every bit either matches or does not, and it would obviously be possible, for example, to sum the numbers of matches and mismatches and use the difference between these sums as a figure of merit for the match:

Figure of merit(*F*) = Σ Number of matches – Σ Number of mismatches

$$F = \sum_i M_i - \sum_i \overline{M}_i \qquad (12.1)$$

The higher the figure of merit, the more exact the match. However, this approach would usually be of insufficient subtlety since, in any real situation, some data bits will embody more significance than others (for example, it is usually true that the first letter of a word is of greatest significance in determining correctness of spelling). It is therefore usually necessary to assign some specific weight (*W*) to each of the matching bits, as shown in the figure. The final formula for the figure of merit therefore becomes:

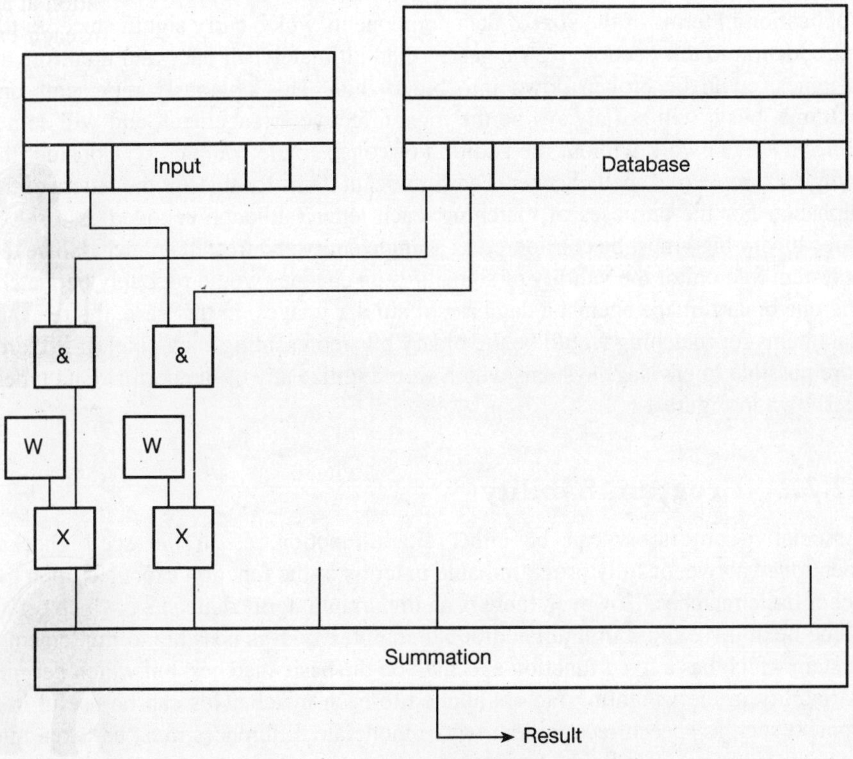

Figure 12.2 An implementation of associative processing.

$$F = \sum_i W_i M_i - \sum_i W_i \overline{M_i} \tag{12.2}$$

As with all the other data-parallel approaches, this concept is subject to a certain amount of flexibility when implemented, and both the design space and the position of any particular system within the design space are determined by the intended field of application. Although it is difficult to generalize from the few examples of this architecture which have so far been constructed, it seems that this factor holds true more forcefully for these architectures than for any other. This is because their most general field of application should be within general business computing, rather than the scientific computing area in which the other architectures covered here will function. This, in turn, implies that specific, fixed, solutions will be the norm, rather than reprogrammable systems. It will therefore be doubly important to correctly determine the required position within the design space. Fortunately, the alternatives are relatively few.

12.2.1 Data precision

One of the most important decisions to be made concerns the data precision used for the basic matching process. This depends crucially on a proper analysis of the application in terms of the size of data components which carry significance. In the introduction to this section, we suggested that, ultimately, all data, and therefore all matches, could be broken down into binary bits. This obviously represents one extreme, but it will not always be the most effective arrangement, and will sometimes not even work without the addition of considerable complexity. Consider the simple example of a spell checker. The significant items for this are the letters of the alphabet. For the purposes of matching, each letter (although encoded as a set of three binary bits) must be considered as a single entity and treated as such. However, a system to monitor the validity of signatures on cheques would probably be matching one binary image against a database of similar images. In this case, the relevant data items for matching would be the binary bits representing each pixel. It is therefore possible to envisage systems which would utilize any of the normal data types, as shown in Figure 12.3.

12.2.2 Programmability

Associative processors can be either single-function, as in the spell checker mentioned above, or fully programmable in terms of the function executed upon the set of basic matches. However, there is an important intermediate stage which offers some flexibility with minimum additional complexity. It is possible to implement a system which has a fixed function executed on the basic matches, but which permits variability in the weighting factors applied to each match. This can be useful in a context such as speech recognition, where moderate differences must be taken into account in terms of individual speech patterns, but where the overall function of word recognition is unvarying. The design space for programmability of associative processors is therefore that shown in Figure 12.4.

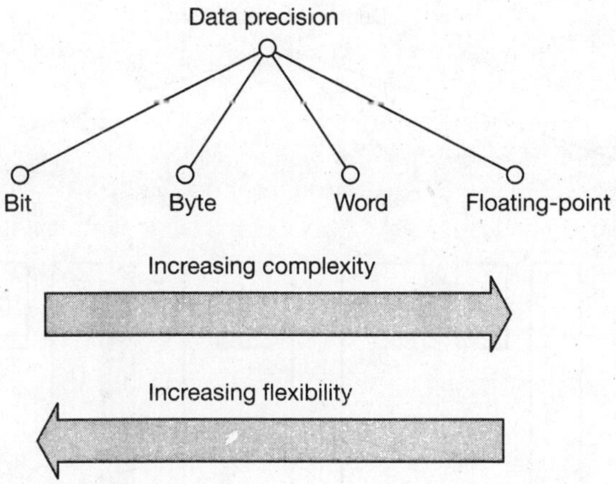

Figure 12.3 The design space for associative data precision.

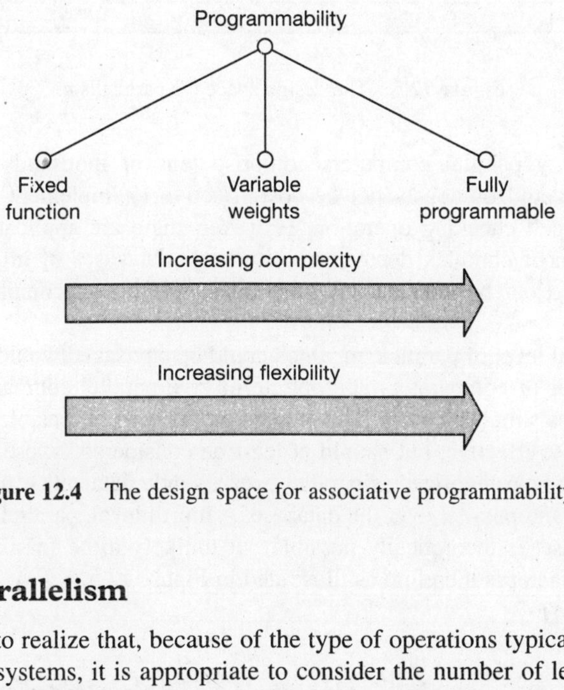

Figure 12.4 The design space for associative programmability.

12.2.3 Parallelism

It is important to realize that, because of the type of operations typically performed by associative systems, it is appropriate to consider the number of levels of parallelism as a design parameter. Consider again the example of the spell checker. At the simplest level, a parallel associative system would check all of the letters of each single word simultaneously. However, there are two further levels of parallelism in the application which could be exploited. Any realistic document whose spelling is being checked will consist of a large number of words. It would be possible to provide a large number of comparators (since each is a simple circuit) so that all words in the document could be checked against one dictionary item simultaneously. This would represent a huge, but not impossible, extension in the degree of parallelism,

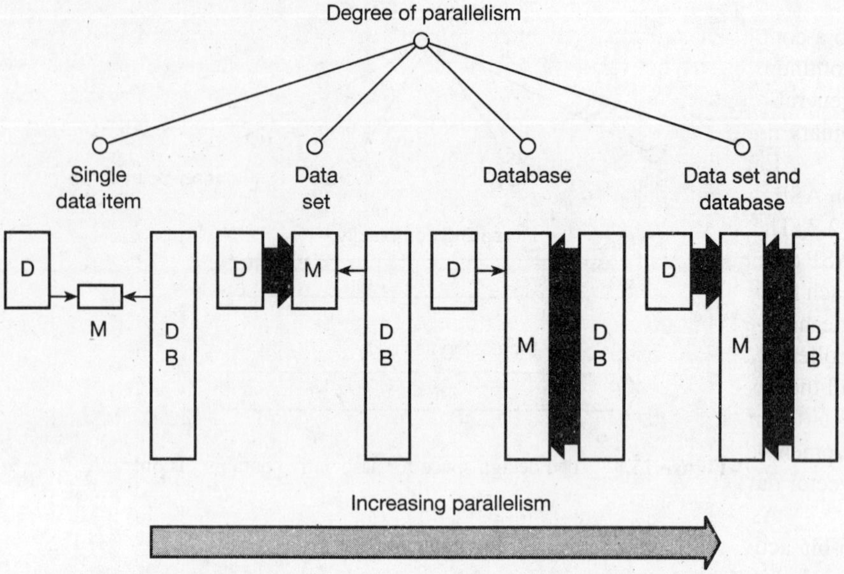

Figure 12.5 The design space for parallelism.

given that many parallel computers comprise tens of thousands of processing elements. (It would obviously not be cost-effective to implement such a system for a simple spell checking operation. However, there are applications involving the comparison of complex documents with large databases of information, such as those carried out by national tax authorities, where such complexity might be justified.)

The final level of parallelism which could be envisaged would be to incorporate the number of comparators appropriate to give parallel comparison of all the dictionary items simultaneously. This is most unlikely to be feasible, and even less likely to be cost-effective, but should at least be considered. These three levels of parallelism can be categorized as parallel over a single data entity, parallel over the data input set, and parallel over the database. A fourth level, parallel over both data set and database, is theoretically possible but unlikely to be feasible. The design space for this factor is therefore as illustrated in Figure 12.5.

12.3 An example – the Associative String Processor

The Brunel ASP is a massively parallel, fine-grain associative architecture, suitable for VLSI and WSI fabrication. It is currently being developed by Aspex Microsystems Ltd, UK, and is described by Jaloweicki (1995).

The fundamental building block of the systems is the ASP module. According to application requirements, an appropriate combination of ASP modules is attached to a control bus and data communications network shown in Figure 12.6. The data communications network is constructed so as to implement a great variety of general-purpose and application-specific topologies, including crossbar, mesh, binary n-cube and shuffle-exchange.

Each ASP module comprises three different components: an ASP substring, an ASP data interface and an ASP control interface, connected as shown in Figure 12.7. The same figure also indicates that the control interface can support a local ASP data buffer or an ASP control unit. System variants can be constructed whereby each control unit is an autonomous microcontroller, under the coordination of a single high-level control unit. Alternatively, the system may comprise no local controllers, where the control interface is a port to a global controller which will provide all the system control.

An ASP substring incorporates a string of identical associative processing elements (APEs), a reconfigurable inter-processor communications network and a vector data buffer for overlapped data input/output, as illustrated in Figure 12.8.

As shown in Figure 12.9, each APE incorporates a 64-bit data register and a 6-bit activity register, a 70-bit parallel comparator, a single-bit full adder, four single-bit registers (representing carry (C), matching and destination (M and D) and active (A) bits) and control logic for local processing and communication with other APEs. In operation, data items are distributed over the data registers. Each ASP substring performs a kind of set processing, in which a subset of active APEs may be programmed to perform scalar–vector and vector–vector operations. Active APEs (denoted by the A-register) are either directly activated by the match data and activity values broadcast from the controller, or are indirectly activated as a result of inter-APE communication initiated by some other matching APE. The match reply

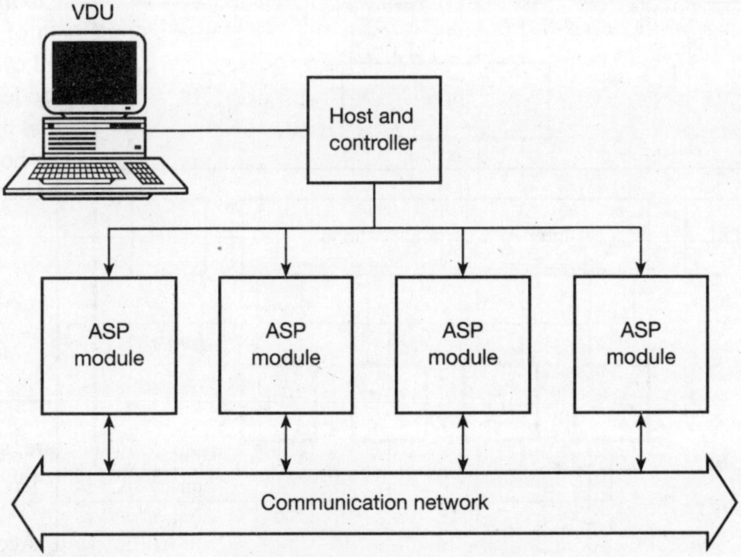

Figure 12.6 An ASP system.

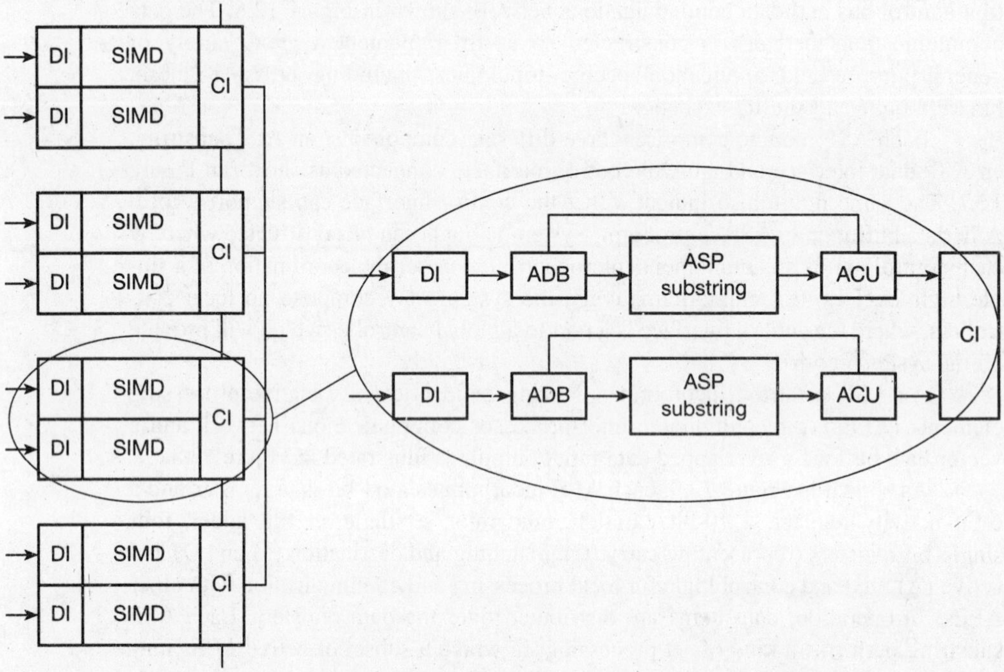

Figure 12.7 The composition of the ASP module.

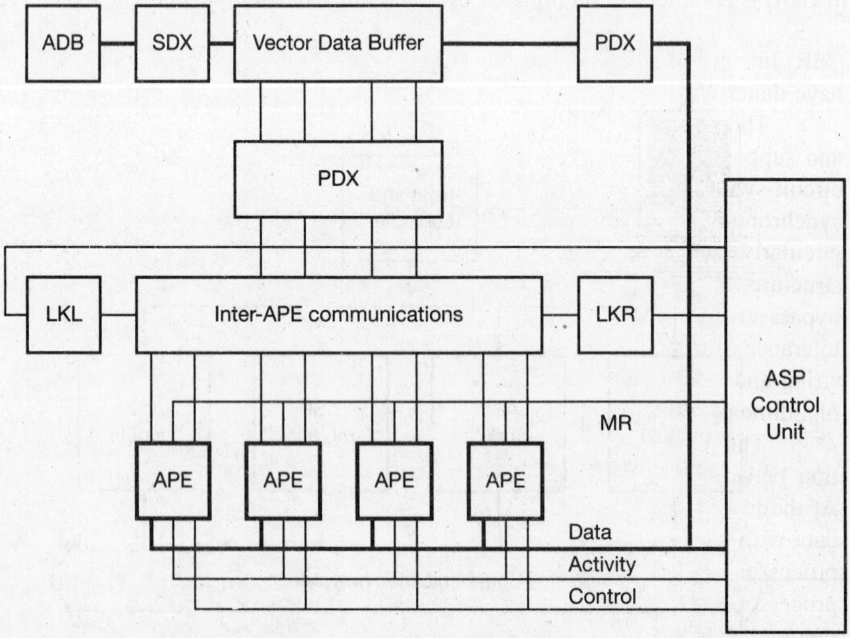

Figure 12.8 An ASP substring.

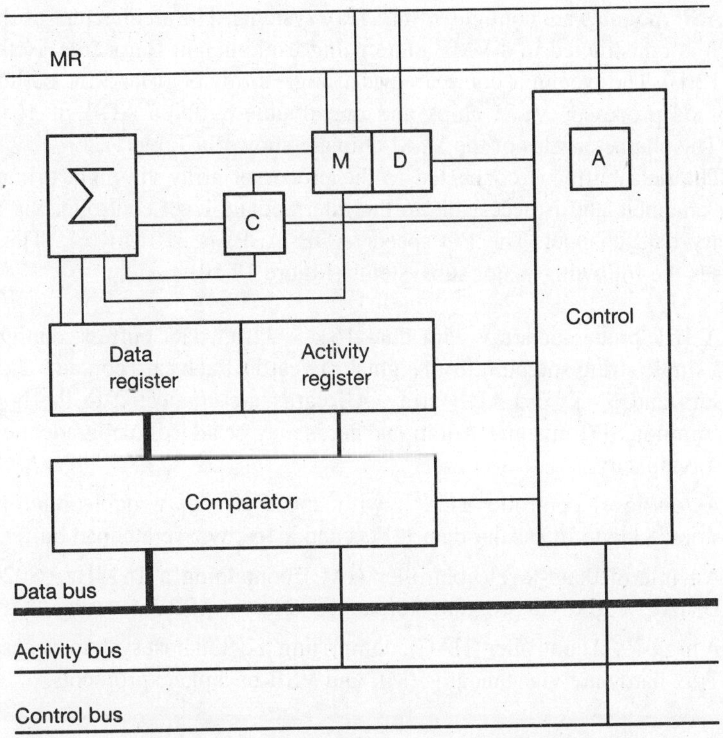

Figure 12.9 An associative processing element.

(MR) line provides the control interface with an indication as to whether any APEs have matched.

The inter-processor communications network is scalable and fault-tolerant, and supports cost-effective emulation of common network topologies. It supports circuit-switched asynchronous communication as well as more conventional synchronous, bi-directional multi-bit communication. At an abstract level, a circularly linked substring can be considered as an hierarchical chordal-ring structure, with the chords bypassing APE blocks (and groups of APE blocks). The bypass structure serves to accelerate inter-APE communications and to provide fault tolerance. Blocks failing in manufacture or service can be simply switched out of the string and bypassed, the content-addressable nature of the string, together with its one-dimensional connectivity, easing the reconfiguration task.

The upper levels of the input/output hierarchy correspond to paging information between an external global memory store and the data buffers (if present). At the lowest level the vector data buffer supports a dual-port exchange of vector data with the APE data registers and with the local memories. The first of these is processor-parallel and therefore is a very high-bandwidth exchange. The second is processor-sequential and provides a slower exchange between local and non-local memory, although this may be fully overlapped with parallel processing and so does not necessarily present a sequential overhead.

ASP modules are configured into Trax systems. The architecture of the Trax-1, which is constructed in a VME crate using triple-height Eurocards, is shown in Figure 12.10. The system is configured as a single string of 16 k APEs, built from an array of 64-processor VLSI chips and one double-buffered ADB of 16 k 32-bit words. The characteristics of the VLSI chip are shown in Table 12.1.

The data buffer is connected to the processor array via eight primary data transfer channels and is accessible to the intermediate-level controller via a single secondary data channel. The I/O speed (ADB–ASP) is 320 Mbyte/s. The system comprises the following major subsystems (Figure 12.10):

- A 16 k processor array with dual 16 k × 32-bit data buffers, configured as a single string and built from eight array cards. Each card contains 2 k processors and a 4 kword ADB array. All cards are connected to the host via a common SDT channel. Additional cards may be added to upgrade the processor capacity.
- A low-level controller (LAC) with 256 kbytes of writable microprogram store, 8 kbyte I/O scalar data FIFOs and a 16 kbyte scratchpad buffer.
- An intermediate-level controller (IAC) containing a 16 MHz 68020 CPU, DMAC, 256 kbyte program store and 512 kbyte ASP data store.
- A high-level controller (HAC), comprising the Sun host system, accessing the Trax hardware via standard VME and VSB backplane protocols.

An application program running on the Trax architecture can be divided into three distinct parts according to the level of the control hierarchy. Procedures targeted at the HAC are grouped in high-level software modules (HAMs), those targeted at the IAC are grouped into IAMs and those for the LAC are grouped into LAMs.

Trax systems provide software support to develop, debug and run applications, including programming tools, debugging tools, system software, run-time libraries and UNIX device drivers. The programming language is based on Modula-2, but interfaces to other programming languages at the high and intermediate expression levels are feasible.

Table 12.1 VLSI APE chip characteristics.

Parameter	*Value*
Chip area	7 mm × 8 mm
Number of pins	120
Clock rate	16 MHz
Number of APEs	64
Transistor count	64 000

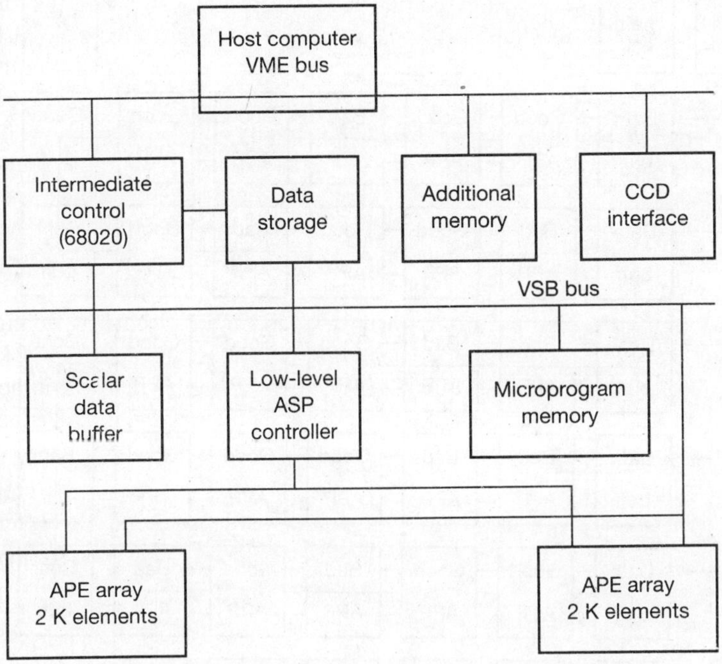

Figure 12.10 The TRAX machine architecture.

The architecture of the Trax systems is shared with the wafer-scale integration ASP (WASP) developed jointly by Brunel University and Aspex Microsystems. As indicated in Figure 12.11, a WASP device is composed from three different VLSI-sized blocks known as data routers (DRs), ASP substrings and control routers (CRs). The DR and CR blocks incorporate routing to connect ASP substring rows to a common data interface and a common control interface respectively. Moreover, both these blocks incorporate ports to effect row-to-row extension of ASP substrings.

Each of the individual blocks has a fault-tolerant design, so that anything between a processor block and a complete WASP device can be bypassed. This hierarchical bypassing arrangement permits both small and large clusters of faults, whether occurring in manufacture or in service, to be bypassed. The power distribution network is also fault-tolerant. Each ASP substring row is independently powered; the power tracks run along the rows and are fed from external connections at both ends, within the DR and CR blocks. Each block contains a power isolator, so that bypassed blocks and rows can be isolated from the power network.

The WASP programme is designed to achieve extremely high performance by combining the advantages of data parallelism and advanced technology. The result is indicated by the figures in Table 12.2, which relate to a single-package, two-substrate system.

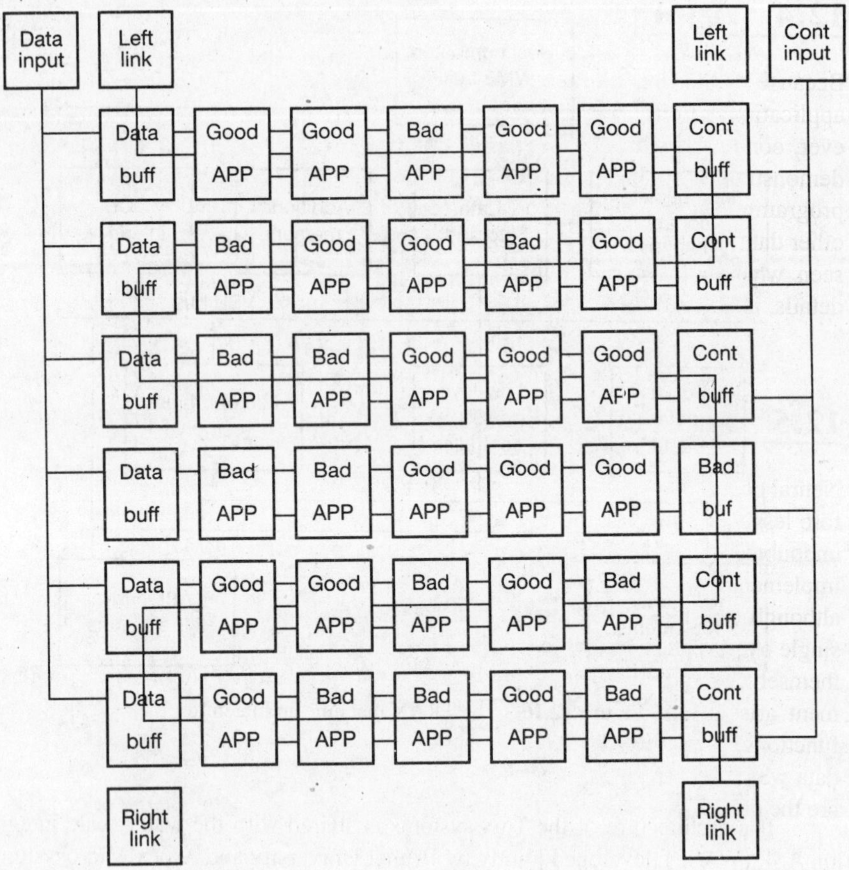

Figure 12.11 Configuration of a WASP device.

Table 12.2 Performance for a two-substrate WASP system.

Parameter	*Value*
Configuration	1 or 2 MIMD arrays
Performance	100 GOPS
I/O bandwidth	640 Mbyte/s
Number of processors	65 536
Package size	$16.25 \times 15 \times 0.75\,\text{cm}^3$
Power dissipation	<100 W

12.4 Application-array mapping

Because of the linear structure of the ASP systems, it is particularly easy to map applications of differing data-set sizes onto the system. This versatility is not, however, connected with the associative paradigm itself. Anyanwu et al. (1994) have demonstrated, by execution of appropriate benchmarks, that their system is fully programmable and competitive in performance with comparable machines utilizing other data-parallel paradigms. In the authors' opinion, however, it still remains to be seen whether the associative paradigm, when divorced from its implementation details, is more or less constraining than straightforward SIMD.

12.5 Neural computers

Neural computing is a comparatively new field, and the design components are therefore less well specified than those of other architectures. Although neural computers undoubtedly implement data parallelism, it is also arguable that, at the same time, they implement functional parallelism. This somewhat confusing situation arises because, although a given neural network is trained, at any given time, to implement only a single overall function, the functions which each node of the network is executing are themselves likely to be somewhat individual. The uncertainty apparent in this statement arises from the fact that such computers are not programmed with specific functions, but combine a specific evolutionary rule with a great diversity of training data which causes the states of the computer itself to be modified. In almost no cases are the details of the modifications which take place known to the user.

This situation requires that the design space for neural computers be specified in a somewhat different fashion from those of other systems. The first area concerns the basic paradigm by means of which the neural network will arrive at its conclusions. It is possible to identify a small number of such paradigms, each of which is examined below.

12.5.1 The paradigms of neural computing

In what follows, it must be borne in mind that neural computers are operated in a way which is completely different from the operation of normal computers. Neural computers are trained (not programmed) so that, given a certain starting state (data input), they either classify the input data into one of a number of classes, or cause the original data to evolve in such a way that a certain desirable property is optimized. Each of the two methods leads to two somewhat different types of functionality.

Classification

First, data about a series of objects (the training set) is fed to the computer. This data includes both the parameters used to describe the object and the specified classification. When the training phase is complete, the computer will decide on categories for new data which include only the parametric description.

The key to the use of this paradigm is the question of implementation. In order to explain how this can be done, it is useful to begin with some of the ideas of multivariate analysis illustrated in Figure 12.12. In each of the three parts of this diagram, a graph has been plotted whose axes are two parameters of a set of objects – perhaps the length and width of rectangles. It is required to classify these rectangles into a small number of classes, based on the values of the parameters. To illustrate the idea, three classes of object are plotted (using a different symbol for each class) in each case.

Figure 12.12(a) shows a set of data which is linearly separable, that is, the three categories can be separated by a set of straight lines, as shown. Such a situation would be quite easy to program on a standard computer – the equations of the lines can be written analytically. However, even in this case, we might introduce another element which the computer would classify wrongly according to our predefined criteria. Furthermore, this type of situation is uncommonly simple. A more realistic case is shown in Figure 12.12(b). Here, the categories are still separable, but not by straight lines. The lines shown follow simple analytic formulae, although this is not necessarily the case. It would obviously be more difficult to program a standard computer to perform the required classification, and any additional data falling outside the designated clusters would require a complete reprogramming exercise. Before proceeding to the third case, a further complication can be introduced. Figure 12.12 plots only two parameters. Suppose there were ten, or a thousand, or a million? The computational complexity of the situation could quickly become overwhelming.

Finally, consider Figure 12.12(c). Here, the data points are intermingled – the data is, in fact, *non-separable* in any meaningful way. We could still make an attempt at a set of lines which gives the best available separation, but the situation is only amenable to an approximate solution.

Considerations of the complexity of this problem led Rosenblatt (1958) to propose a solution called the perceptron. This is a device which accepts two classes of information. The first class are those which correspond to parametric data, while the second set is used, during a training phase, to modify the internal states of the device to produce the required classification. If the design of the device and the

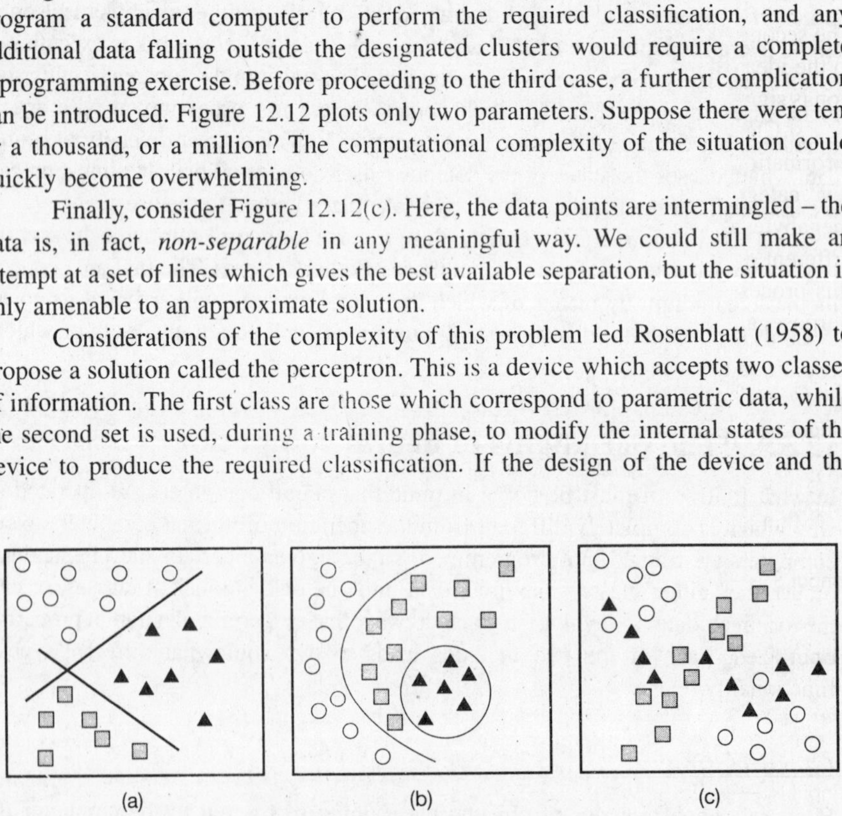

Figure 12.12 Multivariate analysis.

amount and method of training are both satisfactory, new inputs will then be classified satisfactorily. A type of circuit which offers this functionality is shown in Figure 12.13. Although a single perceptron will only accomplish linear separation, multi-layer circuits using perceptrons can produce some sort of answer for all the cases shown in Figure 12.12, and also allow large numbers of inputs to be used.

In its original form, called the single-layer perceptron, the applicability of the circuit is unnecessarily limited. If many are combined into a multi-layer structure, two things become apparent. First, the circuit becomes more flexible, more powerful and therefore more generally applicable, partly because the intermediate (hidden) layers of nodes represent intermediate features which are not those representing the ultimate classification.

The second factor which becomes more apparent as the complexity of the multi-layer perceptron circuits builds up is the similarity to neural structures – there is the same distributed and unspecified functionality and the same complexity and distribution of connections. Even the functioning of the nodes is similar to the way in which neurons work.

Transformation

The second of the neural computing paradigms, transformation, has many similarities to the ideas of classification. However, it seems clear that the intention of the operation is significantly different and this leads to important differences of implementation.

Classification involves, almost invariably, a reduction in the quantity of information. Instead of thousands of instances of data, classification results in just a few categories. In computer terms the amount of data can be reduced from megabytes to bytes – an enormous reduction. The purpose of transformation is quite different. It is concerned with changing one representation of data into another – in this process any analysis of the characteristics of the data is incidental to the real purpose, although it may serve as a useful tool for improving efficiency.

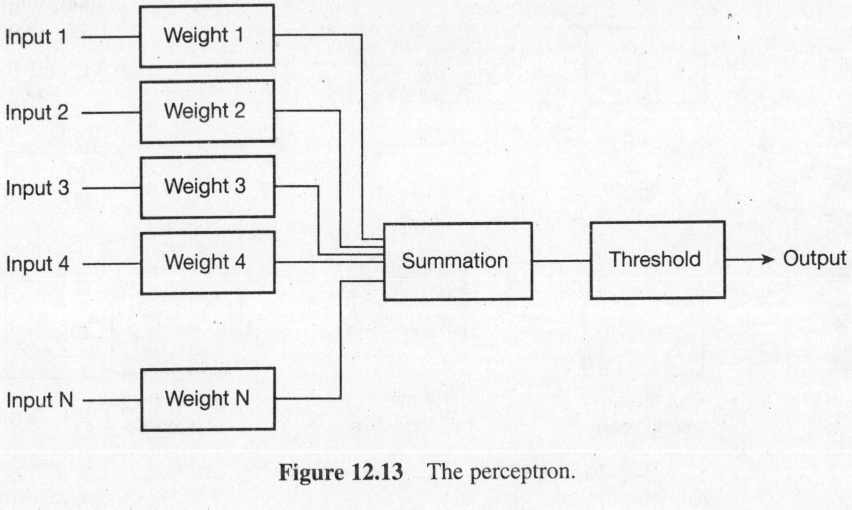

Figure 12.13 The perceptron.

Figure 12.14 depicts a system for converting written material into speech. (Such a system might well be used as an aid for the partially sighted.) Clearly, the amount of data output is of the same order as the amount input, but the representation is quite different. In this example, the internal (hidden) states of a cognitive system designed to implement such a transformation might correspond to the *phonemes* of the language, but this internal classification would be incidental to the purpose of the system.

It is apparent from this example that the transformation paradigm usually employs implementations which are similar to those of classification, with one important difference. Whereas classification implies a many-to-few operation, it is quite likely that transformation will require a many-to-many system, with each data input producing a unique output. For the sake of efficiency, it may be that the output data is itself produced in an encoded form, so that the physical number of output lines from a system may be few, but this does not invalidate the principle of the operation.

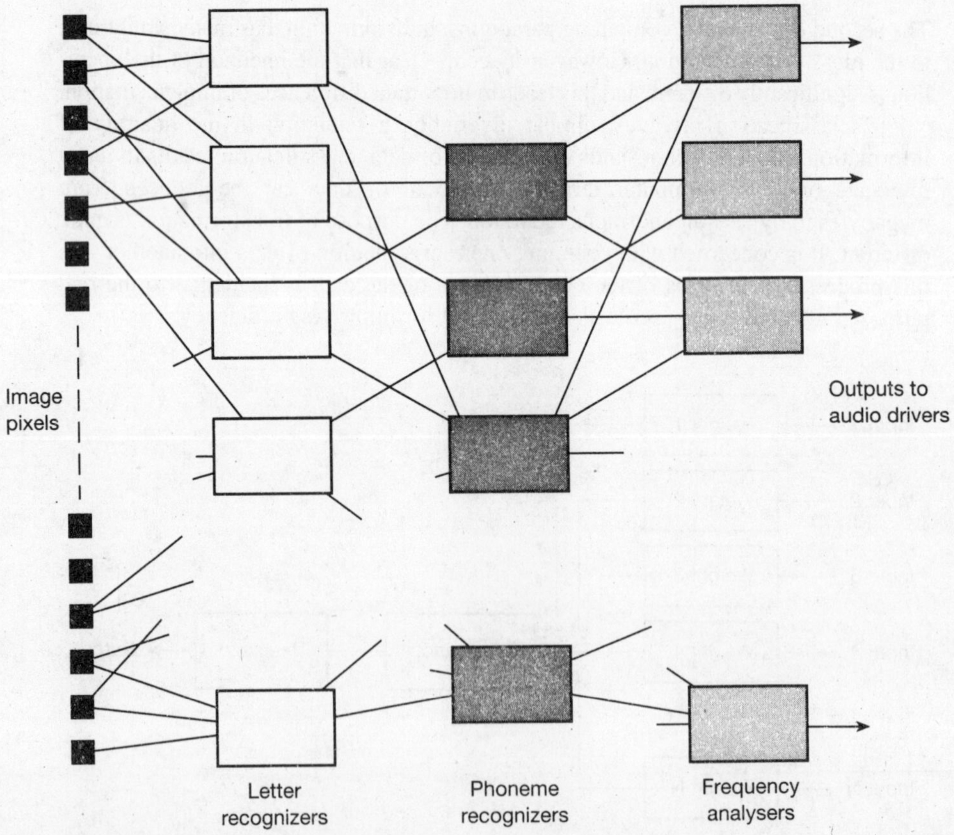

Figure 12.14 A text verbalization system.

Minimization

The third cognitive technique, minimization, is used in a rather different way from the other two, and demands a different starting point in order to arrive at an understanding of its operation. Figure 12.15 is a three-dimensional plot of a surface in parameter space. It can be readily observed that the value of the z-parameter has a number of points which are local minima; that is, starting from one of these points, any small change in either the x- or y-parameters results in an increase in the value of z. It is also observable that there is a global minimum value of the z-parameter – any change in x or y, of whatever magnitude, results in an increase in z.

This representation enables us to visualize two types of problem. The first of these is the problem of recognition. In the sphere of human action, it is apparent that the brain can recognize the face of someone known to it from the most fragmentary glimpse. It appears that the brain can associate the fragmented picture with stored information, and recall the stored information in its entirety. The second is the type of problem where the z-parameter represents a cost function, and we wish to arrive at a solution which will minimize this cost. An example of each of these cases follows.

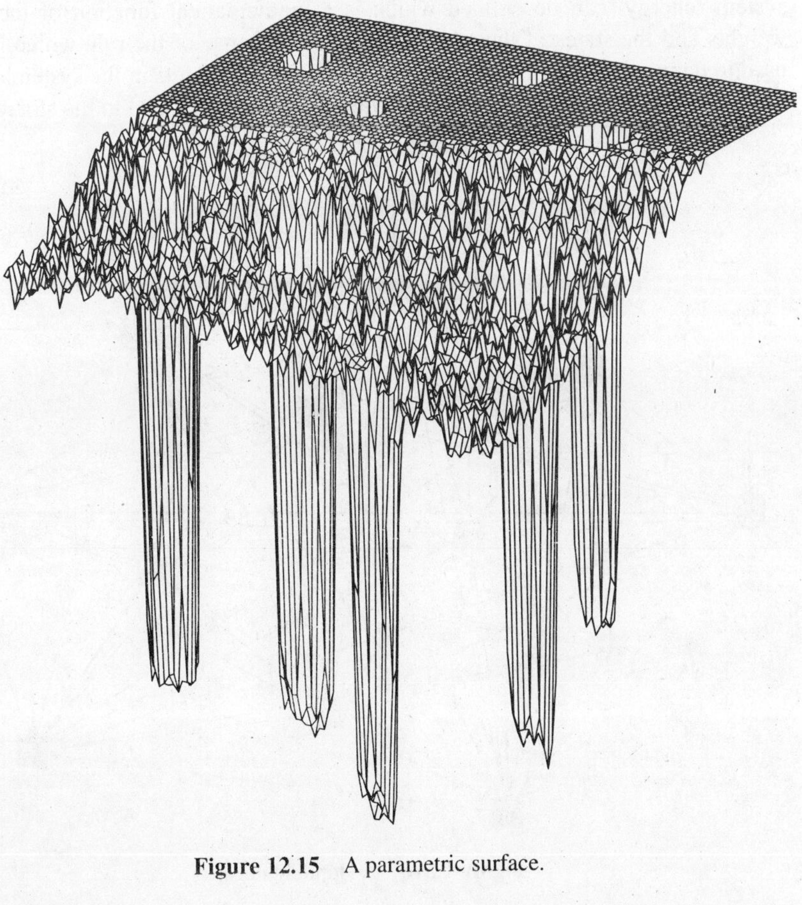

Figure 12.15 A parametric surface.

The classic embodiment of local minimization is the Hopfield network, devised by John Hopfield (1982). The network comprises a set of all-to-all connected binary threshold logic units with weighted connections between the units. The state of each unit of the system can be either one or zero (this is sometimes modified to minus one or plus one). The idea is that a number of patterns are stored in the network, by modifying the weights according to a specific rule devised by Hebb (1949) which defines the weights in terms of the states of the elements of the system. This rule-based approach to defining the interconnection weights is in contrast to the training employed for the same purpose in the two cognitive paradigms described above. The patterns correspond to particular sets of values of the variables of the problem under consideration. Figure 12.16 gives some idea of the complexity of such a network, in which a significant difference from the multi-layer perceptron lies in the presence of feedback. Each connection shown in the diagram represents a two-way path.

The object of the exercise is to present to the network a partial data set (or one corrupted by noise) and allow the network to determine which of its stored data sets is the closest to it. The network achieves this by taking the input pattern as its starting state and evolving by means of serial, element-by-element, updating. A system 'energy' can be defined which is a mathematical function of the system weights and the states of the system elements. Because of the rule which has been used to define the weights in the system, the updating results in the system evolving towards the nearest energy minimum, which should correspond to the stored pattern

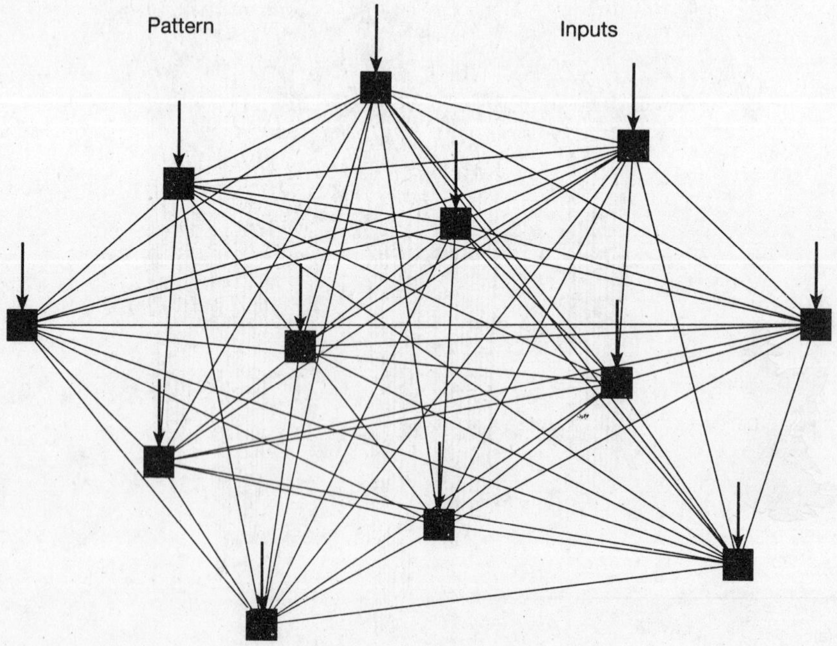

Figure 12.16 A Hopfield network.

which is most like the input. Thus the second important difference from the multi-layer perceptron approach is that the production of the answer is an iterative process (which may take a considerable time).

There are a number of serious difficulties in achieving useful implementations of this technique. The number and quality of the stored data sets are severely limited – if there are too many, or they are too similar, then the energy minima are either too diffuse or too close together, both cases leading to a high incidence of false recognitions. The one remedy for this – a substantial increase in the number of elements – has its own drawbacks. There is a physical problem, in that all-to-all connectivity becomes increasingly difficult to implement as the number of elements increases. A second problem is the added time required to implement the serial updating algorithm over a larger number of elements. For these reasons, amongst others, although there is still considerable theoretical interest in such techniques, an alternative method, global minimization, offers better prospects of applicability.

Hopfield networks, such as those described above, are suitable for discovering local minima. If the global minimum in some set of data is required, then a different technique, known as simulated annealing, can be applied. A classic problem which is amenable to solution by this method is the so-called travelling salesman problem, described in Hopfield and Tank (1985) and illustrated in Figure 12.17. The idea is to find the best route for a salesman travelling between retail outlets in a number of cities and so minimize the cost of the operation, which in this case corresponds to the system energy discussed above. If the number of cities is large, an exhaustive analytical solution to the problem is computationally unrealistic, but the technique of global minimization can offer a solution.

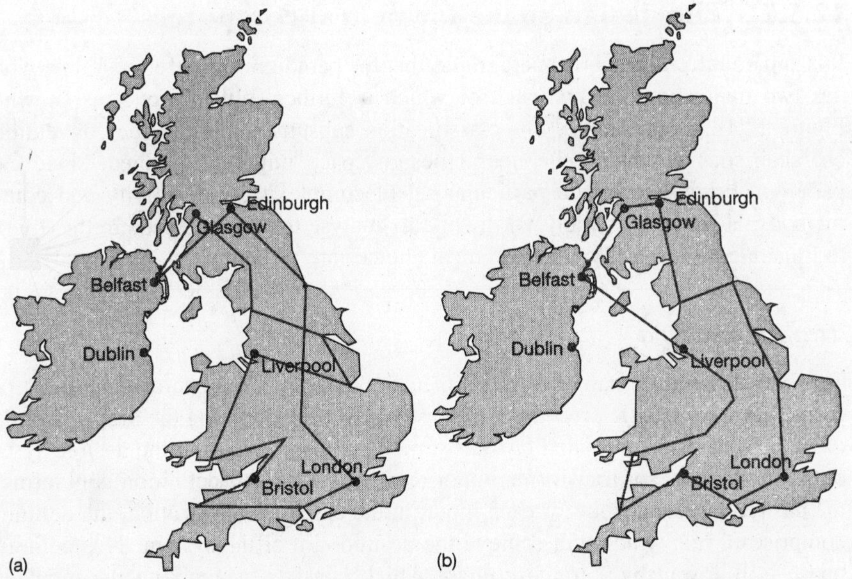

Figure 12.17 The travelling salesman problem.

In this example the parameters of the problem are the distances between cities, and the cost function is the overall distance covered on the chosen route. It is intuitively obvious that some particular route will have the minimum cost, but it is almost equally obvious that many routes will give a reasonable approximation to this minimum. Two possible routes around the same set of cities in the British Isles are suggested in the diagram.

There are a number of significant differences from the local minimization procedure described above. First, the rule for defining the system weights is different. In the present case, the weights are defined as a function of the distance between cities – each specific problem of this type will have its own, unique, definition. Second, the element updating procedure, while still being a serial operation, is no longer deterministic. At every stage of the algorithm, a probabilistic calculation determines whether or not a given alteration (corresponding, here, to a change in routing) is accepted or rejected. Any alteration which reduces the overall cost of the route will be accepted, but there is a finite chance that a change which increases the overall cost of the route will also be accepted. This probability is related to a factor which is often called *temperature* (in continuation of the energy analogy). The higher the temperature, the greater the probability that a higher-cost route change will be accepted. Eventual convergence of the system towards the global minimum usually involves gradually reducing this temperature from an initially high value. Low values are not used from the outset because they can lead to the system becoming trapped in states far from the global minimum.

By allowing the system to evolve under these conditions from some arbitrary starting configuration, solutions very close to the minimum cost can often be found, and in some cases the minimum itself can be achieved.

12.5.2 The design space for neural computers

It is apparent from the above paragraphs that the paradigm space for neural networks has two major components, each of which is further split into two, as shown in Figure 12.18. In one sense, this classification subsumes many of the conventional characteristics by which the neural design space might be defined, since each paradigm brings together a particular set of complexity, connectivity and control methods. However, it is still worthwhile to analyse the design space in these terms to illustrate more clearly what technical choices are available.

Training method

There are three alternative training methods available for neural computers. All execute the same basic procedure. This consists of first defining the set of input data (which is to be discriminated or transformed), and then defining the desired system output. In the case of transformation or discrimination, this definition is in terms of the desired system output for each input; in the case of minimization, the definition comprises a rule which will achieve the desired aim of the system. This definition phase is followed by a training phase which consists of applying the input data set to the network and allowing the states of the system to evolve. The process of

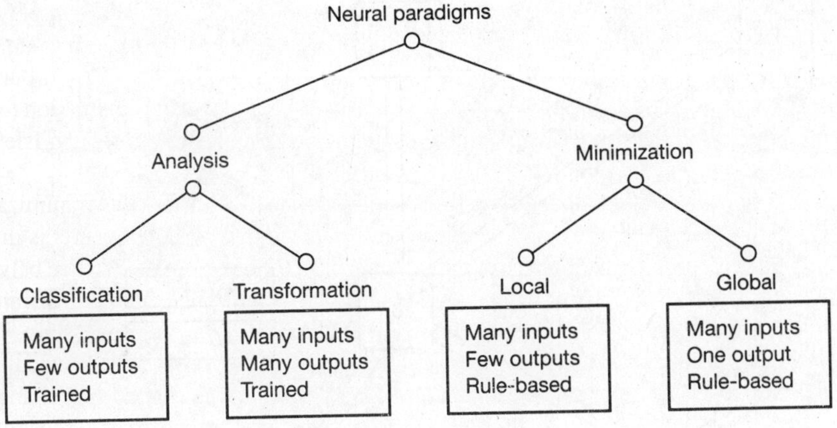

Figure 12.18 Neural computing paradigms.

evolution is automatic, but the rules for modifying the system states must be themselves predefined in each case. The three possible methods for effecting this evolution are described below.

Hebb's rule This technique, described qualitatively in Hebb (1949), takes as its starting point a set of interconnected summing/thresholding nodes in which the connections between any pair of nodes are symmetrical. That is, for two nodes (*i*) and (*j*), there is a connection from (*i*) to (*j*) with weight W_{ij} and a connection from (*j*) to (*i*) with the same weight. Figure 12.19 illustrates an appropriate configuration – for the sake of simplicity, only the connections to node 3 are shown, and only the weights between nodes 3 and 4. W_{34} must equal W_{43} and, similarly, W_{13} must equal W_{31}, and so on.

The approach is used in systems where minimization is the aim, and is derived by considering a parameter of the system equivalent to the energy of (say) a group of atomic particles. In such a context, the energy (*E*) of a particle of mass (*m*) and velocity (*v*) can be defined as:

$$E = \frac{1}{2} mv^2 \qquad (12.3)$$

For one particular state of such a system, an equivalent expression exists:

$$E = -\frac{1}{2} \sum_i \sum_j W_{ij} s_i s_i \qquad (12.4)$$

where s_i and s_j are the (binary) states of the *i*th and *j*th nodes respectively. In order to minimize this expression for a set of *p* independent system states (α_1 -- α_p) we find that:

$$W_{ij} = \sum_{\alpha=1}^{p} s_i^{\alpha} s_j^{\alpha} \qquad (12.5)$$

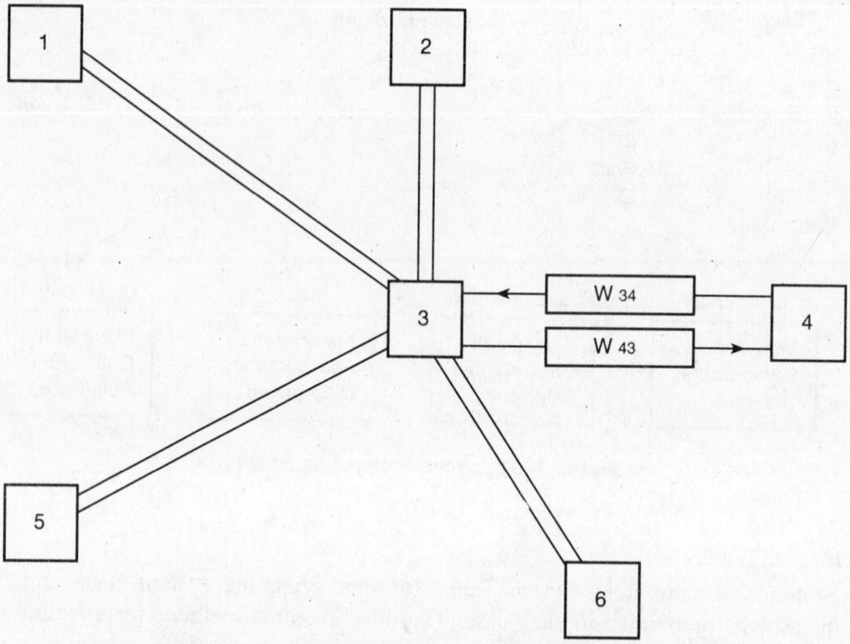

Figure 12.19 A system of nodes to which Hebb's rule can be applied.

Executing this manipulation on the set of system weights will effectively store in the system the set of training patterns. Provided that the training set satisfied a number of important criteria concerning their number and separability, any applied input pattern will then cause the system to settle into the nearest trained pattern.

This technique works well for small data sets which are *almost orthogonal*, that is, where the components are significantly different. However, there are two sets of circumstances, still concerning systems involved in the process of minimization, where some extra help is required. First, with some sets of training data, systems can generate false minima in their energy landscape. This can result in false answers being supplied for some configurations of subsequent input. Second, when global minimization is desired, systems can be trapped in undesirable local minima. Under both these circumstances, the following technique can be of benefit.

Simulated annealing Figure 12.20 depicts a situation in which the energy of a system is plotted against a single, arbitrary, parameter. If the system being represented is a type of Hopfield network such as that illustrated above, then, from any starting state to the left of point A in part (a) of the diagram, the system will end up in the local minimum at point B. If global minimization is desired, this situation is unsatisfactory. The fundamental idea of simulated annealing is as follows. If the system is endowed with a property akin to electrical noise, in which the system energy can randomly increase at any iteration, rather than monotonically decreasing, then, under some circumstances, the system can jump out of shallow, local energy minima and eventually arrive at the global minimum. This situation is depicted in Figure 20(b).

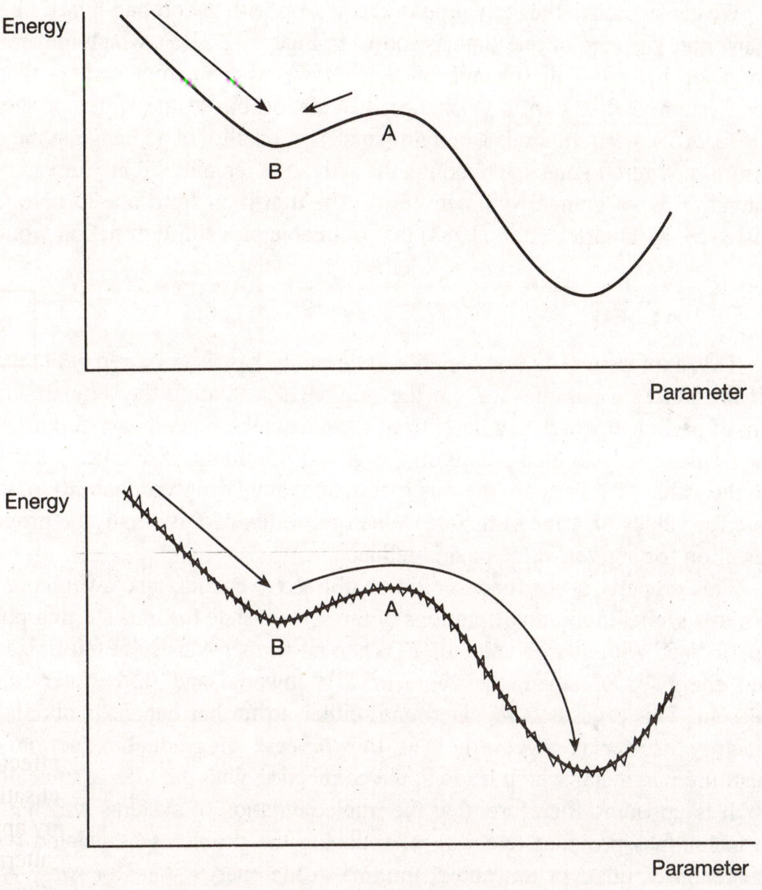

Figure 12.20 Avoiding local minima.

Two problems arise in connection with this technique. First, some method of implementing the idea of a noisy system must be implemented in Hopfield networks. Second, systems must be encouraged to move towards a global minimum, rather than just hopping about between whatever local minima are available.

The first problem can be addressed by expressing the state of a neuron in such a network mathematically.

If: O_i is the output state of the *i*th neuron
T_i is the threshold of the *i*th neuron
W_{ij} is the weight linking the *i*th to the *j*th neuron
A_i is the activation of the *i*th neuron

And if: $A_i = \sum W_{ij} O_j - T_i$

Then, for $i = j$: $O_i = 1$ if $A_i > 0$
and $O_i = 0$ if $A_i < 0$

We can associate the activation of the neuron with the probability of its output being in either the zero or one state as shown in Figure 12.21(a), which illustrates the deterministic nature of the change of state. If we wish to implement a thermally excited system, a first step is to change the relationship to the situation shown in Figure 12.21(b), where there is a certain (small) probability of a change in the output state from, say, zero to one, even though the activation remains slightly less than zero. The situation is, of course, symmetrical for the transition from one to zero. It was suggested by Kirkpatrick et al. (1983) that a suitable probability function would be:

$$p(1) = \frac{1}{1+e^{-A/T}} \tag{12.6}$$

This expression has two benefits. It certainly has the required general shape, and it introduces a parameter T (in the original formulation the temperature of a system of particles) which can be utilized to address the second part of our problem – how to make a system converge on the global minimum. It does this as follows. When the value of T is large, there is a correspondingly high probability of change of state for values of A far from zero. When the value of T is small, the probability of transition for a given value of A is reduced.

This property of the function can be utilized to encourage convergence of the system to a global minimum. Iterations of the system state from its starting point are first performed with a large value of T. When no further consistent minimization of system energy is obtained, the value of T is lowered and further iterations are carried out. This process is repeated until either no further benefit is obtained or a satisfactory answer is achieved. It is this process of gradual reduction of the temperature parameter which leads to the connection with the idea of annealing.

It is apparent, therefore, that the implementation of systems which embody these techniques provides one way of reducing the problems associated with the phenomenon of false, or unwanted, minima in the energy states of some types of neural networks. As described, this approach is relevant to the use of such systems, rather than to their original training. It can, however, be regarded as a training technique if the weights of interconnection are regarded as variables during an annealing process. This approach has been described by Hinton and Sejnowski (1986) as being suitable for the Boltzmann machine. The next training technique uses a rather different approach.

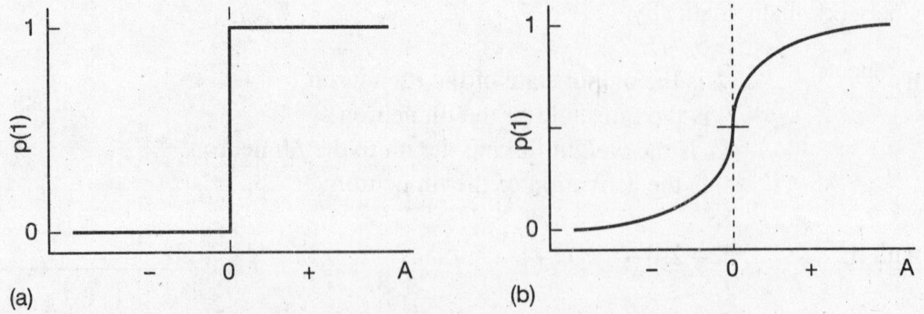

Figure 12.21 Activation probabilities for a neuron.

Back propagation The type of network shown in Figure 12.22 is appropriate for the paradigms of classification or transformation. It comprises a layer of input nodes, an unspecified number of layers of internal nodes and a layer of output nodes. The general technique is as follows. First, the system weights, which are to be modified by the process known as back propagation of errors, are set at their initial (perhaps arbitrary) values. Next, a set of inputs are applied for which the desired outputs are known. The system state is then allowed to evolve, after which the actual outputs are compared with the desired outputs, generating an error value for each node. The weights of the output nodes are adjusted in such a way as to minimize the output errors. This in turn allows error functions to be calculated for the previous layer of nodes, which then allows their weights to be modified. This process is continued until the corrections generated by the original errors are propagated back to the inputs. The whole procedure is then iterated as necessary.

We can express the method in mathematical terms. The object of the exercise is to define a way of altering weights for sets of neural nodes whose output is some general function of the activation states. A method of doing this has been set out by Rumelhart et al. (1986) as follows.

During training, for the *p*th presentation of an input state, the necessary change in weight connecting the output of the *i*th unit to the input of the *j*th is given by:

$$\Delta_p W_{ij} = \beta \delta_{pj} O_{ip} \qquad \textbf{(12.7)}$$

where O_{ip} is the output of the *i*th unit
β is a constant related to the rate of learning
δ_{ip} is some computed error

Then, if O_{ip} is defined by:

$$O_{ip} = \frac{1}{1+e^{-A_{pj}}} \qquad \textbf{(12.8)}$$

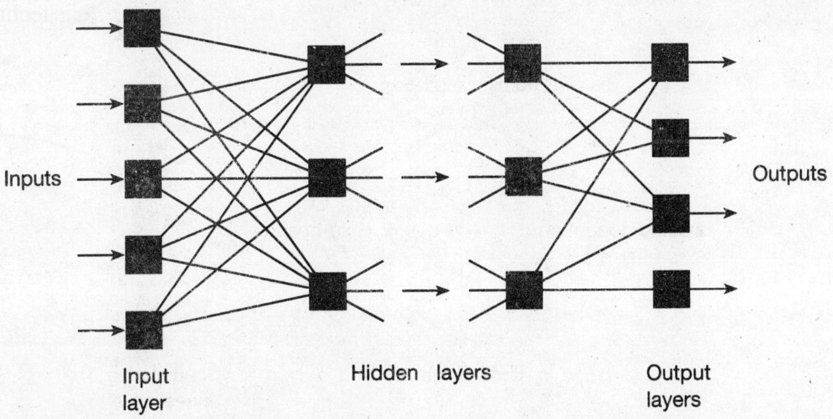

Figure 12.22 A feed-forward network.

where, if T_{pj} are the target outputs, the errors can be stated as:

$$\delta_{pj} = (T_{pj}-O_{pj})\,O_{pj}(1-O_{pj}) \qquad \textbf{(12.9)}$$
$$\delta_{pj} = O_{pj}(1-O_{pj})\sum \delta_{pk} W_{pk}$$

for output and hidden nodes respectively.

These rules form a basis for applying the training technique known as back propagation of errors, but it should be remembered that the fundamentals of the idea lie first in the fact that it is applied only to feed-forward networks; second in the necessity for knowing the desired outputs for all input sets during training; and third in the two-stage process of propagating results forward from the inputs, then propagating corrections back from the outputs. The design space for training techniques is therefore as illustrated in Figure 12.23.

Connectivity

There are two aspects to the design space for connectivity, the first of which concerns the direction of propagation of data within a network. Those systems which are designed for classification or transformation need only to propagate data in one direction, whereas those intended for minimization need to exchange data between nodes in both directions, as shown in Figure 12.24.

The second aspect of connectivity concerns the type of network which is employed between the nodes. Some systems require that each node be connected to every other, and this is only technically feasible for small systems. Where this is not required, or cannot be achieved, alternative methods are used, as illustrated in Figure 12.25, which shows the design space for neural connectivity.

Node complexity

There is little variation in the complexity of neural nodes. That which exists concerns the arrangements for dealing with the inputs from neighbours, and that concerns only the varying numbers of such inputs.

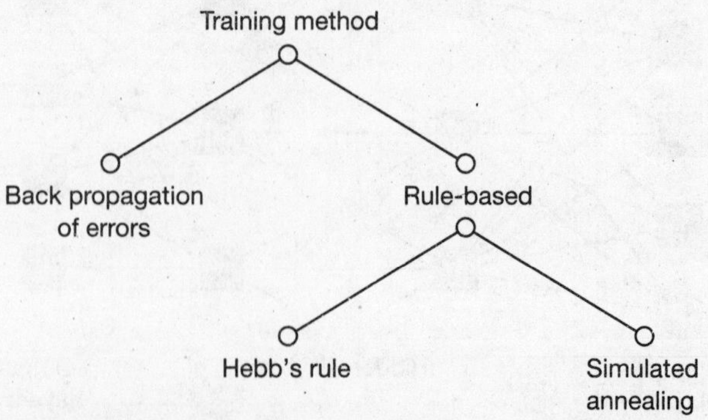

Figure 12.23 The design space for neural system training.

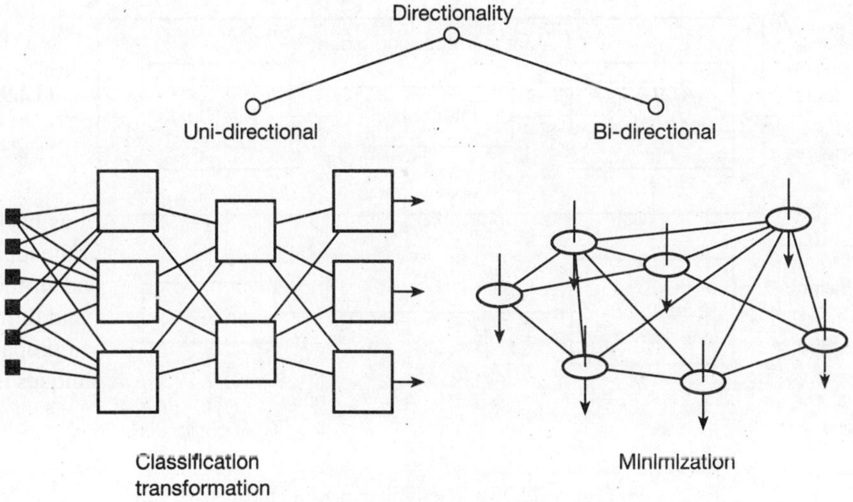

Figure 12.24 Directionality of connections.

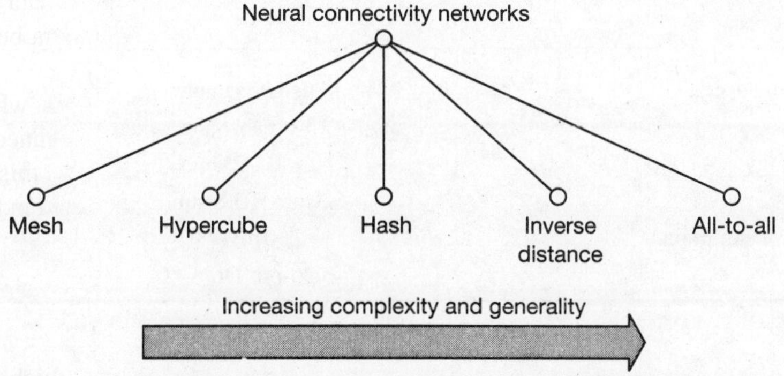

Figure 12.25 The design space for neural connectivity.

12.5.3 Examples of neural computers

Most of the work on neural computing to date has been carried out in simulations. However, a number of hardware devices have been implemented recently, including prosthetic hearing devices from Carver Meade (1989) and a number of chips from Japan.

Masumoto et al. (1993), working at Fujitsu, have developed a multi-purpose analog neuroprocessor which implements one neuron on a single chip. The model of the neuron is the usual weighted summation of inputs followed by a sigmoid threshold function. Weights are stored in digital form in standard memory, and are multiplied by the input signal in a multiplying DAC. This uses the analog input as the reference voltage and the weight as the digital input. Summation of the weighted inputs is achieved by charge accumulation in a capacitor. A piecewise linear

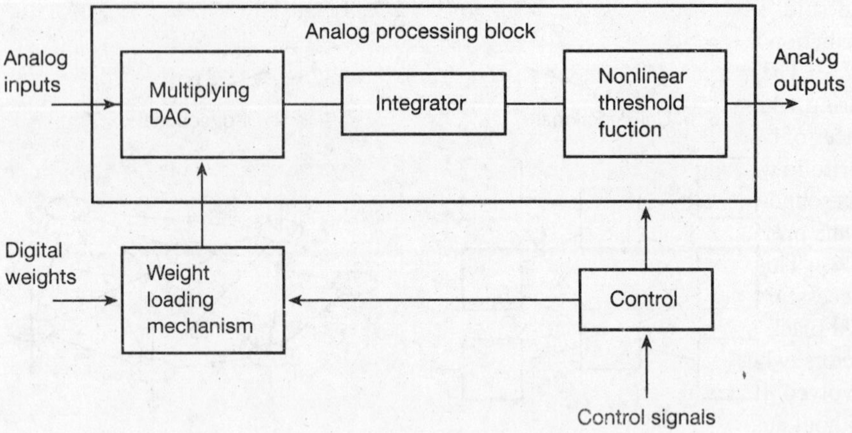

Figure 12.26 The Fujitsu neural chip.

Table 12.3 Fujitsu neural chip parameters.

Property	*Value*
Processing speed	13 μs per sample
Weights	sign + 15-bit absolute value
Technology	2 μm Bi-CMOS
Size	5.3 mm × 3.8 mm
Power consumption	200 mW
Package	20-pin DIP

approximation is made to the sigmoid output function. A block diagram of the chip is shown in Figure 12.26, and the main characteristics of the chip are listed in Table 12.3.

It is intended that the chip should be used to implement multi-layer neural networks, and one such has been constructed on a single card. It comprises two layers, having respectively eight and four neurons, and has 32 inputs. The back-propagation training phase is executed by simulation, followed by writing of weights to on-chip EPROM.

12.5.4 Applications of neural computers

Because of the scarcity of actual hardware, almost all neural network applications are based on simulations. One of the most interesting of these is a system which predicts the optimum times for selling and buying stocks on the Tokyo Stock Exchange. The system is a simulation of a network of several neural modules. These modules are trained with previous market data concerning market indices, technical, political and economic factors, fluctuations of currency and so on, so that they become able to predict the best times at which stocks and shares should be bought and sold. Each module outputs its own prediction, and the overall system output prediction is a weighted average of these, as described by Kimoto and Yoda (1993).

The system was tested over a four-year period before being installed in 1989, during which time it achieved a correct prediction rate for rises and falls in share prices of better than 60 %. These predictions were used in the management of a share portfolio which achieved a per annum return of 1.60 % over the test period. Although this sounds unimpressive, it compares very favourably to the –20.63 % annual figure of the previously regarded best strategy adopted during the test period.

This startlingly successful result demands comment. The development of a successful strategy (by humans) for dealing on stock markets has long been regarded as a black art, not susceptible to analysis. This reflects both the complexity of the factors which drive stock prices and the emotional involvement of all players involved. It appears that, in this application, the neural network strategy of learning without analysis (which may be similar to that employed by humans) has proved to be more successfully implemented by a computing machine than by its designers. This is not unexpected since, at the least, the computer is (presumably) not swayed by emotion or upset by fatigue.

13 Data-Parallel Pipelined and Systolic Architectures

Section 13.1 introduces the basic ideas of data-parallel pipelines and systolic architectures. Section 13.2 describes how pipelines are used in data-parallel architectures, using the DIP-1 system as an example. Section 13.3 discusses systolic architectures in detail.

13.1 Introduction

Data-parallel pipelined and systolic architectures have a number of aspects in common. Both utilize the fundamental idea that, if a defined computation is to be carried out item by item on a large data set, an efficient mechanism can be set up whereby the computation is defined only once, followed by a repeated execution sequence in which no alteration of the control is required. Repeated results can then be obtained as fast as data can be presented to the inputs of the system. Both also use the fact that a supposedly single operation (adding two numbers together or multiplying two matrices) can be subdivided into a number of simpler (and therefore faster) operations which can be cascaded in the manner described in the following sections. It is also true, however, that there are some significant differences between the two approaches, and these are fully described below.

13.2 Pipelines

13.2.1 Introduction

The existence of data-parallel pipeline systems is something of a surprise. In Chapter 5 it was shown that pipelining is usually a function-parallel technique which permits the micro-operations of repeated macro-functions to be overlapped, yielding a consequent increase in speed. The use of pipelining in the data-parallel context is a somewhat specialized consequence of the particular functions which are executed in image processing. The basic idea is illustrated in Figure 13.1.

Many image processing operations share two characteristics which make them suitable for implementation in a pipeline fashion. In the first place, the

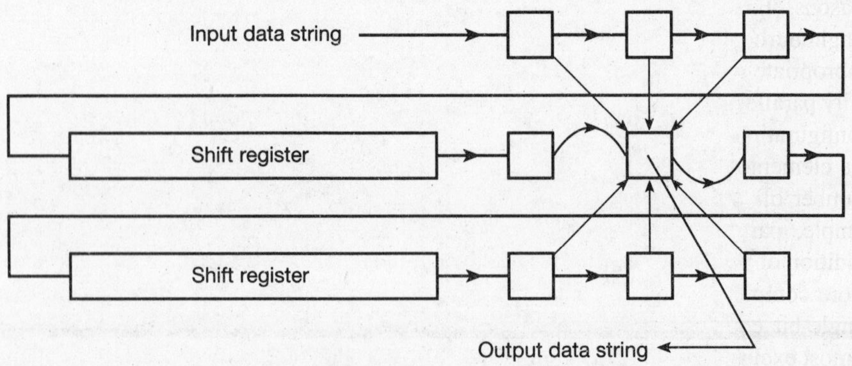

Figure 13.1 A data-parallel pipeline.

identical function must be executed upon a very long stream of data. Secondly, the result which is calculated at each point is a function of the data from a limited neighbourhood of pixels. Figure 13.1 shows how these two properties are utilized to improve the performance of a simple image processing function. The stream of data, representing the pixels of an image, is inserted into a structure which is essentially a long shift register. Data is then tapped off from points on the shift register such that they correspond to the neighbourhood which is required to form the specific function. In the case shown, the classical 3 × 3 local neighbourhood is used. This data is then brought together at a computing element, which repetitively calculates the required result at every time step of the data passing through the shift register. The calculating element is arranged to deal with all the incoming data simultaneously, thus executing a limited amount of data parallelism. In many implementations of this arrangement, the stream of results output from the first computing element itself forms the input to the shift register of a second, similar, pipeline, and so on.

The amount of data parallelism, and hence the increase in performance, is small by comparison with other data-parallel paradigms considered in this chapter, being limited by the number of elements in the required neighbourhood. However, since neighbourhoods of the order of 25 × 25 pixels are sometimes used, the improvements achieved can be worthwhile.

13.2.2 Design space

Designers of such systems have few degrees of freedom open to them. The first and most obvious is the effective picture area over which data elements can be gathered. This is substantially only a question of scale, and the design space is therefore self-evident. This is not so for the other elements of a design.

Programmability

One obvious degree of freedom lies in the programmability of the computing element. However, the provision of a fully programmable unit is not simple, for two reasons. First, different functions are likely to operate upon differently sized neighbourhoods, so that a change in the executed function must be accompanied by appropriate reconfiguring of the neighbourhood-generating shift registers. Second, fully parallel implementations of many functions are likely to require quite different configurations within the computing element. Consider Figure 13.2. Part (a) shows the element which would be required to execute a simple thresholded count of the number of 'on' neighbours in a local pixel surround. While this is comparatively simple, part (b), which illustrates the circuits needed to implement a parallel addition of neighbour grey-values followed by calculation of their average, is much more complex. For this reason, programmable units are usually provided only for single-bit computing elements. Those which act directly on integer data sets are almost exclusively single function. The design space for complexity is therefore that shown in Figure 13.3.

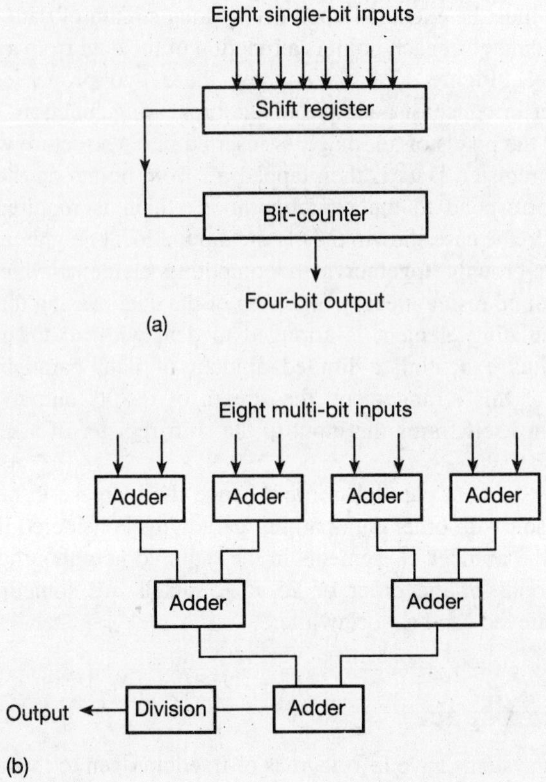

Figure 13.2 Alternative processor functions. (a) Bit counting; (b) multi-bit average

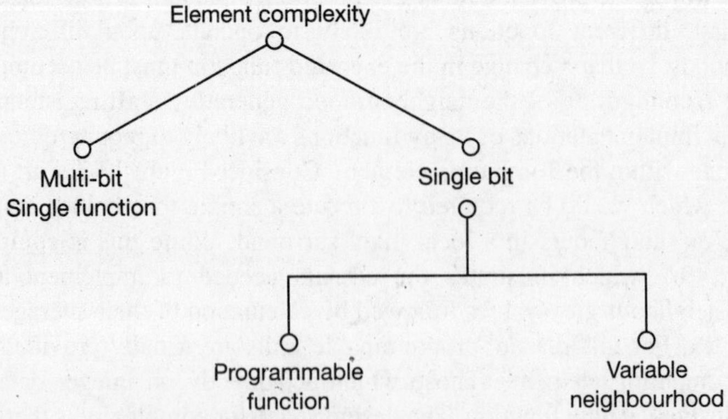

Figure 13.3 Design space for element complexity.

Connectivity

There are obvious degrees of freedom associated with the connectivity arrangements of a data-parallel pipeline system. The first is that mentioned above, concerning the choice of input data neighbourhood. Although this is in theory infinite (up to the full size of the relevant image), in fact it is usually quantized into regular neighbourhoods as illustrated in Figure 13.4, which shows the number of inputs which the processing element must accept for the first few regular neighbourhoods of the first three degrees of dimensionality. This is the second degree of freedom available in the data set. One-, two- and three-dimensional sets are conventionally implemented, but it should be borne in mind that this degree of freedom is orthogonal to that mentioned above concerning size of neighbourhood. The overall design space can therefore be depicted as incorporating both aspects, as shown in Figure 13.4. It is worth noting how rapidly the number of elements in the neighbourhood grows with diameter for the systems of higher dimensionality. Although this offers the opportunity for greater parallelism, it carries a corresponding penalty in terms of technical difficulty.

13.2.3 The DIP-1 system

Modern examples of data-parallel pipelines are hard to find. In general, because the degree of parallelism involved in these systems is relatively small, their performance has been overwhelmed by that of workstations. We therefore describe here one of the classical early developments in the field, the DIP-1 system constructed by Gerritsen (1978) and others at the Delft Institute of Technology.

A block diagram of the central part of the system is given in Figure 13.5. There are a number of unusual and important elements of the design. First amongst these is the generation of the neighbourhoods of input data by computation of RAM addresses, rather than by tapping a shift register. This removes the difficulty which would otherwise exist when altering the neighbourhood specification. It does,

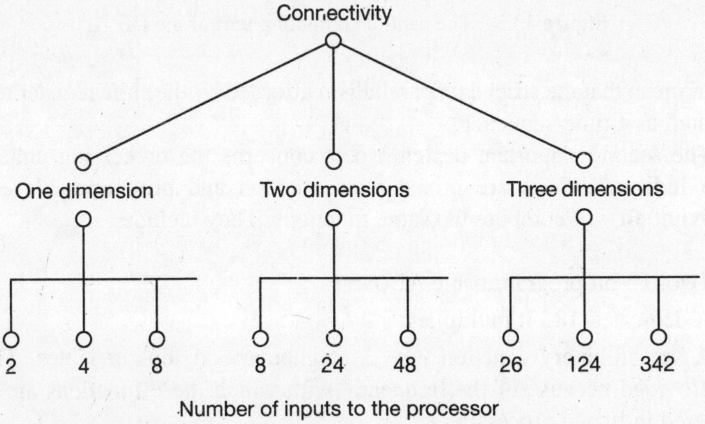

Figure 13.4 The design space for connectivity in pipelines.

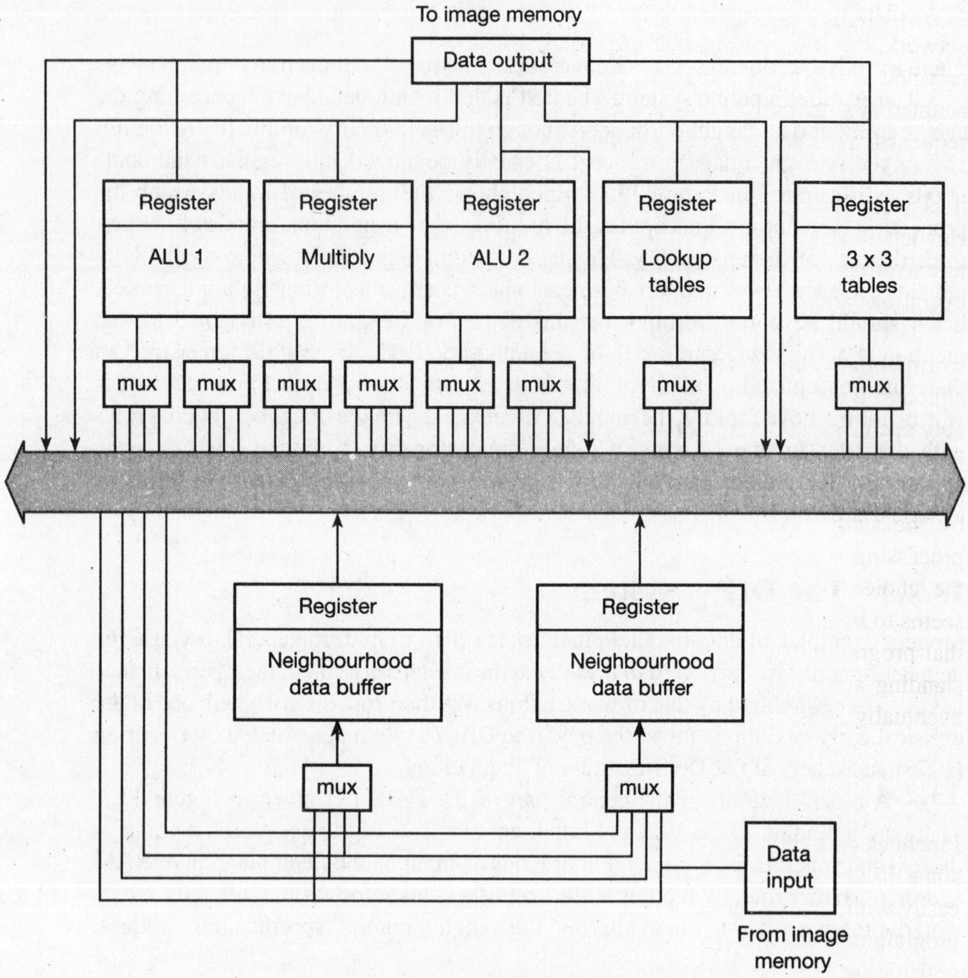

Figure 13.5 The central computing unit of the DIP-1.

however, mean that the strict data parallelism afforded by the shift-register technique is emulated as a time-sequence.

The second important design aspect concerns the processing units. As the diagram indicates, these are mixed fixed-function and programmable elements, although not all will compute the same functions. They include:

- Two, 18-bit programmable ALUs.
- A dedicated 18-bit multiplier.
- A set of binary function 3 × 3 neighbourhood lookup tables. These are provided because of the frequency with which these functions are encountered in image processing.
- Two conversion tables for efficient execution of pointwise operations.

The final unusual element of the design is a reconfigurable interconnection network, based on multiplexers, which permits the output of any pipeline unit to be recycled as the input of one or more further units. Appropriate use of this facility, coupled with the provision of registers in the computing units, permits complex sequences of functions to be executed as required.

Although the performance of the DIP-1 is unimpressive by modern standards, it is worth comparing with that of a contemporary leading-edge workstation (a Hewlett-Packard 1000), in order to illustrate the benefits endowed by the architecture over that of a single processor design. Table 13.1 gives figures for a number of operations and two different neighbourhood sizes.

The table shows that the benefits conferred by the specialized architecture are worthwhile, being typically of the order of 100 times faster than the workstation, although it is of some interest to note that the actual improvement varies considerably according to the specific function being executed. Unfortunately, however, the improvement in performance was insufficient to overcome the drawbacks of the system, which were twofold. First, the functionality, although highly programmable by the standards of such systems, proved to be too limited for more general processing. Second, the system suffered from being microprogrammed. Although the choice between microprogrammed control and state machine cycle control seems to be governed as much by fashion as any other factor, it is undoubtedly true that programming a microprogrammed machine demands a higher level of understanding and effort than would an equivalent assembly-level system. This factor eventually rendered DIP-1 unusable.

13.2.4 Application mapping

Pipelines offer, naturally, some advantages over other data-parallel architectures and some disadvantages. The advantages include relatively low cost and the ability to deal easily with data sets of different sizes. The disadvantages include relatively limited programmability, a limited amount of parallelism and difficulties in implementing scalable increase in performance with increasing size. While it would obviously be

Table 13.1 Performance of the DIP-1.

Operation	*Neighbourhood*	*DIP-1 (secs)*	*Workstation (secs)*
Convolution	3×3	0.8	70
Convolution	15×15	5.8	700
Kuwahara filter	3×3	2.0	220
Kuwahara filter	15×15	10.0	310
Median filter	3×3	1.0	120
Median filter	15×15	4.0	480
Linear relaxation	15×15	5.8	900

possible to program pipelines to execute calculations in many of the fields in which data-parallel computing is appropriate, this has not, in fact, been done. The only real application area for pipelines has been image processing and, even in this area, it is probably the function-parallel aspect, permitted by the ability to pass the output of one pipeline element to the input of another, which has been most effective.

13.3 Systolic architectures

In terms of extracting the maximum possible performance from data-parallel architectures, the SIMD approach suffers the drawback of being, in some sense, general-purpose, and therefore less than optimally efficient for any specific purpose. The class of systolic architectures is intended, by and large, to overcome this drawback. The term systolic array, as applied to computing, was originated by H. T. Kung (Kung and Leisersor, 1978), by analogy with the (systolic) pumping action of the heart. It was intended to convey that data would be pumped through a computing system to produce (usually) a stream of results.

It is perhaps easiest to envisage the principle as it is applied to matrix multiplication, the process illustrated in Figure 13.6. Typically, when two square arrays of data (matrices) are to be multiplied, the result will itself be a square array (of the same dimensions as the two original arrays) whose value at every point is computed by multiplying together elements of the row (from the first input array) by elements of the column (from the second input array) which overlap at the point, and summing these products. The process is expressed mathematically as:

$$C_{mn} = \sum_{ij} A_{in} B_{mj} \qquad (13.1)$$

The application of the systolic principle to this process is achieved by noting the following points:

- The basic computation required at each point of the result matrix is the same.
- Each of the values within a given column (or row) of the array is required at every point of the corresponding column (or row) of the result.
- The data required at each point could conveniently be passed sequentially across or down the array.
- A large number of partial results (the product of one element of a row and one element of a column) could be calculated simultaneously.

When related to the basic idea of data-parallel computation, these considerations result in the type of systolic system shown in Figure 13.7. The design of this system includes the following aspects:

- There is a square array of computing elements whose dimensions are those of the matrices to be multiplied.

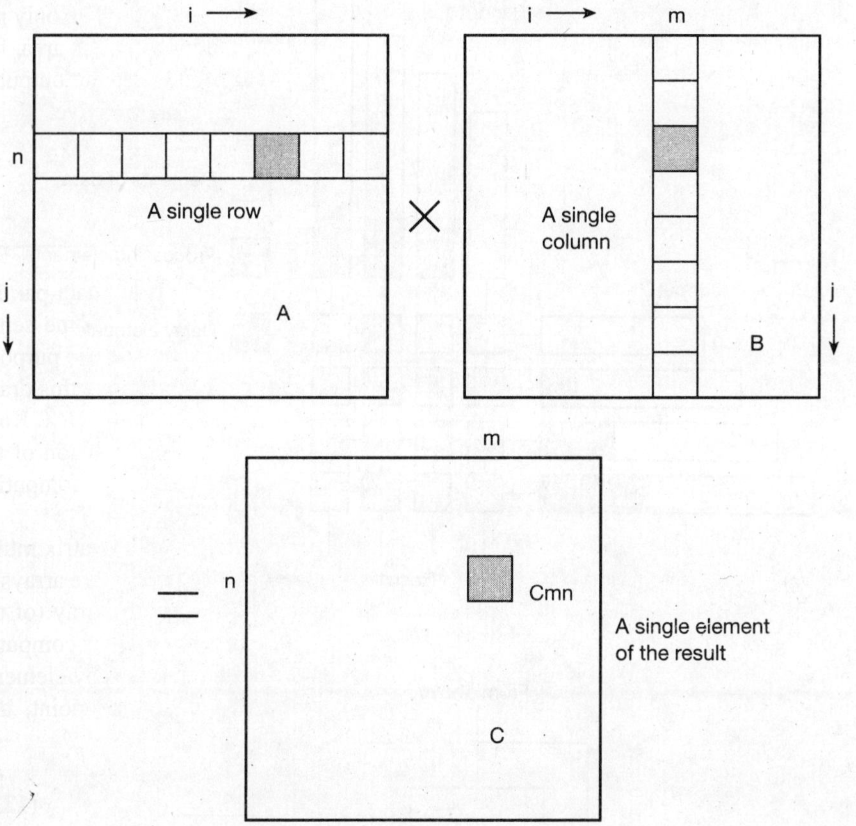

Figure 13.6 Matrix multiplication.

- At each node of the array, the computing element consists of a multiplication unit, an addition unit and a storage unit.
- Each element of the array computes a single, fixed function.
- Each element is connected only to its nearest neighbours in the array, and only by means of a uni-directional data path.
- The only control signal broadcast through the array is a clock pulse, used to synchronize operations
- Input data is inserted at two edges of the array, in sequences which comprise the elements of the input matrices, and passes through the array in two orthogonal directions.
- Output data (the result matrix) can be extracted as a series of elements from either of the two remaining edges of the array.

Figure 13.7(a) indicates that the various rows and columns of the two input arrays are not all inserted into the computing array at the same moment. This is to

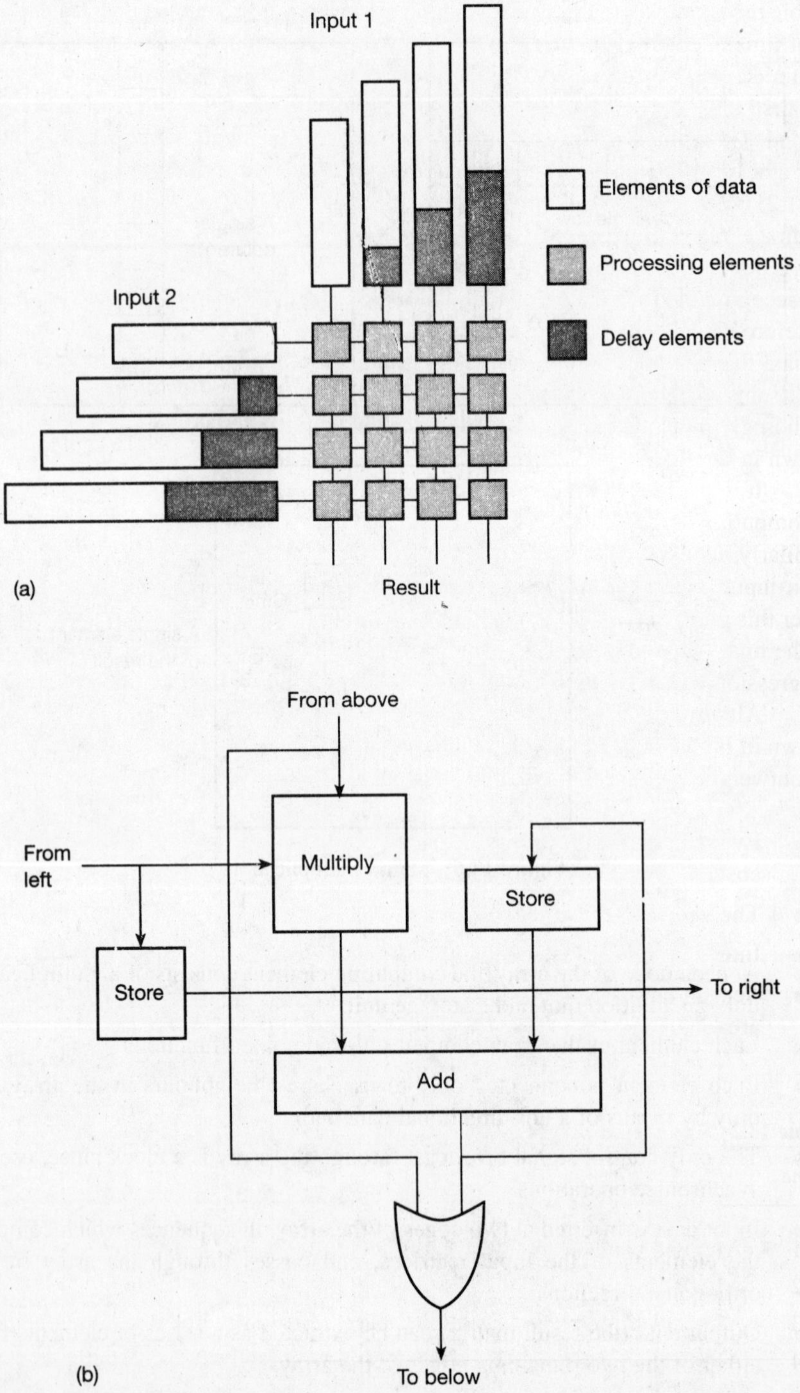

Figure 13.7 (a) System connections for systolic matrix multiplication; (b) the processing element for matrix multiplication.

enable the proper elements of data to arrive at the correct processing elements at the right time. Consider the first row of computing elements. The first partial product required at the first processor (PE1,1) is the result of multiplying the first element of the first row of one input matrix by the first element of the first column of the second. This can be achieved by inputting these two elements simultaneously, at the first clock pulse. However, the first partial product required at the second processor (PE1,2) is the result of multiplying the first element of the first row of one matrix by the first element of the second column of the other. Since the first element of the first row is being used during the first clock pulse by PE1,1, it cannot arrive at PE1,2 until the second clock pulse. The arrival of the first element of the second column must therefore be delayed until the proper time, that is, by one clock pulse. The progress of data through the first row of PEs as time progresses is illustrated in Table 13.2. This same progressive delaying principle applies across all the rows, and correspondingly down the columns, of the array, leading to the skewing of the input data shown in the figure.

It is also worth noting that, at the first clock, only one element of the PE array is computing a useful result, at the second three are active, at the third six and so on. Similarly, there comes a point, after all elements of the first row and column have been input, when the PE which was first active ceases to compute useful results. After this point, fewer and fewer PEs are usefully employed until all of the elements of the final row and column of data have passed completely through the array. This progression of activity and inactivity is shown in Figure 13.8.

Although the inactivity of a proportion of the elements of a systolic array, shown in Figure 13.8, might be regarded as a drawback in terms of efficiency, it can be outweighed by the following advantages:

- Every PE in the array is of the same simple design, reducing design time and costs.
- The layout of the array is extremely regular, reducing LSI layout difficulties.
- Inter-PE connections are all local, reducing interconnection problems.
- Very little data storage is required at each PE, reducing the required silicon area.

Table 13.2 The progression of data through a row of PEs.

Time	*PE1,1*	*PE1,2*	*PE1,3*	*PE1,4*	*PE1,5*	*PE1,6*
T1	A11×B11					
T2	A12×B12	A11×B21				
T3	A13×B13	A12×B22	A11×B31			
T4	A14×B14	A13×B23	A12×B32	A11×B41		
T5	A15×B15	A14×B24	A13×B33	A12×B42	A11×B51	
T6	A16×B16	A15×B25	A14×B34	A13×B43	A12×B52	A11×B61

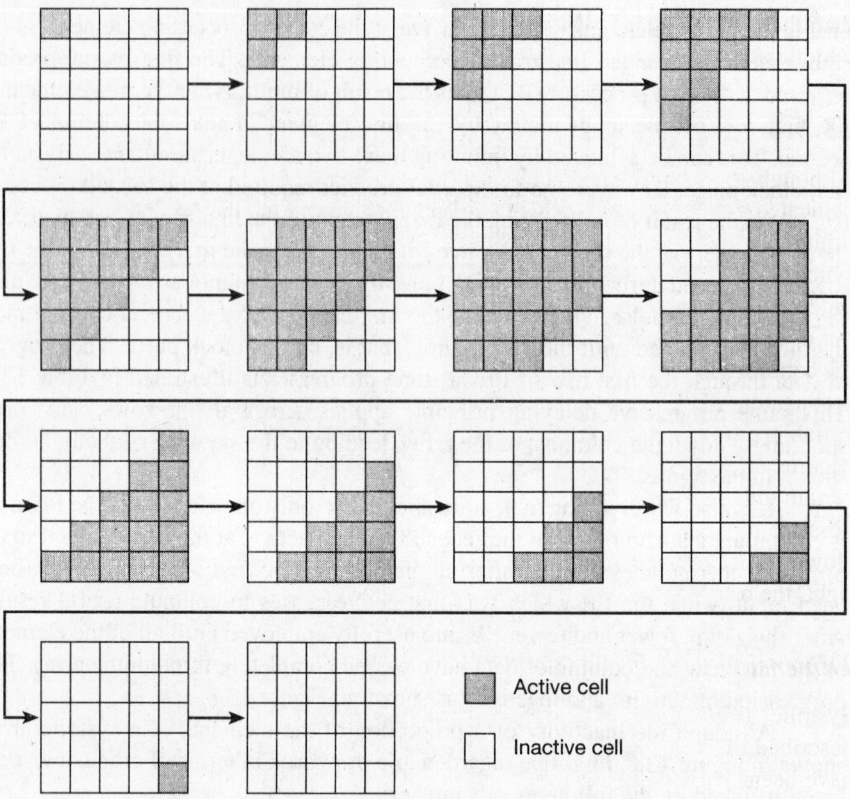

Figure 13.8 The progression of activity in a systolic array.

- Distribution of control lines throughout the array is unnecessary, again reducing silicon area and interconnection problems.
- No control program is needed, enhancing the ease of use.

It is, therefore, apparent that single-function systolic devices such as that outlined above can be simple to construct and use, and cost-effective to build.

The example given above demonstrates the main principles of systolic arrays, but does not illustrate the variety of implementations and applications which can be, and have been, attempted. This variety is described in the following sections. At this point in Chapter 11 it was possible to briefly summarize the early history of the development of SIMD systems and that of the principles embodied in them. The same exercise is scarcely possible for systolic arrays. Partly because of the comparative ease of implementing systolic devices, partly because of the greater interest in and understanding of parallel computing which prevailed during their development, and partly because commercial developments of the idea have been few, the growth of investigation into this area was more diverse, more explosive and shorter-lived than that for the SIMD principle. In the following sections the reader may discover why this has been so.

13.3.1 Design space

Although the basic idea of the systolic paradigm was to have a single-function, dedicated processing chip, designers soon discovered that this was an unnecessarily limiting constraint. It proved possible, while still retaining the basic notion of synchronously propagated data, to incorporate considerable variations on the theme. Indeed, it was realized that the data and function could well be interchanged without upsetting the basic idea, so that the data array could be regarded as static, while the control function was propagated across it, modifying the data (and sometimes the propagated control) as it went. By adopting these ideas, together with those of variable precision and dimensionality, the design space for systolic systems has become almost as diverse as that of SIMD machines. This expansion has led to a certain amount of overlap and convergence with the SIMD area. It might even be possible to argue that systolic systems are a constrained subset of SIMD systems. However, if we consider systolic arrays as a category of architecture in their own right, the design space can be subdivided into a number of areas, as follows.

Dimensionality

Systolic architectures are not confined to the type of two-dimensional system described in the introduction to this section. Many systolic algorithms/architectures have been developed in the application area of image processing. In particular, the operation known as spatial convolution is particularly well suited to systolic implementations. The basic operation, in image terms, is illustrated in Figure 13.9. At every point in an image, a pixel is regarded as being at the centre of a defined area (a three by three pixel area is shown in the figure). If the pixel values in the area are specified as p_{ij} and a fixed set of values, called the weights, are assigned to the defined area and are designated as w_{ij} then the value of the central pixel is replaced by a new value (V) given by

$$V = \frac{1}{n} \sum_{ij} p_{ij} w_{ij} \qquad (13.2)$$

Since this function is a sum of products over an array of values, it is an obvious candidate for a systolic implementation. However, there are two significant differences from the example given in the introduction. First, one of the sets of inputs to the multiplications is a fixed set of values. These could therefore be distributed over an array of processing elements and left in place while data is pumped past permitting, for example, the same operation to be applied to a sequence of images. This would be of marginal but not significant benefit in terms of implementation, but of considerable performance benefit in the multiple image context. Second, and more important, the convolution algorithm itself can be transformed from a two-dimensional operation to a pair of two one-dimensional operations executed in sequence:

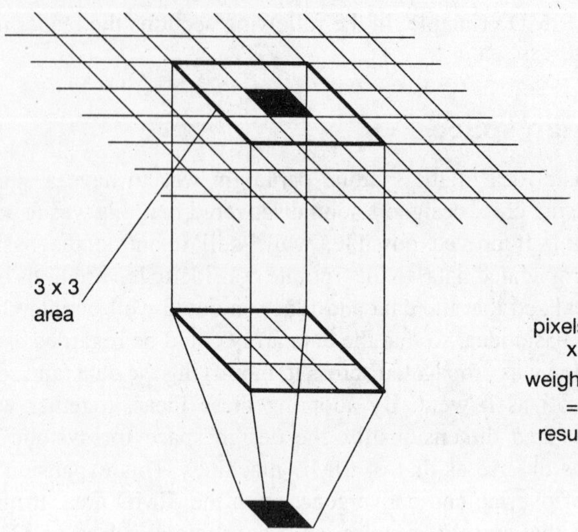

Figure 13.9 The principle of spatial convolution.

$$V_H = \sum_i w_i p_i \tag{13.3}$$

$$V = \frac{1}{2} \sum_j V_H p_j$$

These functions can then be executed by separate devices of considerably reduced complexity, comprising linear strings of elements rather than two-dimensional arrays, as shown in Figure 13.10. Each of these devices is a one-dimensional systolic system.

The design space for dimensionality in systolic design is therefore that shown in Figure 13.11. The figure includes a dotted line for systolic systems of higher dimensions. This reflects an obvious theoretical possibility which has not yet been investigated.

Precision

The question of the design space relating to precision in systolic arrays is not completely straightforward. Clearly, given appropriate complexity at each node of the array, and suitable interconnection between nodes, it would be possible to construct either one- or two-dimensional systolic arrays operating upon any desired precision of data. The only subtlety under these conditions would be the difference between the bit precision of each element and the precision of the input data occasioned by the operations of multiplication and summing carried out by the array. Thus, an array could be designed to process single-bit data. However, at this point a new factor emerges. Many workers have observed that, in a two-dimensional array of elements, each of the dimensions could be made to correspond to the sequence of bit-values which make up a multi-bit datum. Each column and row of the array has

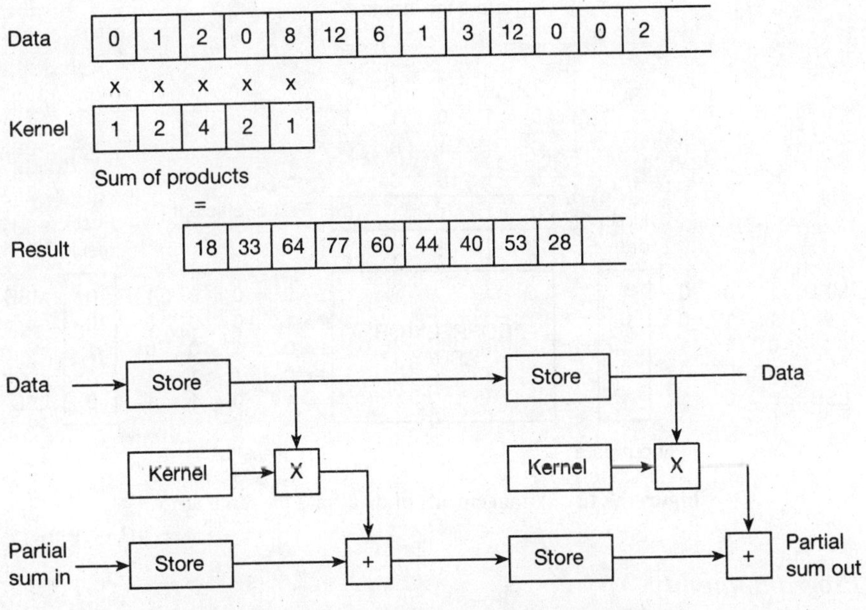

Figure 13.10 One-dimensional systolic convolution.

a different numerical significance in the way shown in Figure 13.12. The inputs to the systolic device now correspond to simple sequences of multi-bit numbers, rather than arrays of such data.

Clearly, such an arrangement demands somewhat different functions to be performed at each element, and differences in the data which are propagated through the array. A specific example of this type of system is given below in Section 13.3.2. The design space for precision within systolic arrays is therefore clearly differentiated between bit-serial and bit-parallel designs, as shown in Figure 13.13.

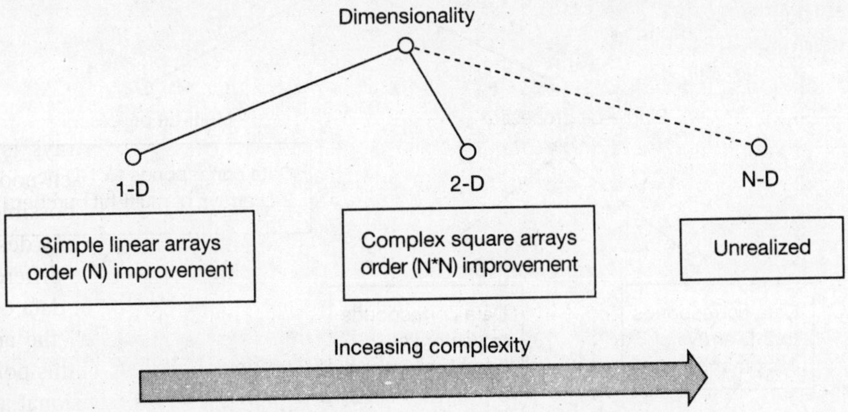

Figure 13.11 The design space for systolic dimensionality.

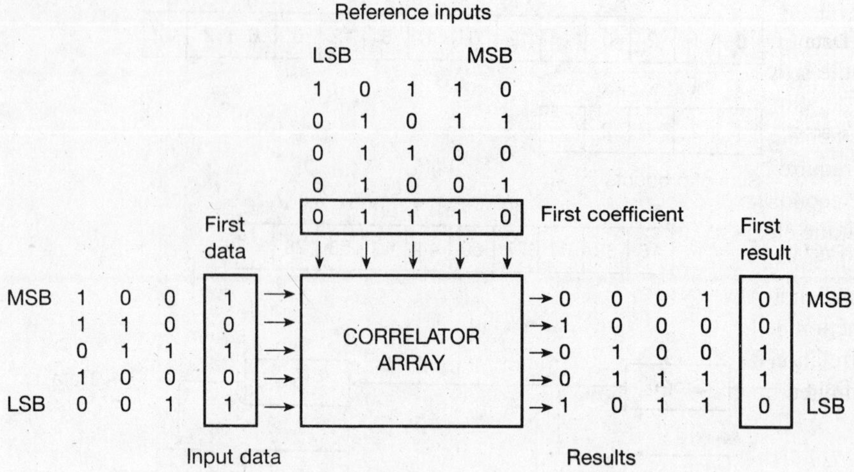

Figure 13.12 Arrangements of data for a bit-serial array.

Programmability

In spite of the remarks made in the introduction to this section of the chapter, programmability is an issue in the design of systolic systems. This has arisen for a number of reasons. First, it is apparent that a number of systolic operations, including matrix multiplication, correlation and convolution, are sufficiently similar that a common architecture could be devised which would permit execution of all the similar functions, so long as a little flexibility in controlling the exact function of each element is included. Second, it is also apparent that in many systolic operations, although the main array of elements executes exactly the same function, a

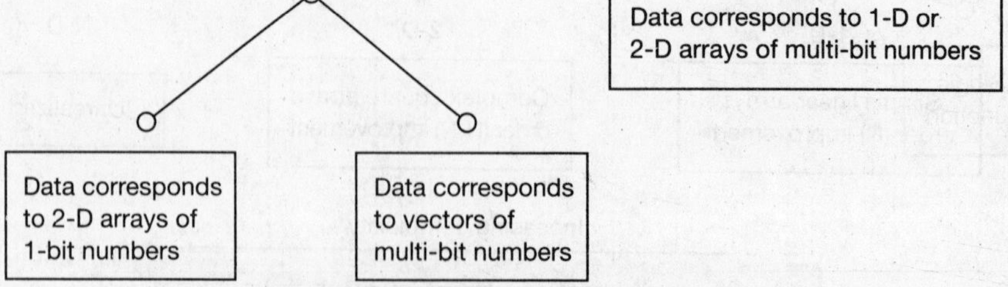

Figure 13.13 The design space for systolic precision.

different function (often rearrangement or scheduling of data) is needed at the edges of the array.

Since the most efficient system is usually constructed from identical elements, it is of obvious benefit to be able to vary the operation of sub-sets of units as required, so as to cause the whole array to execute the complete function. Finally, the economic effectiveness of constructing systems for applications from dedicated systolic elements began to be doubted as the overall functions to be executed within each application became more complex. Taken together, these factors led to the dichotomy in the design space illustrated in Figure 13.14, between single-function dedicated devices and completely programmable systems. There is a close correlation between this choice and that between single-bit and multi-bit precision, exhibited by the two examples described in Section 13.3.2.

Connectivity

There is little variation in the inter-element connectivity of systolic systems. Connections are always made between nearest neighbours, in one or two dimensions according to the configuration of the array. In two-dimensional arrays connections are usually on a square grid, with no corner connections, although a few examples of hexagonal arrangements have been designed, in which case the connections are along three axes, as illustrated in Figure 13.15.

The complexity of the inter-processor links corresponds to the precision of the processor circuits, and connections may be in either one or both directions between each pair of elements. The design space which results from this variability is shown in Figure 13.16.

Synchronicity

Although synchronous operation is one of the bedrocks of the systolic technique, some slight variation in this factor has to be considered. In some algorithms the rates at which various streams of data are propagated across an array of processors are not

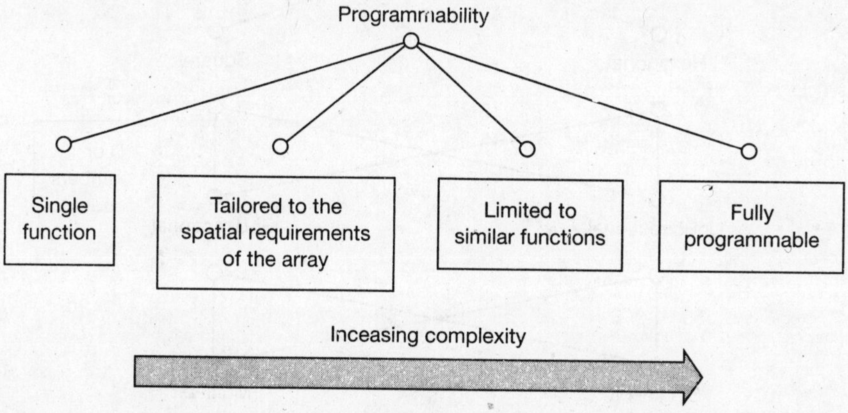

Figure 13.14 The design space for systolic programmability.

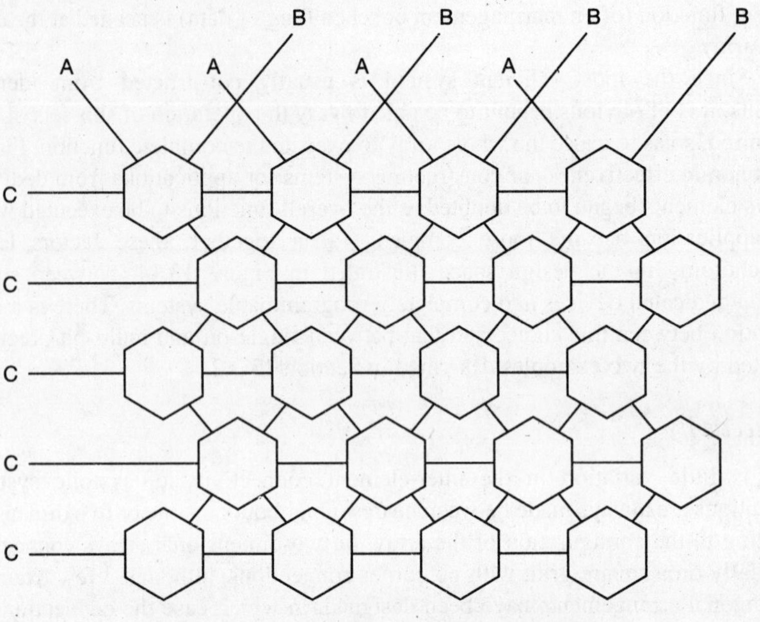

Figure 13.15 Hexagonal systolic connectivities.

the same. This problem can be overcome, however, by introducing into the data streams varying numbers of storage elements whose only function is to delay one element or another until its proper arrival time. This technique is fully explored in the example below (the WARP system). The alternative arrangements might best be described as automatic and programmed synchronicity, as illustrated in Figure 13.17.

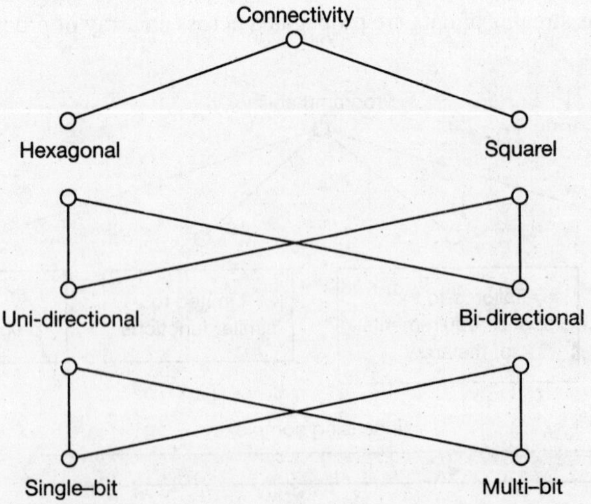

Figure 13.16 The design space for systolic interconnections.

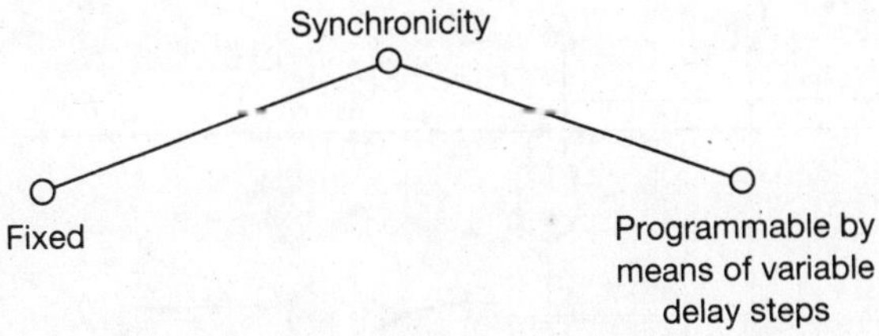

Figure 13.17 The design space for synchronicity.

13.3.2 Examples of systolic systems

Because of the great variety of existing and possible systems, it is impossible to select a single example which epitomizes the systolic idea. Instead, we shall describe two, one from each of the extreme ends of the design spectrum.

A single-function systolic chip

The basic form of a single unit of an array intended to compute a correlation function is shown in Figure 13.18(a). The unit contains a bit-level gated full adder which computes the following functions:

$$Y_{out} = Y_{in} @ (X_{in} . A_{in})$$
$$C_{out} = Y_{in} . C_{in} + Y_{in} . X_{in} . A_{in} + C_{in} . X_{in} . A_{in} \quad (13.4)$$

where

@ = exclusive OR
\+ = OR
. = AND

The arrangement of these cells into an array forming a correlator is shown in Figure 13.18(b), together with the time-skewed arrangement of data which is required. Results also appear in the time-skewed form shown and are, in effect, the set of binary coefficients

$$Y_{in} \quad n = 0,1,\ldots,m \quad (13.5)$$

which taken together form the binary number Y_i given by:

$$Y_i = Y_{i0}2^0 + Y_{i1}2^1 + \ldots\ldots\ldots \quad (13.6)$$

The size of the array is determined by the precision of data and coefficients used, while any real convolver chip would have additional peripheral cells. In general such devices require particular skewing of the data to be presented to the array and in some cases the circuits required to implement this, and the equivalent de-skewing of results, are integrated onto the same very large scale integration

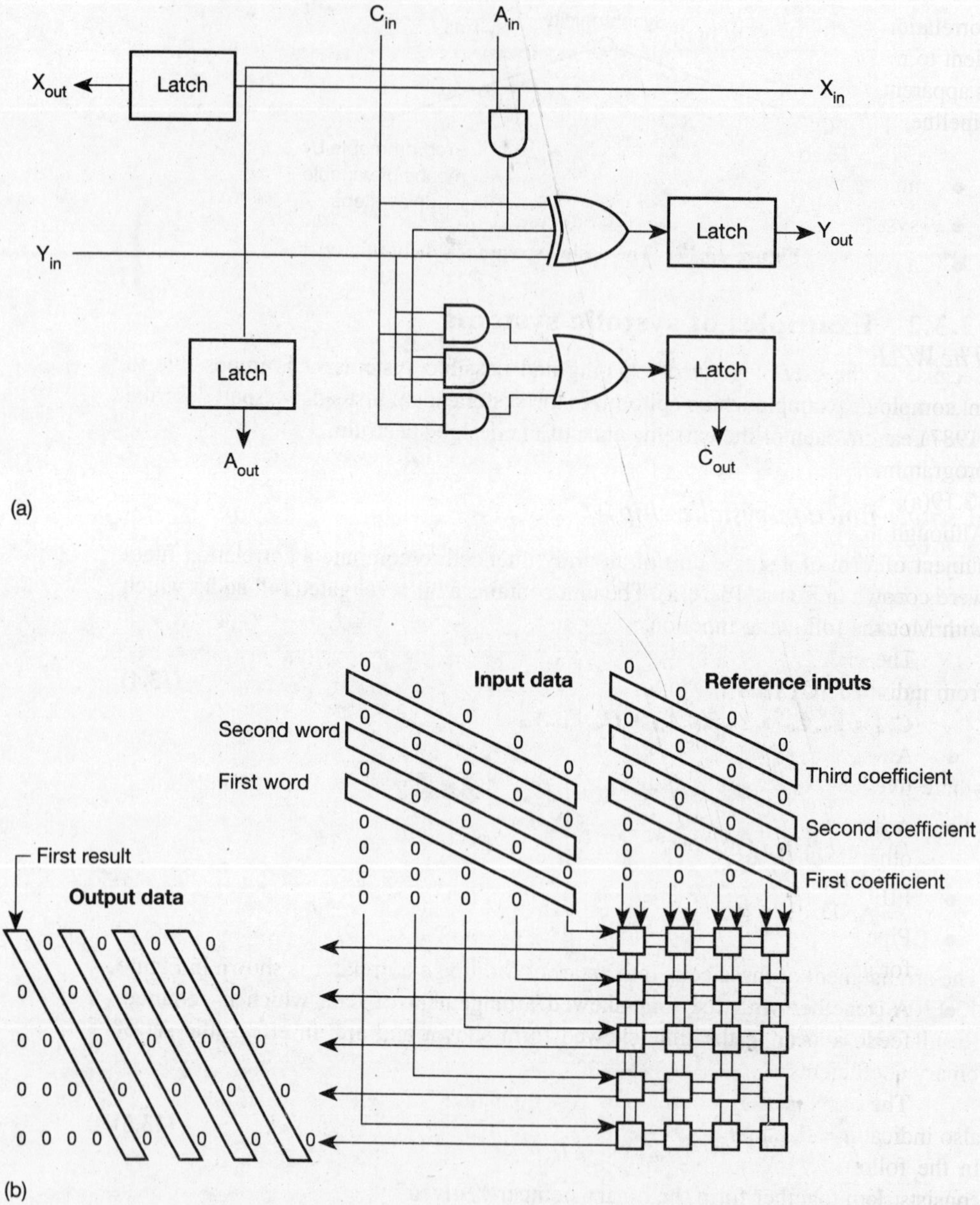

Figure 13.18 (a) A bit-serial inner product circuit element; (b) A bit-serial correlator array.

(VLSI) device. Because the devices are optimized for a particular operation (and are, as a corollary, unable to perform any other) their performance is extremely good. These VLSI devices, described by McCanny and McWhirter (1982), operated at 20 MHz and the correlator chip could therefore execute, for example, a 16-stage correlation on 9-bit data over a 512 × 512 pixel image in about 14 ms. This is sufficient to maintain single-function frame-rate image processing using a single chip. It is apparent, therefore, that a collection of systolic chips of this type, assembled into a pipeline, would provide a reasonable solution in applications where:

- an overall processing algorithm is known;
- systolic algorithms are available for each stage of the process;
- a relatively small number of components make up the overall algorithm.

The WARP programmable systolic computer

In complete contrast to the above is the WARP processor developed by Kung (1987) at Carnegie-Mellon University in the late 1970s. This is a fully programmable system based on the simple linear architecture shown in Figure 13.19(a), which utilizes the complex processing element shown in 13.19(b). Although it would be somewhat of an exaggeration to say that the system was the subject of full commercial exploitation, a number of examples of WARP systems were constructed, for use outside Carnegie-Mellon University, under an agreement with Motorola.

The processor cell, one of which occupies a single Eurocard, is constructed from individual integrated circuits and incorporates the following components:

- An internally pipelined, 32-bit floating-point multiplier and ALU, each with five pipeline stages.
- A data RAM having 4 k 32-bit words, which can be used to store, amongst other data, look up tables of correlation coefficients.
- FIFO registers which ensure proper synchronization of data streams.
- Pipeline registers which can be used for synchronization of data streams or for general storage.
- A crossbar switch which permits a variety of data paths, including internal feedback, to be implemented.

The operation of the system is best illustrated through three examples, which also indicate the range of computations which can be programmed onto the system. In the following examples it will become obvious that programming the system consists largely of configuring the internal processor connectivity. This is in accordance with one of the guiding principles of systolic processing, that the functioning of the array should be, in some sense, automatic.

Convolution Figure 13.20 shows how the system is configured to carry out simple one-dimensional convolution. Each element of the linear array is arranged to carry out the classical inner product computation, utilizing pre-distributed weights and the appropriate insertion of delay units in the data stream to compensate for the internal pipelining in the floating-point units.

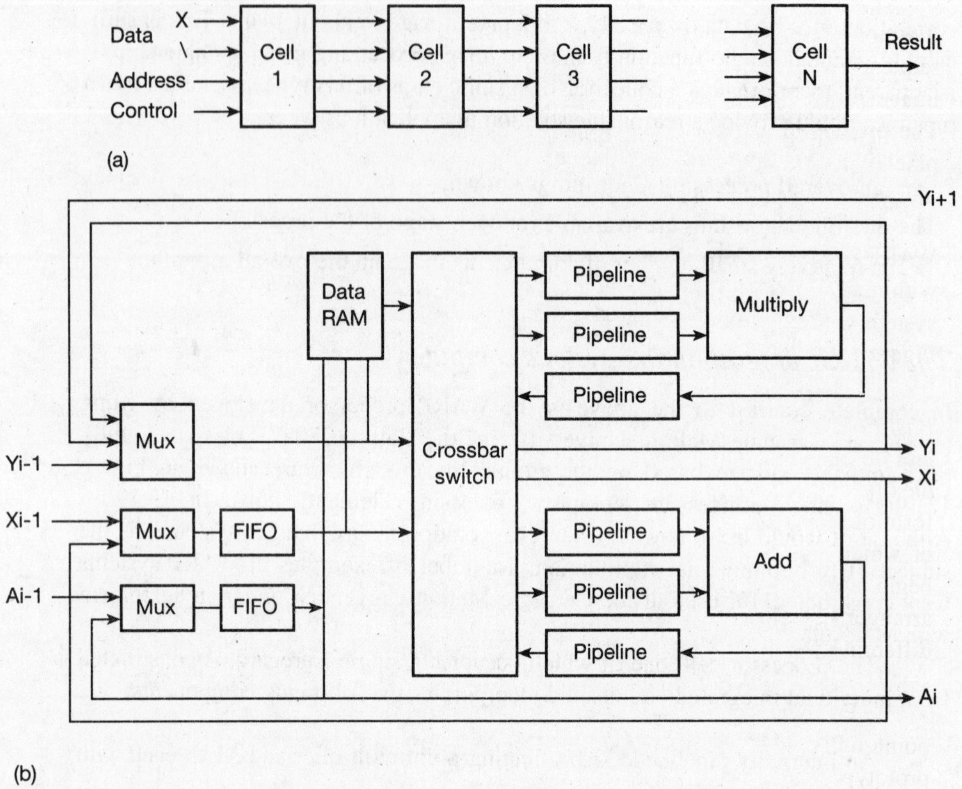

Figure 13.19 (a) The WARP linear systolic architecture; (b) The WARP processing element.

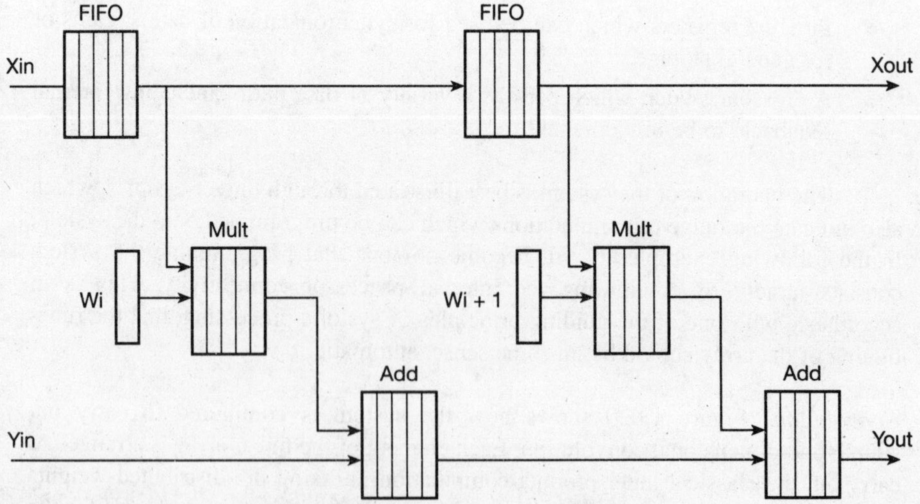

Figure 13.20 Convolution on the WARP system.

Interpolation This function is often required when a discretized data stream (a sequence of pixels, for example) has to be resampled. This happens frequently in image processing when a digitized picture undergoes geometrical transformation. The process is carried out by distributing the original value associated with each pixel over a set of pixels. Thus the new value at each point is a sum of products, each individual product being an original pixel value multiplied by a fractional weight. The distribution of weights need not be the same for each resultant point, and the WARP machine deals with this requirement by storing a variety of sets of weights within the local RAM of each processor and using them as is appropriate. The system configuration required to execute this operation is therefore that shown in Figure 13.21.

Fast Fourier transform Computation of an n-point discrete Fourier transform is a less obvious example for systolic implementation, and utilizes to the full the complexity of each WARP cell. The algorithm employed uses the constant geometry form of the fast Fourier transform, requiring $2n$ stages of butterfly operations, each of which involves four multiplications and six additions. Each cell can therefore begin a new butterfly operation every six cycles, using the two-level systolic arrangement shown in Figure 13.22. Each cell is executing elements of up to four different butterfly operations at any one time.

Principally because of the presence in each cell of two dedicated floating-point units, the performance of the WARP system is impressive, although the prototype was completed in 1980. A 10-cell system has a peak overall computation rate of 100 MFLOPS, all of which can be utilized for appropriate algorithms.

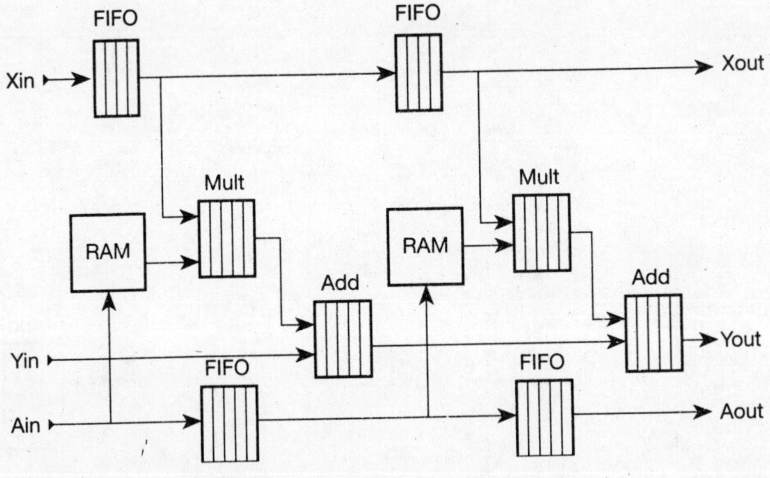

Figure 13.21 Interpolation on the WARP system.

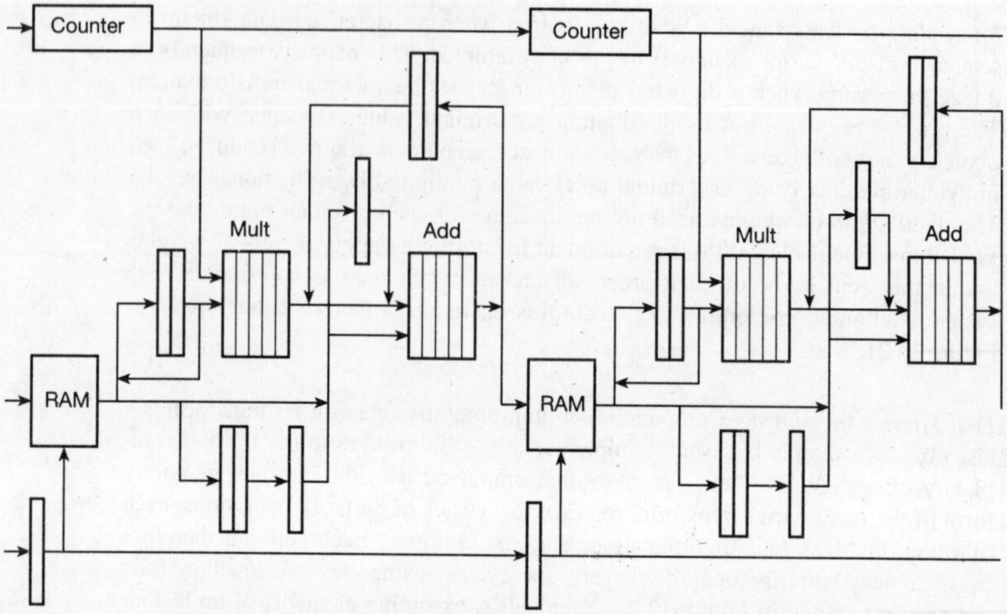

Figure 13.22 The WARP arrangement for executing an FFT operation.

13.3.3 Application-array mapping

Because the function, data precision and data array size of a systolic system are all specified by any given application, the mapping between the two elements of a solution is much closer and, therefore, much more important than is the case for SIMD arrays. It is, perhaps, this factor which has limited the general application of systolic devices.

14 Vector Architectures

Section 14.1 introduces the principles of vector architectures. Section 14.2 describes the two major considerations involved in choosing the word length. Section 14.3 describes how vectorization works and Section 14.4 shows the advantages of pipelining. Section 14.5 discusses how a vectorizing computer can be both data parallel and function parallel. Section 14.6 briefly introduces the technology used in vector supercomputers, before detailed examples using the Cray family (Section 14.7) and the Convex C4/XA system (Section 14.8) are given.

14.1 Introduction

There is no doubt that by far the most successful use of data parallelism during the past decade or more has been in vectorizing supercomputers. Since the first of the Cray machines (the Cray-1) appeared in 1976, until the recent advent of multiprocessor systems such as the CM-5 described in Chapter 11, vector supercomputers were the *de facto* standard for high performance in scientific computing. While this was due in part to the advanced technology employed in such systems, a major part of their success was conferred by the architectural features of vectorization. As illustrated in Figure 14.1, the main components of the vectorizing paradigm are fourfold.

First, a high degree of data-parallelism is applied to the basic computational objects of the paradigm – the words. Vectorizing supercomputers can employ effective word lengths significantly greater than the corresponding parameter for other data-parallel computers, and longer even than those employed in mainstream serial computing. This high word length is echoed in every aspect of the central computational architecture of such systems, including the memory organization and all communication channels.

Second, data words are composed into *vectors*, possibly comprising hundreds of words, which are treated by the control flow as single data entities. Thus, each of these single data items comprises perhaps as much as 64 kbytes of data. Each time an instruction is executed in the main program, it is executed (ideally) on this amount of data. By this means, potential bottlenecks in the control flow are avoided, so there is little necessity for the use of RISC architectures in the control processors of such architectures.

Third, the technique of pipelining is applied to the fullest extent, both micro-pipelining of each appropriate computational element and macro-pipelining of multiple computational elements. Further, pipelining of data input/output is applied to the contents of the data vectors described above, wherever this is appropriate and possible.

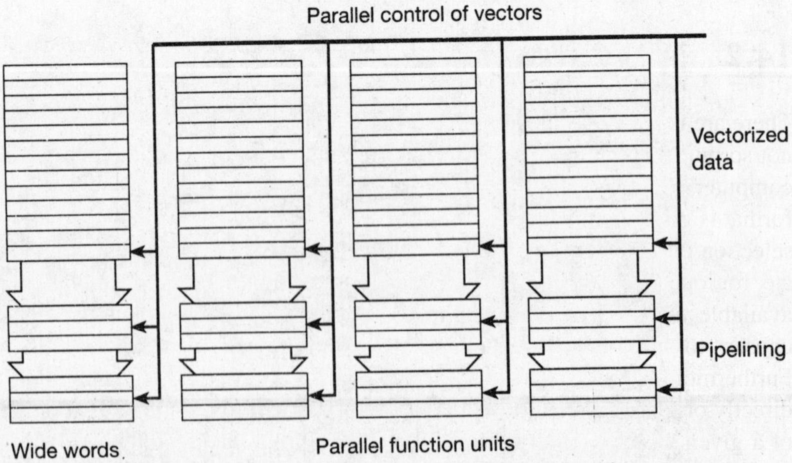

Figure 14.1 Components of a vectorizing supercomputer.

Fourth, parallelism of computational elements, both similar and disparate, is applied whenever possible. Thus, simultaneous streams of vectors may be processed by, for example, several floating-point adders or multipliers and several (very long) integer computing elements.

Although the speed-up obtained from each of these techniques individually is modest by data-parallel computing standards (perhaps an order of magnitude from each element, as opposed to the factors of tens of thousands claimed by the SIMD paradigm), the application of all four together can be, at its most effective, cumulative, resulting in an overall speed-up of 1000 or more over the raw computing power of a single element. It must, however, be realized that this advantage is not obtained at zero effort. The selection of appropriate applications and the compilation of programs and data into appropriate formats are not trivial tasks. Although much of the process is often undertaken by parallelizing compilers, this is only successful when the application is carefully chosen in the first place. Furthermore, just as with computers of the CM5 type, although the peak performance of such systems might be quoted as, for example, 10 GFLOPS, it is generally the case that the typical achieved average performance is an order of magnitude less – 1 GFLOPS.

From the computer architecture viewpoint, vectorizing supercomputers are by far the most complex of the data-parallel systems considered in this part of the book. This is a natural consequence of the multiplicity of techniques which they utilize to achieve high performance, but it means that the task of understanding their architectures is bound to be correspondingly difficult. In the following sections we attempt to separate the various factors as far as possible, but there is inevitable interaction between them. The student should ensure that he or she fully understands each aspect of the system architecture before attempting to consider the two examples which form the last sections of this chapter.

Each of the architectural components of vectorizing supercomputers will now be considered separately. In addition, we include a short section concerning the technology of such systems, since this is an important element of their design.

14.2 Word length

There are two major considerations which affect this element of design. The first is not so much a technical matter as a question of standardization. The bulk of supercomputer programming is carried out in terms of floating-point numbers, whose format is governed by a number of possible standards. One obvious strategy for the selection of word length in a vectorizing computer is to make that length appropriate for one or another of the available standards. There are two basic lengths available as IEEE standards but, unfortunately, a number of manufacturers have chosen to implement their own configurations within those standard lengths. Furthermore, there exists the possibility of implementing the longer word either directly or by concatenation of two shorter words, in order to increase the flexibility of a given system. Finally, it would clearly be possible to implement greater word lengths, even in the absence of an appropriate standard. The design space for this factor is illustrated in Figure 14.2.

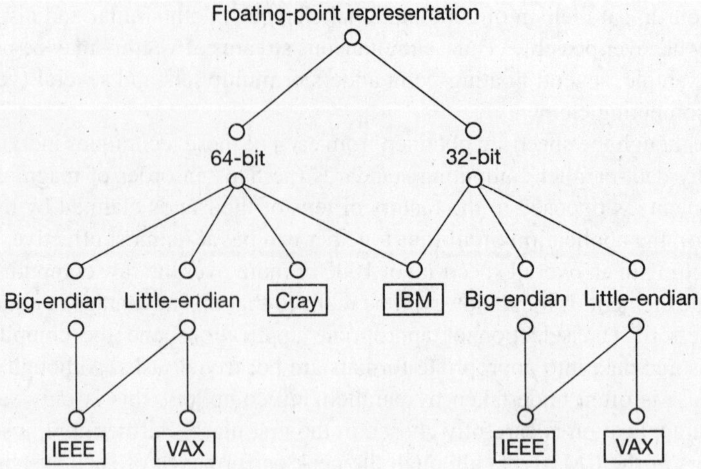

Figure 14.2 The design space for floating-point precision.

The second question arises when considering integer manipulation (even, in the limit, logical Boolean manipulation). If it is assumed that, in integer calculations, no overflow or carry will be generated (not always the case, of course) there is no reason why short integers cannot be concatenated into longer words, up to the limit of practicality. Of course, this may introduce problems of interpretation of results,

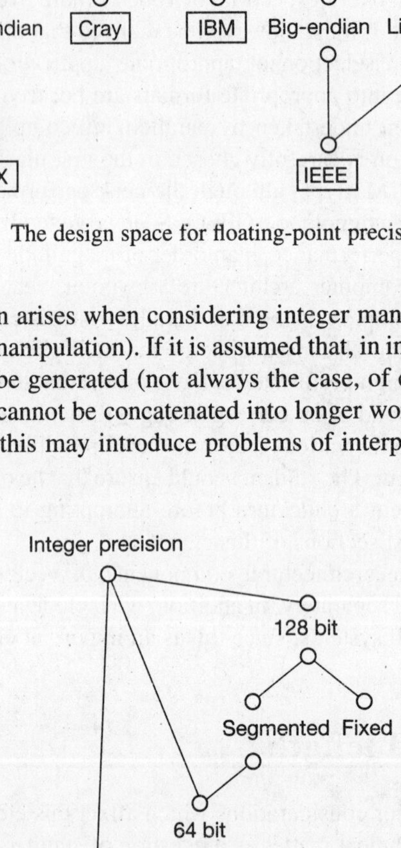

Figure 14.3 The design space for integer precision.

but these are probably no greater than those involved in satisfactory concatenation in the first place. This question really resolves itself into one of segmentation. The smaller the minimum segmentable word length in a system, the greater will be the flexibility of that system in handling small integers. However, the larger the minimum segmentation, the greater is likely to be the computational efficiency for large integers, if only because the hardware complexity need be less. There is a range of possible alternative arrangements, illustrated in Figure 14.3.

The designer of a vector supercomputer must somehow arrive at a compromise solution which is satisfactory for both types of calculation. The most frequently preferred solution is to allow the selection of floating-point precision to take precedence, and thereby to determine the precision of both computational and memory units.

14.3 Vectorization

The principle of vectorization is illustrated in Figure 14.4. The first part of the diagram indicates the timing of various operations required to execute a simple calculation (for example, addition of two integers) in a normal, scalar, computer architecture. It shows that the time required to execute the computation itself in the CPU is far outweighed by the operations of address calculation and data fetching and storing. In the case of repetitive operations of the same sort, although pipelining can improve the speed somewhat, the governing time is still that demanded by the complexities of data manipulation.

Vectorizing the operation (where it is possible) works as indicated in the second part of the diagram. Data is precompiled into blocks (vectors) which require only one set of complex fetching or storing calculations per block. For each instantiation of the function, data is then fetched or stored as though using a FIFO – one datum per clock. The time-consuming scalar data handling appears as an overhead only once per vector, rather than once per instruction, and even this can be hidden by pipelining if the vector length is sufficient. Figure 14.5 illustrates the variation in execution time with number of data elements for scalar and vector implementations of the same function, using typical timings for each micro-operation.

Of course, the success of the operation depends on two principal factors. First, can the data set on which calculation is to be performed be effectively vectorized in the required manner? There is usually little difficulty in doing this for highly data-parallel computation, but programs in which neither computation nor data is sufficiently structured present a formidable challenge. Second, can the vectorizing of the data be carried out in a manner which does not, in itself, slow down the overall operation? This is usually achieved by causing it to be done offline, by some pre-compilation process.

The design space for vectorization, *per se*, is uncomplicated, merely consisting of a decision on the length and number of vectors which can be manipulated. A much more complex question relates to how the vectors will be handled in terms of

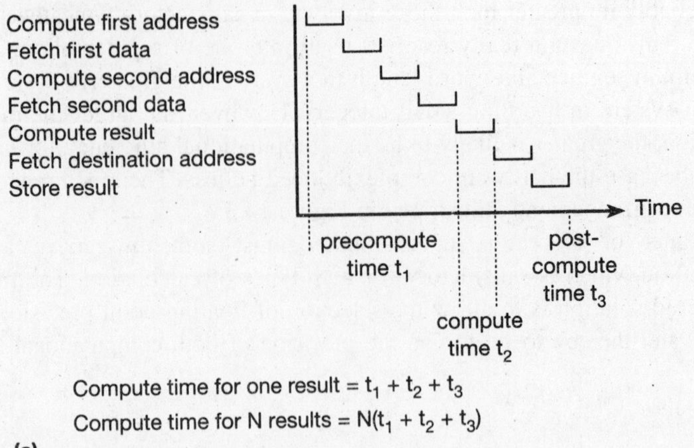

(a)

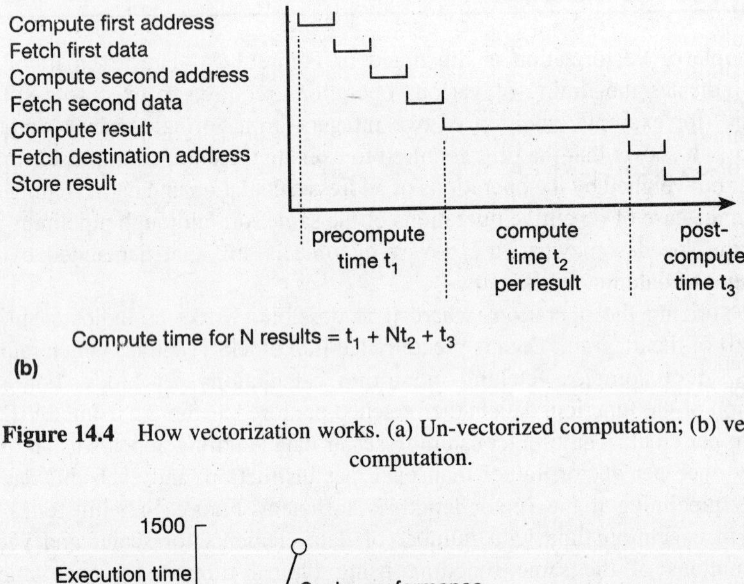

(b)

Figure 14.4 How vectorization works. (a) Un-vectorized computation; (b) vectorized computation.

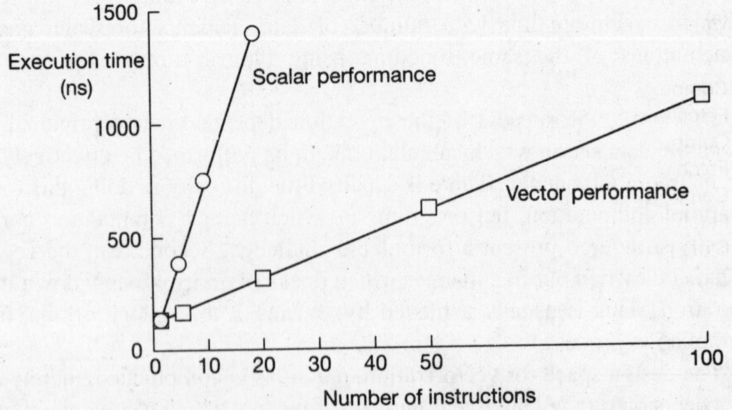

Figure 14.5 How vectorizing speeds up computation.

parallel data streams, vector registers, and so on, but this question really concerns the next two components of the architecture to be considered.

14.4 Pipelining

Pipelining is basically, as described in Chapter 5, a function-parallel technique. However, it forms such an important component of data-parallel vector supercomputers that it is necessary to describe here how the two aspects interact. The basic principle is again best illustrated by a timing diagram. Figure 14.6 shows two possible implementations of a vectorized function, the first embodying no pipelining, the second a fully pipelined implementation.

The essential improvement lies in the repetition rate at which results can be achieved on a stream of data, not in the time taken to achieve the first result. In fact, the time to the first result will be the same in both systems. However, in the pipelined system, subsequent results can be achieved at the same rate at which data is presented to the input – ideally, one result every clock tick. Of course, achieving the highest performance depends on careful design of the pipeline itself. It is likely (indeed, almost certain) that the natural maximum repetition rate of different elements of the pipeline will be dissimilar. If this is so, three approaches can be

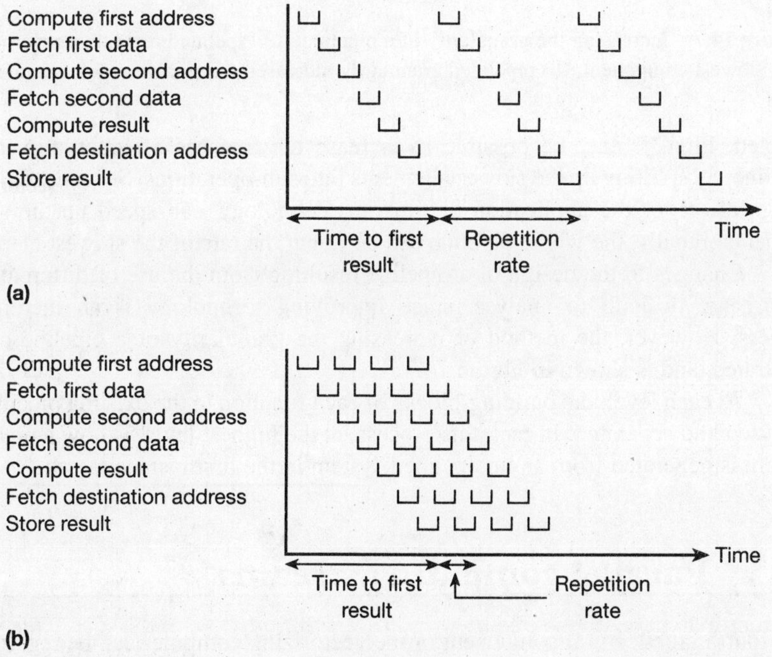

Figure 14.6 Speed improvements achieved by pipelining. (a) Non-pipelined computation; (b) pipelined computation.

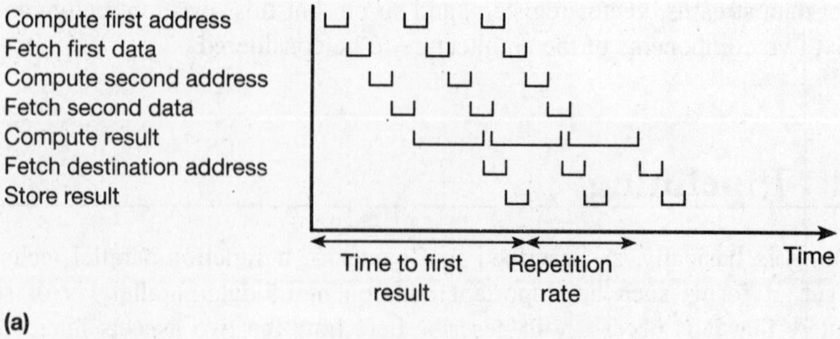

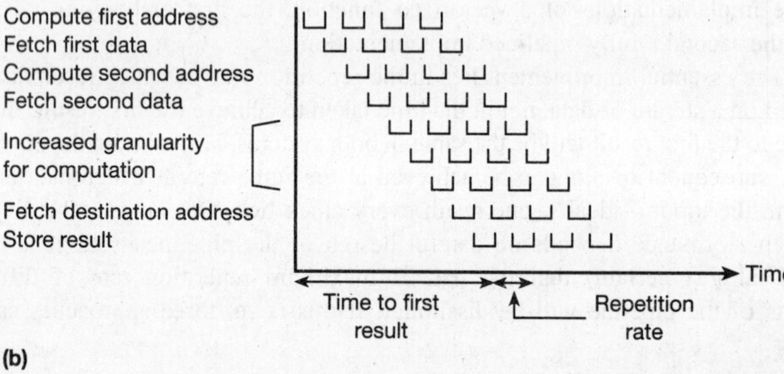

Figure 14.7 Increasing the granularity of a pipeline. (a) Pipelined repetition governed by slowest component; (b) pipelined granularity increased to improve repetition rate.

adopted. First, it may be possible to increase the fineness of granularity of the pipeline, by splitting up the slowest elements into sub-operations. Second, additional design effort, or the application of superior technology, can speed up the slower elements. Finally, the whole pipeline can be run at the rate of the slowest element.

Changes to the design of a pipeline resulting from the use of different technology are difficult to analyse, since improving technology is an incremental process. However, the method of increasing the granularity of a pipeline can be illustrated, and is shown in Figure 14.7.

At each level, the building-blocks of each function in the existing pipeline are analysed and separated. In fact, this process, at the highest level, is how a pipelined system is generated from an unpipelined system in the first instance.

14.5 Parallel computing streams

The fourth architectural component of the vectorizing computer can be regarded as function parallel, data parallel, or both, depending on the particular configuration and on the quantity and type of data which is being applied to the system. The simplest implementation of this principle is illustrated in Figure 14.8. In the system

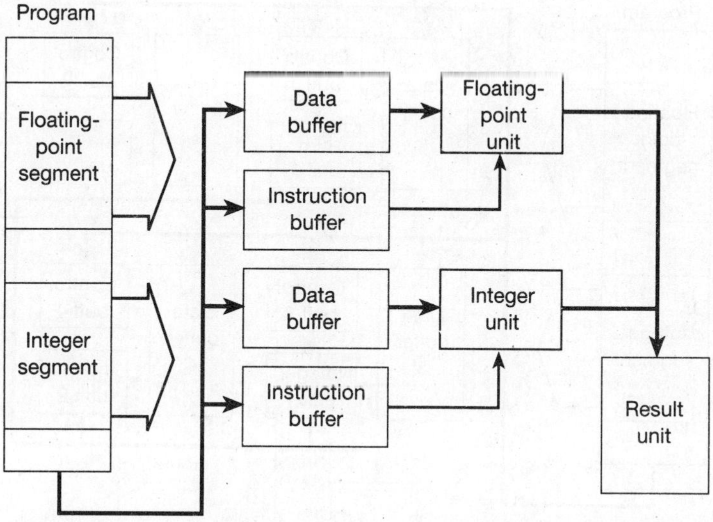

Figure 14.8 Parallel computation of floating-point and integer results.

shown, separate computational elements are provided for floating-point and integer calculation. These can operate in parallel on suitable data types if these appear at appropriate sections of a computational problem, and as long as sufficiently complex means are provided (both physically and in terms of pre-compilation) to supply the correct data at the right time. In the diagram, the physical means provided is that of data buffering, and it is perhaps easy to see at this point how vectorization could be implemented by utilizing the same registers for both purposes.

At this point it is clear that functional parallelism is being implemented. However, at the next possible stage, shown in Figure 14.9, the situation becomes more complex. Here, more than one (in this case, two) versions of each type of unit are implemented, and two different ways of decomposing a problem to take advantage of the architecture can be envisaged. First, four completely separate and independent segments of program and data could be identified and applied to the four units independently. This would involve a higher degree of functional parallelism. Second, long sequences of the same calculation could be split up and applied to the available similar parallel units, thus effectively implementing a degree of data parallelism in addition to the functional parallelism implied by the different units.

The increasing complexity of this situation is already apparent, and the difficulty of utilizing the available complexity effectively is illustrated by the moderate degree of this type of parallelism which is implemented in even the most modern of such systems. It is worth emphasizing this complexity by illustrating the design decision tree which a designer must consider in such cases. This is shown in Figure 14.10.

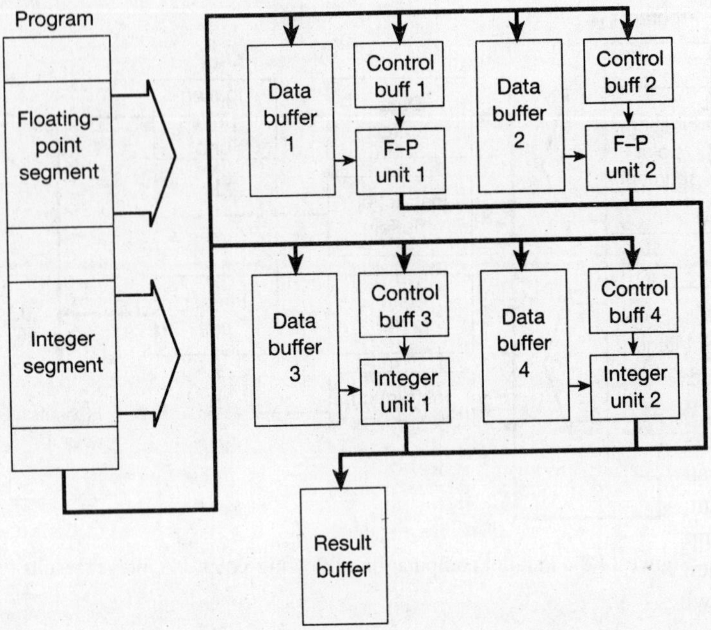

Figure 14.9 Mixed functional and data parallelism.

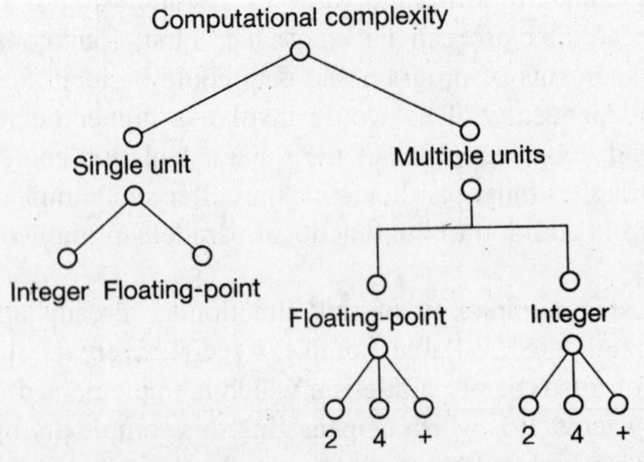

Figure 14.10 The design space for parallel computational functionality.

14.6 Technology

Because, during the period of their ascendancy, vector supercomputers were unchallenged as suppliers of the maximum available computing power, their designers were able to utilize the fastest available technology in order to achieve their ends. When it appeared in 1976, the Cray-1 computer was a technical *tour de force* which combined gates with astonishingly fast switching times (12 ns clock period), a massive power consumption demanding Freon cooling circuits, and a startling physical configuration intended to minimise the length of connecting wires (it takes an electronic signal about 1 ns to pass along 1 foot of wire). This concentration on the use of advanced technology has continued to the present day (see Section 14.7), but the advantage of the supercomputer manufacturers has been eroded over the decades. Whereas in 1976 that advantage could be considered at least an order of magnitude in speed, the enormous effort which has been applied to the development of integrated circuits for the business and domestic computing market has reduced the advantage to perhaps little more than a factor of two in clock rate. That vector supercomputers substantially retain a significant advantage in computing power is due to their architectural sophistication. This factor is illustrated more completely in the following sections.

14.7 The Cray family

During the 1960s, the availability of integrated circuits permitted, for the first time, the construction of reliable supercomputing systems from large numbers of components, when increasing the complexity of systems was necessary to yield higher performance. It therefore became possible to consider approaches involving parallel operation of parts of the system, including techniques such as pipelining and vector processing within the CPU and the movement of some system functions to separate processors.

Beginning in 1976, Cray supercomputers have been at the leading edge of numerically intensive computing. Each succeeding generation has incorporated technological innovation and increasing parallelism to extend the capabilities of the systems. The results of this process are shown in Table 14.1.

Key aspects of these systems include the concept of vector processing, which overcame the instruction issue bottleneck by permitting one instruction to initiate action on a series of data elements. The combination of vector instructions with the use of vector registers allowed the processing of data within the CPU independently of the traffic of data between memory and processor logic. Pipelining is used both in the instruction issue process and within the arithmetic units. Finally, multiple independent functional units, each of which is itself a pipeline segmented at every clock period, further increase parallelism.

The X-MP system was the first multiprocessor supercomputer. It incorporated synchronization logic between the processors in such a way that all processors could be coordinated on one task. It also introduced multiple parallel paths to memory

Table 14.1 Performance of four generations of Cray systems.

System	*CPUs*	*Clock (Mhz)*	*FP results per clock per CPU*	*Words moved per clock per CPU*	*MFLOP rate at 1 data word per clock*
Cray-1	1	80	2	1	80
X-MP	4	105	2	3	840
Y-MP	8	166	2	3	2 667
C90	16	240	4	6	15 360

from each CPU, thereby improving the performance for memory-intensive programs.

In the Y-MP system, the number of processors was increased to eight and the clock cycle time was reduced. Packaging improvements and the use of higher levels of integration allowed the construction of a processor on a single physical module.

In the C90 systems, further increases in the number of processors and the clock speed were achieved. The architecture was modified to employ double-size vector registers and duplicated functional units allowing two results from each logical pipeline in each clock cycle.

14.7.1 System architecture of the Cray C90

The range of C90 systems includes physical frames which can accommodate 2, 4, 8 and 16 processors. The largest of these, the C916 system, has the following major characteristics:

- 16 CPUs.
- More than 8 Gbyte of high-speed central memory uniformly accessible to each CPU.
- A maximum of 256 I/O channels providing up to 13.6 Gbyte/s bandwidth to peripheral devices and networks.
- Connectivity to closely couple the C916 system to a massively parallel Cray T3D.
- Optional solid-state storage device (SSD) containing up to 32 Gbyte of storage with a maximum bandwidth of 13.6 Gbyte/s
- Simultaneous vector and scalar processing.
- Each CPU has two independent vector processing segments.
- Vector processing, the performance of iterative operations on sets of ordered data, provides results at rates greatly exceeding those of conventional scalar processing, while scalar operations complement the vector capability by providing solutions to problems not readily adaptable to vector techniques.

14.7.2 Memory organization

The central system memory is shared by all of the CPUs, any one of which has access to the full memory address space. Each CPU has four double-width ports to central memory, as shown in Figure 14.11. The central memory is organized so that multiple data transfers may proceed in parallel. The following hierarchical arrangement is employed. There are:

- Eight independent sections
- Eight subsections per section
- Two bank groups per subsection
- Eight banks in a bank group
- 1024 total banks.

Each CPU is connected by an independent access path to each of the sections, allowing up to 128 64-bit memory references per clock period.

The central memory contains program code for the CPUs, as well as data for problem solution. A maximum of 1024 Mwords is available, each word comprising 80 bits (64 data bits and 16 bits for error detection and correction), and the memory is shared by the CPUs and the I/O section.

14.7.3 System interconnections

An independent I/O subsystem (IOS) matches the processing rates of the CPUs with high I/O transfer rates for communication with mass storage units, other peripheral devices and a wide variety of other computer systems and networks. It supports a

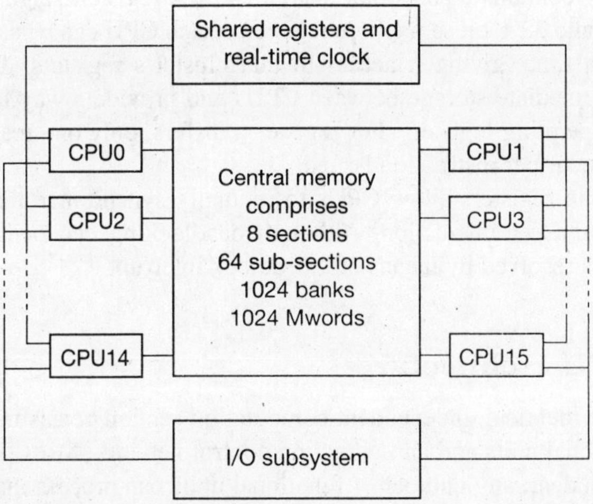

Figure 14.11 Communication between CPUs and memory.

number of 200 Mbyte/s high-speed channels for connection to the massively parallel T3D system and to the solid state disk subsystem (SSD). The IOS is connected to central memory by up to 16 high-speed communication channels. The SSD is connected to central memory with up to four 1800 Mbyte/s channels.

Each CPU is connected to central memory through four ports. Data transfer to and from the operating registers and instruction fetches to the instruction buffers take place through these memory ports. Three are used for register transfers, the fourth for I/O and instruction fetches. Once an instruction is issued to a port, that port is reserved until all references are made for that instruction. If an instruction requires a port that is busy, issue is blocked.

Each port is made up of two independent pipes, each capable of making one memory reference per clock period. The references for all the elements of a block transfer are made through the two pipes of a port. Concurrent block reads and writes are not examined for memory overlap hazard conditions so software must detect the cases where this hazard occurs. Instructions are provided to resolve these cases and assure sequential operation. The inter-processor communication section of the mainframe has three features to pass data and control information between CPUs:

- Shared registers to pass data
- Semaphore registers to synchronize programs
- Inter-processor interrupts to initiate exchange sequences.

These features are employed as the primitives upon which the higher-level parallel software constructs depend. The CPU inter-processor communication section consists of identical groups of clusters. The number of clusters supported depends on the maximum number of CPUs supported in the configuration – there will be one more cluster available than the number of CPUs, up to a maximum of 17. Each cluster contains eight 32-bit shared address registers, eight 64-bit shared scalar registers and 32 1-bit semaphore registers. Each CPU can be assigned to only one cluster at a time, giving it access to that cluster's registers. These registers function as intermediate storage between CPUs and provide a way to transfer data between their operating registers. For register transfers, only one read or one write operation can occur per instruction issued.

Semaphore registers allow CPUs to mutually synchronize their operations, using the test and set instruction. Although deadlocking can occur using these instructions, it is resolved by means of a deadlock interrupt.

14.7.4 CPU architecture

Each CPU is an identical, independent computation section consisting of operating registers, functional units and an instruction control network. Most functional units are fully independent; any number of functional units can process instructions concurrently. The operating registers and functional units are associated with three types of processing: address, scalar and vector.

- Address processing is used on internal control information such as addresses and indices, and on control information related to vector length and shift count. It employs two integer ALUs.
- Scalar processing is the application of arithmetic operations to single numbers or pairs of numbers. Five functional units are dedicated solely to scalar processing, and three floating-point units are shared with vector operations. Scalar and vector processing can execute concurrently except during floating-point operations.
- Most vector functional units perform operations on operands obtained from two vector registers or from a vector and a scalar register. Results from a vector functional unit are delivered to a vector register.

A functional unit receives operands from registers, performs a specific operation on them, and delivers the result to a register when the operation is completed. Functional units usually operate in three-address mode with source and destination addressing limited to register designators. Functional units are fully segmented – a new set of operands for unrelated computation can enter a functional unit each clock period, even though the function unit time can be more than one clock period.

There are two parallel sets of floating-point (FP) functional units with each set containing three functional units. These units perform FP arithmetic for both scalar and vector operations. The vector registers use both sets of functional units, with one set processing the even-numbered elements and the other set processing the odd-numbered elements. For an operation involving only scalar operands, only one set of FP units is used.

14.7.5 Vector processing

A vector is an ordered set of elements. Examples of structures in Fortran that can be represented as vectors are one-dimensional arrays; and rows, columns and diagonals of multidimensional arrays. A long vector is processed as one or more 128-element segments and a possible shorter remainder. The processing of long vectors in Fortran is handled by the compiler and is transparent to the programmer.

In vector processing, two successive pairs of elements are processed each clock period. The dual vector pipes and the dual sets of vector functional units allow two pairs of elements to be processed during the same clock period. As each pair of operations is completed, the results are delivered to appropriate elements of the result register. The operation continues until the number of elements processed is equal to the count specified by the vector length register.

Parallel vector operations allow the generation of more than two results per clock period. They occur automatically either when successive vector instructions use different functional units and different vector registers, or when successive vector instructions use the result stream from one vector register as the operand of another operation using a different functional unit. This process is known as chaining.

Vector processing is usually faster and more efficient than scalar processing because it reduces the overhead associated with maintenance of the loop-control variables (for example, incrementing and checking the count). In many cases, loops processed as vectors are reduced to a simple sequence of instructions without branching backwards. Central memory access conflicts are reduced and functional unit segmentation is optimally exploited. Vectorization typically speeds up a code segment by a factor of about 10.

The contents of a vector register are transferred to or from central memory through a block transfer. This is accomplished by specifying a first-word address in central memory, an increment or decrement value for the address, and a vector length. The transfer proceeds at a maximum transfer rate of two words per clock period, although this can be degraded by central memory conflicts.

14.7.6 Technology

In any significant engineering project there are trade-offs to be made in the choice of technologies used. In the case of vector parallel designs, the basic technology chosen is dictated by switching speed in conjunction with the level of integration available. For this reason the most powerful C916 system is implemented in emitter-coupled logic (ECL). The same architecture has also been implemented in CMOS technology for the Cray EL98 entry-level system, which is air-cooled and significantly lower priced.

In each generation of computer system design, ambition is bounded by practical concerns related to the availability of components which can be used to construct a robust and reliable product. Figure 14.12 shows the increase in complexity of the processors in four generations of Cray systems. The progression in basic component technology makes possible the increasing trend per processor – the overall complexity of the processor part of the system is obviously increasing even faster. Table 14.2 shows the logic component level of integration for each range of systems.

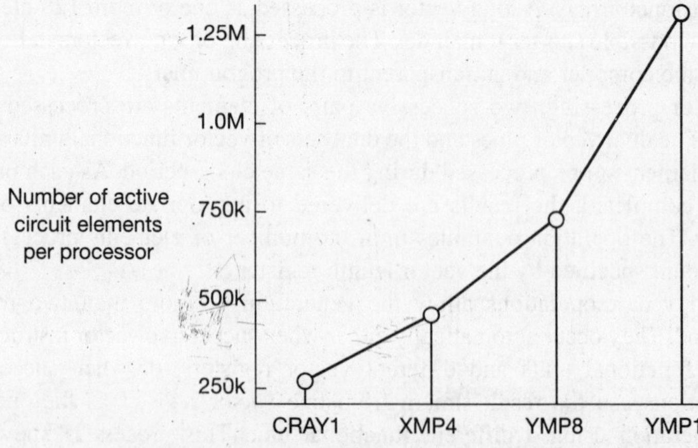

Figure 14.12 The increasing complexity in Cray systems.

Table 14.2 Integration density for four generations of system.

System	*Gates/chip*
Cray-1	2
Cray X-MP	16
Cray Y-MP	2500
Cray C90	10000

As the number of processors rises, an increasing proportion of logic has to be devoted to ensuring the ability of the memory subsystem to deliver data to the CPUs at high rates and low latency. In the case of the C916 system approximately half of the logic within the system is allocated to this task.

14.7.7 Software

Parallel operation of hardware is to no avail unless it can be harnessed by applications software. Cray system software offers a consistent user interface to the functionality and architectural features of the Cray systems.

The operating system UNICOS is based on UNIX System V, and provides interactive, local batch and remote batch interfaces. Several functions of the Fourth Berkeley Software Distribution (4.3 BSD), along with significant Cray extensions, provide additional performance and operational enhancements. UNICOS provides multiprogramming and multiprocessing facilities, and supports the application of multiple CPUs to a single process (multitasking). Multitasking is most effective when it is used on programs that embody a high degree of parallelism.

From the point of view of the programmer seeking performance, specific arrangements are required to support the use of multiple processors to execute a single application. The multitasking facilities provided result in substantial throughput improvements. To achieve this, the three techniques of auto-tasking, micro-tasking and macro-tasking can all be utilized in the same program.

- Auto-tasking automatically partitions parallel Fortran and C codes across multiple CPUs, exploiting parallelism at the loop level. It requires no programmer intervention, but permits experienced programmers to tune programs for optimum performance.
- Micro-tasking also exploits parallelism at the DO-loop level in Fortran and C code. It does not require code modification; rather, users insert directives to indicate where parallelism exists. The synchronization costs of micro-tasking are extremely low, implying that small code segments can be successfully partitioned.
- Macro-tasking allows parallel execution of code at the subprogram level on multiple processors. The user interface is a set of subroutines that explicitly define and synchronize tasks at the subprogram level for Fortran, C or Ada code. The user inserts calls to these subroutines.

14.8 The Convex C4/XA system

The Convex Computer Corporation was founded in 1982 and presently holds a substantial share of the world vector supercomputer market. Their most recent high-end system, the C4/XA, has the general configuration illustrated in Figure 14.13. The main components of the design are as follows.

14.8.1 The crossbar/memory system

This element of the overall system is regarded as the heart of the C4/XA design. The design aim was to prevent bottlenecks in the supply of control and data information from interfering with the prodigious processing power which the system provides. All of the data paths in the subsystem are 64 bits wide.

Each memory module, configured as a single card, includes 32 interleavable memory banks, each of up to 32 Mbyte, giving up to 1 Gbyte per module. The memory access time is 50 ns, and the bank cycle time is only 19 clocks. The transfer rate of each module is 1.1 Gbyte/s, and up to four modules can be incorporated in a system.

The communication mechanism provided between the memory and CPU modules is a 5×5 non-blocking crossbar illustrated in Figure 14.14 (the additional ports to the crossbar are required for external communications and utilities). The crossbar can sustain a bandwidth of 1.1 Gbyte/s per port, up to a total of 4.4 Gbyte/s.

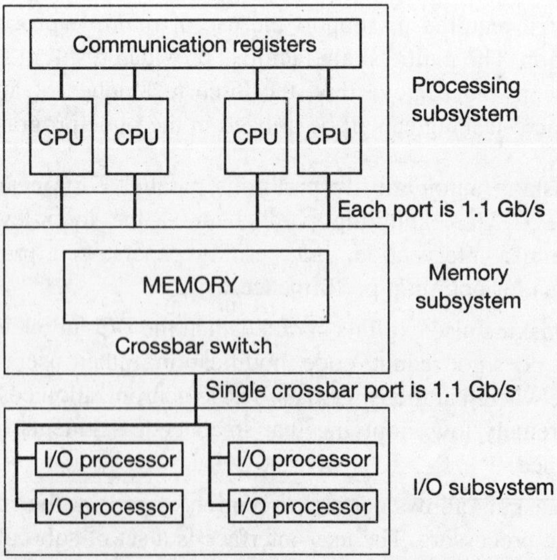

Figure 14.13 The overall architecture of the Convex C4/XA system.

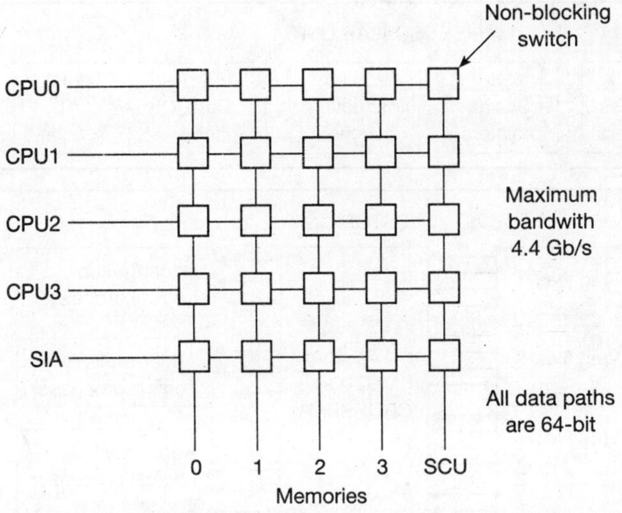

Figure 14.14 The configuration of the crossbar switch.

14.8.2 The processor units

The Convex C4/XA system incorporates up to four processor units. The overall configuration of each unit is illustrated in Figure 14.15. The main features of the design include :

- All data paths within the processor operate at 1 Gbyte/s.
- The system clock runs at 7.5 ns.
- There are separate scalar and vector units which operate in parallel.
- There is very high provision of cache memory (both data and instruction) for the scalar unit.
- There are three, parallel, floating-point pipes, each of which produces two results per clock in 64-bit configuration or four results per clock in 32-bit configuration.
- Both scalar and vector units are supplied with large numbers of registers. In particular, the vector files which feed the floating-point pipelines comprise 16 128-bit registers.
- A crossbar is provided for communication between the vector register files and the floating-point pipes.

When fully utilized, these features permit a maximum computation rate of 1 620 MFLOP/s in each processor unit, in addition to the scalar processing.

14.8.3 The I/O subsystem

Input/output of data is a vital part of any supercomputing system. In the C4/XA system, a dedicated 1.1 Gbyte/s port is provided for this function, and this is

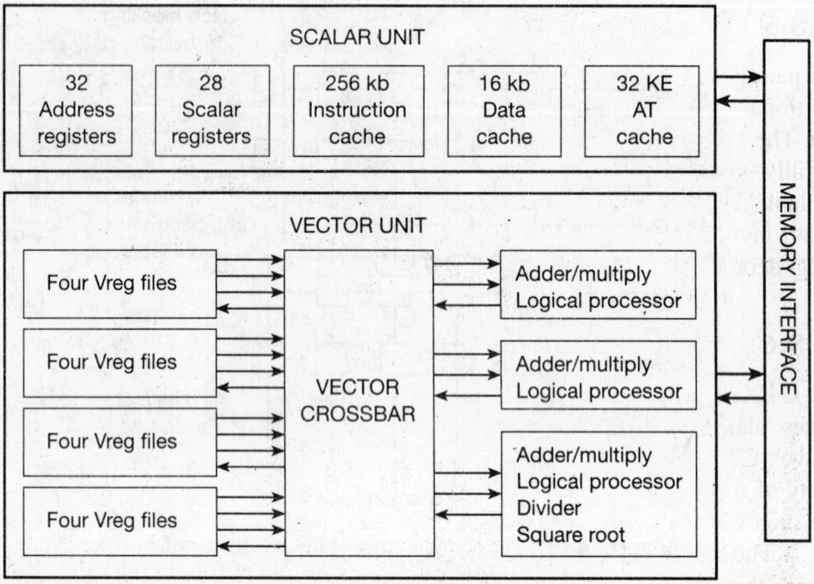

Figure 14.15 The processor configuration.

supported by a full range of data interface formats and protocols including VME, SCSI, FIPS-60 and IPI-2. In particular, provision is made for the installation of substantial disk farms, which can be needed to support the enormous data storage requirements of some applications.

14.8.4 A complex instruction set

In complete contrast to the RISC architectures which are currently fashionable in microprocessors, the C4/XA processor implements a very rich instruction set in order to achieve maximum performance. Important elements of the instruction set include:

- Three-address scalar instruction.
- All scalar instructions can use immediate data.
- Register+register addressing mode is supported.
- There are instructions for all possible data-type conversions.
- 32-bit logical instructions are provided.
- A select instruction reduces unpredictable branches.
- 32-bit vector instructions allow twice the 64-bit rate.
- A 32-bit vector concatenate instruction accelerates complex arithmetic.
- Compound multiply/add instructions accelerate these operations.

14.8.5 System software

The parallelism implemented in the C4/XA system is complex, involving data and functional parallelism, pipelining, memory and process interleaving and vectorization. The system software supports all of these features in either completely hidden or fully visualized mode. Thus, scheduling of processors (on an 'as soon as available' basis), memory interleaving and demand-paged virtual memory handling are all invisible to the user, whereas visualization tools are provided for programming, debugging and performance analysis.

14.8.6 Applications on Convex systems

The C4/XA is the most recently introduced high-end product from Convex, but it shares many architectural features, including its overall architecture, with the Convex C3000 series, on which a wide variety of applications have been studied. Many of these applications involve complex modelling of physical processes, and one such was involved in the deployment of the Hubble space telescope.

The telescope is powered by solar cells which are subject to extraordinarily intense thermal cycling as they pass in and out of sunlight. This cycling generates extreme mechanical stresses in these components, which meant that conventional soldering techniques could not be relied upon in their manufacture. The company tasked with constructing the solar cell panels (Telefunken Systemtechnik of West Germany) needed to model the stress patterns arising in the panels during use of their innovative parallel gap welding technique, used as an alternative to conventional soldering. The required finite-element modelling was carried out on a Convex computer using Automatic System for Kinematic Analysis software from IKO Software Service GmbH.

Seven different three-dimensional finite-element models for both silicon and gallium arsenide cells were developed, the complex non-linear and transient calculations required demanding the full power of a vectorizing supercomputer for successful and timely completion. This application is typical of the operations performed routinely on the installed base of Convex systems, and of those performed by vectorizing supercomputers in general.

References for Part III

References

Anyanwu C. D., Jalowiecki I. and Krikelis K. (1994). Evaluating ASTRA on image processing applications. In *Proc. IEE Coll. on Parallel Architectures for Image Processing*, No 1994/135

Barnes G. H. et al. (1968). The ILLIAC IV computer. *IEEE Trans*, **C-17**, 746–57

Batcher K. E. (1980). Design of a massively parallel processor. *IEEE Transactions on Computers*, **C-29**, 836–40

Blank T. (1990). The MasPar MP-1 architecture. In *Proc. IEEE Compcon Spring 1990*, IEEE, February

Convex Computer Corporation (1990). Supercomputers and space exploration. Application profile

Duff M. J. B. et al. (1973). A cellular logic array for image processing. *Pat. Recog. 5*, pp. 229–34

Fountain T. J. (1987). *Processor arrays – Architecture and Applications*. Academic Press

Fountain T. J. (1983). A survey of bit-serial array processor circuits. In *Computing Structures for Image Processing*, (M. J. B. Duff, ed.), pp. 1–14. Academic Press

Fountain T. J. (1988). Introducing local autonomy to processor arrays. In *Machine Vision*, (Freeman H., ed.), pp. 31–56. Academic Press

Gerritsen F. A. (1978). Design and implementation of the Delft Image Processor DIP-1. *PhD Thesis*, Faculty of Applied Physics, Delft University of Technology

Gregory J. and McReynolds R. (1963). The SOLOMON computer. *IEEE Trans.*, **EC-12**, pp. 774–81

Hebb D. O. (1949). *The Organisation of Behaviour*. New York: Wiley

Hillis W. D. (1985). *The Connection Machine*. MIT Press

Hinton G. E. and Sejnowski T. J. (1986). Learning and relearning in Boltzmann machines. In *Parallel distributed processing*, vols. **1 and 2**. MIT Press

Hopfield J. J. (1982). Neural networks and physical systems with emergent collective computational properties. In *Proc. Nat. Acad. Sci. USA*, **79**, 2554–8

Hopfield J. J. and Tank D. W. (1985). Neural computation of decisions in optimisation problems. *Biol. Cybern.*, **52**, 141–52

Jaloweicki I. (1995). WASP: the associative string processor. In T. Fountain, *Parallel Computing – Principles and Practice*, CUP, pp. 296–308

Kimoto T. and Yoda M. (1993). Buying and selling timing prediction system for stocks based on modular neural networks. *Fujitsu Sci. Tech. J.*, **29**(3), 257–64

Kirkpatrick S., Gellat C. D. and Vecchi M. D. (1983). Optimisation by simulated annealing. *Science*, **220**, 671–80

Kung H. T. (1987). Systolic algorithms for the CMU WARP processor. In *Systolic Signal Processing Systems* (E. E. Swartzlander and Dekker M., eds), pp. 73–95

Kung H. T. and Leiserson C. E. (1978). Systolic arrays for VLSI. In *Sparse matrix Proc. 1978* (Duff I. S. and Stewart G. W., eds), pp. 256–82

Maresca M. and Fountain T. J., eds. (1991). Massively parallel computers, *Special issue Proc. IEEE*, April

Masumoto D. et al. (1993). An analogue neurochip and its applications to multilayered artificial neural networks. *Fujitsu Sci. Tech. J.*, **29**(3), 234–41

McCanny J. V. and McWhirter J. G. (1982). On the implementation of signal processing functions using one-bit systolic arrays. *Electron. Lett.*, **18**, 241–3

McCormick B. H. (1963). The Illinois pattern recognition computer – ILLIAC III. *IEEE Trans.*, **EC-12**, 791–813

Mead C. (1989). *Analog VLSI and Neural Systems.* Addison-Wesley

Reddaway S. F., DAP, A Distributed Array Processor, First Annual Symposium on *Computer Architecture*, IEEE/ACM, Florida

Rosenblatt F. (1958). The Perceptron: a probabilistic model for information storage and retrieval in the brain. *Psych. Rev.*, **65**, 386–408

Rumelhart D. E. et al. (1986). Learning internal representations by error propagation. In *Parallel Distributed Processing*, vols. **1 and 2**. MIT Press

Strong J. P. (1991). Computations on the massively parallel processor at the Goddard Space Flight Center. In *Massively parallel computers* (Maresca M. and Fountain T. J., eds), Special issue *Proc. IEEE,* pp. 548–58, April

Thinking Machines Corporation (1993). *CM-5 Scientific Application Examples*

Turing A. (1937). On Computable Numbers with an Application to the Entscheidungsproblem.

Unger S. H. (1958). A computer oriented towards spatial problems. In *Proc. IRE*, **46**, pp. 1744–50

Von Neumann J. (1951). The general logical theory of automata. In *Cerebral Mechanisms in Behaviour – The Hixon Symposium* (Jeffries L. A., ed.). Wiley

Part IV

Thread and Process-level Parallel Architectures

15 Introduction to MIMD Architectures

Thread and process-level parallel architectures are typically realized by MIMD (Multiple Instruction Multiple Data) computers. This class of parallel computers is the most general one since it permits autonomous operations on a set of data by a set of processors without any architectural restrictions. Instruction-level data-parallel architectures must satisfy several constraints in order to build massively parallel systems. For example, processors in array processors, systolic architectures and cellular automata should work synchronously, controlled by a common clock. Generally the processors in these systems are very simple and in many cases they realize a special function (systolic arrays, neural networks, associative processors, and so on). Although in recent SIMD architectures the complexity and generality of the processors have been increased, these modifications have resulted in the introduction of process-level parallelism and MIMD features into the most recent generation of data-parallel computers (for example, CM-5), too.

MIMD architectures became popular when progress in integrated circuit technology made it possible to produce microprocessors which were relatively easy and economical to connect into a multiple processor system. In the early 1980s small systems, incorporating only tens of processors, were typical. The appearance of the Transputer in the mid-1980s caused a great breakthrough in the spread of MIMD parallel computers and resulted even more in the general acceptance of parallel processing as the technology of future computers. By the end of the 1980s mid-scale MIMD computers containing several hundreds of processors became generally available. The current generation of MIMD computers aim at massively parallel systems containing over 1000 processors. These systems are often called scalable parallel computers.

Section 15.1 introduces the architectural concepts of MIMD architectures. Section 15.2 discusses the two fundamental problems to be solved in scalable computers: how to tolerate and hide the high latency of remote loads, and how to tolerate and hide processor idling caused by synchornization. Finally, Section 15.3 summarizes the main design issues of MIMD computers.

15.1 Architectural concepts

The MIMD architecture class represents a natural generalization of the uniprocessor von Neumann machine which in its simplest form consists of a single processor connected to a single memory module. If the goal is to extend this architecture to contain multiple processors and memory modules, basically there are two alternatives:

- Replicate the processor/memory pairs and connect them via an interconnection network. The processor/memory pair is called a **processing element (PE)** and PEs work more or less independently of each other. Whenever interaction among PEs is necessary they send messages to each other. None of the PEs can ever access the memory module of another PE directly. This class of MIMD machines is called **distributed memory MIMD architectures** or **message-passing MIMD architectures**. Their structure is depicted in Figure 15.1.
- Create a set of processors and memory modules. Any processor can directly access any memory module via an interconnection network as shown in Figure 15.2. The set of memory modules defines a global address space which is shared among the processors. Parallel machines of this type are called **Shared Memory MIMD Architectures** and this arrangement of processors and memory is called the **dance-hall** shared memory system.

Distributed memory MIMD architectures are often simply called **multi-computers** while shared memory MIMD architectures are referred to as **multi-processors**. In both architecture types one of the main design considerations is how to construct the interconnection network so as to reduce message traffic and memory latency. A network can be represented by a **communication graph** in which vertices correspond to the switching elements of the parallel computer and edges represent communication links. The topology of the communication graph is an important property which significantly influences latency in parallel computers. According to their topology interconnection networks can be classified as **static** or **dynamic networks**. In static networks the connection of switching units is fixed and

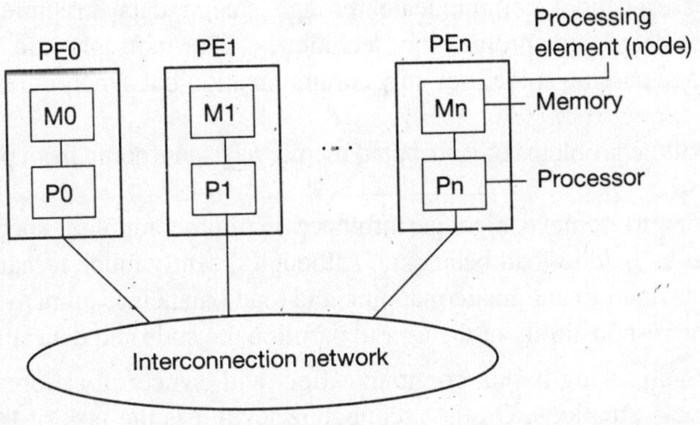

Figure 15.1 Structure of Distributed Memory MIMD Architectures.

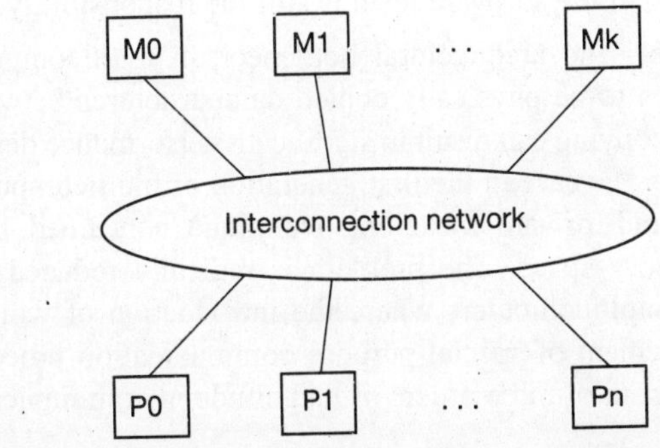

Figure 15.2 Structure of Shared Memory MIMD Architectures.

typically realized as direct or **point-to-point connections**. These networks are also called **direct networks**. In dynamic networks communication links can be reconfigured by setting the active switching units of the system. Multicomputers are typically based on static networks, while dynamic networks are mainly employed in multiprocessors. It should be pointed out here that the role of interconnection networks is different in distributed and shared memory systems. In the former the network must transfer complete messages which can be of any length and hence special attention must be paid to supporting message-passing protocols. In shared memory systems short but frequent memory accesses characterize the typical use of the network. Under these circumstances special care is needed to avoid **contention** and **hot-spot** problems in the network.

There are some advantages and drawbacks with both architecture types. The advantages of the distributed memory systems are:

- Since processors work with their attached local memory module most of the time, the contention problem is not so severe as in shared memory systems. As a result distributed memory multicomputers are highly scalable and good architectural candidates for building massively parallel computers.

- Processes cannot communicate through shared data structures and hence sophisticated synchronization techniques like monitors are not needed. Message passing solves not only communication but synchronization as well.

Most of the problems of distributed memory systems come from programming:

- In order to achieve high performance in multicomputers special attention should be paid to load balancing. Although recently much research effort has been devoted to automatic mapping and load balancing, in many systems it is still the responsibility of the user to partition the code and data among the PEs.
- Message-passing-based communication and synchronization can lead to deadlock situations. On the architecture level it is the task of the communication protocol designer to avoid deadlocks derived from incorrect routing schemes. However, avoiding deadlocks derived from message-based synchronization at the software level is still the responsibility of the user.
- Although there is no architectural bottleneck in multicomputers, message passing requires to be physically copied data structures between processes. Intensive data copying can result in significant performance degradation. This was particularly the case in the first generation of multicomputers where the applied store-and-forward switching technique consumed both processor time and memory space. The problem is radically reduced in the second generation of multicomputers where the introduction of wormhole routing and the employment of special-purpose communication processors resulted in an improvement of three orders of magnitude in communication latency.

The advantages of shared memory systems relate mainly to programming these systems:

- There is no need to partition either the code or the data, therefore uniprocessor programming techniques can easily be adapted in the multiprocessor environment. Neither new programming languages nor sophisticated compilers are needed to exploit shared memory systems.
- There is no need to physically move data when two or more processes communicate. The consumer process can access the data from the place where the producer stored it. As a result communication between processes is very efficient.

Unfortunately there are several drawbacks with shared memory systems, too:

- Although programming shared memory systems is generally easier than programming multicomputers, synchronized access to shared data structures requires special synchronizing constructs such as semaphores, conditional critical regions, monitors, and so on. The use of these constructs results in nondeterministic program behaviour which can lead to programming errors that are difficult to discover. Usually message-passing synchronization is simpler to understand and apply.

- The main disadvantage of shared memory systems is lack of scalability due to the contention problem. When several processors want to access the same memory module they must compete for the right to do so. The winner can access the memory, while the losers must wait. The larger the number of processors, the higher the probability of memory contention. Beyond a certain number of processors this probability is so high that adding a new processor to the system will not increase performance.

There are several ways to overcome the problem of low scalability in shared memory systems:

- The use of a high throughput, low-latency interconnection network among the processors and memory modules can significantly improve scalability.
- In order to reduce the memory contention problem, shared memory systems are extended with special, small-size local memories called as **cache memories**. Whenever a memory reference is given by a processor, the attached cache memory is first checked to see if the required data is stored in the cache. If it is, the memory reference can be performed without using the interconnection network and as a result memory contention is reduced. If the required data is not in the cache memory, the page containing the data is transferred into it. The main assumption here is that shared memory programs generally provide good locality of reference. For example, during the execution of a procedure, in many cases it is enough to access just local data which is contained in the processor cache. Unfortunately, this is not always the case, which reduces the ideal performance of cache-extended shared memory systems. Furthermore, a new problem, the **cache coherence problem**, appears, which further limits the performance of cache-based systems. The problems and solutions of cache coherence are discussed in detail in Chapter 18.
- The logically shared memory can be physically implemented as a collection of local memories. This new architecture type is called a **virtual shared memory** or **distributed shared memory architecture**. From the point of view of physical construction a distributed shared memory machine very much resembles a distributed memory system. The main difference between the two architecture types comes from the organization of the memory address space. In distributed shared memory systems the local memories are components of a global address space and any processor can access the local memory of any other processor. In distributed memory systems the local memories have separate address spaces and direct access to the local memory of a remote processor is prohibited.

Distributed shared memory systems can be divided into three classes based on how local memories are assessed:

- Non-uniform memory access (**NUMA**) machines

- Cache-coherent non-uniform memory access (**CC-NUMA**) machines
- Cache-only memory access (**COMA**) machines

The general structure of NUMA machines is shown in Figure 15.3. A typical example is the Cray T3D machine. In NUMA machines the shared memory is divided into as many blocks as there are processors in the system and each memory block is attached to a processor as a local memory with direct bus connection. As a result, whenever a processor addresses the part of the shared memory that is connected as local memory, access to that block is much faster than access to remote ones. This non-uniform access mechanism requires careful program and data distribution among the memory blocks in order to exploit the potentially high performance of these machines. Consequently NUMA architectures have similar drawbacks to distributed memory systems. The main difference between them is in programming style: while distributed memory systems are programmed according to the message-passing paradigm, programming the NUMA machines still relies on the more conventional shared memory approach. However, in recent NUMA machines like the Cray T3D, a message-passing library is available and hence the difference between multicomputers and NUMA machines is becoming almost negligible.

The other two classes of distributed shared memory machines employ **coherent caches** in order to avoid the problems of NUMA machines. The single address space and coherent caches together significantly ease the problem of data partitioning and dynamic load balancing, providing better support for multiprogramming and parallelizing compilers. They differ in the extent to which coherent caches are applied. In COMA machines every memory block works as a cache memory. According to the applied cache coherence scheme, data dynamically and continuously migrates to the local caches of those processors where it is most needed. Typical examples are the KSR-1 and DDM machines. The general structure of COMA machines is shown in Figure 15.4.

CC-NUMA machines represent a compromise between the NUMA and COMA machines. Like the NUMA machines, the shared memory is constructed as

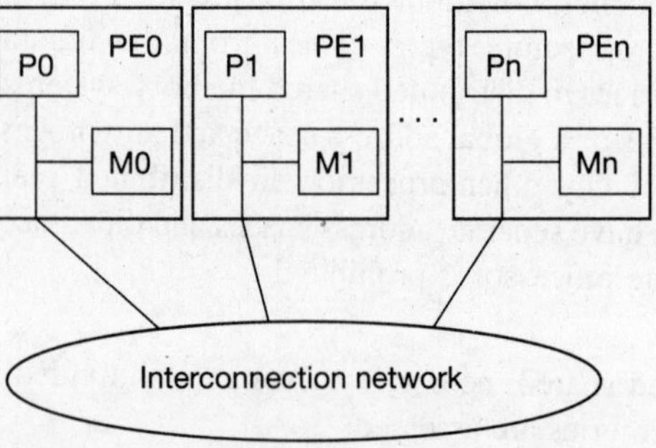

Figure 15.3 Structure of NUMA Architectures.

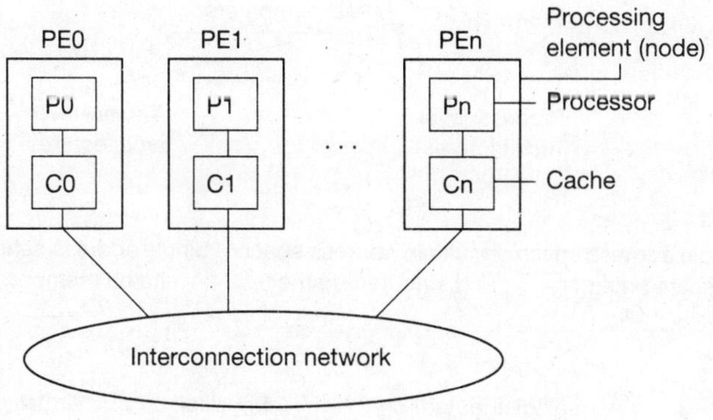

Figure 15.4 Structure of COMA Architectures.

a set of local memory blocks. However, in order to reduce the traffic on the interconnection network each processor node is supplied with a large cache memory block. Although initial data distribution is static as in NUMA machines, dynamic load balancing is achieved by the cache coherence protocols as in the COMA machines. Most of the current massively parallel distributed shared memory machines are built according to the concept of CC-NUMA architectures. Examples are the Convex SPP1000, Stanford DASH and MIT Alewife. The general structure of CC-NUMA machines is shown in Figure 15.5.

Process-level architectures have been realized either by multiprocessors or by multicomputers. Interestingly, in the case of thread-level architectures only shared memory systems have been built or proposed. The classification of MIMD computers is shown in Figure 15.6. Details of multi-threaded architectures, distributed memory and shared memory systems are given in detail in the following chapters.

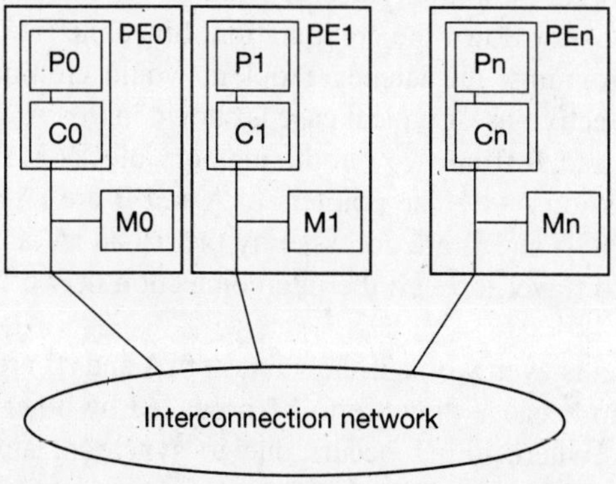

Figure 15.5 Structure of CC-NUMA Architectures.

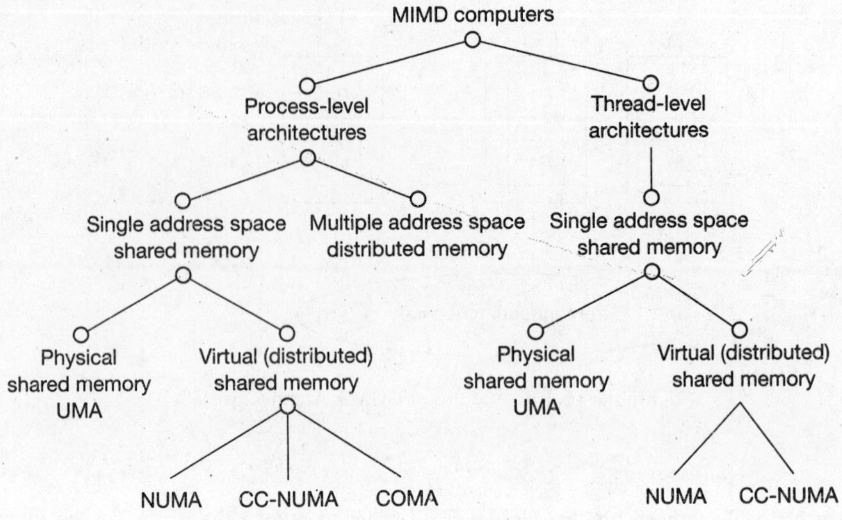

Figure 15.6 Classification of MIMD computers.

15.2 Problems of scalable computers

There are two fundamental problems to be solved in any scalable computer system (Arvind and Iannucci, 1987):

(1) Tolerate and hide the latency of remote loads.

(2) Tolerate and hide idling due to synchronization among parallel processes.

Remote loads are unavoidable in scalable parallel systems that use some form of distributed memory. Accessing a local memory usually requires only one clock cycle while access to a remote memory cell can take two orders of magnitude longer time. If a processor issuing a remote load operation had to wait for the operation to be completed without doing any useful work in the meantime, the remote load would significantly slow down the computation. Since the rate of load instructions is high in most programs, the latency problem would eliminate all the potential benefits of parallel activities. A typical case is shown in Figure 15.7 where P0 has to load two values A and B from two remote memory blocks M1 and Mn in order to evaluate the expression A+B. The pointers to A and B are rA and rB stored in the local memory of P0. A and B are accessed by the 'rload rA' and 'rload rB' instructions which have to travel through the interconnection network in order to fetch A and B.

The situation is even worse if the values of rA and rB are currently not available in M1 and Mn because they are to be produced by other processes to be run later. In this case, where idling occurs due to synchronization between parallel processes, the original process on P0 has to wait for an unpredictable time, resulting in **unpredictable latency**.

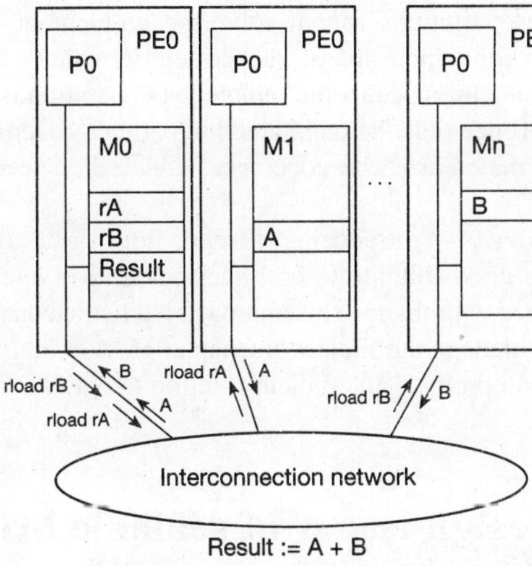

Figure 15.7 The remote load problem.

In order to solve these problems several possible hardware/software solutions have been proposed and applied in various parallel computers:

- Application of cache memory
- Prefetching
- Introduction of threads and a fast context switching mechanism among threads.

The use of **cache memory** greatly reduces the time spent on remote load operations if most of them can be performed on the local cache. Suppose that A is placed in the same cache block as C and D which are objects in the expression following the one that contains A:

Result := A + B;
Result2 := C – D;

Under such circumstances, caching A will also bring C and D into the cache memory of P0 and hence the remote load of C and D is replaced by local cache operations, which cause significant acceleration in the program execution.

The **prefetching** technique relies on a similar principle. The main idea is to bring data into the local memory or cache before it is actually needed. A prefetch operation is an explicit non-blocking request to fetch data before the actual memory operation is issued. The remote load operation applied in the prefetch does not slow down the computation because the data to be prefetched will not be used until later and hopefully, by the time the process needs the data, its value will have been brought closer to the requesting processor, hiding the latency of the usual blocking read.

Notice that these solutions cannot solve the problem of idling caused by synchronization. Even for remote loads, cache memory cannot reduce latency in every case. When a cache miss occurs the remote load operation is still needed and, moreover, **cache coherence** must be maintained in parallel systems. Obviously, the algorithms needed to maintain cache coherence reduce the speed of cache-based parallel computers.

The third approach – introducing **threads and fast context switching** mechanisms – offers a good solution to both the remote load latency problem and the synchronization latency problem. This approach led to the construction of multi-threaded computers, which are the subject of Chapter 16. A combined application of the three approaches can promise an efficient solution to both latency problems.

15.3 Main design issues of scalable MIMD computers

The main design issues in scalable parallel computers are:

- Processor design
- Interconnection network design
- Memory system design
- I/O system design.

The current generation of commodity processors contain several built-in parallel architecture features like pipelining, parallel instruction issue logic, and so on, as shown in Part II. They also directly support the building of small- and mid-size multiple processor systems by providing atomic storage access, prefetching, cache coherency, message passing, and so on. However, they cannot tolerate the remote memory loads and the idling caused by synchronization which are the fundamental problems of scalable parallel systems. To solve these problems a new approach to processor design is needed. Multi-threaded architectures, described in detail in Chapter 16, offer a promising solution in the very near future.

Interconnection network design was a key problem in data-parallel architectures since they aimed at massively parallel systems, too. Accordingly, the basic interconnections of parallel computers were described in Part III. In the current part we reconsider those design issues relevant to the case when commodity microprocessors are to be applied in the network. In particular, Chapter 17 is devoted to these questions since the central design issue in distributed memory multicomputers is the selection of the interconnection network and the hardware support of message passing through the network.

Memory design is the crucial topic in shared memory multiprocessors. In these parallel systems the maintenance of a logically shared memory plays a central role. Early multiprocessors applied physically shared memory which became a bottleneck in scalable parallel computers. The recent generation of multiprocessors employs a distributed shared memory supported by a distributed cache system. The maintenance of cache coherency is a non-trivial problem which requires careful hardware/software design. Solutions to the cache coherence problem and other innovative features of contemporary multiprocessors are described in Chapter 18.

In scalable parallel computers one of the main problems is handling I/O devices efficiently. The problem seems to be particularly serious when large data volumes have to be moved between I/O devices and remote processors. The main question is how to avoid disturbing the work of the internal computational processors. The problem of I/O system design appears in every class of MIMD system. Unfortunately, its solution is not matured enough and hence it is not discussed in this book.

16 Multi-threaded Architectures

Section 16.1 discusses solutions to memory and synchronization latency and the design space of multi-threaded architectures. Section 16.2 introduces the three computational models relevant to these architectures: von Neumann, dataflow and a hybrid von Neumann/dataflow model. Section 16.3 describes three systems based on the von Neumann model: the HEP, Tera and the MIT Alewife Section 16.4 describes dataflow architectures, looking at static dataflow architectures, tagged-token dataflow machines and explicit token-store architectures. Section 16.5 is devoted to hybrid multi-threaded architectures, using the MIT Hybrid Machine as an example of a macro dataflow architecture, the USC Decoupled Architecture and Super-Actor Machine (SAM) as examples of decoupled hybrid dataflow architectures, and P-RISC and *T as examples of RISC-like hybrid multi-threaded architectures. Finally, Section 16.6 summarizes the chapter.

16.1 Introduction

Although current commodity superscalar RISC processors are very successful in exploiting functional parallelism within a chip and can support the building of small-scale multiprocessors, they fail in supporting large-scale parallel systems. Multi-threaded architectures represent a promising new direction in processor design for supporting the construction of scalable, massively parallel computers. In this chapter we provide a detailed study of the main classes and features of multi-threaded architectures. Several prototype machines are also described in order to illustrate the main principles.

16.1.1 Solution for memory and synchronization latency

In Chapter 15 the main problems of scalable parallel computers were described. It was shown that a possible solution for tolerating memory and synchronization latency is the introduction of threads and a fast context switching mechanism among threads. In this chapter this solution is described and explained thoroughly. This approach tolerates both the remote load and synchronization latency problems and, therefore, plays a crucial role in the organization of future processors. Systems that support this technique are called **multi-threaded systems**. In principle, multi-threaded systems are very similar to multitasking systems where processes are descheduled from the processor whenever they have to wait for time-consuming operations like I/O or for synchronization conditions. The general solution in these systems is that processes are temporarily suspended; that is, their contexts are saved in a certain storage area (memory or a register set) and later, when the operation they initiated has been completed, they can resume by loading the processor with the saved context. Although the context switch is usually supported by hardware, the surrounding operations are managed by software (for example, by the explicit use of semaphore operations at program level). This approach works well in coarse-grain operations where the time necessary for context switching is negligible compared with the time spent on the required I/O and synchronization operations.

However, in the case of remote memory access operations, latency varies according to the distance between the requesting and destination PEs. It can often result in low latency which requires a fine-grain, very fast context switching. Therefore, hardware support is needed which can be applied at every remote memory access and which can guarantee that even for the lowest latency the switching time is less than the latency.

For the synchronization problem, again a hardware mechanism is needed that automatically recognizes the situation and can suspend the current thread without causing idle clock cycles in the executing processor.

The processor utilization (U) can be represented as the proportion of the useful processing time (P) and the total time (T) spent on the computation. The total time consists of the processing time, the idle time (I) when the processor is waiting for an outer condition and the switching time (S) which is used for changing the active thread on the processor.

$$U = \frac{P}{T} = \frac{P}{P + I + S} \tag{16.1}$$

The objective of any scalable parallel system is to keep U as high as possible (close to the optimum value 1). Obviously, U is high, if I and S are negligible. The purpose of multi-threading techniques is to reduce I without significantly increasing S. To achieve it, two conditions must be satisfied, First, a very fast context switch mechanism is needed for which S < I even for the shortest latency operations. Second, a sufficiently large number of threads should be available on the processor in order to switch from a potentially idle thread to an active one. Unfortunately, the maintenance of a large set of threads on a processor requires a large register set and therefore a very expensive processor. Finding a reasonable compromise is a crucial problem in designing multi-threaded processors.

16.1.2 Design space

There are several multi-threaded hardware approaches to solve the remote load and synchronization problems. They differ in the computational model applied in the processor design. In chapter 1 the control flow and dataflow model were discussed. These two models represent the two extremes of a range of possible computational models. Between these extremes several other models, called hybrid models, can be found which combine features of both the dataflow and control flow models. Multi-threaded machines typically belong to one of the hybrid models, though there are multi-threaded machines based purely on control flow, too.

Hybrid multi-threaded machines can be classified according to their position in the scale of computational models. Macro dataflow architectures are the closest to the original dataflow machines. Decoupled architectures are based on the control token concept and represent the next step towards control flow machines. Finally, RISC-like hybrid architectures are the closest relatives of the original control flow machines. They work on a parallel control flow model based on parallel control operators. The possible computational models are compared in Section 16.2.

The other important design decision is related to the granularity of thread interleaving. The two main directions are the application of fine-grain and coarse-grain approaches. The fine-grain concept means that threads are interleaved at the level of clock cycles inside the processor pipeline in order to ensure maximal processor utilization. Fine-grain multi-threaded architectures are optimum provided that there are a sufficiently large number of active threads available inside the processor to keep the processor pipeline busy. However, they suffer poor single-thread performance and low processor use when there is not enough parallelism in the program. To avoid this problem coarse-grain multi-threaded machines execute only one thread at a time. When the active thread encounters a remote load or failed synchronization, thread switching occurs and the processor executes the new thread while the preceding one is suspended. Notice that coarse-grain multi-threading is a more conventional approach than fine-grain multi-threading. The former can be derived from commodity superscalar RISC processors as an evolutionary modification of these chips while the latter is typically progressed from the revolutionary dataflow approach.

Multi-threaded parallel computers can also be classified according to their memory system. Some contain physically shared memory, such as the classic shared memory architectures, while others have only physically distributed memory and work as distributed shared memory systems. In both cases an important aspect of designing large-scale multi-threaded machines is the employment of coherent cache memories. Cache memories reduce memory access latency at cache hit, but in order to maintain cache coherency they increase latency at cache miss. (The effect of cache memory is analysed in detail in Chapter 18.) These contradictory features of cache coherent systems require a thorough investigation of how to combine multi-threading with coherent caches. It is worth mentioning that in order to reduce the negative effect of the cache coherence problem, recent scalable parallel computers apply some kind of multi-threading support even if they are not particularly designed as multi-threaded computers.

The fourth design decision should take into consideration the optimum number of threads to be handled by hardware inside a processor. Usually, fine-grain thread interleaving without cache support requires a large number of threads to keep the processor busy all the time. In coarse-grain multi-threaded architectures supported by a coherent cache it is sufficient to handle only a very limited number of threads inside the processor, although the cache coherence problem complicates the processor and system design. Between these two extremes there are various possibilities to tune the number of threads.

The design space of multi-threaded machines is shown in Figure 16.1. The multi-threaded machines studied in this chapter are classified on the basis of the design space described above and their classification tree is shown in Figure 16.2.

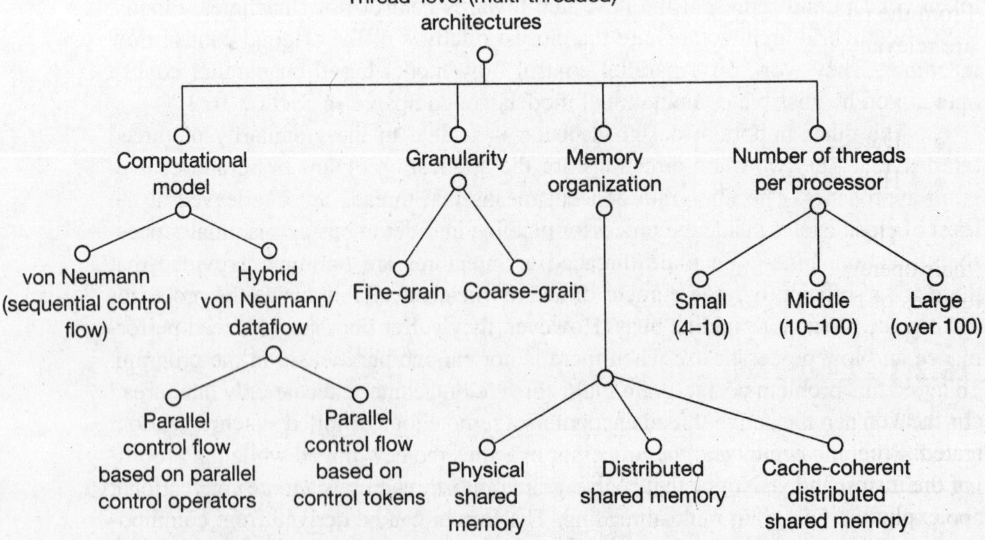

Figure 16.1 The design space of thread-level (multi-threaded) architectures.

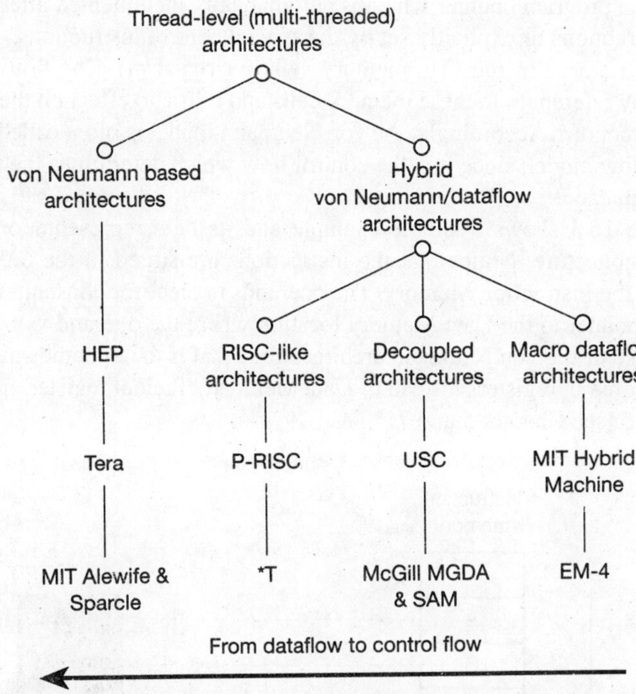

Figure 16.2 Classification of multi-threaded architectures.

16.2 Computational models

From the point of view of multi-threaded architectures three computational models are relevant:

- von Neumann model
- Dataflow model
- Hybrid von Neumann/dataflow model.

Their main characteristics are discussed in Chapter 1; here, we concentrate on their operational semantics in order to explain how they are related to the various classes of multi-threaded machines.

16.2.1 Sequential control flow (von Neumann)

In the von Neumann computational model the flows of control and data are separated. Program instructions should be executed sequentially according to the order of the instructions in the program text. Any deviation from this textual order should be explicitly defined by special control instructions like GOTO, JUMP, CALL, and so on which are generated either by the programmer or by an intelligent compiler using program analysis. The hardware support for this sequential execution scheme consists of the program counter which is automatically incremented after executing ordinary instructions or explicitly set by the special control instructions.

Data is stored in reusable memory cells (or registers). The flow of data is determined by references to these memory cells and it has no effect on the execution order of instructions. Accordingly, the von Neumann model is often called a sequential control flow model, since it is the control flow which determines the instruction execution sequence.

Figure 16.3 shows a simple example and its data representation in a von Neumann architecture. Notice that the instructions are stored in the order of their execution in the Instruction Memory. The operands (except for constants) are represented by a pointer to the Data Memory location where the operand value is stored. The advantage of the von Neumann architecture is that if the operands inside a procedure are stored in registers instead of Data Memory, efficient register optimization could be used (see Chapter 5 and 7).

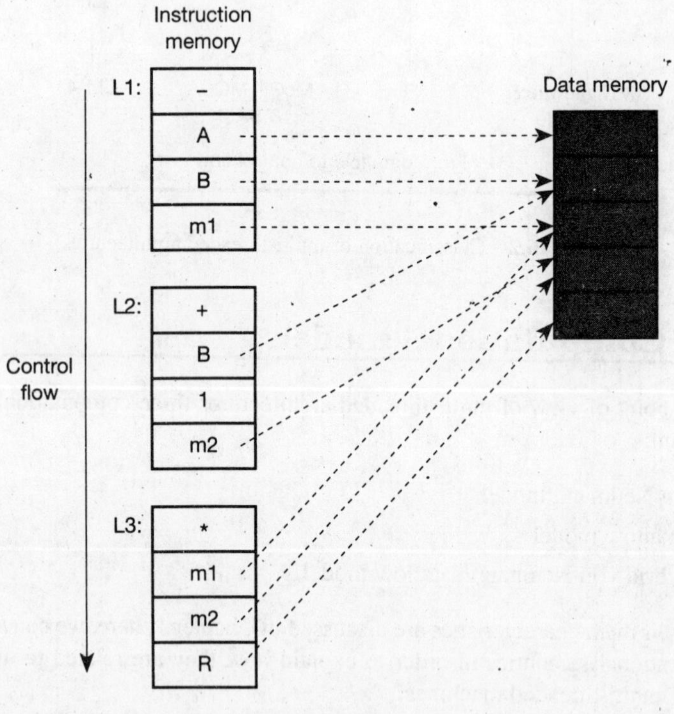

Figure 16.3 Sequential control flow model to compute R = (A–B)∗(B+1).

16.2.2 Dataflow

In the dataflow model control is tied to the flow of data. The order of instructions in the program text has no effect on the execution order. An instruction is executed if all the data needed for execution is available. There is no concept of shared, rewritable data storage. Data is in continuous flow independently of reusable memory cells and its availability initiates instruction executions. Since data can be available for several instructions at the same time, these instructions can be executed in parallel.

The potential parallel computation is reflected by the data dependency or **dataflow graph** whose nodes are the instructions of the program and whose arcs represent data dependency between instructions (see Figure 16.4). Data moves on the arcs of the graph in the form of **data tokens** which contain data values and status information. The asynchronous, parallel computation is determined by the **firing rule** which is expressed by means of tokens: a node of the dataflow graph can fire if there is a token on each input arc. If a node fires it consumes the input tokens, performs the associated operation and places result tokens on the output arcs.

The advantage of the dataflow concept is that nodes of the dataflow graph are self-scheduling based on the firing rule. However, the hardware support to recognize the availability of necessary data is much more complicated than the simple program counter of von Neumann machines. The different generations of dataflow architectures reflect the various solutions applied for solving this problem.

Figure 16.5 illustrates the data representation of dataflow architectures for the same example that was used in Figure 16.3. Notice that there is no separate data memory in the dataflow approach, the operands of instructions are represented as memory slots inside the instruction frames representing the nodes of the dataflow graph. These originally empty slots are filled in by the incoming data tokens. A node can fire (the corresponding instruction becomes executable) if all the tokens have arrived (all the slots in the instruction frame are filled in). No matter how these instructions are distributed in a multiple processor space, their synchronization is solved without any explicit language construct like semaphore. However, register optimization becomes a difficult problem in such dataflow architectures since the processor pipeline constantly requires new data not available in the local registers.

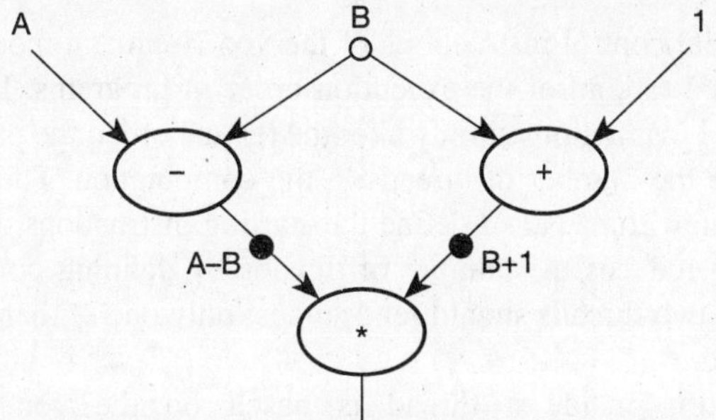

Figure 16.4 Dataflow graph to compute R = (A–B)∗(B+1).

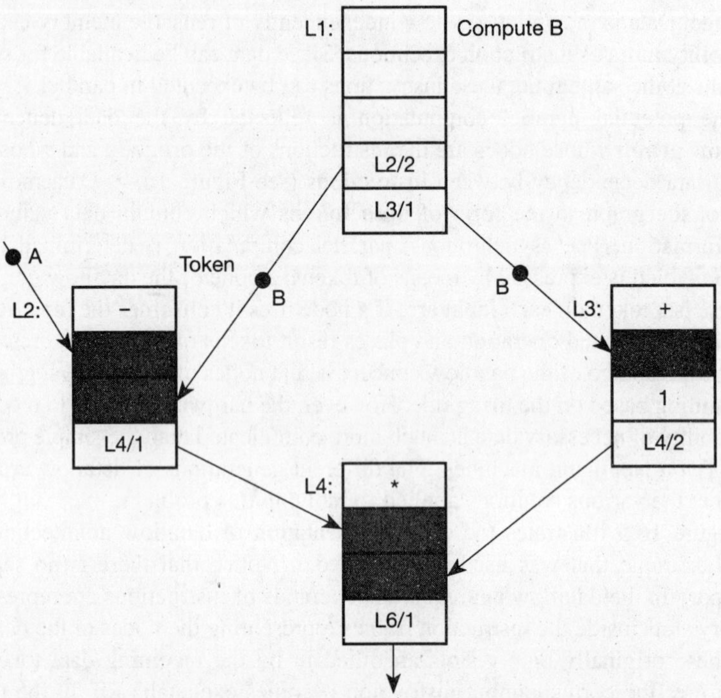

Figure 16.5 Dataflow model to compute R = (A–B)∗(B+1).

16.2.3 Parallel control flow (hybrid) models

Parallel control flow models represent the transition from the sequential control flow model to the parallel dataflow one. The parallel control flow model based on **control operators** is closer to the sequential control flow model, while the model based on **control tokens** resembles the dataflow model in several ways.

Parallel control operators

Like the sequential control instructions of the von Neumann model, parallel control operators are used to control the execution order in programs. However, while the sequential control instructions simply alter the textual order, the parallel control operators can change the number of threads in the computation. The FORK instruction serves to create new threads and define the starting instructions of new threads. The JOIN instruction reduces the number of threads by defining points in the program execution where two threads should rendezvous; only one of them can continue, and the other is killed.

Computation inside a thread is based on the von Neumann model. Communication between threads is realized by reusable memory cells (or registers) which require extra care with synchronization (for example, semaphores). Notice that the flows of control and data are still strongly separated. The simple example shown previously and its internal representation based on the parallel control flow model is depicted in Figure 16.6. Notice that the structure of instruction frames and Data Memory are almost the same as in the sequential control flow model (Figure 16.3). The only difference is that several control threads can exist and progress in parallel. In such systems several instructions from different threads running on different processors can refer to the same memory location which can cause a synchronization problem. In such cases, explicit synchronization constructs (like semaphores, etc.) should be used to solve the memory access conflicts in traditional multiprocessors. It will be shown later in this chapter that in case of multi-threaded architectures such an explicit synchronization control can be omitted. Concerning register optimization, two approaches are possible. In coarse-grain systems where single-threaded instruction pipelines are used, register optimization is possible within each thread (for example, MIT Alewife machine). In fine-grain systems based on multi-threaded instruction pipelines, register optimization requires a very large register set.

Control tokens

The parallel computational model based on control tokens resembles the dataflow model in many ways. The computation is specified by the data dependency graph as in the dataflow model. However, the physical representation of this graph is different

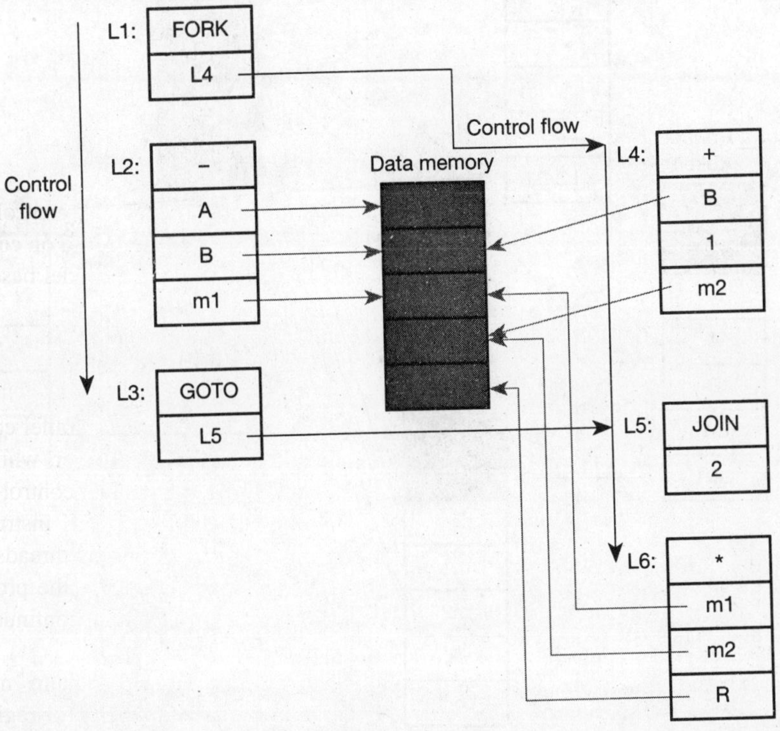

Figure 16.6 Parallel control flow model based on control operators to compute R = (A–B)∗(B+1).

from the representation applied in the dataflow model. Here, the concept of rewritable shared data storage of control flow machines still exists and hence so-called **control tokens** move on the arcs of the graph instead of data tokens. According to the graph each instruction specifies its successor instruction and after execution it sends control tokens to its successors. An instruction can be executed if it has received all the required control tokens (each input arc contains a control token).

Obviously there is a strong analogy between the dataflow model and the parallel control tokens model, although in the latter data and control are separated as in the von Neumann model. This separation means that reusable memory cells are still maintained for data handling. However, if their access is synchronized by the data dependency graph, other synchronization methods, such as semaphores, are not needed. The simple example and its execution scheme based on control tokens is shown in Figure 16.7. Notice that the instruction frames of the sequential control flow model are extended with two types of slot. Control token slots are used to collect the necessary control tokens to enable the execution of the instruction. Next, an instruction address slot defines where to send the control token if the current

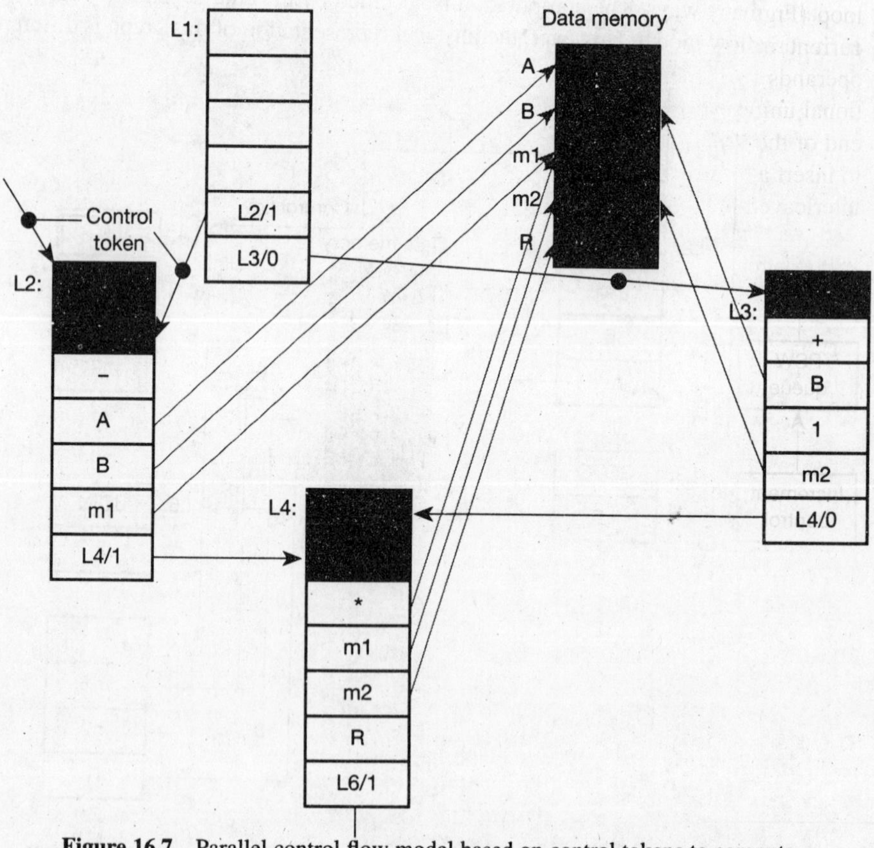

Figure 16.7 Parallel control flow model based on control tokens to compute R = (A–B)∗(B+1).

instruction has been executed. In fact, the control mechanism based on these two types of slot replaces the program counter of von Neumann machines.

16.3 von Neumann-based multi-threaded architectures

16.3.1 HEP

The roots of multi-threaded architectures go back to the Denelcor HEP machine which was a revolutionary novel design in the second half of the 1970s. The HEP was the very first parallel architecture designed with the objectives of tolerating memory latency and synchronization problems. It represents a fine-grain interleaving of threads where the processor pipeline contains eight stages and at each time step a new thread enters the execution pipe. Threads are taken from the Process Status Word queue (PSW queue) which is the fundamental element of the control loop (Figure 16.8). After a thread is taken from the head of the PSW queue, the current instruction of the thread is fetched from the program memory and the operands from the registers. Finally the instruction is executed by one of the functional units and the thread, with an incremented instruction pointer, is placed on the end of the PSW queue. The minimal length of the queue is eight in order to be able to insert a different thread in the pipeline at every clock step. As a result, threads are interleaved at the instruction level.

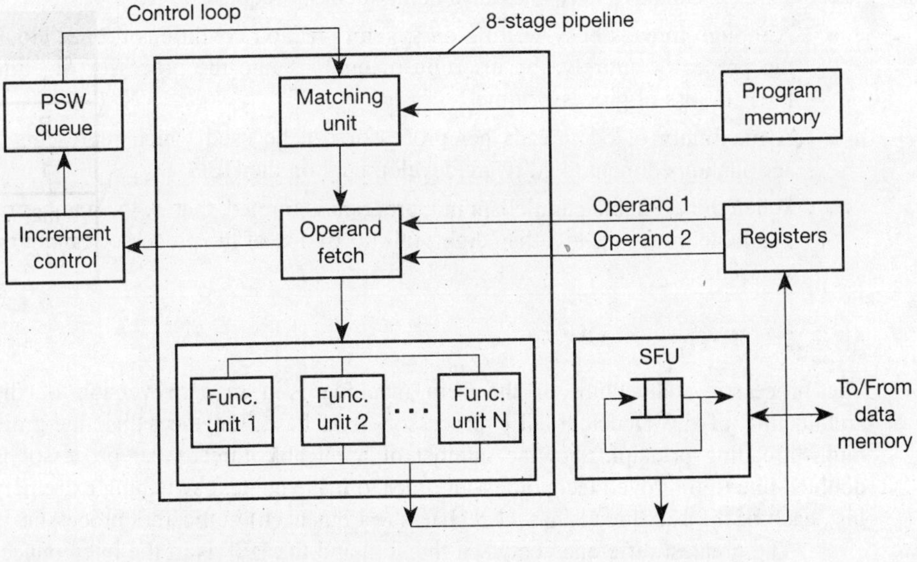

PSW: Process status word
SFU: Scheduler function unit

Figure 16.8 Structure of the HEP processing element.

Memory latency toleration is solved by the Scheduler Function Unit (SFU) and by extending the data memory words with a **Full/Empty bit**. Attempting to read a word whose Full/Empty bit is in the Empty state results in the suspension of the current thread. In order to avoid the useless circulation of such a thread in the control loop, the PSW of the thread is moved from the control loop to the SFU. The PSW of the suspended thread circulates here and reissues the memory request until the required memory access can be fulfilled. At this time the thread is put back in the control loop and can continue its program execution. Notice that suspended threads do not waste execution stages in the processor pipeline if they can be replaced by other active threads of the control loop. A maximum of 64 PSWs (threads) can be handled at each processor in the HEP machine.

Synchronization among threads is realized via register communication. In each processor there are 2048 registers supplied with Full/Empty/Reserved bits for synchronization purposes. An unsuccessful attempt at communication via a register results in a NO-OP operation in the processor pipeline and the thread is placed back on the PSW queue without updating its program counter. Thus thread synchronization is realized in a busy-wait fashion but the processor is not blocked. Other threads can actively use the processor; the waiting thread causes bubbles in the processor pipeline wherever it is taken from the PSW queue and the synchronization condition is not yet satisfied.

The HEP machine was a shared memory multiprocessor. It had up to 16 processors and up to 128 data memory modules which were connected in a 'dance-hall' configuration via a high-speed switching network.

Although the HEP represents a revolutionary step in processor design it has several limitations:

- Threads can have only one outstanding memory request.
- Although threads busy-waiting on synchronization conditions do not block the processor entirely, the insertion of bubbles into the processor pipeline leads to loss of processor time.
- A maximum of 64 threads per processor can be used which represents a serious impediment to software development on the HEP.
- When the available parallelism in a program is limited, that is, the number of available threads is less than eight, full utilisation of the processor cannot be assured.

16.3.2 Tera

The processor architecture of the Tera machine is a modern version of the architecture of the Denelcor HEP processor. It is based on the same fine-grain multi-threading principle, but the number of applicable threads per processor is doubled due to improved technology. In order to make context switching extremely fast, each of the 128 threads has 41 registers (64 bits each) in the Tera processor.

The greatest difference between the Tera and the HEP is in the interconnection of processors and memory modules. While the HEP was a physically shared memory multiprocessor, the Tera machine is a distributed shared memory system. It can have up to 256 processors, 512 memory modules, 256 I/O cache units, 256 I/O processors and 2816 communication nodes which have no functional units or resources attached. The interconnection network contains 4096 nodes arranged in a sparse 16×16×16 toroidal mesh.

The Tera machine is a state-of-the-art distributed shared memory system in which processor design is based on the multi-threading principle in order to tolerate memory and synchronization latency. The clock period is less than three nanoseconds and the architecture is scalable essentially without limit. The multi-threaded Tera processor has the same advantages and drawbacks as the HEP processor.

16.3.3 MIT Alewife and Sparcle

The MIT Alewife machine is a large-scale cache coherent distributed shared memory (CC-NUMA) system. The maximum 512 processing nodes are arranged in a two-dimensional mesh topology. Each node consists of a Sparcle processor, 4 Mbyte main memory, 64 Kbyte cache, 4 Mbyte local memory, floating-point unit, communication and memory management unit (CMMU), and a network router/switch. The 4 Mbyte main memory is part of the distributed shared memory, while the 4 Mbyte local memory contains the cache coherence directory, code and local data. The structure of the Alewife machine is shown in Figure 16.9.

The MIT Alewife is one of the recent state-of-the-art scalable parallel computers that combines the following main features:

- physically distributed memory
- logically shared memory
- hardware-supported cache coherence
- hardware-supported user-level message passing
- multi-threading.

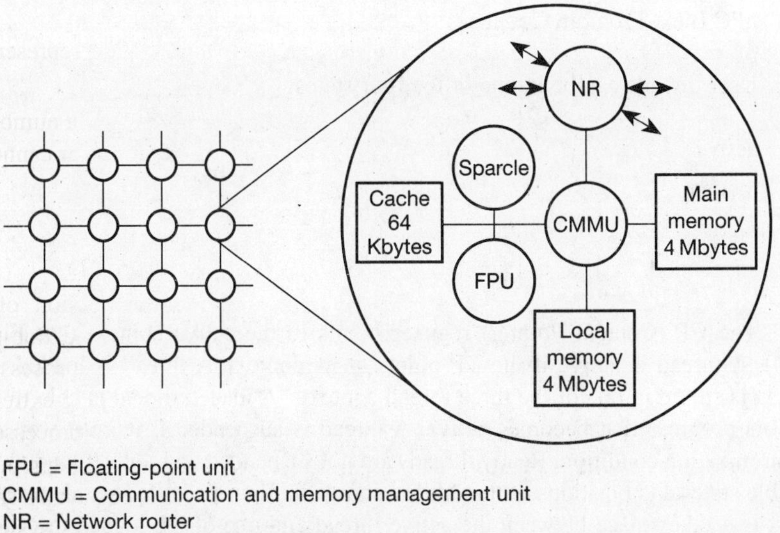

FPU = Floating-point unit
CMMU = Communication and memory management unit
NR = Network router

Figure 16.9 Structure of the Alewife machine (Agarwal et al., 1993). © 1993 IEEE

Unlike the HEP and Tera machines, Alewife realizes coarse-grained multi-threading, i.e. the processor pipeline works on a single thread as long as remote memory access or synchronization is not necessary. This concept has the advantage of being able to exploit register optimization in the processor pipeline. However, thread switching takes more time than in the fine-grained multi-threaded architectures since it requires the flushing of the processor pipeline. Accordingly, the main focus in the design of Alewife was the integration of multi-threading capabilities with hardware-supported cache coherance. Here we concentrate on the multi-threading property of the Alewife machine by explaining Sparcle, the processor chip used in Alewife.

The Sparcle processor

Sparcle is an evolutionary extension of the Sparc architecture designed to solve the problems of scalable parallel computers:

- tolerance of memory latency by means of fast context switching
- fine-grain synchronization
- efficient user-level message passing.

Fast context switching In Sparc there are eight overlapping register windows which are used in pairs by Sparcle to represent four independent, non-overlapping contexts. Three are used for user threads and the fourth for traps and message handlers. Each context contains 32 general-purpose registers and the following three special-purpose registers:

- PSR (Processor State Register)
- PC (Program Counter)
- nPC (next Program Counter).

User threads can be in one of the four states:

- active
- loaded
- ready
- suspended.

The CP (Context Pointer) register points to the active context (see Figure 16.10). A thread is active if the CP points at its context. A thread is loaded if its context is stored in one of the three thread contexts. A loaded thread is able to continue its progress if it becomes active. A thread is suspended if it must wait on a synchronization condition. Ready threads are not suspended and not yet loaded. The possible states and positions of threads are shown in Figure 16.10. Thread switching is fast if it takes place between the active thread and one of the loaded threads. In this case it contains only two main steps:

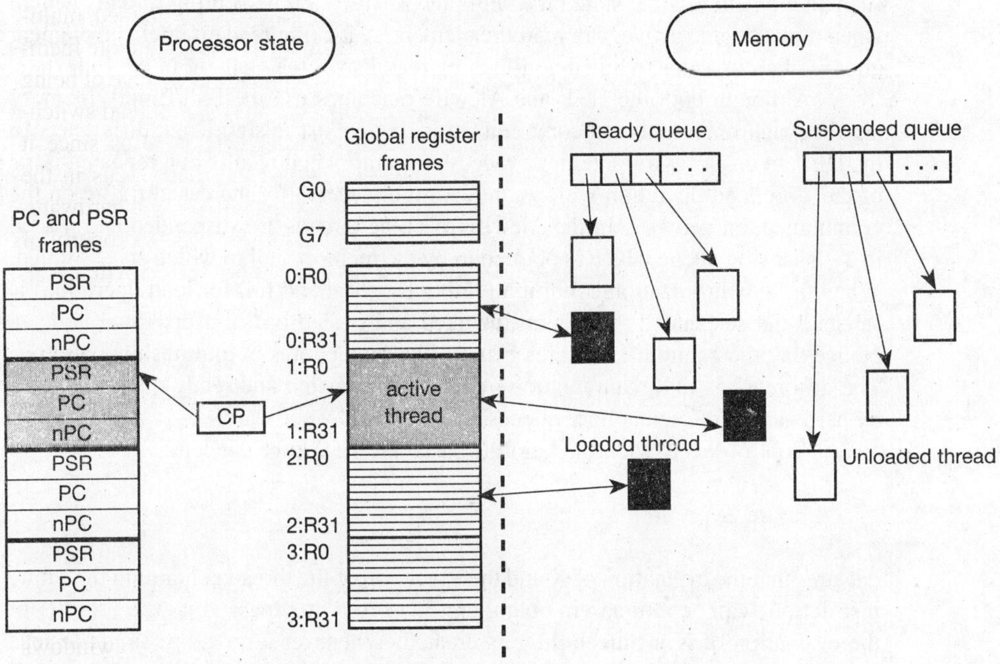

Figure 16.10 Thread states in Sparcle (Agarwal et al., 1993). © 1993 IEEE

(1) changing the value of the CP register

(2) flushing the processor pipeline.

Even the fastest thread switch requires 14 cycles which means a relatively large context switch overhead compared with the fine-grain multi-threading architectures. That is why cache support is used in the Alewife machine: to reduce the frequency of thread switches.

Support for fine-grain synchronization Both data-level and control-level synchronization are available in the Alewife machine. Data-level synchronization is very similar to the I-structure introduced in the MIT Tagged-Token Dataflow Machine (see Section 16.4.2). Two versions, called the **J-structure** and **L-structure**, are applied in the Alewife machine. They are data structures supporting producer–consumer style synchronization by extending memory words by a special state bit (Full/Empty bit). They differ in the types of operations they support. On J-structures only two operation types are allowed: write and non-locking read, while on L-structures, the locking read is also allowed.

When a J-structure or L-structure is allocated, all the state bits are in the Empty state. The content of each element is −1, showing that no reader thread is waiting for a write operation. A read operation in this state results in the requesting thread being suspended; it is put into a suspension queue and a pointer to this queue is placed in the corresponding element of the J- or L-structure. A write operation on such an element sets the state bit to Full and releases all the waiting threads which, when they become active, can read the element. A locking read empties the element after reading its value, while a non-locking read leaves the element in the Full state.

Although both the HEP and Alewife machines use the Full/Empty memory tag for synchronizing thread communication, there exists a significant difference. In the HEP an unsuccessful attempt to access a memory cell results in a repeated issue of the store/load operation which can lead to unnecessarily increased traffic on the communication network. In the Alewife machine threads are suspended and placed in a suspension queue which is pointed to by the memory cell to which access failed. When the synchronization condition (empty for store and full for load operation) is satisfied the suspended threads are invoked and placed back on the Ready queue. Notice that the J- and L-structures behave like semaphores in multitasking systems. The difference is that manipulation of thread suspension and ready queues is done by hardware while semaphore queues are operated by software.

Control-level synchronization is based on the **future** concept:

future X

declares that the evaluation of X and the execution of the thread containing the future instruction can continue in parallel. In order to pass on the result of the evaluation of X a **placeholder** is created. Whenever a thread attempts to read the value of X before its evaluation is completed, the task is suspended on X's placeholder. When the value of X is produced all the threads waiting on the placeholder will be released. The implementation mechanism is similar to data-parallel synchronization, with the low bit of placeholders being used as a state bit.

Communication and memory management unit

As well as the Sparcle processor, the communication and memory management unit (CMMU) of the Alewife machine should also play an active role in supporting latency tolerance and synchronization. For the sake of latency tolerance the CMMU should be able to handle split-phase memory transactions where the memory request is separated from the response. In the case of a cache miss the cache controller initiates the context-switch trap and at the same time sends a request message to the remote processing element holding the requested data item.

An extra storage area must be reserved in the cache system for Full/Empty bit synchronization. A notable feature of the Alewife is that the state bits are stored together with the cache tags, which has several advantages. The physical memory used for cache data can be an ordinary one. Access to the cache tags is faster than to the cache data because the tag file is smaller and it is not necessary to cross chip boundaries.

Assessment of the Alewife architecture

The most important design aspect of the Alewife machine is the combination of coherent caches and multi-threading. The advantage of this combination is that the relatively large context switch overhead does not cause significant performance reduction. Processor utilization depends on the product of context switching overhead and switching frequency. Owing to the presence of the cache the need for remote access is relatively rare and hence the switching frequency is low.

Another advantage of the coarse-grained multi-threaded approach of Alewife is that register optimization can be applied in the processor pipeline as long as the same thread is executed. As a result, the Alewife can work efficiently even if the number of threads per processor is not more than four. Recall that in the HEP and Tera machines large numbers of threads (at least eight per processor) are necessary to achieve high processor pipeline utilization.

The Alewife and Sparcle projects have demonstrated that contemporary RISC processors could easily be modified to support scalable parallel computers, particularly if a large coherent cache (greater than 64 Kbyte) is allocated for each processing node.

16.4 Dataflow architectures

The execution mechanism of dataflow architectures is defined by the dataflow computational model described in Chapter 1 and Section 16.2.2. Dataflow architectures can exploit both instruction- and procedure-level parallelism, depending on the complexity of the functions associated with the nodes of the dataflow graph (DFG). Instruction-level parallelism appears when nodes of the DFG represent single instructions. Procedure-level parallelism is exploited when nodes of the DFG are associated with complete functions. Three generations of dataflow architectures can be distinguished according to their approaches to solving the problem of token matching:

- Static dataflow architectures
- Tagged-token dataflow machines
- Explicit token-store architectures.

The following sections explain the properties of these generations in detail.

16.4.1 Static dataflow architectures

The first generation of dataflow architectures is based on the 1-token/arc principle which is governed by the **static firing rule**: a node can fire if there is a token on each input arc and *there is no token on its output arcs*. A token is represented by a 3-tuple:

<v, <f,n>, a>

where v is the data value conveyed by the token, f represents the current function activation, n is the target node inside the function and a represents the destination arc of the target node. Tokens of a target node match if their <f,n> fields (called the tag) are the same.

The structure of a typical static dataflow architecture is shown in Figure 16.11. The Activity Store consists of two memory units: the Instruction/Data Memory and the Control Memory. A node of the dataflow graph is represented by a frame in the Instruction/Data Memory. Each frame has the following structure:

operation_code
operand_1
:
operand_N
target_node/destination_arc_1
:
target_node/destination_arc_K

A Control Memory frame belongs to each Instruction/Data Memory frame. The Control Memory frame contains presence bits for all operands and target_node/destination_arc fields. The presence bit is set for an operand if the operand is available (an input token has arrived at the input arc of the associated node of the dataflow graph) and for a target_node/destination_arc field if the associated arc does not contain a token. A node can fire (the corresponding instruction can be executed) if all the presence bits in the Control Memory frame are set. When this situation is recognised by the Update Unit, it places an instruction packet on the Instruction Queue. Notice that Instruction Queue plays a similar role to the PSW Queue of the HEP processing element (see Figure 16.8). Based on the instruction packet and the contents of the Activity Store, the Fetch Unit composes an operation

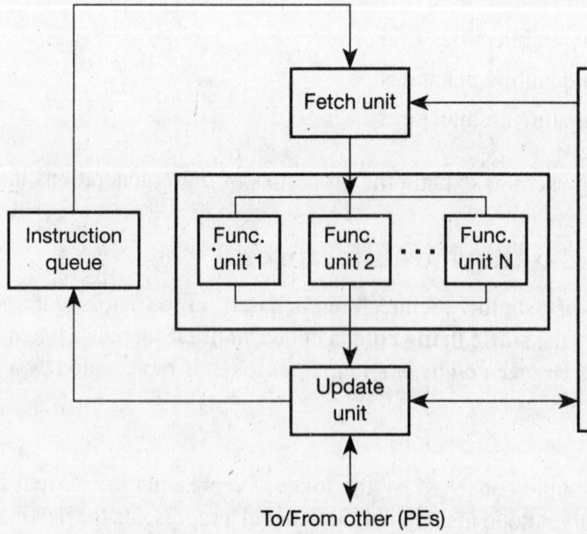

Figure 16.11 Structure of a typical static dataflow PE.

packet and sends it to one of the idle Functional Units. After executing the required operation the Functional Unit creates a result packet and sends it to the Update Unit which updates the Activity Store according to the results.

The parallelism achievable by this generation is strongly limited. For example, when a complex function is to be executed in a loop, the function invocations belonging to different loop cycles must be executed sequentially even if they are independent.

16.4.2 Tagged-token dataflow machines

Tagged-token dataflow machines were introduced to eliminate the problems of static dataflow machines. They do not restrict the number of tokens on the arcs of the dataflow graph and as a result they do not limit the achievable parallelism. However, this concept raises a new problem: tokens belonging to different activations must be distinguished when tokens are matched. For example, a node with two input arcs must consume two tokens belonging to the same cycle of a loop iteration. This is achieved by introducing a **token colouring** scheme. The colour is an index which is carried by the token and to which, in the case of loops, for example, it identifies the cycle of the loop to which the token belongs.

In the tagged-token model the structure of a token is more complex than in the static model:

<v, <f,n,c,i>, a>

where c specifies a code block or loop body within function activation f and i (the index) represents the colour. The **firing rule** of the tagged-token model becomes: a node can fire if there exists a colour 'i' for which tokens of colour 'i' are available on each input arc. Owing to the colour, the matching of tokens becomes a more complex operation than it was in static dataflow machines.

The typical structure of tagged-token dataflow machines is shown in Figure 16.12. Notice that a new unit, the Matching Unit, has to be introduced into the processor pipeline in order to perform coloured token matching. The Matching Unit is a special memory containing tokens which wait for their partner token of the same colour. The Matching Unit receives tokens from the Token Queue and checks if their partner token is already available in the matching store. If the partner token is missing, the received token is placed in the matching store. If the partner token is present, the Matching Unit removes the matching token from the store and passes the two matching tokens to the Fetch Unit. Based on the common tag, the Fetch Unit finds the enabled instruction in the Instruction/Data Memory and composes an operation packet which is sent to one of the idle Functional Units. Finally, the Form Token Unit creates result tokens and places them in the Token Queue.

Another problem to be solved by dynamic dataflow machines is array handling. Since there is no concept of reusable memory cells (or variables) in dataflow models, the single assignment principle is valid even for data structures like arrays. This implies that every time an element is updated the whole array must be

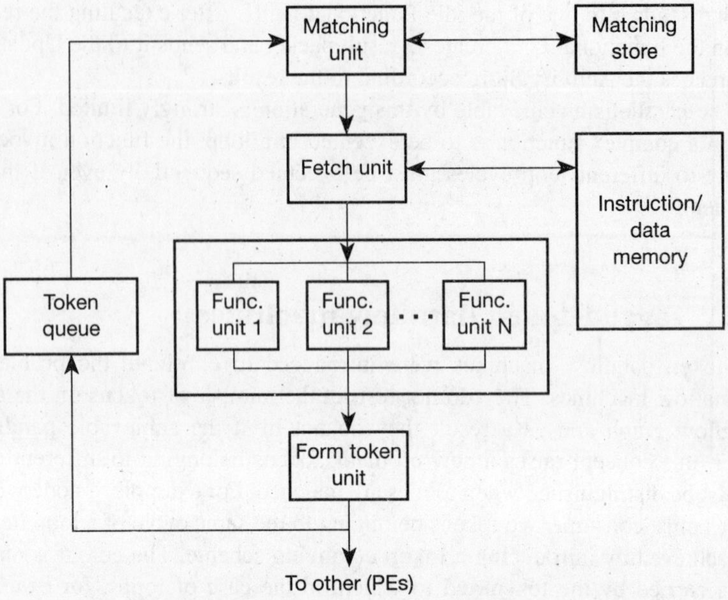

Figure 16.12 Structure of a typical tagged-token dataflow PE.

copied, which is prohibitively expensive. To tackle the problem several schemes have been proposed: heaps, I-structures, token relabelling, HDFM-arrays. The most successful, particularly from the point of view of multi-threading, is the **I-structure** concept introduced by Arvind and Thomas (1980). The I-structure storage consists of two parts: data storage and deferred read lists (Figure 16.13). In the data storage each memory cell is extended by presence bits which indicate the status of the cell:

Present: A store operation has already placed the datum in the cell.
Absent: Neither a store nor a load operation has been executed.
Waiting: One or more load operations have been executed, but no store operation.

When a cell is in the Waiting state the read requests are deferred and placed in the deferred read list whose pointer is stored in the memory cell. When the store operation is performed on a Waiting cell, all the pending read requests are removed from the corresponding deferred read list and the newly arrived datum is sent to its target instructions. The memory cell is updated by storing the datum and modifying the state to Present. Notice that the load operation implemented by the I-structure is a **split-phase transaction**. The dataflow processor can issue multiple, overlapped memory requests and can tolerate out-of-order responses. Accordingly, tagged-token dataflow architectures, supported by I-structure memory, can tolerate latency of remote memory access and therefore represent a good candidate for scalable parallel architectures. It is worth mentioning that the I-structure memory resembles the tagged memory concept of HEP. However, in the HEP unsatisfiable memory requests lead to the busy-waiting condition since the concept of a deferred read list is lacking.

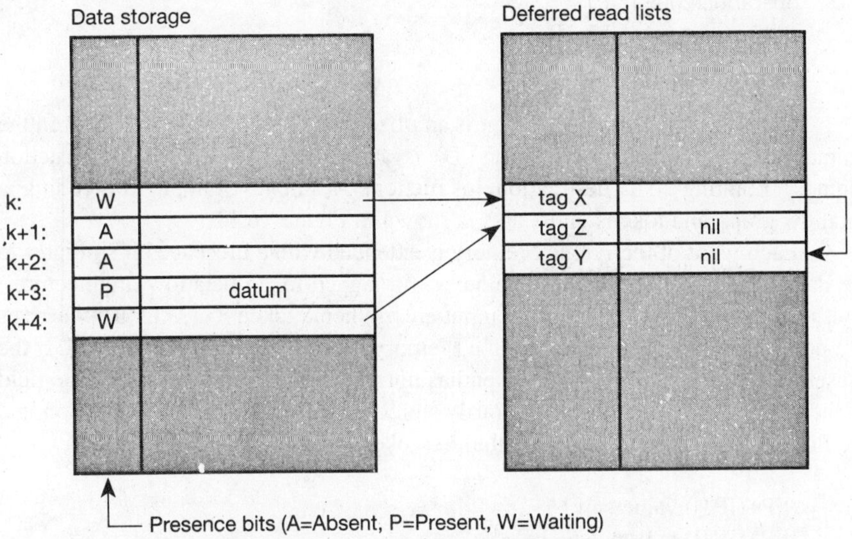

Figure 16.13 Organization of the I-structure storage.

Comparing the static and tagged-token dataflow machines, there are advantages and drawbacks on both sides. The tagged-token model is better than the static model in that it enables much more parallelism to be exploited and, supported by the I-structure, can tolerate memory latency. However, in machine organization terms the price for this enhanced parallelism is the extra Matching Unit which requires either a large-capacity associative memory which is too expensive or a pseudo-associative matching mechanism that needs several memory accesses which renders unbalanced the processor pipeline of the tagged-token dataflow architectures.

16.4.3 Explicit token-store architectures

A significant progression in dataflow architectures was the invention of the explicit token-store mechanism which eliminated the main drawback of tagged-token dataflow architectures. The main idea of this architecture type is the perception that tokens of the same colour belong to the same activation block and, therefore, a separate data memory segment can be created for them when the block is activated. The **Frame Memory** was introduced for this purpose. Whenever a block is activated a frame is allocated in the Frame Memory to hold the tokens belonging to the current block activation. The colour of these tokens is represented by the frame pointer (FP) of the activated block. Similarly, the f, n fields of the <f,n,c,i> tag are replaced by a single pointer, the instruction pointer (IP) which always points into the code block of the activated function in the Instruction Memory. The representation of a token in the explicit token-store architecture becomes:

<v, <FP,IP>>

The instruction format in the Instruction Memory is as follows:

operation code (OP)
frame memory index (I)
destinations (D)

Here, the frame memory index is an offset value to the rendezvous slot in the Frame Memory and the destination (D) is a relative index into the Instruction Memory pointing to a destination instruction. A simple example for coding a dataflow graph and tokens on its arcs is shown in Figure 16.14.

Each word of the Frame Memory is extended with a Presence bit similarly to the data memory of the HEP machine. As in tagged-token dataflow architectures, nodes can have a maximum of two input arcs. When a token <v1, <FP,IP>> arrives at a node the Presence bit of the Frame Memory location FP+(IP.I) is checked. If the Presence bit is reset, the partner token has not yet arrived and hence the value field of the current token must be temporarily stored in this Frame Memory location and the Presence bit set indicating that the first token is already available.

(FP+(IP.I)).value := v1
(FP+(IP.I)).presence := 1

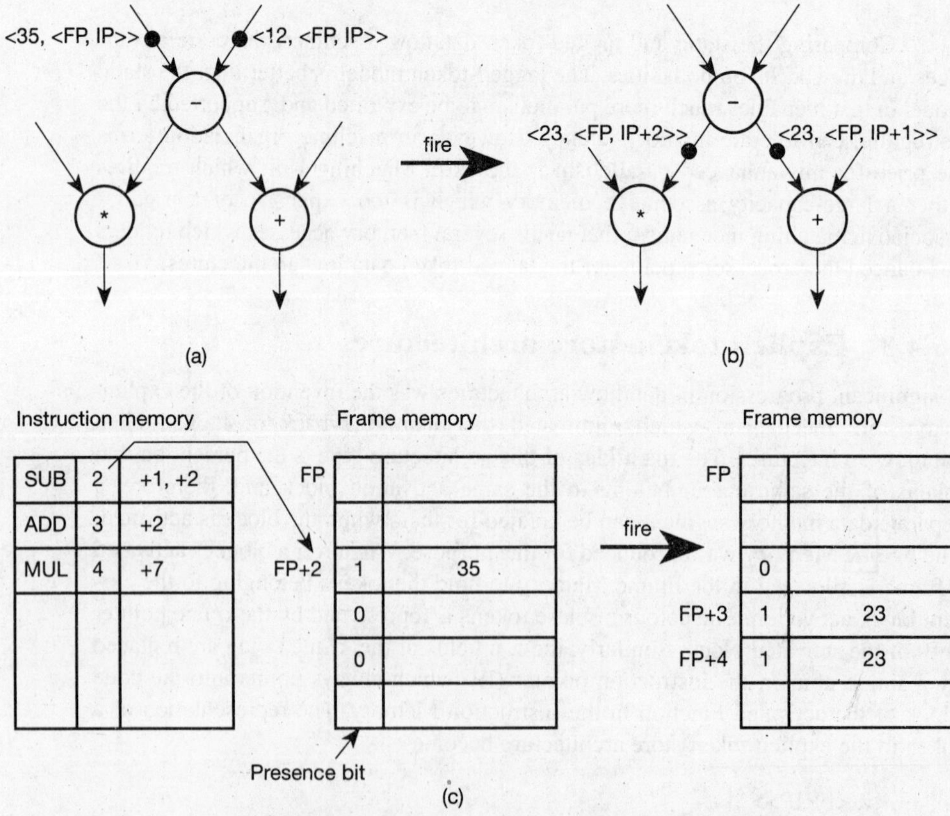

Figure 16.14 Coding in explicit token-store architectures.

This case is shown in Figure 16.14 after the first token <35, <FP,IP>> has arrived at the left input arc of the SUB node.

If a token <v2, <FP,IP>> arrives at a node for which the value v1 of the first token is already stored, the instruction representing the node (at location IP of the Instruction Memory) can be executed with the two values v1 and v2. At this time v1 is fetched from the Frame Memory, the Presence bit is reset and an instruction packet <v1, v2, FP, IP, IP.OP, IP.D> is passed to the Functional Unit which executes the requested operation and passes the result to the Form Token Unit. Figure 16.14 illustrates what happens when the second input token for the SUB node arrives. The SUB operation becomes firable and after its execution the result is passed to the ADD and MUL nodes which require the input token in the position of FP+3 and FP+4, respectively.

The typical structure of an explicit token-store architecture is shown in Figure 16.15. Notice that the token-matching function has become a short operation which makes it possible to introduce a several-stage well-balanced processor pipeline.

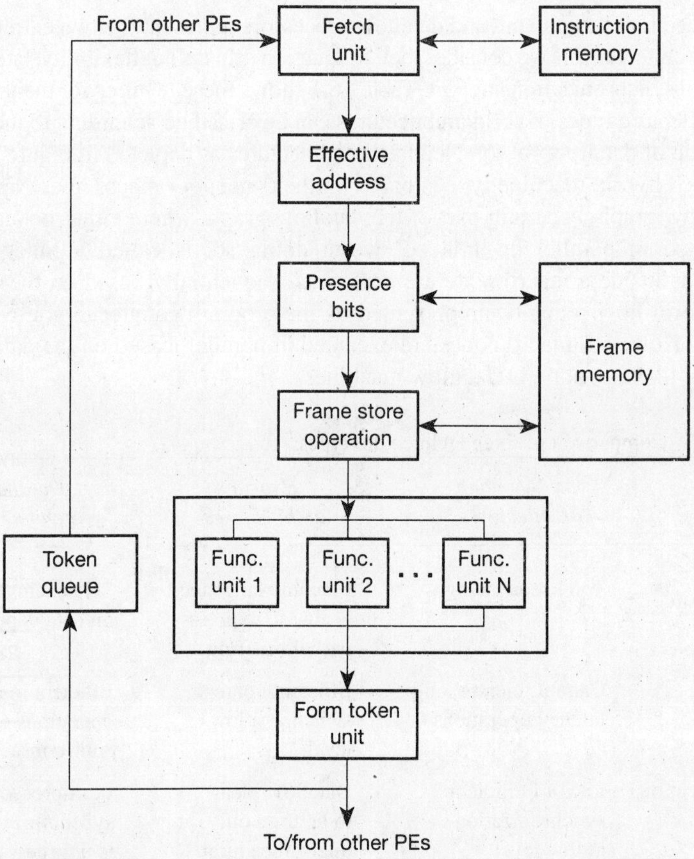

Figure 16.15 Structure of a typical explicit token-store dataflow PE.

Indeed, in the Monsoon explicit token-store architecture an eight-stage pipeline has been applied which significantly increases the processor performance compared with tagged-token dataflow architectures (Papadopoulos and Culler, 1990).

16.5 Hybrid multi-threaded architectures

In dataflow architectures, instructions become self-scheduling based on the dataflow firing rule. Although this is a very useful mechanism for exploiting instruction-level parallelism, it becomes superfluous for processing inherently sequential instruction streams and leads to unnecessary overhead in exploiting parallelism. In order to reduce overhead in dataflow machines an obvious compromise would be to increase the granularity of parallelism and exploit parallelism only among procedures, while inside procedures the sequential execution scheme of von Neumann processors could be applied. The resulting architecture is called the hybrid von Neumann/dataflow architecture and inherits features from both the dataflow and von Neumann processors.

Indeed, von Neumann and dataflow processors represent the two extremes of a range of architectures if we consider their instruction scheduling flexibility, latency toleration and synchronization support. Table 16.1 shows these features for the three possible architecture types. Hybrid architectures can be classified according to their place on the scale of dataflow → von Neumann architectures as depicted in Figure 16.16.

Each hybrid machine type is based on the concept of macro nodes applied in the dataflow graph. A certain part of the dataflow graph, where either nodes cannot be executed in parallel or it is not worth doing so, is called a **macro node**. Instructions inside a macro node are performed sequentially based on the conventional control flow semantics represented by the program counter in von Neumann machines. However, macro nodes are executed in parallel, based on the data-driven semantics, like any node in dataflow machines.

Table 16.1 Comparison of three architecture types.

	von Neumann architectures	*Hybrid architectures*	*Dataflow architectures*
Instruction scheduling flexibility	Total sequencing	Machine language is able to express partial ordering	Sequencing is based on data dependency
Latency toleration	Cannot tolerate long latency operations	Efficient context switch at a low level	Efficient multi-phase operations called split-transactions
Synchronization support	Lack of efficient synchronization at low level	Dataflow ideas to be used only at inter-procedural level	Intra-procedure synchronization is unnecessarily general

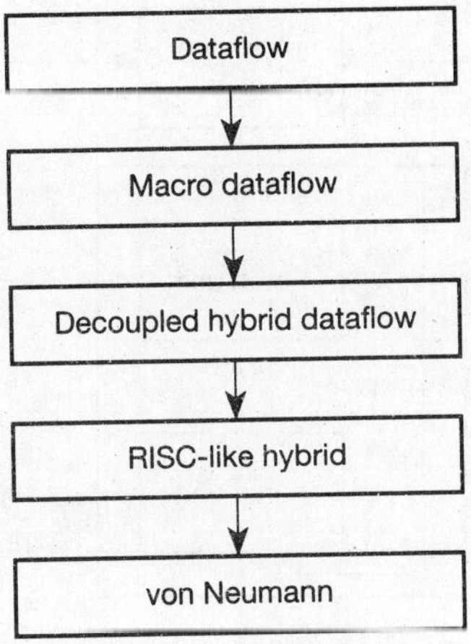

Figure 16.16 Scale of von Neumann/dataflow architectures.

One can consider *macro nodes as threads and hybrid architectures as multi-threaded processors*. The hybrid von Neumann/dataflow architectures represent the fourth generation of dataflow machines. Indeed, they all apply some form of the most developed dynamic, explicit token-store execution scheme for exploiting parallelism among the nodes of the dataflow graph.

16.5.1 Macro dataflow architectures

Macro dataflow architectures represent the first step from conventional dataflow design towards hybrid multi-threaded machines. They resemble a dataflow architecture rather than a von Neumann processor. Their typical structure is depicted in Figure 16.17. The main difference from dataflow machines appears in the organization of the internal control pipeline where the instruction sequence is determined by a simple program counter as in von Neumann processors. Macro nodes of the dataflow graph are executed by this internal control pipeline as a single-threaded (coarse-grain) instruction pipeline in which register optimization is utilized. Parallelism among macro nodes and other nodes of the dataflow graph is exploited by the same execution mechanism that was applied in explicit token-store dataflow architectures.

MIT Hybrid Machine

The MIT Hybrid Machine is a close follower of the Monsoon architecture. It introduces the concept of a **scheduling quantum (SQ)**. An SQ represents a sequential partition in the dataflow graph composed according to any optimality criterion. Ianucci (1988) defines five such criteria:

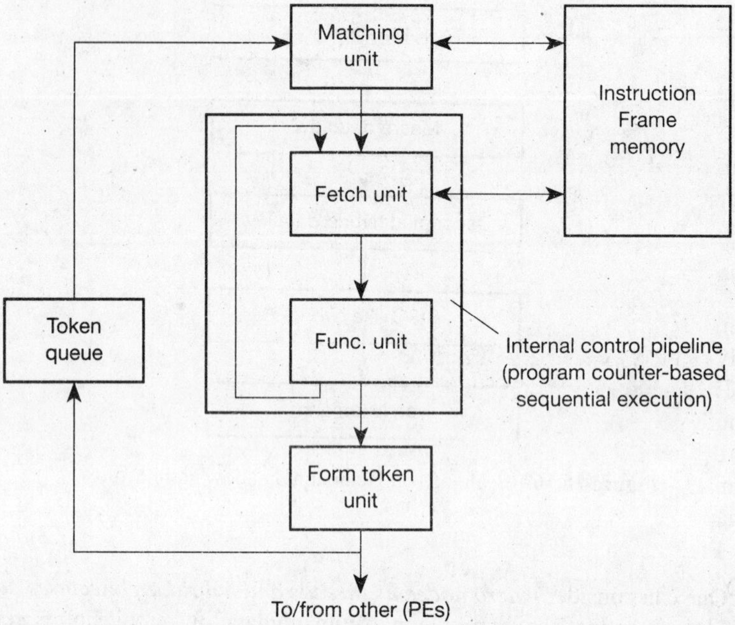

Figure 16.17 Structure of a typical macro dataflow PE (Lee and Hurson, 1994). © 1994 IEEE

- maximization of exploitable parallelism
- maximization of run length in SQs
- maximization of machine utilization
- minimization of explicit synchronization
- deadlock avoidance.

Based on these criteria the compiler can generate SQs in any dataflow graph. An SQ is implemented as a thread and represented as a continuation in the MIT Hybrid Machine. A continuation is a tuple consisting of a program counter (PC) and frame base register (FBR). A continuation (or thread) can be in one of the following states:

Enabled: The continuation is placed in the Enabled Continuation Queue (which corresponds to the Token Queue of dataflow machines).

Running: The continuation is loaded into the Active Continuation Register.

Suspended: The continuation resides in a frame slot waiting for a matching token (similarly to the explicit token store machines).

A continuation remains in the Running state for as long as the necessary input tokens are available and the last instruction has not yet been reached. In the Running state the PC field of the continuation is updated in exactly the same way as in von Neumann processors. An attempt to read an empty memory slot results in the suspension of the thread by saving its continuation in the empty memory slot and updating the presence bit of the memory slot (see the I-structure in Section 16.4.2). The organization of a processing element in the MIT Hybrid Machine is shown in Figure 16.18. Notice that optimized register use is possible in the control pipeline as in von Neumann processors. The I-structure memory is realized as a physically shared global memory in the MIT Hybrid Machine. The interconnection of processing elements and I-structure memory blocks is based on the 'dance-hall' concept similarly to the Denelcor HEP machine.

The architecture of a processing element in the MIT Hybrid Machine is a real compromise between dataflow machines and von Neumann-based parallel computers. On the one hand it resembles the Monsoon dataflow architecture, on the other it shows many similarities with von Neumann PEs like, for example, the Transputer (see Chapter 17). The Enabled Continuation Queue plays the same role as the two Active Process Queues in the Transputer. Communication and suspension on memory slots are very similar to the channel communication and suspension scheme

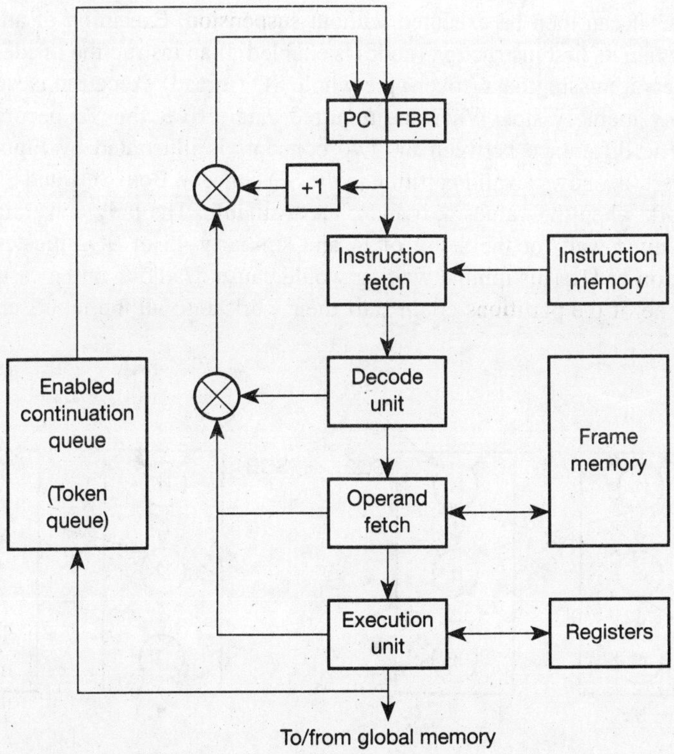

Figure 16.18 Organization of a PE in the MIT Hybrid Machine.

of the Transputer since the channel is implemented as a two-state memory slot in the Transputer, too. The real difference is that the channel can transfer data of any complexity and hence a physical communication phase is needed after the synchronization phase, while in the MIT Hybrid Machine a successful synchronization results in direct access to the required data.

Macro dataflow machines in Japan

The second example of the macro dataflow architecture class is the EM-4 machine developed at ETL of Japan. The EM-4 architecture is based on the **strongly connected arc model** where arcs of the dataflow graph are categorized as normal or strongly connected ones. Nodes inside a macro node – called a **strongly connected block (SCB)** – are connected by **strongly connected arcs** while SCBs are connected by normal arcs. An SCB can fire when all its input arcs contain a token; that is, macro nodes are executed based on dataflow semantics. However, nodes within an SCB are executed sequentially and therefore an SCB behaves as a thread (Sato et al.,1992).

The scheduling quantum (SQ) of the MIT Hybrid Machine and the strongly connected block (SCB) concepts are very similar since the execution of instructions in both kinds of macro node is sequential. The main difference is in the way they are activated. An SCB can be activated only when all of its input tokens are already available. It can then be executed without suspension. Execution of an SQ can be started when its first instruction (node) is enabled. If an instruction inside an SQ later encounters a missing data (token) the whole SQ (thread) execution is suspended on the empty memory slot. When the required data arrives the SQ becomes enabled again. The difference between the two concepts is illustrated by Figure 16.19 in which part (a) shows a valid partition in the SQ concept. Both SQ1 and SQ2 can start their work when the values a, b and c are available. The only constraint is that I2 of SQ1 must wait for the result of I4 and similarly, I5 of SQ2 must wait for the completion of I1. This mutual waiting would cause deadlock in the case of an SCB since none of the partitions could start their work until all the inputs are available,

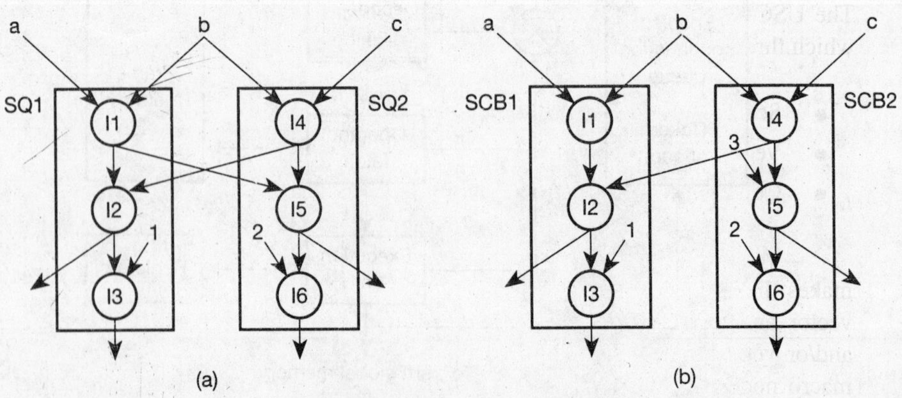

Figure 16.19 Comparison of (a) SQ and (b) SCB macro nodes.

but they each would need input from the other partition. If the mutual dependence is extracted, as shown in Figure 16.19(b), the SCB concept can be applied, too. First SCB2 can start its work and when I4 is completed, SCB1 becomes enabled, too.

The third example of macro dataflow machines is the Datarol-II architecture developed at the Kyushu University of Japan (Kawano et al., 1995). The main advantage of the Datarol-II machine is the introduction of a hierarchical memory system including a pre-loading and an implicit load/store mechanism which results in a very low context switching overhead for threads.

16.5.2 Decoupled hybrid dataflow architectures

Decoupled hybrid dataflow architectures work according to the parallel control flow model based on control tokens (see Section 16.2.3). Since in this model instruction scheduling concerns the collection of necessary control tokens, a natural implementation of the model would require a separate specialized functional unit for this purpose. Indeed, decoupled hybrid dataflow architectures distinguish and decouple a scheduling unit from the computational one. The computation processor can be any RISC processor with a highly optimized processor pipeline which works as a single-threaded (coarse-grain) instruction pipeline. Thread switching is relatively expensive, like in the Alewife machine, and hence they also use cache memory to reduce its frequency. Unlike the dataflow execution model, the control token model does not ensure that the already available operand is placed in the same local memory as that used to store the consumer instruction. As a consequence the employment of cache memory becomes necessary in these architectures to avoid time-consuming remote memory accesses. Two notable examples of this architecture type are:

- USC Decoupled Architecture
- McGill Dataflow Architecture and Super-Actor Machine (SAM).

The USC Decoupled Architecture

The USC Decoupled Architecture is based on the **Multi-level dataflow model** in which three kinds of nodes are distinguished (Evripidou and Gaudiot, 1991):

- Scalar node (one node, one operation)
- Vector macro node
- Compound macro node (CMN).

Vector macro nodes are specialized for vector operations. Their application makes the dataflow graph simpler and it also reduces the size of tags needed for vector and matrix operations. Compound macro nodes are collections of scalar and/or vector nodes. These are generated by the compiler, like the SQ and SCB macro nodes of the macro dataflow architectures. The CMN is scheduled on the same principle as the SCB.

In the USC Decoupled Architecture the computation and scheduling are decoupled. Scheduling is realized by the Data-Flow Graph Engine (DFGE) which fetches enabled macro nodes (threads) from the Graph Memory. A macro node is enabled when all the input tokens have arrived at the node. This is administered by the status word of the node stored in the Graph Memory. The status word is originally set to the number of expected operands and decremented whenever an operand becomes ready. When it reaches zero, the node can fire. Computations within threads are coded in the Computation Memory and processed by the Computation Engine (CE) which is a von Neumann processor based on advanced pipeline techniques. The two engines communicate through two queues: the Ready Queue (RQ) holds descriptors of enabled macro nodes, while the Acknowledge Queue (AQ) contains descriptors of nodes executed by the CE. The DFGE updates the Graph Memory based on the control tokens found in the AQ. The structure of the USC Decoupled Architecture is shown in Figure 16.20.

The processing elements of the USC machine are clustered. There is a shared Graph and Computation Memory for each cluster. Cluster memories are connected via a communication network and constitute a global virtual shared memory. At each processing element two caches (GC = Graph Cache and CC = Computation Cache) assure fast local memory access. The placement and replacement policy of the

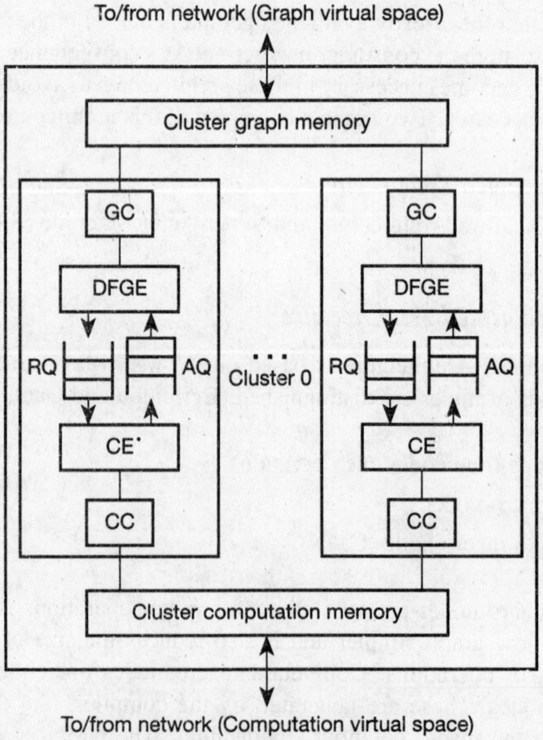

Figure 16.20 Structure of the USC Decoupled Architecture.

caches is based on the contents of the Ready Queue. The aim is to have the context-blocks in the cache for all the instructions which are in the Ready Queue. If this condition cannot be satisfied, the contents of the Ready Queue should be rearranged to give priority to the nodes whose context-blocks are already in the cache. Structure handling and producer/consumer synchronization is based on a combination of the I-structure and token relabelling concepts.

The USC Decoupled Architecture has the following advantages:

- The USC machine supports both thread-level and instruction-level parallelism based on compiler decision.
- The Computation Engine can be any state-of-the-art RISC processor.
- The number of threads per processor is not restricted by a register set. The only limit is the capacity of the Ready Queue.

The Super-Actor Machine (SAM)

The McGill Dataflow Architecture (MGDA) resembles the USC Decoupled Architecture in many ways (Gao et al., 1989). The MGDA concept was developed towards a complete multi-threaded machine, called the Super-Actor Machine (SAM). The novel feature of the SAM is the introduction of a special high-speed storage area called the **register-cache** (Hum and Gao, 1991). It is organized both as a register file viewed from the execution unit and as a fully associative cache memory from the main memory perspective.

In the SAM a thread is equivalent to a **super-actor** which is a macro node of the dataflow graph. Two types of super-actors are distinguished. Within a **sequential super-actor** instructions must be executed sequentially due to data dependencies among them. Instructions in a **parallel super-actor** can be executed at every pipe beat since they are data independent. A super-actor must satisfy two conditions to become enabled:

(1) **The firing rule** of static dataflow models: all the input arcs should contain a token and its output arcs should be empty (that is, its result tokens generated from a previous activation have been consumed).

(2) **Space locality condition**: its input data is physically residing in the register-cache and space is reserved there to store the results.

Owing to the space locality condition, once a super-actor becomes active it will be executed atomically until its completion, without any suspension. The problem of remote load latency simply does not occur since every operation is entirely local to the register-cache. Synchronization with other super-actors takes place in the Actor Scheduling Unit (ASU) based on the dataflow firing rule and hence a super-actor requires no synchronization during its execution in the Super-actor Execution Unit (SEU).

The structure of the SAM is shown in Figure 16.21. The ASU processes the control tokens and decrements the actors' associated enable count. When an actor becomes enabled, the ASU resets its enable count and sends a fire signal containing

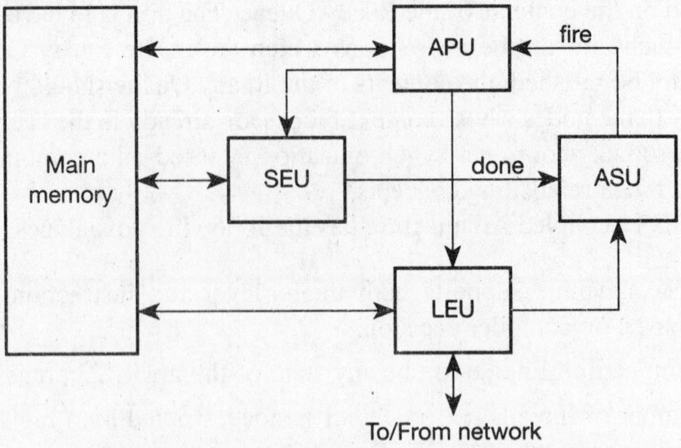

Figure 16.21 Structure of a node in the SAM.

the enabled actor and its attributes to the Actor Preparation Unit (APU). The APU is a new unit in the SAM compared with the MGDA. Its main role is to allocate space in the register-cache for the enabled actors before passing them to the SEU. Notice that the ASU implements the firing rule condition and the APU realizes the space locality condition. By the time an actor arrives at the SEU it satisfies both conditions.

The SAM concept has the following advantages:

- The SAM supports both thread-level and instruction-level parallelism based on compile-time decision.
- The SEU is an optimized pipelined RISC processor enhanced with the register-cache.
- The execution of a thread is atomic without any long-latency operation. By the time a thread becomes active, all the necessary data locations are placed in the local register-cache.

16.5.3 RISC-like hybrid multi-threaded architectures

RISC-like hybrid multi-threaded processors represent the closest architecture type to von Neumann machines. Indeed, the starting point for designing these processors is a 'conventional' RISC processor which is extended towards fine-grain thread-level parallelism support. Their computational model is based on **parallel control operators** (**FORK** and **JOIN**), which represents the closest approach to the sequential control flow model. The main problem with this model, when it is applied at the process level as originally introduced, is that synchronization on reusable memory cells is necessary. Moreover, this synchronization requires significant overhead and special care when applied at the user level. The RISC-like hybrid multi-threaded architecture represents a successful attempt to solve all of these problems.

The main advantage of hybrid multi-threaded architectures is that they are able to solve the synchronization problem in a fine-grain manner with a low overhead as a consequence of inheriting the latency hiding techniques of dataflow machines. Advanced dataflow and control flow compiler techniques make it possible to generate the necessary control instructions (FORK and JOIN) from high-level languages without introducing special user-level notations.

There are two notable milestones in designing hybrid multi-threaded architectures:

(1) the P-RISC processor developed at MIT, and

(2) the *T processor – a joint development by MIT and Motorola.

A detailed description of these two hybrid multi-threaded architecture designs is given below.

P-RISC

P-RISC (Nikhil and Arvind, 1989) inherits the organization of tokens from the macro dataflow machines, particularly from the MIT Hybrid Machine. Each token, called a **continuation**, consists of two fields: frame pointer (FP) and instruction pointer (IP):

context = <FP.IP>

where the context represents a thread, FP represents the local data frame of the thread and IP points to the current instruction of the thread.

The structure of the P-RISC processor is shown in Figure 16.22. The pipeline of conventional RISC processors is easily recognizable in the figure. The main difference between P-RISC and RISC processors lies in how the next instruction is entered into the pipeline. In conventional RISC processors instructions from the same thread are loaded into the pipeline based on the program counter. In P-RISC the

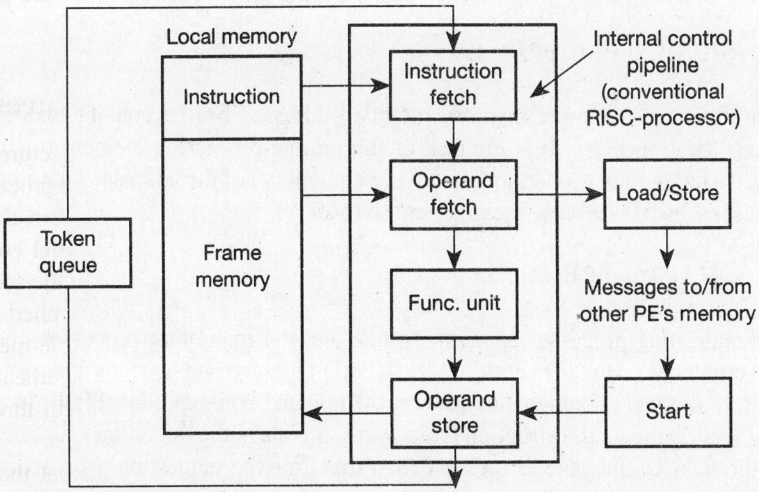

Figure 16.22 Structure of the P-RISC processing element. © 1989 ACM

token queue contains threads and in each clock step a new thread enters the pipeline from the token queue. As a result, different stages of the pipeline process instructions belonging to different threads, similarly to the HEP architecture. One can say that the P-RISC realizes fine-grain thread-interleaving like the HEP. At the end of the processor pipeline P-RISC creates a new token and places it in the token queue. Notice that the control loop based on the token queue and pipeline in the P-RISC is in principle the same as the control loop and pipeline in the HEP architecture.

For most ordinary RISC-like instructions, P-RISC works similarly to RISC processors. For example, an instruction in the form

op s1 s2 d

is executed in the following way:

FP+d := [FP+s1] op [FP+s2]

that is, the Frame Pointer (FP) serves as the base address for fetching the source operands and for placing the result of the instruction. Finally, a new token is created and placed on the token queue:

<FP.IP+1>

Since conventional RISC processors cannot tolerate memory latency when they execute load and store instructions, in the P-RISC design these instructions are implemented in an essentially different way. From a

load a x

instruction P-RISC creates a message in the form

<READ, [FP+a], FP.IP+1, x>

which is sent to a remote memory module addressed by the content of the local memory location FP+a. It is the task of the remote processing element possessing the requested memory location to fetch the content (v) of the addressed memory cell and to send back as a reply message in the form

<START, v, FP.IP+1, x>

to the requesting processor element. Notice that the requesting processor does not create any local token after emitting the READ message and hence it does not place a token in the local token queue. Rather, the updated continuation <FP.IP+1> of the thread issuing the load instruction temporarily travels in the interconnection network until the START message arrives back. At this time the requesting processor stores the fetched value v in FP+x and places the updated continuation <FP.IP+1> back into the token queue.

The remote load operation realized this way has the following advantages:

- Loads are split-phase transactions.
- Any number of loads can be performed in parallel in the distributed system.
- Responses can return in any order without disturbing the original semantics of the program.
- The processor is not blocked during load operations (unlike conventional RISC processors).
- While a thread is travelling in the network other threads from the token queue can keep the processor busy. The only limit on the number of threads handled by one processor is the length of the token queue.

Notice that the Scheduling Function Unit (SFU) of the HEP is replaced by the split-phase transaction model of P-RISC. As a consequence the reissuing of load operations by the SFU is avoided in the P-RISC processor, resulting in a much more efficient waiting mechanism for memory operations. Another advantage of P-RISC compared with the HEP is that bubbles are not inserted into the processor pipeline during the remote memory load operation.

The store operation is also implemented by a message-passing mechanism in the P-RISC based machine. The

store x a

instruction is executed by generating a

<WRITE, [FP+a], [FP+x]>

message directed to the PE that owns the memory location addressed by the contents of FP+a. However, in this case the updated continuation <FP.IP+1> of the thread can immediately be placed back in the token queue. Thread synchronization on memory locations is realized by means of I-structure memories, just as in the MIT Hybrid Machine.

In addition to the ordinary RISC-like instructions, P-RISC implements new instructions to support fine-grain thread-level parallelism. These instructions, used for creating new threads (fork) and removing threads (join), can be derived from the original dataflow graph of programs as shown in Figure 16.23 (Nikhil et al., 1992). The effect of the

fork IPt

instruction is the insertion of two continuations in the token queue. The first is the updated continuation of the current thread <FP.IP+1>, while the second is a newly formed continuation <FP.IPt>. Afterwards the two threads represented by the two continuations can progress independently through P-RISC's execution pipeline. When a node of the dataflow graph requires tokens from independent threads, a join instruction is generated by the compiler to collect the necessary tokens.

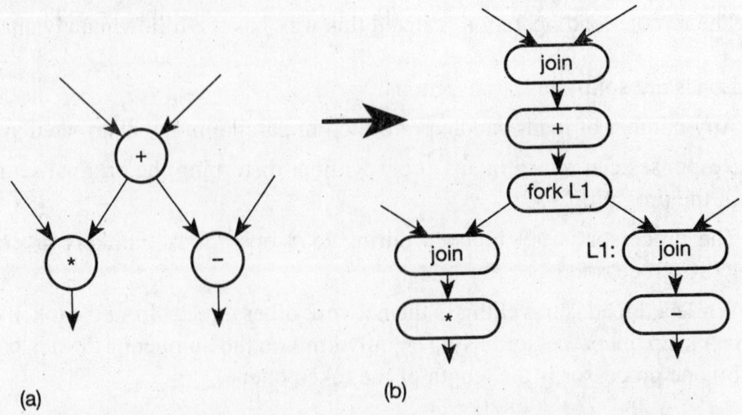

Figure 16.23 Transformation of dataflow graphs into control flow graphs. (a) Dataflow graph; (b) control flow graph. © ACM 1992

join x

represents a competition-based reduction of threads in the machine. The caller thread checks the local memory cell FP+x. If it contains zero (empty), the current thread is removed from the system by not placing its continuation back in the token queue. At the same time FP+x is set to one (full). If FP+x contains full, the current thread can continue and its updated continuation <FP.IP+1> is inserted in the token queue. Notice that the technique is very similar to the explicit token-store (ETS) concept. The difference is that in the P-RISC control tokens are collected in the Frame Memory, whereas in the ETS data tokens are collected there.

*T

The objective of the *T (read as 'start') design was to create a commercial multi-threaded processor chip based on the principles of P-RISC. Careful analysis of the P-RISC model showed that the performance of the *T chip can be significantly improved by introducing functional coprocessors to support remote memory access. The structure of the *T chip is shown in Figure 16.24.

The Data Processor contains the execution pipeline and operates on local instructions as shown in P-RISC. Whenever an instruction requiring remote memory access is fetched, it is passed to the Message Formatter which has the task of forming a message from the instruction and sending it into the network.

The Remote Memory Request Coprocessor handles incoming rload and rstore requests. It accesses the Local Memory to execute the requested services without disturbing the work of the Data Processor. In case of an rload instruction it fetches the information from the memory and passes it together with other parameters of the requesting message to the Message Formatter which composes a reply message and inserts it in the network.

The Synchronization (SP) Coprocessor handles rload responses returning to this node:

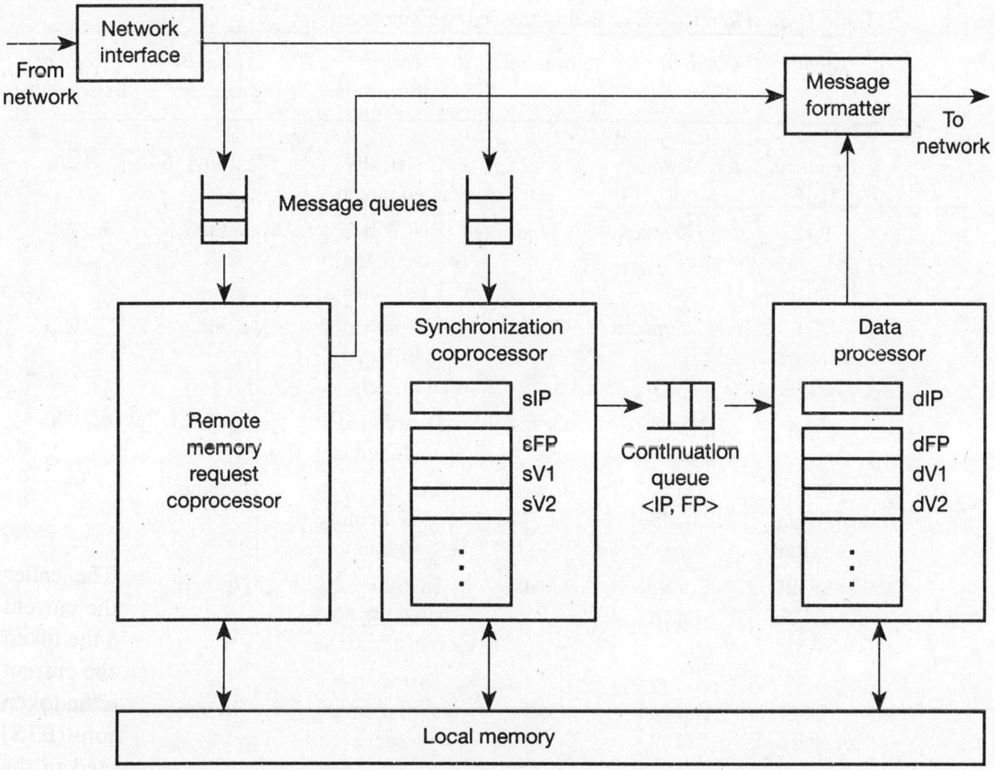

Figure 16.24 Structure of *T node (Nikhil et al., 1992). © 1992 ACM

<START, v, FP.IP+1, x>

SP loads FP+x with the received value v and places the updated continuation <FP.IP+1> in the Continuation Queue from which the Data Processor can resume work on the thread.

16.6 Summary

The multi-threaded architectures studied in this chapter are compared in Table 16.2 according to their design space. Although the very first multi-threaded machine was developed in the late 1970s another decade was necessary to really understand the necessity of the multi-threaded concept in the design of scalable parallel computers. Since 1988 progress in the field of multi-threading has been undiminished and year by year new multi-threaded machines have been designed and even produced for commercial purposes.

Three main directions can be distinguished in multi-threaded machine concepts. The first directly follows the ideas of the first multi-threaded computer, the

Table 16.2 Comparison of multi-threaded machines.

Machine	*Computation model*	*Granularity*	*Memory organization*	*Threads/ processor*	*Yea: of appearance*
Denelcor HEP	von Neumann	Fine	Physically shared memory	Maximum 64	1978
Tera	von Neumann	Fine	Distributed shared memory + I/O cache	Maximum 128	1990
MIT Alewife	von Neumann	Coarse	Cache-coherent distributed shared memory	Maximum 3	1990
EM-4	Macro dataflow	Coarse	Distributed shared memory	No limit	1990
MIT Hybrid Machine	Macro dataflow	Coarse	Physically shared memory + local memory	No limit	1988
McGill MGDA/ SAM	Control token	Coarse	Distributed shared memory + register cache	No limit	1991
USC Decoupled Architecture	Control token	Coarse	Distributed shared memory + cache	No limit	1990
P-RISC	Control operators	Fine	Distributed shared memory	No limit	1989
*T	Control operators	Fine	Distributed shared memory	No limit	1992

Denelcor HEP. The Tera machine is a representative example of this class of multi-threaded machines. The main characteristics of this class are:

- von Neumann-based computational model
- Fine-grain thread interleaving
- A large number of registers to accommodate as many threads as possible in the processor.

The third feature makes this concept very expensive and dependent on the current state of chip fabrication technology. This is an obvious drawback which will lead to the search for new forms of multi-threading.

The second direction is represented by the MIT Alewife machine and has the following main properties:

- von Neumann-based computational model
- Coarse-grain thread interleaving

- Small number of threads/processor
- Coherent cache support to reduce the frequency of thread switches.

This approach combines multi-threading with coherent cache memory in the framework of a CC-NUMA architecture. Since CC-NUMA machines are expected to become very popular as scalable parallel computers, it can be foreseen that the results of the MIT Alewife project will influence the design of future CC-NUMA architectures.

Interestingly, the third direction has grown from the field of dataflow architectures and in the form of the *T processor it has led to a concept very similar to the initial Denelcor HEP. Within this direction two significantly different concepts can be distinguished:

(1) Hybrid von Neumann/dataflow architectures applying coarse-grain thread interleaving.

(2) Hybrid von Neumann/dataflow architectures supporting fine-grain thread interleaving.

Followers of the first concept apply some form of macro nodes in the dataflow graph. They represent a real hybrid design. From the perspective of macro node communication and synchronization they look like a dataflow machine, but inside the macro nodes they behave like von Neumann processors. All of them require sophisticated compiler technology to optimally partition the dataflow graph into macro nodes.

The second hybrid concept gets very close to the original HEP design although significantly improves its disadvantageous features. Introducing the concepts of continuation and a control pipeline based on the continuation queue radically reduces the number of registers required for fast context switching. The split-phase memory access scheme avoids the busy-wait memory access mechanism of the HEP. Thread creation is straightforward by systematically transforming the dataflow graph into the control flow graph based on FORK and JOIN instructions. The recent *T design represents a very promising approach to efficiently supporting latency hiding by multi-threading.

17 Distributed Memory MIMD Architectures

Section 17.1 discusses solutions to memory and synchronization latency and the design space of distributed memory MIMD architectures. Section 17.2 lists the main characteristics of direct interconnection networks and describes several topologies as well as switching techniques and routing. Section 17.3 describes fine-grain systems, using the Message-Driven Processor and J-machine as examples. Section 17.4 uses the Transputer and machines based on it as examples of medium-grain systems, while Section 17.5 looks at coarse-grain systems using the Intel Paragon as an example of homogeneous architectures and the Parsytec GC/PowerPlus and IBM SP2 as examples of hybrid architectures. Section 17.6 summarizes the chapter.

17.1 Introduction

17.1.1 Solution for memory and synchronization latency

Unlike in multi-threaded and shared memory architectures, memory access of a remote memory block is prohibited in multicomputers. Each local memory has the same address space and hence, any address used by a processor will access the local memory of that processor. As a result, processes running on different processing elements cannot communicate through shared data structures. Such processes should send messages to each other via the interconnection network of the multicomputer. Accordingly, distributed memory MIMD architectures are called message-passing computers, reflecting the solution offered by this type of architecture to the problem of accessing remote memory and hiding both memory and synchronization latency. The basic idea is that processes are allocated along with their data areas in local memory and hence remote memory references are avoided. Whenever access to a remote memory location becomes necessary its content is requested by sending a message to the process owning that memory area. While awaiting the response, the requesting process can be handled in two different ways:

- It is suspended and its processor is allocated to another process.
- It can continue (doing other useful computations) until it needs the response. At this point it busy-waits for the reply message.

The first approach requires an efficient process switching mechanism similar to the thread switching in multi-threaded systems and a sufficiently large number of processes per processor to replace suspended processes with active ones. In the second approach, efficient software and hardware support is needed to poll pending communications.

Notice that time requirements of process switching in multicomputers are not as strict as in multi-threaded architectures since the size and frequency of messages are quite different in the two architecture types. In multi-threaded systems, the size of messages is proportional to the access of a single remote memory cell, i.e. very small, and the frequency of issuing such messages is very high. Accordingly, the thread switching time should be comparable to the access time of a single local memory cell. Conversely, in multicomputers, messages can contain data structures of any size, and hence the issuing of such large messages is much less frequent. Owing to the low frequency of issuing messages, the time requirement of switching processes is much less strict than in the multi-threaded systems. Nevertheless, keeping process switching time low is a crucial issue in multicomputers, too.

In order to reduce the frequency of interprocessor communication, message-passing computers raise two important new questions:

(1) How best to partition the parallel program into processes

(2) How to map processes onto processors in order to minimize interprocessor communication.

The answers to these questions are not trivial; they lead to NP-complete problems and although they stimulated many research efforts in the past decade, generally accepted algorithms are not yet available. Even if satisfactory solutions could be found, the problem of load balancing immediately appears. An initial mapping, optimal from the point of view of interprocessor communication, can result in an unbalanced system that has idle and overloaded processors at run time. These problems caused parallel computer designers to turn to distributed shared memory systems where these problems do not occur or, more correctly, they are automatically solved by the underlying hardware/software system. Nevertheless, message-passing computers are still popular and can deliver the best peak performance for problems containing a large amount of parallelism.

17.1.2 Design space

Recall that in multi-threaded machines the main design issue was to reduce the time and frequency of thread switches. Naturally, process switching time and frequency are not negligible in message-passing architectures either, but they are less dominant than the following two factors:

- Frequency of communication
- Processor time spent on communication.

Accordingly, the focus in designing message-passing parallel computers is the organization of the communication subsystem, that is, the interconnection network of processing elements and the hardware support for passing messages among nodes of the multicomputer. The frequency of communication can be reduced only by software technology using efficient partitioning, mapping and load-balancing techniques. From the point of view of hardware design the main concern is the reduction of processor time spent on communication.

A multicomputer consists of a set of nodes and a communication network connecting the nodes. Communication among nodes is typically realized via point-to-point or direct connections called **links** or **channels**. Such networks are called **direct** or **static networks** and can be represented by a **communication graph** in which vertices correspond to the nodes of the multicomputer and edges represent channels. The nodes of message-passing architectures consist of three main components:

- Computation processor + private memory (PE)
- Communication processor
- Router (or switch unit).

The role of both the communication processor and the router is to organize communication among the nodes of the multicomputer. Since the size of messages can vary depending on the application, messages are divided into **packets**. On the sender node, it is the task of the communication processor to packetize messages; similarly the communication processor of the receiving node depacketizes them.

When a message is sent between nodes that are not directly connected (remote nodes), intermediate nodes must transmit the message to the next node of the **communication path** established between the source and destination nodes. Establishing such a path is the task of either the source node communication processor or the router, depending on the actual routing protocol. Transmitting messages via the communication path is always the task of the router.

Multicomputers can be classified according to:

- how the interconnection network is organized;
- how the three components of the nodes are composed and integrated;
- the message-passing computational model supported by the multicomputer;
- the optimal grain of computation supported by the multicomputer.

The interconnection network design has three main considerations. Firstly, the **topology** of the communication graph is an important characteristic of the interconnection network which significantly influences message transmission time in the multicomputer. Accordingly, one of the main design decisions in message-passing architectures is the selection of a proper network topology. Secondly, a strongly related question arises: what kind of **switching technique** is to be used at the nodes of the network? Switching is the actual mechanism by which messages are transmitted from input buffers to output buffers. Finally, **routing protocols** play a crucial role in finding communication paths between non-neighbour source and destination nodes.

Clearly, based on the organization of interconnection networks and nodes, three generations of multicomputers can be distinguished. In first-generation message-passing computers the processing elements were directly connected, so there were no communication processors or switch units (Figure 17.1(a)). Their functions were provided by the processing element via low-level software layers (for example, machines built of Transputers). In second-generation multicomputers independent switch units were introduced and separated from the processor. The generic interconnection schemes of these machines are either decentralized (for example, iPSC/2, Figure 17.1(b)) or centralized (for example, Parsys Supernode, Figure 17.1(c)). In current third-generation message-passing architectures the three main components are clearly distinguishable and for each component a separate, specialized processor is applied (for example, Meiko CS-2). Figure 17.1(d) shows the organization of third-generation multicomputers.

The node computation processor could be either a commodity microprocessor or a custom-designed one. Employing off-the-shelf microprocessors significantly reduces the design cost of multicomputers, though the performance of such machines might be lower than those with custom-designed chips. Another aspect of computation processors, namely whether they are supported by special vector processors, is also related to computing power. Interestingly, only a few commercial multiprocessors were enhanced with vector processors (Intel iPSC/2, Meiko CS-2), though the lack of vector processors obviously reduces their performance compared with other parallel architectures.

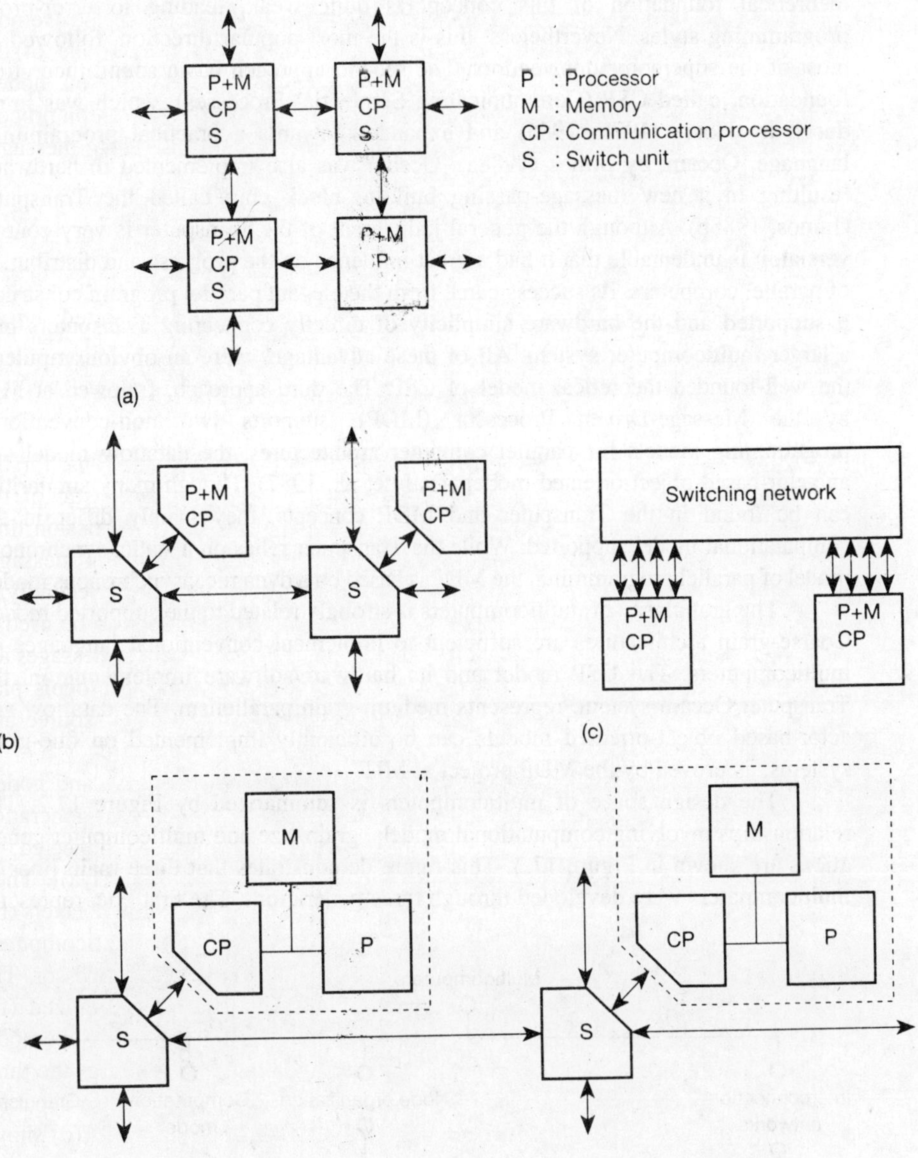

Figure 17.1 Node organization in different generations of multicomputers. (a) First-generation multicomputer organization; (b) decentralized second-generation multicomputer organization; (c) centralized second-generation multicomputer organization; (d) third-generation multicomputer organization.

The third important issue in designing multicomputers is the computational model to be supported. Three main directions can be distinguished. The first, very pragmatic approach intends to apply conventional programming languages (like C and Fortran), extending them by special communication libraries. The theoretical foundation of this concept is quite weak, leading to error-prone programming styles. Nevertheless, this is the most popular direction, followed by most of the supercomputer vendors. The second approach has a sound theoretical foundation, called CSP (Communicating Sequential Processes), which was introduced by Hoare (1978, 1985) and expanded towards a practical programming language, Occam, by Inmos (1988a). Occam was also implemented in hardware, resulting in a new message-passing building-block chip called the Transputer (Inmos, 1988b). Although the general judgement of the Transputer is very controversial, it is undeniable that it had a great influence on the progress and distribution of parallel computers. Its success came from the elegant parallel program constructs it supported and the hardware simplicity of directly connecting Transputers into a larger multicomputer system. All of these advantages were an obvious result of the well-founded theoretical model of CSP. The third approach, followed at MIT by the Message-Driven Processor (MDP), supports two non-conventional programming models for parallel computer architectures: the dataflow model and an actor-based object-oriented model (Dally et al., 1987). Though many similarities can be found in the Transputer and MDP concepts, they mainly differ in the computational model supported. While the Transputer relies on a static, synchronous model of parallel programming, the MDP is based on a dynamic, asynchronous model.

The granularity of multicomputers is strongly related to the supported model. Coarse-grain architectures are sufficient to implement conventional languages on multicomputers. The CSP model and its hardware/software implementation, the Transputer/Occam system, represents medium-grain parallelism. The dataflow and actor-based object-oriented models can be efficiently implemented on fine-grain systems, as proved by the MDP project at MIT.

The design space of multicomputers is summarized by Figure 17.2. The relationships involving computational models, grain size and multicomputer generations are shown in Figure 17.3. This figure demonstrates that three main lines of multicomputers were developed through three generations. The first line, represent-

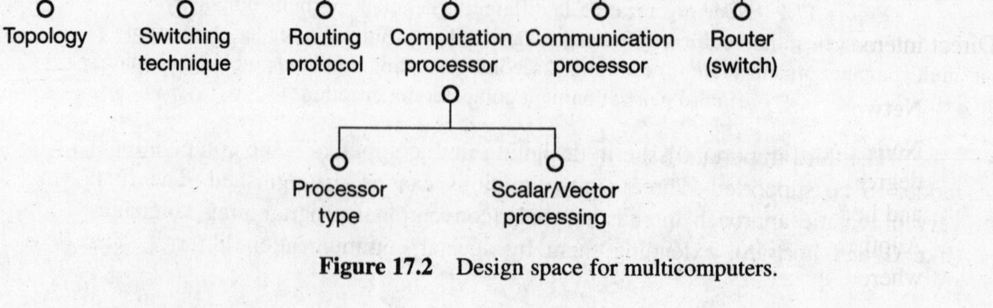

Figure 17.2 Design space for multicomputers.

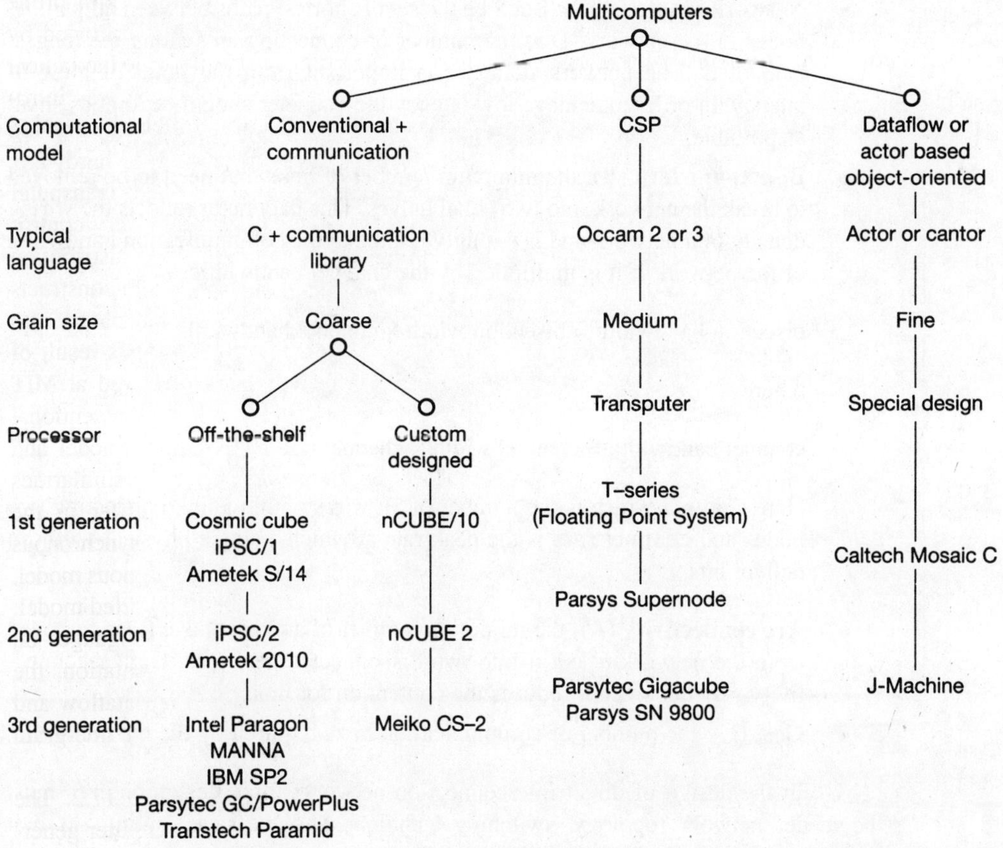

Figure 17.3 Classification of multicomputers.

ing the conventional approach, has two branches: one for computers built using commodity processors and one where custom-designed processors are used. In this chapter we first study the properties of direct interconnection networks, and then investigate the three main directions of multicomputers by concentrating on their third-generation representatives.

17.2 Direct interconnection networks

Direct interconnection networks are characterized by the following main measures:

- **Network size (N)**: the number of nodes in the network.
- **Node degree (d)**: the number of input and output links of a node. The node degree represents the cost of a node from the communication point of view and hence network topologies where the node degree is low are favourable. Another important aspect of node degree is related to scalability. Networks where the node degree does not depend on the network size are scalable.

- **Network diameter (D)**: Let S be the set of shortest paths between all pairs of nodes in the network. D is the number of connecting arcs along the longest path of S. The network diameter is important from the point of view of latency. In order to achieve low latency the diameter should be kept as small as possible.
- **Bisection width (B)**: the minimum number of links that need to be removed to break the network into two equal halves. This parameter reflects the wiring density of a network and is strongly related to the communication bandwidth of the network if it is multiplied by the channel bandwidth:

  bisection bandwidth = bisection width × channel bandwidth

  where

  channel bandwidth = channel width × channel rate

  Here **channel width** is the number of bit wires within a link connecting two nodes and **channel rate** is the peak rate at which a single physical wire can deliver bits.

- **Arc connectivity (A)**: the minimum number of arcs that have to be removed from the network to cut it into two disconnected networks. Higher connectivity is better since it reduces the contention for links.
- **Cost (C)**: the number of communication links required by the network.

In the design of direct interconnection networks three design choices must be made: network topology, switching technique and message routing. At first sight they seem to be largely orthogonal; however, the progress of generations of multicomputers demonstrates that switching techniques have influenced the choice of network topology.

17.2.1 Interconnection topologies

The six parameters listed above represent conflicting requirements. Scalability requires a large number of nodes with a small and constant degree at a low cost, that is, with a small number of links. However, low latency and high bandwidth require a higher node degree and a large number of links. These contradictory requirements lead to a compromise in static network design decisions and particularly in the selection of the interconnection topology.

Static interconnection topologies can be classified according to their dimensions:

- One-dimensional topologies
- Two-dimensional topologies
- Three-dimensional topologies
- Hypercubes.

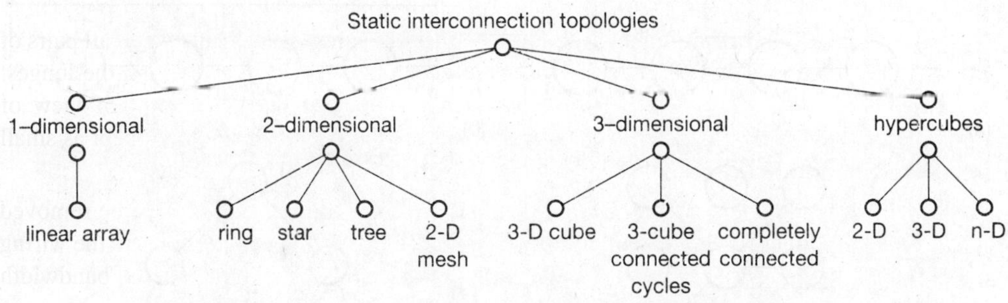

Figure 17.4 Design space of static interconnection topologies.

The design space for direct network topologies is shown in Figure 17.4 and the main static interconnection topologies in Figure 17.5. A brief overview of the main topologies is given below.

Linear array The simplest way to connect nodes is the linear array topology (Figure 17.5(a)) which can be advantageously used in pipelined algorithms. This is a low-cost network (C=N–1) requiring a low node degree (d=2) but has many drawbacks. The diameter is the worst of all the possible topologies (D=N–1) and both the bisection width (B=1) and arc connectivity (A=1) parameters are very poor.

Ring By applying a simple wraparound connection between the processors at the ends of a linear array one can get the ring topology (Figure 17.5(b)) which improves the poor parameters of the linear array by a factor of two: D=N/2, B=2 and A=2. Recently the ring topology has become popular, particularly at various levels of hierarchical topologies. For example, in the KSR1 rings are connected in a hierarchy; in the Convex Exemplar the so-called hypernodes are connected by multiple parallel rings.

Star The star connection is another simple and low-cost (C=N–1) topology (Figure 17.5(c)) which has the same poor bisection width (B=1) and arc connectivity (A=1) parameters as the linear array but the diameter is radically improved (D=2). From the point of view of both scalability and fault tolerance the central node of the star topology represents a critical point.

Tree The **binary tree** topology (Figure 17.5(d)) takes a significant step towards reducing the network diameter (D=2log((N+1)/2)) without sacrificing the constant node degree (d=3). Another advantage of the tree topology is that it fits well with many important parallel algorithm classes. Accordingly, the binary tree architecture gains popularity from time to time. The main drawback of the binary tree network is the poor bisection width (B=1) and arc connectivity (A=1). The **fat tree** network (Figure 17.5(e)) tries to eliminate this problem by duplicating the number of links at each level going upwards in the tree and also duplicating the number of links connecting a node to a higher-level node. The price for this improvement is that the node degree becomes variable and the network cost grows significantly. Nevertheless, recently the fat tree topology has gained popularity. For example, CM-5 and CS-2 employ fat tree networks.

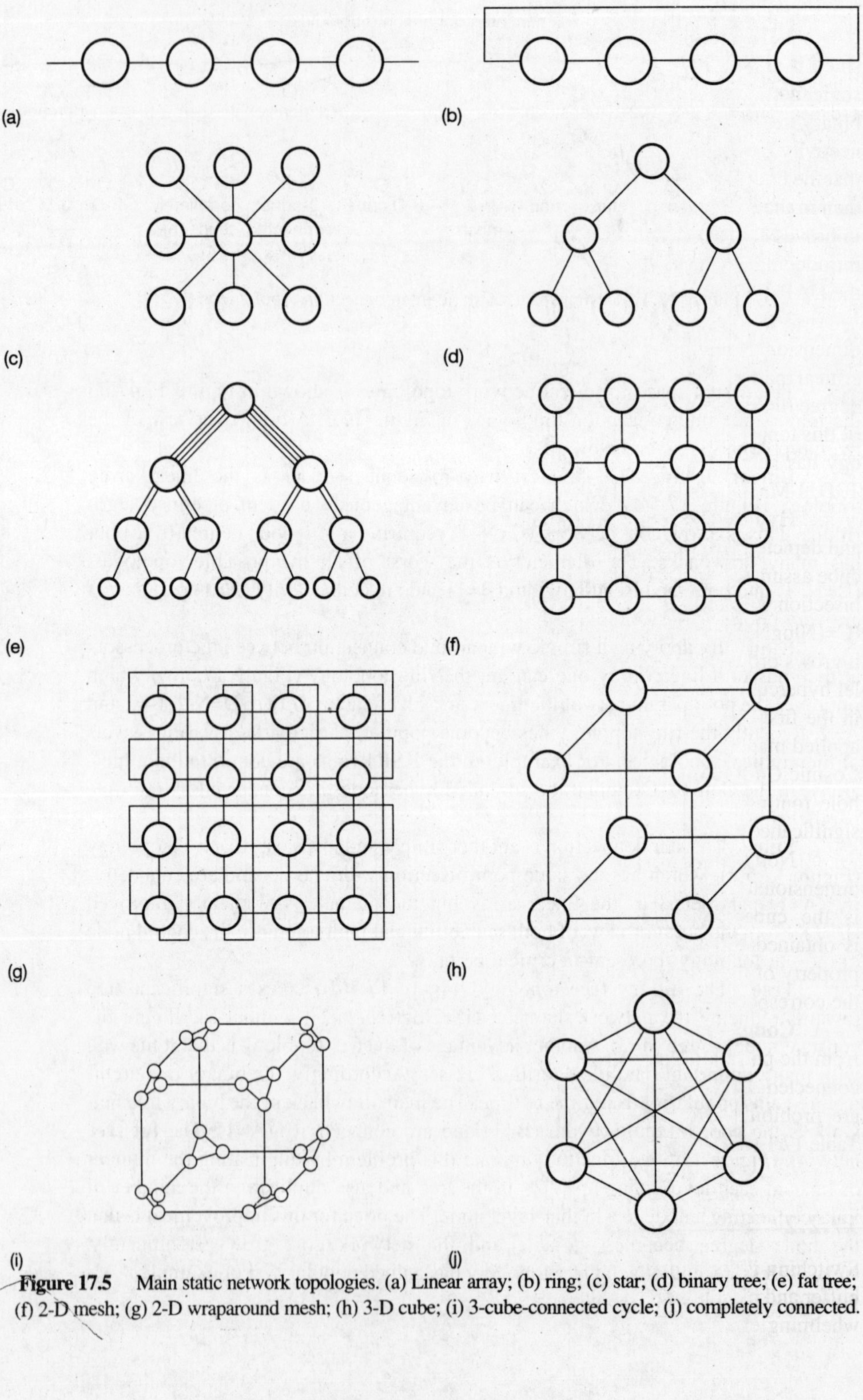

Figure 17.5 Main static network topologies. (a) Linear array; (b) ring; (c) star; (d) binary tree; (e) fat tree; (f) 2-D mesh; (g) 2-D wraparound mesh; (h) 3-D cube; (i) 3-cube-connected cycle; (j) completely connected.

2-D Mesh One of the most popular topologies is the mesh (Figure 17.5(f)) since it represents a good compromise among the contradictory requirements of static network parameters. It assures a shorter diameter ($D=2(N^{1/2}-1)$) than the binary tree and a significantly improved bisection width ($B=N^{1/2}$). Even the arc connectivity (A=2) is doubled compared to the binary tree. The other side of the coin is that the node degree (d=2, 3 or 4) and network cost ($C=2(N-N^{1/2})$) are slightly higher than in the binary tree. The **wraparound 2-D mesh** or torus (Figure 17.5(g)) further improves the most important parameters ($D=N^{1/2}$, $B=2*N^{1/2}$, A=4) at the cost of introducing $2*N^{1/2}$ more links. Examples of 2-D mesh-based parallel computers are the DAP, Caltech Mosaic C, Intel Paragon, MIT Alewife and Stanford Dash.

3-D Mesh (Cube) Another frequently used topology is the three-dimensional extension of the 2-D mesh (Figure 17.5(h)) which further improves the critical parameters ($D=3*(N^{1/3}-1)$, $B=N^{2/3}$, A=3) without causing too high node degree (d=3, 4, 5 or 6) or network cost ($C=2(N-N^{2/3})$). The technological realization of this topology is much more difficult than the 2-D mesh and hence the cube topology has been introduced only in the most recent parallel computers like the Cray T3D, J-Machine and Parsytec GC.

Hypercube The hypercube topology is described in detail in Section 10.2.4 and depicted in Figure 10.7. Here, we consider only its main parameters. The hypercube assures an even smaller diameter (D=logN) than the cube network. It has good bisection width (B=N/2) and arc connectivity (A=logN) but naturally at a higher cost (C=(NlogN)/2). However, its main drawback is that the node degree is not constant; it grows proportionally with logN which renders the fabrication of massively parallel hypercubes tremendously difficult. The hypercube topology was frequently used in the first- and second-generation multicomputers where the switching technique applied made the diameter the most crucial parameter of the network. For example, Cosmic Cube, nCUBE and iPSC employed the hypercube topology. When wormhole routing became generally accepted, the diameter parameter lost its superior significance and the hypercube lost its popularity.

Notice that the 2-D mesh and 3-D cube are actually two- and three-dimensional hypercubes. Another topology that can be derived from the hypercube is the cube-connected cycle. The **3-cube-connected cycle** of Figure 17.5(i) is obtained by replacing each node of a 3-D cube by a 3-node cycle. A notable property of the 3-cube-connected cycle is that each node in a cycle is connected to the corresponding node in another cycle.

Completely connected network This topology (Figure 17.5(j)) is ideal from the point of view of network diameter (D=1) since any two nodes are directly connected. However, the cost (C=N(N–1)/2) and node degree (d=N–1) parameters are prohibitive in building massively parallel computers based on this topology. Table 17.1 summarizes the main properties of the most important static network types.

17.2.2 Switching techniques

Switching is the actual mechanism by which a message is removed from the input buffer and placed in the output buffer. The switching technique applied has an overwhelming effect on message latency and hence the choice of switching method is

Table 17.1 Summary of static network parameters for the main topologies.

Topology	*Node degree*	*Diameter*	*Bisection width*	*Arc connectivity*	*Cost*
Linear array	1 or 2	N – 1	1	1	N – 1
Ring	2	N/2	2	2	N
Star	1 or N – 1	2	1	1	N – 1
Binary tree	1, 2 or 3	2log((N+1)/2)	1	1	N – 1
2-D mesh	2, 3 or 4	$2(N^{1/2}-1)$	$N^{1/2}$	2	$2(N-N^{1/2})$
2-D wraparound mesh	4	$N^{1/2}$	$2N^{1/2}$	4	2N
3-D cube	3, 4, 5 or 6	$3(N^{1/3}-1)$	$N^{2/3}$	3	$2(N-N^{2/3})$
Hypercube	logN	logN	N/2	logN	(NlogN)/2
Completely connected	N – 1	1	$N^2/4$	N – 1	N(N – 1)/2

absolutely crucial in designing any distributed memory computer. The design space of switching techniques is shown in Figure 17.6.

Packet switching (store-and-forward)

In first-generation multicomputers the packet switching mechanism was borrowed from the world of computer networks. The packet switching mechanism behaves in a store-and-forward manner similar to the mail service. A message is divided into packets which are sent independently via the communication network between the source and the destination nodes. A packet consists of a header and the data. The header contains the necessary routing information and, based on that information, the switching unit decides where to forward the packet. The unique feature of the packet switching scheme is that when a packet arrives at an intermediate node, the whole packet is stored in a packet buffer as illustrated in Figure 17.7(a). The packet is forwarded to a neighbouring node if an empty buffer is available in that node.

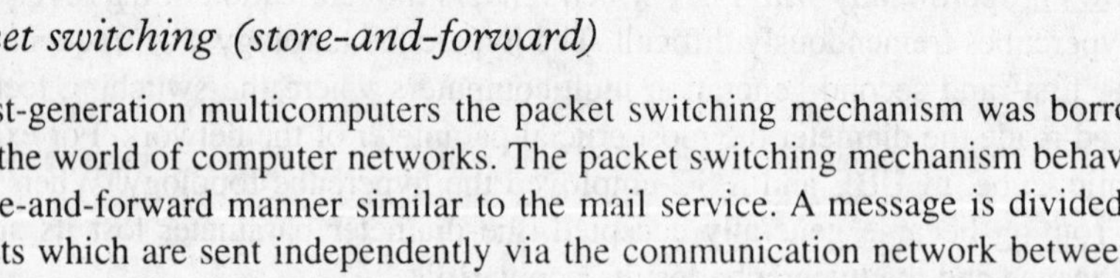

Figure 17.6 Design space of switching techniques.

The network latency (L) in the case of packet switching is:

$$L = \frac{P}{B} * D \qquad (17.1)$$

where P is the packet length, B is the channel bandwidth and D is the distance (number of nodes) between the source and the destination nodes. The timing diagram of the store-and-forward technique shown in Figure 17.8(a). and the latency expression above both reflect the main drawback of packet switching: latency is proportional to the message path length. This is the reason why the diameter was the most important parameter in first-generation multicomputers and why the hypercube topology was so popular. Although the node degree and cost parameters for the hypercube are not the best, its diameter is one of the smallest among the topologies surveyed in

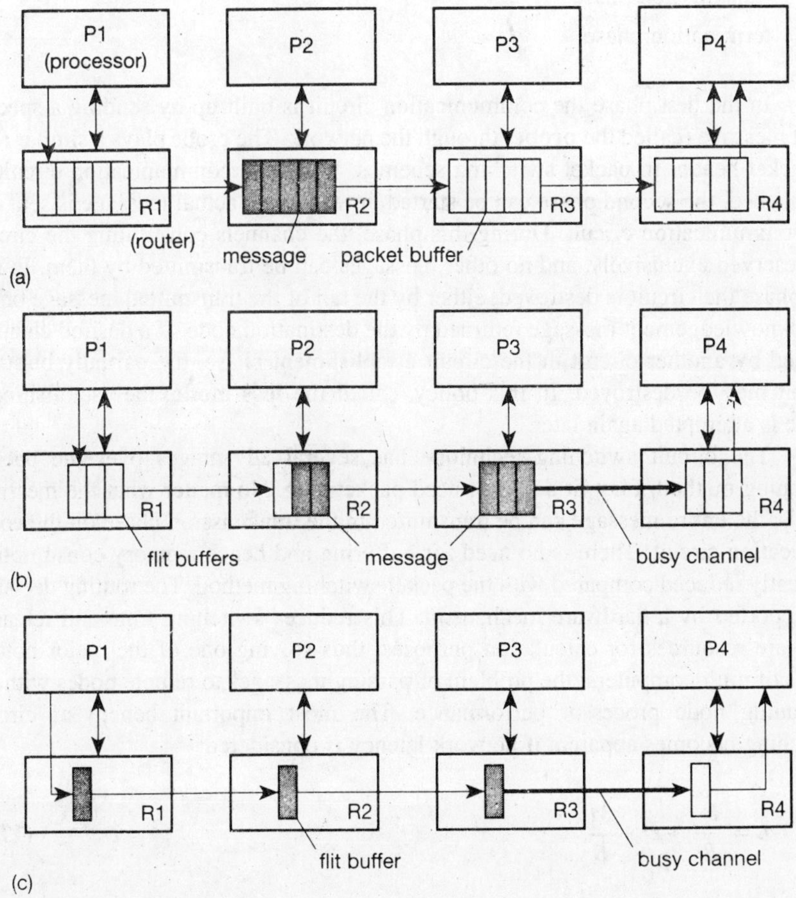

Figure 17.7 Comparing three switching techniques. (a) Packet switching; (b) virtual cut-through; (c) wormhole routing.

Table 17.1. The other drawback of packet switching is that it consumes significant memory space for buffering every incoming packet. Despite these drawbacks, packet switching was used in every first-generation multicomputer (Cosmic Cube, iPSC-1, Ncube 1, Ametek 14, FPS T-series and other Transputer-based machines) because of its simplicity.

Circuit switching

Circuit switching methods behave analogously to telephone systems where a path between the source and destination is initially built up and the circuit is held until the entire message is transmitted. The circuit switching mechanism is realized in three phases:

(1) circuit establishment phase
(2) transmission phase
(3) termination phase.

In the first phase the communication circuit is built up by sending a special short message (called the **probe**) through the network. The probe plays a similar role to packet header in packet switching schemes. When the communication circuit is established, the second phase can be started, in which the actual message is sent via the communication circuit. During this phase, the channels constituting the circuit are reserved exclusively, and no other messages can be transmitted by them. In the last phase the circuit is destroyed, either by the tail of the transmitted message or by an acknowledgement message returned by the destination node. If a desired channel is used by another circuit in the circuit establishment phase, the partially built up circuit may be destroyed. In this policy, called the **loss mode**, the establishment phase is attempted again later.

The circuit switching technique has several advantages over the packet switching method. First, it does not need packetizing. No matter what the message size is, the entire message can be transmitted in the transmission phase on the communication circuit. There is no need for buffering and hence memory consumption is greatly reduced compared with the packet switching method. The routing decision is supported by a hardware mechanism. This reduces switching time and releases software resources for calculation purposes, thus solving one of the major bottlenecks of multicomputers: the problem of passing messages to remote nodes without degrading node processor performance. The most important benefit of circuit switching becomes apparent if network latency is considered:

$$L = \frac{P}{B} * D + \frac{M}{B} \quad \textbf{(17.2)}$$

where P is the length of the probe and M is the length of the message. If P << M, the first component of latency becomes negligible and consequently the network latency becomes independent of the communication distance, as shown in the timing diagram of Figure 17.8(b).

After recognizing the advantages of circuit switching over packet switching, Intel applied the circuit switching technique in the second-generation iPSC-2 machine. This resulted in a ten-fold bandwidth improvement over the iPSC-1 machine. In iPSC-2, sending a message between the two most distant nodes requires only about 10% more time than sending it between neighbouring nodes. Accordingly, mapping algorithms have become much simpler because they do not have to handle communication requirements; only computational load requirements need be considered.

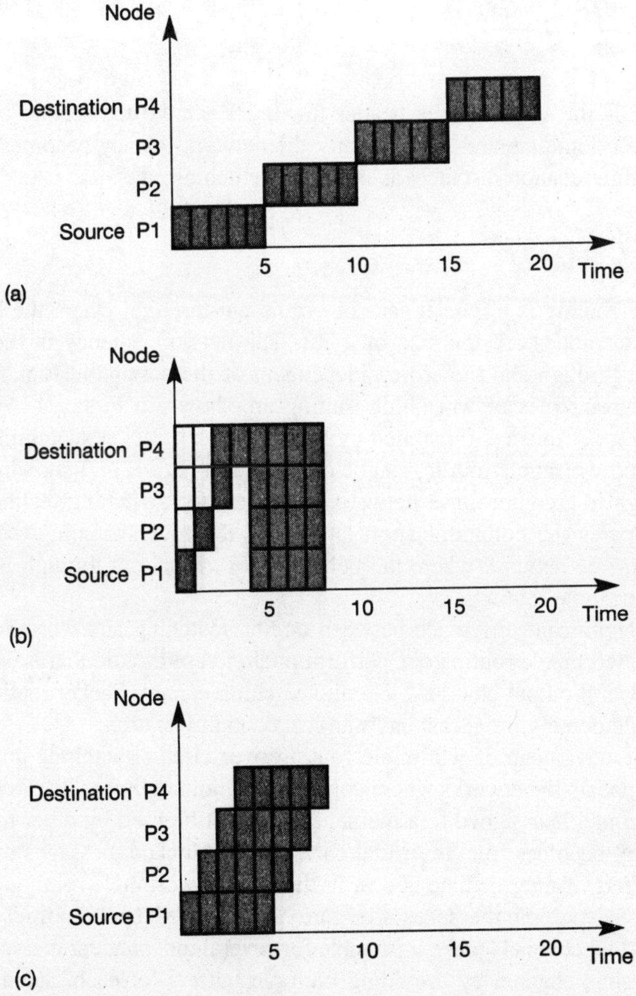

Figure 17.8 Comparing network latency. (a) Packet switching; (b) circuit switching; (c) wormhole routing and virtual cut-through.

Virtual cut-through

Virtual cut-through attempts to combine the benefits of packet switching and circuit switching. The message is divided into small units called **flow control digits**, or **flits**. As long as the required channels are free, the message is forwarded between nodes flit by flit in a pipeline fashion. If a required channel is busy, flits are buffered at intermediate nodes. Depending on the size of the available buffers, virtual cut-through can behave in different ways. If the buffers are large enough, the entire message is buffered at the blocked intermediate node, resulting a behaviour similar to packet switching. If the buffers are not large enough, the message will be buffered across several nodes, holding the links between them as shown in Figure 17.7(b).

The network latency is:

$$L = \frac{HF}{B} * D + \frac{M}{B} \qquad \textbf{(17.3)}$$

where HF is the length of the header flit. If HF << M, the second component of latency will dominate and consequently the network latency becomes independent of the communication distance, as in circuit switching.

Wormhole routing

Wormhole routing is a special case of virtual cut-through, where the buffers at the intermediate nodes are the size of a flit. The network latency is the same as in virtual cut-through and therefore independent of the communication distance. The functional principles of wormhole routing are shown in Figure 17.7(c), while its pipelining mechanism is illustrated by Figure 17.8(c). Packet switching, virtual cut-through and wormhole routing can be compared in Figure 17.7 showing that virtual cut-through is a compromise between the other two switching techniques. Figure 17.8 compares the communication latency of the four switching techniques in a contention-free network where the behaviour of virtual cut-through is the same as that of wormhole routing.

A significant difference between circuit switching and wormhole routing is that while wormhole routing can perform **packet replication**, that is, send copies of flits on several output channels, circuit switching cannot. Packet replication is useful in implementing broadcast and multicast communication.

The advantage of wormhole routing over circuit switching and virtual cut-through appears in networks where contention is not negligible. In circuit switching, once a channel is assigned to a message, it cannot be used by other messages until the channel becomes free. In virtual cut-through, blocked messages must be stored in the buffers of intermediate nodes. In the case of wormhole routing, channels can be shared by multiple messages after introducing the **virtual channel** concept.

Virtual channels make it possible for several independent messages to use the same physical channel by providing multiple buffers for each channel in the network. Virtual channels decouple the allocation of buffers from the allocation of physical channels. A virtual channel consists of a buffer for holding one or more flits.

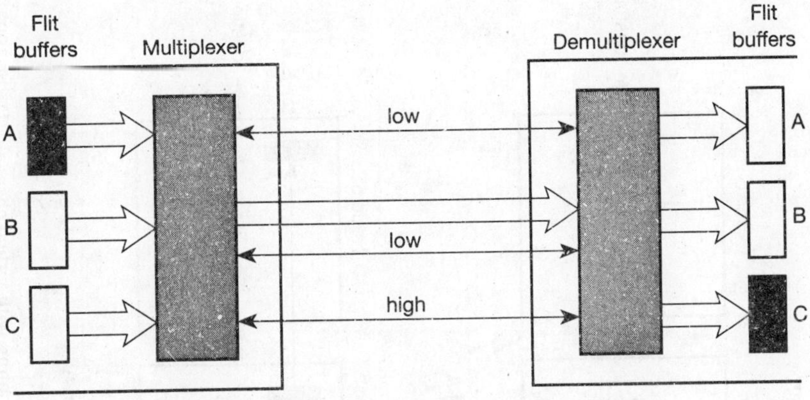

Figure 17.9 Organization of virtual channels.

Several virtual channels share the bandwidth of a single uni-directional physical channel through a pair of multiplexer–demultiplexer units as shown in Figure 17.9 for three virtual channels A, B and C. For each virtual channel a bi-directional control line with a handshaking protocol is employed in order to assure pipeline usage of virtual channels. The low value represents an empty buffer flit on the receiver side. The multiplexer switch can choose any of the virtual channels whose control line is low and whose sender flit buffer is full. After selecting such a channel the corresponding control line is raised, indicating that the channel is ready to send a flit. When the flit arrives, the control line remains high as long as the flit buffer on the receiver is not emptied.

The introduction of virtual channels entails the following advantages:

- Virtual channels increase network throughput by reducing physical channel idle time.
- Virtual channels can be used for deadlock avoidance.
- Virtual channels facilitate the mapping of the logical topology of communicating processes onto a particular physical topology.
- Virtual channels can guarantee communication bandwidth to certain system-related functions, such as debugging and monitoring.

The first advantage of virtual channels can be illustrated by Figure 17.10 that compares routing without virtual channels (Figure 17.10(a)) and with virtual channels (Figure 17.10(b)). In both figures two messages are on their way: message A directed to destination P followed by message B directed to destination Q. In figure (a), message B cannot progress towards destination Q since message A is blocked and holds buffer 3E (3E means the East buffer at node 3). If virtual channels are employed, message B can progress towards destination Q even if message A is blocked, as illustrated by figure (b). The application of the two virtual channels dramatically increases the network throughput: one blocked message cannot block all the following messages using the same route. One can think that the greater the

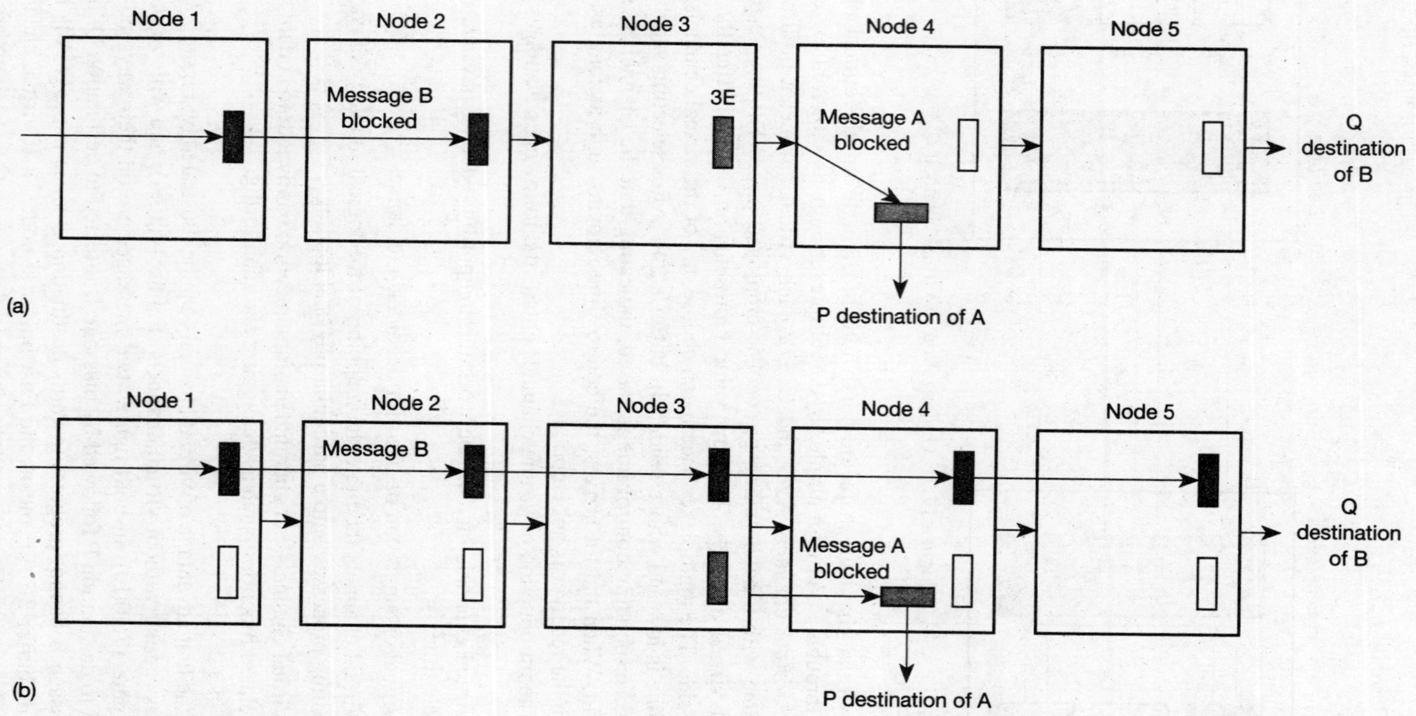

Figure 17.10 Increasing throughput by virtual channels. (a) Routing without virtual channels; (b) routing with virtual channels (Dally, 1992). © 1992 IEEE

number of virtual channels on the same physical link the better. However, as the number of virtual channels increases, the effective bandwidth is proportionally reduced resulting in increasing network latency. The trade-off between higher network throughput and longer latency should be considered when applying virtual channels.

The second advantage of virtual channels appears in avoiding deadlocks in routing networks. **Deadlock** is a situation in the network when a subset of messages is mutually blocked waiting for a free buffer to be released by one of the other messages. Deadlock can typically occur in networks where cyclic dependencies could be formulated. Such a typical case is shown by Figure 17.11. Message A occupies flit buffer 2N and requires buffer 1E to advance. However, buffer 1E is held by message B that requests buffer 4S and so on. Following the chain of messages it turns out that all messages are waiting for buffers held by another message and since none of them can progress until the required buffer is released, the messages are deadlocked.

There are several methods to avoid deadlock:

- Pre-emption of messages by rerouting
- Pre-emption of messages by discarding
- Application of virtual channels.

The first solution leads to an adaptive routing technique where one of the trapped messages is rerouted on an alternative path towards the destination node. In the second approach one of the messages is discarded and retransmitted from the

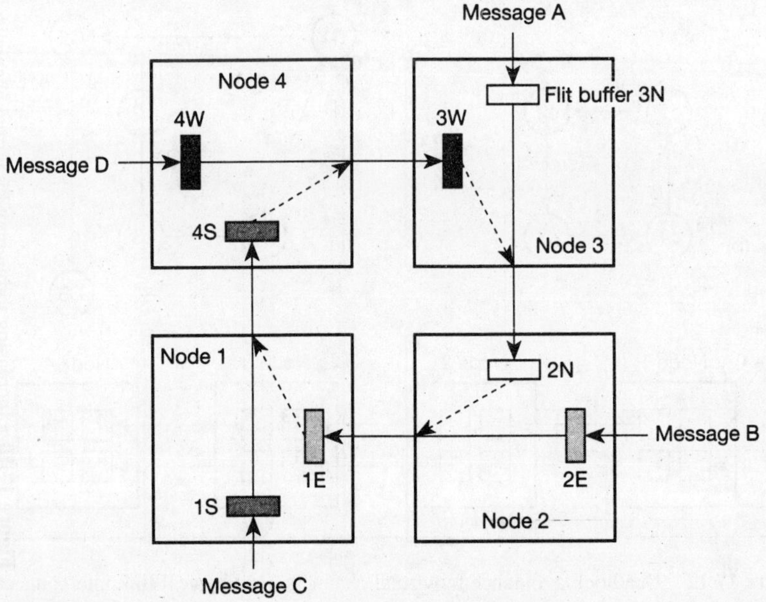

Figure 17.11 A typical deadlock situation (Ni and McKinley, 1993). © 1993 IEEE

source node on an alternative route. Both methods are rarely used in direct network architectures because of the requirements for low latency and reliability.

The third method was proposed in Dally and Seitz (1987) and has become the commonly used technique in wormhole routing networks. The usage of virtual channels for deadlock-free routing algorithms comes from the recognition that a necessary and sufficient condition for deadlock-free routing is the absence of cycles in the **channel dependency graph**. A simple way of eliminating cycles from any channel dependency graph is to split physical channels into groups of virtual channels.

The channel dependency graph of a multicomputer is a directed graph that can be constructed from the interconnection network and the routing algorithm. Vertices of the graph are unidirectional channels of the multicomputer, and the edges are the pairs of connected channels as it is defined by the routing algorithm. Figure 17.12(b) depicts the channel dependency graph for a four-node multicomputer shown in Figure 17.12(a). The graph contains a cycle which means that deadlock can occur. In order to avoid the deadlock we split each physical channel (c1, c2, c3, c4) into two logical channels: lower virtual channels (c1, c2, c3, c4) and upper virtual channels (C1, C2, C3, C4). When routing a message, a processor chooses a

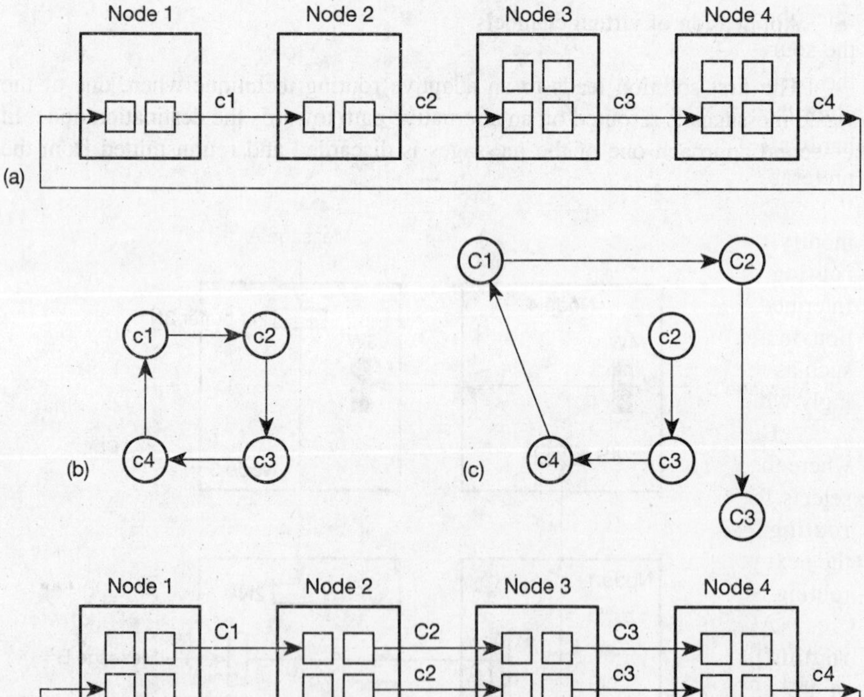

Figure 17.12 Deadlock avoidance by virtual channels. (a) Physical link interconnections; (b) dependency graph for interconnection (a); (c) dependency graph for interconnection (d); (d) virtual channel interconnections.

virtual channel depending on its own address (O) and the destination address (D). If D > O, the message if forwarded on the upper virtual channel if D < O, the message is routed on the lower channel. Notice that c1 and C4 are not needed according to this channel selection policy and we obtain a total ordering of the virtual channels (c2, c3, c4, C1, C2, C3) without any cycle as shown in Figure 17.12(c) and (d). Since there is no cycle in the new channel dependency graph, the routing function is deadlock-free. This method of eliminating cycles in the dependency graph can be used for any direct interconnection network topology.

Another harmful situation in direct networks is **livelock** when messages endlessly propagate in the network without reaching their destinations. It can typically occur in flow control policies where collision on channels and buffers are avoided by misrouting messages to find an alternative path to the destination. Packet switching and virtual cut-through networks are very sensitive to livelock, while circuit switching and wormhole routing are usually live lock-free.

17.2.3 Routing

The third crucial decision point in designing message-passing architectures is the selection of the routing scheme. The task of routing is to determine the path between the source and the destination nodes of a message. Routing has great influence on the performance of the direct network and hence it plays a crucial role. Routing algorithms on the nodes of the multicomputer can be realized by either software or hardware. Obviously, routing algorithms that are easy to implement in hardware are preferable.

Routing algorithms are divided into two classes according to their ability to modify the routing paths based on dynamic network conditions. In **deterministic routing** the path is completely determined by the source and destination nodes. Intermediate nodes are unable to redirect messages even in case of network congestion. In **adaptive routing** intermediate nodes can take the actual network conditions, such as the presence of failures or bottlenecks, into account and determine accordingly which neighbour the message should be sent.

Deterministic routing can be further classified according to the node position where the deterministic path is selected. In **source routing** it is the source node that selects the complete path between the source and destination nodes. **Distributed routing** gives each intermediate node the freedom to independently determine the next node of the path to which the message should be sent. Notice that adaptive routing is always based on distributed routing.

All of these routing schemes can be divided into **minimal** and **non-minimal routing**. A routing algorithm is minimal if the path selected by the algorithm is one of the shortest paths between the source and destination nodes. Otherwise, the algorithm is called non-minimal routing. Notice that in minimal routing the message gets closer to the destination in every hop, which is not true of non-minimal routing. Though theoretically deterministic routing schemes can be non-minimal, in practice they are always minimal. The categorization of routing protocols is summarized in Figure 17.13. Obviously, for each routing algorithm a strict requirement is to guarantee freedom from deadlock and livelock.

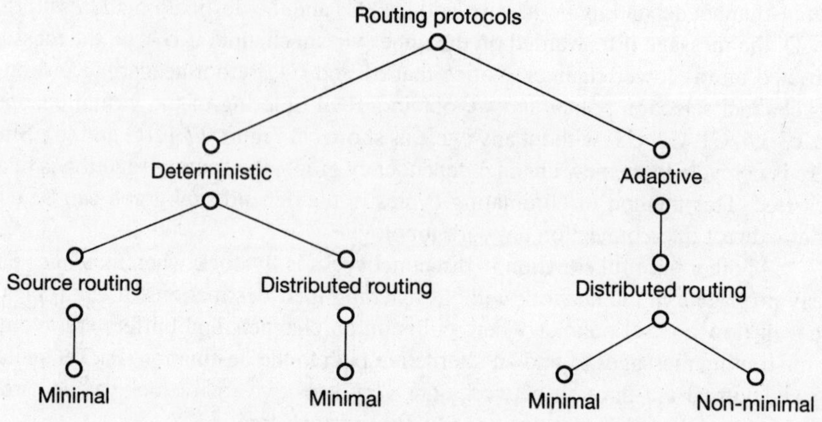

Figure 17.13 Categorization of routing protocols.

Deterministic routing

Three deterministic routing schemes are applied in practice:

- Street-sign routing
- Dimension-ordered routing
- Table-lookup routing.

Street-sign routing belongs to the source routing class and therefore the message header must carry the complete path information. Since the length of the message influences the performance of the system, the header information should be kept as small as possible. In street-sign routing this requirement is fulfilled by introducing the concept of default direction. The message header contains routing information only for those intermediate nodes change direction where the message should turn. Any node receiving a header flit compares the node address with its own address. In the case of a mismatch the message should follow the default direction. If the addresses match the second part of the header flit describes the operation to be done by the node. Either the message is to turn direction or the message has arrived at its destination. In the case of a turn the node and action identifiers are removed from the header which is forwarded to the specified neighbour node. The street-sign routing scheme is used in the Intel iWarp machine.

Dimension-ordered routing is a distributed deterministic routing scheme applied in n-dimensional meshes. The main idea is that messages travel along a certain dimension until they reach a certain coordinate of that dimension. At this node they proceed along the next dimension, and so on (as illustrated in Figure 17.14). Deadlock-free routing is guaranteed if the dimensions are strictly ordered. Dimension-ordered routing is applied in, for example, the J-Machine.

Table-lookup routing, another distributed deterministic routing scheme, can be used in any network topology. At each node a routing table contains the identifier

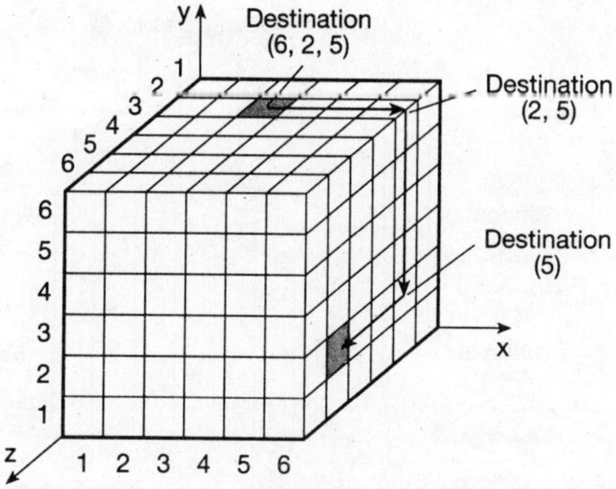

Figure 17.14 Dimension ordered routing.

of the neighbouring node to which the message should be forwarded for each destination node. Table-lookup routing is very advantageous if realized by software but introduces an unnecessary upper limit on the size of the network if it is realized by hardware. Furthermore, a large lookup table reduces the available chip area. Accordingly, the main design concern in table-lookup routing is how to reduce the size of the lookup table. One solution, called **interval labelling**, associates each output channel of the node with an interval. If the destination address carried in the header belongs to this interval, the header should be forwarded on the corresponding output channel. This scheme is employed and realized by hardware in the C104 routing chip of the Inmos IMS T9000 Transputer system.

Adaptive routing

Adaptive routing schemes are much more favourable than deterministic routing since, as their name suggests, they are able to take routing decisions in the presence of faulty and blocked channels. A large number of adaptive routing schemes have been proposed. They are categorized in Figure 17.15.

Adaptive routing schemes can be either **profitable** or **misrouting** according to the selection of the output channel. In profitable routing, only channels that are known to be guaranteed to move closer to the destination are candidates for selection. Profitable routing represents a conservative view. Misrouting protocols rely on an optimistic view and can use both profitable and non-profitable channels for establishing a path between the source and destination. Selecting a non-profitable channel optimistically assumes that it will lead the message to a free set of profitable channels, allowing a further advance towards the destination. The advantages of profitable protocols are:

- They result in a minimum-length path.
- They are free from livelock.
- They make it easier to prove deadlock freedom.

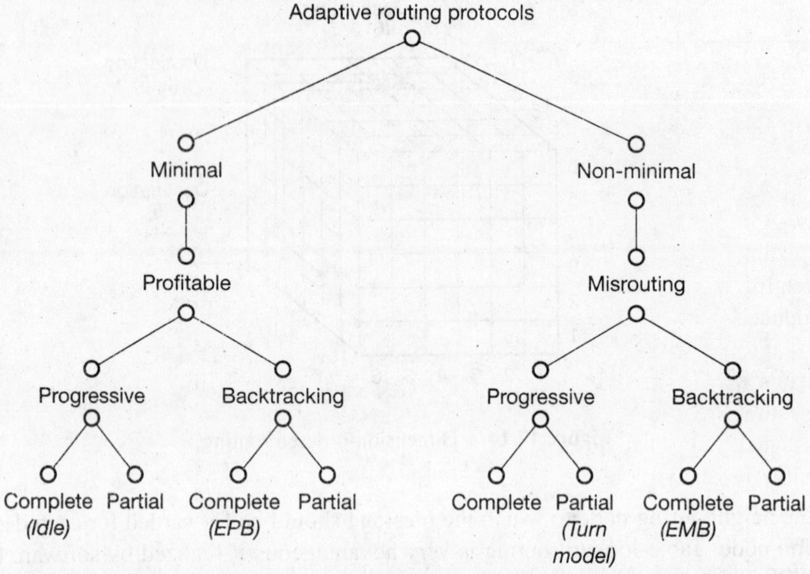

Figure 17.15 Categorization of adaptive routing protocols.

Misrouting protocols are advantageous when faulty channels are present in the network. Under such conditions misrouting protocols have a higher chance of finding an appropriate path.

Adaptive routing schemes can be further divided into **progressive** or **backtracking** protocols. In progressive routing, messages cannot step backwards on the path they have already followed. Conversely, in the backtracking scheme, messages can backtrack and systematically explore all possible paths between the source and destination nodes. The message header must contain some status information to avoid a repetitive search of the same path and hence livelock freedom is assured. Backtracking schemes are also deadlock-free since they do not block holding resources. Notice that in wormhole routing the backtracking protocol cannot be used since the pipelined nature of wormhole routing prevents backtracking.

In order to prevent a repeated search of the same path, backtracking protocols store history information in the message header (or probe). Since the search space can be very large, especially in misrouting protocols, the header becomes too long, which significantly increases the latency time. In circuit switching a hardware support on each node can significantly reduce the header size. Each channel on each node of the multicomputer is supplied with a history bit vector which contains as many bits as there are channels available on the node. If a probe enters the node on channel K, the bits of history bit vector K contain information on the corresponding output channels. If an output channel has been tried the corresponding bit is high, otherwise it is low. An additional history bit vector is used on each node for administrating the probes that were created by the node itself.

If there is no free profitable channel at an intermediate node there are several alternative strategies to follow:

- Progressive profitable routing waits until a profitable channel becomes free.
- A progressive misrouting protocol tries a non-profitable free channel.
- Backtracking routing steps backwards and starts again at a previous node.

All the protocols mentioned above can be **completely** or **partially adaptive** ones. A completely adaptive protocol can choose any channels from its class. For example, a completely adaptive backtracking protocol realizes an exhaustive search for the path. Partially adaptive protocols are used when certain restrictions are introduced in order to guarantee deadlock freedom in the network.

From the many available adaptive routing protocols, only a typical one called the **turn model** (misrouting, progressive, partially adaptive) is described here as a case study. Glass and Ni (1992) recognized that deadlock occurs because the message paths contain turns that form a cycle. They proposed restricting the possible turns by disallowing certain combinations of turns and as a result cyclic dependencies are prevented. Based on this principle several protocols can be defined. All are misrouting, progressive and partially adaptive. One is the **west-first routing** algorithm applied in 2-D meshes. The main idea is that of the eight possible turns, the two to the west are prohibited. This creates the rule: first route the message west, if necessary, and then turn adaptively to other directions. Figure 17.16 shows several west-first paths in an 8×8 mesh.

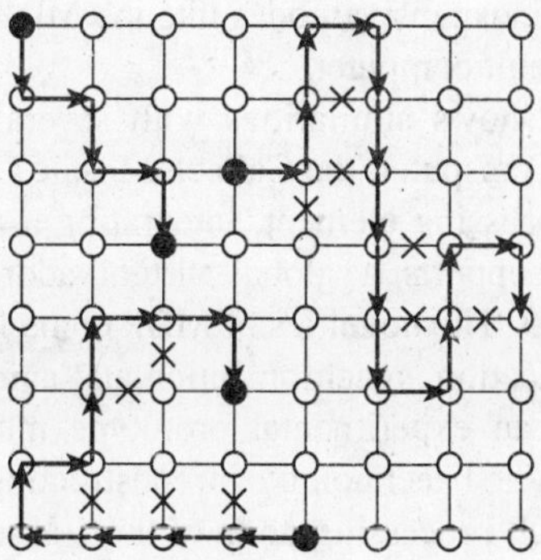

Figure 17.16 Examples of west-first paths (Ni and McKinley, 1993). © 1993 IEEE

17.3 Fine-grain systems

In the 1980s there was a general expectation that massively parallel systems should be built on new computational models that require fine-grain or at least medium-grain parallelism. Many research projects and commercial parallel computers were based on this concept. In Europe the most influential result was the Transputer which was built on a new theoretical concept, called CSP (Communicating Sequential Processes). In the USA one of the main representatives of this direction was the J-Machine project at MIT. The Transputer represents a static, synchronous model realized at medium-grain parallelism, while the J-Machine project represents a dynamic, asynchronous model realized at fine-grain parallelism.

By the 1990s it became clear that big parallel computer manufacturers are not interested in revolutionary new concepts. Rather they follow a cautious evolutionary approach which means that they are more interested in connecting high-performance off-the-shelf microprocessors into a loosely connected network. This approach obviously leads to coarse-grain parallelism. Research on fine-grain and medium-grain systems gradually lost ground. Initially fine-grain commercial products like the Connection Machine have recently become coarse-grain as well. Eventually, there remained only one significant fine-grain research project, the J-Machine project, that is worth describing in this book.

17.3.1 Message-Driven Processor and the J-Machine

The J-Machine was designed at MIT with two primary goals. Firstly, they wanted to create a single-chip processing node in which the communication and synchronization mechanisms can efficiently support several parallel programming models like the dataflow model and the actor-based object-oriented model. The chip is called the Message-Driven Processor (MDP) since it carries out processing in response to messages without having any receive instructions. Secondly, they wanted to prove that connecting plenty of inexpensive nodes like the MDP will result in a powerful, cost-efficient, fine-grain multicomputer.

The MDP design shows similarities with several other parallel computer projects. Like the Inmos Transputer, the Caltech Mosaic C and the Intel iWARP, the MDP is a single-chip processing element, integrating a processor, memory, and a communication unit. It supports a global virtual address space like the BBN Butterfly and the IBM RP3. The novelties of MDP come from its efficient primitive mechanisms for communication, synchronization and naming.

The J-machine is an experimental prototype multicomputer to study the possible exploitation of VLSI technology in constructing massively parallel fine-grain multicomputers. Each processing node of the J-Machine consists of an MDP and 1 Mbyte of DRAM memory (Dally et al., 1992). The nodes are connected into a *3-D mesh network* which uses *deterministic, dimension-ordered, wormhole routing* (see Figure 17.14). A 1024-node J-Machine has been constructed and used at MIT.

17.3.2 The communication subsystem of the J-Machine

The pin layout and inner structure of the MDP is shown in Figure 17.17(a) and (b), respectively. The MDP provides six bi-directional bit-parallel channels, each consisting of nine data and six control lines. The six network ports correspond to the six cardinal directions (+X, –X, +Y, –Y, +Z, –Z) and make possible the direct wiring of MDP chips by connecting opposite direction ports. These connections result in a

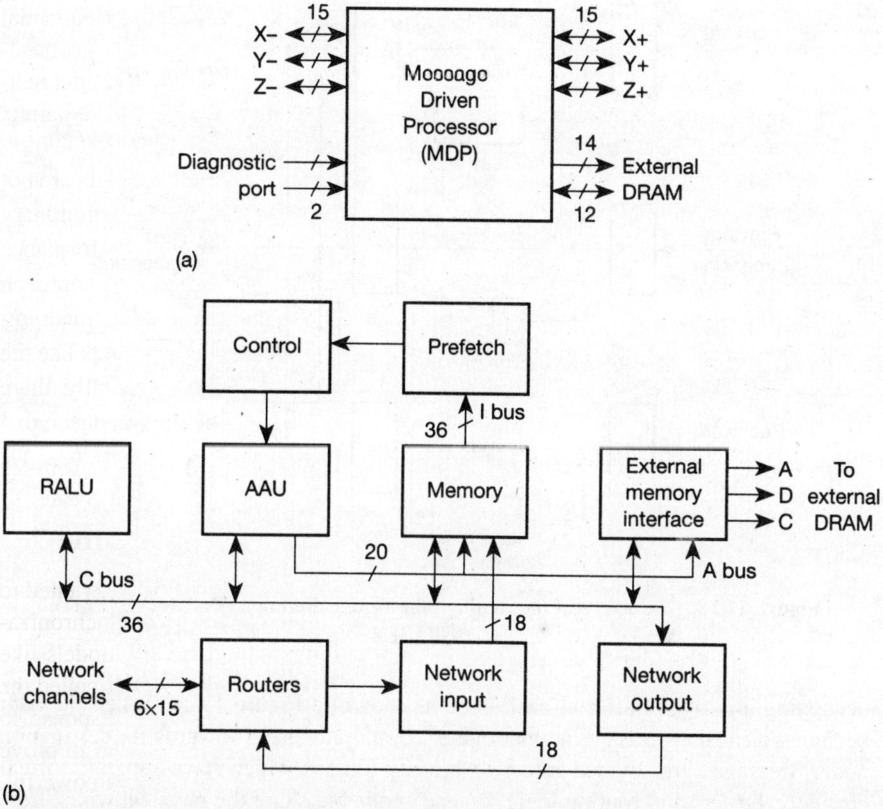

Figure 17.17 The Message-Driven Processor (Dally et al., 1992). (a) Pin layout of the MDP chip; (b) internal structure of the MDP. © 1992 IEEE

3-D mesh topology in which deterministic dimension order routing is realized by routing messages first in dimension X, then Y and finally Z.

Messages are divided into flits. The first three flits contain the X, Y and Z addresses of the destination node. When a message arrives at a node along dimension D, the router unit compares the D address of the node with the first flit of the message. If the two values do not match, the message is forwarded along the same dimension D. If the two values match, the node strips the leading flit from the message and routes the rest along the next dimension (see Figure 17.14). The part of the routing unit responsible for dimension order routing is depicted in Figure 17.18. The MDP contains three such independent routers for each of the three dimensions. Notice that messages entering the new dimension compete with messages continuing in that dimension at a two-to-one switch. The granted message will block the competing message for its duration. The switching scheme used in the J-machine is the wormhole technique, that is, once the head flit establishes the communication path, subsequent flits follow directly behind it.

In the case of contention, the J-machine network applies blocking flow control. The blocked message is compressed in the routers along the message path,

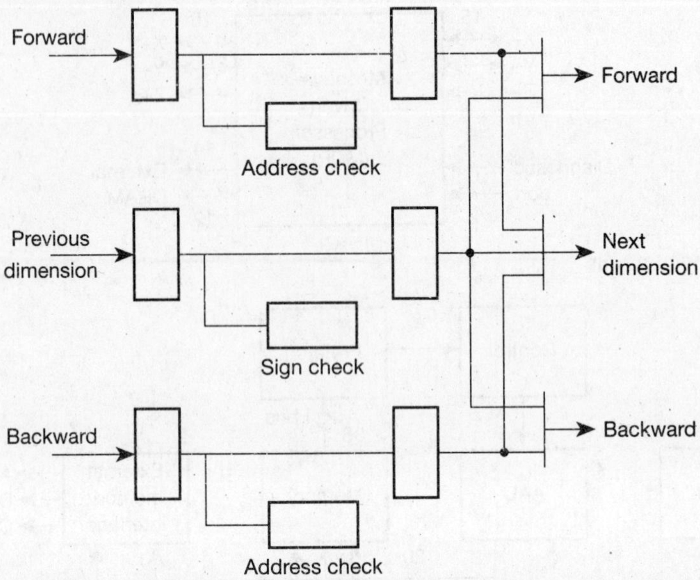

Figure 17.18 Structure of the routing unit for one direction (Dally et al., 1992). © 1992 IEEE

occupying a two-flit buffer at each node as shown in Figure 17.19. When the path becomes clear the message is uncompressed and advanced towards its destination node. Messages are divided into two priority classes which have separate virtual channels (buffers and routing logic) on each node but share the physical wires. Low priority messages cannot block high priority ones, but the high priority network can pre-empt the wires even if the low priority network is congested.

As well as the router, the communication subsystem of the MDP also has a network output and network input unit. The network output unit contains an eight-word FIFO buffer to which the MDP transfers one or two words on each SEND instruction. If a message is complete or the FIFO buffer is full the network output

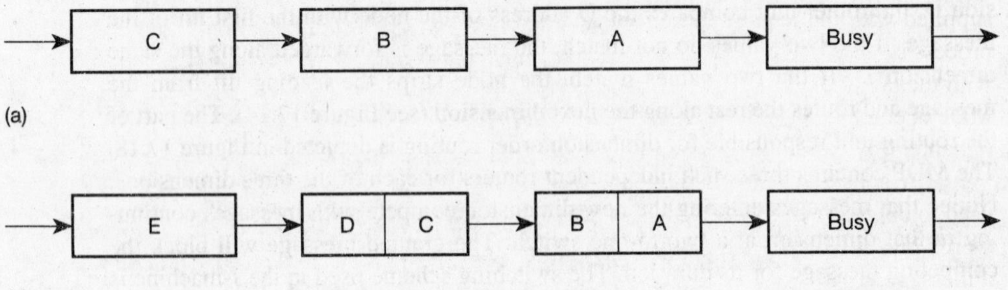

Figure 17.19 Message compression due to busy channels (Dally et al., 1992). (a) Message arrives at a busy channel; (b) message becomes compressed due to the busy channel. © 1992 IEEE

unit launches the message onto the network. Similarly, the network input unit provides a four-word buffer where flits from the network are collected. When the buffer is full, the network input unit writes its contents to the on-chip memory in one cycle.

17.3.3 Architecture of the Message-Driven Processor

The MDP was designed to support fine-grain concurrent programs by:

- reducing the overhead and latency associated with receiving a message;
- reducing context switch time;
- providing hardware support for object-oriented programming.

There are three execution levels in the MDP: background, priority 0 (low priority) and priority 1 (high priority). When there is no message requiring service the MDP works at the background level. For each level a separate register set is maintained, consisting of the following registers:

- R0–R3: general-purpose data registers
- A0–A3: address registers
- ID0–ID3: ID registers
- instruction pointer.

Two sets of ID registers (ID0–ID3) and two sets of queue registers are available for the two priority levels. Each queue register set contains a base/limit register and a head/tail register for administrating the two message queues. Additionally, a translation buffer base/mask register and a status register are shared between the different execution levels. The use of separate register sets for different execution levels assures extremely fast switching between them. Also, the small size of each register set facilitates quick task switching within one execution level.

To make software more efficient and robust, MDP employs hardware support for type checking and synchronization. Each 36-bit word contains a 4-bit tag. Two tags, Fut and Cfut, are used for interprocess synchronization. Fut serves for global synchronization and Cfut for local synchronization. Initially an empty location is supplied with the tag Cfut. If a read attempts to access such a location, the reading process is suspended by the Cfut fault handler. A write access substitutes the Cfut tag with the tag of the final value. Notice that the synchronization scheme applied in the MDP is equivalent to the full/empty bit synchronization of multi-threaded machines (Chapter 16).

A series of network instructions (SEND, SENDE, SEND2, SEND2E) are used to compose and send messages between processors. They can inject one or two words into the network at either priority 0 or 1. A typical code segment for sending a message at priority 1 is the following:

```
SEND      R0,1          ; send destination address
SEND2     R1,R2,1       ; header and receiver
SEND2E    R3,[2,A3],1   ; two words and end of msg
```

The first instruction sends the X, Y and Z coordinates of the destination processor from register R0. The second instruction enqueues two words from registers R1 and R2 for transmission. The third instruction takes a word from R3 and another from memory and, finally, creates an end of message mark.

The MDP contains a Message Unit (MU) as well as the conventional Instruction Unit (IU). When a message arrives, it is the task of the MU to decide whether the message should be executed immediately by pre-empting the IU or be queued. Queuing takes place without interrupting the processor, by stealing memory cycles. The logical structure of a message is as follows:

<priority>, <opcode>, <arg>, ... ,<arg>

If the incoming message has higher priority than the task currently being executed by the IU, its processing is started immediately and the current task is suspended. The message opcode is the physical address of the routine that implements the function required by the message. These routines are stored in a small ROM and realize the following message types:

- READ, WRITE, READ_FIELD, WRITE_FIELD: These messages are used for reading and writing memory locations.
- DEREFERENCE reads the entire contents of an object.
- NEW creates a new object and returns an identifier.
- REPLY, FORWARD, COMBINE, GC are used to implement 'futures', multicast, fetch-and-op combining, and garbage collection, respectively.
- CALL and SEND cause a method to be executed. For CALL the method is defined by the <method-id> parameter of the message. For SEND the method is determined at run time, based on the type of the receiver.

An innovative and unique feature of the MDP is that a dispatch mechanism directly processes messages requiring low latency (for example, FORWARD and COMBINE). When a message reaches the head of the highest priority non-empty message queue, the dispatch mechanism transforms it into a task. The opcode of the message is written into the instruction pointer and the message length (part of the message header) and the queue head are used to create a message segment descriptor.

17.3.4 Assessment of the J-Machine

Experimental work on the J-Machine prototype at MIT proved that the initial design goals were fulfilled; that is, combining fast message injection, automatic message buffering and fast message dispatching resulted in efficient communication and synchronization on a fine-grain level where task sizes are less than 150 instructions. Table 17.2 compares the asynchronous send and receive overheads (excluding network latency) of the J-Machine with those of several other current multicomputers constructed from off-the-shelf microprocessors (Noakes et al., 1993). The first two

Table 17.2 One-way message overhead. T1 is the sum of the fixed overheads of send and receive. T2 is the injection overhead per byte (Noakes et al., 1993). © 1993 IEEE

Machine	*T1: μs/msg*	*T2: μs/byte*	*cycles/msg*	*cycles/byte*
nCUBE/2 (Vendor)	160.0	0.45	3200	9
CM-5 (Vendor)	86.0	0.12	2838	4
nCUBE/2 (Active)	23.0	0.45	460	9
CM-5 (Active)	3.0	0.12	109	4
J-Machine	0.9	0.04	11	0.5

rows are based on the vendor message libraries, while the third and fourth lines report results gained by the Active Message system (Eicken et al., 1992) implemented on the same hardware. The table clearly shows that the J-Machine reduced the overhead per message by up to two orders of magnitude and the overhead per byte by almost an order of magnitude. Further measures showed that threads achieve processor utilization of over 50 % with task length between 25 and 50 cycles; 90 % of the total network bandwidth can be achieved by messages of eight-word length. A barrier synchronization library developed at MIT exceeds the similar libraries of other multicomputers by one to two orders of magnitude.

However, the experimental measures have also revealed some limitations of the J-Machine. The routing protocol is not fair in the sense that messages locked out by a contention can be delayed for an arbitrary time. The register set proved to be too small and hence led to many more memory references than necessary. The external memory bandwidth of the MDP is three times less than the network would require. The external memory latency also limits the sequential performance of the nodes. The naming mechanism is not efficient enough to support the global name space concept of the J-Machine. Finally, the lack of floating-point hardware strictly limits the achievable performance on numerical applications.

Considering both the benefits and limitations of the J-machine architecture, one can conclude that marrying the J-Machine communication and synchronization scheme with a contemporary high-performance RISC processor and 4 Mbyte of high-bandwidth DRAM memory would result in an outstanding multicomputer system.

17.4 Medium-grain systems

The Transputer approach is another attempt to realize multicomputers by directly connecting processor chips. A Transputer is a complete microcomputer integrating a central processor, a floating-point unit (except in the first-generation T212 and T414 chips), static RAM, interface for external memory, and a number of communication links into a single chip. The communication links enable Transputers to be connected directly to each other and to communicate. The appearance of the Transputer in the mid-1980s led to a breakthrough in the spread and acceptance of parallel processing. The Transputer offered a relatively cheap and very modular tool to build parallel computers from a very small size up to massively parallel systems based on the same theoretical and practical platforms.

In contrast to the Message-Driven Processor approach, Transputers were designed to implement a static, synchronous model of parallel programming based on Hoare's CSP concept (Hoare, 1978, 1985). CSP (Communicating Sequential Processes) had a solid theoretical background which resulted in a well-understood concurrent programming paradigm. CSP was further developed and turned into a concurrent programming language, Occam-2, which contains clear programming constructs and concepts (PAR and ALT constructs, channel concept, and so on) to handle processes, communication and synchronization.

Transputers and Occam have two generations. The first generation reflects the requirements of the originally intended application areas, like signal processing and real-time systems. For such applications, relatively small-size systems with fast communication links, basically neighbourhood-oriented communication, and fast context switching seemed to be sufficient. However, it turned out that the Transputer was more than the building block of special-purpose parallel systems. General-purpose multicomputers built from Transputers were comparable in performance with other first-generation multicomputers. Notable first-generation Transputer chips are the T212, T414 and T805 Transputers.

However, when the second-generation multicomputers appeared, it became clear that first-generation Transputers could not compete with these new machines. A thorough redesign was necessary which improved both the Transputer's sequential performance and its communication concept. The Transputer is now supported by a router chip and the processing node structure has become like the one shown in Figure 17.1(b). The first-generation store-and-forward switching technique is replaced by wormhole routing as in other second- and third-generation multicomputers. Another important improvement was the introduction of the virtual channel concept which significantly reduced the mapping problem. The second-generation Transputer is called the T9000 and the router is realized by the C104 routing chip.

Both the first- and second-generation Transputers were designed to support advanced communicating process architectures. Fulfilling this objective was so successful that both generations of Transputers are much stronger in the field of communication than in the field of computing. The first generation was revolutionary, compared to other microprocessors, in supporting direct connection of Transputers without using complicated multibus systems. On the other hand, the numerical performance of the Transputer was no better than other contemporary microprocessors. The very first Transputers (T414 and T212) were even delivered without floating-point units. Similarly, the second-generation Transputer family implements a very advanced communication system but, as far as computational speed in either MIPS or MFLOPS is concerned, the T9000 is left far behind by other modern superscalar chips like the PowerPC, Pentium, and so on. Therefore, the main significance of the Transputer concept lies in its support mechanisms for creating multicomputers and hence these features of the second-generation Transputer family are explained in detail.

17.4.1 Internal structure of the T9000 Transputer

The internal structure of the T9000 Transputer is depicted in Figure 17.20. The main components are the 32-bit integer processor, a 64-bit floating-point unit, 16 kilobytes of CPU cache memory, four serial-communication-link engines, a virtual channel processor (VCP) and a programmable memory interface (PMI). Synchronization with the external world is supported by four pairs of event channels and two control links. All the subunits are connected by an internal crossbar switch that controls four 32-bit data paths which connect the CPU, the VCP, the PMI and the process scheduler to the four banks of the main cache.

17.4.2 Process management in Transputers

One of the most remarkable features of the Transputer is the use of a very small register set and, as a result, a very fast context switching scheme. Each Transputer has only six registers to accommodate the active process. The first three, referred to as A, B and C, make up a small stack for holding the operands of arithmetic operations. Register A is the top of the stack. The fourth register (W) points to the workspace area of the active process. The fifth register plays the role of a program counter (PC). Finally, the sixth register, called the operand register (O), serves for elaborating operands and instructions longer than 4 bits. In Transputers where a floating-point unit is included in the chip, registers FA, FB and FC are added to the register set to support floating-point operations. The register structure of the Transputer is shown in Figure 17.21.

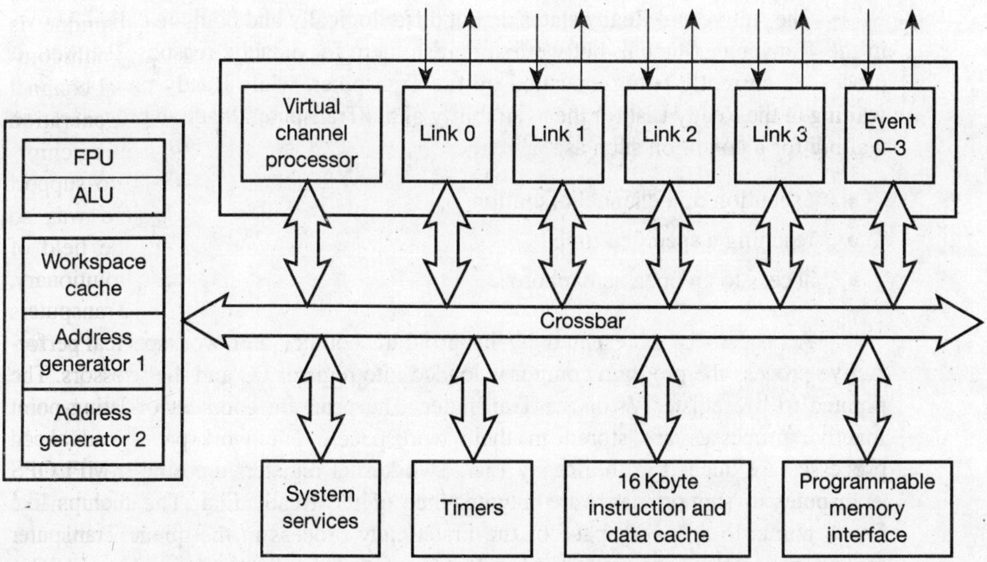

Figure 17.20 Structure of the T9000.

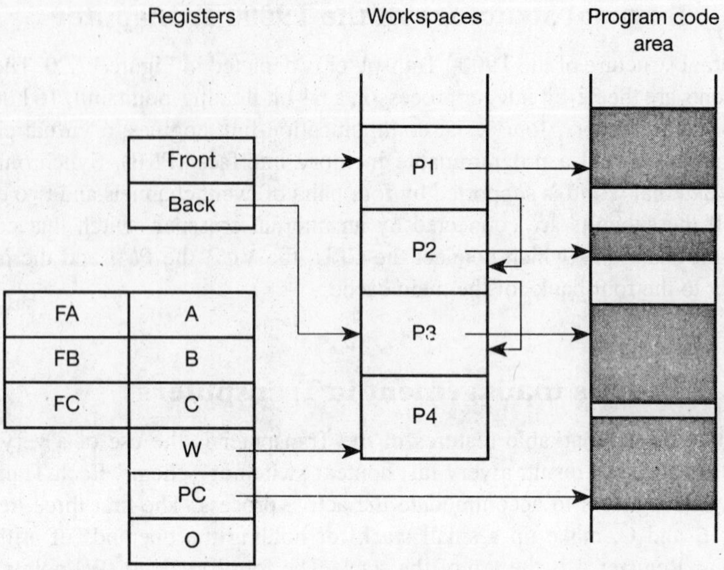

Figure 17.21 Register and Ready List structure of transputers.

Processes can be in one of the three states:

- Active
- Ready
- Inactive.

The Active and Ready states do not differ logically and both are called Active in the Transputer Manual, but we distinguish them for didactic reasons; the Active process is currently being executed by the Transputer, while Ready processes are waiting in the Ready List for the availability of the Transputer. Inactive processes are waiting for a condition such as:

- execution of a channel operation
- reaching a specified time
- access to an open semaphore.

A process is represented by its program counter and workspace. For the Active process the program counter is loaded into register PC and the workspace is pointed to by register W of the Transputer. The program counters of Ready and Inactive processes are stored in their workspaces. The workspaces of Ready processes are queued in the Ready List. Two kernel registers are employed in the Transputer to support hardware maintenance of the Ready List. The first, called Front, points to the workspace of the first Ready process in the queue, while the second, called Back, points to the last Ready process, as illustrated in Figure 17.21. Actually there are two Ready Lists in the Transputer, one for low priority processes and one for high priority processes. Inactive processes are placed in different queues depending on the reason for their suspension. The forthcoming sections will explain how processes waiting for a channel operation are blocked.

Process switching is an extremely fast operation. It requires only the following steps:

(1) Save the PC of the Active process to its workspace.

(2) Add the workspace of the Active process to a waiting queue.

(3) Restore register PC from the workspace of the first process in the Ready List.

(4) Load Register W with the value of register Front and set register Front to point to the second process in the Ready List.

Notice that the other registers (A, B, C and O) do not need to be saved since the Transputer permits process switching only at instructions where the values of these registers are irrelevant.

17.4.3 Channel communication inside a Transputer

Channels always connect two processes: the sender and receiver. Communication on the channel is synchronous; that is, neither the sender nor the receiver can continue after executing a channel instruction until the partner process is ready to perform the transmission. As a result, the first process trying a channel communication must be suspended until the partner arrives at the channel operation.

An ingenious method is applied in every Transputer chip to implement the synchronous channel communication mechanism. The channel itself is realized as a single memory word which is initialized to a special value, 'NotProcess', before using the channel. When a process (Pi) wants to perform a channel operation, three items of data (length, channel, pointer) should be placed in the register stack as shown in Figure 17.22(a). The contents of register B identify the channel to be used in the communication. Register C contains the address of the message in memory, while A defines the length of it. The 'NotProcess' value of channel C means that the partner process (Pj) has not yet arrived at its communication point and hence, Pi should be suspended. This is done simply by overwriting the contents of channel C with the address of the workspace of Pi and saving registers PC and C in the workspace (Figure 17.22(b)).

When Pj reaches its communication point, registers A, B and C contain the message length, channel identifier and message area address, respectively (Figure 17.22(c)). Since channel C contains the identifier of Pi, both partner processes are ready to execute the communication which immediately takes place. When the message transmission is complete, Pi is moved to the Ready List of the Transputer and Pj can continue its progress (Figure 17.22(d)). In the T9000 it is possible to transfer variable length messages, too. In that case the message length parameters of Pi and Pj could be different and hence the length must be saved in the workspace together with the message area address.

Notice that neither a message queue nor an extra process queue was necessary to realize synchronous communication based on the channel concept. This is an advantageous consequence of the Transputer communication concept

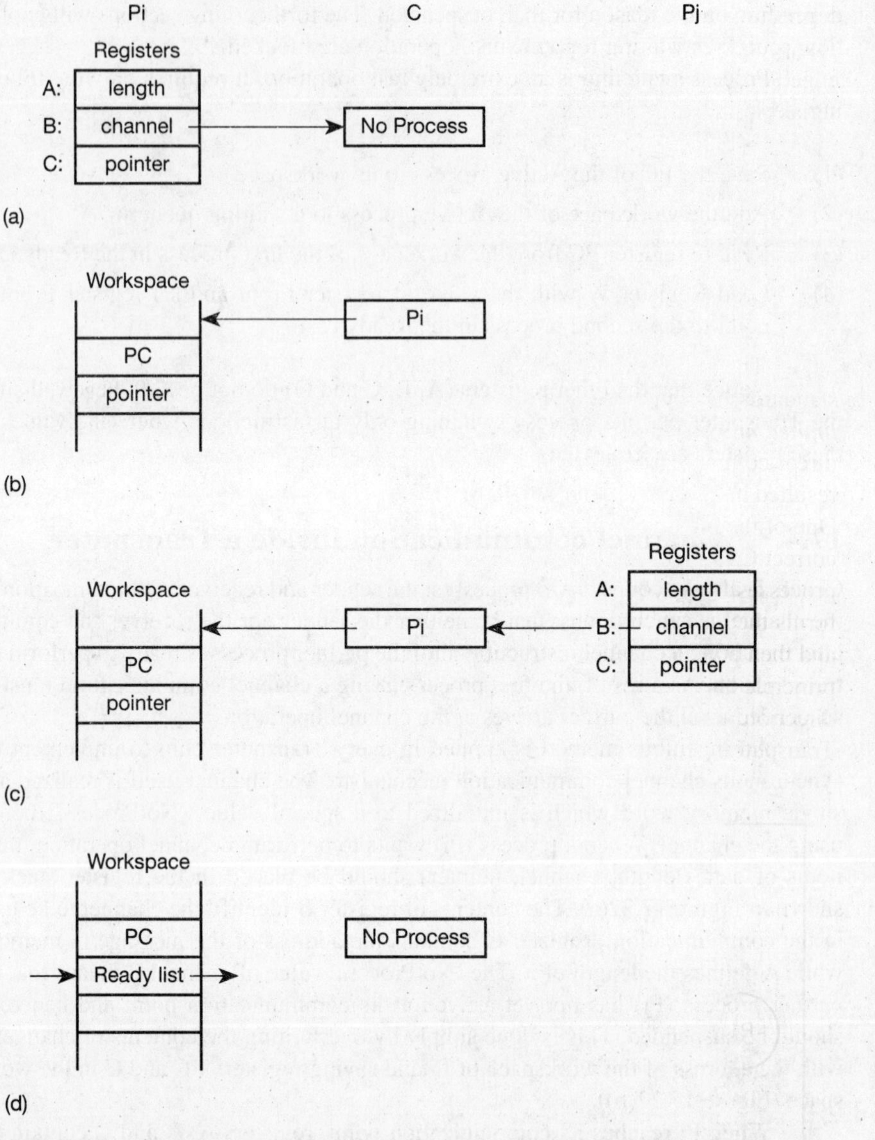

Figure 17.22 Internal channel communication in transputers. (a) Input on empty channel; (b) inputting process is descheduled; (c) output to a ready channel; (d) communication is completed.

17.4.4 Communication between neighbouring Transputers

First-generation Transputers employ serial communication links, called 'OS-Links', as an integral part of the processor chip. Each OS-Link comprises two wires: one for an input channel and one for an output channel. It provides a full-duplex, asynchronous, bit-serial, point-to-point connection between two neighbouring Transputers by connecting a link interface of one Transputer to a link interface of the other Transputer. Data is sent byte by byte. Every byte of data sent on a link is acknowledged on the input of the same link. The quiescent state of a link output is low. The serial bit protocol for a data byte on the link is as follows:

< high, high, <data>$_8$, low >

The ACK signal is:

< high, low >

The OS-Link has an exceptionally low implementation cost, but by today's standards its speed of 20 Mbit/s is relatively low. In first-generation Transputers a *limited number* (typically 2 or 4) *of unsharable physical links* were used to support direct communication between adjacent Transputers. This limited number of links resulted in a serious limitation in the Transputer implementation of the CSP concept. One of the cardinal principles of CSP is **scheduling invariance** which means that a correct CSP program can be executed on any Transputer system, no matter how the processes are actually mapped to the processor space. The scheduling invariance forms the basis of developing Occam programs in a single Transputer environment and then porting the correct program to any multi-Transputer system. However, this principle is violated when processes on a Transputer must communicate in a certain direction (input or output) with more than four processes mapped on other Transputers. Such a case is illustrated in Figure 17.23.

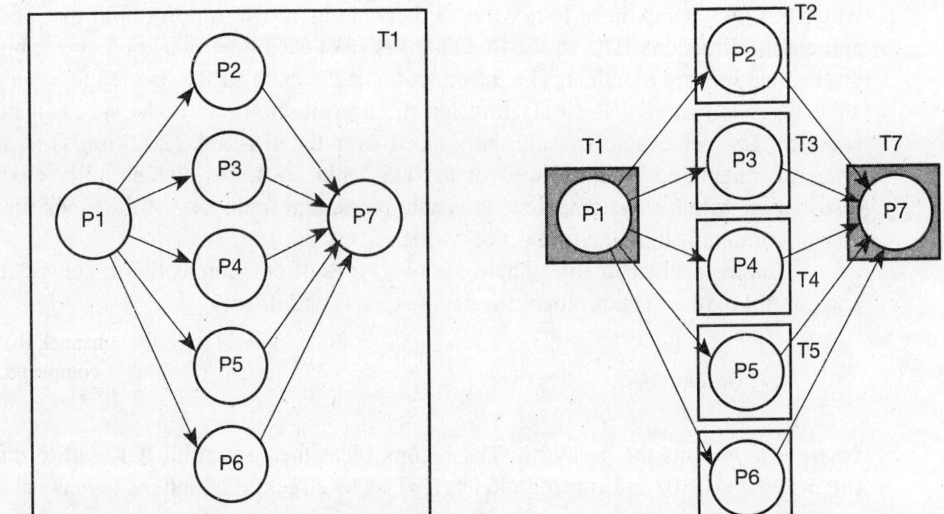

Figure 17.23 Problem with scheduling invariance. (a) Processes mapped on one transputer; (b) processes mapped on six transputers T1 and T6 illegally require five links.

There are several ways of tackling the problem. One obvious solution would be to increase the number of physical links on the Transputer chips. However, this would only defer the emergence of the problem, not solve it. Another possible remedy could be to write multiplexer/demultiplexer processes for each physical channel so that they could each service several 'user' processes. Although this would provide a general solution to the problem, it would be quite tedious for the Occam programmer to write all of these extra processes and, moreover, the program would become significantly slower.

In the second-generation Transputer family the scheduling invariance was retained by means of hardware-implemented multiplexer/demultiplexer processes. The number of links remains four in the T9000 Transputer chip but a new hardware unit called the Virtual Channel Processor (VCP) has been introduced. It allows an *arbitrary* number of processes to use each link. These links, which are now transparently shared by processes, are called **virtual links**. Each virtual link provides two channels, one in each direction. The VCP unit of the T9000 multiplexes virtual links onto the four physical ones. In order to realize virtual links, several layers of link protocols have been introduced:

- Bit-level protocol
- Token-level protocol
- Packet-level protocol
- Message-passing protocol.

Bit-level protocol The OS-Links of first-generation Transputers are replaced with DS-Links which have four wires, a data and a 'strobe' line for both the input and output directions. The strobe line changes state each time two consecutive bits on the data line are identical. The introduction of the extra strobe line led to several advantageous features. The only limit on the transmission rate is the speed of the receiver. The achievable transmission speed over the DS-Link (200 Mbit/s) is an order of magnitude higher than over the OS-Link. DS-Links also simplify clock distribution within a system, since the exact phase and frequency of the clock on a pair of communicating devices is not critical.

Token-level protocol There are two types of communication tokens: data and control tokens. The protocol for data tokens is as follows:

$$< P, 0, <data>_8 >$$

where P represents the parity bit. The second bit is the control bit (C) used to distinguish data (C=0) and control tokens (C=1). The structure of control tokens is:

$$< P, 1, <control>_2 >$$

The control can be:

00: Flow control token (FCT)
01: End of packet (EOP)
10: End of message (EOM)
11: Escape token (ESC)

The FCT token is used to prevent a sender from overrunning the input buffer (at least eight tokens long) of a receiving link. The receiver sends an FCT token to the sender when its input buffer has room to receive another eight tokens. After sending eight tokens, the sender waits until a new FCT token arrives.

Packet-level protocol The VCP unit of the T9000 splits messages of arbitrary length into packets. Each data packet consists of a header followed by the data field and a terminator. The header identifies the virtual channel and specifies the receiver process. The data field can contain up to 32 bytes. The terminator is either an EOP or an EOM token.

Acknowledge messages are used to implement synchronous communication on a virtual channel. After sending a packet, the sender VCP must wait for an acknowledge message. When the acknowledgement of the last packet has arrived the sender process can resume. After receiving the first packet the receiver VCP sends back the acknowledge message if the receiver process is ready to input from the channel. As a consequence of this strict acknowledgement protocol, sequence numbering of packets is not necessary, even when the network applies an adaptive routing scheme.

The acknowledge message is sent as a zero length packet consisting of only a header field and an EOM token. Since virtual links are always built from a pair of virtual channels, it is not necessary to include a return address in packets. The acknowledgements are simply sent back along the other channel of the virtual link.

Message-passing protocol Implementation of the virtual link concept in the T9000 processor requires that each physical link should be associated with a list of virtual links waiting to use it. Virtual links are represented by a pair of virtual link control blocks (VLCBs), one on each Transputer. The organization of virtual link lists is identical to that of the Ready List (Figure 17.21). When a process executes a send or receive message operation, the computation processor of the T9000 delegates the job of transferring the message to the VCP and deschedules the process. The identifier of the process is saved in the control block which is added to the queue of the associated physical link. After completing the message transfer, the VCP reschedules the waiting process. This mechanism allows the T9000 computation processor to run another process while the VCP performs the external message-passing protocol.

The series of diagrams in Figure 17.24 illustrates the activities of the VCP in implementing the external message-passing protocol. Assume that Pi is the sender and Pj is the receiver process on virtual channel C which is associated with physical link L. When either Pi or Pj starts a message operation, registers A, B and C contain the same information as in the case of internal message passing. The only difference is the channel representation which is a VLCB instead of a single word (Figure 17.24(a)). The VCP copies the pointer and length values of the message to the

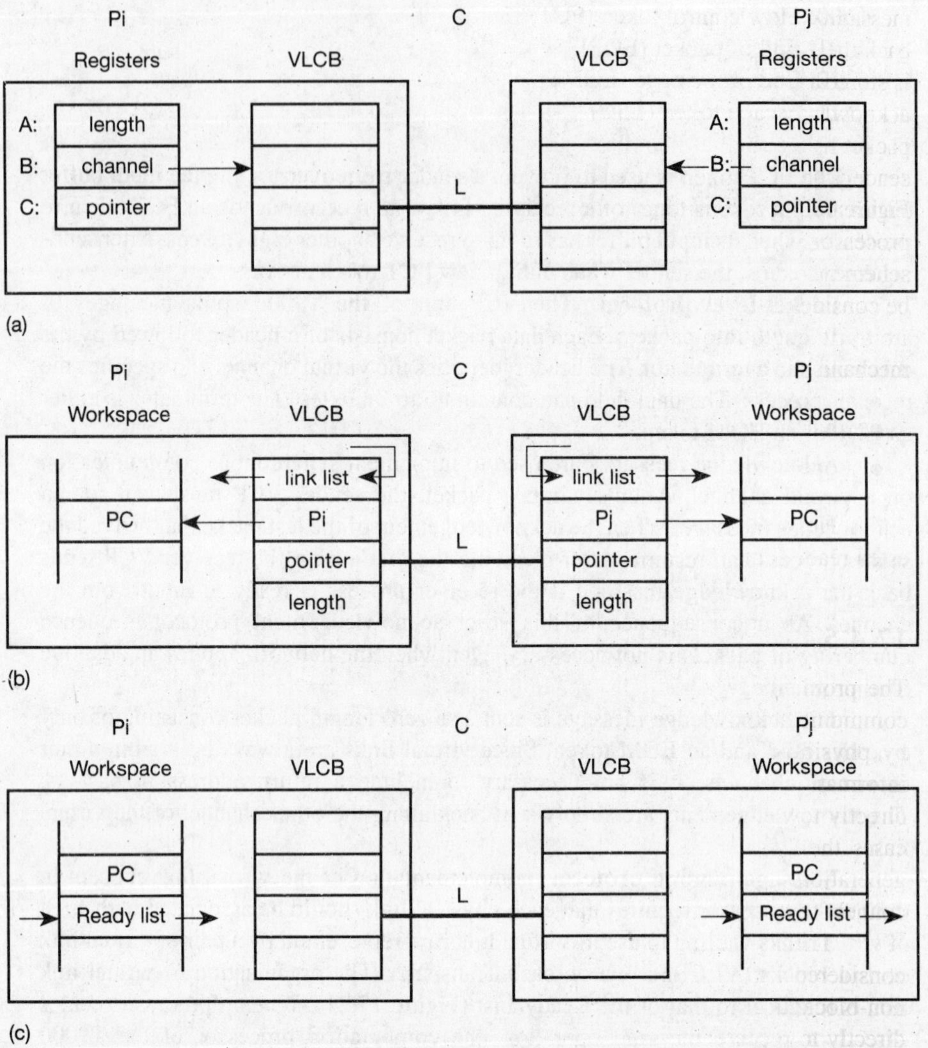

Figure 17.24 External channel communication between transputers. (a) Preparation of external virtual link communication; (b) external virtual link communication in progress; (c) external virtual link communication is completed.

VLCB. The process is descheduled and its workspace is connected to the VLCB by storing the address of its workspace in the VLCB (Figure 17.24(b)). The VLCB is added to the virtual link list of the physical link L.

On the sender side, the first packet of the message is sent via link L when the VLCB becomes the first in the waiting list. Any further packet is sent when the acknowledge message for the previously sent packet has arrived. On the receiver side (Pj), there are two possibilities, depending on the relative speed of the two processes. If the first packet arrives when the receiver is not ready yet to input a

ful, specialized component. Accordingly, they employ commodity superscalar RISC processors as computation processors since these can deliver the highest achievable MFLOPS. The difference between them lies in the choice of communication processor. Some use the same RISC processor for organizing communication as the computation processor. The advantages of this architecture are homogeneity and the fact that, when communication needs are not demanding, the communication processor can support the computation processor by doubling the achievable MFLOPS per node. From now on we call these coarse-grain multicomputers **homogeneous multicomputers**. Notable representatives of this group are the Intel Paragon and machines designed in the framework of the GENESIS and MANNA projects.

The second group employs different processor types for computation and communication purposes. This type of message-passing computers is called **hybrid multicomputers**. Computers in this group are the Parsytec GC PowerPlus, Transtech Paramid, IBM SP1 and SP2. In the Parsytec and Transtech machines the T805 Transputer is used as the communication processor. Although it turned out that the Transputer is not a powerful enough computation processor, its ability to handle four independent asynchronous links efficiently makes it a capable communication processor.

In the third type of multicomputers, custom-designed communication processors are employed in order to achieve the highest possible performance. A representative of this type is the Meiko CS-2 computer which indeed delivers the best performance of all the current message-passing computers. Performance as a specific design issue in the CS-2 is demonstrated by the fact that the CS-2 is the only third-generation coarse-grain multicomputer where vector processor units can be employed in the processing node. Although the application of vector processor units was considered in the GENESIS project too, it was finally rejected due to the time required to develop such a unit. It should be mentioned that the vector unit of the CS-2 was not developed by Meiko; they use the Fujitsu μVP.

Third-generation coarse-grain multicomputers differ in the structure and implementation of the communication switch unit (or router), too. Two concepts are popular. They use either a custom-designed communication switch unit (as in Paragon, CS-2, MANNA, SP2) or the C004 or C104 communication switch units of the Transputer family.

Naturally, a crucial design factor is the choice of the interconnection network topology. From this point of view there is no clear trend as to what the preferred topology of future multicomputers will be. One obvious change from previous generations is that hypercube topology has lost its significance due to the application of wormhole routing where the communication distance between nodes is no longer a crucial feature. Consequently, favourable topologies are those where the implementation cost is radically less than in the hypercube topology and yet good scalability is assured. These topologies are mainly the mesh, cube and fat tree which appear respectively in the Paragon, GC PowerPlus and CS-2 machines. The design space of coarse-grain multicomputers is shown in Figure 17.29. The main representatives of the three groups are reviewed below.

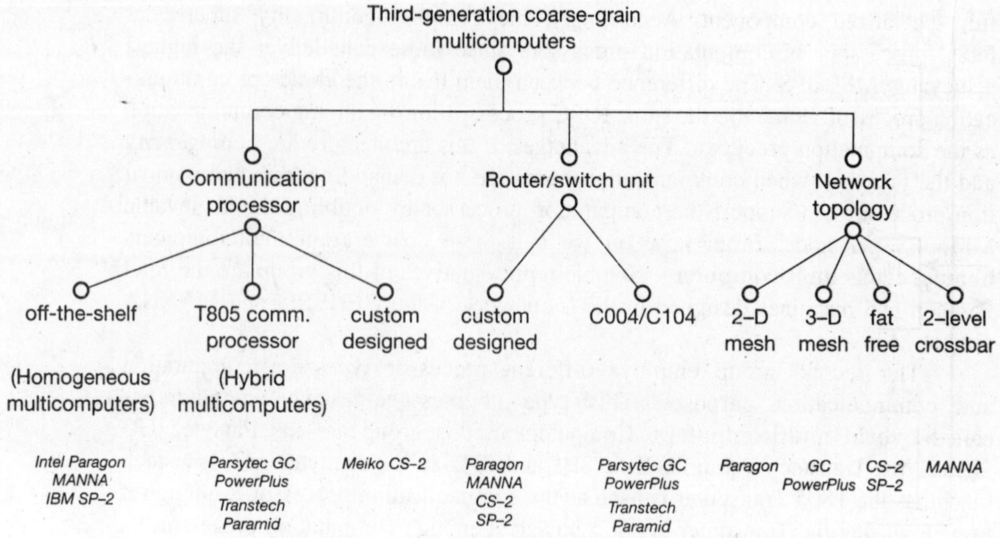

Figure 17.29 Design space of third-generation coarse-grain multicomputers.

17.5.1 Homogeneous architectures

Intel Paragon

The Intel Paragon machine is radically different from the previous Intel multicomputers. All of those machines (iPSC/1, iPSC/2 and iPSC/860) were based on the hypercube topology and none of them applied the wormhole routing technique. In the Paragon machine, nodes are connected in a 2-D mesh topology and communication is based on wormhole routing. Unlike the other machines, the Paragon contains three different node types:

- compute nodes
- service nodes
- I/O nodes

The various nodes are organized into several types of partitions inside the mesh as shown in Figure 17.30. The largest partition is the Compute Partition where compute nodes are employed to perform numeric computation. The service and I/O nodes are realized as general-purpose (GP) nodes, while compute nodes are multiprocessor (MP) nodes.

In the GP node two i860 processors are employed; one is the application processor and the other is dedicated to message processing. GP nodes contain an expansion port for adding an I/O interface such as HiPPI or SCSI. I/O nodes can support input/output connectivity, while service nodes provide interactive use for several users.

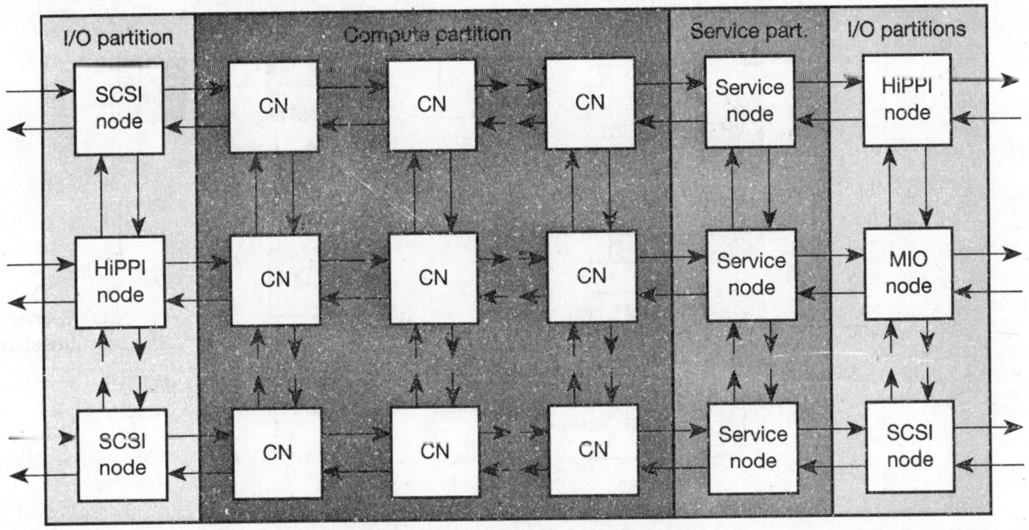

Figure 17.30 Structure of the Paragon machine.

The MP node is organized as a small-size shared memory multiprocessor in which four i860 application processors work together in a symmetric way. The node memory is shared among the four processors and each of them is supplied with a 256 Kbyte second-level cache. (Inside the i860 processor chip a 16 Kbyte instruction and a 16 Kbyte data cache are available as first-level caches.) Besides the application processors, the MP includes an additional i860 chip as a message processor for improving latency and throughput of message passing. The structure of MP and GP nodes is shown in Figure 17.31(a) and (b), respectively.

Message passing is initiated by the application processor but it is actually performed by the message processor which handles message-protocol processing. Message handling software is executed from the internal cache of the message processor. The advantage of this organization is that application processing and communication are overlapped, freeing the application processor from time-consuming context switches. Furthermore, the message processor realizes such global functions as broadcasting, synchronization and global reduction calculations (for example, global sum).

Message routing is realized by the Mesh Router Controller (MRC) of the node. MRC is a custom-designed chip which realizes the third component of multicomputers, the communication switch unit (or router). In the Paragon, MRCs are connected in a two-dimensional mesh and they form an independent routing system for the actual transmission of messages. MRCs route messages between any two nodes at speeds of 200 Mbyte/sec full duplex. The internal structure of the MRC is a 5×5 crossbar switch supplied with flit buffers and input controllers at each direction. The MRC handles four links to the neighbours and one link to the local node.

Communication in a node is further supported by two block transfer engines and by the Network Interface Controller (NIC), a custom VLSI chip. These three

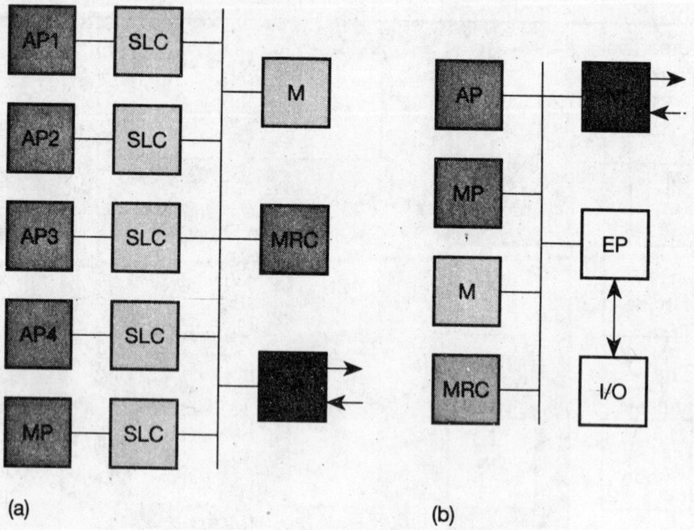

AP: Application processor
SLC: Second-level cache
MP: Message processor
EP: Expansion port
M: Memory
MRC: Mesh router controller
NI: Network interface

Figure 17.31 Structure of nodes in the Paragon. (a) Multiprocessor node; (b) General-purpose node.

units together permit simultaneous inbound and outbound communication at 200Mbyte/sec. NIC also provides a pipelined interface between the node memory and the coupled MRC of the node.

17.5.2 Hybrid architectures

In hybrid architectures, high-performance commodity microprocessors are employed as computation processors while less powerful microprocessors are built into the node as communication processors. In several cases the communication processor is a Transputer, whose internal structure was designed to support communication-intensive applications. Two motivations led to the design of hybrid architectures employing Transputers as communication processors:

- It turned out that the T9000 Transputer cannot compete with the floating-point performance of advanced superscalar processors.
- While superscalar RISC processors generally have hardware support for shared memory parallel architectures, they have no provision for the communication links necessary for a distributed memory system.

In order to combine the advantages of superscalar RISC processors and Transputers, hybrid architectures integrate high-performance superscalar RISC processors with first-generation Transputers in the processing nodes of the multicomputers. The powerful RISC processors play the role of computation processors while Transputers work as communication processors. Several machines were built on these principles: the Parsytec GC/PowerPlus, and the Transtech TTM200 and Paramid. The advantage of such hybrid architectures is that message routing operations are performed on the Transputer and do not detract from the processing power of the computation processor. There are several approaches to distributing the operating system among the processors of a hybrid architecture node:

- The operating system resides on the computation processor and just uses the Transputer as a communication device.
- The operating system and the application code run mainly on the Transputer and the computation processor is used simply as a coprocessor.

Parsytec GC/PowerPlus

In the GC/PowerPlus machine, a node (shown in Figure 17.32) is analogous to a T9000 Transputer (see in Figure 17.20). The two PowerPC 601 CPUs replace the CPU of the T9000 and they have much higher numeric performance than the T9000. Four T805 Transputers are employed instead of the VCP (Virtual Channel Processor) and link interfaces of the T9000. Together they provide 16 bi-directional Transputer

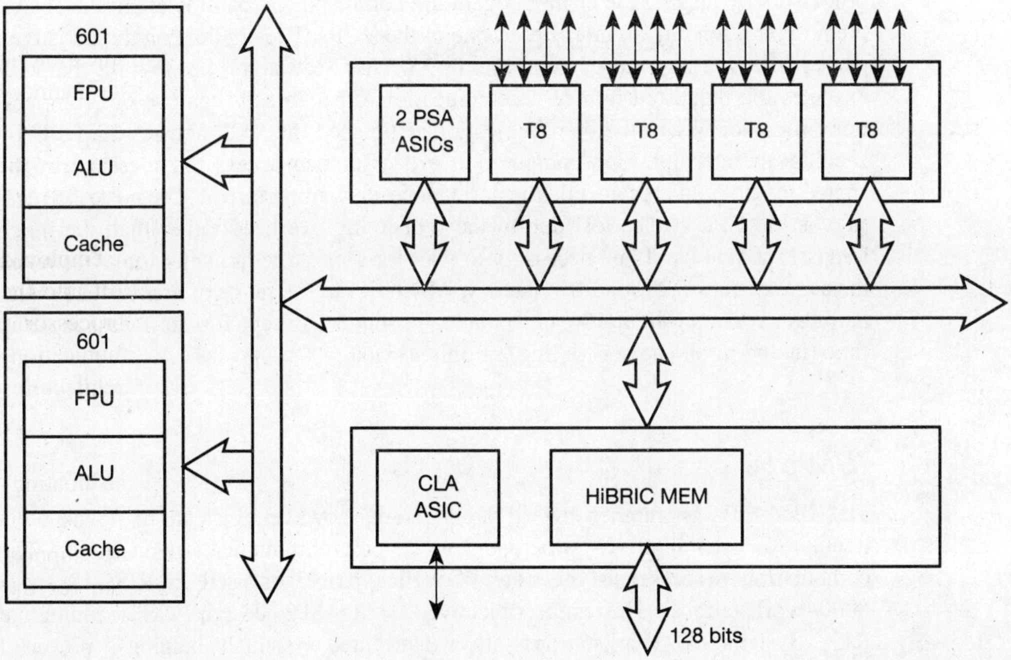

Figure 17.32 Structure of the GC-PowerPlus-Node-CPU.

links instead of the four links of the T9000. They realize virtual channel processing by software over the 16 physical links; for this reason they are also called Virtual Channel Processors (VCP).

The GC/PowerPlus machine implements a variable balance architecture concept whereby the number of CPUs, the number of communication processors, and the amount of memory per node can be configured to customers' needs. The machine node is a multiprocessor whose memory is physically shared among computation and communication processors. The CPUs and VCPs can signal each other incurring only a low overhead and their communication takes place in the user address space. Notice that while the T9000 is a single chip implementation of this concept, the GC/PowerPlus node is a multi-chip implementation in which the balance between CPUs and VCPs can be customized. In the GC/PowerPlus node, an ASIC interface has been designed to turn the four Transputers into efficient bus-masters at the PowerPC bus.

The interconnection network has a 3-D mesh topology derived from the original GC architecture. One GC/PowerPlus cube consists of 4 clusters of 4 + 1 nodes interconnected by 16 C004 switch units. The application of a redundant node in each cube renders the GC/PowerPlus machine fault-tolerant. Like other third-generation multicomputers, the GC/PowerPlus applies wormhole routing.

Although the communication model of the GC/PowerPlus is based on CSP, it involves a coarse-grain multi-threaded concept in the sense that it emulates the virtual channel processor concept of the T9000. Application threads (processes) running on the CPU request communication service from the communication processors by placing the channel operation command and parameters in the shared memory and sending an interrupt to one of the VCPs. The application thread is then placed in a waiting queue, as in the T9000 (see Section 17.4.3). While the VCP executes the requested remote communication, other threads can use the computation processor. When the communication is finished the VCP notifies the CPU by sending an interrupt. The computation processor can access the message in the shared memory and reschedule the corresponding waiting thread. The cost of a message is the CPU cycles lost due to the scheduling overhead rather than the much longer time that would be necessary to wait for a message transmission. As a result the average network round-trip latency, which lies in the range of architectures with hardware routers (about 100 μs), is actually hidden, except for the message setup time (including thread scheduling) of only 4-5 μs.

IBM SP2

The IBM SP2 is another hybrid architecture; however, instead of Transputers it employs Intel i860 XR processors to support communication on nodes. The computation processor is the new POWER2 processor used in RISC System/6000 workstations. The main objective of the SP2 design was to integrate RISC System/6000 workstations into a distributed system by adding a powerful communication subsystem. The innovative features of the SP2 communication subsystem are:

two data paths between any two input and output channels. An unbuffered data path through the crossbar unit requires only five cycles of latency. This data path can be used when the incoming packet encounters no contention for the selected output channel. Otherwise, the receiver module deserializes the incoming packet into eight-flit chunks and sends them to the central queue for temporary buffering.

The central queue can accommodate up to 128 eight-flit chunks in a 128×64 RAM memory which is allocated dynamically for the output channels according to demand. For each output channel a FIFO list is maintained for queuing message chunks waiting for that channel to become available. The bandwidth into and out of the switch chip is eight flits per cycle, which matches the bandwidth of the central queue which can serve one receiver and one transmitter module in each cycle as long as free queue space and message data are available in the central queue memory.

Packet chunks are divided into critical and non-critical chunks in order to prevent starvation. Chunks that are ready for immediate transfer to their destination transmitter are called critical chunks. These have higher priority than non-critical chunks. The transmitter module accepts packet chunks from the central queue, serializes them, supplies them with a CRC and transmits them on the corresponding output channel.

The **unified data and service network** is one of the main innovative features of SP2. The same network is used both for normal data transmission and for network service. Accordingly, the network operates in one of two modes:

- run mode
- service mode.

The two modes apply different communication protocols. In run mode the link protocol is *token based* to tolerate link propagation delays of several cycles. The input port sends token signals to its partner output port. Each token represents the readiness of the input port to accept another flit. The service mode applies a *circuit switching protocol* for reliable communication. The separation of run mode and service mode makes it possible to collect monitoring information without perturbing run mode operations.

17.6 Summary

The three generations of multicomputers clearly show the trends of progress in this class of parallel computer architectures. For applied interconnection networks, the turning point was the discovery of wormhole routing which led to a reduction of three orders of magnitude in communication latency. Another consequence was that communication latency for neighbour nodes and remote nodes became nearly the same. As a result, the network diameter, which was the most important network parameter in first-generation multicomputers, has lost its priority. In third-generation multicomputers scalability became the most crucial issue and hence topologies where the node degree is constant became popular. Thus, gradually the fat tree and the 2-D and 3-D mesh topologies took over from the originally favoured hypercube networks. The changes in communication networks are shown in the first part of Table 17.3 and the sixth column of Table 17.4.

The node organization, too, went through significant changes during the three generations. In first-generation systems the computation processor, communication processors and routers were not separate units, all of these functions being realized by the computation processor via software techniques. In second-generation systems the router became a separate hardware unit and finally, in the third generation the three units are clearly implemented by hardware either within the same chip (for example, computation processor and communication processor in the T9000) or distributed among several chips. In some third-generation multicomputers the node architecture became a small shared memory system where one or more computation processors share the local memory with the communication processor (for example, Intel Paragon). In the next chapter the organizational concepts of such small-size multiprocessors will be described in detail. As a summary, Table 17.4 gives a detailed comparison of the node and network organizations of the most important distributed memory machines.

Table 17.3 Comparison of the three generations of multicomputers (extended from Athas and Seitz, 1988). © 1988 IEEE

	First generation	*Second generation*	*Third generation*
Topology	Hypercube	Hypercube/mesh	2-D and 3-D mesh
Switching technique	Packet (store and forward)	Circuit or wormhole	Wormhole
Comm. latency of 100-byte message			
Neighbour (μsec)	2000	5	0.5
Remote (μsec)	6000	5	0.5
Node organization	Single computation processor	Computation processor + router	Computation proc. + communication proc. + router
Typical node number	64	256	1024
Node memory (Mbytes)	0.5	4	32
MIPS	1	10	100
MFLOPS scalar	0.1	2	40
MFLOPS vector	10	40	200
System memory (Mbytes)	32	1K	32K
System MIPS	64	2560	100K
System MFLOPS scalar	6.4	512	40K
System MFLOPS vector	640	10K	200K

Table 17.4 Summary of multicomputer organizations.

Machine	*Computation processor*	*Communication processor*	*Vector processor*	*Communication switch unit*	*Network topology*
nCUBE 2	Custom designed	–	–	Custom designed	Hypercube
iPSC-2	I386	–	Yes	Yes	Hypercube
Intel PARAGON	I860 (1 or 4)	I860	–	Custom designed	2-D mesh
GENESIS	I870	I870	Custom designed	–	2-level crossbar
MANNA	I860	I860	–	16×16 crossbar	Hierarchical crossbar
Parsytec GC/PowerPlus	PowerPC601 (2)	T805 (4)	–	C004	3-D mesh
Transtech Paramid	I860	T805	–	C004	Variable
IBM SP-2	POWER2	I860	–	Custom designed	Fat tree
Meiko CS-2	SPARC	Custom designed	Fujitsu μVP (2)	Custom designed	Fat tree
Parsys SN9800	T9000	T9000	–	C104	Hierarchical switch
J-Machine	Custom designed (MDP)	MDP	–	MDP	3-D mesh

Obviously, the technological improvements of the past 15 years are also reflected in the size parameters of multicomputers. The typical node number in first-generation systems was 64 which increased to over 1000 after two generations. Similarly, the memory size of nodes has been significantly expanded from 0.5 to 32 Mbyte. The total system memory size developed from 32 Mbyte to 32 Gbyte. Organizational and technological improvements led to enormous advances in the performance of multicomputers. For example, typical system performance in scalar-floating-point operations has reached 40 GFLOPS. All of these parameters of the three generations of multicomputers are summarized in the second part of Table 17.3.

18 Shared Memory MIMD Architectures

Section 1 introduces the main design issues in shared memory and distributed shared memory MIMD architectures. Section 18.2 describes dynamic interconnection networks, dividing them into shared path networks and switching networks. Section 18.3 tackles the problems of cache coherence, describing several hardware- and software-based protocols designed to overcome them, while Section 18.4 is devoted to synchronization and event ordering in multiprocessors. The next four sections describe uniform memory access (UMA) machines (Section 18.5), using the Encore Multimax and Power Challenge as examples; non-uniform memory access (NUMA) machines (Section 18.6), using Hector and the Cray T3D as examples; cache-coherent non-uniform memory access (CC-NUMA) machines (Section 18.6), using the Wisconsim multicube, Stanford Dash, Stanford FLASH and Convex Exemplar as examples; cache-coherent non-uniform memory access (CC-NUMA) machines (Section 18.7); and cache-only memory access (COMA) machines (Section 18.8), using the Data Diffusion Machine (DDM) and KSR-1 as examples. Finally, Section 18.9 assesses interconnection networks, cache coherence schemes, and trends.

18.1 Introduction

The distinguishing feature of shared memory systems is that no matter how many memory blocks are used in them and how these memory blocks are connected to the processors and address spaces of these memory blocks are unified into a global address space which is completely visible to all processors of the shared memory system. Issuing a certain memory address by any processor will access the same memory block location. However, according to the physical organization of the logically shared memory, two main types of shared memory system could be distinguished:

- Physically shared memory systems
- Virtual (or distributed) shared memory systems.

In physically shared memory systems all memory blocks can be accessed uniformly by all processors. In distributed shared memory systems the memory blocks are physically distributed among the processors as local memory units. In the current chapter both types of shared memory system will be discussed.

The three main design issues in increasing the scalability of shared memory systems are:

- Organization of memory
- Design of interconnection networks
- Design of cache coherent protocols.

As shown in Chapter 15, shared memory systems are basically classified according to their memory organization since this is the most fundamental design issue. Accordingly, shared memory systems can be divided into four main classes:

- Uniform memory access (UMA) machines
- Non-uniform memory access (NUMA) machines
- Cache-coherent non-uniform memory access (CC-NUMA) machines
- Cache-only memory access (COMA) machines.

UMA machines belong to the physically shared memory architecture class, while NUMA, CC-NUMA and COMA machines form the class of distributed shared memory architectures. The four classes cover the three generations of shared memory systems. Their first generation contains the UMA machines where the interconnection network was based either on the concept of shared bus in order to construct low-price multiprocessors or on multistage networks in order to build massively parallel shared memory systems. While small-size bus-based shared memory systems became commercially available in the mid-1980s, the massively parallel shared memory machines remained prototypes.

Contention is an inherent consequence of sharing and, by introducing an additional shared hardware resource – the shared bus – it became a critical architectural bottleneck. The whole history of shared memory systems is about struggling against contention. Even in the first generation, local cache memories were introduced to reduce contention. However, despite of the use of sophisticated cache systems, the scalability of first-generation shared memory systems was strongly limited. The number of effectively exploitable processors was in the range of 20–30 in shared bus machines and 100–200 in multistage network-based machines.

The second-generation shared memory systems tried to physically distribute the shared memory among the processors in order to reduce the traffic and consequently, the contention on the interconnection network. A further improvement was the replacement of the single shared bus by a more complex multibus or multistage network. As a consequence, in second-generation shared memory systems hundreds of processors were accommodated even in commercially available machines. For example, in the BBN Butterfly machine 256 processors worked together. However, in order to keep all the processors busy, highly sophisticated software techniques were needed both at the level of operating systems and compilers and of user-written application programs.

The third-generation shared memory systems combine the advantages of the first two generations. CC-NUMA and COMA machines are highly scalable, massively parallel systems where contention is dramatically reduced by introducing large local cache memories. Because of the underlying cache coherence protocols, programming these machines is no more difficult than programming the first generation. Current CC-NUMA and COMA machines can be upgraded in the range of a thousand processors.

Like multicomputers, the quality of the interconnection network has a decisive impact on the speed, size and cost of the whole machine. Since in multiprocessors any processor must be able to access any memory location, even if it physically belongs to another processor, **dynamic interconnection schemes** are usually employed. Dynamic networks can be divided into two main classes according to their mode of operations. Those that provide continuous connection among the processors and memory blocks are called **shared path networks**. In these networks the continuous connection is shared among the processors which have to compete for its use. The shared path was typically a **single bus** in the first-generation multiprocessors. In recent third-generation machines **hierarchical bus systems** are introduced.

The other type of dynamic network does not provide a continuous connection among the processors and memory blocks, rather a switching mechanism enables processors to be temporarily connected memory blocks. The two most popular classes of these **switching networks** are **crossbar** and **multistage networks**. The latter can be further divided according to the structure of the employed switching elements and their interconnection topology.

Dynamic networks have some drawbacks compared with the static networks applied in multicomputers. Dynamic networks are either too expensive (switching networks) or they can support only a limited number of processors (bus connection). Recently, hierarchical multibus systems have been proposed as a compromise between the price and scalability of the network. Another recent approach combines static and dynamic network components in a hierarchy: direct interconnection networks and message passing are used among the nodes of modern scalable distributed shared memory systems, while inside the nodes dynamic networks are employed to connect several processors.

Uniprocessors have successfully demonstrated the benefits of cache memories in order to increase memory bandwidth. Accordingly, most of the shared memory systems employ cache memories, too. However, the application of caches in a multiprocessor environment gives rise to the so-called **cache consistency problem**. In order to solve the problem of maintaining data consistency in the caches, the **cache coherence protocol** must be added to the traffic on the network. The extra traffic deriving from the protocol reduces the benefits of the caches and hence, careful design is necessary to introduce a protocol of minimal complexity.

Cache coherence protocols are divided into two classes: **hardware-based protocols** and **software-based protocols**. Hardware-based protocols are strongly related to the type of interconnection network employed. The **snoopy cache protocol** is employed in single bus multiprocessors, while **directory-based cache coherence protocols** are the most popular in multistage networks. Finally, **hierarchical cache coherence protocols** are applied in hierarchical multibus systems.

The design space and classification of shared memory architectures is shown in Figure 18.1.

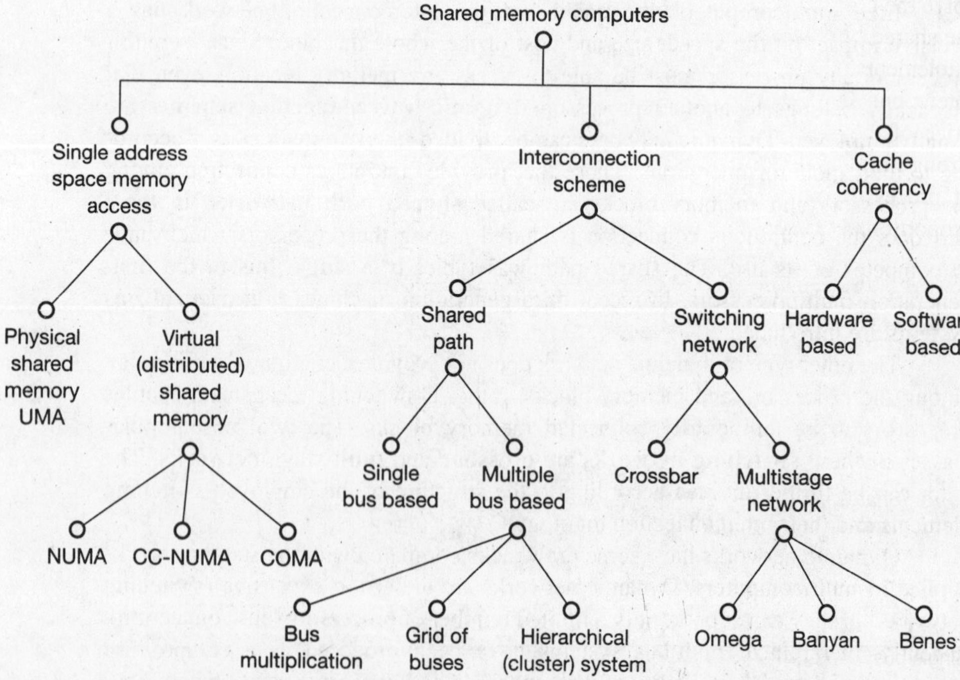

Figure 18.1 Design space and classification of shared memory computers.

18.2 Dynamic interconnection networks

Dynamic interconnection networks enable the temporary connection of any two components of a multiprocessor. This is provided either by a shared path network that can be allocated to any active component of the machine on a competitive basis or by a number of switches that can be set in different ways according to the connection requirements. The former networks are called shared path networks, while the latter are called switching networks. Both dynamic network types can be further classified. Shared path networks can be either single bus or multiple bus systems depending on the number of buses providing interconnection among the components of the multiprocessor. Switching networks are either crossbars or multistage networks. The classification of dynamic interconnection networks is shown in Figure 18.2.

18.2.1 Shared path networks

Single shared bus

One of the most popular interconnection networks is the single shared bus which has several advantageous features. Firstly, its organization is simply a generalization and extension of the buses employed in uniprocessor systems. It contains the same bus lines (address, data, control, interrupt) as uniprocessors and some additional ones to solve the contention on the bus when several processors simultaneously want to use the shared bus. These lines are called arbitration lines and play a crucial role in the implementation of shared buses. Secondly, the shared bus is a very cost-effective interconnection scheme. Increasing the number of processors does not increase the price of the shared bus. However, the contention on the shared bus represents a strong limitation on the number of applicable processors. Obviously, as the number of processors on the bus increases, the probability of contention also increases proportionally, reaching a point when the whole bandwidth of the bus is exhausted

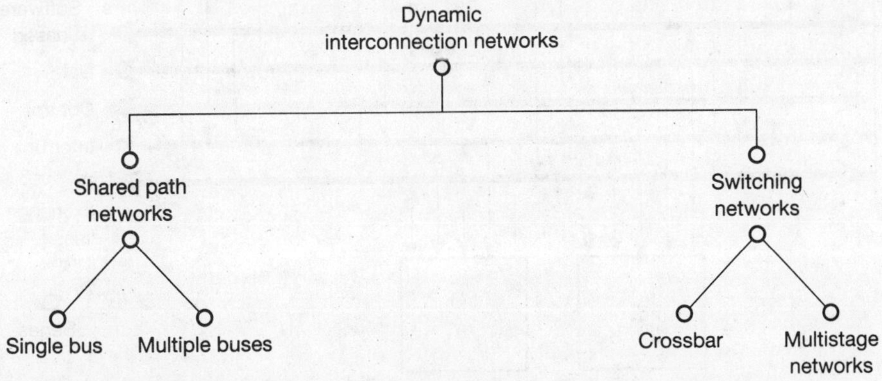

Figure 18.2 Classification of dynamic interconnection networks.

by the processors and hence, adding a new processor will not cause any potential speed-up in the multiprocessor. One of the main design issues in shared bus multiprocessors is the enhancement of the number of applicable processors by different methods. The three most important techniques are:

- Introducing private memory
- Introducing coherent cache memory
- Introducing multiple buses.

Without these improvements the applicable number of processors is in the range 3–5. By introducing private memory and coherent cache memory, the number of processors can be increased by an order of magnitude up to 30 processors. Bus hierarchies open the way to constructing scalable shared memory systems based on bus interconnection. However, the employment of coherent cache memories as well as multiple buses will significantly increase the expense of building such multiprocessors. Section 18.3 deals with the problem of coherent caches while Section 18.7.1 shows an example of scalable multiprocessors with multiple buses.

The typical structure of a single bus multiprocessor without coherent caches is shown in Figure 18.3. The new components of the system, relative to a uniprocessor, is the bus arbiter logic which has the role of allocating the bus in the case of several simultaneous bus requests, and the extra bus exchange lines supporting the work of the arbiter. The bus exchange lines comprise typically one or more bus request lines by means of which the processors or other temporary bus masters can request bus allocation for their transfer. According to the state of the bus request lines and the applied bus allocation policy, the arbiter grants one of the requesters via the grant lines.

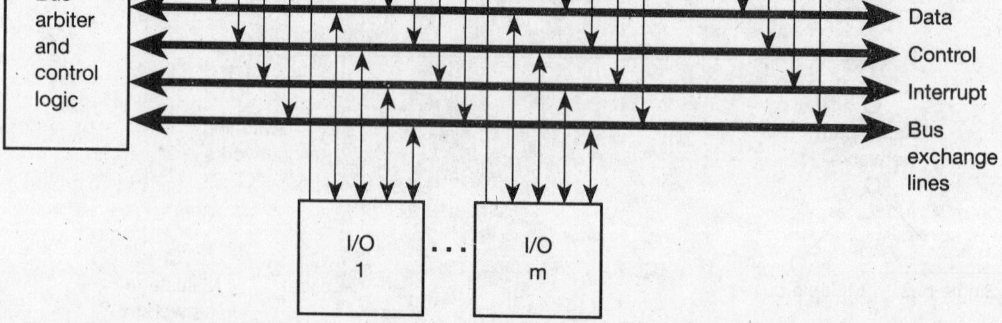

Figure 18.3 Structure of a single bus multiprocessor without caches.

Although, in principle, the uniprocessor and multiprocessor buses are very similar, there is a significant difference in their mode of operation. Uniprocessors and first-generation multiprocessors employ the so-called **locked buses**; examples are the Multibus, VMEbus, etc. Second-generation multiprocessors apply **pended buses**. The difference is in how memory accesses are handled on the bus. A memory write access needs two phases:

Phase 1. The address and data are transferred via the bus to the memory controller.

Phase 2. The memory write operation (including parity check, error correction, and so on) is executed by the memory controller.

The first phase is typically 3–4 times faster than the second. In a uniprocessor system the two phases are executed sequentially, and the bus is locked until the complete memory operation is finished. However, locking the bus in a multiprocessor system is unnecessary and leads to low exploitation of the fast bus. If several processors and several memory units are connected by the bus (and this is the case in single bus multiprocessors), then bus transfers and memory controller operations can be overlapped. After finishing the bus transfer phase for a memory unit, another processor can start a new write operation for another memory unit. Figure 18.4(a)

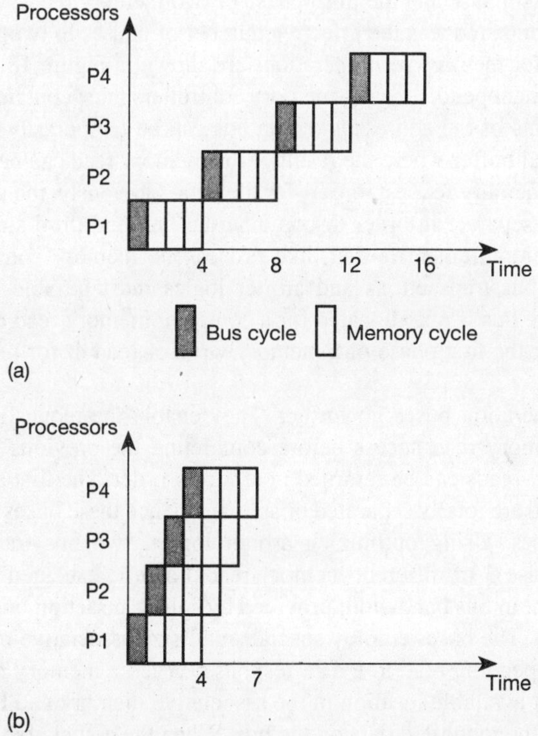

Figure 18.4 Comparison of write bandwidths of various buses. (a) Memory write on locked bus; (b) Memory write on pended and split-transaction buses.

shows the execution time of four write operations launched by four processors on a locked bus, while Figure 18.4(b) demonstrates that the execution time can be radically reduced by a pended bus provided that the memory operation is three times longer than the bus transfer time. The situation is very similar to the introduction of wormhole routing in multicomputers as shown in Figure 17.8. In the case of packet switching the whole packet is stored before executing the routing operation. Separating and overlapping the message head buffering, and routing in the first phase and buffering the message body in the second phase, produces the same effect in multicomputers as pending in multiprocessors.

The exploitation of the fast bus can be further improved by optimizing memory read accesses, too. A memory read access needs three phases:

Phase 1. The address is transferred via the bus to the memory controller.

Phase 2. The memory read operation is executed by the memory controller.

Phase 3. The data is transferred via the bus to the requesting processor.

The three phases must be executed sequentially. However, in a multiprocessor system it is possible to reduce the three phases to, two in practice. Notice that phase 1 does not require the data bus, while phase 3 does not need the address bus. Hence, combining the first phase and the third phase of two memory reads, executed on different memory units, reduces the effective number of phases to two. The locked bus and pended bus for memory read operations are shown in Figure 18.5(a) and (b).

To implement pended buses, memory controllers must contain an input buffer where the contents of the address and data bus can be temporarily stored from the bus, and an output buffer where the result of the memory read can be stored until the bus accepts the memory request to transfer the data. Obviously, the address and data buses should be separate in order to combine the first and third stages of memory reads. A further requirement is that, like processors, memory controllers must be able to request bus transactions and arbiter logics must be able to service their requests, too. The bus is not allocated for a complete memory read or write. Rather, it is allocated for the first phase of a memory write or read or for the third phase of a memory read.

Third-generation buses go further. They enable the requesting processor to issue a new memory read access before completing the previous one. Data from different memory reads can be returned in arbitrary order. The first and third phases of a memory read are totally separated or split and hence these buses are called **split-transaction buses**. Using optimizing arbiter logics, two bus transaction phases (phase 1 and phase 3 of different memory reads) can be executed simultaneously. The improvement in bus bandwidth provided by split-transaction buses is illustrated in Figure 18.5(c). The buses employ special small-size associative memories to link the address of a pending read to a data response. When a memory read is issued, it occupies the first available location in the associative memory and holds it until the memory returns the requested data on the bus. When the associative memory is full, further memory requests must be delayed until a location becomes free.

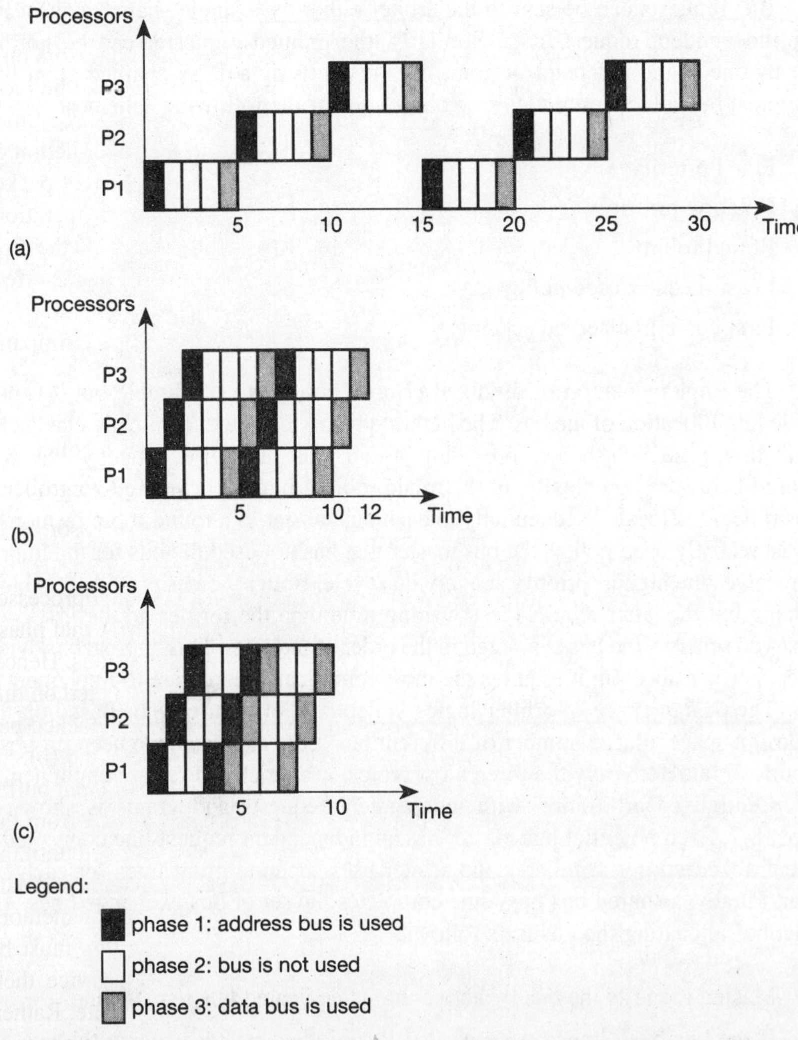

Figure 18.5 Comparison of read bandwidths of various buses. (a) Memory read on locked bus; (b) memory read on pended bus; (c) memory read on split-transaction bus.

Arbiter logics play a crucial role in the implementation of pended and split-transaction buses. These are the so-called 1-of-N arbiters since they grant the requested resource (the shared bus) only to one of the requesters. The design space of arbiter logics is very rich. There are two ways to organise the arbitration logic according to the distribution of its components in the multiprocessor system:

- Centralized arbiter
- Decentralized arbiter.

Bus requests can be sent to the arbiter either by a single shared request line or by independent request lines. Similarly, the granted requester can be notified either by one of the independent grant lines or by using a daisy-chained grant line. The typical bus allocation policies belong to one of the following schemes:

- Fixed priority
- Rotating priority
- Round robin
- Least recently used policy
- First come first served scheme.

The implementation of the fixed priority policy is very simple but it cannot provide fair allocation of the bus. The highest priority can be dynamically changed in the rotating priority scheme, providing a fair bus allocation strategy but with increased hardware complexity. In the round robin arbiter policy, fixed-length slices of bus time are allocated sequentially to each bus master in a round robin fashion. In the least recently used policy, the bus master that has not used the bus for the longest time receives the highest priority at every bus cycle. Both schemes provide good load balancing but the latter requires less waiting time than the former. In the first come first served scheme, the bus is granted in the order of requests. This approach provides the best performance but it requires the most complicated hardware to implement.

The design space of arbiter logics is depicted in Figure 18.6. Based on this rich design space a large number of different bus arbiter logics have been proposed and built so far. Here only the three most typical arbiter structures are explained.

Centralized arbitration with independent requests and grants is shown in Figure 18.7. Each potential bus master has an independent request line connected to the centralized arbiter. Similarly, the arbiter uses separate grant lines for each bus master. Finally, a shared bus busy line completes the set of bus exchange lines. The protocol of allocating the bus is as follows:

(1) $Master_i$ requests the bus by activating its dedicated bus request line.

(2) If the bus busy line is passive, that is, no other master is using the bus, the arbiter immediately allocates the bus to the requester by activating the $grant_i$ line. The requester deactivates its request line and activates the bus busy line, prohibiting the allocation of the bus for other requesters. After completing the bus transaction, the requester deactivates the bus busy line.

(3) When the bus busy line is active, the arbiter does not accept any bus requests.

(4) When several request lines are active by the time the bus busy line becomes passive, the arbiter can use any of the bus allocation policies described above.

The centralized arbiter with independent request and grant lines has two major advantages. Firstly, it can realise any bus allocation policy and secondly, it has faster arbitration time compared with daisy-chained arbiters. However, it requires a large number of bus exchange lines, which is an obvious drawback.

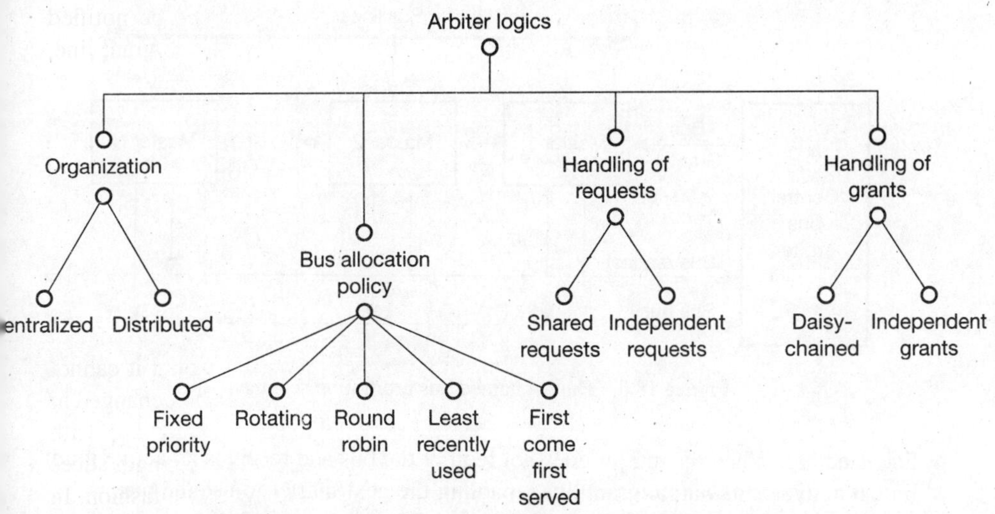

Figure 18.6 Design space of arbiter logics.

One of the most popular organizations of arbiter logics is **daisy-chaining**. The centralized version with fixed priority policy is illustrated in Figure 18.8. There is only one shared bus request line in the daisy-chained bus arbitration scheme. All the masters use this line to indicate their need to access the shared bus. The arbiter passes the bus grant line to the first master and then it is passed from master to master, creating a chain of masters. The priority of a master is determined by its position in the grant chain. The closer it is to the arbiter, the higher its priority. A master can access the shared bus if the bus busy line is passive and its input grant

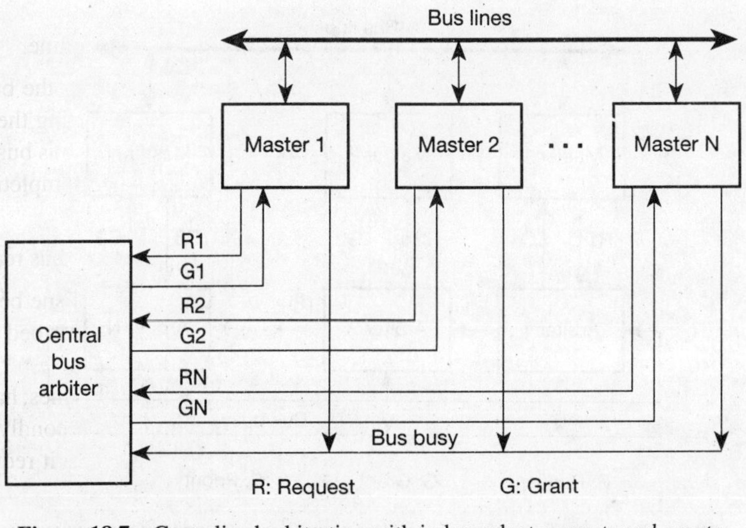

Figure 18.7 Centralized arbitration with independent requests and grants.

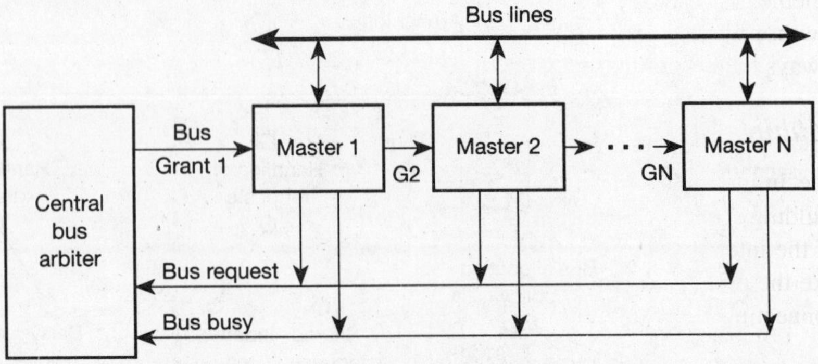

Figure 18.8 Daisy-chained bus arbitration scheme.

line is active. When the master does not require the bus and receives an active grant line, it activates its output grant line, enabling the next master to use the bus.

The implementation of the daisy-chained arbitration scheme is very cost-effective. Adding a new processor module does not require any extension of the existing bus exchange lines. However, the relatively slow propagation of the grant signal on the grant chain is a drawback of the scheme. Another obvious disadvantage is the lack of fairness in the allocation scheme.

In order to eliminate this drawback a modified version, called the **rotating arbiter**, can be employed in shared bus multiprocessors. The structure of a decentralized, rotating arbiter with independent request and grant lines is shown in Figure 18.9. The priority loop of the rotating arbiter works similarly to the grant chain of the daisy-chained arbiter. Arbiter_i is allowed to grant its coupled master unit if master_i has activated its bus request line, the bus busy line is passive and the $\text{priority}_{(i-1)}$ input line is active. If master_i has not activated its bus request line, arbiter_i activates

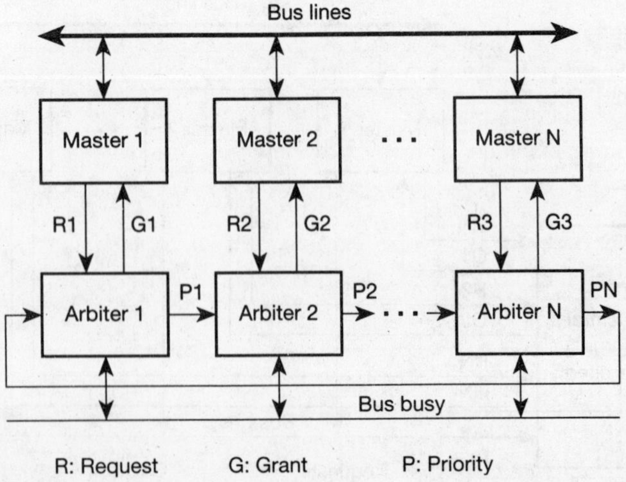

Figure 18.9 Structure of a decentralized rotating arbiter with independent requests and grants.

its output $priority_i$ line. The main difference compared with the daisy-chained scheme is in how the lowest priority unit is selected. In the daisy-chained arbiter the lowest priority unit is always the master farthest away; in the rotating scheme, it is always the master that releases the bus.

Multiple shared bus

The limited bandwidth of the single shared bus represents a major limitation in building scalable multiprocessors. There are several ways to increase the bandwidth of the interconnection network. A natural idea is to multiply the number of buses, like the processors and memory units. Four different ways have been proposed for connecting buses to the processors, memory units and other buses:

- 1-dimension multiple bus system
- 2- or 3-dimension bus systems
- cluster bus system
- hierarchical bus system.

The simplest generalization of the single bus system towards a multiple bus system is the **1-dimension multiple bus system** shown in Figure 18.10. This approach leads to a typical uniform memory access (UMA) machine where any processor can access any memory unit through any of the buses. The employment of the 1-of-N arbiters described in the previous section is not sufficient in such systems. Arbitration is a two-stage process in 1-dimension multiple bus systems. First, the 1-of-N arbiters (one per memory unit) can resolve the conflict when several processors require exclusive access to the same shared memory unit. After the first stage m (out of n) processors can obtain access to one of the memory units. However, when the number of buses (b) is less than the number of memory units (m), a second stage of arbitration is needed where an additional b-of-m arbiter is employed to allocate buses to those processors that successfully obtained access to a memory unit.

Here, a b-of-m arbiter described in Mudge et al. (1987) is shown as an example. The structure of the b-of-m arbiter is depicted in Figure 18.11. It contains a state register and m arbiter modules (A_1, A_2, ..., A_m) for each memory unit. The state register realizes a round-robin arbitration policy; that is, it ensures that the highest priority in the next arbitration cycle will be given to the arbiter module immediately

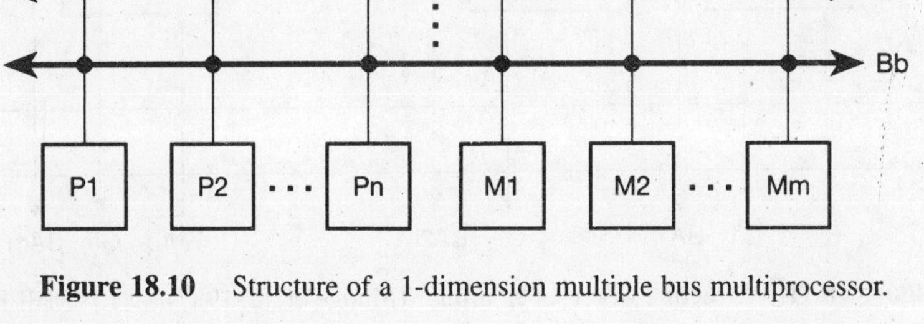

Figure 18.10 Structure of a 1-dimension multiple bus multiprocessor.

following the last one serviced. The highest priority module A_i is selected by activating its e_i input. If the memory unit M_i was selected in the first stage of the arbitration cycle, it activates its request line R_i. If both e_i and R_i are active, the first available bus is allocated to the memory unit M_i (and to the processor that obtained access to M_i in the first stage of the arbitration cycle) by activating the grant line G_i and setting BA_i as the address of the first available bus. The arbiter module A_i passes the right of bus allocation to the next module by activating the C_i line. The bus allocation proceeds sequentially from left to right in the ring of arbiter modules as long as there is free bus in the system. When the last bus is allocated, the corresponding arbiter module A_j activates the s_j line of the state register. Accordingly, in the next arbitration cycle A_{j+1} will have the highest priority. If an arbiter module has no active request from the associated memory unit, it immediately activates its C output and copies the input BA value (the address of the next available bus) to its output.

A further generalization of the 1-dimension multiple buses is the introduction of the second and third dimensions. **Two-dimension multiple buses** are employed in the Aquarius Multi-Multi architecture (Carlton and Despain, 1990), while the use of a **3-dimension multiple bus system** was proposed in the Wisconsin Multicube machine (Goodman and Woest, 1988). In these systems, multiple buses compose a grid interconnection network. Each processor node is connected to a row bus and to a column bus. Processors along a row or column constitute a conventional single bus multiprocessor. The memory can be distributed in several ways. The most traditional approach is to attach memory units to each bus. In the Wisconsin Multicube machine, only the column buses are supplied with memory units (see Figure 18.39). In the Aquarius Multi-Multi architecture the memory units are allocated to processor nodes rather than to buses. The main problem of these architectures is the maintenance of cache coherency. The cache coherence techniques applied in the Wisconsin Multicube are described in Section 18.7.1.

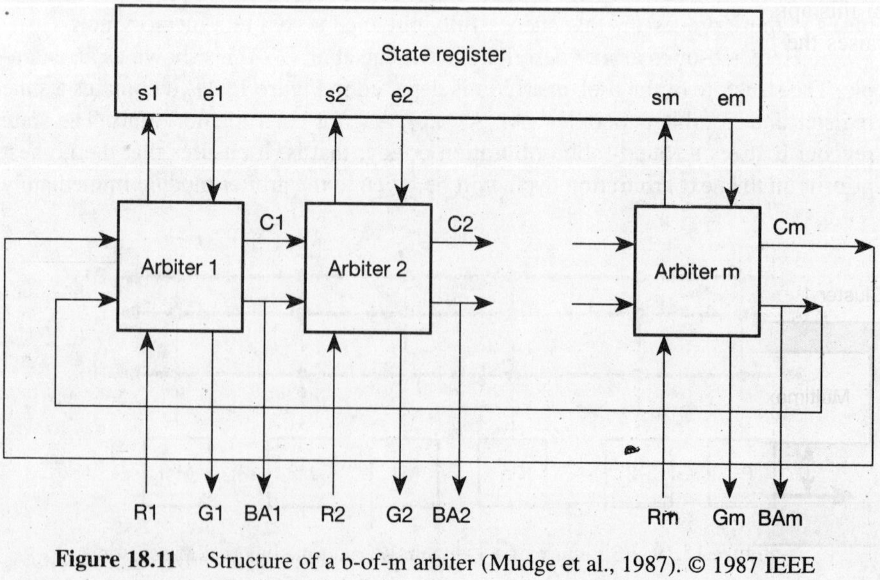

Figure 18.11 Structure of a b-of-m arbiter (Mudge et al., 1987). © 1987 IEEE

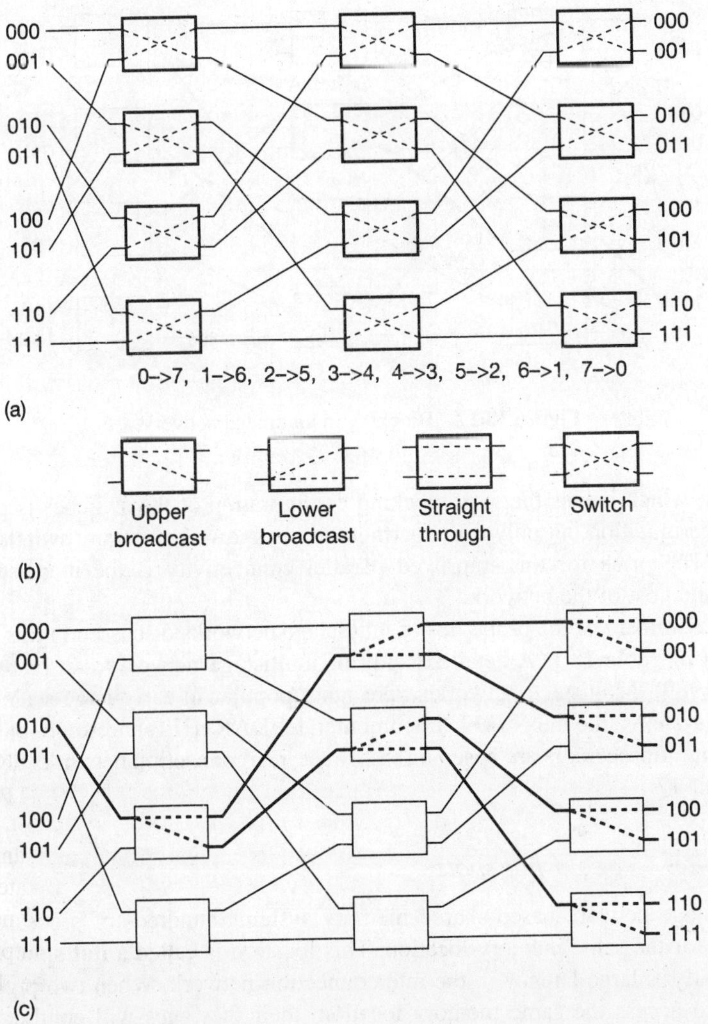

Figure 18.16 Omega network. (a) Omega network topology and set of switches to reverse order; (b) possible switch positions; (c) broadcast in the omega network.

Consider the (0→5, ..., 6→4, ...) permutations. Figure 18.17 shows that no matter how the other inputs are mapped to the outputs, a conflict appears at switch A, resulting the blocking of either the 0→5 or the 6→4 message.

The relevant difference between these multistage networks and the crossbar interconnection is that the crossbar is a **non-blocking network**. For any permutation there exists a configuration of switches in the crossbar that satisfies the permutation, that is, any simultaneous input–output combination is possible. Although this flexibility cannot be achieved in multistage networks there are remedies that can significantly improve the parallel access mechanism of these networks. For example, the **Benes network** contains additional stages to introduce redundant paths in the interconnection scheme. The resulting network is a **rearrangeable non-blocking**

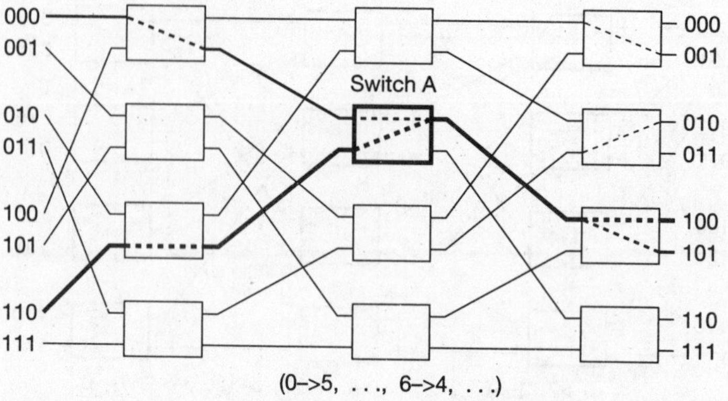

Figure 18.17 Blocking in an omega network.

network, which means that non-blocking configuration of the switches is possible for any permutation but only if the permutation is known before any switch is configured. The price for this improved parallel connectivity is the increased size, latency and cost of the network.

A summary of the properties of multistage networks discussed in this section is shown in Table 18.1. A detailed study of multistage networks can be found in Siegel (1989). Multistage networks were quite popular in early large-scale shared memory systems like the NYU Ultracomputer, CEDAR, HEP, and so on, but recent scalable multiprocessors are based on the direct interconnection networks described in Chapter 17.

Techniques to avoid hot spots

In multistage network-based shared memory systems hundreds of processors can compete for the same memory location. This location is called a **hot spot** and can significantly enlarge latency in the interconnection network. When two processors attempt to access the same memory location, their messages will conflict in one

Table 18. 1 Summary of multistage networks.

Network type	*Number of stages*	*Number of switches at a stage*	*Topology of links between stages*	*Switch size*	*Operation mode*
omega	$\log_2 N$	N/2	2-way shuffle	2×2	Blocking
butterfly	$\log_8 N$	N/8	8-way shuffle	8×8	Blocking
generalized-cube	$S=\log_2 N$	N/2	[0,1]: shuffle [1,S]: exchange	2×2	Blocking
Benes	$S=2*\log_2 N-1$	N/2	[2,S-1]: exchange	2×2	Rearrangeable non-blocking

of the switches no matter which interconnection network is used (crossbar or multistage). They enter at two different inputs to the switch but want to exit at the same output. Obviously, only one of the messages can be forwarded on the required output. According to the way the other message is handled, two kinds of networks are distinguished: queuing networks and non-queuing networks.

Queuing networks temporarily hold the second message in the switch by using a queue store able to accommodate a small number of messages. Despite the switch queues, queuing networks are quite vulnerable to network saturation. Experiments showed that even if only a very small percentage of all accesses are aimed at a particular memory location, the presence of the hot spot will affect not only the processors requesting access to the hot spot but also the other processors trying to use the network. Waiting messages hold switch resources, restricting the availability of such resources for messages coming from other processors. As a consequence, additional messages are blocked, holding yet more resources, and hot spot saturation propagates back through the network in a tree-like fashion as illustrated in Figure 18.18.

Non-queuing networks reject the second message so that unsuccessful messages retreat and leave the network free. It gives other messages requiring different paths a chance to get through the network. However, the rejection of conflicting messages decreases the network bandwidth to O(N/logN).

To compare the effect of the hot-spot problem in queuing and non-queuing networks, consider the case in Figure 18.18. In a queuing network message P7→M4 is blocked and hence message P1→M5 is prevented from getting through. This results in the blocking of message P5→M7, too. This case demonstrates that processors attempting to access different memory modules are delayed by the hot spot. In a non-queuing network the P5→M7 message has no obstacle since P1→M5 would be rejected by the network.

Another way of reducing the effect of hot spots in a switching network is to introduce **combining switches**. These recognize that two messages are directed to the same memory module and in such cases they can combine the two messages into one. This technique is particularly advantageous in the implementation of synchronization tools like semaphores and barriers which are frequently accessed by many

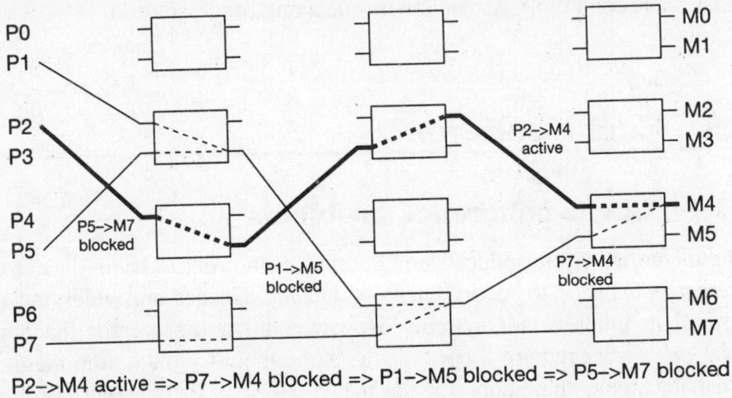

Figure 18.18 Hot-spot saturation in a blocking omega network.

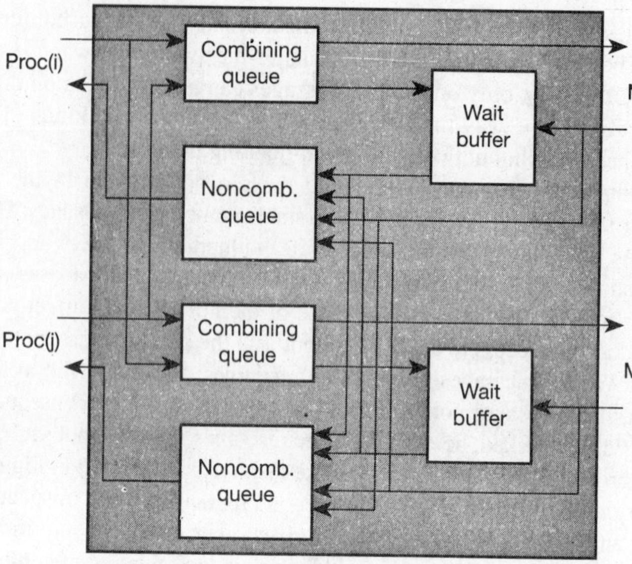

Figure 18.19 Structure of a combining switch.

processes running on distinct processors. Switching networks that employ combining switches are called **combining networks**. Section 18.4.1 explains in detail how the fetch&add primitive can be used in a combining network to implement various synchronization tools.

The structure of the combining switch used in the NYU Ultracomputer is depicted in Figure 18.19. The memory requests from Pi and Pj enter two combining queues, one for the Mk and one for the Ml memory block. If the two requests refer to the same memory address the corresponding combining queue forwards one request to the memory block and places the second request in the associated wait buffer. Replies from memory are directed both to the non-combining queue of the requesting processor and to the associated wait buffer which tries to match the incoming reply with the stored requests. If a match is found, the wait buffer generates a second reply for the other requesting processor, too.

18.3 Cache coherence

18.3.1 Cache coherence problems

Cache memories are introduced into computers in order to bring data closer to the processor and hence to reduce memory latency. Caches are widely accepted and employed in uniprocessor systems. However, in multiprocessor machines where several processors require a copy of the same memory block, the maintenance of consistency among these copies raises the so-called cache coherence problem which has three causes:

- Sharing of writable data
- Process migration
- I/O activity.

Assume that data structure D is a shared writable structure and processes on processors Pi and Pj read the value of D. As a result, D is loaded into caches Ci and Cj and hence both caches contain a consistent value of D. If a process on processor Pi updates D to D', cache Ci will contain D' while the other cache Cj still contains the original D value; that is, the copies of D become inconsistent. A read from Cj will not return the latest value of D.

Assume now that D is a private writable data structure owned by process A running on processor Pi. If A writes D into D', Ci will contain D' while the main memory still contains the original D value. If afterwards A migrates to processor Pj (j<>i) and performs a read operation on the data structure, the original value D will be fetched from the main memory to Cj instead of the updated value D'.

Inconsistency from I/O activity can arise in the case of any writable data structure if the I/O processor is working directly from the main memory. Obviously, if the data structure D is written into D' by any processor, the I/O system cannot see this change of value for D since the main memory contains the stale value of D.

From the point of view of cache coherence, data structures can be divided into three classes:

- **Read-only data structures** which never cause any cache coherence problem. They can be replicated and placed in any number of cache memory blocks without any problem.
- **Shared writable data structures** are the main source of cache coherence problems.
- **Private writable data structures** pose cache coherence problems only in the case of process migration.

There are several techniques to maintain cache coherence for the critical case, that is, shared writable data structures. The applied methods can be divided into two classes:

- hardware-based protocols
- software-based schemes.

Software-based schemes usually introduce some restrictions on the cachability of data in order to prevent cache coherence problems. First the hardware-based protocols are described in detail, then a short introduction to software-based schemes is given.

18.3.2 Hardware-based protocols

Hardware-based protocols provide general solutions to the problems of cache coherence without any restrictions on the cachability of data. The price of this approach is that shared memory systems must be extended with sophisticated hardware mechanisms to support cache coherence. Hardware-based protocols can be classified according to their:

- memory update policy
- cache coherence policy
- interconnection scheme.

Two types of memory update policy are applied in multiprocessors. The **write-through policy** maintains consistency between the main memory and caches; that is, when a block is updated in one of the caches it is immediately updated in memory, too. The **write-back policy** permits the memory to be temporarily inconsistent with the most recently updated cached block. Memory is updated eventually when the modified block in the cache is replaced or invalidated. Figure 18.20(a) shows the effect of the write-through policy while Figure 18.20(b) illustrates the same cache operation but with the write-back policy. The application of the write-through policy leads to unnecessary traffic on the interconnection network in the case of private data and infrequently used shared data. On the other hand, it is more

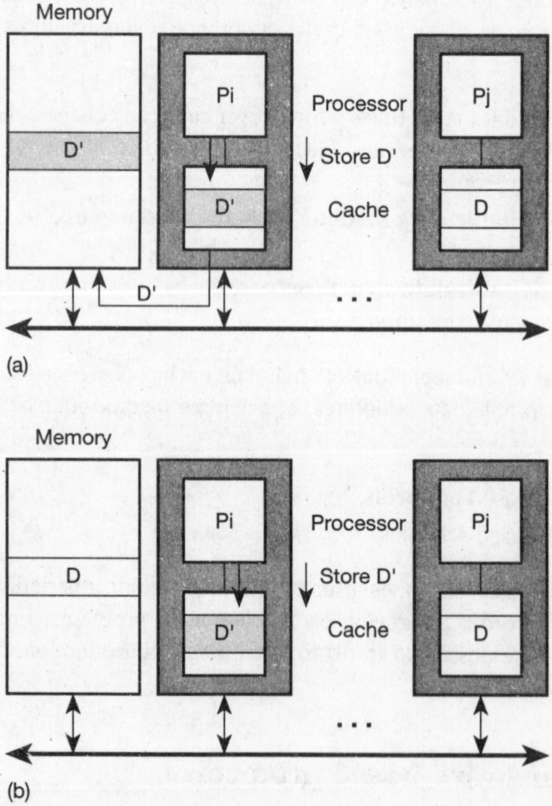

Figure 18.20 Memory update policies in writing shared data structures. (a) Write-through memory update policy; (b) write-back memory update policy.

reliable than the write-back scheme since error detection and recovery features are available only at the main memory. The write-back policy avoids useless interconnection traffic; however, it requires more complex cache controllers since read references to memory locations that have not yet been updated should be redirected to the appropriate cache.

The write-through policy is a greedy policy because it updates the memory copy immediately, while the write-back policy is a lazy one with postponed memory update. Similarly, a greedy and a lazy cache coherence policy have been introduced for updating the cache copies of a data structure:

- write-update policy (a greedy policy)
- write-invalidate policy (a lazy policy)

The key idea of the **write-update policy** is that whenever a processor updates a cached data structure, it immediately updates all the other cached copies as well. Whether the shared memory copy is updated depends on the memory update policy. The mechanism of the write-update policy is illustrated in Figure 18.21(a). Immediate data migration can cause saturation in the interconnection network.

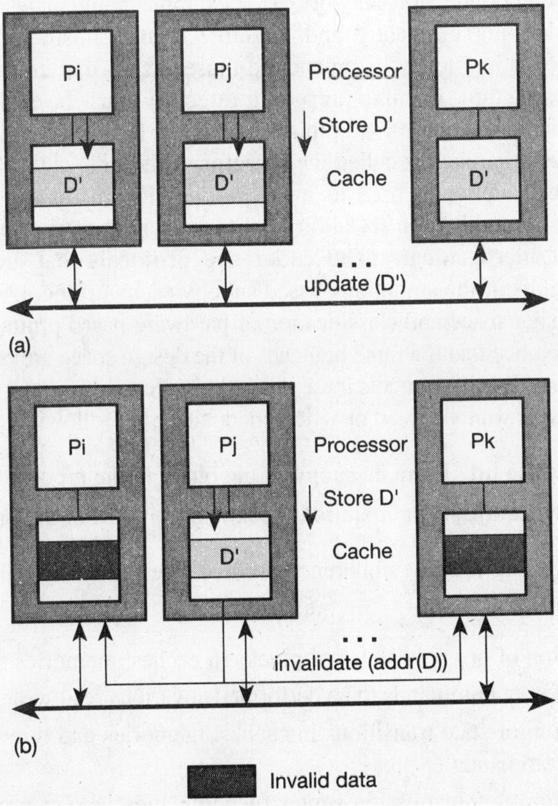

Figure 18.21 Cache coherence policies in writing shared data structures. (a) Write-update cache coherence policy; (b) write-invalidate cache coherence policy.

Moreover, this traffic is unnecessary in the case of infrequently used shared data. Cache controllers must be able to accept requests not only from their own processor but also from other cache controllers.

In the case of the **write-invalidate policy**, the updated cache block is not sent immediately to other caches; instead a simple invalidate command is sent to all other cached copies and to the original version in the shared memory so that they become invalid. If later another processor wants to read the data structure, it is provided by the updating processor. The mechanism of the write-invalidate policy is shown in Figure 18.21(b). The traffic on the interconnection network is significantly reduced compared with the write-update policy since the invalidate command requires sending only the address of the updated data structure. Furthermore, cache controllers have to accept only the invalidate command from other controllers.

Hardware-based protocols can be further classified into three basic classes depending on the nature of the interconnection network applied in the shared memory system. If the network efficiently supports broadcasting, the so-called **snoopy cache protocol** can be advantageously exploited. This scheme is typically used in single bus-based shared memory systems where consistency commands (invalidate or update commands) are broadcast via the bus and each cache 'snoops' on the bus for incoming consistency commands.

Large interconnection networks (for example, multistage networks) cannot support broadcasting efficiently and therefore a mechanism is needed that can directly forward consistency commands to those caches that contain a copy of the updated data structure. For this purpose a directory must be maintained for each block of the shared memory to administer the actual location of blocks in the possible caches. This approach is called the **directory scheme.**

The third approach tries to avoid the application of the costly directory scheme but still provide high scalability. It proposes multiple-bus networks with the application of **hierarchical cache coherence protocols** that are generalized or extended versions of the single bus-based snoopy cache protocol.

The design space and classification of hardware-based protocols are shown in Figure 18.22. Notice that the three branches of the design space are orthogonal, that is, for any hardware-based protocols these three choices can be used in any combination. When a processor wants to read or write a data block the following cases can occur:

- **Read/write hit**: There is a copy of the block in the processor's cache.
- **Read/write miss:** The required block is missing from the processor's cache.

In describing a cache coherence protocol the following definitions must be given:

- Definition of possible states of blocks in caches, memories and directories.
- Definition of commands to be performed at various read/write hit/miss actions.
- Definition of state transitions in caches, memories and directories according to the commands.
- Definition of transmission routes of commands among processors, caches, memories and directories.

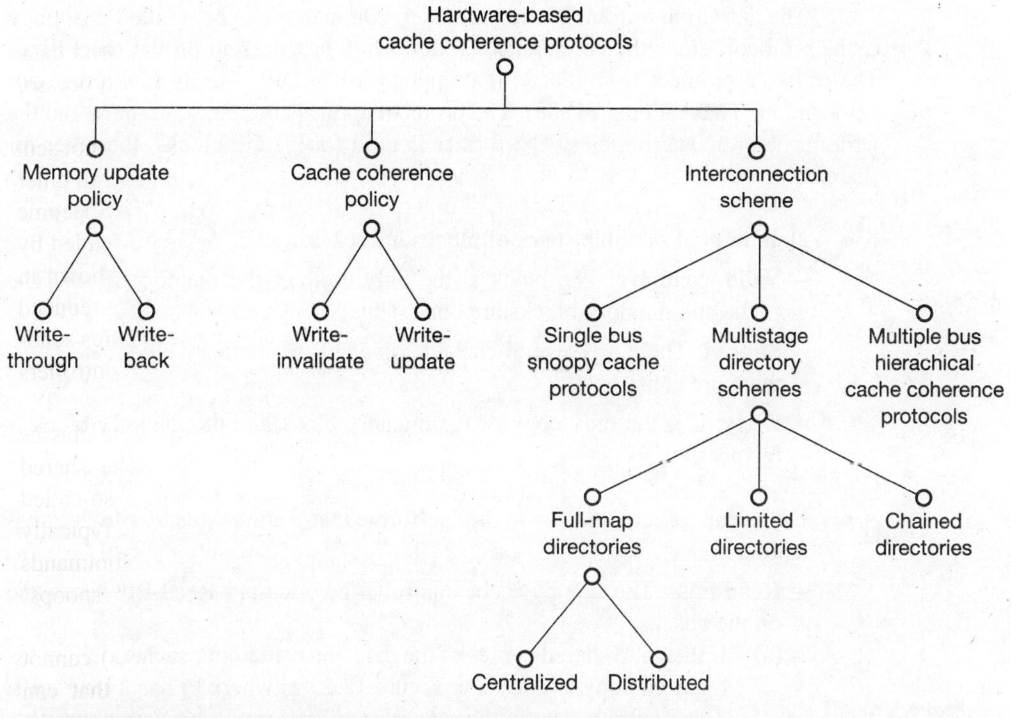

Figure 18.22 Design space of hardware-based cache coherence protocols.

In the next sections a detailed description of the cache coherence protocols related to the interconnection networks is given. The description of protocols is based on the definitions listed above.

Snoopy cache protocols

Snoopy cache protocols are very popular in shared bus multiprocessors due to their relative simplicity. They have both write-update and write-invalidate policy versions. Here, only a write-update snoopy cache protocol is explained in detail. Write-invalidate snoopy cache protocols resemble this protocol in many ways and therefore are also easy to understand after studying a write-update protocol. A good survey of several snoopy cache protocols can be found in Archibald and Baer (1986).

In describing a snoopy cache protocol the following definitions must be given:

- Definition of possible states of blocks in caches.
- Definition of commands to be performed at various read/write hit/miss actions.
- Definition of state transitions in caches and memories according to the commands.

The definition of transmission routes of commands can be omitted in snoopy cache protocols since the commands are uniformly broadcasted on the shared bus. The example protocol is similar to that applied in the DEC Firefly multiprocessor workstation (Thakkar et al., 1988). The protocol applies both the write-back and the write-through update policies. The former is used for private blocks, the latter for shared blocks.

- Definition of possible states of blocks in caches.
  - **Valid-exclusive**: The block is the only copy of the memory block. The cache and memory blocks are consistent.
  - **Shared**: There are several cached copies of the memory block and all of them are consistent.
  - **Dirty**: It is the only copy of the memory block and the memory block is inconsistent.

- Definition of commands to be performed at various read/write hit/miss actions.
  - **Read miss**: The snoopy cache controller broadcasts a Read-Blk command on the bus.
    (a) If there are shared copies of the data, the containing caches deliver the required copy as shown in Figure 18.23(a) where Pj has a read miss. The resulting state in the requester processor will be shared, too.
    (b) If a dirty copy exists, it supplies the necessary copy and updates the main memory, too. All the copies become shared. The mechanism is illustrated in Figure 18.23(b).
    (c) If a valid-exclusive copy exists, it supplies the necessary copy and all the copies become shared.
    (d) If there is no cache copy of the block, the memory sends the block which becomes valid-exclusive.
  - **Write hit**:
    (a) If the state of the block is valid-exclusive or dirty, the write operation can be performed locally (no command is placed on the bus) and the new state will be dirty (write-back policy).
    (b) If the block is shared, the snoopy cache controller broadcasts an Update-Blk command on the bus. The Update-Blk command contains the address and value of the updated data. All copies, including the memory one, will be updated (write-update, write-through policy) and remain shared.
  - **Write miss**: The snoopy cache controller broadcasts a Write-Blk command on the bus. The Write-Blk command contains the address and value of the updated data.
    (a) If only the memory contains the block, it will be updated with the new value of the updated data and the updated block is sent to the requester processor where it becomes valid-exclusive (see Figure 18.24(a)).

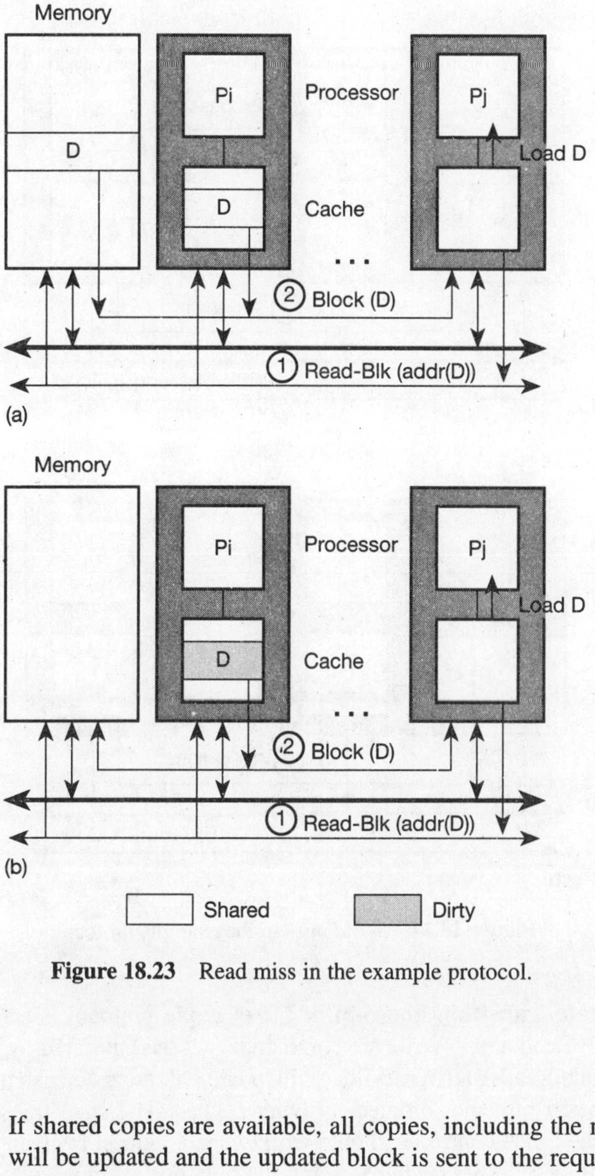

Figure 18.23 Read miss in the example protocol.

(b) If shared copies are available, all copies, including the memory one, will be updated and the updated block is sent to the requester processor as shown in Figure 18.24(b). The resulting state of all copies will be shared.

(c) If a dirty or valid-exclusive copy exists, it will be updated as well as the memory block, and the updated block is sent to the requester processor. The resulting state of all copies will be shared.

– **Replacement**: If the cache is full when a new block should be written into it, one of the blocks should be removed from the cache in order to replace it with the new block. If the block selected for replacement is a dirty one, the memory should be updated, otherwise no further action is necessary.

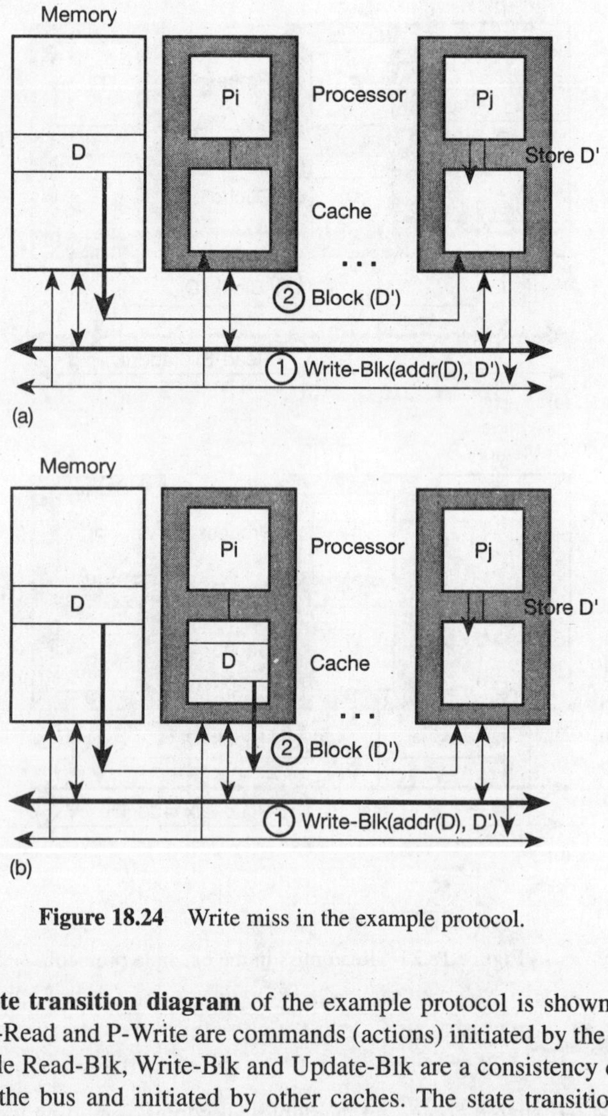

Figure 18.24 Write miss in the example protocol.

The **state transition diagram** of the example protocol is shown in Figure 18.25 where P-Read and P-Write are commands (actions) initiated by the associated processor, while Read-Blk, Write-Blk and Update-Blk are a consistency commands arriving from the bus and initiated by other caches. The state transition diagram defines how the cache controller should work when a request is given by the associated processor or by other caches through the bus. For example, when a Read-Blk command arrives at a cache block in a Dirty state, the cache controller should modify the state of the block to Shared.

The typical structure of a **snoopy cache controller** is depicted in Figure 18.26. It is constructed as a finite state machine which realizes the state transition diagram of the snoopy cache protocol. It comprises three main parts. The snoopy controller implements the snoopy cache protocol by continuously monitoring bus operations through the bus interface. The cache directory contains the state for each block (two bits/block in the case of the example protocol). The directory is often duplicated in order to avoid contention among commands arriving from the associ-

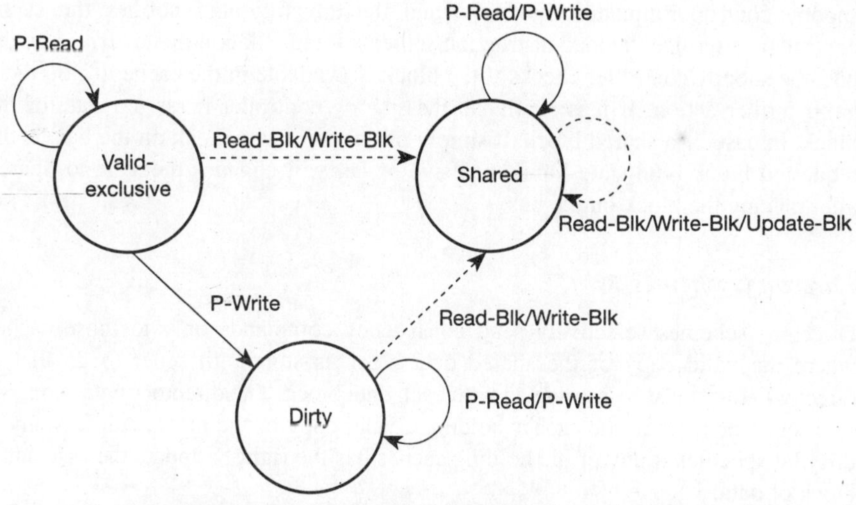

Figure 18.25 State transition graph of the example protocol.

ated processor and from the bus. The cache controller is similar to those employed in uniprocessor systems but it is extended to handle the cache directory, too. It realizes those parts of the state transition diagram of the snoopy cache protocol that are related to processor activity. For example, in the case of a load instruction the cache controller checks if the requested block is in the cache. If it is, it services the request locally. If not, it passes the request to the snoopy controller which generates a Read-Blk command on the system bus. When the requested block arrives, the

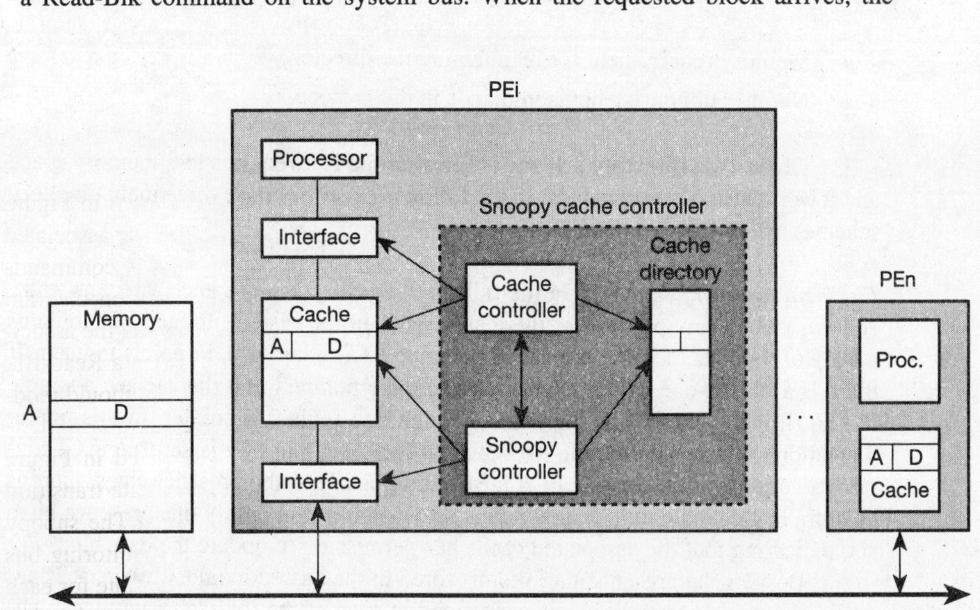

Figure 18.26 Structure of the snoopy cache controller.

snoopy controller updates the cache and the directory and notifies the cache controller to service the load instruction. When a Read-Blk command arrives on the bus, the snoopy controller checks if the block is available in the cache. If not, there is no further action. If it is available, the snoopy controller reads the state of the block. In case of a shared block, it simply places the cache block on the bus. If the requested block is in state Valid-exclusive or Dirty, it changes the state to Shared after placing the block on the bus.

Directory schemes

Directory schemes selectively send consistency commands only to those caches where the valid copy of the shared data block is stored. In order to do that, a directory entry must be associated with each data block. The directory entry consists of a set of pointers to the caches holding a valid copy of the block. Additionally, a dirty bit specifies if any of the holding caches has the right to update the associated block of data.

Three main approaches can be distinguished in the realization of directory schemes:

- Full-map directory
- Limited directory
- Chained directory.

These schemes differ in how the structure of the directories is organized. There are two metrics which should be considered in comparing the three approaches:

- Memory requirement for maintaining the directory
- Number of consistency commands in the protocols.

Obviously, a directory scheme is favourable if it requires less memory space and fewer consistency commands. In the following sections the three main directory schemes are described in detail.

Full-map directory scheme In the full-map directory scheme each directory entry consists of as many pointers as there are caches in the system. If cache Ci contains a copy of the data block, the pointer Pi points to Ci, otherwise, Pi points to itself. If there is a one-to-one correspondence among the pointers and the caches, a simple flag Fi (implemented as a single bit) is enough to replace a pointer. In this implementation structure, called the **presence flag vector**, a flag Fi is set true if Ci contains a valid copy, otherwise, Fi is false. Additionally to the presence flags, there is an extra flag called the dirty flag which is set when one and only one presence bit is set, indicating that the associated cache has permission to update the data block.

Besides the presence flag vector stored in the shared memory, two state flags (valid and write-permission) are maintained in each cache for each data block. The first is set if the block is valid, while the second is set if the cache has permission to write into the block. The cache coherence protocol is complemented by means of these flags and the presence flag vector. Stenström (1989) has proposed a modified version of the full-map directory scheme, where the presence flag vector is associated with the cached copy instead of the memory copy. This scheme has the advantages of both reducing the number of protocol messages via the interconnection network and reducing the necessary bit overhead of maintaining presence flag vectors.

Limited directory scheme The objective of introducing the limited directory scheme was to radically reduce the bit overhead compared with the full-map directory scheme. The observed feature of cache-based shared memory systems showed that in the vast majority of cases only a limited number of caches contained valid copies of the same data block. Therefore, maintaining a presence flag vector which contains a flag for each cache is superfluous in most cases and particularly in highly scalable shared memory systems where hundreds of processors (and therefore caches) are applied. Recoginizing this, Agarwal et al. (1988) proposed the use of limited directories.

From a logical point of view, the structure of the directory entries in the shared memory is very similar to that of the full-map scheme. There are two main differences. The number of pointers (k) in a directory entry is much smaller than the number of processors (n) in the shared memory system and these pointers are dynamically allocated for those caches that contain a copy of the associated data block. As a consequence, simple bits are not enough to represent pointers. In an n-processor system $\log_2 n$ bits are needed for defining a presence pointer and therefore, storing k pointers for each block of memory; the bit overhead of the limited directory is klog2n/block, while in the full-map scheme it is n/block. The bit overhead of the limited directory scheme is less than the full-map scheme if

$$k\log_2 n < n \quad \text{i.e. } k < \frac{n}{\log_2 n}$$

As long as the number of valid copies of a data block does not exceed k, the limited directory-based cache coherence protocol is very similar to the full-map scheme. The difference appears when more than k caches require read access to a data block. When cache Cn sends a read request to the shared memory and all available pointer places in the limited directory entry are filled with valid pointers, one of the copies of X in the caches must be invalidated and then the corresponding pointer can be replaced with a pointer to the requesting cache. This pointer replacement is called **eviction** and obviously needs a **selection policy**, which can be as simple as a pseudo-random eviction policy.

Chained directory scheme The chained directory scheme is a good compromise between the previous two schemes. It preserves the limited size of the central directory frames and even further restricts the number of presence pointers to one, and yet eviction becomes unnecessary. Dynamic extension of the number of presence pointers is achieved by distributing the extra presence pointers among the caches. Each data block in each cache is extended with a pointer that is used to chain the valid copies of a data block. The positive characteristic of this scheme is that it requires exactly as many presence pointers as there are valid copies of the data block. There is no superfluous presence pointers in the directory entries of the shared memory.

The creation of chained cached copies of shared data blocks are explained by means of Figure 18.27. When the first processor (P0) wants to read data block X, the memory sends a copy of X to C0, along with a special chain termination (CT) pointer, and sets a pointer to C0 in X's directory entry in the shared memory. After receiving a second read request for X from cache C1, the memory sends a copy of X to C1, along with the previously stored pointer to C0, which is now replaced by a pointer to C1 in X's directory entry. Cache C1 simply stores the incoming copy of X and the pointer to C0. Figure 18.27(b) illustrates the state of the shared memory and caches after these activities. By repeatedly performing similar activities, arbitrarily long chains can be dynamically constructed in a demand-driven way.

Suppose now that processor Pn wants to write data block X. In this case cache Cn sends a write request to the memory which has to send an invalidate request along the presence chain originating from the pointer stored in X's directory entry in the shared memory. The first invalidate request arrives at C1 which invalidates its copy of X and sends the invalidate request onto cache C0. Since C0 finds a CT pointer, it does not send the invalidate request any further after invalidating its copy of X, but sends an acknowledgement back to the memory. On receiving the acknowledgement from C0, the main memory controller sets X's dirty flag and sets X's presence pointer to Cn. Finally, it sends a copy of X and a write permission to cache Cn which sets the write-permission flag, updates block X and reactivates processor Pn.

Scalable Coherent Interface A concrete example of the chained directory is the Scalable Coherent Interface (SCI) defined by the IEEE standard 1596-1992. The SCI standard does not define a specific interconnect rather than an interface to the interconnection network. However, the point-to-point nature of the interface and the communication protocols fit well to a simple, uni-directional ring as applied in the Convex Exemplar machine (see Section 18.7.4). The major purpose of the SCI

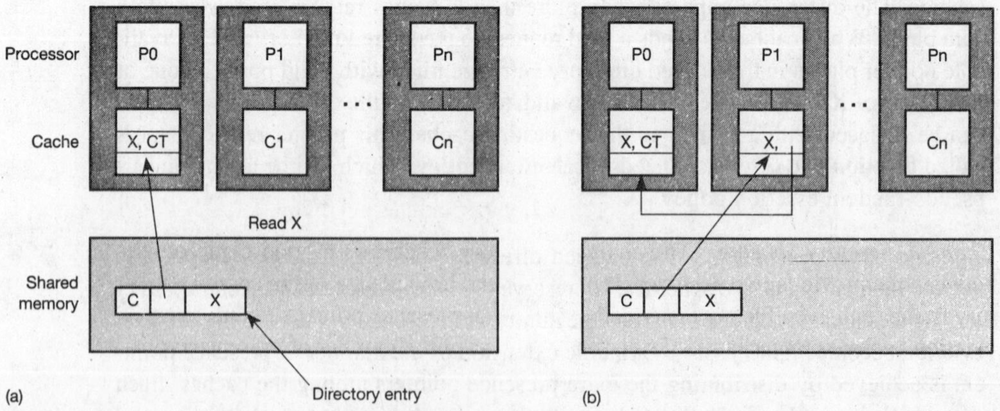

Figure 18.27 Chained directory scheme.

standard is to provide a memory-address-based, cache-coherent communication scheme for creating scalable parallel machines with large numbers of processors.

The SCI coherency protocol provides a scalable **linked list form of distributed directories**. The cache mechanism ensures simultaneous linked list modification by all the processors in a sharing-list for maximum concurrency. There are no locks and no resource choke points in the protocol, enabling it to scale with the number of processors in a linear manner. Any number of nodes can share the same memory line, and the size of the directory is proportional to the number of cache lines. Deletion of nodes from the sharing-list is fully decentralized, not requiring any central directory (memory) operation. Although the insertion is centralized, relying on central directory operations, combining list insertion requests is possible.

All SCI communications are organized in packets. The base protocol is a write-back and invalidate type that supports forward progress, delivery, fairness, basic error detection, and recovery.

The SCI organization is based on the so-called **sharing-list** in which each coherently cached block is chained up. The head element of the list points to the memory block where the associated memory line is stored as shown in Figure 18.28. The memory tag in each block of the memory is extended with the identifier of the head node of the sharing-list (forw_id field) and a 2-bit memory state (mstate field). The cache tags of blocks are extended with two identifiers; one for the previous node (back_id field) and one for the following node (forw_id field) of the sharing-list. Beside those fields, the cache unit contains the cache state (cstate field), too. The first cache element of the sharing-list uses the mem_id field to identify the memory block.

Four main operations are defined on the sharing-list:

- Creation
- Insertion
- Deletion
- Reduction to a single node.

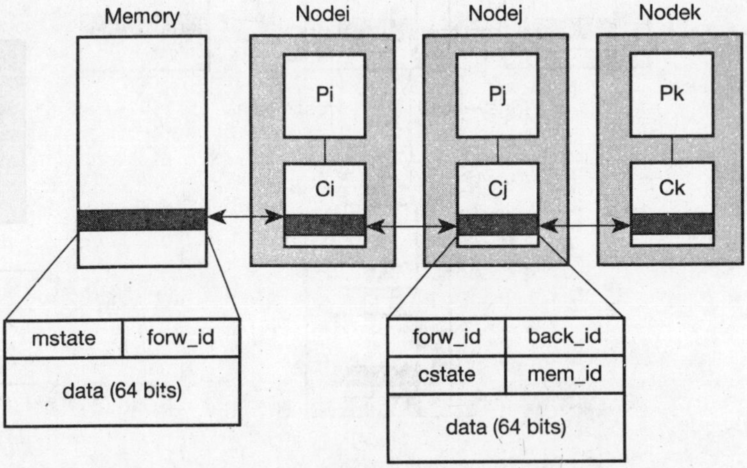

Figure 18.28 Structure of sharing-lists in the SCI.

Creation This is a simplified version of the insertion operation when the associated sharing-list is empty.

Insertion When a cache miss occurs (at Ci in Figure 18.29), the node sends a **prepend request** to the memory which responds with the pointer of the old head node and refreshes its head node pointer with the address of the requester. After receiving the **response** from the memory, the new head (if the sharing-list was not empty) notifies the old head node by sending a **new-head** request. The old head updates its backward pointer and returns its data field. The two transactions are illustrated in Figure 18.29 and the result of the transactions is the sharing-list shown in Figure 8.28.

Deletion When a node wants to remove its cache line from the sharing-list, it sends two messages. First, it sends an update backward request containing its backward pointer (Pb) to its successor. The successor will update its backward pointer by the value received in the request. The second message, an update forward request, is sent to the predecessor. This message contains the forward pointer of the requester and is used by the predecessor to update its forward pointer. The transactions and their result are illustrated in Figure 18.30.

Reduction to a single node When a cache line is written, all the other elements of the sharing-list must be invalidated. Only the head node has the right to update a cache line and to remove the other elements from the sharing-list. This is the reduction process and it is performed sequentially. The head sends a purge request to the second node of the list. This node returns its forward pointer, that is,

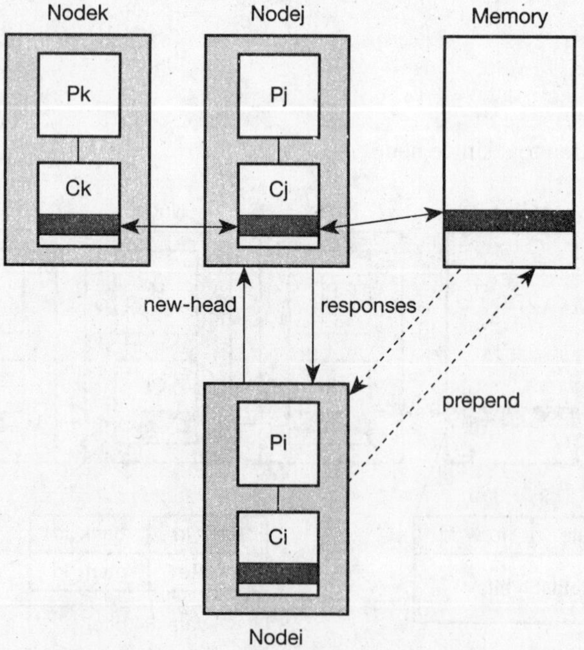

Figure 18.29 Insertion in a sharing-list.

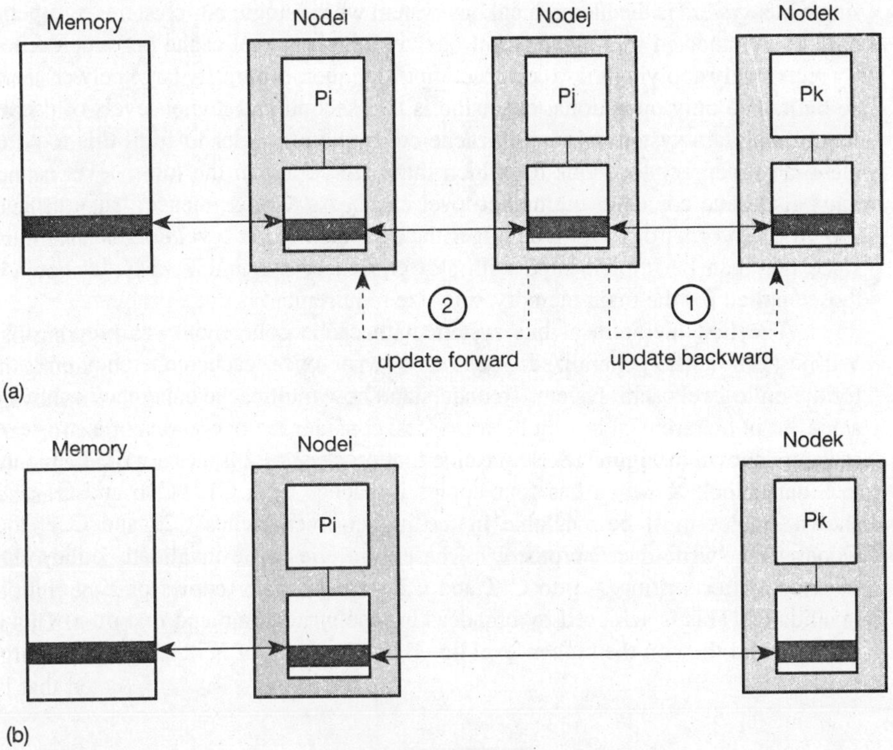

Figure 18.30 Deletion from a sharing-list. (a) Messages for deletion; (b) structure of the sharing-list after deletion.

the address of the next node in the list. Then, the head node sends a purge request to the third node, and so on until the last node receives the purge request. If a node different from the head wants to execute a write on a shared cache line, it has first to remove its cache line from the sharing-list and then to insert it. As a result the node becomes the head of the sharing-list, with the right to update its cache line.

Several insertion and deletion actions can be executed simultaneously on the same sharing-list. In the case of simultaneous prepend requests, the memory immediately responds in the order the requests arrive. However, the new head that won the competition will delay the other new heads until it has prepended itself to the sharing-list. Special precedence rules are applied in the case of simultaneous deletions among adjacent nodes. The node closer to the tail always has priority and is deleted first. A useful feature of simultaneous insertions is that they can be combined and, as a result, hot spots can be avoided. An optional extension of the SCI base protocol can optimize the sequential purge operation by replacing it with a parallel one (Gjessing et al., 1992).

Hierarchical cache coherent protocols

Hierarchical cache coherent protocols are applied in multiple bus multiprocessors which were introduced in Section 18.2.1. One of the natural generalizations of the single bus system is the hierarchical bus system where single bus clusters or 'supernodes' are connected to a higher-level bus via a higher-level cache or 'supercache'. By recursively applying these construction techniques, arbitrarily large networks can be built. The only operational extension is that second and higher levels of caches should maintain system-wide multicache coherency. In order to fulfil this requirement, any memory locations for which there are copies in the lower-level caches must also have copies in the higher-level cache. As a consequence, 'supercaches' should be an order of magnitude larger than the next lower-level caches. However, since they can be implemented with slower, denser dynamic RAMs, identical to those applied for the main memory, this size requirement is not a problem.

The first hierarchical bus system with cache coherency was proposed by Wilson (1987) who generalized Goodman's 'write-once' cache coherency protocol for the multilevel cache system. To understand how multicache coherency control is achieved in hierarchical bus multiprocessors, consider the operations of a two-level structure shown in Figure 18.31. Assume that processor P2 issues a write command to a data block X which has four copies in caches C11, C12, C16 and C17. As shown, copies must be available in the higher-level caches C20 and C22, too. Goodman's 'write-once' protocol is based on the write-invalidate policy and therefore, after writing X into C12 and C20, all the other copies of X should be invalidated. This is achieved by broadcasting the write command first on low-level bus B10 and then on the higher-level bus B20. The copy of X in C11 is invalidated

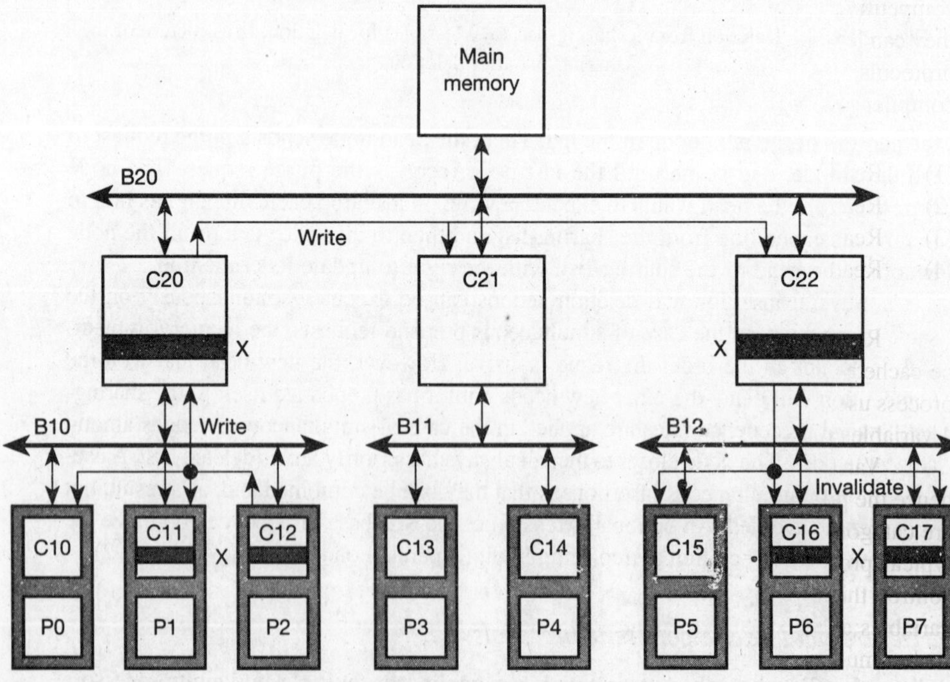

Figure 18.31 Hierarchical cache coherence.

by the write command on bus B10. When the write command appears on bus B20, second-level caches check if they have a copy of X. When C22 detects a write command to X and finds a copy of X, it must invalidate its own copy and send down an invalidate command to bus B12 where copies of X in C16 and C17 must be invalidated. The final result is that only the first- and second-level caches associated with the updating processor (C12 and C20) have copies of X. A subsequent read request issued by another processor (for example, P5) should be broadcasted at the lower level, and since there is no copy at that level it should be propagated up the hierarchy. When C20 detects the read request for X and finds that it has a dirty copy of X, it supplies the dirty copy of X to cache C15 and issues a flush request down to bus B10 where cache C12 will relinquish exclusive access.

Notice that second-level caches that have no copies of the written data block work as filters during the invalidate or read operations. In the current example cache C21 did not send any command to bus B11. As a result, clusters where there is no copy of the updated data block are not affected at all by the hierarchical cache coherence protocol.

18.3.3 Software-based protocols

Although hardware-based protocols offer the fastest mechanism for maintaining cache consistency, they introduce a significant extra hardware complexity, particularly in scalable multiprocessors. Software-based approaches represent a good and competitive compromise since they require nearly negligible hardware support and they can lead to the same small number of invalidation misses as the hardware-based protocols. All the software-based protocols rely on compiler assistance. The compiler analyses the program and classifies the variables into four classes:

(1) Read-only
(2) Read-only for any number of processes and read-write for one process
(3) Read-write for one process
(4) Read-write for any number of processes.

Read-only variables can be cached without restrictions. Type 2 variables can be cached only for the processor where the read-write process runs. Since only one process uses type 3 variables it is sufficient to cache them only for that process. Type 4 variables must not be cached in software-based schemes.

Variables demonstrate different behaviour in different program sections and hence the program is usually divided into sections by the compiler and the variables are categorized independently in each section. For example, a parallel for-loop is a typical program section. More than that, the compiler generates instructions that control the cache or access the cache explicitly based on the classification of variables and code segmentation. Typically, at the end of each program section the caches must be invalidated to ensure that the variables are in a consistent state before starting a new section. According to how invalidation is done, two main schemes can be distinguished:

- Indiscriminate invalidation
- Selective invalidation.

The simplest approach is indiscriminate invalidation in which the *complete cache* is invalidated at the end of each program section. This scheme requires a single hardware mechanism for turning on or off and invalidating the cache. However, it is very conservative, and invalidates variables that could be used in the same cache in the next program section.

Selective invalidation schemes can be further categorized according to the generation of program sections:

- Critical section scheme
- Parallel for-loop scheme.

The **critical section scheme** relies on the assumption that shared read-write variables are always accessed in critical sections guarded by software synchronization tools. These variables are selectively invalidated when the critical section is completed. In order to do that, shared variables belonging to the same critical section are placed on the same page and each page is associated with a one-time identifier. Loading a cache line will also place the associated one-time identifier in the cache. Invalidation is based on the one-time identifiers.

Three parallel for-loop selective invalidation schemes were proposed to eliminate the drawback of indiscriminate invalidation:

- Fast selective invalidation
- Timestamp scheme
- Version control scheme.

The fast selective invalidation scheme (Cheong and Veidenbaum, 1988) relies on a write-through cache policy and introduces three instructions to control cache accesses: Memory-Read, Cache-Read and Cache-Invalidate. Cache-Read is applied to access a variable when it is guaranteed that the variable is stable in the cache, otherwise the Memory-Read command is used. An extra bit, called the change bit, is added to each cache line. The Cache-Invalidate command sets all change bits true. An attempt to read a variable with its change bit set true will lead to a read from memory. As a second effect the change bit is modified to false and hence forthcoming accesses can be satisfied by the cache.

The timestamp scheme (Min and Baer, 1989) allocates a clock to each data structure and a timestamp entry to each cache line. The clock associated with a data structure is updated at the end of each program section when the data structure was updated. The timestamps in the cache directory are set to the value of the corresponding clock+1 when the block is updated in the cache. By comparing the timestamp and the associated clock value, it can be decided whether the variable in the cache is valid (timestamp > clock) or whether it should be loaded from memory.

Notice that in the timestamp scheme, invalidations for variables that are local to a processor in two subsequent program sections can be omitted since the timestamp value of these variables exceeds their clock value.

A similar method called the version control scheme was proposed in Cheong and Veidenbaum (1990) in order to avoid unnecessary invalidations. The main idea of this method is that only one process in a program section is permitted to write a variable and this writing generates a new version of the variable. When the writing process exits its program section, the new version becomes the current version which can be used by other processors, too. In order to recognise whether a variable in the cache of a processor is valid, two new data structures are introduced. First, each processor maintains a counter, called the current version number (CVN), for each variable it can use. Second, each cache line is extended with a tag called the birth version number (BVN). The CVN represents the version of the variable that the processor must use, while the BVN represents a particular version to which the cache copy belongs. A cache miss occurs when the CVN is greater than the BVN; otherwise, the variable can be accessed from the cache.

The categorization of software-based cache coherent protocols is shown in Figure 18.32. Software support to reduce the complexity of hardware necessary to maintain cache coherency is an important active research area in order to reduce the hardware cost of scalable parallel computers.

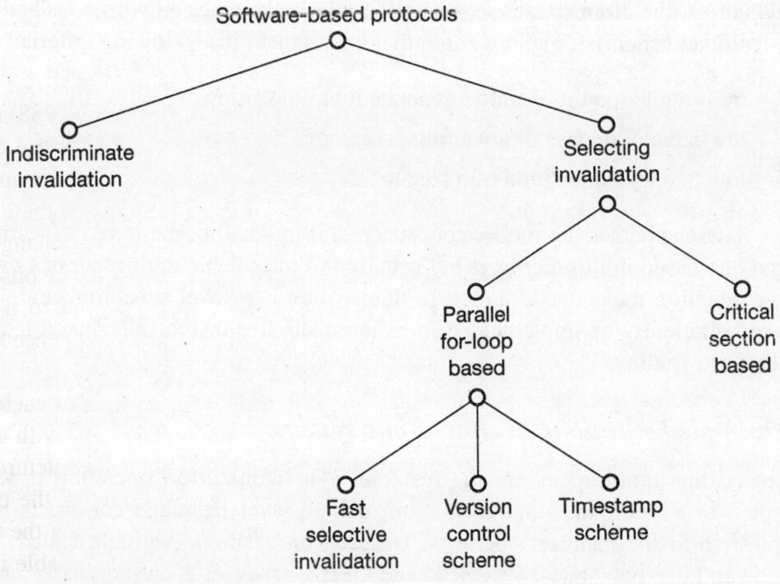

Figure 18.32 Classification of software-based cache coherence protocols.

18.4 Synchronization and event ordering in multiprocessors

There are two levels of exploiting parallelism in a multiprocessor. At the higher level, the program is partitioned into processes that are executed on different processors. This technique is called **concurrent processing**. At the lower level, memory accesses within a process could be overlapped with other accesses in order to reduce load/store latency stemming from cache miss. This technique of hiding latency is known as **access pipelining**. Another form of hiding latency, called **access buffering**, is when memory accesses within a process are overlapped with other computations.

In order to synchronize concurrent processes, special synchronizing software tools are used that are usually supported by hardware mechanisms. The lowest level of these structures is the lock mechanism, the hardware/software implementation of which gives rise to special problems in cache coherent multiprocessors. These implementation techniques are examined in the next two sections.

Access buffering and access pipelining also require special attention in cache coherent shared memory systems. The ordering of load/store events and maintaining the correct order require new memory models which are the subject of Section 18.4.2.

18.4.1 Synchronization mechanisms in multiprocessors

Mutual exclusion and other synchronization problems can be solved by high-level synchronization language constructs like semaphores, conditional critical regions, monitors, and so on. All of these high-level schemes are based on low-level synchronization tools realized or supported by hardware. In cache coherent architectures, the atomic test&set operation is usually replaced with a cached **test-and-test&set** scheme for spin waiting that has to meet the following criteria:

- minimum amount of traffic generated while waiting
- low latency release of a waiting processor
- low latency acquisition of a free lock.

These schemes are moderately successful in small cache-based systems like shared bus-based multiprocessors but usually fail in scalable multiprocessors where high-contention locks are frequent. In this section low-level synchronization tools that can efficiently be implemented in either small-size or scalable shared memory systems are studied.

Lock implementations in shared bus systems

In shared bus multiprocessors the **test&set synchronization** operation is widely accepted to support the implementation of high-level language constructs. In its simplest form the test&set operation is based on a simple variable called 'lock' which can have two states: CLOSED and OPEN. test&set is an indivisible, atomic operation on the lock variable defined by the following C program:

```
char *lock;
while (exchange(lock, CLOSED) == CLOSED);
```

Exchange (value1,value2) is usually a CPU instruction meaning that the value of the second parameter (value2) should be exchanged with the value of the memory location given by the first argument (value1) and the latter value should be returned as a result of the instruction. The instruction exchange requires two memory cycles: the first for reading value1 and the second for writing value2. Atomic operation means that during the execution of these two memory cycles the shared bus must not be granted to any other processor in the system. Since in shared bus systems the bus arbiter logic is responsible for bus allocation, the bus arbiter is also responsible for realizing the atomic exchange operation. For example, in the Intel 80386 family a special LOCK control line forces the arbiter logic to suspend bus arbitration for the second cycle of the exchange instruction. After finishing the exchange instruction, the LOCK control line re-enables the bus arbiter which can now allocate the shared bus to another processor.

One of the main problems of implementing synchronization schemes in cache coherent architectures is in deciding what happens if the test&set operation failed, that is, the lock was in the CLOSED state. Obviously, as the definition of the test&set operation shows, the processor should repeat the operation for as long as the lock is CLOSED. This is a form of **busy waiting** which ties up the processor in an idle loop and increases the shared bus traffic and contention. This type of lock which relies on busy waiting is called a **spin-lock** and is considered to be a significant cause of performance degradation when a large number of processes use it simultaneously.

The use of spin-locks in cache-based multiprocessors gives rise to a new problem, called **thrashing**. Assume that processor Pi successfully executes a test&set operation on lock. As a result, a dirty copy of lock remains in cache Ci (Figure 18.33(a)). A subsequent test&set operation on lock by Pj causes cache Ci to send a copy of lock to Cj and both copies become shared. Notice that fetching a block from a remote cache requires a much longer time than fetching a single byte from main memory. Moreover, the second phase of test&set must write lock, which entails sending an invalidate command on the shared bus and makes the copy of lock in Cj dirty (Figure 18.33(b)). When Pj finishes the test&set operation, a fair bus arbitration policy allocates the shared bus to another processor Pk, which wants to perform test&set on lock, too. Obviously, the same bus operations are required and performed again and finally, Ck contains a dirty copy of lock (Figure 18.33(c)). Since the test&set operation of Pj failed, Pj again attempts to execute test&set. As a result, the block of lock is copied back to Cj, and so on. Cj and Ck play ping-pong with the block of lock as long as Pi holds the lock in state CLOSED.

To avoid this situation spin-locks should be replaced by other types of locks in cache-based multiprocessors. One possible candidate is the so-called **snooping lock** which relies on the same hardware support but is defined by a different software algorithm:

```
while (exchange(lock, CLOSED) == CLOSED)
      while (*lock == CLOSED);
```

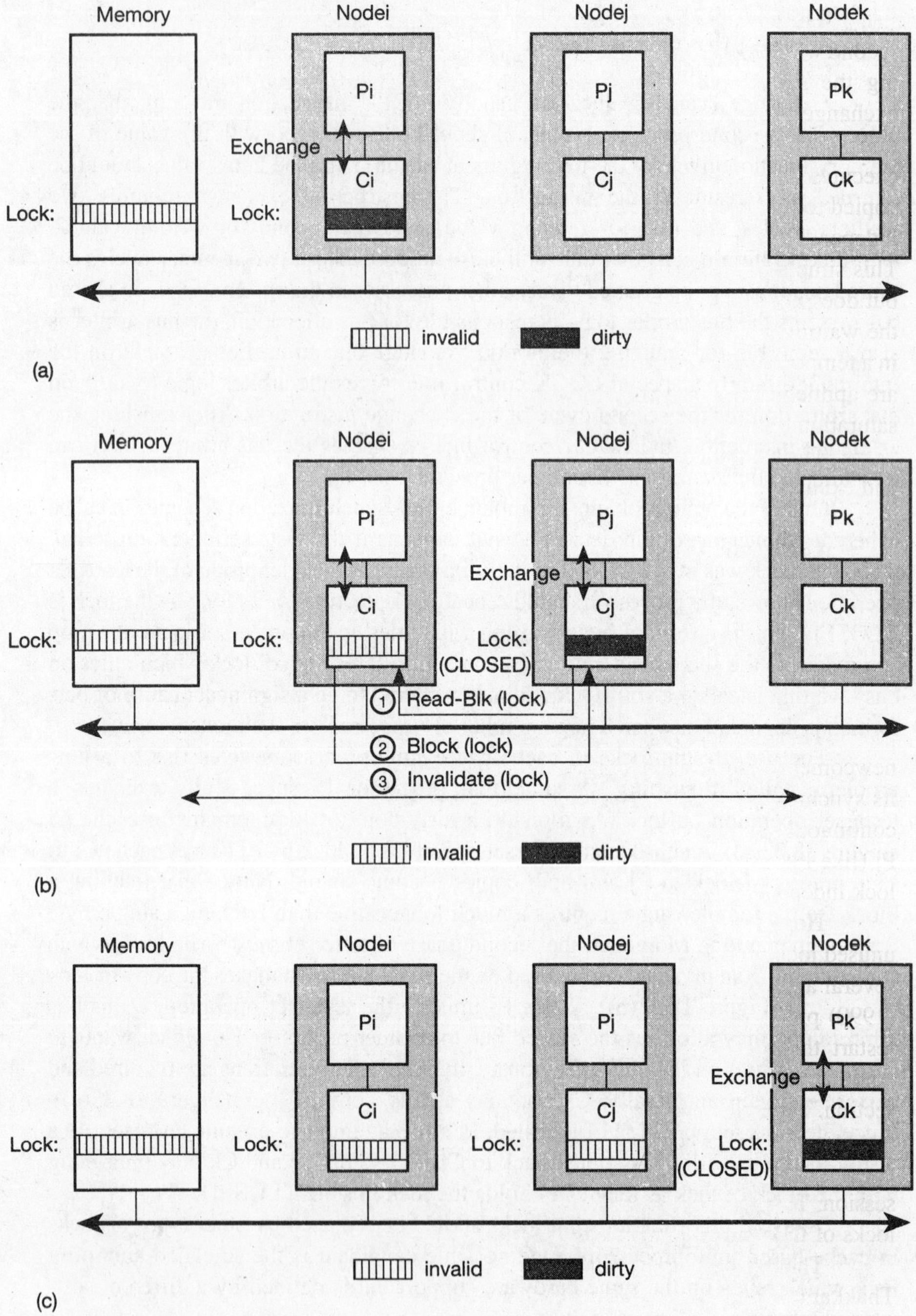

Figure 18.33 Cache implementation of spin-locks. (a) Cache states after Pi successfully executed test&set on lock; (b) bus commands when Pj executes test&set on lock and cache states after; (c) cache states after Pk executed test&set on lock.

The advantage of this approach comes from the introduction of the simplified second while loop which can be executed on the cached copy of lock without accessing the shared bus since it only reads lock. The situation after executing the exchange operations by Pj and Pk is identical to that of the spin-lock implementation shown in Figure 18.33(c). However, the continuation is different. When Pj executes the `*lock==CLOSED` test instruction, the dirty block of lock from Ck is copied to Cj and both blocks become shared. Afterwards the two copies can be read independently and in parallel by Pj and Pk without any access to the common bus. This simple modification of the test&set algorithm eliminates the ping-pong effect but does not solve every problem. When the locking processor Pi releases the lock, the waiting processors compete to execute their exchange operations which results in a temporary bus saturation. The problem is not too serious if large critical sections are applied in the program. However, in the case of short critical sections the bus saturation can become continuous due to the frequent exchange operations.

The solution can be further improved by exchanging the order of the test loop and exchange instruction:

```
for (;;) {
    while (*lock == CLOSED);
    if (exchange(lock, CLOSED) != CLOSED)
        break;
}
```

This variation, called the **test-and-test&set** scheme, has the advantage that a newcomer processor does not disturb the waiting processors. Assume that Pj starts its synchronization action when Pi is already engaged in its critical section and Pk continuously executes its synchronization action in order to enter its critical section. Pj (like Pk) receives a shared copy of the lock on which it can test the state of the lock independently from the other processors.

However, the simple solution shown above introduces extra latency for unused locks and cannot prevent bus saturation when the lock is released. There are several approaches to remedy the bus saturation situation at lock release. Anderson (1990) proposed **collision avoidance locks** which enable the waiting processes to restart the exchange operation after a lock release with a different delay time. Another approach applies a tree of locks in which the root lock protects the critical section. The tree forms a tournament for competitive processes. The winner of a contest at a lower level becomes a contestant at the next level. When finally a process reaches the root lock and wins the contest it has permission to enter its critical session. This kind of aggregate of locks is called **tournament locks**. The individual locks of the tournament are constructed as snooping locks.

The most effective lock type, the **queue lock**, was proposed in Graunke and Thakkar (1990). The structure of a queue lock is more complicated than a single byte representing the CLOSED or OPEN state. It actually contains in an array as many such bytes as there are processes using the lock for synchronization. More than that, each process can define in the array what it specifies as a locking state. The main idea of the queue lock is that processes are waiting for the lock in a queue (represented by the lock array) from which they are served in a first-in-first-out way. Accordingly, there is no competition after an unlock operation; only the 'next' process can relock the lock. Moreover, relocking does not need any write operation and hence, the relocking process enters into the critical section without requiring any shared bus operation for accessing the queue lock.

Lock implementations in scalable multiprocessors

The collision problem on a lock is even more serious in scalable multiprocessors where hundreds of processors can compete for the same lock. The memory location of the lock becomes a hot spot which can significantly enlarge latency in the interconnection network.

In order to reduce the hot-spot problem in the NYU Ultracomputer and in the IBM RP3 multiprocessor a new read-modify-write primitive, called **fetch&add**, was introduced. The definition of the fetch&add primitive is as follows:

```
fetch&add( x, a )
int *x, a;
{   int temp;
    temp = *x;
    *x = *x + a;
    return( temp );
}
```

The fetch&add primitive is by definition atomic, just like the test&set primitive. For the efficient implementation of fetch&add all the memory modules are augmented with an adder circuit. Thus it is sufficient to lock the variable x only for two memory cycles, which otherwise would have required 10–20 cycles. Moreover, to avoid the hot-spot problem the fetch&add operation can also be combined with the applied omega network in which all switches are enhanced with adder circuits.

Consider the implementation of DOALL loops using the fetch&add primitive. The original DOALL loop is:

```
DOALL N=1 to 1000
        <loop body using N>
ENDDO
```

The equivalent implementation the fetch&add primitive is using:

```
i = fetch&add(N,1);
while (i <= 1000) {
     loop_body(i);
     i = fetch&add(N,1);
}
```

After initializing N to 1 each processor executes a fetch&add operation on N before entering the loop. The fetch&add returns with different values which are used by the processors as an index in the loop_body procedure. The work of the combining network in realizing the distributed fetch&add operation for eight processors is depicted in Figure 18.34. For simplicity, only those arcs are drawn that are active during the fetch&add operation. Figure 18.34(a) shows how the combining switches propagate the fetch&add messages towards the memory module. One of the incoming messages is stored in the switch while the other one is forwarded with an increment which is the sum of the original increments. When the last fetch&add message arrives at the memory module it contains the sum of all the increments: fetch&add(N, 8) indicated as F & A (N, 8) in Figure 8.34. The memory block (M6) returns the initial value of N(1) and updates it by the increment of the arriving fetch&add message, i.e. the new value of N will be 9 in the memory. Notice that the switches operate as a distributed parallel adder (their structure is shown in Figure 18.19). The back propagation of the result can be followed on Figure 18.34(b). The result arriving back on the output arc of a switch is copied to one of the input arcs. On the other input arc the sum of the incoming result and the stored increment is forwarded back. Finally, each processor receives a unique value in the range 1–8.

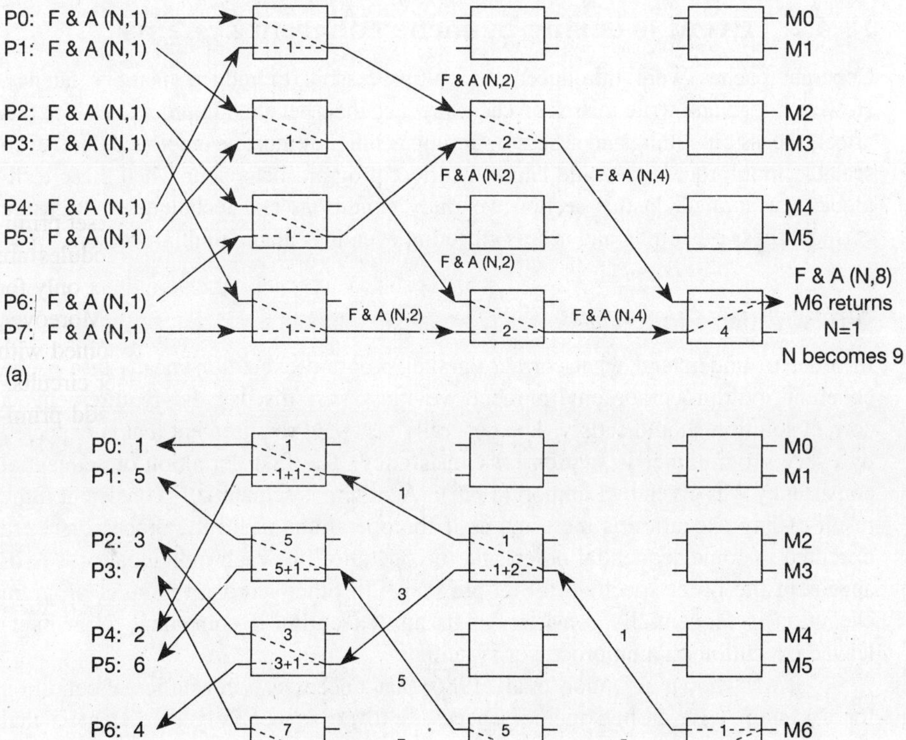

Figure 18.34 Distributed execution of fetch&add in a combining omega network. (a) Propagation of fetch&add operation through combining switches to M6 containing the value N=1; (b) back propagation of results.

One can conclude that when N processors attempt to perform fetch&add operations at the same memory location (potential hot spot), the memory is updated only once (no hot spot) by the sum of the N increments. The returned values are unique and correspond to an arbitrary sequential execution of the N fetch&adds but they are performed in one operation.

Additionally to the fetch&add operation, in the Dash architecture the so-called **queue-based locks** are introduced to support synchronization on high-contention locks. Dash applies a directory-based cache coherent scheme (see Section 18.7.2 for details) which is extended with queue-based locks indicating which processors are spinning on the lock. When the lock is released, only one node (which is actually a four-processor cluster) is chosen at random and informed by the directory. This solution eliminates unnecessary traffic and latency among the nodes. The grant request invalidates only the selected node's caches and enables one of the waiting processors in that node to acquire the lock. A time-out mechanism on the lock grant permits the grant to be sent to another node if the spinning process has been migrated or swapped out.

18.4.2 Event ordering in cache coherent systems

Coherent caches were introduced in multiprocessors to reduce memory latency. However, read and write misses on caches reduce their benefits. In order to reduce this effect, access pipelining and access buffering techniques must be employed. However, scalable multiprocessors could cause incorrect program behaviour when these techniques are applied. In this section we study conditions and techniques that ensure correct access pipelining and access buffering even in scalable multiprocessors.

Strong ordering of events

In order to understand what correct parallel program execution means in a cache coherent multiprocessor environment we must first discuss the requirements a correct solution should satisfy. The generally accepted requirement that is expected by every programmer is **sequential consistency**. The first definition of sequential consistency was given by Lamport (1979): 'A system is sequentially consistent if the result of any execution is the same as if the operations of all the processors were executed in some sequential order, and the operations of each individual processor appear in the order specified by its program.' In other words, a parallel program execution is sequentially consistent if its any execution is equivalent to an interleaved execution on a uniprocessor system.

It was shown in Dubois et al. (1986) that a necessary and sufficient condition for a system with atomic memory accesses to be sequentially consistent is that memory accesses should be performed in program order. Systems for which such a condition holds are called **strongly ordered systems**. A *memory access is atomic* if its effect is observable for each processor of the parallel computer at the same time. It can be shown that memory accesses in parallel systems without caches are always atomic and hence, for them it is sufficient to be strongly ordered in order to maintain sequential consistency.

When caches are added to the processors, memory access can become non-atomic. Fortunately, memory accesses remain atomic in shared bus multiprocessors because of the simultaneous broadcast capability of the buses. In such systems the invalidations are latched simultaneously by all the cache and memory controllers. However, the use of coherent caches in multiprocessors with scalable interconnection networks (for example, packet-switched networks) gave rise to a new problem that did not occur in previous parallel computers: **non-atomic memory accesses**, where the effect of memory accesses spreads through the system at different speeds to different processors, that is, processors can observe the same memory access at distinct times. It has been shown that for such systems it is not sufficient to be strongly ordered to ensure sequential consistency.

To illustrate the problem, consider a simple example shown by Dubois et al., (1988) where three processors want to access the memory cells A and B in the following order:

P1: ..., store A, ...
P2: ..., load A, store B, ...
P3: ..., load B, load A, ...

Assume that each processor executes the memory accesses in the order specified by the program and that each starts a new access when the previously issued one is completely finished with respect to all the processors. Yet, it can happen that a processor Pi can observe an out-of-date memory value even although the indirect effect of the new updated value has already reached Pi. This is an unexpected behaviour contradicting the sequential consistency model upon which current programs are written.

First, examine how this unexpected behaviour can occur in a packet-switched network where processors are equipped with coherent caches that work according to the write-invalidate protocol. Assume that initially each processor has a read-only copy of A and B in its cache.

Step 1. P1 issues a store operation on A that invalidates the other copies.

Step 2. P2 performs a read operation to get the new value of A since the invalidation message has already arrived in its cache. As a result of the read operation, P1 writes back the new value of A into the memory and sends a copy to P2. Since the load operation finished successfully, Processor 2 executes a store operation on B that invalidates the copy of B in the cache of P3.

Step 3. P3 reads the new value of B as updated by P2 because the invalidation message from B has already arrived. However, P3 reads the old value of A because the associated invalidation message has not yet reached P3.

Notice that the reason for not satisfying sequential consistency in the above example is the unequal speed of invalidation messages, that is, the presence of non-atomic memory accesses. If a hardware mechanism could restore the atomicity of memory accesses, sequential consistency could be satisfied in scalable multiprocessors, too. However, the question arises: do we really need sequential consistency?

Before answering the question let us examine what kind of event ordering is necessary to ensure sequential consistency. It has been shown that the following event ordering is sufficient to maintain sequential consistency:

> All previous loads must be globally performed and all previous store accesses must be performed before a load or store is allowed to perform with respect to any other processor.

A load is **globally performed** if it is performed and if the store that is the source of its returned value has been performed. An access (load or store) is **performed** if it is performed with respect to all processors. A load by P_i is **performed with respect to P_k** when the issuing of a store by P_k cannot affect the value returned by the load. A store by P_i is **performed with respect to P_k** when a load issued to the same address by P_k returns the value defined by this store.

Sequential consistency is the strongest possible requirement for the logical behaviour of parallel systems and its strict implementation significantly restricts the achievable parallelism. Fortunately, the condition of strong ordering can be relaxed in order to improve the performance of multiprocessors. A slightly relaxed version of sequential consistency, called **processor consistency**, has been proposed by Goodman (1989). The following event orderings should hold to satisfy processor consistency:

- All previous loads must be performed before a load is allowed to perform with respect to any other processor.
- All previous loads and stores must be performed before a store is allowed to perform with respect to any other processor.

Weak ordering of events

Those systems that are able to further relax the conditions of event ordering by relating memory request ordering to synchronizing points of the program are called **weakly ordered systems**. Two consistency models have been proposed to build weakly ordered systems. The first was introduced in Dubois et al. (1986) and is called the **weak consistency model**; the second, called the **release consistency model**, is described in Gharachorloo et al. (1990). Before the models are explained in detail some definitions and concepts must be described.

First, shared writable accesses should be classified according to their relationships (Figure 18.35). They can be either **competing** or **ordinary accesses**. An access is competing if it includes a pair of **conflicting accesses** that are not ordered and are executed by different processors. Two accesses are conflicting if they refer the same memory location and at least one of them is a store operation. Competing accesses can be either **synchronization accesses** or **non-synchronization accesses**. Synchronization accesses have two distinctive features: (1) they consist of one read and one write access to the same variable; and (2) they serve for ordering conflicting accesses, that is, making them non-competing. Typical

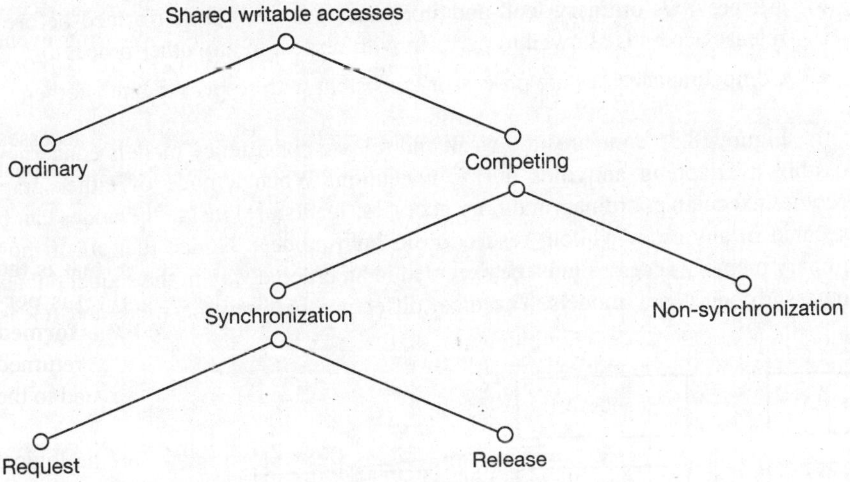

Figure 18.35 Classification of shared writable variable accesses (Gharachorloo et al., 1990). © 1990 IEEE

examples are the lock and unlock operations. Synchronization accesses can be further divided into **request** and **release accesses**. A request is always considered as a read (load) synchronization access, and release as a write (store) access.

The memory consistency models can be categorized according to how deeply they exploit the classification tree of shared writable accesses. The sequential and processor consistency models cannot distinguish shared writable accesses at all. They handle all such accesses in a uniform way. The weak consistency model can exploit all the categories except for the request and release types. Accordingly, the conditions to ensure weak consistency are as follows:

- All previous synchronization accesses must be performed before an ordinary load or store access is allowed to perform with respect to any other processor.
- All previous ordinary load and store accesses must be performed before a synchronization access is allowed to perform with respect to any other processor.
- Synchronization accesses are sequentially consistent with respect to one another.

Notice that weak consistency enables ordinary accesses to be executed in any order, which means a significant improvement in exploiting access pipelining and access buffering. The release consistency model further improves the weak consistency model by distinguishing request and release accesses. The conditions to ensure release consistency are as follows:

- All previous request accesses must be performed before an ordinary load or store access is allowed to perform with respect to any other processor.

- All previous ordinary load and store accesses must be performed before a release access is allowed to perform with respect to any other processor.
- Competing accesses are processor-consistent with respect to one another.

Figure 18.36 compares the weak and release consistency models concerning possible overlapping activities during execution. When a node of either graph becomes executable, ordinary memory accesses (load/store) inside the nodes can be executed in any order without restriction in both models. Notice that all of those ordinary memory accesses must be executed in an ordered way in the sequential and processor consistency models. The main difference between the weak and release

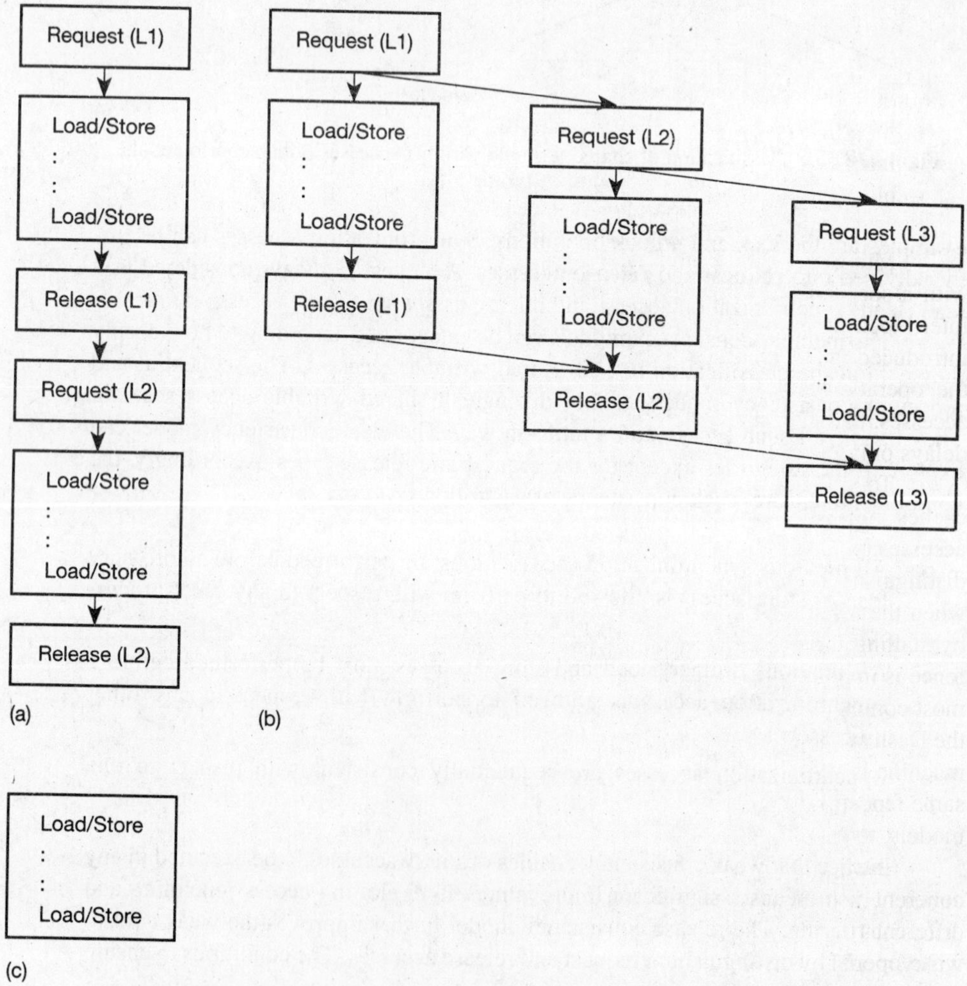

Figure 18.36 Comparison of the weak and release consistency models (Gharachorloo et al., 1990). (a) Weak consistency; (b) release consistency; (c) load and store operations can be executed in any order. © 1990 IEEE

consistency models is in the enabling of the execution of nodes in the graphs. In the release consistency model distinct critical sections (guarded by distinct locks) can be executed in an overlapped way as the figure illustrates, whereas in the weak consistency model the critical sections must be executed in a sequentially ordered way.

Implementation of memory consistency models

We have reached the point where we can answer the question whether we really need to support the realization of sequential consistency in a scalable multiprocessor. It turned out that the release consistency model provides a much higher degree of overlapping than the sequential consistency model and hence, the implementation of the release consistency model is much more preferable. Two cases should be distinguished in the implementation:

- Inter-block access ordering, that is, ordering accesses to distinct memory blocks
- Intra-block access ordering, that is, ordering accesses to the same memory block.

Multiprocessors with scalable interconnection networks must be provided with a special hardware mechanism called a **fence** in order to ensure appropriate inter-block access ordering for release consistency. Several fence operations were introduced in Gharachorloo et al. (1990) according to the operations they delay and the operations they wait upon. The **full fence** delays all future read and write accesses, the **write fence** delays all future write accesses, and the **immediate fence** delays only the access immediately following the fence.

To implement fences, acknowledgement messages from target memories and caches must be introduced. The processor must administrate the outstanding accesses by handling as many counters as there are different kinds of accesses to be distinguished. A counter is incremented when an access is issued and decremented when the associated acknowledgements come back. The full fence is implemented by stalling the processor until the necessary counters become zero, and the write fence is implemented by stalling the write buffer. The immediate fence requires the most complicated hardware support. The fence operations were first implemented in the Dash architecture and their realization is shown in Section 18.7.2 where the Dash machine is described in detail. It was shown in Gharachorloo et al. (1990) that the same fence operations are suitable for realizing the other three memory consistency models, too.

Intra-block ordering of accesses is necessary in an invalidation-based cache coherent multiprocessor where invalidations may reach different processors at different times and acknowledgement messages are necessary to indicate that the write operation has finished. There are two options to handle read and ownership requests to a block with pending invalidates:

- The request is delayed until the invalidations are complete. This solution results in an atomic store operation.

- The request is serviced but the requesting processor is notified that the acknowledgement messages of the pending invalidates should be collected. Although this alternative does not guarantee atomicity of store access, it at least informs the requesting processor when the store has performed with respect to all processors.

The SCI cache coherence protocol (see Section 18.3.2) supports both strong and weak ordering. Since invalidation is realized by the purge operation in the SCI standard, the implementation of strong ordering means that the processor cannot proceed before the purge operation is complete. However, the processor can proceed without waiting for the completion of the purge operation in order to realize weak ordering.

18.5 Uniform memory access (UMA) machines

Contemporary uniform memory access machines are small-size single bus multiprocessors. Large UMA machines with hundreds of processors and a switching network were typical in the early design of scalable shared memory systems. Famous representatives of that class of multiprocessors are the Denelcor HEP and the NYU Ultracomputer. They introduced many innovative features in their design, some of which even today represent a significant milestone in parallel computer architectures. For example, HEP is the starting point for each multi-threaded architecture as shown in Chapter 16. The combining switch approach of the NYU Ultracomputer and the realization of synchronization primitives based on it was a significant step towards scalable shared memory systems (see Section 18.4.1). However, these early systems do not contain either cache memory or local main memory which turned out to be necessary to achieve high performance in scalable shared memory systems.

Although the UMA architecture is not suitable for building scalable parallel computers, it is excellent for constructing small-size single bus multiprocessors. Two such machines are the Encore Multimax of Encore Computer Corporation representing the technology of the late 1980s and the Power Challenge of Silicon Graphics Computing Systems representing the technology of the 1990s. In the next two sections these two representative machines are described based on the design space of single bus multiprocessors shown in Figure 18.37. The figure also illustrates the main design differences between the two multiprocessors.

18.5.1 Encore Multimax

The most advanced feature of the Encore Multimax, when it appeared on the market, was the Nanobus which was one of the first commercial applications of a pended bus. The overall structure of the Nanobus is very similar to the one shown in Figure 18.3. Unlike in many locked buses, the address and data buses are separated in the Nanobus. The address bus initiates both memory read and memory write transfers on the Nanobus. In the case of write transactions the data bus is used together with the address bus, while in a read transaction the data bus can be used by a memory unit to transfer the result of a previous read access.

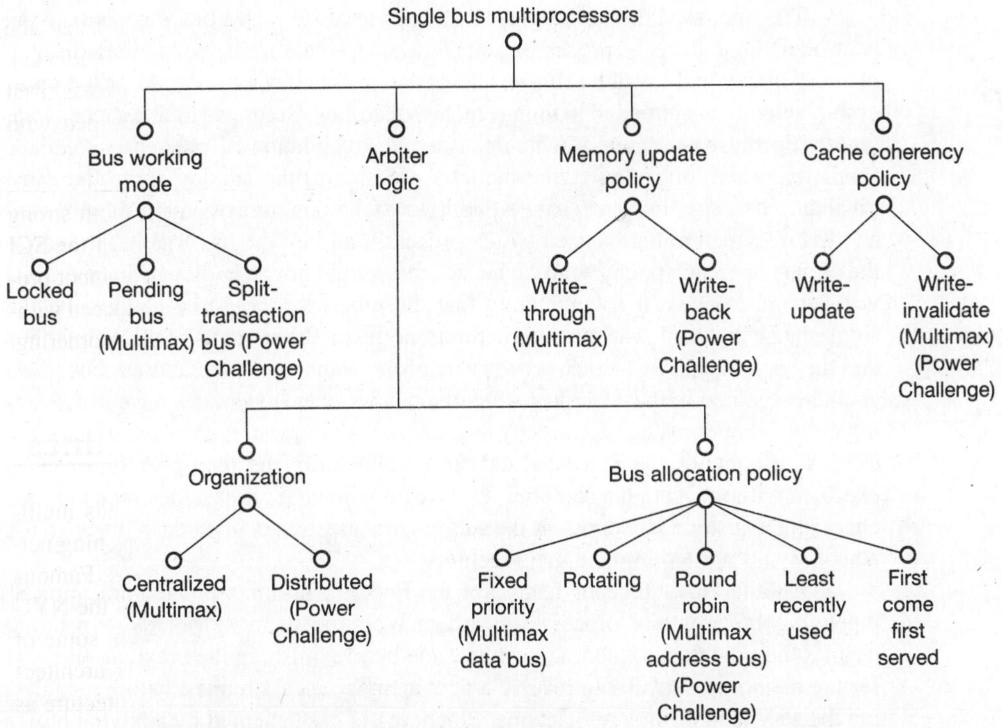

Figure 18.37 Design space of single bus multiprocessors.

Separate but co-operating arbiter logics are employed to allocate the address and data bus among the 20 processors and 16 memory banks. A centralized arbiter is used to realize a fair round-robin arbitration policy for the address bus. However, the work of the centralized address bus arbiter can be influenced by distributed access control mechanisms under certain conditions. If a processor or memory controller cannot gain control over the address bus for a certain number of bus cycles, they can use special bus selection lines to force the central arbiter to deny access to the address bus for other bus masters.

The data bus arbiter is also divided into a central arbiter and a distributed access control. The main difference between the address bus arbitration and the data bus arbitration is in the applied arbitration policy and the scope of users. The data arbitration scheme is used only by the memory controllers, since the processors can obtain access to the data bus implicitly when the address bus is allocated to them in the case of a memory write. Under such conditions the granted memory controller should ignore its grant line. This situation can be detected by observing a special field of the address bus. The data bus arbiter applies a fixed priority arbitration policy among the memory controllers. The priority of a memory controller depends on its physical location on the Nanobus. This fixed priority scheme can lead to the starvation of low priority memory controllers. In order to avoid this situation, the distributed access control can activate special bus selection lines to lock out other bus masters temporarily from the arbitration cycle.

The Encore Multimax employs a 256 Kbyte cache with a bus watcher (snoopy controller) logic for each processor unit. The bus watcher implements write-through memory update policy and write-invalidate cache coherence policy. A special **ownership scheme** is applied to maintain cache coherency. Before writing a cache block ownership must be attained, which causes the invalidation of other cache copies. Similarly, when any other cache requests ownership, the snoopy controller must invalidate its copy. For each cache line, two cache tag stores contain the physical address information that is used by the processor and by the bus watcher to realize the cache coherence policy. One cache tag store would not be sufficient since the bus watcher must access it so frequently that the processor would be blocked on the single cache tag store. The bus watcher must compare the contents of the address bus and the cache tag store at each write cycle of the Nanobus. If the address bus holds an address stored in the cache tag store, the bus watcher invalidates the corresponding cache location. When the processor issues a read request, it checks the cache tag store. If it contains the requested data in a valid form, the read operation can be executed without using the Nanobus. In the case of a write request the processor also checks the tag store. If it contains the address, the location is invalidated through the Nanobus and written into the main memory.

Another advantageous feature of the Encore Multimax is the application of pipelining both on the processor board and on the memory boards. Pipelining enables the processor to start a new bus cycle before finishing the previous one, and for the memory controller to receive a new memory access request before completing the servicing of the previous one. Pipelining is implemented by applying buffer registers on both the processor board and the memory board.

18.5.2 Power Challenge

The Power Challenge has two versions: a deskside configuration, supporting up to six processors, or a rack configuration, supporting up to 18 processors and a very large memory. The MIPS R8000 RISC processor is used in both cases. Since the Power Challenge is a top multiprocessor, the parameters of its maximum system configuration are given in Table 18.2 (Silicon Graphics Computer Systems, 1995).

Table 18.2 Power Challenge maximum system configuration. © 1995 Silicon Graphics Computer Systems

Component	*Description*
Processor	18 MIPS R8000, 6.48 Gflops peak
Main memory	16 Gbyte, 8-way interleaving
I/O bus	4 POWERchannel-2, each 320 Mbyte/sec
SCSI channels	32 fast-wide independent SCSI-2 channels
Disk	3.0 Tbyte disk (RAID) or 960 Gbyte disk
Connectivity	4 HIPPI channels, 8 ethernet channels
VME slots	5 VME64 expansion buses provide up to 25 VME64 slots

The heart of the Power Challenge multiprocessor is the POWERpath-2 split-transaction shared bus. The associative memory used for splitting read transactions is constructed from eight so-called read resources, that is, up to eight reads can be outstanding at any time. The POWERpath-2 bus was designed according to RISC philosophy. The types and variations of bus transactions are small, and each transaction requires exactly the same five bus cycles: arbitration, resolution, address, decode, acknowledge. These five cycles are executed synchronously by each bus controller.

The 40-bit address bus and the 256-bit data bus are arbitrated separately. The only bus transaction which requires simultaneous arbitration for the same processor is the write request, as shown by Table 18.3. Read and invalidate requests need only the address bus; therefore, they can be combined with a simultaneous read response.

Bus transactions are divided into three groups in descending order of priority:

(1) read responses
(2) address operations (read requests, invalidate requests, and interrupts)
(3) write requests.

Within each group a fair, round-robin arbiter policy is applied. Although distributed arbitration needs more logic to implement, POWERpath-2 employs a distributed arbitration scheme since it requires fewer transactions on the bus and hence reduces latency. To prevent starvation a programmable urgent timer is provided for each processor node. When a node is unable to issue requests on the bus for a specified amount of time, its arbiter automatically raises its priority to urgent.

The POWERpath-2 maintains write-invalidate cache coherence by snoopy hardware. The applied cache coherence policy is a slightly modified version of the Illinois Protocol (Papamarcos and Patel, 1984). Each cache line has four states: Invalid, Exclusive, Dirty exclusive, Shared. The memory update policy is write-back. Whenever a read request is satisfied from another processor's cache, the cache read response is used to update the memory as a writeback. Similarly to the Encore Multimax, the processor–bus interface maintains a duplicate set of cache tags to reduce contention between the processor and the snoopy controller.

Barrier synchronization consists of two synchronization activities. First, N processes are started by a fork operation and at the end of the parallel activity the N

Table 18.3 POWERpath-2 bus transactions.

Bus transaction	*Address bus*	*Data bus*
Write request	+	+
Read request	+	–
Invalidate request	+	–
Read response	–	+

participating process must wait for each other in a join operation. Special hardware mechanisms and compiler techniques support both synchronization steps in the Power Challenge. SGI's parallel compilers realize the process forking necessary for barrier synchronization by using a master/slave role distribution among processes. The master prepares a parameter block and sets a start bit in this block. When a fork occurs, slaves can start their work if they find an activated start bit, and hence all the processors simultaneously attempt to read the start bit. To avoid N read accesses to the start bit, the POWERpath-2 bus provides a **piggyback read**. This means that any number of processors can participate in a single read transaction by accepting the read response as their own and indicating that the corresponding cache block is shared.

The join operation is implemented by a counter initialized to 0 at forking. Any time a processor finishes its activity, it decrements the counter. The join operation is completed when the counter reaches N. Without hardware support the join operation would require approximately N^2 bus transactions since each processor must exclusively read the cache line containing the counter to decrement it, and must reread it anytime another processor writes it (due to cache coherence maintenance). To reduce the bus traffic to only N bus transfers, the join mechanism is supported by a special count register at each processor interface. Since the synchronization counter is not in the cache, the extra reads stemming from cache coherence maintenance can be eliminated. When a processor reaches the barrier it issues a single broadcast transaction on the address bus, which increments all of the counters in the system. It then begins reading its own counter until it reaches N, which means all the processors reached their barrier point and hence, the join is completed.

18.6 Non-uniform memory access (NUMA) machines

Non-uniform memory access (NUMA) machines were designed to avoid the memory access bottleneck of UMA machines. The logically shared memory is physically distributed among the processing nodes of NUMA machines, leading to distributed shared memory architectures. On one hand these parallel computers became highly scalable, but on the other hand they are very sensitive to data allocation in local memories. Accessing a local memory segment of a node is much faster than accessing a remote memory segment. Not by chance, the structure and design of these machines resemble in many ways that of distributed memory multicomputers. The main difference is in the organization of the address space. In multiprocessors, a global address space is applied that is uniformly visible from each processor; that is, all processors can transparently access all memory locations. In multicomputers, the address space is replicated in the local memories of the processing elements (PEs). No PE is allowed to directly access the local memory of another PE. This difference in the address space of the memory is also reflected at the software level: distributed memory multicomputers are programmed on the basis of the message-passing paradigm, while NUMA machines are programmed on the basis of the global address space (shared memory) principle.

However, distinguishing these machines becomes more and more difficult in recent parallel computers, like the Cray T3D, where both programming paradigms are provided to the user in the form of library packages. A further aspect that makes the difference even smaller comes from the fact that the actual form of accessing remote memory modules is the same in both classes of MIMD computers. Remote memory accesses are realized by messages even in the NUMA machines, similarly to the message-passing multicomputers.

The problem of cache coherency does not appear in distributed memory multicomputers since the message-passing paradigm explicitly handles different copies of the same data structure in the form of independent messages. In the shared memory paradigm, multiple accesses to the same global data structure are possible and can be accelerated if local copies of the global data structure are maintained in local caches. However, the hardware-supported cache consistency schemes are not introduced into the NUMA machines. These systems can cache read-only code and data, as well as local data, but not shared modifiable data. This is the distinguishing feature between NUMA and CC-NUMA multiprocessors. Accordingly, NUMA machines are closer to multicomputers than to other shared memory multiprocessors, while CC-NUMA machines look like real shared memory systems.

In NUMA machines, like in multicomputers, the main design issues are the organization of processor nodes, the interconnection network, and the possible techniques to reduce remote memory accesses. Typical NUMA machines are the BBN TC2000, the IBM RP3, the Cray T3D and the Hector multiprocessor. Here only the latter two are described as examples to illustrate the realization possibilities of NUMA architectures.

18.6.1 Hector

Hector is a hierarchical NUMA machine consisting of stations connected by a hierarchy of ring networks. Stations are symmetric multiprocessors where the processing modules (nodes) are connected by a single bus. Nodes comprise three main units: a processor/cache unit, a memory unit and the station bus interface which connects the otherwise separated processor and memory buses as shown in Figure 18.38. The separation of the two buses enables other processors to access this memory while the processor performs memory access operations in off-node memory. The processing modules of the machine are grouped into shared bus symmetric multiprocessors, called stations. These are connected by bit-parallel local rings which are, in turn, interconnected by a single global ring. Hector provides a flat, global address space, where each processing module is assigned a range of addresses. The addressing scheme uses r+s+p bits where r identifies the ring, s points to the station, and p addresses the slot inside the station. Although global cache consistency cannot be maintained in Hector, a snoopy protocol provides cache consistency among the nodes inside a station.

Memory accesses take place in a synchronized packet-transfer scheme controlled by a **hierarchy of interface circuits**:

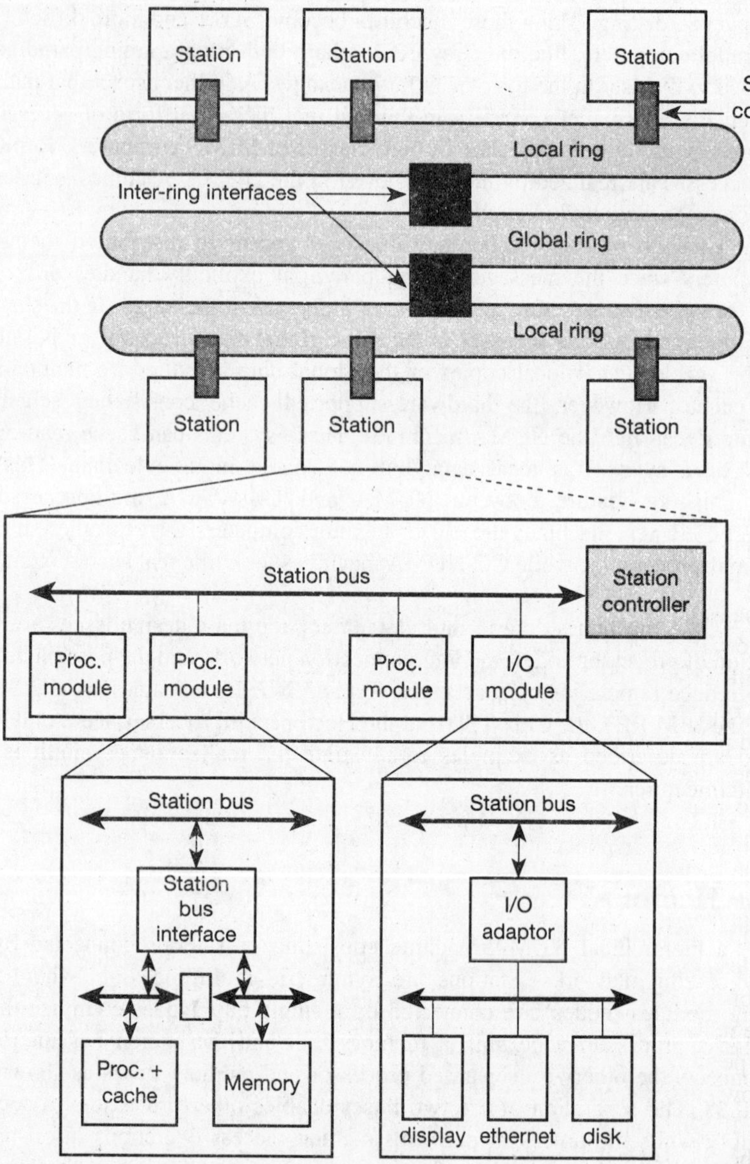

Figure 18.38 Structure of the Hector machine (Vranesic et al., 1991). © 1991 IEEE

- Station bus interface
- Station controller (local ring interface)
- Inter-ring interface.

The station bus interface connects processing modules to the station bus by forwarding station bus requests to the station controller. When a processor requests on-board memory access, it is the station bus interface that connects the processor bus to the memory bus. Off-board memory requests are transformed into request packets and passed by the station bus interface to the station controller. Incoming memory requests are temporarily stored in a two-deep FIFO by the station bus interface until the memory bus becomes free. If the FIFO is full, the station bus interface sends back to the requester a negative acknowledgement.

The station controller has a twofold role. First, it controls the allocation of the station bus between on-station requests, and second, it realises the local ring interface for the station. When a processing module requests the station bus and there is no contention on the bus, the station controller grants the bus at the beginning of the next cycle. The processor module places the data packet on the bus in the same cycle. If the destination module belongs to the station, it acknowledges the reception of the packet in the next cycle. If the acknowledgement is not given, the source module automatically retransmits the request. An on-station transfer requires three cycles but only one of them ties up the bus and hence, by independent requests, the full bus bandwidth can be exploited.

The station controller is responsible for connecting the station to a local ring, as well. The station controller handles three kinds of requests listed in increasing priority: (1) on-station requests (explained above), (2) off-station requests and (3) arriving packets from the ring. Communication on the local ring is performed on a slot-by-slot basis. When the arriving slot on the ring addresses the station, the packet is transmitted to the station bus. When the slot is empty the station controller can fill it with an off-station message. When the arriving slot addresses another station, it is forwarded in the local ring and the station bus is granted to an on-station request.

The inter-ring interface is realized as a two-deep FIFO buffer that gives priority to packets moving in the global ring. It means that whenever a packet travels on the global ring it will reach its destination without delay.

The heart of the Hector design is the realization of memory accesses as packet transfer operations. As was shown, non-local memory requests are transformed to **request packets** by the station bus interface. The request packet contains a 32-bit destination memory address, a source node address, and 32 bits of data in the case of write access. Packets move on the station bus and in the ring networks. When the request packet reaches the destination node the corresponding station bus interface performs the request and sends back a **response packet** that can be a simple acknowledgement for a write access or contain up to 64 bits of data for read accesses. If the request cannot be serviced a **negative acknowledgement** is sent back to the source node. If either a negative acknowledgement or no acknowledgement arrives during a timeout period, the source node retransmits the memory request. The latter case can occur, for example, when a transmission error is detected (by parity bits) and the packet is simply dropped.

This simple timeout-based request–response protocol works well for ordinary read and write operations. However, it can cause serious problem in the case of read-and-write operations like test&set. Assume that no answer arrives in the timeout period after issuing a test&set operation. Two possible scenarios could cause the loss of acknowledgement. First, the test&set request packet was dropped before it could reach the destination. In this case the retransmission of the request does not cause any problem. Second, the request arrived at the destination, the semaphore was closed due to the request, but the acknowledgement packet has been dropped. In this case the retransmission cannot help, and the semaphore remains locked for ever. Obviously, the two scenarios should be visible for the source node to react correctly. In Hector the read-and-write operations are handled in two stages by sending two distinct request packets.

In the first stage, a read-and-lock packet is sent to the destination node which reads the memory cell and sends its value back to the requester. The station bus interface of the destination node maintains a <proc, addr> table to record that the given address is locked for the associated processor and rejects access requests from other processors. In the second stage, when the source node receives the result of the read-and-lock packet, it generates a write-and-unlock packet which makes the destination node write the given memory location and also remove the <proc, addr> pair from its table, unlocking the access of the memory cell. By this time the test&set has finished so other processors can access the semaphore without restriction. If the acknowledgement of the first stage request cannot reach the source node within the timeout period, the retransmission of the read-and-lock does not cause a problem even if the previous one reached the destination node, due to the presence of the <proc, addr> pair. If the write-and-unlock packet is not acknowledged, its retranmission can be handled correctly based on the absence or presence of the <proc, addr> pair.

Three main advantages can be stated in assessing the Hector machine:

- The hierarchical structure enables short transmission lines and good scalability.
- The cost and the overall bandwidth of the structure grow linearly with the number of nodes.
- The cost of a memory access grows incrementally with the distance between the processor and memory location.

The main drawbacks of Hector are typical for all the NUMA machines: lack of global cache consistency and non-uniform memory access time which require careful software design.

18.6.2 Cray T3D

Cray T3D is the most recent NUMA machine that was designed with the intention of providing a highly scalable parallel supercomputer that can incorporate both the shared memory and the message-passing programming paradigms. As in other NUMA machines, the shared memory is distributed among the processing elements in order to avoid the memory access bottleneck and there is no hardware support for cache coherency. However, a special software package and programming model, called the CRAFT, manages coherence and guarantees the integrity of the data.

The Cray T3D hardware structure is divided into two parts:

- Microarchitecture
- Macroarchitecture.

The **microarchitecture** is based on Digital's 21064 Alpha AXP microprocessor which, like other contemporary microprocessors, have three main weaknesses:

- Limited address space
- Little or no latency-hiding capability
- Few or no synchronization primitives.

Cray research has designed a shell of circuitry around the core microprocessor to extend its capabilities in the three areas. The Cray T3D system has up to 128 gigabytes of distributed shared memory that requires at least 37 bits of physical address. In order to extend the number of address bits beyond the 34 provided by the Alpha chip, the Cray T3D employs a 32-entry register set. It is the task of the shell circuitry to check the virtual PE number. If it refers to the local PE, the shell performs a local memory reference.

To improve the latency hiding mechanism of the Alpha chip, Cray introduces a 16-word FIFO, called the **prefetch queue**, which permits 16 prefetch instructions to be performed without executing any load from the queue. The effect of a prefetch for a remote node is that the next free location of the prefetch queue is reserved for the data and a remote load operation is started for the requested data. When the processor needs the prefetched data a load operation on the prefetch queue delivers the requested slot of the queue. If the data has not yet returned from the remote node, the processor is stalled.

The Cray T3D supports four **synchronization mechanisms** by hardware. The **barrier** hardware comprises 16 parallel logical AND trees that enable multiple barriers to be pipelined. When a processor reaches the barrier it must set the associated barrier bit to one. When all the processors have reached the barrier, the AND function is satisfied and clears the barrier bit of each participating processor by hardware, signalling them to continue.

The Cray T3D provides a specialized register set to realise **fetch-and-increment** hardware. The contents of these registers are automatically incremented whenever they are read. **Messaging** is supported by a predefined queue area in the memory of each processing node. Sending a message means a special cache-line-size write to the queue area of the destination node. The shell circuitry interrupts the destination processor when the message is stored in the queue. **Atomic swap** registers are provided to exchange data between a register and a remote memory cell as an indivisible operation. The latency of an atomic swap can be hidden by using the prefetch technique.

The **macroarchitecture** defines how to connect and integrate the nodes of the parallel computer, while the microarchitecture specifies the node organization. One of the main design objectives was to maintain the same macroarchitecture even with varying microarchitectures which will always be designed around state-of-the-art commodity microprocessors.

The two parts of the macroarchitecture are the memory system and the interconnection network. The memory system realises a distributed shared memory where any PE can directly address any other PE's memory. The physical address has two components: a PE number and an offset within the PE. Each PE contains 16 or

64 Mbytes of local DRAM. Access time of the local memory is between 13 and 38 clock cycles (87 to 253 nsec). The latency for accessing remote memory varies between 1 and 2 microseconds. The data cache is resident on Digital's 21064 Alpha AXP microprocessor which applies a write-through, direct-mapped, read-allocate cache technique. Recall that the Cray T3D has no hardware support for ensuring cache coherency; rather, the CRAFT programming model guarantees it.

The topology of the Cray T3D machine is a 3-D torus that was selected on the basis of measurements on global latency and global bandwidth of real-world software packages. The router logic implements a dimension-order, wormhole routing algorithm with four virtual channels (similar to the J-Machine – see Chapter 17). The network moves data in one or four 64-bit word length packets. Each hop through the network requires 1 clock cycle (6.67 nsec at 150 MHz) for the switch and an additional 1 or 1.5 clock cycle for the physical wire. Every node comprises two processing elements. The PEs are independent, supplied with separate memories and data paths. They share only the bandwidth of the network and the block transfer engine which is an asynchronous direct memory access controller.

The CRAY T3D system configuration and its major parts are shown in Figure 18.39. The heart is a 4×4×4 3-D torus that is connected to the Cray Y-MP host (a traditional parallel-vector system) and to the I/O controllers by special I/O gateways.

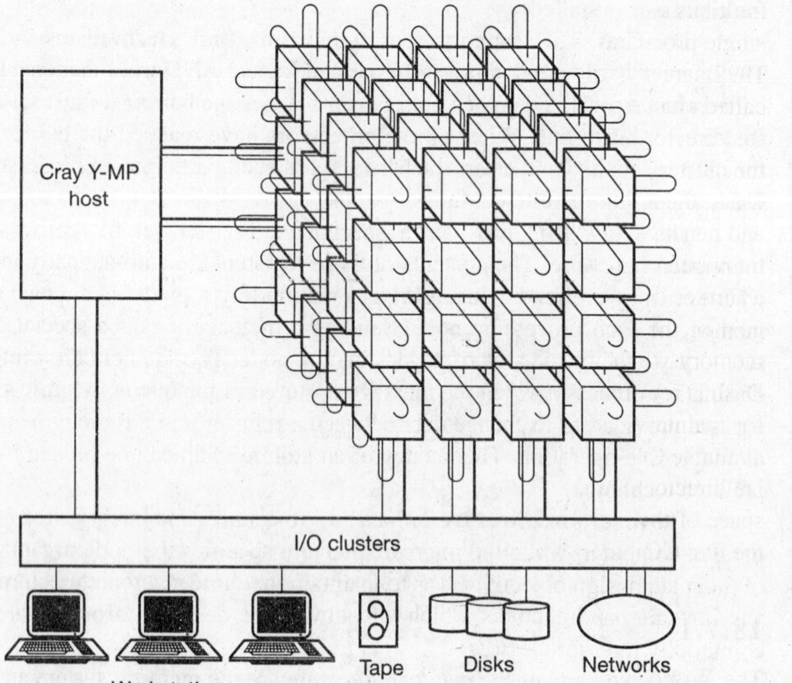

Figure 18.39 Structure of the Cray T3D system (Kessler and Schwarzmeier, 1993). © 1993 IEEE

These gateways are positioned throughout the 3-D torus and have low-speed (LOSP) and high-speed (HISP: 400 Mbytes/sec full-duplex) versions. A typical configuration can have 8×8×8=512 nodes with two PEs in each, that is 1024 PEs overall.

18.7 Cache-coherent non-uniform memory access (CC-NUMA) machines

All the CC-NUMA machines share the common goal of building a scalable shared memory multiprocessor. The main difference among them is in the way the memory and cache coherence mechanisms are distributed among the processing nodes. Another distinguishing design issue is the selection of the interconnection network among the nodes. They demonstrate a progress from bus-based networks towards a more general interconnection network and from the snoopy cache coherency protocol towards a directory scheme.

The Wisconsin multicube architecture (Goodman and Woest, 1988) is the closest generalization of a single bus-based multiprocessor. It completely relies on the snoopy cache protocol but in a hierarchical way. The Aquarius Multi-Multi architecture (Carlton and Despain, 1990) combines the snoopy cache protocol with a directory scheme, but the interconnection network strictly relies on the shared multibus concept. Both the Wisconsin multicube and the Aquarius Multi-Multi have single processor nodes. The nodes of the Stanford Dash architecture (Lenoski et al., 1992) are more complex; they are realized as single bus-based multiprocessors called **clusters**. The Dash architecture also combines the snoopy cache protocol and the directory scheme. A snooping scheme ensures the consistency of caches inside the clusters, while the directory scheme maintains consistency across clusters. In the Dash, the directory protocol is independent of the type of interconnection network and hence, any of the low-latency networks that were originally developed for multicomputers such as the mesh can be employed. The Stanford FLASH architecture is a further development of the Dash machine by the same research group. The main goal of the FLASH design was the efficient integration of cache-coherent shared memory with high-performance message passing. Since the cluster concept of the Dash is replaced with one-processor nodes, FLASH applies only a directory scheme for maintaining cache coherence. Finally, the Convex Exemplar is a commercially available CC-NUMA machine which applies the Scalable Coherent Interface to realize directory scheme-based global cache coherence. Figure 18.40 shows the design space of the CC-NUMA machines and Table 18.4 summarizes the main features of the five CC-NUMA architectures mentioned above.

18.7.1 Wisconsin multicube

The Wisconsin multicube architecture employs row and column buses forming a two-dimensional grid architecture as shown in Figure 18.41. The three-dimensional generalization will result in a cube architecture. The main memory is distributed along the column buses, and each data block of memory has a **home column**. All

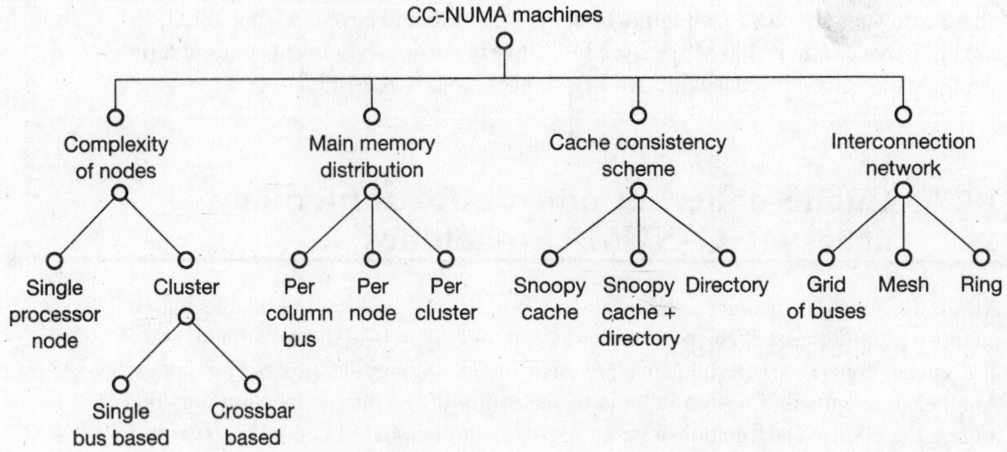

Figure 18.40 Design space of CC-NUMA machines.

Table 18.4 Main features of CC-NUMA machines.

Machine	*Complexity of nodes*	*Memory distribution*	*Cache consistency scheme*	*Interconnection network*
Wisconsin Multicube	Single processor	Per column bus	Snoopy cache	Grid of buses
Aquarius Multi-Multi	Single processor	Per node	Snoopy cache + directory scheme	Grid of buses
Stanford Dash	Bus based multiprocessor (cluster)	Per cluster	Snoopy cache + directory scheme	-Bus inside cluster -Pair of meshes among clusters
Stanford FLASH	Single processor	Per node	Directory scheme	2-D mesh
Convex Exemplar	Hypernode (8 processors)	Per hypernode	Directory scheme (Scalable Coherent Interface)	- crossbar inside hypernode - Multiple uni-directional rings among hypernodes

rows of processors work similarly to single bus-based multiprocessors. Each processing element contains a processor, a conventional cache memory to reduce memory latency and a snoopy cache that monitors a row bus and a column bus in order to realize a write-back, write-invalidate cache coherence protocol. In order to describe the cache coherence protocol of the Wisconsin multicube architecture, the following definitions must be given:

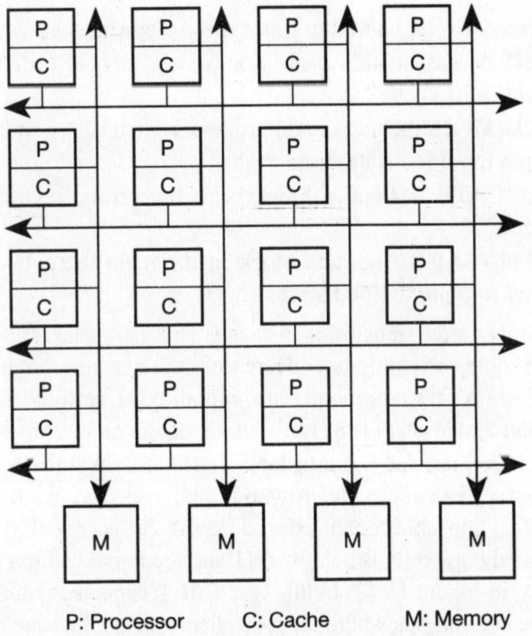

Figure 18.41 Structure of the Wisconsin multicube machine.

- Definition of possible states of blocks in caches and memories.
- Definition of commands to be performed at various read/write hit/miss actions.
- Definition of state transitions in caches and memories according to the commands.
- Definition of transmission routes of commands among processors, caches and memories.

These definitions are as follows:

- Possible states of blocks in memories:
  - **unmodified**: the value in the main memory is correct and it can have several correct cached copies, too.
  - **modified**: the value in the main memory is stale and there exists exactly one correct cached copy.
- Possible states of blocks in caches:

  Data blocks in a particular cache can have three different local states: **shared** (its copy in the main memory is in a global unmodified state), **modified** (its copy in the main memory is in a global modified state), **invalid**. Each cache controller contains a special data structure called the **modified line table**. This table stores addresses of all modified data blocks residing in caches in that column. Notice that all the modified line tables in a given column should be identical.

- A cache controller can issue four types of consistency commands:
  - **READ**: the associated processor wishes to read a data block that is not present in its cache.
  - **READ-MOD**: the associated processor wishes to write a data block that is not in a modified state in its cache.
  - **ALLOCATE**: an entire block is to be written regardless of its current contents.
  - **WRITE-BACK**: the data block in the main memory should be updated and set into unmodified state.
- Definition of state transitions in caches and memories, and definition of transmission routes of commands. Here only the execution mechanisms of READ and READ-MOD commands are explained. Interested readers can consult Goodman and Woest (1988) for details of the other consistency transactions.
  - **READ request for a data block X which is in state modified**. The READ request is issued on the row bus and accepted by the controller whose modified line table contains the address of X. Assume the requester is C00, the modified copy of X is held by C11 and the home column of X is column 2 as shown in Figure 18.42. In this case C01 accepts the request and broadcasts it on the column bus where all controllers change the state of X to unmodified. In parallel, C11 picks up the request and fetches X. Finally, C11 transmits X back on the column bus where C01 accepts the data block and broadcasts it on the row bus. The requesting cache C00 picks up X along with the home column controller,C02 which writes X back to the memory in unmodified state, issuing the Mem-Write (X, unmodified) command on the home bus.
  - **READ request for a data block X which is in state unmodified**. In this case the home column controller C02 accepts the request. If X has a copy in C02, it is directly sent back to C00 on the row bus. Otherwise, C02 transmits the request to the memory on the column bus. On receiving X from the memory on the column bus, C02 transmits X to C00 via the row bus.
  - **READ-MOD request for a data block X which is in state modified**. After the first two bus operations (same as in the READ request) C11 picks up the request, invalidates the copy of X and transmits it on the *row* bus. Here, controller C10 accepts the data block and broadcasts it on the column bus. Finally, C00 picks up X, updates it and stores it in modified state. As a side effect of the last column operations, all the Cx0 controllers add the address of X to their modified line tables. Note that the main memory is not updated (write-back policy).
  - **READ-MOD request for a data block X which is in state unmodified**. In this case the home column controller C02 accepts the request and forwards it to the main memory which sends back an invalidate request along with a copy of X. Each controller on the column bus accepts the invalidate request and broadcasts it on the associated row bus. C02 broadcasts the invalidate request along with the copy of the block containing X on its row bus. Finally, C00 picks up the copy of X and broadcasts a consistency command on its column bus to force the other caches to insert the address of X to their modified line tables.

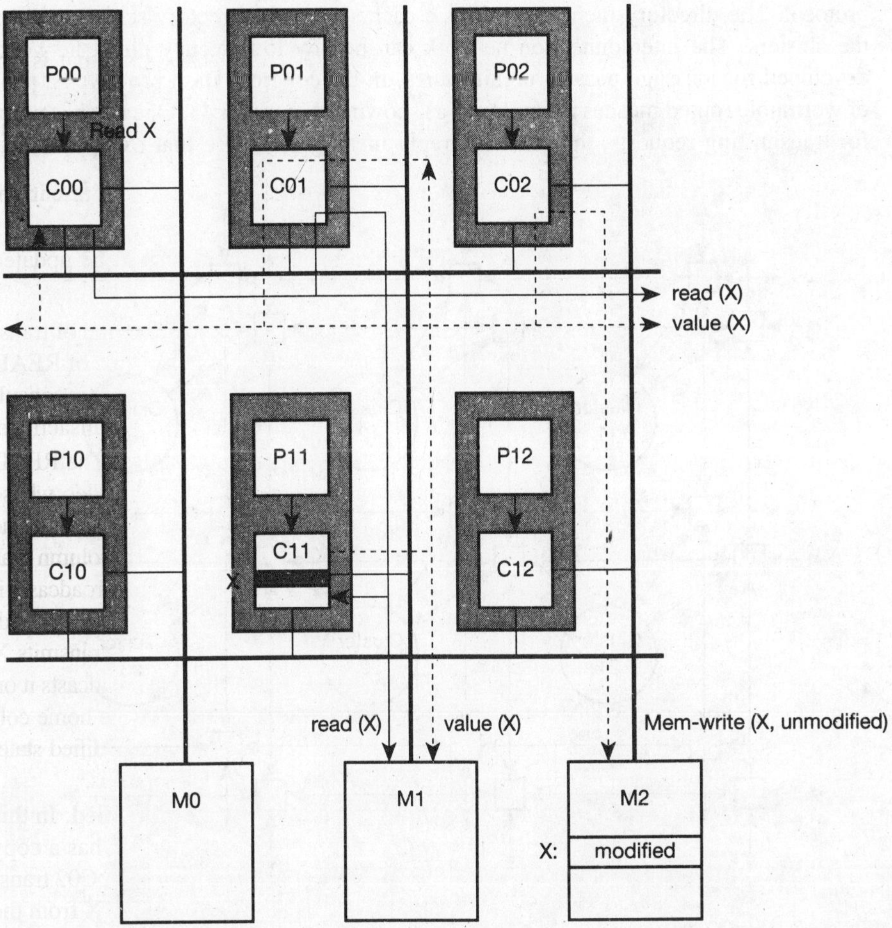

Figure 18.42 The mechanism of reading block X in state modified.

Notice that the symmetry of the multicube's organization distributes bus traffic uniformly among the row and column buses. This symmetry greatly reduces the possibility of communication bottlenecks. Owing to the grid organization, a memory request that results in a cache miss requires, at most, twice the number of bus operations as that of a single bus-based multiprocessor.

18.7.2 Stanford Dash

The nodes of the Dash architecture are single bus-based multiprocessors, called clusters. Each cluster comprises four processor pairs (MIPS R3000 processor and R3010 floating-point coprocessor), I/O interface, first- and second-level caches, a partition of the main memory, and a directory and intercluster interface logic. Notice that the memory is distributed among the nodes of the Dash, reducing the bandwidth demands on the global interconnect. The second-level writeback caches are responsible for maintaining cache coherency inside the cluster by applying a snoopy cache protocol. The directory memory realises a cache coherent directory scheme across the clusters. The interconnection network can be any low-latency direct network developed for message-passing architectures. In the concrete Dash prototype a pair of wormhole routed meshes is employed as shown in Figure 18.43. One mesh is used for transmitting requests, the other for reply messages. Notice that except for the

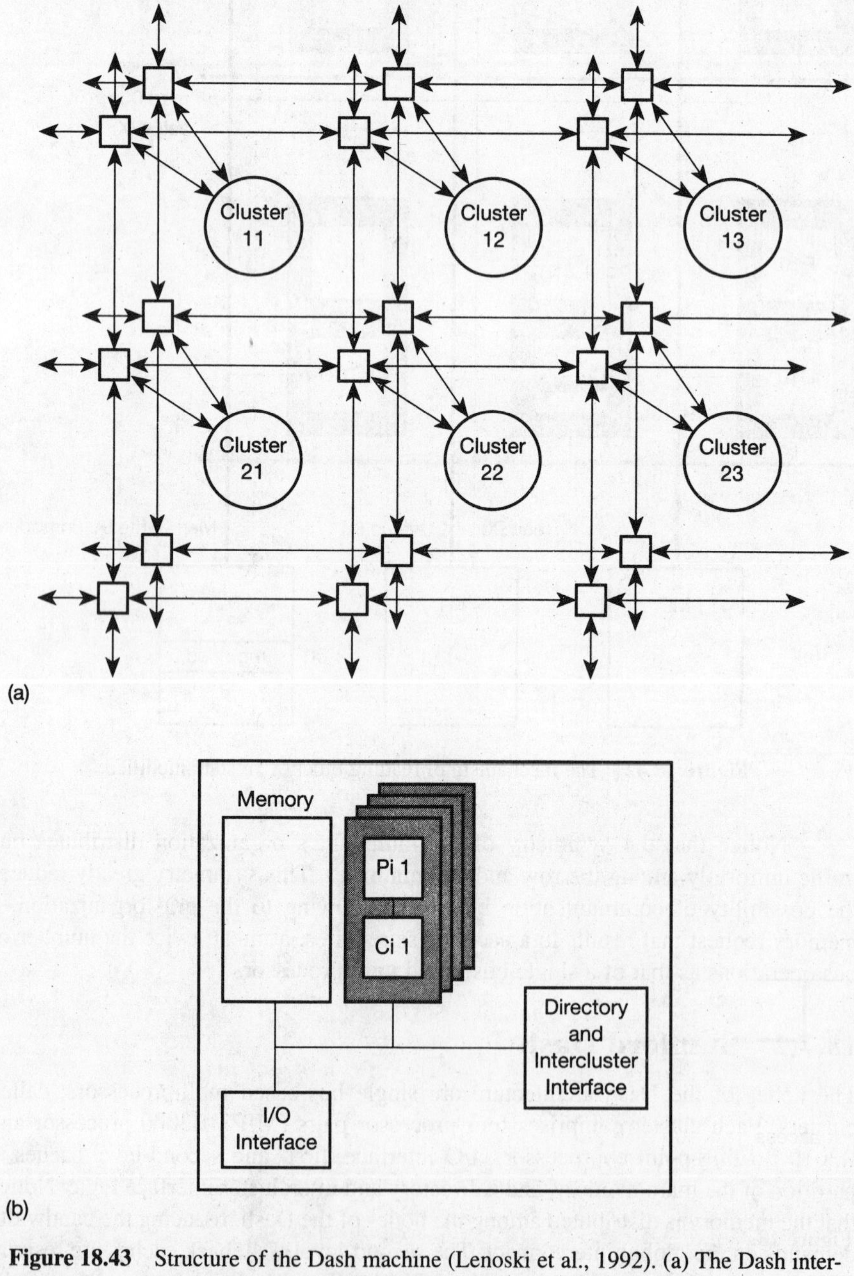

Figure 18.43 Structure of the Dash machine (Lenoski et al., 1992). (a) The Dash interconnection network; (b) structure of a cluster. © 1992 IEEE

cache and directory memory, the Dash architecture is similar to many message-passing systems (see Chapter 17).

The innovative feature of the Dash architecture is the distributed implementation of the directory-based cache coherence scheme. The memory system of the Dash is partitioned into four levels as explained by Figures 18.44(a)–(d). The

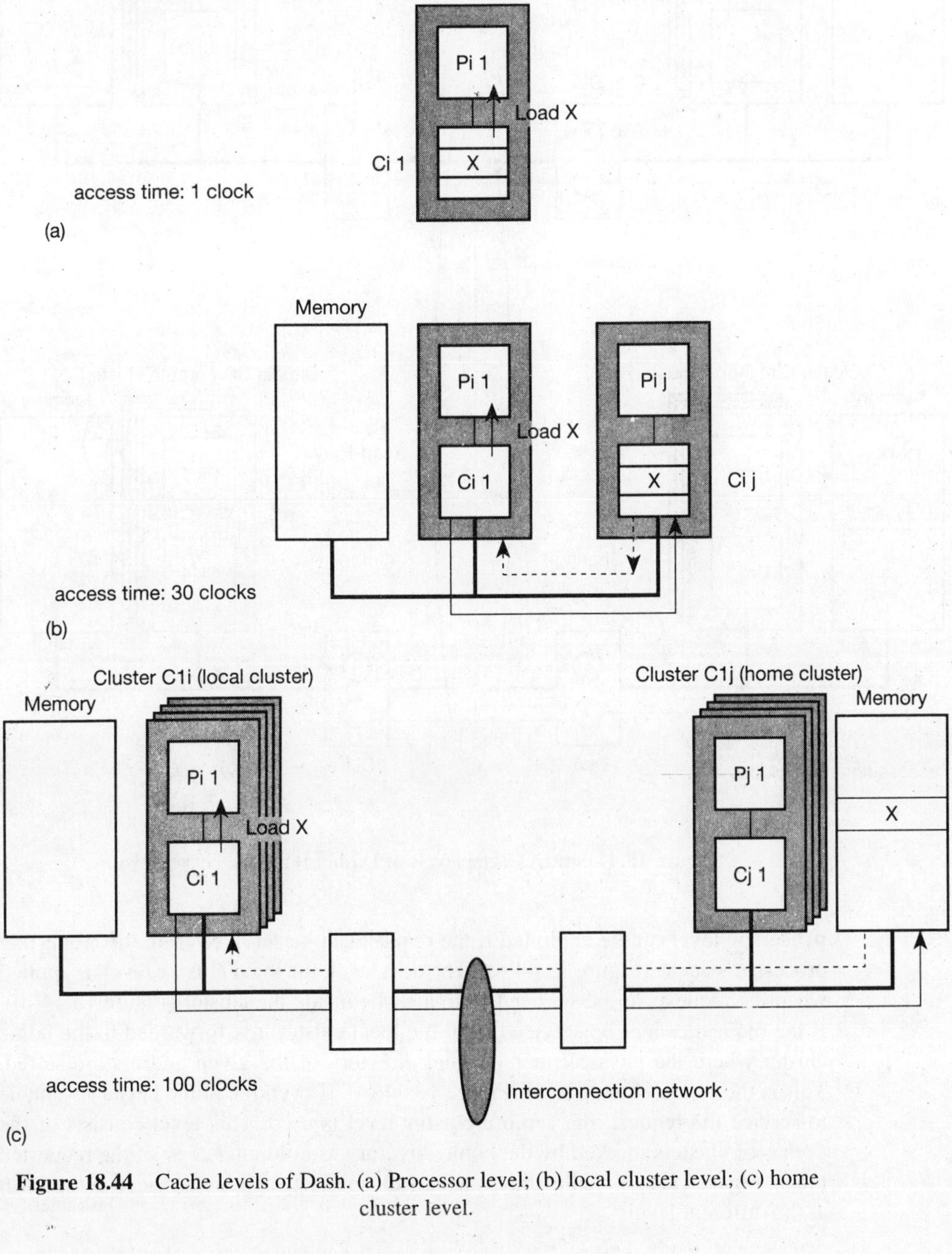

Figure 18.44 Cache levels of Dash. (a) Processor level; (b) local cluster level; (c) home cluster level.

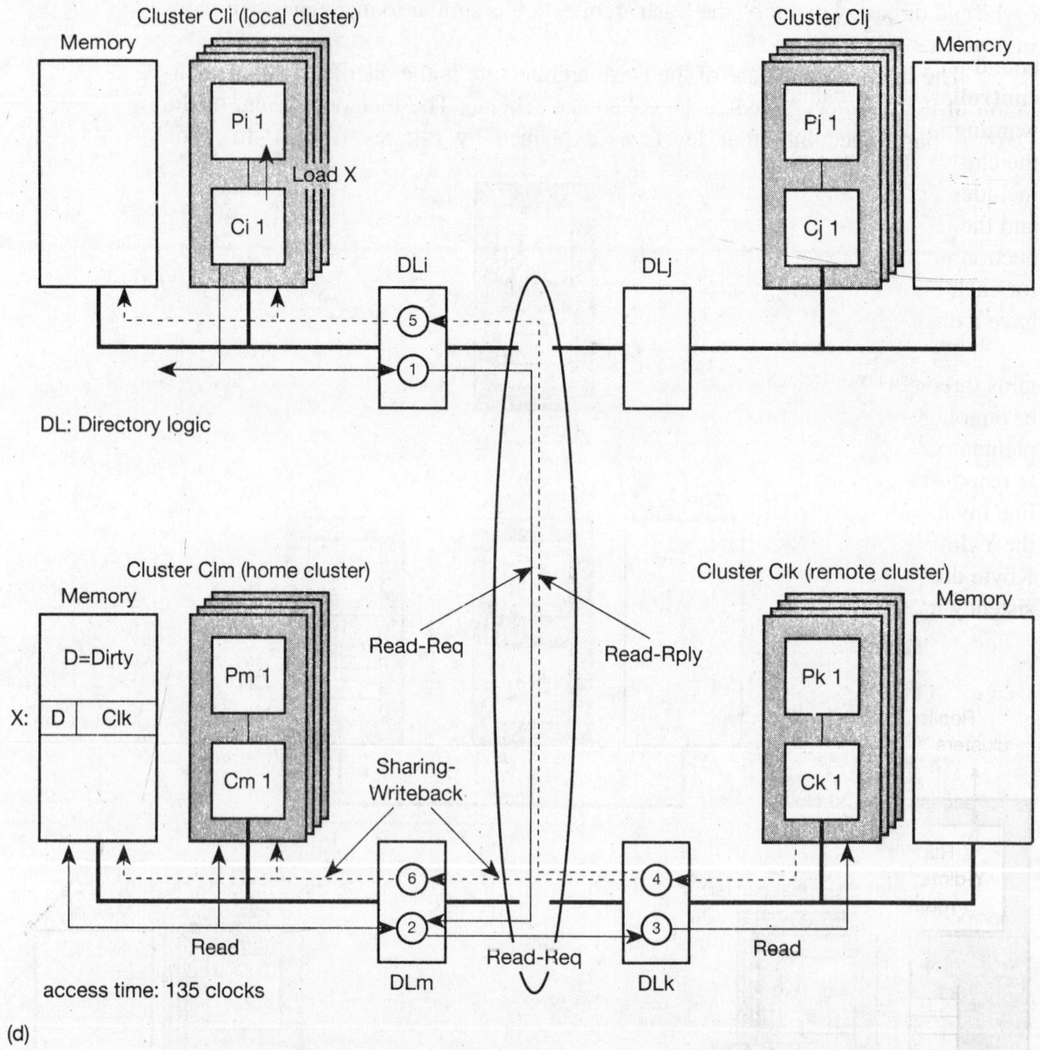

Figure 18.44 cont. Cache levels of Dash. (d) remote cluster level.

processor level can be exploited if the request can be serviced from the requesting processor's cache (Figure 18.44(a)). The next level, the **local cluster level,** is applied when the request can be serviced from a cache inside the cluster (Figure 18.44(b)). If the request cannot be serviced from the local cluster it is forwarded to the home cluster where the physical memory and directory of the given address are stored. This is the **home cluster level** (Figure 18.44(c)). If even the home cluster is unable to service the request, the **remote cluster level** is used. This level consists of the caches of clusters marked by the home directory as holding a copy of the requested block. Figure 18.44 also illustrates the way the read requests are serviced in the Dash at the different levels.

The Dash directory logic (Figure 18.45) is divided into an inbound and outbound part to support intercluster transactions. The outbound part is the **directory controller** (DC) including the directory memory. The DC is responsible for forwarding local requests to remote clusters, replying to remote requests, responding to the cluster bus with directory information and storing locks and lock queues. It also includes a performance monitor for tracing a variety of intra- and intercluster events, and the request and reply network logic handling the X-dimension of the interconnection network. The directory memory is realized as a full-bit vector with one bit for each cluster. Additionally, for each entry, a single state bit shows if the clusters have a dirty or shared copy of the block as explained in Section 18.3.2.

The **reply controller** (RC), the inbound part of the directory logic, also contains three major units. The remote access cache (RAC) is used for storing the state of ongoing memory requests and remote replies, and snooping on the bus. It is supplemented with invalidation counters for each processor. The pseudo-CPU (PCPU) is responsible for forwarding remote requests to the cluster bus and issuing cache line invalidations and lock grants. The third part is the network logic which handles the Y-dimension of the interconnection network. The RAC is implemented as a 128-Kbyte direct-mapped snoopy cache with 16-byte cache lines. It realizes release consistency in the Dash and performs operations such as prefetch. The RAC can handle

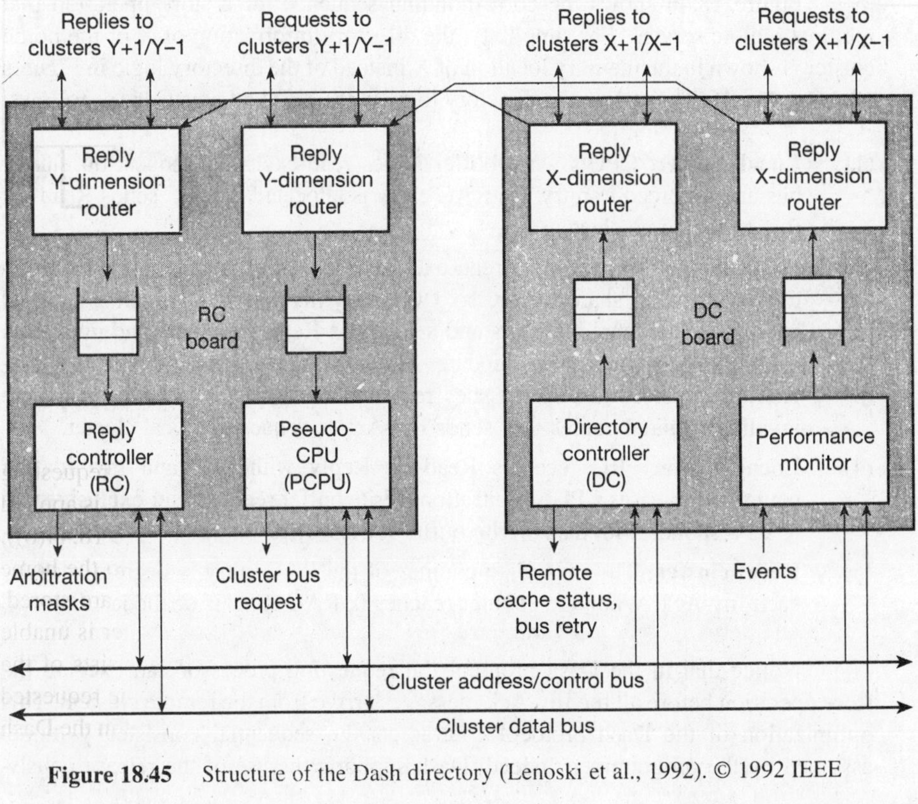

Figure 18.45 Structure of the Dash directory (Lenoski et al., 1992). © 1992 IEEE

several outstanding remote requests from each of the cluster processors and is able to merge requests made to the same cache block by different processors.

Figure 18.44(d) assists in describing the main functions of the directory logic during a read request. The circled numbers in the figure represent the actions of the directory that are described here:

(1) **Local cluster**: An RAC entry is allocated and DC sends a Read-Req message to the home cluster.

(2) **Home cluster**: PCPU issues a read on the cluster bus. Since the directory entry is in a dirty state, DC forwards the Read-Req message to the dirty remote cluster.

(3) **Remote cluster**: PCPU issues a read on the cluster bus.

(4) **Remote cluster**: The cache data is placed on the cluster bus by the dirty cache. DC sends a Read-Rply message to the requester local cluster and a Sharing-Writeback to the home cluster.

(5) **Local cluster**: RC gets reply and releases CPU's arbitration. CPU retries read and RAC responds with data.

(6) **Home cluster**: PCPU issues Sharing-Writeback on the cluster bus. DC updates directory entry to shared state.

Figure 18.46 shows the corresponding sequence for a store operation that requires remote service. For simplicity, the directory information of X of the home cluster is shown in the memory location of X instead of the directory logic in Figures 18.44 and 18.46. The task of the directory logic in the different clusters is as follows:

(1) **Local cluster**: CPU's write buffer issues read-exclusive request on cluster bus and is forced to retry. An RAC entry is allocated and DC sends Read-Ex Req to the home cluster.

(2) **Home cluster**: PCPU issues read-exclusive request on cluster bus. The directory entry is in shared state, so DC sends Inv-Req (invalidation request) message to all shared clusters and a Read-Ex Reply with data and invalidate counter to local cluster. DC updates directory state to dirty.

(3) **Remote cluster(s):** PCPU issues read-exclusive request on cluster bus to invalidate shared copies. DC sends Inv-Ack to requesting local cluster.

(4) **Local cluster:** RC receives Read-Ex Reply with data and invalidation counter. It releases CPU's arbitration. Write buffer repeats read-exclusive and RAC responds with data. Write buffer retries write.

(5) **Local cluster:** The invalidate counter of the RAC entry is decremented by each Inv-Ack. When the counter reaches 0, RAC entry is deallocated.

Notice that in the Dash protocol the requesting processor can execute the store operation before all the Inv-Ack messages arrive from the remote clusters. This optimization of the Dash protocol contradicts the sequential consistency model assumed by the programmer. Indeed, Dash supports the use of the release consis-

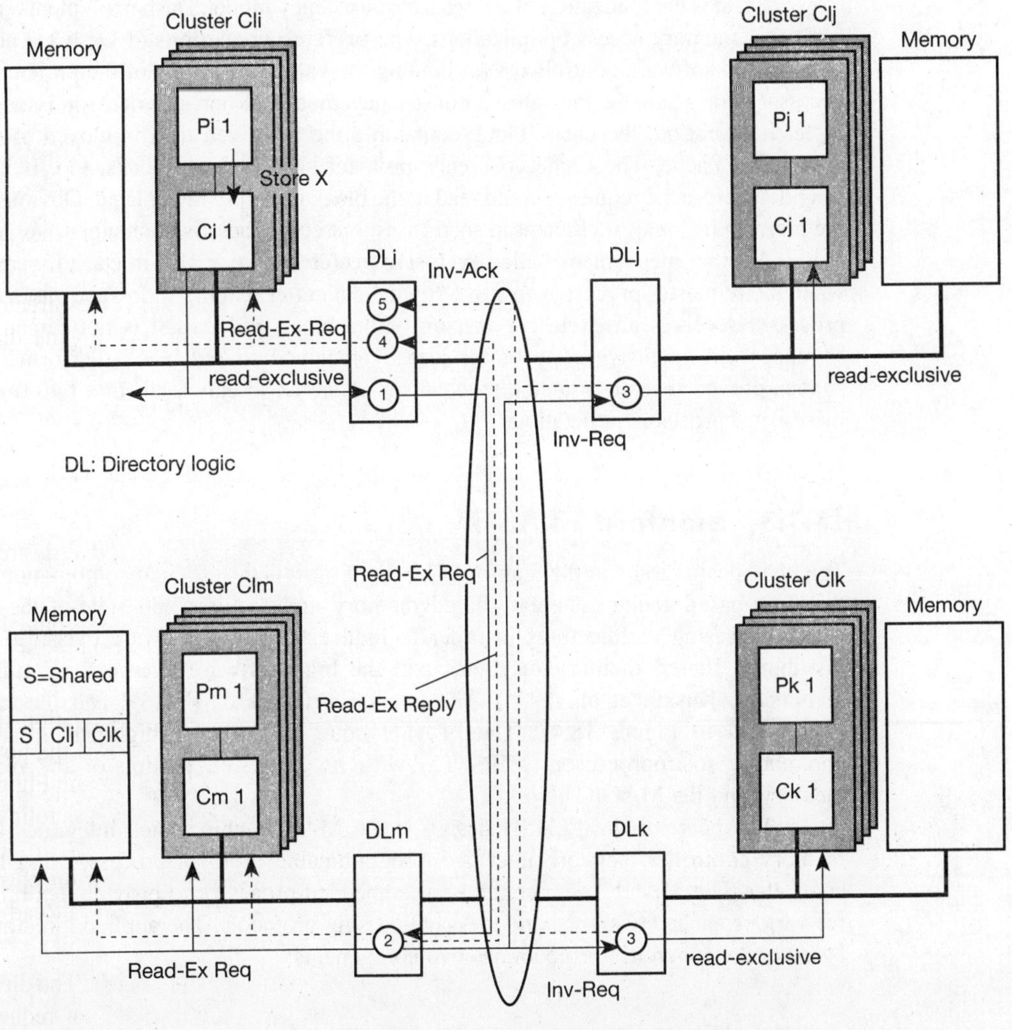

Figure 18.46 Sequence of actions in a store operation requiring remote service.

tency model described in Section 18.4.2. In the case of intercluster ordering fence operations are realized by a per-processor counter that indicates the number of outstanding requests. The fence operation can be completed when the counter reaches zero which means that there is no outstanding request. Two types of fence operations are realized in the Dash: full fence and write fence. In order to reduce hardware complexity, the write fence replaces the immediate fence described in Section 18.4.2.

The lock and unlock synchronization operations are distinguished by their physical address in the Dash. Each unlock operation realizes an implicit write fence operation, preventing the processor from issuing any other writes. It can be shown that this implicit write fence provides a sufficient implementation of the release consistency memory model.

Besides the realization of the release consistency model, Dash implements several other memory access optimizations. The **prefetch operations** of Dash are non-binding and software controlled. Not binding the value at the time of the prefetch is necessary for realizing the release consistency model. When a processor issues a prefetch operation, the cache block containing the requested data is moved to the processor's cache. The cache coherence protocol handles such blocks, too. If it is rewritten before the requester could read it, the block is simply invalidated. Obviously, the prefetch becomes inefficient in such cases, but correctness is maintained.

Another mechanism, called **exclusive prefetch**, is available in Dash for cases when the requester process wants to write the data after reading it. In such cases the processor receives an exclusive version of the block and thus it is not forced to re-request an exclusive copy of the already received shared block. Performance studies proved that the prefetch mechanism of the Dash can result in a two times increase of processor utilization.

18.7.3 Stanford FLASH

The main design issue in the Stanford FLASH project is the efficient combination of directory-based cache coherent shared memory architectures and state-of-the-art message-passing architectures in order to reduce the high hardware overhead of distributed shared memory machines and the high software overhead of multicomputers (Kuskin et al., 1994). The general structure of FLASH and its node is depicted in Figure 18.47. The FLASH node comprises a high-performance commodity microprocessor (MIPS T5) with its caches, a portion of the main memory, and the MAGIC chip.

The heart of the FLASH design is the MAGIC chip which integrates the memory controller, network interface, programmable protocol processor and I/O controller. The MAGIC chip contains an embedded processor to provide flexibility for various cache coherence and message-passing protocols. The applied directory-based cache coherence protocol has two components:

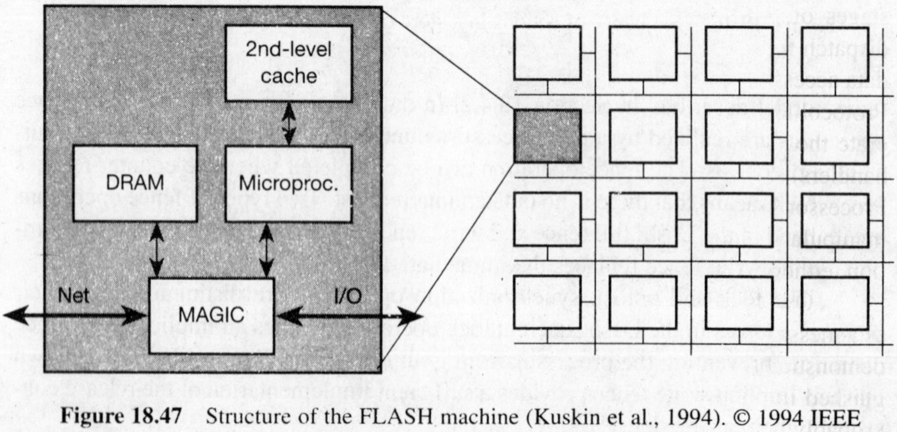

Figure 18.47 Structure of the FLASH machine (Kuskin et al., 1994). © 1994 IEEE

- Directory data structure
- Handlers to realize the cache coherent protocol.

The directory data structure is built on a semi-dynamic pointer allocation scheme for maintaining the list of sharing processors. The protocol is very similar to the Dash protocol with the main difference in collecting invalidation acknowledgements. While in the Dash each cluster collects its own invalidation acknowledgements, in FLASH they are collected by the home node where the directory element of the corresponding block is stored.

Concerning the message-passing protocols of FLASH, it can support different message types. To implement a protocol two components must be defined for the embedded processor of MAGIC: the message type and the executing handler that realises the necessary protocol. Messages are optimized to support cache operations and hence they are cache line sized. User messages are realized as long messages transferred in three stages:

(1) Initiation

(2) Transfer

(3) Reception

Besides long messages, FLASH supports short messages, too, in order to realise synchronization operations like fetch-and-op and tree barriers. These are implemented similarly to the concept of active messages (Eicken et al., 1992) but only at the system level.

The MAGIC node controller separates data and control paths as shown in Figure 18.48. The Message Split Unit divides the incoming messages into header and data part. The header is directed to the Control Macropipeline while the data part is handled by the Data Transfer Logic. The latter contains 16 data buffers each the size of a cache line. Copying the data part is avoided by keeping it in the same buffer as that in which it was received until the header is processed by the control pipeline. Then, the output header and the data part are combined again to form an outgoing message.

The Control Macropipeline comprises three main units representing three stages of a pipeline (Figure 18.49). At the first stage Inbox executes hardware dispatch for message headers and initiates speculative memory operations to reduce data access time. After preprocessing the message headers, Inbox passes them to the Protocol Processor where the actual message handler is executed. In order to accelerate the work of the Protocol Processor its instructions (the code of the message handlers) and data are stored in instruction and data caches. In addition, the Protocol Processor has a specially designed instruction set containing, for example, bitfield manipulation instructions. Finally, Outbox directs message headers to the destination, either the network, the processor or the I/O subsystem.

Owing to the central role of the MAGIC controller, FLASH can be conceived as a message-passing computer, too, extended with coherent caches. Its organization demonstrates well that the two MIMD architecture types that were strictly distinguished in the past, the shared memory and distributed memory architectures, will probably be merged into a single class in the near future.

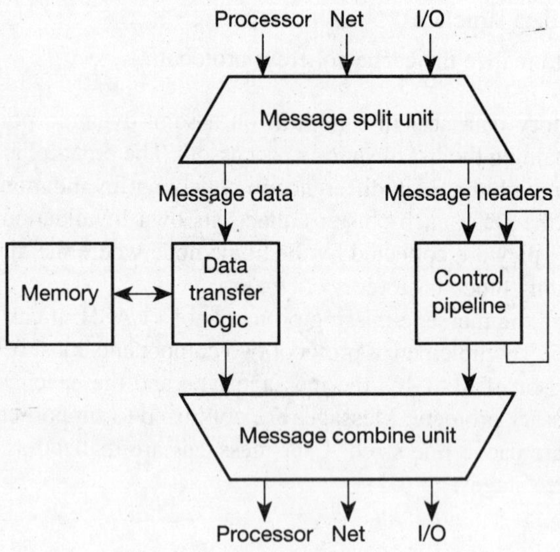

Figure 18.48 Structure of the MAGIC node controller (Kuskin et al., 1994). © 1994 IEEE

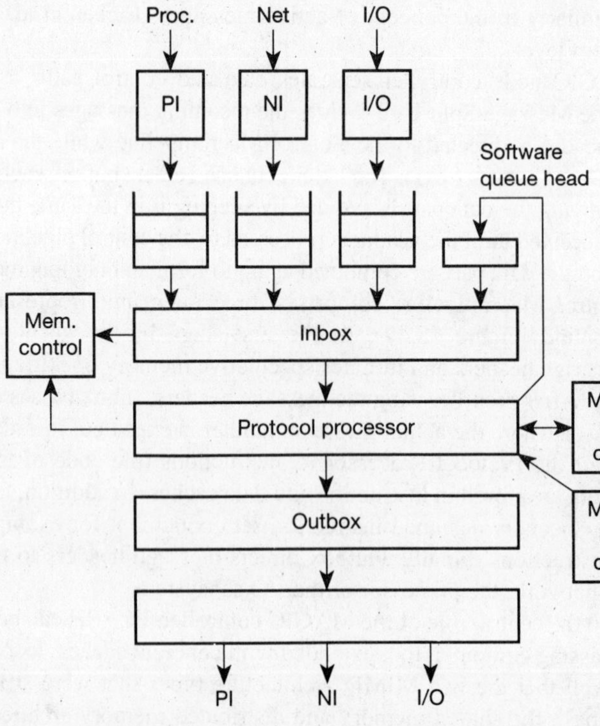

Figure 18.49 Structure of the control macropipeline (Kuskin et al., 1994). © 1994 IEEE

18.7.4 Convex Exemplar

Convex was the first computer manufacturer to commercialize a CC-NUMA machine, called the SPP1000. Here SPP stands for Scalable Parallel Processor and, indeed, the objective of the SPP Exemplar series is to create a family of high-performance computers where the number of processors can easily range from 10 to 1000 and the peak performance would reach the TeraFLOPS. The first member of the Exemplar series, the SPP1000, can be upgraded up to 128 processors (Convex Press, 1994a).

The nodes of the SPP1000 are symmetric multiprocessors, called **hypernodes**. Each hypernode comprises four functional blocks and an I/O subsystem as shown in Figure 18.50. Each functional block consists of two CPUs (HP PA-RISCs) sharing a single CPU agent, and a memory unit holding hypernode-private memory

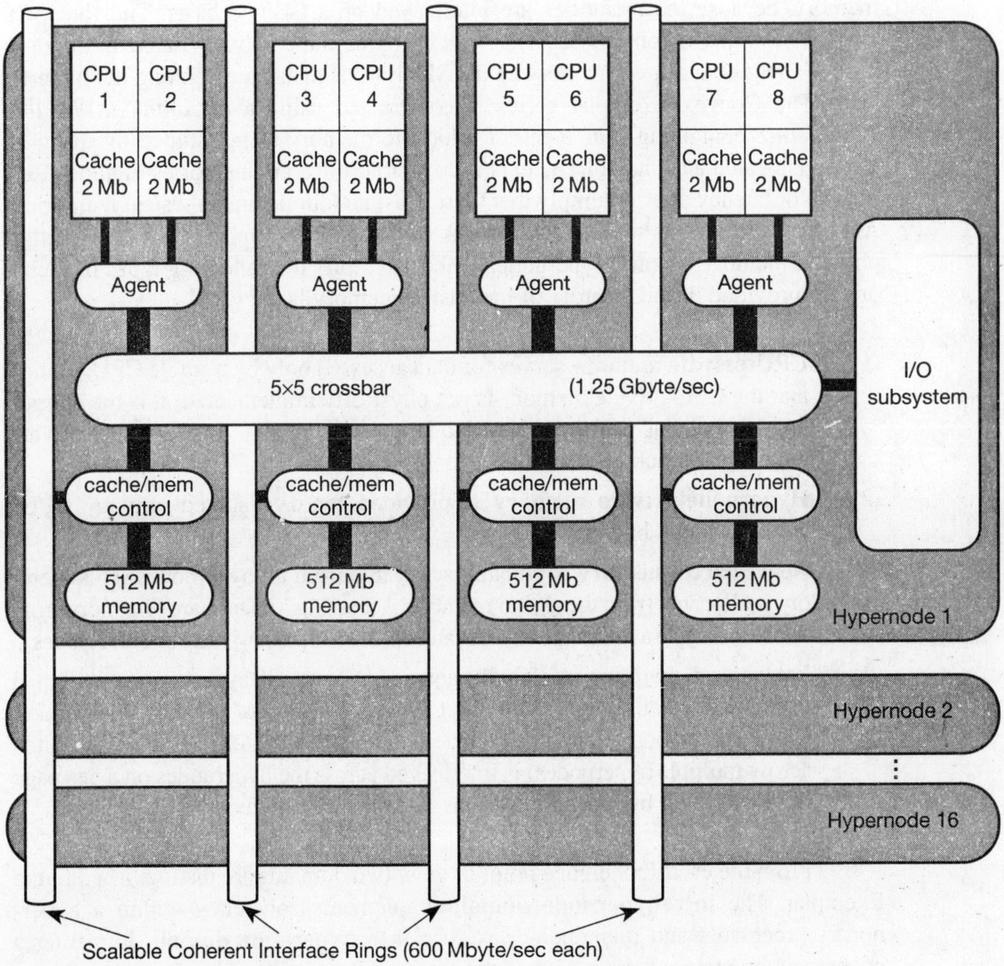

Figure 18.50 Convex Exemplar Architecture.

data, global memory data and network cache data. The four memories in a hypernode are interleaved, providing higher bandwidth and less contention than accessing a single memory. **Interleaving** is a scheme where sequential memory references search the four memories on a round-robin basis. Each memory returns 64 bytes for sequential reads. A five-port crossbar interconnects the four functional blocks and the I/O subsystem. Besides the network cache that is included in the memory unit, each CPU is associated with 1 Mbyte data and instruction caches. The cache/memory control unit realizes cache coherency within the hypernode and across the hypernodes only for the network cache units.

The hypernodes are connected by four SCI (Scalable Coherent Interface) point-to-point, unidirectional rings. As shown in Section 18.3.2, SCI can support several kinds of interconnection network; the unidirectional ring is one of those. Sequential memory references to global memory are interleaved across the four rings. This is accomplished using the ring in the same functional unit as the target memory, because the memories are interleaved on a 64-byte basis. The four SCI rings are interleaved on this basis as well; 64 bytes is the network cache line size.

The global shared memory of the SPP1000 is distributed among the hypernodes. The Convex Exemplar series is constructed using a *hierarchical memory architecture* containing four types of allocable memory differentiated by the way data is allocated and shared. The existence of four different memories in allocation, sharing or latency does not imply that there must be four distinct physical memories. All four memories, as well as the network cache, may be implemented by the same physical memory on each hypernode. In the Exemplar the following types of memory are provided, listed in order of increasing memory latency:

(1) **CPU-private memory** serves for data accessed only by a single CPU. Notice that the CPU-private memory is not physically implemented; it is the operating system that partitions hypernode-private memory used as CPU-private memory for each of the CPUs.

(2) **Hypernode-private memory** is provided for data shared only by CPUs within a single hypernode.

(3) **Near-shared memory** is globally accessible from all hypernodes. This memory is allocated from the global memory. Accessing a near-shared memory from the home hypernode requires less latency than accessing it from other nodes.

(4) **Far-shared memory** is globally accessible from all hypernodes with equal latency. It is allocated from the global memories of several hypernodes. Coherent memory that is designated far-shared (shared by and distributed across multiple hypernodes) is interleaved across the hypernodes on a per-page basis (4 Kbyte) by operating system software allocation of the table entries.

From the cache coherence point of view two domains are distinguished in the Exemplar. The **intrahypernode domain** implements coherency within a hypernode's processors and their memories. The **interhypernode domain** implements coherency among the hypernodes of the system. The two domains are bridged by a special **network cache** that tracks coherency in both domains.

The SPP system applies the write-back, invalidate SCI coherency protocol (see Section 18.3.2) to ensure cache coherence in the interhypernode domain. This is done by maintaining a linked sharing list that contains a list of all the hypernodes sharing each cache line, or the hypernode that exclusively owns the cache line. Within every hypernode a record is kept of which CPUs have encached each line in the network cache so that network coherency requests can be forwarded to the appropriate CPUs.

The cache coherence protocol of the intrahypernode domain satisfies the following requirements:

- Any number of read encachements of a cache line may be made at the same time. The cache line may be read-shared in multiple caches.
- To write data into a cache line, the cache line must be owned exclusively. This implies that any other copies must be deleted.
- Modified cache lines must be written back to memory before being deleted, or the contents can be forwarded directly to the new owner.

To illustrate what the above rules imply, consider the pseudocode of a simple matrix multiply (Figures 18.51 and 18.52). The algorithm calls spawn to fork nCPUs number of threads. Each thread receives a unique thread identifier, itid. Each iteration of the outer do j… loop is only executed by one CPU as determined by the following if statement. The CPUs are allocated in cyclical fashion to the loop iterations. The first code (Figure 18.51) works correctly for a cache coherent machine. The second code (Figure 18.52) shows the applications of those cache-handling and

```
global c(idim, idim), a(idim, idim)
global b(idim, idim), nCPUs
private i, j, k, itid
call spawn ( nCPUs )
do j = 1, idim
  if ( jmod(j, nCPU).eq.itid ) then
      do i = 1, idim
            c(i, j) = 0.0
            do k = 1, idim
                        c(i, j) = c(i, k) + a(i, k) * b(k, j)
            enddo
      enddo
  endif
enddo

call join
```

Figure 18.51 Parallel matrix multiply code for cache-coherent machine.

```
global c(idim, idim), a(idim, idim)
global b(idim, idim), nCPUs
private i, j, k, itid, tmp
semaphore is (idim,idim)
call spawn (nCPUs)
do j = 1, idim
   if ( jmod(j, nCPU).eq.itid) then
         do i = 1, idim
                tmp = 0.0
                do k = 1, idim
                       call flush (a(i,k))
                       call flush (b(k,j))
                       tmp = tmp + a(i,k)*b(k,j)
                 enddo
                 call lock (c(i,j), is(i,j))
                        c(i,j) = tmp
                        call flush(c(i,j))
                 call unlock(c(i,j), is(i,j))
         enddo
   endif
enddo
call join
```

Figure 18.52 Parallel matrix multiply code for non-cache-coherent machine.

synchronizing instructions that are necessary for maintaining cache coherency in a non-cache-coherent machine. The calls to flush on the a and b arrays are required to ensure that the executing CPU gets an up-to-date copy of the input arrays, because they may have been modified on a different CPU after being encached on the current CPU. The call to flush on the c array is needed to write the output array back to memory, so that subsequent operations will see the result of the matrix multiply.

The flush on the c array should be done in a synchronized way in order to prevent two processors from updating different c(i,j) elements in the same cache line at the same time. For that purpose, a semaphore is allocated to each element of the c array. Updating and flushing a c(i,j) element can happen in a critical section that is guarded by the associated semaphore. The lock and unlock functions are defined to compute the corresponding cache line address for their first argument, and to lock or unlock the semaphore in their second argument corresponding to that cache line. The second algorithm is what the cache coherence hardware implements in the Exemplar's intrahypernode domain.

18.8 Cache-only memory access (COMA) machines

COMA machines try to avoid the problems of static memory allocation of NUMA and CC-NUMA machines by excluding main memory blocks from the local memory of nodes and employing only large caches as node memories. In these architectures only cache memories are present; no main memory is employed either in the form of a central shared memory as in UMA machines or in the form of a distributed main memory as in NUMA and CC-NUMA computers. Similarly to the way virtual memory has eliminated the need to handle memory addresses explicitly, COMA machines render static data allocation to local memories superfluous. In COMA machines data allocation is demand driven; according to the cache coherence scheme, data is always attracted to the local (cache) memory where it is needed.

In COMA machines similar cache coherence schemes can be applied as in other shared memory systems. The only difference is that these techniques must be extended with the capability of finding the data on a cache read miss and of handling replacement. Since COMA machines are scalable parallel architectures, only cache coherence protocols that support large-scale parallel systems can be applied, that is, directory schemes and hierarchical cache coherent schemes. Two representative COMA architectures are:

- DDM (Data Diffusion Machine)
- KSR1.

DDM uses a hierarchical cache coherence scheme, while KSR1 applies a distributed directory to maintain cache coherency. In the next sections these machines and their cache coherence schemes are explained.

18.8.1 Data Diffusion Machine (DDM)

DDM is a hierarchical, tree-like multiprocessor where the leaves of the tree represent the basic DDM architecture (Hagersten et al., 1992). The basic DDM is a single bus-based multiprocessor as illustrated in Figure 18.53. It contains a number of processor/attraction memory pairs connected to the DDM bus. An attraction memory consists of three main units:

- State and data memory unit
- Controller
- Output buffer

There are two protocols applied in the controller. The snooping **memory above protocol** provides the cache coherence scheme among the attraction memories, while the **memory below protocol** realises the interface between the processor and the attraction memory. Both protocols consider a cache line of the attraction memory as one unit and a state field is stored in the attraction memory for each unit.

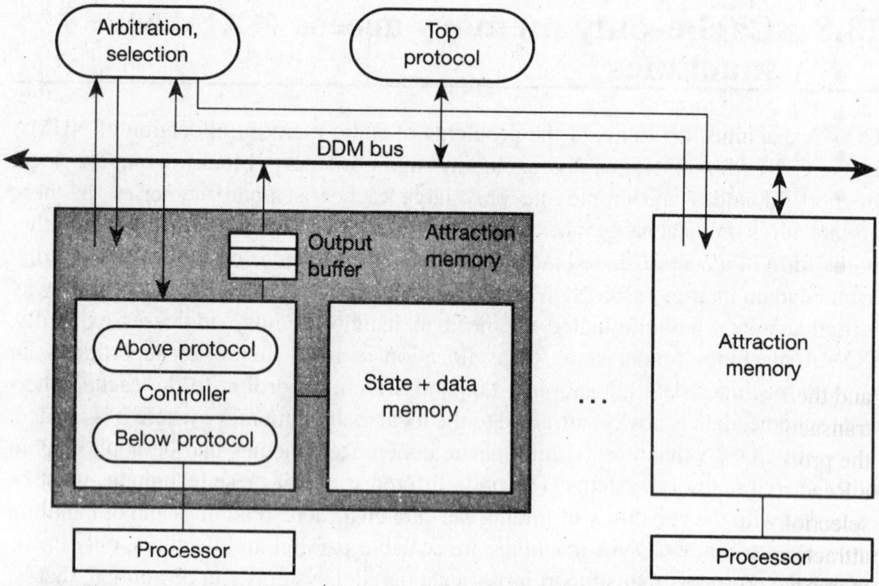

Figure 18.53 Structure of the basic DDM machine (Hagersten et al., 1992). © 1992 IEEE

The DDM employs an asynchronous split-transaction bus, that is, the bus is released between a requesting transaction and its response. This delay time can be of arbitrarily length. Deadlock avoidance on the DDM bus is guaranteed by the introduction of an arbitration/selection logic that makes sure that only one responder will be selected for each bus request.

A write-invalidate snoopy-cache protocol is introduced which limits broadcast requirements to a smaller subsystem and extends with support for replacement. A cache line can occur in any of the following seven states:

- **I (Invalid):** This attraction memory does not contain the cache line.
- **E (Exclusive):** This attraction memory contains the cache line and there is no other copy in the system.
- **S (Shared):** There are several copies of the cache line and one of them is located in this attraction memory.
- **R (Reading):** This node started a read transaction and is waiting for the reply.
- **W (Waiting):** This node started an erase transaction and is waiting to become Exclusive.
- **RW (Reading-and-Waiting):** This node is waiting for a data value that becomes Exclusive later.
- **A (Answering):** This node is supposed to answer a read request.

The last four states are the so-called transient ones which are needed because of the split-transaction bus where outstanding requests must be remembered. The following transactions are permitted on the DDM bus:

- **Erase:** Erases all copies of this cache line.
- **Exclusive:** Acknowledges an erase request.
- **Read:** Reads a copy of the cache line.
- **Data:** Transfers data for an earlier read request.
- **Inject:** Carries the only copy of a cache line and looks for an attraction memory to place it. (Inject is initiated by a replacement.)
- **Out:** Transfers the cache line out of the attraction memory. It will terminate when another copy of the cache line is found. (Out is caused by a replacement.)

The state transition diagram of Figure 18.54 shows the possible transactions and their relationship with the possible states of the attraction memories. Notice that transactions can arrive either from the processor of a node or from the network. If the processor wants to read an invalid cache line (I), the attraction memory initiates a Read transaction on the network and rewrites the state into Reading (R). The bus selection logic will select one attraction memory to service the request. The selected attraction memory places the requested data on the bus and the requesting attraction memory will grab it and place it as a shared cache line in the local cache.

Writing to an invalid cache line results in sending a Read transaction on the bus and changing the state to RW. When the requested cache line arrives, its state becomes Waiting and an Erase transaction is initiated on the bus. Writing to a shared cache line also initiates an erase transaction on the bus and changes the state to Waiting where the Exclusive acknowledgement must be waited for. Notice that simultaneous attempts to write the same cache line will put many attraction memories in Waiting state with pending Erase transactions in their output buffers. In order to solve this write race each output buffer unit should snoop transactions on the bus.

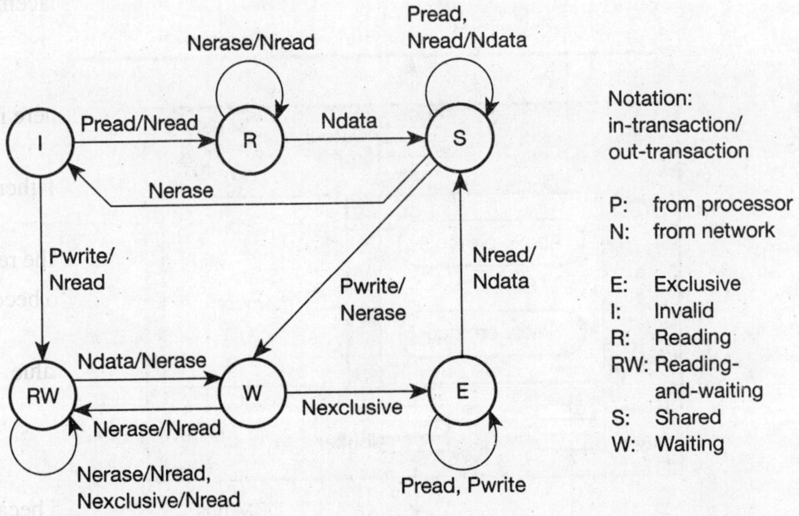

Figure 18.54 State transition diagram of the attraction memory protocol (Hagersten et al., 1992). © 1992 IEEE

The first Erase reaching the bus will win the write race and all the other transactions, bound for the same item, are removed from the output buffers and their related state is changed to RW. The winner receiving the Exclusive acknowledgement may proceed. The other state transitions are easy to follow based on Figure 18.54 and hence they are left to the reader.

Replacement should take place when the attraction memory runs out of space. Under such conditions some cache lines, for example the oldest one in Shared state, should be forced to leave the attraction memory, making room for other cache lines. Replacing a shared cache line generates an Out transaction. The top protocol checks if there is any attraction memory containing the same cache line in state Shared, Reading, Waiting or Reading-and-Waiting. If there is, the top protocol does nothing, otherwise, it converts the Out transaction into an Inject one. The meaning of this transaction is that the last copy of the given cache line should be placed in a new attraction memory. The selection strategy for the new place first tries to find an invalid space and then to replace a Shared cache line.

The single bus-based basic DDM architecture can be expanded to a hierarchical multiprocessor system by simply replacing the top protocol with a directory unit which connects the bus of the basic DDM architecture to a higher-level bus. The structure of the directory unit is shown in Figure 18.55. The directory unit can be used to connect two higher-level buses, resulting in a tree-like hierarchical architecture where the leaves are basic DDM architectures, the root is the top and the other nodes of the tree are directory units as illustrated in Figure 18.56.

The heart of the directory unit is a set-associative state memory containing administrative information for each cache line residing in an attraction memory below it. However, *the state memory does not contain any data*. The controller of the directory units realizes two protocols. The **directory above protocol** is a snooping

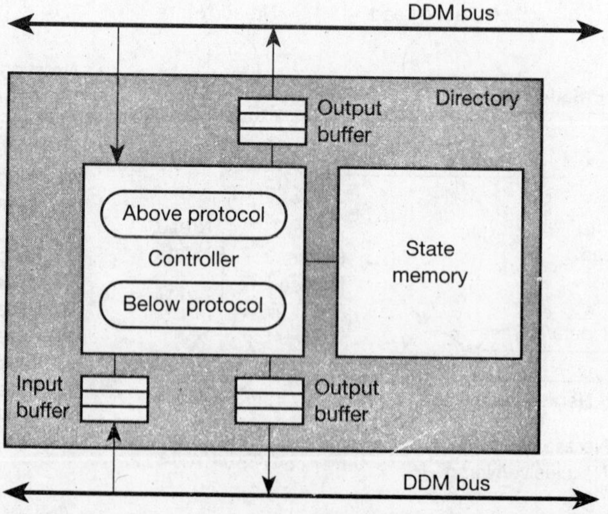

Figure 18.55 Structure of the directory unit (Hagersten et al., 1992). © 1992 IEEE

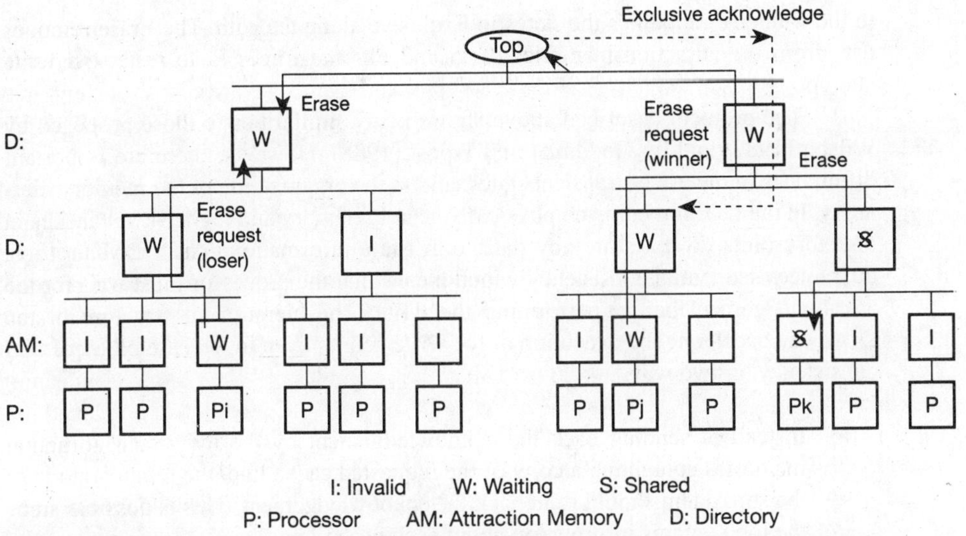

Figure 18.56 Write race in the hierarchical DDM (Hagersten et al., 1992). © 1992 IEEE

one very much resembling the memory above protocol. The **directory below protocol** is compatible with the top protocol for items in Exclusive state.

Trying to read data that is not available in the basic DDM architecture leads to the process of **multilevel read**. In such a case the directory unit passes the read request to the next higher-level bus and changes the status of the cache line to Reading. The read request travels up the tree until a directory is found whose subsystem contains the requested cache line. This directory passes the request down the tree until it reaches an attraction memory containing the requested cache line. The state of the data is set to Answering in the directories passing the request down. When the request arrives at the destination attraction memory a path, containing Reading and Answering directories, indicates the way back to the requester.

A **multilevel write** is needed when the lowest-level directory does not contain the requested item in Exclusive state. In such a case the original Erase transaction is forwarded to the next higher level while all the copies on the current bus level are erased and the state of the item is changed to Waiting in the directory, indicating that an Exclusive acknowledgement is waited for. The propagation of the Erase request ends when a directory in Exclusive state or the top is reached. In this case the Exclusive acknowledgement is sent back along the path marked by Waiting states, changing the states to Exclusive.

A **write race** can occur among processors and is solved similarly to that of the basic DDM. The Erase requests propagate up the tree until they reach the lowest common bus. The winner, the one reaching that bus first, returns with an Exclusive acknowledgement following the path marked by Waiting states, while the loser attraction memory receives the Erase transaction. Upon receipt of the Erase, the loser automatically generates a new write action. A write race between processors Pi and Pj is shown in Figure 18.56. The Exclusive acknowledgement, sent by the top to the winner Pj, modifies the states to Exclusive along the path. The Erase removes data from the attraction memories of Pi and Pk, and forces Pi to restart its write attempt.

The protocol described above shows many similarities to those proposed by Wilson (1987) and by Goodman and Woest (1988). However, there are important differences in the use of transient states, and in the organization of the memory hierarchy. In the DDM, there is no physically shared memory and higher-level caches in directory units do not store any data, only state information. The DDM protocol guarantees sequential consistency which means that the processor must wait for the acknowledgement before performing the write. The hierarchical structure of the DDM can accelerate the execution of the write action, even in the case of sequential consistency, in two ways:

- Instead of sending back the acknowledgement by the individual attraction memories containing a copy of the requested cache line, the topmost node of the subsystem should send back the acknowledgement. This is possible since the top contains information about each cache line.
- Upon receiving the acknowledgement, a write can take place before the other copies of the cache line are actually erased.

18.8.2 KSR1

The KSR1 machine was the first commercially available CCMA machine in which the logically single address space is realized by a collection of local caches and by the so-called **ALLCACHE Engine** (Frank et al., 1993). The **ALLCACHE Engine** realizes a sequentially consistent cache coherence algorithm based on a distributed directory scheme. ALLCACHE stores data in pages and subpages. The unit of memory allocation in local caches is the page containing 16 Kbytes. The unit of data transfer among local caches is the subpage consisting of 128 bytes.

The distributed directory is a matrix in which a row is allocated for each subpage and a column for each local cache as shown in Figure 18.57. A matrix element is empty if the corresponding local cache does not contain any copy of the subpage. Since it is the general case, the matrix is very sparse and therefore stored in a condensed way, excluding those elements that are empty. Non-empty elements can represent any of the following four states:

- **EO (Exclusive Owner):** This is the only valid copy in the whole machine.
- **C (Copy):** At least two valid copies of the subpage exist in the machine.
- **NO (Non-exclusive Owner):** When several copies of the subpage exist, one of them is marked as the non-exclusive owner.
- **I (Invalid):** Although a copy of the subpage exists in the local cache, it is invalid and will not be used.

A read miss will result in sending a request packet to the ALLCACHE Engine which sends back a copy of the requested data from the local cache where the

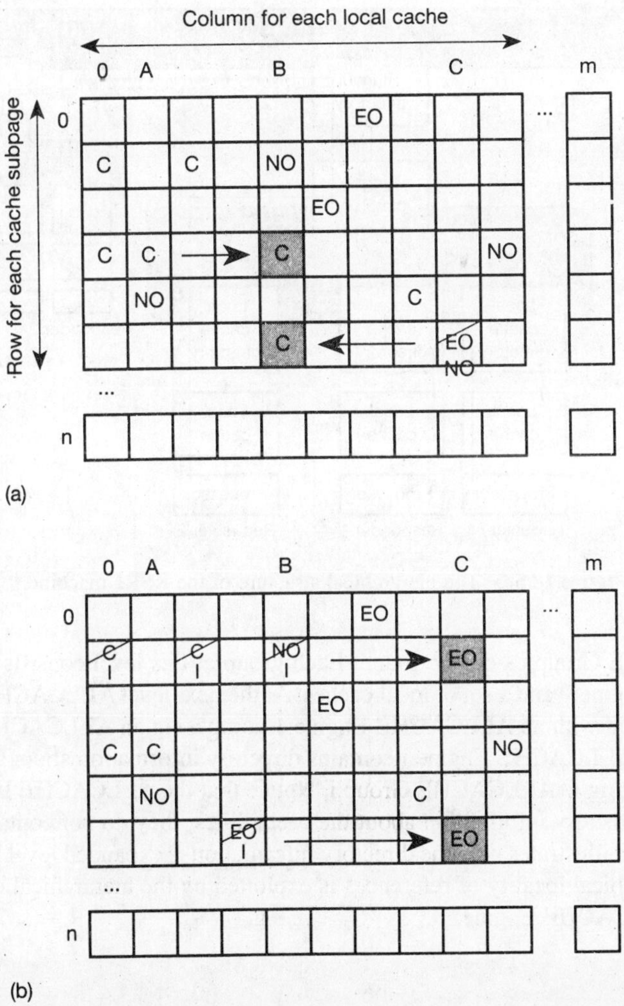

Figure 18.57 ALLCACHE Engine operations in the KSR1 (Frank et al., 1993). (a) Read operations by processor B; (b) write operations by processor C. © 1993 IEEE

exclusive owner is currently situated. At the same time the state of the owner is changed to Non-exclusive Owner. If there is no exclusive owner, the copy of the requested data is taken from any local cache where a valid copy exists as illustrated in Figure 18.57(a).

Writing a non-existent or invalid subpage leads again to the activation of the ALLCACHE Engine. If an exclusive owner exists, the subpage is copied from there to the requester, while the requester becomes the new exclusive owner and the original owner is invalidated. If several copies exist, the exclusive ownership is transferred to the requester while the other copies are invalidated as shown in Figure 18.57(b).

Like the Data Diffusion Machine, the KSR1 has a hierarchical organization, but based on rings instead of buses (Figure 18.58). At the lowest level of this hierarchy

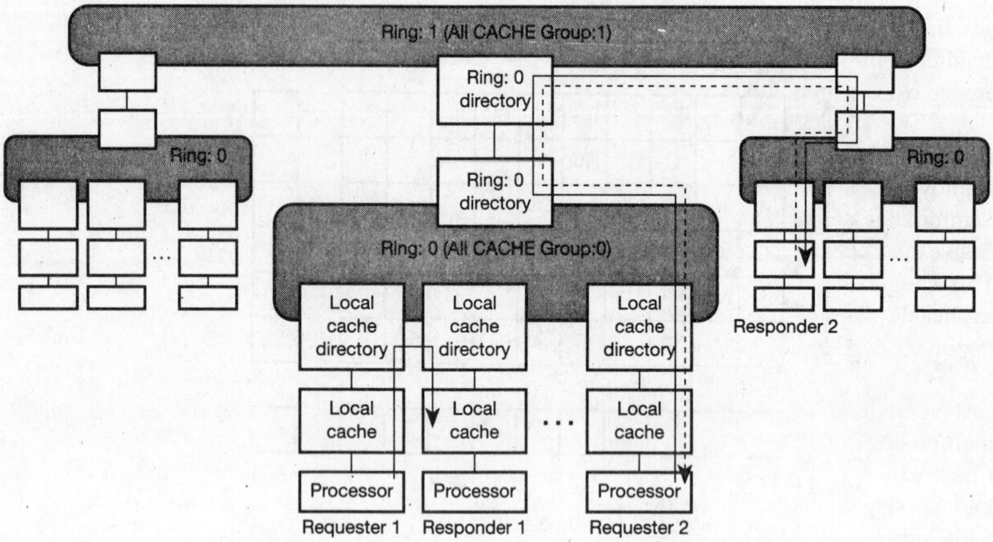

Figure 18.58 The hierarchical structure of the KSR1 machine.

ALLCACHE Group:0s can be found. Each group at this level consists of an ALLCACHE Engine:0 and a set of local caches. At the next level ALLCACHE Group:0s are combined with an ALLCACHE Engine:1 composing an ALLCACHE Group:1, and so on. ALLCACHE Engine:i contains directory information about all the cache lines belonging to ALLCACHE Group:i. Notice that the ALLCACHE Engines contain only directory information about the cache lines; they do not contain any data. Figure 18.58 illustrates how the directory information is expanded level by level and how hierarchical locality of references is exploited by the hierarchical organization of the ALLCACHE Engine.

18.9 Summary

18.9.1 Assessment of interconnection networks

Two main tendencies can be witnessed in the application of interconnection networks. First- and second-generation multiprocessors employed the three main types of dynamic interconnection networks: buses, crossbars and multistage networks. Buses were used for relatively inexpensive small-size multiprocessors like the Sequent Balance, Sequent Symmetry, and Encore Multimax. Crossbars were also used in small-size systems where high performance was a main design issue, such as C.MMP and Alliant FX/8. In the first- and second-generation multiprocessors, the multistage network was the most popular interconnection for building scalable multiprocessors with hundreds of processors since this network had relatively good price and performance properties for that number of processors. The bandwidth of the bus was unsatisfactory, while the price and complexity of the crossbar were intolerable for hundreds of processors. Representative multiprocessors built on multistage networks are the NYU Ultracomputer, Cedar, IBM RP3 and BBN TC-2000.

The significant progress of static interconnection networks of message-passing architectures caused recent, third-generation scalable multiprocessors to employ mesh or ring interconnections instead of multistage networks. Cray T3D, Stanford Dash and Stanford FLASH apply 3- or 2-dimensional meshes, while Convex Exemplar, Hector and KSR1 use rings to connect nodes in the multiprocessor. This shift from multistage networks to static interconnection networks is easily explicable using Table 18.5 which summarizes the main properties of the most important dynamic and static network types.

While multistage networks seemed to die out, buses and crossbars still survive as the internal connection between processors within clusters of scalable multiprocessors. Stanford Dash and Hector apply buses inside their clusters, while Convex Exemplar introduces a crossbar for the hypernode. Current workstations are built as small-size multiprocessors and hence they employ buses to connect their RISC processors. A typical example is the Power Challenge of Silicon Graphics. As chip fabrication technology advances, future RISC chips will be built as multiprocessors and will use buses to connect their multiple CPUs inside the chip (Gwennap, 1994). Crossbars found a new application area in recent vector supercomputers like the Cray Y-MP/816 and Fujitsu VPP500 to connect their powerful but small number of vector processors.

18.9.2 Assessment of cache coherence schemes

The only matured cache coherence scheme is the snoopy cache technique which has been intensively used in single bus-based commercial multiprocessors. Directory-based and hierarchical cache coherence protocols are still under active research. Only

Table 18.5 Comparing the dynamic and static network characteristics.

Network	*Bus*	*Crossbar*	*Multistage*	*Tree*	*Hypercube*	*Mesh*
Minimum latency	const.	const.	log(N)	log(N)	log(N)	$N^{1/2}$
Bandwidth per processor	1/N	const.	const.	const.	const.	const.
Wiring cost	w (width of bus)	N	Nlog(N)	N	Nlog(N)	N
Switching cost	N	N^2	Nlog(N)	–	–	–
Connectivity	Any to any but only one to one at a time	All permutations, one at a time	Some permutations if the network is unblocked	3 nearest neighbours	log(N) nearest neighbours	4 nearest neighbours

Table 18.6 Comparison of six representative commercial supercomputers

	Convex Exemplar	*Cray T3D*	*IBM SP-1/2*	*Intel Paragon*	*KSR-1*	*TMC CM5*
Commodity RISC processor	Yes	Yes	Yes	–	–	Yes
64-bit addressing	Yes	Yes	–	–	Yes	–
All 64-bit data	Yes	Yes	Yes	–	Yes	–
cache coherence	Yes	–	–	–	Yes	–
Virtual shared memory	Yes	Yes	–	–	Yes	–
Explicit message passing	Yes	Yes	Yes	Yes	Yes	Yes
Standalone single OS	Yes	–	–	Yes	Yes	Yes

two commercial scalable multiprocessors have been supplied with hardware-supported cache coherency as shown by Table 18.6: KSR-1 and Convex Exemplar. Other supercomputer vendors consider the directory-based and hierarchical cache coherence protocols too risky to use. Even the most carefully designed Scalable Coherent Interface lacks any mathematical proof of correctness. However, such a complex protocol cannot be considered reliable without exhaustive verification. Under these circumstances it is understandable why supercomputer vendors recently turned their attention to the more tiring but more reliable message-passing paradigm instead of the shared memory programming model. Table 18.6, which compares the main features of six representative commercial supercomputers, justifies this statement. No matter what hardware concept these machines follow (distributed memory or distributed shared memory), all of them provide an explicit message-passing interface to the user.

18.9.3 The trend of merging the three main classes of MIMD architectures

It can be observed quite clearly that the three main directions of MIMD architectures are convergent and that the fourth-generation scalable MIMD computer will demonstrate the most characteristic features of each type in the very close future.

Multi-threaded architectures will dominate the processor design and the computation processor will certainly be a multi-threaded superscalar processor. The computation processor will be supported by some specialized processors such as the communication processor and router inherited from distributed memory computers and by some coprocessors for reducing memory latency like the remote memory request and synchronization coprocessors of the *T node (see Chapter 16). As a result of the shared memory technology, processor nodes will be equipped with coherent caches and directory logics. Such nodes could be extended to a supernode (or cluster) by connecting several multi-threaded computation processors via a shared bus. The FLASH and April machines well represent the first steps in this direction. FLASH tries to combine directory-based cache coherency with message passing, while April integrates multi-threading with cache coherency. Figure 18.59 illustrates how the three generations of different MIMD computers converge to the envisaged fourth-generation scalable parallel computer.

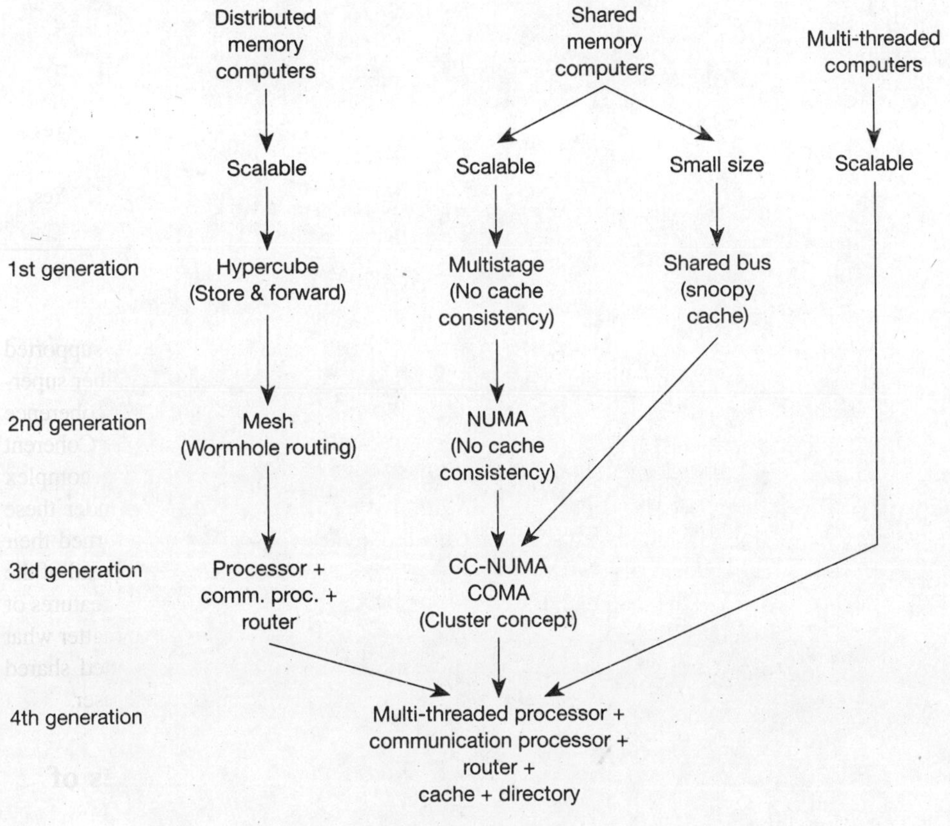

Figure 18.59 The convergence of scalable MIMD computers.

References for Part IV

References

Agarwal A., Kubiatiwicz J., Kranz D., Lim B.H., Yeung D., Souza G.D and Parkin M. (1993). Sparcle: An evolutionary processor design for multiprocessors. *IEEE Micro*, **13**(3), 48–61, June

Anderson T. (1990). The performance of spin lock alternatives for shared-memory multiprocessors. *IEEE Trans. on Parallel and Distributed Systems*, **1**(1), 6–16

Archibald J. and Baer J.L. (1986). Cache coherence protocols: Evaluation using a multiprocessor simulation model. *ACM Trans. Comput. Syst.*, **4**, Nov., 273–98

Arvind and Iannucci R.A. (1987). Two fundamental issues in multiprocessing. In. *Proc. DFVLR Conf. 1987 on Parallel Processing in Science and Engineering*, Bonn-Bad Godesberg, Germany, June LNCS 295 Springer-Verlag

Arvind and Thomas R.E. (1980). I-structures: An Efficient Data Type for Functional Languages. *Technical Report LCS/TM-178*, MIT

Athas, W.C. and Seitz, C.L. (1988). Multicomputers: Message-passing concurrent computers. *Computer*, **21**(8), Aug. 9–24

Carlton M. and Despain A. (1990). Multiple-bus shared-memory system: Aquarius project. *IEEE Computer*, **23**(6), 80–2

Cheong H. and Veidenbaum A.V. (1988). Cache coherence scheme with fast selective invalidation. In *Proc. 15th Annual Int. Symp. on Computer Architecture*, p. 299

Cheong H. and Veidenbaum A.V. (1990). Compiler-directed cache management in multiprocessors. *IEEE Computer*, **23**(6), 39–47

Convex Press (1994a), *Convex Exemplar Architecture*, p. 239

Convex Press (1994b), *Convex Exemplar Programming Guide*, p. 316

Dally W.J. (1992). Virtual-channel flow control. *IEEE Trans. Parallel and Distributed Systems*, **3**(2), Mar., 194–205

Dally W.J. et al. (1987). Architecture of a message driven processor. In *Proc. 14th Int. Symp. Computer Architecture*, IEEE CS Press, June, pp. 189–205

Dally W.J., Fiske J.A.S., Keen J.S., Lethin R.A., Noakes M.D., Nuth P.R., Davison R.E. and Fyler G.A. (1992). The Message-Driven Processor: A multicomputer processing node with efficient mechanisms. *IEEE Micro*, **12**(2), 23–39

Dubois M., Scheurich C. and Briggs F.A. (1986). Memory access buffering in multiprocessors. *In Proc. 13th Annual Int. Symp. on Computer Architecture*, pp. 434–42

Dubois M., Scheurich C. and Briggs F.A. (1988). Synchronization, coherence, and event ordering in multiprocessors. *IEEE Computer*, No. 2, 9–21

Eicken T., von Culler D., Goldstein S. and Schauser K. (1992). Active messages: a mechanism for integrated communication and computation. In *The 19th Annual International Symposium on Computer Architecture*, pp. 256–66. ACM and IEEE, ACM Press, May

Encore Computer Corporation (1987). *Multimax Technical Summary, 726-01759*, March

Evripidou P. and Gaudiot J-L. (1991). The USC decoupled multilevel data-flow execution model. In *Advanced Topics in Dataflow Computing*, pp. 347–79. Englewood Cliffs, NJ: Prentice Hall

Frank S., Burkhardt H. and Rothnie J. (1993). The KSR1: Bridging the gap between shared memory and MPPs. In *Proc. COMPCON 1993*, pp. 285–94

Glass C.J. and Ni L.M. (1992). The Turn Model for adaptive routing. In *Proc. 19th Int. Symp. Computer Architecture*, pp. 278–87. Los Alamitos, CA: IEEE CS Press. Order No. 2940 1992

Gao J.R., Hum H.H.J. and Monti J.-M. (1989). Towards an efficient hybrid dataflow architecture model. In *Proc. PARLE '89*

Gharachorloo K. et al. (1990). Memory consistency and event ordering in scalable shared-memory multiprocessors. In *Proc. 17th Annual Int. Symp. on Computer Architecture*, pp. 15–26

Gjessing S. et al. (1992). SCI cache coherence protocol. In *Scalable Shared Memory Multiprocessors* (Dubois M. and Thakkar S.S, Ed.), pp. 219–38. Kluwer Academic Publisher

Goodman J.R. (1989). Cache Consistency and Sequential Consistency. *Technical Report no. 61*, SCI Committee, March

Goodman J.R. and Woest P.J. (1988). The Wisconsin Multicube: A new large-scale cache-coherent multiprocessor. In *Proc. 15th Annual Int. Symp. on Computer Architecture*, pp. 422–31

Graunke G. and Thakkar S. (1990). Synchronization algorithms for shared-memory multiprocessors. *IEEE Computer*, No. 6, 60–9

Gwennap L. (1994). Microprocessors head toward MP on a chip. *IEEE Micro*, No. 5, 18–21

Hagersten E., Landin A. and Haridi S. (1992). DDM – A cache-only memory architecture. *IEEE Computer*, **25**(9), 44–54

Hoare C.A.R. (1978). Communicating Sequential Processes. *Comm. ACM*, **21**(8), 666–77

Hoare C.A.R. (1985). Communicating Sequential Processes, p. 256. Prentice-Hall International

Hum H.H.J. and Gao J.R. (1991). A novel high-speed memory organization for fine grain multithread computing. In *Proc. PARLE'91*

Iannucci R.A. (1988). Towards a dataflow/von Neumann hybrid architecture. In *Proc.15th Ann. Int. Symp. on Computer Architecture*, May

Inmos Ltd. (1988a). *OCCAM 2 Reference Manual*. Prentice-Hall International

Inmos Ltd. (1988b). *Transputer Reference Manual*. Prentice-Hall International

Inmos Ltd. (1991). *The T9000 Transputer Products Overview Manual* (Inmos Databook Series 72 TRN 228 00). Bristol: Inmos

Kawano T., Kusakabe S., Taniguchi R. and Amamiya M. (1995). Fine-grain multi-thread processor archhitecture for massively parallel processing. In *Proc. First IEEE Symp. High-Performance Computer Architecture*, pp. 308–31

Kessler R.E. and Schwarzmeier J.L. (1993). CRAY T3D: A new dimension for Cray Research. In *Proc. COMPCON 1993*, pp. 176–82

Kuskin, J. et al. (1994). The Stanford FLASH multiprocessor. In *Proc. 21st Annual Int. Symp. on Computer Architecture*, pp. 302–13

Lamport L. (1979). How to make a multiprocessor computer that correctly executes multiprocess programs. *IEEE Trans. on Computers*, **28**(9), 690–1

Lee B. and Hurson A.R. (1994). Dataflow architectures and multithreading. *IEEE Computer*, **27**(8), 27–39

Lenoski D. et al. (1992). The Stanford Dash multiprocessor. *IEEE Computer*, **25**(3), 63–79

May M.D., Thompson P.W. and Welch P.H., eds (1994). *Networks, Routers and Transputers*, p. 210. IOS Press

Min S.L. and Baer J.-L. (1989). A timestamp-based cache coherence scheme. In *Proc. 1989 Int. Conf. Parallel Processing*, vol. I, Aug. pp. 23–32. Los Alamitos, CA: CS Press

Mudge T.N., Hayes J.P. and Winsor D.C. (1987). Multiple bus architectures. *IEEE Computer*, **20**(6), 42–8

Ni L.M. and McKinley P.K. (1993). A survey of wormhole routing techniques in direct networks. *IEEE Computer*, **26**(2), 62–76

Nikhil R. and Arvind (1989). Can dataflow subsume von Neumann computing? In *Proc. 16th Ann. Int. Symp. on Computer Architecture*, pp. 262–72

Nikhil R., Papadopoulos G. and Arvind (1992). *T: A multithreaded massively parallel architecture. In *Proc. 19th Ann. Int. Symp. on Computer Architecture*, pp. 156–67

Noakes M.D., Wallach D.A. and Dally W.J. (1993). The J-Machine multicomputer: An architectural evaluation. In *Proc. 20th Ann. Int. Symp. on Computer Architecture*, pp. 224–35

Papadopoulos G.M. and Culler D.E. (1990). Monsoon: an explicit token-store architecture. In *Proc. 17th Ann. Int. Symp. on Computer Architecture*

Papamarcos M. and Patel J. (1994). A low overhead coherent solution for multiprocessors with private cache memories. In *Proc. 11th Ann. Int. Symp. on Computer Architecture*, pp. 348–54

Pountain D. (1990). Virtual channels: the next generation of Transputers. *Byte*, **15**(4), 3–12

Sato M., Kodama Y., Sakai S., Yamaguchi Y. and Koumura Y. (1992). Thread-based programming for the EM-4 hybrid dataflow machine. In *Proc. 19th Ann. Int. Symp. on Computer Architecture*, May, pp. 146–55, ACM Press

Siegel H.J. (1989). *Interconnection Networks for Large-Scale Parallel Processing: Theory and Case Studies*, 2nd edn. New York, NY: McGraw-Hill

Silicon Graphics Computer Systems. (1995). *Power Challenge*. Technical Report

Stenström P. (1989). A cache consistency protocol for multiprocessors with multistage networks. In *Proc. 16th Ann. Int. Symp. on Computer Architecture*, pp. 407–15

Stunkel C.B. & al. (1994). The SP1 high-performance switch. In *Proc. Scalable High Performance Computing Conf.*, pp. 150–7

Thakker C.P., Stewart L.C. and Satterthwaite E.H. (1988). Firefly: A multiprocessor workstation. *IEEE Trans. on Computers*, **37**(8), 909–20

Vranesic Z.G. et al. (1991). Hector: A hierarchically structured shared-memory multiprocessor. *IEEE Computer*, **24**(1), 72–9

Wilson A.W. (1987). Hierarchical cache/bus architecture for shared memory multiprocessors. In *Proc. 14th Ann. Int. Symp. on Computer Architecture*, pp. 244–52

Further Reading

Agarwal A. (1992). Performance tradeoffs in multithreaded processors. *IEEE Transactions on Parallel and Distributed Systems*, **3**(5), 525–39, September

Agarwal A. et al. (1988). An evaluation of directory schemes for cache coherence. In Proc. *15th Annual Int. Symp. on Computer Architecture*, pp. 280–9

Agarwal A., Lim B.H., Kranz D. and Kubiatiwicz J. (1990). APRIL: A processor architecture for multiprocessing. In *Proc. ISCA-17*, pp. 104–14, Seattle, Wash., May

Alverson G., Alverson R. and Callahan D. (1991). Exploting heterogeneus parallelism on a multithreaded multiprocessor. *Workshop on Multithreaded Computers, Proc. Supercomputing*, ACM Sigraph, Nov.

Alverson R., Callahan D., Cummings D., Koblenz B., Porterfield A. and Smith B. (1990). The Tera Computer System. In *Proc. Intl. Conf. on Supercomputing*, Amsterdam, June

Amamiya M., Takesue M., Hasegawa R. and Mikami H. (1986). Implementation and evaluation of a list-processing-oriented data flow machine. In *Proc. 13th Annu. Symp. on Computer Architecture*, pp. 10–19, June

Ametak (1987). *Series 2010 Product Description*, Ametek Computer Research Division, Monrova

Arlauskas R. (1988). IPSC/2 system: A second-generation hypercube. In *Proc. Third Conf. Hypercube Concurrent Computers and Applications*. pp 33-36. New York: Assn. for Computing Machinery.

Arvind and Culler D.E. (1986). Dataflow architectures. *Ann. Review in Computer Science*. **1**, pp. 225-53

Arvind and Iannucci R.A. (1987). Two fundamental issues in multiprocessing. In *Conference on Parallel Processsing in Science and Engineering*

Arvind and Nikhil R.S. (1987). Executing a program on the MIT Tagged-Token Dataflow Architecture. In *Proc. PARLE (Parallel Architectures and Languages Europe)*, Eindhoven, The Netherlands, June

Arvind and Nikhil R.S. (1989). Executing a program on the MIT Tagged-Token Dataflow Architecture. *IEEE Trans. on Computers*

Bitar P. and Despain A.M. (1986). Multiprocessor cache synchronization issues, innovations, evolution. In *Proc. 13th Annual Int. Symp. on Computer Architecture*, pp. 424–33

Brantley W.C., McAuliffe K.P. and Weiss J. (1985). RP3 processor–memory element. *IEEE Trans. Computers*, **C-34**(10), Sept. 782–9

Buehrer R. and Ekanadham K. (1987). Incorporating dataflow ideas into von Neumann processors for parallel execution. *IEEE Trans. on Computers*, **C-36**(12), Dec, 1515–22

Cheriton D.R., Goosen H.A. and Boyle P.D. (1991). Paradigm: A highly scalable shared-memory multicomputer architecture. *IEEE Computer*, **24**(2), 33–46

Dally W.J. (1990). Performance analysis of k-ary n-cube interconnection networks. *IEEE Trans. Computers*, **39**(6), June 775–85

Dally W.J. and Seitz C.L. (1986). The Torus routing chip. *Distributed Computing*, **1**, 187–96

Dally W.J. and Seitz C.L. (1987). Deadlock-free message routing in multiprocessor interconnection networks. *IEEE Trans. Computers,* **C-36**(5), May 547–53

Dally W.J., Keen J.S. and Noakes M.D. (1993). The J-Machine architecture and evaluation. In *Proc. 20th Annual Int. Symp. on Computer Architecture*, pp. 183–8

Dennis J.B. (1980). Data flow supercomputers. *IEEE Computer*, 48–56, November

Dinning A. (1989). A survey of synchronization methods for parallel computers. *IEEE Computer*, **22**(7), 66–77

Gajski D.D., Padua D.A., Kuck D.J. and Kuhn R.R. (1982). A second opinion of data flow machines and languages. *IEEE Computer*, **15**(2), February, 58–69

Gaudiot J-L. and Bic L. (1991). *Advanced Topics in Dataflow Computing*, pp. 617. Englewood Cliffs, N.J: Prentice Hall

Gaudiot J-L. and Kim C. (1993). Data-driven and multithreaded architectures for high-performance computing. Summer School, Praque, July

Gaughan P.T. and Yalamanchili S. (1993). Adaptive routing protocols for hypercube interconnection networks. *IEEE Computer*, **26**(5), 12–22

Grafe V., Davidson G., Hoch J. and Holmes V. (1989). The Epsilon dataflow processor. In *Proc. 16th Ann. Intl. Symp. on Computer Architecture*, Jerusalem, Israel, pp. 36–45, May

Gupta A., Hennessy J., Gharachorloo K., Mowry T. and Weber W. (1991). Comparative evaluation of latency reducing and tolerating techniques. In *Proc. 18th Intl. Symp. on Comp. Arch.*, Toronto, Canada, May

Hagersten E., Haridi S. and Warren D.H.D. (1990). The cache coherence protocol of the data diffusion machine. In *Cache and Interconnect Architectures in Multiprocessors* (Dubois M. and Thakkar S.S, ed.), pp. 165–88. Kluwer Academic Publisher

Halstead, R.H.Jr and Fujita T. (1988). MASA: A multithreaded processor architecture for parallel symbolic computing. In. *Proc. ISCA-15*, pp. 443–51, Honolulu, Hawaii, May–June

Hayes, J.P. Mudge, T., Stout, Q.F., Colley, S. and Palmer, J. (1986). A microprocessor-based Hypercube Supercomputer. *IEEE Micro*, **6**(10), 6–17

Iannucci R.A (1990). *Parallel Machines Parallel Machine Languages, The Emergence of Hybrid Dataflow Computer Architecture*. Engineering and Computer Science. Kluwer Academic Publishers

James D.V. (1990). SCI (Scalable Coherent Interface) cache coherence. In *Cache and Interconnect Architectures in Multiprocessors* (Dubois M. and Thakkar S.S, ed.), pp. 189–208. Kluwer Academic Publisher

James D.V. et al (1990). Scalable Coherent Interface. *IEEE Computer*, No. 6, 74–7

Jordan H.F. (1983). Performance measurement on HEP – A pipelined MIMD computer. In *Proc. 10th Annual International Symposium on Computer Architecture*, Stockholm, Sweden, June

Koeninger R.K., Furtney M. and Walker M. (1994). A shared memory MPP from Cray Research. *Digital Technical Journal*, **6**(2), 8–21

Kuehn J.T and Smith B.J. (1988). The Horizon Supercomputing System: Architecture and software. In *Proc. Supercomputing '88*, Orlando, Florida, Nov., pp. 28–34

Kurihara K., Chaiken D. and Agarwal A. (1991). Latency tolerance multithreading in large-scale multiprocessors. In *Proc. Int. Symp. Shared Memory Multiprocessing*, IPS Press, Japan, Apr., pp. 91–101

Lamport, L. (1978). Time, clocks, and the ordering of events in a distributed system. *Comm. ACM*, **21**(7), 558–65

Lenoski D. et al. (1990). The directory-based cache coherence protocol for the Dash multiprocessor. In *Proc. 17th Annual Int. Symp. on Computer Architecture*, pp. 148–59

Lin X. and Ni L.M. (1991). Deadlock-free multicast wormhole routing in multicomputer networks. In *Proc. 18th Int. Symp. Computer Architecture*, pp. 116–25. Los Alamitos, CA: IEEE CS Press. Order No. 2148

Nassi I.R. (1987). A Preliminary Report on the Ultramax: A Massively Parallel Shared Memory Multiprocessor. *Report ETR 87-004*, Encore Computer Corporation

Papadopoulos, G.M. and Traub, K.R. (1991). Multithreading: A revisionist view of dataflow architectures. In *Proc 18th Ann. Int. Symp. on Computer Architecture*

Pountain D. (1991). The Transputer strikes back *Byte*, Aug., 265–75

Rettberg R. and Thomas R. (1986). Contention is no obstacle to shared-memory multiprocessing. *Comm. ACM*, **29**(12), 1202–12

Robinson M. (1991). Popular and parallel (But are truly scalable shared-memory architectures possible, probable, and practical?) *Byte*, June, 219–28

Sakai S., Yamaguti Y., Hiraki K., Kodama Y. and Yuba T. (1989). An architecture of a dataflow single chip processor. In *Proc. 16th Ann. Int. Symp. on Computer Architecture*, June, pp. 46–53

Schauser K.E., Culler D.E. and Eicken T.von (1991). Compiler-controlled multithreading for lenient parallel languages. In *Proc. 5th AGM Conf. on Functional Programming Languages and Computer Architecture*, Cambridge, MA, Aug., pp. 50–72. Springer-Verlag LNCS 523

Scheurich C. and Dubois M. (1987). Correct memory operation of cache-based multiprocessors. In *Proc. 14th Ann. Int. Symp. on Computer Architecture*, pp. 234–43

Smith B.J. (1978). A pipelined, shared resource MIMD computer. In *Proc. 1978 Int. Conf. on Parallel Processing*, pp. 6–8

Stenström P. (1990). A survey of cache coherence schemes for multiprocessors. *IEEE Computer*, **23**(6), 12–24

Stenstrom P., Joe T. and Gupta A. (1992). Comparative performance evaluation of cache-coherent NUMA and COMA architectures. In *Proc. 19th Ann. Int. Symp. on Computer Architecture*, pp. 80–91

Steven F.J. (1984). Tightly coupled multiprocessor system speeds memory access times. *Elecronics*, 164–9

Swan R.J., Fuller D.H. and Siewiorek D.P. (1977). Cm* – a modular multi-microprocessor. In *Proc. 1977 National Computer Conference*, pp. 637–44

Thakkar S. et al. (1990). Scalable shared-memory multiprocessor architectures. *Computer*, **23**(6), June, 71–83

Tomasevic M. and Milutinovic V. (1994a). Hardware approaches to cache coherence in shared-memory multiprocessors, Part 1. *IEEE Micro*, **27**(5), 52–9

Tomasevic M. and Milutinovic V. (1994b). Hardware approaches to cache coherence in shared-memory multiprocessors, Part 2. *IEEE Micro*, **27**(6), pp. 61–6

Weber W-D. and Gupta A. (1989). Exploring the benefits of multiple hardware context in a multiprocessor architecture: Preliminary results. In *Proc. 16th Ann. Int. Symp. on Computer Architecture*, IEEE, New York, June

19 Outlook

19.1 Introduction

Parallel computing has historically been a field whose future promise has been characterized by hyperbole, but whose development has been defined by pragmatism. This situation has resulted, on the one hand, from the sheer excitement of the ideas put forward in the early development of the field and, on the other, by the practical difficulties involved in the effective realization of the ideas, coupled with the extraordinary successes achieved in improving the effectiveness of serial computers.

In recent years, however, it has become apparent that some aspects of parallelism have been introduced to mainstream computing. One or another type of parallelism has become the *sine qua non* of high-performance scientific computation, whether the approach is a combination of relatively modest techniques, as in the Cray or Convex supercomputers, or concentration on a high degree of parallelism of one type, as in the Thinking Machine's CM5 system. In this type of computing, the parallel techniques are trumpeted as positive benefits which confer advantages beyond their numerical factors, even though the utilization of these advantages may require additional effort on the part of the user.

In the field of more mainstream computing, however, a different technique has been adopted. Although the existence of moderate parallelism is often quoted as an advantage, its utilization is hidden, as far as that is possible, from the user. Thus, the evolution of single processor workstations (epitomized by the Sun systems) into multiple processor versions of the same architecture has been made almost seamless by the use of appropriate software techniques. This development, in turn, forms one strand in the general evolution in software away from dependence on the architecture of any particular platform and towards user-friendly interfaces which allow problems to be expressed in more natural forms.

Finally, the use of parallel operation in the form of embedded or special-purpose systems is becoming more widespread, again partly because the complexity of mapping problem to architecture is either hidden (in embedded systems) or is accepted as a necessary evil (in the case of image processing, for example).

In the light, then, of this current situation, how might we envisage the future development of the field of parallel computing? Perhaps the easiest area to consider concerns the purely technical developments which may impinge upon parallel systems.

The prediction of future technical developments in parallel computer technology allows of two possibilities – extrapolation and speculation. Extrapolation is straightforward but unexciting, and its validity is increasingly in question the further it is carried. Speculation is, if anything, even easier and certainly more entertaining, but its validity is always in question. In what follows, we attempt to combine the two techniques to provide somewhat informed and sustainable predictions which are, nevertheless, somewhat more interesting than 'a little more of the same'.

19.2 Semiconductor technology

The development of semiconductor devices has followed a similar path for some decades. Devices become gradually smaller, clock rates become higher, and circuits become more complex. At the present time, a leading-edge circuit would be built using a minimum device dimension of about 0.5 μm, would incorporate up to ten million devices, and run at a clock rate somewhat greater than 100 MHz. These parameters are to some extent linked, and we can anticipate modest improvements in them all in the near term. This technology is appropriate to support SIMD systems of tens of thousands of elements and MIMD systems with hundreds of elements.

There are, however, some factors which will have a significant effect on developments. The first of these is Wafer Scale Integration. At present, commercial devices are limited to die dimensions on the order of 1 cm × 1 cm. Work is already being carried out by Jaloweicki (1995) and others to develop the necessary process technology and architectural strategies to permit single circuits which utilize the entire surface of a semiconductor wafer to be made. When these ideas have been developed to the point of commercial viability, single circuits comprising upwards of one billion devices will become possible. These developments will be of particular value in the implementation of memory systems and highly parallel computers such as those considered in earlier chapters. The potential scale of this development is illustrated in Table 19.1, in which the area per device takes into account the reduction in area dedicated to interface functions.

The second major development which is occurring concerns device dimensions. It is perfectly feasible to foresee the development of current technology down to minimum dimensions of about 100 nm (one fifth of today's values), and this will produce worthwhile increments in packing density and performance. However, below this dimension, the physical model of device operation which must be adopted begins to change from the classical to the quantum regime, partly because the number of atoms in a given device drops below the number for which statistical prediction of the device operation is valid. In this so-called nanoelectronic region, devices consist of a few (in the limit as few as one) atoms, with commensurate increases in packing density and decreases in device reliability.

Major programmes are currently being carried out worldwide (for example, the ARPA ULTRA programme 1993–96) to investigate the promise and the problems of such devices. At present, two main classes of nano-devices are being investigated – resonant tunnelling devices and those based on so-called quantum dots. The resonant tunnelling devices operate in a similar way to present-day transistors, but by avoiding the use of depletion layers their dimensions are scalable to a typical parameter of about 10 nm. Quantum dots are devices whose physical dimensions are such as to create a quantum well which can trap (in the limit) single electrons. Again, the typical physical dimensions are between 1 and 10 nm. At present, work is concentrated on attempts to enunciate the physics of such putative devices, and to develop the

Table 19.1 The implications of WSI.

Technology	*Area*	*Area/device*	*Number*
VLSI	1 sq cm	25 sq μm	4×10e6
WSI	100 sq cm	10 sq μm	1×10e9

Table 19.2 Target parameters for nanoelectronic devices.

Parameter	*Value*
Minimum dimension	1–10 nm
Typical device area	100–10 000 sq nm
Number per sq mm	10e8–10e10
Number per system	10e9–10e11
PEs per system (SIMD)	10e6
PEs per system (MIMD)	10e4

technology which will enable them to be made. To illustrate the challenges of this technology, at present single lines of as little as 10 nm width can (sometimes) be defined on the surface of suitable semiconductors. To develop useful systems this will have to be reproducibly achieved over distances of many millimetres, and achieved, moreover, for multilayered structures similar to today's integrated circuits. It is regarded as unlikely that this target will be achieved within the next decade. However, the advantages when it is achieved will be immense. One prediction which has been made by Fountain and Tomlinson (1994) is that an SIMD array of up to a million processors could be constructed on a few square mms of silicon, although significant changes in architecture would be required to achieve this. The relevant parameters of nanoelectronic systems are indicated in Table 19.2.

In addition to simple changes of dimension and performance, some of the proposed nanoelectronic devices, such as the resonant tunnelling transistor, offer the possible of multi-state operation, opening up the possibility of performing arithmetic operations with bases other than two.

19.3 Interconnection technology

One of the practical factors which has limited the complexity of parallel computers is interconnection technology. This becomes particularly apparent when the physical size of an aggregation of circuit elements exceeds some natural barrier such as the available silicon area of a single die, the real estate of a single printed circuit card or the number of cards which can be contained in a single cabinet. An excellent example of this effect is the early Cray system on display in the museum at Los Alamos, which has been opened to show the wiring complexity of the back plane.

The problem is usually twofold. First, interfacing to another module inevitably involves the use of connection techniques which are simultaneously bulky and unreliable. Second, extension of circuits outside a single module means longer signal paths and therefore greater delays (this becomes more important as clock speeds increase). There are a number of methods under investigation to overcome these problems. One technique is to increase the circuit complexity available on a single semiconductor die until a complete system can be implemented in one such unit. The two approaches which offer promise here are the evolutionary – somewhat smaller devices coupled with wafer scale integration – and revolutionary – nanoelectronics, where, in the limit, each atom is an active device.

A second approach is to improve the interconnection technology so module-to-module connections are not a problem. The most promising route here is the use of optical interconnections, in which signal generators (usually lasers) and sensors (photodiodes) are incorporated with the circuits as described by Dowd et al. (1993). Unfortunately, there are problems to overcome. The optical devices must be carefully tuned to avoid interference, which demands significant advances in materials technology. The devices must be either (very) carefully aligned to emulate point-to-point wiring, or must generate significant power (and conversely, detect minimal power) if a broadcast approach is adopted. To be integrated effectively with active circuit elements, the optical devices should be of comparable size, and this sometime contradicts their own design requirements. Finally, there is often some external component such as a mirror or lens required which increases the bulk and unreliability of the system.

19.4 Optical computing

Optical computing is often spoken of as the next leap forward in computing technology (and, as more than one humorist has suggested, it always will be). However, a number of current developments which are of particular promise for parallel computing are described by the Optical Society of America (1993).

The main principle in optical computing involves the recognition that the cross-section of a light beam can be regarded as corresponding to a two-dimensional array of data, of almost arbitrarily fine resolution. In ordinary optics, such arrays usually correspond to images but, in considering their computational significance, this need not necessarily be so. The main components of optical computers are those familiar to us from ordinary optical systems (although they may be used in novel ways):

- **Lasers** are used both because of the coherence of their light and its relative concentration. They are effectively the power supplies of the system.
- **Lenses** distribute or concentrate the light beams as required.
- **Beam splitters** permit the effective duplication of the light beam.
- **Shutters** control activity in the system.
- **CCD arrays** convert images representing output data into electronic signals used either for control feedback or interfacing.
- **Spatial light modulators** encode information into spatially distributed optical patterns.
- **Holographic plates** by means of which data can be stored and retrieved in the form of holographic patterns.

From the above it may be correctly inferred that the present state of optical computing is conceptually fairly simple while being spatially somewhat dispersed. A typical example, a holographic storage system, is described by Brown et al. (1993), and illustrated in Figure 19.1. The system operates as follows. During recording, a pattern representing a database entry is loaded into SLM1. At the same time, a single pixel of SLM2 is selected, corresponding to the data storage address. The resulting hologram is then exposed by the laser and recorded in the holographic plate. To record a second entry, a different pixel of SLM2 is selected. Recording of each entry occurs in parallel.

Data can be retrieved by either address or content. In address mode, the appropriate pixel of SLM2 is selected, causing the appropriate image to illuminate CCD1, and therefore to be output. In content addressed mode, the search argument is loaded to SLM1. For every entry in the plate with a field equal to the search argument, one pixel of CCD1 will be illuminated – usually more than one match will be found. This information can then be passed, pixel by pixel, to SLM2, whence each full entry can be retrieved at CCD2.

This system is typical of present-day optical computing setups, both in its potential for great data parallelism and in its physically cumbersome arrangement. It is readily apparent that increases in the data parallelism can be achieved (by, for example, improved holographic media, larger lenses and more powerful lasers) and that functional parallelism could be introduced by splitting beams where appropriate and inserting different combinations of components in each beam.

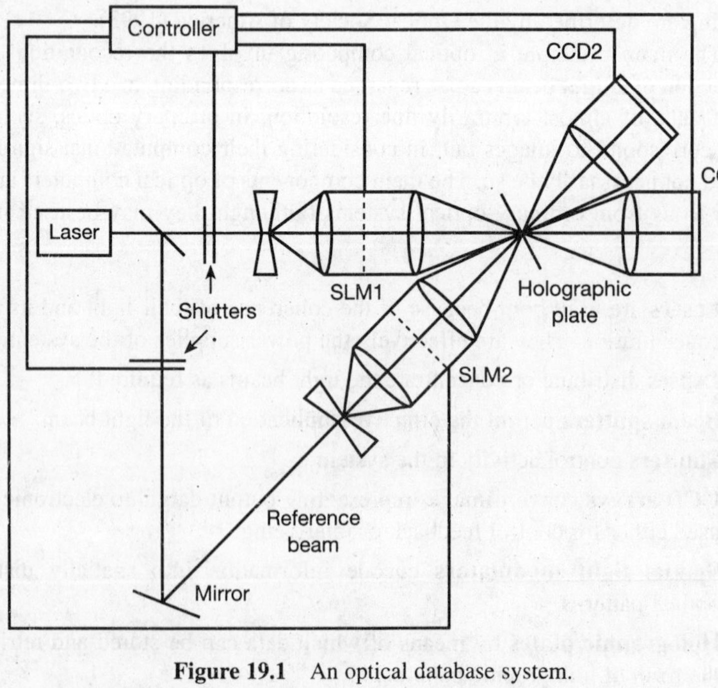

Figure 19.1 An optical database system.

There are, however, two real problems which will need to be overcome in the future if optical computing is to attain viability. The first concerns the physical setup. It is hard to see how the intrinsic physical limitations of the system, such as the focal length of lenses, can be overcome. Further, very accurate physical alignment of, for example, the SLMs and CCD arrays is demanded for accurate operation, and this is not easy to maintain in other than a laboratory environment.

The second problem concerns the control and interfacing of the system by electronic means. It is at least possible that this, rather than any intrinsic difficulty with optical computing *per se* will prove to be the limiting factor in its development.

19.5 Bio-electronic computing

Bio-electronic computing is sometimes spoken of as the next step after optical computing, from which statement its present viability can be inferred. There are two main approaches being considered at present, which might best be described as, respectively, structured and unstructured.

The first draws its inspiration from the way in which the human nervous system, in particular the brain, grows. The idea of Ireland et al. (1987) is to provide an ordered substrate across which growth may occur, and an environment which corresponds, in some way, to goal-oriented training. The second is perhaps more akin to chemistry than biology, and involves the generation of highly parallel ordered structures from solution. It is viewed as an alternative to conventional micro-fabrication techniques and offers the potential advantage of being self-ordering on the molecular scale. At present it is not understood how such structures will be controlled or interfaced, or even initiated, although the chemistry required to implement links and even specific functions is described by Tour (1994).

19.6 Final remarks

The overall implications of the developments suggested above may be summarized in a number of concluding observations, which we offer in the spirit of prophesy.

- A small percentage of systems have always employed significant parallelism; the proportion of current systems which are significantly parallel is surprisingly high (most of this being accounted for by pipelining of one kind or another); eventually most systems will be significantly parallel.
- The perception of the importance of parallelism in computing is gradually increasing, but there will rapidly come a time when parallel architectures of one sort or another are regarded as the norm rather than the exception.
- The overall effectiveness of use of parallelism will decrease in the near future as deployment runs in advance of understanding.

- The maximum number of computing elements which can be effectively employed will continue to increase but, as in the past, the increase will not be smooth, as it tends to depend on the commercial implementation of leaps in technology. It is worth noting that even the advent of nanotechnology is unlikely to raise the number of computing elements in a single system to anywhere near the number of neurons in the human brain. Whether this will ever occur, or what the results would be if it did, are questions best left to the writers of fiction.

19.7 References

ARPA ULTRA Electronics Program Reviews, Presentation Summaries 1993, 1994, 1995.

Brown J. et al. (1993). Volume holographic storage and processing for large databases. In *Optical Computing – Technical Digest Series Vol 7*, Palm Springs, CA, Optical Society of America

Dowd P. W. et al. (1993). Hierarchical scalable photonic architectures for high-performance processor interconnection. *IEEE Trans. on Comp.*, **42**(9), 1105–19

Fountain T. J. and Tomlinson C. (1994). The propagated instruction processor. *University College London Image Processing Group Internal Report No. 94/3*

Ireland G. W. et al. (1987). Effect of patterned surfaces of adhesive islands on the shape, cytoskeleton, adhesion and behaviour of Swiss mouse 3T3 fibroblasts. *J. Cell. Sci. Supp.* **8**, 19–23

Jaloweicki I. (1995). WASP: the associative string processor. In T. Fountain, *Parallel Computing – Principles and Practice*, pp. 296–308. CUP

Optical Society of America (1993). *Optical Computing – Technical Digest Series Vol 7*, Palm Springs, CA

Tour J. M. (1994). Spontaneously-assembled molecular transistors and circuits. In *ULTRA Electronics Programme Review*

Index